The Law of Debtors and Creditors

THE LAW OF DEBTORS AND CREDITORS
Text, Cases, and Problems

Fifth Edition

ELIZABETH WARREN
Leo Gottlieb Professor of Law
Harvard University

JAY LAWRENCE WESTBROOK
Benno C. Schmidt Chair of Business Law
University of Texas

ASPEN
PUBLISHERS

111 Eighth Avenue, New York, NY 10011
http://lawschool.aspenpublishers.com

Aspen Publishers
Attn: Permissions Department
111 Eighth Avenue, 7th Floor
New York, NY 10011-5201

Printed in the United States of America.

1 2 3 4 5 6 7 8 9 0

ISBN 0-7355-5788-8

Library of Congress Cataloging-in-Publication Data
Warren, Elizabeth.
    The law of debtors and creditors : text, cases, and problems /
Elizabeth Warren, Jay Lawrence Westbrook. — 5th ed.
        p. cm.
    Includes index.
    ISBN 0-7355-5788-8
        1. Debtor and creditor—United States—Cases.
I. Westbrook, Jay Lawrence. II. Title.

KF1501.A7 W365 2005
346.7307'7 — dc22

2005026519

About Aspen Publishers

Aspen Publishers, headquartered in New York City, is a leading information provider for attorneys, business professionals, and law students. Written by preeminent authorities, our products consist of analytical and practical information covering both U.S. and international topics. We publish in the full range of formats, including updated manuals, books, periodicals, CDs, and online products.

Our proprietary content is complemented by 2,500 legal databases, containing over 11 million documents, available through our Loislaw division. Aspen Publishers also offers a wide range of topical legal and business databases linked to Loislaw's primary material. Our mission is to provide accurate, timely, and authoritative content in easily accessible formats, supported by unmatched customer care.

To order any Aspen Publishers title, go to *www.aspenpublishers.com* or call 1-800-638-8437.

To reinstate your manual update service, call 1-800-638-8437.

For more information on Loislaw products, go to *www.loislaw.com* or call 1-800-364-2512.

For Customer Care issues, e-mail *CustomerCare@aspenpublishers.com*; call 1-800-234-1660; or fax 1-800-901-9075.

Aspen Publishers
a Wolters Kluwer business

To My Parents,
Donald J. and Pauline Reed Herring

— E.W.

―――――――――――――――――――――

To Polly
Wonderful One Times One

— J.L.W.

SUMMARY OF CONTENTS

CONTENTS

=== CHAPTER 6 ===

CHAPTER 13 BANKRUPTCY   281

═══════════════ CHAPTER 7 ═══════════════

CHAPTER 7 LIQUIDATION   369

══════════════════ CHAPTER 11 ══════════════════

THE FUNCTIONS OF BANKRUPTCY LAW   873

PREFACE

We should start the Preface to the Fifth Edition of this casebook the same way we started the first four: Both of us love to teach. This book is a product of the delight we have found in introducing students to a part of the law that is as filled with human drama as it is with intellectual complexity and social importance.

This preface is a little like the owner's manual that comes with a new car, albeit in abbreviated form. It tells the people who will be using this book how it works and points out some special features available in this new model. Like all owner's manuals, the preface reflects our efforts to see that everyone uses this book to best advantage. It also reflects our fervent hope that people will have as much fun using it as we had writing it.

Our primary objective is to make debtor-creditor law lively, interesting, and intellectually challenging. Our method is to use ample explanatory text to permit readers to understand the law and legal system, coupled with realistic problems to test and expand that understanding. Our principal focus is bankruptcy law, although we also discuss a good deal of non-bankruptcy law, both state and federal.

The fundamental organizing principle of The Law of Debtors and Creditors is the division between consumer and business bankruptcy, rather than a doctrinal organization that lumps together legal principles regardless of the factual context in which they are used. Our experience in practice and our empirical research suggest that both social policy questions and the realities of the functioning bankruptcy system are quite different in consumer and business cases. We have also observed that beginners find the material more accessible when consumer bankruptcy is presented first; it becomes possible to master basic principles and see how they interrelate in a somewhat more familiar setting before tackling the twists of bankruptcy law in a complex business reorganization. In turn, the consumer and business presentations are organized around the basic choice in each—liquidation or payout.

The Law of Debtors and Creditors is organized into four parts: Individual Debt Collection, Consumer Bankruptcy, Business Bankruptcy, and Functions and Boundaries of Bankruptcy Law. Each of the first three parts covers its subject in some detail for those teachers who choose to emphasize that subject. The fourth covers jurisdiction, both domestic and international, along with an introduction to the contemporary debate about the functions of bankruptcy. We do not have the luxury of devoting as much class time to each subject as we would like, so we have designed the book to permit a brief treatment of any of the subjects. Teachers can follow any of several "roadmaps" through the material, selecting a focus on state law, consumer bankruptcy, or business bankruptcy, as they choose.

While we have made every effort to ensure that the materials in the book are current and reflect the most pressing issues, the book is not a treatise designed to reveal every clever twist on a statutory provision. In making the difficult choices about how to use the space and time available, we have chosen not to include extensive citations to the majority rule, the minority rule, and the Virginia rule as recently amended. Instead, we devote our space to explaining difficult concepts and central provisions of the Code as clearly and accurately as we can. We leave the details to the hornbooks and the practitioner services.

New to the Fifth Edition

The Fifth Edition has some significant changes. The state law section has once again been condensed, a victim of riding on the same bus with the ever-expanding bankruptcy laws. The 500 pound gorilla (a description that is apt in more ways than one) of bankruptcy is the 2005 Amendments, which are now integrated throughout the bankruptcy sections, as appropriate. Once again, we do not go over every nit and jot, but we try to cover those issues that will reshape the practice of bankruptcy law. The Fifth Edition has a new section on eligibility for a consumer bankruptcy filing, the much-discussed "means test." The business part has new sections on small business bankruptcy and on big-company Chapter 11s, a reflection both of changes in the Bankruptcy Code and changes in practice. There are enough new problems and new cases in most sections to refresh the interest of teachers who have used the book for years, but many of the old favorites remain. Discussion of some topics has been shortened (for example, modification and dismissal of Chapter 13 plans), some has been reorganized (for example, exemptions), and, of course, some has been expanded (for example, transnational bankruptcy). In this edition, we have continued to expand our references to available empirical studies. Thanks to a growing number of academic studies, we are able to enrich the discussions at more and more turns.

Features

We have structured The Law of Debtors and Creditors to be taught largely through its problems. The cases are primarily designed to show the operation of the statute in a relatively simple context; the students can then attack the more complex analytic and policy issues by working through the problems. While some "leading" cases are included, our case selection depends much more on the teaching value of a case than on the prominence we would give it in a law review article.

We have divided the problems into three categories: statute readers and case extension problems, which help the students through key legal provisions; theoretical and policy problems, which require the students to think about the social and political implications of the law; and transactional problems, which reverse the litigation orientation of most problems to encourage students to think about planning transactions to help clients plan and structure their affairs. The problems also force a certain amount of review and integration. As students learn more about the legal process, problem-solving increasingly becomes a function of putting pieces together and selecting the right legal tool to achieve a certain result or to analyze a policy choice.

It is our intention to make every problem "real," that is, realistic in operation and with a human face—the kind of problem a student might actually confront after graduation. The problems are designed to teach the commercial background of each subject area, as well as the legal rules. Many of the problems are practice oriented, while others put the student in the role of legislative aide, judicial clerk, or empirical researcher. In addition to practice and policy, problems raising ethical issues are woven throughout the materials, and a separate section near the end focuses on the special ethical issues raised in bankruptcy practice. These problems give a combination of perspectives. It is our intention to encourage students to appreciate issues beyond the mechanics of the statute, and we think that the complex realities reflected through a problem approach produce more interesting insights than do neoclassical ruminations.

The Megaproblem

Another important feature is the inclusion of a megaproblem, that is, a large problem involving one debtor—Barney Thornaby—and his closely held corporation. Barney's Problem is divided into sections and runs throughout the book. Each section reviews the material just covered and places it in a growing factual context to show how each of the doctrinal subjects relates to the others in the process of analyzing and solving Barney's Problem. While the megaproblem can easily be omitted in favor of greater coverage, it has met with enthusiasm from teachers who have used it and from their students. The use of the megaproblem was quite unconventional in the first edition, but the approach is now appearing in a number of casebooks, reflecting its success in the classroom.

The Modern Role of Bankruptcy Law

These materials reflect our premises (or prejudices) about the modern role of bankruptcy law and bankruptcy lawyers, so we should declare those that are most important to us:

1.   We believe that several factors have combined to make bankruptcy commonplace in contemporary America. One important factor

has been the enormous growth in international trade competition and the creation of world markets. The consequence has been, and will continue to be, accelerating economic instability and change domestically, with one industrial or geographic sector booming while another is in sharp recession. Bankruptcy is a central part of the painful process through which both small families and big businesses adjust to the effects of rapidly changing world markets.

2.   We believe that bankruptcy will be in the mainstream of commercial and business law and practice for the foreseeable future. It is therefore critical that it be understood by every lawyer and every policy-maker concerned with the functioning of our economic system.

3.   On a microeconomic level, we think that debtor-creditor law has been dominated too long by easy stereotypes and untested assumptions. Calvinistic sneers at deadbeats and populist disdain for money-changers reflect a distorted view of the complexities of financial relationships. Too often these emotional attachments serve as substitutes for detached analysis and careful research. One of the most important things we want to do for our students is to teach against their prejudices and, harder still, our own.

Charles Warren began his 1935 history of American bankruptcy law with the words "Bankruptcy is a gloomy and depressing subject." We reject that proposition. The economic pathology that leads to bankruptcy is indeed depressing, but bankruptcy itself is the process of healing and restoration. Bankruptcy is an integral part of a free market system that permits individuals and businesses to fail; a strong bankruptcy system undergirds a market-based economy. The bankruptcy lawyer and judge help individuals and businesses to pick up the pieces, right the wrongs, and begin anew when old approaches have failed. Bankruptcy is about the future. The bankruptcy scholar searches for a better treatment of economic wounds that is less painful and more permanent. It is good work, the work of the healer, and there is much of it to be done.

Warren & Westbrook
Professors of Law

Cambridge, Massachusetts
Austin, Texas
October 2005

ACKNOWLEDGMENTS

This section is the most fun to write because as we write it we know we are finished. It is also fun to write because it causes us to reflect on how much this book has been the product of wonderful students, helpful colleagues, supportive spouses, tolerant friends, and patient children. For all the help and support, we are grateful.

Some people have given extraordinary help and they deserve a special thanks. For the Fifth Edition we particularly thank Pauline Delk, Sarah Jane Hughes, Melissa Jacoby, Daniel Keating, Kenneth Kettering, Katherine Porter, John Pottow, and Timothy Zinneck for their comments, suggestions, corrections, and advice. The Fifth Edition is built on the hard labor from the preceding four editions, and we gratefully acknowledge help on those editions from Dick McQueen, Ray Nimmer, and Paul Razor, who taught from early versions of the text and pointed out a frightening number of errors. We owe a special debt to Alan Axelrod who taught one of us bankruptcy law, and then read and commented on early outlines and sample chapters. Barry Cass has been a special friend, teaching our classes—and us—a great deal about the tax implications in business bankruptcy. Teresa Sullivan, our sociologist coauthor on empirical research projects, has helped us develop a view of bankruptcy that looks beyond legal doctrine to difficult social and policy implementation issues. Our colleague Doug Laycock has given the best kind of support—always willing to argue a point, challenge a premise, and enjoy a new insight.

Douglas Whaley and Lynn LoPucki have been both tough and generous in their comments from the first wrinkled photocopies of cases to the completion of this Fifth Edition. We are grateful to them both. Most recently, Jim Caher helped us through the trackless forest of the new means test.

We have been blessed with intelligent, dedicated research assistants. For the Fifth Edition we had the able help of Jonathan Hammer of the University of Texas Law School. On earlier editions we also had great help—from the University of Texas, Karen Cheyney, Brian Farney, Bruce James, Catherine Nicholson, and Kimberly Winick—and from Harvard University, Bruce Gottlieb, Dirk Suringa, Derrick Talerico, and Anthony Tu. The students in our classes have remained unfailingly cheerful—even enthusiastic—about helping us with the book, and many of the successful problems and comments in the following pages stem from interesting discussions with them.

One student who is now a valued colleague, Ronald Mann, provided a particularly helpful critique early on.

Our editor, Matthew Seccombe, has been nothing short of miraculous. Not everyone could dive into a book as full of complex statutory references and technically exacting problems as this one, but Matt did it with grace and his own special style. He has brought a level of professionalism to his editing work that leaves us with deepest respect for a fellow professional. We have had excellent technical support from Greg Castell and Dee Wellborn, and we publicly acknowledge our debts to both. We have also shared in the blessings of the Tarlton Law Library and its talented staff.

Finally, thanks to our friends and families who patiently listened to alternative versions of how to teach section llll(b) elections and the merits of learning voidable preferences in a business rather than a consumer context. Polly Westbrook actually read the book and still smiled. Bruce Mann gave more loving support than anyone could reasonably ask. We are richly blessed.

Warren & Westbrook
Professors of Law

Cambridge, Massachusetts
Austin, Texas

We would also like to thank the following authors and copyright holders for permission to use their materials:

Avco Inc. Promises to Tame Debt Collectors, Daily Iowan, Apr. 12, 1982, at B8. Reprinted with permission of the Associated Press, Inc.

Banks Move To Put Curbs on WorldCom, New York Times, July 13, 2002. Reprinted with permission of the New York Times.

Collection Agency Headed by "Thugs" Helps Merchants, Daily Iowan, Apr. 12, 1982, at 8B. Reprinted with permission of United Press International, Inc.

EuroDisney, International Financial Law Review, May, 1994, Vol. XII, No. 5, p. 10. Published with permission of International Financial Law Review (www.iflr.com), the leading provider for banking counsel of regulatory developments and comment on securities and international finance.

A Farmer, 70, Saw No Choice; Nor Did the Sentencing Judge, N.Y. Times, July 20, 1994, at A1. Reprinted with permission.

Happy Holidays from TRW Inc., Natl. L.J. p.6 (Jan. 11, 1993). Reprinted with permission of the Associated Press, Inc.

It was 1961, Cartoon from Punch, Mar. 30, 1983. Published with permission of Punch. Reprinted with permission from the Philadelphia Inquirer, December 7, 1994.

Kale, W., Dressed for Success. Photograph published by permission of the Chicago Tribune.

King of Deadbeat Dads Due in Court Today, Philadelphia Inquirer, Aug. 14, 1995, at A3. Reprinted with permission of the Associated Press.

Lawyer's Methods, Debtors' Nightmare, Philadelphia Inquirer, June 12, 1994, at Al and A8. Reprinted with permission from the Philadelphia Inquirer, December 7, 1994.

LoPucki, The Debtor's Lawyer as Trojan Horse, Debtor Creditor Game (teacher's manual 2d ed. 1986). Reprinted with permission.

McKnight, Protection of the Family Home from Seizure by Creditors: The Sources and Evolution of a Legal Principle, 86 Sw. Hist. Q. 364 (1983). Courtesy Texas State Historical Association, Austin. All rights reserved. Reprinted with permission of the Texas State Historical Association.

Moritz, M. and A. Seaman, Patience and Prudence, chapter 13 from GOING FOR BROKE by Michael Moritz and A. Barrett Seaman. Copyright © 1984 by Michael Moritz and Barrett Seaman. Used by permission of Doubleday, a division of Random House, Inc.

Son Can't Pay, So Father's Body Is Returned, N.Y. Times, Oct. 14, 1993, § A, col. 1, at 16. Reprinted with permission of the Associated Press, Inc.

Sullivan, Warren &. Westbrook, Limiting Access to Bankruptcy Discharge, 1983 Wis. L. Rev. 1091. Copyright 1983 by The Board of Regents of the University of Wisconsin System. Reprinted by permission of the Wisconsin Law Review.

Uncle Sam Is My Collection Agent, Forbes, June 15, 1998. Reprinted by permission of Forbes Magazine © 2000 Forbes 1998.

Whitford, A Critique of the Consumer Credit Collection System, 1979 Wis. L. Rev. 1047. Copyright 1983 by The Board of Regents of the University of Wisconsin System. Reprinted by permission of the Wisconsin Law Review.

Excerpts from A MAN IN FULL by Tom Wolfe. Copyright © 1998 by Tom Wolfe. Reprinted by permission of Farrar, Straus and Giroux, LLC.

SPECIAL NOTICE

The problems in this book are filled with debtors, creditors, lawyers, trustees, and others who are the products of our imaginations. Any resemblance to any real person, solvent or insolvent, is purely coincidental.

We have edited cases and articles for the sake of smoother reading. Citations and footnotes have been deleted without indication. Footnotes that were not eliminated retain their original numbers; asterisks indicate editors' footnotes.

The Bankruptcy Code is referred to as "the Code," and citations to it are by section number only. "The Act" refers to the Bankruptcy Act of 1898.

Citations to various federal consumer law acts may be to the USCA or the original public law number; references are to the public law sections only because this conforms to popular usage.

The Law of Debtors
and Creditors

PART I

INDIVIDUAL DEBT COLLECTION

CHAPTER 1

COLLECTION WITHOUT COURTS

A. NONJUDICIAL COLLECTION METHODS

1. *Leveraging*

This is a book about debtors and creditors. It deals with the laws governing debtor and creditor behavior, laws that prescribe when obligations must be paid, how unpaid obligations can be collected, and how bankruptcy law can change legal obligations. Not surprisingly, this is a book laden with rules, regulations, common law doctrines, state codes, federal statutes, and enough "law" to exhaust even the most diligent student.

Although there is much law in this book, and much that relies on book-keepers, accountants, and actuaries, you will not find here a musty cupboard filled with rules and numbers. This text is filled with stories of shrewd uses of leverage and tragic circumstances. It is sometimes about people who wear pin-striped suits and live without passion, but it is also about self-help and self-defense in a very tough world.

Son Can't Pay, So Father's Body is Returned

Richmond, Tex — The body of a man who died Friday was dumped on his son's doorstep by a funeral home on Monday evening because the son had been unable to pay the full price of cremation.

The bizarre episode, in this town 30 miles southwest of Houston, began Saturday morning when the body of George Bojarski, who had died of esophageal cancer at the age of 66, was picked up by the Evans Mortuary.

Mr. Bojarski's son, Larry, paid the funeral home $299 of the $683 cremation fee and was told that if he failed to pay the balance, the body would be returned.

Gary Geick, the Justice of the Peace for Fort Bend County, quoted Larry Bojarski today as saying that he had not had the money to pay the balance and that he had not believed that the funeral home would follow through with its threat....

But on Monday evening, George Bojarski's body, covered only by a sheet, was found at the door of his son's apartment.

It was unclear why the Evans Mortuary had not given the son more time to pay the fee; a telephone call today seeking comment from the funeral

3

home was not returned. The town's Police Chief, Butch Gore, said there had been no decision on whether to bring criminal charges.

The Hernandez Funeral Home in the nearby town of Rosenberg has now agreed to provide the cremation services at no cost.

"My father's been in the business for 50 years," said one of the owners, Joe Hernandez, "and he's never heard of a case like this. The son was kind of like in shock. Here your dad is laying there on the floor after being dead for three days." [*New York Times*, October 14, 1993, at A16, col. 1.]

The debtor–creditor payment process can best be viewed as a constant balancing — a weighing and leveraging process. A debtor who has bills to pay makes a series of decisions about the costs and benefits of paying each bill. The process may be explicit or vaguely unarticulated, but either way debtors decide when to pay, which bills to pay first, and whether to pay at all.

Creditors engage in another balancing process. They would, of course, like to be paid on all bills. When they are not, they face decisions about how to collect. In a typical cost-benefit analysis, creditors must decide what actions are worth taking to collect a delinquent debt. A creditor might win a lawsuit, but surely it is not worthwhile to go to court to collect a $15 bill from a customer. A creditor might consider nonjudicial alternatives such as telephoning a delinquent customer, but in each case the creditor must weigh both the cost of time expended in such activities and potential loss of customer goodwill against any increase in the likelihood of repayment. Because many creditors have more than one delinquent or potentially delinquent customer, a creditor might derive wider benefits than merely collecting the debt at issue. Perhaps the Evans Mortuary hands out photocopies of the *New York Times* article to relatives who fail to pay for services rendered.

Creditors try to determine how, at the lowest cost, to make it more beneficial — or less costly — for the debtor to pay the money owed. The creditor looks for means to enhance its leverage with the debtor in order to increase the likelihood that the debtor will repay this creditor.

A creditor could, of course, think of all sorts of things to do to increase the odds of repayment. Evans Mortuary thought of a ploy that could be very effective. Harassing phone calls or including the debtor's name and picture in a "Deadbeat of the Month" advertisement in the local paper might be an inexpensive — but effective — means of encouraging debtor repayment. Of course, debtors could try to discourage creditor collection efforts. Keeping a pack of large dogs, having an unlisted phone number and an answering machine, or moving every few weeks might deter certain collection activities.

While the most obvious leverage decisions are made at the collection end of the debtor–creditor relationship, much of the analysis occurs when the loan is incurred. A passage from a Bank of America lending guide that explains why banks take collateral for loans is instructive:

[Term] loans are normally secured by the pledging of all the assets in the business (not just the assets being bought with this money). "Although it generally is insufficient value to pay off the loan," the Bank of America guide intones, "securing capital equipment provides three valuable functions:

1. *Leverage.* As long as the applicant remains in business, the equipment and machinery necessary to his business operation are important....

Therefore, the fact that it is secured gives greater incentive to the borrower to meet his payments.
2. *Collateral Control.* Often a security agreement is taken simply to prevent the applicant from obtaining an additional loan from another lending institution . . . .
3. *Loss Reduction.* When a loan is in default, security can be sold and proceeds applied toward the loan balance . . . ."

Mayer, The Bankers 263-264 (1974). Professor Ronald Mann did an empirical study of secured lending that found that leverage and control are key benefits of security to secured creditors. Ronald J. Mann, Strategy and Force in the Liquidation of Secured Debt, 96 Mich. L. Rev. 159 (1997). Leverage is important to both debtors and creditors, but their activities are necessarily limited by the formal legal system. The scope and degree of the influence of formal law varies. Ordinary civil and criminal laws are not suspended for debtors and creditors engaged in a collection struggle, and they restrain some of the behavior suggested above. Indeed, some collection devices, such as seeking court enforcement of judgments, are governed by formal legal rules that are peculiar to debt collection activities.

Other leverage factors are almost entirely outside the scope of legal regulation, such as the desire of a debtor to repay a loan made by a family member who stood by the debtor during difficult times. Leverage over a debtor typically involves both formal legal rules and informal collection devices, such as the debtor's desire to pay a doctor who may withhold future services to the debtor if the past bills are not paid and who also can make a credible threat of prosecution for theft of services.

Most money owed is repaid without resort to any legal process. Even when there is a dispute about whether a debt is payable, or when a debtor is unable to repay on time, resort to legal devices to avoid or coerce payment is rare. Although state and federal courts regularly hear a substantial volume of debt collection actions, when the number of formal actions is compared with the number of debts collected without such actions, it becomes clear that formal proceedings make up only a tiny fraction of the debt collection process.

After a careful empirical study, Professor William Whitford explained that many creditors are unlikely to use courts for collection because they see litigation as loaded with unnecessary costs. He added that many creditors avoid litigation because of other risks as well:

A risk inherent in almost all litigation is that one party will net nothing by losing the case entirely. For the creditor in consumer credit collection, this risk takes the form either that the debtor will be judgment proof or that the creditor will be judged not to own a valid debt. The creditor can avoid the risk that the debt may be declared invalid by obtaining voluntary debtor payment. Moreover, when the debtor is judgment proof, it does not usually mean that he or she is assetless, but rather that available assets are exempt or encumbered. Nothing in the exemption laws, however, prevents the debtor from making a voluntary payment from otherwise exempt assets. Alternatively, a judgment proof debtor can attempt to borrow from a friend or relative, or to obtain a consolidation loan from a finance company, in order to settle a debt. These sources of payment cannot be reached directly by a creditor through coercive execution, of course, and hence create additional incentives to the creditor for voluntary settlement.

Whitford, A Critique of the Consumer Credit Collection System, 1979 Wis. L. Rev. 1047, 1055.

> *handwritten margin note: - Little use of formal collection process against consumers prior to bankruptcy*

In our own empirical studies of people in bankruptcy, we found remarkably little use of the formal collection process against consumers prior to bankruptcy. In 1981, we found that in two-thirds of the cases, no collection suit had been filed against the debtors before they declared bankruptcy. Even though these debtors doubtless had been in default on most of their obligations, only about 4 percent of the claims were the subject of lawsuits at the time the debtors filed for bankruptcy. Sullivan, Warren, and Westbrook, As We Forgive Our Debtors: Bankruptcy and Consumer Credit in America 305 (Oxford 1989). By 2001, again about two-thirds of the debtors had no legal actions filed against them before they had filed for bankruptcy.

> *handwritten margin note: 2001! 2/3 of debtors had no legal actions filed against them b/4 they had filed for bankruptcy*

You might be thinking that you can close up this book right now because mastery of the legal system is therefore irrelevant, but pause for a minute. The most obvious point, of course, is that attorneys are called to aid in resolving a disproportionate number of debtor–creditor difficulties that involve formal process. An attorney who is unfamiliar with the rules of debtor–creditor law is not in a position to provide effective help. But a larger point is more crucial: Formal debtor–creditor laws are important because of the impact they have on the informal, negotiated debt collection process, whether that process is accomplished with or without an attorney.

> *handwritten margin note: * Formal Debtor-Creditor laws are important b/c of the impact they have on informal, negotiated debt collection process, whether an atty is used or not.*

Collection laws draw the boundaries between debtors who may try to evade paying and creditors who are determined to collect. Some points of leverage are simply left undisturbed. (The cremation story demonstrates the rule of no payment, no service, which the law generally does not alter.) Other points of leverage are defined by detailed legal rules. These debtor–creditor laws have an enormous impact on debt repayment regardless of whether either party invokes the formal rules. Creditor and debtor behavior is shaped by the limits of what actions are legally permissible, and by what remedies the law will grant — at what cost — if the formal process is invoked.

This is not to say that debtors or creditors will never engage in unlawful behavior. They often do. Nor is this to say that debtors or creditors will always seek legal advice before they engage in various debtor collection activities. They usually do not. But it is clear that the boundaries drawn by the debt collection laws affect the kinds of behavior in which most debtors and creditors engage and provide some protection from overzealous adversaries.

Professor Whitford concluded his empirical study:

> [The collection system is] characterized by bargaining and "voluntary" payment of delinquencies rather than by collection through formal legal processes. The bargaining is importantly influenced by each party's ability to exert leverage — usually credible threats of action that will harm the other. The main relevance of legal rules governing formal execution is that they provide leverages to one or the other party to the bargaining.

Whitford, A Critique of the Consumer Credit Collection System, at 1071.

One final note: There is an uneasy tension surrounding the identification of the debtors and creditors affected by these laws. In evaluating rules of debt collection it is necessary to identify the debtors or creditors most likely to be affected by a provision and to make some rational speculations about how they will be affected. This approach encourages a stereotyping of debtors and creditors that is both necessary and helpful. But there are no fixed guidelines to help in deciding who are the good guys and who are the bad guys in debtor–creditor relationships. Debtors and creditors come in a wide variety of shapes, sizes, and sympathies. It is extremely rare for any person or business to be only a creditor or only a debtor. Most people or businesses are both — debtors in some capacities and creditors in others. Studying debtor–creditor law often involves identifying the typical debtor and creditor interests that are affected by a collection rule, then searching out the implications of the rule for atypical debtors and creditors who may suffer unexpected consequences from its implementation.

We make these points to ensure that throughout these materials the rules of debtor–creditor law are evaluated not only in formal operation, but in how they shape the informal debtor–creditor system. In both the consumer and business contexts, a debtor–creditor rule must be understood as it operates "on the street," as well as in the courtroom.

2.   *Indirect Leverage in the Legal System*

Creditors can always sue when a debtor has not paid, but, as Professor Whitford points out, the process is expensive and fraught with the possibility of mistake. Creditors would like to find someone else to help them encourage the debtor to repay, especially if the cost to the creditor is negligible.

The government sometimes shifts the leverage of parties in the debt collection arena in unexpected ways. For example, a California statute governing the payment of wages authorizes a temporary restraining order to be issued to close down any company that twice in ten years either violates the duties to pay its employees under the act or fails to satisfy an employee's judgment for nonpayment of wages. Cal. Labor Code §243 (1996). An employee who has not been paid who knows of another such instance need not bother with attachments and seizing property for the collection of wages. The employee can make a credible threat to close the business if he or she is not paid immediately. The reach of the statute is long: any employer who uses the services of an agent, contractor, or subcontractor who fails to pay or has failed to pay in the past violates the provision if the employer knows of the nonpayment.

An ex-spouse who fails to pay court-ordered child support or alimony may be put in jail for nonpayment, a move that has a way of concentrating the debtor's attention. A bank that hasn't been repaid may report the debtor to the IRS for "income" from the forgiveness of debt.[1] These provisions are

---

1. If a creditor "forgives," a debt — that is, releases the debtor from the obligation to pay, then the tax law treats the release as the same as getting income on which income tax should be paid. The position is logical, but the results can be paradoxical, to say the least. We discuss this point further in the business bankruptcy section.

just a few of the dozens of similar provisions in the state and federal laws that indirectly re-allocate the leverage between debtors and creditors. Few would show up in an index of debtor–creditor laws, but they may have powerful effects on the leverage a party can exercise in collecting a debt.

3.   *The Credit Information Process*

Understanding leverage requires a keen eye on a number of statutes outside those traditionally identified as regulating the debtor–creditor relationship. Credit reporting, long viewed as simply a tool for creditors to decide which applicants to approve or deny, has a prominent position in the collection process. Creditors who can make credible threats to deny access to future credit may increase their collection leverage.

Creditors have long exercised this leverage individually with their debtors by refusing any further extensions of credit until past bills are paid. The problem, of course, is that debtors may find it easy to walk away from a single creditor. Creditors know that their leverage will be stronger if there is nowhere else for the debtor to walk to. If a creditor can influence other providers of goods and services to withhold future credit from a nonpaying debtor, the unpaid creditor has far greater leverage to push a debtor to repay.

To maximize this leverage effect, creditors need an inexpensive, fairly accurate method of tracking and reporting debtors' payment behavior. Well-established credit-reporting services throughout the United States accomplish these ends. These services are usually privately owned reporting companies supported by the creditors who use the service's information. An entrepreneur or a group of creditors form a company, charging an annual fee from each creditor-member and sometimes a per-use charge. The company then maintains credit information on each debtor, such as the number of credit accounts the debtor has, the credit limits for each account, the timeliness and amounts of the debtor's payments, and the number of times a debtor has been delinquent in repayments. This information is garnered from the creditor-members who agree to make their credit information available to the reporting service.

Some reporting services provide more information. They report how often the debtor has moved in the preceding few years or whether the debtor is a homeowner. Most reporting services monitor court dockets to determine when collection lawsuits are pending against certain debtors or when a debtor has filed for bankruptcy.

The creditors may use the data to rate the debtors with a kind of shorthand to indicate, based on the factors available, which debtors are most "creditworthy" — that is, which are most likely to repay their debts. These ratings are often based on credit "score sheets" that assign numbered values to various items listed in the files (number of credit cards, home ownership, frequency of 30-day late payments, and so forth). The numbers are then totaled to produce a single number, most famously known as the FICO score.[2]

_____

2. The term "FICO" stands for "Fair Isaac Company," which is the company that made this scoring system famous.

In the interest of keeping costs low, these scoring systems are designed to be implemented by relatively low-paid clerical employees who do not require extensive training and are not expected to use much personal judgment. When a subscriber of the reporting service is about to extend credit to a customer, the subscriber can call the reporting service to find out the credit-worthiness of the customer. The credit reporting company may offer either the raw information for the creditor to score or a composite score based on factors the creditor has already identified. The subscriber can then make a credit decision based on this information.

Reporting services serve an important function in providing credit information at a low cost to help subscribers identify debtors unlikely to repay. The role of reporting services in the collection process is equally important. By encouraging potential creditors to withhold credit from debtors who are having difficulties with other creditors, these services create powerful leverage to encourage debtors to pay their earlier debts. It is no accident that dunning letters and phone calls frequently begin with exhortations to the debtor to "Protect Your Credit Rating."

Acknowledgment of some industry abuses, fears about privacy in a computer age, and a recognition of the enormous impact of the desire to protect future credit have led to federal regulation of credit information. We offer an excerpt from these statutes, which we suggest you review to see how they draw a boundary between permissible and impermissible debt collection activities. It is also interesting to review the statute to see how the leverage of the debtor and the creditor have been structured under the Act.

The statute has two principal themes: giving the debtor access to the credit report information and prescribing procedures to assure the accuracy of the information in the file. (While the statutory numbering begins with 1681, the provisions in the Act have always been known by the section numbers in the bill as it was originally proposed; accordingly, we use the latter numbers.)

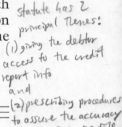

statute has 2
principal themes:
(1) giving the debtor
access to the credit
report info
and
(2) prescribing procedures
to assure the accuracy
of the info in the file

=========== FAIR CREDIT REPORTING ACT ===========

15 U.S.C. 1681i, 1681n, 1681o

§611. Procedure in Case of Disputed Accuracy

(a) If the completeness or accuracy of any item of information contained in his file is disputed by a consumer, and such dispute is directly conveyed to the consumer reporting agency by the consumer, the consumer reporting agency shall within a reasonable period of time reinvestigate and record the current status of that information unless it has reasonable grounds to believe that the dispute by the consumer is frivolous or irrelevant. If after such reinvestigation such information is found to be inaccurate or can no longer be verified, the consumer reporting agency shall promptly delete such information. The presence of contradictory information in the consumer's file does not in and of itself constitute reasonable grounds for believing the dispute is frivolous or irrelevant.

(b) If the reinvestigation does not resolve the dispute, the consumer may file a brief statement setting forth the nature of the dispute. The consumer reporting agency may limit such statements to not more than one hundred words if it provides the consumer with assistance in writing a clear summary of the dispute.

(c) Whenever a statement of a dispute is filed, unless there is reasonable grounds to believe that it is frivolous or irrelevant, the consumer reporting agency shall, in any subsequent consumer report containing the information in question, clearly note that it is disputed by the consumer and provide either the consumer's statement or a clear and accurate codification or summary thereof.

(d) Following any deletion of information which is found to be inaccurate or whose accuracy can no longer be verified or any notation as to disputed information, the consumer reporting agency shall, at the request of the consumer, furnish notification that the item has been deleted or the statement, codification or summary pursuant to subsection (b) or (c) to any person specifically designated by the consumer who has within two years prior thereto received a consumer report for employment purposes, or within six months prior thereto received a consumer report for any other purpose, which contained the deleted or disputed information. The consumer reporting agency shall clearly and conspicuously disclose to the consumer his rights to make such a request. Such disclosure shall be made at or prior to the time the information is deleted or the consumer's statement regarding the disputed information is received.

§615. Requirements on Users of Consumer Reports

(a) Duties of users taking adverse actions on the basis of information contained in consumer reports. If any person takes any adverse action with respect to any consumer that is based in whole or in part on any information contained in a consumer report, the person shall —

(like a lender who turns you down or an Eer doesn't hire you)

(1) provide oral, written, or electronic notice of the adverse action to the consumer;

(2) provide to the consumer orally, in writing, or electronically —

(A) the name, address, and telephone number of the consumer reporting agency (including a toll-free telephone number established by the agency if the agency compiles and maintains files on consumers on a nationwide basis) that furnished the report to the person; and

(B) a statement that the consumer reporting agency did not make the decision to take the adverse action and is unable to provide the consumer the specific reasons why the adverse action was taken; and

(3) provide to the consumer an oral, written, or electronic notice of the consumer's right —

(A) to obtain, under section 612, a free copy of a consumer report on the consumer from the consumer reporting agency referred to in paragraph (2), which notice shall include an indication of the 60-day period under that section for obtaining such a copy; and

(B) to dispute, under section 611, with a consumer reporting agency the accuracy or completeness of any information in a consumer report furnished by the agency.

* * *

(c) Reasonable procedures to assure compliance. No person shall be held liable for any violation of this section if he shows by a preponderance of the evidence that at the time of the alleged violation he maintained reasonable procedures to assure compliance with the provisions of this section.

(d) Duties of users making written credit or insurance solicitations on the basis of information contained in consumer files.

(1) In general. Any person who uses a consumer report on any consumer in connection with any credit or insurance transaction that is not initiated by the consumer, that is provided to that person under section 604(c)(1)(B), shall provide with each written solicitation made to the consumer regarding the transaction a clear and conspicuous statement that—

(A) information contained in the consumer's consumer report was used in connection with the transaction;

(B) the consumer received the offer of credit or insurance because the consumer satisfied the criteria for credit worthiness or insurability under which the consumer was selected for the offer;

(C) if applicable, the credit or insurance may not be extended if, after the consumer responds to the offer, the consumer does not meet the criteria used to select the consumer for the offer or any applicable criteria bearing on credit worthiness or insurability or does not furnish any required collateral;

(D) the consumer has a right to prohibit information contained in the consumer's file with any consumer reporting agency from being used in connection with any credit or insurance transaction that is not initiated by the consumer; and

(E) the consumer may exercise the right referred to in subparagraph (D) by notifying a notification system established under section 604(e).

* * *

(3) Maintaining criteria on file. A person who makes an offer of credit or insurance to a consumer under a credit or insurance transaction described in paragraph (1) shall maintain on file the criteria used to select the consumer to receive the offer, all criteria bearing on credit worthiness or insurability, as applicable, that are the basis for determining whether or not to extend credit or insurance pursuant to the offer, and any requirement for the furnishing of collateral as a condition of the extension of credit or insurance, until the expiration of the 3-year period beginning on the date on which the offer is made to the consumer.

(4) Authority of Federal agencies regarding unfair or deceptive acts or practices not affected. This section is not intended to affect the authority of any Federal or State agency to enforce a prohibition against unfair or deceptive acts or practices, including the making of false or misleading

statements in connection with a credit or insurance transaction that is not initiated by the consumer.

* * *

(f) Prohibition on sale or transfer of debt caused by identity theft.

(1) In general. No person shall sell, transfer for consideration, or place for collection a debt that such person has been notified under section 605B has resulted from identity theft.

(2) Applicability. The prohibitions of this subsection shall apply to all persons collecting a debt described in paragraph (1) after the date of a notification under paragraph (1).

* * *

(g) Debt collector communications concerning identity theft. If a person acting as a debt collector (as that term is defined in title VIII on behalf of a third party that is a creditor or other user of a consumer report is notified that any information relating to a debt that the person is attempting to collect may be fraudulent or may be the result of identity theft, that person shall —

(1) notify the third party that the information may be fraudulent or may be the result of identity theft; and

(2) upon request of the consumer to whom the debt purportedly relates, provide to the consumer all information to which the consumer would otherwise be entitled if the consumer were not a victim of identity theft, but wished to dispute the debt under provisions of law applicable to that person.

* * *

§616.   Civil Liability for Willful Noncompliance

Any consumer reporting agency or user of information which willfully fails to comply with any requirement imposed under this title with respect to any consumer is liable to that consumer in an amount equal to the sum of —

(1) any actual damages sustained by the consumer as a result of the failure;

(2) such amount of punitive damages as the court may allow; and

(3) in the case of any successful action to enforce any liability under this section, the costs of the action together with reasonable attorney's fees as determined by the court.

§617.   Civil Liability for Negligent Noncompliance

Any consumer reporting agency or user of information which is negligent in failing to comply with any requirement imposed under this title with respect to any consumer is liable to that consumer in an amount equal to the sum of —

(1) any actual damages sustained by the consumer as a result of the failure;

(2) in the case of any successful action to enforce any liability under this section, the costs of the action together with reasonable attorney's fees as determined by the court.

Most debtors will deal directly with a credit reporting service only after they have been denied credit. The most frequent source of dispute between the agencies and the debtors is the accuracy of the credit information supplied by the creditor-members. Debtors may complain that debts listed were not owed, that the amounts owed are incorrectly listed, or that the payments sent to the creditor are not accurately listed. The credit report initially contains only the creditor's version of any ongoing debtor–creditor dispute.

— Debtors will typically deal directly w/ a credit reporting service after they have been denied credit.

It is the creditor's ability to make negative reports to the credit reporting agency and thereby influence the debtor's credit rating that creates leverage in debt collection. The Fair Credit Reporting Act offsets some of that leverage by providing procedures to which the reporting agency must adhere when the accuracy of a creditor's report is questioned. A credit reporting agency cannot defend itself by blaming the creditors for any misinformation; both are now responsible and both often find themselves as co-defendants when something goes wrong. On the other hand, there may be a reverse twist: To the extent that the law makes the credit records more accurate and more credible, it may increase the leverage they give a creditor. Moreover, while the FCRA creates penalties for violations, it is also important to note its preemption effects.

FCRA

The credit industry has mushroomed in the past 20 years. Three companies, TRW, Equifax, and Transunion, dominate this multibillion-dollar industry. The Federal Trade Commission reports that they maintain files on 200 million persons and issue around 1.5 billion credit reports per year. It is a rare adult in America who does not have a credit file outstanding at one or more of the big three.

TRW, Equifax & Transunion are the Big 3

As the industry has grown, the number of complaints about the accuracy of the reports has grown as well. Despite the high stakes and the credit industry's self-interest, Congress documented in considering the FCRA amendments that 48 percent of credit reports sampled from the three major credit bureaus contained inaccurate information. S. Rep. 103–209, 103d Cong., 1st Sess., 3 (Dec. 9, 1993). A 2002 study by the Consumer Federation of America found that 20 percent of consumers could have been misclassified as subprime mortgage risks when they were not and 20 percent more could have been misclassified the other way (i.e., as prime when they were really subprime).

Congress: 48% of cr. reports had inaccuracies

While most debtors with a complaint have to fight it out one-on-one with one of the big companies, occasionally a group of debtors encounters the same problem — and garners the leverage to get a fairly impressive settlement.

Happy Holidays from TRW Inc.

TRW really screwed up

Montpelier, Vt. — TRW Inc., a big credit-reporting firm that botched the credit records of 1,200 Vermont residents, has agreed to pay up to $1,000 to each homeowner for wrongly naming them as tax deadbeats. TRW also agreed to pay $125,000 to settle a state lawsuit.

In 1991, TRW falsely recorded tax bills of every property owner in the wealthy town of Norwich and 650 residents in Woodstock as property tax liens, which compromised the residents' credit status.

usury law - a law that prohibits moneylenders from charging illegally high interest rates.

"This settlement marks the first time that TRW has agreed to provide restitution on a broad basis to consumers who were damaged by inaccurate tax-lien reporting," state Attorney General Jeffrey L. Amestoy said.

TRW, one of the nation's three major credit reporting agencies, blamed a subcontractor, National Data Retrieval Inc. of Norcross, Ga., for making the error while tabulating a list of local taxpayers.

TRW also agreed to change its practices to avoid similar mistakes.

The state filed suit against TRW in October 1991, claiming that TRW violated state credit report and consumer fraud law by misrepresenting the tax-delinquency status of many Vermonters and failing to correct it. The case inspired the Vermont Legislature to enact one of the strongest credit reporting reform laws in the nation, which lets consumers see one credit report for free each year.

Julie Brill, an assistant attorney general, said 1,200 Vermonters will be notified by mail that they may be eligible for $250 if their credit report was delayed or damaged because of reporting errors. Anyone with out-of-pocket losses due to botched credit records could receive up to $1,000.

TRW initially thought the problem was an isolated one, company officials said. But in October 1991, they withdrew tax information for consumers in New Hampshire, Vermont, Rhode Island, and Maine because of the problems, an official said then. [*National Law Journal*, p.6 (Jan. 11, 1993).]

B. RESTRICTIONS ON NONJUDICIAL COLLECTION

1. *Usury Laws*

One of the most overt restrictions on collection was blunt and direct: usury laws. If a creditor charged more than a pre-determined rate of interest, the loan would be deemed usurious and the interest, and under some statutes the principal itself, would be deemed uncollectible. Some laws even provided criminal penalties for usury lenders. By regulating the amount of interest that a lender could charge, the government regulated the heart of the debtor-creditor relationship and maintained control over ancillary issues such as service fees and penalty charges.

Usury laws are perhaps the most ancient form of economic regulation. These laws long pre-date the founding of the American republic. Left largely to state law, usury restrictions varied both in the interest permitted and in other details about the application to consumers versus businesses or the methods of calculation. By the late 1970s, only three states had no interest limits.

The high inflation of the late 1970s and early 1980s put a great deal of pressure on many of the usury laws. Rates deemed usurious in times of low inflation looked quite modest when Treasury bills interest rates were pressing into the double digits. Restrictions on consumer credit in low-ceiling states made the disadvantages of usury laws more apparent.

In 1978, the Supreme Court profoundly changed the interpretation of usury laws in Marquette National Bank of Minneapolis v. First Omaha Service Corporation, 439 U.S. 299 (1978). First Omaha was soliciting credit card customers in Minnesota at an interest rate that was lawful in Nebraska

Perhaps the most ancient form of economic regulation.

MNB of Minn v. 1st OSC - 1978 sup ct. case that profoundly changed the interpretation of usury laws.

[handwritten margin note: 4. Held: st. law of customer's location wasn't relevant, instead a bank could charge whatever interest rate was legal in the bank's home state.]

but that exceeded the Minnesota cap. The Supreme Court ruled that the state law of the customer's location was not relevant. Instead, a bank could charge whatever interest rate was legal in the bank's home state. South Dakota and Delaware seized the initiative, deregulating interest and other banking functions to attract banks and other consumer lenders. By 1982, most leading banking states had relaxed or repealed their interest rate ceilings. Retail outlets, such as Sears, established captive banks located in interest-friendly states, then exported their interest rates all over the country.

While some states have more restrictive usury laws and there is occasional litigation over whether some charge violates local usury laws, FDIC analysts and other government officials now characterize interest rates as "deregulated." Credit regulation, to the extent that it survives, has moved to a review of process rather than substance. The deregulation of consumer credit has profoundly altered the world of consumer credit, a point that will be discussed further in the consumer bankruptcy materials.

2. *Federal Statutory Controls on Nonjudicial Collection*

Direct control of debt collection began at the state level with a patchwork of common law decisions and state statutes. In the 1970s, various government agencies collected data documenting credit collection abuses. In response, Congress adopted the Fair Debt Collection Practices Act. The act represents a major effort to acknowledge difficulties with debt collection and to fashion a federal remedy directed specifically toward debt collection abuses. A portion of the act is reproduced below (once again the section numbers are from the original bill). It will be useful to look through these provisions more than once to identify which practices are prohibited, which parties are controlled by the statute, the remedies for wrongful activities, and the amounts and kinds of resources needed by debtors to protect the rights established by the act.

FAIR DEBT COLLECTION PRACTICES ACT

15 U.S.C.A. 1692 et seq.

§801. SHORT TITLE

This title may be cited as the "Fair Debt Collection Practices Act."

§802. FINDINGS AND PURPOSE

(a) There is abundant evidence of the use of abusive, deceptive, and unfair debt collection practices by many debt collectors. Abusive debt collection practices contribute to the number of personal bankruptcies, to marital instability, to the loss of jobs, and to invasions of individual privacy....

§803. Definitions

As used in this title —

(1) The term "Commission" means the Federal Trade Commission.

(2) The term "communication" means the conveying of information regarding a debt directly or indirectly to any person through any medium.

(3) The term "consumer" means any natural person obligated or allegedly obligated to pay any debt.

(4) The term "creditor" means any person who offers or extends credit creating a debt or to whom a debt is owed, but such term does not include any person to the extent that he receives an assignment or transfer of a debt in default solely for the purpose of facilitating collection of such debt for another.

(5) The term "debt" means any obligation or alleged obligation of a consumer to pay money arising out of a transaction in which the money, property, insurance, or services which are the subject of the transaction are primarily for personal, family, or household purposes, whether or not such obligation has been reduced to judgment.

(6) The term "debt collector" means any person who uses any instrumentality of interstate commerce or the mails in any business the principal purpose of which is the collection of any debts, or who regularly collects or attempts to collect, directly or indirectly, debts owed or due or asserted to be owed or due another. Notwithstanding the exclusion provided by clause (F) of the last sentence of this paragraph, the term includes any creditor who, in the process of collecting his own debts, uses any name other than his own which would indicate that a third person is collecting or attempting to collect such debts. For the purpose of section 808(6), such term also includes any person who uses any instrumentality of interstate commerce or the mails in any business the principal purpose of which is the enforcement of security interests. The term does not include —

(A) any officer or employee of a creditor while, in the name of the creditor, collecting debts for such creditor;

(B) any person while acting as a debt collector for another person, both of whom are related by common ownership or affiliated by corporate control, if the person acting as a debt collector does so only for persons to whom it is so related or affiliated and if the principal business of such person is not the collection of debts;

(C) any officer or employee of the United States or any State to the extent that collecting or attempting to collect any debt is in the performance of his official duties;

(D) any person while serving or attempting to serve legal process on any other person in connection with the judicial enforcement of any debt;

(E) any nonprofit organization which, at the request of consumers, performs bona fide consumer credit counseling and assists consumers in the liquidation of their debts by receiving payments from such consumers and distributing such amounts to creditors;

(F) any person collecting or attempting to collect any debt owed or due or asserted to be owed or due another to the extent such activity (i) is incidental to a bona fide fiduciary obligation or a bona fide escrow arrangement; (ii) concerns a debt which was originated by such person; (iii) concerns a debt which was not in default at the time it was obtained by such person; or (iv) concerns a debt obtained by such person as a secured party in a commercial credit transaction involving the creditor.

(7) The term "location information" means a consumer's place of abode and his telephone number at such place, or his place of employment.

(8) The term "State" means any State, territory, or possession of the United States, the District of Columbia, the Commonwealth of Puerto Rico, or any political subdivision of any of the foregoing.

§804.   Acquisition of Location Information

Any debt collector communicating with any person other than the consumer for the purpose of acquiring location information about the consumer shall —

(1) identify himself, state that he is confirming or correcting location information concerning the consumer, and, only if expressly requested, identify his employer;

(2) not state that such consumer owes any debt;

(3) not communicate with any such person more than once unless requested to do so by such person or unless the debt collector reasonably believes that the earlier response of such person is erroneous or incomplete and that such person now has correct or complete location information . . . .

(4) not communicate by post card;

(5) not use any language or symbol on any envelope or in the contents of any communication effected by the mails or telegram that indicates that the debt collector is in the debt collection business or that the communication relates to the collection of a debt; and

(6) after the debt collector knows the consumer is represented by an attorney with regard to the subject debt and has knowledge of, or can readily ascertain, such attorney's name and address, not communicate with any person other than that attorney, unless the attorney fails to respond within a reasonable period of time to communication from the debt collector.

§805.   Communication in Connection with Debt Collection

(a) Communication with the Consumer Generally. — Without the prior consent of the consumer given directly to the debt collector or the express permission of a court of competent jurisdiction, a debt collector may not communicate with a consumer in connection with the collection of any debt —

(1) at any unusual time or place or a time or place known or which should be known to be inconvenient to the consumer. In the absence

of knowledge of circumstances to the contrary, a debt collector shall assume that the convenient time for communicating with a consumer is after 8 o'clock [ante meridian] and before 9 o'clock [post meridian], local time at the consumer's location;

(2) if the debt collector knows the consumer is represented by an attorney with respect to such debt and has knowledge of, or can readily ascertain, such attorney's name and address, unless the attorney fails to respond within a reasonable period of time to a communication from the debt collector or unless the attorney consents to direct communication with the consumer; or

(3) at the consumer's place of employment if the debt collector knows or has reason to know that the consumer's employer prohibits the consumer from receiving such communication.

(b) Communication with Third Parties — Except as provided in section 804, without the prior consent of the consumer given directly to the debt collector, or the express permission of a court of competent jurisdiction, or as reasonably necessary to effectuate a post-judgment judicial remedy, a debt collector may not communicate, in connection with the collection of any debt, with any person other than the consumer, his attorney, a consumer reporting agency if otherwise permitted by law, the creditor, the attorney of the creditor, or the attorney of the debt collector. . . .

§806.   Harassment or Abuse

A debt collector may not engage in any conduct the natural consequence of which is to harass, oppress, or abuse any person in connection with the collection of a debt. Without limiting the general application of the foregoing, the following conduct is a violation of this section:

(1) The use or threat of use of violence or other criminal means to harm the physical person, reputation, or property of any person.

(2) The use of obscene or profane language or language the natural consequence of which is to abuse the hearer or reader.

(3) The publication of a list of consumers who allegedly refuse to pay debts, except to a consumer reporting agency or to persons meeting the requirements of section 603(f) or 604(3) of this Act.

(4) The advertisement for sale of any debt to coerce payment of the debt.

(5) Causing a telephone to ring or engaging any person in telephone conversation repeatedly or continuously with intent to annoy, abuse, or harass any person at the called number.

(6) Except as provided in section 804, the placement of telephone calls without meaningful disclosure of the caller's identity.

§807.   False or Misleading Representations

A debt collector may not use any false, deceptive, or misleading representation or means in connection with the collection of any debt.

Without limiting the general application of the foregoing, the following conduct is a violation of this section:

(1) The false representation or implication that the debt collector is vouched for, bonded by, or affiliated with the United States or any State, including the use of any badge, uniform, or facsimile thereof.

(2) The false representation of —

(A) the character, amount, or legal status of any debt; or

(B) any services rendered or compensation which may be lawfully received by any debt collector for the collection of a debt.

(3) The false representation or implication that any individual is an attorney or that any communication is from an attorney.

(4) The representation or implication that nonpayment of any debt will result in the arrest or imprisonment of any person or the seizure, garnishment, attachment, or sale of any property or wages of any person unless such action is lawful and the debt collector or creditor intends to take such action.

(5) The threat to take any action that cannot legally be taken or that is not intended to be taken.

(6) The false representation or implication that a sale, referral, or other transfer of any interest in a debt shall cause the consumer to

(A) lose any claim or defense to payment of the debt; or

(B) become subject to any practice prohibited by this title.

(7) The false representation or implication that the consumer committed any crime or other conduct in order to disgrace the consumer.

(8) Communicating or threatening to communicate to any person credit information which is known or which should be known to be false, including the failure to communicate that a disputed debt is disputed.

(9) The use or distribution of any written communication which simulates or is falsely represented to be a document authorized, issued, or approved by any court, official, or agency of the United States or any State, or which creates a false impression as to its source, authorization, or approval.

(10) The use of any false representation or deceptive means to collect or attempt to collect any debt or to obtain information concerning a consumer....

§808.   Unfair Practices

A debt collector may not use unfair or unconscionable means to collect or attempt to collect any debt. Without limiting the general application of the foregoing, the following conduct is a violation of this section:

(1) The collection of any amount (including any interest, fee, charge, or expense incidental to the principal obligation) unless such amount is expressly authorized by the agreement creating the debt or permitted by law.

(2) The acceptance by a debt collector from any person of a check or other payment instrument postdated by more than five days unless such

person is notified in writing of the debt collector's intent to deposit such check or instrument not more than ten nor less than three business days prior to such deposit.

(3) The solicitation by a debt collector of any postdated check or other postdated payment instrument for the purpose of threatening or instituting criminal prosecution.

(4) Depositing or threatening to deposit any postdated check or other postdated payment instrument prior to the date on such check or instrument.

(5) Causing charges to be made to any person for communications by concealment of the true purpose of the communication. Such charges include, but are not limited to, collect telephone calls and telegram fees.

(6) Taking or threatening to take any nonjudicial action to effect dispossession or disablement of property if —

(A) there is no present right to possession of the property claimed as collateral through an enforceable security interest;

(B) there is no present intention to take possession of the property; or

(C) the property is exempt by law from such dispossession or disablement.

(7) Communicating with a consumer regarding a debt by postcard.

(8) Using any language or symbol, other than the debt collector's address, on any envelope when communicating with a consumer by use of the mails or by telegram, except that a debt collector may use his business name if such name does not indicate that he is in the debt collection business.

═══════════════

The omitted provisions include a requirement that collection agencies verify the accuracy of debt information and a restriction on the ability of collection agencies to bring lawsuits in fora far from the debtor. The act also provides for both FTC and private enforcement, with the recovery of actual damages, costs, and $1,000 for violations.

Attorneys' cool observation of the application of various consumer protection laws, including the Fair Debt Collection Practices Act, became a little less detached in 1995 when the Supreme Court announced that one of the groups the public would be protected from were the attorneys themselves. The following case produced a whole new round of CLE programs in which the lawyers took very careful notes.

══════════ **HEINTZ v. JENKINS** ══════════
514 U.S. 291 (1995)

BREYER, J., delivered the opinion for a unanimous Court.

The issue before us is whether the term "debt collector" in the Fair Debt Collection Practices Act, 91 Stat. 874, 15 U.S.C. §§1692-1692o (1988 ed. and Supp. V), applies to a lawyer who "regularly," through litigation, tries to collect consumer debts. The Court of Appeals for the Seventh Circuit held that it does. We agree with the Seventh Circuit and we affirm its judgment....

The plaintiff in this case, Darlene Jenkins, borrowed money from the Gainer Bank in order to buy a car. She defaulted on her loan. The bank's law firm then sued Jenkins in state court to recover the balance due. As part of an effort to settle the suit, a lawyer with that law firm, George Heintz, wrote to Jenkins's lawyer. His letter, in listing the amount she owed under the loan agreement, included $4,173 owed for insurance, bought by the bank because she had not kept the car insured as she had promised to do.

Jenkins then brought this Fair Debt Collection Practices Act suit against Heintz and his firm. She claimed that Heintz's letter violated the Act's prohibitions against trying to collect an amount not "authorized by the agreement creating the debt," §1692f(1), and against making a "false representation of . . . the . . . amount . . . of any debt," §1692e(2)(A). The loan agreement, she conceded, required her to keep the car insured "against loss or damage" and permitted the bank to buy such insurance to protect the car should she fail to do so. App. to Pet. for Cert. 17. But, she said, the $4,137 [sic] substitute policy was not the kind of policy the loan agreement had in mind, for it insured the bank not only against "loss or damage" but also against her failure to repay the bank's car loan. Hence, Heintz's "representation" about the "amount" of her "debt" was "false"; amounted to an effort to collect an "amount" not "authorized" by the loan agreement; and thus violated the Act....

There are two rather strong reasons for believing that the Act applies to the litigating activities of lawyers. First, the Act defines the "debt collectors" to whom it applies as including those who "regularly collect or attempt to collect, directly or indirectly, [consumer] debts owed or due or asserted to be owed or due another." §1692a(6). In ordinary English, a lawyer who regularly tries to obtain payment of consumer debts through legal proceedings is a lawyer who regularly "attempts" to "collect" those consumer debts. See, e.g., Black's Law Dictionary 263 (6th ed. 1990) ("To collect a debt or claim is to obtain payment or liquidation of it, either by personal solicitation or legal proceedings.").

Second, in 1977, Congress enacted an earlier version of this statute, which contained an express exemption for lawyers. That exemption said that the term "debt collector" did not include "any attorney-at-law collecting a debt as an attorney on behalf of and in the name of a client." Pub. L. 95-109, §803(6)(F), 91 Stat. 874, 875. In 1986, however, Congress repealed this exemption in its entirety, without creating a narrower, litigation-related, exemption to fill the void. Without more, then, one would think that Congress intended that lawyers be subject to the Act whenever they meet the general "debt collector" definition.

Heintz argues that we should nonetheless read the statute as containing an implied exemption for those debt-collecting activities of lawyers that consist of litigating (including, he assumes, settlement efforts). He relies primarily on three arguments.

First, Heintz argues that many of the Act's requirements, if applied directly to litigating activities, will create harmfully anomalous results that Congress simply could not have intended. We address this argument in light of the fact that, when Congress first wrote the Act's substantive provisions, it had for the most part exempted litigating attorneys from the Act's coverage; that, when Congress later repealed the attorney exemption, it did not revisit the wording of these substantive provisions; and that, for these reasons, some awkwardness is understandable. Particularly when read in this light, we find Heintz's argument unconvincing.

Many of Heintz's "anomalies" are not particularly anomalous. For example, the Sixth Circuit pointed to §1692e(5), which forbids a "debt collector" to make any "threat to take action that cannot legally be taken." The court reasoned that, were the Act to apply to litigating activities, this provision automatically would make liable any litigating lawyer who brought, and then lost, a claim against a debtor. But, the Act says explicitly that a "debt collector" may not be held liable if he "shows by a preponderance of evidence that the violation was not intentional and resulted from a bona fide error notwithstanding the maintenance of procedures reasonably adapted to avoid any such error." §1692k(c). Thus, even if we were to assume that the suggested reading of §1692e(5) is correct, we would not find the result so absurd as to warrant implying an exemption for litigating lawyers. In any event, the assumption would seem unnecessary, for we do not see how the fact that a lawsuit turns out ultimately to be unsuccessful could, by itself, make the bringing of it an "action that cannot legally be taken."

The remaining significant "anomalies" similarly depend for their persuasive force upon readings that courts seem unlikely to endorse. For example, Heintz's strongest "anomaly" argument focuses upon the Act's provisions governing "communication in connection with debt collection." §1692c. One of those provisions requires a "debt collector" not to "communicate further" with a consumer who "notifies" the "debt collector" that he or she "refuses to pay" or wishes the debt collector to "cease further communication." §1692c(c). In light of this provision, asks Heintz, how can an attorney file a lawsuit against (and thereby communicate with) a nonconsenting consumer or file a motion for summary judgment against that consumer?

We agree with Heintz that it would be odd if the Act empowered a debt-owing consumer to stop the "communications" inherent in an ordinary lawsuit and thereby cause an ordinary debt-collecting lawsuit to grind to a halt. But, it is not necessary to read §1692c(c) in that way — if only because that provision has exceptions that permit communications "to notify the consumer that the debt collector or creditor may invoke" or "intends to invoke" a "specified remedy" (of a kind "ordinarily invoked by [the] debt collector or creditor"). §§1692c(c)(2), (3). Courts can read these exceptions, plausibly, to imply that they authorize the actual invocation of the remedy that the collector "intends to invoke." The language permits such a reading, for an ordinary court-related document does, in fact, "notify" its recipient that the creditor may "invoke" a judicial remedy. Moreover, the interpretation is consistent with the statute's apparent objective of preserving creditors' judicial remedies. We need not authoritatively interpret the Act's conduct-regulating provisions now, however. Rather, we rest our conclusions upon the fact that it is easier to read §1692c(c) as containing some such additional, implicit, exception than to believe that Congress intended, silently and implicitly, to create a far broader exception, for all litigating attorneys, from the Act itself.

Second, Heintz points to a statement of Congressman Frank Annunzio, one of the sponsors of the 1986 amendment that removed from the Act the language creating a blanket exemption for lawyers. Representative Annunzio stated that, despite the exemption's removal, the Act still would not apply to lawyers' litigating activities. Representative Annunzio said that the Act "regulates debt collection, not the practice of law. Congress repealed the attorney exemption to the act, not because of attorney[s'] conduct in the courtroom, but because of their conduct in the backroom. Only collection activities, not legal activities, are covered by the act.... The act applies to attorneys when they are collecting debts, not when they are performing tasks of a legal nature.... The act only regulates the conduct of debt collectors, it does not prevent creditors, through their attorneys, from pursuing any legal remedies available to them." 132 Cong. Rec. 30842 (1986). This statement, however, does not persuade us.

For one thing, the plain language of the Act itself says nothing about retaining the exemption in respect to litigation. The line the statement seeks to draw between "legal" activities and "debt collection" activities was not necessarily apparent to those who debated the legislation, for litigating, at first blush, seems simply one way of collecting a debt. For another thing, when Congress considered the Act, other Congressmen expressed fear that repeal would limit lawyers' "ability to contact third parties in order to facilitate settlements" and "could very easily interfere with a client's right to pursue judicial remedies." H.R. Rep. No. 99-405, p.11 (1985) (dissenting views of Rep. Hiler). They proposed alternative language designed to keep litigation activities outside the Act's scope, but that language was not enacted. Ibid. Further, Congressman Annunzio made his statement not during the legislative process, but after the statute became law. It therefore is not a statement upon which other legislators might have relied in voting for or against the Act, but it simply represents the views of one informed person on an issue about which others may (or may not) have thought differently....

For these reasons, we agree with the Seventh Circuit that the Act applies to attorneys who "regularly" engage in consumer-debt-collection activity, even when that activity consists of litigation. Its judgment is therefore affirmed.

═══════════════

Lawyers have complained about the penetration of the FDCPA into routine legal work. In Young v. Citicorp Retail Services, No. 97-9397 (2d Cir., June 29, 1998) (unpublished) the court determined that the lawyer who "oversaw" the collection letters that bore her name and office stationery but that were sent from her office at Citicorp were not "from" the lawyer but were, instead, from Citicorp using the name of another. As a result, Citicorp was subject to the FDCPA and, along with the lawyer, in violation of the FDCPA because of its intent to mislead the debtor into believing the matter had been referred to an attorney for collection. The Seventh Circuit has gone further, by a vote of 6-4 *en banc,* holding that when the law firm's first "communication" with the debtor was a summons and complaint in a lawsuit, the firm was obligated as a debt collector to furnish a "debt validation notice," a statutory notice that advises consumers of certain rights. Thomas v. Simpson & Cybak, 392 F.3d 914 (7th Cir. 2004). On the other hand, a district court has held that a firm whose consumer debt collection activities were less than 5 percent of its cases is not a debt collector within the Act. Camara v. Fleury, 285 F.Supp. 2d 90 (D. Mass. 2003).

Others in the legal profession are content to let collections lawyers sweat out the FDCPA, but they wonder if the provisions could reach into other parts of their practice. Lawyers pressed Congress for an exception to the Act for litigation, and a bill made it to the Senate in 1998 that would have made such an adjustment, but the bill failed to become law.

Even with the Fair Debt Collection Practices Act firmly in place, some debt collectors seem to find effective and creative methods of collection. The following stories indicate some of the more original approaches.

Collection Agency Headed by "Thugs" Helps Merchants

Davenport, Ia. (UPI) — Quad Cities' businessmen, burdened with bundles of bad checks by the faltering economy, are turning to an unconventional collection agency with a pair of tough-looking hombres at the helm.

Dressed in leather jackets over Harley-Davidson T-shirts, Kenneth Fitzpatrick and Maurice Holst don't look like modern entrepreneurs.

But just let someone dare to not pay up on a rubber check. That's when Fitzpatrick, better known as Doc, pushes back the bandanna tied around his head, reaches into his jacket and whips out a worn copy of the Iowa Code.

While he explains the state's penalties for passing bad checks, Holst, who prefers to be called Trammp, scowls and looks menacing. A person might easily get the impression that they'll knock the garbage cans over on the way out.

But they don't. They may look like "Easy Riders," but they never use violence or threatening language. Folks seem to be scared of them anyway and cough up the requested money.

"One person even ran next door to borrow the money to make good on a check," Trammp said.

Local businessmen have welcomed the crusty, street-smart pair with open arms. In less than two months, 2 Outlaws Check Collecting Service has grown into a thriving business.

"They're happy to see us," Doc said of the clients. "They say we're just what they're looking for. It's a crazy world out there where people are scared to collect money for themselves."

"They have to manage their business," Trammp said. "They don't have time for collecting bad checks."

Doc got the idea for the business while working for a liquor store in California, where he made a little extra money collecting the store's bad checks.

Then when he moved to Iowa and ran into money problems with a broken leg, he bounced a few checks of his own.

"I noticed that all these people (collection agencies) do is call you," he said. "That didn't scare me."

Dressed for success: Davenport, Ia., bill collectors Maurice Holst (left front), Ken Fitzpatrick (second from right), and their associates show off their Hell's Angels regalia and Harley Davidsons.

Doc and Trammp decided they could do better. After checking the legalities of such an enterprise, the pair registered their trade name with the Scott County Recorder's Office, printed up business cards and went to work.

"We gave one business card to an alderman and I guess he was pretty shook up about it," Trammp said, describing the reaction of Davenport councilman Larry d'Autremont, who runs a medical supply store.

"They didn't do anything to me," d'Autremont confided. "But they scared the hell out of me."

Doc said the pair started out collecting a $5 check for a local restaurant, but since then, "things started to snowball." About 10 friends have joined the business, which blossomed into rent collection and unpaid charge accounts.

"We work in pairs," Doc said. "That protects us as well. We don't want anybody saying we threatened them."

The collectors begin with a courteous telephone call.

"Most of the time the people say they'll pay up and send a check in the mail," he said. "Maybe 15 to 20 percent will pay just on a phone call. But sometimes you have to investigate them, if they've skipped town or something."

If a phone call doesn't work, Doc and Trammp show up on the offender's doorstep for a personal visit. Sometimes it takes more than one visit, or more than two people.

If that fails, they may institute legal action by filing a suit in small claims court or — if there is a large amount of money involved — talk the county prosecutor into filing criminal charges.

For their services, 2 Outlaws receives half of whatever they collect, whether it is a $5 check or a $1,000 charge account.

"Most people are happy to give it to us," Trammp said. "Half is better than nothing."...[*Daily Iowan*, Apr. 12, 1982, at p.8B.]

But the 2 Outlaws are pussy cats, relatively speaking.

Lawyer's Methods, Debtors' Nightmare

Edwina Rizzo vividly remembers the day her husband was on life support waiting for a heart transplant and Steven B. Zats called demanding payment of an overdue cable television bill.

Rizzo, of Havertown, says she explained her husband's critical condition and the bill collector replied: "Hey, people get sick and die every day. That's not my problem."

Zats told her in another conversation, she says, to bring payment to his office without delay. "You crawl, you walk, you get a bus," Rizzo remembers him saying, "you do whatever you can to get here."

And that, according to many who have dealt with him, is vintage Steven Zats.

A slender man who dresses in sneakers, blue jeans, and T-shirts, Zats, 33, is perhaps the most aggressive — and some say the most unmerciful — small debt collector in the Philadelphia region.

Many of the debtors Zats pursues are poor, unemployed, or disabled. Their debts often involve a single unpaid bill — usually a disputed payment for medical services. Most of his 600 clients are doctors, dentists, or health-care firms.

Zats, a lawyer, routinely obtains judgments against them, freezes their bank accounts, and adds his own fees to their debts, driving up costs hundreds of dollars....

"I was gullible, all right!" says Viola Hartman, of Kensington [a Legal Services client]. "They called and said it was a survey on banks and all this."

Hartman is 63 and a widow. She works as a part-time housekeeper in a Philadelphia public school.

She owed $1,500 for a laser surgery bill which she believed her insurance was supposed to pay.

It didn't.

Zats sued to collect.

When someone from [Zats' corporation] called earlier this year [posing as a telephone survey company], Hartman disclosed that she banked at CoreStates Bank.

In February, Zats froze her account there and cleaned it out.

Hartman bounced checks for her water and telephone bills.

"I didn't even know that they could do such a thing to you," she said. "I'm two months behind on everything now because of it. I'm behind in my mortgage, my gas bill . . . ." [*Philadelphia Inquirer*, June 12, 1994, at pp.A1 and A8.]

Mr. Zats declined to be interviewed for this story, but one of the debtors furnished a letter from Mr. Zats. He wrote: "My goal in business is to please my clients, not to please the debtors. Debtors don't like to have their bank accounts frozen and their personal belongings sold to satisfy the debts. Since the debtors have not been concerned with paying the bill . . . my office cannot be concerned if the debtors can't pay their rent because of a frozen bank account."

Publicity did not help Mr. Zats. A federal prosecutor got interested, and Mr. Zats and his sister Jodi were indicted by a grand jury with eleven counts of mail fraud related to the embezzlement from his clients and four counts of tax evasion. Both entered plea agreements.

Of course, insensitivity and slick tricks are not the monopoly of creditors in this dog-eat-dog game. The following story illustrates that some debtors are willing to go to a lot more effort to evade their debts.

King of Deadbeat Dads Due in Court Today

New York — Jeffrey Nichols is king of the deadbeat dads, owing more than a half-million dollars in support for his three children.

He had tried to hide himself and his money in Florida, Vermont, and Canada, and had set up a bank account in the Bahamas.

He even had denied fathering the daughter and two sons born during the 16 years he lived with his ex-wife.

While there are 7 million cases of parents failing to pay court-ordered child support, Nichols is one of an elite 77 deadbeats whose offenses are so egregious that the federal government has intervened.

He was arrested on a federal warrant last week at his home in Charlotte, Vt. But he was allowed to go free, and he's supposed to bring himself back to Manhattan for a federal court hearing today.

"I've heard of people owing a few hundred thousand," said Elaine Fromm, president of the Organization for the Enforcement of Child Support. "But a half-million? This is the biggest."

Nichols' ex-wife, Marilyn Nichols Kane, said his behavior nearly put her on welfare.

"There was a time when I was six months in arrears on rent, and he was keeping the cash reimbursements for the children's medical expenses," she recalled. "He'd cashed out our life insurance policies, dissipated our retirement funds, and taken our car to Canada."

She is happily remarried and has a career in real estate.

Nichols, an investment adviser on commodities and precious metals, walked out on her and the children in Manhattan in 1990.

She tracked him to Florida, to Ontario, and then to Vermont. And when his second wife filed for divorce, she included an affidavit documenting the lengths to which he had gone to hide income from his first wife.

Nichols' attorney, Mark Kaplan, did not return a phone call.

New York officials lacked authority to have Nichols arrested elsewhere. Vermont initiated its own case, but did not get him to pay up.

Suzanne Colt, who handles child support cases for New York City, finally asked the federal government to intervene under the Child Support Recovery Act of 1992. Nichols was charged with crossing state lines to evade child support, which carries a $5,000 fine and six months in jail.

While Colt is glad the Feds helped out, she complained that their intervention is "pitifully rare."

Assistant U.S. Attorney General Andrew Fois said the federal government can't be expected to take over the tens of thousands of support cases in which a child lives in one state and the parent lives in another.

Nichols' second wife, who never carried out her threatened divorce, died several weeks ago of cancer. She left behind two adopted children.

"He may already be in Canada," Colt said. "He's done it before. Frankly, I'll be amazed if he's in court on Monday." [*Philadelphia Inquirer*, August 14, 1995, at p.A-3.]

Mr. Nichols spent four months in jail in 1995 and another three months in 1996 before he dropped off the news service radar screens. The extraordinary remedy of incarceration is available only to a limited class of creditors — an ex-spouse and minor children.

Since Mr. Nichols was crowned "King of the Deadbeat Dads," others have vied for the title, including a 51-year-old Queens father of three who allegedly ran his various business interests from a jailhouse pay phone and has stayed in prison for more than two months while he refused to pay court-ordered support. Matrimonial Judge Jacqueline Silbermann explains that in almost every case, a few hours or days in jail "shakes the money loose," but we note that some deadbeats are dedicated to their craft.

Problem Set 1

1.1. After graduation from law school you spent two years in a big firm doing SEC securities registration statements. You began to feel like an idiot savant, and you decided that there had to be more variety and interest to the practice of law. So you and two old classmates (one who had hibernated in the library for a litigation department and one who had taken rich people to lunch for a trust and wills department) opened up a general practice firm.

The firm has been in existence for over a year now, and it is becoming solidly established. Over lunch one day, you and your partners reflect on the nature of your practice. It seems that the bulk of your clients are not disputing whether money is owed (ah, those lovely contract and tort hypos you mastered in law school); instead they are engaged in either trying to make someone pay money or trying to avoid paying money themselves. You recognize that much of your time is spent guiding clients in coercing or avoiding payment.

Chatting over lunch today, the three of you are once again exchanging horror stories (as all lawyers do) about what the client didn't tell you and how terrible your legal advice turned out to be because of the key fact the client didn't reveal. You tell of hearing in a deposition for the first time that your debtor-client had a huge asset his creditors could grab or that your creditor-client was about to push a debtor into a bankruptcy, not realizing bankruptcy would invalidate an important security interest your client held in one of the debtor's assets.

This conversation leads you and your partners to revise your standard interview form. Your current form includes a typical question asking debtors to list assets and liabilities. You believe your clients really intend to make a full disclosure to you, but you find that many people do not recognize immediately where they may owe money or where they may have unrealized assets. You conclude that a more particularized list might trigger more complete information from your clients, so you and your partners decide to compile lists of potential debts and assets for both consumer and business clients. What is on each list?

1.2. You work for a major firm in a large city. One of the firm's most important clients is Security Bank. Security is having trouble with collection of an unsecured loan of $83,366 from a local physician, Janille Talis. The firm has asked you to help the bank determine what is the wisest course of action with Talis.

Talis is a pathologist employed by Community Hospital. Her take-home salary is $12,500 per month. She owes $1200 per month to your client. She spends about $1,800 on food, utilities, dry cleaning, and other day-to-day expenses. Her monthly payments are listed below. Her credit report has no late payments, except to Security Bank.

Central Bank, home mortgage	$4,200
USA Savings, car loan	$650
Health Insurance	$950
Pam Harris, veterinarian	$175
Robbie Reich, co-worker	$150
Farmington Country Club, monthly dues	$300
Shell Oil, gasoline card, average monthly	$250
Mastercard, bank card	$400
VISA, bank card	$400
Talbot's Clothing Store	$500
Saks Fifth Avenue Store	$350
John South, alimony payment	$2,325

Before exploring possible legal actions you try to evaluate Security's leverage as it compares with other creditors' positions. Of the creditors on this list, whom is Talis most likely to pay? Why? How can Security try to improve its relative position?

1.3. Mark Watkins has had continuing difficulties with credit charges on his account at Highland Department Store. Apparently, Highland transposed two numbers in recording monthly charges sometime last spring, and it billed Watkins for $4,000 in goods Watkins did not purchase. Watkins notified Highland of the error, but Highland continued to issue bills. After three months Watkins decided he had put enough time into letters and phone calls to Highland and that if they sued he would do all right in court. Watkins simply threw away all correspondence that arrived from Highland and did not go into the store again.

Watkins recently decided to purchase a condominium and he hired you to handle the transaction. When he applied for a mortgage, however, he was turned down. The mortgage company sent him a form letter explaining that he was not "within the range of applicants" to whom the mortgagee made loans.

Watkins, who has a good job and pays his bills on time, was outraged. It suddenly occurred to him that the dispute with Highland could be at the root of his troubles, and he wants you to help him. If Watkins discovers that the credit reporting agency has reported an erroneous version of his difficulties with Highland, what are his remedies? See Fair Credit Reporting Act §§611, 615-617. If Watkins's dispute were for $40 rather than $4,000, what would you advise him?

1.4. The senior partner of your big Wall Street firm explains that one of the pension funds the firm advises is considering a sizeable investment in a payday loan company, but in order to assess the value of the investment, it wants an opinion from the firm that the practices of the company are generally in accord with the law. The partner hands you a copy of a May 31, 2000, story in the *Christian Science Monitor* that begins: "Kesha Gray needed $100 fast. Her credit-cards were at their limit, she had no home equity to fall back on, and her daughter's day-care bill was due. She saw only one alternative. She went to a 'payday lender' and wrote a check for $162, post-dated for two weeks — when she was due to get a paycheck. When two weeks rolled around, more-pressing bills gobbled up her paycheck, and she couldn't muster the $162 she owed. Instead, she paid a $15 fee to roll over the loan. Two weeks later, she paid the debt. Total annualized interest rate 924 percent." Although 14 states outlaw payday loans, the industry reports 20,000 outlets and $40 billion in loans outstanding.

Another publication quoted a typical collection letter:

> "We have contacted the city of Chicago police department. They are aware of your bad check with nationwide budget finance. It is a felony to write a bad check in the state of Illinois. Your failure to respond to this notice within 72 hours will result in us applying for a warrant for your arrest."

The senior partner knows that you will want to review individual practices in detail, but she asks first for your general assessment and an outline of your initial approach. See FDCPA §§803-808.

1.5. Discount retailer K-Market has worked out a collection arrangement with Fiddle Collections. K-Market gives Fiddle all its bad checks, and Fiddle returns 85 percent of everything it collects to K-Market (a much higher percentage than the 50 percent return that is standard in the industry). Fiddle manages this by charging the K-Market customers who bounced a check a fee for its collection efforts, over and above the amount of the check. The fees range from $50 to $400, depending on the amount of work involved, and they give Fiddle a lucrative business. Fiddle consults your company for a "legal check up." You have given them advice about the importance of following the FDCPA rules generally. Is there anything else you need to discuss?

1.6. You decided to forsake the lure of the big firm and go with a small firm in Columbus. You like the eight partners in the firm, and you are eager to make yourself useful. The firm has carved out a practice in what the partners call "Main Street" law — real estate closings, car accidents, contract disputes, unpaid bills for local businesses, and so forth.

Last month you received an assignment for Ms. Chalmers, who owns a small house that she rents out. She is upset that a tenant moved out and left about $2,000 worth of damages beyond the security deposit. You reviewed the case and sent out one of the firm's standard form letters outlining the damages claimed by the client, demanding a quick resolution, and indicating that you will take immediate legal action, including a lawsuit, if the outstanding amount isn't paid promptly. You were shocked to receive a letter this morning from Ms. Chalmers' former tenant charging you with violations of the FDCPA and agreeing to settle the matter if Ms. Chalmers will drop all claims. You do a little investigating and discover that the former tenant is a third-year law student. (It now occurs to you why no one wanted to rent to you when you were in law school.) What should you do?

CHAPTER 2

STATE LAW DEBT COLLECTION

A. COLLECTION REMEDIES

1. *Introduction to Judgment Collection*

When a creditor pursues collection through the court system, the first step is to establish in court that the debt is owed. This may involve a complex trial, rich with factual and doctrinal issues of contract, tort, antitrust, or the like. Then again, the court process may be the more abbreviated UCC Article 3 suit on a check or other negotiable instrument. Or the court process may be a default judgment obtained by the debtor's failure to appear or with a confession of judgment signed by the debtor sometime earlier. In any case, three years of law school have prepared the attorney to master the elements of getting a judgment.

Yet that same attorney may have no idea of what to do if the losing defendant ("judgment debtor") fails to write out a check for the judgment. The attorney may be utterly flummoxed when faced with an enforcement problem in practice, in part because of the strange terminology involved.

The basics of the judgment collection process are quite simple. An introductory caveat is nonetheless in order. The terminology in this area is arcane and varies greatly from state to state, with different words used to describe the same procedures. The details of the rules also vary greatly, and in any particular jurisdiction authority may be scarce and opaque. The object here is to introduce the most frequently used terms and to identify the issues that routinely arise, rather than to survey all the varying results.

We will look primarily at post-judgment collection devices to work through the basics of the process. At the end of this section, we will touch briefly on the remedies available while a lawsuit is pending.

a. Execution

It is important to understand at the outset that the rendition of a judgment in itself produces only a document suitable for framing. The judgment gives the successful plaintiff (now known as the "judgment creditor")

33

no interest and no priority in any of the debtor's property or income. The judgment creditor remains an unsecured ("general") creditor until "execution" is obtained on the judgment. ~~The only improvement in the judgment creditor's position is that the claim has become indisputable by the debtor, that is, it has become "liquidated."~~

The collection process begins with a "writ," which is simply a court order. The first type of writ that concerns us is called an "execution writ" or a writ *fi. fa.* (pronounced "fi fay," from *fieri facias*) or a "writ of attachment." The writ orders the sheriff or marshal to look for non-exempt property of the judgment debtor, to seize it, to sell it, and to pay the proceeds to the judgment creditor, until the judgment is fully paid. The writ is issued routinely by the court clerk upon request of the judgment creditor and is delivered to the sheriff for "execution."

Once the writ is delivered, the sheriff climbs into a pickup truck and goes looking for the debtor's property. Often in practice the lawyer for the judgment creditor will tell the sheriff where to look and may even go along. Ordinarily the sheriff will take physical possession of any property found (e.g., a stereo, a car, some tools), put it in the pickup, and lock it up back at the courthouse. If personal property cannot be seized immediately (e.g., because it is too big for the pickup), the sheriff may tag it with a notice of seizure. Since real property can never be loaded into the pickup, it is always seized by "posting" notice of seizure and sale or some similar method. The entire process of seizure is often called a "levy" and what the sheriff does is "to levy upon" the property. The whole process, from writ issuance to seizure, is often called an "execution." Once the sheriff has seized the property, actually or constructively, it is said to be in the custody of the court or ~~in *custodia legis*~~.

The writ will tell the sheriff to report to the court with a document called a "return," which describes the sheriff's efforts to find property of the debtor. If no property has been found, the sheriff's return may state "nulla bona."

Once the sheriff has levied upon a specific piece of the debtor's property, ~~the judgment creditor becomes a "judicial lien creditor"~~ *as to that property* (such a creditor is often called a "lien creditor" for short). After levy the sheriff will advertise the property for public sale and sell it to the highest bidder. The proceeds of the sale will then be paid to the levying judgment creditor until the creditor is paid in full. Any remaining proceeds will be paid back to the judgment debtor, unless some subsequent judgment creditor levied symbolically upon the property while it was stored at the courthouse. An entry is made in the judgment record noting the partial or complete satisfaction of the judgment. If the proceeds are insufficient to pay the judgment in full, then the sheriff will be commanded to look for more of the debtor's property to seize, and the process will start over.

b.   Turnover Orders

In a modern urban society, the traditional writs have become unsatisfactory. Judgment debtors have property scattered all over the nation and even all over the world. Much of their wealth is not in land or equipment, but in intangible assets for which the traditional remedies work haltingly, if at all. One result has been the adoption in many states of "turnover" statutes. The operation of a fairly typical statute was explained in a 1997 Texas case: *Turnover Statute*

> ...The judgment debtor may be ordered to turn over property he possesses. The judgment debtor can also be ordered to turn over property, no matter who possesses it, if the property is subject to his control. §31.002. The debtor risks imprisonment for contempt if he does not comply. Id.; cf. Ex parte Ramzy, 424 S.W.2d 220, 225-226 (Tex. 1968) (order of contempt for not returning coins upheld as to coins realtor had allegedly given to his children, but reversed as to coins resold by purchaser); Ex parte Green, 603 S.W.2d 216, 217-218 (Tex. 1980) (realtor could not be held in contempt for continued operation of brothel because no evidence showed he exercised control over operation).... Once property is traced to the debtor, the debtor bears the burden of establishing that certain property is no longer in his or her possession.

Parks v. Parker, 957 S.W.2d 666, 668-669 (Tex. App. 1997).

Notice the considerable advantages of this remedy for the judgment creditor. All it has to do is get the necessary information about the asset. Typically, a turnover statute permits examination of the debtor under oath (with attendance required on pain of contempt), so assets can be found. Once that information is in hand, the debtor can be ordered to produce the property, again under threat of contempt and jail. It is particularly significant that this remedy reintroduces the threat of incarceration into the debtor-creditor game, albeit on a fairly narrow basis. The following story illustrates its operation.

O.J. Simpson Ordered to Give up His Car and Piano

Santa Monica, Calif. (Reuters) — A judge ordered O.J. Simpson Monday to hand over his sport utility vehicle and a piano to help pay off the $33.5 million in damages he owes the families of two murder victims.

An angry Simpson later told reporters the items were gifts from his widowed mother and his sister. "They have a right to spend their money any way they want, and Fred Goldman can't dictate that," he said.

Goldman, whose son, Ronald, was murdered in 1994 along with Simpson's former wife, Nicole Brown Simpson, is owed much of the damages the Judge awarded after Simpson was found liable for the deaths in a civil trial that ended this year.

Simpson, a former football player and bit actor, was acquitted of their murders after a highly publicized criminal trial that polarized the country.

He was in court again Monday for a so-called debtor's examination during which lawyers for Goldman asked about his assets to satisfy the judgment.

After the closed-door session, Superior Court Judge David Perez ruled that Simpson's Ford Expedition and his grand piano must be handed over to be sold to pay off some of the $33.5 million in damages.

Earlier, one attorney accused Simpson of making light of the process going on behind closed doors.

"(Simpson) thinks this is a one- or two-month nuisance, that we're just being pests" Gary Carris, who represents Fred Goldman, said. "At one point, he referred to this process as boring."

"This is not a boring process, but it is a long-term process, and Mr. Simpson has to realize that. We're not going away today or tomorrow or the next week or the next month," Carris told reporters.

Simpson says he is broke except for the $16,000 to $17,000 he gets each month from his National Football League pension and other pensions from his two companies.

Court officers recently seized artwork and other valuables, including his 1968 Heisman Trophy as the best college football player, to help pay the damages.

One legal source said lawyers asked Simpson Monday what he did with his pension income, which cannot be touched to satisfy the damage judgment.

"That is none of your business" he reportedly replied during the session, in which he was also asked about his future living arrangements.

Simpson is looking for a new home for himself and his two young children, saying he could afford about $6,000 a month for rent.

Earlier this month, the mansion he owned for 20 years was auctioned off after a savings and loan association foreclosed on it because he had failed to keep up monthly mortgage payments. [Steve James, July 29, 1997.]

c. Other Writs

A variety of other writs are used in various jurisdictions for specific types of property or specific types of claims. For example, many jurisdictions have a writ of "sequestration," which may be used in defined circumstances to seize and hold specific property of the debtor, often property in which the creditor has a security interest. Each state's statutes must be consulted for the details of specific writs.

d. Judgment Liens by Recordation

In nearly every state special recordation procedures exist that make it possible to obtain a lien on a debtor's property quickly and simply, without going through the full-blown execution process just described. In most states these procedures are limited to encumbering the debtor's real estate, but in a handful of states recordation can give a creditor a lien on the debtor's personal property as well.

Judgl. Lien - lien put on debtor's R/E w/in the county.

The "judgment lien" against real property is obtained by recording a judgment in the county land records where deeds of sale and mortgages are filed. (This process is often called "abstracting the judgment" because a summary of the court judgment is actually filed.) The fact of recordation gives the creditor a lien on all of the debtor's real estate located in the county of recordation. In most states the judgment lien also operates against real estate that the debtor may acquire after the judgment is recorded. The judgment lien is available in addition to the execution process.

In most sts. you can't obtain a lien on Pers. Prop. by any form of filing or recordation.

In most states it is not possible to obtain a lien on personal property by any form of filing or recordation. However, a minority of states, including California and Florida, do permit a single filing to put a legally effective lien

- Cali & FL do allow this.

on all the debtor's personal property available for collection anywhere in the state. This recordation process is roughly analogous to a filing of a security interest under Article 9 of the UCC.

Often recording a judgment is the fastest and cheapest post-judgment collection step a creditor can take. Recordation is effective as to the debtor's property even if the creditor spends no time locating or identifying the property. For a nominal filing fee, the creditor effectively ties up the debtor's assets, often preventing any resale because no purchaser would buy property with the title clouded by an earlier judgment lien. As a practical matter, recordation has the greatest effect against real property owners, who cannot move their land to another state and who are unlikely to find a buyer who would not check the local filing records and discover the lien. But creditors in the states recognizing judgment liens against personal property also have some increased leverage by recording a judgment. If debtors find themselves unable to sell personal property or unable to borrow against the property because subsequent buyers or creditors check the public records, those debtors may decide "voluntarily" to settle up on the outstanding debts.

Creditors may see a second benefit from a judgment lien. By recording a judgment and getting a lien against the debtor's property, the judgment creditor can pursue execution at leisure, knowing that in a race against other judgment creditors the recording creditor's position in line has been assured. The judgment creditor who records knows, as to property covered by the recordation, that some later judgment creditor will not be able to swoop in and grab the property just as this creditor reaches for it. Moreover, a judgment lien may give a creditor some protection if the debtor later goes bankrupt, a subject we discuss in much greater detail in Parts II and III.

Creditors often file judgment liens and then wait to see if something turns up. They run some risk of "dormancy" — or even final expiration of the judgment — both of which we discuss in the next section. They also face the obvious risk that the debtor owns no property to be covered by the lien. But for a modest fee the judgment creditor has an *opportunity* to exercise some leverage over a debtor, a more attractive alternative for some creditors than simply waiting and hoping or making more expensive collection attempts.

e. Debt Collection by the Federal Government

For more than 200 years the federal government was satisfied to use the procedures provided by state law, together with some priority and lien advantages, to collect debts owed to it. However, in the wake of the great savings and loan debacle of the 1980s, which left the government holding the bag for billions of dollars, Congress decided to adopt a special set of uniform procedures for collecting debts owed to the federal government. Federal Debt Collection Procedures Act, 104 Stat. 933 (1991), 28 U.S.C.A. §§3001-3308. These procedures are generally similar to those described in this section for collection of debts under state law, so the real point is uniformity. It should be emphasized that the Act does not apply to enforcement of all judgments in federal courts, only to judgments in favor of the federal government.

f. Family Debts

Marriage is an institution with many aspects — social, emotional, spiritual. But it is also a very important financial institution. Other things being equal, married people have a better and more stable economic situation than divorced or single people. Indeed, marriage has been described as "a kind of long-term 'co-insurance' pact between spouses that buffers them against the stresses of life." *Population Today*, June 1995, at 3. The increasing divorce rate and the decline in the marriage rate have left an increasing number of middle-class Americans struggling financially.

The connection between financial difficulty and divorce is revealed in *The Fragile Middle Class*. It shows that bankrupt men and women are far more likely to be divorced and, if divorced, far more likely not to be remarried than Americans generally. Later work shows that single mothers file for bankruptcy at rates that are more than three times higher than debtor households with no children. They also file at rates that are about 50 percent higher than married couples with children. Warren and Tyagi, *The Two-Income Trap*.

Experience has demonstrated that alimony and child support are among the most difficult debts to collect. It has been estimated that less than half of the parents with custody of their children (usually women) are receiving support from the noncustodial parent following divorce. Mr. Nichols (see pp. 27-28) is merely one of the most spectacular examples. In *The Fragile Middle Class*, women in bankruptcy repeatedly cited nonpayment of support as an important cause of their bankruptcies.

In recognition of the importance of family support payments and the difficulty of their enforcement, there have long been specialized rules surrounding collection of this sort of debt. In particular, imprisonment has been retained as an enforcement tool for family support payments, despite the fact that it has been abolished almost everywhere in the United States for all other sorts of debt. Many other special exceptions to debt collection restraints are applicable in the case of family support payments. For example, states often exempt some or all wages from garnishment, but provide an exception for child support. See p. 173 and p. 176 for examples from Texas and Delaware. The Bankruptcy Code also provides special treatment for family support obligations, including major reforms adopted in 1994 and 2005, a matter covered later in this book. As Mr. Nichols learned, federal enforcement legislation, added by the Child Support Recovery Act of 1992, gives ex-spouses more extensive tools for collecting support. In addition, state and federal governments also get involved directly, spending about $3 billion on their own support enforcement efforts.

g. Voluntary Liens

Most of this section deals with judicial collection — the attempt by general creditors to get a judgment and then realize on it by taking some asset of the debtor. Collectively, this system is often referred to as an involuntary lien system because it gives the judgment creditor rights in the debtor's property without any acquiescence or cooperation from the debtor. Before we leave this section, however, it is important to complete the picture of the formal collection system with a very brief overview of the alternative collection system used by many creditors — obtaining mortgages and security interests in the debtor's property. For students who have had a course in real estate financing or in Article 9 of the UCC, this section will be a quick review of what they have already learned about real estate and personal property security, respectively.

Many creditors do not rely on involuntary liens; instead, they make themselves secured creditors by obtaining voluntary liens from their debtors. If a debtor and a creditor can agree in advance of the collection stage to give the creditor a lien against real or personal property, then the creditor has a legally enforceable lien without the assistance (or the resulting expense) of court action. The property on which the debtor grants the lien is called the "collateral." Enforcement of these consensual liens is another important part of the state collection system.

A consensual lien must follow a fairly detailed statutory scheme of agreement and recordation. Consensual liens on real property are usually called "mortgages," and those who lend money and take mortgages are called "mortgagees" or "mortgage lenders." In some states, the local terminology for a consensual lien on real property is a "deed of trust," or "DOT" among the cognoscenti. The law of mortgages is covered in detail in a course on real estate transactions.

Consensual liens on all other property are usually called "security interests." Those who take security interests are called "secured parties" or "secured creditors," as distinct from their creditor counterparts who do not have consensual liens, called "general creditors" or "unsecured creditors." The law of security interests is covered by Article 9 of the Uniform Commercial Code. It too is covered in detail in another course in commercial law.

Most consensual liens require a writing in which the debtor grants the lien and describes the property covered. To protect third parties who may have dealings with the debtor, consensual liens are given legal effect against third parties only if the secured party gives public notice of its interest, usually by some form of recordation in a government office. This filing enables other potential creditors or buyers to find out about the earlier creditor's interest in the property, either directly or through the reports made by credit-reporting services, who search these records routinely. When a creditor has made such a filing, or taken one of the other steps deemed to provide the required public notice, its lien is said to be "perfected" and the making of the filing, or other required step, is called "perfection" of the security interest.

For real estate and most personal property (such as equipment and inventory), recordation is in a county or state filing system where any subsequent creditor or buyer can find out about the interest of the earlier creditor. For some types of collateral, notice is given when the creditor takes possession of the item. (For example, perfection of a security interest in a certificate of deposit or a piece of jewelry can be achieved by taking possession.) Some very special types of collateral have a specialized notice system. (For example, a lien on an automobile can be perfected only by entering it on the certificate of title for that automobile.) The details of notice-giving are fairly complex and exceptions to the various rules abound. But the system generally aims toward an inexpensive and uniform way to inform others who may deal with the debtor about the interest of the creditor who took the consensual lien.

In general, a consensual lien assures the creditor that if the debt is not paid, the lienholder may force the sale of the collateral and use the proceeds to repay its outstanding loan. A consensual lien usually restricts the debtor's disposition of the property, so that the creditor can count on its being available at the time of default. Moreover, a consensual lien will give the secured creditor some ability to "fence off" the property covered by the lien from collection efforts by other creditors. This point is discussed in greater detail in the following section on priorities.

Consensual liens may be "purchase-money liens" — those liens used to furnish the credit necessary for the purchase of the collateral. (These liens are nicknamed "PMSIs" by those in the trade, referring to a Purchase Money Security Interest.) Typically, home mortgages are used to buy houses, car loans are used to buy cars, and the purchases of many kinds of business equipment and home appliances are financed through PMSIs. But debtors also may borrow money and give a lien on property they already own to secure their promises to repay, a "non-PMSI loan." A debtor who owns stock may pledge it to the bank for a cash loan and use the cash in a variety of ways. Many commercial lenders extend operating capital to a company only after taking a consensual lien on all the equipment and other assets the company already owns, instead of limiting themselves only to an interest in the new property to be acquired.

In business transactions, debtors frequently will give a security interest in property they plan to acquire in the future. Typically, the lien will be granted in all the property of a certain type the debtor company owns now and the property of the same type it may acquire in the future. The Article 9 system recognizes such interests, so that a debtor may offer a security interest in "all my equipment, current and after acquired." When the debtor acquires a new piece of equipment, the security interest automatically attaches to the new purchases as well as to the equipment the debtor already owns.

Sometimes more than one creditor may take a consensual lien on a piece of property. One creditor may lend money to help a debtor buy a house and take a mortgage. Some time later the debtor may go to a second creditor to borrow money for a home improvement or a vacation and offer to secure repayment by giving a second mortgage on the home. If there is sufficient value in the home (and a willing supply of creditors), a third mortgage, fourth mortgage, and so on could be placed on property. The same holds true for security interests in personal property, where creditors might take first, second, and third liens on an item if they believed there was sufficient value to justify the effort.

A creditor with a consensual lien often can seize the collateral more quickly and cheaply than a judgment creditor who has to go through all the steps of suit and execution before the sheriff sells the goods. The seizure for sale — called a "foreclosure" in the case of real estate and "repossession" in the case of personalty — is heavily governed by a myriad of state rules that differ in detail but usually cover similar issues.

In some states a mortgage lender must go to court for a decree of foreclosure — a finding by the court that the mortgage is in default and a sale of the property is in order. State law may decree that the creditor then can sell the property, or it may require the sheriff or another official to conduct an auction. In other states the mortgagee may be able to seize and sell the property without the need for court action. In all states detailed regulations govern the notice of foreclosure a mortgagee must give, the details of the conduct of a sale, the time during which the debtor may reclaim the property by paying off the mortgage, and how to get the debtor off the property.

Part Six of revised Article 9 of the UCC governs the seizure and sale of personal property subject to a consensual lien. A creditor with a security interest in personal property has two ways to satisfy the outstanding debt that are not available to the judicial lien creditor: The Article 9 creditor can seize the property without any help from the sheriff ("self-help repossession") or can offer to keep the property in satisfaction of the debt without any sale ("retain in satisfaction"). Both options have some restrictions, including a requirement that self-help repossession not involve a breach of the peace (no fistfights with the debtor, no breaking into the house to grab the property when no one is home). In addition to the special Article 9 remedies, the secured creditor has all the remedies of any other creditor. The secured creditor can sue on the debt, obtain a judgment, and ask the sheriff to seize and sell the collateral.

For both real and personal property, the most important type of dispute that arises in the enforcement process is the problem of a "deficiency judgment." If the collateral is sold for less than the amount still owed on the debt, the difference is called a "deficiency." Because the creditor has exhausted the collateral and thus is effectively unsecured for the amount of the deficiency, it has to sue the debtor for that amount, like any other unsecured creditor. Oftentimes in such a lawsuit the debtor will argue that the sale of collateral was conducted in violation of the complex rules governing such sales and therefore that the debtor should not be responsible for the deficiency. In effect, the debtor claims that if the sale had been conducted properly, the collateral would have sold for enough to pay the whole debt. So, for example, a secured creditor who is owed $10,000 might sell the debtor's inventory at auction for $7,500 and sue the debtor for the $2,500 deficiency. The debtor might defend by claiming that no notice of the sale was given to the debtor, as required by section 9-611 of Article 9 and therefore the creditor should forfeit any right to the remaining $2,500. If the debtor is a consumer and is correct in claiming that proper notice was not given, many states will stick the creditor with the $2,500 deficiency. In non-consumer transactions, there is a presumption against the creditor, but it can be rebutted by showing that the deficiency would have been just as great even if all the procedures had been followed. Section 9-626.

h. Statutory Liens and Trust Funds

In addition to the consensual liens validated by state real estate law and by Article 9 of the UCC, state law also creates liens by operation of law in

Nonconsensual Encumbrances

1) LL's lien
2) Artisan's lien

favor of certain types of creditors. The landlord's lien is perhaps the most common and the most ancient of these nonconsensual encumbrances, but there are many others. One everyday example is the artisan's lien, which is a possessory lien on personal property of the debtor. It entitles a garage mechanic to keep a car until the repair bill is paid or to sell the car if necessary to satisfy the charges. Typically this sort of lien is created by a state statute and the priorities created by such statutes are specifically recognized in Article 9 of the UCC (§9-333).

3) Construction liens

The industry most completely blanketed by statutory liens is construction, where those who provide goods and labor to a prime contractor, and ultimately to a developer, are granted special priorities in the real estate that they help to improve by the construction project. These statutory liens are justified because of the financial volatility of the construction business and the relative lack of legal sophistication of many subcontractors and suppliers, as well as their collective political influence and well-organized trade associations.

The landlord's lien was originally a common law right and remains one in many states. However, most states also have statutes that give a landlord a lien on personal property of the tenant located in the leased premises.

While the foregoing are the most typical statutory liens, every state has a variety of nonconsensual liens in favor of certain creditor groups. One contemporary example is a lien on the proceeds of a personal injury action given to a hospital that treated the plaintiff for those injuries. Closer to home for a law student is the "charging lien," common law or statutory, given to an attorney with respect to the proceeds of a successful litigation.

State laws have also evolved another approach to giving certain creditors special priorities in debtors' property: the trust fund statutes. These statutes make the debtor a "trustee" of certain property for the favored creditors, who, as "beneficiaries" of the statutory trust, effectively get a priority in that property. Most often the property consists of cash or cash equivalents held by the debtor. A common example would be funds paid to a prime contractor by a developer, with the statute making the prime contractor a "trustee" of those funds for the benefit of subcontractors. Of course, as with all priority rules, if the debtor isn't paying, the game is zero-sum. Whatever goes to the beneficiaries of the trust, such as the favored subcontractors, does not go to the general creditors, such as the contractor's own employees.

i.　Property Exempt from the Collection Process

Each state protects some property from seizure. Typical examples are the family home and household goods. Because exemptions are most often important in the context of bankruptcy, we explore them in detail in Chapter 5, along with various contractual devices to protect assets. For now, we just note that there are many approaches to hiding assets from pursuing creditors.

The Wall Street Journal
Copyright (c) 1999, Dow Jones & Company, Inc.
Monday, June 21, 1999
Case of Vanishing Manager and Missing Millions
By Deborah Lohse and Mitchell Pacelle
Staff Reporters of The Wall Street Journal

A cache of burning documents in a hastily abandoned mansion in Greenwich, Conn. A reclusive money manager who has disappeared. At least $218 million, and possibly billions, missing. Money wired to a Swiss bank account. And several insurance companies insolvent and in receivership.

It's all part of a bizarre saga that the Federal Bureau of Investigation and insurance regulators are still trying to unravel.

But what they have discovered so far is worthy of a John Grisham novel. According to the affidavit of an FBI agent filed in federal court in Bridgeport, Conn., the latest chapter of this tangled tale began unfolding on May 5 when a fire alarm sounded at a $3 million contemporary stone home at 889 Lake Ave. in the ultraexclusive "back-country" section of Greenwich, the home and office of Martin R. Frankel.

When firefighters arrived, the home was empty. Two fireplaces were stuffed with burning documents, some of them shredded, a filing cabinet was ablaze in the kitchen, and used fire extinguishers suggested a failed effort to douse the blaze. Among the papers police later rescued from the premises: a handwritten to-do list topped by the task "Launder money." ...

On the other hand, Mr. Frankel was later arrested in Germany, and extradited to the United States, where he is now housed courtesy of the government.

j. Collection in Other Jurisdictions

A host of problems must be faced if it is necessary to enforce a judgment obtained in state *A* (the rendering jurisdiction) against property found in state *B* (the enforcing jurisdiction). Within our own country the process can be difficult, expensive, and frustrating. Enforcement outside the United States is even harder. Nonetheless, enforcement outside the rendering jurisdiction is possible, if the amount involved makes the effort worthwhile. The difficulty of the task is one reason an involuntary bankruptcy may be an attractive alternative for the judgment creditor, since the reach of the bankruptcy court is national and all the debtor's property is effectively "seized" by a single petition. Here we briefly consider the most significant devices used for enforcing judgments outside the rendering jurisdiction.

Common Law. The full faith and credit clause of the Constitution requires each state to recognize and enforce the judgments of sister states, subject to numerous caveats. Even without a statute in the state where enforcement is sought, therefore, a foreign judgment will be given effect. The common law method, which is always available, involves filing a new lawsuit, serving a summons, and so forth. A certified copy of the judgment to be enforced should be attached to the complaint. Once a new "judgment on the judgment" has been obtained, it is enforceable in the enforcing state in the same manner as any other state judgment in that state.

Uniform Enforcement of Foreign Judgments Act. This statute, which has been adopted in a number of states, provides a "registration" system of enforcement, to avoid the necessity of a new lawsuit. While the Uniform Act is helpful, its procedures, especially as modified in some states, are still relatively cumbersome.

Federal Judgments. In general, a Federal District Court judgment is enforceable in the state where it is rendered to the same extent and in the same ways as a judgment of a state court in that state. See 28 U.S.C. §1962 and Fed. R. Civ. P. 64. That judgment can be enforced in other states pursuant to a federal registration scheme. 28 U.S.C. §1963. A certified copy of the judgment filed with a Federal District Court in the enforcing state makes the judgment a judgment of that federal court and therefore enforceable in the state where that federal court is located. The judgment is enforceable even if it is subject to appeal, unless a supersedeas bond has been filed in connection with the appeal, blocking enforcement in the court where it was rendered.

Transnational Enforcement. The United States is not a party to any general convention on the enforcement of judgments transnationally. Our courts, however, have traditionally been quite willing to enforce foreign judgments on the basis of comity and the policies underlying res judicata. Our courts will enforce a foreign judgment if the foreign procedure treated the defendant with fundamental fairness as to the basis of jurisdiction and gave the debtor adequate notice and a fair opportunity to defend, even if the foreign procedure differs substantially from our own. See, e.g., Somportex Ltd. v. Philadelphia Chewing Gum Co., 453 F.2d 435 (3d Cir. 1971), cert. denied, 405 U.S. 1017 (1972).

A substantial debate continues as to whether our federal courts really require a showing of reciprocity for such enforcement, while it seems clear that a majority of states do not. A number of states have adopted the Uniform Foreign Money-Judgments Recognition Act, which provides for enforcement of foreign judgments fairly rendered and does not require a showing of reciprocity.

United States state and federal court judgments have been enforced many times in foreign proceedings. The principal difficulty has been that many foreign courts require a showing of reciprocity. Even though the United States courts are in fact generous in enforcing foreign judgments, many foreign jurisdictions are governed by the civil-law tradition that looks soley to statutes rather than case law for legal rules. They are often reluctant to accept case law decisions that are not supported by a statute. This problem has provided the principal impetus behind adoption of the Uniform Foreign Money-Judgments Act, so that a New York plaintiff, for example, trying to enforce a New York judgment overseas can point to a statute (not merely a case) to prove that New York would enforce a foreign judgment under equivalent circumstances.

The American Law Institute has approved a controversial proposal for a federal statute to preempt the field. American Law Institute, Recognition and Enforcement of Foreign Judgments (2005). While many applaud any effort to make international enforcement of judgments less burdensome, some worry that the ALI proposals will put the United States in the position of enforcing foreign judgments that have few recognized safeguards, while others think that the proposal over-narrows enforcement of foreign judgments, or that the whole subject should be left to state law.

While obtaining recognition of a United States judgment in other countries is important, it is not always necessary to do that in order to collect from assets found outside the United States. Here a Texas court gave a plaintiff effective control over property in Mexico.

═══════════ GERDES v. KENNAMER ═══════════

155 S.W.3d 541 (Corpus Christi App. 2004)

Opinion by Justice CASTILLO.

Appellants Roger Gerdes ("Gerdes") and Carolyn Gerdes (collectively, the "Gerdeses") appeal the terms of a turnover order issued pursuant to section 31.002 of the civil practice and remedies code[1] as well as the trial court's finding of Gerdes' noncompliance with two earlier turnover orders. ****

I.   FACTS AND PROCEDURAL HISTORY

Gerdes is a judgment debtor of Kennamer. Pursuant to section 31.002 of the civil practice and remedies code, the trial court issued three turnover orders to assist Kennamer in collecting the judgment. Tex. Civ. Prac. & Rem. Code Ann. §31.002 (Vernon 1997). On evidence that the Gerdeses each own fifty per cent of a Mexican entity called Inmobiliaria Don Rogelio

---

1. Section 31.002 provides:

(a) A judgment creditor is entitled to aid from a court of appropriate jurisdiction through injunction or other means in order to reach property to obtain satisfaction on the judgment if the judgment debtor owns property, including present or future rights to property, that: (1) cannot readily be attached or levied on by ordinary legal process; and (2) is not exempt from attachment, execution, or seizure for the satisfaction of liabilities.

(b) The court may: (1) order the judgment debtor to turn over the nonexempt property that is in the debtor's possession or is subject to the debtor's control, together with all documents or records related to the property, to a designated sheriff or constable for execution; (2) otherwise apply the property to the satisfaction of the judgment; or (3) appoint a receiver with the authority to take possession of the nonexempt property, sell it, and pay the proceeds to the judgment creditor to the extent required to satisfy the judgment.

(c) The court may enforce the order by contempt proceedings or by other appropriate means in the event of refusal or disobedience.

(d) The judgment creditor may move for the court's assistance under this section in the same proceeding in which the judgment is rendered or in an independent proceeding.

(e) The judgment creditor is entitled to recover reasonable costs, including attorney's fees.

(f) A court may not enter or enforce an order under this section that requires the turnover of the proceeds of, or the disbursement of, property exempt under any statute, including Section 42.0021, Property Code. This subsection does not apply to the enforcement of a child support obligation or a judgment for past due child support.

Tex. Civ. Prac. & Rem. Code Ann. §31.002 (Vernon 1997).

("Don Rogelio"), the trial court issued orders that would effect a turnover of their interest in Don Rogelio. Don Rogelio is valuable because it holds title to a large plot of land in Mexico and represents Kennamer's only avenue to collect on a $915,392.65 judgment against Gerdes. On October 14, 2002, on Kennamer's motion, the trial court signed the first turnover order, requiring Gerdes to turn over to the Matagorda County Sheriff's Department within seven days, "the original stock certificates or any other physical evidence of ownership for all of the shares of stock of (a) Inmobiliaria Don Rogelio S. de RL. de C.V., (b) Hacienda de Aves Inc., and (c) Hacienda de Aves S.A. de C.V. so the same may be sold under execution."

Gerdes produced no documents. On October 28, 2002, the trial court ordered Gerdes to appear on December 2, 2002 to "show cause why he should not be held in contempt for violation of this Court's Turnover Order of October 14, 2002." * * * *

On the same day, the trial court signed the second turnover order, requiring Gerdes to "turn over... any original evidence of ownership of property in the name of Inmobiliaria Don Rogelio S. de R.L. de C.V., including but not limited to [a specific plot of land] so the same may be sold under execution." The trial court then recessed the hearing until January 8, 2003.

When the hearing reconvened, the Kennamers' counsel presented seven documents which, if executed by the Gerdeses, would effect the issuance of the Don Rogelio stock Gerdes claimed was never issued. Also, the documents would authorize the transfer of that stock to the sheriff's office and then to the final purchaser. Over Gerdes's objection that he could not force his wife to sign the documents, the trial court issued a third turnover order requiring Gerdes to deliver originals of the seven documents, executed by both him and his wife, to the Sheriff's office. The order also states "Roger Gerdes, Jr. has failed to comply with the Court's Turnover Order dated October 14, 2002, and the Second Turnover Order dated December 2, 2002." * * * *

II. Standard of Review

Issuance of a turnover order is a statutory remedy grounded in equity. * * * *

III. Analysis

A. *Execution by Carolyn Gerdes*

* * * * Evidence introduced during the trial that resulted in the underlying judgment here showed that the Gerdeses also each owned fifty per cent of Hacienda de Aves, the Texas corporation whose 500 shares Gerdes turned over. Gerdes presented no evidence in response to the turnover order that Carolyn Gerdes's interest in Don Rogelio was not subject to his control. Nor did he tender the documents with his signature only. Accordingly, on these facts we find that the trial court's order that Gerdes deliver originals of documents executed by both himself and his wife to effect a turnover of

ownership in Don Rogelio is not beyond the scope of the turnover statute. *See* Tex. Civ. Prac. & Rem. Code Ann. §31.002(b)(1) (Vernon 1997). * * *

B. Nonexistent Documents

[T]he Gerdeses contend the trial court abused its discretion by ordering them to sign and turn over nonexistent documents. They argue that the Order orders them to turn over "nonexistent documents that were simply made up by the Appellee." They also argue that forcing them to sign the documents is beyond the scope of the trial court's power under the turnover statute.

The evidence before the trial court is undisputed that Roger and Carolyn Gerdes are the sole owners of Don Rogelio, each owning fifty per cent of the company. Contrary to the Gerdeses' assertions, the documents, and the property interest that the documents will effectively convey, exist. The documents comprise seven pages of the appellate record, were in evidence during the hearing, and are included as an appendix in the Gerdeses' own brief. The Gerdeses' argument suggests the relevancy of a line of authority in which trial courts were reversed for ordering debtors to turn over property in spite of a record establishing that the debtors did not possess and had no means of obtaining the property subject to the turnover order. * * * Here, however, the evidence establishes the Gerdeses' ownership interest in Don Rogelio. Gerdes must simply sign the documents, obtain his wife's signature, and deliver the documents to the Sheriff's office. Nothing in the record suggests that Gerdes is unable to comply with the turnover order.

Further, while the turnover statute does not specifically provide that a trial court can compel a judgment debtor to execute documents, the statute does not limit the trial court's powers to ordering only the turnover of property and documents. Rather, the statute provides that a judgment creditor is entitled to aid from a court through injunction "or other means" to reach the debtor's property. *Id.* (citing Tex. Civ. Prac. & Rem. Code Ann. §31.002 (Vernon 1986)). A trial court has authority to compel a debtor to execute documents that will aid in collecting a judgment debt. Accordingly, we hold that the trial court acted in conformity with guiding legal principles and did not abuse its discretion by ordering Gerdes to execute documents effecting a turnover of the Gerdeses' interests in Don Rogelio. We overrule the Gerdeses' first issue.

C. Inadequacy of Ordinary Legal Process

In their second issue, the Gerdeses contend that the Kennamers failed to establish that the property subject to the trial court's turnover order could not be attached readily or levied on by ordinary legal process. We agree that the turnover statute requires the judgment creditor to show that the property could not be attached readily or levied on by ordinary legal process. Tex. Civ. Prac. & Rem. Code Ann. §31.002 (Vernon 1997). However, when a creditor presents evidence that corporate stock is held in the hands of third parties out of the state, the evidence is sufficient to support a finding that the stock could not be attached readily. We hold that the Kennamers established that the Gerdeses' interest in Don Rogelio, a Mexican entity, could not be attached readily or levied on by ordinary legal process. We overrule the Gerdeses' second issue. * * * *

[One judge dissented on the merits of the appeal of the underlying judgment.]

═══════════

Creative lawyers can sometimes forge a new path.

2. The Struggle Among Creditors: Priorities

a. Background

The first concern of a creditor and a debtor is often whether the procedures for judgment, execution, and sale have been properly followed. The debtor hopes that some mistake will make it impossible for the creditor to seize property to collect, and the creditor wants to make sure that no slip-ups occur just as the creditor is about to get some cash out of a losing deal. But debtors in trouble with one creditor are often in trouble with others, and the focus of collection may quickly shift from whether this creditor has a right to collect from this debtor to which creditor gets to collect from which assets first.

When a debtor starts to fail — because the debtor has lost a job, because the business is losing money, because debts have simply outrun income — creditors often frantically compete to get paid. In general, the rule in state collection law is the rule elsewhere in law: "First in time, first in right." The first creditor to levy on a particular piece of property will have the right to be paid in full from the sale proceeds of that property before any other creditor gets even a single dollar from the sale.

The race is almost primal in its simplicity: If a debtor owes three creditors $1,000 each and the debtor has one piece of property worth $1,500, the race is on. The creditor lucky enough to have first priority under the state system gets the full $1,000 he is owed. The creditor who comes in second in the state scheme gets $500, and the third creditor is out of luck. In general, the state law system provides for no sharing, does not listen to hard luck stories about which creditor was out of town or was trying to help the debtor, and makes very little assessment of which creditors are more deserving. Most state court judges will remind unhappy creditors that the state law system is "a race of diligence."

The best way to figure out who will win the race is to identify who is running and what property is the prize. For most debtors, the creditors vying for their property will be one of three types: secured creditors with consensual liens, unsecured creditors who have gotten judgments, and tax creditors, who sometimes have a lien and sometimes do not. Any creditor without a security interest or a judgment or status as a taxing authority hasn't even laced up his sneakers to begin the race. Once the competitors are lined up, specific rules of the race will vary from state to state, but this description shows the pattern.

The key date for determining priority turns on who made some required legal move first, not on who has the oldest loan or who showed up first at the sale of property. This legal move has a lot of different names, but the most generic is "perfection" — that state of grace a creditor reaches when its interest in the debtor's property will prevail over subsequent interests. Generally, the first to perfect wins, but the rules vary depending on the nature of each competitor's interest.

Unsecured Creditor versus Unsecured Creditor. As the prior discussion indicated, an unsecured creditor must first get a judgment and then execute or "levy on" that judgment in order to get an interest in a piece of property belonging to the judgment debtor. The levy perfects the judgment lien on that property. Thus, as between two judgment creditors, the first to levy will win as to the property levied on. In the easiest case, if the Apple Finance Company levies on the debtor's car on Monday, and the Baker Finance Company levies on the car on Tuesday, Apple Finance takes all the proceeds from the sale of the car up to the outstanding amount of its debt. Baker Finance takes any proceeds left up to its outstanding debt. If by some wild chance something remains from the sale of the car, it goes back to the debtor.

Suppose Baker Finance is faster on its feet as to another item of the debtor's property, the living room furniture. If Baker Finance levies on the living room furniture on Tuesday, and Apple Finance does not levy on the furniture until after the sale of the car leaves it with a shortfall, the creditors' positions switch. As to the furniture, Baker Finance takes all the proceeds first, and Apple Finance waits in line. This point is a reminder that in most states there is no *general* levy, but an item-by-item execution.

While order of perfection is clear in the preceding example, real life usually makes it more complicated. One common situation is a case in which Apple Finance's judgment writ was delivered to the sheriff on Monday and Baker Finance's writ was delivered on Tuesday, and the sheriff levied under both writs on Wednesday. It is not always true that it is a tie just because the two writs were levied at the same time. While a levy is essential for perfection and priority, the date of the levy is not always the controlling date for determining priorities. In many states Apple Finance will still win because its perfection — and thus its priority in the proceeds of sale of the collateral — is backdated to the date the sheriff got the writ. Some states use a different rule, however, so that the date of the judgment or the date of the sheriff's levy will be controlling. In states where date of levy is controlling, priority might go to the first one levied, even if they were nanoseconds apart (with Apple Finance winning all), or the levies may be held to have been simultaneous, so the creditors share pro rata. There are a few other local variations as well.

The terminology describing the priority process is arcane and varies from jurisdiction to jurisdiction. Some courts say that the judicial creditor gets an "inchoate lien" as of the priority date (for example, when the sheriff gets the writ), which becomes "choate" on the date of actual levy or seizure of the property and "relates back" to the earlier date. If there is never a completed levy, then the lien never becomes choate and the creditor has no priority against any other creditor. The analysis is roughly the same as the Article 9 situation in which the secured creditor files first and then gets the security interest later.

Sometimes one or more unsecured creditors will get a judgment lien by recordation. If Apple Finance obtains a judgment lien on the debtor's real property by recording its judgment in the county records, it may decide to rest on its laurels. If Baker Finance comes along with a writ of execution and levies on the property, Baker Finance can force a sale, but the first proceeds will go to Apple Finance by virtue of its earlier recorded lien. The same principle applies in the case of personal property in the three states that recognize recordation of judgment liens on such property.

Unsecured Judgment Creditor versus Secured Creditor. When a creditor obtains a consensual lien on the debtor's property, the pattern of priority on collection is functionally similar to that described above: First to perfect wins. With a consensual lien, the critical issue is what constitutes perfection for the secured creditor against the unsecured creditor with a judgment.

The general rule is easy: Ordinarily, the secured creditor or the mortgagee perfects when it records its consensual lien according to the statutory prescription. If the judgment creditor's lien is later, it loses; if the judgment creditor's lien is earlier, it wins. Thus if on Monday Apple Finance takes a consensual lien (a security interest or mortgage) and records it (by filing, by notation on a certificate of title, or by whatever other means are provided at state law) and Baker Finance executes and levies on Tuesday, Apple Finance is first and takes all the proceeds from sale up to the outstanding amount of its debt. If Apple Finance takes the consensual lien on Monday, but fails to record until Thursday, and Baker Finance executes and levies on Tuesday, Baker Finance wins.

Of course, there are hundreds of variations on the pattern described above. (Otherwise, how could there be two other law school courses devoted in large part to explaining how the real estate and secured credit systems work?) Purchase-money transactions in which the secured creditor finances the purchase of the collateral often involve a 20-day grace period during which the secured creditor may record its lien and beat any intervening unsecured creditors with involuntary liens. And, of course, secured creditors who fail to perfect their liens according to the requirements of the state statutes may find that they have no priority over any other creditors. When they eventually perfect, their priority only dates from the date of their perfection.

Judgment Creditors and Secured Creditors versus Buyers. Sometimes the party claiming an interest in the debtor's property is someone who just bought the property from the debtor. Once again, the usual rule is "first in time, first in right" — measured by perfection, usually through some recordation system. If Ann Adams buys the debtor's car on Monday, recording her ownership on the certificate of title (now required in all 50 states), and

Bob Brown executes on his judgment and levies on the car on Tuesday, Ann wins and retains ownership of the car. But if Ann buys after Bob's levy, she generally loses. The details are complicated, especially with regard to who had possession of the car when, but this is a fair general summary.

The general rule for secured creditors is the same: If Ann buys the debtor's car on Monday, and the secured creditor does not try to record a security interest on the car until Tuesday, the secured creditor is out of luck. If the secured creditor makes a notation on Monday, however, and Ann buys on Tuesday, it is Ann the buyer who is usually out of luck. This obviously puts a premium on checking the certificate of title for automobiles and checking the other perfection devices for buyers and creditors seeking an interest in other goods.

Again, there are many points of potential dispute between the warring parties. The secured creditor may not have followed the recordation requirements exactly or the buyer may have had some notice of the creditor's interest. And again, the details are beyond this course. Moreover, exceptions abound in this area so that, for example, an Ann Adams who buys Craftsman tools at Sears will be protected even if Irving Trust Co. has a properly recorded security interest in all of Sears' inventory. People who buy inventory are almost always protected from security interests — if for no other reason than to make sure we fill up the shopping malls on weekends.

Statutory Liens and Trust Funds. We noted earlier that there are a host of nonconsensual liens created as a matter of law in favor of certain favored creditors, such as landlords and subcontractors, as well as "trust fund" statutes with a similar effect. These statutes are designed to give priority over other creditors (e.g., lenders, who might be more successful in getting consensual liens from the debtor). There are so many different types of these liens with so many different effects that it is difficult to generalize about the priorities they confer as against other competing interests.

Some of the areas affected by these statutory priorities have become sufficiently complex and removed from the realities of marketplace bargaining power that innovative industry schemes have developed to create a workable alternative to the statutory scheme. The construction industry, noted for its variety of statutory lien and trust fund protections, is a study in the interaction between statutory requirements and commercial responses. Lenders and others with leverage have created consensual priority systems to avoid the effect of these priority statutes, and subcontractors and suppliers have responded in turn by seeking additional statutory protections in an ever-evolving complexity of competing priorities.

Unsecured Judgment Creditor and Secured Party versus the Trustee in Bankruptcy. The Trustee in Bankruptcy is the most dangerous foe of the judgment creditor who has levied or the secured party with a consensual security interest or even a statutory lienholder. In Parts II and III of this book we consider what happens to those state law creditors when the debtor has declared bankruptcy and the forum has shifted to the federal courts. Because equality among creditors is the fundamental principle of bankruptcy, consensual and statutory creditors will face a rigorous testing of the legal soundness of their priorities. Judgment creditors will usually be even more seriously threatened, to the point that the very existence of the bankruptcy system discourages the use of the judgment-execution process, because judgment liens are so routinely "avoided" in bankruptcy, nullifying all the diligence and expense of the execution process.

b. Competing Unsecured Creditors

Some of the rules concerning priorities are straightforward. The next two cases address who gets priority in proceeds from a judicial sale when two competing judgments have been recorded. The general rule is, of course, first in time, first in right. The first judgment recorded (or "docketed") has priority, regardless of when the competing judgments were rendered. That is, for priority purposes it is the recording or registration of the judgment in a manner deemed to give notice to other parties — especially other creditors and buyers — that creates a priority position.

Even such an apparently simple rule inevitably gives rise to complications, as the next case illustrates. A major advantage of judgment liens is that they can attach to real property that the debtor acquires after the judgment is recorded. If two judgments have been recorded before the debtor acquires real estate, the first-in-time rule would give priority to the judgment recorded first once the debtor does acquire the property. That is the result in most states. A minority follow the New York rule, as in the following case. This case also illustrates a second proposition of more general application: If two creditors enjoy equal priority under the usual rules, a taxing authority usually turns out to be "more equal" than the other creditor. Cf. George Orwell, *Animal Farm* (1946).

================ In re ESTATE OF ROBBINS ================

74 Misc. 2d 739, 346 N.Y.S.2d 86 (N.Y. Sur. 1973)

HILDRETH, Surrogate.

In this accounting the residuary estate is insufficient to pay in full the claims against the sole residuary beneficiary. The executrix and two claimants request the court to determine the priority of their claims.

The decedent died April 24, 1967, and by her will she gave the residuary estate to her son, Edmund C. Robbins, as sole residuary beneficiary. When decedent died said Edmund C. Robbins was indebted to two judgment creditors, one being the State Tax Commission and the other being the Bank of Commerce.

The claim of the State Tax Commission is based upon a warrant in the original amount of $32,030.89 issued against said Edmund C. Robbins pursuant to Article 16 of the tax law for unpaid income taxes for the period from 1953 through 1959, which warrant was docketed as a judgment in the office of the County Clerk of Suffolk County on October 18, 1965, and upon a second warrant in the sum of $687.01 against said Robbins and another, individually and as co-partners, for unincorporated business taxes for 1954, which was docketed as a judgment in the office of the County Clerk of Suffolk County on May 10, 1968. Neither warrant has been satisfied and the amount now due on both is $45,618.32 with interest at 12% from February 15, 1973. Under the provisions of section 380 of the tax law such warrants when docketed became liens upon the real and personal property of the person against whom the warrants were issued in the same manner as a judgment duly docketed in the office of the County Clerk.

The Bank of Commerce claims as a judgment creditor based upon a judgment it obtained against said Edmund C. Robbins which was filed in the office of the Clerk of Suffolk County on September 28, 1962, and on which judgment there is due $12,327.14 with interest from September 28, 1962....

At the time the executrix commenced her accounting on September 17, 1971, by filing her petition (SCPA 203), the State Tax Commission had not made any levy under its warrants. The account showed a balance on hand of $27,102.06 and also a parcel of real estate. Proceedings were thereafter had for a sale of the real property which was consummated June 22, 1972. The supplemental account thereafter filed January 25, 1973, shows a balance on hand of $43,379.26 which, subject to commissions and any unpaid administration expenses, will be available for distribution. The balance is not sufficient to pay the claims in full.

Until the decedent died on April 24, 1967, said Edmund C. Robbins had no interest whatsoever in any property of decedent nor was there any estate of decedent in which he had any interest, nor any assets in the hands of any fiduciary of decedent to which any judgments against Edmund C. Robbins could attach or have any effect. Therefore, in the opinion of the court, questions as to the priority of the judgment creditors of Edmund C. Robbins for payment from his interest in the estate must be considered beginning with the date of decedent's death. A judgment cannot be a charge on property the debtor does not own.

Only upon the death of decedent did said Edmund C. Robbins become possessed of an interest in the estate. He then acquired an asset which he did not previously own. At that time both State Tax Commission and Bank of Commerce had judgments against him, but as to his newly acquired interest in the estate, neither judgment had priority of lien. Both were general liens attaching to such property simultaneously. A judgment will extend to after-acquired property, CPLR §520 l(b), but when a debtor has several judgments against him they become liens on after-acquired property simultaneously even though they were docketed at different times.

As to personal property docketing of a judgment does not create a lien; such a lien upon personal property comes into being only when execution is issued to the proper officer....

The State Tax Commission is, however, entitled to priority under the rule giving priority to claims of the State as sovereign over other general liens. The claim of the State Tax Commission is based upon its warrants which have the same effect as judgments for taxes due from the debtor. Such claims are preferred except where a creditor has obtained a prior specific lien. Witas v. Carlson, 201 Misc. 201, 202, 110 N.Y.S.2d 659, 661 (1952), in which it is stated, "The rule is well settled that monies and taxes due the state have a priority over all other general liens and may be superseded only by a prior specific lien obtained by a creditor."

Accordingly the court determines that the State Tax Commission is entitled to priority over the Bank of Commerce in distribution of the interest of Edmund C. Robbins, in the residuary estate.

The account should be brought up to date and then decree submitted.

The next case yields yet another exception to the first-to-record rule and reflects the fact that inactive judgments, like inactive people, may lose their vitality. It is not surprising that it involves Dr. Dudas, the dentist, because medical providers seem to be aggressive debt collectors, but it is surprising that a dental creditor would let his judgment go numb.

WEAVER v. WEAVER
413 Pa. Super. 382, 605 A.2d 410 (1992)

WIEAND, Judge.

Karen Nannette Weaver (now Swank) and James Hamilton Weaver were divorced by a bifurcated decree entered November 21, 1980. The equitable distribution of marital property, consisting solely of a jointly owned residence having a value of twenty thousand ($20,000) dollars, was referred to a special master. Following the divorce decree but before the marital property had been distributed, three judgments were entered against the husband. The first of these judgments was entered on June 29, 1981, for four hundred and 69/100 ($400.69) dollars in favor of the Pennsylvania Department of Revenue. The second judgment was entered on August 18, 1981, in favor of Martin Dudas, D.D.S., t/a Dr. Dudas Associates, in the amount of seven hundred twenty-seven and 53/100 ($727.53) dollars. The third judgment was entered on October 2, 1986, in favor of Craig A. Miller for three thousand, nine hundred ninety-eight and 46/100 ($3,998.46) dollars. When the master held a hearing on November 19, 1987, the liens of the Department of Revenue and Dr. Dudas had not been revived. The master filed a report in which he recommended that the marital home be awarded to the wife. Exceptions were filed by the husband and by Craig A. Miller and heard by the trial court, which awarded the marital home to the wife free and clear of liens, subject, however, to her payment of three thousand ($3,000) dollars. The trial court also directed the master to hold a further hearing to determine the manner in which the three thousand ($3,000) dollars were to be distributed among husband and his creditors. Only Craig Miller appeared at the subsequent hearing before the master, and the master recommended that the entire three thousand ($3,000) dollars, less certain costs and fees, be awarded to Miller on account of his judgment. He concluded that any liens which Dr. Dudas and the Department of Revenue might have had against husband's interest in the real estate had lapsed when the same had not been renewed at the end of five years. Dr. Dudas filed exceptions, which the trial court dismissed. He then filed the instant appeal.

After husband and wife had been divorced by decree entered on November 21, 1980, the real estate previously owned by them as tenants by the entireties was owned as tenants in common....

When the Dudas judgment was entered on August 18, 1981, it became a lien against the undivided one-half interest of the husband in the real estate which he and his former wife then owned as tenants in common....

The lien of the Dudas judgment continued as a lien against James Weaver's undivided one-half interest in real estate for a period of five (5) years after it had been filed but no longer, unless it was revived. Judgment Lien Law of July 3, 1947, 12 P.S. §878. Because the Dudas judgment was not revived, the lien thereof lapsed and lost its priority to the lien of the Miller judgment, which was entered on October 2, 1986. When the Weaver home was ordered distributed to Karen Weaver Swank, the Dudas judgment did not constitute a lien against the interest of James Weaver in the real estate and was not entitled to participate in the funds paid to James Weaver as part of the trial court's plan of distribution. Therefore, Dudas cannot complain of the trial court's award of the real estate to Karen Weaver Swank free and clear of any lien of the judgment which he held against James Weaver. Similarly, he cannot complain that the moneys due his debtor were ordered paid to Craig Miller.

Order affirmed.

======

c.   The Aging Judgment

A judgment that has not been the subject of enforcement efforts for a long period faces disability in two ways: dormancy and limitations. While both concepts are relatively simple, the distinction between them is somewhat confusing. The following discussion is subject to the usual caveat about the host of varying rules found in different states.

If a judgment creditor fails to seek enforcement of a judgment for a period of time, often a year, the judgment becomes "dormant." Dormancy is a coma-like state in which the judgment still exists but is no longer enforceable without being "revived." One common consequence is that any judgment lien that has been created by recording the judgment lapses. Another consequence is that an execution obtained on a dormant judgment is probably subject to collateral attack. Dormancy can be avoided by regular (typically yearly) attempts to enforce the judgment, even if those attempts are unsuccessful. If, for example, the judgment creditor has an execution writ issued once a year, even though the sheriff searches in vain and returns the writ "nulla bona," the attempts at enforcement will prevent dormancy. If the judgment creditor has permitted a judgment to become dormant, it can be "revived" by a special action brought for that purpose, with service upon the judgment debtor.

Although dormancy can be cured, expiration of the statute of limitations to enforce a judgment is usually terminal. Limitations run regardless of dormancy or attempts at execution. The most common limitations period is ten years, after which the judgment expires and cannot be revived or enforced. A judgment creditor can avoid having the judgment expire by bringing a new action on the judgment within the limitations period. Absent any valid defense by the judgment debtor (e.g., that the judgment has been paid), a new judgment will result from such an action and a new limitations period will begin.

The distinction between dormancy and expiration can be illustrated by the example of a client who comes to you with a judgment obtained nine years ago, but never paid or enforced. Because no attempt at enforcement has been made, the judgment is dormant. In one more year it will be worse than dormant, it will be dead, because the limitations period will have run. Thus you would consider bringing two actions: (1) a "reviver" action, which will cure dormancy and enable you to get enforcement writs issued against the debtor's property during the next year; and (2) a new action on the judgment, which will produce a new judgment you can enforce in the future if your efforts in the next year do not suffice to satisfy the judgment in full.

d. Execution

When multiple creditors are trying to reach the proceeds of a judicial sale, the priority rules are usually clear. In general, the perfected creditors, either judicial lien creditors or consensual secured creditors, take in order of their perfection. Although a levy will usually be the judgment creditor's perfection (often with a relation back to the delivery of the writ), disputes sometimes arise over *when* a judgment creditor's levy actually occurred. The resolution of this issue requires asking, "What must the sheriff do to complete a priority-conferring levy?" The following case illustrates both the basic execution process and the priority analysis.

CREDIT BUREAU OF BROKEN BOW v. MONINGER
204 Neb. 679, 284 N.W.2d 855 (1979)

BRODKEY, Justice.

This is an appeal from an order of the District Court for Custer County which affirmed a judgment entered by the county court of Custer County awarding the proceeds from a sheriff's sale of a 1975 Ford pickup truck to the Broken Bow State Bank (hereinafter referred to as Bank). We reverse and remand.

The facts which give rise to this action are not in dispute. The Credit Bureau of Broken Bow, Inc. (hereinafter referred to as Bureau) obtained a default Judgment against John Moninger (hereinafter referred to as Moninger) in the amount of $1,518.27 on October 20, 1977. No appeal was taken from this judgment. On May 16, 1978, Moninger renewed his prior note to the Bank in the amount of $2,144.74. The renewed note was to be secured by a security agreement on feeder pigs and a 1975 Ford pickup owned by Moninger, but no security agreement was entered into at that time. On June 27, 1978, at the request of the Bureau, a writ of execution was issued on its judgment in the amount of $1,338.50, the balance remaining due on the judgment.

The deputy county sheriff who received the writ examined the motor vehicle title records on July 7,1978, to determine if a lien existed as of that date on the pickup owned by Moninger. Finding no encumbrance of record, the deputy sheriff proceeded to Moninger's place of employment to levy on the vehicle. The deputy sheriff found Moninger, served him with a copy of the writ, and informed Moninger that he was executing on the pickup. Moninger testified he informed the officer that there was money borrowed from the Bank against the pickup, and that the Bank had title to the vehicle. Following this conversation, the officer proceeded to the vehicle, "grabbed ahold of the pickup," and stated: "I execute on the pickup for the County of Custer." The officer did not take possession of the vehicle at that time, nor did he ask for the keys to the vehicle.

On July 10, 1978, after being informed of the events which occurred on the 7th, the Bank and Moninger executed a security agreement on the vehicle which was then filed. Notation of the security interest was made on the title to the pickup truck that same day. The vehicle was seized by deputy sheriffs on July 13, 1978, and sold at sheriff's sale on August 14, 1978, for $2,050.

The sheriff filed a motion in the county court for a determination of the division of the proceeds from the sheriff's sale. The Bank joined the action by application for the proceeds of the sheriff's sale, basing its claim on its alleged status as a secured creditor. Prior to a hearing on these matters, a stipulation was entered into by all parties whereby this dispute was limited to the distribution of the proceeds of the sheriff's sale, the pickup having previously been sold.

Hearing on the motion and the application was had on August 21, 1978. The county court orally ruled that the deputy sheriff had knowledge of the possible lien against the vehicle as of July 7, 1978; that such notice made any execution subject to the lien; that the vehicle was not ponderous and physical possession could have been taken by the officer; that the notice of the possible lien resulted in a valid lien in the Bank as of July 7, 1978; that the proceeds of the sheriff's sale should go to the Bank; and that the sheriff in making a levy "at that time" (July 7, 1978) used due care and acted properly as a stakeholder.

However, the written order entered by the county court differed in certain respects from the oral ruling at the hearing. By its written order, the county court found that the sheriff was a stakeholder; that a valid levy was not made on the vehicle until July 12, 1978; that the Bank's lien was perfected on July 10, 1978; that the sheriff had notice of the claim to a lien on July 7, 1978; that the knowledge of the sheriff was imputed to the Bureau; that the Bank's lien was prior to the Bureau's lien; and that the proceeds of the sheriff's sale should be paid to the Bank.

An objection to the written order was filed on September 8, 1978, and hearing was held thereon, contesting the apparent discrepancies therein, particularly as to the date when levy was made on the vehicle. This objection was overruled. Appeal was had to the District Court assigning as error the finding of the county court with regard to the validity of the execution on July 7, 1978, and the failure of the county court to correct the purported conflict between the oral ruling and the written order. After reviewing the bill of exceptions from the county court, the District Court affirmed the judgment of the county court. This appeal followed.

The Bureau first assigns as error the ruling of the trial court which found the Bank's security interest in the vehicle to be superior to the execution lien of the Bureau. Specifically, the Bureau contends that the actions of the deputy sheriff on July 7, 1978, amounted to a valid levy which bound the vehicle for the satisfaction of the Bureau's judgment against Moninger. §25-1504, R.R.S. 1943. On that date, the Bank held only an unperfected security interest in the vehicle. The Bureau contends that since the levy of execution made the Bureau a lien creditor, and since the lien creditor has an interest superior to that of an unperfected secured party, the trial court was in error in ruling that the Bank had a superior interest in the proceeds.

In effect, the Bureau is relying on section 9-301, UCC, [now §9-317 — eds.] which relates to the relative priorities as between unperfected security interests and lien creditors. "[A]n unperfected security interest is subordinate to the rights of ... a person who becomes a lien creditor without knowledge of the security interest and before it is perfected." §9-301(l)(b), UCC. The correctness of the Bureau's position turns on two issues: (1) Whether the Bureau was in fact a lien creditor on July 7, 1978; and (2) whether the Bureau was a lien creditor without knowledge of the Bank's alleged security interest prior to the perfection of such interest by the Bank.

From an examination of the record, we conclude that the Bureau was a lien creditor on July 7,1978. Section 9-301, UCC, defines a lien creditor as "a creditor who has acquired a lien on the property involved by attachment, levy or the like ...." A lien on personal property is acquired in this state at the time it is "seized in execution." §25-1504, R.R.S. 1943. Therefore, the Bureau became a lien creditor within the meaning of section 9-301, UCC, when the sheriff levied on the vehicle.

The rule by which to test the validity of a levy has been earlier set out by this court. "A manual interference with chattels is not essential to a valid levy thereon. It is sufficient if the property is present and subject for the time to the control of the officer holding the writ, and that he in express terms asserts his dominion over it by virtue of such writ." Battle Creek Valley Bank v. First Nat. Bank of Madison, 62 Neb. 825, 88 N.W. 145 (1901). We believe a review of the record makes it clear that a valid levy did occur before the Bank had perfected its security interest in the chattel.

The deputy sheriff expressly asserted his dominion over the vehicle by virtue of the writ. He likewise exerted control over the vehicle as against all others at the time of levy. At that time the deputy sheriff informed Moninger that he was sorry that he had to execute on the vehicle but that it was his job. He further stated that he hoped Moninger would straighten the problem out with the Bureau. It should be noted that the officer's report, as well as the return on the writ, clearly indicated that the officer "executed" on the vehicle on July 7, 1978. On the basis of this evidence, we conclude that a valid levy took place at that time.

The Bank would have us hold that the pickup should have been physically seized to make the levy valid. We do not believe that failure to take physical possession in this case goes to the validity of the levy. The deputy sheriff did all that was required by the laws of this state with regard to levying under a writ of execution. Whether or not the officer took physical possession after he levied relates to the ability of the officer to produce the property levied on, and to his possible civil liability for failure to do so, not to the validity of the levy. It is, of course, possible that the failure of a levying officer to protect and preserve the property levied upon might give rise to an action between the officer, or his bonding company, and the judgment creditor. We therefore reject the Bank's contention and conclude that the Bureau was a lien creditor on July 7, 1978, by virtue of the deputy sheriff's levy on the writ of execution.

[The requirement that the lien creditor have no knowledge of the security interest, which the court addressed next, was eliminated in the 1972 UCC Amendments. This court reached the same result under the 1962 Code by holding that the sheriff's knowledge is not appropriately imputed to the judgment creditor.]

We hold, therefore, that the Bureau has prior rights to the proceeds of the sheriff's sale . . . .

━━━━━━━━━━━━━━━━━

A number of jurisdictions agree with the *Credit Bureau* approach that it is generally not necessary for the sheriff to remove the goods in order to complete an effective levy. Other jurisdictions disagree, requiring that the sheriff either take possession or appoint an independent custodian. Even when a court will permit the levy to suffice without possession, the subsequent actions of the creditor can vitiate the lien. Because subsequent creditors could be misled, deliberately or otherwise, if goods are left with the debtor, there is a caveat in the situation where no possession is required: If the levied-upon goods are left in the hands of the debtor for an unreasonably long period of time with the consent of the creditor, the lien will be lost. The creditor's permitting the debtor to continue to use the goods in the same way as before the levy is often construed as evidence of fraud, causing the court in any subsequent action to set aside the first judgment lien in favor of subsequent creditors.

Seizure does not end the execution process, although it does give the levying creditor a lien. The property must then be sold by the sheriff, usually at an auction traditionally held on the courthouse steps. After paying the sheriff's fee and other costs of sale, the proceeds go to the judgment lien creditor. If there is more than one such creditor, the payments are in order of priority.

3. *Discovery*

Law school hypotheticals about the collection process typically skip the hardest aspect of collection of judgments by seizure of the debtor's property: getting information about the existence, location, and exemption status of leviable property. Information is crucial not only to permit use of the execution process, but also to avoid mistakes that might expose the judgment creditor to liability, such as damages for attaching exempt property or seizing property in which a third party has a superior interest.

The Federal Rules of Civil Procedure, and most state rules of procedure, permit the judgment creditor to conduct discovery concerning the debtor's assets and affairs. Fed. R. Civ. P. 69.

Problem Set 2

2.1. Rollins Home Appliances is in deep financial trouble. Three of its suppliers have sued and recovered judgments against Rollins, each in the amount of $10,000. Ace Machinery obtained its judgment on November 1. You represent Blake Construction. You got a judgment for Blake on November 10 and delivered a writ of execution to the sheriff on November 15. Cratchett Parts got a judgment on November 20, delivered a writ to the sheriff on November 22, and on November 25 got a deputy to execute the writ by seizing all of the appliances at the Rollins store.

Your client estimates that the appliances will bring $15,000 at the sheriff's sale, which will be held next week. As things stand now, who will get the proceeds from the sale? Can you change that outcome?

2.2. Shoes Below Cost is a local shoe store that discovered too late that volume will not make up for losing money on each sale. Five of its creditors have obtained judgment against SBC, but only one has executed. Each judgment is for $5,000. You represent the executing creditor, Harry Kleson. On November 25, the sheriff went into the store and announced he was seizing all of the shoes pursuant to Kleson's *fi. fa.* However, SBC's lawyer arrived and explained that SBC had a plan for paying all of its creditors, a plan to be discussed at a meeting the next day. Your client agreed to go to the meeting, and you asked the sheriff to forbear actually seizing the shoes pending the results of the meeting.

At the meeting, SBC agreed to pay each creditor so much a month in exchange for each creditor's agreement to freeze its collection actions, leaving each creditor's execution efforts at the points described above. SBC agreed to a faster payment schedule for your client because he had gotten further along in collection. All the creditors went along with the plan.

Brisk Christmas sales completed the financial demise of SBC, which closed its doors on January 5. SBC has just revealed that on December 1 it granted a security interest in all of its inventory to the Solid State Bank to secure a loan of $20,000 additional operating capital. You have confirmed that the security interest was properly perfected on December 5. Your client estimates that the sale of the remaining shoes at the SBC store will produce $20,000. How will those proceeds be divided? How could you have better protected your client while going along with his decision to negotiate rather than shut the business down on November 25?

2.3. Your client, Omar Hassan, has obtained a judgment for breach of contract against Forman Handler. You have been informed that Handler is the beneficiary of a letter of credit in the amount of $35,000 reflecting an obligation owed by Giant Oil Company to Handler. You pore through

Article 5 of the UCC and a treatise or two. You learn that a letter of credit ("LOC") is a promise by an issuer, usually a bank (here Bank of America), to pay a specified sum (here $35,000) to a named beneficiary (here Handler) upon presentation of certain documents (here an engineer's certificate that a certain design job has been satisfactorily completed by Handler). You are also informed that this LOC is payable to "Handler or his assignee." How can you use this knowledge to collect on Hassan's judgment? What will you need to show in court and how can you get the evidence to make that showing?

4.   *Garnishment*

Law generally follows practical necessity, and nowhere is that more evident than in the law of collections. Not all property is physically in the hands of the true owner. (Think of the property in a safety deposit box at the bank; the true owner leaves physical possession with the bank.) In addition, some property exists only in the abstract. The most common example is a debt owed to the debtor by a third party. (Think of wages in the period after the debtor has done the work but before the employer has issued a paycheck or think about an account receivable for goods already delivered.) The law has developed a means by which creditors can direct these third parties to turn over the debtor's property or to divert payments that otherwise would have gone to the debtor.

Traditional forms of creditor actions to seize property held by a third party or intangible property require writs that are different from the standard execution writ. The most common is a writ of "garnishment," which is typically used to "attach" debts owed to the debtor for the benefit of the debtor's judgment creditor. A creditor may garnish a debtor's wages by obtaining a writ directing the employer to pay the wages to the employee's creditor rather than to the employee. Similarly, a creditor might garnish a bank account or obtain an order to turn over the contents of a safety deposit box.

The garnishment writ has two parts: a set of questions designed to determine whether the party served with the writ — the "garnishee," e.g., the employer or the bank — owes any money to the debtor or has any property belonging to the debtor, and a command to the garnishee to withhold payment or return of the debtor's property pending further order of the court. If the garnishee answers the questions falsely or disobeys the command to withhold payment or delivery, it may be liable to the judgment creditor. For example, the employer who pays wages to the debtor after service of the writ of garnishment may owe the judgment creditor an amount equal to the wages paid. The same may be true of the bank that honors the debtor's checks after service of the writ.

As a procedural matter, a garnishment is an ancillary lawsuit against the third-party garnishee. If, for example, the third party denies owing anything to the debtor, a trial may be held on that issue. It more often happens that the garnishee asserts a defense to the writ in the form of some superior right in the debtor's property (e.g., the garnishee may have a security interest in the property held) and there may be a trial on that issue. The judgment debtor receives notice of this process and may well participate in it. If the garnishee is found to owe money to the debtor or to have the debtor's property without any superior rights therein, a judgment will be entered against the garnishee. This judgment is satisfied when the garnishee delivers the debtor's property or pays the debt to the judgment creditor. The delivery or payment also satisfies the garnishee's obligation to the debtor.

While procedures in garnishment actions vary widely, in most states the garnishing creditor gets a temporal "net" — the time between service of the garnishment writ and the garnishee's answer — during which the creditor can hope to "catch" obligations arising in favor of the debtor. Thus garnishment of a bank account will "catch" not only the amount on deposit on the service date but also funds deposited thereafter prior to the answer. If the garnishment is contested and a trial is to be held, the creditor's net may even extend to the time of the garnishment trial.

The following case outlines the obligation of the garnishee — the third party holding the property owed the debtor. Although the garnishee here was able to overturn a judgment against him, it is crucial to note the extraordinary proofs he offered and legal expenses he incurred in his effort to escape the serious consequences of having failed to meet the obligations imposed on a garnishee.

Marginalia (handwritten): Garnishee – the 3rd party holding the prop owed the debtor

Marginalia (handwritten): Ct. Held: given the totality of circumstances, the trial ct. did not abuse its discretion in vacating the default jdgmt. against Bates (Garnishee) by Webb

WEBB v. ERICKSON
134 Ariz. 182, 655 P.2d 6 (1982)

FELDMAN, J.

On August 5, 1975, appellant Webb obtained a default judgment against Carl and Nancy Erickson in the amount of $5,000 plus interest, and $1,500 in attorneys' fees. The judgment was based on two promissory notes and a check for insufficient funds executed by Erickson.

Marginalia (handwritten): 08/05/75: Appt./Webb obtained Def. jdgmt. against Erickson for 5k + 1.5k

During 1975, Carl Erickson earned commissions by acting as the real estate agent in the sale of several houses. In order to collect on his judgment against Erickson, Webb caused several writs of garnishment to be served on parties whose houses had been sold by Erickson. One of these parties was Bates. On November 22, 1975, Webb served a summons and writ of garnishment on Bates at his home. The process served on Bates designated him as a garnishee-defendant in an action which was based upon the Webb/Erickson judgment.

Marginalia (handwritten): 1975: E sold B's house & earned commission

Marginalia (handwritten): 11/22/75 - W served garnishmt on B as Garnishee of E.

In a subsequent affidavit, Bates stated that in November of 1975 he had just been released from the hospital after a seven-week stay resulting from injuries sustained in an industrial accident. During a two-year period, Bates had been hospitalized several times for treatment of pain and depression associated with the injury. In addition to his health problems, Bates was involved in divorce proceedings and subsequently lost custody of his two children.

Marginalia (handwritten): - B had health & divorce problems.

Bates stated that in light of these conditions he did not clearly understand the process served on him in November of 1975. He assumed that the summons was not intended for him because he had never heard of James

Webb and was not connected with any dispute between Webb and the Ericksons. While he probably knew that Carl Erickson was the real estate agent involved in the sale of his home, Bates was under the impression that the entire transaction was in escrow at the Minnesota Title Company at that time and that he had no control over payment of the real estate commission. As a result, Bates never answered the writ.

On February 27, 1976, Webb obtained a default judgment against Bates for the full amount of Webb's underlying judgment against Erickson pursuant to A.R.S. §12.1583 (1956) (amended 1981).[2] No copy of the default judgment was mailed to Bates. No execution was attempted.

Bates did not know that a judgment had been entered against him for the full amount of the Webb/Erickson judgment until more than three years later. In late March of 1979, Bates received a telephone call from Webb's attorney who informed him of the 1976 judgment, that interest had been accruing since that time and that Bates was "in trouble." The attorney told Bates that a reduction of the $6,500 judgment was possible if Bates would be willing to negotiate. Bates immediately contacted an attorney.

The record reflects that some negotiations took place between the parties after Bates was informed of the judgment, but no settlement was reached. On August 7, 1979, Webb served a writ of garnishment on Bates' employer, garnishing Bates' wages on the basis of the 1976 default judgment and seeking to collect the entire amount of Webb's judgment against the Ericksons.

On August 16, 1979, Bates filed a motion to vacate judgment pursuant to Rule 60(c), Rules of Civil Procedure, 16 A.R.S., and a motion to stay the execution of the judgment. After a response and oral argument, the superior court issued an order granting Bates' motion to vacate and set aside the default and quashing the writ of garnishment served on Bates' employer. A formal judgment to this effect was entered on September 19, 1979. Garnisher Webb appealed this decision to the court of appeals, which held that the trial court had abused its discretion, and reversed. Bates then petitioned this court for review. We granted review and now vacate the opinion of the court of appeals and affirm the judgment of the trial court.

[The court expressed concern about the delay in overturning the default judgment, but stated:] extraordinary circumstances justifying relief exist in this case.

Bates was a defaulting garnishee. This court has held that more liberality should be shown in setting aside a judgment against a defaulting garnishee than in setting aside a judgment against a defaulting defendant. The reason for this rule was stated in *Gutierrez* [24 Ariz. 382, 210 P. 470 (1922)]:

The court should be even more liberal in allowing the belated garnishee to answer after default than in granting the privilege to an ordinary suitor defaulter, since he is a disinterested party in the proceedings, so far as any

2. Prior to the 1981 amendment, §12-1583 read:

If a garnishee fails to answer within the time specified in the writ, the court may, after judgment has been rendered against defendant, render judgment by default against the garnishee for the full amount of the judgment against defendant.

prospect of being benefitted is concerned, yet an interested third person so far
as the danger of being injured is concerned.

Id. 24 Ariz. at 387, 210 P. at 472 (quoting Waples, Waples on Attachment and
Garnishment §501 (2d ed.)).

Under Arizona law, a judgment can be entered against a defaulting
garnishee for the full amount of the judgment against the defendant. A.R.S.
§12-1583. The necessary result of such a rule is that a defaulting garnishee
often may become liable for a debt which is significantly greater than the
debt allegedly owed to the defendant. In light of such a result, it is not difficult to see why the principles relating to the setting aside of default judgments are applied more liberally in the case of a garnishee.

The trial court could also have considered the confusing nature of the
entire proceeding as well as the wording contained in the summons and
writ served on Bates, a person who was not involved in and knew nothing
about the dispute between Webb and Erickson.

The summons served on Bates read as follows:

In obedience to the Writ of Garnishment served together with this Summons
I do hereby summon and require you to appear and answer the accompanying
Writ in the manner prescribed by law and within TEN DAYS, exclusive of the
day of service, after service of this summons upon you if served within the
County of Maricopa, or within TWENTY DAYS, exclusive of the day of service,
if served outside the County of Maricopa, and you are hereby notified that in
case you fail to so answer, judgment by default may be rendered against you for
the full amount of the balance due upon the judgment against the defendant and
in favor of plaintiff and not merely for the amount that you may owe to the
defendant, and that such judgment may be so rendered in addition to any other
matters which may be adjudged against you as prescribed by law.

The writ and summons contained no information with respect to how
the garnishee was to "answer" or where and when the garnishee was to
"appear." This may have contributed to Bates' failure to appreciate the significance of the documents and his resulting neglect in failing to answer the writ.

An additional factor that could have been considered by the trial court
was Bates' physical and mental condition in November of 1975. At that
time, Bates was recovering from an industrial accident and suffering from
depression. This condition, added to the confusing nature of the proceedings and notice, could well have contributed to his failure to understand and
answer the writ.

The reasons behind Bates' failure to understand and answer relate to
the question of excusable neglect....

None of the circumstances of this case alone would have been sufficient [to set aside a judgment]. In combination, however, a unique situation
was created and we cannot say that the trial court abused its discretion in
vacating the default....

Meritorious Defense

In his affidavit, Bates stated that while Carl Erickson was the real estate
agent handling the sale of his house, in November of 1975 the entire

transaction was in escrow at Minnesota Title Company. Bates claimed that he had no control over the payment of the real estate commission and never owed Erickson any money. It is difficult to tell what Bates meant when he claimed he had "no control" over the payment of the commission. Interpreting this phrase in its broadest sense, however, it could mean that the commission was being paid by someone else or had already been paid.... These facts, if proved at trial, would constitute a meritorious defense....

Now it is back to court once again for Mr. Bates, the fellow who sort of remembers the real estate agent, Mr. Erickson, and who said he never heard of Mr. Webb.

a. Restrictions on Wage Garnishment

Wage garnishments, like the "secondary" garnishment faced by Mr. Bates in the *Webb* case, present a special issue. If a garnishing judgment creditor could seize the entire salary or wages that an employer owed to a judgment debtor, then the judgment debtor's ability to survive might be seriously jeopardized. The debtor's incentive to work would be sharply reduced, resulting in hardship to the debtor's family or increased social costs. Moreover, such garnishment power would give the creditor excessive leverage to strike a new bargain with a defaulting debtor. A debtor facing garnishment of an entire wage packet might well offer the creditor exempt property or promise to pay a much higher interest rate in the future in return for the creditor's willingness to let the debtor keep some current wages.

The Supreme Court discussed the special difficulties associated with wage garnishments in Sniadach v. Family Finance Corp., 395 U.S. 337, 340-341 (1969).

> A prejudgment garnishment of the Wisconsin type is a taking which may impose tremendous hardship on wage earners with families to support.... As stated by Congressman Reuss:
>
>> The idea of wage garnishment in advance of judgment, of trustee process, of wage attachment, or whatever it is called is a most inhuman doctrine. It compels the wage earner, trying to keep his family together, to be driven below the poverty level.
>
> Recent investigations of the problem have disclosed the grave injustices made possible by prejudgment garnishment whereby the sole opportunity to be heard comes after the taking. Congressman Sullivan, Chairman of the House Subcommittee on Consumer Affairs who held extensive hearings on this and related problems stated:
>
>> What we know from our study of this problem is that in a vast number of cases the debt is a fraudulent one, saddled on a poor ignorant person who is trapped in an easy credit nightmare, in which he is charged double for something he could not pay for even if the proper price was called for,

and then hounded into giving up his pound of flesh, and being fired besides. 114 Cong. Rec. 1832.

> The leverage of the creditor on the wage earner is enormous. The creditor tenders not only the original debt but the "collection fees" incurred by his attorneys in the garnishment proceedings:

> > The debtor whose wages are tied up by a writ of garnishment, and who is usually in need of money, is in no position to resist demands for collection fees. If the debt is small, the debtor will be under considerable pressure to pay the debt and collection charges in order to get his wages back. If the debt is large, he will often sign a new contract of [sic] "payment schedule," which incorporates these additional charges.

In response to various observations, including those outlined above, Congress in the Consumer Credit Protection Act (15 U.S.C. §§1671 et seq.) restricted the access of all creditors to the wages of any debtor. One impetus for the federal restrictions on garnishment was the enormous variation that existed among states. Some states banned garnishments altogether (with the frequent exception of efforts to collect child support and alimony payments), while other states had no restrictions. Many states were scattered between these extremes. The federal garnishment restrictions act as a floor, creating minimal protection, which some states then exceed with their own restrictions.

In the next case, the family support creditors got their garnishment order in first, leaving the other creditors to fight over whatever was left. The others were willing to fight, but they had some trouble figuring out exactly how much was left to fight over.

═══ COMMONWEALTH EDISON v. DENSON ═══

144 Ill. App. 3d 383, 494 N.E.2d 293, 98 Ill. Dec. 859 (Ill. App. 1986)

Justice STOUDER delivered the opinion of the court:

Employer-Appellant, Caterpillar Tractor Company (Caterpillar) appeals from two separate judgments of the circuit court of Will County....

The first action was originally brought by plaintiff-appellee, Commonwealth Edison (Com Ed) to collect monies due and owing to it by defendant, Willie Denson. On June 27, 1984, the circuit court entered judgment in favor of Com Ed and against Denson for $629.54 plus costs. Summons was issued pursuant to an affidavit for a wage deduction order in the amount of the outstanding judgment and Com Ed served interrogatories upon Caterpillar, Denson's current employer....

Caterpillar responded to the interrogatories and forwarded a check to Com Ed in the amount of $139.32. Caterpillar declined to deduct the full 15 percent of Denson's gross earnings, in accordance with the order, as it was already withholding $60 per week from his wages pursuant to a previously filed support order.

The second action was originally brought by plaintiff-appellee, Newsome Physical Therapy Clinic (Newsome) to collect monies due and owing to it by defendant, Dwight Morgan. On October 31, 1984, the circuit court

A. Collection Remedies

67

entered judgment in favor of Newsome and against Morgan for $748.19 plus costs. Summons was issued pursuant to an affidavit for a wage deduction order in the amount of the outstanding judgment and Newsome served interrogatories upon Caterpillar, Morgan's current employer....

Caterpillar contends under Illinois law no garnishment is allowed which would exceed the lesser of 15 percent of gross earnings, or the amount by which the weekly disposable earnings exceed 30 times the Federal minimum hourly wage which was $3.35 per hour at all times relevant to this case....

From our review of the Acts and Regulations involved we have determined the trial court erred and therefore its judgment must be reversed. The contention that payroll deductions required under a support order should not be included when computing the percentage reduction of a debtor's disposable earnings is not a legally supportable interpretation and application of these statutes.

We initially examine the Federal law. Under the Supremacy Clause (Article VI, U.S. Constitution) the garnishment restriction provision of the Consumer Credit Protection Act (CCPA) (15 U.S.C., Sec. 1671 et seq.) preempts state laws insofar as state laws would permit recovery in excess of 25 percent of an individual's disposable earnings. The cardinal provision of the Act is 15 U.S.C., Sec. 1673....

The Federal Act does not pre-empt the field of garnishment entirely, but provides that in those instances where state and federal laws are inconsistent, then the courts are to apply the law which garnishes the lesser amount. (15 U.S.C., Sec. 1677.) In Illinois, Section 12-803 of the Code of Civil Procedure (Ill. Rev. Stat. 1985, ch. 110, par. 12-803) provides:

> 12.803. Maximum wages subject to collection. The maximum wages, salary, commissions and bonuses subject to collection under a deduction order, for any work week shall not exceed the lesser of (1) 15% of such gross amount paid for that week or (2) the amount by which disposable earnings for a week exceed 30 times the Federal Minimum Hourly Wage prescribed by Section 206(a)(1) of Title 29 of The United States Code, as amended, in effect at the time the amounts are payable. This provision (and no other) applies irrespective of the place where the compensation was earned or payable and the State where the employee resides. No amounts required by law to be withheld may be taken from the amount collected by the creditor. The term "disposable earnings" means that part of the earnings of any individual remaining after the deduction from those earnings of any amounts required by law to be withheld.

The Federal Act does not seek to establish any order of priority among garnishments. There being no other Federal statutory provision setting priorities as between support order garnishments and creditor garnishments, the matter of priority is thus determined by Illinois law. Pursuant to Illinois statute, it is clear and unequivocal that as between garnishments of the same type, the prior in time is to be satisfied first. As between judgment creditor garnishments and support order garnishments, Illinois gives priority to those for support regardless of the timing of those garnishments.

Handwritten margin notes:
When Garnishments are sought only by Jdgmt Creditors
— No more than 25% of disposable earnings
— 15% of Gross earnings
— OR Amt by which disposable earnings exceed 30 times the Fed Min. Wage
When Garnishments are sought only to enforce support Orders
— as much as 65% of disposable earnings may be witheld
Ct. Holds! no basis for viewing Support Garnishment & Jdgmt Creditor Garnishment being viewed independently
Reversed & Remanded

... Thus, when garnishments are sought only by judgment creditors, no more than the lesser of 25 percent of disposable earnings, or 15 percent of gross earnings, or the amount by which disposable earnings exceed 30 times the Federal minimum wage may be withheld for that purpose; when garnishments are sought only to enforce support orders, as much as 65 percent of disposable earnings may be withheld for that purpose. The interrelationship, however, between the general rule and the exception, when both creditor and support garnishments are sought, is less clear. Plaintiffs in this case argue support garnishments should be considered entirely independent of judgment creditor garnishments, and that the Acts should be construed under the facts of the case as reserving 15 percent of the employees' earnings for attachment by judgment creditors after the satisfaction of family support orders. We find no basis for this argument either in the language of the statutes or in their legislative history.

Our conclusion is reinforced by the manner in which 15 U.S.C., Sec. 1673 has been construed by the Secretary of Labor. . . .

"...(iv) If 25% or more of an individual's disposable earnings were withheld pursuant to a garnishment for support, and the support garnishment has priority in accordance with State law, the Consumer Credit Protection Act does not permit the withholding of any additional amounts pursuant to an ordinary garnishment which is subject to the restrictions of section (1673(a))." 29 C.F.R., Sec. 870.11 . . . .

We are mindful of the plaintiff's argument that the statutes as thus construed may help debtors to evade payment of their debts if they collusively procure orders of support that exceed the statutory maximums. This point was considered and indeed vigorously debated in Congress prior to the passage of the Act. . . . Thus, we hardly feel free to tamper with the way in which Congress has chosen to balance the interests of the debtor, his family, and his creditors.

Reversed and remanded with directions.

═══════════════

The employer-garnishee, Caterpillar, was defending its employees' interests in the last case, but often the garnishee is defending its own interest against a garnishing creditor. The garnishee may defend its action by arguing that no obligation is owed to the judgment debtor or that any obligation owed is offset by an obligation of the judgment debtor to the garnishee.

A bank account is often the source of this kind of dispute between garnishee and judgment creditor. The law regards the account as a debt the bank owes to the depositor, so garnishment is the way to reach the asset. The account, with its ready cash, is attractive to the judgment creditor as an easy way to satisfy the judgment debt. But banks often have multiple relationships with their depositors. It is not uncommon for a business or individual to maintain a checking account with the same bank where one or more loans are outstanding. The customer then becomes creditor for the deposit account and debtor on the loan accounts. When the deposit account is garnished, the bank rapidly switches hats, agreeing as account debtor that the money is owed to the customer, but arguing that as loan creditor that the customer owes offsetting amounts back to the bank. The bank then offers the judgment creditor in satisfaction of the garnishment order only the amount — if any — left in the account after the bank's own "setoff."

There is often a dispute between the judgment creditor and the bank, with the creditor claiming that its writ was served and a lien attached before the bank had properly accelerated and set off the debtor's obligation to it against its obligation — the account — to the debtor. For the moment, it is enough to say that bank almost always wins.

b. Garnishing "New Property"

As more and more wealth exists in the form of contract rights and other intangibles, and as technology and law combine to create endlessly new forms of property, judgment creditors seek to use garnishment in new and untried ways.

NETWORK SOLUTIONS, INC. v. UMBRO INTERNATIONAL, INC.,
529 S.E.2d 80 (Va. Sup. Ct. 2000)

KINSER, Justice.

I. INTRODUCTION

In this case of first impression, we address the issue whether a contractual right to use an Internet domain name can be garnished. In doing so, we "apply traditional legal principles to [a] new avenue[ ] of commerce," Intermatic Inc. v. Toeppen, 947 F.Supp. 1227, 1229 (N.D. Ill. 1996), and conclude that such a contractual right is "the product of a contract for services," Dorer v. Arel, 60 F. Supp. 2d 558, 561 (E.D. Va. 1999), and hence is not subject to garnishment. Accordingly, we will reverse the judgment of the circuit court holding that the domain name registrations at issue in this appeal are garnishable.

[Handwritten margin note: Ct. Concludes: Utual rights to a domain name is ak for services & is not subject to garnishment — Reversed]

II. FACTS AND PROCEEDINGS

In 1997, appellee Umbro International, Inc. (Umbro), obtained a default judgment and permanent injunction in the United States District Court for the District of South Carolina against 3263851 Canada, Inc., a Canadian corporation (the judgment debtor), and also against a Canadian citizen who owns the judgment debtor. That proceeding involved the judgment debtor's registration of the Internet domain name "umbro.com." In its order, the district court permanently enjoined the judgment debtor from further use of the domain name "umbro.com" and awarded judgment to Umbro in the amount of $23,489.98 for attorneys' fees and expenses. Id. at 8.

[Handwritten margin note: 1997 - Appe/Umbro obtained Def. Jdgmt & injunction against Canada/ Jdgmt Debtor over umbro.com]

* * *

- Umbro named NSI the garnishee & sought to have 38 Domain Names of the Judgmt. Debtor auctioned off

- NSI claimed it held no garnishable property

In the garnishment summons, Umbro named Network Solutions, Inc. (NSI), as the garnishee and sought to garnish 38 Internet domain names that the judgment debtor had registered with NSI. Accordingly, Umbro asked NSI to place those domain names on hold and to deposit control of them into the registry of the circuit court so that the domain names could be advertised and sold to the highest bidder.

NSI answered the garnishment summons, stating that it held no money or other garnishable property belonging to the judgment debtor. Instead, NSI characterized what Umbro sought to garnish as "standardized, executory service contracts" or "domain name registration agreements."

* * *

In opposing the garnishment, NSI submitted an affidavit from its director of business affairs, who stated that domain names cannot function on the Internet in the absence of certain services being provided by a domain name registrar such as NSI. He further stated that NSI performs these domain name registration services pursuant to a standard domain name registration agreement.

Circuit Ct.: held Jdgmt. Debtor's Domain names are Garnishable

After a hearing on Umbro's show cause motion, the circuit court determined that the judgment debtor's Internet domain name registrations are "valuable intangible property subject to garnishment." In a letter opinion, the court concluded that the judgment debtor has a possessory interest in the domain names registered with NSI. The court further found that there are no unperformed conditions with regard to the judgment debtor's contractual rights to use the domain names, that NSI is not being forced to perform services for entities with whom it does not desire to do business, and that the domain names are a "new form of intellectual property."

Circuit Ct.: directed the sale of the Domain names

Accordingly, the court ordered NSI to deposit control "over all of the [j]udgment [d]ebtor's Internet domain name registrations into the [r]egistry" of the court for sale by the sheriff's office. Because of the intangible nature of the domain names, the court directed the sheriff's office to sell the domain names in whatever manner it "deem[ed] appropriate" after consultation with Umbro, and to notify NSI as to the name of the successful bidder for each domain name. According to the court's order, NSI then had to "transfer the domain name registration" to the successful bidder "as soon as commercially practicable following NSI's receipt of a properly completed registration application for the domain name from the winning bidder." This appeal followed.

- Jdgmt. Debtor Appealed

* * *

III.   The Internet and Domain Names

The Internet, which began as a United States military computer network called ARPANET, is now a "vast and expanding," *Intermatic*, 947 F. Supp. at 1230, worldwide network of interconnected computers....

Each method of communicating on the Internet depends on the use of a unique domain name, also known as a "fully qualified domain name," *Intermatic*, 947 F. Supp. at 1230, to locate a specific computer or network, *Lockheed Martin*, 985 F. Supp. at 951. Domain names have been compared to trademarks, addresses, or telephone numbers, but domain names, addresses, and telephone numbers, unlike some trademarks, are unique.

Each "host" computer that is "more-or-less permanently" connected to the Internet is assigned its own "Internet Protocol" (IP) number or address, which specifies the location of the computer....

Because Internet users can more readily remember a name as opposed to a lengthy sequence of numbers composing an IP number, each individual computer or network also has an alphanumeric name called a "domain name." ... For example, in this Court's domain name, courts.state.va.us, "us" is the top-level domain, and is a country code or identifier which signifies that the domain name is registered in the United States...." [V]a," the second-level domain, indicates a sub-network used in the Commonwealth of Virginia; "state," the third-level domain, describes a sub-network used by the state government of Virginia; and "courts" further indicates a computer used by Virginia's judiciary.

* * *

If an Internet user knows the domain name for a particular Web site, such as this Court, the user can type the name into a Web browser and access that site directly without having to conduct what may be a time-consuming search. See also MTV, 867 F.Supp. at 204 n. 2 (noting absence of "satisfactory Internet equivalent of telephone company white pages or directory assistance"). Even when a user does not know the specific domain name for a Web site, the user can often deduce the name and still find the site without performing a search. Most businesses on the Internet use the "com" top-level domain. See *Lockheed Martin*, 985 F. Supp. at 952. Thus, a user could intuitively find a company's Web site by typing into a Web browser the corporate or trade name, such as "umbro.com."[3] Because the second-level domain name, i.e., "umbro" in the example, must be exclusive, a company would obviously want to use its recognized name in the second level of its Internet domain name. See id. See also *Panavision*, 945 F. Supp. at 1299 ("businesses frequently register their names and trademarks as domain names"). The advantage of having such a domain name thus explains the value that is attached to some domain names and the reason why litigation has occurred between trademark owners and domain name holders.[4] Id. See also *Intermatic*, 947 F. Supp. at 1233.

NSI's role in the Internet domain name system is to manage certain domain name registrations. *Lockheed Martin*, 985 F. Supp. at 953. At one time, NSI held the exclusive right, pursuant to a contract with the National Science Foundation, to assign Internet domain names using the top-level domains "gov," "com," "org," "net," and "edu," see id., but it now shares that

---

3. When an Internet user enters a domain name in his or her browser, the browser sends the request through the Internet in a process administered by a computer termed a "top-level server." Top-level servers maintain a registry of each domain name active in a given top-level domain and match requests for domain names to IP numbers in their registries. Intermatic, 947 F.Supp. at 1231; Berne, supra, at 1167.

4. Much of the litigation regarding domain names has focused on trademark infringements. We cite to several of those cases and related law review articles in this opinion, but none of those cases squarely addresses the question before us.

right with other domain name registrars. NSI charges an initial registration fee of $70 for each new domain name. The registration is valid for two years and may be renewed on a yearly basis for a fee of $35 per year.

In assigning the second-level domain names, NSI performs basically two services. NSI first compares applications with a database of existing domain names to prevent the registration of identical second-level domain names. NSI then matches the domain name to the corresponding IP number for the desired Web site. Domain names are available essentially on a first-come, first-serve basis.

NSI performs these services pursuant to domain name registration agreements. NSI does not independently verify a registrant's right to use a domain name, but does require a registrant to make certain representations and warranties, such as certifying that the registrant has the right to use the domain name and that such use does not interfere with the rights of another party.

A registrant also agrees to be bound by NSI's "Domain Name Dispute Policy." In accordance with that policy, when litigation arises with regard to the registration and use of a domain name, NSI deposits control over the domain name into the registry of a court by furnishing the plaintiff in such litigation with a "registry certificate."[5] In such instances, NSI agrees to be bound by the provisions of any temporary or final court orders regarding the disposition of a domain name without being named a party to the litigation, provided the domain name registrant is named as a party. The terms of the "Domain Name Dispute Policy" also authorize NSI, in its sole discretion, "to revoke, suspend, transfer or otherwise modify a domain name registration upon thirty (30) calendar days prior written notice, or at such time as [NSI] receives a properly authenticated order from a court...requiring the revocation, suspension, transfer or modification of the domain name registration."

NSI has also developed a procedure that allows a new domain name registrant to acquire a previously registered domain name with the consent of the former registrant of that name. The old registrant relinquishes its domain name registration, and the new registrant agrees to be bound by the terms of NSI's current "Domain Name Registration Agreement" and "Domain Name Dispute Policy." NSI requires the old and new registrants to execute a form agreement titled "Registrant Name Change Agreement[,] Version 3.0 — Transfers" in order to effect this change.

IV.   GARNISHMENT PROCEDURES

Under Virginia law, a judgment creditor can enforce a judgment for money by requesting the clerk of the court where the judgment was rendered to issue a writ of fieri facias and then by delivering that writ to a

5. The record in this case does not contain any "registry certificate" that was filed in the litigation in the federal district court in South Carolina, but it does contain a "Declaration" by NSI's "Internet Business Manager," which was filed in that litigation. The "Declaration" contains essentially all the elements of a "registry certificate."

"proper person" of the court for execution. Code §8.01-466. See also Code §8.01-465.2 (foreign judgment properly filed with clerk is subject to same procedures as judgments rendered by circuit court). The writ commands the officer "to make the money therein mentioned out of the goods and chattels of the person against whom the judgment is." Code §8.01-474. See also Code §8.01-478 ("writ of fieri facias may be levied on the goods and chattels of the judgment debtor"). When property of a judgment debtor is not capable of being levied on, as in the case of intangible personal property, such property is nevertheless subject to the execution lien upon delivery of the writ to a sheriff or other officer. Code §8.01-501.

Garnishment, like other lien enforcement remedies authorizing seizure of property, is a creature of statute unknown to the common law, and hence the provisions of the statute must be strictly satisfied. As pertinent here, a judgment creditor can institute garnishment proceedings if "there is a liability" on a third person to the judgment debtor. Code §8.01-511. "Liability" in this context means a "legal obligat[ion]," "enforceable by civil remedy," "a financial or pecuniary obligation," or a "debt." Black's Law Dictionary 925 (7th ed.1999). Accord Webster's Third New International Dictionary 1302 (1993) (an "amount that is owed ... [;] pecuniary obligations ... [;] debts").

* * *

V. ANALYSIS

In its first assignment of error, NSI asserts that the circuit court erroneously concluded "that Internet domain names are a new form of intellectual property, separate and apart from the domain name services provided by NSI, in which the judgment debtor has a possessory interest." NSI argues that the registration services agreement is the only source of rights acquired by a registrant and that a "registrant receives only the conditional contractual right to the exclusive association of the registered domain name with a given IP number for a given period of time." In NSI's words, a domain name is "simply a reference point in a computer database ... [or a] vernacular shorthand for the registration services that enable the Internet addressing system to recognize a particular domain name as a valid address." Thus, NSI contends that such services are not subject to the execution lien of a writ of fieri facias.

In response, Umbro contends that, when NSI processes a registrant's application and assigns a specific domain name to the registrant under NSI's first-come, first-serve policy, that registrant acquires the right to use the domain name for an initial period of two years, to exclude others from using the name, and to effect a transfer of the name by using NSI's "Registrant Name Change Agreement." Thus, Umbro posits that NSI not only agrees to associate a particular domain name with an IP number, thus making the domain name an operational Internet address, but also grants to the registrant the exclusive right to use a unique domain name for a specified period of time. That contractual right, according to Umbro, is the intangible property in which the judgment debtor has a possessory interest and that is subject to garnishment.

[Margin notes: NSI claims Circ. Ct. erred by concluding Domain names are a new form of Intell. property, separate from services provided by NSI.

—NSI claims its services aren't subject to execution lien of a writ of fieri facias.

Umbro claims the intangible property of a domain name is that which the judgment debtor has a possessory interest in & is subject to garnishment]

Initially, we must point out that NSI acknowledged during oral argument before this Court that the right to use a domain name is a form of intangible personal property.

* * *

Irrespective of how a domain name is classified, we agree with Umbro that a domain name registrant acquires the contractual right to use a unique domain name for a specified period of time. However, that contractual right is inextricably bound to the domain name services that NSI provides. In other words, whatever contractual rights the judgment debtor has in the domain names at issue in this appeal, those rights do not exist separate and apart from NSI's services that make the domain names operational Internet addresses. Therefore, we conclude that "a domain name registration is the product of a contract for services between the registrar and registrant." *Dorer*, 60 F. Supp. 2d at 561. A contract for services is not "a liability" as that term is used in §8.01-511 and hence is not subject to garnishment. See Sykes v. Beal, 392 F. Supp. 1089, 1094-95 (D. Conn.1975) (analyzing garnishment of services and concluding that automobile insurer's duty to defend is not garnishable); cf. J. Maury Dove Co., Inc. v. New River Coal Co., 150 Va. 796, 827, 143 S.E. 317, 327 (1928) (where "contract contains mutual obligations and liabilities, or involve[s] a relation of personal confidence," one party cannot assign it without consent of other party); McGuire v. Brown, Guardian, 114 Va. 235, 242, 76 S.E. 295, 297 (1912) (holding contract for personal services is not assignable).

If we allow the garnishment of NSI's services in this case because those services create a contractual right to use a domain name, we believe that practically any service would be garnishable. For example, if a satellite television customer prepaid the fee for a particular channel subscription, Umbro's position would allow garnishment of the subscription service. We also are concerned that a decision to uphold the garnishment at issue would be opening the door to garnishment of corporate names by serving a garnishment summons on the State Corporation Commission since the Commission registers corporate names and, in doing so, does not allow the use of indistinguishable corporate names....

Nevertheless, Umbro attempts to draw a distinction between the judgment debtor's contractual right to use the domain names, which came into existence after NSI screened its database to guard against registering identical names and matched the judgment debtor's domain names to the corresponding IP numbers, and NSI's services that continue to make those domain names operational Internet addresses. We are not persuaded by Umbro's argument, although at least two jurisdictions have made a similar distinction with regard to telephone numbers.

The court in Georgia Power Co. v. Security Inv. Properties, Inc., 559 F.2d 1321 (5th Cir.1977), found such a distinction. In discussing the principle that a bankruptcy court cannot exercise summary jurisdiction over property unless the debtor or trustee has actual or constructive possession of the property in question, the court observed that "for a business,... telephone numbers constitute a unique property interest, the value of which increases as the number becomes widely known through publication in guidebooks, posting on billboards, and imprinting on publicity items." Id. at 1324. The court then distinguished the property interest in such numbers "from a subscriber's rights to the telephone utility's service." Id. See also Darman v. Metropolitan Alarm Corp., 528 F.2d 908, 910 n.1 (1st Cir.1976) (approving sale of telephone numbers in order to increase value of bankruptcy estate and noting distinction between "a subscriber's rights derived from a contract for telephone service and a subscriber's possible claim to a possessory interest in the telephone number"). However, other courts have reached different results. See Slenderella Sys. of Berkeley, Inc. v. Pacific Tel. & Telegraph Co., 286 F.2d 488, 490 (2nd Cir. 1961) (finding that telephone numbers were neither property of, nor in possession of, bankrupt subscribers).

We are cognizant of the similarities between a telephone number and an Internet domain name and consider both to be products of contracts for services. See *Dorer*, 60 F. Supp. 2d at 561. In our opinion, neither one exists separate from its respective service that created it and that maintains its continued viability.

*#Ct. does not suggest
Ktual rights can never be
garnished.*

* * *

By our decision today, we do not suggest that contractual rights can never be garnished. We recognized otherwise in *Lynch*. There, a judgment creditor attempted to garnish a sum due and payable under the terms of a fire insurance policy. The judgment creditor claimed that only the judgment debtor was to be indemnified by the insurance policy, that there was a present liability on the part of the insurance company to pay the judgment debtor for the insured loss, and that the funds held by the insurance company were garnishable. This Court determined that the judgment creditor's position would be correct if the judgment debtor had the right to demand payment from the insurance company for his sole benefit. Id.....

Similarly, while applying Virginia law, the United States Court of Appeals for the Fourth Circuit allowed a judgment creditor to garnish money that a builder owed to a judgment debtor under the builder's contract with the judgment debtor. United States v. Harkins Builders, Inc., 45 F.3d 830, 835 (4th Cir.1995). In its discussion of garnishment proceedings under Virginia law, the court stated, and we agree, that "where the property is in the form of a contract right, the judgment creditor does not 'step into the shoes' of the judgment debtor and become a party to the contract, but merely has the right to hold the garnishee liable for the value of that contract right." Id. at 833. Notably, in *Lynch* and *Harkins*, the property that each judgment creditor sought to garnish was a sum of money due under a contract, not the performance of services by a garnishee.

VI. Conclusion

Under Code §8.01-511, a garnishment summons may be issued with respect to "a liability on any person other than the judgment debtor." In a garnishment proceeding, "[o]rdinarily, the only adjudicable issue is whether the garnishee is liable to the judgment[ ] debtor, and if so, the amount due."

Butler v. Butler, 219 Va. 164, 166, 247 S.E. 2d 353, 354 (1978). In the present case, the only "liability" due on the part of NSI is the provision of its Internet domain name services to the judgment debtor. Code §8.01-511. Although, as Umbro points out, domain names are being bought and sold in today's marketplace, we are not willing to sanction the garnishment of NSI's services under the terms of our present garnishment statutes. To do so would allow Umbro to "step into the shoes" of the judgment debtor. *Harkins*, 45 F.3d at 833. Even though the Internet is a "new avenue[ ] of commerce," *Intermatic*, 947 F. Supp. at 1229, we cannot extend established legal principles beyond their statutory parameters.

For these reasons, we will reverse the judgment of the circuit court, dismiss the garnishment summons, and enter final judgment in favor of NSI.

COMPTON, Senior Justice, with whom Chief Justice CARRICO joins, dissenting.

Relying heavily on decisions of federal trial courts, the majority concludes that a domain name registration is the product of a contract for services between the registrar and the registrant.... I disagree that the registration is a contract for services not subject to garnishment.

NSI, the garnishee, correctly acknowledges that the right to use a domain name is a form of intangible personal property. Code §8.01-501 clearly provides for an execution lien on intangible personal property, that is, property not capable of being levied upon. That lien attaches to the extent the judgment debtor has a possessory interest in the intangible property subject to the writ.

Therefore, the question becomes whether the judgment debtor has a possessory interest in the domain names it registered with NSI. In my opinion, the trial court correctly ruled that the judgment debtor, by virtue of the domain name registration agreements with NSI, has a current possessory interest in the use of the domain names, that is, a contractual right to the exclusive use of the names it has registered with NSI.

However, NSI contends that the judgment debtor's contractual rights are not subject to garnishment because they allegedly are contingent, dependent on unperformed conditions, or are like personal services. The majority erroneously has bought into this idea.

NSI's contractual obligation to the judgment debtor already is presently due, not contingent or akin to a personal service agreement. The judgment debtor has submitted its registration forms and paid the registration fees. NSI has completed the registration of the judgment debtor's Internet domain names under NSI's "first come, first served" policy, and the judgment debtor acquired the right to the exclusive use of the domain name for an initial period of two years.

Because NSI has received everything required to give the judgment debtor the exclusive right to use the domain names it registered, the contractual right, a valuable asset, is the intangible personal property in which the judgment debtor has a possessory interest. This right is a "liability" within the meaning of Code §8.01-511 and is subject to garnishment.

In my view, contrary to the majority's conclusion, this right exists separate and apart from NSI's various services that make the domain names operational Internet addresses. These services, as the trial court correctly ruled, are mere conditions subsequent that do not affect the garnishment analysis.

Consequently, I would affirm the judgment of the trial court.

=======

This case is just another in a whole line of judicial opinions in which courts are required to harmonize the quickly changing computerized world with legal principles developed centuries ago.

Problem Set 3

3.1. ***A.*** On February 1 First Finance Co. obtained a $3,000 judgment against Wayne Smettle and delivered a writ of garnishment to the sheriff for service on Amos State Bank, where Wayne had his checking account. On that date the account was overdrawn by $10. On February 5, Wayne deposited $5,000 in the account. On February 7 Second Finance Co. obtained a judgment against Wayne for $3,500 and delivered a writ of garnishment to the sheriff, also for service on ASB. As it happened, the sheriff served both writs on the bank at the same time on February 9. You are ASB's junior counsel, a new attorney from out of state. When ASB calls for advice and explains these facts, what is your preliminary analysis under the general principles discussed so far?

B. As so frequently happens, before you can develop an answer for your client, additional facts emerge. It seems that Wayne didn't know about the garnishments and wrote a $500 check to the telephone company the day of the service of the writs, February 9. The bank paid the check by mistake on February 10. Still ignorant of the garnishment, Wayne deposited $200 in the account on February 11. The bank answered the garnishment writ on February 15, five days before the answer was due under local rules. The day after the bank's answer was filed, February 16, Wayne's employer made an automatic electronic deposit to the account of Wayne's weekly wages, $300. What does your list of issues look like now as you head for the library?

3.2. On October 15 Judgment Collections, Inc. delivered to the marshal a garnishment writ addressed to Chuck Nicholson. Nicholson answered the writ on November 4, saying he had in his possession office equipment belonging to Catherine Baker, the judgment debtor. Nicholson stated that he had leased the equipment from Baker on October 1 for one year and attached a copy of the lease. Alberta Doyle is a neighbor of both Baker and Nicholson. Doyle says the equipment was just being kept for Baker by Nicholson, as a favor. Doyle also says she was present when the lease was executed on October 20, although it was dated October 1. By what process will the matter be resolved? Depending on Doyle's credibility, who is entitled to the office equipment?

3.3. NCP Homebuilders, Inc. employs a sales staff of 18 to 22 people to market their new homes. These employees are salaried, and they work with individual homebuyers to help them purchase NCP homes. The employees must work with the homebuyers' family budgets, mortgage and tax rates, employment plans, etc., to help both the company and the buyer determine what the buyer can afford.

Carlos Valdez is the sales force supervisor. He monitors the work of his employees closely and keeps close tabs on any "image" factors that might reflect on NCP. He trains and educates his staff, advises them on clothing, indicates when haircuts are appropriate, and so on. He fires employees who are not productive enough in sales or whose appearance or sales tactics are not approved by the company.

Valdez consults you on a new matter. He has just received a notification of a garnishment of the wages of one of the sales employees. Valdez would like to fire the employee. What do you advise? If Valdez wrongfully fires the employee, what are the possible consequences? Are there any risks besides an employee suit? See §304 of the Consumer Credit Protection Act, 15 U.S.C. §1674.

5.   *Pre-Judgment Remedies*

Special issues arise when a creditor attempts to seize property prior to obtaining a judgment. Although a pre-judgment attachment obviously precedes the judgment and the liens, executions, levies, and writs we have already studied, we delayed consideration of pre-judgment remedies because they raise special issues best considered once the typical collection process is understood.

The judicial process often takes time — often far too much time. While the judicial machinery is grinding fine, the defendant — especially one with a consciousness of having done wrong — may place assets out of reach, so the plaintiff has a victory without a triumph. Pre-judgment remedies are therefore very important to creditors. On the other hand, in a due-process society, permitting seizure of someone's property before the court has decided the rights and wrongs of the case is a very serious business. The tension between these concerns animates this whole area.

Pre-judgment attachment was traditionally a creature of state law — both statutory and common law — much like other collection procedures. There were many state variations on the prerequisites for pre-judgment remedies, including giving notice to the debtor, swearing affidavits of the debt owed, and posting a bond. Starting in 1969, the Supreme Court focused its attention on the due process requirements of pre-judgment remedies, and within a few years, state laws were reformed to reflect the new constitutional requirements.

Pre-judgment protection for defendant-debtors now falls into two categories: (1) traditional protection under state law by means of special requirements that a creditor must satisfy before being able to get a remedy prior to obtaining a judgment; and (2) procedural requirements in the pre-judgment process that the Supreme Court has found to be necessary to ensure the defendant debtor due process of law.

The state statutes typically require (1) a showing of need — for example, that the putative debtor is decamping with its assets; and (2) a bond, often in twice the amount of the value of the property, to provide a fund for the defendant's damages if the pre-judgment remedy turns out to have been wrongfully employed.

The requirements imposed by the Supreme Court in cases like Mitchell v. W. T. Grant, 416 U.S. 600 (1974), and North Georgia Finishing v. Di-Chem, 419 U.S. 601 (1975) can be roughly summarized as follows. A defendant's property may not be seized without an order issued by a judicial officer (not a clerk) upon a factual showing of need. Once it has been seized, the defendant must be given a hearing and a chance to get the property back very quickly.

The limitations imposed by the Supreme Court have made pre-judgment remedies less attractive for harassment and oppression, but at the same time have also lessened their usefulness for creditors with legitimate concerns, like a creditor pursuing defendants whose assets are relatively liquid and can move quickly from country to country.

The Supreme Court more recently nipped in the bud an attempt to augment the various pre-judgment remedies with a preliminary injunction "freezing" the assets of a defendant pending trial. Grupo Mexicano De Desarrollo, S.A., v. Alliance Bond Fund, Inc., 527 U.S. 308 (1999). Although the Court decided the case as a matter of the limits of the federal equity jurisdiction, its discussion of the inappropriateness of injunctive relief in lieu of the traditional collection remedies may influence state courts as well. Because the case raised important issues of international jurisdiction (the British have a worldwide "Mareva" injunction that works in much the way rejected in *Alliance Bond Fund*), it is discussed in more detail in the section on transnational bankruptcy.

B.   FRAUDULENT CONVEYANCES AND SHIELDING DEBTOR ASSETS

1.   *Origins of Fraudulent Conveyance Law*

Pierce's Gift to twyne was fraudulant to avoid C's jdgmt. against Pierce.

TWYNE'S CASE

3 Coke 806, 76 Eng. Rep. 809 (Star Chamber, 1601)

In an information by Coke, the Queen's Attorney General, against Twyne *C v. Pierce* of Hampshire, in the Star-Chamber, for making and publishing of a fraudulent gift of goods: the case on the stat. of 13 Eliz. cap. 5. was such; Pierce was indebted to Twyne in four hundred pounds, and was indebted also to C. in two hundred pounds. C. brought an action of debt against Pierce, and pending the *Pierce secretly by* writ, Pierce being possessed of goods and chattels of the value of three hundred *deed of gift, all* pounds, in secret made a general deed of gift of all his goods and chattels real *his goods & chattels* and personal whatsoever to Twyne, in satisfaction of his debt; notwithstanding *Real & Personal to* that Pierce continued in possession of the said goods, and some of them he sold; *Twyne to satisfy* and he shore the sheep, and marked them with his own mark: and afterwards *his debt.* C. had judgment against Pierce, and had a *fieri facias* directed to the Sheriff of Southampton, who by force of the said writ came to make execution of the said *C received jdgmt against Pierce*

[margin note: —Twyne resisted the sheriff.]

goods; but divers persons, by the command of the said Twyne, did with force resist the said sheriff, claiming them to be the goods of the said Twyne by force of the said gift; and openly declared by the commandment of Twyne, that it was a good gift, and made on a good and lawful consideration. And whether this gift on the whole matter, was fraudulent and of no effect by the said Act of 13 Eliz. or not, was the question. And it was resolved by Sir Thomas Egerton, Lord Keeper of the Great Seal, and by the Chief Justice Popham and Anderson, and the whole Court of Star Chamber, that this gift was fraudulent, within the statute of 13 Eliz. And in this case divers points were resolved:

[margin note: Ct. held the gift to Twyne was fraudulent.]

1st. That this gift had the signs and marks of fraud, because the gift is general, without exception of his apparel, or any thing of necessity; for it is commonly said, *quod dolus versatur in generalibus.*

2nd. The donor continued in possession, and used them as his own; and by reason thereof he traded and trafficked with others, and defrauded and deceived them.

3rd. It was made in secret, *et dona clandestina sunt semper suspiciosa.*

4th. It was made pending the writ.

5th. Here was a trust between the parties, for the donor possessed all, and used them as his proper goods, and fraud is always apparelled and clad with a trust, and a trust is the cover of fraud.

6th. The deed contains, that the gift was made honestly, truly, and *[margin note: Ct. Held; there was a true debt to Twyne]* bona fide; *et clausulae inconsuet' semper inducunt suspicionem.*

Secondly, it was resolved, that notwithstanding here was a true debt due to Twyne, and a good consideration of the gift, yet it was not within the proviso of the said Act of 13 Eliz. by which it is provided, that the said Act shall not extend to any estate or interest in lands, &c. goods or chattels made on a good consideration and *bona fide;* for although it is on a true and good consideration, yet it is not *bona fide,* for no gift shall be deemed to be *bona fide* within the said proviso which is accompanied with any trust; as if a man be indebted to five several persons, in the several sums of twenty pounds, and hath goods of the value of twenty pounds, and makes a gift of all his goods to one of them in satisfaction of his debt, but there is a trust between them, that the donee shall deal favorably with him in regard of his poor estate, either to permit the donor, or some other for him, or for his benefit, to use or have possession of them, and is contented that he shall pay him his debt when he is able; this shall not be called *bona fide* within the said proviso; for the proviso saith on a good consideration, and *bona fide;* so a good consideration doth not suffice, if it be not also *bona fide:* and therefore, reader, when any gift shall be to you in satisfaction of a debt, by one who is indebted to others also; 1st, Let it be made in a public manner, and before the neighbors, and not in private, for secrecy is a mark of fraud. 2nd, Let the goods and chattels be appraised by good people to the very value, and take a gift in particular in satisfaction of your debt. 3rd, Immediately after the gift, take the possession of them; for continuance of the possession in the donor, is a sign of trust....

2. Development of the Uniform Fraudulent Transfer Act

The Statute of Fraudulent Conveyances, 13 Eliz. c.5, 1571, was passed to protect creditors against debtors who would obstruct collection efforts by conveying away all their property, usually with an intent to have it reconveyed back to themselves at a future date. The statute was supplemented by a second act against fraudulent conveyances, designed to protect purchasers, in 27 Eliz. c.4, 1584-1585. Both statutes imposed fines for fraudulent conveyances and permitted the court to set such conveyances aside.

Much of the subsequent case law turned on whether there had been sufficient proof of the debtor's "intent to delay, hinder or defraud" creditors or purchasers. Courts dealt with the difficult problems of proof by developing "badges of fraud," facts that raised a presumption (rebuttable or otherwise) that the transaction was fraudulent. One key factual setting that raised the presumption of fraud was a sale or gift without transfer of possession. This presumption had an enormous impact on the development of non-possessory security interests, inspiring a judicial hostility to such interests that persisted into the twentieth century until the "secret lien" problem was finally solved.

American jurisdictions adopted the Statute of Elizabeth either by enacting statutes based on it or by treating it in the courts as a part of the accepted common law tradition. A host of issues were litigated, primarily focusing on complicated procedural questions and on classifying the various acts that were presumptively fraudulent. Case law became confused and contradictory. In 1915 the National Conference of Commissioners on Uniform Laws decided to draft a uniform act to clarify the substantive issues and streamline the procedures. The resulting Uniform Fraudulent Conveyance Act (UFCA) was adopted by the Conference in 1918. It subsequently was enacted — essentially without change — in 24 states and used as the model in numerous others.

In 1984 the Commissioners promulgated a new statute to replace the UFCA, the Uniform Fraudulent Transfer Act. The UFTA has been adopted in 41 states. The new statute makes a number of technical changes and improvements but retains all of the basic principles and concepts of its predecessor. It adds one completely new provision governing preferential payments to insiders, something we will discuss later in connection with federal preference law in bankruptcy.

The most important aspect of the original 1918 statute was that it codified in fraudulent conveyance law a concept usually called "constructive fraud" or "presumptive fraud." Both terms are misnomers because the new concept permitted a creditor to avoid — to set aside — a transfer even though the debtor was entirely innocent of any fraudulent intent. The statute defined circumstances in which the transfer was regarded as unfairly disadvantageous to the debtor's creditors, regardless of intent. Such a transfer could be avoided without any showing of fraud, constructive or otherwise, so there was no need for any "presumption" and there was nothing to rebut. Of course, if the attacking creditor could not show the circumstances constituting "constructive" fraud, the creditor could still try to show that the transfer was made with actual intent to defraud creditors.

The more recent uniform statute carries forward these same provisions but with modifications. The key section is section 5(a), which permits a creditor to avoid any transfer made (1) in exchange for an unfairly low consideration (2) at a time when the debtor was insolvent. This section therefore includes transfers in which the debtor was utterly innocent of fraudulent intent. Such a transaction, even though innocent, depletes the assets of an already insolvent debtor by the difference between the true value of the property and the amount the debtor actually received, thereby injuring the debtor's creditors.

The new version covers actual fraud in section 4(a)(1) and, for the first time, codifies in section 4(b) a modern version of the old badges of fraud, updating the list first compiled in *Twyne's Case*. Two other provisions in the updated statute are divided between a type of constructive-fraud test and one that is closer to "quasi-constructive" fraud, subsections 4(a)(2)(i) and (ii), respectively. The first incorporates "undercapitalization" from corporate law, while the second tests for a state of mind that is at least negligent.

The phrase "fraudulent conveyance" and the catch phrases "constructive fraud" and "presumptive fraud" often seemed to deflect courts from the fact that some innocent, although harmful, conduct is regulated by the statute. Of course, sometimes the constructive nature of fraud is exactly right: No one needs to prove outright fraud, but the inference of misbehavior is strong. The case that follows was decided under the UFCA. Our edited version contains bracketed citations to the provisions of the UFTA that approximate the provisions of the UFCA that were applicable in the case.

ACLI GOVERNMENT SECURITIES, INC. v. RHOADES

653 F. Supp. 1388 (S.D.N.Y. 1987)

LASKER, District Judge.

This case concerns the validity of a conveyance of property from defendant Daniel Rhoades to his sister defendant Norma Rhoades, which occurred the day before a judgment of over $1,500,000 was entered against Daniel Rhoades in favor of plaintiff ACLI Government Securities, Inc. ("AGS") in *ACLI Government Securities, Inc. v. Rhoades*, 81 Civ. 2555 (MEL) ("the AGS securities action"). After hearing the testimony of six witnesses and examining a number of documents presented at a three-day non-jury trial, I conclude that the conveyance was fraudulent and that AGS is entitled to judgment accordingly.

The significant facts are not in dispute. AGS is a government securities trader. Daniel and Norma Rhoades, both New York State residents and attorneys licensed to practice in New York, are brother and sister who are also partners in the law firm of Rhoades & Rhoades. After a lengthy jury trial, on May 10, 1983 the jury in the AGS securities action returned a verdict in favor of AGS and against Mr. Rhoades in the amount of $1,285,598.28. On May 20, 1983, a judgment on the verdict against Mr. Rhoades was signed and it was filed three days later. After a technical amendment, the total judgment was for $1,519,898.59, of which $1,385,401.06 plus post-judgment interest remains outstanding and unpaid.

On June 30, 1959, Daniel and Norma Rhoades became the owners of the property which is the subject of this suit, consisting of 68 acres of land located at Route 124 and Turk Hill Road in Brewster, Putnam County, New York ("the Putnam County Property"), as "tenants-in-common, Daniel Rhoades having an undivided three-fifths...thereof...and Norma

Rhoades having an undivided two-fifths...thereof." In 1981-1982 a house was constructed on the property, and as of May, 1983, the property was appraised to have a value of $325,000. On May 19, 1983, the day before the judgment against Daniel Rhoades referred to above was signed, defendants executed a deed in which Daniel and Norma Rhoades conveyed the Putnam County property to Norma Rhoades, for $1.00 and unspecified "other good consideration."[6]

While the parties agree on these facts, they strenuously debate the question at the heart of this action: whether the May 19, 1983, conveyance described above was fraudulent under N.Y. Debt. & Cred. Law §§270–81 (McKinney 1945 and Supp. 1987). AGS argues that the conveyance is fraudulent under (1) N.Y. Debt. &. Cred. Law §273-a (McKinney Supp. 1987), because the conveyance was made without fair consideration by a defendant in a lawsuit who failed to satisfy a final judgment against him; (2) N.Y. Debt. & Cred. Law §273 (McKinney 1945) [see UFTA §5(a)], because the conveyance was made without fair consideration and rendered Mr. Rhoades insolvent; and (3) N.Y. Debt. & Cred. Law §276 (McKinney 1945) [see UFTA §4(a)(1)], because the conveyance was made with actual intent to defraud AGS. Defendants contend that the conveyance of property was a valid transfer, grounded upon the consideration of an antecedent debt owed by Mr. Rhoades to Ms. Rhoades, that the conveyance did not render Daniel Rhoades insolvent and that it was not made with intent to defraud....

Defendants contend that the May 1983 conveyance was based on fair consideration because it was in satisfaction of an antecedent debt owed by Daniel Rhoades to Norma Rhoades. Ms. Rhoades testified at trial that she had entrusted her brother with half a million dollars in treasury bonds so that he could convert them from 4.25 percent to 9 percent treasury bonds via his AGS account, and that the bonds were never returned to her. The only proof offered of this transaction was evidence that Norma Rhoades owned $40,000 of over $350,000 in treasury bonds that Daniel Rhoades had forwarded to his AGS account in August–September 1980.

The burden of proof to establish that a debtor's conveyance was made without fair consideration is on the creditor. However, where the evidentiary facts as to the nature and value of the consideration are within the transferee's control, the burden of coming forward with evidence on the fairness of the consideration shifts to the transferee.

Moreover, in an intrafamily transaction there is a heavier burden on the transferee to establish fair consideration for the transfer.

I find that the May 19, 1983, conveyance of property was not based on fair consideration. While an antecedent debt may provide fair consideration for a conveyance of property, it must be "in amount not disproportionately small as compared with the value of the property...obtained." N.Y. Debt. &

---

6. PX 8 (May 19, 1983, bargain and sale deed to Putnam County property). Although on December 15, 1982, an order was entered in the AGS securities action which directed Mr. Rhoades "not [to] engage (either directly or indirectly) in any transfer of assets which might cause a material change in his financial condition except upon five (5) days written notice to this Court and ACLI's counsel...," PX 5 (Court Order, Dec. 15, 1982), Daniel Rhoades did not notify AGS's counsel or the court of this conveyance.

Bailment - a delivery of personal property by one person (the bailor) to another (bailee) who holds the property for a certain purpose under an express or implied-in-fact

Ct. Holds - can't find evidence of antecedent debt.

Cred. Law §272(b) (McKinney 1945) [see UFTA §§4(a)(2), 5]. The evidence here was not sufficient to establish the existence of *any* antecedent debt, let alone a debt proportionate to Mr. Rhoades' interest in the Putnam County property. First, while on deposition Ms. Rhoades stated that she "loaned" bonds to her brother, at trial she testified that she "entrusted them" to her brother "[t]o return to [her] 9 percent Treasury Bonds or an equivalent amount." Ms. Rhoades' trial testimony, then, suggests the conclusion that the transaction between her and her brother, if any, was a bailment rather than a loan. Furthermore, even if Norma Rhoades did make bonds available to her brother, this would not necessarily have created a creditor-debtor relationship between them. The evidence presented supported the conclusion that defendants' joint partnership and individual personal financial accounts were inextricably mixed: Norma Rhoades stated in her deposition that she and her brother have never balanced their financial accounts, and Daniel Rhoades testified that there has never been an accounting as to their law partnership. The fact that defendants' finances have been commingled for so long makes it impossible to conclude, on the evidence presented, that Daniel Rhoades was in debt to Norma Rhoades. Finally, Daniel Rhoades' own statements and those of his counsel further support the conclusion that he was not in debt to his sister at the time of the conveyance. In December 1982, Mr. Rhoades' then-attorney represented that he was unaware of any significant liabilities faced by Mr. Rhoades, and Mr. Rhoades himself swore out an affidavit on the issue of his financial condition which failed to mention any debt owed to Norma Rhoades.

Ds' joint partnership & fin. accts were inextricably mixed.

Ct. Holds: at best a Bailment was established b/w Ds, & there was no antecedent debt to serve as fair consideration.

In sum, the evidence presented on the transfer of bonds from Norma to Daniel Rhoades established at most a bailment of indeterminate size, and I conclude that there was no antecedent debt owed by Daniel Rhoades to Norma Rhoades which could have served as fair consideration for the conveyance of property in question....

It has already been concluded that the Rhoades conveyance was made without fair consideration, so that if it is found that the conveyance rendered Daniel Rhoades insolvent within the meaning of the statute, the conveyance is fraudulent under §273 [see UFTA §§4(a)(2), 5].

Under New York law,

> [a] person is insolvent when the present fair salable value of his assets is less than the amount that will be required to pay his probable liability on his existing debts as they become absolute and mature.

Ct. Holds: DR was insolvent at time of 05/83 conveyance & .: It was fraudulent

N.Y. Debt. & Cred. Law §271(1) (McKinney 1945) [see UFTA §2]. When a transfer is made without consideration, the burden of going forward with proof of solvency is on the defendants. I conclude that Daniel Rhoades was insolvent at the time of the May 1983 conveyance.

At trial, Daniel Rhoades offered evidence of three assets which he claimed to have owned at the time of the conveyance, the aggregate value of which (without including the Putnam County property) was allegedly sufficient to satisfy ACS' judgment of $1,519,899. The three assets were real property in South Carolina, a securities account at Advest, Inc., and an account receivable of Rhoades & Rhoades.

a)   The South Carolina Property

Daniel Rhoades testified at trial that at the time the May 1983 judgment was entered against him, he was the owner of real property in Anderson County, South Carolina. Karl Kenyon, a South Carolina lawyer who also invests in real estate in Anderson County, testified for Mr. Rhoades that in his opinion the property, which consisted of about 425 acres of undeveloped land, could have been sold as "ranchette" sites for a net of approximately $700,000. However, Kenyon's opinion was undercut in several ways. First, the South Carolina property was actually sold in 1984 or 1985 at auction for only about $200,000, and the actual price which the property brought on the open market is far better evidence of its value than Kenyon's speculation as to what price the land might have brought had it been marketed in a particular way. Second, the only appraisal of the property which was put into evidence was an estimate made in 1983 by a South Carolina real estate broker that the property was worth approximately $475-500 per acre, or about $212,500 in all. Finally, Kenyon's limited experience in the real estate field — which is not his profession — and his business relationship and friendship with Daniel Rhoades, weaken the value of his opinion. I find that the South Carolina property had a value of approximately $212,500 in 1983. [With respect to the remaining two assets that were part of Rhoades's claim to have been solvent, the court found that they were of virtually no value.]

In sum, I find Daniel Rhoades' testimony on his alleged solvency as of May 19, 1983, to be incredible in critical part, and conclude that defendants have failed to establish that at the time Daniel Rhoades transferred the Putnam County property to his sister he had assets whose aggregate fair, salable value was equivalent to the judgment about to be entered against him of $1,519,899. Hence, the conveyance was fraudulent under §273 [see UFTA §§4(a)(2), 5].

Ct. Holds: DR wasn't solvent as of 05/19/83

He had assets equal to $1,519,899

III.   §276

Under §276,

[e]very conveyance made . . . with actual intent . . . to hinder, delay, or defraud either present or future creditors, is fraudulent . . . .

N.Y. Debt. & Cred. Law §276 (McKinney 1945) [see UFTA §4(a)(1)]. The burden of proof to establish "actual intent" is on the creditor who seeks to set aside the conveyance, and he must do so by clear and convincing evidence. Actual fraudulent intent, by its very nature, is rarely susceptible to direct proof, and normally is established by inference from the circumstances surrounding the allegedly fraudulent act. Factors from which fraudulent intent can be inferred include (1) a close relationship among the parties to the transaction; (2) secrecy and haste of the sale; (3) inadequacy of consideration; and (4) the transferor's knowledge of the creditor's claim and his own inability to pay it [see UFTA §4(b)]. In this case, I find and conclude that the conveyance of the Putnam County property was made by Daniel Rhoades with actual intent to defraud AGS, and that Norma Rhoades knew of his intent.

Burden of Proof to estb. "actual intent" is on the creditor who seeks to set aside the conveyance

Ct. Holds: DR intended & NR knew of his intent to defraud AGS

This case has all of the classic indicia of fraudulent intent. Intrafamily transfers are scrutinized carefully, and Daniel and Norma Rhoades are not only brother and sister but have been law partners together for almost forty years. Both defendants knew of the jury verdict against Daniel Rhoades at the time of the conveyance. Indeed, Norma Rhoades testified on deposition that she demanded that her brother turn over his interest in the property to her precisely because she was angry "that a verdict had been rendered in this matter, an unconscionable verdict, which was full of error," and she was concerned that "a sheriff should not come up and try to sell this interest improperly." Second, the conveyance was made in secret, and was contrary to the court order of December 15, 1982, which required Daniel Rhoades to notify counsel and the court before transferring any assets. Moreover, the timing of the transaction, which occurred nine days after the jury verdict against Mr. Rhoades was announced and one day before judgment was signed against him, could not more strongly support the finding of fraudulent intent. Finally to be noted are the inadequacy of consideration involved and Daniel Rhoades' knowledge of his inability to pay the judgment, as discussed in Parts I and II.[7]

In sum, I conclude that AGS has established by clear and convincing evidence that the defendants' joint intent in conveying Daniel Rhoades' interest in the Putnam County property to Norma Rhoades was to defraud AGS, and that the conveyance was fraudulent under N.Y. Debt. & Cred. Law §276 [see UFTA §4(a)(1)]. Norma Rhoades claims that if the conveyance is declared fraudulent she is nevertheless entitled to an equitable lien on the property in the amount of the property taxes, maintenance and utility bills she has paid since the conveyance took place.... Even if Ms. Rhoades were entitled, despite her participation in the fraud, to an equitable lien on the property, a conclusion which is far from obvious, she would be entitled only to reimbursement for expenses essential to the preservation of the property and for tax payments beyond the reasonable value of her use and occupation of the land. Here, there is no evidence that the $50,000 paid by Norma Rhoades in taxes for the Putnam County property for the years 1983 through 1987 exceeds the fair rental value of the estate for four years, nor that payment of the other bills was essential for the preservation of the property.

For these reasons, I find that Norma Rhoades had no right to an equitable lien on the Putnam County property. She retains, of course, her forty percent interest in the property as a tenant in common.

_____

3. Leveraged Buyouts

The next case involves the most controversial aspect of contemporary fraudulent conveyance law: its application to leveraged buyouts (in the argot

7. In fact, if other circumstances warrant a finding of fraudulent intent, the conveyance may be found fraudulent even if it was based on fair consideration, see DeWest, 418 F. Supp., at 1279, or if the debtor remained solvent after the conveyance, see Elliott v. Elliott, 365 F. Supp. 450, 454 (S.D.N.Y. 1973).

of the stock market, "LBOs"). Without LBOs, many marginal corporate takeovers could not be financed.

The essence of the LBO financing device is that the assets of the corporation being acquired are used to secure the purchase price paid for those assets. (When outside investors are doing the financing, it is often through issuance of the aptly named "junk bonds.") Current equity holders are paid off in cash. The financer takes a security interest in virtually all of the company's assets, not just the stock. The acquirers take the equity for relatively little infusion of their own cash. Alternatively, the old equity holders may finance the operation by taking back a security interest in the company's assets to secure the new buyer's promise to pay the selling price, an arrangement referred to as "seller financing." The first generation of LBOs used these devices. When the transactions were later targeted as fraudulent conveyances, the parties began to dress up the transactions — and law firms were called on to issue opinions that they were not subject to set-aside under the UFTA. The next case involves such a "second generation" LBO, along with a lot of "first generation" discussion of the underlying public policies. The case arises in bankruptcy under a section that permits the trustee or the debtor to stand in the shoes of a creditor, here the Shintech Corporation. Just to make things livelier, Shintech sold its bankruptcy claim to an assignee, Nicole Plastics, which owned the bankrupt company (an early clue as to why Alice would have loved bankruptcy law). Later we will discuss the bankruptcy provision, section 544(b), that permits state UFTA law to be used in this way. For now, the focus can remain on how Judge Bufford applied the substantive element of the UFTA.

In re BAY PLASTICS, INC.

187 B.R. 315 (Bankr. C.D. Cal. 1995)

Samuel L. BUFFORD, Bankruptcy Judge.

I.   INTRODUCTION

The debtor has brought this adversary proceeding against the selling shareholders of a leveraged buyout ("LBO") to recover the funds that they received in the buyout transaction. While the action was also brought against the bank that financed the transaction, the bank has settled. The Court grants summary judgment to the debtor on the undisputed facts.

The Court holds that the transaction may be avoided as a constructive fraudulent transfer under the California version of the Uniform Fraudulent Transfer Act ("UFTA"), on which the debtor relies pursuant to Bankruptcy Code §544(b), and that in consequence the debtor is entitled to recover against the selling shareholders. The Court finds that the transaction rendered the debtor insolvent, and that the sellers did not act in good faith.

II. FACTS

The Court finds that the following facts are undisputed. ~~Defendants Bob Younger, Abner Smith and Paul Dodson~~ ("the selling shareholders") formed ~~debtor Bay Plastics, Inc.~~ ("Bay Plastics") in 1979 to manufacture ~~polyvinyl chloride ("PVC") plastic pipe~~ for water well casings and turf irrigation. ~~Bay Plastics filed this bankruptcy case on January 25, 1990.~~

A.   The Buyout

[margin note: 10/31/88 - selling shareholders sold near Bay Plas stock to Milhous for 3.5 mil + 1.8 mil in deferred pmts.]

Because they were nearing retirement, on October 31, 1988 (fifteen months before this bankruptcy filing) the selling shareholders sold their Bay Plastics stock to Milhous Corporation ("Milhous") for $3.5 million in cash plus $1.8 million in deferred payments.[8] Milhous did not acquire the Bay Plastics stock directly. Instead, it caused its subsidiary Nicole Plastics to form its own subsidiary, BPI Acquisition Corp. ("BPI"), to take ownership of the Bay Plastics stock. Formally, the parties to the stock sale transaction were ultimately BPI and the selling shareholders.

[margin note: BP borrowed 3.95 mil from Δ-BT & then loaned $3.5 mil BPI]
[margin note: BPI paid the $3.5 mil directly to selling shareholders]

The sale was unexceptional. The difficulty lay in the financing of the purchase. Milhous put no money of its own, or even any money that it borrowed, into this transaction. Instead, it caused Bay Plastics to borrow approximately $3.95 million from defendant BT Commercial Corp. ("BT") (a subsidiary of Bankers Trust), and then caused Bay Plastics to direct that $3.5 million of the loan be disbursed to BPI. BPI in turn directed that the $3.5 million be paid directly to the selling shareholders in substantial payment for their stock. Thus, at the closing, $3.5 million of the funds paid into escrow by BT went directly to the selling shareholders.

[margin note: BT received 1st sec interest in BP's assets.]

As security for its $3.95 million loan, BT received a first priority security interest in essentially all of the assets of Bay Plastics. In consequence, BT has received all of the proceeds of debtor's assets in this bankruptcy case, and nothing is left for unsecured or even for administrative creditors.

The financing also provided a revolving credit facility for working capital, in addition to the payment for the LBO, up to a total loan of $7 million.[9] A total of just over $4 million was owing to BT at the time of the bankruptcy filing, according to the debtor's schedules. Thus most of the debt (all but approximately $500,000) owing to BT at the time of the filing resulted from the LBO.

[margin note: 10/25/88 - selling shareholders knew of the deal.]

The selling shareholders were not in the dark about the financing. On October 25, 1988 they and their attorney met with Milhous representatives in Los Angeles to finalize the deal. While the Milhous representatives provided rather little information about the Milhous finances, they did disclose the details of the BT secured loan to Bay Plastics to finance the stock purchase. In addition, the selling shareholders received a projected post-transaction balance sheet, which showed a balance of $250,000 in equity

8. Apparently the deferred payments have not been made. All but $100,000 of the deferred payments were designated as compensation for a non-competition agreement.

9. While working capital advances were authorized up to $3.35 million, the Court has received no evidence on whether such advances were actually made.

only because of the addition to the asset side of the ledger the sum of $2,259,270 in goodwill. Both the selling shareholders and their attorney were experienced in LBOs, and the selling shareholders discussed this feature of the transaction, and their exposure on a fraudulent transfer claim, with their attorney on that date. With this information in hand, Younger, Smith and Dodson approved the terms of the sale.

In contrast to the selling shareholders, the industry did not know about the LBO character of the transaction until a number of months later. Shintech Corp., a creditor at the time of the transaction (and continuously thereafter), did not learn of it until ten months later, in August, 1989.

[handwritten margin note: Shintech, a creditor didn't learn of it until 10 mos. later in 08/89.]

B. The Shintech Debt

Some three months before the LBO, on July 22, 1988, Bay Plastics entered into a requirements contract with Shintech to supply PVC resin. Shintech agreed under the contract to supply up to 2.6 million pounds of PVC resin per month on payment terms of 30 days after shipment. To induce Shintech to enter into this contract, Bay Plastics granted Shintech a security interest in all its assets, and the shareholders gave personal guaranties. This arrangement stood in the way of the BT transaction.

In consequence, the selling shareholders, their attorney, and Milhous representatives met with Shintech in late October, 1988 (after Milhous had disclosed to the selling shareholders the terms of the LBO), to arrange a new deal with Shintech. The parties to the LBO persuaded Shintech of Milhous' good credit, and induced Shintech to release both its security interest and the guaranties.[10] However, they did not disclose the LBO character of the transaction, and Shintech did not learn of this until ten months later.

The impact of this transaction on the balance sheet of Bay Plastics was dramatic. Immediately after the transaction, its balance sheet showed tangible assets of approximately $7 million, and liabilities of approximately $9 million. Only the addition of almost $2.26 million in goodwill, which had not appeared on prior balance sheets, and for which no explanation has been provided, permitted the balance sheet to show a modest shareholder equity of $250,000. But for the newly discovered goodwill, there would have been a net deficiency of some $2 million. In contrast, immediately before the transaction Bay Plastics had assets of $6.7 million and liabilities of $5.6 million, and a net equity of $1.1 million.

Bay Plastics was unable to service this overload of debt, and filed its bankruptcy petition fifteen months later. According to the debtor's schedules, at the time of filing its two principal creditors were BT and Shintech: it owed approximately $4 million in secured debt to BT, and $3.5 million in unsecured debt to Shintech. No other creditor was owed more than $20,000. . . .

---

10. In consequence of giving up its security and its guaranties, Shintech now holds more than 99% of the unsecured debt in this case.

III Discussion

a.   GENERAL

The basic structure of an LBO involves a transfer of corporate owner-ship financed primarily by the assets of the corporation itself.[11] Typically the corporation borrows the funds, secured by the assets of the corporation, and advances them to the purchasers, who use the funds to pay the purchase price to the selling shareholders. Kathryn V. Smyser, Going Private and Going Under: Leveraged Buyouts and the Fraudulent Conveyance Problem, 63 Ind. L.J. 781, 784-85 (1988). LBOs have two essential features:

> First, the purchaser acquires the funds necessary for the acquisition through borrowings secured directly or indirectly by the assets of the company being acquired. Second, the lender who provides such funds is looking primarily to the future operating earnings of the acquired company and/or to the proceeds from future sales of assets of the company, rather than to any other assets of the purchasers, to repay the borrowings used to effect the acquisition.

Id., at 785. LBO investors thus generally consider cash flow, the money available for working capital and debt service, as the most important factor in assessing a potential buyout candidate. Id., at 785 n. 12.

The application of fraudulent transfer law to LBOs has generated con-siderable debate among courts and commentators. LBOs were a popular form of consensual corporate takeover in the 1980's. They fell into disuse at the end of that decade for economic reasons. However, the use of the LBO as an acquisition device has recently become popular again.

The LBO dates back long before the 1980's. In earlier years, it was known as a "bootstrap acquisition." Some of these transactions were invali-dated as fraudulent conveyances....

The Court notes at the outset that this case is not determined by the Ninth Circuit case law as set forth in the [Lippi v. City Bank, 955 F.2d 599 (9th Cir. 1992)] and [Kupetz v. Wolf, 845 F.2d 842 (9th Cir. 1988)] cases. Those cases both involved a fraudulent transfer attack on behalf of subse-quent creditors. This case, in contrast, is brought for the principal benefit of a creditor existing at the time of the transaction, which holds more than 99% of the outstanding unsecured debt.

We begin with the elements of the cause of action under the UFTA §5, as adopted in California, for a constructive fraudulent transfer rendering the debtor insolvent. The elements of a cause of action under this statute are as follows: the debtor (1) made a transfer or incurred an obligation, (2) without receiving a reasonably equivalent value in exchange, (3) which rendered the debtor insolvent (or the debtor was already insolvent), and (4) which is attacked by a pre-transaction creditor.

1.   Transfer or Obligation

The selling shareholders do not dispute that, in making the BT loan, the debtor made a transfer or incurred an obligation. In fact, the debtor did both.

---

11. While LBOs have frequently been used by management to buy out existing share-holders and take over the ownership of a business, management is not an essential party to an LBO. Indeed, in this case the purchaser was an outside third party.

The debtor undertook the $3.95 million obligation to BT, it transferred a security interest in essentially all of its assets to BT, and it transferred $3.5 million ultimately to the selling shareholders. Thus the first element of the cause of action is satisfied.

2.   Lack of Reasonably Equivalent Value

The selling shareholders likewise do not contest whether the debtor received reasonably equivalent value for the BT loan. However, this element is not apparent on its face.

Nominally, BT's transaction was only with Bay Plastics. It lent the $3.95 million to the debtor, the debtor promised to repay the loan, and the debtor gave a first priority security interest in essentially all of its assets to secure the repayment. If this were the transaction, creditors likely would have no grounds for complaint, and it would not be vulnerable to fraudulent transfer attack.

However, the foregoing structure obscures the reality of the transaction. The selling shareholders' transaction was formally with Milhous, and eventually with BPI, the new owner of Bay Plastics. BPI purchased their stock, and arranged for their payment with funds that Bay Plastics borrowed from BT. Before Bay Plastics received the funds, it directed that $3.5 million be transferred to its incoming parent, BPI, and BPI in turn directed that the funds be paid out for the stock purchase. Thus in substance $3.5 million of the funds that Bay Plastics borrowed from BT went to pay for the stock of the selling shareholders, rather than to Bay Plastics.

This raises the question whether the Court should collapse the various transactions in this case into one integrated transaction. Under *Lippi* this turns on whether, from the perspective of the selling shareholders, the transaction appeared to be a straight sale without an LBO. [955 F.2d at 612.] If, in contrast, there is evidence that the parties knew or should have known that the transaction would deplete the assets of the company, the Court should look beyond the formal structure. Id. In *Kupetz* the Ninth Circuit found it improper to collapse the transactions where the selling shareholders had no knowledge of the LBO character of the transaction, and there were no pre-transaction creditors.

In this case, in contrast, the selling shareholders had full knowledge that this was an LBO. The Milhous representatives informed them of this at the October 25 meeting before the transaction was finalized, and it was disclosed in the financial projections provided at that time. In addition, the selling shareholders discussed this feature with their legal counsel on October 25, and specifically discussed their exposure to a fraudulent transfer claim. Both the selling shareholders and their legal counsel were familiar with leveraged buyouts, because they had done others previously, and they knew the fraudulent transfer risks.

This knowledge of the selling shareholders distinguishes this case from both *Kupetz* (where the selling shareholders did not know or have reason to know of the LBO) and from *Lippi* (where the evidence was disputed). Instead, this case is like *Richmond Produce, Wieboldt* and *Tabor Court Realty,* where the transaction was collapsed because of the knowledge of the selling shareholders.

In addition, because Shintech qualifies as a pre-transaction creditor, the Court does not need to reach the issue of the knowledge of the LBO feature of the transaction by the selling shareholders: this is material to whether the transaction's various parts should be collapsed only when challenged by post-transaction creditors.

Thus, in this case the Court finds it appropriate to collapse the various pieces of this transaction into one integral transaction, in which the funds went to the selling shareholders, not to Bay Plastics or to its new parent BPI. The loan obligation, in contrast, was undertaken by Bay Plastics, which also provided the security for the loan.

Bay Plastics received no reasonably equivalent value for the security interest in all of its assets that it gave to BT in exchange for BT's funding of the stock sale.

From the debtor's perspective, it is apparent that the $450,000 that Bay Plastics presumably received (the $3.95 million loan less the $3.5 million paid to the selling shareholders) is not reasonably equivalent to the $3.95 million obligation that it undertook. Cf. Shape, Inc. v. Midwest Engineering (In re Shape, Inc.), 176 B.R. 1, 3 (Bankr. D. Me. 1994) (payment of $70,000 for stock worth more than $1.5 million lacks reasonably equivalent value). Thus Bay Plastics did not receive reasonably equivalent value for the loan obligation and security interest that it granted to BT.

3. Insolvency of the Debtor

The third element of the fraudulent transfer cause of action at issue in this litigation is that the transaction rendered the debtor insolvent, if it was not so already. In this case the Court finds the evidence undisputed that the LBO rendered the debtor insolvent.

Insolvency is defined in California Civil Code §3439.02(a) (West Supp. 1995): "A debtor is insolvent if, at fair valuations, the sum of the debtor's debts is greater than all of the debtor's assets." UFTA §2(a) is essentially the same. These statutes adopt the balance sheet test for insolvency: a debtor is insolvent if the liabilities exceed the assets ....

The valuation of assets for insolvency purposes is based on "a fair valuation." This differs from a balance sheet, where most assets apart from publicly traded stocks and bonds are carried at historic cost, rather than current market value. The values of assets must be updated in light of subsequent use and market conditions: in accounting parlance, they must be "marked to market."

In addition, a balance sheet may include intangible assets such as goodwill[12] that may have no liquidation or going concern value, and which thus must be deleted in evaluating the solvency of an entity. Goodwill cannot be sold to satisfy a creditor's claim. Thus, in a liquidation bankruptcy case it

---

12. Goodwill is generally understood to represent the value of intangible factors that are expected to translate into greater than normal earning power. In addition to the advantageous relationship that a business enjoys with its customers, goodwill also includes advantageous relationships with employees, suppliers, lenders and others. Because goodwill has no independent market or liquidation value, generally accepted accounting principles require that goodwill be written off over a period of time. In acquisition accounting, going concern value in excess of asset value is treated as goodwill. Dictionary of Finance & Investment Terms 157 (2d ed. 1987).

must be disregarded in determining solvency of the debtor at the time of an LBO.

Goodwill frequently appears on a balance sheet after the sale of a business, where it represents the excess of the purchase price over the net value of the other assets purchased. It appears that this may be the explanation for the appearance of goodwill on the debtor's balance sheet in this case.

Nominally, Bay Plastic's corporate balance sheet showed the debtor to be solvent after the LBO. But this resulted only from the addition of $2.26 million of goodwill to the asset side of the balance sheet. Bay Plastics had not previously carried any goodwill on its balance sheets.

The parties to this litigation have accepted the debtor's balance sheet immediately after the LBO as a fair presentation of the debtor's financial status, with the exception of goodwill. Thus the Court is relieved of the burden of marking to market the debtor's assets. However, the trustee contends that the goodwill of $2.26 million that first appeared at that time must be deleted in determining the debtor's solvency.

The Court finds that the balance sheet must be adjusted by deleting the unamortized goodwill of $2.26 million. It was not carried on the balance sheet before the LBO, and in any case it could not be sold to satisfy a creditor's claim. Richmond Produce, 151 B.R. at 1019. This is a liquidation case, where goodwill has no other value. This downward adjustment left Bay Plastics with a negative net worth of approximately $2 million immediately after the LBO. For fraudulent transfer purposes, it was rendered insolvent by the transaction.

Indeed, this is exactly the type of transaction that poses the extreme risk of an LBO. No Milhous entity put any funds or assets at risk in the investment at all. In consequence of the structure of the transaction, all of the risks of the enterprise were placed on its creditors. Milhous retained only the right to reap the benefits if the business was sufficiently profitable to avoid bankruptcy. [13]

4.   Attack by a Pre-transaction Creditor

The final element of the cause of action for fraudulent transfer rendering a debtor insolvent is that the transaction must be attacked by a pre-transaction creditor. This element is satisfied in this case.

Shintech, the principal unsecured creditor in this case, which holds more than 99% of the unsecured debt, is the pre-existing creditor. It was secured until this transaction, and in addition it held guaranties from each of the selling shareholders. In this transaction the selling shareholders and Milhous induced it to relinquish its security and guaranties to permit the transaction to be consummated. Although knowing the LBO character of the transaction, both the selling shareholders and Milhous failed to disclose this feature to Shintech.

13. In such a transaction there is a danger that the selling shareholders will be paid more than their stock is worth. With nothing at risk if the business is not sufficiently profitable, the purchaser has less incentive to make sure that the price is not excessive. Absent fraudulent transfer law, there is nothing to deter the buyers, sellers and bank from imposing all of the risks of loss on the creditors, as they did in this case.

The selling shareholders make three arguments against considering Shintech a qualifying pre-transaction creditor. First, they argue that Shintech's account was current at the time of the LBO, and that in consequence all of its debt comes from a later date. Second, they argue that Shintech had an opportunity at the pre-closing meeting, where it agreed to release its security interest and guaranties, to ask any questions that it wanted, and it declared that it was satisfied with the information provided to it. Third, they claim that Nicole Plastic's purchase of Shintech's claim in settlement of a lawsuit by Shintech against Nicole and other Milhous entities disqualifies this claim as a pre-transaction claim: in effect, the shareholders contend, the claim now belongs to the debtor itself. The Court finds all of these arguments unpersuasive.

a.   SHINTECH AS CREDITOR

First, the Court finds that Shintech is a pre-transaction creditor of Bay Plastics, even if the account was current at the time of the LBO. Just three months earlier Shintech had entered into a massive contract with Bay Plastics to provide all of its requirements of PVC, which were monumental — up to 2.6 million pounds (1300 tons) per month. Under this contract Bay Plastics owed a duty to Shintech to buy its PVC from Shintech for the duration of the contract, whether or not the account was current on any particular day. The contract was in place on the day of the LBO, and remained in force until after the bankruptcy filing....

Shintech's contract rights under its requirements contract to provide PVC were certainly not valueless, even if payments were current at the time of the LBO. If Bay Plastics had repudiated the contract on the day after the LBO, it would have owed massive damages to Shintech. [The court found this contract obligation was enough to make Shintech a present creditor under the UFTA]... immediately before the date of the filing of the petition....

In Aluminum Mills Corp. v. Citicorp North America, Inc. (In re Aluminum Mills Corp.), 132 B.R. 869, 888-91 (Bankr. N.D. 111. 1991), the court found that a complaint sufficiently alleged the existence of pre-transaction creditors where it claimed that there were agreements for open trade accounts in place at the time of the LBO and continuing until the bankruptcy was filed.[14] In this case there was more than an open account with Shintech: there was a massive requirements contract for all of the PVC that Bay Plastics needed.

The Court holds that this made Shintech a creditor of Bay Plastics at that time, and that Shintech maintained this status until the bankruptcy case was filed. Thus this element of the cause of action is met.

b.   INVESTIGATION OF THE TRANSACTION

Second, the selling shareholders argue that Shintech, the largest supplier of PVC resin in the industry, had every opportunity to investigate the nature of

---

14. Cf. Unsecured Creditors' Committee v. Banque Paribas (In re Heartland Chemicals, Inc.), 103 B.R. 1012, 1016 (Bankr. C.D. 111. 1989) (creditor does not qualify as a pre-transaction creditor if the indebtedness was paid off after the transaction and then extended new credit).

the LBO transaction, and cannot now be heard to complain about it. The Court finds this is irrelevant to the cause of action for a fraudulent transfer that renders a debtor insolvent....

Shintech did change its position at the time of the transaction, in giving up its security and its guaranties. It apparently could have prevented the transaction from going forward if it had refused to make these concessions. However, the LBO feature of the transaction was hidden from it. Thus, the transaction was a secret transaction as to both Shintech and the industry, of the sort that the Ninth Circuit in *Kupetz* declared to be within the scope of a fraudulent transfer claim, even if brought only on behalf of subsequent creditors.

C. APPLICATION OF FRAUDULENT TRANSFER LAW TO LBOS

The Court finds it appropriate to apply fraudulent transfer law to an LBO. An LBO is different, not just in degree, but in character from the ordinary business and investment transactions engaged in by a corporation's management. An LBO is not a routine business transaction that should normally be given deference by the courts. It is not a corporate investment in a new venture, new equipment or property....

Since an LBO reduces the availability of unencumbered assets, the buyout depletes estate assets available to pay creditors' claims. As the Ninth Circuit has stated:

> Existing unsecured creditors are vulnerable in [an LBO]. From their perspective, a pledge of the company's assets as collateral to finance the purchase of the company reduces the assets to which they can look for repayment.

Kupetz, 845 F.2d at 846; accord, Moody v. Security Pacific Business Credit, Inc., 971 F.2d 1056,1073 (3d Cir. 1992). An LBO is attractive to the sellers, the buyers and the lender because it shifts most of the risk of loss to other creditors of the corporation. The acquired corporation receives little or nothing in exchange for the debt that it incurs.

From a creditor's point of view, an LBO is indistinguishable from a distribution or a gift to shareholders. The harm is quite like the harm imposed on creditors by donative transfers to third parties, which is one of the most traditional kinds of fraudulent transfers. If the value of the security interest given by the corporation does not exceed the shareholders' equity as shown on the balance sheet (after suitable revisions to mark the assets to market and to eliminate intangible assets of dubious value), there is usually no substantial harm to creditors. Indeed, typical corporate distribution statutes permit the payment of dividends in such circumstances, to the extent of the balance sheet equity. See, e.g., Cal. Corp. Code §166 (West Supp. 1995). If the price paid to selling shareholders is higher, however, there may be insufficient assets remaining to satisfy creditors.

The vice of an LBO lies in the fact that the selling shareholders are paid indirectly with assets from the corporation itself, rather than by the purchasers. In effect, in an LBO the shareholders are paid with a corporate dividend or distribution. An LBO enables the selling shareholders to liquidate their equity interests, which are otherwise subordinate to general unsecured claims, without first paying creditors, which a normal liquidation would require. The selling shareholders in the transaction in effect disregard the status of the corporation as a separate entity for their benefit, but insist on respect of the corporation's separate status when it comes to creditors' claims (apart from those of the lender providing the funds for the transaction).

The possible detriment to creditors is exacerbated if the corporation's cash flow is not sufficient to service the loan. The bank eventually proceeds to foreclose on the corporation's assets and sells them at foreclosure prices, and leaves nothing for other creditors. Such foreclosure is frequently interrupted by the filing of a bankruptcy case. So it happened in this case....

Should all LBOs be exposed to fraudulent transfer challenge? Certainly not. Under this Court's analysis, two kinds of LBOs ordinarily escape fraudulent transfer attack. This includes many, if not most, LBOs.

First, in a legitimate LBO, in which the assets mortgaged by a corporation to support an LBO do not exceed the net equity of the business (after appropriate adjustments), the transaction will not make the corporation insolvent, at least according to the balance sheet test. If in addition it has sufficient projected cash flow to pay its debts as they come due, the cash flow solvency test is met, also. This leaves an LBO exposed to fraudulent transfer attack only if the margin of equity is too thin to support the corporation's business.

A second kind of LBO also escapes fraudulent transfer attack, even though it leaves the subject corporation insolvent. If the cash flow is sufficient to make the debt payments, the transaction also is unassailable. This ordinarily turns on two factors: the degree of risk of default undertaken in the first instance, and the degree to which projected economic developments impacting the business are not overly optimistic. These LBOs escape fraudulent transfer attack either because of good financial projections or because of good luck: either factor is sufficient.

The Court's view of the proper application of fraudulent transfer law to LBOs does not make the selling shareholders the guarantors of the success of the LBO. A legitimate LBO, as described supra, shifts the risk of failure off their shoulders. As to subsequent creditors, they should not be required to shoulder the risk if the failure is caused by outside forces not reasonably foreseeable at the time of the transaction.

However, an LBO that is leveraged beyond the net worth of the business is a gamble. A highly leveraged business is much less able to weather temporary financial storms, because debt demands are less flexible than equity interest. The risks of this gamble should rest on the shoulders of the shareholders (old and new), not those of the creditors: the shareholders enjoy the benefits if the gamble is successful, and they should bear the burdens if it is not. This, after all, is the role of equity owners of a corporation. The application of fraudulent transfer law to LBOs shifts the risks of an LBO transaction from the creditors, who are not parties to the transaction, back to the old and new shareholders who bring about such transactions. As Sherwin states:

> These parties, who are directly involved as the principal engineers and beneficiaries of the buyout, should bear the risk of negative consequences if

the transaction does not in fact comply with the standards for creditor protection set out in the fraudulent conveyance statutes. . . . They should be accountable to creditors for the benefits diverted from the corporation if they knew or should have known . . . of facts the court determines to establish a constructive fraud against creditors.

[Emily L. Sherwin, Creditors' Rights Against Participants in a Leveraged Buyout, 72 Minn. L. Rev. 449, at 519 (1988).]

How long should selling shareholders be exposed to the risk that an LBO will go bad? There is a traditional answer to this question: until the statute of limitations runs. Perhaps there should be a shorter statute of limitations for LBOs than the four to seven years that is common under the UFTA. This is a decision for the legislature to make. . . .

Judge Bufford decided that Shintech was a preexisting creditor of the LBO. In many cases, however, the earlier creditors have been paid off and the lawsuit is initiated by a later creditor who claims to have signed on to the *Titanic* without knowing that all the ballast had been removed. The standard for review shifts. It is interesting to contemplate whether Judge Bufford, if pushed, would have declared that the parties initially intended to "hinder, delay or defraud" the creditors, bringing the transaction afoul of UFTA §4. We also wonder whether there is any substantive difference between §4(a)(2) (available to present and future creditors) and §5(a) (available only to present creditors) notwithstanding Judge Bufford's careful notation that he could decide the case under the presumably more creditor-friendly rules of §5.

The use of fraudulent conveyance statutes to attack LBOs has drawn sharp academic criticism. The critics have asserted that current fraudulent conveyance law is too all-encompassing in its effects. See, e.g., Baird and Jackson, Fraudulent Conveyance Law and Its Proper Domain, 38 Vand. L. Rev. 829 (1985). These authors see the state and federal fraudulent conveyance statutes as old-fashioned. They argue that these statutes should be narrowly drawn and interpreted because (1) there are transactions, like LBOs, that are sometimes benign in their effects on a debtor and its creditors; (2) it is relatively easy for a creditor to contract against the risk of a harmful fraudulent conveyance, but difficult for a debtor and its creditors to contract out of fraudulent conveyance law to protect a beneficial transaction; and (3) fraudulent conveyance law may block some beneficial transactions. Because these critics recommend narrowing fraudulent conveyance law, rather than abolishing it, it appears that they believe that there is a point up to which current law blocks more harmful transactions than good ones, but they do not identify that point or provide an approach to its identification, either analytically or empirically.

As Judge Bufford demonstrates, this view has not carried the day. Many experts, both in the academy and in practice, continue to believe that both the technical requirements for fraudulent conveyance and the spirit of the fraudulent conveyance laws have been violated when the old equity bows out with a big payment and the corporation is saddled with high debt and security interests for which it received no discernible value. See, e.g., Preliminary Report of Examiner, Professor Barry Lewis Zaretsky, In re Revco D.S., Inc., 118 B.R. 468 (Bankr. N.D. Ohio 1990) (Appendix).

Problem Set 4

4.1. Adrienne Leiske is insolvent. She owes $50,000 to Family Finance. In order to raise money so she can make her rent payments and eat, she sells her grand piano. Although the piano is valued at $15,000, she runs a want ad asking $10,000. When offered $7,500, Adrienne accepts. Can Family Finance successfully claim a fraudulent conveyance? See UFTA §§4, 5, 8.

4.2. Bonney O'Hare is insolvent, and she feels the tightening web of creditors. She decides to sell her coin collection to her cousin, Susan Mallory. Although the collection would bring $75,000 if she sold it to a dealer, Bonney sells it to Susan for $5,000 so that "it will stay in the family." Bonney also knows that Susan has no real interest in the collection and will undoubtedly be willing to sell it back when Bonney's financial troubles are over. The day after her conveyance to Susan, Bonney uses her American Express card to purchase $25,000 in new furnishings. Can American Express successfully claim a fraudulent conveyance? See UFTA §§4, 5.

4.3. Jeremiah Stoke owns a homestead free and clear worth $100,000. His other assets total $55,000; his debts, all unsecured, total $75,000. He knows that under state exemption law his homestead is safe from his creditors. He has made a mess of his own affairs, but his favorite son has just married, and he'd like to do just one thing right. So Jeremiah conveys the homestead to his son as a gift and settles down to await the battles with his creditors over his debts. Can Jeremiah's current creditors reach the homestead conveyed to the son? See UFTA §§1, 2, 5.

4.4. S. R. Wilson is insolvent. His chief creditor is Lo-Cost Credit Union, to which he owes $100,000. Wilson sells his mobile home, valued at approximately $60,000, to his neighbor Sam for $30,000 cash. Sam moves into the home, cleans it up, spends $5,000 for repairs, and enhances the value of the mobile home by 20 percent. Lo-Cost successfully claims that the conveyance was fraudulent. What can Lo-Cost recover from Sam? See UFTA §8.

4.5. Kim Winick called you this morning about a broken friendship. It was just one year ago that Kim lent $100,000 — the money she had inherited from her mother — to help her friend Pat Rafferty start a dry cleaning business, Magic Clean, Inc. Kim lent the money to the company at a good interest rate, with only the interest payable for six years. At the end of six years, which was Pat's estimate of the time needed for the business to become well established and consistently profitable, the company would repay Kim in full. Two weeks ago Kim got a letter from Pat saying that he had sold all the stock of the company to Rick Lance, a recently retired navy man. Kim knows Lance and says he has no business experience. As Kim put it, "Cash flow is not one of the flows he knows about." The stock sale was entirely on credit, with the company guaranteeing Lance's payments to Pat and all of the company's assets securing the guarantee. A balance sheet that

Pat had prepared was attached to the letter. It shows the value of the company's assets exceeding its liabilities, even if the guarantee to Pat is included as a liability.

Pat's letter explained that the business is struggling and its bills from suppliers are piling up. It concluded, "I have been without a salary for a whole year, Kim, and I just can't go on like this. But I'm proud of the fact that I'm up-to-date on your interest and I'm sure everything will be fine with Rick running the shop." Kim does not feel at all fine and wants to know what she can do "to cancel my ticket on the *Titanic.*" What's your advice? See UFTA §§2, 4, 5.

4.6. Mr. and Mrs. Young are members of the Crystal Evangelical Free Church. They are active in their church, attending services regularly with their children, serving as officers, and contributing their time. They tithe regularly, following the biblical injunction to contribute 10 percent of their income to the church. Last year, their church contributions totaled $13,450, all made while the Youngs were legally insolvent. They have filed for Chapter 7, and their trustee has asked the church to return the contributions. You represent the church; what do you advise? (Once again, we don't make this stuff up. To see a more complete discussion of the case, brought by a trustee named Christians, where the court relied on a case styled In re Moses, see Christians v. Crystal Evangelical Free Church (In re Young), 148 B.R. 886 (Bankr. D. Minn. 1992), aff'd, 152 B.R. 939 (D. Minn.); rev'd, 82 F.3d 1407 (8th Cir. 1996), vacated, 521 U.S. 1114 (1997), on remand, sub nom. In re Young, 141 F.2d 854 (8th Cir.), cert. denied, 525 U.S. 811 (1998).)

4.7. Marcel Du Champs fraudulently conveyed his beloved prize race-horse Jonquil to his friend Travis Winchel for $100 to keep it safe from creditor attachment. The two had an express understanding that when Marcel's business difficulties were over, Travis would reconvey the horse, which is worth about $200,000. Ultimately, Marcel was able to revive his business, become solvent, and pay all his creditors in full. He offers $100 to Travis plus a generous bonus to cover the horse's stable fees, but Travis refuses to reconvey. He has grown fond of the horse and of life in the fast lane, and he doesn't want to sell. Does Marcel have any legal recourse?

C. STATE COLLECTIVE REMEDIES

The state collection system is based on the one-at-a-time race of the diligent that effectively pits every creditor against both the debtor and every other creditor who is trying to press the debtor for repayment. This collection system is premised on the ultimate individual actor and a series of bilateral debtor-creditor negotiations.

Either debtors or creditors may grow weary of the one-at-a-time approach, especially when the debtor seems to be collapsing financially rather than disputing a single debt. Creditors may conclude that in some circumstances they will be better off if they work together. They may want to reduce their individual costs or simply increase the chances that they will receive something from the debtor. Debtors may decide they would rather deal with their creditors collectively instead of individually. State collection laws typically provide for two ways in which creditors can work in concert and debtors can resolve their disputes in a single blow.

In this section we discuss these two state remedies, but we do so more by way of background than for practical application. The state devices are sufficiently limited that in most cases a debtor or creditor seeking a collective remedy will choose the federal bankruptcy statutes. There are certain parts of the country and certain types of situations, however, where there may be an advantage to the state system, which means that any well-educated lawyer should have some familiarity with it. For example, Professor Ronald Mann has found data showing that high-tech companies in Northern California are often liquidated under a state procedure called an assignment for the benefit of creditors, although similar high-tech companies in Texas almost always liquidate in bankruptcy (see Mann, An Empirical Investigation of Liquidation Choices of Failed High Tech Firms, 82 Wash. U.L.Q. 1375 (2004)).

1. Assignment for the Benefit of Creditors

Usually called "ABCs," assignments for the benefit of creditors offer a way for the debtor to "get everyone off my back." The debtor can assign all non-exempt property to a local lawyer, Jones, as assignee and tell the creditors, "Leave me alone and go argue with Jones." The assignee is typically a lawyer who accepts a conveyance of all of the debtor's non-exempt property, liquidates it, and distributes the proceeds pro rata to claimants. The assignee generally operates under the supervision of a court, although there are enormous variations among the states. Many states have statutes regulating this procedure, although a nonstatutory, common law assignment is recognized in a number of jurisdictions as well.

ABCs do not discharge a debtor from the unpaid portion of the outstanding debts. Any such discharge would intrude upon the Bankruptcy Code's supremacy in the field and the state statute would be void. See, e.g., Straton v. New, 283 U.S. 318 (1931). The lack of discharge limits the usefulness of an ABC for any debtor who can consider a bankruptcy alternative.

Once an ABC has been made, the property assigned is generally immune from legal process issued on behalf of individual creditors because it is in the custody of the court (*custodia legis*) and thus no new priorities or other rights in the property can be created after the assignment. The assignee is also a lien creditor under Article 9 of the UCC under UCC section 9-301(3) and Revised 9-309(12) and thus takes priority over unperfected security interests pursuant to UCC section 9-301 (1)(b) and Revised 9-317. As in bankruptcy, this priority inures to the benefit of the general creditor body.

In some states an assignment may prefer certain creditors or groups of creditors, while in others such unequal treatment is forbidden. Various other terms and conditions may invalidate an assignment or be unenforceable in some states, while recognized as legitimate and enforceable in others. In particular, states differ on the validity of an assignment that is conditioned upon creditor agreement to release the debtor from the unsatisfied portion of the debts.

2. Composition and Extension

A "composition" is an agreement between the debtor and all (or virtually all) of the creditors that the creditors will accept a stated partial payment in full satisfaction of their debts. An assignment for the benefit of creditors is sometimes the vehicle for a composition, to obtain the benefits of that proceeding to aid in the composition. (One benefit is priority over unperfected security interests.) Closely related is an "extension," which is a general agreement to give the debtor more time to pay the outstanding debts in full. Extensions and compositions are often brought together in one agreement with creditors. For example, a debtor with $100,000 of currently due debts might propose to pay $50,000 over a period of a year in full satisfaction. The $50,000 payment is a composition and the one-year term is an extension.

These two terms, composition and extension, are often used in a bankruptcy context, although less so today than in times past. In bankruptcy, very different rules apply. State law compositions are entirely voluntary as to each creditor, unlike a bankruptcy reorganization in which some creditors can be forced to go along. By the same token, if a composition fails (for example, the debtor defaults in the promised payment), the original debts may be revived. By contrast, in a Chapter 11 bankruptcy reorganization the original debts are forever discharged when the plan of payment is approved.

State law compositions are valid and enforceable agreements, notwithstanding the apparent lack of consideration, on the theory that each creditor's agreement to accept less binds all other creditors who agreed to accept a reduction of their claims. The consequence of a completed composition is to release the debtor from further payments. A composition can be overturned, however, if the debtor made financial misrepresentations, secretly preferred certain creditors, or engaged in other relevant wrongful conduct.

Although bankruptcy is the legal relief of choice for most debtors and creditors when financial disaster strikes (for a host of reasons that we will study), there are some advantages to the state law remedies. The procedures tend to be faster and less expensive than bankruptcy proceedings. If the special powers and controls of bankruptcy are unnecessary (e.g., because the debtor's assets and liabilities are small and the creditors are agreeable), it may make sense to use the state procedures. In addition, a composition can be done quietly, without court proceedings, which is sometimes critical to the continuing operation of a business or the personal needs of an individual. The very quietness of the procedure, however, and the fact that insiders may manipulate an ABC or a composition provide fewer protections against fraudulent behavior in connection with the agreements, which may account somewhat for the decline in their use. The frequency of use of these state law remedies varies dramatically from place to place around the country.

3. Receiverships

The appointment of a receiver and the consequent creation of a receivership is analogous to guardianship, in which a guardian takes over control of the property of a minor or an incompetent. The receiver appointed by the court becomes the person in legal control of the property of a debtor, with the power to manage the debtor's financial affairs.

Modern receiverships are most often established pursuant to regulatory statutes, notably state and federal securities laws. As the old phrase "went into receivership" suggests, however, receiverships were and are a method of collective action on behalf of creditors of a financially troubled business or individual. Today they have particular importance when the debtor *cannot* be forced into bankruptcy, as where the debtor is a church, a political committee or other nonprofit organization, or where the debtor is a farmer. Bankruptcy Code §§109(b), 303(a).

Financial receiverships are sometimes authorized under state law. A party may ask that a receiver be appointed to aid in the execution of a judgment. If the court agrees, a receiver may take charge of the debtor's assets and preserve them for sale and distribution to the creditors. Regulatory receiverships are sometimes employed when a regulatory agency asks a court to appoint a receiver after discovering that a company or individual is violating a regulatory statute. The proceeding often has a financial purpose, to protect customers by gaining control of assets, but it also has other purposes: for example, preventing further violations and permitting a complete investigation of the debtor's conduct. Another important effect of the appointment of a receiver may be to place the debtor's property in *custodia legis*, preventing execution by particular judgment creditors and halting "the race of the diligent." The receivership thus preserves the debtor's assets to be distributed pro rata to customers and other creditors of the debtor. The receiver acts on behalf of all the creditors to maximize the available assets.

The use of receivership is often limited in effect because companies in recent years have responded to regulatory receiverships by filing bankruptcy petitions under Chapter 11, so that management can regain control from the regulators. See, e.g., In re Cash Currency Exchange, Inc., 762 F.2d 542 (7th Cir. 1985). Much of the current use of receiverships is to deal with failures and mismanagement in banking and insurance. Receiverships in these two industries are particularly important because neither banks nor insurance companies may file for bankruptcy. For the state-chartered companies, this makes state receivership actions the chief tool available for dealing with troubled businesses.

Barney's Problem — Part I

Note: Unless otherwise indicated, the day this part of Barney's Problem is discussed in class is "deemed to be" March 1 of this year. This part of the problem, like the rest, is to be analyzed in "real time," i.e., as if you as counsel obtain the information or take the action indicated on the day (and the deemed date) the problem is to be discussed in class, as if you were a sole practitioner in a town called Aloysius, and this small drama were real.

You have been called today by the Aloysius State Bank. The attorney who has acted as regular counsel has just announced that he is moving to another town to take a job with a large corporation. ASB wants you to pick up its most pressing case while it makes a decision on how to replace its former counsel. You are hopeful that this tryout may give you an inside opportunity for taking on the bank's work.

ASB's case is against Larsene E. Whipsnade, a local rancher, and his company, Whipsnade, Inc. ASB's claims are as follows:

1. Loan to Whipsnade secured by DOT (deed of trust) on ranch — $100,000 (30 years, due February 6, 2016);
2. Loan to Whipsnade, Inc. secured by a lien on all its assets and guaranteed by Whipsnade — $100,000;
3. $50,000 worth of open accounts owed by Whipsnade to local merchants for supplies for his downstate truck farm, which accounts were pledged by the merchants to ASB to secure their own financing. The bank has assumed the accounts for collection.

The bank's former lawyer obtained final judgments on all three claims but, at ASB's request, took no other action pending settlement discussions with Whipsnade. These discussions have broken off, and ASB has directed you to proceed as you think best.

Whipsnade has four other debt actions against him, each for $10,000, three reduced to judgment. Two judgments were entered before ASB's, one (the Anderson judgment) by a lawyer who did everything she could and the other (the Blakey judgment) by a lawyer who did nothing pending discussions with Whipsnade. A third judgment (the Carling judgment) was entered after ASB's and the lawyer was diligent.

On February 5, execution was returned "nulla bona" on the Anderson judgment after Whipsnade charged out of his ranch residence with a shotgun and ran off the sheriff. On February 8, execution on the Carling judgment was levied on Whipsnade's new $50,000 tractor, which was subject to a $20,000 purchase-money lien on the face of the certificate of title. The tractor was sold by the sheriff at public auction over Whipsnade's protest that he would pay. Only judgment creditor Carling appeared at the auction, and he bought the tractor for $30,000. He subsequently resold the tractor for $45,000 to a bona fide purchaser.

On February 10, the plaintiff in the fourth action obtained prejudgment garnishment against Whipsnade's account at ASB in the amount of $12,500.

On February 12, Whipsnade sold all his remaining personal property (including his Mercedes and a Picasso) and the fixtures on the ranch to his son for $50,000, half of which has disappeared and half of which he deposited at your client bank in a preexisting account, "L. E. Whipsnade, Trustee for L. E. Whipsnade, Jr." The account now has $35,000.

The Whipsnade, Inc. balance sheet last given to the bank shows as assets: 5 front loaders ($100,000 cost, 1/2 depreciated); 50 chain saws (new; total cost, $5,000); 3,000 board feet of finished lumber (listed for sale at $1/bd. ft.); a mill and 5 acres of real estate (cost less depreciation equals $50,000); and a partridge in a pear tree (no value given). Whipsnade, Inc. has sold all the lumber to Clearance, Inc., a wood jobber, for $1,800, which is in the corporate account at your client bank. It may have sold the chain saws as well. The balance sheet also shows a $50,000 debt to Barney Thornaby secured by a lien against the loaders, but no liens are shown on the related certificates of title.

What must you do first?
What has the bank failed to do, and how do you protect it now?
Prepare to tell your client:
1. What should be done, what results are likely, and why.
2. What each of the other creditors described above will likely get and why.
3. How other general unsecured creditors will likely come out.

PART II

CONSUMER BANKRUPTCY

"What is a bankrupt, father?" asked Eugenie.

"A bankrupt," replied her father, "is guilty of the most dishonourable action that can dishonour a man."

"It must be a very great sin," said Mme Grandet, "and our brother will perhaps be eternally lost."

"There you are with your preachments," her husband retorted, shrugging his shoulders. "A bankrupt, Eugenie," her father continued, "is a thief whom the law unfortunately takes under its protection. People trusted Guillaume Grandet with their goods, confiding in his character for fair dealing and honesty; he has taken all they have, and left them nothing but their eyes to weep with. A bankrupt is worse than a highwayman; a highwayman sets upon you, and you have a chance to defend yourself; he risks his life besides, while the other — Charles is disgraced in fact."

The words filled the poor girl's heart; they weighed upon her with all their weight; she herself was so scrupulously conscientious; no flower in the depths of a forest had grown more delicately free from spot or stain; she knew none of the maxims of worldly wisdom, and nothing of its quibbles and its sophistries. So she accepted her father's cruel definition and sweeping statements as to bankrupts; he drew no distinction between a fraudulent bankruptcy and a failure from unavoidable causes, and how should she?

Honoré de Balzac, Eugénie Grandet 108 (1833).

CONSUMER BANKRUPTCY

CHAPTER 3

INTRODUCTION TO BANKRUPTCY

A. DEVELOPMENT OF THE CURRENT STATUTE

Although ancient civilizations had laws regulating the treatment of defaulting and insolvent debtors, these antecedents are murky and their connection with modern bankruptcy law is more proclaimed than demonstrated. It is said that in Roman times the creditors did not merely divide the debtor's possessions, but took the debtor to the plaza and divided him. Whether or not it was so (and whether or not "bankruptcy" derives from the Italian "banca rotta" or "broken [merchant's] table"), the clearest origins of United States bankruptcy law are to be found in England.

From the original English bankruptcy statute, adopted in the reign of the first Elizabeth, until the time of the American Revolution, "bankruptcy" was involuntary, a creditor's collection device, a super-attachment of all the debtor's property for equal division among creditors. It unified in a single action all the individual attachments and garnishments that were available at common law and by statute, and that are still part of our state laws today. Generally it could be used only against "traders." The benefit to bankrupts was release from the unpaid portion of their debts.

A separate and later development was "insolvency" law, designed for the relief of debtors. Insolvency was always voluntary. Debtors who placed all their property in the hands of their creditors and the court were "discharged" from debtors' prison — not released from their debts. The debtors' obligations to pay remained, and creditors could still use collection devices other than imprisonment.

In the United States, combining discharge and bankruptcy elements into a unified debtor-creditor statute was a difficult process marked by various unsuccessful attempts. Notwithstanding specific constitutional recognition that a uniform bankruptcy act was vital to national interests, United States Const., art. I, §8, cl. 4, more than a century passed before our legal ancestors could fashion a permanent bankruptcy statute acceptable to competing constituencies. For history buffs and students of social class, Bruce Mann's book, *A Republic of Debtors*, tells a lively tale of debt, bankruptcy, morality, and economy in early America. It also reveals that the most basic questions about the morality of bankruptcy and its place in social policy have been debated from colonial times forward.

Throughout the nineteenth century, there were periodic struggles between mercantile and debtor interests over enactment of "bankruptcy" or "insolvency" laws. The farmers of the South and West detested the idea of involuntary bankruptcy, while the Northern and Eastern merchants wanted a discharge to be contingent on creditor agreement by specified majorities. Many believed that the two bodies of law, insolvency and bankruptcy, could not stand together ("a bill to serve God and Mammon") and the intensity of feeling generated by what is today regarded as a dry and technical subject was quite remarkable:

> [The proposed bankruptcy law] comes from the class of men who are grinding the face of the poor . . . [and from] the same spirit that hung and killed and drew and quartered women for witchery. 31 Cong. Rec. S2362 (daily ed. March 1, 1898) (statements of Senator Stewart, Nev.).

Insolvency and bankruptcy were brought together in a series of short-lived acts. The Acts of 1800 and of 1841 were thought too generous to debtors. The former was repealed within three years and the latter lasted only about a year. The 1867 Act was in some ways too strict and in others too liberal. It was extensively amended in 1874, only to be abandoned four years later. Essentially, then, the bankruptcy "system" for the first 109 years after the adoption of the Constitution was little more than a series of brief legislative fiats, alternately pro-creditor or pro-debtor, accompanied by a growing awareness that a uniform compromise law would better serve everyone. In the meantime, various states enacted their own insolvency laws, which were permitted to stand in the absence of congressional legislation.

The interests of "God and Mammon" were at last accommodated in the Act of 1898, in the aftermath of another economic "panic." The Act answered a need felt by both debtor and creditor interests, who thus compromised more than either had previously been prepared to do. The benefit to debtors was obvious, providing debt relief through discharge. Creditors for their part recognized that a workable bankruptcy system, providing orderliness to the collection process and encouraging debtors to make some payments, even at the cost of permitting debtors a discharge, was in their interest as well.

The legislation enacted in 1898 represented a series of fine compromises on a host of difficult issues. For example, it prohibited involuntary petitions against farmers and thus assuaged the fears of the South and West. Even so, it was thought too liberal by the credit community, which would have pushed for its repeal if the Act had remained unchanged. Reports circulated through Congress that after the Act was passed, some men in large cities had been discharged two or three times in a single year, fueling cries of debtor abuse. Repeal sentiment also stirred in the pro-debtor South, since the generally applicable involuntary provisions of the law remained odious to Southerners. The great backlog of desperate debtors was discharged by 1903, leaving Southerners less anxious to compromise. Nonetheless, in 1903 amendments were adopted that successfully compromised debtor and creditor interests on discharge and a few other issues. With this final series of compromises, the first enduring American bankruptcy law took shape.

The Bankruptcy Act of 1898 was amended a number of times in the following years, but it was not revised extensively until the 1930s, following the greatest "panic" of them all. The Chandler Act, encompassing the most extensive of the changes, was adopted in 1938. That act did not change the fundamental structure of the liquidation provisions of the 1898 Act, although it made a number of detailed changes in response to the lessons of the Depression. From a modern perspective, its most important innovations were the adoption of new procedures for the reorganization of businesses and payment of debt over time by financially troubled wage earners.

The roots of the Chandler Act long pre-dated the Great Depression. Failing businesses and their multiple creditors called on the courts to resolve their disputes over wasting assets and priority of distribution as they tried to leave companies intact while renegotiating their financial obligations. Drawing from state receivership law, the federal courts by the early twentieth century had developed a form of business reorganization called "equity receivership." Based on a host of legal fictions and maneuvers, it served the function of permitting a financially troubled company, especially one with public stockholders and public debt, to "reorganize" (reduce and extend) its debt and to continue operations rather than liquidate. While many of the basic principles of modern bankruptcy reorganization were thus developed in common law fashion, the first forms of the reorganization process had many defects, including expense and frequent fraud. See, e.g., First National Bank v. Flershem, 290 U.S. 507 (1934). The structure crumbled under the assault of the Depression and was hastily replaced in 1933 and 1934 by new bankruptcy enactments, sections 77 and 77B, the former for railroad reorganizations and the latter for businesses generally.

While sections 77 and 77B codified and much improved the equity reorganization, these emergency enactments had many defects of their own. They were replaced in the Chandler Act by Chapter X, which remained the basic corporate reorganization chapter until the adoption of the Bankruptcy Code in 1978. The reorganization of small businesses and of companies with substantial real estate assets were carved out into two more chapters, Chapters XI for small businesses and Chapter XII for real estate companies.

Chapters X and XI diverged from their ancestor in sharply different ways. Chapter XI was designed to be cheap and fast and therefore eliminated many of the procedural safeguards of section 77B. Chapter X, on the other hand, was more elaborate than its parent, containing a number of complex procedures designed to prevent the repetition of serious abuses that had occurred under section 77B with respect to publicly held companies. Among the most important requirements of Chapter X were the appointment of an independent trustee to reorganize the debtor company and the active involvement of the Securities and Exchange Commission to protect the rights of public debtholders and shareholders, who had often been victimized by insiders in equity receiverships and 77B reorganizations.

Chapter XIII was the analogous chapter for individual debtors, providing a way to reorganize a family's finances in much the same way a business could reorganize its obligations. In Chapter XIII debtors could reduce and extend debt as an alternative to Chapter VII asset liquidation and an immediate discharge. Chapter XIII was limited to "wage earners" and was modeled on a proceeding that had enjoyed success in Alabama in the depths of the Depression. Chapter XIII effectively introduced into consumer bankruptcy the debt compositions and extensions of state law, coupled with the unique powers of bankruptcy law, such as the discharge of remaining debt once the debtor completed the repayment plan.

The years that followed saw the Bankruptcy Act amended from time to time, but only in small details. Over time, it became increasingly obvious that the Act was hopelessly out of date. Eventually Congress took two steps to reform the bankruptcy laws: In 1970, it created a National Commission on Bankruptcy to draft a new law and it authorized the Supreme Court to promulgate Bankruptcy Rules analogous to the Federal Rules of Civil Procedure. The bankruptcy system was perceived to be so obsolete that Congress went so far as to make the Rules take precedence over the statute itself in cases of conflict. The Rules were adopted in 1973 and contained many of the reforms that would later be included in the Bankruptcy Reform Act of 1978.

The Bankruptcy Commission reported to Congress in 1973 with a proposed bill. The bill was redrafted after extensive hearings. The House and Senate committees reported two very different versions. An unusually complex legislative history resulted from the process of last-minute compromise. The issues thus created and the compromises that resolved them are discussed in cases and notes throughout the materials that follow.

The 1978 Code was adopted effective as to cases filed on or after October 1, 1979. Although this latest revision of the bankruptcy laws followed the 40-year cycle established by the Chandler Act in 1938, it was the first bankruptcy law in our history not adopted in the immediate aftermath of a great economic debacle. It may be that the short, sharp recession of 1974-1975 served as a sufficient "panic" for an effete generation, or perhaps bankruptcy had become an integral part of the commercial system, important in good times and bad.

Almost as soon as the new Code had been adopted, amendment bills were offered in the House and Senate to correct various mistakes and to reflect some second thoughts about the last-minute policy compromises. In addition, the new Code was attacked by various creditor groups who felt ill-treated under its provisions. Among these groups were the consumer credit industry, which urged adoption of stricter consumer bankruptcy provisions, as well as grain farmers, shopping center landlords, and others who sought exceptions from the generally applicable provisions in the statute.

One of the principal reforms of the Code had been to expand greatly the bankruptcy jurisdiction of the district courts. This expanded jurisdiction was to be exercised primarily by the bankruptcy judges as part of the district court organization. The new bankruptcy judges continued to be Article I judges, appointed for limited terms, unlike their Article III counterparts on the federal bench, who are lifetime appointees. In 1982 the Supreme Court decided Northern Pipeline Construction Co. v. Marathon Pipe Line Co., 458 U.S. 50 (1982). In *Marathon*, the Court held unconstitutional the Code's grant of broad jurisdiction to the bankruptcy judges on the grounds that those judges were not appointed under and protected by the provisions of Article III of the Constitution. (We discuss this case in greater detail in the chapter on jurisdiction, pp. 791-833, infra.)

When the Supreme Court decided the *Marathon* case, it became apparent that Congress would be forced to amend the Code in response, but the houses were divided. The House leadership wanted a "clean" bill creating Article III bankruptcy judges and postponing consideration of any other proposals for changes in the Code. The Senate leadership wanted to adopt a bifurcated jurisdiction approach, allocating jurisdiction between Article I bankruptcy judges and the district judges. The Senate also advocated various proposed changes to the Code, especially amendments to reduce consumer protection. The House ultimately agreed to the overall approach of the Senate, although it insisted on a number of modifications of specific provisions.

Two changes were made between 1984 and 1994 that are worthy of particular mention. One was the adoption in 1986 of a new operating chapter, called Chapter 12, that created a reorganization chapter especially designed to improve bankruptcy relief for hard-pressed family farmers. The 1986 Amendments also made permanent and nationwide a pilot program of "U.S. Trustees" under the supervision of the Office of the U.S. Trustee in the Department of Justice. These local U.S. Trustees were to help administer and monitor bankruptcy cases.

Although Congress passed a number of narrow and often technical amendments from 1984 to 1992, the 1994 Amendments constituted the next extensive batch of changes in the Code. The 1994 statute contained a number of specific changes, but the only overall change was the adoption of an indexing system that tied various dollar amounts in the statute to changes in the Consumer Price Index. 11 UCC §104. For example, adjustments are made to the dollar amounts of property allowed as exempt under section 522, to the threshold limits for eligibility for Chapter 13 under section 109(e), and to the amount of debt required to make a creditor eligible to file an involuntary bankruptcy petition. The first adjustments were announced in the Federal Register on March 1, 1998, and took effect on April 1 of that year. Adjustments are now made at three-year intervals.

One important provision of the 1994 Amendments was establishment of a new National Bankruptcy Review Commission. 1994 Amendments, §§601-610. The Commission, whose Chair was Brady Williamson and whose Reporter/Advisor was Professor Elizabeth Warren, held extensive hearings around the United States and, in 1997, issued a large and comprehensive set of proposals for changes in both consumer and business bankruptcies. The Commission was sharply divided, however, with strong dissents on a number of issues. The minority wanted to impose more constraints on consumer debtors, a position that was supported by the consumer credit industry. The credit industry took its case to Congress, drafting the basics of a bill to cut back sharply on access to consumer bankruptcy. The congressional proposals also included less sweeping, but important changes affecting business bankruptcies and the bankruptcy appeals process. The amendments came close to passing several times, failing by a few votes in the Senate in 1998, encountering a presidential veto in 2000, and failing by a few votes in the House in 2002. In 2005, with another hard push from the credit industry, the bill passed Congress and was signed into law, with an effective date of October 17, 2005. It is the most current version of the amended law that is the subject of this book.

The 2005 Amendments contain the most far-reaching changes since the adoption of the Code in 1978, especially with respect to personal bankruptcy. They leave unchanged the basic structure and processes of American bankruptcy law, but they make important changes of detail that will be discussed throughout the materials that follow. Overall, the amendments reflect the credit industry's view that bankruptcy law needed to be rebalanced in favor of the creditor interest because it was too often abused by debtors. Its proponents were in general suspicious of those specializing in bankruptcy law, including judges, lawyers, and academics. The amendments seek in many ways to decrease the discretion of judges and lawyers in the application of the law and to increase monitoring of their work. On the other hand, many bankruptcy specialists believe that the basic premise of the amendments was wrong, that most debtors who file for bankruptcy do so in the aftermath of a serious economic shock such as a job loss or medical problem, and that a change in the laws will not change the underlying economic realities facing people in serious financial trouble. Many attorneys and judges also note that a number of provisions of the amendments were inartfully drafted, revealing that the drafters were not well-acquainted with their subject. For all these reasons, it can be anticipated that the amendments will affect the bankruptcy process in unexpected ways unfolding over a number of years as the actors in the system gain understanding of the changes and react to them.

Although most of the cases in these materials are Code cases, cases decided under the pre-1978 Act remain important authority in some areas. An easy way to keep Act and Code references straight is to note that Congress kept the same numbers for the most important of the equivalent chapters of Title 11, U.S. Code, in order to help the transition to the new law, but it changed the notational system from Roman numerals to Arabic so that references would be distinct. For example, liquidation, Chapter VII in the 1898 Act, became Chapter 7 in the 1978 Code.

B. BANKRUPTCY COURT ORGANIZATION

Even under the nineteenth century bankruptcy statutes, federal district judges usually had specialized help for bankruptcy cases. Full-time or part-time officials handled much of the work in such cases. Under the 1898 Act, these officials were called "referees," and the referees made many of the everyday decisions in bankruptcy matters. Their position was roughly equivalent to that of a specialized "master" who served on a regular basis. The referees were appointed by the district judges.

As we noted earlier, in the 1978 Code Congress greatly expanded the jurisdiction of the federal courts sitting as bankruptcy courts. Most of this bankruptcy jurisdiction was vested in the bankruptcy judges, who are appointed for 14 years (not for life) under Article I of the Constitution. The *Marathon* decision struck down this allocation of power to the bankruptcy judges on the theory that they had been given plenary jurisdiction, which is reserved in the Constitution for Article III judges. According to the Court, the bankruptcy judges either needed less power or lifetime Article III appointments. Congress responded with the 1984 Amendments Act, which retained broad federal jurisdiction in the bankruptcy system but shifted more of that jurisdiction to the district judges and gave the district judges complete control over the work of the bankruptcy judges. Although the courts of appeal were given the responsibility of appointing bankruptcy judges, the functioning of the bankruptcy court is largely overseen by the district courts. Subject to the district court's discretion, the bankruptcy judges have jurisdiction over "core" proceedings in bankruptcy; their decisions become final unless they are appealed to the district court. With regard to "noncore" proceedings, a bankruptcy judge can hear them only as a "master" who submits proposed findings to the district court, unless the parties involved consent to a binding decision by the bankruptcy judge.

Bankruptcy judges' decisions on matters within their jurisdiction can be appealed to the district court, which reviews them on a "clearly erroneous" basis. If a party is dissatisfied with the district court's resolution of an appeal, it may appeal further to the court of appeals, as with any other district court decision. The Code permits any of the circuit courts to adopt a special appellate procedure whereby the first appeal from a bankruptcy court decision is to a panel of bankruptcy judges and from there to the court of appeals. Code §158(c). These alternatives to the district courts are called "BAPs," referring to their statutory names: Bankruptcy Appellate Panels. An appeal to a BAP sidesteps the district court that otherwise would have heard it. Panel jurisdiction is consensual, however, because any party can insist that the appeal be heard by the district court. Only the Ninth Circuit was using this procedure by 1994, so Congress in the 1994 Amendments added provisions requiring all circuits to do so unless certain adverse findings were made by the judges in a particular circuit. Id. Now BAPs hear cases in the First, Sixth, Eighth, Ninth and Tenth Circuits; the remainder decided against them. Colliers on Bankruptcy 15th ed. Revised, ¶5.02(b)(6).

The unwieldy jurisdictional compromise created by the 1984 Amendments has produced various difficulties and anomalies, which we will consider later in these materials. The Supreme Court has never addressed the constitutionality of the scheme directly, but its general pronouncements on bankruptcy jurisdiction seemed to place the whole system in fundamental jeopardy. Granfinanciera, S.A. v. Nordberg, 492 U.S. 33 (1989). Many in the bankruptcy world are waiting for another jurisdictional shoe to drop. Part IV of this book explores these issues in more detail.

The Supreme Court promulgates the Rules of Bankruptcy Procedure. Since the adoption of the Code, the Rules have been amended a number of times. Unlike the pre-Code rules, the current rules are subject to any controlling provision of the Code. In general, these rules, and the accompanying official forms, prescribe the procedures for administration of the bankruptcy estate, the filing of claims by creditors, the forms and schedules to be filed by each petitioning debtor, the giving of notice to creditors of particular developments in the case, and the like.

It is worth noting specifically the treatment of disputes in the Rules. Part VII of the Rules governs "adversary proceedings," which are defined in Rule 7001. Such proceedings include, for example, actions to void a lien or to recover a preference and actions that have been removed to bankruptcy court from state court. Adversary proceedings are full-blown federal lawsuits within the larger bankruptcy case, so they typically carry two captions: the "In re" bankruptcy caption first and then the more familiar "*A* v. *B*" caption of the dispute. Part VII of the Bankruptcy Rules virtually incorporates the Federal Rules of Civil Procedure. The Federal Rules of Evidence are also applicable to adversary proceedings. Disputes other than adversary proceedings are denominated "contested matters" and are subject to the less elaborate procedures described in Rule 9014.

C. STRUCTURE OF THE BANKRUPTCY CODE

Title 11 of the U.S. Code is divided into "chapters." For historical reasons, all but one of the chapters are odd-numbered: 1, 3, 5, 7, 9, 11, 12, 13, and 15. Chapters 1, 3, and 5 are general provisions that are applicable in all proceedings in bankruptcy unless explicitly made inapplicable in a specific context. Chapters 7, 9, 11, 12, 13, and 15 each govern a different type of bankruptcy proceeding. Except for certain situations in Chapter 15, a debtor is in only one of these chapters at any given time.

Chapter 1 is devoted to structural subjects such as definitions, rules of construction, general powers of the bankruptcy court, and the qualifications of debtors eligible for each of the types of proceedings available. Chapter 3 governs case administration, including appointment and compensation of the Trustee in Bankruptcy (TIB) and of professional persons such as attorneys and accountants, as well as provisions regulating the operation of a bankrupt estate. Chapter 5 provisions include regulation of the claims and distribution process, discharges, and the TIB's avoiding powers.

Chapter 7 governs the classic "straight" bankruptcy liquidation for both consumers and businesses. Chapter 9 has the special provisions for the bankruptcy of a municipality or other governmental unit. Chapter 11 is the chapter most often used by reorganizing businesses. Chapter 13, which excludes corporations, is used by consumers and small businesses. The Chapter 13 dockets include those who wish to save non-exempt property (especially a home), those who wish to try to pay part or all of their debts over time, and those who are ineligible for Chapter 7. Chapter 12 is a specialized version of Chapter 13 governing reorganization bankruptcies filed by family farmers. A Chapter 15 case is a special "ancillary" proceeding in which the United States court assists a foreign court that has the primary bankruptcy jurisdiction over a foreign debtor.

The jurisdictional and procedural provisions governing bankruptcy are found in Title 28 of the U.S. Code. The criminal provisions, which define and establish sanctions for offenses such as bankruptcy fraud, are in Title 18 of the U.S. Code.

Certain provisions of Title 11 are not covered in these materials. For example, there will be only a summary discussion of Chapter 9 municipal bankruptcies, and no coverage of Subchapters III and IV of Chapter 7, which provide special rules for the bankruptcies of stockbrokers and commodity dealers. These are highly specialized and technical areas of an already-technical law.

D.   CONSUMER VERSUS BUSINESS BANKRUPTCY

Traditionally, teaching materials for bankruptcy have been organized conceptually, following the organization of the statute. The basic organization of the materials in this book is different: It divides consumer bankruptcy and business bankruptcy for separate treatment. The traditional approach is consistent with the original Bankruptcy Act. In 1898 there was very little difference between the legal rules that applied to consumers and those that applied to businesses in any area of the law; there was certainly little distinction in the bankruptcy field. This lack of distinction is evident in discussions of bankruptcy in that period.

Modern legal analysis has made the consumer-commercial distinction important throughout commercial law (e.g., the Federal Trade Commission Regulations curtailing the application of the Holder in Due Course doctrine in consumer transactions). The UCC itself was drafted during a transition period in which the need for different treatment of consumer transactions was becoming clear. See, e.g., UCC §2-104 (special definition of "merchant"); Soia Mentschikoff, Reflections of a Drafter, 43 Ohio St. L.J. 537 (1982).

Early English bankruptcy law recognized the distinction and permitted bankruptcy to be employed only against "traders." But the distinction was lost over time in a robust young republic where every man was or hoped to be "in business," if only in land speculation. The distinction began to reemerge in the 1930s with the Chandler Act's adoption of Chapters X, XI, and XII for business rehabilitation and Chapter XIII for "wage earner" payout plans. The Code, with its federal exemptions and its very different rules for Chapter 13, broadened and sharpened the distinction.

The development of formal law lags behind reality even so. Consumer bankrupts are largely served by a different bar than are troubled businesses. Consumer bankruptcies are generally a matter of formbooks, word processors, advertising, routine procedures, and high volume, while a large business bankruptcy often involves extensive litigation, negotiation, and tailor-made plans. Consistent with the general notion of teaching bankruptcy law not as a set of theoretical rules but as an operating force in society and in the lives of those who seek its assistance, we have divided our discussion of bankruptcy into the differing contexts in which it operates.

To make the division sensible and to communicate the materials usefully, we cover each bankruptcy concept in the context in which it most often arises. For example, the TIB's avoiding powers are equally available by law in consumer and business bankruptcies, but their importance is minimal in the former and very great in the latter. For that reason we postpone the discussion of avoiding powers to the business section; their discussion in a consumer context would be almost theoretical. By the same token, we discuss exemptions in the consumer section, because exemptions are vital to an individual debtor but unavailable to a corporation.

The consumer-business distinction is not a sharp line. A large empirical study of bankruptcy has shown that many individuals who file for bankruptcy do so as their small businesses collapse. Elizabeth Warren and Jay L. Westbrook, Financial Characteristics of Businesses in Bankruptcy, 73 Am. Bankr. L.J. 499 (1999) (hereafter cited as *Financial Characteristics*). Until the mid-1980s, government statistics officially classified the collapse of entrepreneurs as business bankruptcies, but administrative changes have resulted in many business cases being reported as if they involved non-business debtors. Robert Lawless and Elizabeth Warren, The Myth of the Disappearing Business Bankruptcy, 93 California L. Rev. 745 (2005). See also, Jennifer Connors Frasier, Caught in a Cycle of Neglect: The Accuracy of Bankruptcy Statistics, 101 Comm. L.J. 307 (1996). Even among the cases officially classified as "business cases," many filings are by small partnerships or individual proprietorships, and in these cases business and personal problems may be thoroughly intertwined. Many small corporate bankruptcies are separated from the owner's personal bankruptcy filing by only one entry on the court docket sheet, because often the owner of the small corporation has personally guaranteed some of its debts. Nonetheless, the great majority of cases are clearly either business or nonbusiness, and a grasp of the two distinct operating systems is critical to understanding the actual operation of the bankruptcy laws.

Two final notes about all the materials in this book, both consumer and business, are in order. Throughout the materials we use cases, text, and problems to illustrate the functioning of the bankruptcy system. We try whenever possible to add to those illustrations with empirical data about the system. We repeatedly cite from a number of studies, including five large studies of the bankruptcy system: The pathbreaking 1964 study, Stanley and Girth, Bankruptcy: Problem, Process, Reform (Brookings 1971) (cited hereafter as *The Brookings Study* or *Brookings*); our own studies in the Consumer Bankruptcy Project, Sullivan, Warren, and Westbrook, As We Forgive Our Debtors: Bankruptcy and Consumer Credit in America (Oxford 1989) (cited hereafter as *As We Forgive*) and The Fragile Middle Class: Americans in Debt (Yale 2000) (cited hereafter as *Fragile Middle Class*); an empirical study of public company bankruptcies in the 1980s done by Professors LoPucki and Whitford reported in a series of law review articles, e.g., LoPucki and Whitford, Bargaining over Equity's Share in the Bankruptcy Reorganizations of Large, Publicly Held Companies, 139 Penn. L. Rev. 125 (1990) (cited hereafter as LoPucki and Whitford); and our current study of business bankruptcy, reported above in *Financial Characteristics*. We also cite data from a number of more discrete studies that have added important insights into the operation of the bankruptcy system and data from the Administrative Office of the Courts, as well as other national data on credit and finance. Finally, we report data from our most recent study of consumer bankruptcy, covering cases filed in 2001 and reported in several articles.

The bankruptcy courts are filled each year with over a million ordinary, middle-class Americans, along with a star-studded cast that has included

Debbie Reynolds, Burt Reynolds, M.C. Hammer, Kim Basinger, Peter Bogdanovich, Merrill Osmond, Mindy McCready, the group TLC, former Texas governor John Connally, famed heart surgeon Michael DeBakey, prizefighter Mike Tyson, and more. The corporate list has its own stars, including recent mega-busts Enron, Worldcom (MCI), Conseco, Global Crossing, Adelphia (cable), Trump Casinos, and numerous major airlines and grocery chains, preceded by classics such as Texaco, Marvel Entertainment, Montgomery Ward, Barney's, Macy &. Company, Dow Corning, Boston Chicken, Southmark Corporation (7-Eleven Stores), Transworld Airlines, Frederick's of Hollywood, Grand Union Company, K-Mart, Kash 'N Karry, Federated Department Stores, Pacific Gas & Electric, Service Merchandise, Continental Airlines, Popeye's Chicken, and Carter Hawley Hale Stores. These individuals and businesses pour into the bankruptcy system looking for a solution to a great variety of problems.

At the intersection of the statutes, the doctrine, the cases, the empirical data, and a host of normative conclusions lies a system that powerfully affects the lives of a legion of our fellow citizens and the economic futures of thousands of businesses each year.

CHAPTER 4

ELEMENTS COMMON TO CONSUMER BANKRUPTCIES

A. BACKGROUND

The next three chapters are devoted to consumer bankruptcy. As always, it is important to understand the context in which the legal rules operate. The key players in the consumer bankruptcy system are the debtors, the professionals, and the consumer creditors.

More than one and a half million households file for bankruptcy each year. The traditional notion of a typical bankrupt was often a housemaid or a day laborer, with the occasional fraudulent financier added for spice. Empirical studies have shown instead that when they are measured by enduring criteria — education, occupation, homeownership — the families in bankruptcy represent a broad cross-section of the middle class, from doctors and lawyers to salesclerks and fast food workers. Elizabeth Warren, Financial Collapse and Class Status: Who Goes Bankrupt?, 41 Osgoode Hall Law Rev. 115 (2003). Although many of them have poverty-level incomes when they file for bankruptcy, few of them are from the long-term poor. They may be down at the moment of filing, but the debtors are solidly in the middle of American society.

Middle Class

The second characteristic of note is that the great majority of the bankrupt debtors are overwhelmingly in debt. The data from the 2001 Consumer Bankruptcy Project, which we organized with our co-author, Dr. Teresa Sullivan, indicate that the average bankrupt debtor or debtor family has a ratio of non-mortgage debt to income of approximately 2.12. That means that it would take them more than two years to pay all their debts, ignoring home mortgages and pretending that interest stopped running during that period, even if they devoted every penny of their current incomes to debt payment and got someone else to support them. About half of them own homes and have mortgages to pay as well. Even the median (middle) bankrupt debtor owes more than a year's income in short-term debt like car loans, credit cards, and utility bills. Very few could make substantial payments from selling their homes and other assets, many of which are subject to mortgages and security interests. For a detailed discussion of the methodology of that study, see Elizabeth Warren and Amelia Tyagi, The Two-Income Trap: Why Middle Class Mothers and Fathers Are Going Broke, 181-188 (2003).

Demographically, the debtors' average age is 41, but filers range across the spectrum. As bankruptcies have grown more numerous for all age groups, bankruptcies among older Americans have grown even faster. Teresa A. Sullivan, Elizabeth Warren, and Deborah Thorne, Young, Old, and In Between: Who Files for Bankruptcy?, Norton Bankruptcy Law Advisor 1 (September 2001). Women filing alone have gone from the smallest group in bankruptcy in 1981 to the largest group by 1999. Teresa Sullivan and Elizabeth Warren, The Changing Demographics of Bankruptcy, Norton Bankruptcy Law Advisor 1 (October 1999). Women heads of households account for 39 percent of all filings, followed by couples at 33 percent and men filing alone at 29 percent. About 14 to 20 percent of the personal bankruptcies follow the failure of small businesses. Robert Lawless and Elizabeth Warren, The Myth of the Disappearing Business Bankruptcy, 93 California Law Review 745 (2005). Most of the rest are filed by people who are used to working for a salary.

Why are these people in bankruptcy? *The Fragile Middle Class* lists income loss (downsizing, layoffs, firings, loss of overtime, or other salary reductions) as by far the most important reason, based on the reports of thousands of debtors in questionnaires gathered at the courthouses. Next in line were medical problems (disabling injuries and medical debt) and the financial squeeze resulting from divorce. Also important has been the rise of a fundamentally different kind of credit represented by all-purpose credit cards, enabling people to get into serious debt one pizza at a time. Finally, the data suggest that many middle-class debtors are homeowners who are using bankruptcy to try to hang on to their homes.

How about financial irresponsibility as a cause? Many of the debtors bitterly concede they have been stupid about money and credit. The evidence is equally clear that many credit issuers have deliberately taken big risks in lending to consumers, because of the large profits available from the difference in interest rates between what a bank has to pay to get money and what it can charge for lending it to willing consumers. Economic historian David Moss and his coauthor Gibbs Johnson analyzed consumer credit and bankruptcy filing data throughout the twentieth century and concluded that lenders' decisions to market to higher-risk consumers drove a sharp increase in bankruptcy filings in the 1990s. David Moss and Gibbs Johnson, 73 Am. Bankr. L.J. 311 (1999). See also, Diane Ellis, Ins. Div., FDIC, The Effect of Consumer Interest Rate Deregulation on Credit Card Volumes, Charge-Offs, and the Personal Bankruptcy Rate (1998). Changes in borrowing and lending patterns surely have affected the number of people who find themselves in need of bankruptcy protection.

We will discuss the consumer bankruptcy professionals as we go through the materials. Suffice it to say here that the lawyers include bankruptcy specialists who advertise to build a high-volume practice as well as those who file only a few cases a year. The consumer debtor specialists have their own organization, the National Association of Consumer Bankruptcy Attorneys (NACBA), which has about 2,000 members. The role of lawyers in consumer bankruptcy was a central focus of the 2005 Amendments to the Code, imposing upon them far greater responsibility for policing the system with a consequent increase in cost.

There are many other players as well. Creditors' lawyers, debtors' lawyers, turnaround professionals, accountants, auctioneers, trustees, academics, judges and other professionals who specialize in bankruptcy, either consumer or business, make up the American Bankruptcy Institute, which numbers its membership at more than 10,000.

Finally, consumer bankruptcy is a financial subsystem, a multibillion dollar portion of a multitrillion dollar consumer credit system. Many, perhaps most, of the debts listed in bankruptcy are owed to large firms that specialize in retailing to consumers or in providing consumer finance. They operate on a high-volume basis in granting credit, with an increasing concentration of millions of transactions running through a small number of special-purpose banks. With the advent of credit cards and Web-based lending, the scale of lending has grown even larger and the process more impersonal.

Throughout the twentieth century and into the twenty-first, the consumer-credit industry has expanded and grown more profitable by steadily extending credit solicitations to include people who were once considered too risky for such loans. With the effective abolition of usury laws, the industry is very profitable and has attracted huge amounts of investment from the capital markets, increasingly secured by pools of consumer debt (a process called "securitization"). Nonetheless, the industry has been increasingly concerned about the rise in consumer bankruptcies and has not been shy in demanding that Congress pass tougher laws.

B. OUTLINE

In both consumer and business bankruptcy cases there are two fundamentally different types of proceedings: liquidations and payout plans. For both consumers and businesses, Chapter 7 is the liquidation chapter in which the debtor gives up all non-exempt assets, the Trustee in Bankruptcy sells these assets, and the proceeds are distributed pro rata to creditors. The benefit of a Chapter 7 liquidation for a consumer debtor is that the debtor receives a discharge of preexisting debts. In this way liquidation achieves the two classic objectives of bankruptcy: fair distribution of the debtor's assets for the benefit of all creditors and a "fresh start" for the debtor.

Both consumers and businesses have an alternative to Chapter 7 liquidation: a payout plan. Under Chapter 13 for consumers and Chapter 11 for businesses and some consumers with very large debts, a debtor can propose to keep all assets in exchange for promising to pay off debts over a period of time out of future income. The payout approach has gained increasing importance in recent years. Not only does it permit the debtor to keep assets instead of liquidating them, often at sacrifice prices, it can also mean much higher returns for creditors. The better result for creditors is particularly important in consumer bankruptcy because most consumer cases are "no asset" cases in which no non-exempt property remains for sale and distribution to pay debts in Chapter 7. Even a modest payout in Chapter 13 looks better to a creditor than no payout in Chapter 7.

The consumer bankruptcy materials in this book begin with a discussion of the concepts and procedures that are typically important both in consumer liquidations and in payout plans. The materials then turn to the special problems found in consumer liquidation cases. The last part of the consumer materials discusses consumer payout cases.

C. GETTING STARTED

In order to begin a bankruptcy case, the debtor files a petition. The petition is the basic request for bankruptcy relief, along with some key certifications, including a requirement that all the information contained in the filing will be true, signed by the debtor under penalty of perjury. The petition is accompanied by schedules in which the debtor must list important financial information. The filing fee for someone in Chapter 7 is $220. The Bankruptcy Code provides a limited form of *in forma pauperis*, permitting anyone whose income is less than 150 percent of the official poverty line to request a fee waiver from the court. 28 U.S.C. §1930(f)(1). Because many of the people who file for bankruptcy have experienced significant interruptions in income — layoffs, cutbacks in hours worked, failing small businesses — a substantial number of people may be eligible for this waiver.

Once the forms are filled out and signed and the necessary fee has been paid, the debtor's attorney usually has a clerk who takes the filing (or a group of filings in a high-volume practice) to the bankruptcy clerk's office, where a clerk will take the filing fee and date-stamp the minute, hour, and day of petition. At that instant, a bankruptcy estate is created and an automatic stay on all collection actions against the debtor, the debtor's property, and the property of the estate is immediately put into place.

While the procedure can be described in fairly summary terms, the details can be excruciating, requiring substantial documentation. The information a person must pull together on assets, debts, and income is substantial. Many debtors will need multiple trips back and forth between home and the lawyer's office to gather the needed paystubs, tax returns, old bills with names of the creditors and outstanding amounts, checkbooks and credit card slips to show how much the family spent in various categories, and the value of real property, cars, household goods, and more.

Even a diligent lawyer with a fairly well organized client may get some of the pieces wrong, and heaven help the lawyer with a client whose recordkeeping is spotty. A critical element of the 2005 Amendments is to step up the pressure on lawyers to verify the accuracy of the debtor's records. A lawyer who fails to do that may forfeit fees in the case, or, even worse, become subject to sanctions. See, e.g., §§526, 707(b). We will return to the specific obligations facing both the debtor and the debtor's counsel as each becomes relevant to the lawyer's efforts to help a debtor through the bankruptcy process.

D.   THE ESTATE

1.   *Property of the Estate*

At the moment a bankruptcy petition is filed (voluntary or involuntary) an "estate" is created by operation of law, just as if a new corporation had been established or a new trust created. The most direct analogy is with the decedent's estate created by law upon someone's death. Bankruptcy is in a sense a financial demise, which creates an estate consisting of all the interests in property previously owned by the pre-bankrupt debtor. At the instant of *§541* filing the bankruptcy petition, all the property owned by the debtor becomes "property of the estate," a deliberately expansive concept, with certain specific exceptions set forth in section 541 of the Code.

The most important exception is for "services performed by an individual *Exception* debtor after the commencement of the case." §541(a)(6). For typical consumer *A* debtors, this provision means that wages, commissions, and the like earned after the petition is filed are not property of the estate and do not have to be surrendered to their creditors. The debtors receive the first benefit of the "fresh start" immediately on filing, an opportunity to put misfortune or irresponsibility behind them and to begin life anew.

Aside from wages, there are a number of expectancies at varying levels of realization or certainty that must be allocated either to the debtors' past (i.e., to the estate) or to their futures (i.e., the fresh start). This problem can be articulated as a determination of the point at which an expectancy becomes "property." The old Act provided a test based on state law: At what point did an expectancy become sufficiently concrete that state law would recognize and enforce its transfer to another? Act §70(a)(5). Since section 541 has substituted a new federal test that is broader and therefore more inclusive, there has been considerable litigation at the margins.

In a trilogy of cases decided under the old Bankruptcy Act, the Supreme *Trilogy of old* Court delineated distinctions between similar types of property that *cases* determined allocation of that property either to the past and therefore to the bankruptcy estate or to the debtor as part of the fresh start.

In the first of those cases, Segal v. Rochelle, 382 U.S. 375 (1965), the *tax Refund = Estate* Court held that a tax refund from a business's prior taxable years was property of the estate, even though the entitlement to receive the refund did not technically accrue until after the bankruptcy was filed. In the second case, Lines v. Frederick, 400 U.S. 18 (1970), the Court held that vacation pay *Vacation Pay ≠ Estate* accrued but not due and owing on the date of bankruptcy was not property of the estate, but rather part of the "fresh start." The distinction from *Segal* seemed to be a special status for wages as opposed to other kinds of property, on policy grounds. But in the third case in the trilogy, Kokoszka v. Belford, 417 U.S. 642 (1974), the Court once again found that an accrued tax *Tax Refund = Estate* refund was property of the estate because the taxes were on prior personal earnings.

Congress expressly overruled Lines v. Frederick in adopting the present *Sec. 541 overrules* language of section 541. Although it is not clear just what Congress had in *Lines v. Frederick* mind in overruling *Lines*, it may be that it intended that the courts include in "property of the estate" *all* interests of value to the estate, regardless of competing policy considerations. The following case is typical of Code litigation on this issue.

SHARP v. DERY

253 B.R. 204 (E.D. MI 2000)

GADOLA, J.

The parties agree upon the following facts. Debtor filed a Chapter 7 petition on December 21, 1998. At that time through February, 1999, Valasis Communications, Inc. employed Debtor. On February 22, 1999, Debtor received an employee bonus of $11,331.63.

The bonus plan was based upon a fiscal year of January 1 to December 31. To receive the bonus under the plan, a worker must have been employed in good-standing when the company issued the bonus checks; i.e., he must not have been fired or resigned during the plan year or before the issuance of the dividend. An exception existed for employees who retired, were disabled, or died during the fiscal year. In those cases, the plan administrator may have, at his discretion, issued the employee a pro rata dividend.

The employer had the right to amend, suspend, or terminate the bonus plan at any time. The timing of any bonus checks under the plan also was at the employer's sole discretion.

* * *

Because of the facts outlined above, Trustee sought a determination from the bankruptcy court that the post-petition bonus was property of the estate. The bankruptcy court decided that it was, and ordered Debtor to turn over the post-petition bonus to Trustee. Trustee is now holding those funds in escrow pending the outcome of this appeal.

* * *

When a debtor files for bankruptcy, an estate is formed. See 11 U.S.C.A. §541(a) (West 2000). From that estate, creditors will attempt to recover at least some of their claims. The bankruptcy estate's property includes "all legal or equitable interests of the Debtor in property as of the commencement of the case," subject to limited exceptions. 11 U.S.C.A. §541(a)(1). Congress intended "property of the estate" to encompass "all interests of the debtor, including a debtor's contract right to future, contingent property." Banner v. Bagen (In re Bagen), 186 B.R. 824, 828 (Bankr. S.D.N.Y. 1995) (citing Rau v. Ryerson (In re Ryerson), 739 F.2d 1423, 1425 (9th Cir. 1984)). Although whether a debtor's alleged interest is estate property is a question of federal law, the Court must look to state law when deciding whether a debtor had a legal or equitable interest in the property when he filed for bankruptcy.

The determinative issue in this case, therefore, is whether Debtor had an enforceable right to receive the bonus check when he filed his petition, December 21, 1998. The bankruptcy court examined the particulars of the bonus plan at bar and noted that the "when an employee receives a dividend is not discretionary" and "the amount of the dividend an employee receives is not discretionary, and is not based upon the employee's work performance. It is based upon a percentage of the employee's salary." (Brief for Appellee, Ex. A at 14-15.) The court below thus reasoned that, because the employer had no discretion as to the amount and timing of any bonus that it decided to pay, Debtor had a right to the bonus as of December 21, and that bonus was therefore the estate's property. (Brief for Appellee, Ex. A at 15.)

The bankruptcy court misconstrued the significance of the above fact. Although the employer may have had no discretion over the amount of any bonus that it actually paid Debtor, as both parties agree, the bonus plan's terms gave the employer discretion as to whether it would pay any bonus at all. (Brief for Appellant at 2; Brief for Appellee at 1.) The question thus becomes whether a bonus plan under which Debtor had no contractual right to payment as of December 21 gave Debtor an enforceable right to the bonus check he would eventually receive in February, 1998.

One case is squarely on point. In Vogel v. Palmer (In re Palmer), 57 B.R. 332 (Bankr. W.D. Va. 1986), the debtor received a bonus from his employer roughly six months after he filed his bankruptcy petition. See *id. at 332.* As the court below noted, there were three salient facts that led the Vogel court to conclude that the debtor had no enforceable interest in the bonus when the case began, and the post-petition bonus thus was not property of the bankruptcy estate: (1) for the debtor to receive the bonus, the employer had to employ him at the time it declared the bonus; (2) "to be eligible for the bonus, the debtor had to satisfactorily perform his job"; and (3) payment of the bonus was solely at the employer's discretion. (Brief for Appellee, Ex. A at 14.)

As explained above, and according to the facts stipulated in this case, all three of the critical factors that led the Vogel court to hold that the post-petition bonus was not property of the estate exist here. The only one that is even arguably absent is the second, requiring that the employee "satisfactorily perform his job" in order to get the bonus.

The bonus plan in this case, however, requires that "an employee must be currently employed in good standing." (Brief for Appellant at 1.) It is hard to imagine how an employer who does not "satisfactorily perform his job" could be "employed in good standing." Even if there were a difference between those two terms, however, both the bonus plan at bar and the one at issue in Vogel share the same dispositive characteristic: the employer, as of the date the debtor filed for bankruptcy, could have decided not to pay any bonus at all under the terms of the bonus plan itself. That was the chief reason that the Vogel court held that bonus plan it addressed was not property of the estate. See *Vogel, 57 B.R. at 336-37.*

This case might be distinguishable from Vogel if, despite the bonus plan's terms, Michigan law held that a worker had an enforceable right in bonus dividends before payment. In those circumstances, the bonus dividend would have been a legal interest of Debtor when he filed for bankruptcy, and thus part of the bankruptcy estate. But Michigan law embraces the opposite principle: an employee who ends his employment before the closing date of a bonus period, thereby failing to establish a contractually-mandated condition for receipt of the bonus, forfeits eligibility for the bonus dividend. As of December 21, therefore, Debtor would have had no legally-recognized interests in the bonus check he later received on February 22.

Although Vogel is not binding on this Court, its reasoning is consistent with the well-established principle that when post-petition income "is dependent upon the continued services of the debtor subsequent to the petition, the amounts do not constitute property of the estate." *Vogel, 57 B.R.* at 334; see also In re Kervin, 19 B.R. 190, 193-94 (Bankr. S.D. Ala. 1982) (holding that an insurance salesman's right to renewal premiums was not part of the estate because it was contingent upon generating new business and providing policy-holder services); McKracken v. Selner (In re Selner), 18 B.R. 420, 421-22 (Bankr. S.D. Fla. 1982); cf. Tennessee Valley Authority v. Kinzer, 142 F.2d 833, 838 (6th Cir. 1944) (holding that at the time of filing for bankruptcy debtor had no interest in contributions he could not enforce).

The post-petition services that a debtor need perform in order to trigger this rule are, moreover, exceedingly slight. In Matter of Haynes, 679 F.2d 718 (7th Cir. 1982), for example, the Seventh Circuit held that the pay of a military retiree was not part of the bankruptcy estate, because it was conditioned on his obligation to perform certain military duties if called upon to do so. The Haynes court cited no example of the debtor ever actually having had to perform such an obligation. It merely reasoned that because the debtor "remained subject to the Uniform Code of Military Justice... and could be recalled to active duty" in an emergency, his retirement pay was dependent upon continued services subsequent to the petition, and thus did not constitute property of the estate. Id. at 719.

In this case, Debtor had to labor for his employer more than two months after the date of filing in order to be eligible for his bonus pay. In light of cases such as Haynes, it is apparent that his bonus check was "dependent upon the continued services of the debtor subsequent to the petition," such that it does "not constitute property of the estate." *Vogel, 57 B.R.* at 336-37

Attempting to refute this conclusion, Trustee cites Towers v. Wu (In re Wu), 173 B.R. 411 (B.A.P. 9th Cir. 1994) for the proposition that the bonus check "will constitute property of the estate if it is sufficiently rooted in pre-petition activities." (Brief for Appellee, Ex. A at 3.) Trustee argues that the rationale of Wu would lead the Court to apportion the bonus between the parts that Debtor earned pre-petition and post-petition, the former going to Trustee and the latter to Debtor. (Brief for Appellee, Ex. A at 4.) * * * The Court rejects this argument....

First, apportionment would be contrary to the plain language of §541. That statute, in pertinent part, dictates that only "legal or equitable interests of the debtor in property as of the commencement of the case" are included in the bankruptcy estate. 11 U.S.C.A. §541(a)(1). Regardless of how rooted Debtor's bonus might have been in pre-petition activities, he had, for reasons discussed above, no "legal or equitable interests" in that dividend when the case began on December 21, 1998. Under the clear language of the statute, therefore, the Court cannot apportion any part of that bonus dividend to the estate.

Even if the text were unclear, legislative history would provide a second reason for this Court's conclusion. As both the House of Representatives and Senate Reports make plain, §541 "is not intended to expand the debtor's rights against others more than they exist at the commencement of the case." H.R. Rep. 95-595, at 367 (1977); S. Rep. No. 95-989, at 82 (1977). A trustee, moreover, "could take no greater rights than the debtor himself had" on the day of filing the bankruptcy petition. H.R. Rep. 95-595, at 367 (1977); S. Rep. No. 95-989, at 82 (1977).

Applying Congress's rationale, as revealed through the House and Senate reports, to these facts, the Court notes that at the "commencement of the case," neither the terms of the bonus plan nor Michigan law gave Debtor an enforceable part of the bonus dividend. Section 541 of the Bankruptcy Code does nothing to change that. It follows, therefore, that Trustee, who could take no greater rights in the property than Debtor had, also had no enforceable interest in the bonus dividend at the case's beginning. The Court, accordingly, may apportion no part of the bonus plan to pre-petition services and allot that portion to the estate.

* * *

IT IS HEREBY ORDERED that the court below is REVERSED and that Trustee will transfer the $11,331.63 in bonus-dividend funds that it holds in escrow to Debtor within seven days of receipt of this order.

SO ORDERED.

———————

Conceptually, disputes about the inclusion of certain expectancies in "property of the estate" under section 541 can be divided into three main categories. The first, illustrated by Sharp v. Dery, involves legal interests that are not enforceable at the date of bankruptcy but may be enforceable at a future time. The question is whether they are sufficiently matured and certain to be included in the estate. A subsidiary point is allocation of their value to the past or the future, where some of the value of the contract payments might arise from personal services performed by the debtor after bankruptcy.

The second type of dispute in this area is created by certain entitlements, such as permits or licenses that are nontransferable, which may or may not be "property." (The distinction between "property" and a mere "license" is analogous to the constitutional distinction between a "right" and a mere "privilege.") One illustration is the debtor's driver's license: It represents a very valuable legal right that is of no value to anyone but the debtor. It cannot be property of the estate. On the other hand, a taxicab license or a permit to run a television station may be technically nontransferable, but the reality may be that such licenses are bought and sold all the time. If that is true, the license may be held to be property of the estate. (For example, is a domain name on the Internet property of the registrant when it files for bankruptcy?)

The third issue frequently encountered under this heading is the problem of restrictions on transferability imposed by contract or by law. The debtor clearly owns valuable property, but the debtor may have no legal right to transfer the property or may be able to transfer only under sharply restricted circumstances. If such restrictions were valid in bankruptcy, then nontransferable property could not pass to the bankruptcy estate under section 541 and thus would not be available for sale for the benefit of creditors. For that reason, such restrictions are not generally favored in bankruptcy, and provisions such as section 541(c)(1) make most of them unenforceable.

Congress has permitted a few specific restrictions on alienation to be effective to keep property out of the bankruptcy estate. The most important example of a permitted restraint on transfer exception is not at all obvious on reading the Bankruptcy Code: the "spendthrift" trust exception, section 541(c)(2). By this provision, debtors are often able to keep retirement accounts out of their bankruptcy estates.

The spendthrift trust provision is discussed in the following case under both federal and state law. The debtor claims that his retirement account is not part of his bankruptcy estate by operation of section 541(c). But Mr. Orkin had two bites at the apple, one under federal law and one under state law. If the account is ERISA-qualified, then federal law protects it from his creditors and the Supreme Court has ruled that it will not be part of the estate. If it is not so qualified, the debtor can try again with state law. If, under applicable Massachusetts law, the plan has a valid spendthrift trust provision preventing alienation and thus protecting it from creditors, it will not become part of his estate. But even with two bites, notice that Mr. Orkin has some trouble keeping his plan.

In re ORKIN

170 B.R. 751 (Bankr. D. Mass. 1994)

William C. HILLMAN, Judge.

Donald J. Orkin ("debtor") was the sole proprietor of a real estate business. On June 22, 1992, he established the Donald J. Orkin Retirement Plan (the "Plan"). In the same month he transferred $271,000 into the Plan, representing the proceeds of an individual retirement account ("IRA"). Under the terms of the Plan, debtor was the employer, sole employee, and sole participant. Debtor filed a voluntary petition under Chapter 7 of the Code on February 24, 1994. His schedules indicate that the Plan had a value of $295,000 on the petition date . . . . [The debtor claimed that the plan was not property of the estate under §541(c)(2); the trustee disagreed.]

APPLICABILITY OF §541(C)(2)

The trustee . . . argues that the Plan's assets are property of the estate and not eligible for the §541(c)(2) exclusion because the Plan does not contain a transfer restriction enforceable under either state or federal non-bankruptcy law.

Section 541(c)(2) validates restrictions upon transfer of a debtor's beneficial interest in a trust that are enforceable under "applicable nonbankruptcy law" by excluding property from the estate. Until 1992 the Circuit Courts of Appeal were divided over whether "applicable nonbankruptcy law" referred only to state spendthrift trust law or included federal law as well. The question was important with respect to retirement trusts because federal regulations under the Employee Retirement Income Security Act of 1974 ("ERISA"), which regulate the vast amount of retirement plans, require the presence of a clause restricting transferability of retirement benefits. 29 U.S.C. §1056(d)(l). Thus, the presence of these anti-alienation clauses would seem to qualify most retirement plans for §541(c)(2) exclusion if federal law was included within the term "applicable nonbankruptcy law."

In 1992, the Supreme Court decided Patterson v. Shumate, holding that "applicable nonbankruptcy law" under §541(c)(2) includes both state spendthrift law and federal law including ERISA. 119 L. Ed. 2d 519, 112 S. Ct. 2242, 2246 (1992). The result of *Patterson* is that employee retirement benefits under ERISA-qualified pension plans are excluded from a debtor's bankruptcy estate. In light of this, the Court must next determine whether debtor's Plan is "ERISA qualified."

ERISA

In 1974, Congress enacted ERISA to regulate the operations of employee benefit plans. The statute imposes various reporting, vesting, funding, and insurance requirements on employers. See 29 U.S.C. §§1021-1309. To encourage compliance with ERISA, Title II of the statute is composed almost entirely of amendments to the Internal Revenue Code ("IRC"), providing tax benefits to both employers and employees. See 29 U.S.C. §§1201–1242. To comply with ERISA[1] and qualify for tax benefits, a pension plan must, among other things, include a restriction prohibiting assignment and alienation of pension benefits.[2]

The term "ERISA-qualified" articulated in *Patterson* is not defined in the Bankruptcy Code, the Internal Revenue Code, in ERISA itself, or in *Patterson.* Arguably the *Patterson* Court left an ambiguity as to whether the term "ERISA-qualified" is meant to designate: (1) plans which are subject to ERISA; (2) plans which are subject to I.R.C. §401(a)[3]; (3) plans which contain enforceable anti-alienation clauses; or (4) plans that have combinations of any of these three features. In re Hall, 151 B.R. 412, 418 (Bankr. W.D. Mich. 1993) (quoting Christy & Skeldon, Shumate and Pension Benefits in Bankruptcy, 2 J. Bankr. L. & Prac. 719, 725 (1992)) (hereinafter "Christy & Skeldon").

Some courts have held that "ERISA qualified" means that a plan satisfies both ERISA and the IRC. However, this approach has been criticized because creditors could reach plan benefits if an employer fails to amend a plan to comply with a change in the tax law. In re Hall, 151 B.R. at 418, n.17 (quoting Christy & Skeldon at 725). Notwithstanding this possibility, the *Hall* court held that a plan is "qualified" when it satisfies both the IRC and ERISA. Id. at 419.

I find the best view to be that a plan is "ERISA qualified" only when it complies with the requirements of both ERISA and the IRC. I believe that the third requirement which other courts impose, that a plan must also

1. ERISA provides: "Each pension plan shall provide that benefits provided under the plan may not be assigned or alienated." 29 U.S.C. §1056(d)(l).
2. The IRC provides: "A trust shall not constitute a qualified trust under this section unless the plan of which such trust is a part provides that benefits provided under the plan may not be assigned or alienated." 26 U.S.C. §401 (a)(13)(A) (passim).
3. I.R.C. §401 (a) contains thirty-one requirements that a plan must comply with in order to be a "tax qualified" plan.

have an enforceable non-alienation provision, is unnecessary as that is already a prerequisite to ERISA compliance. See 29 U.S.C. §1056(d)(l). This is consistent with the controlling First Circuit authority discussed below.

The trustee asserts two challenges to debtor's claim that his Plan is ERISA qualified. First, he contends that the debtor as employer, sole employee, and sole participant under the Plan cannot be an "employee" as that term is used in ERISA. Alternatively, he argues that the Plan's anti-alienation clause is unenforceable under IRC §401(a)(13).

The controlling law in this circuit is found in Kwatcher v. Mass. Service Emp. Pension Plan, 879 F.2d 957 (1st Cir. 1989), in which the court held specifically that a person functioning as the employer cannot be a covered employee under ERISA. "Since Kwatcher is an 'employer' under 29 U.S.C. §1002(5), pension payments to him would 'become of advantage to [an] employer' thereby violating the law." 879 F.2d at 960 (citing Amato v. Western Union Intl., Inc., 773 F.2d 1402, 1414 (2d Cir. 1985), cert, dismissed, 474 U.S. 1113 (1986)). In addition, the court stated that by its terms 29 C.F.R. §2510.3-3(c)(l) "unambiguously debars a sole shareholder... from 'employee' status, notwithstanding that he may work for the corporation he owns, shoulder to shoulder with eligible (non-owner) employees. No amount of mental gymnastics can avoid the plain meaning of the regulation...." Id. at 961.

I find that debtor's interest under the Plan is not ERISA qualified. In light of this, the transfer restriction contained in §12.4 of debtor's Plan is not a restriction enforceable under federal law which will serve to exclude the assets of the Plan from debtor's estate. I need not reach the issue of whether the Plan complies with §401(a) of the IRC.

STATE LAW ISSUES

A debtor can exclude a pension plan from the estate if he or she can demonstrate a restriction on transfer enforceable under applicable state law. *Patterson*, 112 S. Ct. at 246. Debtor has specifically reserved his right to amend his schedules to claim the state exemptions. The following discussion will be helpful if he should do so.

Debtor is the "trustee" of his Plan as that term is defined in §1.85 of the Plan. Section 15.3 of the Plan entitled "Termination" states: Employers shall have the right to terminate their Plans upon 60 days' notice in writing to the Trustee. If the Plan is terminated, partially terminated, or if there is a complete discontinuance of contributions under a profit sharing plan maintained by the Employer, all amounts credited to the accounts of the Participants shall vest and become nonforfeitable. In the event of termination, the Employer shall direct the Trustee with respect to the distribution of accounts to or for the exclusive benefit of Participants or their beneficiaries.... The terms of the Plan allow the trustee (in this case debtor as his own employer) to terminate the Plan on sixty (60) days' notice with the funds reverting to him as beneficiary.

I had occasion to discuss the vitality of spendthrift trusts for purposes of §541(c)(2) in In re Herzig, supra. I noted there that "the conclusion of many courts was that where the debtor has the power to amend or terminate the trust, the debtor has such absolute authority over the trust that it must be included as property of the estate." Id. at p. 7.

Although debtor's Plan does contain a restriction on transfer, the Plan is still easily terminable by him on 60 days' notice, with all funds reverting to him. Under those circumstances I find that the Plan does not contain a restriction on the transfer of a beneficial interest of the debtor in a trust that is enforceable under Massachusetts spendthrift trust law and, hence, the Plan's assets cannot be excluded if state law exemptions were claimed.

...Absent an amendment, an order will enter sustaining the trustee's objection to the claimed exemption.

═══════════════

Retirement funds, it would clearly seem, are part of what a debtor earned in the pre-bankruptcy past and should therefore be part of the estate. On the other hand, what kind of fresh start will the debtor have if stripped of any protection for old age? It is interesting to observe how the policy issues surrounding the spendthrift trust provision are similar to those relating to protection for future wages.

In the 2005 Amendments, Congress further expanded protection for retirement and other savings accounts. Section 541(b)(7) was added to exclude from the estate employee contributions to any ERISA-qualified retirement plans, deferred compensation plans, tax-deferred annuities, and health insurance plans. Of course, the impact of these changes will not be felt uniformly across the spectrum of people filing for bankruptcy: Half of all Americans do not have a single dollar in a retirement account, and tax-deferred annuities and the like are held by even fewer people. To take advantage of these protections in the Bankruptcy Code, someone needs to have the property.

Another change in the 2005 Amendments went even further, protecting the educational accounts of the debtor's children or grandchildren. If a debtor set money aside in the certain kinds of tax-sheltered accounts to pay for the education of children in the family, then such accounts are not property of the estate, even though the debtor may be the named owner of the account, manage the account, and have a right of withdrawal. There are restrictions on the amount to be contributed and the timing, but the idea is clear: the creditors shall not reach the children's educational trust funds. Again, of course, only a handful of those who show up in bankruptcy will have such accounts.

In 2005, the Supreme Court also expanded protection for retirement funds. Instead of claiming an exclusion from the estate, Mr. and Mrs. Rousey claimed that their IRA was part of the estate, but was exempt property under section 522(d). The Supreme Court backed them up in Rousey v. Jackoway, 125 S. Ct. 1561 (2005), holding that Congress intended to include IRAs in its alphabet soup list of retirement account exemptions, even though IRAs are not specifically mentioned in the laundry list of exempt retirement plans. The case is a reminder of the one-two approach to dealing with property of a bankrupt debtor: One, if the property is excluded from the estate, the debtor keeps it. Two, if the property is part of the estate but deemed exempt from creditor attachment, the debtor keeps it. Exemptions are coming up soon.

Lest you conclude that all property-of-the-estate questions are the stuff of technical provisions and pocket calculators, we close this section with the following case:

=========== In re BURGESS ===========
234 B.R. 793 (Bank. D. Nev. 1999)

REED, District Judge....

BACKGROUND

Since 1983, the debtor has operated a legal brothel (or "house of ill fame") in Storey County, Nevada. On July 30, 1997, the debtor filed a voluntary petition for bankruptcy under Chapter 11 of the Bankruptcy Code. On June 2, 1998, the Storey County Commission and the Sheriff of Storey County held a hearing to express their displeasure with the debtor's continuing association with the Hell's Angels motorcycle "club" (or, in the County's terminology, "outlaw motorcycle gang"). At the hearing, the Commissioners revoked the debtor's brothel license....

[The bankruptcy court denied the debtor's request to undo the County's attempt to revoke his license and the debtor appealed to the district court. Under section 362 of the Code, which we consider in the next section, whether the debtor was entitled to a reversal of the revocation of his license and damages depended upon whether the license was property of the estate.] In denying relief to the debtor, the bankruptcy court held that the brothel license was not "property," but rather a "personal privilege."...

DISCUSSION

When a bankruptcy petition is filed, an "estate" is created, consisting of all of the debtor's interests, both legal and equitable, in all property, both tangible and intangible. 11 U.S.C. §541 (a). Although "property" is not defined in the Code, it has been interpreted liberally in order to further the policies underlying the bankruptcy laws. See United States v. Whiting Pools, Inc., 462 U.S. 198, 202-04, 103 S. Ct. 2309, 76 L. Ed. 2d 515 (1983). "[T]he congressional goal of encouraging reorganizations ... suggest[s] that Congress intended a broad range of property to be included in the estate." Id. at 204, 103 S. Ct. 2309....

...As noted above, the County did not provide any insight into the "property" issue. Likewise, we have not been overwhelmed with citations to cases involving the issue of whether a license to operate a legal brothel is "property" or not. The County cites to cases from the Nevada Supreme Court and this Court which indicate that Nevada law views prostitution as an activity that can be heavily regulated or forbidden altogether. From this, the bankruptcy court reasoned that the license was not property, but merely "a personal privilege granted to certain counties" — a "state matter ... subject to discretionary control of the county."

Unfortunately, this analysis is incorrect. The fact that Nevada law may not consider brothel licenses to be property is not dispositive. The fact that the right/privilege to operate a brothel is defined by state law does not matter — most property rights are defined by state law. That does not mean that those rights receive no protection from federal law, bankruptcy and otherwise. In fact, state-created "rights" expressly denominated by the state as "privileges" have often been treated as "property" for purposes of the bankruptcy laws. While state law creates the right, federal law determines whether it is "property" for purposes of the federal bankruptcy laws, tax laws, etc. In re Nejberger, 934 F.2d at 1301-02 ("[W]hile state law creates legal interests and defines their incidents, the ultimate question whether an interest thus created and defined falls within a category stated by a Federal statute, requires an interpretation of that statute which is a Federal question." (internal quotations omitted)); In re Terwilliger's Catering, 911 F.2d at 1171-72 ("While the nature and extent of the debtor's interest are determined by state law 'once that determination is made, federal bankruptcy law dictates to what extent that interest is property of the estate.' " (quoting In re N. S. Garrott & Sons, 772 F.2d 462, 466 (8th Cir. 1985)).

While we have found no published bankruptcy decisions regarding brothel licenses, numerous cases have held that similar licenses issued by state agencies are property for bankruptcy purposes. Most of these cases involve liquor licenses, rather than brothel licenses, but the principle is the same. Most states or local governments require businesses that wish to sell alcoholic beverages to be licensed, and regardless of how the issuing state characterizes such licenses, most courts have held that they are property under the bankruptcy laws. Courts have also held that a license to operate a racetrack or a casino is property of the estate. In addition, many other cases have held similar licenses and certifications to be property. E.g., Ramsay v. Dowden (In re Central Arkansas Broadcasting Co.), 68 F.3d 213, 214-15 (8th Cir. 1995) (FCC license); Federal Aviation Admin, v. Gull Air, Inc. (In re Gull Air, Inc.), 890 F.2d 1255, 1260 (1st Cir. 1989) (airport landing slots); Shimer v. Fugazy (In re Fugazy Express, Inc.), 124 B.R. 426, 430 (S.D.N.Y. 1991) (FCC license), appeal dismissed, 982 F.2d 769 (2d Cir. 1992); Nu-Process Brake Engineers, Inc. v. Benton (In re Nu-Process Brake Engineers, Inc.), 119 B.R. 700, 701 (Bankr. E.D. Mo. 1990) (right to pursue reinstatement of a sales tax license); Brizendine v. Humboldt Express, Inc. (In re Brown Transport Truckload, Inc.), 118 B.R. 889, 893 (Bankr. N.D. Ga. 1990) (trucking certificate); In re Draughon Training Institute, Inc., 119 B.R. 927, 930-31 (Bankr. W.D. La. 1990) (state and federal certifications of eligibility to receive educational funding); Beker Indus. Corp. v. Florida Land & Water Adjudicatory Comm'n (In re Beker Indus. Corp.), 57 B.R. 611, 621-22 (Bankr. S.D.N.Y. 1986) (permission to truck phosphate ore); In re American Central Airlines, Inc., 52 B.R. 567, 571 (Bankr. N.D. Iowa 1985) (airport landing slots); Coben v. LeBrun (In re Golden Plan of California, Inc.), 37 B.R. 167, 170 (Bankr. E.D. Cal. 1984) (corporate name).

Of course, some courts have gone the other way. In In re Gammo, for instance, the court held that a state-issued license to sell lottery tickets was not property. In re Gammo, Inc., 180 B.R. 485, 487 (Bankr. E.D. Mich. 1995); see also Pension Benefit Guaranty Corp. v. Braniff Airways, Inc. (In re Braniff

Airways, Inc.), 700 F.2d 935, 942 (5th Cir. 1983) (holding that airport landing slots are not property); Geiger v. Pennsylvania (In re Geiger), 143 B.R. 30, 35-36 (E.D. Pa. 1992) (holding that a "driver's license is a privilege and not property"), aff'd, 993 F.2d 224 (3d Cir. 1993). Clearly, though, the majority of cases examining the issue have held that liquor and similar licenses are property for bankruptcy purposes. The case that most concerns us, however, is Wade v. State Bar of Arizona (In re Wade), 115 B.R. 222 (9th Cir. BAP 1990), aff'd, 948 F.2d 1122 (9th Cir. 1991). In In re Wade, the Bankruptcy Appellate Panel of the Ninth Circuit held that an attorney's license to practice law was not property. In re Wade, 115 B.R. at 228. While the B.A.P.'s decision was affirmed by the Ninth Circuit, that court did not address the property question at all. The only question before the Circuit was whether the state bar was a government agency for purposes of the government exception. Thus the Ninth Circuit's decision is not particularly strong authority for the proposition that a license to practice law is not property. Nonetheless, we are convinced (although we suspect there may be some who would argue to the contrary) that a brothel license is more like a liquor license than a license to practice law.

Beyond the bankruptcy context, the Ninth Circuit has held that, for instance, a property right exists in license tags required for coin-operated "crane" games. Further, we note that the very license at issue here has recently been held by Judge Hagen, in the debtor's civil rights case, to constitute a property right for purposes of procedural due process analysis. Thus, we hold that the brothel license at issue here is "property." . . . The license has enormous value to the estate — in fact, without the license to operate as a brothel, there would essentially be no business left to reorganize. To hold that the license is not property would be to contravene the broad definition of property meant to further "the congressional goal of encouraging reorganizations." United States v. Whiting Pools, Inc., 462 U.S. 198, 204, 103 S. Ct. 2309, 76 L. Ed. 2d 515 (1983). . . .

. . . [T]he order of the bankruptcy court . . . is reversed and remanded. . . .

The study of bankruptcy allows many new perspectives on the world.

2. The Trustee

Continuing the analogy with trusts and estates (remember that bankruptcy began in equity), the new estate and its property are managed by a "Trustee in Bankruptcy" typically (although not invariably) a local lawyer who specializes in bankruptcy work. In general, the TIB's duties are to gather all the debtor's property, protect and maintain it (e.g., make certain it is insured), sell the property for the highest possible price, and distribute the proceeds among creditors according to the statutory priorities. §704. The TIB is also required to scrutinize claims and oppose those that may be invalid or overblown, to challenge any improper exemption claims by the debtor, and to investigate the debtor's affairs to the extent necessary. Id.

In theory in a Chapter 7 case, the TIB may be elected by the creditors, but such elections are very rare because creditors are typically uninterested in taking the necessary steps in return for the paltry payouts they are likely to receive. §702. Instead, a government official from the Office of the U.S. Trustee generally selects the TIB from a panel of potential appointees that the U.S. Trustee has chosen as qualified to serve as TIBs. §701(a); 28 U.S.C. §586(a)(1).

Panel usually selects the Tee.

The TIB has a special obligation, by custom and common law, to unsecured, general creditors and therefore is especially charged with scrutinizing the debtor's reports to discover any wrongdoing that might result in a failure to get a discharge or to locate any concealed property. The TIB is also careful to be sure that no one creditor is getting more than its share, so the TIB challenges security interests, preferences, and priority claims for the benefit of unsecured creditors. In effect, the TIB stands for the proposition that equity is equality, which means that unless a creditor can clearly demonstrate that it deserves some priority in the bankruptcy payout, the TIB will try to enlarge the estate for distribution to all unsecured creditors. In addition to this obligation, the TIB has an incentive to maximize recoveries for unsecured creditors. The TIB collects fees calculated in part as a percentage of the funds distributed and that distribution is primarily to unsecured creditors. §§326, 330.

The great majority of consumer Chapter 7 bankruptcies are "no-asset" cases, in which the debtor has no non-exempt assets—a fact that has been true for many years. Stanley and Girth, Bankruptcy: Problem, Process, Reform 87 (1971); Herbert and Pacitti, Down and Out in Richmond, Virginia: The Distribution of Assets in Chapter 7 Bankruptcy Proceedings Closed in 1984-1987, 22 Rich. L. Rev. 303 (1988). Typically creditors are advised of this fact and advised not to bother filing a claim, although if non-exempt property turns up, they will receive notice of that happy (but rare) development.

While trustees are ostensibly compensated with a percentage of their recoveries on behalf of the creditors, the economic realities of consumer bankruptcy cases pushed Congress to compensate them in another way. The trustee receives $60 from the $220 of fees that every Chapter 7 debtor must file. No-asset cases are obviously not lucrative individually, but a high-volume practice can make such work well-paid. Moreover, the trustee can hope that the U.S. Trustee will bear service and expertise in mind when the occasional high-asset case comes up for assignment.

It is important not to confuse the TIB, a private citizen who serves as trustee in a particular bankruptcy case, with the U.S. Trustee (the "UST"), a government official appointed by the Attorney General for a five-year term to serve various administrative and monitoring functions in the bankruptcy courts of a particular region. 28 U.S.C. §581.

TIB ≠ UST

The UST's office, like a U.S. Attorney's office, serves as a local branch of the Department of Justice. One difference is that there is not a UST for each federal judicial district; only 21 USTs cover the entire country. While some USTs are responsible for only one judicial district, most have jurisdiction over more than one district, and several have more than one state to supervise. 28 U.S.C. §581(a). The UST's responsibilities are detailed in the statute. 28 U.S.C. §586. In addition to appointing Chapter 7 trustees and performing general monitoring functions, these responsibilities include appointing and supervising trustees for Chapter 13 cases, appointing the members of

Creditors Committees in Chapter 11, monitoring abuse of consumer bankruptcy, certifying credit counseling agencies, and approving debtor education programs, all of which are discussed later in these materials. The UST also serves a major role in supervising the compensation granted to TIBs and attorneys in bankruptcy cases. 28 U.S.C. §581(a)(3)(A). The 2005 Amendments added greatly to the responsibilities and authority of the UST and represented a major extension of the power of the Executive Branch in bankruptcy matters.

Problem Set 5

5.1. You have just been appointed TIB for the estate of Donald Lapman, whose flaky other-worldliness has long charmed his friends and has now brought him into Chapter 7 bankruptcy. Donald had some connection with the following property on the day he filed his bankruptcy petition:

(a) his parakeet, Toto;

(b) a 1999 Ford Taurus he bought used, which is still subject to a purchase-money security interest in an amount exceeding its value;

(c) candid snapshots of hundreds of his friends, some of them quite intimate;

(d) two tickets to a U2 concert;

(e) household furniture, including dishes, pans, chairs, a couch, and the like;

(f) twenty-five shares of Monumental, Inc. left to him by his Uncle Rufus;

(g) an undivided 3/48ths interest in a producing oil well, also left by Rufus;

(h) 3,214 bubble gum baseball cards, some dating back to 1948;

(i) an arrangement with his younger brother: When Donald left home for college years ago, he lent his brother his catcher's mitt, with the understanding Donald could get it back whenever he wanted it;

(j) a bank account on which Donald is the named trustee for the benefit of his little niece Sherry, in the amount of $2,750;

(k) his salary for the month prior to the petition, which he received just hours after filing;

(l) his retirement account, which he cannot touch until he retires.

A month after the petition was filed, the parakeet unexpectedly laid two eggs, which have since become two little parakeets. Seven months later, Donald received from Monumental an annual dividend in the amount of $225. In addition, in the two months since the petition was filed Donald continued working and was paid his salary; his employer also made a contribution to his retirement fund. Which of the above items are "property of the estate" under §541(a)? See also §541(d).

5.2. On January 15, Leslie "Lucky" Lewis purchased a ticket in the New York State Lottery. On January 20, his gambling passion having finished him financially, he filed for bankruptcy. On February 1, ironically, he won $50,000 in the Lottery. If he owed $50,000 prior to bankruptcy, who gets the lottery money?

5.3. On March 1 a local farmer, Frances Alleta, contracted to sell her winter wheat crop of 10,000 bushels to a local grain warehouse for the market price prevailing on May 1. Unable to make it financially, Frances filed a bankruptcy petition April 1. The immature wheat had no market value at that moment. On March 1 the market price for wheat was $10 a bushel, but a severe drought in Argentina raised world prices so that it was worth $15 a bushel on April 1 and $20 a bushel on May 1, when Frances harvested it. When the buyer pays the $200,000, who gets what?

5.4. Your client is Bartholomew Harrington Moss IV. He is broke and owes more than $100,000 to various creditors. His only income is $1,000 per month from a $250,000 trust that his mother established for him. He can get only the income from the trust until she dies, at which time he will get the corpus of the trust. The trust instrument says that his rights to the income and corpus are not assignable. His mother is quite ill. The doctors say she may last six months, but almost certainly not a year. What do you advise?

5.5. On March 1, Robert Cratchet, a charming but impecunious law teacher, filed for bankruptcy. On April 1 he won the $1,000 Teaching Excellence Award for the school year. Who gets the $1,000?

5.6. Although a liquor license is considered a license to print money in the state where Happy Harrison has his liquor store, Happy managed to run his store so badly that he was forced to file for bankruptcy. (Happy's sole proprietorship is a good example of a "personal business bankruptcy," mixing business and consumer elements.) Liquor licenses are issued by the state and are expressly nontransferable, although the State Alcohol Control Commission always has issued a new license to someone who buys a liquor store from a prior licensee, unless the new owner is disqualified, for example, for being an ex-felon. If a person does not buy an existing store, it is very hard to get a new liquor license because the state does not wish to see more liquor stores opened. Can Happy's TIB make any claim for the license? Why would she want the license? (Assume for this purpose that a "license" is not a contract; you will see why later.)

E.   THE AUTOMATIC STAY

Filing a bankruptcy petition not only creates a new estate, it also triggers an "automatic stay" that prohibits any creditor's attempt to continue to collect from the debtor or the debtor's property. The automatic stay is often likened to "closing the windows and locking the doors" to prevent any property from leaving the newly formed estate. Eventually the court will oversee the gathering and distribution of the assets, but until that time or until the stay is lifted, creditors are generally precluded from taking any individual action against the debtor or the debtor's bankruptcy estate. Section 362(a) details the prohibitions of the stay, while section 362(b) provides exceptions that permit certain types of actions against the debtor to continue.

The automatic stay is the first intrusion of federal bankruptcy laws into the state actions that a creditor would ordinarily be entitled to do. As the following cases illustrate, the power of the automatic stay is broad.

══════ ANDREWS UNIVERSITY v. MERCHANT ══════
958 F.2d 738 (6th Cir. 1992)

JOHNSTONE, District Judge....

I

Weiner Merchant, a citizen of Great Britain, came to the United States to attend Andrews University. Merchant received a loan from Michigan National Bank to pay a portion of her educational expenses. The Bank made the loan in connection with a student loan program arranged with the University. The program included a provision to give the Bank full recourse against the University in the event a student defaults on the debt.

In addition to the Bank loan, Merchant received assistance for educational expenses which are evidenced by promissory notes payable to the University.

After graduation, Merchant defaulted on both her obligations to the Bank and the University. The University, pursuant to the guaranty agreement, paid the Bank, took assignment of the note, and became the sole student loan creditor for Merchant's educational expenses.

One year after graduation, faced with $28,892.40 in debts, of which $23,614.00 was attributable to these educational loans, Merchant filed a Chapter 7 bankruptcy. Soon thereafter, in an effort to gain citizenship, Merchant asked the University for a copy of her academic transcript. When her request was refused she filed an adversary proceeding against the University claiming its refusal violated the automatic stay provision, 11 U.S.C. §362(a). The University claimed that both the educational loan and credit extensions are excepted from discharge under 11 U.S.C. §523(a)(8) and thus it had a right to withhold the transcript....

Three issues are raised in this appeal. First, whether educational loans, made by commercial lenders and guaranteed by private educational institutions, are dischargeable under 11 U.S.C. §523(a)(8). Next, whether extensions of credit for educational expenses are dischargeable under 11 U.S.C. §523(a)(8). Finally, whether a school may withhold the transcript of a student who has defaulted on educational loans and filed for bankruptcy under Chapter 7.

[The court held that the loans were nondischargeable, so that Merchant would continue to owe full repayment to the University following bankruptcy. See pp. 254-255.]

The final issue presented in this appeal is whether in refusing to provide a student-debtor their educational transcript because they are in default on a prepetition debt, a school violates the automatic stay provision, 11 U.S.C. §362....

We held in In re Smith, 876 F.2d 524 (6th Cir. 1989), that this provision was to be broadly interpreted and that it is self executing. Thus it automatically takes effect when a petition is filed in bankruptcy.

Various courts have found that the withholding of a debtor's transcript or the refusal to issue a transcript until a debtor pays a prepetition debt is an act to collect, assess, or recover a prepetition debt and thus a violation of section 362(a)(6).

We follow the reasoning of these decisions and hold a violation of 11 U.S.C. §362(a) arises when a prepetition creditor withholds a student-debtor's transcript. Given this determination, we must now determine if Congress made it an exception to the automatic stay provision.

Section 362(b) sets forth the exceptions. While many of the exceptions to discharge found in 11 U.S.C. §523 are exceptions from the automatic stay found in 11 U.S.C. §362(b), educational loans are not. Thus, the automatic stay applies to creditors of education loans and remains in effect until (1) the case is closed, (2) the case is dismissed, or (3) a discharge is granted or denied. 11 U.S.C. §362(c)(2)(C).

Merchant filed a petition for bankruptcy under Chapter 7 and later the University failed to turn over her transcript. Although there is a presumption that the educational debts are not dischargeable, as stated above, they are not listed within the exceptions to the automatic stay found in 362(b). Accordingly, the University violated section 362(a). Having found the student loan debt excepted from discharge, the stay will terminate when the district court enters an order consistent with this opinion. See 11 U.S.C. §362(c)(2)(C).

We affirm the77 Bankruptcy Court and District Court in finding the University in violation of 11 U.S.C. §362(a)(6). As the violation was not willful, sanctions are not merited.

CONCLUSION

In summary, Congress enacted 11 U.S.C. §523(a)(8) in an effort to prevent abuses in and protect the solvency of the educational loan programs. The transactions in issue here were educational loans funded in whole and in part by Andrews University, a nonprofit educational institution. The financial assistance programs made possible by the University enabled Merchant to obtain an education which she might otherwise have been denied. Congress, by excepting educational loans from discharge, has determined that the continued solvency of educational funding and financial aid programs override the need to provide debtors with a fresh start in their financial affairs. Congress, however, has not excepted educational loans from the automatic stay provision.

Accordingly, the judgment of the district court holding the indebtedness dischargeable is reversed. The judgment of the district court refusing to hold the appellant in contempt is affirmed.

====

Merchant illustrates both the power and the impermanence of the automatic stay, which is primarily designed to maintain the status quo while the court sorts things out. The opinion strongly suggests that the school's obligation to send out a transcript will conclude with the termination of the stay, which for a debtor in a Chapter 7 case occurs upon the discharge of the debtor. §362(c)(2). At that point the post-discharge injunction arises (see pp. 254-255), but it would not protect Merchant here because the debt is not dischargeable. Thus there is a window during which the stay protects the debtor and permits a certain amount of sorting (e.g., is this a nondischargeable student loan?), but then the debtor is left without bankruptcy protection as to the obligations that have not been discharged.

===== NISSAN MOTOR ACCEPTANCE CORP. v. BAKER =====
239 B.R. 484 (N.D. Tex. 1999)

KENDALL, District Judge.

This is an appeal from a judgment entered by the United States Bankruptcy Court for the Northern District of Texas, Dallas Division, on February 6, 1996. The Bankruptcy Court held that various actions of Appellant-Creditor Nissan Motor Acceptance Corporation ("Appellant") violated the terms of the automatic stay provided by 11 U.S.C.A. §362(a) (West 1998). The Bankruptcy Court awarded actual and punitive damages for Appellees Debtors ("Appellees") in the amount of $23,000, and reasonable attorneys' fees and expenses in the amount of $4,981.75. The Bankruptcy Court granted Appellant the option of satisfying the actual and punitive damages portion of the judgment by delivering to Appellees a new 1996 Nissan Pickup Truck B, Model SE, together with its title free and clear of any liens. For the reasons stated below, the judgment of the Bankruptcy Court is affirmed.

I. FACTUAL BACKGROUND

Appellees filed a Chapter 7 bankruptcy petition on December 30, 1993. At the time of filing, Appellees listed their 1991 Nissan Pickup ("Vehicle"), for which Appellees were in arrears to Appellant by more than two monthly payments. In their Statement of Intentions submitted with their petition, Appellees stated an intent to reaffirm the debt to Appellant for the Vehicle. On January 4, 1994, Appellant, without knowledge of Appellees' bankruptcy, repossessed the Vehicle. Both sides admit that Appellees' counsel contacted Appellant following the repossession to inform Appellant of Appellees' bankruptcy. Appellant disputes Appellees' assertion that they requested the return of the Vehicle. Nonetheless, the Bankruptcy Court found that as of January 4, 1994, Nissan had notice of Appellees' bankruptcy.

Appellant did not turn over the Vehicle upon notice of Appellees' bankruptcy, but retained possession of the Vehicle. On February 23, 1994, almost two months after the bankruptcy was filed and over six weeks after

Appellant received notice of the bankruptcy, Appellant filed its motion for relief from stay, or, in the alternative, adequate protection. However, while this motion was pending before the Bankruptcy Court, Appellant sold the Vehicle on March 16, 1994. The Bankruptcy Court, which did not know of the sale of the Vehicle, eventually granted Appellant's motion on June 1, 1994.

In November 1994, Appellees filed the adversary proceeding subject to this appeal seeking damages for violation of the automatic stay provided by §362....

II.   Analysis

The bankruptcy court's findings are reviewed under the clearly erroneous standard, and its legal conclusions are reviewed de novo. See Fed. R. Bankr. P. 8013.

Nissan's first assertion on appeal is that the Bankruptcy Court erred in holding that Appellant's exercise of control over the Vehicle after notice of the automatic stay was a willful violation of the stay. Interwoven in Nissan's argument is the issue of adequate protection — whether a secured creditor is required to turn over its collateral, which is property of the estate, without first receiving adequate protection....

...At particular issue here is §362(a)(3), which states that the automatic stay prohibits "any act to obtain possession of property of the estate or of property from the estate or to exercise control over property of the estate."

Numerous cases have held that a creditor's continued retention of estate property after notice of a bankruptcy filing constitutes an "exercise of control" over property of the estate in violation of the automatic stay....

...There is nothing in §363(e) that grants a creditor like Appellant the authority to engage in self-help to retain estate property as adequate protection, which is exactly what Appellant did in this case. Moreover, contrary to Appellant's argument, §542(a) provides that a creditor like Appellant "shall deliver to the trustee, and account for, [estate] property or the value of such property" (emphasis added). Section 542(a) has been construed to establish an affirmative obligation on the creditor to return estate property unless it is of inconsequential value to the estate, and nothing in §542(a) requires the debtor to provide the creditor with adequate protection as a condition precedent to turnover. Appellant's action is a violation of its obligation under §542(a) to turn over estate property, and subverts the authority of the Bankruptcy Court as specified in §363(e) to order adequate protection when the Bankruptcy Court, not the creditor, deems such protection necessary.

Appellant's second issue on appeal is whether Appellant's sale of the Vehicle was a willful violation of the stay.... Appellant knew that the stay was in effect when it filed its motion on February 23, 1994. Appellant cannot "play dumb" and rely on its "records," which inexplicably indicated to Appellant that the stay had lifted on March 5, 1994, when there was no order from the Bankruptcy Court relating to Appellant's motion until June 1, 1994. Appellant's disregard of the Bankruptcy Court's authority is inexcusable, and the Bankruptcy Court did not err in finding that Appellant's sale of the Vehicle was a willful violation of the stay....

Appellant's fourth issue on appeal is whether there was sufficient evidence to award actual damages.... Appellant ignores the ample testimony offered by Appellees on their actual damages. In addition to Appellees' testimony that they paid their daughter-in-law to drive them when necessary, Appellees testified that the Vehicle was the only reliable source of transportation that they had, that Appellee Baker's daily commute to and from his work was ninety miles, that Appellees struggled to secure reliable transportation after the Vehicle was repossessed by Appellant, and that Appellees had to purchase and finance a used Honda Civic in May 1994, as a replacement for the Vehicle. This evidence belies Appellant's contention that there was no other proof of actual damages. Thus, the Bankruptcy Court's award of actual damages was not clearly erroneous.

Appellant's fifth issue on appeal is whether the Bankruptcy Court erred and abused its discretion in awarding punitive damages.... In light of Appellant's willful violation of the stay by exercising self-help to possess and sell estate property, the Bankruptcy Court did not err, nor did it abuse its discretion, in awarding punitive damages....

Finally, Appellant's seventh issue on appeal is whether there is sufficient evidence to support the Bankruptcy Court's award of "excessive" attorneys' fees under §362(h).... Under the facts and circumstances of this case, the Court finds that the Bankruptcy Court's award of $4,860.00 in attorneys' fees per §362(h) is not clearly erroneous.

III.   CONCLUSION

For the reasons stated above, the judgment of the bankruptcy court...is AFFIRMED.

Notice that the court was willing to lift the stay, which means that Nissan could have had the car. But when Nissan acted on its own without approval from the bankruptcy court, it ran up nearly $30,000 in damages. There's a message here.

Another Pothole on the Way to the Automatic Stay

Before the enactment of the 2005 Bankruptcy Amendments, the automatic stay was just that — automatic. When the debtor filed the bankruptcy petition and paid the filing fee, the clerk date-stamped the petition and the stay was automatically in place. Notice went out in the next few days, according to the list of creditors and addresses supplied by the debtor's lawyer. The creditors' addresses were generally where the creditor did business or received payments. Creditors rarely got in trouble for violations of a stay that they didn't know about, although they might have to give back property seized or a payment extracted. If the creditor was in the middle of repossessing the debtor's car or foreclosing on the debtor's home, the debtor's attorney often called the creditor or sent a photocopy of the petition to the creditor so that the creditor would know to stop the action.

The very big creditors with business offices scattered across the country or around the globe were concerned about where the notice for the debtor's bankruptcy might be sent. They persuaded Congress, as part of the 2005 Amendments, to authorize them to file a "notice of address" with the court where all notices in Chapter 7 and Chapter 13 cases must be sent. §342(e). This provision would appear to be mere housekeeping, but for the addition of a provision that any notice sent elsewhere will not be effective until the notice has been "brought to the attention" of the creditor. If the creditor "designates a person or organizational subdivision" to receive bankruptcy notices and has a reasonable procedure to deliver notices to such person or subdivision, a notice is not effective until it reaches that person or subdivision. §342(g)(1).

If the notice is not effective, then no creditor can be charged with any monetary penalty until the notice is delivered to the right party. After a while, of course, the big law firms that do a volume practice will know the designations for Sears, Citibank, Ford Motor Credit, and a few dozen other places. Smaller practitioners may have to work harder to protect their clients, searching the records for specific places to send the notices. For large and small practices, however, creditors that appear less frequently in consumer cases will present additional challenges to notify. The risks associated with delays in notification fall squarely on the debtor.

Preliminary Procedures

A bit more detail about the administrative matters comprising the debtor's first interactions with the bankruptcy process may help complete the picture of what happens when the debtor files for bankruptcy. Along with a voluntary bankruptcy petition, the debtor is required to file various detailed forms called "schedules," all of which are set forth in Official Forms as part of the Bankruptcy Rules. The schedules include detailed lists of debts, assets, income, and expenses. The debtors must also provide a complete list of creditors and their addresses, and they must identify what property they claim as exempt. Before they can file, debtors must produce a certification that they have attended a debt counseling session. §§109(h), 521(b). Other filing requirements will be discussed as they become relevant.

It is crucial that a debtor's schedules be accurate and complete. Failure to list a debt may make the debt nondischargeable. §523(a)(3). In addition, any false statement in the petition or schedules may result in a complete denial of discharge as to all the debtor's debts, §727(a)(4), and may open the debtor to a perjury prosecution as well. The new amendments to the Code require that a certification be filed along with the petition stating that the debtor has been given information about the other chapters of the Code and about credit counseling, and the debtor has been warned that false information in the files can lead to penalties and jail time. 11 U.S.C. §521(b).

In order to police the debtors even more aggressively, the Bankruptcy Code now requires debtors to do more than sign their petitions under penalty of perjury. They must now file copies of their pay stubs for the two months before they filed, a statement of their monthly income and an explanation of how that was calculated, and a statement disclosing any anticipated increase in income over the next 12 months. 11 U.S.C. §521(a)(1)(iv)–(vi). In addition, the debtor must file a tax return for the prior year and a copy must be furnished to any creditor that requests one. 11 U.S.C. §521(e)(2). Tax returns filed after commencement of the bankruptcy must also be filed with the bankruptcy court. 11 U.S.C. §521(f). Failure to produce these documents will result in dismissal of the debtor's case, even if the debtor is otherwise eligible for bankruptcy. 11 U.S.C. §521(i).

To turn the heat up under debtors even more, Congress has instructed the Attorney General and the Judicial Conference of the United States to establish procedures for random audits. Lest the relevant parties be slack in the execution of their duties, Congress has specified the minimum sampling interval (at least one in every 250 cases). PL 109, sec. 256 (2005).

Finally, Congress deputized the debtor's own counsel to police the debtors. The attorney must sign the debtor's petition. Among other things, by signing the attorney represents that the attorney has performed a "reasonable investigation" and has no knowledge that the information in the schedules is incorrect. 11 U.S.C. §707(b)(4)(C), (D). In a turn of phrase that only a legislator could love, consumer bankruptcy lawyers have been renamed "debt relief agencies," and they are specifically prohibited from making any statement in any document filed in a case that is "untrue or misleading, or that upon exercise of reasonable care, should have been known by such agency to be untrue or misleading." §§101(12A); 526(a)(2). Attorneys who fail to abide by these rules can lose their fees, pay actual damages, or be forced to pay the fees of opposing counsel. §§526(c)(2); 707(b)(4)(A). Surely Congress has made it clear that they really and truly want the petition and the schedules to be rock-solid reliable and accurate, but the lawyers' duties are to be measured under somewhat amorphous standards. In later sections, we will continue consideration of the implications of these provisions for the debtor's lawyer, who must at the same time zealously represent the debtor and also police the debtor for any failure to comply with the laws — a new breed of Deputy Lawyer. We will also look into the costs of using the system and how those costs affect outcomes.

The first time a consumer debtor would normally see the inside of the federal courthouse would be at the First Meeting of Creditors (often called the "section 341 meeting" from the Code section that mandates it). This meeting is held at a date set by the court within 40 days after the petition is filed. §341. The meeting is ordinarily at the courthouse, but may be held elsewhere. Rule 2003(a). The presiding officer will be someone from the U.S. Trustee's office. Rule 2003(b). The primary function of the meeting in most consumer cases is to permit an examination of the debtor by the trustee and any interested creditors. Sometimes in a large case the creditors may choose to elect a Trustee in Bankruptcy (§§702, 1104(b)), or they may elect a Creditors' Committee (§§705(a), 1102(a)(1)). In a typical consumer case, however, the trustee appointed by the Office of the United States Trustee is in charge for the remainder of the case.

A debtor's life may be greatly changed at the moment the attorney files a bankruptcy petition. The automatic stay gives the debtor some breathing room and puts virtually all creditor collection attempts into one forum. On the other hand, some creditors may move quickly to seek relief from the stay.

The following problems illustrate imposition of the automatic stay from the perspective of both debtors and creditors.

Problem Set 6

6.1. Joe Weiner has come to see you about getting some help with his staggering debt burden. Joe makes about $34,000 per year as a meat cutter, but he hurt his arm last year and was out of work for nearly eight months. His current wages are reduced by $100 per week because they have been garnished in an action by a finance company. Joe owes about $68,000 in unsecured debt, including gasoline credit cards, medical bills, credit union loans, finance company loans, past due alimony and child support, store credit cards, and overdue utility bills. He also owes $4,500 on his car loan and another $750 to an auto repair garage. Joe adds that he has been receiving dunning letters and phone calls, his doctor's collection agency has threatened legal action if he doesn't come up with some money by tomorrow, the utility company has sent a notice that service will be discontinued at midnight, and both the car lender and the garage have threatened repossession.

To try to hold things together, Joe takes each paycheck and makes small payments to each creditor. When the car lender threatened to repossess his car, Joe wrote him a check for the balance due even though he had only $44.12 in the bank. He has just received a summons from the district attorney to appear in court tomorrow morning on a bad check charge. Joe is late on his rent again, and his landlord has threatened to evict him if he doesn't pay his past-due rent by Friday. His credit counselor has run out of suggestions.

Joe's assets consist of his car, clothing, kitchen utensils, and a few small pieces of furniture. He will get paid tomorrow morning for the two-week pay period that ended yesterday. He has filled out all the necessary paperwork and produced the required documentation. You have satisfied yourself that he is qualified for a Chapter 7, which he has asked you to file later today. Joe wants to know what he can expect to happen in the next few weeks. He especially wants to know if he will get his full paycheck, undiminished by the garnishment, tomorrow and every two weeks thereafter. See §§362(a), (b)(2), (b)(22), (b)(23), 366.

6.2. Puja Seam arrives in your office in tears. She shows you a notice that her house has been posted for sale by foreclosure at noon tomorrow. She explains that she has been in the middle of a divorce, and that her ex-husband claimed that he was making mortgage payments when he was not. She had called him about the earlier notices, but he had said that the notices were "mistakes" and he would "straighten them out." For the past month she has been unable to find him, and she fears he has fled the state. She tried calling the mortgage company, but her loan had been sold from one servicer to another and she could never track down the holder of the note. Now the sheriff's department says the sale is going forward. You know that if it does, she and her children will lose their home.

Puja has filled out all the schedules in your conference room today, but she did not know to bring paycheck stubs, tax returns, or any other paperwork with her, nor has she sought credit counseling. She lives an hour away and isn't sure where all that paperwork is at home. What can you do for her today? Make a list of what you need from Puja and how you can get it. See 11 U.S.C. §§521(a), (b), (i); 101(12A); 526; 707(b)(4)(C), (D); 109(h). When your paralegal points silently to the value she listed for the car ($250), does that raise an issue beyond asking her if she is sure of it?

6.3. Your neighbor Eric Van Horn saw you watering your backyard this afternoon and asked you for some bankruptcy advice. He sold his classic car, a 1937 Cadillac, to Rathbone Robertson, scion of a local family of some prominence. He took back a note for the purchase price secured by the car and properly perfected, along with an agreement covering things like the maintenance of insurance until the full price is paid. Rathbone occasionally misses a payment, but he let the insurance drop only once before. When he did, Eric repo'd the car himself (he had kept a set of keys) and wrote Rathbone a nice letter asking him to bring payments up to date and reinstate the insurance. Both things happened right away. (Eric thinks Rathbone hits up his brother when he really needs money.) Eric returned the car, but last week it happened again — no payment and a notice from the insurance company that the policy had been canceled for nonpayment of premiums. Eric took the car again and it now sits in his driveway.

Yesterday Eric got a notice that Rathbone had filed for bankruptcy, followed by a call from Rathbone's lawyer demanding return of the car. Eric wants to drop Rathbone a polite note or call him on the phone to ask for payment and insurance reinstatement as before, but he doesn't want to have any legal problems. He also doesn't want to hire a lawyer "who'd cost me more than I'm owed on the car." Do you have any good free advice for your neighbor? See 11 U.S.C. §362(a).

6.4. Christy von der Ahe has worked hard to get her chiropractic practice launched, but cash flow problems have caused her to fall behind on several payments. She came to see you a month ago, and last week you filed her Chapter 13 bankruptcy. You have a good plan that will permit her to repay a substantial portion of her debts.

This morning she called you in a panic. It seems that a crew sent out from her bank managed to gain entrance to her office last night, and they took all of her equipment. Without it, she is out of business. She can't even meet today's clients, and once the word spreads, she fears her practice will be destroyed. She desperately wants that equipment back right now.

You called the loan officer at Christy's bank. He said yes, he knew about the bankruptcy, he had seen the proposed plan, and he didn't like the plan. He would like Christy to sell some equipment right now, give that cash to the bank, and then pay more to the bank over time. You know the plan is legal and confirmable as is, and you start sputtering about the automatic stay. "Sorry," said the officer, "our official notice place and person doesn't have anything from you." You quickly look at your files and see that you sent the notice to the bank's main office, but you don't know if the bank has a "designated place" for receiving notices. You ask the loan officer where it should be sent, and he laughs and says, "Figure it out, smart guy. But if that lady doc wants her equipment back today, I suggest we talk changes in the plan right now."

What do you do? How much do you charge Christy? See 11 U.S.C. §342(e), (f), (g).

CHAPTER 5

LIQUIDATION BANKRUPTCY

A. INTRODUCTION

A Chapter 7 bankruptcy is the classic "straight" or liquidation bankruptcy. A Trustee in Bankruptcy (TIB) is appointed to gather all the debtor's property, to sell it, and to distribute the proceeds to creditors. At the end of the process, the creditors have their proportional share of whatever the debtor had, and the debtor receives a discharge of the remaining outstanding debts. The creditors can tote up their losses and move on. The debtor can get back to work or start a new business, flat broke and without much in the way of assets, but knowing that the benefits of tomorrow's hard work will not go to the creditors.

The distribution process in liquidation is governed by section 726. Although the basic principles of bankruptcy distribution are simple, the process can become quite complex. It is therefore useful to set out the basics by way of introduction, then return to it later with more detail. The discussion that follows is necessarily simplified for introductory purposes.

As the TIB prepares to sell each piece of property in which the debtor has an interest, it must first be determined if some other person or company has any interest in that property. For example, such an interest could be that of a co-owner or, more often, a secured party. If another party has a recognized interest, then the TIB must pay that party the part of the proceeds to which it is entitled, with only the remainder available for distribution to creditors generally. In the typical case, the trustee will have to deduct from the sale proceeds the trustee's own fee and costs of sale, and then the amount of the claim of a secured party and pay that amount to the secured party. Any proceeds in excess of those owed to the secured party go into the general distribution fund. So, for example, if the debtor owned a Toyota Camry, the trustee might seize it, sell the car, take a fee for the sale, and pay off the secured lender. If money remains, it would go into the pool for general unsecured creditors.

The trustee must also consider any valid exemption claimed by the debtor in a particular item of property. Exemptions, which are discussed below, will determine what property of the estate is exempt from sale for the benefit of the creditors and reserved for the debtor's fresh start. If, for example, the debtor had a valid exemption for the car, the trustee might still seize and sell it, and the trustee and the secured creditor would be paid, but the debtor would get the dollar value of the exemption. Only if the car brought more money than all of those would there be anything left to go into the pool for the general unsecured creditors.

Once the proceeds from the sales of all property have been obtained and the secured parties and other entities with property interests have been paid, the TIB distributes the remaining funds among the general creditors. General creditors are in turn divided into three principal groups: "priority creditors," "general, unsecured creditors," and "subordinated creditors." None of these creditors is secured, although some of them may have been partially secured and are now in line to collect only on that part of their claims that was not satisfied by the proceeds of the sale of their collateral.

If the TIB is pictured as sitting behind a distribution table with piles of money ready for payment, then the statute sets forth specific rules determining who stands where in the line of unsecured creditors gathered in front of the table. Those who are among the first in line are the "priority" creditors. These creditors are entitled to get paid, in full or up to the dollar limits of their statutory priorities, before the other creditors get anything. Even among these priority creditors, some get paid before others. §507(a). At the very back of the line are "subordinated creditors," who are paid last because they have been "equitably subordinated" to everyone else, usually because of some wrongdoing. All the remaining creditors are general, unsecured creditors who get paid after the priority claimants, but before those who are subordinated. (Some of the unsecured creditors have agreed to be subordinated by contract; their special circumstances are discussed later.)

There are also some distinctions among general, unsecured creditors, but ordinarily they are paid pro rata from the remaining funds, in proportion to the amounts owed to each: If there is $10,000 left and the unsecured creditors are collectively owed $100,000, then each one will get 10 percent of its claim (the infamous "10 cents on the dollar" that springs up in thousands of bankruptcy examples).

B. ELIGIBILITY

1. A Change in Philosophy

Chapter 7 liquidation bankruptcy is the baseline, the central idea behind the bankruptcy system — liquidate property, distribute the proceeds, discharge the debts, and leave the debtor with a reason to keep working. At some level, this cycle of debt forgiveness and re-entry into the marketplace is quite extraordinary. Using a largely administrative process, many kinds of legally enforceable obligations simply dissolve. Bankruptcy is a world turned upside down in which a debtor freely admits owing money to many creditors, but payment will never be made.

At the same time, bankruptcy is not very extraordinary at all. Any free market economy will produce both winners and losers. The winners will pay their debts and count their profits, but there must also be some way to deal with the losers. Even if the law provided no bankruptcy system, many of the losers would never pay — they simply don't have the money. Creditors might press for repayment, and some might get it. Perhaps the biggest creditor would take everything the debtor had left. Perhaps an outlaw creditor would break the debtor's legs unless some family member paid up. Perhaps corporate insiders would loot the business before the creditors showed up. And perhaps creditors would hound the debtor for decades to come, seizing wages or grabbing business assets, unless the debtor fled to another country or to the underground economy where all transactions are in cash. Bankruptcy substitutes an orderly process under a uniform federal law for these other approaches to collection, with Chapter 7 as the central arbiter between debtors and creditors.

The power of the bankruptcy system and its starting point, Chapter 7 liquidation, is so great that Congress has revisited the question of when debtors should be eligible for bankruptcy relief a number of times. The first bankruptcy laws were available only to "traders," an early recognition that debt relief was essential to encouraging entrepreneurial undertakings. By the mid-nineteenth century, bankruptcy laws accommodated both troubled businesses and families in financial distress, all following the liquidation model. When repayment schemes were added during the Great Depression, Chapters X, XI, and XII for businesses and Chapter XIII for wage earners, a new choice was born: liquidate or pay creditors over time.

When Congress enacted the 1978 Bankruptcy Code, it kept access to liquidation bankruptcy broad, making it available to both individuals and businesses, with only the smallest exceptions. But Congress wanted more of the people in trouble to repay if they could, so the 1978 Code substantially revised Chapter 13 to make it a more workable alternative. In order to attract more users, Congress built incentives into the Chapter 13 option. So, for example, Chapter 13 provided carrots such as a unique opportunity to get current on a home mortgage that was in default, a chance to keep more property, and a discharge that covered certain debts that could not be discharged in Chapter 7. Around the country, a number of bankruptcy judges embraced the new system, working with trustees and attorneys to try to make the Chapter 13 system feasible for people who needed bankruptcy relief and who might eventually discharge many of their debts, but who might be able to make payments along the way.

The changes worked. In a short period of time, Chapter 13 spread from a regional oddity to a nationwide system. By the mid-1980s, about 30 percent of all the families that filed for bankruptcy chose Chapter 13. It appeared that Congress had its wish: a two-level bankruptcy system that provided liquidation for people in the worst financial trouble, but a repayment alternative that a sizeable portion of the debtors would attempt.

But there it stalled out. Chapter 13s were half the filings in some districts, but in other districts Chapter 13 remained a rarity. In 20 years, from 1985 to 2005, the proportion of debtors choosing Chapter 13 changed little. Moreover, data began to emerge that showed that only a third of the debtors who filed for Chapter 13 were able to complete their repayment plans. Two-thirds either converted their cases to Chapter 7 or they dropped out of bankruptcy altogether, with no discharge and facing a mountain of interest that piled up on their debts in the meantime.

At the same time that the proportion of debtors filing for Chapter 13 stabilized at about 30 percent, the total number of bankruptcy filings continued to rise dramatically. From the early 1980s to the early 2000s, the number of bankruptcy filings quadrupled. By 2004, about one in every 75 households across the country filed for bankruptcy. With more than 1.5 million cases filed (and more than 2 million people filing, counting husbands and wives who file jointly), bankruptcy had become far more common than our forebears could have imagined (see Warren and Tyagi, *The Two-Income Trap*, p. 13). Now in a single year more people file for bankruptcy than are diagnosed with cancer. More declare bankruptcy than graduate from college. And, as a reminder of the fallout from these bankruptcy decisions, we note that more children live through their parents' bankruptcy than their parents' divorce.

What does it mean when the number of bankruptcies rises so sharply? Could it be that families are in a lot more financial trouble? Could the rise in the number of families with no health insurance or the increasing instability of American jobs be causing some of the increase? Could a deregulated credit industry that aggressively markets consumer debt and sub-prime mortgage financing bear on the failure of these families? Could more small businesses be failing, dragging down the entrepreneurs who owned them? Could increased attorney advertising have increased the number of filings? Or could it be that those in modest financial trouble are simply more willing to seek a bankruptcy alternative than they were a generation ago? Or perhaps more people are spending wildly because they know they have a bankruptcy backstop?

Depending on which answer (or answers) is correct, the rise in bankruptcy filings, and particularly the rise in the number of people who choose to discharge their debts through Chapter 7 liquidation, is either a symptom of other serious problems or it is a problem itself. Congress, spurred on by a highly vocal credit industry, decided it was the latter. In their view, the rise in bankruptcy filings was the fault of wildly spending debtors or of debtors who could pay their debts if they really tried.

In 1984, as the rise in bankruptcy filings began to gather steam, the credit industry lobbied Congress for changes in the laws. In response, Congress gave the bankruptcy judges the power to dismiss Chapter 7 cases if the filing involved "substantial abuse." Over time, a number of debtors were denied access to Chapter 7. Some of those debtors had engaged in bad acts before bankruptcy that made their filings offensive to a sense of fair play. They might meet all the technical requirements for bankruptcy, but they were engaging in criminal activities or cheating their creditors, so the bankruptcy judges tossed them from the system. More often, the debtors who were pushed out were those who had the ability, with a modest amount of sacrifice, to repay their creditors. Debtors who had substantial incomes were told to convert their cases to repayment plans or to leave the bankruptcy system altogether. Published opinions added some flesh to the statutory bone of "substantial abuse" as the trustees and courts monitored which debtors would be eligible for Chapter 7.

Over time, some debtors pushed the boundaries of bankruptcy relief, and some courts pushed back. Notice in the opinion below how the court reshapes the debtors' budget and requires a minimum three-year repayment plan if the debtors want any bankruptcy relief.

===================== In re SHAW =====================

311 B.R. 180 (Bankr. M.D.N.C. 2003)

OPINION BY: Catharine R. CARRUTHERS

* * *

The Debtors, Gregory and Martha Shaw, filed for Chapter 7 bankruptcy on May 27, 2003. The Debtors are a married couple in their early 50s with two grown children, ages 21 and 24. The Debtors' assets include a house that they listed on Schedule A with a value of $415,000.00, but testified that they believed it was actually worth less than $400,000.00. The Debtors listed personal property in the amount of $56,265.00.

The Debtors have been continuously employed for at least the past five years. The Debtors' 2001 Federal tax return shows adjusted gross income of $138,554.00, with an increase in 2002 to $157,024.00. At the time of the bankruptcy filing, Mr. Shaw worked for Shelco, Inc., where he has been employed for the past five years, and Mrs. Shaw worked for R.J. Reynolds Tobacco Company. On their bankruptcy schedules, Mrs. Shaw listed monthly income of $3,080.70 and Mr. Shaw listed income of $4,723.41 for a total combined monthly income, after taxes and other payroll deductions, in the amount of $7,804.11.

Mrs. Shaw has since lost her job, though she will receive severance pay at full salary until April 2004. Mrs. Shaw must now pay for health and dental insurance, which she estimated at $192.00 per month, such that her income should be adjusted down accordingly. Therefore, according to her pay stubs her monthly income is $2,763.89 per month.[1] Mrs. Shaw stated that she obtained many skills from her employment at R.J. Reynolds Tobacco Company and that she is also a licensed cosmetologist. She intends to seek new employment next month, and will continue to receive severance pay at full salary even if she obtains new employment prior to April. Mr. Shaw recently received a raise, such that his income has increased to $5,126.08 per month after taxes. Therefore, the Debtors combined monthly income, after deductions for payroll taxes and health insurance, is currently $7,889.97.

---

1. This monthly figure is based on earnings in the amount of $1,818.50 less $454.24 in taxes paid 26 times a year. The court deducted $192.00 per month for health and dental insurance. Mrs. Shaw also has deductions from her paycheck for a 401(k) loan and a car loan that the court has included in her income.

The Debtors listed net monthly expenses of $7,517.59. The breakdown is as follows:

Home Mortgage	$3,349.28
Electricity and heat	$200.00
Cable	$40.00
Telephone	$95.00
Water	$16.00
Internet	$29.95
Trash service	$16.00
Home maintenance	$30.00
Food	$525.00
Clothing	$75.00
Laundry	$40.00
Medical and dental	$75.00
Transportation	$435.00
Recreation, newspapers	$14.00
Charitable contributions	$165.00
Auto insurance	$227.00
Life insurance	$41.36
Property taxes	$50.00
Auto payments	$944.00
College expenses for daughter	$1,105.00
Miscellaneous	$100.00
TOTAL	$7,517.59

At the hearing on this matter, the Debtors testified as to some adjustments to their scheduled budget. First, the Debtors understated their automobile payments on their petition. The Debtors own a 2002 Oldsmobile Bravado with a payment of $598.00, a 2001 Oldsmobile Alero with a payment of $458.00 per month, and lease a 2000 Mitsubishi Montero for $349.00 per month for a total of $1,404.00 per month. Second, the Debtors monthly telephone expense is $220.00, including two cell phones and two lines for their home. Finally, the Debtors did take out a student loan for their daughter's college tuition, so their college expenses have dropped to $520.00 per month. Even with these changes, the Debtors' monthly budget appears to remain at approximately $7,500.00 per month.

The Debtors' financial problems have been ongoing for over ten years. Prior to filing for bankruptcy, the Debtors had amassed a substantial amount of both secured and unsecured debt consisting primarily of credit card debt. The Debtors have a first mortgage in the amount of $338,000.00 and a second mortgage in the amount of $60,329.00 on their home. The Debtors total secured debt, including three car loans and two mortgages is $469,074.50. The Debtors also owe $131,476.26 in unsecured credit card debt. The Debtors had at least fifteen credit card accounts including credit accounts with stores such as Dillards, Hecht's, JC Penney's, Sears, Belk and Home Depot.

Despite their consistent income during the last several years, the Debtors have been unable to make a dent in the repayment of their debts and have consistently spent more money than they were able to earn. The Debtors contend that they need a fresh start in a Chapter 7 so that they can retain their home and three vehicles.

DISCUSSION

The court scheduled this matter to determine if dismissal was [appropriate] for substantial abuse under Bankruptcy Code Section 707(b)...

The Debtors stipulate that their obligations are "primarily consumer debts" in that they are debts "incurred by an individual primarily for personal, family, or household purposes." 11 U.S.C. §101(8). Congress, however, did not provide a definition for the term "substantial abuse." The Fourth Circuit has adopted a test for substantial abuse that requires that the court look at the "totality of circumstances." In re Green, 934 F.2d 568 (4th Cir. 1991). Under the Green test, an important factor to be considered is whether the debtor has the ability to repay the debt, including consideration of the relation of the debtor's future income to his future necessary expenses. Id. at 572. The court must also examine (1) whether the debtor filed his bankruptcy petition because of sudden illness, calamity, disability, or unemployment; (2) whether the debtor's schedules and statement of current income and expenses reasonably and accurately reflect his true financial condition; (3) whether the debtor incurred cash advances and made consumer purchases in excess of his ability to repay; (4) whether the debtor's proposed family budget is excessive or unreasonable; and (5) whether the petition was filed in good faith. In re Smurthwaite, 149 B.R. 409, 411 (Bankr. N.D.W. Va. 1992).

The facts in this case illustrate that the Debtors can repay a meaningful portion of their unsecured debt over a period of 36 months based upon their projected income and necessary future expenses. Conversely, if the debtors remain in chapter 7, this case will be a no asset case and unsecured creditors will receive nothing. The Debtors' proposed family budget as listed on Schedule J in the amount of $6,312.52 is excessive and unreasonable. While their scheduled budget appears to leave no disposable income, the Debtors' overall expenses can be reduced significantly and still provide the Debtors with adequate food, clothing, shelter and other necessities of life. See In re Engskow, 247 B.R. 314 (Bankr. M.D. Fla. 2000).

The court finds that the Debtors' proposed family budget is excessive and unreasonable within the context of a Chapter 7 bankruptcy. First, the Debtors' mortgage payment expense is clearly unwarranted. The Debtors purchased the home in 1993. At the hearing, the Debtors explained that they needed a large home so that there would be sufficient space for Mrs. Shaw's mother to live with them and yet not interrupt their children's lives. Mrs. Shaw's mother passed away in 1998. The Debtors currently pay $3,349.28 to maintain a home with approximately 3200 square feet as well as a finished basement. The Debtors' children are now grown, however, their 24-year-old son lives at home and contributes nothing to the monthly housing payment. If the Debtors wish to take advantage of the protections afforded by the Bankruptcy Code, they simply must obtain less expensive housing. The Debtors could easily reduce their monthly housing expense by $1,000.00 per month and still have over $2,000.00 per month available for housing.

In addition, the court finds that the vehicle lease payments of $349.00 per month and college expenses of $520.00 per month for the Debtors' daughter are not reasonable and necessary expenses under these circumstances. While supporting a daughter in college is an admirable goal, the Debtors propose to do so at the expense of their creditors. Therefore, the Debtors' budget can be further reduced by $869.00 per month. Further reductions can be made by trimming the Debtors' telephone expenses for two home lines and two cell phones and by eliminating the ongoing expenses for the swimming pool. The court finds that the transportation cost, exclusive of car payments and insurance, is unreasonable and excessive. With just these adjustments alone, the Debtors could be able to contribute approximately $2,000.00 per month to a Chapter 13 plan. The Chapter 13 Trustee estimates a dividend of 29% over 36 months.

The Debtors admit that their bankruptcy was not the result of a sudden illness, calamity, disability, or unemployment. These Debtors were not forced into bankruptcy as the result of a tragic event. While the Debtors have experienced some short period of unemployment, their road to financial distress was the result of lifestyle choices they made. Their debts have been accumulating for years. This *Green* factor weighs in favor of dismissal.

The Debtors admit they have incurred cash advances and consumer purchases beyond their ability to pay such debts. The Shaws have been living beyond their means for years. The Debtors made purchases in anticipation of future bonuses and were unable to pay off those purchases when bonuses were not received or were smaller than expected. For example, Mrs. Shaw testified that she purchased a bedroom suite less than two years ago for approximately $4,000.00 with the expectation that Mr. Shaw would get an anniversary bonus. Mr. Shaw did not receive that bonus. The Debtors also paid for maintenance and repairs on their home through cash advances on credit cards. Mrs. Shaw testified that for years, they managed to keep up with their bills only by relying on bonuses and income tax refunds to catch up payments, and by pushing out payments by consolidating debts or refinancing.

The Debtors contend that they have never incurred debt maliciously or with an intent not to pay, and that their enormous debt has accumulated over a period of years. The fact that these debts accumulated over a long period of time makes it all the more difficult for the court to understand why the Debtors did not change their spending behavior years ago. According to the Debtors' testimony, they have been struggling to make payments on their debts for years, and yet continued to make expensive decisions, such as purchasing a 2002 Oldsmobile Bravado and a 2001 Oldsmobile Alero, and a $4,000.00 bedroom suite and contributing over $1,000.00 per month towards their daughter's college expenses. Thus, the Debtors have clearly been aware of their inability to pay their ever-increasing debt for years, and continued to incur cash advances and consumer purchases beyond their ability to pay.

This brings the court to the question of whether the Debtors filed the case in good faith. The Debtors have incurred over $130,000.00 in unsecured credit card debt. The Debtors have clearly stated that they are seeking the court to discharge this unsecured debt so they can use their income to make their vehicle and mortgage payments. Clearly the Debtors have been quite forthright and honest, however, the Debtors' desire to retain their $415,000.00 home and three vehicles, and maintain a lifestyle they cannot afford at the expense of their creditors weighs against a finding of good faith.

Finally, the court notes that the Debtors' schedules are reasonably accurate and the Debtors were credible at the hearing when questioned by counsel and the court. Therefore, the court will find that the errors in the schedules were not made with the intent to mislead any parties and therefore do not weigh in favor of dismissal.

In evaluating all of the *Green* factors and looking at the totality of the circumstances, the court must take into account that there is a presumption of granting the debtors the relief requested under Chapter 7. Even with this presumption, the court finds that this case should be dismissed for substantial abuse. The Debtors elected to file a Chapter 7 petition to maintain their present lifestyle. They have the ability to repay a substantial portion of the debt with their high income. The Debtors incurred cash advances and made consumer purchases far in excess of their ability to repay and their proposed family budget is both excessive and unreasonable given their current circumstances.

The court concludes that based upon the totality of the circumstances these debtors do not satisfy the criteria to be Chapter 7 debtors. To allow such would be a substantial abuse of the bankruptcy system and goals; and therefore, this Chapter 7 case should be dismissed under 11 U.S.C. §707(b) of the Bankruptcy Code. The Court will delay entry of the Order for ten days to provide the Debtors with an opportunity to consider whether to convert this case to a case under Chapter 13 of the Bankruptcy Code.

With an income about six times higher than the typical debtor filing for bankruptcy, Mr. and Mrs. Shaw are not likely to provoke a great deal of sympathy. Even so, we find ourselves wondering about the creditors that offered all those mortgages, car loans, and new credit cards and that, according to the court, refinanced and consolidated all those debts on multiple occasions. Didn't anyone notice that the Shaws were just a wee bit overextended?

Despite the courts' willingness to crack down in cases such as *Shaw*, most debtors didn't have high incomes and big expenses to cut back on. Even as the bankruptcy judges and trustees screened the debtors, bankruptcy filings continued to skyrocket. A solid 70 percent of the filers were liquidating their debts in Chapter 7, and the failure rate in Chapter 13 remained high. The credit industry lobbied hard for more changes in the law to make it harder for debtors to get bankruptcy relief, launching a public relations campaign about bankruptcy abuses. Empirical studies, including our own, showed that most people filed for bankruptcy following job losses, serious medical problems, and family break-up, but that did not slow down credit industry lobbying. The debate over why so many people were filing for bankruptcy rapidly intensified.

Historically there were two big deterrents to filing bankruptcy: the risk of losing property and the stigma associated with a public declaration of insolvency. As bankruptcy filings rose, critics claimed that these two determinants were obviously inadequate — otherwise how could anyone explain the rise in bankruptcy filings? Most debtors had no non-exempt property and, they argued, an increasingly decadent population no longer regarded bankruptcy as shameful. Therefore there was no real cost to filing bankruptcy and no return to creditors. Debtors should be made to pay at least something from future income in exchange for a discharge.

In 2005, nine years after the bill drafted by the credit industry was first introduced, Congress took steps to make bankruptcy less accessible. Instead of keeping the doors to the bankruptcy courthouse open wide for any person in financial trouble, the 2005 Amendments put new mechanisms in place to screen the debtors seeking relief more aggressively than the courts and trustees had done. Only those who could make it past the screens would be permitted to file for Chapter 7 bankruptcy. The rest must adopt a payout plan in Chapter 13 or struggle along outside of bankruptcy without its fresh start.

2.   The Presumption of Abuse

The 2005 Amendments follow the basic idea of the 1984 Amendments — scrutinize the debtors to see which ones should be denied access to Chapter 7 liquidation because they are abusing the system. As in the 1984 Amendments, Congress embraced the position that only one kind of debtor could engage in abuse: the consumer. For someone whose debts are mostly business debts there is no screening for abuse. §707(b)(1). This means, for example, that someone who runs a small business and is loaded with debts to suppliers, tradespeople, and the like is not subjected to section 707(b). scrutiny. (We note, however, that section 707(a) may still provide a creative court with some chance to review a business petition.) Of course, another small businessperson, with more modest business debts, but a home mortgage and credit card charges run up for family needs, may be barred from Chapter 7. Similarly, the consultant who is self-employed may face a business crisis and file for bankruptcy, but the debts he incurred to support himself will likely be declared "consumer debts," thus requiring him to run the gauntlet of the means test in order to file for Chapter 7.

One place where the 2005 Amendments part company from earlier efforts to scrutinize debtors who might be abusing the bankruptcy process is in the role of the judges. The 1984 Amendments authorized the judge to dismiss cases on any finding of abuse, leaving what constituted abuse in a particular circumstance to the judge who weighed all the facts and circumstances of the individual case. Instead of leaving discretion with the court, however, the new Chapter 7 screen is semi-automated, employing a fixed formula to determine which debtors should be deemed ineligible.

The test is complex. In the 2005 legislation, it filled two printed, single-spaced pages. Like a big meal that can't be digested all at once, the new formula is best understood when broken into smaller parts. The first such part appears in 11 U.S.C. §707(b)(1), instructing the courts to dismiss a case or to convert it to a repayment plan in Chapter 13 or Chapter 11 if the Chapter 7 filing constitutes an "abuse."

The real action, of course, is in the provisions that determine which factors make up "abuse." Those provisions are in section 707(b)(2)(A), which creates a presumption of abuse based upon a formula. The instruction to the courts is now clear: "the court shall presume abuse exists" according to an intricate formula of income minus expenses. The debtor must also supply extensive documentation for the calculation. The starting point is unambiguous: No more weighing and measuring what constitutes abuse under the highly individualized circumstances of each person who files for bankruptcy relief. Instead, under the 2005 Amendments, the judges have their marching orders from Congress: Apply the formula to all Chapter 7 filers, then dismiss or convert the cases that the formula identifies as abusive.

Congress left a sliver of judgment with the courts in the next major subsection, 707(b)(2)(B). "Special circumstances," such as serious medical conditions or service in the armed forces, may justify adjustments to the calculations to determine which debtors are presumed to have abused the bankruptcy system. But the exceptions themselves require extensive documentation and the adjustments to income or expenses must be cranked back into the mechanical formula to determine whether the debtor can overcome the presumption that this bankruptcy filing is abusive. Suffering or distress is not enough; the special circumstances must have an effect on income or expenses that can be quantified and documented.

Although Congress left little room for a court to determine that a filing that failed the formula was not abusive, Congress permitted courts to exercise discretion in the opposite direction. Even a debtor who was deemed "not abusive" under the formula could nonetheless be deemed an abuser by the court in section 707(b)(3). The grounds are "bad faith" and "totality of the circumstances," a catch-all category for any unworthy debtors not captured by the payment formula.

3. The Formula: Income and Expenses

The key to the reform was to determine which debtors could make any meaningful repayment of their debts — and in the process to define "meaningful." Congress was obviously dissatisfied with the judges' efforts since 1984 to determine which debtors could repay. Instead, Congress instituted a formula widely known as the "means test," a mechanical formula to determine who can and cannot (as a matter of law) repay some debt. Debtors who cannot pass the means test are presumed to abuse the bankruptcy process, and the judges are instructed to dismiss their filings without further ado. The core idea is to define income and expenses and subtract the second from the first. If the difference (the surplus of income over expenses) would pay at least "X" amount of debt, the debtor is barred from Chapter 7, absent special circumstances.

a. Income

The formula for the means test begins with the debtor's current monthly income and a threshold test for Chapter 7 eligibility. If the debtor's income is low enough, the debtor is exempt from the means test and therefore eligible for Chapter 7. Otherwise, the rest of the formula must be worked out to determine eligibility. In general, the threshold test is whether the debtor's income exceeds the median income for similar families in the state where the debtor filed. If the debtor's income is equal to or lower than the median, then the debtor has passed through the median-income screen and no presumption bars the way to Chapter 7. If the income is higher than the state median, more calculations await. §707(b)(2))(A). Note it is the median (middle) income that is used, not the mean (average) income, which is pulled way up by really big earners.

What counts as current monthly income is defined in section 101(10A). The court is instructed to calculate the average monthly income for the six months preceding the bankruptcy filing. Income from all sources is included. This means wages, of course, but it also includes other earnings, such as interest on a checking account, stock dividends, unemployment compensation, income tax refunds, or, in the case of a debtor who runs a small business, revenues and accounts receivable. Income also includes amounts paid by others toward household expenses.

Obviously, the median-income screen is the most crucial step in the process, since data show that many debtors will fall below that threshold (see below). This screen depends upon comparison with state median income figures compiled by the Census Bureau, yet the Bankruptcy Code and Census definitions of income are mismatched in several important ways. For example:

A.   Is "income" pre-tax or post-tax? The Bankruptcy Code defines current monthly income as "income received." This distinction might suggest that the test uses only post-tax income, the take-home pay of the debtor after federal, state, and local taxes, Social Security, and Medicare have all been deducted. The Census Bureau bases its data collection on pre-tax income.

B.   On the other hand, the Census Bureau income does not include sources such as capital gains; money received from the sale of property (unless the recipient was engaged in the business of selling such property); the value of income "in kind" as in food stamps; tax refunds; exchange of money between relatives living in the same household; gifts and lump-sum inheritances, insurance payments, and other types of lump-sum receipts. Some or all of these items are included in the definition of income from the Bankruptcy Code in section 101(10A) for income received.

C.   Heading back in the other direction, the Bankruptcy Code excludes Social Security benefits from the calculation of income, even though the Census Bureau includes them.

What if the debtor has other paycheck deductions, such as savings bonds or retirement contributions? Those deductions create assets for the debtor, so they presumably would not be included. What about deductions for health insurance? What about a wage garnishment? It should become increasingly clear that in the flotsam and jetsam of the lives of millions of families, even the simple parts of this means test are going to get pretty complex.

Although the Bankruptcy Code specifically requires a comparison of the debtor's income with that of the state median, the various definitions of income in the Code make it clear that there can be no apples-to-apples comparison. Instead, Congress has determined that two things that are defined differently should be compared to determine whether the debtor has sufficient income to go on to the next steps of the means test.

The Census Bureau collects data on median incomes by state and by family size, reporting what families actually earn, and Congress instructs the court to use the Bureau's data, although the language of section 707(b)(7) uses the Census terminology in an odd way, creating additional questions. §101(39A). The reports are available online at www.census.gov/ hhes/www/income/statemedfaminc.html. The Bureau does not collect new data annually, but it offers estimates. Whether such estimates meet statutory muster is an open question. When there are no current data, the Code instructs the courts to adjust the most recent Census reports for inflation. Even the inflation adjustment presents challenges. Inflation adjustments come from the Consumer Price Index, which is based on expenses — not incomes. The CPI is also national. In any given year, median incomes in a particular region may rise or fall somewhat faster or slower than the national prices for the goods making up the CPI. One place to get data on cost of living adjustments is www.aier.org/cgi-aier/ colcalculator.cgi. Because judges will be required to review thousands of cases to determine whether they pass the means test, data about the current median incomes in the state will likely be posted and revised on a regular basis.

The data from our 2001 Consumer Bankruptcy Project study shows that only about 8 percent of the Chapter 7 debtors would have income above their state medians. Even among these 8 percent, some would not be blocked from Chapter 7 by the means test because their expenses relative to their incomes would leave them with too little money to trigger a presumption of abuse. Using somewhat different median-income and means tests than the ones that finally passed, the 1998 Culhane and White study showed that 24 percent of the debtors had above-median incomes, but only 3 to 4 percent of them would have been blocked from Chapter 7 after working through the remaining elements of the means test. Thus, as one lawyer put it, for the great majority of debtors the problem with the means test is calculating it and litigating it, not living within it.

On the other hand, even if most debtors are below the income threshold, the means test cannot be dismissed as unimportant. The substantial costs it will impose on all Chapter 7 debtors and on their lawyers may reshape bankruptcy practices. Moreover, 6 percent of Chapter 7 individual filers amounts to about 60,000 debtors and their families each year. Furthermore, there are critical public policy implications of the means test. Congress decided to incur enormous public costs to enforce the means test (see above concerning the U.S. Trustee's duties in that regard) despite empirical evidence that it would affect few debtors, because it wanted to reduce Chapter 7 filings. If filings do not drop, will the next step be to adjust the test downward to block more Chapter 7 filings? Or will the data showing that most families are already living below the median income convince Congress that it has misdiagnosed the problem?

b. Expenses

For debtors who failed the median-income screen, the next step is to determine what expenses the debtor may deduct. Government data show what families actually spend in various categories, but Congress wanted families in bankruptcy to spend less — and produce more for their creditors. Here Congress faced a serious challenge. It wanted to force debtors to tighten their belts and pay if they could, but it also wanted a uniform repayment standard, applicable like a rubber stamp to every family. It found its answer in the IRS. For many years the IRS has negotiated with people who failed to pay their taxes. Instead of simply prosecuting and putting these people in jail or seizing their homes and other property, the IRS would sometimes offer a repayment alternative. If the tax delinquent would pay a certain amount toward past-due taxes, penalties, and interest, then the IRS would delay asset seizure or prosecution and, if the miscreant paid up in full, let the person go. The IRS negotiated around a family budget, leaving some for the taxpayer and taking the rest for the IRS. In order to develop some consistency from office to office and agent to agent on how much money to demand that each tax delinquent pay, the IRS developed a series of guidelines. Those guidelines include expense allowances for the tax delinquents.

The IRS guidelines include what they term National Standards. These National Standards use a sliding scale for various expenses based on income. So, for example, when the IRS negotiates with a woman and child whose household income is just under $10,000 a year, it allows $336 a month to feed the two of them. But a woman and child whose household income is $70,000 a year gets $691 a month for food. Whatever the differences between the rich and the poor, it is clear that the IRS thinks the rich need to eat better.

Adding further support to the statement that you can find anything on the Internet, the current IRS expense allowances are now available online at www.irs.gov/individuals/article/0,,id=96543,00.html. The National Standards cover clothing, food, personal grooming, laundry, and miscellaneous. The National Standards apply nationwide, except for Alaska and Hawaii, which have their own tables. When they are figuring out what they have to pay to the IRS, taxpayers are allowed to deduct the National Standards amounts allocated for their family size and income level, regardless of what was actually spent. The Bankruptcy Code similarly permits debtors to deduct these amounts without further proof. §707(b)(2)(A)(ii).

The origin of the National Standards is not entirely clear. The IRS website explains that the numbers are based on numbers from the Bureau of Labor Statistics and Consumer Expenditure Survey, but the IRS makes the decision on how much the families can deduct in the various categories. How much hardship should be imposed on the tax delinquents who are avoiding seizure or prosecution is within their province.

One other note about the National Standards is in order. The IRS uses them as a guideline for agents when they negotiate with people who haven't paid their taxes, not as a hard and fast rule. On its website, the IRS explains:

> If the IRS determines that the facts and circumstances of your situation indicates that using the scheduled allowance of necessary expenses is

inadequate to provide for basic living expenses, we will allow for your actual expenses. However, you must provide documentation that supports a determination that using national and local expense standards leaves you an inadequate means of providing for basic living expenses.

Because these are guidelines for negotiations, the IRS can revise them as they see fit. This power raises the specter that the IRS — not Congress and the courts — will be developing and changing the basic bankruptcy rules.

In other words, the IRS uses these guidelines as a floor. The IRS then leaves some room for agents to use their discretion to permit people to spend more for their basic living expenses if there seems to be a good reason to do so. The Bankruptcy Code also permits some discretion, but in keeping with the automated nature of the means test, even the discretion is tightly controlled. The 2005 Amendments provide that the court may increase the allowance for food and clothing by up to 5 percent, if the debtor can demonstrate that such expenditures are reasonable and necessary. §707(b)(2)(A(ii). But for expenses above that 5 percent or for any amounts in categories other than food and clothing, the Bankruptcy Code seems to leave the courts with no discretion to consider how families actually spend their money.

The National Standards cover food and clothes. In addition, the Bankruptcy Code specifies other expenses that can be subtracted from the monthly income. So, for example, the courts are instructed to include deductions for health insurance, disability insurance, and health savings accounts. (§707(b)(2)(A)(ii)(I)); expenses of caring for the elderly (§707(b)(2)(A)(ii)(II)); and private schools, up to $1,500 per child per year. §707(b)(2)(A)(ii)(IV). Through another IRS allowable-expense list ("Other Necessary Expenses"), the Bankruptcy Code permits the courts to deduct actual expenses for certain items such as childcare, legal fees, life insurance, union dues, taxes, and several other items already specifically covered by the Bankruptcy Code. The IRS has guidelines for many of these items. So, for example, the taxpayer may have Internet service if it is necessary for the production of income. For a look at the whole list, see www.irs.gov/irm/part5/ch14s01.html#d0e122933.

Finally, under the category of general expenses, the debtor is permitted to deduct any expenses to pay arrearages on "priority debts." §707(b)(2)(A)(iv). Priority debts are listed in section 507(a), and they will be covered later in this section. The main ones that appear in consumer bankruptcies are alimony, child support, and taxes. This means that if a debtor owes $5,000 in past-due child support, for example, the amount of the arrearage, divided by 60 (or $83.33), is deductible from the monthly income.

c. Secured Debts

In addition to buying food and clothes, a big monthly expense for many people is the car (or cars). Although some people will lease a car, and others will use public transportation, many debtors will have substantial payments due on a car loan, plus insurance, maintenance, and gasoline. When it adopted the means test, Congress was concerned that the application of the IRS guidelines for transportation would require many debtors to give up their cars, to the distress of the car lenders. (Without the support of the car lenders, the proposed Amendments would likely have never made it into law.) At the urging of the car lenders, Congress made a special provision for lenders who have a security interest in the debtor's property. These loans — such as car loans — can be deducted in full, no matter how large, along with any payment arrearages. §707(b)(2)(A)(iii). The gasoline, insurance, and maintenance then follow the Local Standards in the IRS tables. §707(b)(2)(A)(ii)(I). Gotta protect those wheels!

Home mortgages present an even greater problem because the IRS housing guidelines make no distinction between ownership expenses and operating costs. If the house payment amount is capped, then the debtor might have to give up the house — and that could mean losses for the mortgage companies. Congress decided that the debtor can deduct the payment to the mortgage lender, whatever it may be. §707(b)(2)(A)(iii). But what to do about the other costs of running a home, such as utilities and maintenance, is unclear. The IRS combines all housing costs — rent, mortgage, and incidentals — in a single allowable amount. There is no way to break out the mortgage costs from the other housing costs. It might make sense to deduct the debtor's actual expenses, but there is no apparent statutory authority for such a move. Or it might make sense for the debtor to take the higher (or lower) of his actual house payment and expenses or the IRS housing allowance. Once again, however, what makes sense and what is in the statute seem to be at odds. Congress seems to have made it very clear that it wants the courts to turn very square corners on these deductions. In this case, the statute seems to give the debtor both the actual amount of the home mortgage in section 707(b)(2)(A)(iii) and the full Local Standard deduction in section 707(b)(2)(A)(ii)(I). Of course, the IRS may change its numbers again.

While car purchasers and home buyers seem to get a real break, renters are out of luck. The IRS standard deduction for cars makes room for car leases as part of the ownership costs and home or apartment rentals as part of the housing allowance, but the bonus in the Bankruptcy Code for payments on secured debts makes extra allowances for car payments and mortgage payments, but gives no extra bump for car leases and home rentals. In Washington, it seems that those who buy are rewarded far more generously than those who rent.

d. Income after Expenses

Even if a debtor has some surplus after allowed expenses are deducted from income, Chapter 7 might still be available. To do the final calculation, it is necessary to know (a) the total size of the surplus of income over expenses over 60 months (five years); and (b) how much general unsecured nonpriority debt, such as credit cards and medical bills, that the debtor owes. The Bankruptcy Code has one of those confusing less-than/more-than calculations. The translation into English follows.

Abuse is presumed:
   (1) If the debt is greater than $24,000, and
       (a) the surplus is at least

(i) $10,000 or
(ii) 25% of the debt; OR
(2) If the debt is $24,000 or less, and the surplus is at least $6,000.

Another way to understand this tangle is to note that if the surplus is less than $100 per month, the debtor passes. If it is between $100 and $166.66 he passes if the surplus is less than 25 percent of his unsecured debt divided by 60. If the surplus is greater than $166.66 he flunks no matter how much he owes. Thus, for example, if a debtor owed $28,000 and the monthly surplus was $120 ($7,200 over 60 months), the presumption of abuse would arise, because $7,200 is greater than 25 percent of $28,000 ($7,000). §707 (b)(2)(A)(i)(2).

Whew! A lot of work to shake the money out of the pockets of the people who want to file bankruptcy. With well over a million consumer filings annually we can be sure that both attorneys and courts are struggling to computerize the undertaking. With substantial variations around the country because of the many open legal issues created by the statutory language and the variations presented by each debtor in the classification of non-standard income, expenses, and debts, they will face an extraordinary challenge.

4.   *Policing the New Standards*

a.   **Procedure**

Two important procedural points should be mentioned. The drafters of the Amendments sought to ensure that in processing over a million cases a year, the abuse issue is not overlooked. In every case filed by an individual, the statute requires the debtor to calculate the means test for that case in the form required to be filed under section 521. In turn, the U.S. Trustee's office is required to look at every case filed by an individual debtor to see if the presumption of abuse is triggered and to file a statement reporting its finding that is sent to every creditor. §704(b)(1). In addition, for an above-median debtor, the office must also file a motion to dismiss or convert the case if presumptive abuse is present or file a statement explaining why it has not done so. At this point, the observer understands more clearly why the Congressional Budget Office estimated that taxpayers will pay over $100 million to carry out the requirements of the new law.

On the other hand, the 2005 Amendments follow the 1984 Amendments in limiting standing to raise the question of abuse. Abuse can be alleged against an above-median debtor by the judge, the U.S. Trustee's office, or any creditor. §707(b)(1). A creditor cannot raise the abuse issue against a median-or-below debtor under either section 707(b)(1) (general abuse) or section 707(b)(2) (means test). Only a judge or the U.S. Trustee's office can raise a claim of general abuse. §707(b)(6). Even those officials cannot raise abuse under the means test under section 707(b)(2)(A)(i) if the debtor's income is equal to or below the state median.

Also notice the difference in how a spouse's income is treated. If the couple files jointly, both incomes are included for all purposes, and that is that. If only one files, the non-filing spouse's income is nonetheless included for purposes of determining whether the debtor is above or below the median income for purposes of continuing the inquiry. §707(b)(7). But if the debtor fails the test — that is, if the debtor and the debtor's spouse have income above the median — only the debtor's income and not that of the debtor's spouse is used for working through the budgets and the means test. §§101(10A); 707(b)(2)(A)(i).

b. Many Roles for Debtors' Lawyers

Debtors have always had to file a great deal of information with their bankruptcy petitions. Detailed reports on assets, debts, security interests, income, and the like must accompany every petition. The section 707(b)(2) means test adds a new layer of required information about income and expenses — and it requires documentation for much of that income and expenses for six months preceding the filing.

At the same time that Congress required that debtors filing for bankruptcy provide substantially more information, Congress also increased the scrutiny of the information provided. Debtors have always signed their petitions under penalty of perjury, and their attorneys sign as well. We noted in the preceding section that the 2005 Amendments also require the debtor's attorney to certify that the lawyer has made some investigation of the accuracy of the data. §707(b)(4)(C), (D). In addition, sections 526(a)(4) and 707(b)(4)(A) seem to impose new duties on the attorney regarding the advice the attorney gives the debtor in helping the debtor decide whether to file for Chapter 7.

If a debtor files for Chapter 7 and a court later determines that the debtor was ineligible, the attorney may be litigating with a creditor, the trustee, or even the bankruptcy judge over the advice given. Section 707(b)(4)(A) authorizes the court to award costs and reasonable attorneys' fees to a trustee who prevailed on a motion to dismiss the debtor's Chapter 7 filing as a violation of section 707(b)(2) if the attorney violated Rule 9011 of the Bankruptcy Rules by such filing. Rule 9011 requires that any petition be made only after reasonable inquiry that the allegations have a factual basis, which reinforces the duties of the debtor's attorney to inquire into the underlying facts. In addition, Rule 9011 requires that legal contentions be warranted by existing law or by non-frivolous extension. The standard for charging debtor's counsel may be high, but surely many attorneys will notice that if they advise the debtor to file for Chapter 13 instead of Chapter 7, the likelihood of ending up as a defendant in a lawsuit will disappear.

What if the creditor or trustee files a motion to dismiss under section 707(b)(2) and loses? In other words, what if the court determines that the debtor was eligible to file? Can the debtor's attorney then collect costs and attorneys' fees from the creditor or trustee? Section 707(b)(5) gives the debtor the power to recover (and presumably to collect the money to pay the attorney) if the court finds that the creditor or trustee violated Rule 9011 or brought its motion "solely to coerce the debtor to waive" other rights guaranteed under the Bankruptcy Code. Since the debtor is not the client of the creditor or trustee, we confess to wondering what a creditor or trustee would have to know in order to violate Rule 9011 and thus be charged with costs and attorneys' fees. Can trustees and creditors simply say to every debtor, "prove you are eligible to file for Chapter 7 or I will move to dismiss"? If so, we wonder if this "balancing" provision has much real meaning.

Problem Set 7

7.1. Marissa Allegretti comes into your office in Detroit to see you about filing for bankruptcy. She explains that when the accounting firm she worked for closed, she scraped by on $650 a month unemployment for nearly six months, running up a pile of bills. Three months ago, she found another job. With a base pay of $3,800 a month and overtime adding up to another $2,200 each month, she is catching up on her mortgage payments. Even so, she says that she is struggling with her credit cards and other debt. She doesn't want to file for bankruptcy, but she isn't sure if she has any option.

You ask about her personal circumstances, and Marissa explains that she and her ex-husband effectively share custody of their son Jamal. At the divorce ten years ago, Marissa was granted an award of $1000 a month in child support. Her ex hasn't paid for years, but he buys clothes for the boy and he has been paying the $3,000 each semester for tuition at the local Catholic school, and Marissa hasn't pushed the point.

Can you tell if Marissa is eligible for Chapter 7? See §§101(10A), 707(b)(6), (b)(7). What advice do you give her at this point? Marissa can barely scrape together your standard $800 fee; how aggressive can she afford for you to be?

7.2. Jason and Evie Spitalnik came to see you about filing for bankruptcy. They live near your office in Montgomery County, a suburb of Philadelphia. Jason earns $5,600 a month as an auto mechanic, and Evie's job as a fourth-grade teacher brings in another $4,200. They have three children. The third was born with a serious heart problem. The baby has had three major surgeries, and now lives on a regimen of drugs and monitoring. Even though they have health insurance, the out-of-pocket expenses for medical care for the baby have left Jason and Evie with more than $100,000 in debt. Some of it is medical co-pays and services, supplies and drugs that weren't covered, and some was ordinary credit card debt they ran up when Evie took a seven-month leave from her job during the surgeries and recuperations and Jason also missed a lot of time from work. By skipping other payments and falling behind on everything else, Jason and Evie have been paying about $600 a month on these bills, but that doesn't even cover the interest on the credit cards. Every month, the pile of bills gets higher.

You ask Jason and Evie for a list of their monthly expenses. After working for a while with your paralegal, here's what they identify:

Home mortgage (principal, interest, taxes & insurance)	$1,600
Utilities (water, gas, sewage)	190
Internet	35

Satellite television	75
Ford Bronco (principal, interest)	610
Insurance for Bronco, required by contract	140
Gas, maintenance for Bronco	190
Gas, maintenance, for seven-year-old Corolla	110
Liability insurance for Corolla	90
Food	1,000
Cleaning supplies	20
Personal care (haircuts, etc.)	25
Clothing	500
Laundry and dry cleaning	10
Miscellaneous (newspapers, dog food, etc.)	50
Public school fees, library fees for two older children	50
Lunch money, club dues, transportation, allowances for older children	200
Daycare for baby	800
Expected drugs, other health care supplies for baby	200
Health insurance	820
Contributions to church	400
Social Security and income taxes	2,400
Total	9,515

Can you tell if Jason and Evie are eligible for Chapter 7? Would it make a difference if they rented their home for $1,600 instead of purchasing it and leased their car for $610? §707(b)(2).

7.3. You have worked through the numbers for Michael Negron, a competitive skateboarder who seems to have run up $30,000 in general unsecured debt after he broke his leg last year. Michael is really upset about his debts. He rents a modest apartment and he drives an old clunker ("hey, it's paid for"). His income over the past six months puts him above the median for a one-earner family in his state, and after allowable expenses, Michael seems to have available about $150 a month. His income has been very erratic as he tries to make a comeback, and he's not sure if the leg is OK. He is very reluctant to commit to a Chapter 13 plan. Do you have any advice to make him eligible for Chapter 7? §§707(b)(2)(B)(iv); 707(b)(2)(A)(iii); 707(b)(1); 101(12A); 526(a)(4).

7.4. Ken Lyarre was a phenomenally successful CEO, twice featured on the cover of *Business Week*. The first time was when his privately owned string of diet counseling centers took the health and fitness market by storm, and the second when he lost a class action lawsuit against him for common law fraud and the jury returned a verdict of $1 billion. Ken's lawyers are planning an appeal, but they can't seem to make eye contact with him when they discuss his chances of winning.

Ken thinks he has a better strategy: Chapter 7 liquidation. He has about $1 million in assets that aren't already tied up in various spendthrift and offshore trusts, and he says he is glad to give that up. Because of the trusts his income now and into the future will be about $2 million annually. Is Ken eligible for Chapter 7? See §707(a), (b)(1), (b)(2).

7.5. You and your three partners run a large consumer practice in Tulsa. More than 95 percent of the people you see have incomes below the state median, adjusted for family size. That makes the means test easy, but it doesn't seem to make the reporting any easier. Your paralegals used to be able to help a client fill out all the necessary schedules in about half an hour, and most clients either brought enough information with them or had to make one trip back home for the necessary information. Now the paralegals usually spend more than two hours with each client, and the clients themselves are making an average of three trips before their petitions are complete. The main problem seems to be with listing all the deductible expenses for the means test. Since this information is irrelevant to the debtor's case, you would like to skip it or let the debtor just estimate the amounts. Is either approach a sensible response? §§707(a)(3); 707(b)(4)(C), (D); 521(a)(1); 18 U.S.C. §152(3).

C. PROPERTY EXEMPT FROM SEIZURE

1. *Introduction*

If you have ever seen a cartoon of a skinny little guy who is broke and wearing only a barrel, you may have wondered why the creditors left the barrel. The law in every state makes at least some property exempt from execution and other legal process so that no debtor can be reduced to absolute destitution. The policy reasons include a desire to avoid results so draconian as to threaten the social fabric of the community (the same rationale forbids taking a pound of flesh). In addition, exemption policies also express a healthy dose of self-interest for those with assets. The concern that a creditor not leave the debtor with so little property that the debtor and the debtor's family will become a charge on the community means that exemption laws are often directed toward making certain that every debtor retains enough basic property to have a chance to get out of the hole and make a fresh start (applicants cannot go to most job interviews nude). Another policy reason for some property exemptions is that some items of personal property, such as clothes, have little resale value for the creditor, but are crucial to the debtor. Although the line between the two is fuzzy, the law distinguishes between seizing property to satisfy a debt and seizing property solely to inflict more pain on the debtor.

When property is defined as "exempt" under state law, general creditors cannot seize it to satisfy their judgments. But consensual agreements, such as mortgages on homes, security interests on cars, or pawnshop possession of jewelry, are not so constrained. As part of the granting of a security interest, the debtor waives the exemptions as to these creditors. This means they are entitled to seize the property for nonpayment of their outstanding loans even when the property is otherwise declared exempt. Note the neat divide among creditor groups: home mortgage lenders, car lenders, and pawnbrokers care little about the scope of exemption laws, while credit card issuers, health care providers, tort victims, and others who cannot get a security agreement in advance feel the teeth in the exemption statutes.

All property not listed as exempt is denominated non-exempt and will be sold by the trustee so that the proceeds can be distributed to the creditors. This is often the general unsecured creditor's last chance to get paid.

2. A State/Federal System

Every state has exemption laws, although the amount of protection varies widely. Once a debtor files for bankruptcy, federal law preempts state collection efforts with the automatic stay, but the question about which property to declare as exempt becomes even sharper. After all, the deal in Chapter 7 is that the debtor will give up all non-exempt property. So what property will federal bankruptcy laws protect?

The 1898 Bankruptcy Act deferred to the states on exemption issues. This meant, for example, that a Texas debtor in bankruptcy could protect whatever a Texas debtor outside bankruptcy could protect, while a Delaware debtor in or out of bankruptcy could protect whatever property Delaware exempted. The fact that Texas and Delaware protected very different items or values was irrelevant.

When the bankruptcy laws were modernized in 1978, many experts believed that it was time to develop uniform national exemptions, but that proposal drew fire from two camps: those in Congress who represented states with much smaller exemptions who thought the uniform proposals were too generous and (you guessed it) those in Congress who represented states with far more generous exemptions who thought the federal exemptions were too stingy. A compromise was born: the federal Bankruptcy Code would establish uniform federal exemptions, but states would be permitted to opt-out of those exemptions, denying their own citizens the benefits of the federal protection when they filed for bankruptcy. 11 U.S.C. §522(b)(2). Thirty-five states have opted out. 14 Collier ¶Intro.03. The constitutionality of opt-out has been challenged, has been affirmed, and has ceased to be a widely disputed issue. See, e.g., In re Lauch, 16 B.R. 162 (Bankr. M.D. Fla. 1981).

We reproduce two sets of state exemption laws. The first is from Texas, and the second is from Delaware.

═══════ TEXAS EXEMPTION STATUTES ═══════

Texas Property Code Annotated (Vernon 2005)

§41.001. INTERESTS IN LAND EXEMPT FROM SEIZURE

(a) A homestead and one or more lots used for a place of burial of the dead are exempt from seizure for the claims of creditors except for encumbrances properly fixed on homestead property.

(b) Encumbrances may be properly fixed on homestead property for

(1) purchase money;

(2) taxes on the property;

(3) work and material used in constructing improvements on the property if contracted for in writing....

(c) The homestead claimant's proceeds of a sale of a homestead are not subject to seizure for a creditor's claim for six months after the date of sale.

§41.002. DEFINITION OF HOMESTEAD

(a) If used for the purposes of an urban home or as both an urban home and a place to exercise a calling or business, the homestead of a family or a single, adult person, not otherwise entitled to a homestead, shall consist of not more than 10 acres of land which may be in one or more contiguous lots, together with any improvements thereon.

(b) If used for the purposes of a rural home, the homestead shall consist of

(1) for a family, not more than 200 acres, which may be in one or more parcels, with the improvements thereon; or

(2) for a single, adult person, not otherwise entitled to a homestead, not more than 100 acres, which may be in one or more parcels, with the improvements thereon.

(c) A homestead is considered to be urban if, at the time the designation is made, the property is

(1) located within the limits of a municipality or its extraterritorial jurisdiction or a platted subdivision; and

(2) served by police protection, paid or volunteer fire protection, and at least three of the following services provided by a municipality or under contract to a municipality

(A) electric;

(B) natural gas;

(C) sewer;

(D) storm sewer; and

(E) water.

(d) The definition of a homestead as provided in this section applies to all homesteads in this state whenever created.

§41.003. TEMPORARY RENTING OF A HOMESTEAD

Temporary renting of a homestead does not change its homestead character if the homestead claimant has not acquired another homestead.

§42.001. PERSONAL PROPERTY EXEMPTION

(a) Personal property, as described in Section 42.002, is exempt from garnishment, attachment, execution, or other seizure if

(1) the property is provided for a family and has an aggregate fair market value of not more than $60,000, exclusive of the amount of any liens, security interests, or other charges encumbering the property; or

(2) the property is owned by a single adult, who is not a member of a family, and has an aggregate fair market value of not more than $30,000, exclusive of the amount of any liens, security interests, or other charges encumbering the property.

(b) The following personal property is exempt from seizure and is not included in the aggregate limitations prescribed by Subsection (a)

(1) current wages for personal services, except for the enforcement of court-ordered child support payments;

(2) professionally prescribed health aids of a debtor or a dependent of a debtor; and

(3) alimony, support, or separate maintenance received or to be received by the debtor for the support of the debtor or a dependent of the debtor.

(c) This section does not prevent seizure by a secured creditor with a contractual landlord's lien or other security in the property to be seized.

(d) Unpaid commissions for personal services not to exceed 25 percent of the aggregate limitations prescribed by Subsection (a) are exempt from seizure and are included in the aggregate.

§42.002.   PERSONAL PROPERTY

(a) The following personal property is exempt under Section 42.001(a)

(1) home furnishings, including family heirlooms;

(2) provisions for consumption;

(3) farming or ranching vehicles and implements;

(4) tools, equipment, books, and apparatus, including boats and motor vehicles used in a trade or profession;

(5) wearing apparel;

(6) jewelry not to exceed 25 percent of the aggregate limitations prescribed by Section 42.001(a);

(7) two firearms;

(8) athletic and sporting equipment, including bicycles;

(9) a two-wheeled, three-wheeled, or four-wheeled motor vehicle for each member of a family or single adult who holds a driver's license or who does not hold a driver's license but who relies on another person to operate the vehicle for the benefit of the nonlicensed person;

(10) the following animals and forage on hand for their consumption

(A) two horses, mules, or donkeys and a saddle, blanket, and bridle for each;

(B) 12 head of cattle;

(C) 60 head of other types of livestock; and

(D) 120 fowl; and

(11) household pets.

(b) Personal property, unless precluded from being encumbered by other law, may be encumbered by a security interest under Section 9.203, Business & Commerce Code, or Subchapter F, Chapter 501, Transportation Code, or by a lien fixed by other law, and the security interest or lien may not be avoided on the ground that the property is exempt under this chapter.

§42.003. Designation of Exempt Property

(a) If the number or amount of a type of personal property owned by a debtor exceeds the exemption allowed by Section 42.002 and the debtor can be found in the county where the property is located, the officer making a levy on the property shall ask the debtor to designate the personal property to be levied on. . . .

§42.005.   Child Support Liens

Sections 42.001, 42.002, and 42.0021 of this code do not apply to a child support lien established under Subchapter G, Chapter 157, Family Code.

§42.0021.   Additional Exemption for Certain Savings Plans

(a) In addition to the exemption prescribed by Section 42.001, a person's right to the assets held in or to receive payments, whether vested or not, under any stock bonus, pension, profit-sharing, or similar plan, including a retirement plan for self-employed individuals, and under any annuity or similar contract purchased with assets distributed from that type of plan, and under any retirement annuity or account described by Section 403(b) or 408A of the Internal Revenue Code of 1986, and under any individual retirement account or any individual retirement annuity, including a simplified employee pension plan, and under any health savings account described by Section 223 of the Internal Revenue Code of 1986, is exempt from attachment, execution, and seizure for the satisfaction of debts unless the plan, contract, or account does not qualify under the applicable provisions of the Internal Revenue Code of 1986. A person's right to the assets held in or to receive payments, whether vested or not, under a government or church plan or contract is also exempt

* * *

(b) Contributions to an individual retirement account, other than contributions to a Roth IRA described in Section 408A, Internal Revenue Code of 1986, or an annuity that exceed the amounts deductible under the applicable provisions of the Internal Revenue Code of 1986 and any accrued earnings on such contributions are not exempt * * * * Amounts treated as qualified rollover contributions * * * are treated as exempt amounts under Subsection (a). * * *

§1108.0531.   Exemptions for Certain Insurance and Annuity Benefits

(a) Except as provided by Section 1108.053, this section applies to any benefits, including the cash value and proceeds of an insurance policy, to be provided to an insured or beneficiary under:

   (1) an insurance policy or annuity contract issued by a life, health, or accident insurance company, including a mutual company or fraternal benefit society; or

(2) an annuity or benefit plan used by an employer or individual.

(b) Notwithstanding any other provision of this code, insurance or annuity benefits described by Subsection (a):

(1) inure exclusively to the benefit of the person for whose use and benefit the insurance or annuity is designated in the policy or contract; and

(2) are fully exempt from:

(A) garnishment, attachment, execution, or other seizure;

(B) seizure, appropriation, or application by any legal or equitable process or by operation of law to pay a debt or other liability of an insured or of a beneficiary, either before or after the benefits are provided; and

(C) a demand in a bankruptcy proceeding of the insured or beneficiary.

§1108.053. EXCEPTIONS TO EXEMPTIONS

The exemptions provided by Section 1108.051 do not apply to:

(1) a premium payment made in fraud of a creditor, subject to the applicable statute of limitations for recovering the payment;

(2) a debt of the insured or beneficiary secured by a pledge of the insurance policy or the proceeds of the policy; or

(3) a child support lien or levy under Chapter 157, Family Code.

DELAWARE EXEMPTION STATUTES
10 Del. Code Ann. (2004) §4902

EXEMPT PROPERTY

(a) Every person residing within this State shall have exempt from execution or attachment process, or distress for rent, the following articles of personal property: The family Bible, school books and family library, family pictures, a seat or pew in any church or place of public worship, a lot in any burial ground, all the wearing apparel of the debtor and the debtor's family.

(b) In addition to the articles specifically named in subsection (a) of this section, each person residing in this State shall have exempt the tools, implements and fixtures necessary for carrying on his or her trade or business, not exceeding in value $75 in New Castle and Sussex Counties, and $50 in Kent County.

(c) All sewing machines owned and used by seamstresses or private families, shall be exempt from levy and sale on execution or attachment process and also from distress and sale for rent. This provision shall not apply to persons who keep sewing machines for sale or hire.

(d) All pianos, piano playing attachments and organs leased or hired by any person residing in this State, shall be exempt from levy and sale on execution or from distress for rent due by such person so leasing or hiring any such piano, piano playing attachment, or organ in addition to other goods and chattels exempt by law. The owner of any such piano, piano playing attachment or organ or such owner's agent, or the person so leasing or hiring the same shall give notice to the landlord or the landlord's agent that the instrument is hired or leased.

§4913. EXEMPTION AND ATTACHMENT OF WAGES

(a) Eighty-five percent of the amount of the wages for labor or service of any person residing within the State shall be exempt from mesne attachment process and execution attachment process under the laws of this State; but such limitation shall be inapplicable to process issued for the collection of a fine or costs or taxes due and owing the State.

(b) On any amount of wages due, only 1 attachment may be made. Any creditor causing such attachment to be made shall have the benefit of priority until the judgment with costs for which the attachment was made has been paid in full.

(c) Wages shall include salaries, commissions and every other form of remuneration paid to an employee by an employer for labor or services, but shall not include payment made for services rendered by a person who is self-employed.

§4915. EXEMPTION OF RETIREMENT PLANS

(a) In addition to the exemptions provided in §§4902 and 4903 of this title, there shall be exempt from execution or attachment process assets held or amounts payable under any retirement plan.

* * *

(e) A participant or beneficiary of a retirement plan is not prohibited from granting a valid and enforceable security interest in the participant's or beneficiary's interest under the retirement plan to secure a loan to the participant or beneficiary from the plan, and the right to assets held in or to receive payments from the plan is subject to execution and attachment for the satisfaction of the security interest or lien granted by the participant or beneficiary to secure the loan.

(f) "Retirement plan" means any retirement or profit sharing plan that is qualified under §401, §403, §408, §408A, §409, §414 or §457 of the Internal Revenue Code of 1986 [26 U.S.C. §401, §403, §408, §408A, §409, §414 or §457], as amended.

* * *

═══════18 DELAWARE CODE ANNOTATED (1999)═══════

§2725. EXEMPTION OF PROCEEDS, LIFE INSURANCE

(a) If a policy of insurance, whether heretofore or hereafter issued, is effected by any person on his/her own life, or on another life, in favor of a person other than himself/herself, or, except in cases of transfer with intent to defraud creditors, if a policy of life insurance is assigned or in any way made payable to any such person, the lawful beneficiary or assignee thereof, other than the insured or the person so effecting such insurance or executors or administrators of such insured or the person so effecting such insurance, shall be entitled to its proceeds and avails against the creditors and representatives of the insured and of the person effecting the same.... [Group and health insurance and annuities are also exempted, absent an intent to defraud creditors.]

19 DELAWARE CODE ANNOTATED (1999)

§2355. ASSIGNMENT OF COMPENSATION PROHIBITED; EXEMPTION FROM CREDITORS' CLAIMS; CHILD SUPPORT EXCEPTION

Except for attachments pursuant to child support orders entered under Chapters 4, 5 or 6 of Title 13, claims or payment for compensation due or to become due under this chapter shall not be assignable and all compensation and claims therefor shall be exempt from all claims of creditors.

The opt-out provision offers yet another place for ironic observation. Texas, with its generous exemptions, did not opt out, leaving a Texan to choose between an unlimited homestead and $30,000 in value in other property and a federal homestead exemption of $16,150 and about $16,000 or so in other property. The choice can sometimes be valuable, however. For example, the federal exemptions allow for an $850 wildcard exemption that could be used to protect cash in a checking account (more realistically, a tax refund), while the Texas exemptions protect no cash. For someone with no home and only modest assets, being able to protect a few hundred dollars in cash would make the federal exemptions more attractive than the state exemptions.

While Texas lets it citizens choose between federal and state exemptions, Delaware says no. The state opted out of the federal exemptions. To make its views on bankrupt families a little clearer, Delaware added another provision:

DELAWARE EXEMPTION STATUTES
10 Del. C. §4914 (1999)

§4914. EXEMPTIONS IN BANKRUPTCY AND INSOLVENCY

(a) In accordance with §522(b) of the Bankruptcy Reform Act of 1978 (11 U.S.C. §522(b)), in any bankruptcy proceeding, an individual debtor domiciled in Delaware is not authorized or entitled to elect the federal exemptions as set forth in §522(d) of the Bankruptcy Reform Act of 1978

(11 U.S.C. §522(d)) and may exempt only that property from the estate as set forth in subsection (b) of this section.

(b) In any federal bankruptcy or state insolvency proceeding, an individual debtor domiciled in Delaware shall be authorized to exempt from the bankruptcy or insolvency estate, in addition to the exemptions made in §4915 of this title, property having an aggregate fair market value of not more than $5,000.

(c) This section shall apply separately with respect to each debtor in a joint proceeding.

The latest amendments to Section 4914 were signed by the governor on May 22, 1997, making it clear that Delaware's limited exemptions were not a matter of oversight, but of deliberate choice. The fact that Delaware changes its permissible exemptions when a debtor files for bankruptcy might mean that the state statute has impermissibly encroached on the federal bankruptcy powers. The federal exemptions allow for opt-out, but they do not invite state legislatures to select one set of exemptions to operate at state law and a different set under the federal bankruptcy laws. So far, we have seen no challenges to the Delaware laws. Perhaps debtor advocates are worried that the legislature will respond by imposing the $5,000 cap both in and out of bankruptcy.

The federal exemptions cover a wide variety of property, including payments from crime reparations laws and unmatured life insurance. §522(d). As part of the 2005 Amendments, Congress expanded the federal exemption for retirement funds regardless of whether the debtor lived in a state that opted out of the federal exemptions. §522(b)(3)(C), (d)(12). The action is a little bit of a belt-and-suspenders move since most of those retirement accounts were not property of the estate anyway because they had spendthrift trust provisions. §541(c). To the extent the federal exemptions are limited to specific dollar amounts, such as the $2,950 exemption in a car, those amounts are adjusted every three years for inflation. §108(d), (e).

All states and the federal government must wrestle with the same set of issues about what a debtor can keep and what a creditor can demand that the debtor give up to satisfy unpaid debts. Every set of exemption statutes has at least some provisions that are tied to specific kinds of property — household goods, homesteads, rights to receive disability payments, and so on.

Exemptions amounts may range from non-existent to unlimited. Nowhere is that disparity more evident (or more hotly debated) than with homesteads. The Texas statute cited above limits a homestead in terms of acreage. So long as the home is on less than ten acres in a city or 200 acres in the country, the debtor is entitled to exempt that property from attachment, regardless of its dollar value. At the other end of the spectrum is Delaware with no homestead exemption at all. A homeowner in Delaware cannot keep even the most modest home if the debtor has built up any equity. Federal exemptions are somewhere in between, setting a dollar value on the homestead for each debtor — an amount that can be doubled for married couples filing jointly.

According to our empirical research, about half of the families who file for bankruptcy won't care about the homestead exemption because they are not homeowners. Some have never owned a home, but about 12.2 percent of the non-homeowners had already lost their homes for financial reason before they filed for bankruptcy. No homestead exemption will help either group.

As generous as they are, the Texas exemptions add no special protection for renters to match the protection available to homeowners. By comparison, the federal statutes give a special boost. Anyone who does not claim a homestead exemption under section 522(d)(1) is permitted to claim half the value of the unclaimed homestead exemption in any property at all under section 522(d)(8). Why half? It looks like another perfect compromise — halfway between those who believed only homes should be protected and those who believed that renters should have the same chance to protect value, whether it is in a home or checking account.

Not all homeowners in bankruptcy need to use a homestead exemption. When a home mortgage — or a second mortgage or even third mortgage — is as large as the total value of the property, then the debtor has no equity to protect. Our study of 2001 debtors found that about 30 percent of the homeowners had no equity in their houses. We found that, on average, a debtor family that owns a home reports a mortgage-to-value ratio of about .94, meaning that the mortgage is equal to about 94 percent of the value of the house.

For those debtors who have some equity in their homes, the homestead exemption becomes a matter of critical focus, the determinant of whether they can keep their homes or will be forced to give up the lives they have built. The median amount of home equity (home value minus mortgage) in our 2001 sample was about $12,000, which means half the debtors had more equity than that and half had less. In many cases, of course, a house estimated to have a small equity like $12,000 would not bring more than the mortgage amount in a forced sale. Given these figures, the $16,150 in home equity exemption in the federal exemptions ($32,300 for a couple) is of great importance to a large proportion of the debtors who own homes. §522(d)(1). The homestead exemption is further explored in the next section of this chapter.

Other exemption types carry much the same punch but for fewer debtors. For an office worker with no tools of the trade, the state and federal exemptions for tools are irrelevant. But for a plumber trying to hold on to the tools that make it possible for him to earn a living, the availability of an exemption is a critical part of the protection offered in the bankruptcy system.

It should be noted that both Texas and Delaware, like most states, exempt various domestic support obligations and liens from the exemption laws, so that child support, for example, may be enforced by the seizure of otherwise exempt property. Certain other exemptions from exemptions may also apply in some states.

3. *Classification of Property*

Because exemption statutes are often written to exempt only listed types of property, disputes between debtors and creditors frequently center on classification issues. Debtors argue that the property they intend to keep fits within the statutory classifications, and judgment creditors, who are permitted to reach only non-exempt property, argue that the property does not.

The following cases arose in bankruptcy, a sharp reminder that although the exemptions the debtor may claim are creatures of state law, the federal bankruptcy courts will be called on to determine their meaning — often more regularly than the state courts themselves.

===================== In re JOHNSON =====================

14 B.R. 14 (Bankr. W.D. Ky. 1981)

DEITZ, Bankruptcy Judge.

Is a bus a bus, or is it a car?

Reluctantly we conclude that it is a car.

Bankruptcy petitioner, Theodore Roosevelt Johnson, Sr., has claimed as exempt his 1969 Dodge bus. The bus has a seating capacity of 60 passengers. Upon it are occasionally transported members of Johnson's church congregation.

The trustee vehemently objects. He points to the state exemption statute, KRS 427.010, which in pertinent part permits the exemption of "one motor vehicle and its necessary accessories, including one spare tire, not exceeding $2,500 in value...."

The trustee patiently explains that the legislature intended the term "motor vehicle" to be synonymous with "automobile."

Enacted in 1980, the statute excluded earlier statutory limits upon the *uses* to which a motor vehicle might be put, so we must cast altogether aside the trustee's concern with the voluminous seating capacity of the behemoth. The record is silent on the size of the petitioner's family and their transportation needs.

Is a Moped a motor vehicle? What would the licensing arm of the state Department of Transportation say to the contention that a bus is not a motor vehicle? What would Gertrude Stein have to say about what a motor vehicle is?

Such rhetorical questions having been considered, we are bold to say that a bus is a motor vehicle.

In our dialectic, during this era of motorized evolution, we are inclined to regard the "bus" and the "automobile" as species of the genus, "motor vehicle."

This Bankruptcy Court is answerable to an appellate forum of literal bent. That is good, for it gives us guidance and certainty in ascribing to the legislature the ability to express its intent in clear, simple, precise English.

As this trustee will recall, District Judge Thomas Ballantine, in reviewing a decision of this court, recently held that a statutory 15-day limitation upon the recording of chattel mortgages imposed a recording limitation *not* of indeterminate length, as was contended, but a limitation of 15 days.

Guided by that clarity of perception, we find with conviction that a motor vehicle is a motor vehicle, and not necessarily an automobile.

We expressly reserve, until it is properly presented, any consideration of the reverse proposition that an automobile is neither a bus nor a motor vehicle.

Abundantly confident that this opinion will find its way alongside Marbury v. Madison and McCulloch v. Maryland in the lasting library of legal logic, it is hereby ordered that Theodore Roosevelt Johnson, Sr., is entitled to the claimed exemption, and the trustee shall comport his activities accordingly in administration of the estate.

The only near competitor to Johnson as our favorite classification case is In re Hall, 169 B.R. 732 (Bankr. N.D. Okla. 1994), in which the debtor claimed a tractor-lawnmower exempt under the category "household furniture." The Oklahoma bankruptcy court held that lawnmowers are not furniture. One of us was surprised.

In the next case, the property in dispute is of considerable value.

In re PIZZI

153 B.R. 357 (Bankr. S.D. Fla. 1993)

Robert A. MARK, Bankruptcy Judge.

April 19, 1985, was a good day for Kathleen Pizzi. The Connecticut State Lottery drew the numbers on her ticket converting her one dollar purchase into a prize worth $3,202,624.20. Despite her good fortune, Ms. Pizzi incurred substantial debt in the years that followed, ultimately resulting in the filing of this Chapter 7 case.

Ms. Pizzi seeks to discharge her substantial debts without giving up her right to receive twelve more annual payments of $128,105.17 from Connecticut to complete the twenty (20) year payout of her prize. She claims that this income stream is an annuity contract protected from creditors under Florida law and thus an exempt asset in this bankruptcy case. Her exemption claim is challenged by the Trustee and two bank creditors. The Court sustains the objections. The unpaid lottery winnings are nonexempt assets which must be liquidated to pay creditors....

Based upon the stipulation of the parties and the documents in the record, the relevant facts are as follows:

...3. The lottery winnings had a present money value of $1,003,747.79 after payment of her first of twenty installments.

4. The prize was payable in twenty (20) annual installments each in the amount of $160,131.21. After withholding tax, the net payment to Ms. Pizzi each year is $128,105.17.

5. On or about April 19, 1985, the State of Connecticut, Division of Special Revenue, purchased an annuity contract from Met Life bearing certificate number 512 for the sum of $1,003,747.79, for the benefit of Kathleen G. Pizzi....

[5. Stipulated Documents] c. A letter dated April 22, 1985, from the State of Connecticut to Ms. Pizzi officially confirming her winning ticket, enclosing her first check for $128,105.17 and advising her that the State

Comptroller would be issuing checks in the like amount to her each year for the next 19 years;

    d. The annuity contract issued by Met Life. The State of Connecticut, Division of Special Revenue is named as the "Owner" and "Beneficiary" of the Contract. . . .

    9. The Debtor's schedules reflect secured claims in the amount of $828,540.07, unsecured priority claims in the amount of $28,000 and general unsecured claims of $380,119.29. The unsecured claims include Connecticut National's $310,518.28 claim.

[The debtor's other assets] consist solely of $4,000 realized from the sale of a vehicle (CP #65 — Trustee's Report, November 23, 1992).

DISCUSSION

. . . [T]he sole issue in this case is whether the proceeds from the lottery winnings are exempt from the claims of creditors under Florida law. . . .

C. The Payments from the State of Connecticut to Ms. Pizzi are not Annuity Payments

The Court must alternatively consider whether the yearly payments paid by the State of Connecticut to Kathleen Pizzi should be considered annuity payments. Does this income stream fall within the definition of annuity under Fla. Stat. §222.14?

The definition of an annuity under Florida law has been recently addressed by the Florida Supreme Court. In re McCollam, 612 So. 2d 572 (Fla. 1993). McCollam involved another tragic automobile accident and the damage settlement stemming from the wrongful death action. Under the terms of the agreement Travelers Insurance Company purchased an annuity contract. The debtor was listed as the beneficiary and payee under the contract. Travelers' debt obligation to the debtor is liquidated and discharged by the amount of each successive annuity payment.

. . . In a four to three decision, the Florida Supreme Court employed the plain meaning doctrine and concluded that, on its face, the statute applies to all annuity contracts. The Court rejected the dissent's resort to legislative history stating that "legislative history is irrelevant where the wording of a statute is clear." Utilizing a broad definition of "annuity," the Court concluded that the contract at issue was within the statutory exemption.

. . . In McCollam the court analyzed an annuity contract purchased to settle a personal injury lawsuit. Although the reasons for purchasing the annuity are unique, the facts remain that what was bought was an annuity in the name of the debtor. Here, the income stream flowing directly to the Debtor is not an annuity at all. The monies are prize winnings stemming from the winning of the lottery. The Connecticut Lottery regulations never refer to the winnings as proceeds of an annuity, and the winner is never referred to as the beneficiary or payee of an annuity. . . .

POLICY ARGUMENTS

The Debtor argues that exemptions should be liberally construed in favor of debtors....

The banks argue that §222.14 is intended to protect annuity contracts which provide life insurance and retirement benefits. To broadly interpret the statute and allow lottery winnings to be claimed as exempt would, they argue, be unfair and beyond the intended purpose of the exemption.

This Court agrees that it would be inequitable for a Debtor to obtain loans in reliance upon her lottery winnings and then discharge these obligations without turning over the winnings to her estate. The exemption laws were not intended to protect instant millionaires from paying their legitimate debts.

...Notwithstanding strong policy arguments to include lottery winnings in the estate, the Court's decision today does not and could not rest on policy grounds given the Florida Supreme Court's broad interpretation of §222.14 in *McCollam*. Inequitable or not, if a lottery winner is specifically named as a beneficiary of an annuity contract purchased to fund a state's obligations, the winnings may be exempt.

...By separate order, the Court will sustain the objections to the Debtor's claim of exemption filed by the Trustee, the Bank of New York and Connecticut National.

As these cases demonstrate, whenever a statute exempts property by classification, rather than by total dollar value, there will be hard questions at the margin about what property does and what property does not fall within the classification. The legislator has a mythical typical family in mind, but reality is seldom so neat.

4. *Valuation of Exempt Property*

In addition to determining whether property claimed as exempt fits within the allowed categories, it is often necessary to determine whether the property fits within the permitted valuations as well. The following cases illustrate the disparity in courts' resolutions of these disputes.

=========== In re WALSH ===========

5 B.R. 239 (Bankr. D.D.C. 1980)

WHELAN, Bankruptcy Judge.

This matter came before the Court for hearing on an application for appraisal, pursuant to Local Bankruptcy Rule 24(b), filed by the trustee in bankruptcy, Robert O. Tyler, Esq., and the opposition thereto, filed by the debtor, Charles J. Walsh. Although an application for an appraisal by the trustee may ordinarily be granted without a hearing, a dispute has arisen in the instant case with respect to the standard of valuation to be applied to property claimed by the debtor as exempt under 11 U.S.C. 522. The trustee's application seeks an appraisal of these assets at fair market value, rather than liquidation value, on which basis a previous appraisal was made.

There is no dispute as to the "disinterestedness" or qualifications of the appraiser....

The court ... is of the opinion that the application in this case, although not captioned as an objection to the claimed exemptions, is, in substance, an objection, because it calls into question the amounts claimed as exempt on the basis of their valuation. If the assets claimed as exempt exceed the monetary limits set forth in 522(d), then only to that extent, they are non-exempt assets....

"Value," for the purposes of the exemption section, is defined as "fair market value as of the date of the filing of the petition." [11 U.S.C. §522(a)(l).] This definition governs the meaning of "value" only for purposes of this section, and differs from the definition applicable in other sections of the Code. [11 U.S.C. §102(8).] The legislative history does not elaborate on the purpose or significance of this specific definition in Section 522.

The rules of statutory construction dictate that, where the language of a statute is clear, the Court should interpret it according to its "plain meaning." However, a statute is to be interpreted as a whole, and one provision should not be construed in a manner inconsistent with the whole.

Thus, in construing the meaning of the definition of value in Section 522, the Court must look to the usual and accepted meaning of "fair market value," while taking into consideration the liquidation context and the goals of the Code as a whole. Fair market value has been defined as the "price at which a willing seller and a willing buyer will trade." Fair market value "assumes agreement between owner willing but not obliged to sell for cash and buyer desirous but not compelled to purchase." Black's Law Dictionary 716 (4th Ed. 1968). In ascertaining fair market value, "there should be taken into account all considerations that fairly might be brought forward and reasonably be given substantial weight in bargaining." Karlson v. U.S., 82 F.2d 330, 337 (8th Cir. 1936), citing Olson v. U.S., 292 U.S. 246, 257(1934).

The definition is "not invariable," but "varies with the circumstances surrounding a given object and situation to which it is sought to apply the term." McDougall Co. v. Atkins, 201 Tenn. 589, 301 S.W.2d 335, 337 (1957) (valuation for sales tax purposes, of air ducts installed in buildings, held not equivalent to scrap value). "A valuation is always a stage in some proceeding which has a practical purpose." McCormick, The Law of Damages, §43 at 163 (1935). Thus, the Courts have viewed fair market value in the context in which the valuation question has arisen.[2]

2. The term's meaning in the exemption provision would thus not necessarily be consistent with its meaning in the determination of insolvency under the Old Act, for instance. Cf. 1 Collier on Bankruptcy, paragraph 1.19 at 122-125 (14th ed.).

In light of the rules of statutory construction, this contextual approach to the definition of "fair market value" appears particularly appropriate where the term appears in a statute.

In the instant case, the trustee argues that the §522(a)(l) definition of value should be construed literally and independently of the Ch. 7 context, rather than as "liquidation value." Counsel for the debtor, on the other hand, argues that the definition of "market" on the day a bankruptcy petition is filed, is, invariably, an eventual bankruptcy sale. Thus, he submits that the assets claimed as exempt should be appraised according to their liquidation value.

Inasmuch as the purpose of valuation under the exemption provisions is ultimately to determine whether such property is subject to liquidation by the trustee because it is in excess of specified monetary amounts, the Court believes that the term "fair market value," as it is used to define "value" in Section 522, must be interpreted in the liquidation context in a Chapter 7 case.[3]

Therefore, the Court finds that, in the instant case, "fair market value," as the term is used in Section 522, is equivalent to liquidation value. Accordingly, the trustee's application for an appraisal is denied.

The Texas exemptions cited in the next case have been changed since it was decided. Jewelry is now an exempt category, albeit with a dollar limitation, which it was not in 1989. On the other hand, an indulgent legislature has doubled the total personal property exemption available to a couple, to $60,000. The changes do not affect the basic issue, the proper standard for valuation of property claimed as exempt.

=============== In re MITCHELL ===============
103 B.R. 819 (Bankr. W.D. Texas 1989)

DECISION AND ORDER ON OBJECTIONS TO CLAIM
OF EXEMPT PROPERTY

Leif M. CLARK, Bankruptcy Judge.
A hearing was held before this court on January 11, 1989, regarding the objections of First City National Bank of Austin to the claimed exemptions of the debtors in this case. The objections focused on the debtors' claim to

---

3. This is illustrated by the following hypothetical situation. A debtor owns an automobile, free and clear of any lien, which, if sold under ordinary market conditions — the willing buyer and willing seller approach to the fair market value — would yield $2,000. The debtor, pursuant to 11 U.S.C. 522(d)(2), claims the auto as exempt to the extent of $1,200. If the Court deems the asset to be worth $2,000 because of a theoretical fair market value standard and authorizes a sale by the trustee, the resulting sale, of necessity, in the actual forced sale setting, may bring only $1,200 — the amount which the debtor is entitled to claim as exempt. Obviously, in this situation, no benefit to the estate is gained because the only amount realized is subject to the debtor's claim of exemption. Accordingly, the only conclusion that can be logically drawn is that fair market value, as defined in 522(a), is subject to bankruptcy market conditions.

certain jewelry, including in particular a 6.18 carat diamond ring worn rather regularly by Mrs. Mitchell....

The bulk of the controversy centers on the valuation issue.... First City says that this court should simply apply a fair market standard of valuation, consistent with the language used in both section 522 of the Bankruptcy Code ("Code") and section 42.001 of the Texas Property Code. The debtor argues for applying a distress or liquidation valuation, in keeping with the fresh start policy of the Code and in recognition of the asserted realities of bankruptcy that, if the property is not retained by the debtor, it will realize for the estate only what the Chapter 7 trustee can get for it anyway, which is generally a liquidation price....

BACKGROUND FACTS

The evidence focused largely on the valuation issue, though some evidence regarding use and intent to use was also submitted. All of the jewelry pieces, including the 6.18 carat diamond ring, are worn regularly by the debtors (indeed, some of the pieces show a substantial amount of wear, detracting from their value). The debtors acquired all of the pieces for the purpose of wearing them, and many of the pieces included such comparatively utilitarian items as watches and earrings.

The evidence suggested mixed motives for acquiring the 6.18 carat diamond ring. On the one hand, the ring was purchased on the occasion of the Mitchells' twenty-fifth wedding anniversary. Mr. Mitchell had not been able to buy his wife much of an engagement ring when they were wed, so this was actually her first real wedding diamond. He paid in excess of $30,000 for the ring in 1978, evidently believing the ring to be a good investment at the time.

... The court finds the testimony regarding use and intent to be credible and believes that, notwithstanding a clear investment purpose, expressed in both the size of the diamond and the testimony of Mr. Mitchell, other factors, such as continuous wear and sentimental attachment, carry considerable weight sufficient to qualify the ring as "clothing reasonably necessary for the family."

The valuation testimony differed dramatically. First City's expert assigned an "estate value"[4] to the 6.18 carat diamond ring, of approximately $6,800.00 per carat, or $42,024.00. He gave the ring a fair market value of $36,000.00. The debtors' expert (the same man who wanted to buy the ring and who had also originally sold it to Mr. Mitchell) said that, in situations such as this, where the debtor had to sell, he would offer no more than $7,800.00 for the ring, as that would take into account the risk he would be taking in trying to re-market the ring to someone else. The latter value represented little or no "holding period" while the former assumed a reasonable exposure to the market of a period of months. The court finds both witnesses' testimony credible insofar as they are consistent with an assumed valuation

---

4. The estate value is what a jewelry company would have to pay on the diamond market to acquire the stone, as opposed to the retail market, which is what one would ask the customer to pay for the item.

standard, leaving the court to decide which valuation standard should be adopted.

The debtors will be hard-pressed to keep the 6.18 carat diamond ring should this court find that the fair market valuation standard controls. The debtor has already claimed household goods worth $12,000.00 (by stipulation, which this court accepts), other jewelry of $4,500.00, other clothing of $1,000.00, and the cash surrender value of a life insurance policy ($30,857.00). If the diamond ring is indeed worth $36,000.00, the debtors will be forced to choose between the ring and their household furnishings.[5]

The argument advanced in favor of the fair market valuation standard ("FMV") is that both the state and federal exemption statutes expressly stipulate to that standard....

The debtor appeals to logic, public policy, and practicality. The most elegant expression of the argument is found in In re Walsh, noted above. There, then Bankruptcy Judge Roger Whelan, after acknowledging the express language of the statute, fled to the panoply of canons of statutory construction for relief from the plain meaning of the statute....

...Judge Whelan then added, as illustration, that using fair market value in the traditional sense only hurts the debtor without augmenting the return to creditors....

...It is technically incorrect to say that *Walsh* favors the use of a liquidation valuation per se. The case instead encourages a focus on the applicable market when one speaks of "fair market value." Urging that the applicable market is the one available to a bankruptcy trustee, the values generated in that market will reflect the sale circumstance by being somewhat depressed.

There are a number of difficulties with this position, however. The argument is essentially circular and turns the generally accepted definition of fair market value on its ear.... By focusing on "market," *Walsh* ignores the "fair" in fair market value....

There is also another (and what I consider to be a more fundamental) difficulty with the *Walsh* position, and that is that it is out of step with what I conceive to be the overriding function of the "cap" which Texas places on personal property exemptions. Section 42.002 of the Property Code sets out what Texas finds to be the "approved list" of items which Texans should be allowed to retain, no matter how much they owe creditors. Some of these items assure the survival of the individual or the family in some station above abject poverty.[6] Thus, we will not let creditors take away the debtor's means of transportation in this, the largest state among the lower forty-eight....

In short, Texans cannot simply keep $30,000.00 worth of anything they want. Instead, they must pick items off an approved list of items which, according to the legislature, are the sort of things sufficiently important for

5. First City points out that, even at the debtors' value, the exemptions claimed exceed the $30,000 cap by $26,157.00....

6. Our exemption laws attempt to strike a balance between the rights of creditors and the survival of debtors. They do not assure the preservation of a debtor's station in life, but rather act as a "safety net" to prevent debtors and their families from being left destitute, wards of the state as a result of creditor collection activity. *Leva*, 96 B.R. at 728. Exemptions are in fact a limit on a creditor's right to satisfaction of its claim out of the debtor's assets. The limitations are imposed for reasons of public policy. There is no public policy served in preserving the lifestyles of the rich and bankrupt.

a Texas debtor to keep regardless of the claims of creditors. Once debtors have "gone shopping" from this approved list and picked out what they want to keep, however, they must "go to the checkout line," as it were, to see how much can actually be "purchased" out of the "budget" allowed by the Texas Legislature in section 42.001(a) of the Property Code. This second step in the process balances out the competing concerns of assuring a debtor a fresh start and assuring creditors a fair recovery on their legitimate claims. Letting the debtor have everything off the approved list without limitation offends the sensibilities of the common man (and woman) whom the legislature represents. . . .

The appropriate valuation standard is thus "fair market value," incorporating as it does an exposure of the item to the appropriate market for a reasonable period of time. In this case, the court adopts the fair market valuation suggested by First City's expert and finds the value of the 6.18 carat diamond ring to be $36,000.00.

The debtors are directed to file a new schedule B-4 listing their exemption claims in light of this decision. . . .

═══════

Although this decision gives the debtors a broad license to exempt property, the lower courts have seen to it that debtors who try to be too clever are apt to be sorry, as in one Virginia case in which the debtor claimed two partnerships exempt at a valuation of $1.00. The trustee did not object, but simply found a purchaser more than happy to purchase the partnerships for their market value, which was obviously far greater. In re Grablowsky, 149 B.R. 402 (Bankr. E.D. Va. 1993). The court held that the trustee may have been barred from objecting to the exemption, but only to the extent of the value claimed. The stay was lifted to permit the sale, with a full dollar to go to the debtor for each partnership interest. (Trustee: "Would you prefer cash or a check?")

5. Proceeds and Tracing

Exemptions are typically by category of property — wages, tools of the trade, motor vehicles, household furniture, alimony, etc. — but property is not static in nature. Wages may be deposited in checking accounts, property may be sold, contract obligations may be satisfied. Whenever the form of property changes, it raises issues about proceeds — that is, issues that focus on the application of an exemption to property that would not meet the classification requirements except that it constitutes proceeds from exempt property. The following case illustrates the difficult and sometimes inconsistent resolution of proceeds questions.

═══ In re PALIDORA ═══

310 B.R. 164 (Bankr. Ariz. 2004)

OPINION BY: Randolph J. HAINES

* * *

When Frank and Sondra Palidora ("Debtors") filed their chapter 7 petition they had $2,194.80 in their bank accounts. The Chapter 7 Trustee ("Trustee") moved for turnover of these funds less the $300 exemption provided by Arizona law for funds in a joint debtors' bank account.[7] Debtors objected to the Trustee's motion by asserting that all of the monies in the bank account had derived either from Frank's wages or from a $1,000 check for child support that was paid to Sondra and deposited into her account.

Arizona's Wage Exemption Does Not Apply to Paid Wages

Arizona law exempts 75% of a debtor's disposable earnings. "Disposable earnings" are defined by A.R.S. §33-1131(A) to be "that remaining portion of a debtor's wages, salary or compensation for *his* personal services, including bonuses and commissions," after deducting state and federal withholdings.

The question, therefore, is whether "wages, salary or compensation for personal services" means only what is payable, or includes what has been paid, either by cash, check or direct *deposit* to a debtor's bank account. The meaning of a state exemption is controlled by the applicable state law, and a bankruptcy court is bound by the state's construction of a state statute. Applying the laws of other states, some bankruptcy courts have concluded that exempt wages retain their exempt status once paid and deposited in a debtor's bank account.

The Arizona Court of Appeals, however, has held that "the earnings protection of [A.R.S.] §§33-1131 and 12-1598.10 does not extend to monies disbursed to the debtor's bank account." Frazer, Ryan, Goldberg Keyt & Lawless v. Smith, 184 Ariz. 181, 186, 907 P.2d 1384, 1389 (App. Div. 1 1995). It did so for a number of cogent reasons. Most importantly, it relied on the statute governing garnishment procedures, n6 which expressly provides that "Earnings become monies, as defined in §12-1570, paragraph 6, upon their disbursement by the employer to or for the account of the employee, except disbursements into a pension or retirement fund." A.R.S. §12-1598.01(A). This necessarily means that "earnings" are only earnings until they are paid, and thereafter they are no longer earnings but are "monies." Although that definition is found in a different title of the Arizona statutes than the exemption provisions, the Court of Appeals concluded the statutes are "closely intertwined" and "must be given a consistent interpretation." Smith, 184 Ariz. at 185, 907 P.2d at 1387-88. Indeed, a later provision of the garnishment procedure statute relating to the continuing garnishment lien on earnings expressly cross references the exemption provision. A.R.S. §12-1598.10(F). The *Smith* opinion also noted that Arizona has other exemptions for monies in A.R.S. §33-1126, but nowhere do the statutes "suggest that exempt monies include those that were formerly exempt earnings."[8] Id. Finally, the Court of Appeals noted that Arizona's statute partially exempting disposable earnings was modeled after the federal Consumer Credit Protection Act, 15 U.S.C. §§1672-73, and that courts construing the federal garnishment exemption uniformly hold that it does not extend to earnings disbursed to a debtor's bank account. Id., citing, e.g., Usery v. First Nat'l Bank, 586 F.2d 107, 110(9th Cir. 1978).

Because an Arizona court's construction of the Arizona exemption laws is binding on this Court, we must conclude that the Arizona wage exemption ceases to apply upon the debtor's receipt of those wages, whether paid in cash, by check, or by direct deposit in the debtor's bank account. In short, the wage exemption statute only limits what a creditor could obtain by garnishment of the employer, not what could be attached in the hands of the debtor.

Child Support Payments are Trust Funds

But for different reasons, paid child support is different from paid wages. In a case under the Bankruptcy Act, the Ninth Circuit held that where state law provides that child support payments are held by the custodial parent in a fiduciary capacity, such funds do not become property of the estate. Boston v. Gardner (In re Gardner), 365 F.2d 242 (9th Cir. 1966) (applying Oregon law). In that case, the debtor's ex-husband had fallen behind in making child support payments. When he made the payments postpetition, the trustee sought to claim them on behalf of the estate because the debtor had a right to reimburse herself from those funds for the expenses she incurred in supporting the child while the payments were not being made. The Ninth Circuit held that the funds at issue "have their origin as trust assets for the child's support" and that because of that "origin and the mother's own support obligation, in our judgment her right of reimbursement cannot prevail over the child's claims." Id. at 243. Consequently the Ninth Circuit concluded the trustee had no claim to such funds unless it could clearly be shown that they were not necessary to satisfy the debtor's obligations to the minor child, "either present or during the future period of his minority." Id.

Because Bankruptcy Code §541(d) defines property held in trust not to constitute property of the estate, the holding of Boston v. Gardner should still be good law under the Code, at least with respect to states that define child support payments to be trust funds or funds held in a fiduciary capacity....

---

8. Although the *Smith* opinion did not note it, these provisions also distinguish "monies received by or payable to" a debtor from money "to be paid" a debtor. For example, A.R.S. §33-1126(A)(3) exempts "All monies received by or payable to a person entitled to receive child support or spousal maintenance pursuant to a court order," whereas A.R.S. §33-1126(A)(4) exempts only "money, proceeds or benefits of any kind to be paid" under an employer's health, accident or disability insurance. And there is a distinct $150 exemption for money held in a single bank account. A.R.S. §33-1126(A)(8). These distinctions also indicate that the Arizona legislature did not regard "earnings" as any form of money but rather as the compensation to be paid. They also suggest that the legislature did not intend the exemptions to continue to apply when the asset changes character unless the statutory language expressly so provided. Such an express provision was made for the homestead exemption, A.R.S. § 33-1101(C), which continues to apply for eighteen months to the "identifiable cash proceeds" from the sale of a homestead.

Although there does not appear to be an Arizona statute or judicial decision expressly declaring child support payments to be trust funds, they do imply as much. "Every person has the duty to provide all reasonable support for that person's natural and adopted minor, unemancipated children, regardless of the presence or residence of the child in this state." A.R.S. §25-501(A). "The obligation to pay child support is primary and other financial obligations are secondary." A.R.S. §25-501(C). "All duties of support as prescribed in this chapter may be enforced by all civil and criminal remedies provided by law." A.R.S. §25-501(D). Little v. Little, 193 Ariz. 518, 522, 975 P.2d 108, 112 (1999) (Arizona law prescribes that "the obligation to pay child support is primary and other financial obligations are secondary."); Jorgensen v. Jorgensen, 131 Ariz. 271, 273, 640 P.2d 202, 204 (App. Div. 2 1981) ("A parent obligated to pay child support may not avoid that obligation by voluntarily incurring debts that reduce the ability to pay, since the ability to pay such support must be determined by viewing the child support obligation as a primary obligation superior to all other financial obligations." (Citations omitted)); Beck v. Jaeger, 124 Ariz. 316, 317, 604 P.2d 18, 19 (App. Div. 2 1979) ("Other financial obligations are secondary..."). Arizona courts have held that former spouses may not "bargain away custody and child support provisions of a divorce decree in exchange for interests in real property which serve only to enhance the financial interests of the parties themselves and completely disregard the welfare of the children." Evans v. Evans, 17 Ariz. App. 323, 325-26, 497 P.2d 830, 832-33 (Div. 2 1972). "A parent may not form a valid and enforceable contract which releases the parent from all obligation to support his or her minor children." Smith v. Saxon, 186 Ariz. 70, 73, 918 P.2d 1088, 1091 (App. Div. 1 1996).

From these authorities this Court concludes that an Arizona court would find that money paid by a former spouse to a custodial parent for child support pursuant to a court order are trust funds held by the custodial parent for the benefit of the child. Under Bankruptcy Code §541 and Boston v. Gardner, such funds are not property of the estate.

Moreover, even if the funds paid as child support are not trust funds, they are exempt under Arizona law. A.R.S. §33-1126(A)(3) exempts "All monies received by or payable to a person entitled to receive child support or spousal maintenance pursuant to a court order." Unlike the wage exemption statute, this exemption provision expressly includes not only such money payable to a debtor, but also such money received by a debtor. Consequently the exemption would continue in the funds when deposited in a bank account, provided they are traceable to the exempt source.

There is an important proviso to these conclusions, however. The exemption statute makes clear that the child support payments must have been made pursuant to a court order. And the trust fund analysis does not apply to parents who are still married to each other. "A.R.S. §12-2451 [currently 25-501] imposes a general duty on parents to support their children, but there is no duty on one parent to pay a certain sum to the other parent for child support." Lamb v. Superior Court, 127 Ariz. 400, 402, 621 P.2d 906, 908 n.1 (1980). On this record, it is not possible to determine whether the alleged $1000 check to Sondra for child support was paid by the debtor husband Frank or was paid by a former husband pursuant to a valid court order for child support. The former would be nonexempt property of the estate, while the latter would be both exempt and not property of the estate.

CONCLUSION

For the foregoing reasons, the Trustee's objection to the Debtors' claim of exemption of the bank account based on the wage exemption is sustained. The Court is not in a position to rule on the claim of exemption for child support payments pending further factual development....

━━━━━━━━━━━━━

In a feat of financial planning that may give some clue as to why he ended up in bankruptcy, Kenneth Dasher cashed out every last nickel in his retirement account to buy a pick-up truck. In re Dasher, 2002 U.S. Dist. Lexis 10563 (Neb. 2002). His retirement account was fully exempt and he made the purchase after he had filed for bankruptcy (surely not on advice of counsel). He amended his schedules to claim his new pick-up as exempt, pointing out that it was just his retirement account in a little more tangible form. The court said no, and in a deeply insightful opinion, pointed out some of the key differences between a "retirement account" and a "pick-up truck." The trustee seized the pick-up and sold it, all for the benefit of the creditors. Note that if Mr. D had just waited to cash in his retirement account *after* his bankruptcy case was closed, he would have discharged his debts and owned the pick-up outright. But sometimes a man can't wait.

6. Partially Exempt Property

One exemption issue is often confusing: If there is a dollar limit on an exempt category, does property of a greater value cease to be exempt? The answer is that such property is partially exempt. In most cases the property can be levied on and sold. If that happens, the exemption attaches, up to its dollar limit, to the cash from the sale. Following a judicial sale of exempt property, the proceeds are allocated first to the debtor to the full amount of the exemption. The remainder goes to the judgment creditors.

An example will illustrate: If a state recognized an exemption of $1,000 for a car for each individual, a debtor who owned a car worth $800 would be able to protect the car from any creditor attachment. A debtor who owned a car worth $2,800 subject to no consensual liens would be subject to having the car seized and sold for the benefit of a judgment creditor. If the creditor was owed $3,000 and the car brought $2,800 at a judicial sale, the proceeds would be divided between the debtor ($1,000 in satisfaction of the exemption) and the judgment creditor ($1,800 as non-exempt value).

7. Security Interests in Exempt Property

The debtor's exemption is relatively easy to determine when only the TIB (acting on behalf of all the unsecured creditors) claims an interest in potentially exempt property. If, for example, a debtor owns a car valued at $1,000 that is eligible for a federal exemption of $1,200, the debtor keeps the car. If the car were worth $5,000, the TIB would sell the car, the debtor would keep the first $1,200, and the TIB would take the remainder for distribution to the creditors.

When potentially exempt property is encumbered by a security interest valid in bankruptcy, the secured party moves ahead of both the debtor and the TIB. If the car mentioned above were worth $1,000 and the secured creditor's claim were for $2,000, the secured party would take the car. (Computation of the secured creditor's allowed claim in bankruptcy is covered in the next section.) The debtor would have no exemption and the TIB would have nothing for distribution. If the car were worth $3,000, the car would be sold, the secured party would take $2,000 (the full amount of the allowed secured claim), and the debtor would keep the remaining $1,000. Only when the value of the car exceeds the sum of the allowed secured claim and the debtor's exemption would the TIB be able to reach any value from the property.

8. Avoiding Judicial Liens and Non-PMSI Liens

In addition to personal exemptions, Congress fashioned another protection to improve the economic position of post-bankruptcy debtors. Section 522(f) permits the avoidance of certain kinds of liens on certain categories of exempt property listed therein. Two kinds of liens are made avoidable: judicial liens (that is, liens that are imposed by a court after a judgment has been rendered and a defendant has not paid) and nonpossessory, nonpurchase money consensual security interests (when, for example, a creditor lends money and takes a security interest in the household goods the debtor already owns). In order to void the liens, the collateral must be exempt property. In addition, to void a consensual security interest, the property must also be of a kind of "household good" that is specified in 522(f)(4). The effect of these provisions is that creditors who hold these judicial liens or security interests can be treated like any other general unsecured creditor, entitled only to a pro rata share of the debtor's entire estate — not a special claim to some of the debtor's property. In effect, the law here says that these creditors cannot push their claims ahead of the debtor's exemption, as creditors with regular security interests or liens can.

In general, a debtor may avoid all judicial liens on exempt property, regardless of the nature of the debt secured by the lien. One important exception, however, is that a judicial lien that secures a debt for a domestic support obligation is exempt. §522(f)(1)(B). Those judicial liens remain intact no matter what.

Section 522(f)(1)(B), which voids certain voluntary security interests, was adopted largely in response to a growing concern about the use of security interests by certain finance companies to prey on the poor. Several studies documented established practices of taking security interests in all of a debtor's clothing, in children's toys, in household linens, in family photographs. Many critics pointed out that these security interests were not taken to provide alternate resources to satisfy the loan if the debtor should become unable to pay. Instead, the security interests were taken for their "hostage value," for the likelihood that threatened repossession would cause the debtor to make any sacrifice to find a way to pay. Section 522(f) was adopted in the 1978 Code to defeat these practices in the context of bankrupt debtors.

When section 522(f) was added to the Bankruptcy Code back in 1978, the FTC soon followed suit by imposing similar restraints on creditors outside bankruptcy. The rule was adopted in part to respond to the charges of abuse and in part to limit any special incentive to file bankruptcy. The FTC rule makes it an unfair practice for a company to take a nonpossessory, nonpurchase money security interest in certain listed goods. FTC Trade Regulation Rule on Credit Practices, 16 C.F.R. §444.1 (1985). The 2005 Amendments to the Bankruptcy Code bring the enumerated lists of protected goods into closer alignment.

The FTC was careful to make these rules apply only to security interests created after the effective date of the rules, thereby avoiding a controversy that arose in the application of section 522(f). In United States v. Security Industrial Bank, 459 U.S. 70 (1982), the Court was faced with a constitutional attack on section 522(f) by secured creditors holding the kind of nonpossessory, nonpurchase money liens that the section permits the debtor to void. The secured creditors did not try to claim that Congress could not ban, or make voidable, such liens, but contended that an application of the section 522(f) voiding power to a preexisting lien, i.e., one obtained prior to passage of the Code, would be an unconstitutional deprivation of property under the Fifth Amendment. The United States intervened in the case to defend the constitutionality of the statute.

The six-member majority opinion managed to avoid a square ruling on the constitutional issue. The majority strongly intimated that a retroactive application of the section 522(f) voiding power might violate the Fifth Amendment property rights of secured creditors, but stopped short of so holding. Instead, the majority held that the serious constitutional question involved required a strict reading of the statute so as to avoid the constitutional issue if possible. On such a reading, the majority concluded that Congress did not intend to apply section 522(f) to preexisting liens and therefore the constitutional issue did not have to be addressed.

Three justices concurred in the judgment on the basis of a 1902 precedent holding that the bankruptcy statutes should not be construed as affecting preexisting rights unless Congress clearly so intended. The concurring justices would have held section 522(f) to be constitutional had they reached that issue.

Security Bank raised, but did not resolve, fascinating and recurring problems concerning the extent of Congress's power under the bankruptcy clause of the Constitution to disappoint the expectations of the marketplace. For example, it is said that Congress has considerable power to displace otherwise enforceable "contract rights," but not to deprive persons of "property" under the Fifth Amendment. That can be a very tenuous distinction to maintain. In many contexts, such as enforcement of security agreements in accounts receivable under Article 9 of the UCC, "contract rights" are treated as property. See generally Michelman, Property, Utility and Fairness: Comments on the Ethical Foundations of "Just Compensation" Law, 80 Harv. L. Rev. 1165 (1967).

Even if it were clear which rights are "property" protected by the Fifth Amendment and which are not, there would remain the question of the limit on Congress's power to restrict those rights short of that "deprivation" requiring compensation. Michelman, supra.

It seems clear that Congress can redefine property prospectively. It can say that henceforth those who acquire certain property interests will not enjoy certain rights that existing holders of such interests now enjoy. It is also clear that Congress can limit existing property rights to some considerable degree in the name of regulation or taxation without the limitation being a "deprivation." Such limitations in the bankruptcy context can include a temporary withdrawal of certain property rights, as with the prevention of foreclosure or repossession by the operation of the automatic stay. On the other hand, it seems equally clear that at some point a bankruptcy rule could so undermine existing property rights that the Fifth Amendment's protection would come into play. The issue has arisen many times in bankruptcy and will no doubt arise again.

Problem Set 8

8.1. Harv and Lois Hughes live in an apartment in Houston, Texas. They are unable to pay several of their debts and are worried about which of their assets may be vulnerable to creditor attachment. Their largest creditor is the IRS, to whom they owe about $5,000 in back taxes. They list their assets as follows:

Item	Value
Household furniture and appliances	$8,000
Clothing	2,000
Lois's law books	2,400
Lois's Moped	800
Harv's 1970 MGA (left over from high school, now up on blocks)	500
Cash value on Lois's insurance	2,000
Lois's wedding ring	1,000
Lois's computer	1,200
100 shares Disney Co. (Lois's Dad knew Walt)	5,000
Joint checking account	200
Harv's computer set up	7,500
Joint checking account	200
15-year-old, 25-foot Friendship Sloop (with rebuilt depth finder)	6,000
Harv's motorized wheelchair	18,000
Fluffy (Persian cat, nasty temper but very beautiful)	200
Soccer ball	2

Harv, who is a computer programmer, was injured last year when his car was struck by a train. He has been rated at a 40 percent disability as a result. His lawyer says he can likely settle with the railroad for about $50,000 (there were some serious contributory negligence issues). What can Harv and Lois protect as the creditors begin to move in? What could they protect if they lived in Wilmington, Delaware?

8.2. Harv's cousin Suzan Hughes is also in financial trouble, but Suzan has always been a bit more aggressive than Harv. She works as a computer programmer, but she decided her fortune would ride on her ability to spot valuable rare books. She sold nearly everything she had to acquire a stunning old book and manuscript collection. The collection now includes a fine thirteenth century illuminated-text Bible. The Bible is worth about $500,000 and the remainder of the library is worth another $600,000. Her other assets are worth about $50. Suzan's creditors are closing in. What can she keep if she lives in Odessa, Texas? What can she keep if she lives in Dover, Delaware?

8.3. Kim Sung owns a home in a state that permits an individual debtor to exempt $25,000 in value of the debtor's homestead from creditor attachment. Kim bought the house in 1990. He paid $5,000 down and signed a mortgage obligation for $45,000, which he has paid down to $40,000. Similar houses are now selling for about $75,000 when they are put on the retail market for two or three months and listed with a real estate broker, who charges a 6 percent commission. A similar house sold in a sheriff's auction last month for $29,428. (It was bought by the creditor for whom the sale was being held for exactly the amount of the debt owed the creditor. The creditor was the only one who showed up at the sale.)

Kim owes a judgment creditor $25,000. Assuming the court is not bound by any precedential decisions, what are the court's options in determining whether to order a judicial sale? Explain the rationale for each option and pick the best. Be sure to note how the proceeds of any sale will be distributed. Should the decision on forcing a sale differ if the judgment creditor is a victim of an accident in which Kim was driving drunk or if the creditor is the legal alter-ego of an aluminum siding company that swindled Kim so cleverly that he'll never be able to prove it? Should it matter if it is the mortgagee rather than a judgment creditor that is attempting to have the property sold in satisfaction of the debt? See §522(a)(2).

8.4. Charley Wilson has worked for 12 years on construction sites, most recently as a crane operator. Charley has purchased and completely paid for a 1994 three-quarter-ton Dodge pick-up. When the local construction industry entered yet another slump, Charley used the pick-up as collateral for a $6,500 loan from his credit union. After three months with no work, Charley decided to go into business for himself, and he began work as "Charley's Trash Hauling and Light Deliveries." His new business has not been very successful, and Charley filed for bankruptcy two months after opening, although he was still trying to make the business go. The credit union has filed to lift the stay on the pick-up so that it can repossess and sell it. Assuming the federal exemptions apply, should the stay be lifted? See §522(f). Would it matter if Charley were doing light hauling and working on the crane part-time? If Charley were just driving the pick-up back and forth to the construction sites? If he drives it to collect unemployment checks?

Is there any way his creditor can tell how he uses it? Does that matter? What result for Charley if his state's law (a) opts out of the federal exemptions; (b) makes tools of the trade exempt up to $1,000; (c) makes motor vehicles exempt up to $2,000; and (d) says that all consensual liens on exempt property are fully enforceable? See §522(f)(3).

D. HOMESTEADS, TRUSTS, AND EXEMPTION PLANNING

You have learned the basics about exemptions as they affect most debtors. Because the great majority of debtors have few assets of any value, apart from a heavily mortgaged home, exemptions are important to them only at the "barrel" level — that is, enough protection to cover their clothes, basic household goods, vehicles necessary to daily transportation, and the like. For just that reason, attempts to show that exemption levels are fundamental to bankruptcy policy (or credit availability) have failed. Exemptions beyond a very basic floor don't matter to most middle-class debtors. (See infra pp. 216-217).

On the other hand, exemptions matter a good deal to the small minority of more affluent debtors most likely to need more sophisticated legal advice. Exemptions also serve as a check on affluent debtors who might exploit too liberal a system, as demonstrated by the debates about unlimited homestead exemptions. Part of that debate includes public perceptions of the bankruptcy system that may be soured by well-publicized instances of debtors escaping their legal obligations by manipulating luxury property to keep it from the legitimate claims of their creditors, including fraud victims. Thus the higher levels of exemption policy matter, even though they do not much affect most debtors.

This section addresses the exemption issues surrounding that minority of debtors who have assets of substantial value. The section is not limited to exemption rules, because there are two ways that more affluent debtors protect assets from their creditors: some take advantage of large exemptions and others count on excluding certain assets from their estates. Property may be excluded by operation of law (e.g., most retirement funds are excluded from the estate in section 541). Other property may be excluded by use of trusts that show that the debtor has no remaining legal interest in property the debtor nonetheless seems to control and enjoy. Either device — exemptions or exclusion — puts the debtor's assets beyond the reach of unpaid creditors.

The struggle over what property debtors may and may not keep when they are unable to pay all their creditors as promised has deep social and economic implications. The stakes in these questions can be quite high. Nowhere do they come into greater collision than in the protection afforded homeowners.

1. Homestead Exemptions

The most important type of exempt property for many debtors is the homestead, which is typically the real property occupied by the debtor as a residence. Financially, homes are the most significant assets owned by most Americans. More than 60 percent of all wealth held by individuals is in the form of homes. Homeownership is a cumulative phenomenon, with about 68 percent of the total population owning their own homes, and an astonishing 90+ percent of all Americans over the age of 50 owning the homes they live in. For many, a home represents not only their accumulated wealth, but also their hold on a middle-class lifestyle.

The homestead exemption as we know it developed largely in the nineteenth century. In his very interesting article, Protection of the Family Home from Seizure by Creditors: The Sources and Evolution of a Legal Principle, 86 S.W. Hist. L.Q. 364, 369 (1983), Professor Joseph McKnight examined the sources of the modern homestead exemption laws. He found:

> In popular as well as legal parlance, homestead means not only family home but property that is accorded particular protection because it is the family home. From one American state to another, and elsewhere as well, the most significant protection of the home is that which is accorded it against seizure by the owner's creditors for payment of general, private debts. The term homestead was also once used to refer to a sovereign grant of western lands where the frontiersman and his family made their home. But it is in the sense of a home protected from creditors that the concept of homestead is one of the most significant later contributions to family jurisprudence. Legal tradition has long acknowledged that this notion of homestead emerged on the Mexican-Texan frontier. But the sources and development of the concept have never been clearly demonstrated. Simply stated, the tradition is that an 1829 act of the Mexican state of Coahuila y Texas recodified Castilian exemption principles and extended them to sovereign grants of land. Carrying this development forward, a Texas act of 1839 defined exempt lands in terms of the family home, and from this model the principle of homestead exemption from the claims of creditors spread throughout the United States and beyond.

Professor McKnight bases his analysis on dual themes: the Anglo-American and Hispanic legal traditions of the time, and the continuing political concerns of the independent government of Coahuila y Texas to attract settlers and to protect resident debtors. Professor McKnight explained one interaction between debtor-creditor laws and migration during the nineteenth century.

> Moving West was a frequent early nineteenth-century response to the series of economic crises in the new American nation. A move to Texas where land was cheap was particularly attractive to venturous spirits in the southern United States. The Texas colonists were by no means generally insolvent, but there were some who came to Texas with the hope of leaving debts permanently behind them, and those debts were sometimes large. By the mid-1820s Texas had achieved the reputation as a haven for debtors. First in 1826 and again in 1828 the United States Congress directed questions to the president concerning the obvious irritant to American creditors whose debtors had removed themselves to Mexican territory. The perception of Texas as a refuge for debtors was a consequence of several factors: Texas's primitive judicial system, the difficulty of finding debtors there, and, most particularly, the reluctance of local judges to enforce foreign debts against fellow colonists.

The American financial crisis of 1837, which precipitated the movement of so many distressed debtors into Texas, was a likely catalyst to the 1839 Texas enactment.

Id. at 375, 393.

By 1829, generous homestead and family property exemptions were firmly established in Texas law. The homestead exemption, born of a blending of two legal cultures, soon took root in several states. Professor McKnight traces the spread of the homestead exemption beyond Texas:

> The Hispanic and Anglo-American traditions of exempt property thus interacted to produce the lasting concept of protecting the family home and certain movables from the claims of creditors. These ideas came to full flower in the formulation of the homestead and chattel-exemption provision of the Texas Constitution of 1845. Forceful minds, well versed in the Hispanic concepts of exempt property and their further development in the decree of 1829, composed and passed the constitutional provision that would publish the expanded concept of exempt property in louder tones to the rest of the United States. The idea had already spread, on the apparent inspiration of the 1839 act, to Mississippi, Georgia, and Florida; within a few years more, similar provisions were enacted in a number of other states and were added to some state constitutions. Well before the end of the century the family home had been extended protection from creditors in almost every American state.

Id. at 396.

Homestead exemptions are now available in a large number of jurisdictions. Even so, not every homeowner is protected. Twenty states protect less than $20,000 equity in a homestead, and four more states (including Delaware) offer no homestead protection of any kind. In addition, a number of states have a doctrine known as "tenancy by the entirety" that has some effect in protecting a homestead. By application of this principle of property law, the courts prohibit a creditor of only one spouse from foreclosing on a homestead held by the entirety — that is, jointly owned by the married couple. See, e.g., Patterson v. Hopkins, 247 Pa. Super. 163, 371 A.2d 1378 (1977). This effectively stops a general unsecured creditor from forcing a sale of a home to satisfy a debt if the creditor is owed an obligation by only one spouse, regardless of the value of the home. It does not, of course, have any restraining effect if the creditor has extended credit to both husband and wife or if the debtor is a single person.

Typically, the homestead is exempt from execution by creditors up to a given dollar amount. But seven states and the District of Columbia now offer homestead protection based on area or some other test. As we noted in the preceding section, for example, Texas law exempts a homestead that covers up to 10 acres in a city and 200 acres in the country. Arkansas protects homesteads up to a quarter-acre in a city and 80 acres in the country. At the legislative level policy debates continue over how generous the exemptions should be and what class of debtor should be favored by them. The debate is particularly loud in Florida, where a homestead of unlimited value can be protected, a circumstance that is said to have attracted former baseball commissioner Bowie Kuhn, former ambassador Marvin Warner, and convicted inside-trader

Martin A. Siegel, all of whom were able to protect multi-million-dollar homes from their very angry creditors. The other states with unlimited homestead exemptions evidently have not been so attractive to those fleeing their creditors, so the debates elsewhere have not been so lively.

2. Exemption Planning

Because Texas and states like it protect unlimited value in a homestead, the debtor has the opportunity to do some careful planning before filing for bankruptcy to discharge his debts. Mr. Reed seems to be one of these careful planners.

=============== In re REED ===============

12 B.R. 41 (Bankr. N.D. Tex. 1981)

BRISTER, Bankruptcy Judge.

The debtors filed petition for order for relief under Chapter 7 of Title 11, United States Code, on December 21, 1979. During the two week period preceding the filing of the petition the debtors, obviously engaging in pre-bankruptcy planning, sold nonexempt personal property for approximately 50% of the value which they had assigned to those properties and applied the proceeds of $34,500.00 towards liquidation of liens against their residence homestead. The trustee filed a complaint challenging entitlement to the exemptions. The following summary constitutes the findings of fact contemplated by Rule 752 after nonjury trial.

Since his childhood Hugh D. Reed had collected approximately 35 guns, some of them commemorative guns or otherwise having collector's value. On a financial statement dated April 1, 1979, he had valued the gun collection at $20,000.00. On December 11, 1979, ten days prior to filing the petition in bankruptcy, he sold the entire gun collection to a friend, Steve Gallagher, for $5,000.00 cash.

Reed had been an antique collector, also. On the April 1, 1979, financial statement he had valued his antiques at $3,000.00. Three months later, in August, 1979, he purchased additional antiques from an estate for $11,000.00. In late November, 1979, he sold three items from the antique collection to an acquaintance, Charles Tharpe, for $3,500.00, applying the proceeds to payment of a note to Bank of the West. On December 11, 1979, he sold the remaining antiques to the friend, Steve Gallagher, for $5,000.00 cash.

In November 1979, approximately one month prior to the commencement of the bankruptcy proceedings, he purchased for $15,000.00 an interest in a corporation with the intriguing name of Triple BS Corporation. He sold that interest to the friend, Steve Gallagher, on December 11, 1979, for $5,000.00 cash.

In three separate transactions between October 5, 1979, and November 13, 1979, Reed had purchased gold coins — Krugerrands and Mexican Pesos — for the total sum of $22,115.00. On or about December 10, 1979, he sold those coins for $19,500.00 cash.

Thus, ten days prior to bankruptcy debtors sold nonexempt assets with aggregate value of $68,500.00 (according to their financial statements or based upon the amount actually paid by them on recent purchases), receiving as proceeds the sum of $34,500.00. They received market value for the gold and when that transaction is not considered they received less than 20% of the apparent value of the guns, the antiques and the interest in Triple BS Corporation.

In October 1978, the debtors had executed a note and mechanic's lien to a lending institution in the sum of $20,000.00 to pay for improvements to their residence, consisting of a sun-deck room, swimming pool and pool facilities. On December 11, 1979, $19,892.00 from the proceeds of sale of nonexempt assets were applied to pay off that improvement loan. The balance of $15,000.00 was applied by the debtors towards the vendor's lien note against the residence, reducing the balance of that note to approximately $28,000.00.

The scope of this memorandum is narrow. The trustee insists that the homestead exemption on the residence should be avoided, because of the flagrant prebankruptcy planning in which they engaged. As evidence of fraudulent intent, the trustee contends that the debtors received less than a reasonably equivalent value for the nonexempt assets. Mr. Reed very candidly testified that had he received more money for the nonexempt assets he would have applied those additional monies to the homestead liens.

The issue as to whether the homestead exemptions may be set aside under those facts is clearly drawn.

The debtor, in support of his contention that he could properly pay the liens with proceeds of nonexempt property, and thus engage in obvious exemption planning, cites a comment in the legislative history following §522(b):

> As under current law, the debtor will be permitted to convert nonexempted property into exempt property before filing a bankruptcy petition. See Hearings, pt. 3, at 1355-58. The practice is not fraudulent as to creditors, and permits the debtor to make full use of the exemptions to which he is entitled under the law.

While that language may express the law in some jurisdictions, it is not universally true. Certainly it is not an accurate expression of Texas law because Texas law specifically prohibits the retention of an exemption in personal property so acquired with proceeds of nonexempt property where there was intent to defraud, delay or hinder a creditor or other interested persons.

In this case, however, there was no proof that the debtors had applied the proceeds to acquisition of exempt personal property. All of the evidence indicates that the entire proceeds of $34,500.00 were applied on the real estate liens. The Texas legislature, at the time it adopted V.A.T.S. Article 3836(b), [predecessor to §42.004 supra] had the opportunity to include the same language in V.A.T.S. Article 3833, [predecessor to §41.002, supra p. 61] which provides the homestead exemption in real estate. It failed to do so, and had it included that type of language it is doubtful that it would have passed constitutional muster. Historically Texas law has jealously protected the homestead from forced sale except under very limited conditions. Article 16, §50 of the Texas Constitution prohibits forced sale for any purpose except for purchase money liens, improvement liens, or taxes.

That provision in the Texas constitution prohibits the granting of the relief sought by the trustee in this case and the challenge to the homestead exemption in the residence is denied.

———

But Mr. Reed was not home free. Remember, he is in bankruptcy in order to discharge his outstanding debts. When the trustee appealed the bankruptcy court decision, the Fifth Circuit took a hard look at Mr. Reed and the Triple BS Corporation and did not like what they saw.

In re REED
700 F.2d 986 (5th Cir. 1983)

RUBIN, Circuit Judge.

We hold that a debtor who converts nonexempt assets to an exempt homestead immediately before bankruptcy, with intent to defraud his creditors, must be denied a discharge in bankruptcy because of the provisions of Section 727 of the Bankruptcy Code, 11 U.S.C.A. §727 (West 1979), and, therefore, we affirm the decision of the district court.

I

Hugh D. Reed, as sole proprietor, opened a shop using the trade name, Reed's Men's Wear, in Lubbock, Texas. He financed the venture in part by obtaining from the Texas Bank &. Trust Company a $150,000 loan which was guaranteed by the Small Business Administration (SBA). Three months later, the bank gave Reed a $50,000 line of credit, and the SBA agreed that the original loan would be subordinated to the line of credit. The store showed a profit for the first nine months of operation in 1977, but began to lose money in 1978.

By February 1979, Reed knew that his business was insolvent. After meeting with the bank, the SBA, and his major trade creditors, he signed an agreement to turn over management of the store to a consulting firm for the year 1979. In turn, Reed's trade creditors agreed to postpone collection efforts and Reed promised to resume payments in January 1980. Despite management by the consultant, the business continued to fail, and on December 15, 1979, Reed and his wife, Sharon Marcus Reed, signed a fore-closure agreement surrendering the store to the bank. Six days later, the Reeds filed voluntary petitions for bankruptcy.

* * *

Reed had catholic interests and much energy. He found time to collect antiques, gold coins, and guns, and to make other investments. In a financial statement provided to the bank and to the SBA on April 1, 1979, Reed valued his gun collection at $20,000 and his antiques collection at $3,000. In the four months prior to bankruptcy, Reed augmented each of his collections. He caused Reyata [Corporation, which Reed owned] to borrow $11,000, which he used to purchase more antiques. In three separate transactions during October and November, Reed accumulated, at a cost of $22,115, a collection of Krugerrands and Mexican fifty-peso pieces. One month before filing for bankruptcy, Reed purchased, for $15,000, a one-third interest in a business known as Triple BS Corporation.[9]

Two months before bankruptcy, Reed opened an account at the Bank of the West without the knowledge of his creditors. From that time until the store closed in mid-December, he deposited the daily receipts from Reed's Men's Wear in this separate account. From this account, in late November Reed repaid the loan Reyata made to purchase the antiques.

Reed began selling his personal assets in late November. He first sold three items from his antiques collection to an acquaintance, Charles Tharpe, for $3,500. He sold the remainder of his antiques on December 11 to a friend, Steve Gallagher, for $5,000. Whether this represented their fair market value was not established, but the total realized on the antiques was $8,500, while the original value plus the cost of recent purchases was $14,000. On December 10, he sold his gold coins through a broker for $19,500 cash, their approximate market value. The next day, on December 11, Reed sold to Gallagher for $5,000 each both his gun collection and his Triple BS stock. Whether or not Gallagher paid fair market value for the items was not established, but the stock had been purchased only one month earlier for $15,000.

Reed applied all of the proceeds to reduce the mortgages on his family residence, which was exempt from creditor's claims under Texas law, with the objective, the bankruptcy court found, of reducing the value of his nonexempt assets and increasing the value of his homestead exemption prior to bankruptcy. Thus he raised about $35,000, applying about $30,000 [should read "$20,000" — eds.] to wipe out a second mortgage home improvement loan and applying the balance of approximately $15,000 to reduce the first mortgage on his home to about $28,000.

Reed cavalierly justified his sale of assets for what appeared to be less than their fair market value. This was of no concern to his creditors, he testified, because, if he had received more for the assets, he would have simply applied the additional sum to reduce the mortgage on his homestead. No matter how much he got, there would be nothing for his creditors.

Reed also failed to account for the disposition of $19,586.83 in cash during the year preceding filing. Reed attempted to explain the "unaccounted for" cash by testifying that he habitually carried huge sums of money in cash on his person and frequently made purchases and payments in cash without obtaining receipts. He argued that the amount of "unaccounted for" cash represents only a small percentage of the amount of money which went through his hands in 1979.

The bankruptcy judge found that Reed had effected transfers designed to convert nonexempt property into exempt property less than two weeks

---

9. The significance of the initials is not elucidated in the record.

before bankruptcy with the intent to hinder, delay, or defraud creditors. 11 U.S.C.A. §727(a)(2) (West 1979). He found that, regardless of the amount of money that might have passed through Reed's accounts, $19,586.83 is a significant sum, and that Reed had failed satisfactorily to explain its loss. This constituted an additional basis for denying discharge. 11 U.S.C.A. §727(a)(5) (West 1979).

The district court affirmed the judgment.

II

The Bankruptcy Code provides that a debtor may be denied discharge if he has transferred property "with intent to hinder, delay, or defraud a creditor," 11 U.S.C.A. §727(a)(2) (West 1979), or has "failed to explain satisfactorily... any loss of assets...." 11 U.S.C.A. §727(a)(5) (West 1979). Reed was denied discharge on both bases. Though either would suffice, we review the grounds seriatim.

In considering the effect of Reed's transfers of assets, we distinguish, as did the careful opinion of the bankruptcy court, the debtor's entitlement to the exemption of property from the claims of his creditors and his right to a discharge from his debts. The Bankruptcy Code allows a debtor to retain property exempt either (1) under the provisions of the Bankruptcy Code, if not forbidden by state law, 11 U.S.C.A. §522(b) and (d) (West 1979), or (2) under the provisions of state law and federal law other than the minimum allowances in the Bankruptcy Code, 11 U.S.C.A. §522(b)(2) (West 1979).

Under the Bankruptcy Act of 1898, most courts, applying state exemption laws, had held property that would otherwise have been exempt to be deprived of its immunity if there was evidence other than the simple act of conversion showing that the debtor had acquired it with the intention of defrauding his creditors. If intent to defraud was not proved, however, and it was shown only that granting the exemption would defeat the creditor's claim, the exemption was granted. As stated in 3 Collier on Bankruptcy, ¶522.08[4] (15th ed. 1982): "Under the Act, the mere conversion of nonexempt property into exempt property on the eve of bankruptcy was not of itself such fraud as will [sic] deprive the bankrupt *of his right to exemptions*." (Emphasis supplied.)

Before the Bankruptcy Code was adopted in 1978, it had been urged that property obtained in such last-minute conversions be ineligible for exemption. Id. The Code, however, adopts the position that the conversion of nonexempt to exempt property, without more, will not deprive the debtor of the exemption to which he would otherwise be entitled. 3 Collier, supra, ¶522.08[4]. Thus, both the House and Senate Reports state:

> As under current law, the debtor will be permitted to convert nonexempt property into exempt property before filing a bankruptcy petition. The practice is not fraudulent as to creditors, and permits the debtor to make full use of the exemptions to which he is entitled under the law.

H.R. Rep. No. 595, 95th Cong., 1st Sess. 361 (1977), reprinted in 1978 U.S. Code Cong. & Ad. News 5963, 6317; S. Rep. No. 989, 95th Cong.,

2d Sess. 76, reprinted in 1978 U.S. Code Cong. & Ad. News 5787, 5862. The rationale behind this congressional decision is summed up at 3 Collier, supra, ¶522.08[4]: "The result which would obtain if debtors were not allowed to convert property into allowable exempt property would be extremely harsh, especially in those jurisdictions where the exemption allowance is minimal." Nonetheless, the phrase, "[a]s under current law," qualifies the apparently blanket approval of conversion, since as noted above, courts denied exemptions under the Act if there was extrinsic evidence of actual intent to defraud (and if the state law permitted disallowance of the exemption for fraud).

Reed elected to claim his exemptions under state law. The bankruptcy judge, therefore, referred to Texas law to determine both what property was exempt and whether the exemption was defeated by the eleventh-hour conversion. Texas constitutional and statutory protection of the homestead is absolute, and the bankruptcy judge interpreted Texas law to allow the exemption in full regardless of Reed's intent.

While the Code requires that, when the debtor claims a state-created exemption, the scope of the claim is determined by state law, it sets separate standards for determining whether the debtor shall be denied a discharge. The debtor's entitlement to a discharge must, therefore, be determined by federal, not state, law. In this respect, 11 U.S.C. §727(a)(2) is absolute: the discharge shall be denied a debtor who has transferred property with intent to defraud his creditors. The legislative history of the exemption section, as noted above, does not mean that conversion is never fraudulent as to creditors, but simply that, as under prior law, mere conversion is not to be considered fraudulent unless other evidence proves actual intent to defraud creditors. While pre-bankruptcy conversion of nonexempt into exempt assets is frequently motivated by the intent to put those assets beyond the reach of creditors, which is, after all, the function of an exemption, evidence of actual intent to defraud creditors is required to support a finding sufficient to deny a discharge. For example, evidence that the debtor, on the eve of bankruptcy, borrowed money that was then converted into exempt assets would suffice to support a finding of actual intent to defraud. Only if such a finding is made may a discharge be denied.

The evidence amply supports the bankruptcy court's finding that Reed had an actual intent to defraud. Reed's whole pattern of conduct evinces that intent. Cf. Farmers Co-op. Assn. v. Strunk, 671 F.2d 391, 395 (10th Cir. 1982) ("Fraudulent intent of course may be established by circumstantial evidence, or by inferences drawn from a course of conduct"). His rapid conversion of nonexempt assets to extinguish one home mortgage and to reduce another four months before bankruptcy, after arranging with his creditors to be free of payment obligations until the following year, speaks for itself as a transfer of property in fraud of creditors. His diversion of the daily receipts of Reed's Men's Wear into an account unknown to his creditors and management consultant and his subsequent use of the receipts to repay a loan that had been a vehicle for this conversion confirm his fraudulent motivation....

The fact findings of the bankruptcy judge, affirmed by the district court, are to be credited by us unless clearly erroneous.... [A]nd the finding of actual intent to defraud, based on evidence other than the fact of the conversion, patently was not permeated with error. The denial of a discharge on this ground alone was appropriate. It would constitute a perversion of the purposes of the Bankruptcy Code to permit a debtor earning $180,000 a year to convert every one of his major nonexempt assets into sheltered property on the eve of bankruptcy with actual intent to defraud his creditors and then emerge washed clean of future obligation by carefully concocted immersion in bankruptcy waters.

Reed asserts that denial of a discharge makes the exemption meaningless. This is but fulmination. Reed may retain his home, mortgages substantially reduced, free of claims by his creditors. In light of the ample evidence, aside from the conversion itself, that Reed had an actual intent to defraud his creditors, he simply is not entitled to a discharge despite the fact that a generous state law may protect his exemption.

The argument that we should reject the other ground for denying discharge gets but the short shrift it deserves. . . .

III

The district court found that Sharon Marcus Reed benefited from the "prohibited activities" and possibly had knowledge of them but that she did not participate in them. Accordingly, he granted her discharge. The evidence showed that Sharon Reed made out the daily reports of the sales receipts of Reed's Men's Wear during the time that Reed was surreptitiously diverting those receipts to a bank account unknown to his creditors and management consultant. From this, it would have been possible to infer that Sharon Reed shared her husband's fraudulent intent, but the bankruptcy judge's findings to the contrary are not clearly erroneous. . . .

========================

The dual *Reed* opinions show how the courts have tried to negotiate a line that provides protection for a debtor and yet does not permit debtors to take undue advantage. It also illustrates how courts may see themselves bound by the legislature, as Judge Brister did in the bankruptcy court in *Reed*, or how they can read extremely open-ended language to craft what they believe is a more sensible solution, but one that defies precise definition.

In the debates leading up to the 2005 Amendments, Congress made its dissatisfaction with this approach evident. To respond to repeated complaints about millionaires who protect too much money in a homestead, Senator Herb Kohl, D-WI, proposed an amendment to cap permissible homestead exemptions at $250,000. States could continue to provide unlimited homestead exemptions to govern all state law collection suits, but anyone who wanted a federal discharge in bankruptcy would be limited to protecting no more than $250,000 in equity in a home. The amendment had widespread support, and during the long course of the bankruptcy bills, it passed the Senate more than once. But the then-governor of Texas, George W. Bush, and the senators from Texas threatened to block any bankruptcy bill with such a cap. In the final version of the amendments, the cap was dropped.

Congress rejected a homestead cap, but it did put some restrictions on the value that a debtor could protect in a homestead. The 2005 Amendments included a provision to reduce the dollar value of the homestead protection by any amount that is attributable to otherwise non-exempt "property that the debtor disposed of ... with intent to hinder, delay or defraud a creditor." §522(o). To catch even long-time planners, the provision has a ten-year reach-back period. This means, for example, that if the next court finds that the next Mr. Reed disposed of those non-exempt coins with an "intent to hinder, delay or defraud a creditor," then in bankruptcy his equity in his homestead would be reduced by an equivalent amount.

Notwithstanding the change in bankruptcy law, the real joker in the deck remains: Not all debtors will be as forthcoming as Mr. Reed, especially after they (or their lawyers) read about the outcome of *In re Reed*. Many conversions of non-exempt to exempt property are done with no intent to defraud anyone (think about paying on your mortgage with cash — technically a conversion of non-exempt property to exempt property under the Texas exemptions). Besides, the question remains whether planning activities to take maximum advantage of statutory exemptions are fraudulent or just plain sensible. Recall that even though the Fifth Circuit nabbed Mr. Reed with intent to defraud, not even Mr. Reed's own bankruptcy trustee who took the appeal to the Fifth Circuit claimed that he could prove actual intent to hinder, delay, or defraud his creditors — and Mr. Reed was a man who named his corporation "Triple BS."

Congress added other restrictions to make it more difficult for well-heeled debtors to hide money in homesteads. It clearly signaled that it read the newspapers. In the wake of the mega-fraud Chapter 11 cases, reports emerged that former officers of Enron were building some scrumptious homes in River Oaks and other upscale Houston neighborhoods, perhaps with an eye on that Texas homestead exemption. Some newspapers even started running pictures of the luxurious — and exempt — homes of some of these executives. So Congress added another provision for an absolute cap on the homestead for people who were convicted of securities law violations, fraud in a fiduciary capacity, and a handful of other related bad acts. §522(q). If necessary, the discharge can be delayed to see if the debtor is subject to a proceeding that might give rise to a limitation of the homestead exemption. §§727(a)(12); 1121(d)(5)(C); 1328(h). Thus the bankruptcy law was "Enron-ized" to cut off protection for former big-time executives who might otherwise seek personal bankruptcy protection and try to shield assets in a huge home.

3. Unlimited Exemptions and Asset Trusts

The sound and fury over homestead exemptions overlook other unlimited exemptions. Courts around the country have been struggling with those for years.

One example came out of Minnesota. Dr. Tveten, a physician who dabbled in more than the healing arts, managed to amass $19 million in debts in a real estate partnership that went south. He consulted his attorney, who had two pieces of advice: convert your assets to protect as much as you can and file for bankruptcy. The good doctor took the advice, using 17 transfers to sell off his land and liquidate his non-exempt life insurance and retirement accounts. All the transactions were for fair value. Dr. T put the money into about $700,000 of life insurance and annuity contracts with the Lutheran Brotherhood, a fraternal benefit association. Under Minnesota law, creditors could not attach these contracts. Best of all, the exemption has no dollar limit.

Dr. T conceded that the purpose of these transfers was to shield his assets from creditors. He wasn't trying to cheat anyone, he said. He was just trying to meet the legal requirements of how he should best hold his assets. When Dr. T came up for a discharge in bankruptcy court, the bank that had financed the real estate deal and obtained his unsecured guarantee objected to his discharge. Norwest Bank Nebraska, N.A. v. Tveten, 848 F.2d 871 (8th Cir. 1988). The bankruptcy judge, following the analysis of the Fifth Circuit in *Reed,* denied the discharge, and both the district court and the Eighth Circuit affirmed.

But there was a stinging dissent in *Tveten* by Judge Arnold:

> The Court reaches a result that appeals to one's general sense of righteousness. I believe, however, that it is contrary to clearly established law, and I therefore respectfully dissent.
>
> Dr. Tveten has never made any bones about what he is doing, or trying to do, in this case. He deliberately set out to convert as much property as possible into a form exempt from attachment by creditors under Minnesota law. Such a design necessarily involves an attempt to delay or hinder creditors, in the ordinary, non-legal sense of those words, but, under long-standing principles embodied both in judicial decisions and in statute, such a purpose is not unlawful. The governing authority in this Court is Forsberg v. Security State Bank, 15 F.2d 499 (8th Cir. 1926). There we said:
>
> > It is well settled that it is not a fraudulent act by an individual who knows he is insolvent to convert a part of his property which is not exempt into property which is exempt, for the purpose of claiming his exemptions therein, and of thereby placing it out of the reach of his creditors.
>
> Id. at 501. Thus, under the controlling law of this Circuit, someone who is insolvent may convert property into exempt form for the very purpose of placing that property beyond the reach of his creditors.... The same principle was confirmed by Congress when it enacted the Bankruptcy Code of 1978. The report of the House Judiciary Committee states as follows:
>
> > As under current law, the debtor will be permitted to convert nonexempt property into exempt property before filing a bankruptcy petition. See Hearings, Pt. Ill, at 1355-58. The practice is not fraudulent as to creditors, and permits the debtor to make full use of the exemptions to which he is entitled under the law.

In re Tveten, 848 F.2d at 877.

What made the *Tveten* case particularly noteworthy was that on the very day that it was announced the same court also announced the unanimous opinion in Hanson v. First Natl. Bank in Brookings, 848 F.2d 866 (8th Cir. 1988). The Hansons were South Dakota farmers who, on similar advice of counsel, sold all their non-exempt property, two vans, a car, a motor home, and all their household goods to family members. On agreement with the purchasers, the Hansons retained possession of many of the goods. They received the market value of the goods, $27,115, which they promptly used to pay down their mortgage and to buy exempt life insurance policies. Their lender bank objected to the Hansons' exemptions, wanting to reach the assets they had secreted. The court explored the same questions about whether the debtors had engaged in fraudulent conduct. The bankruptcy judge said the Hansons got their discharge and kept their newly exempt property. Both the district court and the court of appeal affirmed.

Judge Arnold sided with the majority in the second case, but he used the *Hanson* decision to sharpen his outrage in *Tveten*:

The Court is entirely correct in holding that there is no extrinsic fraud [in *Hanson*]. The money placed into exempt property was not borrowed, the cash received from the sales was accounted for, and the property was sold for fair market value. The fact that the sale was to family members, "standing on its own, does not establish extrinsic evidence of fraud." Ante, at 869.

With all of this I agree completely, but exactly the same statements can be made, just as accurately, with respect to Dr. Tveten's case. So far as I can tell, there are only three differences between Dr. Tveten and the Hansons, and all of them are legally irrelevant: (1) Dr. Tveten is a physician, and the Hansons are farmers; (2) Dr. Tveten attempted to claim exempt status for about $700,000 worth of property, while the Hansons are claiming it for about $31,000 worth of property; and (3) the Minnesota exemption statute whose shelter Dr. Tveten sought had no dollar limit, while the South Dakota statute exempting the proceeds of life-insurance policies, is limited to $20,000. The first of these three differences — the occupation of the parties — is plainly immaterial, and no one contends otherwise. The second — the amounts of money involved — is also irrelevant, in my view, because the relevant statute contains no dollar limit, and for judges to set one involves essentially a legislative decision not suitable for the judicial branch. The relevant statute for present purposes is 11 U.S.C. §522(b)(2)(A), which authorizes debtors to claim exemptions available under "State or local law," and says nothing about any dollar limitations, by contrast to 11 U.S.C. §522(d), the federal schedule of exemptions, which contains a number of dollar limitations. The third difference — that between the Minnesota and South Dakota statutes — is also legally immaterial, and for a closely related reason. The federal exemption statute, just referred to, simply incorporates state and local exemption laws without regard to whether those laws contain dollar limitations of their own.... If there ought to be a dollar limit, and I am inclined to think that there should be, and if practices such as those engaged in by the debtor here can become abusive, and I admit that they can, the problem is simply not one susceptible of a judicial solution according to manageable objective standard.

As if the problem of fraudulent intent did not already have enough twists, a third case in the trilogy provides the O. Henry ending. It seems that more than one Minneapolis physician had bought into the bad real estate partnerships (had there been a targeted marketing to Minneapolis doctors?). Dr. Robert Johnson converted about $400,000 in assets into the same kind of exempt property as did Dr. T, on the advice of the very same attorney who advised Dr. T. The same bank made an objection to discharge based on the same facts. But Dr. J drew a different bankruptcy judge, and Dr. J got his discharge. Affirmed in the district court and affirmed by the Eighth Circuit. In re Johnson, 880 F.2d 78 (8th Cir. 1989). Equal justice under law.

The Eighth Circuit trilogy is notable for another feature that does not play a prominent part in the opinion. Both states let people squirrel away as much cash as they want in a Fraternal Benefit Association fund, free from the reach of their creditors.

Fraternal Benefit Associations? What's going on with those? They sound so, um, *pokey*, but some lawyers have seen real potential in the idea of hiding all of a client's assets so that they cannot be reached by creditors — whether the debtor eventually files for bankruptcy or not.

The *device de jour* is called an asset protection trust. The operation is fairly simple. For example, Ryan Spear transfers a big batch of his property to The Ryan Spear Trust, names himself as both trustee and beneficiary, then sits back and smiles. Ryan keeps right on using the property — driving the car, sailing the boat, dropping in on the winter place in Aspen and the summer place in Maine. If Ryan runs over someone with his Hummer or lets his attention wander and commits malpractice during open-heart surgery or does some other thing that gets him sued, the victim can take a judgment, but when she tries to seize the cars/boats/condos, Ryan smiles and says, "Sorry, but those aren't mine. They are the property of the Ryan Spear Trust. The trustee lets me use them sometimes."

The idea of a self-settled trust (self-settled because Ryan gave assets to a trust for which Ryan was the beneficiary) was anathema to trust law. Anything like this looked like a plain old fraud on the creditors. And that remains the law in most places. But the key word is "most."

A few years back, Alaska made self-settled asset protection trusts legal. Never one to pass up something that might generate legal fees, Delaware immediately jumped in and made them legal as well. (Yes, Delaware, the state that says ordinary folks can't even keep a two-bedroom-one-bath home in a bad part of town said that debtors could establish asset protection trusts to place millions of dollars of assets out of reach of creditors.)

Competition for legal business in the emerging field of "asset protection" has heated up. *Accounting Today*, that sizzling magazine that covers all the sexy new trends in accounting, reports that eight states now permit asset protection trusts: Alaska, Delaware, Missouri, Nevada, Oklahoma, Rhode Island, South Dakota, and Utah. Best of all, many of these states make the trusts available to out-of-state residents. Ryans of the world start smiling. Unlike the Texas or Florida homesteads, the asset protection trusts are available without leaving home.

How widespread are these trusts? Click on Nexis and search for "asset protection trusts," and you will probably turn up a batch of advertisements and notices like the one we saw in the June 27, 2005, *Pittsburgh Post-Gazette*. Nestled right in between announcements for the meetings of the Kiwanis Club of McKeesport and the Rotary Club of Pittsburgh, was this little gem:

Wealth Management Roundtable LLC, seminar, noon, law office of ****, Jr., Suite ****, U.S. Steel Tower. Topic: "The Combined Use of Private Annuities,

Life Insurance and Asset Protection Trusts in Estate Planning." Call Mary at
412-201-****.

How much value is tucked away in these accounts? In fact, how many of
them are there? So far, we haven't seen any numbers. We doubt that the
typical cosmetologist has one, but we're less sure about the average plastic
surgeon.

A more exotic and expensive cousin is the offshore trust, established in
the Cook Islands or other sun-kissed locales. (For extra credit, where are the
Cook Islands?) Trusts are offered that purport to become unresponsive to
the settlor's instructions if those instructions are the product of "coercion."
The coercion might be provided, we suspect, by a federal judge. That way a
debtor who is held in contempt for not producing the assets from a foreign
trust can shrug and say, in all honesty, "Gee, your honor, even if I wanted
to produce the assets, I couldn't." These trusts are being increasingly
marketed to the risk-inclined and jury-wary across America. To the benefits
of the self-settled trust they add distance and the fortress of national
sovereignty.

What happens to asset protection trusts in bankruptcy? If they are
structured right, including a spendthrift provision and an automatic
appointment of a third party as trustee if the trustee-debtor is sued, the
debtor will claim that the property in such a trust is not property of the
estate. §541(c)(1). The reference in section 541(c)(1) to state law seems to
give the trusts full protection, at least in eight states. Of course, in the same
way that the funds placed with fraternal orders are exempt in Minnesota,
the states intent on sheltering those who establish asset protection trusts
can also make the property in them exempt from any creditor attachment,
which would also be recognized in bankruptcy through section 522(b).
In other words, excluding property from the estate and exempting property
from creditor attachment meet in devices that are separated more by paper
forms than by any reality.

Asset protection trusts and their fraternal order cousins in exemption
law could always be set aside by the approach taken in *In re Reed* by the Fifth
Circuit: Even if the trust works at state law, the debtor will be denied the
protection of a discharge in bankruptcy. This might work, but there remains
a lot of room for debtors to litigate over intent. As the Eight Circuit indicated
when it affirmed a discharge for Dr. Tveten's colleague Dr. Johnson, what
looks like fraud is far from certain. As a result, many people have begun to
raise concerns about the possible use of these trusts and thought that the law
should be amended to make it clear that this loophole was stitched up.

When the 2005 Amendments were pending, Senator Charles Schumer,
D-NY, proposed that all assets in asset protection trusts be brought into the
estate, and that the exempt portion be limited to a $125,000 cap. His amend-
ment failed. Later, Senator James Talent, R-MO, introduced an amendment
that passed in which he claimed to have fixed the asset protection trust
problem. Others were less sure that the fix really works.

Senator Talent's amendment is a ten-year reach-back for transactions
made with intent to hinder, delay, or defraud creditors. §548(e). It is, of
course, the basic approach of *In re Reed, In re Tveten,* and *In re Johnson,*

with a long reach-back period (if needed). The problem once again is that determining intent is tricky. It is made trickier by the language in the Code that describes such transfers as fraud when they are "in anticipation of any money judgment" or to escape judgments in connection with securities fraud. These examples may limit the courts' application of a fraud standard to those cases in which the debtor was clearly trying to avoid a particular claim. By negative inference, would this make other asset protection trusts all right?

So far as we know, the change in the bankruptcy laws has not slowed down traffic in asset protection trusts, and, just for good measure, the various state fraternal benefit associations remain open for business.

4. Moving to Better Exemptions

There is another way that debtors can plan to protect their property in advance of a bankruptcy filing: They can move from a state with stingy exemptions to one that is more generous. The problem, as in so many other areas of the law, is that some pesky judge may decide the move was not motivated by a strong desire to become a Buckeye, a Sooner, or even a Longhorn, and may treat the move as a form of impermissible exemption planning.

=========================== In re COPLAN ===========================
156 B.R. 88 (Bankr. M.D. Fla. 1993)

C. Timothy CORCORAN, III, Judge.

These contested matters test the limits of what some euphemistically call "pre-bankruptcy planning" by new Floridians who seek to benefit from Florida's nationally recognized liberal exemption laws. In this case, the debtors incurred substantial indebtedness in their home state of Wisconsin, moved to Florida, converted their non-exempt assets into property that is exempt under Florida law, and then filed a Chapter 7 petition here. They thus seek to discharge their debts and keep their newly "exempted" property. Upon the objection of their largest creditor and the Chapter 7 trustee, the court is required to call a foul, holding that the debtors have exceeded permissible limits....

II. FACTUAL BACKGROUND

Before November of 1989, Lee and Rebecca Coplan resided in the state of Wisconsin where Mr. Coplan was engaged in business. Mr. Coplan had been employed for approximately 14 years by a Chapter S corporation known as Coplan's Super Appliance and TV, Inc., a company that owned and operated a retail appliance store conducting business under the name Coplan's Appliance & Home Entertainment Superstore. AT&T provided financing to the business through a line of credit and was the primary creditor of the business. Sometime in 1988, Mr. Coplan acquired a one-half ownership interest in the business from his father. In May of 1989, Mr. Coplan executed a personal guaranty in favor of AT&T Credit Corporation in replacement of the personal guaranty previously executed by his father.

By September of 1989, the business had deteriorated substantially. In fact, the debtors' 1989 tax return reflects that Mr. Coplan's 50 percent interest in the business resulted in a loss to him of $44,264 with a net loss to the business, as a whole, of $88,528 that year.

Mr. Coplan resigned his position with the business in November of 1989. He testified that he had decided to resign his position with the business in August of 1989, citing as reasons unhappiness with what he had been doing, a dishonest business partner, emotional stress relating to the job, problems with his parents, and deterioration in the performance of the company. Although Mr. Coplan interviewed with several companies in Wisconsin and received offers prior to his resignation, he did not accept employment with any company in Wisconsin. Mr. Coplan further testified that he relocated to Florida in pursuit of "job opportunities" with Amana and Disney, although he had no job offer from either of those companies and none was forthcoming until a considerable time after he moved here.

Subsequently, on November 29, 1989, the debtors closed the sale of their home in Wisconsin. The successful bid for the home was received and accepted almost immediately after the house was placed on the market. One day after the completion of the sale of the Wisconsin home, the debtors closed the purchase of the house located in Winter Park, Florida. They paid $228,000 in cash for the house, using virtually all of the proceeds obtained in the sale of the Wisconsin house. Thus, the Coplans completed the entire process of selling one home and purchasing another half way across the country in the space of less than one month. The Coplans then moved to Florida in December of 1989. Mr. Coplan's partner continued to run the business in Wisconsin. In June, 1990, the business ceased operations.

On December 26, 1989, Mr. Coplan purchased an annuity from Pacific Fidelity Life Insurance Company for $20,932.29 with funds held by him in his individual retirement account (IRA). On the same day, Mrs. Coplan also purchased an annuity from Pacific Fidelity Life Insurance Company for $14,741.53 with funds held by her in her IRA. Mrs. Coplan did not work outside the home, and she had no earnings or compensation. She testified that her IRA had been funded in part by gifts made by her parents.

Sometime in early 1990, Park State Bank obtained a judgment in Wisconsin against the debtors jointly for approximately $50,000. In April of 1990, AT&T filed suit against Mr. Coplan in the United States District Court for the Eastern District of Wisconsin to collect on the guaranty. In July of 1990, AT&T obtained a consent judgment in its favor and against Mr. Coplan in the amount of $1,081,839.69.

In August of 1990, Mr. Coplan obtained full-time employment with Amana in Florida. Prior to that time, his only employment had been on a part-time basis as an appliance sales representative for Sears and Roebuck at a Sears retail store. During this extended period without regular employment, the Coplans liquidated nearly all of their non-exempt assets and used the proceeds on which to live.

On December 5, 1990, the debtors filed their petition under Chapter 7 of the Bankruptcy Code in this court. The schedules reflect that there was little or no non-exempt property available to the estate.

III. THE HOMESTEAD ISSUE

Pursuant to Section 541 of the Bankruptcy Code, the filing of a bankruptcy petition creates an estate that consists of all property of the debtor. The exemption of property which is ordinarily subject to administration by the estate is governed by Section 522 of the Bankruptcy Code. In this case, no one disputes that the debtors are bona fide Florida residents. Thus, the relevant exemption statutes are found in Florida law....

Article X, Section 4(a)(1), of the Florida Constitution provides that homestead property may be claimed as exempt to its full value and may thus be protected from the reach of creditors. The objectors do not take issue with this general proposition but argue that the debtors' right to exempt their homestead is subject to qualification where the exempt property has been impermissibly converted from non-exempt assets....

The central question in the instant case... is whether, considering all the circumstances, the debtors' relocation to Florida with the attendant purchase of the Winter Park home was for the specific purpose of shielding their assets from creditors. The court concludes that it was.

If the debtors had retained their Wisconsin home, the judgments entered in favor of Park State Bank and AT&T would have attached to the property. Further, the house would have become an asset of the bankruptcy estate had the debtors filed for bankruptcy in Wisconsin. In addition, under Wisconsin law, the debtors would have been limited to an exemption of only $40,000 on their homestead, rather than its full value.

The objectors argue that the Coplans relocated to Florida solely for the purpose of obtaining the benefit of the generous Florida exemptions. In contrast, the debtors contend that their primary objective in relocating was to pursue job opportunities for Mr. Coplan and to alleviate stress. The debtors have suggested that Mr. Coplan, despite the knowledge that the business was operating at a loss and had an uncertain future, refused one or more job offers in Wisconsin because of low salary and the desire to move and instead came to Florida in the bare hopes of obtaining better employment.

The Coplans' testimony on these points is not credible.[10] The evidence clearly establishes that the business was deteriorating in the months

10. Following the completion of the evidentiary hearing held on the objections to claims of exemptions, AT&T filed a motion to reopen the evidence (Doc. No. 43). AT&T alleged that the debtors perjured themselves in giving this testimony. AT&T sought the opportunity to present evidence to contradict the testimony the debtors gave. The debtors filed a responsive motion to strike (Document No. 47). The court heard the motions on December 4, 1991, and the court took the motions under advisement.

The court deems the motions to be moot and unnecessary because the court does not find the debtors' testimony, especially that complained about in the AT&T motion to reopen, to be credible. In addition to the internal inconsistencies in the testimony that were highlighted during adverse examination, the court carefully observed the demeanor of the debtors as they testified. The court is satisfied, therefore, that the debtors' testimony is unworthy of belief on immediately preceding the move. In fact, the business posted a substantial loss for the 1989 year. Mr. Coplan was painfully aware that, in the event the business defaulted on its obligation to AT&T, he was personally liable. In addition, Mrs. Coplan admitted the debtors knew their house in Wisconsin was subject to forced sale to satisfy the claims of their creditors and that a homestead in Florida was fully exempt. More importantly, she acknowledged on adverse examination that the move to Florida was for the purpose of obtaining the more generous homestead exemption.

The debtors have further argued that the fact that the house was purchased more than one year before the date of the filing of their Chapter 7 case insulates the claim of exemption from objection. The foundation for their argument appears to be Section 548 of the Bankruptcy Code. That section provides a one year statute of limitations for actions to set aside fraudulent transfers. This matter, however, is not a fraudulent conveyance action, and Section 548 does not therefore apply. Instead, this matter is being decided on the basis of Section 522 [the exemption provisions]; in that section of the Bankruptcy Code, there are no strictures in regards to time as there are in Section 548.

In considering issues of this sort, however, the timing of the conversion of assets from non-exempt to exempt status is a factor to be considered in determining whether there was a specific intent to shield assets from creditors. As a general rule, all other things being equal, the more distant the conversion, the less likely the court will be to find that the conversion was part of a specific plan to exclude the property from the reach of creditors. Nevertheless, timing is just one factor to be considered in examining this question.

In the circumstances of this case, the fact that the debtors purchased the Winter Park house one year and five days before the filing of the Chapter 7 bankruptcy petition fails to save the exemption. The debtors are financially sophisticated; they were fully able to appreciate the personal financial ramifications of a faltering business. As soon as it became apparent that the business was failing, the debtors undertook a well considered and carefully orchestrated series of maneuvers for the purpose of shielding their assets from the reach of their creditors. They had the foresight and the resources to wait one year following the conversion of their Wisconsin homestead to a Florida homestead before filing their bankruptcy petition. In fact, although the debtors paid cash for the house, they systematically liquidated their non-exempt assets during that year. Because Mr. Coplan was unemployed for much of that time, the family lived on the results of this liquidation.

The fact that the filing so closely fell upon the expiration of the one year anniversary of the conversion of the property to a fully exempt form itself adds support to the court's conclusion that this was part of a well planned scheme. The debtors sold their home in Wisconsin in a rush. They selected

---

these key points so that no purpose would be served by reopening the evidence. The court has therefore not considered for purposes of the motion to reopen, the responsive motion to strike, or on the merits of the contested matters the affidavits filed by AT&T and the debtors in support of their respective motions.

For these reasons, the court is contemporaneously entering a separate final order denying as moot the motion to reopen the evidence and the responsive motion to strike.

and purchased the home in Florida in an equally fast fashion. The purchase price was, almost to the penny, the same as the net proceeds received from the sale of the Wisconsin home. The debtors then moved to Florida without any job commitment for the only breadwinner for the family, having rejected job offers in Wisconsin. Indeed, it appears the Coplans rushed here once they recognized the hopelessness of their business enterprise so they could put the maximum amount of time between the conversion of their assets and their inevitable bankruptcy filing. This case is plainly unlike the situation where, following conversion of assets, an unexpected disaster occurs that pushes a debtor into bankruptcy and thus necessitates a different treatment.

The actions of the debtors suggest a concerted effort to defeat the ability of their existing creditors to be paid the monies owed them by maximizing the exemption protections offered under Florida law.... [T]he court may not permit this manipulation. Thus, the exemption should be denied to the extent that the debtors achieved a benefit greater than their entitlement under Wisconsin law.

In this case, had the debtors not engaged in this pre-bankruptcy planning, or had they stayed and filed bankruptcy in Wisconsin, they would have been entitled to an exemption of $40,000 from the proceeds of the sale of their home. Accordingly, the court will allow $40,000 of the Florida home as exempt and will deny the exemption as to the remainder. The Florida home is therefore property of the estate subject to administration, although the trustee will be required to recognize that the amount of $40,000 is the exempt property of the debtors. Pursuant to the provisions of Section 363(f) of the Bankruptcy Code, the trustee may sell the property and distribute the net proceeds, after payment of ordinary and necessary expenses and costs of sale and closing, between the debtors and the estate as determined here. The court has previously utilized this methodology when a debtor has a legitimate homestead claim to some but not all of indivisible property....

We haven't seen any evidence that Bowie Kuhn, Marvin Warner, and Martin Siegal are giving up their multimillion-dollar mansions, but the days of debtors fleeing to Florida to take advantage of the superior exemptions may be numbered. On the other hand, if Mr. and Mrs. Coplan had stayed out of bankruptcy and fought with their creditors through the Florida state courts, they might still have their home today.

In this area, Congress decided it did not want to rely on the bankruptcy judges to exercise discretion in weeding out bad cases, so the 2005 Amendments include a provision to limit the ability of a debtor to move to take care of better exemptions. In effect, the new provisions are a sort of choice-of-law provision for exemptions.

What exemptions will govern a debtor's filing? According to section 522(b)(3), the applicable exemptions will be wherever the debtor resided for 730 days (two years in the parlance of ordinary speakers of English). What if the debtor moved during that time? Then go back to the 180 days that precede the 730 days and see where the debtor was for the majority of that time (e.g., the six months before two years before filing). People who move a lot might find themselves in bankruptcy, governed by exemption laws from three or four moves previously. Our data show that debtors in bankruptcy have moved around more than most people.

Not all state exemption laws were written for the twists and turns of federal bankruptcy law, however. Many protect only a homestead "in the jurisdiction" or property held locally. That could mean that a debtor who left the state a year or two ago would be eligible for exemptions nowhere — the debtor's property would all be in the new state and the debtors' exemptions under section 522(b)(3) would be only for property in the previous state — of which there was none. In such a case, the statute commands the debtor to use the federal exemptions, even in states that do not permit such use. It seems that the unlimited homestead exemptions will remain available to real Texans, except those who left and returned.

The consequences of this provision should provide some unusual entertainment as the bankruptcy judge in the Middle District of Tennessee must suddenly learn to interpret the state exemption laws for Alaska for someone who moved to Nashville from Anchorage a year-and-a-half ago. Moreover, the question of where someone was domiciled two-and-a-half years ago now has the potential to become yet another hotly litigated question — even for debtors who can barely scrape together enough money to hire a lawyer to prepare a bare-bones bankruptcy petition. The latter is a reminder that sometimes these attempts to sweep in the abusers also round up a lot of other folks as well.

5.   *Who Cares About Exemptions?*

We began the section on exemptions with the guy in the barrel, thinking about why he might get to keep his clothes. We end the chapter with a Congress not willing to prevent multimillionaires from protecting unlimited assets, if they can negotiate a carefully laid out chicane. The policy grounds for this result remain elusive.

With all the talk about gluttonous exemptions, we cannot leave without one final note. Michelle White, Professor of Economics at the University of California at San Diego, studied state exemptions and entrepreneurial start-ups. She concluded that the likelihood of a homeowner owning a business was 35 percent higher in states with unlimited homestead exemptions. Michelle White, Bankruptcy and Small Business, Regulation 18 (Summer 2001). She concluded that changing bankruptcy laws and narrowing exemptions would "discourage many entrepreneurs from going into business and some of the discouraged businesses would inevitably involve innovative new ideas that would have generated jobs and economic growth."

And what about all the creditors who, at least in theory, recover less money in the high-exemption states? Surely they are charging debtors more in those states than in the ones that will let the creditors strip the debtor almost to his skivvies. A group of economists claimed to answer the empirical question with a yes, but they compared the rates on secured car loans that aren't likely to be much affected by exemption levels. See Reint Gropp,

John Karl Scholz, and Michelle J. White, Personal Bankruptcy and Credit Supply and Demand, 112 Quarterly Journal of Economics 217-51 (February 1997). (Indeed, the fact that they report finding something of statistical significance on secured car loans leaves us scratching our heads — we don't know what is going on, but we're pretty sure it isn't the sort of rationality assumed in many law-and-econ models.)

In his dissertation at MIT, economist Fredrick Link examined the cost and availability of general unsecured credit (the debt that should have been affected by exemption levels) in states with high exemptions and those with low exemptions. He determined that the differences among the states were statistically indistinguishable. Fredrick Link, The Economics of Personal Bankruptcy (MIT June 2004). He also found that homestead exemptions were negatively correlated with homeownership, suggesting that state protection seems to yield fewer, not more, homeowners. His data make it clear that easy assumptions about how exemptions will affect incentives and market effects are likely to be wrong.

There has been a great deal of press about unlimited homestead exemptions and the unsavory characters who seem to be attracted to expensive homes. Interestingly, the stingy homestead exemptions that will cost people their homes in low- or no-exemption states has drawn little press attention. During the debates over the 2005 Amendments, Senator Russell Feingold, D-WI, proposed a floor on homestead protection for older Americans. Anyone 65 or older could protect equity in a homestead up to $125,000 in value, regardless of state exemption laws or state opt-outs. The amendment was defeated, but the issue is likely to arise again. With exemptions, it seems, the debate is never quite over.

Problem Set 9

9.1. Kevin LoVecchio has been battling with a host of angry former partners in a real estate business scheme, and it appears they are closing in. Last week they got a $10 million judgment in a contract law action against him.

Kevin, a law school grad who never wanted to settle down and practice law ("too boring"), has a gorgeous penthouse condo in Chicago, very near The Donald, and not much else ("temporary slump"). He has lived in the condo for five years, except for a period about two-and-a-half years ago when he rented an apartment in Texas for 91 days ("moved there for business, but I couldn't take the heat") and a period last year when he moved to Wisconsin for a couple of months ("thought it would be cheaper, but it really wasn't"). In both Texas and Wisconsin he applied for a drivers' license, registered to vote, and changed his address for all his magazine subscriptions. Kevin came to see you yesterday to ask that you file his petition for Chapter 7. Can he keep his condo? (Illinois permits a debtor to protect $7,500 in a homestead.) Does he face any other obvious problems?

9.2. You are a specialist in tort litigation. Caleb Wiley asks for your advice. He had a very unfortunate car accident that injured two people and completely destroyed a 1996 Jaguar. The accident occurred 19 days after his car insurance had expired. From the facts Caleb recites, you are certain he will lose any lawsuit, and the only question will be how much the plaintiffs will win.

As part of your consultation do you inquire into what property your client currently owns? Do you give a detailed explanation of the law before asking any questions?

9.3. One of your best clients, Dr. Panoply, is an ob-gyn who is known and beloved throughout your community as a fine doctor and a community leader who always has time for charities. He comes to you and says, "I have never had a malpractice claim and don't know of any that might be coming, but I've heard so many frightening things and the malpractice premiums have become so extraordinary, I think I should try an asset-protection plan, like the kind my friends have." He wants to set up a trust to hold all his investments safe from juries "who apparently don't understand that medicine is an art, not a science." What suggestions could you make to him? What sort of state remedies should he fear and how would your advice help? Are there collection remedies that might threaten him no matter what? And so on.

After you discuss things with him awhile, he says, "I have to admit it's not just the malpractice thing. I have been in this terrible dispute with Stock, Lock, and Barrel, the well-known brokerage firm, and it's in arbitration and I am afraid they may win, to the tune of a million dollars." Does this fact change your advice?

9.4. You are the new legislative aide to Virginia Bethania Herring, the ranking member of the Judiciary Committee. Two amendments to the bankruptcy laws have just been dropped in the hopper, and she asks you to give her a preliminary assessment on each.

- Drop the categories in 522(d) and simply put in a dollar amount. Debtors can protect any value up to that amount, regardless of how they hold the asset.
- Establish uniform federal exemptions that do not permit state opt-out.

What do you tell her?

E. CLAIMS AND DISTRIBUTIONS

1. The Claims Process

Once it is clear what property belongs in the debtor's estate and what property the debtor may properly exempt, the trustee begins to assemble any non-exempt property for sale. The proceeds will be distributed pro rata to the creditors. In order to give each creditor the appropriate share of the bankruptcy estate, the trustee's attention now turns from the debtor to the creditors.

Ordinarily a creditor will receive a proof of claim form (Official Form No. 10) with the notice of the bankruptcy. The form is a simple one. Its completion and filing are governed by Rules 3001-3008, Fed. R. Bankr. P.

The most notable requirement is that a claim based on a writing must have a copy of the writing attached.

In Chapter 7 and Chapter 13 cases a claim must be filed within 90 days after the first meeting of creditors, with certain exceptions. Fed. R. Bankr. P. 3002. In Chapter 11 cases, the court fixes a "bar" date before which claims must be filed. Fed. R. Bankr. P. 3003. A creditor must file a claim in Chapter 7 or 13 cases in order to receive a dividend, even if the creditor was listed on the debtor's schedules. Fed. R. Bankr. P. 3002. In Chapter 11, a creditor who is scheduled by the debtor is not required to file a proof of claim to receive payment. Fed. R. Bankr. P. 3003.

To receive any distribution, each Chapter 7 or Chapter 13 creditor must submit a proof of claim. The proof is simple, but practitioners say that some creditors inevitably fail to file in consumer cases. In Chapter 7 cases the habit of non-filing might be understandable since so few cases involve non-exempt assets and any dividend for distribution to the creditors. In Chapter 13 cases, however, where there is typically some payout for all creditors, failure to file is more surprising, but evidently still quite frequent.

A claim is allowed unless a party in interest makes an objection. §502(a). If a party objects, the dispute is resolved as a "contested matter" under Rule 9014, unless the objection also makes a demand for a type of relief that converts the matter into an adversary proceeding under Rule 7001. An example of the latter is a demand to void a preference, which we discuss later.

Later in this book we take a look at more complex claims questions, including warranties and other contingent obligations and future claims based on past wrongdoing. For now — for the average consumer case — we stick to the most recurrent issues: calculation of a claim, resolution of disputed claims, and the different treatments available for secured, unsecured, and priority claims.

2.   *Disputed Claims*

Most claims in a consumer bankruptcy are presented for payment and are paid pro rata without objection by the trustee. It is worth a moment's reflection to note the remarkable thing that has happened: A number of claims are satisfied through the court without any state or federal adjudication that the money is owed. The parties simply agree, and the trustee, representing the interests of all the creditors, ratifies the claims of each creditor. This event illustrates the efforts taken in bankruptcy to spend the available money on distribution to the creditors rather than on litigation about which creditors are entitled to collect. Parties often agree in bankruptcy when they might continue to disagree in a non-bankruptcy context. Because the distributions are often modest, many creditors find that their enthusiasm to pursue a claim is also modest. Similarly, once a debtor has filed for bankruptcy, if the claim is to be discharged anyway, the debtor may have little incentive to spend money fighting rather than settling a claim. Of course, the debtor's lack of interest is precisely why the TIB must review the claims and make the final decisions on whether to challenge them.

In some instances, a TIB may object to paying certain creditors. Most often the trustee argues that there was no valid debt under state law or that the amount of the debt was lower than claimed. These instances are rare, but the threat of their arising serves to police creditor claims and to give the trustee negotiating leverage on doubtful claims. As the following case illustrates, resolution of the claim dispute sometimes requires an evidentiary hearing, much like the trial of a lawsuit. One twist in the case is that although the trustee usually brings such an objection while acting on behalf of the estate, here the debtor brought the objection, for reasons we can safely ignore.

In re LANZA
51 B.R. 125 (Bankr. E.D. Pa. 1985)

Emil F. GOLDHABER, Judge:

The pivotal inquiry brought before the bench on the debtor's objection to a bank's proofs of claim, is whether the evidence supports a bank's entitlement to the three claims at issue, notwithstanding its apparent gross deviations from standard banking practice. After carefully weighing the evidence, we will reduce the amount of the first claim but uphold the remaining two in full. First Peoples National Bank ("the Bank") filed three proofs of claim. In support of the first proof of claim (No. 15) it appears that the debtors conveyed a mortgage on a parcel of real estate to the Bank in exchange for a construction loan with which to improve the subject property. This mortgage was executed for a denominated indebtedness of $200,000.00, although only $125,000.00 was advanced at settlement. The Bank later advanced $170,000.00 to the debtors through a series of unsecured loans, none of which, the Bank concedes, were charged against the original mortgage. Apparently, after some criticism of these advances from its auditors, the Bank convinced the debtors to grant another mortgage for $350,000.00 using the now improved property as collateral and allocating $125,000.00 of the proceeds to satisfy the original mortgage and $177,520.00 to discharge the unsecured indebtedness and interest. The mortgage was then properly filed and recorded. At the hearing the Bank presented conflicting testimony on the outstanding balance remaining on the mortgage and, weighing this discrepancy against the bank, we adopt the lowest figure presented by the Bank — namely, $300,000.00.

The second proof of claim (No. 14) is based on a demand note and a properly recorded mortgage which secures a principal debt of $24,500.00, plus interest to date, for a total sum of $40,282.60. No evidence refuting this claim was introduced and we adopt this figure.

Under the third proof of claim (No. 13) the Bank asserts an outstanding unsecured indebtedness of $27,639.62.[11] The parties are in apparent agreement that this claim accurately expresses the outstanding indebtedness and we so find.

---

11. Plaintiff's exhibit of the original demand note includes a notation that interest was paid to May 7, 1981.

Apparently finding the expansive relief of the automatic stay insufficient succor in this creditor-ridden world, the husband-debtor met his ultimate demise during the pendency of this proceeding.... Not a scintilla of first hand testimony on the transactions under scrutiny was offered. The wife-debtor professed ignorance of all her husband's financial dealings. The Bank, possibly cowering under the far graver spectre of intentional malfeasance, offered shockingly little evidence in support of loans totaling approximately one-third of a million dollars. The examples of so-called bookkeeping for a public financial institution that were presented to us as evidence could easily warrant for a half-dozen or so loan officers an other-worldly judgment[12] of perdition, forever condemning them to scramble about the floor of Pandemonium, each looking for the missing beads of his shattered abacus.

Notwithstanding her apparent ignorance, the wife-debtor, nonetheless, failed to present any evidence to undercut the Bank's moribund case. Although it is said that, "You can't take it with you," the husband-debtor apparently did take with him every financial record of "it" that he ever possessed. Not so much as a check stub supported the debtors' case.

As a preliminary point in our brief discussion, the Bankruptcy Rules state that a "proof of claim executed and filed in accordance with these rules shall constitute prima facie evidence of the validity and amount of the claim." Bankruptcy Rule 3001(f). "It follows, that the burden of going forward with the proof is on the objecting [party], not the claimant. That burden is not satisfied by the mere filing of an objection." In re Trending Cycles for Commodities, Inc., 26 B.R. 350, 351 (Bankr. S.D. Fla. 1982). All parties are in apparent agreement that monies were lent and liabilities incurred and, thereby, the principles underlying Rule 3001, and its applicability to the case before us, are bolstered. In short, as will be seen below, the Bank did not win this case; the debtors lost it.

On the first claim, the debtors argued that the lack of supporting documents and mismanagement of the file should invalidate the Bank's claim. However, as stated above, the burden of proof is not on the Bank to substantiate its claim with extensive documentation, the onus is on the debtor to overcome the presumption of validity. Although the court recognizes the wife-debtor's hardship in supplying this evidence, without guidance or her husband's records, the law is clear that with no evidence offered by the debtors to invalidate the loan or the properly recorded mortgage, the claim must be upheld. However, because of conflicting statements by the Bank's own employees on the balance of the indebtedness, we adopt the Bank's lowest figure of $300,000.00. The Bank should rightfully bear the burden of the ambiguity in light of its abysmal bookkeeping.

We found above that on the second claim the Bank has a secured indebtedness of $40,282.60 and on the third claim the Bank holds an unsecured indebtedness of $27,639.62. The facts on these claims are virtually undisputed, rendering any further analysis unnecessary.

On the debtor's objection to the Bank's three proofs of claim we will accordingly enter an order to reduce the first claim to the secured amount of

---

12. We of the bankruptcy court could enter no such final judgment, the subject matter not being a core proceeding since that power is justifiably reserved to a higher "judicial" authority.

$300,000.00, uphold the second secured claim in the sum of $40,282.60, and uphold the third claim in the unsecured amount of $27,639.62.

═══════════

This kind of detailed fact-finding and dispute resolution is routinely handled by the bankruptcy courts in a relatively short time. Courts will usually consider the papers filed by the parties and schedule an hour or two to hear evidence. A disputed claim that might drift through the state court for years may be resolved within a matter of weeks in a bankruptcy forum.

But here, as elsewhere, a changing world is putting different pressures on the bankruptcy courts. Today, the thought of a bank making a loan and keeping that loan while the debtor repays is, in some circles, charmingly quaint. Instead, many lenders package up their loans, almost as they would box up radios from an assembly line, and ship them off to investment consortia that will discount the face value of the loans and pay in cash for the future stream of income from the loans. Of course, those consortia may not hold on to the debts for long either. In the case of mortgages, for example, so-called "servicers" may collect from the customer and return the cash to an ever-changing group of investors. The difficulties arise, of course, when a customer claims that payments have not been properly recorded or charges have been added that should not have been. The scramble to find a paper record may prove as fruitless as it did in *Lanza*.

Yet another practice has complicated the claims procedures. Creditors may sell accounts after the debtor files for bankruptcy, further complicating the claims process because the paper they buy has the total amount due, but not the breakdown of the claim between principal and interest, fees, and other add-ons that are required in the bankruptcy rules. John Rao, of the National Consumer Law Center, explains:

> The [claims filing rule] has become a "hot topic" primarily because of the rapid expansion in the market for sale of charged-off debt.[13] Preferring not to deal directly with customer bankruptcies, many credit card companies and other creditors are increasingly selling their bankruptcy accounts to debt buyers for pennies on the dollar.[14]
>
> This growth of the debt buying industry has transformed the bankruptcy claims process. Driven by the economics of the assignment process, debt buyers in particular have given short shrift to the Bankruptcy Rules. Rather than attaching cardmember agreements, promissory notes and account statements to proofs of claim, and providing itemized statements of interest and additional charges,

13. In comments submitted to the Federal Trade Commission, the Debt Buyers Association reported that the amount of debt sold had grown from $1.3 billion in 1993 to $25 billion in 2000. See http://www.ftc.gov/os/comments/dncpapercomments/04/debtbuyersassociation.pdf. In 2003, out of the estimated $75 billion in total debt sold, $43 billion was charged-off credit card debt. See Debt Buyers in the Public Eye, Darren Waggoner, http://www.creditcollectionsworld. com/cgi-bin/readstory2.pl?story= 20040601CCRU262. xml.

14. For example, one debt buyer purchased $8 billion of consumer bankruptcy debt last year, paying between a fraction of a cent to 3.5 cents on the dollar for chapter 7 debt and between 6 to 12 cents on the dollar for chapter 13 debt. *See* "Firm Finds Gold in Heaps of Debt," *Puget Sound Business Journal* (Feb. 4, 2004).

debt buyers have been attaching to the claim form a one-page "Accounting Summary" that provides the debtor's name and account number and merely restates the balance owed listed in paragraph 4 on Official Form 10.[15] Proofs of claim are filed in this manner without any actual review of loan documents or account statements because the supporting documents required by Rule 3001 are not provided to debt buyers.[16]

John Rao, Debt Buyers Rewriting of Rule 3001: Taking the "Proof" Out Of The Claims Process, 23-6 ABI Journal 16 (July/August 2004). It seems that bankruptcy will remain an ever-changing system and that the judges will continue to have plenty of disputes to resolve.

3.   Unsecured Claims

a.   The Claim

The typical claim is not disputed by the trustee or the debtor. Section 501 lays out the procedure for filing the claims, and section 502 explains the mechanics of calculating a claim. All pre-petition claims, secured and unsecured, must begin with a §502 calculation. This section is the beginning point for claims against the debtor.

An example may illustrate: A debtor had a charge account with Sears. The terms were cash in full within 30 days or interest thereafter at an annual rate of 12 percent (unrealistic, but it keeps the calculations easy). Sears was also entitled under the agreement to attorneys' fees and costs of collection equal to 20 percent of the debt if it had to take any legal action to collect (a fairly standard clause in credit agreements). At the date of bankruptcy the debtor had made one charge for $1,000 and was three months late in paying, and Sears had begun collection efforts. Sears would file a proof of claim for $1,000, plus $30 interest for three months before bankruptcy (simple interest, not compounded, which is also unrealistic, but again it keeps the calculations easy). Sears would claim the $200 it spent on collection costs, for a total of $1,230. Under section 502 Sears is entitled the full amount as an allowed claim because all of the amounts are treated as having accrued before bankruptcy and therefore are pre-petition claims.

After the non-exempt assets have been sold, if there are proceeds equal to 10 percent of the total unsecured claims (10 cents on the dollar), the TIB will send Sears a check for $123. The difference between what Sears will be "allowed" — the same amount as in a nonbankruptcy lawsuit — and what it gets — a percentage of what it had coming — is the amount to be discharged at the conclusion of the case. In this case, the debtor would discharge $1107.

---

15. See In re Henry, slip. op., Bk. No. 03-25104 (Bankr. W.D. Wash. filed Apr. 14, 2004).

16. Debt buyers are given a computer disk from the selling creditor containing the account summary information used to generate the proof of claim. Documentation and other information may be provided only upon request.

b. Interest

It will probably take some time for the estate to be liquidated and Sears to get paid. If five months elapse between the bankruptcy filing and the distribution, does Sears get another $50 interest? If Sears is an unsecured creditor, the answer is no. Assuming someone objects, Sears will be denied the opportunity to collect any interest on its unsecured claim after the filing and while the bankruptcy is pending. §502(b)(2). In the terms of the statute, that would be interest that was "unmatured" on the date of bankruptcy. Admittedly, "unmatured interest" is like "unfallen rain" — a concept only a lawyer could love. Nonetheless, the phrase emphasizes that unsecured creditors get no post-petition interest, even if someone tries to claim that the interest was somehow owing before bankruptcy although "unmatured." When might someone claim unmatured interest? A loan that provided for a lump sum of interest rather than interest calculated over time would be reanalyzed by a bankruptcy court to determine the portion of interest that was mature and the portion that was unmature as of the instant of filing.

There is no doubt that the delay in distribution is costly to Sears. It loses the time value of money, and yet it can make no claim for interest after the bankruptcy is filed. The reason for this provision is based on the pro rata distribution among unsecured creditors in bankruptcy. The amount available for distribution doesn't increase, and each unsecured creditor will get the same proportion of the estate regardless of whether or not interest is granted. Some creditors will have high interest rates by contract and others will have low or no interest running. By treating all unsecured creditors the same — that is, all collect a pro rata share of whatever remains of the estate — bankruptcy reinforces the goal of equality among these unsecured creditors.

c. Accelerated Claims

The overwhelming majority of claims are obvious, undisputed obligations that the debtor incurred before filing. But because all of the debtor's obligations are about to be resolved in a single forum, once and forever, there exists a need to accelerate all pre-bankruptcy claims whether they have matured or not. This acceleration of claims has few parallels outside bankruptcy law. As a result, sometimes the claims process can involve much more difficult and esoteric questions than resolution of disputed claims or calculation of the amounts owed. A debtor who has guaranteed a loan before the bankruptcy filing, for example, has an undisputed pre-petition obligation. But the debtor may or may not have to pay, and the amount to be paid will change depending on how many payments the primary obligor made before defaulting. Figuring out how to value the guaranty claim can be difficult. Or a debtor may have engaged in some conduct that will injure another, but the injury has not yet manifested itself. Or perhaps the debtor has polluted, and both the pollution and its effects remain unknown. These valuation questions all end up in the lap of the bankruptcy judge to be sorted out.

4. Secured Claims

a.   The Claim

If Sears has a secured claim the first part of the calculation remains the same. Sears can show what it is owed pre-bankruptcy through the calculation of a section 502 claim, and the TIB can raise any contract defense. But as creditors line up for payment in a liquidation bankruptcy, initiates rapidly find that the oft-repeated maxim "equity is equality" takes on unexpected meanings. The largest differentiation among creditors is the distinction between the treatment afforded creditors with valid security interests and that given to their unsecured companions. Section 502(b) governs the permissible nature and extent of an allowed pre-petition claim, while section 506 sets forth the special post-petition and collection rights of secured creditors. An unsecured claim that is established as valid is an "allowed unsecured claim" while a valid secured claim is an "allowed secured claim" (perhaps you detect a pattern here).

Section 506(a) grants a secured creditor an allowed secured claim up to the value of its collateral. If the claim is less than or equal to the value of the collateral, then the entire claim is secured, or in the parlance of bankruptcy professionals, "fully secured." If the claim is greater than the value of the collateral, then the claim is "partially secured." The remaining portion of the initial claim continues as an unsecured claim against the estate.

The typical treatment of a secured creditor is illustrated by another purchase from Sears. The debtor bought a top-of-the-line riding lawnmower from Sears, and Sears took a security interest in it. In the first example, the debtor has made substantial payments and at the time of filing Sears is still owed $5,000 on a lawnmower that is worth $6,500. The TIB sells the lawnmower and clears $6,000, after deducting advertising expenses and other costs of sale. §506(c). Sears has an allowed secured claim under section 506(a) for $5,000, the amount of its claim against the estate, and it gets $5,000 from the proceeds of the lawnmower sale. Sears is paid in full, and the remaining $1,000 goes to the general fund for distribution to unsecured creditors.

If, however, the lawnmower had been ridden hard and wrecked a time or two, it might bring only $3,500. In that case, if the TIB sells it and clears $3,000 after expenses, then Sears will have an allowed secured claim for $3,000 with an unsecured claim for $2,000 (the difference between the section 502 claim and the allowed secured claim). In that case, Sears would get $3,000 from the distribution following the sale. The entire distribution of the sale of the lawnmower would have gone to Sears, leaving nothing for the general fund. In addition (assuming ten cents on the dollar pro rata distribution to the unsecured creditors), Sears would have received another $200 on the unsecured portion of the claim, for a total of $3,200. In effect, an undersecured creditor gets a bifurcated claim under section 506: a secured claim equal to the value of the collateral and an unsecured claim for the deficiency. This isn't nearly as good as if Sears had been fully secured and collected the full $5,000, but it isn't nearly as bad as if the claim were unsecured and Sears had collected only $500.

b. Interest

Another important difference between secured and unsecured creditors is in their entitlement to interest for the period following the filing of the bankruptcy petition. Both secured and unsecured creditors are entitled to interest accrued prior to bankruptcy, assuming that their agreements with the debtor so provided. As we have seen, however, an unsecured creditor cannot claim any interest for the period following bankruptcy. §502(b)(2). Some secured creditors, however, may be able to get post-bankruptcy interest under section 506(b). If the secured creditor is oversecured, i.e., if the value of the collateral exceeds the pre-bankruptcy debt (including pre-bankruptcy interest), then the secured creditor can receive post-bankruptcy interest at its contract rate, until the value of the collateral is exhausted.

In the two examples above, Sears could have collected interest in the first, but not in the second. Where the value of the lawnmower ($6,500) exceeded the allowed claim ($5,000), Sears would have had an allowed secured claim for $5,000 and it would have collected interest on that amount during the pending bankruptcy. The amount would have continued to grow and compound until it reached the amount that could be realized from the sale of the collateral, which means that in our example Sears could have collected up to another $1,000. If the bankruptcy dragged on after that point, it would have collected no more interest. In the second example in which the claim exceeded the value of the collateral, Sears could not have collected any interest.

c. Attorneys' Fees

Attorneys' fees incurred prior to the filing of the bankruptcy petition are treated the same as pre-petition interest: If a creditor, secured or unsecured, is entitled to pre-petition attorneys' fees by contract or state law, then the fees are part of the creditor's secured or unsecured claim. However, the situation as to post-petition attorneys' fees is less clear.

Secured creditors who are oversecured are clearly entitled to post-petition attorneys' fees, until the total claim exceeds the remaining value of the collateral. §506(b). In our view, unsecured creditors should not be able to claim post-petition attorneys' fees, just as they cannot claim post-petition interest, because section 502(b) is limited to pre-petition claims, while section 503, which governs post-petition claims, permits post-petition attorneys' fees only under special circumstances. This conclusion is supported by section 506(b), which grants post-petition fees to oversecured creditors, thus showing that Congress knows how to grant post-petition fees when it so desires. Notwithstanding what we believe to be a fairly clear statement in the Code, the case law is somewhat more confused. The Second Circuit in In re United Merchants and Manufacturers, 674 F.2d 134 (2d Cir. 1982) granted post-petition fees and costs to an unsecured creditor in a case decided under the old Act but with language that strongly suggests that the results would be the same under the Code. The result in *United Merchants* is supported by the absence of a prohibition of post-petition attorneys' fees in section 502(b).

Because post-petition interest is expressly prohibited by section 502(b)(2), the lack of a similar provision barring post-petition attorneys' fees suggests that they may be claimed by unsecured creditors under section 502. We would respond that the reason for the prohibition in section 502(b)(2) is that unmatured interest is often claimed outside of bankruptcy, while no one has yet asserted a right to unmatured (i.e., unearned) attorneys' fees, so Congress would not have thought to prohibit them specifically.

Other courts, such as the Third Circuit in Adams v. Zimmerman, 73 F.3d 1164 (3d Cir. 1996) explicitly reject the result in *United Merchants*, summarizing the law:

> Pre-petition attorneys' fees of unsecured creditors against an insolvent debtor are generally allowed under the bankruptcy code to the extent the applicable state law so provides, and post-petition attorneys' fees are generally not allowed [citations omitted]. Plaintiffs are entitled to attorneys' fees that had accrued as of the date of the insolvency but are not entitled to attorneys' fees following the insolvency.

We are told by our friends in the bar that attorneys routinely claim post-petition fees, then wait to see if trustees object — which they nearly always do. Sometimes the dance among the repeat players in bankruptcy takes on the stylized elements of kabuki theater, but without the cool costumes.

d. Exemptions

Finally, it is worth repeating that valid, unavoidable consensual security interests trump exemption claims, so that a debtor may claim only an exemption in the "equity," the value remaining after the secured creditor has been paid in full.

5. *Post-petition Claims*

Before leaving this example, we can anticipate a distinction that will be important in the next section. Suppose the TIB had decided to repaint some of the debtor's non-exempt furniture before selling it (in order to get a better price) and bought the paint at Sears on credit. Sears would have a claim, but it would be a post-petition claim and therefore made under section 503 — "expenses of administration" — not section 502. Ordinarily Sears would be paid in full on its section 503 claims because these are administrative claims with a first priority in payment. §507(a)(1)-(2). We will explore priority claims in the next section when we discuss distribution.

Problem Set 10

10.1. Corinne Zeppo lost her job last month and filed a Chapter 7 liquidation bankruptcy this month. One creditor, Miller Plumbing Co., claimed

$3,000, plus (a) $200 in past-due interest accrued prior to bankruptcy; and (b) another $100 in interest accrued since the bankruptcy began. Interest was calculated for the pre-bankruptcy period according to the contract between Zeppo and Miller Plumbing and according to the state law judgment rate for the post-bankruptcy period. Miller Plumbing, however, has no security interest in any of Corinne's property. What is the amount of Miller's allowed unsecured claim in bankruptcy? See §502 (a), (b).

10.2. Corinne had only two non-exempt assets: her car, worth $10,000, and 1,000 shares of MicroSoft stock, worth $15,000. At the time of filing, she owed the bank $8,000 on the car and the bank had a valid and enforceable security interest in the car to secure its loan. In addition to the $8,000 principal, the bank claimed (a) past-due interest that accrued prior to bankruptcy of $500, (b) interest since the bankruptcy was filed of $400, and (c) attorneys' fees of $1,000 expended in trying to collect. The bank was entitled to collect all these amounts under its loan and security agreement and under state law. What is the amount of the bank's allowed secured claim in bankruptcy? §§502(b); 506(a), (b).

10.3. If, contrary to the pre-sale estimates, the car had brought only $5,000 when it was sold, how would the bank stand? See §§502(b); 506 (a),(b).

10.4. Ten other creditors of Corinne are owed a total of $20,000, but none of them are claiming any interest. If you were appointed TIB in Corinne's bankruptcy and collected $5,000 for the car and $15,000 for the stock, how should you distribute the money (ignoring other expenses, including your own cut as TIB)?

6. *Priority Among Unsecured Creditors*

After the secured creditors have been satisfied by the sale of their collateral, the unsecured creditors begin the process of dividing the remaining assets. The undersecured creditors, to the extent that the sale of the collateral did not satisfy their allowed secured claims, also join in this process.

Section 507 determines the order and amount of the payout to unsecured creditors. The unsecured creditors again find that "equity is equality" is not strictly the rule.

Problem Set 11

Harold Smith declared Chapter 7 bankruptcy in March 2005. His non-exempt assets consisted of his condo in Kitty Hawk, which the TIB sold for $400,000 but which was subject to a $365,000 mortgage, and miscellaneous personal property that sold for $25,000. All his other property was exempt. The claims filed in bankruptcy court were the following:

1. John Harry, a private duty nurse whom Harold hired while his father was quite ill: $11,000
2. Social Security Administration, Social Security and withholding from Harry's earlier pay checks: $534

3.   City of Eden, property taxes: $3,000 per year for the last three years, plus $500 per year penalties for each of the three years
4.   George Nartowski, down payment against a tractor lawnmower Harold had agreed to sell to George: $300
5.   State Department of Revenue and IRS, income taxes: state $4,000, federal $14,000
6.   Telephone, utility, and other regular bills following bankruptcy: $5,000
7.   Sara Fleet, Harold's attorney: $1,250 in fees ($500 for a will; $750 for preparing this bankruptcy filing)
8.   Suzan Smith, Harold's ex-wife, negotiable note: $25,000
9.   TIB as trustee and as trustee's counsel: $4,000
10. Insurance premiums for insurance on the non-exempt personal property prior to its sale by the TIB: $750
11. Costs of sale of Harold's non-exempt real estate and personal property, including advertising: $2,800
12. Other unsecured, general claims: $17,000

Who will get what under sections 507 and 726(a)(4), (b)?

F.   DISCHARGE

1.   Exceptions to Discharge

From an individual debtor's perspective, the purpose of a liquidation bankruptcy is almost always to discharge outstanding debt. Once the creditors' claims have been paid, the debtor anticipates discharge from all remaining debt. In those courts that still require the debtor to attend, the discharge hearing is the second (and final) time the debtor will come to the courthouse. This time the debtor will appear before the judge, who will review the bankruptcy file, sign the papers declaring the debtor discharged from all listed debts, and close the case. Such hearings are usually mass affairs, with the judge making a few remarks to dozens of debtors gathered for the occasion. Nearly all courts now dispense with the hearing, instead mailing the discharge papers to the debtor on the theory that requiring a struggling debtor to lose a day's pay to attend a discharge ceremony is wasteful.

The debtor is not entitled to the discharge as a matter of right, but the discharge will be granted unless it is challenged by the trustee or a creditor. The trustee or creditors may object to the debtor's discharge of particular debts under section 523 or of all debts under section 727. It is important to remember the distinction between a section 523 denial of discharge and one made under section 727. The former renders only one debt nondischargeable (a "rifle shot"), while a denial of discharge under section 727 renders all of the debts nondischargeable (a "global" denial). Global denial of discharge leaves a debtor who has turned assets over to the trustee for sale and distribution with no relief from debt other than the actual payments made. Even a rifle shot denial leaves the debtor without complete relief and, if the debt was substantial, it may leave the debtor in almost as bad shape as before. For a creditor, of course, prevention of a discharge is usually the creditor's last remaining hope to receive any payment on the debt. As a result, when the grounds for denial of discharge arise they are more often hotly disputed than are other points of potential conflict in consumer bankruptcies.

The list of nondischargeable debts or the events for which a debtor can be denied any discharge at all continues to grow. In some cases the growth comes in response to unanticipated abuses that Congress wants to stop. In other cases, special interest groups have lobbied for an exception to the bankruptcy discharge. The categories of nondischargeable debts now number 19, a variety that now includes debts obtained by lying on a credit application, debts for luxury goods worth more than $500 obtained within 90 days of bankruptcy, fraud by a fiduciary, alimony and child support, and judgments resulting from drunk driving (or drunk boating) accidents. The grounds for total denial now number 11, starting with the declaration that corporations do not receive discharges in Chapter 7 and continuing with denials of any discharge for debtors who have lied or filed false documents in connection with the bankruptcy case or failed to complete a personal finance course. The following cases reflect a sampling of the grounds for denial of discharge and a flavor of the courts' analyses.

First, a case involving a global challenge to the discharge.

In re ROBERT W. McNAMARA, DEBTOR

310 B.R. 664 (Bankr. D. Conn. 2004)

Alan H. W. SHIFF, Bankruptcy Judge.

* * *

BACKGROUND

The debtor was the only witness at the trial. He testified that he had $150,000 in a briefcase as a result of numerous withdrawals from bank accounts during the summer of 1998 and that immediately after he was ordered to deposit the money in an escrow account, he gambled $130,000 in a winner-take-all stud poker game at a private residence in Brooklyn, New York. He was not able to provide any further details about the poker game except that someone, who no longer lives in the country, drove him there. In an effort to explain his failure to remember details, the debtor claimed that he was under the influence of alcohol and medication for severe depression. He further stated that he had just lost his job and had been taken to a hospital in New York with what he initially thought was a second heart attack. He did not, however, produce any evidence to corroborate that claim, such as medical or hospital records or the testimony of anyone who witnessed his condition. The debtor testified that he reserved enough money to pay for a Caribbean vacation, which was supported by receipts from that trip. He denied that he deposited any money into offshore bank accounts.

Apart from his difficulty to recall the details of the poker game, the debtor's credibility was also challenged by an unlikely difficulty recalling the details of significant bank account deposits and withdrawals prior to and concurrent with the alleged gambling losses. For example, he was unable to remember the source of an October 14, 1998 deposit of $44,247.87. He speculated that it was either from life insurance policies, despite testimony that other deposits were from those policies, or from his salary, even though it was a single large deposit, and he claims to have lost his job more than a month earlier. The debtor was also unable to credibly testify how he spent over $200,000 between June 1998 through February 1999. For example, he claimed that he spent a part of that money on renovations to his former marital residence, but the trustee reminded him that the property was sold in May 1998.

The evidence justified the trustee's suspicion that the debtor's claimed gambling loss in a fictional attempt to hide money that he considered to be his and not subject to his former wife's claims. He testified that he had an agreement with her that they would separate for five years rather than get divorced, so that he could maintain his health insurance through her employment. That issue was prompted by the debtor's claim that he was told he would require a heart transplant in the future. In return for her agreement, he claims to have agreed to give her custody of the children and repair the marital residence. The debtor testified that after she repudiated the agreement, he believed he was entitled to the $150,000:

> I told her that if that was the case, that if she would not change her mind and go along with the agreement, that I would be forced to sell the house, take the $150,000 that I felt was mine....

> . . .

> I told her that I would take my monies — if she would not go along [with his plan to set up a trust]..., that I would be forced to sell the home, take the $150,000 that I felt ... was my part....

(Tr. of 11/8/00 at 56).

> I had taken my 150 that I thought was mine.

(Tr. of 11/8/00 at 60).

DISCUSSION
11 U.S.C. §727(a)(5)

11 U.S.C. §727(a)(5) provides that the debtor shall be granted a discharge unless "the debtor has failed to explain satisfactorily, before determination of denial of discharge under this paragraph, any loss of assets or deficiency of assets to meet the debtor's liabilities."

The plaintiff has the burden of introducing evidence of the disappearance of assets or of unusual transactions. The burden then shifts to the defendant to satisfactorily explain the loss or deficiency of assets. The test under this subsection relates to the credibility of the proffered explanation, not the propriety of the disposition. An explanation is not satisfactory if it is not offered in good faith or if it is vague, indefinite and uncorroborated. In re Maletta, 159 B.R. 108, 116 (Bankr.D.Conn.1993) (citations omitted).

The standard of proof is a preponderance of the evidence. Id. at 111.

The trustee satisfied her burden by her effective cross-examination of the debtor, which demonstrated that he could not recall any details to support his claim that he lost $130,000 in a winner-take-all stud poker game. A person who loses $130,000 in a poker game would be expected to have some recollection of the details of the event which could be corroborated, or at least a credible explanation for why he did not.

For the same reasons that the trustee has satisfied her burden of proof, the debtor has not. Although the debtor attempted to excuse his inability to recall any details on the claim that he was suffering from depression, he did not provide a scintilla of evidence to support that claim, such as a medical report or a witness testifying that he was in poor health. Apparently, his alleged condition did not interfere with his decision to reserve at least $11,000 for a Caribbean vacation, which supports the trustee's suspicion that he deposited money in offshore banks. The fact that the debtor withdrew the money over a period of months further supports the conclusion that he was formulating a plan to hide it from his wife.

* * *

11 U.S.C. §727(a)(2)(A) provides in relevant part:

The court shall grant the debtor a discharge, unless —

. . .

(2) the debtor, with intent to hinder, delay, or defraud a creditor or an officer of the estate charged with custody of property under this title, has transferred, removed, destroyed, mutilated, or concealed, or has permitted to be transferred, removed, destroyed, mutilated, or concealed — (A) property of the debtor, within one year before the date of the filing of the petition. . . .

A plaintiff under §727(a)(2)(A) must demonstrate that the act in question "occurred within one year prior to the commencement of the case; was performed with the actual intent to defraud a creditor or officer of the estate; was the act of the debtor or an agent of the debtor; and involved concealing, destroying, transferring, or removing any property of the debtor or permitting any of these acts to be done." Maletta, 159 B.R. at 115-16.

The debtor's schedules listed his former wife as a creditor, with a debt that is nearly all of his total liabilities. The parties agree that the alleged gambling occurred within one year of the bankruptcy filing.

[T]he debtor's testimony demonstrated he was angered by his former wife for breaking an alleged agreement not to divorce him, and he believed he was entitled to the $150,000. So, he took money he had been ordered to turn over to a state court escrow fund . . . and lost it in a poker game.

In the best light, it was his intention to take a chance on either increasing the money, which would enable him to satisfy the court order and still keep the original amount, or lose it all. He cavalierly explained that his plan "didn't work out":

> [A friend] told me about this gambling situation. I went to try to double the money so that I would have money for my medical and pay them off [his former wife and/or the court ordered escrow] before the 25th. It didn't work out. I lost. I then went on that vacation for ten grand or whatever it was.

(Tr. of 11/8/00 at 78). The debtor's testimony demonstrated he did not care that he lost the money because he believed it was his to lose and that his wife had no right to it.

Bankruptcy is a privilege, not a right.

* * *

For the foregoing reasons, IT IS ORDERED that the debtor's discharge is denied under 11 U.S.C. §727(a)(2)(A) & (5).

As with the cases discussed earlier in the homestead section 196-206, these discharge cases involve a great deal of judgment and discretion. In a case in Texas involving an elderly couple, the court in a thoughtful opinion accepted their explanation for the disappearance of large amounts of cash on the basis that South Texas ranchers often carry around a lot of cash to hire day laborers for work on the land. The fact that the debtors had disclosed everything was a major factor in the decision. In re Lee, 309 B.R. 468 (Bankr. W.D. Tex. 2004). In the opinion the court quoted a famous test to be applied to the phrase "explain satisfactorily" in section 727(a)(5):

> The word "satisfactorily"...may mean reasonable, or it may mean that the court, after having heard the excuse, the explanation, has that mental attitude which finds contentment in saying that he believes the explanation — he believes what the bankrupts say with reference to the disappearance or shortage. He is satisfied. He no longer wonders. He is contented.

In re Shapiro & Ornish, 37 F.2d 403, 406 (N.D.Tex.1929).

Very different from a global denial is denial of discharge of just one debt. For certain kinds of rifle-shot denial under section 523(a), the creditor must object to discharge in bankruptcy court or the debt will be discharged automatically. §523(c).

In re DORSEY

120 B.R. 592 (Bankr. M.D. Fla. 1990)

Alexander L. PASKAY, Chief United States Bankruptcy Judge.

This is a Chapter 7 case and the matter under consideration is the dischargeability vel non of a debt admittedly due and owing by Dixie Lee Dorsey

(Debtor) to American Express Travel Related Services, Inc. (American Express). * * *

The Debtor is a widow and has two minor daughters. According to the Schedule of Current Income and Expenditures, she had no income during the relevant time period other than $480 per month received from Social Security. The fact of the matter is that the Debtor has not been gainfully employed since 1978 when she worked as a nurse's aid[e].

It appears that during the past four years the Debtor became involved with a gentleman known only as "Jimmy Jones," which she later learned turned out to be a fictitious name. According to the Debtor, Jimmy Jones supplemented her income by paying her bills and giving her between $2,500 and $6,000 per month as spending money. * * *

The Schedules filed by the Debtor reveal that over the years the Debtor obtained seven American Express credit cards beginning with what is referred to as a personal card, i.e. the green card, a gold card, each with a credit limit, and an Optima card, which apparently has no credit limit at all. Not being satisfied that the credit extended to her through these cards would be sufficient to meet her need for credit, she also collected various other credit cards, which resulted in, according to her schedules, unsecured debts totaling $106,922.39.

It appears that the Debtor, at the suggestion of her mysterious boyfriend, Jimmy Jones, embarked on an extensive overseas journey with her children visiting every country in West Central Europe, including a side trip to the Greek Islands. The cost of this trip was charged by her on a program established by American Express referred to as "Travel & Sign." It appears that under this program, a cardholder is not required to pay the entire balance of the invoice submitted but is permitted to make only minimum monthly payments. Needless to say, incidental expenses, including purchases, on this trip were charged against her American Express credit cards. These charges included, among other things, perfume purchased in Paris for $784.21. In an attempt to explain this purchase she explained that she always liked to smell good. The purchase of this item, no doubt, triggered a not-too-well smelling sour note in the not very sensitive nostrils of American Express credit card department when it received notice of the filing of the Chapter 7 Petition by this Debtor.

* * *

At the time relevant, the Debtor resided in a mobile home in Winter Haven which, according to the Debtor, was burglarized while she was in Europe. * * *

In defense of these undisputed facts, the Debtor claims that she incurred the American Express charges in good faith believing that Jimmy Jones would continue to furnish the funds necessary to meet these obligations. * * *

This Court would be amiss not to make some initial remarks concerning this very unusual case. It is absolutely appalling to this Court and it is difficult, if not impossible, to comprehend how a responsible business enterprise like American Express would grant seven credit cards to a widow with two minor children who had no gainful employment since 1978 and whose sole regular income was, and still is, the munificent sum of $480 per month from Social Security. In defense of this astounding practice, the representative of American Express stated that as long as the cardholder meets the payment obligations, regardless of how many, they have no problem and do not care. This explanation obviously only begs the question and never furnishes a satisfactory answer to the question, why on earth American Express issued initially seven credit cards to a person like this Debtor or any other person in a similar financial situation. Card issuers, including American Express, should not be surprised that from time to time individuals who are bombarded with unsolicited credit cards decide that so long as they have the card, they can use them and go on a charging spree without giving any thought to the fact that one day they will be called upon to repay the charges incurred.

The Court of Appeals of this Circuit had the occasion to consider the claim of nondischargeability based on misuse of credit cards in the case of First National Bank of Mobile v. Roddenberry, 701 F.2d 927 (11th Cir. 1983). This Court is not unmindful of the comments by Judge Hill, speaking for the Court, where it was stated that: "the element of risk is inherent in the issuance of bank credit cards. Our 'credit-card economy' encourages widespread voluntary risk-taking on the part of those issuing cards. Once credit cards are issued (if not fraudulently obtained), the bank has agreed to trust the cardholder and to extend credit, and once credit is extended, the bank must decide when and if credit will be revoked. It is not the function of courts to determine when a bank ought to revoke credit. It also is of little consequence that the bank can show that the terms and conditions said to apply to use of the card have been violated. The mere breach of credit conditions is of minimum probative value on the issue of fraud because banks often encourage or willingly suffer credit extensions beyond contractual credit limits. Indeed, banks have a definite interest in permitting charges beyond established credit limits because of the high finance charges typical in such transactions. In re Talbot, 16 B.R. 50, 52 (Bkrtcy. M.D. La. 1981). Banks are willing to risk non-payment of debts because that risk is factored into the finance charges." Notwithstanding these comments, while this Court agrees that merely exceeding the credit limit would not by itself be sufficient to form the basis of a claim of nondischargeability, fraudulent use of credit cards is another matter. Thus, if it is shown that at the time the Debtor incurred the charges he or she knew that they would be unable to live up to the obligation and pay the charges, or if it appears that they had no intention to pay the charges when the charges were incurred, that would clearly be an actual fraud thus rendering the debt incurred by using the credit card nondischargeable under Section 523(a)(2)(A)....

If the Guinness Book of World Records would include the misuse of credit as a category of records in its publication, this Debtor certainly would have a fighting chance to get the first prize considering what happened in this instance. As indicated earlier, she is a widow with no income of any consequence on which she is to support two minor children, whereby using seven credit cards from American Express [and] from others, i.e. Visa and Mastercharge, she incurred unsecured debt in excess of $106,000. There is hardly any doubt that this Debtor was fully aware that she could never meet these obligations on her income even if she lived to be 100 years old, and her reliance on the continuing generosity of her mysterious boyfriend was unrealistic and unjustified to say the least. Although this relationship lasted four years, she claims they never lived together during those four years and she was not able to find out his real identity, she has no idea where he lives, and she certainly had no basis to believe that his generosity would continue forever.

Thus, it should be evident that this is not merely a claim of nondischargeability based on misuse of a credit card by exceeding the credit limits unlike the fact pattern in *Roddenberry*, supra, but involves obtaining money by actual fraud when she had no intention to pay these charges. The fact of the matter is, when questioned about her European trip, she stated, with some pride, that she had a grand time on her trip and enjoyed every minute of it.

Based on the foregoing, it is clear that whether the burden of proof required to prove a claim of nondischargeability is clear and convincing or merely preponderance of the evidence, American Express did establish with the requisite degree of proof that the outstanding balances of Account No. 1 and Account No. 2 should be excepted from the overall protection of the general bankruptcy discharge by virtue of Section 523(a)(2)(A). * * *

A separate final judgment shall be entered in accordance with the foregoing.

One particular debt that has been singled out for special protection against discharge in bankruptcy is the student loan. While most people think of soon-to-be-rich doctors and lawyers waltzing into bankruptcy to discharge the debts they incurred through college and professional school, many people are struggling with loans incurred to learn to acquire skills that do not pay nearly so well.

In re GERHARDT

348 F.3d 89 (5th Cir. 2003)

Edith H. JONES, Circuit Judge:

Over a period of years, Jonathon Gerhardt obtained over $77,000 in government-insured student loans to finance his education at the University of Southern California, the Eastman School of Music, the University of Rochester, and the New England Conservatory of Music. Gerhardt is a professional cellist. He subsequently defaulted on each loan owed to the United States Government.

In 1999, Gerhardt filed for Chapter 7 bankruptcy and thereafter filed an adversary proceeding seeking discharge of his student loans pursuant to 11 U.S.C. §523(a)(8). The bankruptcy court discharged Gerhardt's student loans as causing undue hardship. On appeal, the district court reversed, holding that it would not be an undue hardship for Gerhardt to repay his student loans. Finding no error, we affirm the district court's judgment. * * *

I.   Undue Hardship Test

This circuit has not explicitly articulated the appropriate test with which to evaluate the undue hardship determination. The Second Circuit in Brunner crafted the most widely-adopted test. To justify discharging the debtor's student loans, the *Brunner* test requires a three-part showing:

> (1) that the debtor cannot maintain, based on current income and expenses, a "minimal" standard of living for [himself] and [his] dependents if forced to repay the loans; (2) that additional circumstances exist indicating that this state of affairs is likely to persist for a significant portion of the repayment period of the student loans; and (3) that the debtor has made good faith efforts to repay the loans. *Brunner*, 831 F.2d at 396.

Because the Second Circuit presented a workable approach to evaluating the "undue hardship" determination, this court expressly adopts the Brunner test for purposes of evaluating a Section 523(a)(8) decision.

A.   Minimal Standard of Living

Under the first prong of the *Brunner* test, the bankruptcy court determined that Gerhardt could not maintain a minimal standard of living if forced to repay his student loans. Evidence was produced at trial that Gerhardt earned $1,680.47 per month as the principal cellist for the Louisiana Philharmonic Orchestra ("LPO"), including a small amount of supplemental income earned as a cello teacher for Tulane University. His monthly expenses, which included a health club membership and internet access, averaged $1,829.39. The bankruptcy court's factual findings are not clearly erroneous. Consequently, we agree with the bankruptcy court's conclusion of law, which we review de novo, that flows from these factual findings. Given that Gerhardt's monthly expenses exceed his monthly income, he has no ability at the present time to maintain a minimal standard of living if forced to repay his loans.

B.   Persisting State of Affairs

The second prong of the *Brunner* test asks if "additional circumstances exist indicating that this state of affairs is likely to persist [for a significant period of time]." *Brunner*, 831 F.2d at 396. ***

Under the second prong of the test, the district court correctly concluded that Gerhardt has not established persistent undue hardship entitling him to discharge his student loans. Gerhardt holds a masters degree in music from the New England Conservatory of Music. He is about 43 years old, healthy, well-educated, and has no dependents, yet has repaid only $755 of his over $77,000 debt. During the LPO's off-seasons, Gerhardt has collected unemployment, but he has somehow managed to attend the Colorado Music Festival. Although trial testimony tended to show that Gerhardt would likely not obtain a position at a higher-paying orchestra, he could obtain additional steady employment in a number of different arenas.

For instance, he could attempt to teach full-time, obtain night-school teaching jobs, or even work as a music store clerk.[17] Thus, no reasons out of Gerhardt's control exist that perpetuate his inability to repay his student loans.

In addition, nothing in the Bankruptcy Code suggests that a debtor may choose to work only in the field in which he was trained, obtain a low-paying job, and then claim that it would be an undue hardship to repay his student loans. Under the facts presented by Gerhardt, it is difficult to imagine a professional orchestra musician who would not qualify for an undue hardship discharge. Accordingly, Gerhardt "has failed to demonstrate the type of exceptional circumstances that are necessary in order to meet [his] burden under the second prong" of Brunner. Finding no error, the judgment of the district court is AFFIRMED.

―――――

The Bankruptcy Court judge saw the case differently, noting that Mr. Gerhardt's full-time job with the Louisiana Symphony Orchestra netted $14,609 — his best year in five years. At the time he filed, Mr. Gerhardt was 43 years old, and he lived in a 600-square-foot apartment, drove a six-year-old car, had no retirement plan and no savings. His mother owned his cello. The recovery arm of the student educational loan group that opposed his discharge was demanding more than $1,000 of his monthly $1,200 pay.

The following case reviews the legal standards applied by the courts to determine dischargeability, but permits a remedy not found in section 523.

===== In re PATRICIA M. MILLER, DEBTOR =====
377 F.3d 616 (6th Cir. 2004).

OPINION

GIBBONS, Circuit Judge.

Miller received a Bachelor of Arts degree from Juniata College in 1988, a Masters of Arts in Philosophy from the University of Tennessee-Knoxville ("UT") in 1992, and worked towards a Doctorate of Philosophy at UT from 1992 to 1997. She failed to complete the requirements for the doctoral degree. To pay for her education, Miller received various student loans that are presently guaranteed by the Pennsylvania Higher Education Assistance Agency ("PHEAA"). After leaving UT, she requested and received forbearances and deferments on her student loans.

On May 30, 2001, Miller filed a Chapter 7 bankruptcy petition. Shortly thereafter, she filed an adversary action in the United States Bankruptcy Court for the Eastern District of Tennessee against PHEAA seeking discharge of all of her outstanding student loan debt, which totaled $89,832.16, as of April 26, 2002. At the time that she filed the adversary action, Miller had

17. This is not meant to be an exhaustive list of possible employment opportunities for Gerhardt, but instead merely seeks to illustrate other viable avenues for income.

made payments of only $368.00 towards her student loans, an amount that represented less than half of one percent of her student loan obligations. Miller described her monthly expenses as follows:

rent	$395.00;
utility payments	$75.00;
cable television:	$45.00;
telephone charges:	$90.00;
cell phone expenses:	$40.00;
internet service expenses:	$25.00;
food:	$275.00;
clothes:	$75.00;
laundry:	$30.00;
prescriptions, herbs, medical expenses:	$65.00;
magazines/books:	$15.00;
transportation (not including auto payments or repair work)	$110.00;
auto payment with insurance:	$250.00;
auto repairs and maintenance:	$100.00;
and other expenses:	$115.10.

Miller is single and has no dependents. As of 2001, her gross annual income was $26,464.00. In that same year, she received a gift of $3,000.00 from a friend and a $300.00 adjustment from the Internal Revenue Service. At the time of her adversary action, Miller was employed full-time as an administrative assistant at a construction company and part-time as a call center representative.

The bankruptcy court held a trial on April 30, 2002. The court found that all of Miller's student loan debts were not dischargeable pursuant to 11 U.S.C. §523(a)(8) because the full amount of the debts did not impose an undue hardship upon her. Notwithstanding this finding, the bankruptcy court granted Miller a partial discharge of her student loan indebtedness. The court decided that Miller's nondischargeable student loan obligation was $34,200.00 and accordingly dismissed the balance of her student loans, an amount of approximately $55,000.00. PHEAA appealed the judgment of the bankruptcy court to the United States District Court for the Eastern District of Tennessee. Miller cross-appealed. The district court adopted the opinion of the bankruptcy court and dismissed the appeals of both parties. PHEAA then filed a timely notice of appeal of the district court's decision.

II.

A discharge in Chapter 7 bankruptcy does not discharge an individual debtor's student loan obligations "unless excepting such debt from discharge . . . will impose an undue hardship on the debtor and the debtor's dependents." 11 U.S.C. §523(a)(8). In this case, the bankruptcy court found that Miller had not made a showing of undue hardship. Nevertheless, the court relied on 11 U.S.C. §105(a), which provides that a court "may issue any order, process, or judgment that is necessary or appropriate to carry out the provisions of this title," to grant Miller a partial discharge of her student loan obligations.

PHEAA argues that a showing of undue hardship — as provided by §523(a)(8) — is the only means by which a court can discharge student loan indebtedness. According to PHEAA, since Miller has not made a showing of undue hardship, none of her educational loan debt is dischargeable. The central issues of this appeal are, therefore, whether a bankruptcy court can rely on §105(a) to grant a partial discharge of student loan indebtedness and whether, before a bankruptcy court grants such a discharge, it must first find that the portion being discharged satisfies the "undue hardship" requirement of 11 U.S.C. §523(a)(8). ***

Although the bankruptcy court found that Miller was not entitled to a complete discharge of her educational loans, the court utilized its §105(a) powers to partially discharge her student loans. This court has sanctioned such a procedure. See Hornsby v. Tenn. Student Assistance Corp. (In re Hornsby), 144 F.3d 433, 439–40 (6th Cir.1998). In Hornsby, we disagreed with the bankruptcy court's finding that Chapter 7 debtors had shown that repayment of the entire balance of their student loans would impose an undue hardship upon them. While we concluded that the debtors were not entitled to a full discharge of their student loans pursuant to §523(a)(8), we found that §105(a) empowered the bankruptcy court "to take action short of total discharge." Id. at 438-39. As will be explained below, we view Hornsby as authorizing the grant of a partial discharge of a debtor's student loans but only when certain requirements are met.

Our holding in *Hornsby* was that, "pursuant to its powers codified in §105(a), the bankruptcy court…may fashion a remedy allowing the Hornsbys ultimately to satisfy their obligations to [their loan guarantor] while at the same time providing them some of the benefits that bankruptcy brings in the form of relief from oppressive financial circumstances." Id. at 440. ***

Hornsby also explained the need for taking action short of full discharge of a debtor's student loans in this way: "In a student-loan discharge case where undue hardship does not exist, but where facts and circumstances require intervention in the financial burden on the debtor, an all-or-nothing treatment thwarts the purpose of the Bankruptcy Act." Id. at 439.

We construe the language of these passages as providing guidance to bankruptcy courts in circumstances where granting a full discharge of student loan indebtedness is unwarranted because the debtor cannot show that excepting the entire balance of her student loans from discharge would impose undue hardship but where some form of relief seemed warranted — the precise factual conclusion reached about the Hornsbys. Therefore, when a debtor does not make a showing of undue hardship with respect to the entirety of her student loans, a bankruptcy court may — pursuant to its §105(a) powers — contemplate granting the various forms of relief discussed in *Hornsby*, including granting a partial discharge of the debtor's student loans. ***

The limiting condition placed on this discussion — "[w]here a debtor's circumstances do not constitute undue hardship as to part of the debt but repayment of the entire debt would be an undue hardship" — supports the notion that bankruptcy courts discharge the portion of student loan debt for which payment would impose an undue hardship on the debtor. For example, assume that a debtor owes $100,000 in student loans, and repayment of the full amount would impose undue hardship on the debtor but repayment of $40,000 would not. *Hornsby* indicates that a bankruptcy court would discharge $60,000 of the debt, the amount for which repayment would impose an undue hardship. The citations quoted by *Hornsby* also support the conclusion that undue hardship must be shown for the discharged amount. * * *

We acknowledge that this understanding of *Hornsby* is at odds with the unpublished opinion of this court in DeMatteis v. Case Western Reserve University, a decision that we are not bound to follow. The court in *DeMatteis* rejected the conclusion of the bankruptcy appellate panel in that case that, in the context of discharging student loans, §105(a) acts as an "overlay on" on §523(a)(8). Rather, the *DeMatteis* court reasoned that *Hornsby* should be read as advocating an "independent §105 equitable grounds theory."

This determination in *DeMatteis* suggests that the grant of a partial discharge of student loan indebtedness pursuant to §105(a) need not be made upon a showing of undue hardship with regard to the amount discharged. We cannot accept this conclusion. * * *

While the undue hardship requirement applies to any discharge of student loan indebtedness, the bankruptcy code itself does not define "undue hardship." As a result, this court has looked to the test enunciated by the Second Circuit in Brunner v. New York State Higher Education Services Corp., 831 F.2d 395 (2d Cir.1987), to decide if a debtor has made the requisite showing of undue hardship. * * *

This court, however, has not formally adopted the Brunner test and may look to other factors, including "the amount of the debt ... [and] the rate at which interest is accruing" as well as "the debtor's claimed expenses and current standard of living, with a view toward ascertaining whether the debtor has attempted to minimize the expenses of himself and his dependents." *Hornsby*, 144 F.3d at 437 (quoting *Rice*, 78 F.3d at 1149) (first alteration in original). In addition, "the debtor's income, earning ability, health, educational background, dependents, age, accumulated wealth, and professional degree" may also be considered. *Rice*, 78 F.3d at 1149. Finally, a court may inquire into "whether the debtor has attempted to maximize his income by seeking or obtaining stable employment commensurate with his educational background and abilities." Id. at 1149–50.

In considering whether to discharge Miller's student loans, the bankruptcy court first analyzed whether Miller had shown by a preponderance of the evidence that she satisfied all three *Brunner* factors. The court found that Miller did not satisfy the second and third factors of the *Brunner* test. According to the bankruptcy court, Miller did not show that her financial situation was more than temporary because she is intelligent and well-spoken, albeit underemployed. The court also concluded that Miller had not satisfied *Brunner*'s good faith prong because in the five years since she had left school, she had contributed only $368.00 towards repayment of her student loans, which totaled almost $90,000, while using such "non-essentials" as personal internet service, long distance telephone service, cell phone service, and cable television.

Despite not meeting the *Brunner* factors for undue hardship, the court relied on its "§105(a) powers" to partially discharge her student loans:

> The Debtor, for the most part, leads a modest lifestyle. PHEAA's sought-after reduction of the Debtor's phone expenses and the total elimination of her cable and internet services would barely generate a third of the funds necessary to meet even the most basic loan consolidation schedule. Further, earnings from additional hours worked at the Debtor's second job are not a permanent solution to this dilemma. The court will not require the Debtor to work 56 hours per week for the next 25 years in order to repay her student loans. To do so would make her a slave to the loans and would deprive her of any future hope for financial independence. The court also cannot place total reliance on the funds freed up by the discharge of the Debtor's credit card bills. Those funds, while substantial, are partially offset by automobile payments and the inevitable maintenance and replacement costs associated with an older used car.

Consequently, when determining whether Miller's student loans should be partially discharged, the court did not apply the Brunner factors, or any other factors relied upon by this court in making a finding of undue hardship, but rather constructed its own framework for granting a partial discharge.

In so doing, the bankruptcy court impermissibly used its equitable authority.

* * *

III.

For the foregoing reasons, we reverse the decision of the district court affirming the order of the bankruptcy court and remand this case to the district court with instructions to remand to the bankruptcy court for proceedings consistent with this opinion.

Not all courts have accepted the idea that a partial discharge of student loans can be written into the Bankruptcy Code, but a Congress fervent in protecting creditors did not attack the *Miller* line of cases in the 2005 Amendments.

We conclude with a case that was decided under the old Act, rather than the Code, but it contains so many eternal truths that we could not resist offering it to a new generation of bankruptcy students.

In re MILBANK
1 B.R. 150 (Bankr. S.D.N.Y. 1979)

SCHWARTZBERG, Bankruptcy Judge.

Plaintiffs are father and daughter who seek a nondischargeable determination with respect to their claims against the bankrupt, who is the ex-son-in-law of plaintiff, Howard Schulman, and ex-husband of plaintiff,

Ann C. Milbank. The essence of their complaints is that the bankrupt obtained money from the plaintiffs at a time when he was having an adulterous affair with his next door neighbor and that he thereafter ran off with her. Since both complaints are based upon the same allegations of fraud the following determination will cover both cases.

The parties appeared at the trial and submitted evidence resulting in the following Findings of Fact and Conclusions of Law:

FINDINGS OF FACT

1. The bankrupt, Mark A. Milbank, filed his voluntary petition in bankruptcy with this court on October 13, 1978, and was thereupon adjudicated. He had been engaged in the business of designing and fabricating custom furniture in Port Chester, New York.

2. Plaintiff, Ann Milbank, was married to the bankrupt on August 20, 1966, and resides in Nassau County, New York. She has three children from this marriage.

3. Plaintiff, Howard Schulman, is the father of plaintiff Ann Milbank and is an attorney at law with offices in New York City. He is a member of the firm of Schulman & Abarbanel, attorneys for both plaintiffs with respect to these proceedings against the bankrupt.

4. During the Spring of 1977, plaintiff, Howard Schulman, learned from his daughter and his former son-in-law, the bankrupt, that their marital relationship was in trouble and that they were trying to put it together again. The bankrupt had moved out of his house and left his wife for a period of five months, commencing January, 1977.

5. In September, 1977, after the bankrupt returned to the marital home, he requested that the plaintiff, Howard Schulman, lend him the sum of $10,000 as a partial payment for the purchase of a building in Port Chester, New York where the bankrupt could conduct his custom-made furniture business. The plaintiff, Howard Schulman, then believed that the bankrupt's marital relationship with the plaintiff's daughter had stabilized; the bankrupt had talked about building another house for his family. Plaintiff, Howard Schulman, was given to understand that the acquisition of the Port Chester location would enable the bankrupt to obtain greater production and alleviate some of his business problems so that the bankrupt could spend more time with his wife and children.

6. Plaintiff, Howard Schulman, advised the bankrupt that the purchase of the Port Chester building was a bad business investment because of the unique nature of the building which impaired its resaleability. However, plaintiff, Howard Schulman, advised the bankrupt that he would make the loan in the interest of the family and his grandchildren. He advanced the money in the belief that the new business location would afford the bankrupt more time to spend with his family.

7. On September 27, 1977, plaintiff, Howard Schulman, paid to the seller's attorney as a down payment for the purchase of the building on behalf of the bankrupt the sum of $5,750. Thereafter, on November 15, 1977, plaintiff, Howard Schulman, advanced to the bankrupt an additional

$4,250 which was used by the bankrupt to enable him to acquire the building in the name of the bankrupt's wholly owned corporation.

8. In August, 1977, the bankrupt requested his then wife, the plaintiff, Ann Milbank to advance to him $5,000 for the purchase of a new Honda automobile to be used in connection with his business. Repayment was to be made from the funds received by the bankrupt in connection with a business project then pending. Plaintiff, Ann Milbank, said that the bankrupt requested this money as a showing of her faith in their marriage and in him.

9. The bank account from which the $5,000 was taken was in the name of the plaintiff, Ann Milbank. She had formerly been a school teacher. Her salary went into this account. They lived on the bankrupt's earnings, although the bank account had been placed in their joint names until December, 1977, when the plaintiff, Ann Milbank, caused it to be put back into her name alone.

10. On or about November 11, 1977, the plaintiff, Ann Milbank, withdrew $7,500 from her bank account which she advanced to the bankrupt at his request in connection with his acquisition of the building in Port Chester, New York.

11. During the period when the plaintiff, Howard Schulman, advanced $5,750 to the bankrupt in September, 1977, and $4,250 on November 15, 1977, and when the plaintiff, Ann Milbank, advanced $5,000 to the bankrupt in August, 1977, and $7,500 in November, 1977, the bankrupt admittedly maintained an adulterous relationship with the wife of his next door neighbor.

12. During this time the bankrupt and his neighbor's wife registered at various motels and admittedly engaged in sexual activities. In October, 1977, the bankrupt rented an apartment in Long Beach, New York where the consorting neighbor visited him and had sex.

13. In December, 1977, plaintiff, Ann Milbank, first learned of the bankrupt's extra-marital affair when the husband of the next door neighbor telephoned to inform her that the bankrupt was having an affair with the neighbor's wife.

14. In January, 1978, the bankrupt left home, abandoning the plaintiff, Ann Milbank.

15. On October 4, 1979, the New York State Supreme Court, Nassau County, entered a decision granting the plaintiff, Ann Milbank, a divorce based on adultery committed by the bankrupt and the neighbor's wife, with whom he is now living.

16. The bankrupt did not repay any portion of the funds borrowed from the plaintiffs, with the result that they seek to have their claims determined to be nondischargeable.

17. There was no proof that when the bankrupt borrowed the funds from the plaintiffs he did not intend to make repayment. Hence, the central issue is even if the bankrupt intended to repay the loans, did he obtain the money under false pretenses?

18. The bankrupt made the stability of his marriage an issue in August, 1977, when he advised his former wife, plaintiff Ann Milbank, that her response to his request for the $5,000 loan for his purchase of a Honda automobile would be a reflection of her faith in their marriage.

19. Similarly the bankrupt's request for loans from his then father-in-law, plaintiff Howard Schulman, and the bankrupt's former wife, plaintiff Ann Milbank, were predicated on a joint effort by the bankrupt and his former wife to attempt to make their previously troubled marriage work. The bankrupt caused plaintiff, Howard Schulman, to believe that the acquisition of the Port Chester building would enable him to spend more time with his family. The plaintiff, Ann Milbank, advanced the sum of $7,500 from her bank account at the bankrupt's request as an expression of faith in their marriage. Thus, the stability of the bankrupt's marriage was a material fact in inducing the loans.

20. Although the bankrupt accepted the funds which the plaintiffs advanced in reliance upon a faithful attempt by the bankrupt and his then wife to repair their marital difficulties, the bankrupt was then unfaithful.

21. During the period when the bankrupt accepted the loans from his then wife and father-in-law he was having an affair with the wife of his next door neighbor. Indeed, the bankrupt even went so far as to rent an apartment in Long Beach, New York where he continued his extra-marital affair until he finally abandoned his wife in January, 1978. Obviously, if the plaintiffs had been aware of the bankrupt's conduct they would not have made the loans. Surely, the bankrupt was aware of the fact that he could only obtain these advances under the pretense that he was making an effort to strengthen his marriage.

22. The bankrupt therefore pretended to his then wife and father-in-law that he was making a good faith effort to stabilize his marriage, when in fact, he was rending it asunder. This false pretense was instrumental in obtaining the loans because the plaintiffs made the advances in reliance upon the bankrupt's express request for a display of faith, at a time when he was faithless.

DISCUSSION

It does not follow that every family loan made concurrently with the commission of adulterous acts can be characterized as having been obtained as a result of fraud in the bankruptcy sense. In this case the bankrupt and his then wife had experienced previous marital difficulties. The bankrupt became restless; he felt he was cut out for better things, notwithstanding his marriage of over ten years which resulted in three children, one of whom was adopted. In January of 1977, he abandoned his wife and family for approximately five months. The bankrupt thereafter returned to his marital home in the Spring of 1977, with the hope of stabilizing his marriage; both husband and wife consulted marriage counselors in this effort. They intended to make a good faith effort to strengthen their marriage.

The plaintiffs, who are the bankrupt's then wife and father-in-law, made loans to the bankrupt to enable him to purchase an automobile for his custom-made furniture business and a building in which the business was to be conducted. These loans were made in reliance upon the bankrupt's representations that he and his wife would make a good faith effort to strengthen their marriage. After the bankrupt returned to his marital home, and unbeknownst to the plaintiffs, from whom the bankrupt requested loans for his business, the bankrupt was then engaged in an extra-marital affair with the wife of his next door neighbor. This conduct was thereafter admitted by the bankrupt in the plaintiff, Ann Milbank's suit for a divorce on the ground of adultery. Hence, the loans were made in reliance upon the bankrupt's expressed representation that he and his then wife would make a good faith effort to strengthen their marriage, when in fact, the bankrupt's conduct was a sham; his extra-marital affair evidenced the bankrupt's false pretenses with respect to a display of marital stability. . . .

It is not essential that the bankrupt's pretenses be expressed in words. A deliberately created falsehood is the same as a spoken falsehood.

Manifestly, the plaintiffs would not have made the loans in question had they known that the bankrupt was not only not working at keeping his marriage together, but that he was at that time engaged in an extra-marital relationship with his neighbor's wife, for whom he later abandoned his wife and children. The stability of the bankrupt's marriage to the plaintiff, Ann Milbank, and her faith in him were factors expressed by the bankrupt in order to induce the original loan. Accordingly, the stability of the marriage was a condition upon which the plaintiffs relied to their detriment as a result of the bankrupt's false pretenses.

CONCLUSIONS OF LAW

1. The plaintiff, Ann Milbank, was induced by the bankrupt's false pretenses in August, 1977, to loan him $5,000 for his purchase of a Honda automobile.

2. The bankrupt's indebtedness to the plaintiff, Ann Milbank, for the $5,000 loan to purchase a Honda automobile was obtained by false pretenses within the meaning of §17a(2) [now §523(a)(2)] of the Bankruptcy Act and, therefore, is nondischargeable.

3. The plaintiff, Ann Milbank, was induced by the bankrupt's false pretenses in November, 1977, to loan him $7,500 for the purchase of a building in Port Chester, New York.

4. The bankrupt's indebtedness to the plaintiff, Ann Milbank, for the $7,500 loan to purchase the Port Chester building was obtained by false pretenses within the meaning of §17a(2) of the Bankruptcy Act and, therefore, is nondischargeable.

5. The plaintiff, Howard Schulman, was induced by the bankrupt's false pretenses in September and November, 1977, to loan him $10,000 for his purchase of a building in Port Chester, New York.

6. The bankrupt's indebtedness to the plaintiff, Howard Schulman, for the $10,000 loan to purchase the Port Chester building was obtained by false pretenses within the meaning of §17a(2) of the Bankruptcy Act and, therefore, is nondischargeable.

The entwining of moral and legal judgments has gotten too deep for us.

2.   Tax Priorities and Discharge

The protected position for tax obligations raises important policy questions, while the nondischargeability of taxes sometimes has a powerful impact on other creditors and the post-bankruptcy situation of the debtor.

The kinds of taxes specified in section 507(a)(8)(A)-(G) are not only given priority in payment, but any unpaid portion of those taxes is exempted from discharge by section 523(a)(1)(A). In effect, the debtor is obligated to pay most income taxes and a raft of other taxes notwithstanding any declaration of bankruptcy. If the estate generates any money, the tax payment will receive a priority distribution. If the tax obligation remains, then the debtor will remain personally obligated after the bankruptcy until the taxes are paid in full.

Pre-petition interest on section 507 (a)(8) priority claims shares the priority of the claims themselves and enjoys their nondischargeable status. Collier on Bankruptcy ¶523.07[7] (15th ed. rev. 2000). Post-petition interest does not accrue on unsecured tax claims against the TIB and the property of the estate, §502(b), but post-petition interest does accrue against the debtor as to any unpaid, undischarged tax debts that survive the bankruptcy. Id.

Penalties on nondischargeable taxes are also nondischargeable, §523(a)(7), even though such penalties do not get priority in payment under section 507(a)(8). In other words, a penalty is dischargeable only if the related tax is dischargeable.

Not only are these tax debts nondischargeable, but the Internal Revenue Service has the right to satisfy them by seizing property that is otherwise exempt under state law. See United States v. Rodgers, 461 U.S. 677 (1983). No wonder most bankruptcy lawyers advise financially troubled clients to pay their taxes if nothing else.

The statute has many other wrinkles and twists, but these will suffice for now.

3.   No Discharge, and Worse — Bankruptcy Crimes

In the basic course on bankruptcy there is insufficient time to deal with bankruptcy crimes. Nonetheless, it is important to note that the acts that trigger denial of discharge may also put the debtor in jeopardy for criminal sanctions. Concealment of assets, false oaths, false claims, fee fixing, and a number of other bankruptcy-specific actions are made crimes in 18 U.S.C. §§151-155.

No doubt most debtors who lose their discharge or their liberty (and perhaps some of those who do not) are the least appealing of those who use the legal system. Some of them are famous frauds who have victimized thousands of people. Yet sometimes a debtor reminds lawmakers that broadly written laws, in and out of bankruptcy, cast a wide net. The following story gives one more picture of the diversity of misfortunes that pass through the bankruptcy courts and are not successfully resolved there.

A Farmer, 70, Saw No Choice; Nor Did the Sentencing Judge

Pawnee City, Neb. — Ernest Krikava, wearing bib overalls caked with the dust of the Nebraska fields he was struggling to save after 50 years on the farm, would trudge past the hog pens and cringe at the frantic sound of his hungry pigs: a pained, high-pitched wail. It was the sound of starvation.

But there was no money for feed. The 70-year-old Mr. Krikava was behind on his loan payments, and the bank, which held a lien on his assets, including his hogs, was keeping the bulk of his income toward repayment of his debt of $240,000, releasing little to maintain his 1,000-acre farm.

In the spring of 1991, as some of the pigs began to die, Mr. Krikava became ever more desperate to buy feed. In a series of transactions, he sold about $35,000 worth of livestock under the name of his sister-in-law, a violation of his trust agreement with the bank. Later, when he sought protection from the bank in Federal bankruptcy court, he denied that any such sale had ever occurred.

Because of that lie, he was convicted of perjury at a 1993 trial and now sits in a minimum-security unit at the Federal prison in Leavenworth, Kan., where he is serving a five-month term. His case is one that critics of Federal mandatory sentencing say illustrates absurd consequences of stripping judges of much of their discretion when they mete out punishment.

In imposing sentence, Judge Warren K. Urbom of Federal District Court in Lincoln expressed reluctance to send Mr. Krikava to prison but noted that he had little choice: guidelines created by the United States Sentencing Commission, established by Congress in 1984 to bring consistency to haphazard Federal sentences, require a prison term of at least five months for a perjury conviction.

"I'm stuck with these guidelines," Judge Urbom said in an interview. "For a nonviolent offender, I'm not sure prison does much good."

Mr. Krikava's wife, Carol, and son, Kevin, pleaded guilty of perjury and received only probation, since the guidelines allow leniency for defendants who plead guilty. Mr. Krikava's not-guilty plea made him ineligible for any such consideration, a rule that civil libertarians say effectively punishes a defendant for exercising his right to trial. . . .

The imprisonment of Mr. Krikava (pronounced KRICK-uh-vuh), who reported to Leavenworth early in July to begin serving his sentence, has astonished his friends and neighbors here in this quiet countryside near the Kansas border. They talk in hushed tones of the family's devastation.

The Krikavas' farm was auctioned off in pieces. Carol Krikava, who stopped going to the doctor for a respiratory problem after the family's health insurance lapsed, died of that ailment in January. Kevin Krikava, 29, now works as a hired hand on another farm.

The family's lawyer, Bill Chapin, expresses outrage. "If they'd ripped off $35,000 and gone to the Cayman Islands, it would be different," he said. "But they used it to buy feed for hogs. I'm not saying they were right. But they were desperate. And something is wrong with our society when we can't see the larger picture here. This is a man who worked more than 50 years to build up the farm. Now he's lost his wife, lost his farm. But that isn't enough. He's got to go to prison. What was gained here?" . . .

But Thomas J. Monaghan, the United States Attorney in Omaha, whose office prosecuted the perjury case, said Mr. Krikava had been justly convicted of a "serious white-collar crime," and noted that he could have been spared prison had he pleaded guilty.

"Even today, he hasn't accepted responsibility," Mr. Monaghan said. "If you're going to avail yourself of the bankruptcy courts, you have certain obligations. And one of them is to tell the truth. He didn't do that."

Mr. Krikava insists he did no wrong, given the circumstances.

"It was going to be a crime either way," he said in a telephone interview from prison. "It was a crime to sell those hogs out of trust, and it would have been a crime to let them starve."

He chafes at the notion that he could have avoided prison by pleading guilty. "I thought I had the right to go to a trial," he said bitterly.

His son still lives in the family's old farmhouse, on a nameless gravel road south of town. But now he pays rent to its new owner, a doctor in Lincoln, who has agreed to sell back a parcel of the land if the Krikavas can raise the money.

"We did do some wrong things," Kevin Krikava said. "We were scared, and we panicked."...

The family's lawyers say that the Krikavas' financial situation worsened after they obtained their $250,000 loan, for farm operations, in 1990, but that even then the farm's assets outweighed the debt. Later, though, Mr. Krikava was required to pay the legal fees that the bank incurred as a result of the bankruptcy hearings.

Mr. Chapin, the lawyer for Mr. Krikava, says these fees exceeded $60,000 and ate up much of the Krikavas' equity in the farm. And when Mr. Krikava was convicted of perjury, the bankruptcy was moved from a Chapter 11 proceeding, which provides for the restructuring of debt, to Chapter 7, which calls for liquidation of assets.

Don Leuger, the president of the Community National Bank in Seneca, Kan., which held the lien on the Krikava farm, said the bank had given the family ample opportunity to renegotiate the loan.

"We tried to work with them," he said, "but they weren't satisfied."

But Mr. Krikava and his son say the bank ignored their warnings that hogs were dying for lack of feed. At times, Mr. Krikava says, he would simply open the gate to the hog pen and let the pigs graze on weeds, which would not fatten them but at least quelled the pangs of hunger for a time.

And things were not much better for the family than for the hogs. "For about a week, we didn't even have any food in the house," Kevin Krikava said. "We were literally surviving on popcorn and canned peaches for a while."

Before sentencing, Judge Urbom received dozens of letters that praised the character of the Krikava family. Herbert Klepper, a former hired hand for the family, wrote of Ernest Krikava's kindness and patience: "I hope that someday Ernie will get back on his feet and need a hired hand again, because I would give up my job to go back to work for him. He was like a father to me."

United States Representative Jim Slattery, Democrat of Kansas, has sent a letter to President Clinton asking him to consider clemency for Mr. Krikava.

"He simply found himself backed into a hole and did what he thought he had to do to survive financially," Mr. Slattery wrote.

On July 3, Kevin Krikava drove his father to Leavenworth, where the elder Mr. Krikava surrendered and began serving his sentence. Kevin said his father had never before spent more than two nights away from the farm.

Ernest Krikava said he planned to "start all over" in farming once he leaves prison. "It's all I know," he said.

The son has sent a letter to the President, six pages, handprinted. "Please help me," he wrote. "I think you are the only one who can."

[*New York Times*, July 20, 1994, at p.A1.]

═══════════

The next crime scene ends this section with a very different kind of tale, that of a mendacious lawyer who discovers poetic justice.

=========== UNITED STATES v. CLUCK ===========
143F.3d 174(5thCir. 1998)

E. Grady JOLLY, Circuit Judge:
Elwood "Jack" Cluck appeals his conviction and sentence for commit-
ting bankruptcy fraud in violation of 18 U.S.C. §152(1) & (3). Finding no
merit in any of Cluck's multitudinous and niggling points of error, we
affirm....

A

Before the events in this case, Cluck was an attorney who specialized,
by his own admission, in the legal avoidance of income, estate, and gift
taxes.[18] His practice was, by all accounts, quite successful, allowing Cluck
to enjoy many of the finer things in life. In his case, the finer things ranged
from an assortment of properties located throughout the state of Texas,
to his own Beechcraft Bonanza airplane, to a collection of classic Jaguar
automobiles.

Smooth travel sometimes comes to an abrupt halt, however, and so it
was in the case of Cluck. In October 1989, the road ahead worsened considerably when a state court rendered judgment against him in the staggering
amount of $2.9 million.[19] Although Cluck had high hopes that an appellate
detour would shortly return him to his golden highway,[20] he soon found
that the detour itself would require a steep toll of 10 percent in the form of
the supersedeas bond necessary to forestall execution. Short of funds and in
need of a cul de sac in which to safely park his troubled vehicle for a while,
Cluck turned to the refuge of the bankruptcy court, as many a similarly
threatened sojourner had done before him.

Unlike these other voyagers, however, Cluck apparently concluded
that his resources would need more protection than the bankruptcy court
could provide until his appellate travels had reached their final destina-
tion. Thus, before invoking the power of Title 11, he perceived that it
might be useful to keep some Jaguars in reserve, some money within easy
access, and, maybe, just for good measure, a few of his favorite things
beyond the reach of his creditors and the bankruptcy court. To this end, on
March 26, 1990, Cluck returned a note for $50,000 to its grantor, Perfect
Union Lodge. Perfect Union was one of Cluck's clients, and the note had
been originally tendered in payment of certain legal services. Three days
later, on March 29, Cluck pawned three Jaguars, a 1983 Chevrolet truck,
his airplane, a Lone Star boat, and a Winnebago camper shell ("the Jaguars,
etc.") to a used car dealer for $32,000,[21] retaining for himself and his

18. An undoubtedly satisfying profession that we do not disparage. See Estate of
McLendon v. Commissioner of Internal Revenue, 135 F.3d 1017, 1025 n.16 (5th Cir. 1998).
19. The suit was based on alleged fraudulent conduct by Cluck in his handling of the
estate of Booney M. Moore, one of his tax planning clients. It was brought pursuant to Texas's
Deceptive Trade Practices Act, whose punitive damage provisions gave rise to the large
award.
20. As well he should have. The judgment entered on the jury's verdict was reversed....
21. A price that was, needless to say, significantly below the assets' fair market value.

designee a right to reacquire at a set price[22] within thirty to ninety days of the sale.

B

His affairs now in preliminary order, on March 30, Cluck filed his petition for Chapter 7 liquidation in the United States Bankruptcy Court for the Western District of Texas. As part of the standard Chapter 7 procedure, Cluck was required to file a Schedule of Assets and a Statement of Financial Affairs. These documents required, among other things, disclosure of all accounts receivable, rights of acquisition, and asset transfers during the prior year. On his forms, Cluck made no mention of the assets recently pawned to the used car dealer or of his right to reacquire. He also did not disclose his return of the $50,000 note or the corresponding account receivable from Perfect Union Lodge. In addition, Cluck failed to list a transfer of 351 acres of land in McMullen County, Texas, that he had made on June 21, 1989. Finally, and significantly for this appeal, Cluck also neglected to include a further $150,000 in pre-petition accounts receivable from another of his clients, the O. D. Dooley Estate.

On July 31, Cluck's bankruptcy came to its first purported close, and the bankruptcy court entered an order discharging him from all dischargeable debts. Thinking his plan to have succeeded, on November 9, Cluck collected $48,000 from the O. D. Dooley Estate in partial payment of that client's aforementioned pre-petition account receivable. On November 16, the remaining $102,000 followed. About seven months later, on June 28, 1991, Cluck collected $35,000 from Perfect Union in settlement of its still-outstanding $50,000 account receivable. Of these funds, a portion was deposited into the account of First Capitol Mortgage, a Nevada corporation owned by Cluck's wife, Kristine. By this time, First Capitol had also reacquired all of the assets that had been pawned to the used car dealer. As might be suspected, neither the receipt of the money nor the reacquisition of the assets was revealed to the bankruptcy trustee. . . .

II

The bankruptcy court's finding of intentional concealment apparently aroused the interest of the U.S. Attorney, and on March 27, 1995, Cluck was charged with eight counts of bankruptcy fraud in violation of 18 U.S.C. §152(1) & (3). The counts were essentially as follows:

[False statements and fraudulent concealment].

On January 16, 1997, a jury found Cluck guilty on counts one, three, four, five, six, seven, and eight, and not guilty on count two. On May 22, 1997, Cluck was sentenced to concurrent terms of twenty-four months imprisonment on each count, and ordered to pay restitution in the amount of $185,000. Cluck appeals his conviction, sentence, and restitution order on multiple grounds. . . .

---

22. About $38,000.

C

Cluck next attempts to persuade us that the evidence was insufficient on all the counts of his indictment with respect to intent. Under §152(1) & (3), the prosecution must show that the concealment or false statement was made "knowingly and fraudulently." Cluck argues, essentially, that the evidence showed only that he was careless in providing information to his bankruptcy attorney, not that he committed intentional fraud. . . .

. . . It is well established that " '[c]ircumstances altogether inconclusive, if separately considered, may, by their number and joint operation, especially when corroborated by moral coincidences, be sufficient to constitute conclusive proof.' " United States v. Ayala, 887 F.2d 62, 67 (5th Cir. 1989) (quoting The Slavers (Reindeer), 69 U.S. (2 Wall.) 383, 401, 17 L. Ed. 911 (1864)).

In this case, it is manifestly clear that Cluck's repeated omissions and history of coincidental and questionable transfers formed just the sort of "circumstances" that the Supreme Court had in mind in the Reindeer case. Based on our review of the record, we are convinced that a rational jury could have inferred the existence of an intentional plan to defraud from the bare facts of Cluck's systematic concealment and false statements. We therefore find no merit to his argument that the evidence was insufficient on this point. . . .

Having found no merit in any of Cluck's numerous points of error, for the foregoing reasons, the judgment of the district court is AFFIRMED.

Denial of discharge is one form of discipline, and prison is another. While our consumer bankruptcy laws may fairly be characterized as generous to troubled debtors, it is important that debtors be fair with the system. The threat of jail is useful in keeping the system in balance. Unfortunately, not many U.S. attorneys are prepared to invest resources in this kind of prosecution. In the *Cluck* case, it may be that the spectacle of a fellow lawyer behaving as he did was enough to produce action.

Problem Set 12

12.1. Wallace Laymon has held a variety of jobs during the past ten years. He is restless and has some difficulty getting along with co-workers. He sometimes walks off jobs, gets fired, abruptly moves, or just "gets tired." Laymon's financial records are a complete disaster. He has no checking statements, no bill receipts, and no clear record of any of his financial dealings except a handful of bills and dunning notices that have arrived in the past two months. Does Laymon face any difficulties in bankruptcy? Should he? Was Laymon required by any law to keep better financial records? See §727.

12.2. Gordon Gram was in serious financial difficulty for several months before he sought your advice. During this time he gave a financial statement to his principal creditor, Dina Chapman, to persuade her to hold off on enforcing the judgment she had gotten against him. The statement falsely stated that he owned 1,000 shares of AT&T stock, which he promised he would deliver to Dina as security for the debt. In the meantime, he also conveyed his only significant asset, his ski chalet, to his daughter. When the stock was not forthcoming, Dina started searching for property to grab. She found out about the chalet deal and initiated execution on the judgment and a levy against the chalet, a collection suit, but before she could collect, Gram filed for Chapter 7. Aside from the question of whether Dina's judgment lien survives in bankruptcy, will Gram have any difficulty discharging the debts he owes to Dina or to his other unsecured creditors? Should he? See §§523, 727. If Dina has an option, under which provision should she file her objection?

12.3. Gerry and Beth were divorced in Iowa. The court order provided that Beth would have custody of the three children (ages four, nine, and ten), that Gerry would take the homestead and specified furnishings, and that Gerry would pay Beth $10,000 in a lump sum now from his separate assets, $2,500 per month for the next five years, then $1,000 per month for the next nine years, and then $200 per month after that time until Beth dies. The day after the divorce was final, Gerry declared a Chapter 7 bankruptcy. Beth's divorce lawyer called you to ask what Beth will get. Would your answer change if the parties lived in Texas, which now permits only a very limited form of alimony? Would it matter whether Beth were a wealthy veterinarian with an active practice or a woman who had not completed high school and who only sporadically held a paying job? Would it matter whether Gerry were a wealthy veterinarian with an active practice or a man who had not completed high school and who only sporadically held a paying job? See §523(a)(5), (15).

12.4. Chickie Narduchi makes his living through "creative debt collection services." Chickie has been very successful, but recently he has encountered a series of financial reverses that have forced him into bankruptcy. Among Chickie's creditors is a tort claimant who owed money to one of Chickie's clients. The claimant has an $800,000 judgment against Chickie for breaking four of his fingers, a favorite kneecap, and his big toe. Will the judgment creditor be discharged in bankruptcy? (Keep in mind that you might later discover that Chickie secretly owns 5 percent of the Forbidden Pleasures Casino, so he is not without assets worth pursuing.) See §523(a).

12.5. Shortly after Reynaldo and Maria Lujan were married, they purchased a rambling old home advertised as a "handyman's special." With visions of creating a quaint and charming nest, they bought a home that sucked up virtually all their cash. During the next three years, they worked constantly on the house and added such decorator touches as replacing the septic tank and rewiring the entire second floor. During that time, they carried maximum amounts on their credit cards, using the cards to support purchases for their house and to meet as many personal needs as they could finance through extended credit. Four months ago Maria was laid off and Reynaldo's income could not support the house and all the credit cards. Unfortunately, during that time their reliance on credit cards increased rather than decreased, so that their cards now represent $16,000 in unsecured debt.

Reynaldo and Maria have filed for Chapter 7 bankruptcy and sold the house, which brought just enough to pay off all the mortgages and home improvement loans and leave them with a small amount of exempt cash. As their attorney, you have looked over their credit card charges, and you see purchases of wallpaper ($450), plane tickets ($1,200), and clothes from a nice men's store ($400) within the three months preceding the filing. The card issuers have filed exceptions to discharge. What will you do at the hearing? See §523(a).

12.6. Craig O'Connor is a struggling young law student who has coped with inadequate parking facilities near his law school by parking wherever he wanted to, thereby collecting 122 parking tickets over three years. If O'Connor declares bankruptcy, will the parking tickets be discharged? See §523(a).

12.7. Congresswoman Herring has heard from an irate constituent about the nondischargeability of student loans, and so the good Congresswoman has promised to investigate. She can surmise the reasons behind the nondischargeability policy, but she has read recently that student loans actually have a lower default rate than other consumer loans, and that there is no empirical evidence of widespread abuse. If what she has read can be supported in congressional testimony, should that persuade Congress to amend the section so that student loans are treated like all others?

G.   THE DEBTOR'S POST-BANKRUPTCY
POSITION: REAFFIRMATION

Discharge is a legal milestone in a bankruptcy case, but often it is merely the beginning of an elaborate end game in which disappointed creditors may retaliate and shrewd ones may maneuver. The most common consequence of this end game is that, despite the language of financial rebirth and fresh start that pervades the bankruptcy literature, post-bankruptcy debtors are not like new babies — low on assets and free from any debt. The financial status of post-bankruptcy debtors is often surprisingly tangled with some of the same debt that sank them the first time around.

The legal key to this post-bankruptcy game is section 524 of the Code. At the moment of an individual debtor's Chapter 7 discharge, the section 362 automatic stay dissolves, §362(c)(2)(C), and the section 524 discharge injunction slides into its place. §524(a). The two injunctions are the book-ends of a Chapter 7 case. The discharge injunction forbids any attempt to collect a dischargeable debt. Like the automatic stay, it has potentially unlimited penalties and is enforced summarily by contempt. It provides a powerful incentive to creditors to permit the debtor a fresh start.

However — in bankruptcy law, there is always a "however" — subsection 524(c) goes on to give the discharged creditor an opening by way of seeking that the debtor "reaffirm" the soon-to-be-discharged debt. That section provides that the debt can become once again legally enforceable, notwithstanding the discharge, if the debtor signs a reaffirmation agreement subject to the procedures and terms specified in that subsection. Of course, a debtor can always repay a creditor voluntarily after bankruptcy, but a properly obtained reaffirmation agreement goes much further, reviving the debt and making the debt (and any future penalties and interest provided in the agreement) fully enforceable in a court of law. The procedures required in subsection 524(c) include a requirement that the agreement be filed with the court and that it contain a option for the debtor to rescind the agreement for a period of 60 days.

The 1898 Act said nothing about reaffirmations. This bounced the question of the enforceability of a promise to pay a debt discharged in bankruptcy back to the common law of contracts. The common law was quite clear: such debts would be enforced. The result, according to the 1973 Report of the Bankruptcy Commission, was that debtors were preyed upon by their most aggressive creditors and many left bankruptcy owing nearly as much as they did before they filed. The commission recommended a complete ban on reaffirmations, but under pressure from the industry Congress opted instead to permit reaffirmations under very limited and closely monitored conditions. The 1978 Code required that the bankruptcy court make an independent inquiry into whether a reaffirmation was in the "debtor's best interests." If it was, the court approved the reaffirmation; if it was not, the court denied it. The 1978 reform apparently reduced the number of reaffirmations. Although little hard data were available, various estimates, including the Brookings Study from the 1960s, suggested that about 70 percent of debtors were signing binding reaffirmations under the old Act. The data from As We Forgive indicate that reaffirmations had slipped to about one in five debtors in the early 1980s after the new bankruptcy laws were in effect.

The consumer credit industry was unhappy about losing access to this alternative payment opportunity, and it pressed for a change in the law. The 1984 Amendments to the Code dropped the requirement of bankruptcy court approval in all cases in which the debtor was represented by a lawyer. Instead, in order to create a legally enforced reaffirmation, the lawyer would need to certify that the reaffirmation was in the debtor's best interest and to file an affidavit to that effect. As the authors of an important empirical study of reaffirmation have noted, "The new reaffirmation routine placed debtors' attorneys in a difficult position. They were to be decision-makers for, rather than advisors to, their clients." Marianne B. Culhane and Michaela M. White, Debt After Discharge: An Empirical Study of Reaffirmation, 73 Am. Bankr. Inst. L. Rev. 709, 716 (1999) [hereinafter "Culhane and White, Reaffirmation"]. There is reason to think that reaffirmations have increased as a result, although they have not reached the levels observed prior to 1978.

The sweeping protection of the discharge injunction and the powerful exception provided by a well-wielded reaffirmation agreement interact in two distinct contexts, secured debt and unsecured debt. We will discuss reaffirmations under each heading. As the discussion evolves, we will encounter the three most important incentives the creditor can use to attract a debtor into a reaffirmation. The first incentive relates to secured debt. It is the creditor's agreement not to repossess collateral that the debtor wants to keep, often collateral such as a car or a home that is exempt from other creditors but vulnerable to the holder of a valid security interest or mortgage. The second and third incentives relate to unsecured debt. They are an offer of future credit and the threat of an objection to discharge.

1. *Reaffirmation of Secured Debt*

The first point worth noting is deceptively simple: Debts are discharged, but liens are not. §506(d). The discharged debtor has no personal liability on any debt, so unsecured debts are effectively vaporized. But a secured debt remains attached to its collateral and can be enforced against the collateral after bankruptcy, even though the debtor cannot be sued for any deficiency. The discharge injunction forbids only an attempt to collect a debt "as a personal liability" of the discharged debtor. Collection by seizure of collateral is not forbidden. If a Chapter 7 debtor has any secured debts, the statute on its face offers only two alternatives to avoid surrendering the collateral to the creditor: redeem the collateral or negotiate a reaffirmation agreement with the creditor. Emerging case law has created a third option, which we may call "ride-through" (also known as "retention").

The first alternative, redemption, requires the debtor to pay the creditor the full loan or the full value of the collateral in cash, whichever is less. §722. The second alternative, reaffirmation, requires a cooperative creditor willing to agree to let the debtor keep the collateral. The agreement may be informal, allowing the debtor to keep the collateral so long as the debtor continues to make satisfactory payments on the loan. Other creditors may demand that their debtors formally reaffirm their debts through the bankruptcy court. §524(c). The consequence of reaffirmation of a secured debt is that debtors sign a legally binding agreement to waive the discharge on a given debt, subjecting themselves once again to losing the collateral and being sued for a deficiency claim if the debt is not paid off according to the terms of the reaffirmation. Unlike a redemption, which a debtor can force on an unwilling creditor if the debtor has the cash to redeem, a debtor cannot force a reaffirmation on a creditor who wants to terminate any relationship with the debtor. The third alternative, ride-through, which requires only maintenance of the contractual payments, has been permitted only in some federal circuits. In this section, we will consider each of the methods by which the debtors can keep the Maytag or the Ford, starting with reaffirmation.

The role that secured debt plays in the post-bankruptcy financial lives of debtors should not be underestimated. In *As We Forgive*, a study of 2,200 consumer debtors reported that more than three-quarters listed some secured debt in their bankruptcy filings, a figure that has remained about the same among our 2001 debtors. In 2001 about half of all the debtors in the sample were buying their own homes, reporting median home mortgages of about $82,000, a figure that was about 17 percent higher than the median mortgage for nonbankrupt homeowners during the same time period. In addition, 78 percent of the debtors had loans secured by their cars, their furniture, their appliances, and other personal property. Most debtors either made substantial repayments following bankruptcy, or they found another place to live, another way to get to work, and so on.

The importance of secured debt is emphasized by the findings of the Consumer Bankruptcy Project for cases originally filed in 1991 and 2001. On average, in 1991 and 2001 debtors owed secured debt equal to more than three-quarters of their total assets. While that does not mean that the debtors would lose all that property absent redemption or reaffirmation (many secured debts are undersecured and other property may be unencumbered), these data demonstrate the overwhelming importance of secured debt in the financial lives of bankruptcy debtors.

The following case illustrates the application of the current version of the reaffirmation provisions of the Code as applied to a secured debt. The case is interesting not only for what it says about the application of the law but also for how it illustrates the tension between the debtor and the creditor — what each wants, and how much leverage each has to get it.

In re PENDLEBURY

94 B.R. 120 (Bankr. E.D. Pa. 1988)

Richard S. STAIR, Jr., Judge.

The debtors in these four Chapter 7 cases each filed a motion requesting an order striking a provision in a proposed reaffirmation agreement with Leader Federal Savings and Loan Association (Leader Federal). The reaffirmation agreements at issue purport to make the respective debtors, individually or jointly, as the case may be, responsible for the payment of attorney's fees in the amount of $250.00. By the execution of reaffirmation agreements, the debtors desire to retain possession of mobile homes financed through Leader Federal. The debtors do not, however, acquiesce in Leader Federal's insistence that each reaffirmation agreement contain the provision requiring payment of a $250.00 attorney's fee.

The trustee in each case has abandoned the mobile home as a burdensome asset of the estate. The court has withheld granting the discharges of the respective debtors pending resolution of the issues raised by their motions.

I

The Bankruptcy Code sanctions two methods by which debtors may retain possession of secured property: redemption or reaffirmation.[23] Redemption, authorized under 11 U.S.C.A. §722 (West 1979), permits the debtor to redeem tangible secured personal property from a lien securing a consumer debt upon a lump-sum payment to the creditor of the fair market value of the property or the amount of the claim, whichever is less.

---

23. 11 U.S.C.A. §524(f) (West Supp. 1988) makes it clear that a debtor may voluntarily repay debts, secured and unsecured, even if a reaffirmation agreement is not obtained. However, voluntary post-petition payments do not reobligate a debtor on the original debt nor is a secured creditor, by accepting voluntary payments, deprived of its right to repossess the secured collateral upon termination of the automatic stay.

Redemption may be voluntary where the debtor and secured creditor stipulate the redemption value of the secured property. Redemption can also be involuntary. Reaffirmation contemplates a voluntary post-petition agreement between the debtor and creditor. In discussing reaffirmation under §524(c), the Court of Appeals for the Sixth Circuit has stated:

> Section 524(c) authorizes a Chapter 7 debtor to seek renegotiation of the terms of the security agreement with the creditor thereby creating an alternative method pursuant to which a debtor may attempt to retain possession of secured collateral. Such an alternative, obviously attractive to the debtor financially unable to redeem the secured collateral through a lump-sum payment, is the equitable complement to §722. Simply, a debtor incapable or unwilling to tender a lump-sum redemption and redeem the secured collateral for its fair market value may reaffirm with the creditor; contra wise, a debtor confronted with a creditor unwilling to execute a renegotiation may retain the secured collateral by redeeming it for its fair market value, which value may be substantially less than the contractual indebtedness. However, 524(c) facially contemplates that the creditor, for whatever reason, may reject any and all tendered reaffirmation offers; §524(c) envisions execution of an "agreement" which, by definition, is a voluntary undertaking....

In re Bell, 700 F.2d at 1056 (citations omitted).[24] ...

Procedurally, debtors in the Northern and Northeastern Divisions of this district are required to file reaffirmation agreements with the clerk prior to expiration of the bar date fixed in the order for meeting of creditors for filing complaints objecting to discharge under 11 U.S.C.A. §727 (West 1979 & Supp. 1988). At the reaffirmation hearings held pursuant to §524(d), this court does not interject itself into the reaffirmation process other than is required under §524(c)(5) and (6) and (d). The court recognizes that debtors' attorneys are in the best position to evaluate the effect of reaffirmation on their clients. Clearly, an attorney by affixing his signature to the declaration or affidavit required by §524(c)(3) certifies that attorney's participation in the reaffirmation process and the accuracy of the representations contained therein to the best of the attorney's knowledge, information and belief.

Notwithstanding the relaxed provisions of §524(c) under the 1984 Amendments respecting court approval, this court would in no way countenance overreaching by a secured creditor. The court would not hesitate in appropriate circumstances to utilize its equitable powers and interject itself into the reaffirmation process. Such a situation should, however, never occur where a debtor is represented by counsel. Congress' intent that the court rely upon the declaration and affidavit filed by counsel is made manifest under the 1984 Amendments by removal of the requirement of court approval except as to reaffirmation agreements entered into by pro se debtors.

---

24. The *Bell* court considered §524(c) as enacted by the Bankruptcy Reform Act of 1978. As originally enacted, §524(c) required every reaffirmation agreement to be approved by the court. The Bankruptcy Amendments and Federal Judgeship Act of 1984 substantially revised the reaffirmation provisions of the 1978 Act. Chief among these revisions is the requirement of the attorney declaration and the removal of court approval except as to debtors filing pro se. Notwithstanding the 1984 Amendments, the principles enunciated in *Bell* remain applicable to §524(c) as presently enacted.

In practice, reaffirmation hearings presently serve no useful purpose except for debtors filing pro se. Attorneys are rightly charged with the responsibility for advising their clients during the reaffirmation process. As is noted in the legislative history to the present §524(c):

> In all, the new section is designed to encourage the prompt execution and implementation of good faith reaffirmation agreements by eliminating the cumbersome and unnecessary prior approval procedures which inhibited debtors and creditors from consummating mutually acceptable debt retirement arrangements.

S. Rep. No. 98-65, 98th Cong. 1st Sess. 59, 60 (1983) (Senate Report accompanying S. 445, Omnibus Bankruptcy Improvements Act of 1983, the forerunner to the Bankruptcy Amendments and Federal Judgeship Act of 1984).

II

The debtors in the instant proceedings are asking the court to intervene in the negotiation of their respective reaffirmation agreements for the purpose of limiting the terms of those agreements. They argue, though incorrectly, that their original contracts executed with Leader Federal do not provide for attorney's fees in these circumstances.

Debtors fail to recognize that the reaffirmation process involves negotiation. Even if debtors were correct in their assertions respecting the lack of a clause providing for attorney's fees in their original contracts, Leader Federal is nonetheless not prohibited from negotiating a provision for the payment of attorney's fees in its reaffirmation agreements. Likewise, the debtors are not prohibited from endeavoring to negotiate reaffirmation agreements with terms differing from those contained in their original contracts.[25]

Clearly, as in any negotiation process, give and take will be required. It appears to the court that, under circumstances involving reaffirmation, a debtor has considerable bargaining power. In the first place, the creditor must recognize that in the absence of reaffirmation its debt will be discharged leaving recourse against its collateral as its sole remedy. Secondly, the creditor must consider reaffirmation in terms of expenses associated with repossession and foreclosure. It must also consider the resale value of its collateral. Merchants and secured lenders are in business to make a profit. They recognize the impact of bankruptcy and realize the advantage of negotiating a reaffirmation agreement which maintains an existing security interest, retains personal liability on the debtor and continues an uninterrupted stream of payments. Foreclosing a security interest in property whose value is generally

---

25. For example, it would appear that interest rates, term of payment, amount of installment payments, methods for curing an arrearage, and the total amount of indebtedness to be reaffirmed are all factors to be considered by the debtor during the negotiation process. The latter is of special importance. Surely debtors and their attorneys would not dispute the wisdom of endeavoring to negotiate a reaffirmation agreement to reduce the amount of prepetition indebtedness to a sum more commensurate with the value of the collateral which is to secure the reaffirmed debt.

speculative would, in this court's opinion, be a creditor's least desirable option.

Debtors must also recognize that a secured creditor might well expect to recover attorney's fees for the trouble and expense it has encountered in protecting its secured interest during bankruptcy proceedings. This court over the years has had occasion to review a considerable number of reaffirmation agreements and is comfortable in stating that for the most part attorney's fees negotiated by secured parties and debtors are fair and reasonable.[26] During the course of negotiating a reaffirmation agreement, a debtor's attorney may determine that attorney's fees requested by a secured party are not fair and reasonable and will impose an undue hardship on the debtor or a dependent. Under such circumstances, that attorney cannot in good faith execute the declaration or affidavit required by §524(c)(3).

The court is mindful that the mobile homes at issue in the instant proceedings probably constitute the residences of the respective debtors. This factor does not, however, change the reaffirmation process required under §524(c). Whether the debtors desire to retain possession of an automobile, household furnishings, mobile home, or other item of property, the statutory requirements involving reaffirmation remain constant. It behooves debtors and their attorneys to thoroughly consider and discuss the redemption and reaffirmation options available prior to filing a case under Chapter 7. Redemption is, of course, the most attractive alternative as the debtor can force the secured creditor to accept payment of the fair market cash value of its collateral or the amount of its claim, whichever is less. High dollar consumer items such as automobiles and mobile homes do not lend themselves to redemption which requires a lump-sum cash payment. This is not to say that redemption cannot be achieved through installment payments for it most certainly can: (1) if the debtor and creditor agree that the debtor may redeem by installments and the parties comply with the reaffirmation provisions of §524(c);[27] (2) by the debtor's filing of a petition under Chapter 13 of title 11.

Chapter 13 is designed to provide a debtor a fresh start through rehabilitation. On the other hand, Chapter 7 provides a debtor a fresh start through liquidation. As reaffirmation envisions the retention of debt beyond discharge it is to some extent inconsistent with the fresh start provisions of Chapter 7. No doubt this factor influenced Congress to include the Miranda warning approach mandated by §524(c) as originally enacted under the Bankruptcy Code of 1978. The Congressional philosophy has not been abrogated by the 1984 Amendments. Its implementation has implicitly been shifted to the debtor's attorney. In effect, the debtors now invite the court to join the reaffirmation process and dictate to Leader Federal what it can and cannot include in its agreements in order to make those agreements palatable to the debtors and their attorneys. Not only is such a procedure not sanctioned by §524(c), its implementation could, it appears, make the court the chief architect of all future reaffirmation agreements. If debtors were

26. Many reaffirmation agreements do not contain provisions providing for payment of attorney's fees associated with the debtor's default or the preparation and execution of the reaffirmation agreement.

27. In which event the debtor has not redeemed the property pursuant to 11 U.S.C.A. §722 (West 1979), but has reaffirmed the debt pursuant to 11 U.S.C.A. §524(c) (West Supp. 1988).

entitled to call upon the court to determine the propriety and amount of attorney's fees requested by secured creditors would they not also be entitled to call upon the court to determine appropriate interest rates, lengths of extensions of contract payment terms, default provisions, and other terms all of which are the proper subject of negotiation under §524(c).

III

The debtors' motions seeking to strike the attorney's fee provision of the four reaffirmation agreements at issue will be denied.

═══════════

As *Pendlebury* demonstrates, reaffirmation is a free-market activity. The creditor may demand what it chooses in exchange for permitting the debtor to keep the collateral. Apparently creditors regularly demand reaffirmation of the entire debt (with or without accrued interest and penalties), regardless of the value of the collateral. If Joe Debtor agrees to pay $2,000 to keep a car worth $5,000, it is easy for his attorney to sign the best-interest affidavit, assuming Joe can make the payments. But if Joe's car is worth $5,000 and the outstanding loan is $7,500, the creditor will probably demand he agree to repay the entire $7,500, plus future interest. Is it in Joe's best interest to pay so much more than the car is worth?

The answer may turn in part on Joe's alternatives, discussed below, but it is obvious Joe would rather pay only $5,000 for a $5,000 car. That alternative may be available under section 722 of the Code, "Redemption." Under Article 9 of the UCC a debtor is allowed to redeem collateral after default by paying the full amount owed, including late charges and other costs. UCC Revised §9-623. Redemption is available only if the collateral is exempt property or has been abandoned by the trustee. The leverage created by permitting the creditor to demand more than the value of the collateral ($7,500 for a car worth $5,000 in the prior example) was too much for Congress to sanction in consumer bankruptcy cases, so section 722 of the Code provides that the debtor may keep the collateral by paying the amount of the allowed secured claim, the value of the collateral. In the previous example, the debtor could redeem the $5,000 car by paying $5,000 in cash, with the remaining $2,500 being treated as an unsecured and dischargeable claim, just as it would have been if the car had been repossessed and sold.

The rub in the real world is that the debtor does not have $5,000 cash. For most debtors, section 722 might as well base redemption on the debtor successfully running a three-minute mile. Perhaps the most practical possibility for a few debtors is a loan from a friend or relative, in which case the debtor emerges from bankruptcy still greatly encumbered by debt. In the past few years, a business aptly named 722 Redemption has popped up in some states, offering to lend money to debtors (at high interest rates) so that they can redeem their cars. The math is simple: any debtor who is better off with the terms offered by 722 Redemption now has at least one alternative to reaffirming with the original creditor. As we will see, Chapter 13 is another possible method of keeping the car or the washing machine, but it may require substantial long-term payments that the debtor cannot make. Thus the statutory alternatives to reaffirmation are often unavailable or unattractive.

The case law had developed a controversial third alternative: ride-through. Ride-through means keeping the collateral by continuing to make the pre-bankruptcy payments, without redeeming or reaffirming. The effect is to permit the debtor to keep and use the car or the washing machine after a Chapter 7 bankruptcy, while discharging any personal liability on the debt. If the collateral is damaged or destroyed, the debtor can simply abandon it, without being legally responsible for any deficiency. On the other hand, if the debtor keeps paying, the creditor will be repaid in full notwithstanding the debtor's bankruptcy and the fact that the collateral might not have satisfied the debt in full. Because the Bankruptcy Code made no specific reference to ride-through, the issue of whether a debtor could make such a move had reached the level of the courts of appeals, with a number of decisions each way.

It appears that Congress may have settled the argument as a matter of federal law in the 2005 Amendments. It does so in two separate provisions that clash with each other in detail. §§362(h); 521(a)(2), (6). The former section is the stronger of the two. It simply removes the collateral from the estate and lifts the stay unless the debtor complies with the command in section 521(a)(2) to state an intention to do one of three things and then to do them: surrender the property, reaffirm the contract with the secured party on that collateral, or redeem pursuant to section 722. Section 521(a)(6) is similar in overall intent, but has a savings clause for the debtor if the creditor demands more than the original terms. It remains to be seen, however, whether a state court would permit a creditor to foreclose or repossess property of a post-bankruptcy debtor if the debtor was making all payments on the contracts, particularly if the creditor accepted any of those post-petition payments. It seems that the very state-law collection issues that persuaded some courts that ride-through is permissible may survive the 2005 Amendments.

One point that has been missed in all the legal analysis of the retention issue is that de facto retention is in fact the most frequent way in which debtors and creditors deal with collateral following a Chapter 7 bankruptcy. The study reported in *As We Forgive* found hints that retention was widespread as to home mortgages and the Culhane and White study of reaffirmations suggests that retention is widely used across the board. In effect, debtors just keep up their payments and creditors just keep taking the money, preferring an uncertain income stream to a repossession and sale that would be guaranteed, in most cases, to produce a substantial loss.

The parties' legal rights are important, no doubt, but it is also important to understand how the system actually functions most of the time.

2. *Reaffirmation of Unsecured Debt*

The secured creditor has an obvious advantage in negotiating a reaffirmation agreement because it can always threaten to take back the collateral.

The unsecured creditor is in a much less advantageous legal position. There are few obvious reasons a debtor would want to reaffirm an unsecured debt. One might be gratitude (e.g., to a doctor) and another affection (e.g., to a friend), but Sears and Federated Stores will not find many such opportunities. The most obvious incentive that might benefit a merchant or lender would be the debtor's desire to protect a co-debtor, agreeing to pay off the loan that Mom had cosigned, as the next case illustrates.

══════════════ In re PAGLIA, Debtor ══════════════
302 B.R. 162 (Bankr. W.D. Pa. 2003).

Bernard Markovitz, Bankruptcy Judge.

* * *

FACTS

Debtor was the sole principal of a business known as F & M Fabricators until it ceased operating some time in 1990.

On January 24, 1990, debtor borrowed the sum of $13,000.00 from First National Bank of Western Pennsylvania, defendant's predecessor, for use in his business. He executed and delivered that same day a promissory note in favor of First National in the amount of $13,000.00 plus interest. The total amount due under the note, which was payable in full by March 31, 1990, was $13,282.08.

Irene Paglia, debtor's mother, did not execute the promissory note but pledged her interest in an annuity to secure payment of debtor's obligation. She executed an assignment of her interest in the annuity to First National on January 24, 1990.

* * *

Debtor filed a voluntary chapter 7 petition on September 19, 1991. First National was identified on the schedules as having an undisputed general unsecured claim in the amount of $12,544.97 for a "loan obtained on behalf of employer on January 24, 1990."

First National sent a letter to Irene Paglia on November 15, 1991, informing her that debtor had defaulted on the above promissory note and demanding payment from her in the amount of $13,484.63. It further demanded that she liquidate the annuity she had pledged as security for debtor's obligation and use the proceeds to satisfy debtor's unpaid obligation. Legal action was threatened if the matter was not fully resolved by November 29, 1991.

On January 10, 1992, before debtor had received a discharge in his ongoing bankruptcy case, debtor executed a second promissory note in favor of First National in the amount of $13,635.00 plus interest. The total amount due under the note, which was payable in 108 monthly installments beginning on February 1, 1992, was $21,134.52.

As security for this new obligation, Irene Paglia once again pledged her interest in the annuity on January 10, 1992, and executed another assignment of her interest in the annuity to First National.

Debtor received a discharge of all his pre-petition obligations on April 16, 1992. Included among the discharged obligations was the debt arising out of the promissory note debtor had executed on January 24, 1990. His bankruptcy case was closed on April 23, 1992.

Debtor continued making monthly payments due under the second promissory note until March of 1999. The amount of the payments, including interest, he made to First National during this period totaled $23,119.82. No further payments were made after March of 1999.

On May 20, 2002, more than ten years after he had executed the second promissory note, debtor commenced this adversary action against Sky Bank, successor to First National. The complaint alleges, among other things, that First National had violated the discharge injunction — found at §524(a)(2) of the Bankruptcy Code — as well as the automatic stay — found at §362(a) — when it coerced him to execute the second promissory note. * * *

Almost five months later, on October 25, 2002, debtor brought a motion to reopen his closed bankruptcy case so the adversary action could be heard and decided in this court. The motion was granted on December 3, 2002.

DISCUSSION

With certain exceptions not relevant here, the discharge of a pre-petition debt owed by a debtor in bankruptcy does not affect the liability of any other entity or their property for that debt. 11 U.S.C. §524(e). Furthermore, a debtor is not prohibited from voluntarily repaying any debt. 11 U.S.C. §524(f).

Unless a specific debt is expressly excepted, a debtor in bankruptcy is relieved of personal liability for all pre-petition debts upon receiving a discharge. See Johnson v. Home State Bank, 501 U.S. 78, 82-83, 111 S.Ct. 2150, 2153, 115 L.Ed.2d 66 (1991). Where a creditor has a security interest in property, a discharge extinguishes only the personal liability of the debtor in bankruptcy. The right of a secured creditor to proceed in rem against the collateral survives the debtor's discharge. Id.

The purpose of §524(a) is to afford a debtor a "fresh start" by ensuring that a debtor will not be pressured in any way to repay a debt after it has been discharged.

* * *

Merely permitting a debtor to execute a new note which makes the debtor personally liable for a discharged debt, Mickens concluded, suffices for there to be an "act to collect" for purposes of this provision of the Bankruptcy Code.

We take issue with this reasoning because it postulates what effectively amounts to a per se principle of law that a creditor violates §524(a)(2) merely by passively permitting a debtor to execute another note and thereby to become personally liable once again for a discharged debt. A creditor, in other words, violates §524(a)(2), without regard for how active or passive it was prior to debtor's execution of another note and without regard to whether it actively sought to collect the discharged debt. Such a per se principle drains the phrase "act to collect" of all content and effectively renders it vacuous.[28] It is difficult, if not impossible, utilizing this principle to conceive of a situation in which a creditor that passively permits a debtor to become liable once again for a discharged debt has not violated §524(a)(2).

Turning to the case now before us, nothing in the evidence presented at trial suffices to warrant the inference that defendant undertook in any way to collect a soon-to-be discharged debt from debtor or that it even advised him that he had to execute the second note. To the contrary, the evidence indicates that, acting out of filial loyalty, defendant himself took the initiative and volunteered to execute the second note so defendant would not take legal action against his mother's annuity. Defendant was not willing to let this happen.

The most that can be said of defendant is that it accepted debtor's offer to execute the second note. Standing alone, this is a far cry from concluding that it undertook or acted to collect the debt from debtor. Debtor's contention that defendant coerced him into executing the second note is without merit.

* * *

Were the second note debtor executed on January 10, 1992, a "reaffirmation agreement" for purposes of §§524(c) and (d) of the Bankruptcy Code, the note would not be enforceable due to the absence of compliance with the requirements set forth in these provisions. The second note, which was not filed with the court, did not advise debtor that he could rescind it within a specified period of time, and did not advise him that he did not have to execute it. See 11 U.S.C. §§524(c), (d).

The obligation arising under the second note unquestionably bore a relationship to the first. The second note, however, was not a reaffirmation for purposes of these provisions of the debt arising under the first note. Debtor instead incurred a different obligation in return for different consideration. As consideration for the first note, debtor received money from defendant. As consideration for the second note, defendant agreed to forgo its lawful right to take action against the annuity pledged by debtor's mother which secured repayment of the obligation arising under the first note.

While he did not actively pursue it trial, debtor asserted in his complaint that defendant's conduct also violated the automatic stay provision of the Bankruptcy Code as well as 15 U.S.C. §1691. Defendant violated neither of these provisions.

* * *

This assertion is without merit for reasons stated previously The reasoning underlying our previous determination that defendant did not commit an "act to collect" for purposes of §524(a)(2) applies *pari passu* with respect to the same phrase for purposes of §362(a)(6). Defendant therefore did not violate

---

28. This is *not* to say that inactivity on the part of a creditor can never constitute an "act to collect." We can envision situations in which inactivity on a creditor's part could so qualify. It is only to say that inactivity on a creditor's part need not do so. Whether it does depends on the particular facts and circumstances present in a specific case and cannot be determined *a priori*.

the automatic stay by undertaking an act to collect a pre-petition claim against debtor when it threatened to take legal action against the annuity belonging to debtor's mother and then instead permitted debtor to execute the second promissory note as an alternative.

* * *

One argument the court ignored rests on the fact that Chapter 13 has a special stay to protect co-debtors like Irene Paglia. §1301. Thus it can be argued that the absence of any such provision in Chapter 7 makes it unlikely Congress would disapprove of a "passive" reaffirmation like the one in Paglia in which the debtor wished to protect a co-debtor. The larger point is that the case demonstrates the tension between the strict restraint of creditors under both the automatic stay and the discharge injunction — to do absolutely nothing to collect a debt except as the court permits in advance — and Congress's friendly attitude toward reaffirmations.

It may make sense to reaffirm a loan signed by a co-debtor, but Culhane and White found relatively few reaffirmations of cosigned debts. Instead, most reaffirmations are the product of creditors' judicious use of a stick or a carrot: a threat to object to discharge or an offer of future credit.

Next we explore a far more direct challenge to the rules regulating reaffirmation. It seems from the case reports that objections to discharge have risen greatly in recent years, primarily because large national retailers and other credit grantors have developed systematic national programs to object to discharge in search of reaffirmation agreements. There are also programs that contact debtors (often by-passing their lawyers) with letters that offer continued use of the creditor's credit card if the debtor will agree to continue paying the old debt. Several bankruptcy judges reacted to these developments by inserting themselves in various ways into the reaffirmation process, despite the statutory language assigning debtor protection to the debtors' lawyers through the affidavit process. Reacting to that development, and perhaps to the awkwardness of the statutory procedures required for reaffirmation under subsection 524(c), a surprising number of national firms decided to take a bolder path. In the case that follows, Sears was owed both secured and unsecured debts and used both the threat of repossession and the incentive of new credit, although it did not threaten the debtor's discharge.

In re LATANOWICH

207 B.R. 326 (Bankr. D. Mass. 1997)

Carol J. KENNER, Chief Judge. . . .

The Debtor, Francis M. Latanowich, acting pro se, filed his petition under Chapter 7 of the Bankruptcy Code on December 7, 1995. In his bankruptcy schedules, he listed total assets of only $375 and unsecured debts totaling $12,805.20, all in the nature of consumer credit. This sum included an unsecured, nonpriority debt to Sears in the listed amount of

$1,073.64 for consumer purchases. In his schedule of current income and expenditures, he disclosed that he was married and unemployed, that he received total monthly income of only $500, consisting entirely of Social Security disability benefits, and that he had monthly expenditures of $1,449. The Chapter 7 Trustee in the case reported that the estate had no assets to distribute.

On April 1, 1996, with no objection to discharge or to the dischargeability of any debt having been filed, the Court entered a discharge....

On November 14, 1996, the Debtor, again acting pro se, filed a motion (in the form of a letter) to reopen his case. In his motion, he states that when he filed his bankruptcy petition in December, 1995,

> I took advice from a lawyer friend and he told me to keep some of my debts so I could start getting my credit back. I receive 518 dollars a month on social security for a disability I have. I have tried to meet the payment every month but it is keeping food off the table for my kids. I would like to know if you could reopen my case so I could get rid of all my debt forever.

Below, he listed four debts from which he sought relief, totaling approximately $12,000, including the previously-listed debt to Sears, which now he quantified at $1,330.58.

...Sears initiated contact with the Debtor by mailing him a letter, accompanied by a proposed reaffirmation agreement. The letter informed the Debtor that Sears had received notice of his bankruptcy filing and that his account balance was $1,161.34. It also informed him that Sears had a security interest in the merchandise represented in the account balance, including an automobile battery and a television set. It set forth the dates of purchase for these items, their purchase prices, and their (then) current values as follows:

Item	Date of Purchase	Purchase Price	Current Value
Battery	7/17/95	$75.33	$75.33
Television	6/1/95	$503.87	$403.10

The letter then asked the Debtor to inform Sears of his intention as to his account. It listed three options:

A.   Sign Reaffirmation Agreement as to account balance, to be paid in monthly installments.
B.   Redeem merchandise, by making lump sum cash payment only.
C.   Return merchandise to Sears.

The letter then stated that "should you elect to reaffirm for the account balance, a line of credit in the amount of $1,161.00 will be granted immediately to assist you in the establishment of a favorable credit history."...

On January 29, 1996, after receiving the letter, the Debtor called a representative of Sears, who informed the Debtor that unless he agreed to pay the full balance due, he would have to return the merchandise that was subject to Sears's security interest. When the Debtor indicated that he needed additional credit to purchase clothing for his children, the representative stated that if the Debtor did agree to reaffirm the debt, Sears would increase his credit limit to $200 above the amount then due. Believing he had no choice if he wanted to retain the merchandise, the Debtor indicated that he would sign the agreement. He also asked the representative whether Sears would notify the Court of the agreement. The representative answered, "All you have to do is sign the paper. We'll take care of the rest."

On January 29, 1996, the Debtor signed the reaffirmation agreement and returned it to Sears. Sears received the agreement but did not file it in the Debtor's bankruptcy case. This was not an oversight but a matter of policy on the part of Sears. Sears did not inform the Debtor that the agreement would not be binding unless submitted to the court. Nor did it inform him that it did not and would not file the agreement in the Bankruptcy Court.

After the Debtor called in February, 1996 to complain that his credit had not been restored, Sears did restore the Debtor's credit, though not in the full amount that had been promised. From March through November, 1996, the Debtor used this credit to purchase clothing, tools, and automotive services, all totaling $338.91. From March, 1996 through January of 1997, Sears billed the Debtor on a monthly basis, not only for the new debt but also for the prepetition debt, including postpetition interest thereon, which in itself averaged $21.50 per month during this period....

Sears produced no witnesses or evidence of its own at the hearing. However, through its attorney, Mr. Harris, it explained that it did not file the reaffirmation agreement because, in another case in this district, Judge Hillman had entered an order of civil contempt under which Sears would incur sanctions if it filed further reaffirmation agreements containing certain prohibited language....

[The court subsequently held that this reason was a "half truth" and that Sears's second reason for not filing was to avoid the constraints of section 524(c).]

At the close of the hearing, the Court took the matter under advisement and shortly thereafter issued two procedural orders. The first afforded interested parties an opportunity to file briefs in connection with the order to show cause. Sears filed a brief in defense of its actions, which it has now withdrawn; and the United States Trustee has filed a brief in support of sanctions.

★ ★ ★

On April 9, 1997, Sears withdrew the memorandum of law it had filed in response to the order to show cause and informed the Court that "the company no longer intends to contest the Court's order to show cause."

A discharge order operates as, among other things, an injunction against the commencement or continuation of any act to collect, recover, or offset any debt to which it applies — in this case, any prepetition debt — as a personal liability of the debtor, even if discharge of the debt was waived. 11 U.S.C. §524(a)(2)....

The purpose of the permanent injunction set forth at §524(a)(2) and reiterated in the discharge order is to effectuate one of the primary purposes of the Bankruptcy Code: to afford the debtor a financial "fresh start."...

The Code permits debtors to reaffirm debts that would otherwise be discharged, but only under conditions, set forth in §524(c)....

Section 524(c) provides that a reaffirmation agreement is enforceable only if certain requirements are met. Two are pertinent here: the agreement must be filed with the bankruptcy court, §524(c)(3); and, in instances where the debtor was not represented by counsel in the course of negotiating the agreement, the court must approve the agreement as (i) not imposing an undue hardship on the debtor or a dependent of the debtor and (ii) in the best interest of the debtor. §524(c)(6)(A). The first makes the second possible, and the second protects debtors from reaffirming debts improvidently — because they do not understand their rights and options, because they fall victim to overreaching creditors, or for whatever reason — by interposing the independent review and judgment of the court. These requirements are mandatory; and, as they exist to protect a debtor from his or her own bad judgment, the debtor cannot waive them.

* * *

For lack of filing and court approval, the agreement is void and never became effective or enforceable. Upon entry of the discharge order, the Debtor's prepetition obligation to Sears was discharged, and Sears was thereby enjoined from engaging in any act to collect it as a personal liability of the Debtor. Nonetheless, Sears did engage in acts to collect it as a personal liability of the Debtor....

Sears took these actions deliberately, with full knowledge that the agreement had not been filed and, consequently, that the debt was subject to the discharge injunction. Through Mr. Harris, Sears admitted that its failure to file the agreement was not inadvertent but deliberate....

Moreover, Sears's action in this case was no isolated incident. Sears admits that from January 1, 1995, through January 29, 1997, in over 2,700 cases in this district alone, it solicited and obtained a reaffirmation agreement that it then failed to file. That fact underscores Sears's willful and intentional flouting of the Bankruptcy Code....

RELIEF, SANCTIONS, AND ENFORCEMENT MEASURES

a. Declaratory Relief and Compensatory Damages

The Debtor is entitled to a declaration that his prepetition debt to Sears is discharged, that the reaffirmation agreement is void and never became effective, that Sears remains enjoined from taking any action whatsoever to recover its claim as a personal liability of the Debtor, and that the balance owing on his Sears account as of November 13, 1996, was zero.

The Debtor is also entitled to compensation for his post-petition payments of principal and interest on the prepetition debt, a total of $375....

The Debtor is also entitled to a reasonable sum, which I fix at $200, for his time and effort and for the travel and other incidental expenses he incurred in finally securing the benefit of his discharge. He would also be entitled to reasonable attorney's fees, but, fortunately for Sears, he was not represented by counsel in this matter. In sum, Sears shall pay the Debtor compensatory damages of $236.09, and it shall do so not by setoff and not in the form of an account credit or of a Sears gift certificate, but by cash.

b. Punitive Damages

The consequential damages in this case do not begin to reflect the magnitude of Sears's offense against Mr. Latanowich and against the bankruptcy law. Sears here made a conscious decision to disregard the clear requirements of the law because it was more expeditious and profitable to do so.[29] Its conduct toward the Debtor was predatory: Sears preyed on the Debtor when he was financially most vulnerable and powerless; and in doing so it deprived him of the fresh start that Congress intended that he should have....

In this case, the consequential damages do little more than dispossess the contemnor of its ill-gotten gains, which leaves it in no worse a position than if it had not violated the law at all. This gives Sears no incentive to discontinue its unlawful practice. In the form of punitive damages, the Court will supply this incentive by making it significantly more costly for Sears to do business by illegal methods than by legal ones.... However, the Court will refrain from issuing an order of punitive damages today, since doing so might arguably impair the government's authority to impose criminal penalties. As soon as that issue is clarified, the Court will sanction Sears in an amount payable to Mr. Latanowich....

c. Other Measures

The Court has issued an order to show cause why compensatory and punitive damages should not enter in each of the 2,733 other cases in which Sears has admitted that it obtained a reaffirmation from the debtor that it then failed to file.

Not surprisingly, the fallout from these events was extensive. Of particular interest to lawyers and law students was the fact that the Massachusetts court called in many of the lawyers involved in the Sears cases to find out why they had signed affidavits approving reaffirmations that were obviously not in the debtor's interest. In the course of some grilling from the bench, the court discovered that the lawyers often had failed to make the disclosures to the debtors required by the statute, even though in their affidavits they had sworn they had. The court joined an increasing number of courts in laying down detailed and rigorous standards for a lawyer to approve a reaffirmation.

---

29. The findings of fact on which the award of punitive damages have been established by proof beyond a reasonable doubt.

In addition, a recommended Reaffirmation Agreement has been adopted, Official Form 240B.

As for Sears, these revelations were naturally followed by civil and criminal investigations and class-action lawsuits. The final bill for its conduct was between $300 and $500 million dollars and an incalculable amount of bad press. Why would a major corporation take such a risk? Culhane and White, who have called the Sears-type procedures "rogue reaffirmations," provide the answer. With some important caveats, they estimate from their data that reaffirmations may represent $2.75 billion per year in potential recovery for creditors. Although Sears is only one creditor, because of its enormous size in the consumer market, Culhane and White estimate that Sears is involved in one-third of all the consumer bankruptcies filed in the United States each year. It had a lot to gain. But Sears was not alone. Federated Department Stores, G.E. Credit, and a number of other major companies had been engaged in similar activities, although on a smaller scale. Each consumer bankruptcy is a small event, except for the family involved, but consumer bankruptcy is a major component of the vast financial structure of consumer credit in America.

Perhaps in reaction to these cases or perhaps as a nod to debtor interests, the 2005 Amendments have inserted in section 524(c) an elaborate series of disclosures to debtors, reminiscent of the Truth In Lending Act disclosures. It seems unlikely that the addition of this boilerplate will have much effect, although it may help some consumers understand better what they will be required to do under a reaffirmation agreement and may force some to focus on their actual ability to make the payments they have promised. §524(c)(2), (k)(6)(A). Among the other weaknesses in these provisions, Congress gave creditors a safe harbor against any failure to abide by the rules by requiring only a good faith attempt to do so. §524(l)(3).

3. *Debts to Sovereign States*

The concept that bankruptcy is a universal proceeding, binding all creditors through Congress's plenary Article I power under the bankruptcy clause is subject to a major and growing exception: When the creditor is a state or local government, the federal courts have very limited powers of enforcement, whatever the theoretical rights of the parties might be under the Bankruptcy Code. If the debtor has stopped all the creditors except a state or local government, the scope of the debtor's bankruptcy protection will be sharply narrowed.

The limitation grows out of a case far from bankruptcy law, a dispute between the State of Florida and the Seminole Tribe over an obligation imposed on the state by a federal gaming statute. Seminole Tribe of Florida v. Florida, 517 U.S. 44 (1996). The tribe sued the state, and the state defended on Eleventh Amendment grounds. As the majority and dissent in *Seminole* issued competing views of the scope of the Eleventh Amendment, the debate specifically included the effect on the bankruptcy laws, among others.

Following *Seminole*, the courts have engaged in a far-ranging effort to determine the boundaries of the opinion as it applies in bankruptcy.

The case that follows reflects the general uncertainty surrounding the extent to which federal bankruptcy law can affect a state. The uncertainty is especially great and especially important as to the state's right to collect debts from a discharged debtor. Where will questions about discharge be resolved? Does the discharge injunction apply or must the debtors duke it out in state court? Many such questions are in active litigation. Because debts owed to states are involved in many consumer bankruptcy cases, the result may be to leave the debtors' fresh start very stale. As a result of *Seminole*, many debtors may leave bankruptcy only to head straight into state court to litigate the effects of their bankruptcy discharge, often with a state judiciary unfamiliar with the Code. Some debtors will find that before they can stabilize their economic circumstances, they must incur substantial additional expenses to finance substantial post-bankruptcy litigation.

═══ TENNESSEE STUDENT ASSISTANCE CORPORATION, ═══ PETITIONER v. HOOD

541 U.S. 440 (2004)

Chief Justice REHNQUIST delivered the opinion of the Court.

Article I, §8, cl. 4, of the Constitution provides that Congress shall have the power "[t]o establish...uniform Laws on the subject of Bankruptcies throughout the United States." We granted certiorari to determine whether this Clause grants Congress the authority to abrogate state sovereign immunity from private suits. Because we conclude that a proceeding initiated by a debtor to determine the dischargeability of a student loan debt is not a suit against the State for purposes of the Eleventh Amendment, we affirm the Court of Appeals' judgment, and we do not reach the question on which certiorari was granted.

I

Petitioner, Tennessee Student Assistance Corporation (TSAC), is a governmental corporation created by the Tennessee Legislature to administer student assistance programs. TSAC guarantees student loans made to residents of Tennessee and to nonresidents who are either enrolled in an eligible school in Tennessee or make loans through an approved Tennessee lender. §49-4-203.

Between July 1988 and February 1990, respondent, Pamela Hood, a resident of Tennessee, signed promissory notes for educational loans guaranteed by TSAC. In February 1999, Hood filed a "no asset" Chapter 7 bankruptcy petition in the United States Bankruptcy Court for the Western District of Tennessee; at the time of the filing, her student loans had an outstanding balance of $4,169.31. TSAC did not participate in the proceeding, but Sallie Mae Service, Inc. (Sallie Mae), submitted a proof of claim to the Bankruptcy Court, which it subsequently assigned to TSAC. The Bankruptcy Court granted Hood a general discharge in June 1999. See 11 U.S.C. §727(a).

* * *

Hood filed a complaint against the United States of America, the Department of Education, and Sallie Mae....

In response, TSAC filed a motion to dismiss the complaint for lack of jurisdiction, asserting Eleventh Amendment sovereign immunity.***

II

By its terms, the Eleventh Amendment precludes suits "in law or equity, commenced or prosecuted against one of the United States by Citizens of another State, or by Citizens or Subjects of any Foreign State." For over a century, however, we have recognized that the States' sovereign immunity is not limited to the literal terms of the Eleventh Amendment. ***

States, nonetheless, may still be bound by some judicial actions without their consent. In California v. Deep Sea Research, Inc., 523 U.S. 491, 118 S.Ct. 1464, 140 L.Ed.2d 626 (1998), we held that the Eleventh Amendment does not bar federal jurisdiction over *in rem* admiralty actions when the State is not in possession of the property. In that case, a private corporation located a historic shipwreck, the S.S. *Brother Jonathan*, in California's territorial waters. The corporation filed an *in rem* action in federal court seeking rights to the wreck and its cargo. The State of California intervened, arguing that it possessed title to the wreck and that its sovereign immunity precluded the court from adjudicating its rights. While acknowledging that the Eleventh Amendment might constrain federal courts' admiralty jurisdiction in some instances, we held that the States' sovereign immunity did not prohibit *in rem* admiralty actions in which the State did not possess the res, 523 U.S., at 507-508, 118 S.Ct. 1464.

The discharge of a debt by a bankruptcy court is similarly an *in rem* proceeding. Bankruptcy courts have exclusive jurisdiction over a debtor's property, wherever located, and over the estate. See 28 U.S.C. §1334(e). *** If a creditor chooses not to submit a proof of claim, once the debts are discharged, the creditor will be unable to collect on his unsecured loans. Rule 3002(a); see 11 U.S.C. §726. The discharge order releases a debtor from personal liability with respect to any discharged debt by voiding any past or future judgments on the debt and by operating as an injunction to prohibit creditors from attempting to collect or to recover the debt. §§524(a)(1), (2); 3 W. Norton, Bankruptcy Law and Practice 2d §48:1, p. 48-3 (1998) (hereinafter Norton).

A bankruptcy court is able to provide the debtor a fresh start in this manner, despite the lack of participation of all of his creditors, because the court's jurisdiction is premised on the debtor and his estate, and not on the creditors. ***

Under our longstanding precedent, States, whether or not they choose to participate in the proceeding, are bound by a bankruptcy court's discharge order no less than other creditors. *** At least when the bankruptcy court's jurisdiction over the res is unquestioned, cf. United States v. Nordic Village, Inc., 503 U.S. 30, 112 S.Ct. 1011, 117 L.Ed.2d 181 (1992), our cases indicate that the exercise of its *in rem* jurisdiction to discharge a debt does not infringe state sovereignty.[30]

TSAC concedes that States are generally bound by a bankruptcy court's discharge order, but argues that the particular process by which student loan debts are discharged unconstitutionally infringes its sovereignty. Student loans used to be presumptively discharged in a general discharge. But in 1976, Congress provided a significant benefit to the States by making it more difficult for debtors to discharge student loan debts guaranteed by States. That benefit is currently governed by 11 U.S.C. §523(a)(8), which provides that student loan debts guaranteed by governmental units are not included in a general discharge order unless excepting the debt from the order would impose an "undue hardship" on the debtor. ★ ★ ★

No matter how difficult Congress has decided to make the discharge of student loan debt, the bankruptcy court's jurisdiction is premised on the res, not on the persona; that States were granted the presumptive benefit of nondischargeability does not alter the court's underlying authority. A debtor does not seek monetary damages or any affirmative relief from a State by seeking to discharge a debt; nor does he subject an unwilling State to a coercive judicial process. He seeks only a discharge of his debts.

★ ★ ★

We find no authority, *in fine*, that suggests a bankruptcy court's exercise of its *in rem* jurisdiction to discharge a student loan debt would infringe state sovereignty in the manner suggested by TSAC. We thus hold that the undue hardship determination sought by Hood in this case is not a suit against a State for purposes of the Eleventh Amendment.[31]

III

Lastly, we deal with the procedure that was used in this case. Creditors generally are not entitled to personal service before a bankruptcy court may discharge a debt. ★ ★ ★ The current Bankruptcy Rules require the debtor to file an "adversary proceeding" against the State in order to discharge his student loan debt. The proceeding is considered part of the original bankruptcy case, see 10 Collier on Bankruptcy ¶ 7003.02 (15th ed. rev. 2003), and still within the bankruptcy court's *in rem* jurisdiction as discussed above. But, as prescribed by the Rules, an "adversary proceeding" requires the service of a summons and a complaint. Rules 7001(6), 7003, and 7004.

Because this "adversary proceeding" has some similarities to a traditional civil trial, Justice THOMAS contends that the Bankruptcy Court can-

---

30. *Missouri v. Fiske*, 290 U.S. 18, 54 S.Ct. 18, 78 L.Ed. 145 (1933), is not to the contrary. ★ ★ ★ There, we noted the State might still be bound by the federal court's adjudication even if an injunction could not issue. 290 U.S., at 29, 54 S.Ct. 18. ★ ★ ★

31. This is not to say, "a bankruptcy court's *in rem* jurisdiction overrides sovereign immunity," *United States v. Nordic Village, Inc.*, 503 U.S. 30, 38, 112 S.Ct. 1011, 117 L.Ed.2d 181 (1992), as Justice THOMAS characterizes our opinion, *post*, at 1919, but rather that the court's exercise of its *in rem* jurisdiction to discharge a student loan debt is not an affront to the sovereignty of the State. Nor do we hold that every exercise of a bankruptcy court's *in rem* jurisdiction will not offend the sovereignty of the State. No such concerns are present here, and we do not address them.

not make an undue hardship determination without infringing TSAC's sovereignty. * * *

If Justice THOMAS' interpretation of *Federal Maritime Comm'n* were adopted, *Deep Sea Research, Van Huffel,* and *Irving Trust,* all of which involved proceedings resembling traditional civil adjudications, would likely have to be overruled. We are not willing to take such a step.

The issuance of process, nonetheless, is normally an indignity to the sovereignty of a State because its purpose is to establish personal jurisdiction over the State. We noted in *Seminole Tribe,* "The Eleventh Amendment does not exist solely in order to prevent federal-court judgments that must be paid out of a State's treasury; it also serves to avoid the indignity of subjecting a State to the coercive process of judicial tribunals at the instance of private parties." 517 U.S., at 58, 116 S.Ct. 1114 (citations and internal quotation marks omitted).

Here, however, the Bankruptcy Court's *in rem* jurisdiction allows it to adjudicate the debtor's discharge claim without *in personam* jurisdiction over the State. See 4A C. Wright & A. Miller, Federal Practice and Procedure §1070, pp. 280-281 (3d ed.2002) (noting jurisdiction over the person is irrelevant if the court has jurisdiction over the property). Hood does not argue that the court should exercise personal jurisdiction; all she wants is a determination of the dischargeability of her debt. The text of §523(a)(8) does not require a summons, and absent Rule 7001(6) a debtor could proceed by motion, see Rule 9014 ("[I]n a contested matter...not otherwise governed by these rules, relief shall be requested by motion"), which would raise no constitutional concern. Hood concedes that even if TSAC ignores the summons and chooses not to participate in the proceeding the Bankruptcy Court cannot discharge her debt without making an undue hardship determination.

We see no reason why the service of a summons, which in this case is indistinguishable in practical effect from a motion, should be given dispositive weight. As we said in Idaho v. Coeur d'Alene Tribe of Idaho, 521 U.S. 261, 270 (1997), "[t]he real interests served by the Eleventh Amendment are not to be sacrificed to elementary mechanics of captions and pleading."

We therefore decline to decide whether a bankruptcy court's exercise of personal jurisdiction over a State would be valid under the Eleventh Amendment. * * * The judgment of the United States Court of Appeals for the Sixth Circuit is affirmed, and the case is remanded for further proceedings consistent with this opinion.

Justice THOMAS, with whom Justice SCALIA joins, dissenting.

We granted certiorari in this case to decide whether Congress has the authority to abrogate state sovereign immunity under the Bankruptcy Clause. Instead of answering this question, the Court addresses a more difficult one regarding the extent to which a bankruptcy court's exercise of its *in rem* jurisdiction could offend the sovereignty of a creditor-State. I recognize that, as the Court concludes today, the *in rem* nature of bankruptcy proceedings might affect the ability of a debtor to obtain, *by motion,* a bankruptcy court determination that affects a creditor-State's rights, but I would not reach this difficult question here. Even if the Bankruptcy Court could have exercised its in rem jurisdiction to make an undue hardship determination by motion, I cannot ignore the fact that the determination in this case was sought pursuant to an adversary proceeding. Under Federal Maritime Comm'n v. South Carolina Ports Authority, 535 U.S. 743, 122 S.Ct. 1864, 152 L.Ed.2d 962 (2002), the adversary proceeding here clearly constitutes a suit against the State for sovereign immunity purposes. I would thus reach the easier question presented and conclude that Congress lacks authority to abrogate state sovereign immunity under the Bankruptcy Clause.

* * *

I

[A]lthough the adversary proceeding in this case does not require the State to "defend itself" against petitioner in the ordinary sense, the effect is the same, whether done by adversary proceeding or by motion, and whether the proceeding is *in personam* or *in rem*. In order to preserve its rights, the State is compelled either to subject itself to the Bankruptcy Court's jurisdiction or to forfeit its rights. And, whatever the nature of the Bankruptcy Court's jurisdiction, it maintains at least as much control over nonconsenting States as the FMC, which lacks the power to enforce its own orders. *Federal Maritime Comm'n* rejected the view that the FMC's lack of enforcement power means that parties are not coerced to participate in its proceedings because the effect is the same — a State must submit to the adjudication or compromise its ability to defend itself in later proceedings. Here, if the State does not oppose the debtor's claim of undue hardship, the Bankruptcy Court is authorized to enter a default judgment *without making an undue hardship determination*. See Fed. Rules Bkrtcy. Proc. 7055, 9014 (adopting Fed. Rule Civ. Proc. 55 in both adversary proceedings and in contested matters governed by motion). The Court apparently concludes otherwise, but, tellingly, its only support for that questionable proposition is a statement made at oral argument.

As I explain in Part I-B, *infra*, I do not contest the assertion that in bankruptcy, like admiralty, there might be a limited *in rem* exception to state sovereign immunity from suit. Nor do I necessarily reject the argument that this proceeding could have been resolved by motion without offending the dignity of the State. However, because this case did not proceed by motion, I cannot resolve the merits based solely upon what might have, but did not, occur. I would therefore hold that the adversary proceeding in this case constituted a suit against the State for sovereign immunity purposes.

* * *

================================

Subjecting the states to the discharge was the most important limitation the Court could impose on the *Seminole* doctrine as applied to bankruptcy, but many other effects remain. The thin distinction offered by the majority in *Hood* leaves open the possibility of a number of other areas in which an ordinary creditor would be stopped in its tracks, but a state government may violate the bankruptcy laws with impunity. So, for example, if a state or local government seizes a driver's license because the debtor failed to pay traffic tickets and offers to return the license if the debtor repays in full, that would seem to be a clear violation of the automatic stay, but it is not clear that the *Hood* majority would permit a bankruptcy court to issue an injunction that would require return of the license as opposed to the defensive use of the discharge in a lawsuit against the debtor. If not, then the protection offered by the bankruptcy laws has been significantly reduced. See In re Raphael, 238 B.R. 69 (D.N.J. 1999) for a pre-*Hood* discussion of these facts and a ruling that left the debtors to the mercy of the state courts.

The Supreme Court took an important step toward protecting bankruptcy jurisdiction in *Hood*, but the dance with state and local creditors is not yet over.

4. Nondiscrimination

Aside from creditors trying to avoid the effects of the discharge, discharged debtors seeking a fresh start also face the risk that employers or government agencies will look askance at someone who has been bankrupt and will refuse a job, a license, or a permit crucial to the debtor's livelihood or well-being. Conscious of that risk, Congress included in the Code section 525, which forbids discrimination of that sort. On the whole, however, the reported cases find the courts interpreting these provisions narrowly. It appears more debtors have lost such suits than have won them. Once again, the reported death of the stigma of bankruptcy seems a bit premature.

Problem Set 13

13.1. The Muscle Mart is the only complete bodybuilding gym in Missoula, Montana. It charges a monthly membership and adds assessments for use of the sauna and items ordered at the juice bar. MM has a firm policy (would they have flabby policies?): If two months of dues or sauna fees are left unpaid, the membership is revoked, and the former member is not permitted to use any of the equipment until the unpaid balance is paid in full.

Peter Lanier has just filed for a Chapter 7 bankruptcy, discharging among his other debts two months' worth of MM dues. MM has revoked Peter's membership, and Peter is frantic to get back to his workouts. He has offered to pay a month in advance, but MM refuses. What would you advise Peter? See §524(a).

13.2. Two months ago, you handled a routine Chapter 7 bankruptcy for Kevin James. Kevin is a gentle soul, and the bankruptcy has been bothering him. Last week, he was in a former creditor's store when a clerk made a remark about "stiffing your friends." Kevin said he felt terrible and offered to repay the debt. The store manager, an enterprising young man, got this promise in writing. Now Kevin fears this was not very smart. He is struggling with his current obligations and is not sure he can pay this creditor. He calls you to ask if that written agreement is enforceable. What do you tell him? See §524(c).

13.3. Chauncy "Big Moon" Mooney supports his wife and five children at a marginal level with his job as a dishwasher at a local bar. Big Moon lives for weekends, when he cruises with his old club, the Ramblers. Big Moon has the meanest machine in the club, a Fat Boy with Porker pipes and a Revteck high performance engine. Big Moon still owes $18,000 on the cycle; notwithstanding Big Moon's loving care, he wrecked it twice, so the cycle would appraise for about $15,000.

Because of ever-increasing costs of maintaining his family and cycle, Big Moon has been overwhelmed with unsecured debt and decides to declare bankruptcy. He has only one valuable asset — a very small home with a 4.5 percent mortgage. His equity in the home will yield about $16,000 after the costs of sale, all of which would be exempt. Monthly rent on an apartment will be more than double his present house payments. Big Moon proposes to sell the home and use the money to redeem his hog. Will you sign an "undue hardship" affidavit for Big Moon? See §722.

13.4. Tawanda Johnson is a single mother of two children who until recently has managed to keep the family in reasonable shape after her husband's death in a car-train accident. Her skills as a die etcher in the local microchip plant produced a decent income until a year ago, when the plant headed for somewhere in Asia. She held out for a technical job for quite a while, running up some substantial bills, but has been waiting tables and working a night-shift cleaning job the last four months to keep food on the table. Her big worry is holding on to her house and her car. The credit union has the mortgage. You've dealt with them before and know their policy: They'll happily agree to a reaff on the mortgage, but only if Tawanda also reaffs in full all her other debts to the credit union, which include three loans. Two are unsecured "signature" loans. The third is a car loan. The car is a four-year-old Hyundai the couple bought used almost three years ago. It is worth $5,900 bluebook on which she owes $7,300. She is desperate to keep it, because it works pretty well (her husband was a mechanic and knew cars). If she had to buy a new one, "they could sell me trash and I wouldn't know it." Without a car, she couldn't get to either job. The house was their dream home and Tawanda says she'd work three jobs to keep it. What do you advise her? What are you able and willing to do for her in this situation? §524(c).

13.5. You are about to file a routine Chapter 7 for the Perez couple, Juan and Sally. Juan drives a truck and Sally pilots an EMS ambulance. There is nothing special about the Chapter 7, except you notice a debt for state taxes from a few years ago. Although it seems clear the taxes are dischargeable under section 523, the state tax authority is very aggressive and you have heard of them going after debtors following bankruptcy, even though they never file claims in no-asset cases like that of the Perez family. What steps should you consider taking and why? What if your research shows that your state has recently adopted drivers-license suspension for failure to pay taxes?

13.6. You have just been hired by a medium-sized firm that has had little previous bankruptcy practice beyond representing creditor banks in a few actions. The partners have decided that in hiring you they are making a significant commitment to developing a bankruptcy practice. They have asked you for some suggestions on what will become the firm's policies regarding consumer bankruptcies, and today you have scheduled a presentation on reaffirmation. What will you propose should be the firm's practice on the attorney reaffirmation affidavit required in section 524(c)? Keep in mind during your presentation that the partners will be concerned about the number of attorney hours spent in relatively low-fee consumer cases, how consumer cases can be processed by lower-paid paralegals or new firm associates, and how to maintain good relations with all their clients.

13.7. Your firm represents Peoples State Bank, which does a substantial amount of consumer lending. With the rise in the number of consumer bankruptcies, PSB has decided it needs help in determining what to do when it holds a security interest in an automobile and the debtor declares bankruptcy. Because your firm has taken care of PSB's legal work for years, you know that PSB has a very protective lending agreement that includes a provision that the debtor's declaration of bankruptcy is an automatic default under the contract.

PSB brings its first case to you: The debtor, Jansen, has gone into bankruptcy owing PSB $7,899. The loan is at slightly better than average market rates. The loan is secured by a valid PMSI on a car worth $6,000. It would cost PSB about $500 to repossess and resell the car. Assuming average depreciation of the car and maintenance of the current payment schedule, if payments are continued the loan balance would decrease faster than the value of the car will decline. Jansen is not in default on the payments. He has a good job and says he plans to continue to pay on schedule.

PSB has three questions, two specific and one general: (1) can it get the car back in this situation, if it wants to; (2) if Jansen keeps the car, what portion of the amount owed will it get paid; and (3) what is your overall advice about how to handle this sort of problem? Keep in mind as you deal with PSB that they want you to develop some generalized principles that they can give to a loan officer so the loan officer can deal with bankrupt debtors without having to call you for expensive individualized analyses each time.

13.8. Carlos Valdez, the sales force supervisor from NCP Homebuilders, is back in your office today. He reminds you that it is his responsibility to monitor the work of the employees closely and to make certain that the sales representatives reflect the image of steadiness and integrity that NCP wishes to promote. Valdez tells you that he followed your advice and did not fire the employee whose wages were garnished (problem 3.3), but he is certain that the employee's problems have gotten worse. The employee could not struggle along on reduced take-home pay, and he has now filed for a Chapter 7 bankruptcy. Valdez has heard that agents in two other firms have mentioned "the kind of people NCP has," and he is apoplectic. Valdez is determined to fire him now. What is your advice? See §§524, 525.

CHAPTER 6

CHAPTER 13 BANKRUPTCY

A. ELEMENTS OF AN ACCEPTABLE PLAN

1. An Overview of Chapter 13

In the preceding chapters of this part, we have seen elements common to all consumer bankruptcies — enforcing the automatic stay and deciding what is property of the estate — and we have taken a consumer debtor through the steps of a Chapter 7 bankruptcy. The Bankruptcy Code provides an alternative for consumer debtors in financial trouble: a Chapter 13 Adjustment of Debt, or "Wage Earners' Plan" as it is often known.

— Wage Earners' Plan

The Chapter 13 option differs significantly from the Chapter 7 liquidation. In Chapter 7 debtors essentially freeze their assets and debts when they file for bankruptcy. Their assets become the property of the bankruptcy estate. The debtor keeps assets within the exemption limits and turns the excess over to the trustee for sale and distribution to the creditors. In return for liquidating all non-exempt assets, the debtor is relieved of any future obligations to pay dischargeable, pre-bankruptcy debts, and all the debtor's subsequent earnings are free from the reach of pre-petition creditors. The debtor either relinquishes property subject to a valid security interest or continues to make payments and keeps it.

Ch. 7

By contrast, Chapter 13 focuses on using future earnings, rather than accumulated assets, to pay creditors. The debtor keeps all assets, regardless of whether the assets exceed exemption levels, but the debtor agrees to turn over a portion of all future income for a minimum of three years. The trustee takes a percentage of the debtor's income for each pay period, deducts a percentage to cover administrative expenses, and then distributes the remainder to the creditors according to a court-approved plan. When the debtor has completed the agreed payout, the debtor's remaining obligations are discharged.

Ch. 13 focuses on future earnings — Tees take a % of Dor's income for each pay period

As a result, every debtor who is eligible for both Chapter 7 and Chapter 13 must make a fundamental choice: To seek an immediate discharge in Chapter 7 or to try to pay some or all debts in installments under a Chapter 13 plan. The debtor who chooses Chapter 13 must prepare a plan detailing the amounts to be repaid and the terms of repayment in accord with certain

Ch. 7 — immediate discharge. Ch. 13 — installment plan

statutory requirements. As we have seen, there are a number of provisions in Chapter 7, including section 707(b), that bar a debtor from that Chapter, leaving a choice of Chapter 13 or no bankruptcy relief at all.

From a creditor's standpoint, the difference between Chapters 7 and 13 is the prospect of payment obtained by selling the debtor's assets versus payment from the debtor's future income. From the debtor's viewpoint, the supervision of the court will last from the day of filing until plan payments are completed, generally three to five years. No discharge from debt will be granted until the debtor makes the very last payment on the plan. This is a marked contrast to the Chapter 7 debtor who is generally under the jurisdiction of the court only from the filing to the day of the discharge hearing, which is usually held within six months. The timing of the Chapter 13 discharge also differs from a corporate discharge in Chapter 11, under which the approval of a plan generates an immediate discharge, even before the payments begin, unlike the delay in Chapter 13.

The Chapter 13 trustee has a somewhat different role from that of the Chapter 7 trustee. In Chapter 13 the debtor retains control of the property of the estate, although the statutory provisions are confused and have a number of gaps. §§1303, 1306. Thus the Chapter 13 TIB does not have the function of collecting, preserving, and selling the property of the estate. §1302(b)(1). Instead, the debtor remains in possession of the property.

Nonetheless, the Chapter 13 trustee has several important functions. The trustee is charged with objecting to improper creditor claims. The trustee is also responsible for ensuring that the debtor gives up the required amount of income, and the trustee asserts any objections to the debtor's discharge. At the same time the trustee has a duty to assist the debtor in the performance of the debtor's duties. §1302(b)(1), (4). In short, the trustee scrutinizes everyone connected with the case — debtor and creditors — to be sure they are following the rules set down in the Bankruptcy Code. The trustee's main duties, however, are in connection with confirmation of the plan and distribution of payments.

The trustee is generally expected to recommend approval or denial of confirmation of a debtor's plan. §1302(b)(2)(B). The trustee is obligated to ensure that payments are commenced within 30 days after the plan is filed and that the payments are properly distributed to creditors. §§1302(b)(5), 1326. Ordinarily, the plan provides that debtors will make a lump-sum monthly payment to the trustee and the trustee will then distribute the funds to the creditors, although some creditors may be paid directly (a procedure known as payment "outside the plan"). If the debtor's payments fall behind, it is usually the trustee who monitors the debtor's performance, urges compliance, and, if need be, files to dismiss the debtor's case for nonpayment. When a debtor misses a payment or two, trustees often seek wage attachment orders, which are routinely granted, so that a portion of the debtor's wages goes directly to the trustee for plan payments. Because the attachment is made pursuant to federal bankruptcy law, state restrictions on wage garnishment are inapplicable.

Most urban districts have "standing" Chapter 13 trustees who serve in a large number of cases. Some districts have more than one standing trustee because of the volume of business. 28 U.S.C. §586(b). The trustees are appointed by the United States Trustee. §1302(a); 28 U.S.C. §586(b). In more populous districts, many millions of dollars are distributed to creditors through the standing Chapter 13 trustees each year. In those districts, the position of standing trustee is not just a full-time job, but an active business relying on a highly sophisticated, computerized system of receipts and disbursements. The fees of standing trustees are fixed by the court, subject to statutory maximums. 28 U.S.C. §586(e).

If a trustee's office is often an active small business, Chapter 13 nation-wide is Big Business, as the following report demonstrates.

Uncle Sam Is My Collection Agent
Forbes Magazine, **June 15, 1998**
By Brigid McMenamin

Last year 400,000 Americans filed for Chapter 13 personal bankruptcy, nearly three times the number a decade ago. Bad news? Not for Bear Stearns Cos.

While banks and credit card firms grumble about deadbeats, those clever folks at the $3.5 billion . . . New York City–based investment bank and securities firm have found a way to cash in on them.

Bear Stearns is snapping up Chapter 13 debts of individuals, through . . . Max Recovery. Max pays creditors like Chase or Household Finance 8 cents to 15 cents on the dollar for claims against individuals going through a Chapter 13 bankruptcy. . . .

When the debtor starts sending monthly checks to the trustee under his payback plan, Bear Stearns gets the creditor's share, typically 20 cents to 70 on the dollar, sometimes more. Many debtors, however, never complete their payment plan. . . .

The key to this business is volume. The market is big: The combined unsecured debts of Chapter 13 filings come to some $6 billion a year. . . . It's just the latest example of the growing multibillion dollar trade in personal debt, from car loans and credit card balances to tort judgments and time shares. . . .

Creditors who opt to sell their claims simply don't think they'll net as much as Max Recovery can pay. . . . Union Bank of California, for one, sold $3 million of Chapter 13 accounts last year to Max Recovery. Bank officials figured they'd never beat 10 cents on the dollar.

What are the sellers thinking? "I don't think they [creditors] fully under-stand the value of what they're selling," says Jack Dennison [a seller of software to Chapter 13 trustees]. . . .

The business promises to grow, as legislation pending in Congress would force more consumers to choose Chapter 13 and pay off a bigger percentage of their debt. The politicians see some kind of moral imperative here. Bankers just see good business.

We will return to the financial and policy questions surrounding Chapter 13, but first we focus on how it works, starting with the required elements of a Chapter 13 plan, followed by a discussion of the eligibility requirements for declaring Chapter 13 bankruptcy. The consumer bankruptcy part concludes with a section exploring why a debtor might choose a Chapter 13 plan or feel forced to do so. At that point, we will have reviewed the details of most of the consumer bankruptcy options, and it will be possible to begin to develop an idea of what choices debtors realistically have and what factors might guide those choices.

Because the process of a Chapter 13 payout is very different from that of a Chapter 7 liquidation, we begin with a sketch of how the Chapter 13 case is filed and how the plan is proposed and confirmed.

A typical case is In re Foster, 670 F.2d 478, 482-483 (5th Cir. 1982). The court described how the Fosters initiated their Chapter 13 case:

> On November 26, 1980, John W. Foster, Jr. and Myrtha D. Foster filed a petition and plan in bankruptcy pursuant to Chapter 13 of the United States Bankruptcy Code. According to the plan, the Fosters would pay to the bankruptcy trustee $350 per month for thirty-six months, which payments were to be used to pay 100 percent of the priority claim of the Internal Revenue Service, the full value of the collateral of all secured creditors whose claims were timely filed and duly proven and allowed (with the exception of the mortgage claims separately provided for), and 49 percent on the claims of the unsecured creditors whose claims were duly proven and allowed. . . .
>
> A Chapter 13 case is commenced by the filing of a Chapter 13 petition. §301. Only the debtor may commence a Chapter 13 proceeding; there is no provision for an "involuntary" Chapter 13. The commencement of the case creates an estate which includes, among other things, "all legal or equitable interests of the debtor in property as of the commencement of the case," §541, and property and earnings acquired after commencement of the case but before the case is closed, dismissed or converted, §1306(a), with the debtor remaining in possession of the property of the estate, except as provided in the confirmed plan or the order confirming the plan, §1306(b). The confirmation of a plan vests all of the property of the estate in the debtor. §1327(b). From the time of the filing of the Chapter 13 petition, the "automatic stay" provisions of §362 restrict the actions of creditors against the property of the estate or of the debtor, "prohibiting most acts and the commencement or continuation of most civil actions to collect a consumer debt." Again, a major concern is the protection of both debtor and creditor. Besides being a fundamental debtor protection, the stay provisions prevent some creditors from obtaining payment in preference to and to the detriment of other creditors. The automatic stay provisions remain in effect as concerns most acts until the case is closed or dismissed or a Chapter 13 discharge is granted or denied. §362(c). In addition to filing a petition, the debtor files a plan providing for the repayment of all or a portion of the claims against the debtor out of the debtor's future income (or out of the estate).
>
> The key hurdle for the debtor is the development of an acceptable Chapter 13 plan. The plan is essentially the price the debtor agrees to pay for the protection of Chapter 13, and it is the debtor's responsibility to develop a plan that conforms to the statutory requirements.

The Fosters then began the process of having their plan confirmed by the bankruptcy court:

> A creditors' meeting was held on February 11, 1981, at which the Fosters appeared and submitted to examination. Also in attendance were the bankruptcy trustee, appointed by the bankruptcy court, and the Fosters' attorney. The trustee recommended that a confirmation hearing be held and that the Chapter 13 plan proposed by the Fosters be confirmed.
>
> At the confirmation hearing, held on February 26, 1981, the bankruptcy court noted that the Fosters' plan "met all requirements for confirmation and was recommended for confirmation by the trustee." . . .

Id. at 482. The Fosters' plan was ultimately approved by the court, although with some modifications.

The debtor's attempt to formulate an acceptable plan — and the legal hurdles the debtor encounters — is the subject of the several sections of this chapter. The Code provisions that tell us what may or must be in a Chapter 13 plan are somewhat arbitrarily distributed between sections 1322 and 1325. Section 1322(a)(2) gives the debtor the power to use a plan to modify the rights of creditors, both secured and unsecured. This power includes, for example, reduction of the amount to be paid and stretching out the period of time over which payment is to be made. Other provisions in the two sections then substantially constrain the debtor's power, especially with regard to secured creditors. These two sections will be our primary focus in the next portion of this chapter.

2. Payments to Secured Creditors

One of the most common reasons for choosing a Chapter 13 bankruptcy is the debtor's desire to keep property that is subject to a security interest. When a significant asset, such as a car or furniture, is subject to a valid security interest, the Chapter 13 plan is often built around satisfying the legal requirements for retaining that property and structuring a new payment schedule.

Just as secured creditors in Chapter 7 enjoy enhanced status and are entitled to greater repayment than unsecured creditors, the secured creditor in Chapter 13 enjoys substantially better protection than the unsecured creditor. The debtor's attempts to fashion a Chapter 13 plan to retain property subject to a security interest will often provoke a dispute with the secured party who declares the debtor in default and wants the collateral back. Whether the creditor can exercise its right to repossession and sale, realizing the value of the collateral and terminating its contract with the debtor, will depend on whether the debtor can comply with the provisions of Chapter 13 that are designed to protect secured creditors.

Courts must solve two separate but related issues when a secured creditor wants to repossess and sell the collateral. The first issue is protection of the secured party's interest in the collateral while the case is going on. Because the debtor proposes to keep the property, the secured party is naturally concerned about the risk that the collateral will lose its value. If the debtor defaults later on, the secured party could be left with collateral worth considerably less than when bankruptcy was originally filed. This problem is usually cast in terms of providing "adequate protection" for the secured party under section 362(d). The two principal types of risks that concern the secured creditor are a loss of the collateral (e.g., by fire, theft, or simple neglect) and a decline in its value (such as depreciation over time).

The second issue is adequate payment to the secured party. There is a statutory formula, discussed below, that calculates the minimum amount the debtor must pay in order to keep the collateral.

In Chapter 11 business cases the two issues are fairly distinct, with the first (adequate protection) focusing on immediate payments even while the plan negotiations are proceeding and the second (total payments) ensuring that the long-term payments will compensate the secured creditor to the extent of its legal protection in bankruptcy. Chapter 11 plans are often proposed months after filing, so that the first issue must be dealt with instantly while the second can await plan negotiations. In a Chapter 13, by contrast, the debtor's plan is usually filed with the bankruptcy petition and the two issues are often considered together. The next case and the text that follows it discuss the adequate protection problem. The two cases that follow after that discuss the payment requirement. In *Radden* the creditor sought to lift the automatic stay, and the court's focus is on adequate protection. In *Rash* and *Hollins*, the creditor objected to the provisions of the debtor's plan, and the court addresses the total payment problem.

As we noted at the beginning of the section on bankruptcy, when a debtor files for bankruptcy all collection attempts against the debtor — including repossession of collateral — are automatically stayed under section 362(a). A creditor can, however, move to have the automatic stay lifted under section 362(d), claiming that its interest in the collateral is not adequately protected. The creditor could move to lift the stay in any proceeding — Chapter 7, 13, or 11. In Chapter 7, because the parties are moving toward immediate liquidation, adequate protection is rarely argued. The debtor is usually about to surrender the property to the creditor or to keep it via redemption, reaffirmation, or ride-through as we discussed in the materials on Chapter 7. A reaffirmation, redemption, or ride-through makes an adequate protection motion unnecessary or unavailable in Chapter 7. In Chapter 13 or Chapter 11, by contrast, the debtor proposes to retain the collateral and pay over a long time, often on terms different from the original contract. Creditors may respond with a claim that the debtor has failed to protect the creditors' statutory rights.

In the following case, creditor GMAC had already repossessed the car before the bankruptcy filing, and it wanted to retain and sell the car to pay off its outstanding loan balance. With the automatic stay in place, GMAC could not proceed with a sale, so it moved to lift the stay, arguing the application of both subsection 362(d)(1) and (2). Because GMAC had possession of the car, the debtor had to make two arguments in his response: one against the lifting of the stay, to prevent GMAC from selling the car immediately, and the other for return of the car to the debtor. The second argument relied on section 542 of the Code, which requires "turnover" of property to the trustee. Because the debtor in this Chapter 13 case retains possession of the estate's property, the debtor has the right to use the trustee's power to recover property.

In re RADDEN

35 B.R. 821 (Bankr. E.D. Va. 1983)

SHELLEY, Bankruptcy Judge.

These matters involve the proper disposition of a 1979 Ford Mustang automobile (the "property"). The debtor, along with Priscilla Coe, purchased the property from Hechler Chevrolet, Inc. ("Hechler") on October 17, 1981.

The property was titled in the debtor's name alone. Hechler financed this purchase by a retail installment sales contract secured by the vehicle. This installment sales agreement was assigned to GMAC pursuant to its agreement with Hechler entered July 3, 1980....

The debtor failed to make the contractually required payments to GMAC for the month of June, 1983. This constituted the first default under the assigned installment sales contract. The debtor did not cure the default and also failed to make the required monthly payment in July, 1983. [Apparently GMAC lawfully repossessed the car prior to bankruptcy.] GMAC notified the debtor and the cobuyer, Priscilla Coe, of their right to redeem the property and of a proposed sale of the property on August 12, 1983, if they did not redeem the property prior thereto.

On August 10,1983, the debtor filed for relief under Chapter 13 of the Bankruptcy Code. In his Chapter 13 plan the debtor lists the value of the property as $2,700.00 and the balance due on the contract as $4,400.30. The Chapter 13 plan proposes to pay, through the standing Chapter 13 trustee, GMAC in full to the extent of the value of the collateral plus interest thereon at the rate of 5 percent per annum in deferred monthly cash payments of $89.68 over a period of 36 months. To the extent that the amount on the contract exceeds the value of the collateral, the obligation owing to GMAC is treated as an unsecured claim. Under the plan, unsecured claims are to receive seventy cents on the dollar.

The debtor lives about a mile and a half from his place of employment and about three blocks from a food store. He has been able to get groceries without difficulty since the time GMAC obtained possession of the property. He has gotten to and from work either by obtaining rides from friends, by using his mother's automobile, or by walking. The debtor testified that (1) he is presently working from 3:00 until 11:00 and that a friend with an automobile in the same apartment complex works the same shift; (2) that he has missed very little work in the past five years at Western Electric, except that on at least one occasion he was absent because of inability to get to work; (3) that when he must walk home he does so on a street that is busy with traffic, is not lighted, and does not have a sidewalk; (4) that he has not yet been required to walk home from work in cold weather; (5) that he seeks a turnover of the property to enable him to get to and from work; (6) that although the property is not presently insured by him for collision and liability, he would re-obtain insurance on the property; (7) that he has the present finances to procure such insurance; and (8) that he has presently a valid driver's license.

CONCLUSIONS OF LAW

... GMAC here seeks relief based both on the lack of adequate protection, id. §362(d)(1), and on the grounds that the debtor does not have any equity in the property and that such property is not necessary for the debtor's effective reorganization. Id. §362(d)(2).

As to the latter basis for obtaining relief from the stay, this Court needs to find only that the property is necessary for an effective reorganization to deny

GMAC relief pursuant to §362(d)(2). The debtor admits in his Chapter 13 plan and his memorandum in support of his adversary proceeding and in opposition to GMAC's adversary proceeding that he lacks equity in the property. Therefore, if the property questioned here is not necessary for the debtor's effective reorganization, the creditor is entitled to relief from stay.

The debtor bears the burden of proving that the property is necessary for his effective reorganization. §362(g). This Court is satisfied that an automobile is necessary for an individual's effective reorganization in today's society. As the debtor testified, he needs the property to get to and from his place of employment. Moreover, individuals need transportation to obtain medical as well as other necessary services. Having found that the property is necessary for an effective reorganization, this Court will not grant GMAC relief from the stay pursuant to §362(d)(2).

As an alternate basis for obtaining relief from the stay, GMAC alleges that it has an interest in property that is not adequately protected. Lack of adequate protection is sufficient "cause" pursuant to §362(d)(1) for a court to grant a creditor relief from the automatic stay. The resolution of GMAC's claim in this regard turns on the issue of what is GMAC's "interest in property."

[The court discussed and rejected GMAC's theory that it must be protected against any loss under its "recourse" or repayment agreement with the car dealer. The court then discussed GMAC's interest in the car itself.]

The Court notes initially that the property in which GMAC has an interest is currently in GMAC's possession, therefore, GMAC is in the best position to protect its interest in the property from the likelihood of theft, vandalism, or destruction by natural cause.

Second, under the provisions of the debtor's plan, GMAC will retain their lien on the collateral and receive the amount of their allowed secured claim with interest and, therefore, its interest in property will be adequately protected if the plan is effectively consummated. GMAC has not demonstrated that the debtor's chances of rehabilitation are remote. To the contrary, the debtor has established that he has a stable employment record and that he is capable of meeting the payments to the standing trustee under the plan. The debtor has a reasonable likelihood of having his plan confirmed and consummated and, therefore, GMAC will likely receive the allowed amount of their secured claim through deferred cash payments. Recognizing this likelihood, GMAC's interest in property is adequately protected under the Chapter 13 plan and, therefore, GMAC requires no relief from the automatic stay to protect said interest....

Finally, this Court now addresses the issue of the debtor's turnover complaint. The debtor seeks to recover the property that was returned voluntarily to GMAC prior to the filing of bankruptcy. The debtor seeks this turnover pursuant to §542....

The debtor here has filed a petition pursuant to Chapter 13 of the Bankruptcy Code. Section 1303 provides the debtor with the rights and powers that a trustee would have under Chapter 7 or the debtor in possession would have under Chapter 11. Consequently the debtor is a proper party to seek turnover pursuant to §542(a) because the property that the debtor seeks to have turned over is property that he as debtor may use in the ordinary course of business. See §363.

Having found that the debtor is the proper party to bring a §542 turnover complaint, this Court notes the elements of §542 include (1) an entity has possession, custody, or control of property (2) that the debtor may use the property pursuant to §363 and (3) that the property has value or benefit to the estate....

For the reasons discussed above, this Court should and will order that GMAC return possession of the property to the debtor. The Court will not, however, order such turnover without providing adequate protection to the creditor of his interest in the property. The debtor's "use of the vehicle pursuant to §363(b) will presumably cause the value of the vehicle to decline." In re Williams, 6 B.R. at 792. This Court is satisfied, however, that if the debtor (1) procures adequate insurance on the property at the time of recovering possession and (2) makes monthly payments under the contract with GMAC until the time that a plan is confirmed, GMAC's interest in the subject property will be adequately protected and, therefore, the requirements of §361 and [§362(d)] will be satisfied.

---

a. Adequate Protection

For Mr. Radden, Chapter 13 became an extraordinarily powerful tool. He was able to restructure his loan payments (more on that in the next case) and to reclaim a car from a creditor that had lawfully repossessed it after default. Once Radden filed, GMAC could sell the car and realize the value of the collateral immediately only if it moved to lift the stay and the court granted the motion under section 362(d). Failing that, GMAC would be off down the path of the three- to five-year Chapter 13 payout.

GMAC lost on both section 362(d) arguments. The court rejected application of section 362(d)(2). It conceded that the debtor had no equity in the property, but it concluded that the property was necessary for an effective reorganization. The court's conclusion about the necessity of the car seemed a bit tongue in cheek, particularly since Radden had indicated that he had had little difficulty getting to work and that he was within walking distance of shopping. Concluding that an item of collateral is necessary for an effective reorganization is always a bit attenuated in a consumer setting, but it will take on far more significance later in business cases when we return to this issue in the Chapter 11 materials.

In its second argument, GMAC argued that the stay should be lifted because its interest in the car was not adequately protected as required in section 362(d)(1). The debtor would have possession of the car if the stay were not lifted, and the possibility existed that the car would decline in value or even be destroyed. In this case, the court found that the debtor's payments and agreement to arrange for adequate insurance met these risks so that GMAC was adequately protected.

b. Modifying the Secured Creditor's Contract

For the secured creditor that loses its move to lift the automatic stay, the next battle will likely shape up over how much the creditor will be paid under the Chapter 13 plan. As we discussed in the Chapter 7 materials, a secured creditor is far better protected in bankruptcy than an unsecured creditor, and the differences between the secured creditor's and unsecured creditor's payments under the Chapter 13 plan reflect this distinction. Nonetheless, even a secured creditor may find that its contract with a debtor has been modified in bankruptcy.

The general rule about required payments to secured creditors is contained in section 1325(a)(5). There are two requirements: A secured creditor must be paid its allowed secured claim in full and it must be paid interest on that claim. For the moment, we put the question of interest to one side and focus on the amount of the principal debt that must be paid.

We discussed previously the calculation of an allowed secured claim (see pp. 225-227) and saw that an undersecured claim is bifurcated by section 506(a) to yield two claims: a secured claim equal to the value of the collateral and an unsecured claim for the remainder (at state law, this would have been called the "deficiency"). Under the general rule of section 1325(a)(5), often called the "cramdown" section, the debtor can promise to pay the allowed secured claim (that is, the value of the collateral) in full, while treating the unsecured portion of the debt like any other unsecured debt.

Suppose a debtor couple who two years before bankruptcy granted a security interest for a loan on their office equipment. At the time of filing, the loan was $10,000 but the collateral was worth only $5,000. Assuming they have promised to pay 50 percent of their unsecured debt, they will pay $5,000 (secured claim) plus $2,500 (unsecured claim) to the creditor with the security interest in the equipment. If the debtors in this example complete the plan, they will discharge the remaining debt. For $7,500 total, they can keep the equipment during and after bankruptcy.

This treatment of an undersecured claim is often called "cramdown," because it can be imposed over the secured creditor's objection. If the debtors fail to complete the plan, they will lose the benefits of cramdown. The debt will not be discharged and following bankruptcy the secured creditor will once again be able to enforce its security interest with regard to all the unpaid debt. §1325(a)(5)(B)(i). But if they make it through, the unsecured portion of the creditor's lien will be partially discharged along with all other unpaid, unsecured debt.

This approach traditionally applied to every type of secured debt except home mortgages, which we discuss in more detail below. The 2005 Amendments added language at the end of section 1325(a) that may have exempted certain security interests from the cramdown rule, although the added language is inartful, to say the least. If so, then two types of security interests granted fairly recently before bankruptcy are exempt from cramdown. Instead of being stripped to the value of the collateral, they must be paid in full — plus interest. First, any security interest granted within the year before bankruptcy is exempt. If the secured creditor objects to the plan, a debtor who wants to keep the collateral must promise to pay the debt in full. Second, for one specially favored secured creditor — the holder of a purchase money security interest in a motor vehicle — the time period is rolled much further back, to exempt security interests granted within two and a half years (910 days) prior to the bankruptcy petition.

For any security interest to which the general rule applies, the key question is the value of the collateral because that number will determine the amount of the allowed secured claim that must be paid in full. In the following case the Supreme Court addressed this problem, which had split six circuits at least three ways, proving once again that this stuff is hard for everyone.

════════ ASSOCIATES COMMERCIAL CORP. v. RASH ════════
520 U.S. 953 (1997)

Justice GINSBURG delivered the opinion of the Court. *

We resolve in this case a dispute concerning the proper application of §506(a) of the Bankruptcy Code when a bankrupt debtor has exercised the "cram down" option for which Code §1325(a)(5)(B) provides. Specifically, when a debtor, over a secured creditor's objection, seeks to retain and use the creditor's collateral in a Chapter 13 plan, is the value of the collateral to be determined by (1) what the secured creditor could obtain through foreclosure sale of the property (the "foreclosure-value" standard); (2) what the debtor would have to pay for comparable property (the "replacement-value" standard); or (3) the midpoint between these two measurements? We hold that §506(a) directs application of the replacement-value standard.

I

In 1989, respondent Elray Rash purchased for $73,700 a Kenworth tractor truck for use in his freight-hauling business. Rash made a downpayment on the truck, agreed to pay the seller the remainder in 60 monthly installments, and pledged the truck as collateral on the unpaid balance. The seller assigned the loan, and its lien on the truck, to petitioner Associates Commercial Corporation (ACC).

In March 1992, Elray and Jean Rash filed a joint petition and a repayment plan under Chapter 13 of the Bankruptcy Code (Code), 11 U.S.C. §§1301-1330. At the time of the bankruptcy filing, the balance owed to ACC on the truck loan was $41,171. Because it held a valid lien on the truck, ACC was listed in the bankruptcy petition as a creditor holding a secured claim. Under the Code, ACC's claim for the balance owed on the truck was secured only to the extent of the value of the collateral; its claim over and above the value of the truck was unsecured. See 11 U.S.C. §506(a).

To qualify for confirmation under Chapter 13, the Rashes' plan had to satisfy the requirements set forth in §1325(a) of the Code. The Rashes' treatment of ACC's secured claim, in particular, is governed by subsection (a)(5).

---

* Justice SCALIA joins all but footnote 4 of this opinion.

Under this provision, a plan's proposed treatment of secured claims can be confirmed if one of three conditions is satisfied: the secured creditor accepts the plan, see 11 U.S.C. §1325(a)(5)(A); the debtor surrenders the property securing the claim to the creditor, see §1325(a)(5)(C); or the debtor invokes the so-called "cram down" power, see §1325(a)(5)(B). Under the cram down option, the debtor is permitted to keep the property over the objection of the creditor; the creditor retains the lien securing the claim, see §1325(a)(5)(B)(i), and the debtor is required to provide the creditor with payments, over the life of the plan, that will total the present value of the allowed secured claim, i.e., the present value of the collateral, see §1325(a)(5)(B)(ii). The value of the allowed secured claim is governed by §506(a) of the Code.

The Rashes' Chapter 13 plan invoked the cram down power. It proposed that the Rashes retain the truck for use in the freight-hauling business and pay ACC, over 58 months, an amount equal to the present value of the truck. That value, the Rashes' petition alleged, was $28,500. ACC objected to the plan and asked the Bankruptcy Court to lift the automatic stay so ACC could repossess the truck. ACC also filed a proof of claim alleging that its claim was fully secured in the amount of $41,171. The Rashes filed an objection to ACC's claim. The Bankruptcy Court held an evidentiary hearing to resolve the dispute over the truck's value. At the hearing, ACC and the Rashes urged different valuation benchmarks. ACC maintained that the proper valuation was the price the Rashes would have to pay to purchase a like vehicle, an amount ACC's expert estimated to be $41,000. The Rashes, however, maintained that the proper valuation was the net amount ACC would realize upon foreclosure and sale of the collateral, an amount their expert estimated to be $31,875. The Bankruptcy Court agreed with the Rashes and fixed the amount of ACC's secured claim at $31,875; that sum, the court found, was the net amount ACC would realize if it exercised its right to repossess and sell the truck. The Bankruptcy Court thereafter approved the plan, and the United States District Court for the Eastern District of Texas affirmed. . . .

On rehearing en banc . . . the Fifth Circuit affirmed the District Court, holding that ACC's allowed secured claim was limited to $31,875, the net foreclosure value of the truck. In re Rash, 90 F.3d 1036 (1996).

In reaching its decision, the Fifth Circuit highlighted, first, a conflict it perceived between the method of valuation ACC advanced, and the law of Texas defining the rights of secured creditors. See id., at 1041-1042 (citing Tex. Bus. & Com. Code Ann. §§9.504(a), (c), 9.505 (1991)). In the Fifth Circuit's view, valuing collateral in a federal bankruptcy proceeding under a replacement-value standard — thereby setting an amount generally higher than what a secured creditor could realize pursuing its state-law foreclosure remedy — would "chang[e] the extent to which ACC is secured from what obtained under state law prior to the bankruptcy filing." 90 F.3d, at 1041. Such a departure from state law, the Fifth Circuit said, should be resisted by the federal forum unless "clearly compel[led]" by the Code. Id., at 1042.

The Fifth Circuit then determined that the Code provision governing valuation of security interests, §506(a), does not compel a replacement-value approach. Instead, the court reasoned, the first sentence of §506(a) requires that collateral be valued from the creditor's perspective. See id., at 1044. And because "the creditor's interest is in the nature of a security interest, giving the creditor the right to repossess and sell the collateral and nothing more[,] . . . the valuation should start with what the creditor could realize by exercising that right." Ibid. This foreclosure-value standard, the Fifth Circuit found, was consistent with the other relevant provisions of the Code, economic analysis, and the legislative history of the pertinent provisions. Judge Smith, joined by five other judges, dissented, urging that the Code dictates a replacement-value standard.

Courts of Appeals have adopted three different standards for valuing a security interest in a bankruptcy proceeding when the debtor invokes the cram down power to retain the collateral over the creditor's objection. In contrast to the Fifth Circuit's foreclosure-value standard, a number of Circuits have followed a replacement-value approach.[2] Other courts have settled on the midpoint between foreclosure value and replacement value.

II

The Bankruptcy Code provision central to the resolution of this case is §506(a), which states: "An allowed claim of a creditor secured by a lien on property in which the estate has an interest . . . is a secured claim to the extent of the value of such creditor's interest in the estate's interest in such property, . . . and is an unsecured claim to the extent that the value of such creditor's interest . . . is less than the amount of such allowed claim. Such value shall be determined in light of the purpose of the valuation and of the proposed disposition or use of such property. . . ." 11 U.S.C. §506(a).

Over ACC's objection, the Rashes' repayment plan proposed, pursuant to §1325(a)(5)(B), continued use of the property in question, i.e., the truck, in the debtor's trade or business. In such a "cram down" case, we hold, the value of the property (and thus the amount of the secured claim under §506(a)) is the price a willing buyer in the debtor's trade, business, or situation would pay to obtain like property from a willing seller. Rejecting this replacement-value standard, and selecting instead the typically lower foreclosure-value standard, the Fifth Circuit trained its attention on the first sentence of §506(a). In particular, the Fifth Circuit relied on these first sentence words: a claim is secured "to the extent of the value of such creditor's interest in the estate's interest in such property." See 90 F.3d, at 1044 (citing §506(a)). The Fifth Circuit read this phrase to instruct that the "starting point for the valuation [is] what the creditor could realize if it sold the estate's interest in the property according to the security agreement," namely, through "repossess[ing] and sell[ing] the collateral." 90 F.3d, at 1044.

We do not find in the §506(a) first sentence words — "the creditor's interest in the estate's interest in such property" — the foreclosure-value

2. In re Taffi, the Ninth Circuit contrasted replacement value with fair-market value and adopted the latter standard, apparently viewing the two standards as incompatible. By using the term "replacement value," we do not suggest that a creditor is entitled to recover what it would cost the debtor to purchase the collateral brand new. Rather, our use of the term replacement value is consistent with the Ninth Circuit's understanding of the meaning of fair-market value; by replacement value, we mean the price a willing buyer in the debtor's trade, business, or situation would pay a willing seller to obtain property of like age and condition.

meaning advanced by the Fifth Circuit. Even read in isolation, the phrase imparts no valuation standard: A direction simply to consider the "value of such creditor's interest" does not expressly reveal how that interest is to be valued.

Reading the first sentence of §506(a) as a whole, we are satisfied that the phrase the Fifth Circuit considered key is not an instruction to equate a "creditor's interest" with the net value a creditor could realize through a foreclosure sale. The first sentence, in its entirety, tells us that a secured creditor's claim is to be divided into secured and unsecured portions, with the secured portion of the claim limited to the value of the collateral. To separate the secured from the unsecured portion of a claim, a court must compare the creditor's claim to the value of "such property," i.e., the collateral. That comparison is sometimes complicated. A debtor may own only a part interest in the property pledged as collateral, in which case the court will be required to ascertain the "estate's interest" in the collateral. Or, a creditor may hold a junior or subordinate lien, which would require the court to ascertain the creditor's interest in the collateral. The §506(a) phrase referring to the "creditor's interest in the estate's interest in such property" thus recognizes that a court may encounter, and in such instances must evaluate, limited or partial interests in collateral. The full first sentence of §506(a), in short, tells a court what it must evaluate, but it does not say more; it is not enlightening on how to value collateral.

The second sentence of §506(a) does speak to the question. "Such value, that sentence provides, "shall be determined in light of the purpose of the valuation and of the proposed disposition or use of such property." §506(a). By deriving a foreclosure-value standard from §506(a)'s first sentence, the Fifth Circuit rendered inconsequential the sentence that expressly addresses how "value shall be determined." As we comprehend §506(a), the "proposed disposition or use" of the collateral is of paramount importance to the valuation question. If a secured creditor does not accept a debtor's Chapter 13 plan, the debtor has two options for handling allowed secured claims: surrender the collateral to the creditor, see §1325(a)(5)(C); or, under the cram down option, keep the collateral over the creditor's objection and provide the creditor, over the life of the plan, with the equivalent of the present value of the collateral, see §1325(a)(5)(B). The "disposition or use" of the collateral thus turns on the alternative the debtor chooses — in one case the collateral will be surrendered to the creditor, and in the other, the collateral will be retained and used by the debtor. Applying a foreclosure-value standard when the cram down option is invoked attributes no significance to the different consequences of the debtor's choice to surrender the property or retain it. A replacement-value standard, on the other hand, distinguishes retention from surrender and renders meaningful the key words "disposition or use."....

...If a debtor keeps the property and continues to use it, the creditor obtains at once neither the property nor its value and is exposed to double risks: The debtor may again default and the property may deteriorate from extended use. Adjustments in the interest rate and secured creditor demands for more "adequate protection," 11 U.S.C. §361, do not fully offset these risks....

Of prime significance, the replacement-value standard accurately gauges the debtor's "use" of the property. It values "the creditor's interest in the collateral in light of the proposed [repayment plan] reality: no foreclosure sale and economic benefit for the debtor derived from the collateral equal to . . . its [replacement] value." In re Winthrop Old Farm Nurseries, 50 F.3d, at 75. The debtor in this case elected to use the collateral to generate an income stream. That actual use, rather than a foreclosure sale that will not take place, is the proper guide under a prescription hinged to the property's "disposition or use." See ibid.[4] . . .

Nor are we persuaded that the split-the-difference approach adopted by the Seventh Circuit provides the appropriate solution. Whatever the attractiveness of a standard that picks the midpoint between foreclosure and replacement values, there is no warrant for it in the Code.[5] . . .

In sum, under §506(a), the value of property retained because the debtor has exercised the §1325(a)(5)(B) "cram down" option is the cost the debtor would incur to obtain a like asset for the same "proposed . . . use."[6]

For the foregoing reasons, the judgment of the Court of Appeals is reversed, and the case is remanded for further proceedings consistent with this opinion. It is so ordered.

Justice STEVENS, dissenting.

Although the meaning of 11 U.S.C. §506(a) is not entirely clear, I think its text points to foreclosure as the proper method of valuation in this case. The first sentence in §506(a) tells courts to determine the value of the *"creditor's* interest in the estate's interest" in the property. 11 U.S.C. §506(a) (emphasis added). This language suggests that the value should be determined from the creditor's perspective, i.e., what the collateral is worth, on the open market, in the creditor's hands, rather than in the hands of another party.

The second sentence explains that "[s]uch value shall be determined in light of the purpose of the valuation and of the proposed disposition or use of such property." Ibid. In this context, the "purpose of the valuation" is

4. We give no weight to the legislative history of §506(3), noting that it is un-edifying, offering snippets that might support either standard of valuation. The Senate Report simply repeated the phrase contained in the second sentence of §506(a). That Report, however, appears to use the term "replacement cost" to mean the cost of buying new property to replace property in which a creditor had a security interest. In any event, House Report excerpts are not enlightening, for the provision pivotal here — the second sentence of §506(a) —did not appear in the bill addressed by the House Report. The key sentence originated in the Senate version of the bill. . . .

5. As our reading of §506(a) makes plain; we also reject a ruleless approach allowing use of different valuation standards based on the facts and circumstances of individual cases.

6. Our recognition that the replacement-value standard, not the foreclosure-value standard, governs in cram down cases leaves to bankruptcy courts, as triers of fact, identification of the best way of ascertaining replacement value on the basis of the evidence presented. Whether replacement value is the equivalent of retail value, wholesale value, or some other value will depend on the type of debtor and the nature of the property. We note, however, that replacement value, in this context, should not include certain items. For example, where the proper measure of the replacement value of a vehicle is its retail value, an adjustment to that value may be necessary: A creditor should not receive portions of the retail price, if any, that reflect the value of items the debtor does not receive when he retains his vehicle, items such as warranties, inventory storage, and reconditioning. Nor should the creditor gain from modifications to the property — e.g., the addition of accessories to a vehicle — to which a creditor's lien would not extend under state law.

determined by 11 U.S.C. §1325(a)(5)(B). Commonly known as the Code's "cram down" provision, this section authorizes the debtor to keep secured property over the creditor's objections in a Chapter 13 reorganization, but, if he elects to do so, directs the debtor to pay the creditor the "value" of the secured claim. The "purpose" of this provision, and hence of the valuation under §506(a), is to put the creditor in the same shoes as if he were able to exercise his lien and foreclose.[7]

It is crucial to keep in mind that §506(a) is a provision that applies throughout the various chapters of the bankruptcy code; it is; in other words, a "utility" provision that operates in many different contexts. Even if the words "proposed disposition or use" did not gain special meaning in the cram down context, this would not render them surplusage because they have operational significance in their many other Code applications. In this context, I also think the foreclosure standard best comports with economic reality. Allowing any more than the foreclosure value simply grants a general windfall to undersecured creditors at the expense of unsecured creditors. As Judge Easterbrook explained in rejecting the split-the-difference approach as a general rule, a foreclosure-value standard is also consistent with the larger statutory scheme by keeping the respective recoveries of secured and unsecured creditors the same throughout the various bankruptcy chapters.

Accordingly, I respectfully dissent.

Interestingly, the security interest in *Rash* would not have been exempted from lien-stripping even had the 2005 Amendments applied, because the debtors had purchased the truck three years before they filed for bankruptcy. In re Rash, 31 F.3d 325, 327 (5th Cir. 1994).

In the 2005 Amendments Congress codified something like the *Rash* rule. §506(a)(2). As we have seen before, however, valuation is at best a difficult and sometimes chancy process. In part because of footnote six, the *Rash* decision failed to reduce the number of valuation disputes. The language since added to section 506(a)(2) will undoubtedly provoke considerable new interpretive litigation, but the effort is worthwhile. A good attorney who can marshal the best valuation arguments will have a far more significant financial impact than an attorney who concentrates solely on doctrinal issues. All the provisions delineating the position of the secured creditor rest on the

---

7. The Court states that "surrender and retention are not equivalent acts" from the creditor's perspective because he does not receive the property and is exposed to the risk of default and deterioration. I disagree. That the creditor does not receive the property is irrelevant because, as §1325(a)(5)(B)(ii) directs, he receives the present value of his security interest. Present value includes both the underlying value and the time-value of that interest. The time-value component similarly vitiates the risk concern. Higher risk uses of money must pay a higher premium to offset the same opportunity cost. In this case, for instance, the creditor was receiving nine percent interest, well over the prevailing rate for an essentially risk-free loan, such as a United States Treasury Bond. Finally, the concern with deterioration is addressed by another provision of the Code, 11 U.S.C. §361, which authorizes the creditor to demand "adequate protection," including increased payments, to offset any derogation of his security interest during a cram down.

assumption that the valuation of the collateral has been established, but valuation will remain the most difficult part of the process.

c. Computing the Amount the Secured Creditor Must be Paid

Once a court has determined that the security interest in the car was a secured claim, it has to make two factual determinations in order to establish the correct amount for the debtor to pay under the Chapter 13 plan:

1. The amount of the allowed secured claim under section 506(a); and
2. The present value of the allowed secured claim under section 1325(a)(5)(B)(ii).

Once the allowed secured claim is determined, the court can establish a payment schedule that permits the creditor to recover the present value of the claim. The concept of "present value" (in statutory terms, "value, as of the effective date of the Plan," §1325(a)(5)(B)(ii)) reflects the elementary proposition that a dollar paid a year from now is worth less than a dollar paid now. Absent bankruptcy, the secured creditor would be allowed to repossess and sell the collateral today. The creditor would then have that money available for another investment. Because the creditor receives deferred payments over time, the Code gives the creditor the right to receive interest on that amount. The total received by the creditor over time is then equal to the "present value" of the collateral.

Before you conclude that present value is simple in principle but hopelessly complex to compute, we should note that virtually all accounting texts and bankers' manuals carry present value tables, so that once the principal amount, the time for repayment, and the rate of discount are known, the correct monthly payment can be determined from a table. In addition, cheap calculators can now perform the computation. For the math whizzes in the group, a number of formulas can be used to calculate present value. One is given here:

$$PV_a = \left(\frac{1-1/(1+i)^n}{i}\right) \times (a)$$

where a = a dollar amount of installment payment
i = a current annual interest rate
n = the number of annual payments
(Computations for other than annual payments require corresponding adjustment of 'i' — e.g., monthly payments use i/12.) But perhaps that is a bit much.

Any formula requires the insertion of the factual predicates, value and interest rate. The interest rate that will fix the present value is nowhere in the Code. Years of divided case law on this point finally brought it to the attention of the Supreme Court. This time even more circuits were split even more ways than in *Rash*.

======= TILL v. SCS CREDIT CORPORATION =======
541 U.S. 465 (2004)

Justice STEVENS announced the judgment of the Court and delivered an opinion, in which Justice SOUTER, Justice GINSBURG, and Justice BREYER join.

I

On October 2, 1998, petitioners Lee and Amy Till, residents of Kokomo, Indiana, purchased a used truck from Instant Auto Finance for $6,395 plus $330.75 in fees and taxes. They made a $300 down payment and financed the balance of the purchase price by entering into a retail installment contract that Instant Auto immediately assigned to respondent, SCS Credit Corporation. Petitioners' initial indebtedness amounted to $8,285.24 — the $6,425.75 balance of the truck purchase plus a finance charge of 21% per year for 136 weeks, or $1,859.49. Under the contract, petitioners agreed to make 68 biweekly payments to cover this debt; Instant Auto — and subsequently respondent — retained a purchase money security interest that gave it the right to repossess the truck if petitioners defaulted under the contract.

On October 25, 1999, petitioners, by then in default on their payments to respondent, filed a joint petition for relief under Chapter 13 of the Bankruptcy Code. At the time of the filing, respondent's outstanding claim amounted to $4,894.89, but the parties agreed that the truck securing the claim was worth only $4,000. In accordance with the Bankruptcy Code, therefore, respondent's secured claim was limited to $4,000, and the $894.89 balance was unsecured.

* * *

The proposed plan . . . provided that petitioners would pay interest on the secured portion of respondent's claim at a rate of 9.5% per year. Petitioners arrived at this "prime-plus" or "formula rate" by augmenting the national prime rate of approximately 8% (applied by banks when making low-risk loans) to account for the risk of nonpayment posed by borrowers in their financial position. Respondent objected to the proposed rate, contending that the company was "entitled to interest at the rate of 21%, which is the rate . . . it would obtain if it could foreclose on the vehicle and reinvest the proceeds in loans of equivalent duration and risk as the loan" originally made to petitioners.

At the hearing on its objection, respondent presented expert testimony establishing that it uniformly charges 21% interest on so-called "subprime" loans, or loans to borrowers with poor credit ratings, and that other lenders in the subprime market also charge that rate. Petitioners countered with the testimony of an Indiana University-Purdue University Indianapolis economics professor, who acknowledged that he had only limited familiarity with the subprime auto lending market, but described the 9.5% formula rate as "very reasonable" given that Chapter 13 plans are "supposed to be financially feasible." [7] Id., at 43-44. Moreover, the professor noted that respondent's exposure was "fairly limited because [petitioners] are under the supervision of the court." Id., at 43. The bankruptcy trustee also filed comments supporting the formula rate as, among other things, easily ascertainable, closely tied to the "condition of the financial market," and independent of the financial circumstances of any particular lender. App. to Pet. for Cert. 41a-42a. Accepting petitioners' evidence, the Bankruptcy Court overruled respondent's objection and confirmed the proposed plan.

The District Court reversed. It understood Seventh Circuit precedent to require that bankruptcy courts set cram down interest rates at the level the creditor could have obtained if it had foreclosed on the loan, sold the collateral, and reinvested the proceeds in loans of equivalent duration and risk. Citing respondent's unrebutted testimony about the market for subprime loans, the court concluded that 21% was the appropriate rate. Id., at 38a.

On appeal, the Seventh Circuit endorsed a slightly modified version of the District Court's "coerced" or "forced loan" approach.... [T]he majority held that the original contract rate should "serve as a presumptive [cram down] rate," which either the creditor or the debtor could challenge with evidence that a higher or lower rate should apply. Accordingly, the court remanded the case to the Bankruptcy Court to afford petitioners and respondent an opportunity to rebut the presumptive 21% rate.

Dissenting, Judge Rovner argued that the majority's presumptive contract rate approach overcompensates secured creditors because it fails to account for costs a creditor would have to incur in issuing a new loan. Rather than focusing on the market for comparable loans, Judge Rovner advocated either the Bankruptcy Court's formula approach or a "straight-forward...cost of funds" approach that would simply ask "what it would cost the creditor to obtain the cash equivalent of the collateral from an alternative source."....

II

The Bankruptcy Code provides little guidance as to which of the rates of interest advocated by the four opinions in this case — the formula rate, the coerced loan rate, the presumptive contract rate, or the cost of funds rate — Congress had in mind when it adopted the cram down provision....

...A debtor's promise of future payments is worth less than an immediate payment of the same total amount because the creditor cannot use the money right away, inflation may cause the value of the dollar to decline before the debtor pays, and there is always some risk of nonpayment. The challenge for bankruptcy courts reviewing such repayment schemes, therefore, is to choose an interest rate sufficient to compensate the creditor for these concerns.

Three important considerations govern that choice. First, the Bankruptcy Code includes numerous provisions that, like the cram down provision,

---

7. The requirement of financial feasibility derives from 11 U.S.C. §1325(a)(6), which provides that the bankruptcy court shall "confirm a plan if...the debtor will be able to make all payments under the plan and to comply with the plan." See *infra*, at 480.

require a court to "discoun[t]...[a] stream of deferred payments back to the[ir] present dollar value," *Rake v. Wade,* 508 U.S. 464, 472, n. 8 (1993), to ensure that a creditor receives at least the value of its claim. We think it likely that Congress intended bankruptcy judges and trustees to follow essentially the same approach when choosing an appropriate interest rate under any of these provisions. Moreover, we think Congress would favor an approach that is familiar in the financial community and that minimizes the need for expensive evidentiary proceedings.

Second, Chapter 13 expressly authorizes a bankruptcy court to modify the rights of any creditor whose claim is secured by an interest in anything other than "real property that is the debtor's principal residence." 11 U.S.C. §1322(b)(2). Thus, in cases like this involving secured interests in personal property, the court's authority to modify the number, timing, or amount of the installment payments from those set forth in the debtor's original contract is perfectly clear. Further, the potential need to modify the loan terms to account for intervening changes in circumstances is also clear: On the one hand, the fact of the bankruptcy establishes that the debtor is overextended and thus poses a significant risk of default; on the other hand, the postbankruptcy obligor is no longer the individual debtor but the court-supervised estate, and the risk of default is thus somewhat reduced.

Third, from the point of view of a creditor, the cram down provision mandates an objective rather than a subjective inquiry. That is, although §1325(a)(5)(B) entitles the creditor to property whose present value objectively equals or exceeds the value of the collateral, it does not require that the terms of the cram down loan match the terms to which the debtor and creditor agreed prebankruptcy, nor does it require that the cram down terms make the creditor subjectively indifferent between present foreclosure and future payment. Indeed, the very idea of a "cram down" loan *precludes* the latter result: By definition, a creditor forced to accept such a loan would prefer instead to foreclose. [8]

* * *

III

These considerations lead us to reject the coerced loan, presumptive contract rate, and cost of funds approaches. Each of these approaches is complicated, imposes significant evidentiary costs, and aims to make each individual creditor whole rather than to ensure the debtor's payments have the required present value. For example, the coerced loan approach requires bankruptcy courts to consider evidence about the market for comparable loans to similar (though nonbankrupt) debtors — an inquiry far removed from such courts' usual task of evaluating debtors' financial circumstances and the feasibility of their debt adjustment plans. In addition, the approach

8. We reached a similar conclusion in *Associates Commercial Corp. v. Rash,* 520 U.S. 953 (1997), when we held that a creditor's secured interest should be valued from the debtor's, rather than the creditor's, perspective. Id., at 963 ("[The debtor's] actual use, rather than a foreclosure sale that will not take place, is the proper guide...").

overcompensates creditors because the market lending rate must be high enough to cover factors, like lenders' transaction costs and overall profits, that are no longer relevant in the context of court-administered and court-supervised cram down loans.

* * *

IV

The formula approach has none of these defects. Taking its cue from ordinary lending practices, the approach begins by looking to the national prime rate, reported daily in the press, which reflects the financial market's estimate of the amount a commercial bank should charge a creditworthy commercial borrower to compensate for the opportunity costs of the loan, the risk of inflation, and the relatively slight risk of default. Because bankrupt debtors typically pose a greater risk of nonpayment than solvent commercial borrowers, the approach then requires a bankruptcy court to adjust the prime rate accordingly.

* * *

Thus, unlike the coerced loan, presumptive contract rate, and cost of funds approaches, the formula approach entails a straightforward, familiar, and objective inquiry, and minimizes the need for potentially costly additional evidentiary proceedings.

* * *

We do not decide the proper scale for the risk adjustment, as the issue is not before us. The Bankruptcy Court in this case approved a risk adjustment of 1.5%, and other courts have generally approved adjustments of 1% to 3%.... If the court determines that the likelihood of default is so high as to necessitate an "eye-popping" interest rate, the plan probably should not be confirmed.

V

The dissent's endorsement of the presumptive contract rate approach rests on two assumptions: (1) "subprime lending markets are competitive and therefore largely efficient"; and (2) the risk of default in Chapter 13 is normally no less than the risk of default at the time of the original loan. Although the Bankruptcy Code provides little guidance on the question, we think it highly unlikely that Congress would endorse either premise.

First, the dissent assumes that subprime loans are negotiated between fully informed buyers and sellers in a classic free market. But there is no basis for concluding that Congress relied on this assumption when it enacted Chapter 13. Moreover, several considerations suggest that the subprime market is not, in fact, perfectly competitive.

* * *

Second, the dissent apparently believes that the debtor's prebankruptcy default — on a loan made in a market in which creditors commonly charge the maximum rate of interest allowed by law and in which neither creditors nor debtors have the protections afforded by Chapter 13 — translates into a high probability that the same debtor's confirmed Chapter 13 plan will fail. In our view, however, Congress intended to create a program under which plans that qualify for confirmation have a high probability of success. Perhaps bankruptcy judges currently confirm too many risky plans, but the solution is to confirm fewer such plans, not to set default cram down rates at absurdly high levels, thereby increasing the risk of default.

* * *

Even more important, if all relevant information about the debtor's circumstances, the creditor's circumstances, the nature of the collateral, and the market for comparable loans were equally available to both debtor and creditor, then in theory the formula and presumptive contract rate approaches would yield the same final interest rate. Thus, we principally differ with the dissent not over what final rate courts should adopt but over which party (creditor or debtor) should bear the burden of rebutting the presumptive rate (prime or contract, respectively).

* * *

If the rather sketchy data uncovered by the dissent support an argument that Chapter 13 of the Bankruptcy Code should mandate application of the presumptive contract rate approach (rather than merely an argument that bankruptcy judges should exercise greater caution before approving debt adjustment plans), those data should be forwarded to Congress. We are not persuaded, however, that the data undermine our interpretation of the statutory scheme Congress has enacted.

The judgment of the Court of Appeals is reversed, and the case is remanded with instructions to remand the case to the Bankruptcy Court for further proceedings consistent with this opinion.

It is so ordered.

Justice THOMAS, concurring in the judgment.

This case presents the issue of what the proper method is for discounting deferred payments to present value and what compensation the creditor is entitled to in calculating the appropriate discount rate of interest. Both the plurality and the dissent agree that "[a] debtor's promise of future payments is worth less than an immediate payment of the same total amount because the creditor cannot use the money right away, inflation may cause the value of the dollar to decline before the debtor pays, and there is always some risk of nonpayment." *Ante,* at 1958; *post,* at 1968. Thus, the plurality and the dissent agree that the proper method for discounting deferred payments to present value should take into account each of these factors, but disagree over the proper starting point for calculating the risk of nonpayment.

I agree that a *"promise* of future payments is worth less than an immediate payment" of the same amount, in part because of the risk of nonpayment. But this fact is irrelevant. The statute does not require that the value of the *promise* to distribute property under the plan be no less than the allowed amount of the secured creditor's claim. It requires only that "the value . . . of *property* to be distributed under the plan," at the time of the effective date of the plan, be no less than the amount of the secured creditor's claim. 11 U.S.C. §1325(a)(5)(B)(ii) (emphasis added). Both the plurality and the dissent ignore the clear text of the statute in an apparent rush to ensure that secured creditors are not undercompensated in bankruptcy proceedings.

* * *

The dissent might be correct that the use of the prime rate, even with a small risk adjustment, "will systematically undercompensate secured creditors for the true risks of default." *Post*, at 1968. This systematic undercompensation might seem problematic as a matter of policy. But, it raises no problem as a matter of statutory interpretation. * * *

The final task, then, is to determine whether petitioners' proposed 9.5% interest rate will sufficiently compensate respondent for the fact that instead of receiving $4,000 today, it will receive $4,000 plus 9.5% interest over a period of up to 36 months. Because the 9.5% rate is higher than the risk-free rate, I conclude that it will. I would therefore reverse the judgment of the Court of Appeals.

Justice SCALIA, with whom THE CHIEF JUSTICE, Justice O'CONNOR, and Justice KENNEDY join, dissenting.

* * *

Our only disagreement is over what procedure will more often produce accurate estimates of the appropriate interest rate. The plurality would use the prime lending rate — a rate we *know* is too low — and require the judge in every case to determine an amount by which to increase it. I believe that, in practice, this approach will systematically undercompensate secured creditors for the true risks of default. I would instead adopt the contract rate — *i.e.*, the rate at which the creditor actually loaned funds to the debtor — as a presumption that the bankruptcy judge could revise on motion of either party. Since that rate is generally a good indicator of actual risk, disputes should be infrequent, and it will provide a quick and reasonably accurate standard.

I

The contract-rate approach makes two assumptions, both of which are reasonable. First, it assumes that subprime lending markets are competitive and therefore largely efficient. If so, the high interest rates lenders charge reflect not extortionate profits or excessive costs, but the actual risks of default that subprime borrowers present. Lenders with excessive rates would be undercut by their competitors, and inefficient ones would be priced out of the market. We have implicitly assumed market competitiveness in other bankruptcy contexts. Here the assumption is borne out by empirical evidence: One study reports that subprime lenders are nearly twice as likely to be unprofitable as banks, suggesting a fiercely competitive environment. See J. Lane, Associate Director, Division of Supervision, Federal Deposit Insurance Corporation, A Regulator's View of Subprime Lending: Address at the National Automotive Finance Association Non-Prime Auto Lending Conference 6 (June 18-19, 2002) (available in Clerk of Court's case file). * * *

The second assumption is that the expected costs of default in Chapter 13 are normally no less than those at the time of lending. This assumption is also reasonable. Chapter 13 plans often fail. I agree with petitioners that the relevant statistic is the percentage of *confirmed* plans that fail, but even resolving that issue in their favor, the risk is still substantial. The failure rate they offer — which we may take to be a conservative estimate, as it is doubtless the lowest one they could find — is 37%. See Girth, The Role of Empirical Data in Developing Bankruptcy Legislation for Individuals, 65 Ind. L.J. 17, 40-42 (1989) (reporting a 63.1% success rate).[9] In every one of the failed plans making up that 37%, a bankruptcy judge had found that "the debtor will be able to make all payments under the plan," 11 U.S.C. §1325(a)(6), and a trustee had supervised the debtor's compliance, §1302. That so many nonetheless failed proves that bankruptcy judges are not oracles and that trustees cannot draw blood from a stone.

* * *

II

The defects of the formula approach far outweigh those of the contract-rate approach. The formula approach starts with the prime lending rate — a number that, while objective and easily ascertainable, is indisputably too low. It then adjusts by adding a risk premium that, unlike the prime rate, is neither objective nor easily ascertainable. * * * When the risk premium is the greater part of the overall rate, the formula approach no longer depends on objective and easily ascertainable numbers. The prime rate becomes the objective tail wagging a dog of unknown size.

* * *

III

Justice THOMAS rejects both the formula approach and the contract-rate approach. He reads the statutory phrase "property to be distributed under the plan," 11 U.S.C. § 1325(a)(5)(B)(ii), to mean the proposed payments *if made as the plan contemplates*, so that the plan need only pay the risk-free rate of interest. *Ante*, at 1966 (opinion concurring in judgment). I would instead read this phrase to mean the right to receive payments that the plan vests in the creditor upon confirmation. Because there is no guarantee that

---

9. The true rate of plan failure is almost certainly much higher. The Girth study that yielded the 37% figure was based on data for a single division (Buffalo, New York) from over 20 years ago (1980-1982). See 65 Ind. L. J., at 41. A later study concluded that "the Buffalo division ha[d] achieved extraordinary results, far from typical for the country as a whole." Whitford, The Ideal of Individualized Justice: Consumer Bankruptcy as Consumer Protection, and Consumer Protection in Consumer Bankruptcy, 68 Am. Bankr.L.J. 397, 411, n. 50 (1994). Although most of respondent's figures are based on studies that do not clearly exclude unconfirmed plans, one study includes enough detail to make the necessary correction: It finds 32% of filings successful, 18% dismissed without confirmation of a plan, and 49% dismissed after confirmation, for a post-confirmation failure rate of 60% (*i.e.*, 49%/(32% + 49%)). See Norberg, Consumer Bankruptcy's New Clothes: An Empirical Study of Discharge and Debt Collection in Chapter 13, 7 Am. Bankr.Inst. L.Rev. 415, 440-441 (1999). This 60% failure rate is far higher than the 37% reported by Girth.

the promised payments will in fact be made, the value of this property right must account for the risk of nonpayment.

* * *

Circuit authority uniformly rejects the risk-free approach. While Circuits addressing the issue are divided over *how* to calculate risk, to my knowledge all of them require some compensation for risk, either explicitly or implicitly. * * *

There are very good reasons for Congress to prescribe full risk compensation for creditors. Every action in the free market has a reaction somewhere. If subprime lenders are systematically undercompensated in bankruptcy, they will charge higher rates or, if they already charge the legal maximum under state law, lend to fewer of the riskiest borrowers. As a result, some marginal but deserving borrowers will be denied vehicle loans in the first place. Congress evidently concluded that widespread access to credit is worth preserving, even if it means being ungenerous to sympathetic debtors.

* * *

Today's judgment is unlikely to burnish the Court's reputation for reasoned decisionmaking. Eight Justices are in agreement that the rate of interest set forth in the debtor's approved plan must include a premium for risk. Of those eight, four are of the view that beginning with the contract rate would most accurately reflect the actual risk, and four are of the view that beginning with the prime lending rate would do so. The ninth Justice takes no position on the latter point, since he disagrees with the eight on the former point; he would reverse because the rate proposed here, being above the risk-free rate, gave respondent no cause for complaint. Because I read the statute to require full risk compensation, and because I would adopt a valuation method that has a realistic prospect of enforcing that directive, I respectfully dissent.

══════

If someone put us on the Supreme Court we would promise not to be grumpy (at least in print) and to try to give the lower courts a reasonably clear idea of what we want them to do.

Cramdown is one of two processes by which a debtor can reduce an undersecured claim to the value of the collateral. The other is redemption under section 722, which we discussed earlier in the book. (Another term used by the cognoscenti for either of these processes is lien-stripping.) A Chapter 13 plan has a great advantage over redemption because in Chapter 13 a debtor can pay the value of the collateral over time, in installments. Notice, however, that the same result is obtained under the retention cases. Retention by a Chapter 7 debtor is actually better than a Chapter 13 plan in one respect, because the Chapter 7 debtor discharges personal liability. A Chapter 13 debtor gets no discharge until the plan is completed (with a rarely used exception in section 1328(b)). If the Chapter 13 debtor defaults, all the personal liability for a deficiency remains with the debtor. Chapter 13 does have an advantage over retention, however, because the automatic stay in Chapter 13 also lasts until that late discharge, which means that a defaulting debtor is protected from repossession by the automatic stay while the debtor makes the required payments. If a post – Chapter 7 debtor wants to retain the collateral, a secured creditor may be able to repossess without going to court, but the creditor must seek to lift the stay against a Chapter 13 debtor. These differences aside, lien-stripping is yet another area in which we find that Chapter 7 and Chapter 13 are not dichotomous, but simply different places on a continuum.

3. *Payments on the Home Mortgage*

The preceding section covered the determination of the allowed secured claim for a creditor with a security interest in personal property. For more than half the debtors in Chapter 13, however, their single biggest asset is their home. These debtors structure their plans around their home mortgage payments to avoid foreclosure. The debtors in many homestead Chapter 13 cases have delayed seeking legal help and often their financial circumstances have deteriorated significantly. By the time they see a bankruptcy lawyer, many of these debtors face imminent foreclosure proceedings. For such debtors, filing for Chapter 13 may be the only way to save a home that is slipping into the creditor's hands.

We mentioned earlier that one type of security interest has always been exempted from the cramdown rule: the home mortgage. Some courts had attempted to work around this exemption, and permit home mortgage cramdowns, but the Supreme Court in Nobelman v. American Saving Bank, 508 U.S. 324 (1993) made it clear that cramdown would not apply to home mortgages. The result is that the only relief in Chapter 13 as to a home mortgage is to "cure and maintain," that is, to catch up on the past-due *arrearage* while making current payments on the mortgage as they come due. §1322(b)(5).

While the lien-stripping question was important for the debtors with mortgages that exceeded the value of their homes, for many debtors the home represents an asset even in bankruptcy. Debtors often have some equity in their homes either because the lender has financed less than 100 percent of the value of a home, or because residential real estate prices have risen rather than declined in value over time. As a result, in the Chapter 13 cases that center on saving the debtor's home, the issue of adequate protection may be less important than in the personal property area. Whenever the value of the home exceeds the mortgage, the mortgagee will nearly always be adequately protected.

Litigation in these Chapter 13 cases is more likely to involve two other problems: (1) in the short term, saving the home from foreclosure sale, and (2) in the long term, proposing a plan to comply with the strict limitations imposed by the provisions of Chapter 13 to protect the rights of mortgage lenders.

In the following case, the debtors propose a Chapter 13 plan in order to save their home from foreclosure. Note two elements in this case: (1) the difficulties the debtors face in stopping their creditor's foreclosure actions, and (2) the amount they must pay on their mortgages during the period of the plan in order to satisfy the Code provisions.

============= In re TADDEO =============
685 F.2d 24 (2d Cir. 1982)

LUMBARD, Circuit Judge.

Joseph C. and Ellen A. Taddeo live at 6 Ort Court, Sayville, New York. Three years ago they defaulted on their mortgage to Elfriede Di Pierro. Di Pierro accelerated the mortgage, declared its balance due immediately, and initiated foreclosure proceedings. The Taddeos sought refuge under Chapter 13 of the new Bankruptcy Code, staying the foreclosure action under the automatic stay, §362(a), and proposing to cure the default and reinstate the mortgage under §1322(b)(5). Di Pierro is listed as the Taddeos' only creditor. She rejected the plan to cure the default, and applied for relief from the automatic stay in order to foreclose. Di Pierro contended that once she accelerated her mortgage, the Taddeos had no way to cure the default under the Bankruptcy Code except to pay the full amount as required by state law. Bankruptcy Judge Parente held that the Taddeos could cure the default and reinstate their mortgage, and denied Di Pierro's motion for relief from the stay. In re Taddeo, 9 B.R. 299 (Bankr. E.D.N.Y. 1981). Judge Pratt affirmed, 15 B.R. 273 (Bankr. E.D.N.Y. 1981). We affirm. We do not believe that Congress labored for five years over this controversial question only to remit consumer debtors — intended to be primary beneficiaries of the new Code — to the harsher mercies of state law.

Di Pierro originally owned the house at 6 Ort Court. On June 14, 1979, she sold the house to the Taddeos, taking in return a "purchase money second mortgage" to secure a principal balance of $13,000. The property is subject to a first lien held by West Side Federal Savings & Loan Association, which is not involved in this case. Di Pierro's second mortgage was payable over 15 years at 8.5 percent in equal monthly installments of $128.05.

Upon taking occupancy, the Taddeos notified Di Pierro that they had discovered defects in the property. On advice of counsel, the Taddeos said they would withhold mortgage payments, depositing the money instead with their attorney. The Taddeos and Di Pierro corresponded for several months without reaching an agreement. On October 5, 1979, Di Pierro wrote that she was accelerating the mortgage and declaring the entire balance due immediately. The mortgage contained the acceleration clause specifically approved in N.Y. Real Prop. §258 Schedule M (McKinney 1968), which gives the mortgagee the option to accelerate after a default in mortgage payments.

Di Pierro commenced foreclosure proceedings in state court on October 19, 1979. The Taddeos tendered full payment of their arrears by check on October 31, 1979, but Di Pierro refused to accept payment. The state court granted summary judgment to Di Pierro and ordered a referee to determine the amount owed. After a hearing on June 30, 1980, the referee found the Taddeos liable for $14,153.48 in principal and interest, plus interest subsequent to the award.

Before Di Pierro could obtain final judgment of foreclosure and sale, the Taddeos filed a Chapter 13 bankruptcy petition in the Eastern District on July 10, 1980.... The petition listed Di Pierro as the only creditor, and stayed Di Pierro's foreclosure action. The Taddeos filed a plan proposing to pay off arrears on the mortgage in installments of $100 per month. The plan further proposed to restore the mortgage and its original payment schedule, with payments through [the] trustee to Di Pierro during the 3-year life of the plan and directly to Di Pierro after the plan ended. Di Pierro objected to the plan, and petitioned for relief from the automatic stay so that she could proceed with her foreclosure action. Di Pierro contended that her rights as mortgagee could not be affected by the Chapter 13 plan....

When Congress empowered Chapter 13 debtors to "cure defaults," we think Congress intended to allow mortgagors to "de-accelerate" their mortgage and reinstate its original payment schedule. We so hold for two reasons. First, we think that the power to cure must comprehend the power to "de-accelerate." This follows from the concept of "curing a default." A default is an event in the debtor-creditor relationship which triggers certain consequences — here, acceleration. Curing a default commonly means taking care of the triggering event and returning to pre-default conditions. The consequences are thus nullified. This is the concept of "cure" used throughout the Bankruptcy Code. Such legislative history as there is supports a similar reading of §1322(b)(5). Both the Bankruptcy Commission's Bill ... and the Bankruptcy Judges' Bill ... plainly permitted the cure and de-acceleration of residential debt accelerated prior to petition....

H.R. 6 adopted language almost identical to §6-301(2) of the Commission's Bill, which accomplished just what the Judges' Bill did, albeit in different language. In fact, H.R. 6 went beyond either of its predecessors and permitted the *modification* of debt secured by a debtor's residence. Although the Senate later adopted a prohibition against modification of the rights of holders of secured real estate debt, S. 2266, 95th Cong. 2d Sess. §1322(b)(2), which the House accepted insofar as it related to debt secured by a debtor's principal residence, 124 Cong. Rec. H.R. 106 (September 28, 1978), the cure and maintain powers of paragraph (b)(5) remained unchanged. This history and the policy discussed above compel the conclusion that §1322(b)(5) was intended to permit the cure and de-acceleration of secured long-term residential debt accelerated prior to the filing of a Chapter 13 petition.

Policy considerations strongly support this reading of the statute. Conditioning a debtor's right to cure on its having filed a Chapter 13 petition prior to acceleration would prompt unseemly and wasteful races to the courthouse. Worse, these would be races in which mortgagees possess an unwarranted and likely insurmountable advantage: Wage earners seldom will possess the sophistication in bankruptcy matters that financial institutions do, and often will not have retained counsel in time for counsel to do much good. In contrast, permitting debtors in the Taddeos' position to de-accelerate by payment of the arrearages will encourage parties to negotiate in good faith rather than having to fear that the mortgagee will tip the balance irrevocably by accelerating or that the debtor may prevent or at least long postpone this by filing a Chapter 13 petition.

Secondly, we believe that the power to "cure any default" granted in §1322(b)(3) and (b)(5) is not limited by the ban against "modifying" home mortgages in §1322(b)(2) because we do not read "curing defaults" under (b)(3) or "curing defaults and maintaining payments" under (b)(5) to be *modifications* of claims.

It is true that §1322(b)(5)'s preface, "notwithstanding paragraph (2)," seems to treat the power to cure in (b)(5) as a subset of the power to modify set forth in (b)(2), but that superficial reading of the statute must fall in the light of legislative history and legislative purpose. The "notwithstanding" clause was added to §1322(b)(5) to emphasize that defaults in mortgages could be cured notwithstanding §1322(b)(2). See 124 Cong. Rec. H.R. 106 (Sept. 28, 1978); S. 17,423 (Oct. 6, 1978). But the clause was not necessary. The Senate protected home mortgages from *modification* in its last bill, S. 2266, 95th Cong., 2d Sess.; it evinced no intent to protect these mortgages from cure. Cf. Hearings on S. 2266 Before the Subcommittee on Improvements in Judicial Machinery of the Senate Committee on the Judiciary 95th Cong., 1st Sess. 836 (1977) (Statement of Charles A. Horsky, Chairman, National Bankruptcy Conference (S. 2266 "is completely unclear as to whether the plan can provide for the curing of defaults and the making of current payments.")). Indeed, earlier Senate bills along with House bills and the present statute listed the power to cure and the power to modify in different paragraphs, indicating that the power to cure is different from the power to modify. Testimony submitted on behalf of secured creditors distinguished between modifying a claim (by reducing payments due thereon) and curing a default (and maintaining those payments). See Hearings Before the Subcommittee on Civil and Constitutional Rights of the House Committee on the Judiciary, 94th Cong., 1st Sess, 1027 (Statement of Walter W. Vaughan on behalf of the American Bankers Association); Hearings Before the Subcommittee on Improvements in the Judicial Machinery of the Senate Committee on the Judiciary, 94th Cong., 1st Sess. 130 (idem). Finally, the few cases under Chapter XIII of the old Bankruptcy Act distinguished between modifying a claim and maintaining payments thereon and indicate that curing a default and maintaining payments on a claim did not modify that claim.

Our reading of the statute disposes of Di Pierro's major contentions on appeal. Di Pierro argues that the Taddeos cannot use §1322(b)(5) to cure their default and maintain payments on her mortgage because (b)(5) applies only to claims whose last payment is due after the last payment under the plan is due. Di Pierro maintains her acceleration of the mortgage makes all payments due now. But we hold that the concept of "cure" in §1322(b)(5) contains the power to de-accelerate. Therefore the application of that section de-accelerates the mortgage and returns it to its 15-year maturity. Alternatively, we hold that the ban on "modification" in §1322(b)(2) does not limit the Taddeos' exercise of their curative powers under either §1322(b)(3) or (b)(5). Therefore the Taddeos may first cure their default under (b)(3) and then maintain payments under (b)(5)....

Di Pierro argues further that §1322(b)(5) requires the Taddeos to cure their default "within a reasonable time" and that under New York law that time has passed. But clearly the "reasonable time" requirement refers to time after a Chapter 13 petition is filed. Otherwise Chapter 13 debtors would forfeit their right to cure merely by negotiating with their creditors, or, as in this case, litigating the right of their creditor to declare a default. The bankruptcy courts which have allowed Chapter 13 debtors to cure defaults under §1322(b)(5) have assumed that "reasonable time" refers to time after the petition was filed. We find no support for Di Pierro's contention that state law must govern what constitutes a reasonable time.

Di Pierro's argument reduces in the end to an assertion that because she can accelerate her mortgage under state law, the Taddeos can cure only as provided by state law. This interpretation of §1322(b) would leave the debtor with fewer rights under the new Bankruptcy Code than under the old Bankruptcy Act of 1898. Defaulting mortgagees would forfeit their right to cure even before the start of foreclosure proceedings, before they have hired lawyers and therefore before they knew anything about their rights under Chapter 13. Such a result would render the remedy in §1322(b) unavailable to all but a select number of debtors. Such a result would be totally at odds with the "overriding rehabilitative purpose of Chapter 13." In re Davis, 15 B.R. 22, 24 (Bankr. D. Kan.), aff'd, 16 B.R. 473 (D. Ran. 1981).

Affirmed.

———————

As *Taddeo* makes clear, the Code did not originally address the de-acceleration question, leaving it instead for the courts to fashion this important exception to section 1322(b)(2). Following *Nobelman*, some courts thought that the plain meaning of §1322(b)(2) meant that if the contract said "no de-acceleration" then the debtor could not force de-acceleration on an unwilling mortgagee, although Justice Thomas had indicated that de-acceleration was probably allowed. Evidently, some meanings are plainer than others. In any case, Congress intervened with the 1994 Amendments, giving homeowners the right to de-accelerate by statute at any time prior to the foreclosure sale. §1322(c).

The recent growth in second mortgages may affect the use of Chapter 13. Notwithstanding the restriction imposed by section 1322(b)(2), some courts have read sections 506 and 1325 to permit a strip down for a second or subsequent home mortgage that is entirely unsecured. A second mortgage would be entirely undersecured if, for example, the home were worth $200,000 and the first mortgage was for $210,000. Any subsequent mortgages would be wholly — not just partially — unsecured. The courts that permit strip down in such circumstances take the position that a wholly unsecured second mortgage is no longer under the protection afforded mortgages "in real property that is the debtor's principal residence." Because these subsequent mortgages could not be removed at state law, Chapter 13 becomes an attractive device for stripping down a home mortgage in some limited cases.

Problem Set 14

14.1. Fran Belinsky is a graphic artist with an income in excess of $52,000 per year. Last year she guaranteed a large business loan for her brother. Her brother skipped town, and now Fran is left to pay the loan. She has filed a Chapter 13 and plans to make a substantial repayment.

Fran's only asset of significant value is an 18-month-old Apple G5 computer with high-end peripherals that is subject to a valid $4,600 purchase money security interest from InterNet CompFinance. She testified at her 341 meeting that it is worth about $5,000. The IC people think that value is about right for now, but IC wants the computer back so that it can resell the computer before Apple announces a new, cheaper model with enhanced features. IC asks for your help in repossessing the computer. What can you do? See §§361, 362(d).

14.2. George Grey has suffered a series of financial reversals. He was laid off from his job as a steel worker for 17 months, he has incurred medical bills for over $20,000 for his younger daughter, and his son just wrecked the car. But things may be looking up for George now. He has been rehired and is working nearly 20 hours per week overtime. Recognizing that he needs some protection from his creditors, he is prepared to file a Chapter 13.

His chief concern at this point is his hunting cabin. Before he was laid off, he had bought the land from LeisureLand, Inc. for no money down and a $40,000 five-year note. During the time he was unemployed, he went out to the site almost every day. He cleared the land and built a one-room cabin with the materials he found on hand. The place has no plumbing or electricity, but George loves it. And now he is afraid he will lose it.

George made only four payments on the land; the principal balance owed is $39,980. In addition, LeisureLand claims $12,300 in past-due interest, penalties, and attorneys' fees provided for under the contract. They have begun foreclosure proceedings, and the land is scheduled for sale next week. The contract interest rate is now running at 14 percent on the principal balance and 21 percent on all accumulated past-due payments and penalties. Because the area where George lives is in a serious economic slump, even with George's improvements the land would not sell for more than $41,000. What can LeisureLand demand in a Chapter 13? See §§506, 1322(b)(2), 1325(a) (5)(B)(ii).

14.3. Jewel Snitz has filed a Chapter 13 bankruptcy. She owns a Ford Explorer she bought about a year ago to haul around her real estate clients and to take to the beach on weekends. The outstanding loan balance, together with accumulated interest and penalty payments, is $30,000. During the period between filing the Chapter 13 and the confirmation of the plan, another $250 in interest will accumulate. The local bankruptcy court has settled on 10 percent as a market interest rate for fully secured car loans in Chapter 13.

The Dealer's Bluebook (retail value) lists the value of the car as $32,100. The Dealer's Redbook (wholesale value) lists its value as $28,400. At a liquidation sale the car would probably bring $26,300. Through a private want ad it would likely sell for $33,300. How much will Jewel have to pay for her car in a Chapter 13? If the car has some unusual scratches, chipped paint, and a funny little knock in the engine, who will want to point that out? See §§506(a), 1325(a).

14.4. Eric Van Horn is a skilled workman who has been in high demand during the local housing boom of the last three years. He is also a devoted soccer coach and a year ago couldn't resist buying a Suburban into which he can get the entire soccer team, even though "it was quite a stretch for me financially." Unfortunately, the local housing crash followed and the Suburban wasn't his only financial stretch. He is considering a Chapter 13 to get his debt load under control and needs to know how much it will cost him each month to hold on to the Suburban.

He bought the vehicle for $2,000 down and $40,000 on a 60-month, 8 percent note. The various value references (bluebook retail, newspaper ads, etc.) suggest it is now worth about $28,000 (Eric mentioned the big chocolate stain on the middle seat), so it has depreciated about 30 percent in its first year. Prior experience with Suburbans suggests that it will depreciate roughly another 20 percent by next year ($22,400), 15 percent in year three ($19,000), 10 percent in year four ($17,100), and 10 percent in year five ($15,400). He's been paying $841 a month on the vehicle and is up to date on his payments so far. The balance on the note is about $34,000. How much principal debt will he have to pay in total, ignoring interest?

The prime rate is 7.5 percent at the moment and the going rate for a fully secured car loan in the area is still around 8 percent. What interest rate will the court likely approve?

Eric is anxious to match his obligations under a plan with his likely cash flow, "as far as I can guesstimate it." See §§506(a), 1325(a). Once he files, when must he make his first car payment? To whom? See §1326(a)(1). Can he figure his payment by simply consulting a loan table for the principal payment at the given interest rate or is a further calculation required? See §1325(a)(5)(B)(iii). (For an example of a loan table, see www.freemortgageanalyzer.com/mortgage/mortgage.html.)

14.5. Donnie Rhodes bought a house seven years ago and took out a 30-year mortgage to finance the purchase. The home is now valued at $155,000, and the outstanding mortgage is $182,000. Rhodes is required to make monthly payments of $250.

Rhodes sells farm machinery, and as the farming industry took a nosedive, so did Rhodes's sales. He went for eight months with no income, but now things have picked up and he is back to his regular earnings. He has decided to go into Chapter 13 to restructure his debts, but he remains worried about his home. After seven years of regular mortgage payments, Rhodes missed six payments in a row. What must his plan provide? See §1322(b)(2), (b)(5).

14.6. Joe and Ethel Gertz have come to see you for help. They fell behind in the payments on their home after Joe was laid off. They received a notice of acceleration and foreclosure from the savings and loan, but they have lost the notice itself, and the man at the savings and loan hasn't returned their calls. Ethel remembers that today's date was in the notice, but doesn't remember what it said would happen today. What do you advise? What should you do? §§109(h), 521(b).

14.7. Mr. and Mrs. Poltz are a small, neat couple who have sat in front of your desk for an hour and a half without a single smile. They are hoping you can save their home. Mr. Poltz was an inventory control clerk for the Phoenix school district, but was hurt about two years ago and has been "on disability" since that time. Because the school district has good disability benefits, he is receiving about $2,900 a month. They have only modest personal possessions worth about $4,000, all of which would be exempt. The small equity they have in their house would also be exempt.

Mrs. Poltz is not employed. After paying their spartan expenses and their mortgage, they have about $150 a month left over. After Mr. Poltz was injured, they ran up credit card bills and borrowed some money unsecured from a local finance company, "always thinking Mr. P would be back to work in just a little time." They have $10,750.42 in unsecured debts. They missed three payments on the house when Mr. Poltz's disability checks were stopped because of a computer error. The bank filed a foreclosure suit and an answer is due tomorrow, but the bank officer called last week and said they would be willing to work things out. The Poltzes say they can pick up the current payments on the mortgage and pay the arrears within three months. They have heard about Chapter 13 being used for saving a home, and they are willing to pay the full $150 a month to a plan "for as long as you say." You have no doubt you could get their Chapter 13 plan confirmed. What is your advice?

4.   Payments to Unsecured Creditors

To deal with the secured creditors and prevent repossession of the property subject to the security interests, a debtor in Chapter 13 must make payments that satisfy the statutory requirements for the present value of the allowed secured claim. In addition, all priority claimants under section 507 are entitled to payment in full. §1322(2). The general unsecured creditors do not have any similar protection for their claims. Instead, these creditors are pooled together for pro rata treatment.

The unsecured creditors can best enhance their position by arguing that the debtor should be required to make larger payments under the plan. By forcing the debtor to increase the amount available to all creditors, each creditor can share pro rata in a larger pie. Unsecured creditors can make that argument under two provisions of section 1325. The first provision, the "best interests" test, requires that each creditor, secured or unsecured, receive at least as much as that creditor would have received if the debtor had gone into Chapter 7. §1325(a)(4), (a)(5)(B). The second provision is that the debtor must devote all "disposable income" to plan payments during the life of the plan. §1325(b). In addition, a plan must be proposed in "good faith and not by any means forbidden in law." §1325(a)(3).

a.   Disposable Income

In 1984, when Congress added the requirement that debtors in Chapter 13 devote all their disposable income to their Chapter 13 plans, the legislators left it to the courts to sort out how to count both income and expenses in order to determine a debtor's disposable income. As with "substantial abuse" screening in Chapter 7, however, the credit industry was unhappy with the results, arguing that the judges were being too easy on debtors who could not only pay, but pay more. In response, Congress included provisions in the 2005 Amendments delineating a disposable income test that parallels the means test it had fashioned for Chapter 7 (see above pp. 158-165).

As with the Chapter 7 means test, the screening starts with a median-income test. For the purposes of this screening, a married debtor who files alone must nonetheless include spousal income in determining whether the debtor's income is above the state median. §1325(b)(4)(A)(ii). Debtors who have incomes below the median and who choose nonetheless to file for Chapter 13 are past the threshold test, so they are governed by a slightly modified version of the "reasonably necessary" test for disposable income adopted in 1984.

Those debtors who have income in excess of the applicable median suffer two adverse consequences. First, they must propose to keep paying for five years under their Chapter 13 plan, rather than the three-year minimum required of below-median debtors. §1325(b)(4). Second, because the Chapter 7 means test applies here too, if the debtors would have been barred from Chapter 7 because of a surplus of income over expenses, the amount of that surplus is what they are required to pay to unsecured nonpriority creditors in a Chapter 13 plan. §1325(b)(2)-(3). These are two separate tests, so that a debtor with income over the median must pay for five years, whether or not the debtor has a surplus of income over expenses under the means test.

i. Below-Median Debtors

Consistent with the dichotomous treatment created by this structure, we begin with the general disposable income test for confirmation of a Chapter 13 plan for below-median debtors and then address the situation of above-median debtors. Keep in mind that below-median debtors are seeking Chapter 13 even though they would have been eligible for Chapter 7 liquidation — much like the situation for most debtors regardless of income who filed before October 2005. The 2005 Amendments made only small changes in the Chapter 13 rules that would affect below-median debtors, so the caselaw that once governed every debtor who filed for Chapter 13 would seem to continue to govern the debtors with below-median incomes.

Our data from the 2001 study of the Consumer Bankruptcy Project indicate that 11 percent of the Chapter 13 debtors in 2001 would have had incomes at or above their state median. As with the Chapter 7 debtors, that would still represent a substantial absolute number: almost 50,000 debtors and their families per year. Nonetheless, the converse is that most Chapter 13 debtors will continue to be governed by the prior case law unless, of course, they decide to go to Chapter 7.

To calculate a debtor's disposable income, there are two obvious components: income and necessary expenses. If it would seem to be a simple matter to determine a debtor's income, the following case highlights an unexpected complication.

=========================== In re CARTER ===========================

205 B.R. 733 (Bankr. E.D. Pa. 1996)

Diane Weiss SIGMUND, Bankruptcy Judge....

The Debtor, Christine Ann Carter, is a married woman residing in Delaware County, Pennsylvania, with her husband, Charles S. Carter, in a house they own as tenants by the entireties. Prior to the filing of the bankruptcy, Styskal [an unsecured creditor of Carter] filed a foreign judgment in Delaware County entered against the Debtor and her husband in the amount of $255,970.27.... The case was filed by her alone, without her husband. By December 18th the Debtor filed her schedules, statement of financial affairs and Chapter 13 plan. On the schedules, the Debtor listed monthly income of $600 and monthly expenses of $500 for herself alone, excluding the income and expenses of her husband.

...The plan calls for payments from the Debtor in the amount of $75 per month for 36 months.

On April 24, 1996, Styskal filed the present objection to the Debtor's plan. The objection raised a number of issues, including whether the plan provided for the payment of all of the Debtor's projected disposable income under 11 U.S.C. §1325(b) and whether it was filed in good faith. Styskal's objection to confirmation calls into question the role of a nondebtor spouse's income when a married person individually files a petition for relief under Chapter 13.

On July 24, 1996, at a hearing on confirmation of the Debtor's plan, Styskal pressed her objection and pointed out that the Debtor failed to provide full disclosure of her family's financial status by neglecting to list the income and expenses of her husband. Although Styskal presented no evidence on the issue, she alleged that Charles Carter had a high income, in the range of $90,000, which should have [been] disclosed on the Debtor's schedules. We took the matter under advisement and requested the parties to submit memorandums in support of their positions.

DISCUSSION

Upon objection by an unsecured creditor or the trustee, a Chapter 13 plan that does not repay the allowed claims of unsecured creditors in full may only be confirmed if it provides for the debtor to commit all of his disposable income for a 36 month period to plan payments. 11 U.S.C. §1325(b)(1)(B). Disposable income is defined as income received by the debtor that is not reasonably necessary for the support of debtor or his dependents. 11 U.S.C. §1325(b)(2)(A). Although the Code does not define what is reasonable and necessary, case law holds that the standard is directed toward the debtor's basic need for support, unrelated to the debtor's former status and lifestyle. Ordinarily, expenditures for necessary non-luxury items are not questioned, but the existence of expenditures on such items raises concerns as to the propriety of the debtor's budget. To apply these provisions to a married debtor who files individually, courts base their calculation of the debtor's disposable income on the debtor's family budget, including the income and expenses of the nondebtor spouse. Consideration of the nondebtor spouse's income is seen as necessary because a portion of that spouse's income is likely to be applied to the basic needs of the debtor, potentially increasing the share of the debtor's own income that is not reasonably necessary for support. As stated by one court:

> Most courts include the debtor's spouse's income in the budget for purposes of calculating projected disposable income under §1325(b) notwithstanding that

the spouse is not a debtor in the Chapter 13 case. The theory is that the nonfiling spouse's income is available to defray the debtor's reasonably necessary expenses, thus freeing a larger portion of the debtor's separate income for satisfaction of unsecured claims. Creditors have argued successfully that it would be unfair to allow the debtor's separate income to be used for the family necessities and not count a nonfiling spouse's income which would remain "disposable" to the debtor and uncommitted to the plan.

This view recognizes the reality that married couples live as a unit, pooling their income and expenses. This reality is also reflected in the Official Bankruptcy Forms which require a married debtor in Chapter 13 to report the income and expenses of herself and her spouse. Official Form No. 6, Schedules "I" & "J." The Official Forms, moreover, are mandatory for debtors to follow pursuant to Bankruptcy Rule 1007(b)(l) which instructs debtors to file a schedule of income and expenditures as prescribed by the Forms. F.R.B.P. 1007(b)(l).

Turning to the present case, then, it is evident that the Debtor's plan is not yet ready for confirmation. The Debtor has not satisfied her burden of demonstrating that all of her projected disposable income is being committed to the plan. Without income and expense information from the Debtor's husband we are unable to make a determination of the Debtor's disposable income. If Mr. Carter's income is as large as it is alleged to be, it may be that Debtor's basic needs are satisfied therefrom, thus freeing a larger portion of her own money for use in the plan. In any event, we are unable to render a judgment on this issue until all of the information is provided. The schedules as presently filed are misleading, giving the impression that the Debtor, with a monthly income of only $600, is impecunious when in fact she may enjoy a lifestyle of considerable comfort. While the instructions on the schedules unambiguously require that income and expense information be included for a nonfiling spouse, we will assume for the purpose of this decision that the Debtor's omission of material information was based on a misunderstanding of her obligations and not a reflection of bad faith on her part. Honesty and full disclosure are the most basic hallmarks of good faith. Good faith also requires the Debtor to rethink her proposed plan to the extent she may have had an unreasonably narrow view of the disposable income required to be dedicated to a Chapter 13 plan. This is especially so where, as here, the Debtor's husband stands to benefit substantially from the Debtor's bankruptcy filing. The filing will have the effect of converting a joint debt, for which all of the Carters' jointly owned property is liable, to a debt owed only by the husband. In the latter instance, all of the Carters' entireties property, such as their house, will be immune from execution. It is, thus, fair and equitable for Mr. Carter's income and expenditures to be included in the schedules and have an effect upon the level of payment expected from the Debtor in order to achieve confirmation.

CONCLUSION

For the reasons stated above, confirmation of the Debtor's plan is denied without prejudice.

Even if the income portion of the calculation is clear, there remains the question of what expenses can be deducted as "reasonably necessary." Payments required to satisfy the secured creditors and the priority creditors are usually deducted from the debtor's income, and then the court reviews the debtor's proposed expenses to determine which ones are "reasonably necessary." The following case illustrates some of the inquiries courts may make.

IN THE MATTER OF WYANT

217 B.R. 585 (Bankr. D. Neb. 1998)

John C. MINAHAN, Jr., Bankruptcy Judge.

This case is before the court to consider confirmation of the debtor's Amended Plan, Debtor's Counsel's Application for Attorney Fees, and the Resistance by the Chapter 13 Trustee. The plan is not confirmed, the debtor shall file an amended plan within 21 days hereof.

The amended plan is not confirmed because the debtor does not propose to pay disposable income to the trustee as required by §1325(b)(1)(B).

This has become a complex case. The complexities are attributable to the debtor's attempt to preserve assets through extensive pre-bankruptcy planning, to manipulate expenses to minimize payments to unsecured creditors, and to provide for the payment of excessive attorney fees.

This case was filed on August 2, 1996. A few days earlier, on July 25, 1996, the debtor borrowed $10,000.00 from his employer and granted a security interest in 6 vehicles, a trailer, a lawnmower and a tractor to secure the loan. On July 31, 1996, the debtor purchased an annuity contract for $10,000.00. These transactions resulted in the encumbrance of the motor vehicles and the placement of $10,000.00 in an annuity which is claimed as exempt property.

On June 6, 1996, about 5 weeks before this bankruptcy case was filed, the debtor and Christel Wyant were divorced by a decree of the District Court of Cass County, Nebraska. The debtor appealed the divorce decree to the Nebraska Court of Appeals asserting that the $1,100.00 monthly alimony and pension awarded Ms. Wyant was excessive, that the court improperly awarded a pickup truck to Ms. Wyant, that Mr. Wyant should have been awarded a number of items of personal property, and that when the court allocated the marital property it did not properly consider a lump sum worker's compensation settlement that Ms. Wyant received. On September 24, 1996, Christel Wyant died which terminated the alimony and pension payments. Mr. Wyant has continued to pursue his appeal of the divorce decree in the Nebraska Court of Appeals, although there is now a limited amount in controversy.

Mr. Wyant's original Schedule J, filed August 20, 1996, showed that his projected monthly income was $3,587.13, that his projected monthly expenses were $3,284.00, which included alimony of $1,100.00, and that his excess income was thus $303.13. Mr. Wyant's original Chapter 13 plan proposed payments of $300.00 per month to the Chapter 13 Standing Trustee. After Christel Wyant died, the debtor filed an amended Schedule I which showed that his after-tax income had decreased because his income tax withholding increased by $323.21 per month when he stopped paying alimony. He also filed an amended Schedule J showing that he no longer had an $1,100.00 monthly alimony expense. However, the debtor increased his other monthly expenses by an aggregate of $408.00 per month. Under amended schedules I and J, the debtor has excess income of $858.72, and he proposes to pay $850.00 per month to the Chapter 13 plan.

Considering the debtor's amended schedules, in light of his original schedule J, and the facts and circumstances recited above, I conclude that the increases in projected monthly expenses are attributable to an unwarranted attempt to offset his increase in income, and that the increase in expenses is not reasonable. Some of the amended expenses are for sums which are certain, such as an increase from $497.00 to $505.00 to reflect the correct amount of the debtor's mortgage payment. Such an increase is appropriate. However, the majority of the increase is for items that are discretionary in nature. It is not necessary for the debtor to make these increased expenditures in order to maintain himself and his dependents. Three hundred seventy-five dollars ($375.00) of the increase in monthly expenditures after the discontinuance of his alimony obligation is disallowed.

I further conclude that the debtor's proposed expenditures on veterinary expenses and livestock feed are unreasonable. The debtor is in the unfortunate position of owning several horses and dogs, which are elderly and which require extraordinary veterinary expenses. It is commendable that the debtor is willing to care for these animals and to attend to their feed and medical needs. On the other hand, this is a bankruptcy case in which the debtor is seeking to be discharged from his obligations to pay creditors. As between the debtor's elderly horses and dogs and his creditors, I think that the creditors should be paid first. The proposed expenditures on these animals are excessive, unreasonable, and not necessary for the maintenance or support of the debtor or his dependents.

On the other hand, the debtor should be encouraged to proceed in Chapter 13 in order that his creditors will receive payments over time. The disposable income analysis should not be so strict as to deprive the debtor of all discretionary income. Accordingly, I conclude that it is appropriate for the debtor to expend $100.00 per month for feed and veterinary expenses. This means that the proposed payments under the plan shall be increased and that for the 36 months of the plan, the debtor shall pay the trustee $1,300.00 per month. This sum represents proposed payments of $850.00 a month, plus disallowed expenses of $450.00 ($375.00 plus $75.00)....

By separate order, the proposed Amended Plan is not confirmed, the Chapter 13 Trustee's Objection to Confirmation is sustained, and the Application for Attorney Fees is denied.

Was confirmation at the Pet Cemetery? Did the Visa representative volunteer to waive in favor of Rover? Is Mr. Wyant a cynical manipulator or a man struggling as he loses the core pieces of his life? Judges are thus forced into intensely personal moral decisions by a provision that appears merely financial.

The disputes over what debtors may and may not deduct from their income under the 1984 Amendments' reasonably necessary test reveal a staggering array of choices. A case that communicates the flavor of the kinds of decisions the court must make is Univest-Coppel Village, Ltd. v. Nelson, 204 B.R. 497 (E.D. Tex. 1996). Mr. and Mrs. Nelson paid $395 a month to keep their 15-year-old daughter in Liberty Christian School. When they filed for Chapter 13, one of their creditors objected to the expense, saying that this money should be counted as disposable income. Dad pointed out that the girl was "adamant" about not changing schools, and, in what he thought would be the clincher argument, he noted that she was the "only freshman to make the cheerleading squad." The bankruptcy court allowed the expense, but the district court said no, send the kid to public school. We wondered if there would be a protest from the pompom crowd.

ii. Above-Median Debtors

As noted earlier, debtors with incomes above their state median are required to propose five-year plans. Their lawyers must also determine if these debtors have a surplus of income calculated according to the presumptive-abuse test of section 707(b)(2)(A)-(B).

If the debtors have a surplus of income under the means test, section 1325(b)(3) requires that they pay unsecured nonpriority creditors an amount equal to that surplus over the 60 months of their plan. That is, the statute in effect establishes their Chapter 13 expense budget at the IRS guidelines level, as modified by the Bankruptcy Code under sections 101(10A) and 707(b)(2)(A)-(B). In effect, the debtors are permitted the same expense allowances they had in the means test. In Chapter 13 they have to write a check to their Chapter 13 trustee every month for the difference between their income and those allowed expenses.

If the debtors are above the median but do not have a surplus according to the presumptive abuse test, it appears they are treated like the below-median debtors for determining how much to pay. That is, they must pay over five years whatever is required by application of the 1984 disposable income test as elaborated by the case law in each circuit and district. §1325(b)(2). Like their above-median counterparts with statutorily defined surplus income, they will be sending a check to their Chapter 13 trustees, but the amount will be determined by a different test.

The implications of using different tests may not be exactly what Congress had in mind. An above-median debtor with $75 per month surplus is not required to use the IRS guidelines for expenses. (Recall that the presumptive-abuse test applies only if the defined surplus is at least $6,000, which is $100 per month for 60 months. See pp. 164-165.) Instead, that debtor must promise to pay unsecured nonpriority creditors over five years whatever amount equals income minus reasonably necessary expenses. That excess could be considerably more or considerably less than $75 per month. The above-median, no-surplus debtor may have a powerful incentive to file in Chapter 7 to avoid having to complete a five-year plan, so long as no other provision in the law pushes him toward Chapter 13.

On the other side, the Chapter 13 debtor with above-median income and a $125 surplus seems to get a different kind of bonus: the amount that that debtor pays is limited to the means-test surplus. The protection of secured debt can sop up a great deal of income, as the above-median debtor continues to pay the big house payment and big car payments after filing for Chapter 13, leaving only a modest amount for the unsecured creditors. §1325(b)(3). By substituting the automated features of the means test, the 2005 Amendments once again oust the court from its discretionary role. Instead, that discretion — making people count a non-filing spouse's income or giving up a pricy car, for example — is reserved for below-median income debtors and for above-median income debtors who have no surplus debt. Bankruptcy has always had a bit of a Wonderland flavor, but Alice might have seen the 2005 bankruptcy revisions as a surprising new path to the rabbit hole.

Section 1325(b)(2) establishes additional deductions for domestic support payments (for example, child support) and certain charitable contributions, both items that may overlap with the deductions allowed under the current-income and presumptive-abuse tests. It also permits deduction of the costs of doing business for those debtors who continue to operate their businesses.

b.   Competition Among Creditors

The *Wyant* case illustrates the creditor-versus-creditor aspect of bankruptcy. The trustee challenged Mr. Wyant's veterinary bills, and we wondered if the trustee might also have joined Mr. Wyant in his challenge to the ex-wife's alimony — if she had survived. For every dollar that did not go to Mrs. Wyant, there would presumably be another dollar for distribution to the unsecured creditors. That certainly gives another cast to the divorce proceedings.

The previous two sections of this chapter focused on the amount to be paid to secured creditors. While the secured creditor wants every penny of what it can collect as payment of its claim, the trustee as representative of the unsecured creditors may press to reduce those payments. The interrelated nature of Chapter 13 payments is sharply illustrated by the 2005 Amendments' requiring full payment to undersecured creditors whose security interests were granted in the recent past, as discussed above. During the debates on these provisions, a group of Chapter 13 trustees examined their records to determine the effects of the that provision as it related to automobile lenders alone. The study reported that adoption of full payment for all auto loans would mean about one in five (20.79 percent) of existing Chapter 13 cases could not be confirmed at all and nearly half of the cases (44.78 percent) would be confirmed with a substantial reduction in distributions to general unsecured creditors. This conclusion suggests that the 2005 provisions favoring secured creditors will substantially reduce the opportunities for repayment of unsecured creditors through Chapter 13. The data are a grim reminder that because the debtors in Chapter 13 often have modest incomes, a dollar that goes to one creditor is a dollar less for another. It is a simple but arresting instance of the general truth that bankruptcy policy is not a simple debtor versus creditor affair, but involves substantial conflicts among creditors (and other interested parties) as well, a point that we will discuss further in the business bankruptcy materials.

c. Family Support, Taxes, and Other Priority Claims in Chapter 13

The third leg of the repayment scheme in Chapter 13 is the special set of rules for repaying priority creditors. As we noted in the preceding section, creditors with claims that would receive a priority under section 507(a) are entitled to payment in full in Chapter 13. §1322(a)(2). Many debtors owe no priority repayments. For them, Chapter 13 is defined by the required treatment of secured and unsecured creditors. But some debtors are obligated to pay debts that would qualify as section 507(a) priorities and must therefore adjust their plans to account for these obligations.

i. Priority Repayments in General

Some debtors pay section 507(a) administrative expenses in their Chapter 13 plans. A debtor who did not have enough cash to pay the filing fee, for example, may pay the filing fee as a priority repayment in Chapter 13. (Under Bankruptcy Rule 1006(b), the filing fee must be paid within 120 days of filing, which means that the filing fee is to be paid in installments in the first four post-filing payments.) Similarly, some debtors pay their attorneys in Chapter 13, although practices on this vary widely from jurisdiction to jurisdiction. Some courts hold that because the attorney's services are rendered pre-petition and do not benefit the estate, they cannot be paid in Chapter 13. Other courts see the attorney's work as creating the estate and therefore entitled to repayment in full as a priority in Chapter 13. Once a court's views are known on this subject, local practice can be expected to adjust, requiring payment up front or payment in installments as a function of what the courts will permit.

Many debtors, like Mr. Wyant in the preceding section, owe alimony or child support at the time of their filing. Because those obligations are entitled to priority repayment in section 507(a)(1), they also enjoy full repayment priority in Chapter 13. §1322(a)(2). Indeed, many Chapter 13 trustees point with pride to an unexpected benefit of having an ex-spouse in bankruptcy: The trustee will take over the function of collecting child support and distributing it to the intended recipients. Trustees frequently use wage orders so that money is diverted directly from the employer to the trustee. Although a support recipient could seek a garnishment order outside bankruptcy, some recipients are glad to have a trustee in bankruptcy take care of the matter and supervise the payments on their behalf. Moreover, the bankrupt ex-spouse who owes support obligations may face a different set of incentives after a bankruptcy filing. Failure to make payments will involve potential dismissal of the Chapter 13 case, which can mean loss of a car or resumption of various other creditor collection actions; the option of paying everyone else and stiffing the ex will no longer be available. A debtor who continues plan payments will, by necessity, have to be current on all support obligations.

Because repayment in full of all priority debts is a requirement for confirmation of the plan, priority creditors are no longer placed in the competitive position they sometimes suffer in Chapter 7. Each and every priority debt must be paid in full, unless the party entitled to repayment waives this right. In addition, the debtor must pay secured creditors the full amount to which they are entitled. If the debtor cannot pay, the plan cannot be confirmed. Disposable income is a floor — a minimum amount that a debtor must pay. It does not act as a cap on the total a debtor must pay. If, for example, a debtor does not have enough money to pay his house payment, his allowed secured claim on his car, his outstanding administrative expenses, his child support, and have enough left to live on, then he cannot confirm a Chapter 13 plan. In such a case a debtor may want to consider giving up some of his property that is collateral for the secured debt obligations, and thus reducing the level of payments required in a Chapter 13. Alternatively, the debtor may file for Chapter 7.

ii. Tax Claims

In addition to administrative and support claims, consumer debtors may face substantial tax claims. Because taxes are nondischargeable, a debtor with a tax problem rarely receives much direct relief in his dealings with the taxing authorities from a Chapter 7 filing, but Chapter 13 offers two advantages. One is paying the taxes over time, with the automatic stay holding off the IRS. (Remember the stay lasts until discharge, which in Chapter 13 isn't until the plan is completed. §362(c)(2)(C).) Second, the denial of post-petition interest on unsecured claims will lock the tax claim at its value as of the date of the bankruptcy filing. §502(b)(2). We have already covered this point, but it bears repeating here. Stopping the relentless accrual of interest may be the only way the taxpayer has a chance to catch up on what he owes. For some, the chance to pay off the taxes over time without interest is the principal motivation for a Chapter 13 filing.

If the debtor gets into bankruptcy before the IRS files a lien, the tax claims will be unsecured. Similarly, if the tax claim exceeds the value of the lien or if the lien secures some taxes but not others, there will be an unsecured tax claim as well. The automatic stay will prevent the IRS from taking any further collection actions — including securing a new lien on the debtor's property.

Once the priority tax claim is determined by reference to section 507(a)(8), the debtor can then work out a plan for regular payments. Priority claims, unlike allowed secured claims, are not paid in present value dollars. Instead, the debtor is required to pay the nominal amount of the claim, without interest. The language in section 1325(a)(4) and (a)(5) requires payment to unsecured and secured creditors based on "the value, as of the effective date of the plan," which the courts uniformly understand to mean present value or interest. But the language in section 1322(a)(2) governing the payment of priority debt refers only to "full payment, in deferred cash payments," an amount the courts have determined does not include interest. See, e.g., In re Pitt, 240 B.R. 908 (N.D. Cal. 1999), discussing Bruning v. United States, 376 U.S. 358 (1964) and In re Pardee, 218 B.R. 916 (9th Cir. BAP 1998). This means that when the interest payments on tax debts stop at the time of filing, they really stop — they do not recommence under a present value analysis in the Chapter 13 plan.

The interconnected nature of the Bankruptcy Code comes into sharper relief with a review of dischargeability. The Chapter 13 debtor ultimately hopes to discharge all the unpaid debts at the conclusion of the plan. This provides a neat set of bookends for the debtor with tax troubles: At one end is repayment in full for all taxes subject to a lien under section 506(a) or entitled to a priority under section 507(a)(8) and an explicit requirement in Chapter 13 to pay these claims ahead of all other claims; at the other end is the discharge of most of the remaining taxes and all other dischargeable debt. By the operation of these combined provisions, a debtor in trouble with the taxing authorities may have a way out.

d. Good Faith

The construction of a Chapter 13 plan begins with dividing up the debtor's income among necessary expenses and payments to secured creditors. After this division is made there is sometimes nothing left. Can a debtor confirm a plan that pays nothing to the general unsecured creditors? Or, to ask the question another way, if all the debtor's disposable income has been used up, can Chapter 13 be used merely to restructure secured debt without making some provision for the unsecured creditors?

To parse out an answer, it is necessary to sift back through the multiple versions of the Code. (We know you just want to cut to the answer, but the problem is that no one knows the answer for sure, so we're stuck with working through the reasoning.) The best interests test was the only explicit statutory requirement for plan payments to unsecured creditors in the 1978 Code. Because so many consumer cases would have been "no asset" cases in which creditors would get nothing in a Chapter 7, the best interests test provided no floor on the amount that debtors would be required to pay. In response to debtor plans proposing to pay little or nothing to unsecured creditors, some courts developed a "good faith" test to force a higher level of payments. When the new disposable-income test was added in the 1984 Amendments, these courts had to determine whether there remained a good faith review that could be used to toss out a debtor who proposed a low-payment plan that otherwise satisfied the disposable-income test.

Prior to the 2005 Amendments, the courts divided on this issue. Some said the disposable-income test had pre-empted cases that used a lack of good faith as a ground for rejecting plans that paid too little to the general unsecured creditors. Others argued that minimal payment could still be used as one element in a "totality of circumstances" test for good faith if other facts suggested abuse of the bankruptcy system. As we have seen, the 2005 Amendments have gone much further in defining disposable income and abuse, and have retained the totality test only as an alternative where the presumptive-abuse doctrine does not apply. §707(b)(2)(B), (3). Those changes may or may not persuade the courts that they should continue to apply an additional, ad hoc standard of good faith, especially in the cases involving below-median debtors to whom the presumptive-abuse standard does not apply (once again with the ironic twist that it may be the lowest-income debtors who get hit with the harshest standards).

The following case is one example of the impact of the good faith issue under the pre-2005 disposable-income standard.

In re LEONE

292 B.R. 243 (Bankr. W.D. Pa. 2003)

Warren W. Bentz, Bankruptcy Judge....

Facts

Debtors own real property located at 4308 Alison Avenue, Erie, Pennsylvania, which serves as their princip[al] residence (the "Property"). The Property is valued at $138,380.

U.S. Bank, N.A. as Trustee ("US Bank") holds a first mortgage secured by the Property with a balance of $205,796. *** The Plan provides for the Debtors to keep the Property valued at $138,380, cure arrearages of $18,957 to U.S. Bank, and to continue regular monthly payments of $1,325.58 which will result in a cure and reinstatement of the U.S. Bank mortgage. In other words, Debtors propose to maintain and pay the principal balance of $205,796 over time for the Property which is valued at no more than $138,380. The Plan also proposes full payment of delinquent real estate taxes in the amount of $6792.79 plus interest.

The Debtors have two vehicles. Debtors have modified the balance due to the lenders on the vehicles under §506 and propose to pay the modified balances in full over the 36 month term of the Plan.

The Plan provides that Debtors will pay $2,850 per month for 36 months. Unsecured creditors will receive a dividend of approximately 11%. Debtors contemplate a monthly housing expense of $2,347.88 [including mortgage payment, insurance, maintenance, and so on]. ***

Debtors list as dependents on Schedule I a 21 year old son and an 18 year old daughter.

Issue

The issue which the Court raises sua sponte is whether it is appropriate to confirm a 36 month Plan of reorganization where Debtors seek to pay $205,264 plus delinquent real estate taxes for a house admittedly worth $138,380 with a total monthly housing expense of $2,347.88 when unsecured creditors receive a dividend of 11%.

DISCUSSION

The Bankruptcy Code requires that a Chapter 13 Plan be proposed in good faith. §1325(a)(3). *** Whether a plan is filed in good faith is a question of fact based on the totality of the circumstances. In re Smith, 286 F.3d at 466; See also In re PPI Enterprises (U.S.), Inc., 324 F.3d 197, 211 (3d Cir.2003) (In considering the good faith requirements in a Chapter 11 filing context, the court states that there is no list that is exhaustive of all the factors which could be relevant when analyzing a particular debtor's good faith.).

"There is no requirement per se that a Chapter 13 Plan provide for substantial repayment of unsecured creditors." In re Hines, 723 F.2d 333 (3d Cir.1983). Plans are routinely confirmed by this Court and others where debtors lack an ability to provide unsecured creditors with a significant distribution. In re Rice, 72 B.R. 311 (D.Del.1987) (and cases cited therein).

Here, the Debtors have an ability to make significant distributions to unsecured creditors. A good faith effort would require that Debtors find replacement housing for themselves and their two adult children at a cost of less than $2,347 per month, or it may require that Debtors give up the idea of paying more than $205,000 for a $138,000 house; neither of which would impose a significant burden. If Debtors elect to maintain their Property, it is they that should bear the cost of the unusual and improvident expenses which unfairly discriminate against unsecured creditors. As an alternative, the Debtors could elect to extend the payments under their Plan for a term of up to 60 months. We are unable to find that the proposed Plan is filed in good faith.

Confirmation of the Plan will be refused.

═══════════════

The 2005 Amendments removed secured debt entirely from the calculation of income and expense, possibly overruling cases like this one on the argument that Congress now intends that all secured debt be paid before any consideration of the required payments to unsecured creditors. §§1325 (b)(1)(2); 707(b)(2)(A)(i), (iii). Moreover, the 2005 Amendments evidently contemplate the confirmation of some plans that will leave nothing for the general unsecured creditors. Section 1322(a)(4) permits a plan to be confirmed without paying all the priority debts only if all disposable income has been dedicated to that task; if all disposable income is going to the priority claimants, there is nothing left for the general unsecured creditors, which suggests that a zero-payment plan is acceptable.

Unsecured creditors may complain that the debtor who is giving them little or no payments, but instead diverting substantial amounts to secured creditors or to pay off priority debts, is not in good faith, but it seems that Congress had in mind to confirm such plans. Once again, we may see the unintended consequences of promising protection to a variety of interest groups. Here the promises to security and priority creditors may mean there is nothing left for the unsecured creditors.

e. Modification and Dismissal of Chapter 13 Plans

A Chapter 7 liquidation involves only the liquidation of already-acquired assets. By contrast, a Chapter 13 plan relies on projections of future income and living expenses to extrapolate the amount the debtor can pay. Often debtors in Chapter 13 bankruptcies already have had significant financial disruptions, and these projections of income and expenses frequently are not borne out. When that occurs, the debtor or the creditor may move to have the plan modified or dismissed. §1329(a). Most often, the debtor is seeking modification because of a lost job or other event that has made payment of the originally promised amounts much more difficult. The 2005 Amendments specifically permit a modification to permit the debtor to purchase health insurance. §1329(a)(4).

Modification hits another bump — the statutory limits on the length of a plan. The Bankruptcy Code limits any Chapter 13 plan to a maximum of 60 months. §1322(d)(1). When a plan is modified, it must still meet all the Chapter 13 requirements, including the five-year limit. When the 2005 Amendments required that all above-median-income debtors file 60-month plans, they wiped out any flexibility in reworking plans when the debtor fell behind. For an above-median-income debtor who loses a job or otherwise stumbles in trying to repay, the two sides of the trash compactor now touch — the plan may not be longer than 60 months nor shorter than 60 months, which means the debtor has to find a way to make up for the missed payments despite an income for which all spare change has already been fully committed.

Not all new events are bad events. Some debtors will get a raise, work a little overtime, or sell the car. But the good news may be short lived for the debtor. Instead, creditors or the trustee are allowed to trumpet good news for the debtor and to argue that the plan should be modified to permit higher payments. Creditor demands for modification may become more common because the 2005 Amendments require the debtor to file annual financial updates if the judge or any party in interest requests them. The update must describe the debtor's income and expenditures for the last tax year — under penalties of perjury. (How many law students or their teachers could produce such a document?) §521(f)(4). Thus creditors can discover any monetary joy that has touched the debtor's life and ask to take it all. Because the debtor is already in "disposable income" territory, any new income would seem to flow directly to the creditors.

Problem Set 15

15.1. You are filing your first Chapter 13 plan since entering practice. In your jurisdiction, judges are randomly assigned as cases are filed. The three bankruptcy judges seem to have rather different views about the requirements for confirmation of a Chapter 13 plan — two are very strict and one is quite lenient. All three permit the debtor to amend if a plan is not confirmed. Your first client, Maria Jackson, is a single parent who supports herself and three children on the salary she earns as a department store clerk in Atlanta.

Ms. Jackson earns $23,000 a year. She is left with $60 per week after she has paid her rent, utilities, insurance, food, gas, and $10 each Sunday to her church. This amount would give her creditors about 50 percent of their outstanding debt over three years or 80 percent over five, but it would not leave any cushion. Giving $60 to the trustee would also require termination of the piano lessons one child has already begun and prevent another child from starting needed orthodontic treatment. What kind of a plan do you propose for her? Does your malpractice insurer have an opinion on what you should do? See §§1322, 1325, 1329; IRS Expense Guidelines.

15.2. A. You represent Todd Cooper, a fast-food store manager in Orlando. With incentive bonuses and income from his accumulated stock, Todd's total income is slightly over $150,000. Todd lives as if it were even higher. He has a home with a mortgage larger than the annual income of some Third World nations, three cars on which he owes more than most people owe on their homes, two children in private school, and so on. In short, after he pays all these fixed expenses, plus a reasonable amount for food and clothing, he has about $30 per week for his unsecured creditors in his Chapter 13 plan. He owes these creditors almost $95,000. His total three-year payout at $30 per week will be $4,680, about 3 percent of his debt. Because most of his assets are subject to heavy liens and his state has generous exemptions, the unsecured creditors would get nothing in Chapter 7. Can you get Todd's plan confirmed? What are the weaknesses in your case? See §1325.

B. In an alternative universe you represent two of Todd's creditors, Perfection Motors, the Mercedes dealer who holds a $35,000 PMSI on one of his cars, and Divine Cuisine, his caterer, who is owed $5,600 for a series of business receptions Todd gave for bosses and coworkers in the fast-food chain. What position will you take regarding Todd's plan?

15.3. Christopher Paulus got his engineering degree from the University of Illinois and is doing well working for a worldwide construction firm. He earns over $60,000 per year. He lives in a nice apartment in Chicago with his girlfriend Frieda, who works as a physical therapist and shares the rent and other household expenses. When he first got out of college he went a little nuts with his credit cards and is carrying a $40,000 credit card debt. However, he has settled down and until recently was steadily reducing the debt by living frugally, driving the old family car his parents gave him, eating at home, shopping at Costco, and so on. Unfortunately, his elderly dad got very ill and even with Medicare payments had substantial out-of-pocket medical expenses. Chris co-signed for the necessary charges to the day his dad died and now finds himself with $60,000 in medical debt in addition to the credit cards, so he is contemplating some form of bankruptcy filing. Chris wants to know what his options are. Tell him what other information you need to know in order to answer his question. §1325.

15.4. Rebecca Nordhaus is a nurse who is rearing a small son while she works in a metropolitan trauma center. She was already carrying too much consumer debt when a serious car accident left her with more than $60,000 in bills that were not covered by insurance. Last year her base salary was $33,000, which would yield about $400 a month in disposable income, but her pay with overtime was $45,152. She says the overtime is exhausting her and she wants to spend more time with her son. What do you list for her disposable income in her Chapter 13 plan? See §1325(b).

15.5. You are completing preparation of a Chapter 13 plan for Jason D'Angelis. He wants to file but his wife, who is not employed outside the home, does not. Their income is $45,000. After you have computed his expenses, it appears that he will have about $425 a month that would be available for distribution to his creditors. Mr. D is very reluctant to pay any-one, and he keeps asking if he can't claim some more expenses. Finally, he looks at the expense list and says, "I want to make contributions to my church." You ask the amount, and he says, "$425 a month." You ask if he has made regular contributions in the past, and he says "No, but I'm turning over a new leaf." Can Mr. D confirm a plan that pays nothing to his unse-cured creditors? What do you advise him? §1325(b)(2)(A)(ii).

15.6. Last year you represented Doris Frankel in her Chapter 13 bankruptcy. You regard it as one of your most satisfying cases. When you met Doris she was a recently widowed, middle-aged woman who had never worked outside the home. At her husband's death, she was left with huge bills incurred during his final illness and a load of debts from his business for which she was jointly liable. After she used all the insurance and sold the business, she was still $120,000 in debt. Her creditors included some hostile and aggressive former business partners of her deceased husband. Doris took a job as a clerk at the local Mega-Lo-Mart, and she asked for your help in keeping her creditors from taking everything she and her husband had built up.

You took her into a Chapter 13, and she insisted on a 25 percent repay-ment of her unsecured debt. You thought that amount was too high and that she would have nothing left over, but she said it was important to her self-esteem.

Today, Doris is back in your office. She hardly looks like the same woman. While she worked at the Mega-Lo-Mart and another part-time, evening job, she began real estate classes. She has passed her exams, quit her other jobs, and has been selling commercial real estate for four months.

She has come to share some wonderful news with you. Last night she got a call from a well-known real estate developer. It seems that he had met Doris and liked her quiet, sincere style. He checked her background and decided she was just the woman he wanted to be in charge of the completion and leasing of his latest office building. She recognizes the enormous work that she will have to do. She must supervise all finishing work, find tenants, negotiate leasing arrangements and customizing work, etc. Doris estimates that she will be working 60 hours a week, at least. But if she can pull it off, the bonuses for 95 percent leasing in the first year could be as much as $50,000. You are delighted for her, but do you have any free advice? See §1329.

B.   THRESHOLD ELIGIBILITY FOR CHAPTER 13

Section 109(e) limits access to Chapter 13 to natural persons with limited debts and regular income. Congress may want more debtors in Chapter 13, but sometimes a creditor would rather deal with the debtor either under state law or in Chapter 7. In that case, the creditor may contest Chapter 13 eligibility. The following case illustrates the liberal attitude of many courts on letting people who want to try a Chapter 13 repayment to have their chance. Some judges, however, might not go as far as Judge Lundin, a widely acknowledged expert in Chapter 13 law.

==================== In re MURPHY ====================

226 B.R. 601 (Bankr. M.D. Tenn. 1998)

Keith M. LUNDIN, Bankruptcy Judge.

I

For 11 years, the Debtor has shared a household with Sam Hambrick. The home is owned by Mr. Hambrick and his elderly mother.

Mr. Hambrick's twin daughters (now 16 years old) live with the Debtor and Mr. Hambrick and have been raised by the Debtor. One of the twins has asthma and needs special medical attention. The Debtor also takes care of Mr. Hambrick's and her own elderly parents.

Mr. Hambrick is a self-employed businessman. He nets $3,800 per month from his businesses. At times during the past 11 years, the Debtor worked at a market owned by Mr. Hambrick. The market closed two or three years ago and the Debtor has not worked outside the home since then.

Throughout their relationship, Mr. Hambrick has deposited money into the Debtor's bank account each month from which the Debtor pays her separate bills. Mr. Hambrick pays all of the utilities and other household expenses for "their family" and typically deposits $800 a month into the Debtor's account.

The Debtor owns a 1994 Cadillac. The monthly installment note on this car was paid before bankruptcy from the bank account funded by Mr. Hambrick. At the petition, the holder of this note, First Indiana National Bank, was owed $5,700. The car was scheduled by the Debtor with a value of $14,750.

In July of 1998, Constance Morris took a default judgment against the Debtor in the General Sessions Court for Davidson County, Tennessee for $15,000. Ms. Morris executed on this judgment during the first week of August 1998 and the sheriff seized the Debtor's 1994 Cadillac. This Chapter 13 case was filed on August 12, 1998, after seizure but before sale of the car to satisfy the judgment. The statements and schedules show current income and expenses of the Debtor's household with Mr. Hambrick. Attached to the schedules is an "affidavit of Samuel Hambrick" which recites "I hereby agree to make [Brenda Jean Murphy's] Chapter 13 plan payment on her behalf, in a timely manner, and in the court order amounts, until completion of the plan."

Under the proposed plan, the Chapter 13 trustee will receive $600 per month for three years. The first lien holder on the car will be paid in full with interest. Constance Morris is treated as a partially secured creditor and the plan provides that the Debtor will avoid the judicial lien "to extent of $4,000 exemption." The portion of Ms. Morris's lien that remains after lien avoidance will be paid in full with interest. Unsecured creditors will receive at least 20% on allowed claims.

The Debtor filed a motion to partially avoid the Morris lien and a motion for turnover of the 1994 Cadillac. Ms. Morris objected arguing that the Debtor is not eligible for Chapter 13 because the Debtor does not have "regular income" as required by 11 U.S.C. §§109(e) and 101(30)....

II . . .

That §101(30) defines individual with regular income by reference to stability and regularity suggests that the existence of regular income is predominantly a fact question answered by examining the flow of money available to the debtor. Put another way, the Bankruptcy Code does not specifically exclude any source of funding from the regular income calculus; the Code does require that whatever source of income is claimed by a debtor, it must be regular and stable enough to fund a plan. The stable and regular focus of §101(30) has led several courts to state that "the test for 'regular income' is not the type or source of income, but rather its regularity and stability."

If the monthly contribution of money committed by Mr. Hambrick to the Debtor is income, the facts overwhelmingly support the finding that this Debtor's income is sufficiently regular and stable to fund a Chapter 13 plan. For 11 years Mr. Hambrick has maintained unbroken financial support to the Debtor. The Debtor has raised Mr. Hambrick's twin daughters and taken care of Mr. Hambrick's elderly parent while maintaining a home for herself, Mr. Hambrick, and Mr. Hambrick's children. Mr. Hambrick's income is substantial and regular and for many years has produced at least the amount he has committed to funding this plan. The expenses in the budget for the Debtor and Mr. Hambrick are comprehensive, modest and appropriate. Mr. Hambrick has signed an unconditional written commitment to provide the Debtor with money sufficient to fund the proposed Chapter 13 plan. Mr. Hambrick was forthright and honest in his testimony. Both Mr. Hambrick and the Debtor presented undisputed and convincing evidence of their commitment to each other and to their collective family and of their intent and ability to fund a Chapter 13 plan.

If Congress intended the word "income" in §101(30) to exclude the money Mr. Hambrick will pay to the Debtor, that less inclusive definition is not apparent in the Bankruptcy Code or its legislative history. The Code easily could but does not restrict the notion of income to wages, salary, return on investment or any of the other restrictions suggested in reported cases. The legislative history of what is now 11 U.S.C. §101(30) is unusually clear that Congress intended to expand and broadly define "individual with regular income" to include funding from diverse and nontraditional sources. As explained in the Senate Report:

> Paragraph [(30)] defines "individual with regular income." The effect of this definition, and of its use in section 109(e), is to expand substantially the kinds of individuals that are eligible for relief under chapter 13, Adjustment of Debts

of an Individual with Regular Income. Chapter XIII is now available only for wage earners. The definition encompasses all individuals with incomes that are sufficiently stable and regular to enable them to make payments under a chapter 13 plan. Thus, individuals on welfare, social security, fixed pension incomes, or who live on investment incomes, will be able to work out repayment plans with their creditors rather than being forced into straight bankruptcy. Also, self-employed individuals will be eligible to use chapter 13 if they have regular incomes.

S. Rep. No. 95-989, at 24 (1978). See also H. Rep. No. 95-595, at 311-12 (1977)....

Some courts have narrowed the definition of income for §101(30) purposes by requiring that the debtor have a "legal right" to the funding or that the source have a "legal duty" to make payments to the debtor. In cases involving contributions by a significant other of the debtor, some decisions use the absence of a "legal duty of support" as the basis for finding the debtor ineligible.

What does legal duty or legal right mean in this context? By statute or common law spouses, for example, have a mutual duty or right of support. But the absence of similar law with respect to the support obligations of unmarried couples hardly proves the absence of income for §101(30) purposes. In states like Tennessee, in the absence of a contrary contract or overriding public interest, an employer has the right to fire an employee at will and without cause. There is no "legal right" in Tennessee to continued employment — it depends on the pleasure of the employer, the quality of a debtor's work, the success of the employer's business, the weather, the economy in Asia — conditions to a debtor's right to wages that are in many ways less within a debtor's control than this Debtor's relationship to Mr. Hambrick. Yet, no one would seriously contend that the money a debtor expects to receive from employment is not income for §101(30) purposes just because the debtor has no legal right to continued employment. A definition of income for Chapter 13 eligibility purposes cannot be bottomed alone on the presence or absence of statutory or common law support obligations.

Maybe these courts mean that there is income only if a debtor has a remedy through the courts if payments stop. This notion is also too narrow for §101(30) purposes. Entitlements such as welfare and social security are income for eligibility purposes in a Chapter 13 case yet such benefit programs can be limited or abolished at the will of the legislature. And once (constitutionally) altered by the legislature, there is no recourse through the courts to force the payment of benefits.

Mr. Hambrick could employ the Debtor to take care of his twin teenagers and that employment would most likely be found to produce income for §101(30) purposes. In Tennessee, Mr. Hambrick could also fire the Debtor from that employment at any time, with or without cause. Mr. Hambrick's written promise to fund this Chapter 13 plan coupled with Mr. Hambrick's convincing testimonial commitments is at least as formal and concrete as legislative largess in a welfare program or as an employer's promises of work in the typical Chapter 13 case.

Mr. Hambrick's promise to fund this plan together with continued performance by this Debtor may generate rights and obligations that are every bit as enforceable as an employment contract. Reported decisions from many jurisdictions confirm that on theories of unjust enrichment, quantum meruit, restitution and express or implied contract, unmarried individuals sharing a household have successfully enforced financial commitments by their significant others. These cases are not based on marital support obligations found in statutes. Rather, recoveries typically are allowed on contract theories. If there is an amorphous requirement of legal rights or legal duties as predicate to a finding of income for §101(30) purposes, such rights and duties are found in the promises and performance by unmarried couples like this Debtor and Mr. Hambrick.

III

The Debtor can use §522(f) to partially avoid the judgment lien of Constance Morris. It is undisputed that the debtor has a $4,000 exemption in the car. The statements and schedules value the car at $14,750. There is a first lien of $5,700. The sum of the first lien and the Debtor's $4,000 exemption is $9,700, resulting in equity in the vehicle of $5,050.... The Debtor's lien avoidance right is limited by the $4,000 exemption and the lien remains in place to the extent of value in the car above the sum of the first lien plus the Debtor's exemption.

Lest anyone draw the wrong conclusion about bankruptcy as a haven for those with irregular living arrangements, we hasten to point out that some bankruptcy judges are more traditional. In Montana, the court said that a debtor who had been getting an allowance from her "live-in boyfriend" did not have REGULAR income. In re Duval, 226 B.R. 117 (Bankr. D. Mont. 1998). The fact that he had been paying for ten years did not make it REGULAR. We begin to suspect that for some courts, "regular" means something other than once-a-month.

Identifying Types of Claims

In the next case, the court addresses the second eligibility requirement for Chapter 13 under section 109(e): that the debtor have *noncontingent, liquidated* debts under the statutory maximums. These terms are slippery and even the courts sometimes get them wrong. Note that the debt limits for Chapter 13 have been raised since this case was decided.

In re HUELBIG

299 B.R. 721 (D.R.I. 2003).

Arthur N. VOTOLATO, Bankruptcy Judge.

Before the Court is Allstate Insurance Company's (Allstate's) Motion to Dismiss the Huelbigs' Chapter 13 case, on the ground that their unsecured debt exceeds the limits proscribed in 11 U.S.C. §109(e). The Debtors argue that Allstate's claim is unliquidated and therefore may not be counted in determining their eligibility for Chapter 13. For the reasons discussed below, I find, for jurisdictional purposes, that Allstate's claim is noncontingent and liquidated, and should be counted in determining the Debtors' eligibility for Chapter 13. Having said that, the Debtors clearly do not qualify for Chapter 13, and Allstate's Motion to Dismiss is GRANTED.

Background

During the early 1990s, Raymond Huelbig operated an auto body repair shop which did business with many insurance companies, including Allstate. In September 1999, Allstate filed a civil complaint in United States District Court in Providence against the Huelbigs and twenty other defendants, alleging Civil RICO violations, including a conspiracy to defraud Allstate out of $337,000 by filing false insurance claims, and on February 20, 2001, Raymond Huelbig plead *nolo contendere* to certain state criminal charges relating to fraudulent insurance claims. As part of the plea bargain, Huelbig received a ten year suspended sentence, with two years to serve in home confinement, and was ordered to pay restitution to Allstate in the amount of $2,480. On the same date as the plea, the Huelbigs filed a joint Chapter 13 case. During the course of these contentious proceedings, the Debtors have proposed two Chapter 13 plans, to which Allstate objected after conducting lengthy discovery. Allstate also filed a motion for relief from stay and for leave to continue its litigation against the Debtors in District Court.

* * *

Discussion

* * *

Together with Allstate's claim of $330,505, the Debtors have unsecured debts totaling $357,469. If Allstate's claim is either contingent or, to the extent that it is unliquidated, it would not count towards the Section 109(e) debt limit, and the Debtors would be entitled to proceed in Chapter 13.

"*Debt*" is defined by the Code as "liability on a claim," and *claim* is defined as a "right to payment, whether or not such right is reduced to judgment, liquidated, unliquidated, fixed, contingent, matured, unmatured, disputed, undisputed, legal, equitable, secured, or unsecured...." 11 U.S.C. §§101(12) & 101(5)(A). * * *

While not conceding the issue, the Debtors do not seriously contest that Allstate's debt is noncontingent. The case law uniformly holds that "if all events giving rise to liability occurred prior to the filing of the bankruptcy petition," the debt is not contingent. Here there is no dispute that all events giving rise to the Debtors' liability occurred in the 1990s, well before the petition was filed. The dispositive question is whether the claim is liquidated.

A claim is liquidated if it is subject to "ready determination and precision in computation of the amount due." In re Sylvester, 19 B.R. 671, 673 (9th Cir. BAP 1982), quoting In re Bay Point Corp., 1 B.C.D. 1635 (Bankr.D.N.J.1975). A variety of tests have evolved to ascertain whether a debt is subject to ready determination or is readily calculable. One court has suggested that if a precise computation can be accomplished after a simple hearing, the debt is liquidated; however, if an extensive, contested evidentiary hearing is required, the debt should be treated as unliquidated. The Bankruptcy Appellate Panel for the Eighth Circuit has stated: "The key factor in distinguishing liquidated from unliquidated claims is *not* the extent of the dispute nor the amount of evidence required to establish the claim, but *whether the process for determining the claim is fixed, certain, or otherwise determined by a specific standard.*" In re Barcal, 213 B.R. 1008, 1014 (8th Cir. BAP 1997) (emphasis in original). Recently, the Ninth Circuit Bankruptcy Appellate Panel clarified its approach, requiring courts to consider the debtor's liability on a debt as part of the process in determining whether a debt is liquidated. Ho v. Dowell (In re Ho), 274 B.R. 867, 872-75 (9th Cir. BAP 2002).

Not surprisingly, the Debtors urge the approach used in *Ho*, i.e., to consider the issue of the Debtors' liability to determine whether the claim is liquidated. Because they deny liability so loudly, the Debtors argue that an extensive hearing would be required to determine whether Allstate's claim is liquidated. As further proof of the magnitude of this dispute, the Debtors point out, with little relevance, that Allstate's District Court complaint consists of 108 pages, 342 numbered paragraphs, and weighs in at over one pound, even without the voluminous exhibits.

I decline the Debtors' invitation to adopt the 9th Circuit BAP approach and to take into account the issue of liability in determining whether or not this claim is liquidated. Considering liability in this context has been widely criticized, and is followed by only a few courts. A noted Chapter 13 commentator has stated: "Including consideration of disputed liability to determine whether a debt is liquidated is confusing and has been appropriately criticized." K. Lundin, *Chapter 13 Bankruptcy*, 3d ed. §16.1 at 16-8 (2002). *** Judge Feeney... concluded that: "the amount of [the creditor's claims] are readily calculable. Therefore, the claims are liquidated regardless of whether the Debtors dispute the liability. This Court specifically rejects the reasoning [that liability should be considered] as it represents a discredited minority view." [In re Mitchell, 255 B.R. 345, 360 (Bankr. D.Mass. 2000)].

Allstate has appended to its proof of claim a list of checks which were funds paid on putative fraudulent claims made by alleged co-conspirators, including the Debtors. While it concedes that liability is vigorously denied, Allstate argues that the dollar amount of its claim may be calculated by simple arithmetic. Following those courts which have so held in similar situations, I also rule here that the claim is liquidated, and that it should be counted in determining the Debtors' eligibility for Chapter 13. See In re Vaughn, 276 B.R. 323 (Lawsuits were pending in federal district court against the debtor alleging RICO violations, conspiracy, and fraud, based on the debtor's failure to tender rare coins to purchasers after accepting non-refundable deposits. Purchasers were seeking in excess of $600,000 plus treble damages and costs, and the bankruptcy judge found the debt to be liquidated, notwithstanding the fact that the debtor disputed his liability on these claims); In re Sitarz, 150 B.R. 710 (Bankr.D.Minn.1993) (Claim for fraud against the debtor is liquidated where a trial exhibit containing false credit card charges and unauthorized checks written by the debtor allowed for simple computation, although the process would be lengthy).

For the foregoing reasons, I find and/or conclude that the Debtors' unsecured debts exceed $269,250, and GRANT Allstate's Motion to Dismiss.[1]

═══════════

The court in *Huelbig* gave good explanations of the terms *contingent* and *liquidated*, but a few more examples might be helpful. The clearest case of a contingent claim is a bet in a state where betting creates legally enforceable obligations. If Jay and Liz bet a huge sum on who will win next year's OU-Texas game, in the days before the game both Jay and Liz have a contingent liability. When Oklahoma wins, Jay owes Liz a huge sum and, of course, Liz owes nothing. The point is that until the occurrence of the event — the game — no liability for either party has been established and the claim of either party against the other is contingent. Another example is a negotiable promissory note (like when mom guarantees a car loan for son). When a person indorses a note (mom), the indorser agrees to pay only if the maker of the note (son) does not. The indorser's liability then is contingent. A third example arises when a dealer sells goods with a 30-day warranty. For 30 days, the warranty obligation is contingent. If no one has trouble with the goods within 30 days, the dealer owes nothing and the obligation disappears. If there is trouble, the obligation is to comply with the warranty. The obligation, one might say, is contingent on the occurrence of a future event that brings the liability into being.

As the court held in *Huelbig*, unliquidated claims are those in which liability may have been admitted, but the amount of the debt is in dispute. When a driver admits responsibility for a car accident, but argues that the amount of damage to the plaintiff is considerably less than the plaintiff claims, the claim is no longer contingent, but it is unliquidated. When a court determines that a company has violated the antitrust laws but the court has not yet determined the scope of the damages, the damages are unliquidated. When a buyer purchases oil on a complicated pricing formula that includes future spot prices, until the price can be determined the amount owed is unliquidated. An obligation may be certain but the amount due may be unliquidated until the parties or the courts take further action.

There are multiple combinations. A claim may be contingent and unliquidated, as is the case with a breach of warranty before liability attaches or the amount of damage can be calculated. A claim may be contingent but liquidated, as is an indorsement on a note — the amount is known

---

1. Note that the fraud debt, if proved, was dischargeable under section 1328, but is not after the 2005 Amendments, a point we discuss in the next section. — eds.

but liability has not been established. A claim may be noncontingent, but unliquidated, as in the example of the yet-undetermined amount of money due for an established antitrust violation.

The only debts that count toward the eligibility cap are those that are both noncontingent and liquidated. Of course, the liquidated or contingent status of a claim is seldom relevant in any context other than bankruptcy. Only in bankruptcy are claims accelerated for settlement. In a non-bankruptcy claim the plaintiff pursues the lawsuit until it is neither contingent nor unliquidated; then the plaintiff begins collection. In bankruptcy, however, the debtor's financial position and the discharge of debts depend not only on what is currently owed but also on what may be owed in the future, based on actions from the past.

The problem with the rule announced in *Huelbig* is that the rule on its face would permit a purely spurious claim by a creditor to block a debtor's access to Chapter 13. Other cases have suggested that the courts will consider the merits of the claim at the threshold in a limited class of cases where the claim is "farfetched." See, e.g., In re Ho, 274 B.R. 867 (BAP 9th Cir. 2002) (cited and rejected in *Huelbig*).

The Chapter 13 restrictions on eligibility limit the kinds of debtors who will use Chapter 13. Those owing large amounts of debt (perhaps those running substantial businesses as sole proprietorships) will be denied access to Chapter 13 and must choose between Chapter 7 liquidation and reorganization through Chapter 11. Both options have, however, become more problematic. Chapter 7 access has been limited through the means test and other devices, while use of Chapter 11 by natural persons is now sharply limited as well.

Section 1129(a)(15) requires application of a Chapter 13 disposable-income test in a Chapter 11 case involving a natural person. Like Chapter 13, everything the debtor earns after filing belongs to the estate, not the debtor, with the debtor receiving an allowance for living expenses. §§1115; 1306(a). But unlike Chapter 13, the Chapter 11 reorganization plan must provide for five years of disposable income regardless of whether the debtor's income is above or below median. Disposable income is defined with reference to the section 1325(b)(2) standard, so the preexisting case law clearly applies to below-median Chapter 11 debtors, with the important difference of a five-year payout requirement. But section 1129(a)(15) does not mention section 1325(b)(3). Thus for above-median debtors it could be interpreted as applying the preexisting disposable-income caselaw under section 1325(b)(2) or the IRS budget means test under section 1325(b)(3), which some might argue is incorporated into section 1325(b)(2). As we have seen, which of those two tests is actually best for a given debtor in a given judicial district will depend on how the courts slice and dice the statutory requirements. As we will see in the business section, the Chapter 11 debtor must do more than meet the five-year requirement. To confirm a plan, the debtor will need both the votes of creditors and the approval of the court, making Chapter 11 less attractive than Chapter 13, if other things are equal. Indeed, an individual debtor facing a hostile creditor holding a large percentage of the debt could find it difficult or impossible to use Chapter 11.

Nothing in the Bankruptcy Code explicitly requires that access to some form of bankruptcy be available to every person in financial trouble. Following the 2005 Amendments, it may be that some debtors will find themselves caught between chapters — unable to use Chapter 7, Chapter 13, or Chapter 11.

Problem Set 16

16.1. Harold Hunt is an oil well firefighter, a specialist in fighting run-away fires in oil wells. Harold is very good, but because he is afraid to fly he limits his work to the California area. He fights only three or four fires per year, but he earns about $40,000 per fire. Some years there are no fires, while other years there are seven or eight.

He is current on his bills, but he has come to you because of a judgment he has just suffered. Two years ago while on a visit to his mother's house he heard an argument between his mother and the plumber who was doing some work in the kitchen. The plumber called Harold's mother a number of very vile things. Harold says, "I lost my head." So did the plumber — at least a good portion of it. The plumber sued Harold and recovered a $360,000 judgment last week, despite Harold's plea of provocation. Harold has no money for an appeal bond and is afraid the plumber will attach his non-exempt house and other property. What do you advise him? See §§1328(a), 109(e).

16.2. Myrtle Tundra owes over $120,000 to banks, credit card issuers, and stores, and she has a $250,000 mortgage on her house. She has about $50,000 in non-exempt personal property. Her legal practice is doing well, and she makes about $100,000 a year. Myrtle has come to see you as a bankruptcy expert because she is nervous about a debt that she guaranteed for her former law firm.

The debt was the mortgage on the small office-building that the firm owned and in which it maintained its office. Her former partner, John Ice, kept the building as part of their agreed wind-up of the former firm's affairs. The mortgage is presently about $775,000, payable over 18 more years. The building is currently worth about $600,000, but it is in a rapidly developing area. A reliable real estate agent has told Myrtle that when a nearby freeway and shopping center are completed in about six months, the property will easily be worth $900,000.

John is having some trouble making the payments and may have missed this month's payment already. The mortgage is held by Loraine Ice, John's former wife, who hates both John and Myrtle for reasons Myrtle does not wish to discuss. Myrtle says Loraine would viciously exploit any default in an effort to hurt John and Myrtle. What is your advice? See §109(e).

16.3. Nino Riccini has been a successful computer design analyst for 16 years. Two years ago, Nino struck off on his own. He took advantage of the boom in Silicon Valley and the free-flowing capital to start a small firm, LectraFuture, Inc. After the investment absorbed $800,000, the first production run failed to sell out.

Nino has given up on the business and decided to go back to working for a larger company, but he finds that getting a good job is taking longer than he had expected. There is a temporary lull in the industry, and many older, higher paid design people have been laid off. Nino is sure he will find something soon. He doesn't want to appear panicked and reduce his bargaining leverage.

In the meantime, Nino's creditors are closing in. Nino has some cash in savings, but he needs help to prevent a foreclosure on his home, seizure of his car, and a host of minor but troublesome state law actions. What do you advise?

16.4. Julio Rodriguez is a technical wizard who left a high-paying job with Microsoft to found his own business. He developed a cell phone add-on that a couple of majors have marketed with varying degrees of success. When he first attracted their business, he expanded his production capacity quickly, then found that interest was cooling. He now has almost $400,000 in unsecured debt owed to suppliers and investors as against inventory, machinery, and a couple patents worth altogether about $200,000. He is making about $65,000 a year from the business, but doesn't think it has more than three years of viability unless he can come up with a new patent. He has lots of new ideas, but each one will take new money to develop. He has little personal debt, except a mortgage just over $500,000 on a small home in Palo Alto worth about $550,000. The housing bubble has begun to shrink a bit and he guesses he'd be lucky to pay off the mortgage if he sold, but for that reason he thinks the mortgage company would be glad to work with him. What are his alternatives under various chapters? As to Chapter 11, ignoring the other requirements for confirmation of a Chapter 11 plan, is section 1129(a)(15) a problem? Balancing it all out, what should you recommend to him? §§101(3), (4A); 526-528; 707(b); 1115(a); 1306(a); 1325(b); 1129(a)(15).

C.   CHAPTER 12 FOR FAMILY FARMERS AND FISHERMEN

In the early 1980s a variety of economic developments struck hard at American farmers. Farmland bought on credit at high prices in the 1970s plummeted in value in many parts of the country, and crop prices were inadequate to permit farmers to service their mortgages. An increasing number of farmers turned to bankruptcy for relief, but those who wanted to keep their farms under a payment plan found themselves straddled uncomfortably between Chapter 11 and Chapter 13. Many family farmers were not eligible for Chapter 13 because they had too much debt in the form of mortgages on their farms and equipment. Yet the provisions of Chapter 11 are designed for businesses with more regular cash flow and involve a large degree of creditor control. Farmers felt they were being forced to conform to requirements that were inappropriate for them and were much more stringent than those imposed on salaried consumers making the same income.

The farmers' discontent became law in the form of a new chapter in Title 11, Chapter 12. The new chapter was modeled on Chapter 13, so that it can be summarized by simply describing the principal differences between Chapter 13 and Chapter 12. The most important difference is in eligibility. A debtor can be eligible for Chapter 12 with far higher debts than for Chapter 13. Reflecting the economic realities of running even a modest farming operation, Chapter 12 has much higher debt limits than Chapter 13, totaling over $3 million. §§101(18)(A), 109(f).

Only "family farmers" are eligible for Chapter 12, a family farmer being defined by reference to percentages of income or debt related to farming. Yet Chapter 12 is more liberal than Chapter 13 in that a partnership or corporation can be a Chapter 12 debtor, in contrast to Chapter 13's strict limitation to natural persons, so long as the legal entity is owned by a single family and meets certain additional "family farmer" tests. §101(18), (21). The definition of family farmer is not the same as the definition of "farmer." §101(20). "Farmers" have some other special provisions scattered through the Code, such as the limitation on the ability of a farmer's creditors to force an involuntary bankruptcy. §303(a). As with a Chapter 13 debtor, the family farmer must have "regular income" to qualify for Chapter 12, but, again, in recognition of the special economics of farming, it may be regular *annual* income. §§101(19), 109(f).

Chapter 12 makes a major change in the standard for adequate protection in section 362 stay-lifting proceedings. The section 361 definition of adequate protection does not apply in Chapter 12. Instead, section 1205 sets forth modified standards for farmers. In particular, section 1205(b)(3) makes payment of a "reasonable" and "customary" rent sufficient for adequate protection regardless of any threatened decline in the value of mortgaged land.

Chapter 12 also changes the Chapter 13 plan requirements and constraints in important ways. It expressly permits the family farmer to modify a residential mortgage along with all other secured debt. It also permits the plan to last for more than five years to deal with secured debt. These two provisions in combination make it possible for the family farmer in Chapter 12 to address unsecured debts in the usual three- to five-year plan, while modifying (presumably decreasing) payments on secured debt by stretching them out over many years. §§1222(b)(2), (9); 1222(c). As with Chapter 13, the debtor must devote all "disposable income" to the plan during the three- to five-year period, but disposable income is determined after deducting business expenses. §1225(b)(1), (b)(2)(B).

One aspect of Chapter 12 makes it less attractive to debtors than Chapter 13. The Chapter 12 discharge is somewhat narrower than the Chapter 13 provisions. After a Chapter 12 case, an individual debtor remains liable on the same debts made nondischargeable in Chapter 7 by the provisions of section 523(a).

The 2005 Amendments extended Chapter 12 eligibility to family fishermen as well. The applicable provisions are similar, except that the total debt limit is $1.5 million, subject to inflation adjustment. §101(19A)-(19B).

D. THE CONSUMER BANKRUPTCY SYSTEM

1. Overview

At this point, anyone who has worked diligently through the materials should have a good grasp of the technical aspects of personal bankruptcy as well as its strategic uses. The reader should also have some sense of the policy issues that lurk in the structure of consumer bankruptcy. To complete the exploration of consumer bankruptcy, we offer here a reexamination of the system that assumes mastery of the details but that adds some new (and not merely legal) perspectives on the system.

The debtor–creditor relationship has been one of the most important social and political relationships throughout history in every society in which credit has been widely granted. Ancient Athens and the Roman Republic provide familiar examples of political and social upheaval associated with widespread burdens of debt. In America, bankruptcy is the dramatic focus of those tensions, even though the bankruptcy process is only part of a much larger system of consumer credit and consumer debt collection.

Consumer bankruptcy policy is today being debated around the world. The debates oscillate in the tension between the traditional idea of the fresh start and a pervasive fear of abuse. In a number of developed countries the growth of modern consumer credit practices has occasioned a great increase in the number of wage earners and small proprietors who find themselves staggering under mountains of debt, leading to demands for a system that will relieve their distress and permit these citizens to begin their financial lives anew. At the same time, in every society there is a deep-seated concern that a relaxation of the traditional commitment to legal enforcement of promises to pay (traditionally, *pact sunt servandum*) may represent a decadent trend that will undermine the commercial basis for a successful community. See generally, Jay Lawrence Westbrook, Local Legal Culture and the Fear of Abuse, 6 Am. Bankr. I. L. Rev. 463 (1998).

The discussion of each of these twin concerns has been divided between the two stages in the consumer credit process — before debts are incurred and afterwards. The debt-incurrence stage engages some who are concerned with debtors who will irresponsibly incur debts beyond their ability to pay, while others decry the irresponsible marketing of credit by financial companies. The post-incurrence stage, when the bankruptcy decisions are made, is the focus of some who fear that debtors will file for bankruptcy who could have paid their debts. Others are more concerned at that point that debtors who cannot pay will be left indefinitely in an unproductive and pointlessly cruel financial quagmire.

a. Theories

Until fairly recently there was little scholarly debate about the purposes of consumer bankruptcy or the overall approach of the United States system. See, e.g., Thomas Jackson, *The Logic and Limits of Bankruptcy Law*, chapter 10 (inter alia, discharge leaves the risk of decisions about extending credit to creditors, who are best able to judge).

A few scholars have come forward in the last several years to suggest that a different approach should be taken. Some have argued that consumers should be freer to waive the protection of the bankruptcy laws and to contract with creditors for individual post-default regimes. See, e.g., Barry Adler, Ben Polak, and Alan Schwartz, Regulating Consumer Bankruptcy: A Theoretical Inquiry, 29 J. Leg. Stud. 585 (2000) (arguing that mandatory bankruptcy laws for consumers are inefficient). On the whole, however, there remains a broad consensus that supports some version of the present system, even as scholars have put forward a number of conflicting proposals for reform of that system.

Scholarly interest has focused primarily on the first aspect of the problem (*ex ante* as professors like to say). One widely discussed theory of consumer bankruptcy treats it as analogous to insurance. The idea is that the cost of credit may be greater because creditors must account for the risk of the bankruptcy discharge at the time credit is extended, although it must be said that this increase is assumed rather than demonstrated. The insurance concept is that any increased cost of credit is the premium all borrowers pay for protection from the direst consequences of financial misfortune. The result is to spread the risk of financial misfortune across a large class of persons subject to the risk. As with any mandatory insurance scheme, however, the argument is made that it creates a "moral hazard" akin to the risk of carelessness about a possible fire arising from issuance of fire insurance.

Closely related is the assertion by many scholars that bankruptcy is a form of social safety net, supplementing unemployment insurance, public medical care, and the rest. It is argued that a country like the United States, which has chosen to have a much weaker set of protections for those who are less successful in economic competition, has more need for consumer bankruptcy laws than other countries where universal medical care, subsidized housing, and generous unemployment benefits provide greater protection against the inevitable risks of a free-market economy. See, e.g., *The Fragile Middle Class*, 258-260.

It appears that the reason the scholarly discussion has focused on the pre-incurrence stage is that most of the empirical research shows conclusively that the debtors who file bankruptcy simply cannot pay. Once the debts are incurred, there is little to be done. Thus it has perhaps seemed more profitable to scholars to focus on the ex ante process. A major problem with that focus, however, is the lack of empirical data to support the theories, perhaps because of the difficulty of obtaining data about the ex ante effects of law. In any case, one result is that scholars have mostly ignored the political policy proposals because those proposals have been devoted largely to getting the debtors to pay after they file for bankruptcy. Professor Feibelman has collected and discussed much of the literature in his article, Defining the Social Insurance Function of Consumer Bankruptcy, 13 A.B.I. L. Rev.1 (2005).

b. Policy Debates

The last few decades have seen an explosion in consumer bankruptcy filings, including a four-fold increase in the rate of filings from 1981 to 2000. Although business bankruptcies have also increased, there remains a strong sense that business cases are somehow different, that they do not implicate the moral and social issues found in personal bankruptcy. The great increase in consumer bankruptcies has driven a continuing policy debate about the role of personal bankruptcy in the consumer credit system and whether substantial reform is required. As with the theoretical literature, the debate involves two questions. Has this great increase been caused by some change in the economic system or is it the result of a change in the attitude of borrowers that causes people to load up on debts? Or are there more filings because debtors who are actually able to pay are flocking to bankruptcy? Again, the first question focuses on pre-bankruptcy conduct and economic conditions, while the second scrutinizes the debtors who seek bankruptcy relief.

While the questions may be phrased in a number of different ways and they may focus on the moment of taking on debt or much later on the time for declaring bankruptcy, the questions always seem to revolve around a central moral dispute: Do bankruptcy filings result primarily from irresponsibility or from misfortune?

Some argue that credit irresponsibility, whether it is the irresponsibility of the debtors who incur the bills or the irresponsibility of the lenders who extend credit, is the leading cause of bankruptcy, while others say that bankruptcies are more often the consequence of economic forces beyond an individual's control, such as layoffs on the income side or the cost of protracted illness on the debt side. The likely reason that the impact of these arguments has been largely rhetorical is that scrutinizing debtors' pre-bankruptcy conduct for irresponsibility, as opposed to fraud, is simply too laden with normative conundrums and practical difficulties. Finding fault in the complex mass of semi-predictable misfortune and debtors' quotidian decisions about incremental increases in debt is a far more difficult task than most researchers, legislators, or judges are prepared to take on. The credit industry's own behavior is laden with ambiguities, as creditors applaud the "democratization of credit" that has them lending to the poor and the unemployed, while others characterize their actions as preying on the vulnerable and unsophisticated.

There is a case for the proposition that credit irresponsibility on someone's part is a major part of the problem. Consumer debt during the 1980s doubled from $300 to $600 billion. By 2004, it had more than tripled again, to more than $2 trillion, exclusive of almost $7 trillion in home mortgages. Federal Reserve Statistical Release Series G.19. The rise has been accompanied by credit-granting horror stories on the pages of the *Wall Street Journal* and elsewhere. We have read about the mass mailing of credit cards to all the inmates in a Louisiana prison. There was the Dallas man who came home from the foreclosure sale of his house to find a MasterCard Gold Card waiting for him. A dog got his Andy Warhol fifteen minutes of fame when the newspapers reported his receipt in the mail of a national credit card with a generous credit limit, only to be eclipsed by a credit card–holding cat a few weeks later. VISA now markets a credit card for the 13- to 17-year-old crowd, suggesting that serious credit scoring does not lie behind the issuance of every credit card, and the new "Hello Kitty" credit card seems aimed for an even younger set. There seems to have been an extraordinary lowering of credit standards in the mass-marketing of credit. That fact has combined with often-mindless automation. (It turned out the prisoners got the credit cards because the computer saw that "they had stable addresses.")

The ads on pages 343-344 are found around the country. One mailing that was sent directly to bankruptcy lawyers offered credit cards to their clients who had completed a bankruptcy. The client could sign up for the card with nothing more than a photocopy of his Chapter 7 discharge papers, and the attorney would receive a $10 finder's fee. What a deal.

Aggressive marketing of credit has a close cousin — default rates of interest and penalty fees that make it nearly impossible for a debtor who has stumbled to catch up. In re McCarthy, 10493-SE (E.D. Va. 2004) (unpublished), illustrates what can happen to someone who falls behind. The opinion reveals that exactly two years before she landed in bankruptcy court Ms. McCarthy owed Providian $2,021. During the intervening 24 months, she charged an additional $203, and she made payments totaling $2,006, so her net payments to Providian were $1,803. How much did she owe Providian? The company said that with interest and fees, she now owed $2,608, which meant that she could make substantial payments month after month, with minor additional charges, and yet, as each month went by, she would end up owing more than the month before. Ms. McCarthy was in about the same shape with four other credit cards. For debtors who get caught in this debt nightmare, bankruptcy may be the only alternative.

Many pieces make up the consumer bankruptcy puzzle, but a very important factor is the explosion of consumer credit. Grasshopper consumers willing to live on the plastic edge of financial collapse have met a credit industry all too willing to oblige. The credit industry spends billions to make debt attractive, only to profess dismay over what results.

On the other hand, evidence also exists that increasing economic volatility in the modern American economy and the vulnerability of the American family as an economic unit put an ever larger share of the middle class at risk for economic collapse. Data reported in *The Fragile Middle Class* show that debtors report layoffs, serious medical problems, and the disastrous aftermath of divorce as principal reasons for their filings. A more recent study shows that about half of all families file bankruptcy in the aftermath of a serious illness or injury. Himmelstein, Thorne, Warren, and Woolhandler, Illness and Injury as Contributors to Bankruptcy, *Health Affairs* (February 2, 2005). By 2001, nine out of ten bankruptcies were tied in to job losses, medical problems, or family breakups, with many families reporting two or all three problems. Warren and Tyagi, *The Two-Income Trap*, p. 13.

Part of the explanation is that the economy that has generated so much wealth has rested upon a greater volatility of employment (especially downsizing and temporary workers) and much greater debt — personal, corporate, and governmental. Both unpredictable employment and spiraling debt are important factors in producing bankruptcy filings. Even in times of economic prosperity and low unemployment, families bear economic risk one household at a time, and the losers often find themselves in bankruptcy.

Critics of the present system have suggested one other cause for the great increase of filings, that bankruptcy has lost its stigma. Judge Edith H. Jones & Todd J. Zywicki, It's Time for Means-Testing, 1999 BYU L. Rev. 177. No empirical support has been offered for this hypothesis, while the interviews with debtors who explained how they were hiding their bankruptcies from family members, friends, neighbors, and coworkers seem to suggest otherwise. See *Two-Income Trap*, p. 13. Moreover, the fact that many of the debtors reported going without needed medical care (54 percent), not having prescriptions filled (43 percent), enduring utility shut offs (30 percent), and even going without food (22 percent) to try to pay their bills before they filed for bankruptcy suggests that bankruptcy was not the first-choice option that the critics claim. See "Illness and Injury as Contributors to Bankruptcy," figure 4.

One factor that has clearly contributed to the increase of bankruptcy filings has been the explosion of consumer bankruptcy advertising following Bates v. State Bar of Arizona, 433 U.S. 350 (1977). Every Sunday TV guide in America (or at least every one we've checked) has multiple ads for consumer bankruptcy help. Some will regard this fact as a perfect illustration of lawyer self-interest promoting unnecessary and counterproductive legal actions, while others will see it as contributing to a great awakening in average people to their legal rights.

In light of all these variables and uncertainties about the causes of the great increases in bankruptcy filings, the ex ante question has seemed too hard to answer. Thus the political debates have focused on the ex post question: Can these debtors pay?

As we saw earlier (see pp. 161, 256–257), the empirical data relevant to this question are not ambiguous. Most debtors are heavily indebted and most are unable to pay any substantial amount of their debts. Yet disagreements about appropriate legal constraints continue because of differing normative views about what conclusion to draw from the facts. For example, it has been suggested that it is an abuse for a family to file for Chapter 7 if they could pay a substantial part of their debts by living at the poverty level for five years. (This was the test employed by the credit industry–sponsored Credit Research Center in its first report to Congress.) Some will regard that conclusion as self-evidently correct, while others will think it an outrageous suggestion. The first group will say those debtors "can pay" and the second will say "you've got to be kidding." The data do have an impact, as discussed below, but naturally they have their effect in the context of normative beliefs.

There is another important but often ignored question that is highly relevant to the policy debate: "Do creditors suffer significantly greater losses in bankruptcy than outside it?" The answer to that question is not obvious, even if many commentators assume that it is. Credit card companies have conceded that about half of the debts listed in bankruptcy were already written off as noncollectible before the debtor filed. Of the remaining half, it isn't clear how much would have been paid absent bankruptcy. Moreover, the debts that credit card companies list in bankruptcy often include penalty interest and late fees, along with credit actually extended.

If creditors are suffering greater losses in bankruptcy, then the question is whether bankruptcy could be reformed to require greater payment to creditors consistent with other normative values. If debtors could pay more under socially acceptable conditions, then reform would be appropriate. But if creditors are not being paid because debtors have so much debt relative to their incomes and assets that they could never repay — with or without bankruptcy — then it may be appropriate to look outside the bankruptcy system for a solution.

2. The Evolution of Consumer Bankruptcy Law

The fresh start was the dominant objective of the Bankruptcy Act of 1898. In 1938, the Chandler Act added Chapter XIII as a payout chapter for wage earners, but its stated purpose was not to coerce "can pay" debtors into mandatory repayment plans, but instead to provide legal breathing room for voluntary repayments by debtors who wanted to pay their debts.

The fresh start policy remained dominant in the Bankruptcy Reform Act of 1978, but with a much greater push for consumer payouts. Personal bankruptcies had increased considerably in the preceding years, and Congress wanted to encourage debtors to try to pay. In addition to expanding the scope of Chapter 13 to include debtors who were operating businesses, Congress offered a set of incentives for filing Chapter 13, including an opportunity to save one's home and a much broader discharge, which even covered fraud and other intentional torts. Following the adoption of the 1978 Act, the percentage of bankruptcy cases that were filed in Chapter 13 rather than Chapter 7 jumped sharply, to about 30 percent overall. There remained, however, wide variations from district to district. Chapter 13 filings then stalled at that level for the next 25 years.

By 1984, the credit industry blamed the increase in bankruptcies on the provisions of the 1978 Act and pressed for more pro-creditor balance. The industry was successful to a limited, but important, extent. Under the 1984 Amendments, section 707(b) for the first time blocked access to Chapter 7 in cases of substantial abuse. Section 523 added a provision presuming fraud (and therefore nondischargeability) for certain debts incurred shortly before bankruptcy. The reaffirmation rules in Chapter 7 were rewritten so that it was easier for creditors to get enforceable promises to repay debts notwithstanding the bankruptcy, and in Chapter 13 the industry was able to add a requirement that all disposable income be devoted to paying creditors for at least three years. The importance of these provisions lay in the fact that they emphasized that debtors should pay more, even if they could not pay all they owed.

In 1994, the industry returned for more benefits, but the most important provision in that legislation established the National Bankruptcy Review Commission with nine commissioners and a law professor, Elizabeth Warren, in the role of Advisor. At each Commission meeting, consumer issues were hotly debated, often drawing substantial attendance and testimony that spanned several volumes. Its proposals were announced on October 7, 1997. The supporting discussions and dissenting views are available online at http://govinfo.library.unt.edu/nbrc/index.html. The majority's recommendations focused on such abuses as repeat filings by debtors and state exemptions that vary widely from stingy to excessive. The report did not embrace the changes that the credit industry thought important, and the Commission Report was denounced before it was delivered. Members of Congress sympathetic to the industry viewpoint turned away from the Commission recommendations, introducing bills with sweeping changes in the consumer bankruptcy system. The credit industry began a public relations campaign and well-financed lobbying effort. An eight-year effort by the industry led to adoption of the 2005 Amendments.

From a policy perspective, the role of empirical studies in this process is especially interesting. It is fair to say that these studies had an important — but far from dispositive — role. See generally, Jay Lawrence Westbrook, Empirical Research in Consumer Bankruptcy, 80 Tex. L. Rev. 2123 (2002). In general, work done in the 1980s, including *As We Forgive*, showed that the overwhelming majority of debtors were unable to pay their debts. That work apparently convinced the industry that it required empirical refutation, so it funded a study from the Credit Research Center at Georgetown University that claimed that its data showed that many debtors could pay their debts. Although the actual study was never published nor were the data made available to government agencies that requested them, it provided a platform for legislation that introduced for the first time a means test for entering Chapter 7. On the other hand, the detailed study by law professors Marianne Culhane and Michaela White had a substantial influence in narrowing the means test to its present form. A study of women in bankruptcy by Teresa Sullivan and Elizabeth Warren led to the substantial preference shown domestic support obligations in the 2005 Amendments. On the broader issues, however, many in Congress made up their minds that a significant number of debtors were guilty of abuse and could pay; no amount of academic data to the contrary would prevent the legislation passing each house several times by gaudy majorities. Of course, the industry's political generosity made its data more persuasive.

3. A Comparative Look

We often have a foolish tendency to assume that conditions and attitudes unique to ourselves govern our policy debates. That is even less true in a globalizing world than it used to be. It remains true, of course, that different cultures address similar problems in different ways, but there is often common ground that makes the differences illuminating for us.

Until the 1980s, the world of personal bankruptcy was easily, if roughly divisible into three main camps: the United States, the common law countries other than the United States, and the civil law countries. The common law countries generally permitted personal bankruptcy of both merchants and consumers and provided for a discharge. However, the discharge was much harder to get in those countries than in the United States, usually requiring years of payments under court supervision. Only in the last two decades have those countries begun to move in the direction of a faster discharge, led by Canada and the United Kingdom. The latter has now gone to a system that permits discharge within a year with minimal payments, a dramatic change from its law 20 years ago.

Traditionally, civil law countries have not permitted any form of personal bankruptcy for anyone other than merchants. In the last 20 years, however, a revolutionary change has occurred in Northern Europe and Japan, largely coinciding with the growth of deregulated, wide-open consumer credit à l'amèricaine. VISA and MasterCard have, no doubt unwittingly, taken the idea of a discharge with them as they have globalized their businesses. The consumer bankruptcy laws as first adopted in Europe and Japan were generally very restricted and as applied often granted few discharges. See, e.g., Rafi Efrat, Legal Culture and Bankruptcy: A Comparative Perspective, 20 Emory Bankr. Dev. J. 361, 390 (2004) (Israel). But governments in these countries have found over and over again that the debtors are unable to pay under the strict rules initially imposed. The legislatures have responded in many countries by relaxing the payment rules and lessening the time to discharge. See Jason Kilborn, *La Responsabilisation de l'Economie:* What the U.S. Can Learn From the New French Law on Consumer Overindebtedness, 26 MICH. J. INT'L L. XXX (forthcoming 2005). See also Junichi Matushita, Comprehensive Reform of Japanese Insolvency Law and Personal Insolvency, __ Theoretical Inquiries in Law XXX (forthcoming 2005); Soogeun Oh, Law and Policy of Personal Bankruptcy in Korea — Challenges and Responses, __ Theoretical Inquiries in Law XXX (forthcoming 2005). The consumer bankruptcy regimes in these countries remain stricter than in the United States, but with a definite trend in our direction.

On the other hand, an emerging theme in several countries is that "the debtors should pay something." That is, even as lawmakers around the world come to realize that most debtors can pay little, there has been support for the idea that they should pay something because even symbolic payment and some time suspended in bankruptcy will deter abuse of the system and maintain commercial morality. So far, that proposition has not been put forward in the United States, but given the increasingly irrefutable evidence that our debtors cannot pay, it may prove to be tomorrow's justification for tougher restrictions on discharge. Or the pragmatic American response might be, "We don't make people suffer for symbolism if there ain't no dollars."

There is a strong connection between modern credit-granting methods and an increased need for personal bankruptcy laws. Indeed, an intriguing new study suggests a powerful correlation between rising personal bankruptcy rates in a nation and the growth of credit card use in that nation, quite apart from the growth of consumer debt generally. Ronald Mann, Charging Ahead: The Growth and Regulation of Payment Card Markets Around the World (forthcoming). Thus we can expect to see a continued convergence of consumer bankruptcy laws around the world, although with the inevitable differences arising from different cultures and circumstances.

4. *The Consumer Bankruptcy System Before and After the 2005 Amendments*

Both anecdote and empirical evidence have demonstrated that the consumer bankruptcy system has always operated in ways not easily deduced from its statutory provisions, so we can be sure that it will take several years for the full range of effects of the 2005 Amendments to be established and several years more for practice manuals and empirical studies to report the changes. In this section, we look at the way in which the system worked prior to the amendments and consider how they may alter the process. Of one thing we can be sure, however: some changes that caught no one's eye will turn out to be important.

With that humbling thought in mind, we can start with the fact that the 2005 Amendments did not make fundamental structural changes in the system. The discharge and fresh start remain the heart of the system and there are still two doors to the discharge: Chapter 7 and Chapter 13. Nonetheless, the amendments do represent a turning of a page in the long history of consumer bankruptcy in the United States and we can anticipate some important modifications in the way the system works. Note that we are not covering all the important changes, but only those that seem likely to have a systemic effect.

a. Abuses

The amendments are likely to constrict or to eliminate two practices that many considered abuses of the existing system. One was beyond doubt an abuse. Especially in California, many debtors repeatedly filed bankruptcy cases to use the automatic stay to block eviction by landlords even though the debtors had no intention of following through with the bankruptcy. Indeed, it was often true that the debtors did not know that bankruptcy was filed for them. They were just told, "There's a legal way to hold up your eviction if you'll just sign right here." And, of course, pay a certain amount to the outfit offering the advice. The new provisions blocking use of the stay through serial filings of either Chapter 7 or Chapter 13 will reduce this abuse. §365(c)(3).

A number of debtors have filed so-called "Chapter 20" cases, in which the debtor files Chapter 7 and Chapter 13 in close succession. The Chapter 7 case discharges all debts dischargeable under section 523. The debtor can then put the nondischargeable debts (e.g., recent taxes) into a payment plan and pay them over time in Chapter 13. It was also sometimes used for debtors ineligible for Chapter 13 who nonetheless wanted to deal with home mortgages or car loans that were badly in default: The debtor would file for Chapter 7 and wipe out the credit card debt that put the debtor above the unsecured debt limits, then file for Chapter 13 and pay off the mortgage arrearage or car loan over time. Although the effect of a Chapter 20 was simply to prevent the dischargeable creditors from riding the Chapter 13 coattails of the tax authorities, mortgage companies, or car lenders, many people saw it as an abuse. It is made impossible by section 1328(f), which denies a Chapter 13 discharge for a debtor who has gotten a Chapter 7 discharge within the prior four years.

b. Recoveries for Creditors

The central premise of the 2005 Amendments was that steering debtors into Chapter 13 would generate greater recoveries for creditors. But that is a factual assertion that is highly problematic. Even before the effects of the 2005 Amendments are known, it is hard to say that the pay-back in Chapter 13 greatly exceeds the repayment made by Chapter 7 debtors. Of course, most Chapter 7 cases are "no-asset" in terms of formal distribution, but, as

Culhane and White found, more than 40 percent of the 1997 debtors formally reaffirmed one or more debts. In addition, Chapter 7 debtors make all sorts of other payments, including redemptions, payments against secured property that the debtors retain, and voluntary repayments.

On the other side, the promise of Chapter 13 is often unfulfilled. It now seems fairly well established nationwide that about 30 percent of the Chapter 13 cases filed actually result in completed payment of whatever was promised in the Chapter 13 plan. It is also clear that most plans propose substantially less than full payment, so that even completed plans do not mean full recoveries for creditors.

But Chapter 13 practice is marked by enormous variability. Data from the Office of the United States Trustee show that success rates in West Virginia and Oregon, for example, run at about 46 percent, while success rates in Florida are about 11 percent. Gordon Bermant and Ed Flynn, Measuring Projected Performance in Chapter 13: Comparisons Across the States, 19 ABI Journal 22, 34-35 (July/August 2000). Per-case yields to unsecured creditors varied from a mean of $4,603 in South Dakota to $443 in Connecticut. Unsecured creditors got only a small fraction of the disbursements to creditors. The Trustee study showed, for example, that Tennessee returned more money to unsecured creditors through its Chapter 13 program than any other state, in part because it leads the nation in the number of Chapter 13 filings, but the return to the unsecured creditors was only about 17.3 percent of all the creditor disbursements made through the program; secured creditors, who presumably would have collected either payments or property in Chapter 7 picked up the lion's share of the Chapter 13 distributions. A single-district study in Mississippi in 1997 by Professor Scott Norberg showed even lower proportional repayments, with 89.5 percent of all payments going to secured creditors. Half of all the debtors he studied paid less than $146 total over the life of the plan to be divided among all of their unsecured creditors. Scott F. Norberg, Consumer Bankruptcy's New Clothes: An Empirical Study of Discharge and Debt Collection in Chapter 13, 7 ABI L. Rev. 415 (1999).

In short, Chapter 7 and Chapter 13 do not represent no-payment versus payment. Instead, there is a spectrum of payment, most of it partial, and it is likely that the two chapters significantly overlap in the center of that spectrum.

It is hard to know if creditors' recoveries will increase over the next several years. As noted earlier, unsecured creditors may actually do worse in bankruptcy after the 2005 Amendments because of the new Chapter 13 rules requiring many secured debts to be paid in full, regardless of the value of the collateral, leaving less for unsecured creditors. The best hope for unsecured creditors may be outside of bankruptcy. If increased costs and other factors cause fewer debtors to file for bankruptcy, then unsecured creditors may be able to collect something more from those debtors. In that connection, if the United States Trustee approves as credit counselors primarily those nonprofit counselors supported by credit industry contributions, unsecured creditors may benefit from counselors who squeeze out additional payments through informal plans and who discourage the debtors from filing bankruptcy.

Another hope for unsecured creditors lies in a greater number of reaffirmations. New subsection 524(l) provides a bit of a safe harbor for the creditor. Perhaps more importantly, provisions such as the tightening of the presumption of fraud for eve-of-bankruptcy transactions in section 523(2)(C) and other such objections to discharge may provide the creditors with more occasions for plausible claims of objection to discharge, and those claims can be settled with reaffirmations.

All of these possibilities are speculative, however, so only time will tell if unsecured creditors will actually realize more recoveries after the 2005 Amendments.

c. Domestic Support

As noted above, recent empirical studies about the economic vulnerability that makes women more likely to file bankruptcy, along with pressure from women's groups, resulted in stepped up protection for domestic support obligations found in our bankruptcy laws. Among other things, those obligations are given top priority in Chapter 7, and they must be current in order for a debtor to confirm or maintain a Chapter 13 plan. The improved priority position in Chapter 7 may amount to little because only a small fraction of consumer cases generate enough funds to pay any of the priority creditors. Moreover, the improvement in position moved alimony and child support creditors ahead of other classes of creditors (such as American fishermen collecting from fisheries) who had never given them much competition for the ex-spouse's dollar. (In the process it created some serious complications in administering the statute. §507(a)(1)(C)). The Chapter 13 provisions may have more impact, but Chapter 13 already required that these debts be paid in full. Whether the impact of the change — demanding that past-due payments be made as a condition of confirming a plan — will be to get those owing domestic support obligations to pay up faster or simply to make them ineligible for Chapter 13 is not yet clear.

d. Bankruptcy Rates

There are several changes that might lower the number of bankruptcies filed. Some of them are discussed separately below. One that stands out is cost and delay. The amendments require vastly more paperwork, plus debt counseling before bankruptcy and post-filing financial counseling as a condition of discharge (see pp. 142–144). All these steps will increase the cost of bankruptcy by some amount, depending, inter alia, on the policies adopted by the United States Trustee's Executive Office as to the counseling requirements. The various requirements imposed on consumer bankruptcy lawyers require additional work and increase their exposure to liability for malpractice or for sanctions, likely increasing their fees. (See below.)

The increased delays may mean that some debtors will lose their property to creditors before filing. Having lost their immediate reason for seeking bankruptcy relief and being in most cases otherwise judgment proof, those debtors may decide not to file at all. Because of the dilution of the automatic stay (e.g., section 362(b)(22)-(23), (c), (g)(2), (h)), other debtors may lose property shortly after a bankruptcy filing and accept dismissal for the same reasons, making it difficult for them to file again for a year. §362(c).

The drafters of the 2005 Amendments were clearly aware of the important role advertising has played in the increase in consumer bankruptcies. The amendments require various new disclosures by bankruptcy attorneys that may or may not make such advertising more expensive or less effective in advising debtors of the possibility of bankruptcy.

The credit industry's position in the bankruptcy debates implied that the means test would also reduce bankruptcy rates by making bankruptcy less attractive to debtors who could after all pay their debts. Given that the data show that there have been very few such debtors in the past, we estimate that that change is unlikely to have much effect. But increased costs and attorney liability may do the trick.

e.   Chapter Choice

Once a debtor considers filing for bankruptcy, the central question remains choice of chapter. Chapter 13 has always been voluntary. As we discussed earlier, until 1984 Congress attempted to influence debtors to choose Chapter 13 by offering carrots, such as a broader discharge and the ability to deal with secured creditors over time. In 1984 the adoption of the 707(b) substantial abuse standard introduced the first stick to prod debtors into Chapter 13. The length of the stick varied from circuit to circuit, depending on the extent to which ability-to-pay was considered a sufficient factor in a substantial abuse finding, but for the most part substantial abuse was found where debtors had ability to pay plus some wrongful conduct such as failure to disclose income or assets.

There may be a number of factors that influence filing rates in various localities, but we begin with the formal legal factors, starting with the fact that most debtors will retain a completely free choice, at least in theory. The means test will apply to only 10 to 15 percent of potential debtors, based on the profiles of those who now file. Among potential Chapter 7 debtors, the above-median debtors affected by the means test will likely be less than 5 percent of the total. (See p. 16.) On the Chapter 13 side, almost 90 percent of those who now file in Chapter 13 are below-median debtors who could have filed in Chapter 7 despite the means test, so their choice will not be much affected either.

Chapter 7 will be available marginally less often than it is now, but eight years between discharges versus seven is not likely to influence many desperate debtors. Most of the onerous new paperwork and delay requirements apply to Chapter 13 debtors as well as those filing Chapter 7, so they are not likely to influence debtors' choices to any great extent.

Thus it is the changes in Chapter 13 that are the place to look for probable changes in current patterns. Ironically (for a bill that was supposed to encourage repayment) the 2005 Amendments raised barriers to filing Chapter 13 as well. So, for example, a debtor who does not have enough cash to catch up on two years' of child support payments cannot confirm a plan. A debtor who bought a car within the preceding two years or who has furniture or appliances bought on credit within the past year won't have access to the stripdown, and that means the bare minimum of cash flow required to confirm a plan will be higher.

Resolution of certain open questions will determine the extent of further impediments to Chapter 13. A key question is whether the courts will permit zero payment or low-payment plans for debtors who are essentially restructuring secured debt only. In those districts that have always permitted such plans if the disposable income test was satisfied, we will see little change. Some districts that required some substantial level of payment as a matter of good faith, over and above the disposable income requirement, may look at the new structure and conclude that secured-debt restructurings are now encouraged by Congress. They may decide therefore that low-payment plans can be accepted following the amendments. In that case, there may be more Chapter 13s of that sort in those districts.

More generally, given that most potential Chapter 13 filers will be below-median debtors, the prior disposable income standard may continue to apply in most districts, reducing the likelihood of change. On the other hand, in some districts that standard will be higher than the new means test and those courts may decide Congress could not have intended such a result. They may lower their disposable-income bar and thus encourage more Chapter 13 filings.

Several other changes will cut against the attractiveness of Chapter 13 filings. Debtors who are above-median in income, but are not barred from Chapter 7 by the means test will face the IRS budget for five long years in Chapter 13. They may decide that Chapter 7 looks much more attractive. The new rules requiring full payment of secured debts as a condition of retaining collateral even though the creditor is undersecured will leave many debtors with little money to pay unsecured creditors. As a result, in districts that continue to refuse to confirm zero payment or low payment plans, many debtors both below and above the median will be unable to propose a feasible Chapter 13 plan without surrendering the collateral. Most of those debtors will be below-median and eligible to file for Chapter 7, and many may choose to do so. By the same token, the fact that the Chapter 13 discharge has been narrowed to be almost the same as in Chapter 7 eliminates that incentive for filing for Chapter 13.

Finally, for all debtors, the cost of failure in Chapter 13 has risen substantially under the 2005 Amendments. Both anecdote and data suggest that most Chapter 13 cases fail. Under the pre-2005 system, it has been possible to refile fairly soon and try again. The new rules limit the automatic stay in such situations, sections 362(c)(3) and 109(g)(2), meaning, inter alia, that a failed plan may mean the loss of a home, while a Chapter 7 linked to a reaffirmation of the mortgage debt might save it. The below-median debtors who are eligible for Chapter 7 — about 9 out of 10 of all debtors in the pre-2005 system — may therefore be safer in opting for liquidation rather than risk a failed payout. The same will be even more true for above-median debtors who qualify for Chapter 7 (because they are not caught by the means test) but who would face paying for five years in Chapter 13 while living on the IRS budget.

f. Lawyers

Study after study has confirmed that the key actor in each consumer bankruptcy is the debtor's lawyer. See, e.g., Jean Braucher, Lawyers and Consumer Bankruptcy: One Code, Many Cultures, 67 Am. Bankr. L.J. 501 (1993). While the client has the ultimate right to decide, the complexity of the bankruptcy system, a complexity increased by the 2005 Amendments, means that the lawyer has an overwhelming influence over the decisions of most clients to file or not and which chapter to choose.

The drafters of the 2005 Amendments understood this particular point and set out to impose substantial responsibilities — and liabilities — on consumer bankruptcy lawyers. §§526-528. First, these lawyers are required to call themselves in any bankruptcy advertisement "debt relief agencies," lumping them under that title with bankruptcy petition preparers who are not attorneys. This requirement presumably had two purposes. Along with a variety of required disclosures to the client, it ensures that lawyers must discontinue the shady practice in which some had engaged of advertising in ways that obscured the fact that bankruptcy was the help they were offering. (Thus they avoided the allegedly nonexistent stigma thereof.) The phrase also demeans all the lawyers who engage in the consumer bankruptcy practice, good and bad.

Every consumer bankruptcy lawyer has made a post-amendments list of all the reports that have to be prepared for a consumer bankruptcy and a list of all the sanctions that can be imposed for any mistake, including professional sanctions, court fines, and damage suits by the United States Trustee or the client. §§526-528, 707(b). These include provisions that may make the lawyer liable and sanctionable for failing to confirm the accuracy of the debtor's valuation of assets, as well as to predict the interpretation of ambiguous terms, like the test for determining the replacement value of an asset. Some attorneys believe that the new rules also come perilously close to saying that the lawyer is liable if the court ever disagrees about a client's eligibility for Chapter 7 and eventually tosses the case out. These sanctions and liabilities are concentrated in Chapter 7.

There are several possible effects of these provisions. One is that a certain number of lawyers, especially nonspecialists, will exit the practice. Those who remain will likely raise their fees, perhaps substantially. Those who are most concerned about liability, especially in the first years following the amendments when so many questions remain unanswered, may set up as owners of bankruptcy petition preparing companies, rather than lawyers. They might train others to give the advice. They might also be called in after filing to represent the debtor in an objection to discharge or lift stay motion, being separately paid for post-petition services. Or clever and experienced lawyers may come up with yet other devices for avoiding exposure.

There are some aspects of the present system likely to continue to attract lawyers to one chapter or the other for their clients. In the case that follows, a close-reading practitioner saw a benefit for his client in Chapter 13. The court, however, was not so enthusiastic about the innovation.

In re SAN MIGUEL

40 B.R. 481 (Bankr. D. Colo. 1984)

GUECK, Bankruptcy Judge.

The above matters were consolidated for hearing with respect to the good faith of proposed Chapter 13 Plans. Each of the plans proposes to pay unsecured creditors minimal payments of $1.00 each over a period of sixteen (16) months. The primary reason for selecting a Chapter 13 approach as opposed to Chapter 7 is to spread the attorney's fees over the sixteen month period. Otherwise, the individual circumstances of each case vary to one degree or another.

No creditor objected to the proposed plan in any of these cases. However, the Court, *sua sponte*, raised the issue of good faith due to the very short duration of each plan and the minimal payment afforded to unsecured creditors.

Each of the debtors is represented by the same counsel, Ed Cohen. Mr. Cohen argues forcefully and persuasively that the debtors are economically deprived persons who are entitled to a fresh start and whose good faith ought not to be questioned simply because they choose the avenue of Chapter 13 rather than Chapter 7. He argues that each of the proposed plans constitutes the best efforts of the debtors, that payments to creditors are capitalized over the sixteen month period to receive as much as they would receive in any Chapter 7 liquidation and that the plans were necessitated so that attorney's fees could be paid over the period of the plan rather than in advance as, he contends, is customarily required by lawyers who accept Chapter 7 debtors.

The Chapter 13 Trustee, while not objecting to any of the proffered plans, does point out that in a liquidation the creditors will receive their money upon liquidation. In the Chapter 13 adjustment, the payments are spread out over a period of many months, and the creditors always run the risk of default under the plans. Further, the Chapter 13 Trustee suggests that if debtors are to receive the advantages of Chapter 13, they should be expected to make a greater effort to comport with the Congressional intent of repayment to creditors, generally adhering to the Congressionally sanctioned period of 36 months as the normal duration of a plan.

Mr. Cohen counters that under the circumstances of the three cases presented herein, there is no real "advantage" to Chapter 13 as opposed to Chapter 7, except for the payment of attorney's fees over a period of time. He further states that, in his experience, no greater creditworthiness results from Chapter 13 than from Chapter 7.

A review of each of these three cases should be accomplished and examined in light of the history and purpose of Chapter 13.

Rivera

Mr. and Mrs. Rivera owed approximately $10,000.00 in unsecured indebtedness. Mr. Rivera is an airman first class in the United States Air Force. His enlistment terminates in 18 months. He does not know if he will be eligible to reenlist, or whether he will desire to do so. He occupies an administrative position, and there is no indication that future raises, bonuses or promotions will be forthcoming in the foreseeable future.

The schedules submitted by the parties appear to be complete and accurate. There are no debts which are alleged to be nondischargeable in liquidation. The combined total net income of the parties is $1,002.00 per month. Their budget reflects expenses in the amount of $948.00. Mr. and Mrs. Rivera have proposed to pay the sum of $50.00 per month for a period of 16 months into the Plan so that attorney's fees in the amount of $690.00 can be defrayed over that period of time. Twenty-two unsecured creditors will receive $1.00 each. Mr. Rivera testified he feels this is their best effort.

Lopez

Mr. and Mrs. Lopez moved from Albuquerque, New Mexico to Denver in August, 1983. Mr. Lopez has been employed by Continental Airlines for 14 years. He was given 72 hours to move to Colorado or lose his job. Mrs. Lopez is employed by Sears, Roebuck & Co. as a customer service clerk.

Upon arriving in Colorado, the debtors purchased a home. Continental Airlines then declared bankruptcy and Mr. Lopez' salary was cut by one-half.

Several attempts were made to secure legal representation for the Chapter 7 liquidation. Mrs. Lopez testified that all lawyers whom they contacted wanted their fees in advance, together with the $60.00 filing fee. They contacted Mr. Cohen who suggested the Chapter 13 approach, with attorney's fees of $690.00 to be paid over the period of the plan. The schedules submitted on behalf of Mr. and Mrs. Lopez appear to be accurate and complete. There are no debts allegedly nondischargeable in a liquidation. The plan provides for $1.00 to each of the 8 unsecured creditors, extinguishing an indebtedness of $6,014.03. Payments of $50.00 per month are contemplated under this plan.

No changes in income are anticipated in the near future. Mrs. Lopez felt the proposed plan over 16 months was their best effort. The combined net monthly income of these debtors is $1,451.00. Their budget reflects expenses in the amount of $1,399.00. Mr. and Mrs. Lopez have three children. One daughter, age 16, desires to further her education beyond high school. The debtors wish to assist her, financially, in this regard. The daughter is reluctant to make plans for further schooling until it is determined that the parents will be free to assist her after the 16 month period.

The total secured indebtedness of these debtors consists of one secured creditor, secured by a first deed of trust on the family home, in the amount of $66,930.36. The value of the home is $71,610.00. This creditor will be paid outside the plan.

San Miguel

Mr. and Mrs. San Miguel have four children living with them, three of whom were Mr. San Miguel's children by a previous marriage. At the time of filing the Chapter 13 proceeding, Mr. San Miguel was in debt to the Department of Social Services in the approximate amount of $1,000.00 as a child support arrearage. He now has custody of the children. No support monies are owed directly to the mother. Nevertheless, Mr. San Miguel indicated he knew this debt may not be dischargeable. He intends to amend the Chapter 13 Plan to specifically provide for this indebtedness.

Mr. San Miguel is now on unemployment as a result of a back injury. However, this does not materially affect the scheduled income of the parties. Their combined net monthly income is approximately $1,689.00 with a budgeted expense of $1,610.00.

Mr. San Miguel indicated that, as experienced by the two previous debtors, his efforts to secure representation without the payment of advance fees for a Chapter 7 liquidation were futile. The Chapter 13 proceeding was chosen as a means to pay attorney's fees over the period of the plan. They propose to pay $75.00 per month into the plan for the 16 month period. This will discharge unsecured indebtedness of $4,021.60 to 6 unsecured creditors, including the aforementioned support obligation.

Opinion

No explanation was given by Mr. and Mrs. San Miguel for choosing not to exceed 16 months in their plan. No evidence is presented to indicate an inability to contribute funds beyond that period. In the case of Mr. Rivera, there is no evidence to indicate what type of employment or earnings he may achieve after his enlistment expires in 18 months. The only explanation given by Mr. and Mrs. Lopez for not exceeding 16 months was that they wished to help their daughter with her education.

In this District, we are guided in our determination of "good faith" by Flygare v. Boulden, 709 F.2d 1344 (10th Cir. 1983). While the Tenth Circuit set forth various different criteria to be reviewed, the basic question to be determined is whether the plan constitutes an "abuse of the provisions, purpose or spirit of Chapter 13." If it does not, the plan should be confirmed. Flygare v. Boulden, supra....

The Tenth Circuit, however, did not intend that plans which pay to creditors at least what would be afforded by a Chapter 7 liquidation should be summarily rubber-stamped as being in "good faith."...

In the matters under consideration there are no malevolent motives in the selection of 16 month plans. However, there is no demonstrated desire for repayment of creditors in any of these plans either. There is the stated desire of achieving a fresh start in all three cases.

One of the Congressional purposes of Chapter 13, as expressed in *Flygare*, is the repayment of creditors. If a debtor simply desires relief from his or her debts, Chapter 7 provides an adequate remedy in most cases. The debtors would also achieve a fresh start sooner in a Chapter 7 liquidation, as attorney's fees are usually smaller and the financial affairs of the debtor are resolved much earlier.

In each of the cases now under consideration, the plan is careful to terminate immediately upon the final installment of attorney's fees. Only secured indebtedness and priority claims are paid to any real extent. There will remain at least as much excess in the budget after the expiration of 16 months as there is now.

The real purpose of the 16 month, minimum repayment plans here is to avail debtors of the opportunity to defer attorney's fees, since it appears difficult to obtain counsel in Chapter 7 without payment of fees in advance. While I understand the practical problems of securing counsel for Chapter 7 liquidations, I cannot modify the Congressional intent of Chapter 13, as expressed by the Tenth Circuit Court of Appeals, because of the local practice of attorneys regarding their fees. It does not appear to me that any of these plans promote the purpose of repayment of creditors. I am mindful that the failure to promote the purpose of legislation may not necessarily be tantamount to an abuse of the spirit and purpose of that legislation. Yet, where, as here, the true purpose of the proposed plan is simply to provide creditors, over a period of time, what they could achieve under Chapter 7 now, while paying the expenses of administration over a period of time, that seems to me to be an abuse (though not a "bad faith" subversion) of the spirit and purpose of Chapter 13, as promulgated by the Congress.

It is therefore ordered that confirmation of the three plans under consideration herein, as proposed, is denied. Each of the debtors is afforded an opportunity within fifteen (15) days to move to convert or to dismiss or to submit modified proposed Plans of arrangement for consideration by the Court and creditors.

The practice condemned in *San Miguel* is widespread, and some courts believe it is a legitimate use of Chapter 13. Even so, many attorneys do not press the issue, offering plans that are not so blatant about their intent. In conversation, attorneys routinely point to the debtor's need for time to pay the legal fees as a good reason to put a debtor into Chapter 13. A few creditors pick up some incidental repayment, and no one complains. This alternative has become even more attractive since the Supreme Court ruled that a debtor's attorney cannot be paid under the literal language of section 330(a). Laime v. U.S. Trustee, 540 U.S. 526 (2004).

The twist (and there always seems to be a twist in bankruptcy) is that in a case in which the attorney puts the debtor in Chapter 13 so that the debtor can pay the attorney's fees over time, the debtors may end up paying all of their disposable income to their creditors for three years, when a Chapter 7 would have been the right answer if they had only had the money for a legal fee. It seems to get things backward when the system puts debtors into Chapter 13 because they have so little money they cannot scrape together enough for the legal fees while their somewhat better-off counterparts can get immediate discharges in Chapter 7. There is a whole body of legend about how some consumer bankruptcy lawyers advise their clients to get the necessary fee for a Chapter 7 and thus avoid this problem, but no one has so far done the empirical study. It seems likely to us that this particular incentive to file in Chapter 13 will continue and, if fees rise, perhaps even be enhanced under the 2005 Amendments.

It may be that any substantial effect on Chapter 7 filing rates will be found here, in the pressure on the lawyers. Although we would like to think that lawyers' concerns for clients would trump their own interests, the statute creates strong incentives for lawyers to put their clients into Chapter 13, both to avoid all the sanctions associated with a Chapter 7 filing and to get their fees paid under a Chapter 13 plan. The statute even goes so far as to forbid lawyers to suggest to debtors that they borrow money to pay the lawyer's fee. §526(a)(4). Whether this includes borrowing from your mother or your brother, with full disclosure, is not clear, but these rules add to the incentive to use Chapter 13 to protect the lawyer's fee.

Provisions so designed to put lawyer and client in confrontation are quite unusual in our law, so it is difficult to predict the results. There is a risk that the overall effect of the amendments is to increase the desirability of Chapter 7 for many debtors while making it harder and more expensive for them to find a lawyer who will file one.

g.   Local Legal Culture

The current authors, along with their long-time co-author sociologist Dr. Teresa Sullivan, have raised the possibility that a major influence on consumer bankruptcy law as it is actually practiced is local legal culture. The Persistence of Local Legal Culture: Twenty Years of Evidence from the Bankruptcy Courts, 17 Harv. J.L. & Pub. Policy 801 (1994). The thesis was that each judicial district has a distinct legal culture sustained by bankruptcy judges, lawyers, and officials and that this culture determines many of the key variables in bankruptcy filings in that district. Thus, for example, the percentage of cases filing in Chapter 7 versus Chapter 13 varies greatly from one district to another even within a state. Moreover, the differences among districts in proportions of 7s and 13s have persisted over long periods of time despite major changes in the economy and in the governing law. The idea was that this culture went well beyond the inclinations of a given judge or a given time, because it persisted among the actors in the district over long periods. The thesis could not be proven, but was plausible in light of long-term trends in the bankruptcy courts not readily explicable by other factors, like variations in state laws. Since then, scholars from other countries have found similar phenomena. See Hans Peter Graver, Consumer Bankruptcy: A Right or a Privilege? The Role of the Courts in Establishing Moral Standards of Economic Conduct, 20 J. Consumer Pol'y 161 (1997) (Norway); Rafi Efrat, Legal Culture and Bankruptcy: A Comparative Perspective, 20 Emory Bankr. Dev. J. 361, 390 (2004) (Israel).

Chapters 4 through 6 have identified many examples of new and ambiguous concepts and terms in the 2005 Amendments. It takes considerable time for bankruptcy questions to make their way to the higher courts, in part because having a specialized bankruptcy trial court adds an extra layer of review. The numerous ambiguities and anomalies combined with the powerful effects of local legal culture makes us confident that substantial variations in practices across the 90-odd federal districts of the United States will continue for at least several years and perhaps long thereafter. The primary element in the system cutting the other way is the United States Trustee's Executive Office, which has been given broad new powers to administer and monitor certain aspects of the system. An aggressive administration in that office could serve to some extent to bring greater uniformity, but it will be contending with powerful centrifugal forces.

h. Conclusion

It can be argued that the genius of the Western democracies has been in maintaining the lively edge of capitalism while preserving social stability and productivity through various devices that cushion the market's inevitable shocks to individuals and communities. Bankruptcy is an integral part of that machinery.

The changes made by the 2005 Amendments were important, but not fundamental. The bankruptcy system in the United States has always been the most pro-debtor in the world and it remains so. That system confounds a number of superficial economic analyses because it has helped to nurture a consumer credit market that is the largest, broadest, and deepest anywhere on the planet. The recent changes in detail are unlikely to alter that fact.

Based on past experience and the empirical data we have, the choices to file bankruptcy or not and which chapter in which to file will be much more controlled by the economics of the consumer credit system than by consumer bankruptcy law. We mentioned earlier the free granting of credit to those who have been recently discharged in Chapter 7. The growth of the market for "bad debtors" is sufficiently lively that credit counselors say they can no longer tell debtors in trouble that a reason to avoid bankruptcy is to protect their future access to credit. By the same token, no debtor need feel that the credit industry will treat a Chapter 7 filing worse than a Chapter 13, despite the years of sacrifice paying out a Chapter 13 plan. (Most credit bureaus apparently just enter "bankruptcy" in their files, regardless of the chapter and regardless of the amount paid in a Chapter 13.) The lessons taught by the market are likely to be much more powerful than those offered by the law.

Other influences may overwhelm any changes in the legal system. The great increase in "subprime" lending, which means lending to people who previously would have been denied credit, is reshaping credit in America. Harvard Business School researchers David Moss and Gibbs Johnson examined bankruptcy filings throughout the twentieth century. They document increased lending to families in the lowest income decile in the 1990s and argue that much of the rise in consumer bankruptcy filings can be attributed to lenders' aggressive push into much riskier — and more profitable — markets. David Moss and Gibbs Johnson, The Rise in Consumer Bankruptcy: Evolution, Revolution, or Both?, 73 American Bankruptcy Law Journal 311 (1999). To be sure, the credit industry has suffered much greater losses from uncollectible debts, but at the same time, it has enjoyed record profits. It seems that 29.9 percent interest and $50 late fees can offset a lot of bad debt losses and leave the companies making record profits. These sorts of developments are likely in the long run to have much greater impact than the details of a means test or the caselaw defining "abuse," even though these developments are highly important to lawyers and their clients.

It is a much-debated question whether it is or is not a sound state of affairs to have many millions of people so highly indebted as in the United States. (A similar debate is ongoing about the high debt levels of our corporations and our governments.) But one cannot argue with the fact that our consumer bankruptcy laws have failed to inhibit the accumulation of more than a trillion dollars of consumer debt, most of which is paid when due. The changes made in 2005 will provide interesting and illuminating data about the effects of law, but as always much larger economic and financial trends will govern the system as a whole.

Having said that, the law does have a lot to do with the distribution of pain and gain in any financial system. The recent amendments are likely to pain consumers while reallocating wins and losses among creditors. They are also nearly certain to stimulate demands for further change. Bankruptcy, like any system for treating the ill and injured, can never do enough.

Problem Set 17

17.1. You are developing the consumer side of your bankruptcy practice, to go along with a flourishing small-business side. One morning while you are working on the management aspects of a bankruptcy practice, especially the expansion of the consumer side, Judge Carnes invites you to lunch. The Judge, as he is known around town, is one of the founding partners of your firm. He has been a highly respected member of the bar for 35 years.

The Judge spends some time asking how you like practice and complimenting you on developing an entire department at the firm when you are still so young. The Judge reflects on how the practice of law has changed through the years, and he asks about whom the firm serves in the bankruptcy practice. It seems that the Judge has heard from more than one source that the firm has had to turn away people in financial trouble because they couldn't pay in advance the $850 fee required for a Chapter 7. Yesterday he saw your memo suggesting that the fee will have to be raised substantially to cover the costs of the amended bankruptcy procedures. The Judge is convinced that some of these people are good people who happen to be in financial distress and asks if there isn't "something we can do to help out." What do you tell him? See §330.

17.2. After lunch you return to the office and begin to develop a checklist of the reports and certificates that the debtor and the lawyer must file in Chapter 7 cases and in Chapter 13 cases. You also list the sanctions available against a debtor and the lawyer in each chapter, making two columns for comparison. What's on your lists? Given the need to control costs by controlling the amount of paralegal and lawyer time spent on each case, what rules of thumb will guide you in advising clients concerning choice of chapter?

17.3. As you continue to sketch out expansion of your consumer bankruptcy practice, you put together a memo for the management committee explaining the need to advertise. What reasons will you give? You also need to explain the requirements for consumer bankruptcy ads and to justify the costs. Assuming you will use newspapers and not radio or TV, you must lay out what will be in your proposed ad. What will your memo say in each regard? §§526-528. Should you anticipate another lunch with Judge Carnes?

17.4. Frank Forsythe is the beneficiary of a spendthrift trust that pays him $275,000 per year. Frank was a very strange child and he hasn't changed. Last year he was apprehended in City Park savagely beating Alice Harris. She was out jogging about 6:30 in the evening and he attacked her for no apparent reason. He struck her no fewer than 100 times with a claw hammer. She was in intensive care for three weeks. She has survived, but she is permanently disabled. Frank, who is currently out on bail awaiting trial, has debts to unsecured creditors of about $4,000 and about $10,000 of non-exempt personal property. He has been referred to you by his brother, an old friend of yours from college. The family is prepared to give you a $100,000 retainer. What will you do? See §§109(e); 1325(a)(3),(b); 1328(a).

17.5. You have gotten a call from Suzie MacIntire, who is the producer of Capital Issues, a program that runs on public TV stations all over the state. She is teeing up a show on bankruptcy. She's heard that you are a well-known practitioner and also active in State Bar policy development in the field. She wants you to start the show with a discussion of the basic purposes of bankruptcy law and an evaluation of the bankruptcy laws as they exist today in the United States. What notes will you make for your presentation?

17.6. Congresswoman Herring is back again. After the dust settles on the 2005 Amendments, she thinks there will be a lot of tweaking to be done to the statute and perhaps a backlash demanding additional changes. She wants your recommendation of one concrete consumer bankruptcy reform that she could introduce and push through, believing that it would really improve things. Longer term, there is a good think tank in her district that needs more government work, and she would like to push a consumer bankruptcy study that would be really useful. For that purpose, she wants to know the best, most important factual question that could be answered by empirical research, as well as some idea of what kind of study would be necessary to answer it. She's a practical woman, so suggest something that can actually be done.

Barney's Problem—Part II

Note: Unless otherwise indicated, the day this part of Barney's Problem is discussed in class is "deemed to be" March 1 of this year. This part of the problem, like the rest, is to be analyzed in "real time," i.e., as if you as counsel obtain the information or take the action indicated on the day (and the deemed date) the problem is to be discussed in class. All previous parts of the problem are incorporated into this part as of the day (and the deemed date) it is discussed in class, as if you were a sole practitioner in a town called Aloysius, and this small drama were real.

Your friend Barney Thornaby has consulted you this morning in a moment of panic about his rapidly declining financial affairs. As the discussion progresses, you manage to extract from him a partial idea of his deteriorating financial position.

On the personal side, he is still a licensed real estate broker and is worried about losing his license, because he knows he can always make a decent living selling real estate. He remembers from the exam he took that under state law the license of any broker who goes into "bankruptcy or any other liquidation proceeding" is revoked.

Barney's antique Packard was attached on January 2 in connection with a pending lawsuit seeking $250,000 in damages. In that lawsuit, a man named John Harris has charged Barney with fraud in the sale of a farm to Harris last year. Barney says that he is entirely innocent, but is concerned because "John Harris is the most accomplished liar I have ever known; he could sell shoes to snakes." Barney's deposition is set for next week, and he still hasn't consulted a lawyer about the case.

His main focus is on his construction company. In the past few years it has made about $300,000 per year after taxes, but it lost $250,000 during the past year. It is in trouble for two main reasons: (1) an enormous cash drain from its subsidiary, Barney's Auto Mow, Inc., and (2) weather delays on pending projects. While the business has some very profitable contracts and decent long-term prospects, the company is entirely out of cash.

The business is Barney's sole source of income, and he has personally guaranteed $50,000 of the company's loan from the Aloysius State Bank. The guarantee is secured by a lien on all his personal property. He has guaranteed an additional $75,000 of the business's debt to the bank, but this second guarantee is unsecured. ASB's president told Barney yesterday that she was very, very sorry, but she had reluctantly concluded that she would have to pull the plug on him. He assumes the bank will "foreclose" soon. He is behind on his personal bills, but aside from the mortgage they only total about $40,000. This amount includes about $4,500 he borrowed from his sister, Fortunata.

Barney bought his home on the edge of town in 1999 for $280,000. It is subject to a $250,000 purchase money mortgage held by the Farmer's State Bank.

Barney has a $1,000,000 whole life insurance policy that he purchased in 1999. He also owns a half-interest in a farm outside of town. The other half is owned by his brother, who lived on the place until he moved to Atlanta last fall. That farm is worth about $950,000, but is subject to an $800,000 mortgage. The Thornabys' other personal property includes two late-model cars, some antiques in the house, 100 shares of AT&T, and miscellaneous property such as silver, clothing, and jewelry. Barney estimates that it would cost about $100,000 to replace all this personal property. Your experience would suggest a liquidation value of about half the replacement value.

Barney shook his head and laughed grimly, thinking of how secure their life had seemed so recently. He gave his daughter a $10,000 diamond ring for her last birthday. He bought the ring from Cheryl Thornaby, his second cousin by marriage. The ring had been in the family for many years, but she needed money and had to sell it.

Although you have gotten Barney to see that he must consider bankruptcy because of his obligations to his wife and children, he keeps saying "Decent people don't go bankrupt. Decent people pay their debts. I'll never be able to hold up my head again. As a matter of fact, who would even deal with a realtor who is a deadbeat? God, I wish I'd shot myself."

Barney is tired, emotionally spent, and getting incoherent, so you tell him to go home and rest. However, he won't leave without your initial analysis and plan.

What else do you have to learn concerning each of the foregoing matters? What is your overall approach and advice?

Assume that Barney and his wife are both liable for all debts and that all their property is jointly owned. Also assume Barney's wife will follow your advice if you suggest she file for bankruptcy. Finally, unless you are told otherwise, assume the federal exemptions are available and are more desirable than the state exemptions.

PART III

BUSINESS BANKRUPTCY

"It was 1961. Boom times, stability, easy credit . . . and of course none of the other entering classmen at law school thought of specializing in insolvency claims."

CHAPTER 7 LIQUIDATION

A. INTRODUCTION

As we turn from consumer to business bankruptcy, we cross the central divide in bankruptcy law and practice. While businesses have the same choice between sellout (liquidation) or payout (reorganization) as consumers do, the considerations are very different for both creditor and debtor. There are actually two dichotomies of fundamental importance in the world of bankruptcy: consumer versus business, and natural persons versus legal entities (the latter we often call "personal" versus "corporate" bankruptcies for convenience). These categories greatly overlap, but are not by any means perfectly congruent.

All consumer cases involve natural persons, while many business bankruptcies are filed by corporations. The great majority of consumer cases are smaller than most business cases measured by assets or income. For the most part, consumer bankruptcies must be handled by the lawyers, judges, trustees, and court personnel on a mass or volume basis; otherwise the costs to process them would be prohibitive. Therefore, consumer cases do not lend themselves to substantial litigation, elaborate financial maneuvers, or custom lawyering, all things characteristic of many business cases.

Because all consumer cases are personal bankruptcies, the differences between personal and corporate bankruptcy divide the prototypes of consumer and business cases. Personal and corporate bankruptcies involve most of the same Code sections and legal doctrines, but there are a number of important differences. One fundamental distinction between a corporate liquidation and a personal liquidation lies in the fact that there is no discharge for a Chapter 7 debtor that is not an individual. §727(a). When a corporation enters liquidation, it is not loosed from its chains of debt, but instead it quietly expires under state corporate law following its financial demise in bankruptcy. In addition, there are no exemptions for corporate debtors; all property is available for repaying the creditors. The effect is that the debtor in a typical corporate liquidation has no interest in the result—no exemptions to claim, no property to redeem, no discharge to protect, no life after bankruptcy to think about, and so forth. This is in marked contrast to the debtor in an individual bankruptcy who is powerfully interested in exemptions, redemptions, and a discharge. This difference also affects choice of chapter. Individuals often get a quick discharge and get back on their feet in Chapter 7. By contrast, because it has so little to gain from a Chapter 7, a corporate debtor almost never seeks liquidation except in final, exhausted resignation.

For all these reasons and more, the dichotomy between the typical consumer case and the typical business case is the most crucial in bankruptcy law. Nonetheless, as in most things in life, there is a substantial intermediate ground. The prototype of a business that might find itself in bankruptcy is a corporate concern with too much debt, but many bankruptcies involving business assets and business debts are filed by natural persons.

In the business materials we will refer to various empirical studies, as we did in the consumer section, including the work of the Business Bankruptcy Project, which is yet another collaboration between the present authors and Dr. Teresa Sullivan, who is a demographer as well as Vice-Chancellor of the University of Texas System. The BBP was a five-year (1994–1999) longitudinal study of business bankruptcies in 23 federal districts around the United States. One of the most startling findings from the study is that natural persons filed 75 percent of the Chapter 7 cases that are designated business cases and, perhaps more surprisingly, they filed 25 percent of the Chapter 11 cases that were designated as business cases.[1] Elizabeth Warren and Jay L. Westbrook, Financial Characteristics of Businesses in Bankruptcy, 73 Am. Bankr. L.J. 499 (1999) (hereafter Financial Characteristics). A narrower study of business cases from 2002 has been conducted by Warren and Westbrook and some of those data will be discussed below as well.

The overlap between business and consumer cases can also be studied from the other direction. According to data gathered for the 2001 Consumer Bankruptcy Project, about 13.5 to 19.5 percent of all the debtors listed as "consumers" had operated a small business. Robert Lawless and Elizabeth Warren, The Myth of the Disappearing Business Bankruptcy 93 California L. Rev. 745 (2005). The Administrative Office reports many fewer business bankruptcies, now officially down around 2 percent of all filings; these entrepreneurs would have been listed as business bankruptcies back in the mid-1980s, but as attorneys began to use computer programs to fill out the bankruptcy forms, and those programs defaulted to make every live human being a "non-business bankruptcy," the AO stats became more and more removed from reality. Regardless of the "official" numbers, in many of these cases there are both consumer and business assets and consumer and business debts. Some of them will be consumer cases with a business caveat, so to speak, and conversely some will be business cases with a consumer twist.

Thus we have a distinction between consumer and business bankruptcy that is fundamental, but also blurs over a significant margin. From this point on, most of the discussion will assume that a business bankruptcy is a corporate bankruptcy. One important reason for this

---

1. The Chapter 11 percentage may have been somewhat higher in the sample year than in other years. A number of the Chapter 11 cases, both personal and corporate, will fail and will be "converted" to Chapter 7 for final internment, a point we will explore in greater detail later. §1112. The figures just given refer to cases originally filed in Chapter 7.

assumption is that this rather technical material is easier to learn in that way. A personal business bankruptcy inevitably involves consumer debt and consumer issues in addition to the kinds of issues that are important in the business context. By focusing on corporate bankruptcy, it is possible to construct a more distilled and less confusing exposure to the questions characteristic of business bankruptcy. It is also true that most of the largest and most intellectually interesting business bankruptcies are those in which the debtor is a corporation or, most often, part of a group of affiliated corporations. Nonetheless, it should always be borne in mind that a human being is the debtor in a large number of small business cases, and in a small number of large ones, even if the AO classifies them all as "non-business." The principles discussed here may apply both to multinational consortia and the guy who has been running a one-man Tupperware distributorship.

One other dichotomy is important in business bankruptcies: the difference in the operation of the bankruptcy system depending on the size of the debtor's business and whether it is a public company.[2] Like toothpaste, companies are often characterized as small, medium, or large, although there is no standard metric for these distinctions. In the bankruptcy literature, there is not even a standard for the relevant characteristic for measuring size. Assets, debts, or number of employees are the most commonly used measurements for this purpose. A frequent distinction is between small and medium sized companies (often abbreviated "SMEs" for Small and Medium Enterprises) and large companies. Further complicating the picture is the fact that discussions of large companies in the bankruptcy literature are limited almost entirely to large public companies; very little research has been done into the bankruptcies of large privately held companies. As a result, analysis of "large" company bankruptcies usually refers to public companies.

Some Code sections that were discussed previously, such as priorities in distribution under §507, will not require specific additional coverage in the business materials, while others, such as the automatic stay, will be covered again, this time highlighting the kinds of stay issues that arise primarily in the business context. In addition, a number of important aspects of the Code will be considered for the first time in the business materials, because it is in business cases that they have their most common and most important functions.

B. BUSINESS LIQUIDATIONS

This chapter and its discussion of business liquidations will be relatively brief. Most of the issues that are significant in business bankruptcies will be

---

2. A "public" company is one that has sold its stock or bonds to public investors, in the process registering those securities with the Securities and Exchange Commission and acquiring a host of duties concerning public disclosure of its finances. Information concerning these companies, especially financial information, is readily available and highly computerized and they are regularly covered by the financial media. The LoPucki database, which is a national treasure of data about big business bankruptcies, includes data on all publicly traded companies with more than $100 million (in 1980 dollars) in assets on the last annual report the company filed before declaring bankruptcy. Take a look at the data (and do your own data runs) at http://lopucki.law.ucla.edu.

covered in the next chapter, business reorganization. The reason is not that there are no important business Chapter 7 cases. Chapter 7 cases made up 59 percent of about 34,000 cases that the AO denominated as business filings in calendar year 2004. Some of those cases were substantial both in size and in the complexity of the legal issues. The key point is not numbers or size in Chapter 7, but the fact that reorganization bankruptcy is the central focus of modern business bankruptcy law and practice. Not only are almost all large business cases begun in Chapter 11, but a large number of small cases are filed there as well. There are a number of issues that arise only in reorganization cases or that have their greatest importance there, while most of the substantial Chapter 7 issues also are found in Chapter 11. For example, even the liquidation of a company — the raison d'etre of Chapter 7 — is today often performed in Chapter 11, for reasons discussed later in the materials. It is better to study all these issues interacting in a reorganization case as events unfold and lawyers and judges make crucial choices. We will do that in the next chapter.

In this chapter, we discuss two conceptual aspects and two practical aspects of business liquidation in Chapter 7. The first conceptual point is that Chapter 7 is primal bankruptcy, the original creature. A similar form of corporate liquidation exists under the laws of virtually every country. Thus Chapter 7 reflects the most basic purposes and devices of bankruptcy as a legal response to the circumstance of general default. For centuries, all over the world, it has been understood that there is a profound difference between a debtor unable or unwilling to pay a particular debt and one who defaults generally on most or all debts. The latter situation gives rise to a collective-action problem and to a social problem. Chapter 7 bankruptcy, the classic straight liquidation proceeding, represents society's collective response to the economic crisis that has thus overtaken the debtor, its creditors, its employees and stockholders, and often the community it serves.

The second conceptual importance of Chapter 7 arises from the fact that many SME Chapter 11 cases collapse into Chapter 7, as does the occasional public company case. Because Chapter 7 is the end game, the place where an unsuccessful reorganization goes to die, its rules and procedures, strengths and weaknesses, provide the central structure of all of bankruptcy law.

All Chapter 11 negotiations are held in the shadow of Chapter 7. The debtor usually has an absolute right to convert the case to Chapter 7, §1112(a), and the creditors can do so on a proper showing, §1112(b). Furthermore, conversion will be required if the creditors do not approve a plan by the majorities specified in section 1126(c). For this reason, each side will be threatening the other with Chapter 7 even though both really want to avoid it. We can think of a Chapter 11 negotiation as taking place in a conference room with the debtor standing in the window threatening to jump ("stand back or I'll do it for sure") while the creditors threaten to push ("we've had enough and we're coming over right now to end this mess").

Because the negotiations take place with Chapter 7 as the alternative, the substance of the negotiations depends on what would happen to each party if a Chapter 7 resulted. For example, a creditor whose security interest was unperfected on Bankruptcy Day (the day the Chapter 11 petition was filed) must face the reality that in Chapter 7 it would be just another unsecured creditor. Such a creditor can expect to have no more leverage than an unsecured creditor in the Chapter 11. If there is a question, legal or factual, about its perfection, the creditor will have more leverage in the bargaining than a clearly unsecured creditor, but less than a creditor whose interest is not subject to serious challenge. The amount of leverage will be a function of the perceived strength of the legal arguments each way.

In this context, the parties and their counsel must always work through the likely outcome in a liquidation for each of them and then work backward from there to determine a reasonable settlement position in the Chapter 11.

In the interwoven world of business negotiations, there is another layer to the chess game. A nonbankruptcy workout similarly takes place in the shadow of Chapter 11. Each party's willingness to agree to a voluntary reorganization will be a function of that party's analysis of the position it would occupy in Chapter 11. In turn, as we have seen, analysis of the hypothetical Chapter 11 position requires analysis of the hypothetical Chapter 7 position, since the hypothetical 11 would play out in the shadow of the hypothetical 7. Therefore, in any workout situation, in or out of bankruptcy, each of the parties will do what is called a "liquidation analysis," which shows the likely financial result for that party in a Chapter 7 liquidation. Working backward from that analysis, the party will determine how strong a position it can take in the nonbankruptcy workout or in the Chapter 11 case.

The first practical point about Chapter 7 is related to its collective nature and its national scope. Chapter 7 is often a much better place to liquidate a business than a state law proceeding is. State law strongly encourages each creditor to grab what it can as fast as it can ("first in time, first in right"), while the automatic stay in Chapter 7 brings everything to a halt and ensures an orderly sale of the assets. Among other things, such a sale permits offering a whole group of assets together, rather than in bits and pieces, and therefore it can sometimes achieve realization of greater value. When a restaurant fails, for example, the lease, the refrigeration equipment, the ovens, and the tables may be more valuable when sold as a group than when they are sold piecemeal. In addition, bankruptcy does not have the rigid timetables and procedures (typically auctions) that are characteristic of state execution laws. The TIB can negotiate with buyers and, with court approval, pick the best method of disposition. For example, it is common in larger cases to appoint professional liquidators who may have substantial experience in maximizing the payoffs from "going out of business sales." The bankruptcy court is in a position to supervise such sales, which can be the occasion of serious abuses, and therefore is in a position to authorize them subject to appropriate conditions and safeguards.

In addition, the special powers granted the TIB on behalf of the creditors to reverse certain pre-bankruptcy transactions may make bankruptcy very useful for some creditors. For example, the creditor that is losing the race of the diligent to other creditors may want to turn to bankruptcy to get the race called off. In addition, the bankruptcy court imposes some supervision on the debtor, with the creation of an estate, disclosure of assets and payments made, nationwide simultaneous control of all the debtor's property, and so on. The creditor that isn't being paid and that suspects the debtor might be moving assets out of reach might find bankruptcy an attractive alternative.

Bankruptcy law also permits an orderly distribution based on legal rights rather than the imperatives of a mad scramble. Creditors in bankruptcy, in effect, pool their resources to discover what the debtor has and to pursue options to enlarge the debtor's estate for distribution. Not only can this save collection costs (no longer does every creditor have to conduct discovery to find assets or get a judgment and a writ to collect), but it also means that distribution is made according to a democratically structured set of priorities (for example, a societal allocation of proceeds among employee salaries, environmental cleanup costs, and utility bills). The theoretical and practical implications of these characteristics of bankruptcy law will be discussed further in the next chapter and in the chapter on bankruptcy theory (coincidentally, Chapter 11 of this book).

Of course, the change in the distribution of losses in bankruptcy from the way they would have been distributed at state law will pain some creditors as much as it will please others. The creditor that has received a preferential payment will lose it in bankruptcy, and the creditor that has recently won a race of the diligent may find its victories turned to dust. This is a reminder that the debtor versus creditor orientation of state law has been sharply modified in bankruptcy. As a practical matter, many of the disputes — especially in a Chapter 7 — are really creditor versus creditor.

For the reasons just discussed, among others, bankruptcy liquidation is likely to provide much more satisfactory results for the creditors collectively than state collection law when the debtor is in general default.

Another practical aspect of Chapter 7 is that it is most often the chapter in which an involuntary bankruptcy petition is filed. The shape and effect of bankruptcy law depends greatly on the process by which the law is invoked, so a consideration of involuntary bankruptcy and its alternative, voluntary filing, is also key. Chapter 7 is the best place to begin to discuss the problem.

C.   INITIATION

In the wave of bankruptcy reform that is rising in countries around the world, it is generally acknowledged that a central problem is initiation of a bankruptcy proceeding — that is, how does a bankruptcy case get started? Does the debtor declare itself bankrupt? Do the creditors bring an action to have the debtor declared bankrupt? Or does some independent regulatory body or police agency investigate and initiate a proceeding? See Legal Department, International Monetary Fund, Orderly and Effective Insolvency Procedures: Key Issues at 22, 52 (1999) (hereinafter "IMF Report"); Elizabeth Warren, Bankruptcy Policymaking in an Imperfect World, 92 Mich. L. Rev. 336 (1992). Bankruptcy always leads to a debtor's loss of control, partial or complete, over the assets and operations of a company and may hurt the business itself through loss of credit from suppliers and general reputational damage. Therefore debtors have a strong incentive to resist filing for bankruptcy. That disincentive added to the natural optimism of a risk-taking entrepreneur who runs the business makes it likely that bankruptcy will be sought only as a last resort. There is a consensus that far too often companies do not file until it is too late to save them and most of their value has been dissipated.

On the other hand, initiation by creditors often fails to fill the gap. Creditors typically lack the necessary information to make a sound and efficient decision about the appropriateness of a bankruptcy remedy. If involuntary bankruptcy is too easy to commence, creditors have too much leverage and a single aggressive creditor may destroy a viable business. Yet if the law imposes stringent requirements for proof of serious financial distress as a precondition for an involuntary bankruptcy, creditors will find it difficult to initiate a case before debtors are completely moribund. The differences among legal systems are reflected in the fact that in some countries, such as the United States, involuntary filings are rare, while in other countries, such as England, they are commonplace.

The ideal solution is that the party with the best information, the debtor, should open a bankruptcy proceeding while there is still substantial value in the company that can be distributed in liquidation or used to rescue the company in reorganization. This solution has been sought in other countries with various carrots or sticks. The United States and some others provide a substantial incentive for a troubled business to file bankruptcy by providing a reorganization procedure that leaves the debtor in control, a point further discussed in the next chapter. The United States adds a generous discharge for individual proprietors who file for personal bankruptcy. Other countries, especially the other common-law countries, use sticks to encourage voluntary filings, including penalties and personal liability imposed on the company's directors if they do not initiate bankruptcy promptly after they know or should have known that the company was in serious financial trouble. Ian Fletcher, The Law of Insolvency 661–664 (Sweet & Maxwell 2d ed. 1996); Harry Rajak, Company Liquidations 309–322 (CCH Ed. Ltd. 1988). Both law and practice relating to initiation are changing in the United States and elsewhere. These developments are discussed in the materials that follow.

D. INVOLUNTARY BANKRUPTCY

Section 303 of the Code reflects the decision in the United States to protect debtors by making involuntary bankruptcy relatively difficult. Involuntary petitions have been rare — so rare, in fact, that the Administrative Office of the Courts ceased any report of the relative proportions of voluntary and involuntary petitions in the mid-1980s. There was speculation in the early 1980s that the proportion of involuntary petitions might rise, especially as more and more lawyers who were not specialists became familiar with the enormous power of bankruptcy law, in particular the power to defeat security interests and other transactions. In a study of involuntary petitions, however, Professor Susan Block-Lieb explained that the proportion of involuntary petitions has remained low — and argued that it should continue to do so. Susan Block-Lieb, Why Creditors File So Few Involuntary Petitions and Why the Number Is Not Too Small, 57 Brooklyn L. Rev. 803 (1991).

Block-Lieb discusses competing bankruptcy policy goals, including a desire to encourage nonbankruptcy workouts that is in tension in some respects with the desire to encourage creditors to file earlier while a debtor still has value. She suggests that the somewhat cumbersome involuntary procedures probably keep the filing numbers in about the right place. Since 1991, there has been no systematic study of involuntary petitions, leaving open the question of whether they continue to remain tiny in number.

Despite the rarity of involuntary proceedings, they have some real significance. The Code encompasses important creditor-protection provisions. It not only restricts the post-bankruptcy conduct of the debtor, it also permits the creditors to dismantle various pre-bankruptcy transactions. These legal devices, which are discussed in detail in the next chapter, create a number of circumstances in which forcing a debtor into bankruptcy is an important option for creditors that may need the protection given by these unique bankruptcy powers. For example, an involuntary petition might be filed out of concern that the debtor is wasting assets or paying certain favored creditors while ignoring the rest. Another common reason is the hope of invalidating any security interests that might be unperfected when the petition is filed and thereby increasing the size of the pie available to all the unsecured creditors.

The rarity of involuntary petitions in the United States, in sharp contrast with other countries, reflects the initiation problem discussed earlier. In his landmark article, A General Theory of the Dynamics of the State Remedies/Bankruptcy System, 1982 Wis. L. Rev. 311, Professor LoPucki argues, based on his research of Chapter 11 filings in Kansas City, that managers have too much personal interest in avoiding bankruptcy and therefore delay too long, using up the asset base necessary for successful reorganization. As a solution he recommends incentives for creditors to bring involuntary Chapter 11s. The database for the study was relatively small, and the businesses in the sample were small, owner-operated outfits. Although the study may have limited applicability nationally, and one may be concerned about the risk of creditors making unsound judgments that push businesses into possibly fatal reorganization proceedings, LoPucki's argument has considerable force.

Involuntary petitions are most often filed by unsecured creditors. Secured creditors usually do not need Chapter 7 bankruptcy help because they have already negotiated for their own preferred collection rights. Indeed, secured creditors typically fear attack by the TIB on their security interests and see bankruptcy as a threat to the exercise of their collection rights.

It may be that the primary use of the involuntary filing provisions of the Bankruptcy Code is as a credible threat during negotiations for a workout. A notable example of such a situation was Baldwin-United, a small piano company that became a huge investment company and then foundered. The company tried to work out its financial problems outside of bankruptcy and negotiated with its creditors. In the midst of these discussions, the company disclosed that it had given a security interest in most of its assets to its previously unsecured institutional lenders ("institutional" meaning banks, insurance companies, and the like). The company's other unsecured creditors were faced with the necessity of filing an involuntary bankruptcy petition to invoke the preference power to set aside the security interest (see pp. 484–522). If they did not, then the institutional lenders would have had most of the assets and the unsecured creditors would have been out in the cold. Under the threat of an involuntary petition, an interim agreement was made among the creditor groups. The various powers of the creditors in bankruptcy await discussion in the following chapter, but the Baldwin-United case illustrates the importance of being ready to use involuntary bankruptcy to protect a creditor client against a debtor or against other creditors.

Traditionally an involuntary bankruptcy was always a Chapter 7 case, but the Code permits a creditor to put a debtor into an involuntary Chapter 11 as well. §303(b). A creditor might elect to put a debtor into Chapter 11 to obtain disclosure of important financial information and court supervision of the debtor's activities while permitting the business to continue operations.

Even though involuntary petitions can serve salutary purposes, they can also be used to bully and threaten a debtor whose business may be destroyed by the mere filing of a petition. This danger explains the presence of section 303(i), which grants attorneys' fees and costs (and sometimes punitive damages) against an unsuccessful involuntary petitioner. Another protection is the three-creditor requirement, under which three creditors must join in most involuntary petitions. §303(b)(1).

3 creditors must join in most Invol petitions. §303(b)(1)

The following cases discuss the requirements for filing an involuntary bankruptcy and the protection these requirements are designed to provide. Although the first case, In re Gibraltor Amusements, is getting quite old (it was decided before the 1978 Bankruptcy Code was in effect), the policy discussions in the majority and dissenting opinions are among the most cogent ever written on the subject. They remain powerfully relevant today.

Ct. Here: Wurl & WAC are 2 separate entities even though WAC is an owned subsidiary of Wurl.

In re GIBRALTOR AMUSEMENTS

291 F.2d 22 (2d Cir.), cert. denied, 368 U.S. 925 (1961)

Smith, Circuit Judge.

Gibraltor Amusements, Ltd., the alleged bankrupt, is the operator of numerous "Juke Box" routes on Long Island. The Wurlitzer Company, principal creditor of the alleged bankrupt for a sum exceeding $1,000,000, filed an involuntary petition in bankruptcy against Gibraltor in March of 1960. The petition alleged insolvency, numerous acts of bankruptcy and that the debtor had fewer than twelve creditors. [Among the points of contention raised by Gibraltor's answer was Gibraltor's assertion that it had more than twelve creditors, which meant that Wurlitzer must be joined by two other creditors for a successful involuntary petition. Wurlitzer was then joined by the Wurlitzer Acceptance Corporation (WAC) as one of the three required petitioning creditors.]

03/60 Wurl filed Invol bankruptcy petition for $1 mil.

-since Gib had less than 12 cr, Wurl had to be joined by 2 other CRs for Invol. petition.

-WAC joined Wurl

On appeal to this court . . . [t]he only substantial question raised is the standing of WAC as a separate petitioning creditor.

Wurlitzer Acceptance Corporation is a wholly owned subsidiary of the Wurlitzer Company. It was incorporated in 1957 and its business has been the financing of sales of the parent's products. Although WAC appears to have dealt solely in the commercial paper of Wurlitzer, it has obtained its own bank financing — on the strength of its own credit. It has been a separate corporate taxpayer for the purposes of the Federal income tax. The evidence indicates that both parent and subsidiary have scrupulously honored the separate corporate form of the latter. WAC's claim is for almost $17,000 on two notes guaranteed by Gibraltor. The notes had been purchased from Wurlitzer long before the filing of the petition; there is absolutely no evidence of attempted subversion of the Bankruptcy Act.

For most purposes, the law deals with a corporation as an entity distinct from its shareholders. Traditionally courts will pierce the corporate veil "when the notion of legal entity is used to defeat public convenience, justify wrong, protect fraud, or defend crime." Although courts will sometimes disregard the separate entity where it has been used as a "front" or a "mere conduit" — the so-called alter ego doctrine — the present case with its complete absence of fraud and strict honoring of the corporate form as to assets and intercorporate transactions is not a proper one for the invocation of that rule.

Since ordinary principles of the law of corporations do not warrant the disregard of WAC's corporate identity here, it remains only to ascertain whether anything in the language or policy of the Bankruptcy Act demands such a result. Section 59, sub. b, 11 U.S.C.A. §95, sub. b provides simply that "Three or more creditors who have provable claims liquidated as to amount and not contingent as to liability against any person . . . may file a petition to have him adjudged a bankrupt." . . .

The aforecited language, far from being restrictive in its definition of the scope of permissible petitioners, is virtually all encompassing. The emergence of the wholly owned corporate subsidiary as a common business instrumentality is not a brand new phenomenon. While Congress has repeatedly added to and amended the Federal taxing laws to deal with problems posed by the multiple corporation means of doing business, it has not seen fit similarly to tinker with the Bankruptcy Act. The detailed ground rules for "counting creditors" laid down by §59, sub. e, 11 U.S.C.A. §95, sub. e indicate that the principal Congressional fear of abuse was not that a debtor would be too easily petitioned into bankruptcy — rather that through connivance with friendly creditors the insolvent debtor might be able unfairly to hamstring one or two large creditors. The courts have long evinced a disposition to honor the separate corporate entity in bankruptcy matters. If Congress meant to alter ordinary judicial rules governing corporations, it should have so provided specifically.

Whether the policy of the Act calls for a more narrow construction of qualified "creditors" is a closer question. The present requirement of three petitioning creditors, inserted in the Act of 1898, is a compromise between the quite liberal provision of the Act of 1841 and the restrictive requirements of the 1867 Act. 3 Collier on Bankruptcy 548. In the process of "counting to three," the courts have perhaps been overly liberal in allowing the holders of assigned claims to qualify as petitioners. . . .

It may be conceded to be highly questionable whether Congress meant to sanction traffic in claims merely for the purpose of creating a sufficient number of petitioning creditors. . . . [N]o such machinations have been presented in the instant case. Even though WAC took the notes in the due course of business, without reference to any future bankruptcy proceeding, it is urged that the mere fact of "control" by Wurlitzer disqualifies the subsidiary's claim. This argument merely raises, in a slightly different guise, the question of the disregard of the subsidiary's separate entity. There has been no showing, however, that Wurlitzer has abused the distinct corporate form nor that it has used it fraudulently to subvert the Bankruptcy Act. Lacking such a showing, WAC's claim should be honored. Such an approach to this question is not a purely conceptual one; it must be kept in mind that protection of the separate creditors of WAC, who cannot reach the assets of Wurlitzer, can only be accomplished by the recognition of the subsidiary as an independent legal entity.

[handwritten margin note: ct Here: Will consider Wurl & WAC 2 separate entities.]

Affirmed.

FRIENDLY, Circuit Judge (dissenting).

With some regret as regards this particular bankrupt, I respectfully dissent from the conclusion that Wurlitzer and its wholly owned subsidiary, Wurlitzer Acceptance Corporation (WAC), may be regarded as two separate creditors for the purpose of §59, sub. b of the Bankruptcy Act, 11 U.S.C.A. §95, sub. b.

Assuming as I do that WAC had sufficient independence of its parent to be regarded as a separate corporation under state law . . . or under federal law for income tax purposes, it does not follow that it is a creditor separate from its parent under §59, sub. b. Although my brothers recognize that the requirement of three petitioning creditors in the Bankruptcy Act of 1898 (save where the bankrupt had less than twelve creditors) was a compromise by Congress between the divergent provisions of earlier statutes, that bland statement scarcely conveys the flavor. "In law also the emphasis makes the song," Bethlehem Steel Co. v. New York State Labor Relations Board, 1947, 330 U.S. 767.

[handwritten margin note: Required to have 3 petitioning CRs where bankrupt had less than 12 CRs.]

The first three bankruptcy acts, all repealed after relatively short periods, permitted a single creditor to initiate involuntary proceedings if his claim met the prescribed minimum. Widespread sentiment against the 1867 Act, which not only allowed a single creditor to institute involuntary proceedings but provided for numerous acts of bankruptcy and, in the absence of creditor consent, denied a discharge from debts to a bankrupt who could not pay fifty cents on the dollar, MacLachlan, Bankruptcy (1956), p. 11, caused Congress to amend it in 1874, 18 Stat. 178, 181. In addition to making discharges less difficult to obtain and narrowing the acts of bankruptcy, the amendment provided that an involuntary petition could be filed only by one fourth of the total number of creditors with aggregate claims amounting to one third of the dollar amount of the total debts. Still the statute was too harsh for debtor sentiment, and it was repealed in 1878, see 3 Collier on Bankruptcy, p.548.

The impulse for a new bankruptcy law came from the 200,000 business failures in the United States between the 1878 repeal of the 1867 Bankruptcy Act and 1898. Hardship had been particularly acute in the West, where a great land boom had raged from 1883 to 1889, followed by a sharp collapse. Southern and Western Populists began a crusade for at least a temporary voluntary bankruptcy law to relieve the large numbers of honest debtors from oppressive burdens and give them a fresh start in life. See Representative Sparkman of Florida, 31 Cong. Rec. 1850.

Although Eastern congressmen were willing to concede that voluntary bankruptcy was a good idea, see Representative Parker (N.J.), 31 Cong. Rec. 1852, many of them were unwilling to enact a voluntary bill without accompanying involuntary features designed to insure an equitable distribution of a bankrupt's assets among his creditors, and, to that end, to abolish preferences. This the Populists opposed. They argued there was no need to infringe on state rights by creating a federal remedy for the collection of debts: State laws were adequate for the purpose. Bankruptcy was viewed as a stigma difficult to erase; it was one thing to allow a hopelessly burdened debtor to choose this disagreeable alternative as preferable to eternal debt but quite another to permit blood-thirsty creditors, with only their own interests at heart, to plunge an unwilling debtor into disgrace — the more so since in many cases the debtor reasonably might hope that the upturn in his fortunes was just around the corner, and bankruptcy would deprive him of the right to keep his business alive in the meantime. See 31 Cong. Rec. 1793 (Underwood, Ala.), 1838 (Settle, Ky.), 1863 (Linney, N.C.), 2313 (Sen. Stewart, Nev.). This position was summed up by Representative Lewis of Georgia, 31 Cong. Rec. 1908: "Voluntary bankruptcy is the means of the redemption of the unsuccessful and fallen debtor. Involuntary bankruptcy is a weapon in the hands of the creditor to press collections of debt harshly, to intimidate, and to destroy."[2] Thus the Populists denounced the bankruptcy bill as an "engine of oppression" (Sparkman, Fla., 31 Cong. Rec. 1851), "intended to bind hand and foot the debtors of this country and place them in the vise-like grip of the greedy cormorants of the country" (Henry, Tex., 31 Cong. Rec. 1803), and even tied the issue to the silver question, haranguing the "conspiracy of gold and monopoly" (Sen. Stewart, Nev., 31 Cong. Rec. 2359–2360). Easterners countered that a properly restricted involuntary bankruptcy law was a benefit not only to creditors but to debtors as well. In the absence of such a law creditors become nervous; whenever the debtor's assets seem less than his liabilities, they are likely to grab them precipitously, thereby forcing the debtor to the wall, lest other creditors beat them to the draw and they get nothing. 31 Cong. Rec. 1789 (Henderson, Iowa), 1852 (Parker, N.J.).

The provisions of the statute with respect to involuntary bankruptcy were the resulting vector of these opposing forces, an attempt to make involuntary bankruptcy less unpalatable to the Populists by surrounding such proceedings with careful safeguards for the debtor. . . . This bill was bitterly debated in the House for more than 100 pages in the Record. Its proponents attempted to sugar-coat the pill by repeated reference to a number of safeguards inserted to protect debtors from oppressive use of the weapon

2. Seventy years earlier, in 1827, Martin Van Buren, denouncing an attempt to provide for voluntary and involuntary bankruptcy in a single statute, had said "It is an erroneous idea . . . that this bill can be made to serve God and Mammon by combining two things totally at variance." 3 Cong. Deb. 279.

of involuntary bankruptcy: to be insolvent one must have assets insufficient to pay his debts, not merely insufficient liquid funds to meet debts as they fall due; oppressive costs of proceedings under the 1857 act had been drastically pruned; petitioning creditors were required to post bonds to cover not only the costs of the proceedings but any damages that might result from a wrongful filing; widows, minors and the insane were protected; the bankrupt could be taken into custody only if he showed signs of departing to avoid examination; he might not be required to travel over 100 miles to testify; criminal offenses and acts of bankruptcy were reduced; and three creditors must join if there were twelve or more in all. H.R. Rep. No. 65, 55th Cong., 2d Sess. 25–27 (1897). . . . The House passed this version; a conference committee toned it down in several respects to make it more favorable to the debtor; and both houses enacted the conference bill.

Thus, the entire process that resulted in the enactment of the Act of 1898 was a pitched battle between those who wanted to give the creditor an effective remedy to assure equal distribution of a bankrupt's assets and those who were determined to protect the debtor from the harassment of ill-considered or oppressive involuntary petitions, including those by a single creditor interest. The requirement of three creditors was one of many provisions reflecting a compromise between the two opposing positions. It is not doing justice to this history to suggest that if Congress had meant to prevent a wholly owned subsidiary from being counted as a petitioning creditor separate from its parent, it should have explicitly said so. We must "remember that statutes always have some purpose or object to accomplish, whose sympathetic and imaginative discovery is the surest guide to their meaning." [Cabell v. Markham, 148 F.2d 737 (2d Cir. 1945).] Here the purpose to require three separate creditor interests, separate in reality and not merely in legal form, is not difficult to discern. With the temper of the 55th Congress on this subject, it would have required a bold man to arise on the floor of the House of Representatives and ask that the bill be clarified to insure that a corporation with a financing subsidiary could be counted as two creditors if each unit held a claim against the debtor; it is hard to suppose the House managers would have imperiled the bill by sanctioning any such proposal and quite impossible to believe it would have been enacted. Yet, where the words permit either interpretation, our duty is to determine "which choice is it the more likely that Congress would have made." Burnet v. Guggenheim, 1933, 288 U.S. 280, 285.

. . . I cannot believe it consistent with that policy to hold that a single creditor corporation may insure its ability to initiate an involuntary bankruptcy by the simple expedient of organizing two financing subsidiaries — perhaps with independent creditors — and seeing to it that claims against each debtor are parceled out in advance of bankruptcy. Whether a wholly owned subsidiary with independent creditors might be deemed separate from its parent in a case where, as a result of its own financial difficulties, the subsidiary was in effect acting for its creditors rather than its stockholders, need not be now determined; no such case is presented here.

More recently, three bonding companies got together and filed an involuntary petition against their common debtor, Iowa Coal Mining. In re Iowa Coal Mining Co., 242 B.R. 661 (Bankr. S.D. Iowa 1999). The court said, "Let's count the creditors." Because the claims were interwoven and full of subrogation and joint obligations, the court concluded that the three bonding companies were just one creditor with one claim, and that was not enough to sustain the petition. Although Judge Friendly has long since passed away, we think we heard him chuckling somewhere.

The Bankruptcy Act had two principal safeguards against an unjustified involuntary petition. The first was the three-creditor requirement, retained in section 303(b)(1). The second was the requirement that the creditor allege and prove that the debtor had committed an "Act of Bankruptcy" within a specified period prior to the filing of the petition. Bankruptcy Act §3. Of the six specified acts of bankruptcy, two amounted to an admission by the debtor of his financial collapse, such as making a general assignment for the benefit of creditors. Bankruptcy Act §3a(4). The other four required a showing of insolvency coupled with a potentially voidable transfer, such as a fraudulent conveyance or the appointment of a receiver for the debtor's property. Bankruptcy Act §3a(1), (5). The "insolvency" requirement usually meant "bankruptcy" insolvency but sometimes referred to "equity" insolvency. Bankruptcy insolvency was defined as balance sheet insolvency, an excess of liabilities over assets, as it remains defined as such in the new Code. §101(32). Insolvency in a court of equity — hence the term "equity insolvency" — traditionally meant that the debtor was "unable to pay his debts as they mature."

The concept of acts of bankruptcy was drawn from English law and was part of every American bankruptcy law until 1978. See Israel Treiman, Acts of Bankruptcy: A Medieval Concept in Modern Bankruptcy Law, 52 Harv. L. Rev. 189 (1938); see also Note, 67 Harv. L. Rev. 500 (1954). The concept was subjected to heavy criticism for many years. See, e.g., Report of the Commission on the Bankruptcy Laws of the United States, H.R. Doc. No. 137, 93d Cong., 1st Sess., pt. I at 14; pt. II at 75 (1973); Treiman, supra. The principal grounds for abolition of the requirement were that it focused on a fault concept, an act of the debtor, rather than on the debtor's financial condition, and that it unnecessarily delayed the case, primarily because the debtor had a right to jury trial of the involuntary petition.

Congress followed the recommendation of the 1973 Bankruptcy Commission. The 1978 Code abolished the required showing of an act of bankruptcy for an involuntary bankruptcy, instead substituting a test of the debtor's financial condition. §303(h)(1). Congress might have adopted the bankruptcy insolvency test (liabilities greater than assets), but chose instead a variation on the equity insolvency test (inability to pay). One advantage of the bankruptcy test would have been protection of a debtor from involuntary bankruptcy so long as the debtor's non-exempt assets that could be attached under state law were sufficient to satisfy the creditors. Use of the equity test could force a debtor into bankruptcy merely because of a cash-flow or liquidity problem even though the creditors were arguably protected by available state remedies. On the other hand, the bankruptcy test could pose difficult valuation questions and could be almost impossible for unpaid creditors to measure before filing, while failure to pay bills is a more visible event. Moreover, the possible harshness of the equity standard is ameliorated by the debtor's absolute right to convert to a reorganization proceeding and pay the debts over time under a plan of reorganization. §706(a).

The "generally not paying" standard as originally adopted by Congress was more creditor-oriented than the traditional "inability to pay" test, since it encompassed the debtor who refused to pay as well as the debtor who could not pay. The standard resembles the standards long applied to involuntary bankruptcy in European courts, where an analogous test is generally called "cessation of payments." Those courts enjoy varying levels of discretion in determining whether a "cessation" of payment by a particular debtor has actually taken place, in light of the debtor's general financial circumstances. See generally, J. Dalhuisen, 1 International Insolvency and Bankruptcy §1.02(4) (1984).

The experience in Canada may be the most helpful reference for American courts applying the involuntary standard. Although Canada retains the concept of "acts of bankruptcy," one of the acts that justifies an involuntary bankruptcy occurs when the debtor "ceases to meet his liabilities generally as they become due." See American Law Institute, Transnational Insolvency Project, International Statement of Canadian Bankruptcy Law at 15 (2003). See also, J. D. Honsberger, Failure to Pay One's Debts Generally As They Become Due: The Experience of France and Canada, 54 Am. Bankr. L.J. 153 (1980).

Of course, "generally not paying" could stem from a number of causes, ranging from cash flow difficulties to stubbornness to a dispute over whether anything was owed. Perhaps as a result, much of the litigation in involuntary bankruptcies prior to the 1984 Bankruptcy Amendments Act involved disputed debts. In the 1984 Amendments Act, Congress tried to lay that problem to rest by specifically excluding from the test debts in bona fide dispute and by making the holders of such debts ineligible to join in an involuntary petition. §303(b), (h). In the 2005 Amendments, Congress further clarified the standard. Some courts had held that if liability were established, a debt was not "disputed" if the debtor was arguing only over the amount owed. Congress amended the statute to make it clear that a dispute about either the fact of liability or the amount owed would be adequate to classify the debt as "disputed."

Even as Congress keeps adding detail, the standard leaves open many questions about the proper test to apply. What is a bona fide dispute? Is "general" failure to pay to be measured by the number of debts paid and unpaid, the amount of such debts, the nature of such debts, or some weighted combination of factors? If the amount of unpaid debts is controlling, should one creditor with a large debt be able to throw into bankruptcy a debtor who is otherwise current or should we leave that creditor to the remedies of state law? Litigation of these matters has been entertaining. See, e.g., In re B. D. International Discount, 701 F.2d 1071 (2d Cir. 1982), cert. denied, 464 U.S. 830 (1983) (in which the fun began when Chase Manhattan bank accidentally credited the debtor's account with $7.3 million, which quickly found its way to Switzerland). The courts continue to wrestle with the issues, as the next two cases demonstrate.

In re FABERGE RESTAURANT OF FLORIDA, INC.
222 B.R. 385 (Bankr. S.D. Fla. 1997)

A. JAY CRISTOL, Chief Judge. ...

FACTUAL BACKGROUND

The three original petitioners to this involuntary Chapter 7 petition are the following corporations:

G.S.P.C. Enterprises, Inc.	$528,000.00
A.R.T., Inc.	$2,230.00
Keystone Creations, Inc.	$4,502.50

On June 11, 1997, a motion to dismiss was filed by Faberge which disputed the debt owed to Keystone Creations, Inc. and A.R.T., Inc. and claimed those creditors were the subject of a bona fide dispute. No defense was raised as to G.S.P.C. Subsequently, three more creditors joined this petition:

Marina Polvay Associates	$4,777.19
Entertainment News & Views, Inc.	$480.00
Millward & Co.	$380.80

Subsequent to the joinder, but prior to the completion of the hearing, which commenced on July 2, 1997 at 1:45 p.m., Faberge approached three creditors and paid them. First on or about July 1, 1997, Faberge paid $2,700.00 to Keystone as a settlement of the dispute between the parties. Second, on July 2, 1997, a Faberge check was delivered to Entertainment News & Views for the sum of $480.00. Third, on July 2, 1997, cash was received by Millward & Co. for $380.80.

None of the creditors who were paid withdrew their joinder in the petition.

CONCLUSIONS OF LAW

Section 303 of the Bankruptcy Code governs the filing of involuntary petitions and provides stringent tests which must be satisfied before a debtor may be adjudicated and an order for relief be entered by the Court.

First, the Court must determine whether the Debtor has generally not been paying its debts as they become due. . . . The principal of the Debtor, Giulio Santillo, stated that he could not make payments to numerous creditors because he didn't have the money. . . .

Second, if the Debtor has more than twelve creditors, then standards under 11 U.S.C. §303(b)(1) require that there be three creditors who are not the subject of a bona fide dispute or holders of contingent claims. . . . There is no doubt that more than twelve creditors exist pursuant to the accounts payable ledger. . . .

G.S.P.C. is an undisputed creditor. G.S.P.C.'s debt also provides the requisite debt of $10,000.00 as required under 11 U.S.C. §303(b)(1). Therefore,

[handwritten margin note: 2 of the 5 CRs must qualify.]

the only issue for the Court to review as to the other five (5) petitioners is whether or not two of the five other creditors qualify to file an involuntary petition. Two are listed on the accounts payable ledger and were paid July 2, 1997 ("Entertainment News and Views" and "Millward &. Co."). One was not listed on the accounts payable ledger, but was paid on or about July 1, 1997 ("Keystone"). . . .

Keystone, Entertainment News & Views, and Millward & Co. . . . received payment after the filing of the bankruptcy. It is the contention of Faberge that payment to those creditors eliminated those parties' standing or eligibility to be creditors under 11 U.S.C. §303(b)(1). This issue has been reviewed by numerous courts. Policy reasons, and other considerations, dictate that the postpetition payments will not deprive the court of jurisdiction or require dismissal of the petition. . . .

The Debtor's July 1, 1997 and July 2, 1997 payments evidence that there was an existing debt on May 23, 1997, the date of the filing of the involuntary petition, to Keystone, Entertainment News & Views, and Millward &. Co. . . .

[handwritten margin note: Debtor's motion to Dismiss is Denied]

. . . Ordered and adjudged that the Motion to Dismiss as filed by the Debtor in the above-captioned involuntary is denied and a separate order for relief shall be entered by this court and this order, as issued, shall be immediately delivered to the U.S. Trustee's Office to assure that a panel trustee be appointed in all due haste to handle the affairs of this restaurant.

A "panel" trustee is simply a TIB appointed by the U.S. Trustee from the standing panel of persons who have been qualified to serve as trustees. Note the possibility that the restaurant would continue to operate in Chapter 7 until it could be sold as a going concern. The data reported in Financial Characteristics suggest that more than half of the businesses in Chapter 7 had at least one employee other than the proprietor and were apparently still operating — a pretty surprising finding in the liquidation section of the Bankruptcy Code.

In re SILVERMAN
230 B.R. 46 (Bankr. D. N.J. 1998)

STEPHEN A. STRIPP, Bankruptcy Judge.

I. FINDINGS OF FACT

In the instant case, a single petitioning creditor, Michael Cantor ("Cantor" or the "petitioner") filed an involuntary chapter 7 petition on October 24, 1997 under section 303 of title 11, United States Code ("Bankruptcy Code" or "Code") against Eugene Silverman ("Silverman" or the "alleged debtor"). Cantor and Silverman had been friends and business associates for many years. They had engaged in many business ventures. Cantor has a stipulated net worth of $30,000,000. Silverman is a person of considerably more limited means. For reasons which are unclear from the record, their relationship turned sour and Cantor sued Silverman in the Superior Court of New Jersey on a $200,000 promissory note. Cantor moved for summary judgment, and in the alternative for partial summary judgment. That motion was denied on August 22, 1997.

As that case continued, Cantor prepared to file the involuntary bankruptcy case against Silverman. Cantor ordered a Uniform Commercial Code (U.C.C.) search and a judgment search against Silverman. Cantor did not inform the court, however, of the results of those searches. Although the standard under section 303(h)(l) of the Bankruptcy Code for entry of an order for relief in an involuntary case is that the debtor is generally not paying his debts as they come due, Cantor did not order a credit report on Silverman. Had he done so, Cantor would have discovered, as Silverman did by obtaining a credit report on himself on October 22, 1997, that of 31 reported accounts, every one reported the history as "never late" or "paid as agreed." Moreover, a creditor does not have standing under Code section 303(b)(l) to file an involuntary bankruptcy petition if his claim is the subject of a bona fide dispute. Although Cantor's motion for summary judgment or for partial summary judgment was denied in state court on August 22, 1997, he nevertheless filed an involuntary bankruptcy petition against Silverman. . . .

. . . On December 29, 1997, Silverman filed a motion to dismiss the involuntary bankruptcy and for the imposition of sanctions and damages based on the allegations stated in the answer.

. . . Cantor [argued] that the superior court had not ruled that there was a genuine issue of material fact as to the entire amount of the debt. He sought to convince the court that at least $10,000 of the alleged debt was undisputed, so that Cantor would have standing under Code section 303(b)(1) to file an involuntary petition. The transcript of that hearing in the superior court plainly discloses, however, that Cantor did request partial summary judgment and that such request was also denied. This court held that the petitioner had no standing to file the involuntary petition and on February 13, 1998 the court entered an order dismissing the petition. Since dismissal was warranted based upon a finding of a bona fide dispute, the court did not decide whether the numerosity requirements of section 303(h)(l) of the Code were satisfied, although Silverman contends that he had more than 12 creditors at that time as well.

The court held that Silverman was entitled to all costs and attorney's fees associated with the involuntary proceeding under Code section 303(i)(l), including those incurred after dismissal of the petition. The court further concluded that Cantor acted in bad faith by filing the petition after the state court held that genuine issues of material fact existed with respect to the alleged debt. The court dismissed the involuntary petition, but retained jurisdiction to determine fees, costs and damages.

Cantor filed a motion for reconsideration in which he argued that the claim was not the subject of a bona fide dispute, alleging that Silverman admitted in a deposition taken on March 24 and 25, 1998 that money was currently due and owing and that he was fairly confident that the amount was greater than $50,000. However, the court held that whether a bona fide dispute exists is evaluated at the time the involuntary petition is filed. . . .

On August 10, 1998, a hearing was held on Silverman's request for fees, costs and damages pursuant to sections 303(i)(1) and 303(i)(2). . . . The court awarded attorney's fees and costs to the alleged debtor totaling $45,264.75 and $1242.90 respectively through August 4, 1998. On August 25, 1998, the court signed an order, entering judgment against Cantor in favor of Silverman in the amount of $46,507.65.

The court acknowledged in the hearing on the request for damages that Silverman requested sanctions against the petitioner's former counsel in the letter memorandum dated August 4, 1998. Since the request for sanctions pursuant to Fed. R. Bankr. P. 9011 was not made by way of separate motion, it is not properly before the court and the court therefore declines to consider the issue at this time. . . .

Silverman's Position

Silverman asserts that punitive damages are warranted in the amount of $900,000. . . . Silverman's request of $900,000 represents 3% of Cantor's net worth, which Silverman contends is an appropriate amount to effectuate the dual policies of deterrence and punishment without being unduly harsh. . . .

II. Conclusions of Law

Section 303(i) of the Bankruptcy Code authorizes the imposition of fees, costs and damages if an involuntary petition is dismissed without the consent of the debtor and all of the petitioning creditors. The Code section is permissive, however, leaving the assessment of fees, costs and damages to the exclusive discretion of the court. . . .

. . . Following the majority approach under section 303(i)(1), this court noted in the hearing on the alleged debtor's motion to dismiss that although the court is not required to impose fees and costs on the petitioning creditor, typically they are awarded upon dismissal.

The imposition of punitive damages, unlike fees and costs, must be predicated upon a finding of bad faith, as the plain language of Code section 303(i)(2)(B) states. Having found that the petitioner's claim was the subject of a bona fide dispute by virtue of the state court's denial of summary judgment and partial summary judgment, the court held that the bad faith component of section 303(i)(2) was satisfied. The court cited BDW Associates v. Busy Beaver Building Centers, 865 F.2d 65, 66–67 (3d Cir. 1989) in which the Third Circuit, applying an objective standard, held that the existence of a bona fide dispute, for purposes of standing under Code section 303(b) to file an involuntary bankruptcy, is measured by the summary judgment standard. Principles of issue preclusion compelled this court to conclude that a bona fide dispute exists with respect to the petitioner's claim, as the superior court already had determined that genuine issues of material fact existed. . . .

Examination of the many cases addressing imposition of punitive damages under section 303(i)(2) reveals that the factors which support a finding of bad faith also justify imposition of punitive damages. Although punitive damages are not automatically imposed upon a finding of bad faith, a punitive damages award is predicated upon a finding of bad faith. Consequently, once the court has found bad faith, the court must decide whether punitive damages are appropriate and, if so, in what amount. This court agrees with the Landmark court's view that the totality of the circumstances must be considered in fashioning an appropriate award under section 303(i)(2). Therefore, although this court found that bad faith is established per se by filing an involuntary petition after denial of summary judgment in another forum, all mitigating or aggravating factors are nonetheless relevant in assessing punitive damages. . . .

In the instant case, the petitioning creditor commenced the involuntary bankruptcy shortly after the superior court ruled that genuine issues of material fact existed with respect to the existence and amount of the alleged debt. Rather than awaiting resolution of the state court proceeding, the creditor filed the involuntary petition with knowledge of the bona fide dispute, thereby using the bankruptcy court as a tool for collection in disregard of the section 303 requirements. This egregious bad faith was exacerbated by the petitioning creditor's blatant denial that partial summary judgment as to the existence of the debt was requested in the state court proceeding when it had been requested. . . .

. . . Cantor maintains that he believed that Silverman's assets were dissipating. These arguments are utterly without merit as Silverman's credit report, dated one week after commencement of the involuntary bankruptcy but before notification of the involuntary case to the credit reporting agency, indicated that Silverman had numerous creditors and that he was paying his debts as they came due. The court is not deciding the actual number of Silverman's creditors, and whether he had 12 or more creditors for purposes of the numerosity requirement for an involuntary petition. Regardless of the actual number of creditors, however, review of Silverman's credit report by Cantor would have disclosed no basis for an argument that Silverman was generally not paying his debts as they came due. Had Cantor truly examined Silverman's financial position diligently, the absence of a basis for an involuntary bankruptcy case would have been readily apparent.

Finally, Cantor offers an advice of counsel argument. He alleges that his counsel stated that despite the state court's denial of summary judgment, as long as $10,000 or more was undisputed, the court would not find bad faith. He also stated that he was never informed that punitive damages could be awarded upon a finding of bad faith. . . . In any event, the court declines to accept that defense here. If Cantor relied with naive innocence on his attorney's advice to file an involuntary bankruptcy petition against Silverman, which this court does not believe, Cantor and his attorneys can deal with the consequences between themselves.

The court concludes that Cantor filed the petition with intent to harass Silverman and with knowledge that his claim was the subject of a bona fide dispute. He employed an improper litigation tactic, failed to conduct an adequate inquiry into Silverman's financial position and made false statements about the state court proceedings. A substantial award of punitive damages is therefore warranted. . . .

Attorney's fees and costs have been awarded in the amounts of $45,264.75 and $1242.90 respectively. After reviewing the totality of the circumstances and in light of the egregiousness of Cantor's behavior, his net worth of $30,000,000, and all other circumstances, punitive damages are awarded in the amount of $50,000.

═══════════

A lawyer reading this opinion should notice that the court avoided the issue of sanctions against the creditor's former lawyer, but then invited a presumably furious millionaire to sue his counsel if he was really misadvised. The next lawsuit could be even more fun than the one resolved in the case.

We should not leave this subject without noting that creditors in the United States are not without means to force a "quasi-involuntary" bankruptcy filing. In particular, secured creditors may provide the necessary pressure for a debtor to file bankruptcy by threatening or actually initiating repossession or foreclosure. When creditors are not secured, their options are much more limited. The background to understanding the following story is found in the capital markets, specifically the commercial-paper market, where large corporations can borrow money on an unsecured, very short-term basis at lower interest rates than those offered by banks. Often, however, a company cannot sell its commercial paper (that is, unsecured promissory notes) unless the paper is backed by quasi-guarantees issued by large banks. Without getting into the details, the banks more or less promise to lend enough to pay off the paper if the company has a problem doing so. The result is that often the banks involved may find themselves with a huge unsecured loan to the company just at the moment when no banker would want to lend the company a dime.

Banks Move to Put Curbs on WorldCom
By Riva D. Atlas and Jonathan D. Glater

An aggressive effort yesterday by a group of banks to protect billions of dollars that they lent to WorldCom greatly increases the likelihood that the company will have to seek bankruptcy protection.

A group of 25 banks asked a judge to block WorldCom from spending any of the $2.6 billion they had lent to WorldCom in May, a lawyer for WorldCom said yesterday. The banks contend that WorldCom committed fraud by drawing down that credit line roughly a month before the company disclosed that it had overstated its revenue by about $3.8 billion in 2001 and early 2002.

Judge Helen E. Freedman in New York State Supreme Court declined to issue the order yesterday, but agreed to review the request at a meeting on Tuesday, said Joseph S. Allerhand, a partner at Weil, Gotshal & Manges.

The banks' aggressive move bodes poorly for WorldCom's hopes of obtaining financing outside of a Chapter 11 filing, some bankruptcy lawyers and advisers said. This week, WorldCom executives voiced some optimism that they would be able to obtain the necessary credit and avoid a bankruptcy filing.

Banks tend to parcel out a loan among a group of lenders, to reduce the risk of default to any one member of the group. The fact that so many banks are sufficiently concerned about WorldCom's ability to repay them that they filed a request for an injunction indicates it would be hard to gather a group for a syndicated loan.

Mr. Allerhand said that WorldCom was still talking to its lenders. "We are talking with all constituents all the time," he said. A spokesman for WorldCom, Bradford Burns, declined to comment on the banks' action. A spokesman for Deutsche Bank, Ted Meyer, declined to comment after confirming the bank was participating in the suit.

The move indicates the desperation of the lenders to obtain some kind of collateral for their loans. The $2.6 billion loan is unsecured, meaning the lenders would have a claim on WorldCom's assets in the event of a bankruptcy filing equal to that of holders of WorldCom's $28 billion in bonds.

A bankruptcy filing may be exactly what WorldCom's creditors are trying to force, said Lynn LoPucki, who teaches bankruptcy law at the University of California at Los Angeles. ✶✶✶✶✶✶

[New York Times, July 13, 2002, late edition, section C, p. 1]

Problem Set 18

18.1. Ramsco is a mud supply company serving the United States, Mexico, and Canada. It supplies the compound that is injected under high pressure into oil and gas drilling lines for lubrication. Ramsco has been hard hit by a recent recession in the oil business. Not only are orders off, but some customers who used Ramsco's mud are now as much as 20 months behind in payments.

As part of its attempt to collect more of the past-due debts, Ramsco consults your firm about one of its largest debtors, Greenhill, Inc. Greenhill is an independent drilling company in Louisiana. It has used Ramsco's mud for three years now, and it is currently $2.1 million in debt to Ramsco. It has not made a payment in ten months, and informal collection efforts do not seem to have worked. Ramsco is concerned that Greenhill may not survive the recession, and that if it does not, the local creditors will get Greenhill's assets if Ramsco doesn't act soon. Ramsco is sure that it can get at least two other creditors who have not been paid recently to join it in a petition for an involuntary bankruptcy.

Your firm has scheduled you to make a presentation at a planning session on whether to file for Greenhill's involuntary bankruptcy. The concern at this meeting is the kinds of facts the firm would have to uncover to demonstrate that Greenhill is "generally not paying" its debts. You should develop several different theories of what constitutes generally not paying and which facts one might be able to uncover about a medium-sized firm in a high-risk industry that would support these theories. Be sure that you can tell your firm the strengths and weaknesses of each theory. See §303(h). It might be a good idea to be prepared to identify the risks, if any, if your theories don't bear fruit. See §303(i).

18.2. Gerald Barr is a personal injury lawyer who also invests in real estate. Over a period of years he has acquired limited partnership interests in a number of local real estate projects, all of which are profitable and have steadily increased in value. Unfortunately, his most recent real estate investment was less favorable, and he was forced to drain his savings to meet repeated calls for additional cash by the developer, who eventually failed anyway and filed for bankruptcy. Gerald is behind on all of his normal bills and is over his limit on his credit cards. Recently he wrote his creditors explaining his problem and assuring them that he would pay everyone in full, with interest, with contingent fees he expects to get in the next year, together with the sale, if necessary, of some of his successful real estate investments. Gerald furnished the creditors with a complete financial statement showing that his assets comfortably exceeded his liabilities and promised them complete cooperation if they wished to check on assets or liabilities for themselves.

All his creditors agreed to wait for payment, except the Solid State Bank, to which he owes $200,000 on a note that became due about two weeks ago. For some years he had a good relationship with SSB, but SSB became indirectly involved in a lawsuit Gerald brought last year, and the president felt Gerald acted in a very unprofessional manner toward SSB. Gerald has come to you because he fears that SSB might bring an involuntary bankruptcy petition against him and that such a proceeding might destroy or severely harm his law practice even if it could be defeated. Ask him key questions, give him your analysis of the situation, and describe the action you might take on his behalf. See §303(h).

18.3. Harold Ruthbort has been appointed TIB for Lucky's Lectronics, a local appliance dealer that recently failed. Your client, the Solid State Bank, was a lender to Lucky's on an unsecured basis and was scheduled as a creditor in the bankruptcy filing. The responsible officer at the bank has just called. She is very upset because she has just read an ad in this morning's paper for "Bankruptcy Sale at Lucky's — 75% off." You explain you know nothing of the sale. The officer says the bank has been negotiating to sell the inventory to another local store for a better price. What can you do and why? See §§363(b)(1), (c)(1); 102(1).

18.4. Your client, Rodney Dudley, has called you from a pay telephone at the federal courthouse. He is attending a sale of heavy equipment that was advertised by a TIB for a failed company. So far, only three potential bidders have shown up, although the sale hasn't started yet. Naturally the three fell to talking as they waited and one of the other bidders has suggested that they go in as partners on a bid, splitting any resale profits equally. Rodney has never been to a bankruptcy sale before and wants to be sure there aren't any legal potholes here that he doesn't know about. Advise him. See §363(n).

18.5. One of your firm's regular clients is Universal Tires, Inc. Universal would like to file an involuntary bankruptcy petition against Wetumka Automotive, a small company that sells tires and other car accessories in eastern Oklahoma. Wetumka Automotive has been very dilatory in paying Universal, and it currently owes Universal $130,600. It has made no payments on this balance for four months. Wetumka Automotive now carries Federated tires as its primary line, and it shows little inclination to send Universal any money.

In Universal's latest conversation with the owner of Wetumka Automotive, Universal threatened to file an involuntary Chapter 7 bankruptcy. Wetumka Automotive's owner laughed, saying, "I wondered when you might get around to that. But my brother-in-law — he's a lawyer — tells me you can't do that without some help. I got myself twelve other creditors, including a little running bill at the hardware, another at the five-and-ten, and, of course, my brother-in-law's bill."

Universal acknowledges that in a small town such as Wetumka, where everyone is related to everyone else and there is a lot of support for the local man over the city fellow, they will probably not get two other creditors to join them. So Universal proposes to file as Universal, Inc., the parent company to whom money is owed for the direct purchase of tires; as Universal Finance, the financing subsidiary to whom money is owed for short-term loans that were used to make some cash purchases from Universal, Inc.; and as Universal Service Body School, a subsidiary to whom money is owed for consultation fees for installation classes. What advice will you give Universal? See §303(b), (h).

18.6. Harry Hopkins has come to see you about $50,000 he is owed by the Yearning for Mayor Campaign Committee. Hopkins is in the printing business and provided all the printed material for the Yearning campaign last spring, as well as some loans for other expenses. As it turned out, Fred Yearning was defeated in his mayoral bid. Even more distressing is the fact that Yearning, in defeat, turned to an "alternative lifestyle" and appears to have no interest in trying to pay his campaign debts. The Yearning Committee had a treasurer and a secretary, as required by state law. The treasurer was George Simple, a small businessman (4'11" and 98 lbs.), and the secretary was Simple's own secretary. Hopkins doesn't know if the committee had any other members, although he is sure it was never incorporated. He believes that the committee still has a substantial amount of unspent money, but fears that Simple may contribute it to another candidate or pay off campaign creditors who are friends of his. Do you have any suggestions for him? See §303(a).

18.7. Your client, the Third State Bank, has for years provided unsecured financing to Alexander's Fine Furs, Inc. AFF is vertically integrated, raising its own fur animals and then manufacturing and retailing their fur as coats and capes. Its best year was 1988, with gross revenues of $25 million. AFF has encountered serious problems since, largely because of animal rights protests, and its manufacturing and retailing business has been greatly reduced, although it has maintained its profits on the animal raising operation by selling pelts to other companies here and abroad. Third State is concerned because AFF has fallen behind in its obligations to the bank, and there are rumors about transfers of AFF assets to favored suppliers and to members of the family who control the corporation. The bank would like to know if there are any actions it could take under the bankruptcy laws to protect its position. See §303(a).

18.8. Congresswoman Herring was intrigued by a law review article by Professor Lynn LoPucki, which was given to her by a staff member. Lynn

LoPucki, A General Theory of the Dynamics of the State Remedies/
Bankruptcy System, 1982 Wis. L. Rev. 311. In that article LoPucki discusses
implications of his empirical study of business bankruptcy in Kansas City.
He found that often the owners of small businesses were so reluctant to
relinquish their hopes for and control over their businesses that they tended
to hang on to the failing businesses far beyond the economically viable
time, thus dissipating the assets that would have been available to creditors
had they filed earlier. LoPucki argues that creditors should be encouraged to
intervene earlier, through the filing of involuntary bankruptcy petitions.
While the "generally not paying" standard for filing petitions would remain
in effect, under LoPucki's proposal petitioning creditors would be granted a
priority repayment in bankruptcy to compensate them for the risks they
must take in filing an involuntary petition. Explain to the congresswoman
why you would or would not recommend an amendment to the Code along
the lines suggested by Professor LoPucki.

CHAPTER 8

CHAPTER 11 REORGANIZATION

A. INTRODUCTION TO BUSINESS REORGANIZATIONS

1. Overview

"Reorganization" in the business context is a somewhat vague and forbidding word to many students. Traditionally, it has described a process much the same as the one in Chapter 13: The debtor wants to "reorganize" its debt by extending the time in which to pay it and reducing the total amount to be paid. A "plan of reorganization" in Chapter 11 might typically provide that the debtor will pay only 75 percent of its bank loans and will have five years to do so rather than the two-year period contemplated in the original loan agreement. (In the jargon of the trade, the 25 percent "forgiveness" of the principal amount of the loans is called a "haircut," although the lender may feel the hair is being cut below the scalp.)

Chapter 11 is often called the reorganization chapter. It was originally designed to facilitate the reorganization process just described, and that remains its central focus. But it has evolved over a quarter century, producing subspecies that are rather different from the parent. The very flexibility that permitted it to serve as a mechanism for reorganization has also permitted the creation of procedures that do not follow the traditional lines. In general terms, the traditional model seems to remain dominant for many SMEs and a significant number of large companies, public and private, as they use Chapter 11 to reorganize their businesses. But a substantial number of Chapter 11 proceedings, especially those involving public companies, are following one of the new models that include liquidations, sale of a going concern, and pre-packaged bankruptcies. In this introduction to Chapter 11, we will outline the traditional Chapter 11 process and then introduce some of the principal spin-offs. The description of the traditional Chapter 11 includes a brief summary of its background and history, which help to explain why and how it is moving in new directions.

While the basic idea of reorganization in Chapter 11 is similar to Chapter 13, the debt of a business debtor is often much more complicated than that of a consumer. Elizabeth Warren and Jay Lawrence Westbrook, Contracting Out of Bankruptcy: An Empirical Intervention, 118 Harv. L. Rev. 1197 (2005). Debt structures may include public bondholders or note-holders, subordinated levels of debt, suppliers from around the country and the world, and institutional lenders such as banks, insurance companies, and pension funds. While these factors make the extension and composition much more complex and technically difficult, in principle the reorganization of business debt is similar to the Chapter 13 process. Indeed, Chapter 11 is available for individuals as well as corporations; our data reported in *Financial Characteristics* suggests that in a typical year about 16 percent of Chapter 11 business filers are natural persons. Although that is a fascinating and unexpected niche of debtors, worthy of further research, the typical Chapter 11 debtor is corporate. Most individual debtors are better off in Chapter 13, which is less complex and less costly. Nearly all of our discussion of Chapter 11 will assume that the debtor is a corporation.

Some reorganizations are purely financial. That is, the business operations remain the same, while the debts are written down or eliminated. A business that has loaded up on debt may be operationally sound in the sense that revenues comfortably exceed marginal costs, but that business may have no hope of meeting its debt service. There is no reason in such a case to change the business operations. Instead, all that takes place is that the rights of various stakeholders must be readjusted. Old equity may be wiped out, for example, while the unsecured creditors become the new stockholders. These reorganizations are sometimes called "balance sheet reorganizations" to reflect the fact that they take place on paper rather than by shifting operations.

Other reorganizations involve a wholesale reshuffling of the business operations. The debtor will use the breathing room provided by the automatic stay to close or to sell money-losing divisions, trim excess staff, refocus product lines, cut back on the number of company cars, and so forth. In the retail clothing industry, for example, reorganization often involves closing the unprofitable stores while sprucing up the rest. Steel companies have reorganized by dropping peripheral lines of business and closing their most out-of-date plants. A business reorganization Chapter 11 will usually produce a smaller, leaner company with a reduced debt (and interest) burden, once again able to concentrate on the type of business that it does well.

The key point in either type of reorganization is that all or some large part of the business is preserved as a going concern rather than sold off one piece at a time in an old-fashioned courthouse-steps sort of sale. Experience and economic theory combine to reinforce the old saw that the whole is greater than the sum of its parts.

a. The Debtor in Possession

As we noted earlier, the business debtor almost never wants to liquidate because, unlike the individual debtor, there is no advantage for the company in liquidation. In corporate liquidation there are no exemptions and no discharge from debt. Liquidation is, as the term suggests, death. In bankruptcy reorganization, on the other hand, there can be many advantages.

On an altruistic level, managers may have a very strong personal commitment to retaining as many jobs for employees as possible and to avoiding the calamitous effects that a liquidation can have on a community. Management may also feel that there is a good chance in the long run to save something for equity shareholders.

On a personal level, the incentives to keep the business going may line up the same way. The managers of the debtor company who would face the certain termination of their jobs in Chapter 7 retain the hope that their jobs and benefits may survive a Chapter 11 reorganization. The managers also retain control of the business so long as they can hang on, giving them a final chance to show that they can manage it successfully. If the reorganization works, their prospects may be dim, but they are at least brighter than they would have been in a liquidation. No manager would hope for the circumstances that make consideration of a Chapter 11 necessary, but if it comes to the choice between reorganization or liquidation, the decision is relatively easy for current management.

Sometimes the management that makes the decision to file for Chapter 11 is not the same management that rode the business downhill, especially in public companies. Turnaround management firms are consultants who manage troubled businesses, often taking them through bankruptcy for a thorough cleaning before the businesses are stabilized and the management team flies off to another crisis. These specialists have become a sufficiently important part of the overall restructuring dynamic that they have even developed their own trade association, Turnaround Management Association (TMA). We will discuss this phenomenon further below.

For smaller companies, where there is less creditor involvement and where there may be no business without the personal involvement of the owner-operator, there is little reason to believe that managers are routinely replaced. This difference highlights a distinction between small and large Chapter 11s that is largely ignored in the policy debates, but that may make general statements based on one set of experiences completely inapplicable to Chapter 11s of a different size.

b. A Brief History of Business Reorganization

The statutory basis for reorganization was constructed in the aftermath of the Great Depression of the 1930s. The Chandler Act provided two separate business reorganization chapters, Chapter X for publicly held companies and Chapter XI for "Mom and Pop" businesses. As we noted earlier, Chapter X grew out of the "equity reorganizations" of the late nineteenth and early twentieth centuries, appropriate for large, publicly held corporations. Chapter XI, by contrast, grew out of the experience that the elaborate procedures of such reorganizations made no sense for small, privately owned businesses.

Nonetheless, for 40 years, large public companies tried desperately to use Chapter XI rather than Chapter X. Critics of Chapter X pointed to the many failed proceedings under that Chapter and blamed its cumbersome procedures. In particular, they attacked the requirement of a full-scale investigation by the Securities and Exchange Commission into the reasons for the company's failure. The delays required by SEC review and approval of any proposed plan of reorganization were perceived as ensuring the demise of a faltering business. Critics also insisted that Chapter X's requirement that a TIB take over operations was a great mistake, since experienced management was crucial to the survival of a troubled company. They contrasted these difficulties with the relative speed of Chapter XI, which did not require SEC participation, and the particular advantage that Chapter XI permitted the old management to remain in control of the business, exercising both the rights *and the duties* of the TIB.

Cynics argued that the real reason for companies' dislike of Chapter X was the fact that managers lost control of their companies and frequently lost their jobs as well. Cynics also wondered if management feared the searching scrutiny of the SEC concerning past dealings between the managers and the company. There is some evidence that, in fact, old management was not pushed out in Chapter X, but that a trustee took over and quickly retained the old management team. Elizabeth Warren, The Untenable Case for Repeal of Chapter 11, 102 Yale L.J. 437, 452-455 (1992). Whatever the effects on prior management, it is certainly clear that companies were very reluctant to enter Chapter X.

Over and over again the courts held that public companies could not reorganize in Chapter XI except under the rarest of circumstances. Nonetheless, public companies in trouble persistently filed in Chapter XI. By the mid-1970s a pattern was developing in which the company would file in Chapter XI, the SEC would move for conversion to Chapter X, and then the company and the SEC would negotiate about the treatment of public debt holders and shareholders, with the commission in effect offering to permit the case to remain in Chapter XI if the stockholders and bondholders were given good treatment. Institutional lenders, such as banks and insurance companies, increasingly felt that this process was working to their disadvantage and that value was being diverted from creditors to shareholders in the failing company.

To add to the complexity, businesses whose only asset was real estate, such as a venture formed to own and operate an apartment complex or an office building, were segregated into Chapter XII. This chapter was modeled after Chapter XI in form, but it was designed to deal with long-term real estate mortgages and other real estate finance devices.

Congress profoundly changed the structure of business reorganization in the new Code. In effect, Chapters X, XI, and XII were merged in the new Chapter 11. The distinction between a "Mom and Pop" operation and a billion-dollar company was largely abolished. SEC participation was dramatically reduced and the presumption was established that the debtor (i.e., existing management) should remain in control absent strong reasons for appointment of a TIB. No other factors are more responsible for the increased willingness of troubled companies to use bankruptcy reorganization in the 1980s.

A case can be made that the benefits of the new provisions outweigh the obvious loss of protection for widely scattered and relatively powerless public debt holders and stockholders. The principal benefit might be that companies will enter Chapter 11 earlier and therefore will be healthier and more likely to survive when they do. As we noted in the last chapter, companies (and individuals as well) often wait too long to enter bankruptcy, so that the patient's condition is hopeless by the time it enters the hospital. To the extent that Chapter 11 eliminates the main disincentives to seeking legal help while the company still has some cash and operating assets, there may be an important benefit in jobs saved and investments protected. Of course, there may also be more abuse of this less painful reorganization procedure, as some claim there has been in cases such as In re Ionosphere Clubs, Inc. and Eastern Airlines, Inc., 922 F.2d 1005 (2d Cir. 1990) and In re Johns-Manville Corp., 36 B.R. 727 (Bankr. S.D.N.Y. 1984), appeal denied, 39 B.R. 234 (S.D.N.Y. 1984). These policy tensions have become even more acute with the increasing use of Chapter 11 as a liquidation device in lieu of Chapter 7.

The small-case/big-case distinction that was obliterated in 1978 reemerged in 2005. As part of its large package of amendments, Congress added a provision to treat small business cases differently from their big business cousins — but the direction is the opposite of the old Chapter X/Chapter XI distinction. For the first time, small businesses will be denied Chapter 11 benefits that are available to big business. A new "small business case" definition was added that will apply to most businesses with debts less than $2 million at the time of filing. 11 U.S.C. §101(51D)(A). Such businesses will face increased reporting requirements, greater U.S. Trustee supervision, shorter deadlines, and more drop-dead points at which they can be forced out of Chapter 11. So far as we know, this is the first federal statute to discriminate against small businesses as such. We will go over more of these provisions later on.

Big-business reorganization did not escape unscathed in the 2005 Amendments, however. Provisions giving suppliers greater leverage and reducing management's control of the reorganization-plan process were among those that will likely increase the cost of reorganization and make it more difficult.

c. High Theory and Personal Trauma

Far from being the dreary subject of business failure, Chapter 11 has engendered some of the most heated debates in the business and legal worlds. Economists and lawyers, businesspeople and academics continue to argue over the role served by Chapter 11. As more data about the Chapter 11 process become available the debates may not subside, but they may involve more joinder of issue and a better understanding of the pressures facing both debtors and creditors in the reorganization process.

Theory and policy aside, there is a human side to the process that is at least as important as legal doctrine and economic policy. The businesses that once were courted as the valued customers of banks and lending consortia see a different side of their lenders when the business begins to slip. For nearly every case and problem discussed in the following chapters, there was once an amicable relationship that both parties sought and both hoped to preserve.

The recent wave of fraud revealed by the collapse of the stock market bubble in 2000 has made the general public aware of the personal trauma of financial failure. Perhaps the most vivid example was the sight of Enron employees in shock after learning that their life savings had been lost in its scandalous collapse, but many other business bankruptcies are filled with stories of personal tragedy.

The problem of corporate fraud leading to bankruptcy will come up again later in this chapter. It raises interesting questions about the role of bankruptcy law, along with SEC investigations and criminal trials, in the policing of our financial markets and corporate boardrooms. The Enron collapse has received the most attention. The interested student may want to read Bethany McLean and Peter Elkind, The Smartest Guys in the Room (2003) and the reports issued by Neal Batson, who was appointed an examiner in the Enron bankruptcy. http://www.enron.com/corp/por/examiner final.html. Both include a number of salutary lessons for lawyers and other professionals who advise public companies.

For a bitter and highly critical view of Chapter 11 from the perspective of a man who lost his family business, see S. Stein, A Feast for Lawyers (1989). Although many of the author's criticisms will seem wrongheaded or misdirected to knowledgeable lawyers and law students, the book should serve as the occasion for some genuine soul-searching about the bankruptcy process. Another book that raises serious questions at the intersection of reorganization and mass tort cases is R. Sobel, Bending the Law (1991), which criticizes the Chapter 11 case of the A.H. Robins company from the perspective of the victims of its Dalkon Shield IUD.

Business in the twentieth and twenty-first centuries has yet to find its Balzac or its Dickens, but Tom Wolfe has come closer than most in his novel *A Man in Full*. We offer the following excerpt because it captures some of the human dynamics of a financial restructuring in a traditional Chapter 11. In this excerpt, the focus is on the time that the relationship between debtor and creditor changes, a time that precedes the bankruptcy but that may color the emotional background for much of what follows both in and out of court. Not all "workouts" are like this, but the debtor's fall from grace often yields similar emotions, on both sides of the table.

The protagonist of the novel is Charlie Croker, a larger-than-life Atlanta real estate developer who finds his empire in serious financial trouble. He is invited to a meeting with the bankers at his lead bank. (The developer, and the author's prose, are earthier and more vivid than this excerpt reveals. A full reading is highly recommended.)

════════════ TOM WOLFE, THE SADDLEBAGS ════════════
From *A Man in Full* (1998)

. . . Just then Croker's gaze wandered toward a far corner of the room and a doubtful, puzzled look came over his face.

Peepgass's colleague, Harry Zale, the workout artiste, leaned his huge head over and said out of the corner of his mouth:

"Hey, Ray, check out the big boffster. He just noticed the dead plant."

It was true. Croker's eyes had drifted over to the corner where, in a dismal gloaming, there stood a solitary tropical plant, a dracaena, in a clay pot, dying. Several long, skinny yellowish fronds drooped over like the tongues of the dead. The pot rested on an otherwise empty expanse of Streptolon carpet pocked with the mashed-in depressions of desk feet, chair casters, and office machines that had been moved somewhere else. The old man had to squint to make it out. He was puzzled. He could hardly see a thing. From where he was sitting, he should have been able to look out through the plate-glass wall and seen much of Midtown Atlanta . . . the IBM tower, the GLG Grande, Promenade One, Promenade Two, the Campanile, the Southern Bell Center, Colony Square, and three of his own buildings, the Phoenix Center, the MossCo Tower, and the TransEx Palladium. But he couldn't. . . . It was the glare. He and his contingent had been seated so that they had to look straight into it.

Oh, everything about this room was cunningly seedy and unpleasant. The conference table itself was a vast thing, a regular aircraft carrier, but it was put together in modular sections that didn't quite jibe where they met, and its surface was not wood but some sort of veal-gray plastic laminate. On the table, in front of each of the two dozen people present, was a pathetic setting of paperware, a paper cup for the orange juice, a paper mug with fold-out handles for the coffee, which gave off an odor of incinerated PVC cables, and a paper plate with a huge cold, sticky, cheesy, cowpie-like cinnamon-cheddar coffee bun that struck terror into the heart of every man in the room who had ever read an article about arterial plaque or free radicals. That, in its entirety, was the breakfast meeting's breakfast.

To top it off, on the walls a pair of NO SMOKING signs glowered down upon the Croker Global crew with the sort of this-means-you lettering you might expect to find in the cracking unit of an oil refinery, but not at a conference of twenty-four ladies and gentlemen of banking and commerce in the PlannersBanc Tower in Midtown Atlanta.

* * *

Harry began speaking in a softer, lower voice. "Listen, Mr. Croker, don't get me wrong. We're on your side here. We don't want this to turn into a free-for-all with nine lenders, either. And we wouldn't particularly look forward to the press coverage." He paused to let that terrorist threat, the press, stalk the room. "We're the agent bank in this setup, and that gives us the privilege of looking out for PlannersBanc first of all. But we gotta come up with something *concrete.*" He extended his right fist up in the air as high as it would go and said, "Where's the money gonna come from? It ain't gonna come . . . *poof*!" — he sprung his fist open — "from outta the air! Mr. Stroock assures us you got a lot of sound assets. Okay . . . good. The time has come to make them liquid. The time has come to pay us back. The time has come to sell something. I'm with you — the tailgate has dropped."

At that point young Stroock jumped in, evidently to give his boss, Croker, time to get his breath back and his battered wits together. Just "selling something," said Stroock, was not such an easy proposition. Croker Global had considered this particular option. But in the first place there was a complex of interlocking ownerships. Certain corporate structures within Croker Global's real estate portfolio actually owned certain independently structured divisions of Croker Global Foods, each of which was a corporation in its own right, and —

"I'm aware of all that," said the Artiste. "I've got your organization chart. I'm entering it in the Org-off."

"The Org-off?" said Wismer Stroock.

"Yeah. That's a contest we have at PlannersBanc for the worst-looking organization chart. I thought nobody was gonna be able to beat Chai Long Shipping, out of Hong Kong. They got three hundred ships, and each ship is a separate corporation, and each corporation owns a fraction of at least five other ships, and each ship has a color code, and the chart is ten feet long. Looks like a Game Boy semiconductor panel, blown up. I thought Chai Long was a sure thing in the Org-off until I saw yours. Yours looks like a bowl of linguine primavera. You just gotta untangle it and sell something."

"Unh-huh. I see. Do you mind if I finish?"

"No, I don't mind, but why don't we entertain a few modest proposals first."

The Artiste turned to an assistant on his other side and said in a low voice, "Gimme the cars, Sheldon." The young man, Sheldon, snapped open a ring binder and handed Harry a sheet of paper.

The Artiste studied it for a moment, then looked up at Croker and said, "Now, in your last financial statement you list seven company automobiles, three BMW 750:L's valued at . . . What's it say here? . . . $93,000 each . . . Two BMW 540:A's valued at $55,000 each, a Ferrari 355 valued at $129,000, and a customized Cadillac Seville STS valued at $75,000. By the way, how'd you get here this morning?"

Croker gave the Artiste a long death-ray stare, then said, "I drove."

"What'd you drive? A BMW? The Ferrari? The Customized Cadillac Seville STS? Which one?"

Croker eyed him balefully but said nothing. The steam was coming back into his system. His mighty chest rose and fell with a prodigious sigh. The dark stains were inching closer, from either side of his chest, toward the sternum.

Harry said, "Seven company cars . . . Sell 'em."

"Those cars are in constant use," said Croker. "Besides, suppose we sold 'em — to the distinct disadvantage of our operations, by the way. What are we talking about here? A couple of hundred thousand dollars."

"Hey!" said the Artiste with a big smile. "I don't know about you, but I have great respect for a couple of hundred thousand dollars. Besides, your arithmetic's a little off. It's five hundred and ninety-three thousand. A thousand more insignificant items like that and we've got half a billion and plenty to spare. See how easy it is? Sell 'em."

He turned to his assistant again and said, "Gimme the airplanes." The ring binder snapped open, and the assistant, Sheldon, gave him several sheets of paper.

"Now Mr. Croker," said Harry, looking at the pages, "you also list four aircraft, two Beechjet 400A's, a Super King Air 350, and a Gulfstream Five." Then he looked up at Croker and, in a voice like W. C. Fields's, repeated: "a Gulfstream Five . . . a Gee-Fiiiiiiive . . . That's a $38 million aircraft, if I'm not mistaken, and I see here that yours has certain en*hance*ments . . . A Satcom telephone system, $300,000 installed . . . a Satcom telephone enables you to telephone, while you're aloffffft from anywhere in the world, isn't that correct?"

"Yeah," said Croker.

"How many of Croker Global's operations are overseas, Mr. Croker?"

"As of now, none, but — "

"And I see you've also got a set of SkyWatch cabin radar display screens, worth $125,000 installed, and a cabin interior custom designed and furnished by a Mr. Ronald Vine for $2,845,000. And it says here there's a *painting* installed on that airplane worth $190,000." The Artiste raised his great chin and looked down his nose at Croker with a mixture of incredulity and disdain. "Are those figures correct? They come straight from your financial statement. You presented these items as collateral."

"That's right."

"That's $40 million tied up in that one aircraft." He turned to his assistant. "What's the total value of the other three planes, Sheldon?"

"Fifteen million, nine hundred thousand."

"Fifteen million, nine hundred thousand," said Harry. "So now we're talking about $58 million worth of airplanes. Where do you keep those airplanes, Mr. Croker?"

"Out at PDK," said Croker, referring to the airport for private aircraft in DeKalb County, just east of the city. PDK was short for Peachtree-DeKalb.

"You lease hangar space there?"

"Yeah."

"How many pilots do you employ?"

"Twelve."

"Twelve . . ." The Artiste arched his eyebrows and whistled through his teeth in mock surprise. He smiled. "We're gonna save you a whole *lotta* money." He smiled again, as if this was all great fun. Then the smile vanished, and he said with a toneless finality, "Sell 'em."

"That we could always do," said Croker, "but it would be totally self-defeating. Those aircraft are not used in a frivolous manner. In Global Foods we got seventeen warehouses in fourteen states. We got — "

"Sell 'em."

"We got — "

"Sell 'em. From now on we're gonna be like the Vietcong. We're gonna travel on the ground and live off the land."

2. *The Traditional Chapter 11*

a. Mechanics of Chapter 11

A traditional Chapter 11, as you would expect, resembles in broad conceptual outline the other rehabilitation chapter, Chapter 13. When a debtor files a petition, the section 362(a) automatic stay is imposed. The business continues to operate "in the ordinary course," §363(c), under the control of the debtor in possession, usually called the "DIP."

It is important to remember that the DIP only looks like the old debtor. Even though its president is wearing the same blue pinstripe suit and lives at the same address, the DIP controls a new legal entity — the estate — and has most of the rights and duties of a TIB. §1107. Thus, for example, even though a debtor-transferor in a fraudulent conveyance does not have the right to attack its own conveyance and get the property back at state law, the DIP can do so because it is acting on behalf of *all of its creditors*, not merely for itself. Since the DIP has these rights, duties, and powers, ordinarily no TIB is appointed in Chapter 11.

While the DIP can operate in the ordinary course without court approval of each routine transaction, it is limited in the use of its assets if those assets are subject to a security agreement. §363(c), (e). The business also faces the prospect that secured creditors will seek court approval for lifting the automatic stay as to their collateral, unless the DIP can provide "adequate protection" of their interests. §§361, 362(d).

The DIP may also obtain financing and other credit during bankruptcy with the approval of the court. §364. The Code makes it possible for the debtor to offer post-petition creditors relatively attractive terms, which is important because further financing is often vital to the debtor's survival. On the other hand, these provisions also increase the risk that a debtor's overly optimistic attempt to survive will merely consume what few assets might otherwise have been left for preexisting creditors.

As we noted above, a TIB or DIP has "avoiding powers," which include the power to recover preferences (payments or transfer of property to favored creditors within 90 days of bankruptcy), §547; the power to assume or to breach outstanding executory contracts, §365; the power to void fraudulent conveyances, §§548 and 544(b); and the power to set aside unperfected or late-perfected security interests in the debtor's property, §§544(a) and 547. The TIB or DIP also has the power to require turnover of property of the debtor being held by another entity. §§542 and 543. All of these powers are equally available in consumer or business bankruptcies, but they are much more often used in business cases where the stakes are higher and there are more resources to support both the investigation and the litigation that may be required to recover these assets on behalf of the estate. These powers are important in business liquidations, but their use — more often the threat of their use — is even more important in the negotiations that lead to reorganization of a business. We study them in the context in which they most often arise.

After a business files a Chapter 11 petition, an initial period of chaos typically follows in which the debtor is obtaining financing, getting approval for the use of cash collateral, arguing about "adequate protection" of secured creditors, firing employees, reassuring customers, closing money-losing facilities, and so forth. Once some stability has been achieved, the debtor then goes about the business of negotiating a plan with its major creditors. A creditors' committee is appointed (although in smaller cases this often does not happen) to scrutinize the debtor's activities on behalf of all creditors and to negotiate with the debtor. §1102. As the negotiations draw to a close, the debtor enters another whirlwind of activity as the plan is confirmed. Corporate counsel for a major retailer that entered and successfully emerged from bankruptcy described the experience as being similar to flying through a hurricane — initially chaotic and frightening, followed by a period of unreal calm, followed in turn by another period of chaos in which the survival of the enterprise was once again very much at stake.

To conclude the bankruptcy, the debtor will propose a plan of reorganization, in which it will offer to pay each "class" of creditors a certain percentage of their claims over a stated period of time, with payment to be made in cash, in property, or in securities issued by the reorganized debtor. The plan and an explanatory disclosure statement are distributed to all creditors who have filed claims. If the plan is approved by the specified majorities of creditors in each class, §1126(c), it will be confirmed by the court, provided that it also conforms to the requirements of section 1129, including the requirement that every creditor who has not accepted the plan will get at least as much as that creditor would have gotten in a liquidation. §1129(a)(7) (the analog to the "best interests" test, §1325(a)(4)). Upon confirmation of the plan, the debtor is discharged from all its pre-petition debts except as provided in the plan, §1141(d). The discharge of debt in Chapter 11 stands in sharp contrast to Chapter 13, where there is no discharge until the plan has been completed, and in contrast to Chapter 7, which gives no discharge at all to a corporate debtor.

b. The Logic of a Traditional Chapter 11

A Chapter 11 petition is an invitation to a negotiation. Therefore, it would be reasonable to ask why a court proceeding is necessary at all. Why can't the debtor sit down and negotiate with the creditors without the very substantial expense and delay of bankruptcy proceedings? In fact, it can and often does just that, especially when the debtor's business is one that might be destroyed if its customers and suppliers heard the terrible word "bankruptcy." For some companies, however, formal bankruptcy proceedings may be the only route to successful negotiations for a variety of reasons. One is panic; in the 1970s the Chapter 11 of a billion-dollar company was provoked by an offset by one nervous bank, which in turn stampeded the company's other banks into setting off the company's bank accounts against its unpaid loans. Left with no cash whatsoever in the bank, the company was forced to go into Chapter 11, although many observers thought bankruptcy should never have been necessary for that company. It ultimately confirmed a plan to pay 100 percent of its debt.

Another problem is that not all creditors want to sit down to the negotiating table. Creditors who are oversecured, for example, may have no interest in negotiating a rearrangement of the debtor's obligations because they know that they are well protected and see no reason not to be paid in full and on time. Other creditors may themselves be hard pressed financially (especially in a general recession) and unable to contemplate a delay in payment. Still other creditors may be involved in substantial disputes with the debtor and there may be bad blood between them on a personal level (such things are more significant in big business than most people realize). Sometimes there simply may be so many creditors in so many different circumstances that the sheer logistics of negotiation are difficult and bankruptcy becomes the mechanism to force all the parties to the table at once.

Sometimes most creditors would go along with an out-of-court restructuring, but only if the pain is shared equally among all those to whom the debtor owes money. If a few creditors hold out for better treatment and defeat the deal, bankruptcy may be necessary to force the minority to go along, as explained below.

Above all, some creditors may not share the optimism of the debtor's management about the future of the business. They may believe that the debtor's projections of future profits are pipe dreams and that creditors generally would be better off if the debtor were sold or liquidated immediately. In some instances such creditors may themselves file an involuntary Chapter 11 petition. §303(a). They may do so even if they seek liquidation of the debtor, since a liquidating plan is permitted in Chapter 11. §1123(b)(4). In this last instance they could choose Chapter 11 rather than Chapter 7 because they believed a more measured and orderly liquidation could be achieved in Chapter 11 than in Chapter 7.

How, then, can bankruptcy offer any hope? For one thing, many creditors do want to "work things out" (in and out of bankruptcy the jargon for a reorganization is a "workout"). Some of them, for example, will be suppliers for whom the debtor is a significant customer whose survival is more important than full payment of past debts. Many others will accept the simple logic that a payout will produce more payment than a liquidation. Hope — sometimes false hope — lies at the heart of the reorganization process.

Given those facts, bankruptcy offers the debtor a number of powerful aids in its negotiations, notably:

- the automatic stay and the breathing room it brings;
- the possibility of adopting a plan that will legally bind all creditors, even though a minority reject it;
- the turnover and avoiding powers, which can greatly augment the assets available and provide powerful leverage over certain creditors.

These new tools, available only in bankruptcy, will change the negotiating leverage of every party dealing with a troubled debtor.

c. Analysis of a Chapter 11 Negotiation

If a Chapter 11 petition is an invitation to a negotiation, it is issued in most cases at the eleventh hour. Most debtors are *in extremis* when they enter Chapter 11, and a fair number fail before they ever develop and offer a plan of reorganization to their creditors. The failure rate in Chapter 11 has been the subject of much speculation and several researchers have made a stab at trying to pin down the number of Chapter 11 successes. Here, however, the problem of definition is more acute than almost anyplace else in the bankruptcy system.

The conventional claim is that about 30 percent of Chapter 11 cases produce plans confirmed by the court, and the data support that claim. Many researchers use the confirmation of a plan as the measure of "success," thereby implying that the 70 percent of cases dismissed or converted to Chapter 7 were failures. But there are several other outcomes that may be considered successes. For example, under the shelter of the automatic stay the creditors may have worked out a suitable arrangement with the debtor and the parties may have agreed to dismiss the case. That case would better be designated a success than a failure, if only a researcher could find an easy way to capture that information — the court records would list the case as simply one more "dismissal." Simple confirmation rates don't give a nuanced view of success.

Even looking at confirmation rates alone, the conventional view is a bit simple-minded. The data from the Business Bankruptcy Project ("BBP") permit a more sophisticated understanding. The data strongly suggest that a great many bankrupt corporate debtors file in Chapter 11, even if they plan to liquidate. The data reported in *Financial Characteristics* show that about 95 percent of all the businesses with assets in excess of $1 million or more file in Chapter 11. By contrast, more than half the debtors with less than $100,000 in assets went directly into Chapter 7. The percentage choosing Chapter 7 liquidation from the start goes steadily downward as the size of the business increases. This creates a peculiar distortion in the data. Smaller businesses sort themselves out between Chapter 7 and Chapter 11, with the weakest cases presumably going directly into liquidation without taking a spin in Chapter 11. As cases get larger, the sorting effect at the time of filing seems to wane and it seems that many obvious liquidations are initially filed in Chapter 11.

Two implications follow from the fact that many cases doomed to liquidation are filed in Chapter 11. The first is that the courts have an important gatekeeper role in Chapter 11 proceedings, to dispose of such cases as quickly as possible by dismissal or conversion to Chapter 7. Second, if the gatekeeping turns out to be efficient and timely, then it may be plausible to measure the confirmation-rate success of Chapter 11 by the percentage of cases that produce confirmed plans from among those that survive the initial sorting. Data soon to be reported by the BBP suggest that the gatekeeper role is being well executed. Looking at data from both 1994 and 2002, of the cases that are ultimately dismissed or converted, over 60 percent were booted out of Chapter 11 in less than nine months and three-quarters within a year. Against that background of efficient sorting, the confirmation rates were quite high. In both 1994 and 2002, Chapter 11 cases that were still alive nine months after filing, had a confirmation rate of almost 50 percent.

The companies that get past the gatekeeper and succeed in achieving a measure of business stability in the first frenzied weeks or months of the case can then begin the process of negotiating a feasible plan with the creditors' committee and other creditors. Negotiations with the creditors become the focus of their survival.

Although different perspectives on the business prospects of the debtor are a major obstacle in plan negotiations, legal disputes are also important in many cases. One reason that nonbankruptcy agreements sometimes cannot be achieved or that negotiations for a plan in Chapter 11 fail is that the parties have quite different perceptions of the likely outcomes in Chapter 7. Often they evaluate differently the answers to key legal questions (and related factual ones). If the debtor believes that there is a 75 percent probability that creditor *A*'s security interest will be voided in Chapter 7 and creditor *A* believes there is only a slight chance it will lose its security interest, the debtor and creditor *A* will find it hard to reach agreement on the amount that creditor *A* should receive relative to other creditors, secured and unsecured. Once in bankruptcy, the DIP might institute avoidance litigation challenging the validity of the security interest to get a ruling in its favor, so that creditor *A* will accept less. On the other hand, litigation is time consuming, and the debtor will often want to propose a plan within the 120 days in which it has the exclusive right to do so, suggesting even more reasons to negotiate. §1121(b).

The problem of different legal opinions grows even more complex when creditor *B* may think that creditor *A*'s security interest is likely voidable, even where the debtor thinks the security interest is probably valid. In that case, creditor *B* will insist that *A* receive less (leaving a larger pie available for *B* and the other creditors) while creditor *A* will insist on the enhanced treatment due a fully secured creditor. Either way the debtor will lose the vote of one creditor or another, whether it treats the claim in the plan as a secured claim or as an unsecured one. Again, litigation may be necessary to clarify the parties' rights, but protracted litigation, including perhaps years of appeals, can destroy the possibility of a successful Chapter 11.

Because of the problem of litigation delay, it sometimes happens that a plan will provide, in effect, an escrow of money or property pending resolution of the litigation. Thus a plan might provide that if *A*'s security interest is vindicated, the withheld money will go to it, while if the security interest is voided as unperfected, then it will be a further dividend for unsecured creditors. A whole new creature, the "litigation trust," has been born of the effort to confirm a reorganization plan quickly while continuing litigation that may eventually yield assets for the creditors of the reorganized business.

This approach creates its own difficulties, however, including the fact that it leaves creditors without a "bottom line." When they vote on the plan of reorganization, they often have no concrete idea of how much they are giving up and how much they are getting, making more than one creditor refer to the decision to accept a plan as like buying a pig in a poke. Its value is more speculation than reality.

As we noted earlier, one of the great advantages that Chapter 11 gives the debtor is the right to use, or to threaten to use, the avoiding powers that the DIP may exercise in the shoes of the TIB who would exercise them in liquidation. Sometimes adversary proceedings are brought in Chapter 11 to avoid liens or other transfers. More often the threat of such proceedings, in Chapter 11 or a subsequent Chapter 7, is a source of powerful leverage for the DIP and other creditors.

3.   *Control*

As we will discuss at more length in the chapter on theory, control is a central concept in all bankruptcy laws. The law's immediate responses to the filing of a bankruptcy petition — the automatic stay, the automatic transfer of ownership of the debtor's property to a new legal entity, and the appointment of a trustee in bankruptcy — put the courts in overall charge of the debtor and its business and therefore empower these agents of government to impose socially mandated policies on the process of sorting out the effects of a debtor's general default. Whatever economic or social policies might be adopted in a particular bankruptcy system, it is this control that ensures that those policies (for example, priorities) will be applied to the value to be obtained from the distressed business. Jay Lawrence Westbrook, The Control of Wealth in Bankruptcy, 82 Tex. L. Rev. 795 (2004).

In Chapter 11, that control is exercised by the debtor in possession or DIP. The idea of DIP control came from the old Chapter XI, designed for small proprietorships and closely held companies where the management and owners were largely the same people. When Congress in 1978 put the DIP in charge of every Chapter 11 case as the legal stand-in for the trustee in bankruptcy, the DIP concept was applied to much larger public companies in which management and ownership are routinely separated. The stockholders who own these companies are not the people who manage them and the managers usually hold a very small percentage of the stock. The classic discussion is found in A. Berle and G. Means, The Modern Corporation and Private Property (1932).

The effect of the DIP concept was to put the existing pre-bankruptcy management of the company in charge of the Chapter 11 debtor, but with no congressional definition of management's role. As a result, the flexible provisions of Chapter 11 permit management of a public corporation to exercise that control on behalf of several possible constituencies. It may act on behalf of stockholders, creditors, or other constituencies like employees and communities, given the fact that Congress has seemed to indicate that it is concerned to protect the interests of a number of different constituencies of a business following a general default. Elizabeth Warren, Bankruptcy Policymaking in an Imperfect World, 92 Mich. L. Rev. 336 (1992). Finally, experience and economic theory combine to suggest that management will give considerable attention to protecting its own interests.

The control point is greatly complicated by management turnover. A number of studies show that the typical annual management turnover for CEOs is about 3 to 5 percent, but that for public companies in bankruptcy about 90 percent of the CEOs resign within two years of the filing date. LoPucki and Whitford, Corporate Governance in the Bankruptcy Reorganization of Large, Publicly Held Companies, 141 U. Pa. L. Rev. 62 (1992); Betker, Management Changes, Equity's Bargaining Power and Deviations from Absolute Priority in Chapter 11 Bankruptcies, 68 Journal of Business 161 (1995).

Some scholars have claimed that today's public-company Chapter 11 cases are controlled by creditors, a result that they applaud. Douglas G. Baird and Robert K. Rasmussen, The End of Bankruptcy, 55 Stan. L. Rev. 751 (2002). Although they do not explain the mechanics of that control, it is apparent that they believe it is exercised through security interests and through influence over management as DIP. Others have commented on the increasing power of secured creditors in business bankruptcies. Elizabeth Warren and Jay L. Westbrook, Secured Parties in Possession, 22 Am. Bankr. Inst. J., 12 (2003).

Control of smaller businesses in Chapter 11 is not without controversy. Professor LoPucki has suggested that too often the owners of those businesses as DIPs use Chapter 11 for their own purposes while abusing those powers vis-à-vis creditors. Lynn LoPucki, A General Theory of the Dynamics of the State Remedies/Bankruptcy System, 1982 Wis. L. Rev. 311. See also Douglas G. Baird and Edward R. Morrison, Serial Entrepreneurs and Small Business Bankruptcies, University of Chicago Law & Economics, Olin Working Paper No. 236; Columbia Law and Economics Working Paper No. 265 (January 4, 2004).

Thus throughout the business bankruptcy materials it is important to keep an eye on the question of control: who exercises it for whose benefit? Because the DIP is given the sweeping legal powers of a trustee in bankruptcy, the answer goes to the heart of the public policy debates about Chapter 11.

4. Large Public Companies and Nontraditional Chapter 11 Cases

New approaches to the Chapter 11 process have been emerging over the last decade or so. These new structures and procedures are found in both publicly and privately held companies, but are more prevalent in public company cases because of certain characteristics of those companies. Two nontraditional Chapter 11 approaches that bear special mention in this introduction are auctions and prepackaged plans.

a. Auctions

It is increasingly common for companies in Chapter 11 to resolve their financial difficulties by a sale of the entire business (or what remains after closing down losing operations). That sale is quite often through an auction process, although nothing like the old-fashioned, piecemeal liquidation with a fast-talking auctioneer. These sales are negotiated by the lawyers and investment bankers in the merger and acquisition departments of large firms. We will discuss how these auctions work later in this chapter. For now, it is enough to note the key points. First, it appears that an auction approach almost always means there will be no meaningful recovery for shareholders of the business. Second, the auction may be held pursuant to a confirmed plan, but often is not. In the latter case, the sale is completed under section 363 of the Code prior to any creditor vote and the plan is simply a mechanism for allocating and distributing the proceeds of the sale.

b. Prepackaged Plans

This term is used to describe a case in which the debtor has negotiated the deal with its creditors before the petition is ever filed, but needs the help of the bankruptcy law to close the deal. An example would be if one large creditor refuses to accept the proposal. Outside of bankruptcy, that creditor presents an insurmountable obstacle, but in Chapter 11 it can be outvoted by the accepting creditors in the same class and effectively forced to go along. Prepackaged bankruptcies among large companies have risen and fallen, with about 4 percent of all publicly traded companies in Chapter 11 filing as a "prepack" in 2003. New Generation Research, Inc., The Bankruptcy Yearbook and Almanac 162 (2003). Under local rules adopted in some of the federal court districts around the country, including the key districts of Delaware and Southern New York, these cases can proceed with far less public disclosure of information in bankruptcy court than the ordinary Chapter 11. Prepackaged plans may or may not be liquidating plans as discussed below.

5. *Single Asset Real Estate Cases (SARE)*

When Congress created Chapter 11 in 1978, it abolished Chapter XII, which was a separate reorganization chapter for real estate cases, but it could not abolish the economic factors that make such cases quite different from the typical Chapter 11. SAREs are defined in section 101(51B) of the Code. A typical example would be a corporation or partnership whose only real asset is an apartment house or office building and whose only substantial debt is the mortgage on it. Such a case often amounts to a two-party struggle between the owner and the mortgage lender, with few other creditors or employees involved.

Nonetheless, such cases stirred a lot of controversy in the first two decades after the adoption of the Code. Despite their unusual nature, these cases were also the context in which much of the Chapter 11 common law of those years was forged. In recent years, following a tightening of the SARE rules by Congress and the courts, they have appeared much less often in published opinions, perhaps because they are more often being resolved out of court. Or perhaps recent years have seen fewer such cases because real estate markets have generally been quite strong. Perhaps over the next few years the need to think about how to reorganize the debtors of real estate entities will surge to the foreground. Either way, SAREs often present some of the most challenging intellectual and policy problems in the Chapter 11 field. For a penetrating discussion of SAREs in bankruptcy, see Kenneth N. Klee, One Size Fits Some: Single Asset Real Estate Bankruptcy Cases, 87 Cornell L. Rev. 1285 (2002).

6. *Liquidation in Chapter 11*

The ultimate proof that Chapter 11 is no longer synonymous with reorganization is the fact that it is increasingly used for liquidation of companies.

Although conversion to Chapter 7 is the traditional method for liquidating a company unable to reorganize, the data from the BBP show that 20 percent or more of the confirmed plans in Chapter 11 cases are liquidating plans. The Code has always permitted use of Chapter 11 for liquidation, but the traditional mindset remains that Chapter 11 is for reorganization, Chapter 7 for liquidation. In fact, nowadays very few companies of substantial size liquidate in Chapter 7. Again, the leading contemporary example is Enron Corporation, whose liquidating plan is estimated to pay around 20 cents on the dollar. For current information, visit www. Enron.com.

Liquidating plans are often, although by no means always, associated with auctions and with prepackaged plans, as noted above. We will discuss them in more detail in the plan section of this chapter. We note here two points for subsequent discussion. On the one hand, Chapter 11 provides a highly flexible approach to maximizing the sale value of the debtor's assets, especially in a sale of the whole business as a going concern. On the other hand, Chapter 11 is a negotiated resolution of a debtor's general default and therefore permits much more flexibility in the realization and distribution of value than do the relatively fixed rules of Chapter 7 supervised by a disinterested trustee in bankruptcy. Whether these two types of flexibility are good or bad in public policy terms are questions that will recur as we proceed.

7. *Costs of Chapter 11*

Law is not free. That axiom is nowhere more true than in bankruptcy, where angry creditors and disappointed investors are facing the danger of losing some or all of their investments in a failing enterprise. More than once throughout this book it has been clear that the legally correct answer was not one that the parties could afford to reach. A right that will yield only a few dollars is often one not worth pursuing. The need for low cost, mass-produced solutions in the consumer bankruptcy area shapes much of the legal policy. But in the Chapter 11 field there are often substantial assets at stake, along with jobs, embedded business relationships, and ongoing legal obligations. Unlike their mass-produced cousins on the consumer side of the house, business bankruptcies are often individually crafted solutions of profound complexity. And "individual crafting" and "profound complexity" are terms that, in the legal world, are synonymous with "costly."

The debates over Chapter 11 have raised the question of whether use of a Chapter 11 is a high-priced delaying tactic or a model for lower-cost negotiation. Determining the costs of a Chapter 11 is a staggeringly complex operation. There are lawyers' fees, accountants' fees, and appraisers' fees. There are creditors who must deal with accelerated debts, claim forms, and demands for repayment of earlier transactions. There is the time that management spends on bankruptcy issues rather than the operation of the business. There are, in effect, the direct costs of Chapter 11, including attorneys' fees, and the indirect costs, including lost value in the company.

Several researchers have looked at direct costs in the reorganization of the largest Chapter 11 cases. Professor Lynn M. LoPucki and Joseph W. Doherty examined data collected from all of the largest cases, reporting that the average ratio of fees and expenses to assets was 2.2 percent. The Determinants of Professional Fees in Large Bankruptcy Reorganization Cases, 1 J. Empirical L. Stud. 111, 140 (2004). Professor Stephen Lubben looked at a somewhat different sample of large cases and concluded that direct costs in large reorganizations are approximately 2 percent of firm assets. The Direct Costs of Corporate Reorganization: An Empirical Examination of Professional Fees in Large Chapter 11 Cases, 74 Am. Bankr. L.J. 509, 515 (2000). Similarly, Brian Betker finds a ratio of direct costs to assets of 3.9 percent for 75 big Chapter 11 cases. Betker, The Administrative Costs of Debt Restructuring: Some Recent Evidence, 26 Financial Management 56 (1999). While these percentages seem small, the absolute values can be quite high. In Enron, for example, professional fees alone have exceeded one-half billion dollars with the case far from over.

Unlike the previous researchers who concentrated on the largest Chapter 11 cases, which comprise only a tiny fraction of all the business cases filed in a given year, Stephen Ferris and Robert Lawless have conducted several studies of routine business cases. They find that the costs are proportionately much higher. Robert M. Lawless, Stephen P. Ferris, Narayanan Jayaraman, and Anil K. Makhija, A Glimpse at Professional Fees and Other Direct Costs in Small Firm Bankruptcies, 1994 U. Ill. L. Rev. 847, 868, finding that the average professional fees in a small-business Chapter 11 proceeding amounted to 8.66 percent of all assets. In a later study, Ferris and Lawless reported: "The average Chapter 11 in our study incurred $73,050 in direct costs. (The median figure was $21,174.) Whether these amounts are excessive depends on one's perspective. These direct costs may be trivial for a large, publicly traded company but may be a significant portion of the assets for a small sole proprietorship." Stephen P. Ferris and Robert M. Lawless, The Expenses of Financial Distress: The Direct Costs of Chapter 11, 31 University of Pittsburgh L. Rev. (1999). The direct costs represented about 17.6 percent of the assets of the business, and about 30 percent of the distributions to general unsecured creditors. These data suggest that Chapter 11 may entail an irreducible core of costs, even in small cases, and that these costs can consume a significant fraction of a Chapter 11 payout.

To add to the complications of analyzing the costs of Chapter 11, it is important to consider the alternatives. Is a Chapter 11 reorganization expensive? Compared to what? Undoubtedly, it is less expensive for a debtor to succeed in business than to reorganize in Chapter 11, but that option has usually been lost by the time parties are brushing up on their understanding of Title 11 of the U.S. Code. What about an out-of-court workout or a complete financial restructuring outside bankruptcy? Professor Gilson finds that when the two are compared for large, publicly traded companies, Chapter 11 is the cheaper alternative. Stuart Gilson, Transactions Costs and Capital Structure Choice: Evidence from Financially Distressed Firms, 52 Journal of Finance 161; Stuart Gilson, John Kose, and Larry Lang, Troubled Debt Restructurings: An Empirical Study of Private Reorganization of Firms in Default, 27 Journal of Financial Economics 315 (1990).

The good news is that more researchers are learning more about how the Chapter 11 system actually works. The bad news is that every study suggests it is more complicated than previously imagined.

In the following sections we will study the details of the provisions mentioned here and several other technical provisions as well. It is important to keep in mind a dual purpose in studying these Code provisions: The technical law must be mastered, but its true function lies in how it can be used in the constant negotiation and leveraging in the informal workout or the going-concern sale, whether in Chapter 7 or in Chapter 11.

B. THE AUTOMATIC STAY AND ADEQUATE PROTECTION

1. *General Considerations*

Among all the advantages to a debtor of bankruptcy reorganization, the most immediate is the automatic stay. As lawsuits proliferate, as suppliers threaten to reclaim their goods, as bankers mutter "setoff" in increasingly unpleasant meetings, the "great freeze" of the automatic stay becomes immensely important and attractive. By the same token the mere threat of the bankruptcy stay acts as a strong incentive for secured creditors, usually the largest and most powerful of creditors, to hold off foreclosure or repossession. They know that stay-lifting litigation is difficult, time consuming, and expensive, and that the stay is unlikely to be lifted in the early days of a Chapter 11. Creditors are equally aware that a repossession immediately preceding (and perhaps triggering) bankruptcy will not improve the creditor's position. The TIB or DIP can force return of the property to the debtor.

On the other hand, the debtor and its counsel must realize that stay litigation will be filed by creditors early in the case and that the court must act on a request to lift the stay within 30 days or the stay will automatically be lifted as to the requesting creditor's collateral. §362(e). They must be aware, too, that the burden will be on the DIP to show the existence of "adequate protection" of the secured party's interest in the collateral. §362(g).

The cases that follow cover issues first introduced in consumer bankruptcy: the effect of the automatic stay and what must be proven to have the stay lifted. The same sections of the Code apply, but the business context presents issues that differ from those raised in most consumer cases.

2. *Scope of the Stay*

It is important to emphasize the power and comprehensiveness of the automatic stay, as well as its central place in the bankruptcy process. Neither the maximization of values in an orderly liquidation nor any attempt at reorganization has any real hope of succeeding unless the court obtains immediate and complete control over the debtor and all of its assets. For that reason the stay must be nationwide (or even worldwide — see pp. 836–872) and it must be strictly enforced. The stay comes into effect automatically and instantly against a large number of people who had no prior notice or opportunity to contest it. Unlike the normal injunction, the stay is imposed by operation of law ex parte. Furthermore, even actions taken in innocent violation of the stay, without notice of the bankruptcy filing, are void or voidable. A majority of circuit courts say "void." Even the minority that holds that any action in violation of the stay is only voidable nonetheless concludes that such actions should almost always be voided. E.g., Easley v. Pettibone Michigan Corp., 990 F.2d 905 (6th Cir. 1993).

Naturally creditors do all they can to avoid the effect of the stay, but they have to remember that the Bankruptcy Code protects an "estate" that represents a host of creditors and other interests, not just the debtor.

The following case involves a debtor and creditor who saw the possibility of bankruptcy on the horizon as they negotiated an arrangement to try to get the mortgage paid. The question is whether their two-party deal binds the post-petition estate and all the other creditors.

═══ FARM CREDIT OF CENTRAL FLORIDA, ACA v. POLK ═══
160 B.R. 870 (M.D. Fla. 1993)

KOVACHEVICH, District Judge. . . .

I

Polk and Farm Credit entered into a Forbearance Agreement on May 1, 1992, whereby Farm Credit agreed to extend the date of the foreclosure sale in exchange for Polk agreeing not to contest a motion for relief from stay by Farm Credit in the event that Polk filed for bankruptcy protection. The Bankruptcy Court found that a prepetition agreement that entitled Appellant to an immediate lifting of the automatic stay, in and of itself, is not sufficient to lift the stay unless there is a showing of other criteria, such as bad faith.

Farm Credit contends that while Polk cannot contract away his right to file for protection under the bankruptcy laws, he can enter into a prepetition agreement limiting and/or waiving rights available to him under those laws. Further, Farm Credit asserts that the Bankruptcy Court erred because Polk cannot be allowed to circumvent the contractual terms he voluntarily entered into under the Forbearance Agreement. Farm Credit relies on a series of single asset bankruptcy decisions to support its argument that a prepetition waiver of rights should be enforceable. . . . A review of the underlying facts of the cases cited by Farm Credit does confirm that in each case the Bankruptcy Court, expressly or impliedly, determined that the debtor could not effectively reorganize. This Court agrees that the fact patterns existing in this line of cases are not present in the instant case.

Unlike the debtors in that line of cases, Polk has operated significant business enterprises since the mid-1950's. These business enterprises include ranching operations, management of substantial commercial and investment properties and a major heavy machinery repair business. These business enterprises employ a number of people, generate substantial income and involve the types of activity for which Chapter 11 was designed.

Additionally, Polk has a significant number of creditors, both secured and unsecured, and his proposed plan of reorganization provides for the treatment of 17 separate classes of claims and the payment in full of $12,000,000.00 in obligations. This Court concurs with Appellee, Polk, that courts that have held that a prepetition waiver of the §362 automatic stay provision is valid and enforceable have done so in single asset bankruptcy cases where bad faith existed and the court determined that there was no prospect for a successful reorganization. Those cases do not support the claim of Farm Credit.

This Court also agrees with Appellee, Polk, that the automatic stay is a key component of federal bankruptcy law. In a Chapter 11 reorganization proceeding, the stay prevents the dissipation or diminution of the debtor's assets while rehabilitative efforts are undertaken. The stay goes into effect without regard to conduct by the debtor or his creditors. Relief from the automatic stay must be authorized by the Bankruptcy Court. The stay prevents certain creditors from gaining a preference for their claims against the debtor and, in general, avoids interference with the orderly liquidation or rehabilitation of the debtor. . . .

. . . The secured creditor in In re Sky Group Intl., Inc., 108 B.R. 86, 88 (Bankr. W.D. Pa. 1989), argued that the debtor had waived the stay pursuant to an agreement. . . . The Bankruptcy Court reasoned that granting a creditor relief from stay simply because the debtor elected to waive protection afforded to the debtor by the automatic stay ignores the fact that the stay is designed to protect all creditors and to treat them equally. Since the purpose of the stay is to protect the creditors, as well as Polk, Polk could not have unilaterally waived the automatic stay against the interest of his creditors. It is the opinion of this Court that the Bankruptcy Court's holding that prepetition agreements providing for the lifting of the stay are "not per se binding on the debtor, as a public policy position," is consistent with the purposes of the automatic stay to protect the debtor's assets, provide temporary relief from creditors and promote equality of distribution among the creditors by forestalling a race to the courthouse. The automatic stay provision is intended to preclude the opportunity of one bankruptcy creditor to pursue a remedy against the debtor to the disadvantage of other bankruptcy creditors and thus, to promote the orderly administration of the bankrupt's estate. No other creditors were involved in the prepetition agreement, nor did the Bankruptcy Court approve this agreement. The policy behind the automatic stay is to protect the debtor's estate from being depleted by creditors' lawsuits and seizures of property before the debtor has had a chance to marshal the estate's assets and distribute them equitably among creditors. The Bankruptcy Court correctly determined that the agreement to waive the automatic stay was not self-executing. . . .

[The district court went on to uphold on the merits the Bankruptcy Court decision refusing to lift the stay under section 362(d).]

[A]ffirmed.

================================

Notwithstanding the sweep of the Code language, the automatic stay provision is not absolute. A long list of exceptions to the stay is provided in section 362(b) and Congress substantially lengthened the list in the 2005 Amendments. But, as the following case demonstrates, the exceptions are often narrowly construed. In addition, the broad powers of section 105 may be invoked to extend the reach of the stay even further.

═══════════ UNITED STATES v. SEITLES ═══════════
106 B.R. 36 (S.D.N.Y. 1989)

KRAM, District Judge.

On January 12, 1988, the United States (hereinafter "government") commenced this action against defendant Westbrook [Publishing Co.] and its president and sole remaining executive, defendant [Victor] Seitles, under the False Claims Act, 31 U.S.C. §3729 et seq. The government seeks treble damages and civil penalties against the defendants, jointly and severally, in the amount of $1,666,769.00, comprising $278,923.00 in actual damages trebled ($836,769.00) plus civil penalties of up to $830,000.00.

[After the corporate debtor filed Chapter 11, the debtor and its president Seitles asked the court to stay the pending government case in federal district court in order to permit the bankruptcy court to adjudicate the government's claim in bankruptcy.]

BACKGROUND

This claim arises under the same set of facts and circumstances that led to the conviction by guilty plea of defendant Seitles for conspiring with and bribing an officer of the United States Government Printing Office. In that criminal action, United States v. Victor Seitles, S 86 Cr. 1007 (PKL), the government sought restitution in the amount of approximately $278,000.00, the figure alleged to be the amount of actual damages in the present case. In sentencing defendant Seitles in the criminal matter, Judge Peter K. Leisure heard argument by both government and defendant as to the actual amount of damages suffered. Judge Leisure ordered defendant Seitles to pay $44,000.00 restitution to the Government, representing Seitles' approximate profit realized from the illegally-obtained printing jobs.

On January 20, 1989, Defendant Westbrook filed a petition for reorganization in the United States Bankruptcy Court for the Eastern District of New York pursuant to the Bankruptcy Code, Chapter 11 of the United States Code. Defendants now move this Court to stay Plaintiff's False Claims Act claim against Westbrook in light of the pending bankruptcy proceedings. They argue that, as to Westbrook, this action is subject to the automatic stay provision of the Bankruptcy Code (11 U.S.C. §362(a)) and that, as to Seitles, this action should be stayed in the exercise of this Court's discretion. The government argues, on the other hand, that the automatic stay does not apply to claims brought by the government under the False Claims Act, and furthermore, that there is no good reason to grant a stay to non-debtor codefendant Seitles.

DISCUSSION

I.   Automatic Stay Provision

The purpose of a voluntary petition for Bankruptcy under Chapter 11 is to enable debtors to obtain the court's protection against their creditors.[1] To that end, the federal reorganization provisions call for an automatic stay of most judicial proceedings against debtors. . . .

One purpose of the automatic stay is to allow debtors a "breathing spell" from their creditors. Another purpose of §362(a)(l) is to protect creditors by providing for the orderly resolution of their claims.

Subsection (b) provides for a few exceptions to the Automatic Stay. . . .

[Section 362(b)(4) and (5)] function to "permit governmental units to pursue actions to protect the public health and safety" even when the target of such enforcement actions is in bankruptcy. In re Greenwald, 34 B.R. 954, 956-57 (Bankr. S.D.N.Y. 1983) (quoting 124 Cong. Rec. H 11092 (daily ed., Sept. 28, 1978), reprinted in 1978 U.S. Code Cong. & Ad. News 5787, 6436, 6444-45). In carving out these exceptions, Congress intended to combat the risk that defendants could frustrate "necessary governmental functions" by seeking refuge in bankruptcy court.

The question that arises before this Court is whether the present governmental action under the False Claims Act is a "necessary governmental function" geared towards the "protect[ion of] the public health and safety," or instead, whether this claim is a proprietary governmental function aimed at the protection of pecuniary interests. The government asserts that the "public policy and deterrent" purposes of this action are to "recover damages resulting from [defendants'] fraud upon the government and bribery and corruption of a public official, and to deter other similar conduct." Debtor-defendant alleges that "Plaintiff is attempting to circumvent the automatic stay in order to protect its pecuniary interest in the property of the debtor."

Courts examining the legislative history of §362 usually construe the police and regulatory powers exception narrowly, see, e.g., In re Wellham, 53 B.R. 195, 197 (Bankr. M.D. Tenn. 1985). . . . False Claims Act claims are usually thought to be subject to the automatic stay provisions of §362(a)(l). Most recently, in In the Matter of Chateaugay, et al., No. 86 B 11270 (Bankr. S.D.N.Y., Sept. 29, 1988), the Court approvingly quotes the findings of judges in two other jurisdictions to the effect that the False Claims Act may not "properly be characterized as an enforcement of police or regulatory powers but is merely an action for damages." Id., Slip Op. at 51.

The *Chateaugay* Court followed the two tests laid out in *Commonwealth* and *Wellham*, the "pecuniary purpose" test and the "public policy"

---

1. Section 301 of the Bankruptcy Code provides:

A voluntary case under a chapter of this title [11 USCS §§101 et seq.] is commenced by the filing with the bankruptcy court of a petition under such chapter by an entity that may be a debtor under such chapter. The commencement of a voluntary case under a chapter of this title constitutes an order for relief under such chapter.

test, to determine whether a government claim falls within the §362(b)(4) exception to the automatic stay. The pecuniary purpose test examines

> "whether the government's proceeding relates primarily to the protection of the government's pecuniary interest in the debtor's property and to matters of public safety. Those proceedings which relate primarily to matters of public safety are excepted from the stay."

Chateaugay at 47 (quoting In re Commerce Oil Co, 847 F.2d 291, 295 (6th Cir. 1988)). The "public policy" test "distinguish[es] between proceedings that adjudicate private rights and those that effectuate public policy. Those proceedings that effectuate a public policy are excepted from the stay." Id. As a guide, the *Chateaugay* and *Wellham* courts recommend examining whether the government in the action in question is "engaging in an action which affects the immediate parties to the action or whether it concerns a wider group subject to the authority of the governmental unit." *Chateaugay*, supra, Slip Op. at 48.

The Pecuniary Purpose Test

Wellham involved a False Claims Act suit against a supplier of substandard metals to an agency of the United States Department of Defense. In that case, by the time the False Claims Act claim was filed, the debtor had already reached an agreement with the U.S. Attorney and was no longer providing the government with metal supplies. The *Wellham* court found that those facts did not satisfy the tests for excepting the automatic stay because the government's claim did not relate to a continuing threat to public safety. "The civil action . . . does not purport to stop any continuing misconduct by the debtor, who is no longer providing material to the government." 53 B.R. at 198.

By contrast, in In re Commerce Oil Co., 847 F.2d 291 (6th Cir. 1988), the Tennessee Commissioner of Health and Environment successfully obtained an exception to the automatic stay under the police power exception. In that case, the State sought an injunction against defendant company for illegally discharging brine into a creek and sought damages and civil penalties against the company. The Sixth Circuit found that the primary purpose of the State's suit was the protection of public health and safety, and the proprietary or pecuniary reward in assessing penalties was only of secondary importance.

According to these precedents, the presence or absence of continuing harm as well as a threat to public health is relevant in determining the applicability of §362(b)(4). Similarly to *Wellham* and in contrast to *Commerce Oil*, the present case involves no threat to public health or safety. The fraudulently obtained printing contracts posed only a monetary, not a safety, threat to the government. Furthermore, as in *Wellham*, defendants no longer suppl[y] printing services to the United States Government Printing Office and in fact Seitles has already been convicted and sentenced in connection with the underlying fraud. This civil action thus does not serve to stop any continuing misconduct by the debtor. Because the harm caused by Seitles and Westbrook is neither continuing nor health-related, the government may not obtain an exception to the automatic stay in this case under the pecuniary interest test.

The Public Policy Test

Neither does the "public policy" test indicate that this suit should be excepted from the automatic stay. The government contends that there are public policy reasons to pursue this False Claims Act suit, namely, reimbursement of damages incurred by the government because of defendants' actions and deterrence of other similar conduct by defendants and others. Under similar facts, the *Chateaugay, Commonwealth Cos.,* and *Wellham* courts disposed of this issue without hesitation. "While the government has articulated a public policy reason for continuing the action, the Court is not convinced that the reason propounded is the government's primary motivation." *Chateaugay,* supra, Slip Op. at 6.

Several factors in the present case point to the same conclusion. As to reimbursement of loss, defendant Seitles has already been ordered by Judge Leisure in the related criminal matter to pay to the government restitution in the amount of $44,000.00. As to the deterrent value of the government's present civil action, that purpose has been served to a significant degree by the criminal action in which defendant Seitles was sentenced to a suspended prison term, community service and restitution. Finally, it is noted that the amount that the government alleges in actual damages, $278,000.00, is approximately the same amount it sought, unsuccessfully, in Judge Leisure's courtroom. The similarity of those figures suggests that the government in this case is attempting to recover the damages that it could not obtain in the prior matter, a purely pecuniary endeavor which may be addressed after the orderly settlement of the bankrupt Westbrook estate. . . .

Therefore, this Court grants defendants' motion and holds that the stay of 11 U.S.C. §362(a) applies to the government's claim.

II.　Stay of Proceeding Against Defendant Seitles

Defendant Seitles has moved the court for a stay of these proceedings pursuant to 11 U.S.C. §105 pending a final resolution of plaintiff's claims against Westbrook in Bankruptcy Court. The government contends that a stay is inappropriate as to Seitles.

The automatic stay provision of §362(a) stays actions only against those who have filed for bankruptcy. It is well established that non-debtors, even non-debtor codefendants such as Seitles, are not entitled to §362 relief.

Section 105(a) of the Bankruptcy Code states that

> The Court may issue any order, process, or judgment that is necessary or appropriate to carry out the provisions of this title.

Section 105 enables this court, in the exercise of its equity powers, to stay proceedings not covered by the automatic stay provisions of 11 U.S.C. §362(a). However, non-debtor stays are not to be granted freely; Bankruptcy Judge Lifland cautions: "Section 105 does not have a life of its own and this extension may only be accomplished within the proper boundaries of Section 362." *Johns-Manville,* supra, 26 B.R. at 414-15, quoted in *Anje Jewelry,* [47 B.R. 485, 486-87 (Bankr. E.D.N.Y. 1983)].

The primary considerations for determining when a non-debtor codefendant may properly be granted a stay under §105 are: "(a) irreparable harm and (b) either (1) likelihood of success on the merits or (2) sufficiently serious questions going to the merits to make them a fair ground for litigation and a balance of hardships tipping decidedly toward the party requesting the preliminary relief."

One element of irreparable harm is "interference with the rehabilitative process," 2 Collier on Bankruptcy ¶362.05 (15th ed. 1982). This test is met when the action against the non-debtor codefendant is so "inextricably interwoven" with the affairs of the debtor that it would "substantially hinder the debtor's reorganization effort."

In *Ms. Kipps,* the codefendant was the non-debtor president of two bankrupt companies which continued their operations as debtors in possession. The bankrupt companies were sued by a labor union for certain unpaid employee benefit contributions. The court extended the companies' §362 stay to the debtor's principal pursuant to §105. It found that "requiring him [the president] to maintain a defense in another forum will necessarily detract from his efforts to operate and rehabilitate the debtor corporations." Id. at 93. Similarly, in the present case, Seitles is the president and sole remaining executive officer of Westbrook. He is responsible for overall management and supervision of the company, which operates as a debtor-in-possession. The government's action against him is "inextricably interwoven" with its claims against Westbrook such that defending himself against it would necessarily detract from his ability to continue Westbrook's printing operations. Therefore, a §105 stay is necessary and appropriate to enable Seitles to devote his full attention to rehabilitating Westbrook.

The government urges that §105 relief not be granted to Seitles. It cites In re Anje Jewelry Co. as an example of a case where the non-debtor president of a debtor corporation was denied a stay under the court's equitable powers. That case, however, is distinguishable on its facts. There, the president of Anje Jewelry allegedly signed a bad check issued by the company. The complexity of the action and the amount in dispute was considered "relatively insignificant" by the court.

Here, by contrast, the amount of damages actually suffered by the government remains hotly disputed. . . .

The complexity of the issue of damages in this case also persuades the Court to find the presence of "sufficiently serious questions going to the merits" plus a weighty "balance of hardships" tipping towards defendant Seitles. . . .

Finally, it is most efficient for the claims against Seitles and Westbrook to be heard together, because the issues are identical as to each of the defendants. The government admits that "any effort Seitles will have to expend to defend himself personally will be essentially identical to that necessary to defend his company, Westbrook. Principles of judicial economy dictate that all the claims against Westbrook and Seitles be settled in one proceeding." Government's brief at 22-23. Therefore, because this Court has determined that these proceedings are automatically stayed as against defendant Westbrook pursuant to 11 U.S.C. §362, the interest of judicial economy is served by staying these proceedings as to defendant Seitles as well.

CONCLUSION

For the reasons stated above, this Court grants defendant Westbrook's motion for a stay of this action under 11 U.S.C. §362(a), and grants defendant Seitles' motion for a stay pursuant to 11 U.S.C. §105.

This action is hereby placed on the suspense docket for the duration of the stay.

So ordered.

Notice what happened here: Not only did the umbrella of the automatic stay protect the corporate debtor from prosecution under the False Claims Act, its extension through section 105 also protected the corporate president who did not even file for bankruptcy. Not a bad deal. On the other hand, this is only a stay — not a permanent release. The music may have stopped for the company and its president long enough to let them get the business's affairs in order, but it will resume.

3. Lifting the Stay

Most creditors readily acknowledge that the stay applies to them, but they ask the court to lift the stay under section 362. The most important point to have in mind in reading the next case is that section 362(d) lists three alternative tests for lifting the stay, and the secured party can win by successfully invoking any of them. The first alternative, lack of "adequate protection," requires the court to go outside section 362 to section 361, where "adequate protection" is defined.

In re ROGERS DEVELOPMENT CORP.
2 B.R. 679 (Bankr. E.D. Va. 1980)

SHELLEY, Bankruptcy Judge.

On November 1, 1979, the Debtors filed their petition for relief pursuant to Chapter 11 of the Bankruptcy Code. As a result, the automatic stay provisions of Bankruptcy Code §362 (§362) became applicable. On November 9, 1979, the Plaintiffs commenced this adversary proceeding by filing two complaints, one against Rogers Development Corp. (Rogers) and one against Beaverdam Farms, Inc. (Beaverdam) in which complaints the

Plaintiffs sought relief pursuant to Bankruptcy Code §362(d)(1) and (2) from the automatic stay. . . .

STATEMENT OF THE CASE

The pertinent facts as established by the pleadings, stipulations and the evidence at the hearings are as follows. Rogers and Beaverdam are Virginia corporations which were incorporated on January 18, 1972, and May 17, 1971, respectively. Rogers and Beaverdam (hereinafter referred to as the Debtors) are engaged in the real estate development and home construction business in the Richmond metropolitan area.

In approximately mid-1976 the Debtors formulated a plan for a development of an 89.7, more or less, acre parcel of unimproved property located in Hanover County, Virginia (hereinafter referred to as the Property). The Property was to be developed for single and multi-family dwellings and was to be called the Villages of Beaverdam Park. Rogers owns an undivided 75 percent interest in the fee simple title to the Property and Beaverdam owns a 25 percent undivided interest. Pursuant to the loan commitments dated October 26, 1976, made by Heritage Savings & Loan Association (Heritage) to the Debtors, Heritage committed to make a $520,000 acquisition and development loan and a $360,000 line of credit construction loan. These loans were closed simultaneously on December 30, 1976. . . .

. . . In approximately May 1978 the Debtors went into default under the acquisition and development loan. Notwithstanding the default on the acquisition and development loan, advances were made by Heritage under the construction loan and construction at the Property site continued and homes were completed and sold. In approximately July 1979 they went into default on the construction loan. As of the date of the preliminary hearing, the Plaintiffs took the position that the total indebtedness of the Debtors to Heritage was $548,188.41. This amount includes total principal and interest, late charges, appraisal fee, and legal fees. This indebtedness the Plaintiffs contend is increasing as a result of interest continuing to accrue at the rate of approximately $63,000 per year. The Debtors, only for purposes of this proceeding, have accepted the validity of Heritage's figures. . . .

Aside from general background information concerning the Debtors and their relationship with Heritage, the main thrust of both the Debtors' and the Plaintiffs' evidence at the preliminary hearing concerned the present fair market value of the Property. The Plaintiffs introduced their evidence as to value through the testimony of Joseph B. Call, III, who qualified as an expert real estate appraiser who does business in the Richmond area. Mr. Call is the appraiser that Heritage had previously employed in November of 1976 to appraise the Property when the loan commitments were made by Heritage. Mr. Call testified that in his opinion the current fair market value of the Property was $704,200. Ronald E. Martin, also qualified as an expert appraiser of real estate and an appraiser in the Richmond area, testified on behalf of the Debtors that in his opinion the Property had a fair market value of $801,000. The Debtors also introduced testimony of a Mr. Phillip N. Duhamel which indicated that Mr. Duhamel's company,

Hanover Craftsman, Incorporated, was currently interested in purchasing some of the Property of the Debtors. The final witness to testify for the Debtors was William D. Bayliss, Esq. Mr. Bayliss is a member of the creditors' committee appointed by the United States Trustee and was speaking for four of the seven creditors represented on the committee. Mr. Bayliss stated that the creditors' committee regards the Property as being essential to the successful reorganization of the Debtors. . . .

CONCLUSIONS OF LAW

Heritage has asserted two grounds for relief from the stay. Heritage has alleged a lack of adequate protection of its interest in property, and alternatively that the Debtors do not have equity in the Property and that the Property is not necessary to an effective reorganization.

In considering the issue of adequate protection the Court notes that the phrase "adequate protection" is not defined in §362 or in any other section of the Bankruptcy Code. Instead §361 of the Bankruptcy Code offers three non-exclusive methods of providing adequate protection to an entity with an interest in property of the debtor. The methods offered in §361(1) (periodic payments) and in §361(2) (additional or replacement lien) have not been proposed by the Debtors. The third method, which is contained in §361(3), is a "catch all," permitting such other means of providing adequate protection "as will result in the realization by such entity of the indubitable equivalent of such entity's interest in such property." Although the Debtors contend that they are providing adequate protection pursuant to §361(3), the Court does not believe that maintenance of the status quo is "granting such other relief" nor is it the "indubitable *equivalent*" (emphasis added) required under that subsection. However, it is the opinion of the Court that a debtor may provide adequate protection by an equity cushion since §361 does not preclude other forms of adequate protection. The District Court in In re Blazon Flexible Flyer, Inc., 407 F. Supp. 865 (N.D. Ohio 1976) found that a bank was "adequately protected" despite the bankruptcy judge's order allowing the debtor in possession to use and consume accounts receivable, because of the surplus of security over debt. Further an "adequate cushion" can itself constitute adequate protection with nothing more. Collier on Bankruptcy, 15th ed. §361.02[3] at pp. 361-369.

Therefore, since an equity cushion can be adequate protection, the amount of the debt and the value of the property must be determined to establish whether an equity cushion in fact exists. The amount of the debt owing to Heritage from the Debtors has been stipulated for purposes of this proceeding by the parties as $548,188.41. However, the fair market value of the Property is in doubt because of the conflicting evidence of the parties as presented by their respective appraisers. Furthermore, conflict exists on which standard of value, i.e. the liquidation value, the full going concern value, or some value in between, is the proper valuation standard for purposes of this proceeding.

Turning first to the standard of valuation to be used, the Court notes that there is no clear direction to the Court by statute. Therefore, at this juncture, the legislative history of §361 is important. It reveals a clear intent to not utilize liquidation value in every bankruptcy proceeding. In 1973 the Commission on the Bankruptcy Laws of the United States had recommended that "a benchmark in determining adequate protection is the liquidation value of the collateral at the date of the petition." Commission on the Bankruptcy Laws Report, House of Representatives Document No. 137, 93rd Cong., 1st Session Part II at 237 (1973). Congress specifically rejected that recommendation. The Senate Report states:

> Neither is it expected that the courts will construe the term value to mean, in every case, forced sale liquidation value or full going concern value. There is wide latitude between those two extremes although forced sale liquidation value will be a minimum. In any particular case, especially a reorganization case, the determination of which entity should be entitled to the difference between the going concern value and the liquidation value must be based on equitable considerations arising from the facts of the case. Finally, the determination of value is binding only for the purposes of the specific hearing and is not to have a res judicata effect. Senate Report No. 95-989, 95th Cong., 2nd Session (1978).

The House Report was substantially the same, rejecting liquidation value in every case and leaving the issue to be decided on a case by case basis. House of Representatives, Report No. 595, 95th Cong., 1st Session 339 (1977). Judge Conrad Cyr noted in In re American Kitchen Foods, Inc., 9 C.B.C. 537, 553 (N.D. Me. 1976) that "the most commercially reasonable disposition practicable in the circumstances should be the standard of value universally applicable in all cases and at every phase of each case." Further, "the nature of the debtor's business, the prospects for rehabilitation, and the nature of the collateral all enter into the determination of the standards of value to be applied." 2 Collier on Bankruptcy, 15th ed. §361.02.

In this case the collateral is primarily real property which by all testimony is appreciating in value. While there was some evidence that the partially completed houses were suffering some deterioration because of weathering and vandalism, the impact of this deterioration in value loses significance when measured against the value of the Property as a whole. Further, the Court realizes that while there is no guarantee that real property will sell, both appraisers stated that given a commercially reasonable time, the Property should sell at or near the fair market value. The Court finds, therefore, that a standard of valuation approximating the fair market value should be and is the "commercially reasonable" standard required given the circumstances of this case.

Since the standard of valuation for purposes of this proceeding is the fair market value it is now necessary to determine what is the fair market value of the Property. The parties, Heritage and Rogers, each presented its valuation evidence through an expert appraiser. The Court finds both experts to be credible with no major discrepancies of significant import in their testimony to tender one more reliable than the other. Both experts were testifying as to the fair market value and were using the same definition provided by the American Institute of Real Estate Appraisers and the Society of Real

Estate Appraisers.[3] The only important difference between the testimony of the two appraisers was the value they attributed to the Property. As the Court has no reason to place greater credence on one expert's testimony than the other's, and recognizing that valuation of property is not an exact science, the Court finds the difference in the values is properly attributable to a difference of professional opinion. The Court, therefore, finds the fair market value as somewhere in between the $801,000 value attributed to the Property by the Debtors and the $704,000 value attributed to it by Heritage. The Court further finds valuation of $750,000 for the purposes of this proceeding is reasonable. However, even if the Court were to find that the value of the Property for purposes of this proceeding is as low as $700,000, as counsel for Heritage argues both in his brief and in oral argument, the Court could still conclude that the Debtors have proven that Heritage is adequately protected by the equity cushion that presently exists between the amount of the loan commitment and the value of the property. . . .

Since the Court has concluded that the value for purposes of this proceeding is approximately $750,000 rather than $700,000 as the Plaintiffs have argued, the equity cushion may well be over $130,000. Although the Plaintiffs are correct that interest and other costs are accruing daily, thereby increasing the amount of the encumbrances against the Property, both appraisers testified that the value of the Property would probably increase over time. This increase in value will help maintain the equity cushion that presently exists by, at least, partially offsetting the increasing amount of indebtedness due to interest and cost continuing to accrue. "Of course in some instances where collateral is appreciating, nothing needs to be done by the trustee as the mere passage of time constitutes adequate protection." 2 Collier on Bankruptcy, 15th ed. §361.01 at 361-366. . . .

The Court is of the opinion that it should conclude that the Plaintiffs are currently adequately protected by the equity cushion that presently exists between the amount of the Debtors' obligation to Heritage and the value of the Property.

Plaintiffs argue in the alternative that they should be granted the relief from stay pursuant to subsection (d)(2) of §362. Section 362(d)(2) is an avenue for relief only from a stay of an action against property and in order for the secured creditor requesting relief to prevail two facts must be proved. First that the Debtor has no equity in the property and second that the property is not necessary to an effective reorganization. It is clear in this

---

3. The definition of fair market value, as defined by the American Institute of Real Estate Appraisers and the Society of Real Estate Appraisers is: "The highest price in terms of money which a property will bring in a competitive and open market under all conditions requisite to a fair sale, the buyer and seller, each acting prudently, knowledgeably, and assuming the price is not affected by undue stimulus." Implicit in this definition is the consummation of a sale as of a specified date in the passing of title from seller to buyer under conditions whereby:

1. Buyer and seller are typically motivated.
2. Both parties are well informed, are well advised, and each acting in what he considers his own best interest.
3. A reasonable time is allowed for exposure in the open market.
4. Payment is made in cash or its equivalent.
5. Financing, if any, is on terms generally available in the community at the specified date and typical for the property type in its locale.

case that the Debtors have no equity in the Property as claims of over a million dollars are outstanding against the Property which has been determined for the purpose of this hearing as having a value of $750,000. The Debtors, however, claim that since the real estate is the only asset and that the intended purpose of their business is the developing and selling of real estate, the Property is necessary to an effective reorganization. The Debtors' present financial condition effectively precludes them from acquiring other real estate. If they are denied the use of the real estate they currently own, it becomes abundantly clear that the Debtors' reorganization potential is extinguished.

The commentator in Collier on Bankruptcy, 15th ed. makes the following comments concerning relief pursuant to the requirements of §362(d)(2):

> This alternative [362(d)(2)] will be of little practical value to creditors in reorganization cases since in most cases the property will be needed for an effective reorganization, although the argument may exist that not every asset will be necessary for an *effective* reorganization. The reference to an "effective" reorganization should require relief from the stay if there is no reasonable likelihood of reorganization due to creditor dissent or feasibility considerations. The lack of equity test should be most relevant in liquidation cases where rehabilitation is not being sought and where if there is no equity to be realized for junior interest there is no reason to continue the stay. 2 Collier on Bankruptcy, 15th ed. ¶362.07[2] at pp. 362-368 (footnotes deleted — emphasis in original).

The Plaintiffs presented no evidence that the Property is not needed for an effective reorganization. The Debtors have shown that without this Property there cannot be a reorganization. The Court cannot determine that there is no reasonable likelihood of reorganization due to creditor dissent. The junior creditors do not dissent in this case. In fact the majority of the creditors' committee oppose the relief from stay being granted and desire that the Debtors be allowed an attempt to reorganize. The Court at this time cannot find that a reorganization is not feasible. It is early in the case. The plan has not been submitted. There is no other evidence before the Court that would allow it to determine that a reorganization is not feasible for the Debtors. Therefore, although the Debtors have no equity in the Property, the Property is necessary for the Debtors to effectively reorganize and relief from stay pursuant to §362(d)(2) should not be granted.

Although relief is being denied at this time (and properly so because of a finding of adequate protection to the Plaintiffs and the need of the Property for an effective reorganization), the safeguards of adequate protection to the secured creditor must remain paramount and thus denial in no way precludes subsequent similar complaints, nor does it portend a successful reorganization. The Debtors cannot ignore the rights of the Plaintiffs because any disposition of the real estate by the Debtors involves the disturbance of the security interest of the Plaintiffs which of necessity will require compliance with §363(f). In addition, the ultimate test of an acceptable and confirmable plan must be met. §§1126, 1129.

Once again, the court reminds the parties that stay litigation is about the immediate move. It will not insulate the debtor from a subsequent effort to lift stay if something changes nor will it relieve the debtor from the need to get a plan confirmed. Even so, staying alive to fight another day always feels good to the prevailing party.

4.   *Payments While the Chapter 11 Is Pending*

Not all adequate protection litigation is a direct attack on the automatic stay. Instead, such litigation often focuses on how much the debtor must pay to the creditor during the proceeding in order to provide adequate protection to the secured creditor. Only if the debtor cannot make the adequate protection payments does the litigation lead to lifting the stay.

There may be a conflict between expert appraisers on property valuation or a battle of the crystal balls over what will happen to the local economy. If a court requires an adequate protection payment, and the amount of that payment is too high for the business's cash flow to cover, the reorganization effort is usually over. The debtor faces immediate repossession of critical assets, and the business generally folds. As a result, the determination of what is required for adequate protection, much like the motion to lift the stay, is often a life-or-death struggle for a post-filing debtor. (You may have noticed by now that Chapter 11 is a bit like a video game: nearly every point along the path toward reorganization presents some challenge that can result in the death of the business trying to reorganize.)

As we have seen, there can be little question about the need to provide adequate protection against a decline in the value of collateral during the proceeding. Once the difficult questions of valuation, depreciation rates, and future market probabilities have been resolved, the debtor must provide protection against the secured creditor's anticipated loss of collateral value. The hard legal questions in those cases turn on the nature of the adequate protection to be provided. In particular, whether an equity cushion or additional lien will suffice or whether the debtor must make cash payments to balance the decline in value is often a critical question to a cash-squeezed debtor.

Adequate protection payments can sometimes be confused with interim interest payments. All creditors — oversecured, undersecured, and unsecured — add pre-petition interest to their claims, according to the terms of their contracts or applicable nonbankruptcy law. §502. The secured creditor who has excess collateral is also entitled to add interest to its allowed secured claim under section 506(b) during the pendency of the bankruptcy. Its claim grows until it hits the value of the collateral. Undersecured creditors, like their unsecured cousins, are denied that opportunity. §§502, 506(b). That point was hotly disputed for years, but settled by the Supreme Court in United Savings Association v. Timbers of Inwood Forest, 484 U.S. 365 (1988).

When a Chapter 11 plan is confirmed, the calculation of interest is like that in Chapter 13: Secured creditors will be entitled to the present value of their allowed secured claims, while unsecured creditors will be entitled to the present value of what they would have received in a

Chapter 7 liquidation. §1129(a)(7). A moment's reflection shows that the test is the same for each in economic substance: The creditor must be no worse off in a reorganization than it would have been if there were a liquidation. This means that oversecured creditors will receive the full amount of their claims, including post-petition, pre-confirmation interest (up to the value of the collateral) and they will then earn interest post-confirmation on the allowed amount that has accrued up to the time of the confirmation. Undersecured creditors will get the value of their collateral at the time of filing, plus post-confirmation interest on that amount, plus payment for the deficiency part of their claim at whatever rate the unsecured creditors get — but no post-petition interest. Unsecured creditors will get at least the amount they would have gotten in a liquidation, plus interest on that amount — but once again, no post-petition interest. In effect, these constraints mean that a business cannot confirm a Chapter 11 plan if it does not at least match, in present value dollars, the liquidation distribution to all the creditors.

One critical question for a business is whether the interest payments that accrue post-filing and pre-confirmation on oversecured debt are due as the case progresses or whether they are added to the allowed secured claim and the amount that must be paid at confirmation. Obviously, if a court holds that a debtor must service the debt at current interest rates or face lifting the stay, the reorganizing business will face an immediate and usually significant cash drain that may seriously dim its reorganization prospects. If the debtor is not required to make such payments, it is in a far better position to mount a successful reorganization without immediate pressure on its cash flow, but the creditor remains at some risk, notwithstanding the guarantees, that something could go wrong.

One class of cases that we singled out for special mention in the introduction to this chapter is the single asset real estate case or SARE. In the 2005 Amendments, Congress expanded a special adequate protection rule for SAREs that it had first applied only to small cases. §§101(51B), 362(d)(3). The special rule responded to complaints that real estate cases were often abusive, filed only to gain delay while a local real estate market turned around. The new rule was designed to ameliorate the problem by forcing the debtor in such cases either to propose a workable plan promptly or to start paying interest on the value of the collateral. Failure to do either would lead to lifting or modifying the stay. In the 2005 Amendments, Congress made the rule applicable to all SAREs. It also adopted some important changes to the rule, giving something to each side. In particular, the single-asset real estate debtors got the right to use rents to make adequate protection payments, an area where case law had often gone against them, while mortgage lenders got the interest rate set at the preexisting contract rate, which helps them in the typical falling market.

5. *Good Faith*

For the most part, only a secured creditor is in a position to seek a lifting of the automatic stay. For other creditors, any hope of an early escape from a

Chapter 11 case is limited to a motion to convert to Chapter 7 or a motion to dismiss. The former will succeed in the first months of a case only if the futility of a Chapter 11 plan is demonstrated. The best hope for the latter may be a claim that the case was filed in bad faith. It appears that such motions rarely win. When they are successful, they may raise fundamental questions about the purposes of bankruptcy that Congress has never explicitly addressed.

One important reason such questions arise is that the United States is unusual in permitting a solvent company to go bankrupt. Most countries require insolvency as a predicate for invocation of the bankruptcy laws. One reason for the United States rule is that it is difficult and expensive to prove insolvency, because it requires valuing the assets and estimating the liabilities. The latter task is especially difficult as to contingent, disputed, or unliquidated liabilities. A second reason is the benefit of early initiation of bankruptcy without waiting until a financial crisis has reached the point of insolvency. It can be argued there is a third reason: preservation of value for the benefit of equity owners. On the other hand, the lack of an insolvency requirement may create occasions for abuse, which the court found in the next case.

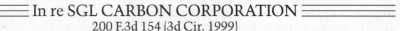

In re SGL CARBON CORPORATION
200 F.3d 154 (3d Cir. 1999)

SCIRICA, Circuit Judge.

* * * * *

I.

SGL Carbon is a Delaware corporation that manufactures and sells graphite electrodes used in steel production. In 1997, the United States Department of Justice commenced an investigation of alleged price-fixing by graphite electrode manufacturers, including the SGL Carbon Group. Soon thereafter, various steel producers filed class action antitrust lawsuits in the United States District Court for the Eastern District of Pennsylvania against SGL Carbon and other graphite electrode manufacturers.

* * * * *

In June 1998, SGL Carbon's German parent SGL AG recorded a charge in Deutschmarks of approximately $240 million as its "best estimate" of the SGL Carbon Group's potential liability in the criminal and civil antitrust litigation. On December 16, 1998, at the direction of SGL AG, SGL Carbon filed a voluntary Chapter 11 bankruptcy petition in the United States District Court for Delaware. In SGL Carbon's Disclosure Statement, in a section addressing "Factors Leading to [the] Chapter 11

Filing," SGL Carbon only discussed the antitrust litigation. The bankruptcy filing contained a proposed reorganization plan under which only one type of creditor would be required to accept less than full cash payment for its account, namely the antitrust plaintiffs who obtained judgments against SGL Carbon. Under the plan, potential antitrust judgment creditors would receive credits against future purchases of SGL Carbon's product valid for 30 months following the plan's confirmation. The proposed plan also bars any claimant from bringing an action against SGL Carbon's affiliates, including its parent SGL AG, "based on, relating to, arising out of, or in any way connected with" their claims against SGL Carbon.

The next day, on December 17, in a press release, SGL Carbon explained it had filed for bankruptcy "to protect itself against excessive demands made by plaintiffs in civil antitrust litigation and in order to achieve an expeditious resolution of the claims against it." The press release also stated:

> SGL CARBON Corporation believes that in its case Chapter 11 protection provides the most effective and efficient means for resolving the civil antitrust claims. . . .
>
>   . . . . .
>
> "SGL CARBON Corporation is financially healthy," said Wayne T. Burgess, SGL CARBON Corporation's president. "If we did not face [antitrust] claims for such excessive amounts, we would not have had to file for Chapter 11. We expect to continue our normal business operations."
>
>   . . . . .
>
> However, because certain plaintiffs continue to make excessive and unreasonable demands, SGL CARBON Corporation believes the prospects of ever reaching a commercially practicable settlement with them are remote. After much consideration, SGL CARBON Corporation determined that the most appropriate course of action to address the situation without harming its business was to voluntarily file for chapter 11 protection.

* * *

Contemporaneous with the press release, SGL AG Chairman Robert Koehler conducted a telephone conference call with securities analysts, stating that SGL Carbon was "financially healthier" than before and denying the antitrust litigation was "starting to have a material impact on [SGL Carbon's] ongoing operations in the sense that . . . [it was] starting to lose market share." He also stated that SGL Carbon's Chapter 11 petition was "fairly innovative [and] creative" because "usually Chapter 11 is used as protection against serious insolvency or credit problems, which is not the case [with SGL Carbon's petition]."

[The court first followed a number of prior decisions in holding that a Chapter 11 case is subject to dismissal if not filed in good faith.]

i.

[T]he District Court found SGL Carbon's Chapter 11 petition was filed in good faith for two reasons: first, because the distractions caused by the antitrust litigation "posed a serious threat to [SGL Carbon's] continued successful operations," and second, because the litigation might result in a judgment that could cause the company "financial and operational ruin," SGL was required to file when it did. *SGL Carbon*, 233 B.R. at 291. Although mindful of the careful consideration given by the able District Court, we believe each of these findings of fact was clearly erroneous.[11]

Although there is some evidence that defending against the antitrust litigation occupied some officers' time, there is no evidence this "distraction" posed a "serious threat" to the company's operational well being.

* * *

We also find clearly erroneous that SGL Carbon's Chapter 11 petition was filed at the appropriate time to avoid the possibility of a significant judgment that "could very well force [SGL Carbon] out of business." There is no evidence that the possible antitrust judgments might force SGL Carbon out of business. To the contrary, the record is replete with evidence of SGL Carbon's economic strength. [A]t the time SGL Carbon filed its petition, that is, before SGL AG paid its $135 million criminal fine, the $240 million reserve was untouched. In documents accompanying its petition, SGL Carbon estimated the liquidation value of the antitrust claims at $54 million. In contrast, no evidence was presented with respect to the amount sought by the antitrust plaintiffs beyond SGL Carbon's repeated characterization of their being "unreasonable."

Whether or not SGL Carbon faces a potentially crippling antitrust judgment, it is incorrect to conclude it had to file when it did. As noted, SGL Carbon faces no immediate financial difficulty.

The District Court was correct in noting that the Bankruptcy Code encourages early filing. It is well established that a debtor need not be insolvent before filing for bankruptcy protection. It also is clear that the drafters of the Bankruptcy Code understood the need for early access to bankruptcy relief to allow a debtor to rehabilitate its business before it is faced with a hopeless situation.[14] Such encouragement, however, does not open the door to premature filing, nor does it allow for the filing of a bankruptcy petition that lacks a valid reorganizational purpose.

SGL Carbon, therefore, is correct that the Bankruptcy Code does not require specific evidence of insolvency for a voluntary Chapter 11 filing. But SGL Carbon cites no case holding that petitions filed by financially healthy companies cannot be subject to dismissal for cause. At any rate, as we explain more fully, SGL Carbon's ability to meet its debts is but one of

---

11. Although we conclude these findings were clearly erroneous, we do not hold that under the proper circumstances managerial distraction and other litigation harms may not constitute factors contributing to good faith.

14. See, e.g., Alan N. Resnick, Bankruptcy As a Vehicle for Resolving Enterprise-Threatening Mass Tort Liability, 148 U. Pa. L.Rev. ____ (forthcoming 2000) M12.

many factors compelling the conclusion it did not enter Chapter 11 with a valid reorganizational purpose.

We do not hold that a company cannot file a valid Chapter 11 petition until after a massive judgment has been entered against it. Courts have allowed companies to seek the protections of bankruptcy when faced with pending litigation that posed a serious threat to the companies' long term viability.

Although SGL Carbon may have to file for bankruptcy in the future, such an attenuated possibility standing alone is not sufficient to establish the good faith of its present petition.

ii.

We also consider whether other evidence establishes the good faith of SGL Carbon's petition, that is, whether the totality of facts and circumstances support a finding of good faith. Courts have not been unanimous about what constitutes "good faith" in the Chapter 11 filing context.

Courts, therefore, have consistently dismissed Chapter 11 petitions filed by financially healthy companies with no need to reorganize under the protection of Chapter 11.

The absence of a valid reorganizational purpose and the consequent lack of good faith by SGL Carbon is evident here. SGL Carbon's financial disclosure documents give no indication the company needed to reorganize under Chapter 11 protection. Prior to filing, SGL Carbon had assets of $400 million and liabilities of only $276 million, or a net worth of $124 million. In addition, there is no evidence that SGL Carbon had difficulty meeting its debts as they came due, that it had any overdue debts, or that it had defaulted on any debts. Nor is there any evidence that SGL had any difficulty raising or borrowing money, or otherwise had impaired access to the capital markets.

Statements by SGL Carbon and its officials confirm the company did not need to reorganize under Chapter 11.

We are not convinced by SGL Carbon's claim that a Chapter 11 filing was necessary because we see no evidence the antitrust litigation was significantly harming its business relationships with the antitrust plaintiffs. For example, none of SGL Carbon's officers stated that any customer terminated its purchases from the company because of the litigation. As noted, SGL AG Chairman Koehler denied the litigation was having a material impact on SGL Carbon's customer relationships.

Based on the facts and circumstances of this case, we conclude SGL Carbon's Chapter 11 petition lacks a valid reorganizational purpose and consequently lacks good faith making it subject to dismissal "for cause" under 11 U.S.C. §1112(b).

C.

In reaching our conclusion, we are cognizant that it is growing increasingly difficult to settle large scale litigation. We recognize that companies that face massive potential liability and litigation costs continue to seek ways to rapidly conclude litigation to enable a continuation of their business and to maintain access to the capital markets. As evidenced by SGL Carbon's actions in this case, the Bankruptcy Code presents an inviting safe harbor for such companies. But this lure creates the possibility of abuse which must be guarded against to protect the integrity of the bankruptcy system and the rights of all involved in such proceedings. Allowing SGL Carbon's bankruptcy under these circumstances seems to us a significant departure from the use of Chapter 11 to validly reorganize financially troubled businesses.

IV.

For the reasons stated, we will reverse the judgment of the District Court and remand to the District Court so that it may dismiss SGL Carbon's Chapter 11 petition.

By contrast, some bankruptcies have happy endings at the very start.

Tarver: From Bankruptcy to Champ in 8 Days

Antonio Tarver's stunning victory over Roy Jones Jr. on Saturday night could not have come at a better time for him.

Just eight days before winning the WBC light heavyweight title, Tarver went broke, filing for Chapter 11 protection in federal bankruptcy court in Tampa.

Tarver earned more than $2 million for the fight, the biggest payday of his career, plus a $100,000 bonus that promoter Don King paid him at a post-fight party. And the opportunities for him now will be limitless after his second-round TKO of Jones.

King, who promoted the rematch and has three heavyweight title holders — Chris Byrd, John Ruiz and Lamon Brewster — under contract, said, "Antonio is certainly a candidate for a heavyweight fight."

"I fought for peanuts for years," Tarver told The Washington Post. "I fought in all these small places, like the Blue Horizon [in Philadelphia], and I more than paid my dues." (ESPN.com news services, May 17, 2004.)

Problem Set 19

19.1. Phoenix American Commercial Bank has a perfected security interest in all the equipment of Big City Bike Repair Shop, to secure a loan at prime plus 6 percent with a current balance of $180,000. Big City is currently in a Chapter 11, and Phoenix American wants your help.

The equipment consists mostly of specialized repair tools. The tools were purchased one year ago for $200,000 and have an expected life span of ten years, with no salvage value. Big City took a depreciation deduction on the tools of 20 percent for tax purposes last year. The wholesale value of similar new tools would be $140,000 and the retail value of such tools this year is $220,000. The owner of Big City thinks that he could sell the tool set to a bike repair shop just getting under way in another city for $160,000, but once this buyer has bought his tools, the Big City owner doesn't know anyone else who could use similar tools.

What do you advise Phoenix American to ask for in the Chapter 11? See §§361, 362.

19.2. Cameron Cohen is a major player in the high stakes game of family entertainment. Cameron's World Inc. ("CWI") now operates a number of theme parks in secondary markets. A series of nasty accidents on the roller coaster in Tulsa, combined with a lengthy labor dispute, caused revenues to plummet, sending the company into Chapter 11. Cameron is convinced he can turn things around, but cash is tight. He is furious when AtlantaFirst moves to lift the stay so that it can sell the corporate jet. At the time of the bankruptcy filing, AtlantaFirst was owed $1.8 million on a 12 percent note secured only by the jet. Cameron loves that jet, and he insists (his word) that you keep it for him. You had the jet appraised, and discover that it is worth about $1.1 million. According to the appraiser, a four-year-old jet has an expected lifespan of about 40 years, and if it is properly maintained, its value isn't likely to change much for at least a couple of years. What will you argue at the hearing, and what will likely happen? See §§361, 362.

19.3. Your client is Sam Sager, a well-to-do businessman who has just completed his multi-million dollar dream house. He bought most of the lamps and light fixtures from Roy Resendiz, Inc. (RRI), a corporation owned by Roy who has used his flair for design to develop a good business. Sam and Roy got into a major dispute about many of the fixtures, each of which was unique and expensive. Sam hired you to sue Roy for breach of warranty and fraud, which you did about six months ago. Sam told you, "I want you to drive him into the ground." When you demurred, saying it was not your practice to use litigation to harass people, Sam replied, "I'm not asking you to do anything you think is wrong, but go after him as hard as the law allows. He deserves it."

You agreed you would be aggressive in the litigation, and you have been. Roy just finished his third deposition session and you are going to court to complain about gaps in his answers for the third time. You expect to bring him back for more. You have filed three motions for partial summary judgment on various aspects of the case and otherwise kept Raul Smith, RRI's lawyer, in court every week. You've just given notice of three experts you've hired for testimony at the trial. RRI made an offer of settlement last week, but Sam will settle for nothing less than the full amount he has demanded. He said, "Roy could sell RRI's inventory and equipment and have just enough to pay me and his lawyer in full. Then I'd be paid, he'd be out of business, and that would be that."

This morning you got a notice that RRI has filed in Chapter 11. It lists just two debts, about $50,000 owed to his lawyer Raul and the disputed debt to Sam. You call Raul who explains that RRI had to file because the legal expenses were out of hand and Roy couldn't run his business while spending so much time in court and in deposition. Plus Raul claims the stress and anxiety made it impossible for Roy to come up with new designs and the business was falling off as other customers heard about the case.

What should you tell Sam about the effect of the RRI filing? What steps can you tell him you will take to get his case back on track? §§362, 1112(b).

19.4. American Slide, Inc. is a slide rule manufacturer. With the advent of the pocket calculator, the slide rule has fallen into almost total disuse, but owner Sharon Johnson-Cramer has some great ideas for launching ASI into the computer age. American Slide has recently filed a Chapter 11, and its creditor, Heathe Manufacturing, is trying to repossess the only remaining collateral of value, a $50,000 metal stamping machine. Heathe Manufacturing has a valid purchase money security interest in the press for $35,000, and Commerce Bank has a non-PMSI security interest in the press for another $20,000. Can Heathe get the machine? See §362(d).

19.5. Billy D. Woodward has been engaged in Denver commercial development for a dozen years. When the Denver real estate market crashed, Billy D. was badly over-committed and his fortune was wiped out. Billy D. now has $2.5 million in unsecured debt and deficiency judgments against him and $40 million in debt secured by his remaining assets.

Billy D.'s last remaining asset is a Denver office building that is 30 percent occupied. The building cost $45 million to build three years ago, and occupancy was at 50 percent within the first year. But a crash in the regional economy forced many of the tenants out of business or to cheaper quarters, and the building occupancy dropped off to 15 percent last year. Billy D. has scoured the town for tenants and is having some success, as the 30 percent rate reflects. Rather than sell the building for $20 million earlier this year ("a giveaway price," said Billy D.), he filed Chapter 11 a month ago.

Billy D. says that the building occupants now generate enough cash to pay the marginal cost of maintaining the building, but there is no extra income. As occupancy rises, deferred maintenance costs will consume the initial rise, and marginal costs will increase somewhat. At a 65 percent occupancy rate, Billy D. estimates that the building will generate a sufficient profit to begin paying interest on the secured debt. At 80 percent there will be enough to begin paying the unsecured creditors in full.

You represent the FDIC, which has taken over the Atlanta bank that made the loan to Billy D. You recognize that if the Denver market rebounds, you will be paid in full. But you also recognize that if the market does not come back within a year, deferred maintenance will make the building less desirable and more expensive to repair. Moreover, the market could slip even further, especially with many foreclosed properties coming into the market, so that in a year the FDIC might not get more than $12.5 million.

The bookkeeping for Billy D.'s business is complex, so you are not even sure that Billy D. is right about "breaking even" on a cashflow basis. You also can't remember the last time Billy D. made eye contact with you. Furthermore, Billy D. shows no progress toward developing a plan of reorganization. You are beginning to sense that Billy D.'s idea is to park this building in the shelter of a Chapter 11 for as long as possible and wait to see what happens to the market. What strategy do you suggest for the FDIC? See §§361, 362.

19.6. To finance her heavy equipment leasing business, Reenah Kim borrowed $12 million from Bank of the West (BoW), giving the bank a security interest in her long-term leases and underlying equipment. The loan was set up with interest-only payments at 10 percent annually, or $1.2 million in interest each year. Last year, Reenah filed for Chapter 11. Her payments were up to date at the time of filing, and she immediately struck a deal with BoW to make monthly payments of $100,000 in return for BoW withdrawing its adequate protection motion. Reenah was getting the business stabilized when a serious problem last month caused her to miss the eleventh payment to BoW. She believes that she can soon propose a plan, but BoW is unpersuaded. It has moved to lift the stay.

The leases and equipment were valued at $12.2 million at the time of filing, but the equipment is a little older and some of the time on the leases has been used up, so they are now worth about $11.4 million. What will you argue at the hearing? What should happen? §§361, 362(d), 506(b).

C.   OPERATING IN CHAPTER 11

1.   *Who's Running the Show?*

In a liquidation bankruptcy, the debtor and creditors are chiefly concerned with calculating past debt and liquidating non-exempt assets for distribution to creditors. In a Chapter 13 the focus is usually on the debtor's new budget — how much of the debtor's income will be dedicated to paying creditors and whether the payments are adequate. The attention in a Chapter 11 reorganization is fundamentally different. The DIP retains control of the business (now known as the estate) and continues running it. Often, debtor and creditors alike focus on the operation of the business as the central concern of the ongoing Chapter 11.

The amount to be paid to the creditors in Chapter 11 depends in large part on the success of the business. Creditors may complain that the debtor is not running the business in a way that will enhance its likely survival and therefore increase the chance that the creditors will be repaid. Whether they admit it or not, debtors and creditors in almost all contexts are economic partners hoping for the success of the debtor's business, but there's nothing quite like a bankruptcy filing to bring that point home. The creditors' dependence on the debtor, who retains control over the business after demonstrating some degree of business failure, can produce an acrimonious environment for the interim operation of the business. Alternatively, if a new management has taken over at the insistence of one of the creditors (usually the largest and most powerful), then the other creditors may worry that the business is being run to increase the likelihood of repayment to that particular creditor, not all the creditors collectively.

The range of disputes that can arise between debtor and creditors during the operation of the business can run the spectrum from disputes over minor aspects of daily operations to allegations of dishonesty and unfair dealing. In some circumstances creditors complain because the DIP is making business choices that are hostile to the creditors' interests. Some creditors may be interested in asset protection or liquidation, while the DIP may wish to gamble assets in the hope of a long-range comeback. Some debtors will respond to pressure from the chief creditor while other creditor interests suffer. The DIP may be honest, working hard to try to save the business, but at the margins there are often a series of decisions to make that will unavoidably favor one party or another. Jay Lawrence Westbrook, The Control of Wealth in Bankruptcy, 82 Tex. L. Rev. 795 (2004).

Consider a wholesale food distributor. Its hard assets consist of its refrigeration equipment, trucks, computers, and various office equipment, worth perhaps $500,000. Its real value is in its customer relationships, its supply lines, and its knowledge of the retail food industry. The bank that has a security interest in the hard assets looks at its outstanding debt of $400,000 and sees an easy solution for this company: liquidate the business, sell off the hard assets, and pay the bank in full. Whatever is left over can go to the costs of administration and, if there is anything left after that, to pay something to the general unsecured creditors. The unsecured creditors — the suppliers who have sent vegetables and canned goods on credit — see this rather differently. They know that they will make something if the business is liquidated, but they may make much more if the business succeeds. Besides, they can keep a customer, so future profits may offset current losses. The employees will have much the same interests and concerns. The investors in the debtor company are at the opposite end from the secured creditors. They may have subordinated debt or only equity, which means they will see no return on their investment unless the business succeeds. They are often enthusiastic about high-risk, high-reward options, something that may take them from no recovery to a meaningful ownership stake in the business. Finally, the community where the business is located may have a strong interest, generally in the continuation of the business. The community sometimes has leverage in the form of promised infrastructure for real estate and other benefits, but often does not.

If the disputes between the DIP and a group of creditors become really serious, the creditors may seek appointment of a trustee to run the business. §1104. Although a DIP and a trustee have largely coextensive legal duties and powers, the appointment of a trustee has enormous practical importance.

This struggle can be a fight for both the direction and the survival of the business. The following case illustrates one circumstance in which a creditor demands that the DIP be replaced by an outside TIB for the purpose of thwarting the DIP's reorganization plans. The debtor's president is Victor Posner, a well-known takeover specialist of the 1980s.

In re SHARON STEEL CORP.
871 F.2d 1217 (3d Cir. 1989)

GIBBONS, Chief Judge:
Sharon Steel Corporation manufactures steel in a facility located near Sharon, Pennsylvania. The Sharon facility includes two blast furnaces. By

April, 1987, only one of these — number 3 — was operational. Sharon's most efficient blast furnace, number 2, was shut down pending $18 million in repairs. Furthermore, furnace number 3, which was three years overdue for relining, faced imminent shutdown. On April 17, 1987, confronted with $742 million in liabilities, only $478 million in assets, and pressing creditors, Sharon filed a voluntary petition for reorganization under Chapter 11 of the Bankruptcy Code.

Sharon management remained in control of the corporation's operations as debtor-in-possession. At all times relevant to this case, appellant Victor Posner served as Sharon's chairman, president, and chief executive officer. Appellant DWG, under common control with Sharon, provided financial management services to Sharon and other Posner-controlled companies. It operated out of a Miami office building owned by Posner and provided 13,000 square feet of office space to Sharon to house its executive offices, charging Sharon $24 per square foot.

Some five months after Sharon filed for reorganization, the committee, dissatisfied with the progress — or lack thereof — made by Sharon's management, petitioned the bankruptcy court for appointment of a trustee pursuant to 11 U.S.C. §1104. . . .

The bankruptcy court's Opinion on Appointment of a Trustee, dated May 2, 1988, 86 B.R. 455, sets forth its reasons for granting the motion for appointment of a trustee. . . . It cited numerous prepetition transfers of Sharon assets that amounted at best to voidable preferences and at worst to fraudulent conveyances, none of which had been questioned by the debtor-in-possession.[9] Not only had Sharon failed to sue for recovery of these transfers, but the bankruptcy court questioned the current management's ability

---

9. These either preferential transfers or fraudulent conveyances include a $3.7 million wire transfer made by Sharon to DWG on April 16, 1986, apparently in payment of a $3.58 million annual charge including $122,433.21 rent for the chairman's office, $74,465.53 for use of a yacht that Sharon owned, $170,483.26 for airplane usage (although the plane also was owned by Sharon), $230,422.28 for use of the guest apartments in Miami, and $100,833.21 for accommodations in the Waldorf-Astoria; a December 1986 transfer by Sharon to NPC Leasing Company, under common control with Sharon, of title to a yacht and airplane, each minimally valued at $750,000; a March 16, 1987, transfer of 141,000 common shares in Chesapeake Financial Corporation, valued by the trustee at $24 million, to Insurance and Risk Management, also connected to Sharon by interlocking directors, in satisfaction of an antecedent debt of $1,512,493.75; and approximately $16 million in compensation paid to Victor Posner between 1983 and September 1987, including $4.4 million paid by Sharon for his defense in a criminal action for individual tax evasion and conspiracy, and approximately $1.8 in compensation paid to Stephen Posner.

In its conclusions of law, the bankruptcy court held the transfers of the $3.7 million to DWG, the yacht and plane to NPC Leasing, and the 141,000 shares of Chesapeake Financial Corporation to Insurance and Risk Management constituted prima facie voidable preferences. It also held that the 1985 through March 1987 transfers of $9.8 million to Victor Posner and $940,000 to Stephen Posner "were not shown to be for an adequate consideration, and prima facia [sic] constitute fraudulent conveyances." The bankruptcy court also credited expert testimony that valued the Miami office space at $12.50 per square foot and noted that DWG charged Sharon $24.

The trustee has instituted several actions to recover various of these assets for the estate. He has sued Posner in United States district court for reimbursement of the criminal defense costs, excessive compensation paid to him, and damages caused by his mismanagement of the debtor. The trustee also has brought two actions in the bankruptcy court: on August 19, 1988, to obtain books, records and financial information from DWG, Posner, and others; and on March 11, 1988, to recover the 141,000 shares of Chesapeake Financial

to fulfill its fiduciary duty to pursue these claims since Sharon shares common management with the recipients of the transfers, who also owe conflicting fiduciary duties to the recipients. Disclosure of the transfers did not cure the preferential or fraudulent transfers.

The bankruptcy court also faulted Sharon's day-to-day management of the estate. Sharon, which continued to rely on DWG for financial services, had not yet closed out its books for the period preceding reorganization. Thus, not only was the debtor continuing to hemorrhage money at an estimated $2 million per month at a time when steel prices were rising, but the debtor could not even measure the precise size of these losses since it had no postpetition profit and loss statements.

Similarly, the court also criticized Sharon's failure to renegotiate its $30 million working capital loan from the 28% to 30% interest rate originally agreed to a reasonable 14% to 15% — an action that would save Sharon $4 million a year. It also impugned the wisdom (and the propriety) of Sharon's repayment during 1985 and 1986 of $294 million in secured bank loans "in order to facilitate new loans from those banks to other Posner companies." Given Sharon's blast furnace crisis and the fact that the payments left Sharon so cash-poor that it was forced to enter into the $30 million, high-interest working capital loan, it concluded such actions amounted to gross mismanagement.

Last, the bankruptcy court raised an even more fundamental issue when it questioned the $279,872.50 in attorneys' fees expended during the last quarter of 1987 to fight the appointment of the trustee:

> While the equity owners are entitled to representation and to assert their rights, one must speculate whether the expenditure of such resources was appropriate, and whether Sharon's counsel in doing so was fulfilling its fiduciary duty to the debtor's estate, or was defending the private position of the equity owners. The funds expended come from the estate, and in view of the admitted insolvency, will likely be borne chiefly by creditors.

The bankruptcy court determined that the sum of the above behavior amounted to cause under section 1104(a)(1). It also demonstrated the necessity of new management just to keep Sharon operating, therefore implicating the interests of the creditors and equity holders alike specified for appointment of a trustee under subsection (b). . . .

It is settled that appointment of a trustee should be the exception, rather than the rule. H.R. Rep. No. 595, 95th Cong., 1st Sess. 233 (1977), reprinted in 1978 U.S. Code Cong. & Admin. News 5787, 5963, 6192 ("[V]ery often the creditors will be benefitted by continuation of the debtor-in-possession, both because the expense of a trustee will not be required, and the debtor, who is familiar with his business, will be better able to operate it during the reorganization case."). While 11 U.S.C. §1104(a) mandates appointment of a trustee when the bankruptcy court finds cause — seemingly requiring

---

Corporation stock from Insurance and Risk Management. The trustee also filed suit against Posner in the bankruptcy court on June 3, 1988, for the return of 14 original Norman Rockwell oil paintings that belonged to Sharon. In October 1988, the bankruptcy court approved without prejudice a stipulation requiring Posner to return the paintings.

plenary review, "a determination of cause . . . is within the discretion of the court," Committee of Dalkon Shield Claimants, [828 F.2d 239, 242 (4th Cir. 1987)].

Subsection (a)(2) also creates a flexible standard, instructing the court to appoint a trustee when doing so addresses "the interests of the creditors, equity security holders, and other interests of the estate." . . . Because subsection (a)(2) envisions a flexible standard, an abuse of discretion standard offers the most appropriate type of review for this subsection as well. . . .

The bankruptcy court opinion conveys the image of a titanic industrial vessel foundering on the shoals of bankruptcy, steered there by at best careless management practices. These practices include payment of $294 million to secured creditors and $9.8 million and $970,000 without consideration to Victor and Stephen Posner respectively during a period when Sharon was so cash-poor that it could not afford to reline the vital number 2 blast furnace — so cash-poor that to continue operations on a daily basis it borrowed $30 million at 28% to 30% interest.

Other questionable management actions cited by the court include the petition-eve payment of $3.7 million to DWG, transfer of Sharon's yacht and plane to NPC, and transfer of the 141,000 shares of Chesapeake Financial Corporation stock to Insurance and Risk Management. At no time did Sharon's postpetition management try to recover any part of these transfers (or any part of the sums paid to Victor and Stephen Posner).

DWG and Posner claim that the court's November 1988 authorization for the committee to sue for recovery of these transfers cures its failure and eliminates any management conflicts of interest, rendering the court's determination erroneous. In fact, they claim that all of the alleged prepetition incidents of gross mismanagement have been corrected, forcing the court to rely on postpetition mismanagement, which they claim falls short of providing clear and convincing proof that a trustee is required. Specifically, they point to the appointment of Walter Sieckman as chief operating officer, and the court-acknowledged management improvements he had wrought since coming aboard. They also claim that Sharon's bylaws, in compliance with Pennsylvania law, authorized payment of Posner's $4.4 million in legal fees. According to Posner and DWG, these factors make the court's reliance upon the prepetition management problems improper.

For support, they rely on three cases that they contend stand for the proposition that appointment of a trustee is inappropriate where prepetition gross mismanagement has been corrected and no postpetition gross mismanagement has occurred: . . .

These cases present very different scenarios than does the case at hand. . . . [M]anagement here is extremely sophisticated. This sophistication colors interpretation of their actions. While DWG and Posner cite other case law holding that business dealings between a debtor and its subsidiaries or related entities does not per se create a conflict of interests, they ignore the presence of "something more" in this case.

Unlike *General Oil*, Sharon's management appears to have engaged on the eve of bankruptcy in a systematic syphoning of Sharon's assets to other companies under common control. Despite DWG and Posner's contention to the contrary, such behavior raises grave questions about current management's ability to fulfill its fiduciary duty as debtor-in-possession to Sharon's creditors. Judicial intervention enabling the committee to sue for recovery of per se voidable preferences and fraudulent conveyances may have solved that isolated management problem, but it has not cleared up the question about current management's fitness to continue running Sharon Steel and its commitment to see it through to a successful reorganization. See In re Concord Coal Corp., 11 B.R. 552 (Bankr. S.D. W. Va. 1981) (trustee appointed under 11 U.S.C. §1104(a)(2) on grounds that debtor's many competing business interests rendered questionable his commitment to rehabilitation and that debtor could not secure and maintain lenders' and creditors' trust). . . .

Believing that they had cleared the prepetition gross mismanagement determinations, Posner and DWG hoped to sail past the trustee appointment by arguing that the court's remaining determinations of postpetition gross mismanagement do not satisfy the heavy burden of proof imposed on the movants. The court concluded that current management's failure to negotiate a reduction in the interest rate on the $30 million operating loan, to obtain up-to-date, comprehensive postpetition financial statements from DWG, and to cut or eliminate the estimated $2 million lost monthly despite the protection of the bankruptcy laws satisfied both subsections of section 1104(a). Furthermore, it held "[t]he ongoing problem of fair allocation of costs of the Miami offices among Sharon and other Posner-owned businesses is exacerbated by the conflicts of interest, and only an independent trustee can make a proper investigation and determination of the best interests of Sharon."

Once again, we cannot say that the bankruptcy court abused its discretion. Under the discretionary determination of cause required by 11 U.S.C. §1104(a)(1) and the flexible standard embodied in (a)(2), the court acted within its discretion in concluding that the totality of the circumstances signaled the need for a trustee. Despite improvements instituted by Walter Sieckman, too many major problems remained — problems symptomatic of potential bankruptcy despite the calm harbor provided by Chapter 11. Failure to force closure of the prepetition books and production of current financial statements nine months after filing, combined with continued losses exacerbated by the failure to cut a major expense like the approximately $4 million in added interest on the operating loan, signaled the court that as captain, the debtor-in-possession had continued to steer Sharon toward bankruptcy rather than to turn her about toward solvency. Corrective measures that are too few too late cannot defeat a change in command. The bankruptcy court's opinion clearly indicates it felt appointment necessary to save Sharon from bankruptcy. We agree. . . .

The fight over control of a Chapter 11 debtor through the appointment of a trustee or otherwise may become a life-or-death struggle over whether the business will be given the opportunity to survive and over its future direction if it does survive. In some cases the creditors explicitly seek liquidation of the business in Chapter 11, a goal usually accomplished through a variety of other devices but speeded up and better controlled when a recalcitrant management is ousted. Courts are notably reluctant to accede to such uses of a trustee, but occasionally they see the facts as justifying such a move.

Another reason for a creditor motion for a trustee occurs when dealings between the creditor and management have themselves become a source of the debtor's troubles. The bitter feud between manager Frank Lorenzo and the airline unions tore Eastern Airlines asunder. After months in bankruptcy and numerous attempts at refinancing and restructuring the business, the parties continued to struggle over whether Lorenzo, widely perceived as a flamboyant union-buster, would be left in charge. Judge Lifland, who presided over the case, finally concluded that Eastern's only opportunity to survive intact was to oust Lorenzo from control and hope for union peace and better cooperation from the creditors. Eventually, the case ended in Eastern's liquidation. The case is notable for several events, including the reminder that leverage lines are redrawn somewhat in bankruptcy, and that a debtor with union problems may face those problems in new forms after bankruptcy as its employees become powerful creditors. We also note that Lorenzo was not ousted immediately, but was given a chance — albeit limited — to reorganize the company.

Sharon Steel, another large and highly controversial Chapter 11 case, is one of the few in which a trustee has been appointed. In other cases, even the suspected existence of fraudulent conveyances and concealment of assets did not justify removing the DIP and substituting a trustee. For example, the case of In re Rush, 10 B.R. 518 (Bankr. N.D. Ala. 1980), involved a professional engineer who had a number of large government engineering contracts. The debtor had engaged in several suspicious transactions prior to bankruptcy, including transfers of very valuable property to his children and transfers of a yacht and a condominium to a corporation the debtor controlled. Nonetheless, the United States Air Force and the debtor's bonding company, among others, opposed appointment of a trustee on the grounds that the debtor's control was vital to the continued operation of the business. The court agreed and the DIP remained in control.

This might seem pretty shocking to those of us who read bankruptcy court opinions, but policymakers did not seem to care very much until Enron broke into the news, quickly followed by Worldcom and Adelphia, among others. The actions of the insiders in these companies were headline news, along with their subsequent criminal indictments. But no one moved for the appointment of a trustee. As Professor LoPucki pointed out in his book, Courting Failure: How Competition for Big Cases Is Corrupting the Bankruptcy Courts (2005), Ken Lay and the other Enron insiders were given time to appoint their own replacement management, a manager whose first announcement was that he would be looking forward, not spending time investigating the former officers.

When the 2005 Amendments were added to the Bankruptcy Code, a Congress intent on clamping down on what it saw as "abuse" in consumer bankruptcy cases couldn't very well do nothing about such abusers who had fled with their companies to Chapter 11. To remedy the questions raised by the failure to appoint a trustee in Enron, Congress pushed the U.S. Trustee to get more involved. It ordered that the U.S. Trustee *shall* move for the appointment of a trustee if there are "reasonable grounds to suspect" that those currently in control of the business participated in "actual fraud, dishonesty or criminal conduct" as they managed the debtor or made financial reports. §1104(e). It also gave the court additional grounds to appoint a trustee: If there is a reason to dismiss the case, then the court may replace the DIP with a trustee if such a move is "in the best interests of creditors and the estate." 1104(a)(3). Because the court already had such power under the general trustee appointment provisions of §1104(a)(2), this seems to be less about equipping the courts with tools they need and more like a nudge to appoint trustees more often.

It isn't hard to see why most people think a trustee should be appointed in a case like Enron where the allegations of fraud and mismanagement were thicker than the hair on a bunny, but it is always important to look both ways in bankruptcy. *Rush* illustrates one difficulty the courts must face when a creditor requests appointment of a trustee. There will be little doubt about the trustee's honesty, but the price for that assurance is that the trustee will probably be less capable of running the business. Even in bankruptcy, it is the current operator of the business who is most likely to know how to run it and who usually has the greatest incentive to succeed. Finding a trustee skilled in the particular business to be reorganized (juke box operator or steelmaker — just to name two businesses we have seen so far) can be a daunting task. The trustee is brought in when the business is in crisis, so the trustee must learn the operations rapidly to give the business any chance to survive. When the business is not mired in scandal and the management is struggling to bring a successful business out of the ruins, appointment of a trustee is an unattractive option to most courts. On the other hand, when it is evident, as it was in Enron, that the business will be sold off, division by division, it is unclear how important any special knowledge of old management would be and, in any case, why a turnaround manager would serve better as a DIP than as a TIB.

Nonetheless, the presumption against a trustee has become so embedded in Chapter 11 practice, even in liquidating Chapter 11 cases, that the courts have increasingly turned to a middle option offered by the Code: the appointment of an examiner. §1104(c). The central function of an examiner is to investigate the affairs of the debtor. The investigation can have many purposes, including identification of pre-bankruptcy fraud and mismanagement, discovery of causes of action that should be brought against various parties by the estate, and monitoring of the DIP's performance. The examiner option is attractive to creditors and the court because it permits experienced and knowledgeable management to continue to run the business while providing the comfort of a disinterested examination and monitoring of the debtor's past and present activities.

In recent years, courts have ventured far outside the statutory guidelines in appointing examiners. On the one hand, they have assumed they could appoint an examiner to perform a remarkable range of duties, all the way from acting as the United States negotiator in a worldwide bankruptcy case to performing as a mediator and facilitator to help the parties agree on a plan. In re Maxwell Communication Corp., 93 F.3d 1036, 1051 (2d Cir.

1996); In re Big Rivers Electric Corp., 233 B.R. 754 (Bankr. W.D. Ky. 1999). On the other hand, the courts have regularly assumed, without much discussion, that they could define and limit the examiner's powers pretty much as they chose. In re Gliatech, Inc., 305 B.R. 832 (Bankr. N.D. Ohio 2004). The courts have dealt with this provision as if the examiner were a sort of special counsel appointed to do some discrete job rather than to do the job the language of the statute and its history suggest: to provide a replacement for the investigation and recommendations of a trustee in an appropriate case.

In large public-company cases, the resistance to a trustee amounts to a privatization of the process. In their empirical study of large business bankruptcies, Professors Lynn LoPucki and William Whitford note that the price that current management of a large publicly held company often pays for crashing a business into Chapter 11 is that they must give up management control. LoPucki and Whitford, Corporate Governance. See also Gilson, Management Turnover and Financial Distress, 25 J. Fin. Econ. 241 (1989). Rarely is the process of divesting management as fiery as in the Eastern case, but LoPucki and Whitford note that in the overwhelming proportion of large Chapter 11 cases, the CEO leaves office shortly before or after the filing of a bankruptcy. They conclude that when something goes wrong, someone has to pay the price — and the CEO is the likely candidate. It is important to note, however, that these studies were of large corporations, often those with powerful institutional investors, sometimes strong unions, and sophisticated creditors with substantial resources.

The change in control is a public-company phenomenon. In an earlier study of smaller, closely held companies, LoPucki found that if the small company survived the Chapter 11 filing, the owner-managers virtually never lost control. LoPucki, The Debtor in Full Control: Systems Failure Under Chapter 11 of the Bankruptcy Code?, 57 Am. Bankr. L.J. 247, 263-266 (1983).

In public companies, the development of turnaround management (TM) specialists has further changed the dynamics regarding when and whether to seek either a trustee or an examiner. TM specialists advertise their successes in temporarily taking over failing businesses on short notice in a wide variety of industries, providing stability, vision, and leadership to get the company out of its present hole.

Whether or not new management is a TM specialist, what does not happen is an election of that new controlling person by the creditors under section 1104(b)(2). Why should the controller be selected in some other way when the statute has such a clear provision? We will discuss all these questions in a section devoted to large public companies near the end of this chapter.

TM is a business that is not for the faint of heart, and, despite some claims, the practitioners cannot turn dross into gold. TM is also very expensive, which limits its application to businesses of substantial size. But the presence of TM means that courts and creditors have somewhere else to turn when they lose faith in current management, and turnaround managers have served as trustees, as examiners, and as consensual replacement management in some of the largest business reorganizations.

Sometimes the wind blows from the other direction: No one seeks to push the old management out. Instead, the managers are on the verge of fleeing to more successful businesses. Talented people often have many options, and many ambitious people will not see staying with a business in Chapter 11 as a good career move — particularly if that business faces the possibility of liquidation. We also discuss this aspect of the management problem in the section on public companies.

2.   What Happens to the Cash?

Although in most circumstances the court is not likely to permit the creditors to wrest control of the business from the debtor by the appointment of a trustee, the debtor is not given the same free rein to run the business that it had before the bankruptcy. The Code is replete with both DIP powers and restrictions on those powers, striking a balance between the debtor's need to run the business without undue constraint and the creditors' need for reassurance that the assets of the business are not dissipated.

The vast majority of businesses in Chapter 11 are there in part because they are having cash-flow difficulties — that is, they have insufficient cash on hand to meet present operating expenses. For many businesses seeking Chapter 11 reorganization, the first critical step to survival is to keep the business going until longer-range plans for enhanced profitability can be developed. To keep the business going requires cash — often in amounts greater than the business needed before the Chapter 11, because many of the usual sources of short-term credit dry up at filing. The debtor needs to be able to use the cash; otherwise, the business — and the Chapter 11 reorganization — will be effectively shut down before it begins.

Despite this overwhelming need, Congress has also recognized the danger of DIP control of an asset so volatile as cash. The danger is the special concern of lenders who lend on an "asset basis," that is, lend on the security of inventory and accounts, because their collateral turns quickly into cash and may as quickly disappear.

In balancing these considerations, Congress has placed few constraints on the DIP's use of cash that is not subject to a lien, so long as the cash is used "in the ordinary course of business" under section 363(c)(1). On the other hand, the debtor is much more constrained in its use of cash that is subject to a lien, which is usually cash derived from the sale of inventory or the collection of accounts subject to an Article 9 proceeds claim by a lender secured by inventory or accounts. This encumbered cash is called "cash collateral" in section 363 and cannot be used by the DIP without the permission of the bankruptcy court.

The next case requires several introductory observations. First, the court refers to a "lock box" arrangement. Briefly, such an arrangement involves giving directions to those who owe money to the debtor to send their payments to a certain post office box. Although the debtor's customers do not know it, the post office box is under the control of the lender or of a third party acting as a sort of escrow agent for the lender and the debtor. The parties have an agreement as to how much of the money in the "lock box" is distributed to the debtor and how much goes to the lender in payment on the loan.

Second, we should note that the "cash collateral" problem normally arises at the very start of a Chapter 11. In the following case, the parties had agreed on the use of cash collateral and other matters at the start of the case, then the debtor defaulted on that agreement and the parties went before the court for a new resolution of their rights to cash collateral.

Finally, the case demonstrates how the struggle over the use of the cash may be a struggle over whether the business is to be given a chance to reorganize under Chapter 11 or forced to liquidate.

============================ In re EARTH LITE ============================
9 B.R. 440 (Bankr. M.D. Fla. 1981)

PASKAY, Bankruptcy Judge.

This is a business reorganization case and the specific matter under consideration is presented for resolution both by the Debtor, Earth Lite, Inc. (Earth Lite) and by the Plaintiff, Sun Bank and Trust Company of St. Petersburg, Florida (Sun Bank). Sun Bank sought relief from the automatic stay imposed by §362 of the Bankruptcy Code, but not satisfied with the 30-day time frame designed by Congress by §362(e), Sun Bank moved on 24 hours notice, and sought an immediate hearing in order to get a preliminary injunction to prevent Earth Lite from using any of its collateral, i.e., the inventory and the monies received from the collection of accounts receivable. Earth Lite, faced with this challenge of its right to use its inventory and cash obtained from collection of accounts receivable, which challenge, of course, meant a kiss of death if successful, filed a Motion and sought leave to use cash collateral and other collateral pursuant to §363.

The historical background of this controversy and the relationship of the parties is telling and is relevant to the matter under consideration. Earth Lite is engaged in processing glassware products, although in the conventional sense [it] is not a manufacturer. It buys finished glassware of different shapes and sizes and decorates and dresses up the glass containers and then sells the finished product to gift shops and department stores. Prior to the commencement of the case, Earth Lite financed its operation, at least in part, through Sun Bank and received a loan from Sun Bank in the original amount of $350,000. This was a secured loan, collateralized by the inventory and the accounts receivable of Earth Lite. Earth Lite filed its petition for an order for relief under Chapter 11 of the Bankruptcy Code on June 27, 1980. On the same date, Earth Lite was authorized to remain in possession and to operate its business under certain specific terms and conditions.

Shortly after the commencement of the case, Earth Lite and Sun Bank entered into a new agreement. According to the relevant terms of the agreement, Sun Bank agreed to lend to Earth Lite an additional $75,000 in exchange for some additional collateral, and for personal guarantees of insiders. The agreement called for periodic payments to be applied not only to interest, but also to principal. In addition, Earth Lite was required to pay attorney fees. The agreement called for the establishment of a "lock box" system designed to handle the collection of accounts receivable, to be supervised by an independent warehousing firm, Lawrence Warehouse, Inc. appointed by the parties to monitor the arrangement.

There is no question that the parties operated amicably under this arrangement until February of 1981 and Sun Bank received monthly not only the amount stipulated in the agreement, but also approximately $8,000, a reimbursement for attorney fees.

At the time of the commencement of this case, Earth Lite had on hand approximately $500,000 in inventory and approximately $90,000 in account receivables. [T]he value of the inventory of Earth Lite as late as February 6, 1981, was far in excess of the debt owed to Sun Bank and secured by the inventory. Most importantly, this debt which has been reduced since the commencement of these proceedings from $425,000 to $288,000 is also secured by the accounts receivable of Earth Lite, and by additional collateral furnished by insiders to the Bank.

This additional collateral securing the personal guarantee of the insiders consist of a second mortgage on the principal residence of the president, a collateral assignment of a mortgage receivable, a mortgage lien on a condominium and on a cemetery lot. According to the schedules submitted by Earth Lite in connection with its Motion to Allow Use of Cash Collateral and Other Collateral the net equity of the insiders in these assets is in excess of $180,000,000 [sic].

There is no question that Earth Lite defaulted on the post-petition financing agreement in that it did not make the February payment to Sun Bank. It is equally clear that Earth Lite, as noted earlier, paid to Sun Bank more than $137,000 since the commencement of the proceeding.

Sun Bank seeks an immediate relief on the emergency basis because Earth Lite defaulted on the post-petition financing agreement and that the outlook of Earth Lite to survive, according to Sun Bank, is hopeless. Therefore, it should be entitled to sequester all funds currently in the special account which was set up to handle funds obtained through collection of receivables and is entitled to prevent Earth Lite [from using] these funds and its inventory immediately.

Of course, it does not take any imagination to conclude that if the relief sought by Sun Bank is granted, and Earth Lite is put out of business, the economic future and the life of Earth Lite as a functioning viable entity is doomed and Earth Lite would end up as just one more statistic in the great graveyard of ailing debtors who sought, but failed to obtain, rehabilitation under this Chapter.

The apprehension of a secured lender, especially one who has advanced additional funds after the commencement of a proceeding and who is already soured because of past unkept promises by the borrower is understandable. This is especially so if it appears that the economic health of the Debtor is shaky and steadily deteriorating. This reaction is not unusual and not surprisingly triggers the very type of litigation under consideration. This apprehension also tends to lead the secured lender astray and in the haste to obtain immediate relief, it loses sight of facts which are, and which are not, relevant to the matter under consideration.

To be fair, it is not only the secured lender who is led astray by the haste, but also the Debtor who understandably fears the possibility of immediate doom and the loss of its business and pleads for understanding on equitable grounds, relying on its valiant past efforts to live up to its obligations and pleads an excuse for its failure due to circumstances beyond its control, none of which are relevant to the matter under consideration.

Section 363 of the Bankruptcy Code provides that "cash collateral" means cash or other cash equivalents in which the estate and an entity other than the estate has an interest. Whenever non-cash collateral is liquidated, the resulting proceeds are cash collateral so long as the proceeds continue to remain subject to the original lien. Congress, in enacting §363 of the Code, gave a special treatment to "cash collateral" for the obvious reasons that cash collateral is highly volatile, subject to rapid dissipation and requires special protective safeguards in order to assure that a holder of a lien on "cash collateral" is not deprived of its collateral through unprotected use by the Debtor. On the other hand, it is evident that if a Debtor who seeks relief under Chapter 11 is deprived of the use of cash, its chances to secure rehabilitation are immediately destroyed and very few, if any, entities could survive and effectuate a reorganization without cash. The interests of the parties which, by their very nature, are irreconcilable and conflicting must be balanced according to the circumstances and the equities of the case, in order to achieve the possible protection of both interests and in order to carry out the aim and the purpose of this Chapter which is rehabilitation of ailing, but not yet dead business enterprises.

The Code provides certain protective devices designed to assure that the rights of a secured party are safeguarded. This could be accomplished by any method which furnishes "adequate protection" to the secured party. The term "adequate protection" is not defined in §361 of the Bankruptcy Code which Section merely sets forth examples which include giving an additional or replacement lien to the secured party to compensate the secured party for the diminution of its cash collateral.

The Debtor points out that Sun Bank is amply secured and the Debtor has a very substantial "equity cushion" even without the security granted by the insiders to back up their personal guarantee. According to the Debtor, the "equity cushion" alone is sufficient adequate protection which would warrant the use of cash collateral. This is, however, an overstatement and oversimplification of the problem especially when one deals with the use of cash collateral. The cases cited by Earth Lite dealt with the concept of adequate protection in connection with a complaint which sought a modification of the automatic stay under §362(d)(1), (2). This Court is satisfied that due to the different nature of the proceeding and due to the different collateral involved, the cases cited are not controlling and a debtor, before it is authorized to use cash collateral, cannot rest on its equity cushion, but must offer more to the secured party before it is entitled to use cash collateral.

The Debtor, in addition, in order to bolster his position, relies on the fact that as part of the post-petition agreement Sun Bank urged personal guarantees of the insiders. Therefore, that alone by itself would justify this Court to authorize Earth Lite to use the cash collateral. Sun Bank points out in opposition of this contention that a personal guarantee is not an adequate protection and does not warrant an order authorizing a debtor to use cash collateral. In support of this proposition, Sun Bank cites the case of In re Kenny Kar Leasing, 6 BCD 677, 5 B.R. 304 (Bankr. C.D. Calif. 1980), where the Court, discussing the nature of a personal guarantor, concluded that the personal guarantee is not legally sufficient to furnish adequate protection. While the Debtor's reliance on the personal guarantee of the insiders is misplaced, so is the reliance of Sun Bank in *Kenny*, supra. The personal guarantee in *Kenny*, supra, was a totally unsecured obligation and the only evidence in that record, presented in support of the soundness of the personal guarantee, was an unverified statement of assets and liabilities of the guarantor. In addition, the values allocated to the assets of a guarantor came solely from the data submitted by the guarantor himself. It is not surprising that under these conditions the Court accorded no persuasive force to the personal guarantee of the insiders and totally disregarded it in the valuation of the adequate protection offered by the debtor.

In contrast, in the present case, the personal guaranties of the insiders are amply secured by properties of the insiders which are valued in excess of $300,000 against which there is an indebtedness of less than $150,000. The guarantor in the Chapter 11 does not enjoy the automatic stay protection accorded to a guarantor in Chapter 13 by virtue of §1301 of the Bankruptcy Code. Thus, Sun Bank can, in the event there is an additional default in the agreement, proceed to establish the liability of the prime obligor and then proceed, in the event it fails to obtain satisfaction, to foreclose its security interest on the property pledged as security for the indebtedness. Thus, neither the proposition urged by the Debtor nor the proposition urged by Sun Bank meets with pragmatic precision of the elusive concept of "adequate protection."

There are a variety of means by which this could be accomplished and the Court must fashion an appropriate "adequate protection" for a secured party after consideration of all facts involved and circumstances of the case.

For instance, this Court is satisfied that the Debtor should not be permitted to use cash collateral without making some payments to the secured party just because it has, at the commencement of the case, a meaningful equity cushion in the collateral. To accept this proposition would mean that a debtor may freely use cash collateral until the collateral is reduced to the amount of indebtedness during which time the secured party is deprived of income, for which it bargained when the loan was granted. In the present instance, the Debtor agreed to pay Sun Bank $12,500 a month. The Debtor is now in default on the February payment. The fact that the Debtor has an equity cushion, because on this record Sun Bank is oversecured, is not sufficient to relieve the Debtor of this monthly obligation, although it should be given an opportunity to cure this default within a reasonable time.

It is clear that a debtor as a general proposition must demonstrate with convincing proof that the Sun Bank is adequately protected without resorting to the crutch furnished by a personal guarantee of third parties. This is so because if it is attempted to be used to justify the use of cash collateral, due to the highly volatile nature of the cash collateral this is not enough since at the time the Sun Bank is able to resort to the enforcement of its claim on the guarantee both the cash collateral and the secured or unsecured assets of the guarantor may be dissipated leaving the secured party with no property which could be subjected to satisfy its claim.

Since this Court is satisfied that Sun Bank is more than adequately protected at this time if the Debtor is required to resume the contractual payments and makes provisions for curing the default even without considering the value of the personal guarantee, it is clear on this record that Sun Bank is not entitled to a preliminary injunction and the Debtor is entitled to have immediate access to the monies in the "lock box" and shall be permitted in the future to use some of the proceeds of the collections to the extent that it is necessary to cure the existing default and to make the monthly payments agreed upon, commencing May 1, 1981. . . .

As we have seen, the use of cash on hand at the time of filing is constrained if it represents the proceeds of assets subject to a security interest. The availability of this cash is subject to yet another constraint, a bank's right of "setoff."

The Bankruptcy Code recognizes the right of any creditor to offset a debt it owes to the debtor against a debt owed to the creditor by the debtor, subject to some qualifications and limitations. §553. The right to setoff is a very valuable one, since it enables the creditor to obtain, in effect, full payment for its claim up to the amount of its debt to the debtor. For example, a supplier who is owed $1,000 in a case where unsecured creditors will get 20 percent will get only $200 on its claim. Another creditor who owes the debtor $1,000 will be sued by the trustee and forced to pay the full $1,000 to the estate. If, however, the same creditor owes $1,000 to the estate and is owed $1,000 by the estate, that creditor will pay nothing and will have gotten full payment for its claim by cancellation of the amount it owed.

The right to setoff is especially important in the case of banks. In legal contemplation, Mary's checking or savings account (or a certificate of deposit) is merely a loan that Mary has made to the bank, payable on demand when she writes a check or presents her passbook (or at a stated date on a CD). If Mary has borrowed money from the bank where she has her account, in the event of her default on the loan the bank has a right to set off its debt to her — the checking account — against her debt to the bank — the unpaid loan.

The right to setoff is not technically a security interest and is expressly excluded from the general rules of Article 9 of the UCC, except to the extent that the setoff rights of depositary institutions are specifically acknowledged. Revised UCC §§9-109(d)(10), 9-340. Nonetheless, a setoff has much the same effect as a security interest and is treated as one for most purposes under the Bankruptcy Code. In particular, a creditor with a right of setoff is treated as secured for the amount of its setoff right, §506(a), and the account subject to setoff is cash collateral and governed by the rules set forth in section 363(c). On the other hand, the creditor with a setoff right is also subject to the automatic stay, just like a secured creditor, and may not exercise a setoff without the permission of the court. §362(a)(7).

The chances are good in most businesses that the cash on hand at the time of filing is held in a checking account with a bank that is also a major creditor of the business. Typical business practices (and sometimes the insistence of the major lender) make this very likely. When the debtor files bankruptcy, the cash already in the account becomes subject to the bank creditor's desire to grab the cash. Sometimes the creditor wants the cash to pay down the balance on the bank creditor's loans to the debtor, while sometimes it wants only to make certain that the debtor will not dissipate the cash contrary to Code provisions. In either case, the debtor is usually desperate for cash, and the creditor's freeze seriously hampers attempts to use the cash in the ongoing business.

For many years banks and debtors wrangled over the cash in the debtor's checking account immediately post-filing. Businesses want that cash to pay ongoing operations; indeed, their need for cash may be more acute following a bankruptcy filing when many small vendors will refuse to do business except on a cash basis. They claimed that a bank's efforts to hold their cash and make an offset against the loans to the bank violated the automatic stay provision of section 362 as an attempt to collect from the debtor. Many courts agreed with the debtors. Banks argued their view at full voice as well, noting that the right of setoff would be worthless if they had to wait for an order from the court that did not come until long after the debtor had cleared all of the cash out of the checking account. Many courts agreed with the banks.

With the courts badly split on the issue, the issue was ultimately resolved by the United States Supreme Court in Citizens Bank of Maryland v. Strumpf, 516 U.S. 16 (1995). The Court held that the creditor could not set off without violating the stay, and therefore it needed to seek court approval to have the stay lifted before it acted, but (and this was a very big but) the creditor could protect itself with an "administrative freeze" by holding the money in the checking account pending its application to the bankruptcy court for the lift-stay motion.

With that area of ambiguity cleared up, a sizeable fraction of the litigation between banks and their bankrupt depositors disappeared. But the desperate desire to keep the money did not go away, and sophisticated debtors today frequently drain their checking accounts in the last days before they file for bankruptcy.

Strumpf emphasized that the Bankruptcy Code did not create a right of setoff; it merely enforced rights that might exist under nonbankruptcy law. Litigation over the requirements of a setoff continues. One limitation on setoffs under nonbankruptcy law that arises in the bank–customer relationship is on the ability to set off against a special purpose account. If a business had two accounts in a bank, a regular checking account and an escrow account in which funds were being held pending the closing of a business deal, common law holds that the bank may set off against the general purpose account but not against the special purpose escrow account. Business debtors frequently have segregated accounts, such as accounts that hold the proceeds of cash withheld from employee paychecks. If the business gets into trouble, the bank cannot reach any such "special account" for a setoff. It is no surprise that there is substantial litigation over what constitutes a "special account."

Not all setoffs arise in the context of private parties. The government can be both the debtor and the creditor of a business, as it is in the next case. The case raises two issues: Is the government one party or two, and when are equitable restrictions imposed on setoff rights?

=== In re HAL, INC. ===
196 B.R. 159 (9th Cir. BAP 1996)

JONES, Bankruptcy Judge: . . .

I.   FACTS

On September 21, 1993, Hawaiian Airlines, along with related entities HAL, Inc. and West Maui Airport, Inc. (collectively referred to as "Debtors") filed chapter 11 petitions. Prior to bankruptcy, Hawaiian Airlines remitted quarterly payments of Air Transportation Excise Taxes ("Excise Taxes") to the IRS. After the Debtors filed bankruptcy, the IRS conducted an audit and concluded that Hawaiian Airlines had committed errors in the reporting and paying of the Excise Taxes. After seeking relief from the stay, the IRS assessed the correct Excise Taxes, readjusted Hawaiian Airlines' pre- and postpetition payments, and determined that Hawaiian Airlines had made overpayments totaling $215,000.

On September 9, 1994, the United States filed a Motion For Relief From Stay To Effectuate A Setoff. The United States sought an order allowing it to use the $215,000 overpayment to offset the claims of other agencies.[2] Under the terms of the confirmed plan, creditors with non-priority unsecured claims receive stock of the reorganized Debtors as payment in full of their claim. Therefore, if setoff were not allowed, the government agencies would receive stock in full payment of their claims. . . .

IV.   DISCUSSION

The Bankruptcy Code states that the filing of a bankruptcy petition does not (except in certain circumstances not applicable in this appeal), "affect any right of a creditor to offset a mutual debt owing by such creditor to the debtor that arose before the commencement of the case . . . against a claim of such creditor against the debtor that arose before the commencement of the case. . . ." 11 U.S.C. §553(a) (1994). Section 553, therefore, recognizes in

---

2. The United States proposed to use the money to setoff the following claims in the following order:

Federal Aviation Administration:	$94,500
United States Air Force:	$51,121
Department of Agriculture:	$55,101
Immigration and Naturalization Service:	$299,375

bankruptcy a party's nonbankruptcy right to setoff mutual prepetition debts, but does not itself create such a right. Citizens Bank of Maryland v. Strumpf, 116 S. Ct. 286, 289 (1995).

To enforce a setoff right, "[a creditor] must establish that (1) it has a right of setoff under nonbankruptcy law; and (2) this right should be preserved in bankruptcy under §553." In re County of Orange, 183 Bankr. 609, 615 (Bankr. C.D. Cal. 1995). The principal element of setoff is mutuality, which requires that the debts are "in the same right and between the same parties, standing in the same capacity and same kind or quality." Boston and Maine Corp. v. Chicago Pac. Corp., 785 F.2d 562, 566 (7th Cir. 1986). Both sides agree that all relevant debts arose prepetition. Therefore, the only issues presented on appeal are whether the United States has a nonbankruptcy right to setoff (which in turn requires a finding that mutuality is satisfied), and if so, whether the bankruptcy court abused its discretion in permitting setoff.

A.   Does the United States Have a Nonbankruptcy Right of Setoff?

The notion of "setoff" dates back to early Roman and French law. Buckenmaier, 127 Bankr. at 237; In re Hancock, 137 Bankr. 835, 840 (Bankr. N.D. Okla. 1992). Because setoff was not recognized as a legal right in early English common law, it was first used by the courts of equity as a discretionary procedural device in order to prevent multiplicity of actions. 4 Collier on Bankruptcy ¶553.01 at 553-3 (15th ed. 1991); Hancock, 137 Bankr. at 840. In other words, the use of setoff prevented a court from having to entertain two separate lawsuits, enter two separate judgments, and require the parties to try and collect on their individual judgments. Instead, the court merely netted out the amounts owing and entered one judgment, "thereby avoiding 'the absurdity of making A pay B when B owes A'" Strumpf, 116 S. Ct. at 289 (quoting Studley v. Boylston Nat'l Bank, 229 U.S. 523, 528, 57 L. Ed. 1313, 33 S. Ct. 806 (1913)). Gradually, however, setoff has also come to be recognized as a legal right, both under statute[3] and as a "latter-day common-law doctrine derived from the equitable doctrine." Hancock, 137 Bankr. at 840.

Courts have consistently recognized this broad common law right to setoff amongst government agencies outside of bankruptcy. "The government has the same right 'which belongs to every creditor, to apply the unappropriated moneys of his debtor, in his hands, in extinguishment of the debts due to him.'" United States v. Munsey Trust Co. of Washington, D.C., 332 U.S. 234 (1947) (quoting Gratiot v. United States, 40 U.S. (15 Pet.) 336, 370 (1841)).

---

3. The federal government, for example, has enacted various statutory setoff provisions in title 31 of the United States Code. One section authorizes government agencies to setoff "past-due legally enforceable debt[s]" with the unpaid federal tax refunds of the debtor. 31 U.S.C. §3720A (1994). However, in order to use this section, the government agency has to formally enter into an agreement with the IRS, notify the IRS of any deficiency, and conform to the procedural due process requirements contained in the statute. Another setoff provision requires the Comptroller General to "withhold paying that part of a judgment against the United States . . . that is equal to a debt the plaintiff owes the Government." 31 U.S.C. §3728 (1994).

The seminal case on the issue of government agency mutuality is Cherry Cotton Mills, Inc. v. United States, 327 U.S. 536 (1946). In *Cherry Cotton Mills*, the plaintiff was owed a tax refund for taxes paid under the Agricultural Adjustment Act ("AAA"). In turn, the plaintiff owed the Reconstruction Finance Corporation ("RFC") on a promissory note. The General Accounting Office was instructed to apply the AAA tax refund to the balance owing on the RFC promissory note. The plaintiff sued for the tax refund in the Court of Claims. When the government filed a counterclaim on behalf of the RFC, the plaintiff argued that the Court of Claims did not have jurisdiction to hear the counterclaim. The plaintiff reasoned that because the RFC was a "corporation" it should not be treated as a government agency subject to the Court of Claims' jurisdiction.

In rejecting this contention, the Supreme Court stated that just because the RFC was called a "corporation" did not alter the fact that "its activities are all aimed at accomplishing a public purpose; all of its money comes from the Government; its profits, if any, go to the Government; its losses the Government must bear." . . .

This reasoning was applied in the bankruptcy context in Luther v. United States, 225 F.2d 495 (10th Cir. 1954). In *Luther*, a bankruptcy referee entered an order allowing the government to offset the debtor's income tax refund against a debt owed by the debtor to the Commodity Credit Corporation, which is part of the Department of Agriculture. On appeal, the Tenth Circuit held that "it [is] implicit in the *[Cherry Cotton Mills]* opinion that the right of setoff exist[s]. That case is controlling here and leads to the conclusion that the overpayments of income tax were properly offset against the amount which the bankrupt owed Commodity." *Luther*, 225 F.2d at 498.

Recent decisions interpreting §553 of the Bankruptcy Code have resulted in a split of authority.

Only two circuit courts have addressed the issue of mutuality, and they came to different conclusions. The minority position was adopted by the Tenth Circuit in In re Turner, 59 F.3d 1041 (10th Cir. 1995). In *Turner*, the Tenth Circuit distinguished its previous holding in *Luther* because it arose under the Bankruptcy Act and occurred in a liquidation, not a reorganization case. The court concluded that:

> While we recognize that the United States normally has a right to setoff, see Cherry Cotton Mills v. United States, 327 U.S. 536, 66 S. Ct. 729, 90 L. Ed. 835 (1946), we agree . . . that setoff should be given a narrow meaning in the reorganization context. . . . This narrow interpretation of setoff is best accomplished by strictly construing the mutuality requirement.
>
> We acknowledge that all federal agencies draw from or contribute to a common pool of money, the U.S. Treasury. This familial relationship between the SBA and the ASCS does offer some support for a finding of mutuality. The general rule, however, holds that triangular setoffs among related parties do not meet the mutuality requirement. Thus, in the corporate context, "it is well-established that one subsidiary may not set off a debt owed to a bankrupt against a debt owing from the bankrupt to another subsidiary." We think the transaction attempted in this case to be closely analogous to a triangular setoff between related corporate entities. To treat government

agencies more favorably than comparable private parties would run counter to the principle that all like creditors should be treated equally.

We note, moreover, that, notwithstanding familial ties, government agencies frequently squabble in court. Separate agencies have distinct budgets and interests, and occasionally sue each other to protect their budgets and interests. More important to the question analyzed here, *bankruptcy* law does not treat individual agencies as a single unit when multiple agencies are creditors in the same case. Rather, some agency claims are given priority over others based on general principles of bankruptcy law, such as whether the debt was secured. We see no reason to accord agencies more favorable treatment in this context.

Turner, 59 F.3d at 1045-46 (citations omitted) (emphasis in original).

The Ninth Circuit reached the opposite conclusion in *Doe*, holding that government agencies are, as a matter of law, a single entity.

The organization of the agencies of the United States government supports a finding of mutuality. Title 5 of the United States Code defines Executive departments, Government corporations, and independent establishments, all of which are classified as "Executive agencies." 5 U.S.C. §§101, 104-105 (1994). Each of the agencies involved in this appeal were established as Executive departments of the United States, not as separate juristic entities. See 5 U.S.C. §101 (1994). As *Turner* recognizes, "all federal agencies draw from or contribute to a common pool of money, the U.S. Treasury." 59 F.3d at 1045. Although *Turner* goes on to characterize federal agencies' relationships as that of corporate subsidiaries, we feel the more appropriate analogy is that of separate departments within a single corporation. Just as a large corporation has different departments — marketing, sales, accounting, personnel, etc. — with individual budgets and separate interests, so does the federal government. In both situations, each separate department must compete against the others for its share of the overall budget. Such is not necessarily the case with corporate subsidiaries, who are often expected to be self-sustaining, and whose fortunes are not necessarily tied to the parent's profitability.

For the foregoing reasons, we hold that as a matter of law, federal government agencies, with the exception of those acting in a distinctly private capacity, are a single entity for purposes of setoff under §553. . . .

B. Did the Bankruptcy Court Abuse Its Discretion in Allowing Setoff?

Hawaiian argues that even if mutuality is found, the bankruptcy court abused its discretion by permitting the setoff. Courts which have denied setoff have done so for a variety of reasons. First, courts have denied setoff in cases where the creditor has acted inequitably. See *Cascade Roads*, 34 F.3d [756, 763-64 (9th Cir. 1994)] (affirming bankruptcy court's denial of setoff because the U.S. Forest Service had "stonewalled" on discovery and, "with knowledge of the merits of the debtor's position," caused eight years of litigation in numerous courts before "capitulating" on the eve of trial). Second, courts often deny setoff if setoff would jeopardize a debtor's ability to reorganize. *Turner*, 59 F.3d at 1045. This is especially true in cases involving farmers who have filed a chapter 12 petition. Third, courts may deny setoff in a liquidation context because it results in either a preference or priority over other unsecured creditors. See *Hancock*, 137 Bankr. at 841. Hawaiian's only argument against allowing setoff in this case is that it is unfair to other unsecured creditors who will only receive stock in satisfaction of their claims.

This argument was considered, and rejected, by the bankruptcy court. We hold that this finding was not an abuse of discretion. First, §553 clearly states that bankruptcy law does not affect a creditor's nonbankruptcy right to setoff. Therefore, Congress knew when it drafted the Code that §553 would allow some creditors to receive a de facto priority over other creditors. If Congress thought that allowing setoff was per se unfair to other creditors, it would not have allowed discretionary use of setoff under §553.

Second, §553 actually reduces the scope of setoff available under pre-Code bankruptcy law. Before enactment of the Code, the only limitation on setoff was a denial of setoff if a creditor purchased a claim against the debtor after the filing of the petition for the purpose of obtaining a right of setoff. See Section 20 of the Bankruptcy Act of 1867. The current version of §553 not only maintains that limitation, but extends it to claims obtained or debts incurred within 90 days of the filing of the petition. 11 U.S.C. §553(a). In addition, §553 prevents a creditor from improving his setoff position during the 90 days prior to bankruptcy. 11 U.S.C. §553(b)(1) (1994). Congressional limitations on the right of setoff indicate that Congress is aware of the preferential and priority potential of setoff and has placed specific limitations on it. Aside from those specific limitations, however, Congress has left equitable setoff determinations to the bankruptcy court's discretion because, "the Code recognizes the possible injustice in compelling a creditor to file its claim in full and accepting possible dividends thereon, while at the same time paying in full its indebtedness to the estate." 4 Collier on Bankruptcy ¶553.02 at 553-11 (15th ed. 1996).

V. CONCLUSION

For the foregoing reasons, we affirm the bankruptcy court's decision that the agencies involved have a nonbankruptcy right to setoff and its decision to allow setoff.

═══════════════

The reference to equitable limitations in the preceding case illustrates the unease some courts express when happenstance gives one party a much higher priority over other creditors of the same "class." Of course, the key to setoff is that it routinely benefits some parties, especially banks, which may rely on it when they assess the risk associated with a loan. The benefit of setoff to other parties is sometimes more-or-less accidental and incidental. Given that, the courts have followed the congressional mandate to enforce setoff rights, but they have expressed some uncertainty about whether that means the right should be read to its fullest extent in a bankruptcy context in which full payment to everyone is unlikely.

Problem Set 20

20.1. Fredrick Fredrick is the president of Tiny Telephones, which is about to enter Chapter 11. The Maine State Bank was the company's principal lender and has a security interest in its inventory. Fredrick wants to know if he can operate the business normally after filing without having to go to court. What do you tell him? See §363; UCC Revised §9-315.

20.2. The First National Bank has always been the principal bank of Teddy's Toasters, a local kitchen appliance dealer. Teddy's has always kept its checking accounts at the bank and has gotten its working capital and equipment loans there. As of June 1, Teddy's owed the bank about $150,000. The bank's loan was unsecured. By July 1, Teddy's was obviously in some financial trouble, and for the first time the bank demanded that Teddy's maintain a 10 percent "compensating balance," i.e., that it keep in its checking account at the bank (and never withdraw) an amount of money equal to at least 10 percent of its debt to the bank. From July 1 on, Teddy's complied by never letting its checking account balance fall below $15,000.

On September 5, Teddy's came to you for bankruptcy advice, and you filed a Chapter 11 petition on September 10 on Teddy's behalf. On that date Teddy's had $40,000 in its checking account at the bank. Is that money "cash collateral"? See §§506(a) and 363(a). If a setoff right is cash collateral, how much, if any, right to a post-petition setoff does the bank have and why? See §553(a)(3).

20.3. Gretchen Deaton is the owner of Funtime Vehicles, Ltd., a dealership for Winston motorbikes. Funtime is in severe financial difficulty and has sought your advice. You have recommended a Chapter 11. On the day before the planned filing, Funtime has $61,000 in Citywide Bank, ready to meet its monthly payroll that is due four days later.

As part of her explanation of Funtime's financial affairs, Gretchen tells you that she buys the motorbikes on unsecured credit from Winston, and that she owes them about $50,000. Gretchen said that last month she received a bill from Citywide Bank for the regular payment on the line of credit. She called the bank and learned that Winston had approached Citywide, saying it would continue to ship to Funtime on credit only if the bank agreed to "buy" Funtime's outstanding debt to Winston, i.e., to pay them $40,000 for the Funtime account. The bank did so.

How much of the cash in the checking account would Gretchen be able to use without getting court permission? What is your advice? See §§553(a)(2), 363(a). (Later we will discuss section 553(b) in connection with section 547(c)(5) and voidable preferences. At that point we will explore how a setoff is somewhat like a preference, just as we have looked at how a setoff in these cases is something like a security interest.)

20.4. You are counsel to the equity security holders of eBump, the dazzling new technology firm that dazzled its way right through $52 million of your clients' investment and right into Chapter 11. The business filed owing another $20 million in debt and with hard assets valued at about $10 million. The reorganization has been pending for about eight months and talk of a plan is in the wind. The plan, as best you can figure it out from the negotiations, will give all the outstanding equity to the current creditors in return for forgiveness of their debts — wiping out your clients completely. Your clients think a better deal could be cut in which old equity invests a little more money and the current creditors take cash and some equity and forgive some debt, but they can't seem to get a seat at the negotiating table. It seems that the current management team thinks that VentureLoan, the company that owns the biggest share of the outstanding debt, will be in the power position, and they are doing everything they can to make VL happy. Your clients are also disgusted with management's free-spending ways and have heard rumors about playhouses on Padre Island. They are also outraged because management's new-found loyalty may come from the fact that VL has also announced that after the plan is confirmed, there will be a 5 percent stock distribution to this fine management team.

Your client says, "I know that to you it looks like this business is a loser, but I'm telling you that they have a great idea. I want to hang on to a piece of the equity, but they won't even talk to us. Do something." You know the plan as described can be confirmed if the creditors vote for it, so you need to find another lever to push on behalf of your clients. What is your best idea? If you need to investigate for more information, what will you look for? See §§ 503(c), 1104.

3. Post-petition Financing

Even if the debtor were given unfettered access to the cash already in the business and the cash generated by its post-filing business operations, most businesses in Chapter 11 would not have adequate resources for an effective reorganization. For some businesses already suffocating from an inadequate cash flow, an increase in operating capital is essential for survival. For others, interim financing to keep the present operations afloat must be secured until other measures can be taken to streamline business operations and enhance profitability.

Attorneys often must remind their clients that although the Bankruptcy Code can do a great deal for debtors in trouble, filing alone will not produce any cash. Typically the debtor must find someone who is willing to make new infusions of cash in order for the business to survive.

Finding such a lender can be a challenge. The debtor's current lenders — those who have the most to lose if the business cannot survive — are often the most likely source of new funds. There are also lenders who specialize in high-risk business loans, such as those made to reorganizing companies. When sufficient assurances can be offered, even very conservative institutions may be persuaded to lend. The likely success of any attempt to secure financing will, of course, depend on what inducements the debtor can offer, such as new security interests or priority repayments. The Bankruptcy Code is designed to encourage post-petition lending by giving these creditors special protection.

Perhaps the most important protection a DIP can offer to a post-petition lender is a security interest in its property. In that connection, it is important to understand that pre-petition security interests with after-acquired property clauses cease to operate at the instant bankruptcy is filed.

While a security interest may lock up all property the debtor owns at the moment of filing, under section 552(a) pre-petition security interests do not attach to property acquired by the DIP after bankruptcy. The underlying conceptual basis is, once again, that the estate is a new entity, not bound by the old security agreement. New property created by the estate or purchased by the estate after filing does not automatically feed the lien of the secured lender who has an after-acquired property clause; instead, it belongs to the estate, which represents the interests of all the creditors collectively. So, for example, if Drug-Store has $100,000 in inventory on hand on the day of its bankruptcy filing, the creditor with a perfected security interest in inventory can lay first claim to this inventory. But the inventory DrugStore acquires after it files for bankruptcy will be property of the estate, no longer subject to the secured creditor's after-acquired property clause.

Of course, the secured creditor can — and often does — claim a security interest in post-petition property by way of a proceeds argument under UCC §9-315. For example, if the secured creditor can trace the purchase of the new, post-petition inventory back to the sale of the old, pre-petition inventory in which it held an interest, the secured creditor could claim a continuing security interest. Note, however, that this is claiming the interest by way of proceeds, not by way of after-acquired property, and so the creditor must be able to trace the value in an unbroken chain directly from the property in which it held an interest to the new property. With the exception of any property locked up through tracing, the post-filing debtor will be able to offer as security for a post-petition loan both an interest in property that was not encumbered before bankruptcy plus an interest in any new property it acquires after bankruptcy.

The following cases illustrate the circumstances in which post-petition financing may be negotiated and the legal protection for those who become post-petition creditors. The cases should also be read with a view toward identifying which creditors might object to post-petition financing and the basis for their complaints.

In re GARLAND CORP.
6 B.R. 456 (Bankr. App. D. Mass. 1980)

Cyr, Chief Judge.

An emergency appeal has been taken from various orders of the bankruptcy judge entered during the early stages of these chapter 11 reorganization proceedings. The Garland Corporation and its subsidiaries [debtor] manufacture and sell clothing, principally knitted goods and sportswear for women. From its earliest beginnings, the debtor achieved financial success as a sweater manufacturer. Severe financial difficulties later developed in the wake of its operation of thirty-six retail stores and a factory producing clothing principally for Levi Strauss, and its entry into the field of sportswear design and manufacture.

Upon the commencement of its reorganization proceedings, the debtor sought authorization to borrow operating funds from New England

Merchants Bank [Bank] and Prudential Insurance Company [Prudential]. Following an ex parte hearing the same day,[2] the bankruptcy judge authorized an immediate borrowing from the Bank and Prudential, fixing May 7, 1980, after the formation of the Creditors' Committee, for further hearing on the application. At the conclusion of the May 7 hearing, the Creditors' Committee having appeared without interposing objection, the bankruptcy judge authorized the debtor to borrow an additional $700,000 and to enter into a line-of-credit agreement with the Bank and Prudential for up to $1.4 million in postpetition borrowings. These post-petition loans were later deemed priority costs of administration under Bankruptcy Code §507(b) and a first encumbrance on all assets of the debtor.[6]

On May 16, the Creditors' Committee appeared in opposition to the request of the debtor to borrow an additional $500,000. . . . After hearing, the bankruptcy judge approved the $500,000 borrowing, [and] increased the line of credit to $1.7 million. . . . The Creditors' Committee appeals. . . .

The appellant challenges the May 16 order authorizing a third borrowing in the amount of $500,000 on grounds that the evidence did not demonstrate a reasonable likelihood that the debtor could be successfully rehabilitated, and because the borrowing of operating funds secured by theretofore unencumbered assets requires adequate protection of the interest of unsecured creditors, within the meaning of Bankruptcy Code §361, in the absence of which the borrowing constituted a taking of property without just compensation, contrary to the fifth amendment to the Constitution of the United States. . . .

. . . The appellant did not deny that significant reductions in employee and executive payrolls and the sale of the retail outlets would produce beneficial results. The likelihood that substantial benefits would result from an aggressive implementation of these initiatives was substantiated by the appellant's own witness.

2. The record reveals that only the debtor, the Bank and Prudential received notice of the application. However, it was suggested during oral argument that the U.S. trustee was informed. While the April 30, 1980, order has not been appealed, it was to have been entered only "after notice and a hearing." Bankruptcy Code §364(c)(1) and (2). The flexible notice formula prescribed by Bankruptcy Code §102(1)(A) is not so relaxed as to permit ex parte relief in the absence of specific findings substantiating its appropriateness in the circumstances. The exigent nature of the circumstances may have warranted ex parte relief, but not without reasonable efforts to provide advance notice to parties in interest. 2 B.R. at 356. The nonexistence of an official Creditors' Committee does not excuse the failure to attempt notification of the twenty largest unsecured creditors. See Interim Local Bankruptcy Rule 1007(a), District of Massachusetts. The Panel opines that there has been no sufficient showing of reasonable efforts to notify other parties in interest. The right to be heard "has little reality or worth unless one is informed that the matter is pending and can choose for himself whether to appear or default, acquiesce or contest." Mullane v. Central Hanover Bank and Trust Co., 339 U.S. 306, 314 (1950).

6. The order signed by the bankruptcy judge on May 12, 1980, provides as follows: Any loans made pursuant to such line of credit and pursuant to the order of May 1, 1980 will be secured by a lien on all the assets of the debtors, including, without limitation, a first lien on postpetition receivables, inventory and leasehold rights and a lien junior to the Bank's and Prudential's security interest in prepetition receivables, machinery and equipment, and such loans shall constitute a cost of administration pursuant to §507(b). . . .

The May 12 order was not appealed.

. . . While the debtor's own projections clearly evidenced the near certainty of short-term operating losses, the bankruptcy judge concluded, appropriately in our view, that there existed a reasonable likelihood that the debtor could be rehabilitated.

Appellant next challenges the authorization under section 364(c)(2) to borrow operating funds secured by unencumbered assets. The appellant insists that it was an abuse of discretion to permit the May 16 loan to be secured by unencumbered assets of the debtor, without first determining that the debtor was unable to obtain unsecured credit, as required by Bankruptcy Code §364(c).

The May 16 borrowing was authorized under Bankruptcy Code §364(c)(2), after notice and a hearing, upon a sufficient showing that the debtor was unable to obtain unsecured credit. The debtor was in urgent need of operating funds with which to meet its payroll. Its 1,300 employees had been instructed not to report for work without calling in advance to learn if the plant would open. The appellant's own witnesses and committee members confirmed that essential raw materials were available only on a cash-on-delivery basis and that other trade creditors would not produce the needed yarns without assurances of payment. The record substantiates the finding that the urgently needed operating monies were otherwise unavailable.

There is no express statutory requirement that holders of unsecured claims be provided "adequate protection." Adequate protection within the meaning of Bankruptcy Code §361 need be provided only as expressly required under section 362, section 363, or section 364. There is no requirement of adequate protection in respect to credit obtained under Bankruptcy Code §364(c)(2). . . .

[The court rejected the unsecured creditors' claim of constitutional violations in taking property without just compensation.] Since there are no other constitutional or legislative requirements, the court may permit the use of unencumbered assets as collateral to secure postpetition indebtedness upon compliance with section 364(c)(2).

Affirmed.

=========

Sometimes the post-petition financing pushes a pre-petition secured creditor out of the way. In the following case, note the shifting views of the different creditors with pre-bankruptcy interests in the real estate.

===== In re HUBBARD POWER & LIGHT, INC. =====
202 B.R. 680 (E.D.N.Y. 1996)

Opinion by: Dorothy EISENBERG

This case comes before the Court pursuant to an Order to Show Cause and Application made by Hubbard Power & Light, Inc., the debtor (the "Debtor" or "HPL") seeking authorization for HPL to incur $750,000 of post-petition financing from Enron Capital & Trade Resources Corp. ("Enron") pursuant to sections 364(c) and (d) of the Bankruptcy Code. The Debtor filed a Memorandum of Understanding executed by both Enron and the Debtor memorializing the proposed loan transaction which proposes to provide to Enron a super-priority lien in exchange for the loan to the Debtor. Opposition was interposed by the New York State Department of Environmental Conservation ("DEC"); Oak Re, who represents the bond-holders holding a lien on all of the Debtor's real and personal property, and who is the Debtor's senior secured creditor; and Hubbard Sand & Gravel Corp. (the "Landlord"). In addition, the County of Suffolk, New York (the "County"), an alleged lienholder on the Debtor's real property, strongly objected to the proposed financing. . . .

BACKGROUND

HPL is a New York corporation engaged in the production of electrical power under an agreement entered into in 1988 with the Long Island Lighting Co. ("LILCO") called the Parallel Generation Agreement (the "PGA"). The Debtor's president and sole shareholder is James Solano ("Solano"). HPL's power generation facility is located on approximately two (2) acres of land in Bay Shore, New York (the "Bay Shore property"), which real property is owned by the Debtor. In conjunction with its operations, it also leases adjoining property from the Landlord. HPL's main business activity is the collection of wood debris which it sorts, cuts and makes into wood chips and then burns at its plant to produce steam which, in turn, generates electricity that HPL sells to LILCO under the PGA.

In early June 1995, the DEC inspected HPL's power producing plant and found that the Debtor was in violation of the special conditions of its operating permit issued by the DEC. Under the DEC permit, HPL was required to separate and remove all painted or treated wood chips and burn only clean, unadulterated wood chips. On June 28, 1995 the DEC commenced an action in New York State Supreme Court, Suffolk County to enjoin the Debtor from burning adulterated wood in violation of the New York State Environmental Conservation Law. HPL and the DEC later agreed to a Consent Order including a temporary restraining order that effectively shut down HPL's plant. The Debtor's plant has been non-operational since July 1995.

In August 1995, the wood chip piles that had accumulated at the Bay Shore property prior to the shut down caught fire and burned for several days. The fire spread to the adjacent pieces of property as well. The Town of Islip, the municipality in which HPL's facility sits, expended over $1,000,000 to fight the fire and for emergency clean-up costs on the Debtor's property and on the adjoining property. To secure repayment of the fire-related and cleanup expenses, the Town of Islip assessed a real property tax lien against the Debtor's Bay Shore property for the entire amount of the clean-up costs. Pursuant to various local legislative requirements, the County later reimbursed the Town of Islip for the clean-up costs and has now asserted its rights as lienholder on the Bay Shore property, in place of the Town of Islip.

On September 11, 1995, the Debtor agreed to a Consent Order with the DEC which, inter alia, requires the Debtor and its related entities to develop a work plan to clean up its site. HPL and its related entities filed a clean-up plan with the DEC on October 17, 1995.

Because of the injunction that resulted from the DEC's litigation and the subsequent Consent Order entered into by the Debtor, the Debtor was required to expend substantial sums to do the necessary clean-up. However, the Debtor had ceased operating and did not have the necessary funds to adequately clean-up the property so as to remove the injunction obtained by DEC. The Debtor filed its Chapter 11 petition on November 14, 1995.

The DEC approved HPL's work plan on November 17, 1995.

As part of its overall attempt to reorganize, the Debtor has sought financing from several entities in the energy producing field in order to obtain sufficient funds to clean-up its property and recommence operations. Though many firms expressed initial interest in making a loan, or a purchase of the Debtor's business, only Enron has made an offer to lend funds to the Debtor. The necessity for substantial sums of money to be expended to perform the cleanup before the Debtor can resume its operations appears to have inhibited any other lender from coming forward.

Among other provisions, the pertinent terms of the financing, as outlined in the Memorandum of Understanding, are as follows. Enron will loan the Debtor a maximum of $750,000. HPL will be able to draw down money against the $750,000 fund pursuant to a mutually agreeable draw down schedule. The loan is payable one year from the date on which HPL recommences operations. The rate of interest, to be set two days before the closing, will be 820 basis points over the 1 year United States Treasury Rate. There will be a 3 % structuring fee (of the total loan amount) for the making of the loan, payable to ECT Securities Corp. on the closing date from the loan proceeds. There is also a 0.5 % commitment fee on any unused amount of the loan. As security for the loan, Enron will receive a super priority administrative claim under §364(c) of the Code and pursuant to Section 364(d), a priming lien on all of the Debtor's assets, as well as an assignment of and a first priority security interest in all revenues the Debtor receives from the sale of electric power. In addition to other conditions set forth in Attachment A to the Memorandum of Understanding, the closing of the contemplated transaction is subject to satisfactory resolution of the Debtor's disputes with LILCO and its landlord and entry of a final non-appealable order providing for the consent of the DEC to the resumption of HPL's power producing business. . . .

Out of the loan proceeds the Debtor has budgeted approximately $300,000–$400,000 for the clean-up of the Debtor's Bay Shore property to the satisfaction of the DEC, and the balance shall be used for Debtor's start-up operational needs.

The bondholders are represented by Oak Re and its counsel. Oak Re has a valid perfected first lien on all of the Debtor's property, real and personal. Although Oak Re initially objected to the proposed financing, following the Debtor's amendment of the Enron financing by the filing of a supplemental application and revised Memorandum of Understanding, it has agreed to subordinate its claim to Enron pursuant to the Financing Agreement, and support its approval. Though papers were also submitted in opposition by the DEC and the landlord, the only party that raised significant opposition to the approval of the financing arrangement was the County which claims a lien on the Debtor's property in a sum in excess of one million dollars. They did not file papers in opposition, but orally raised substantial objections claiming that their one million dollar lien should not be subordinated to the loan being made by Enron as they are not being provided with adequate protection for their lien. . . .

FINDINGS OF FACT

The Debtor filed a voluntary petition for reorganization relief under Chapter 11 of the Bankruptcy Code on November 14, 1995. The Debtor thereafter continued in possession and control of its assets as a debtor-in-possession in accordance with 11 U.S.C. §§1107 and 1108.

The Debtor's primary assets consist of an approximate two (2) acre parcel of real property and a pre-fabricated type building with equipment therein located at Bay Shore, New York, together with a cogeneration agreement that it has with Lilco.

This cogeneration agreement with Lilco is not assignable.

All of the Debtor's property, real and personal, is subject to a validly perfected blanket lien held by Oak Re on behalf of the bond holders in the sum of $4,500,000.00 and there is no equity in any of the Debtor's property.

Subsequent to the perfection of Oak Re's lien, the County holds a lien filed in Suffolk County against the Debtor's real property for the sum of $1,000,000.00.

By operation of law, the County's lien primes the lien of Oak Re on the Debtor's real property.

The value of the Debtor's raw land is $275,000.00.

The Debtor has no other assets, and no other source for funding the clean-up of the sites; for operating or for expenses.

The Debtor is prohibited from operating its business pursuant to an injunction obtained by the DEC which requires the Debtor to clean-up the premises pursuant to DEC regulations before the Debtor can operate and generate any income.

The cost of the required clean-up is estimated to be between $300,000 and $400,000.

The Debtor's need for financing if it is to continue to operate and reorganize is not in dispute.

If the Debtor is not able to clean-up the premises and remove the injunction imposed by the DEC, the Debtor cannot operate and will have to cease operations and the case will thereafter be dismissed or converted to a Chapter 7. The secured creditors would then be entitled to foreclose. . . .

The real property upon which the County has its lien would remain encumbered by the cost of clean-up.

Oak Re does not oppose the subordination of its secured claim. Only the County of Suffolk is vehemently opposed to the requested relief claiming it is not adequately protected.

The real property is encumbered with a pre-fabricated type building, and equipment which are of little value and subject to the first lien of Oak Re. According to testimony presented, the only valuable items of personalty are turbines, which would probably be removed by Oak Re. The balance of the machinery, equipment and building is purportedly of very little value and probably would be abandoned by Oak Re rather than have Oak Re incur the costs of removal.

In the event of a foreclosure by the County and an abandonment, Suffolk County would have the following choices: it could either sell the real property (a) subject to the cost to clean it up to the satisfaction of the DEC, or (b) at a reduced amount based on the necessary cost of clean-up of the premises, and the cost of removal of whatever may have been abandoned by the Debtor and the secured creditor.

It is not likely that any purchaser of the property would wish to keep and use the machinery that would be abandoned since it was specially created for the generation of steam for the purposes of creating electricity. No purchaser of the property would be entitled to obtain any of the Debtor's rights in its cogeneration agreement.

The loan by Enron to the Debtor would enable the Debtor to expend the funds necessary to clean up the property to the satisfaction of the DEC and to commence operation of its business. Without the clean-up of the property, the injunction imposed by DEC would inhibit any potential purchaser from being able to utilize the property for any purpose, even if it found the building and abandoned equipment to have some use. In fact, without a clean-up of the property sufficient to satisfy the injunction placed on it by the DEC, the property has no monetary value.

The loan is ear-marked for the clean-up and start-up of the Debtor's business. The investment by the Debtor of $300,000–$400,000 to clean-up the property enhances the value of the collateral as to both the County and Oak Re.

The testimony reveals that the Debtor has made adequate attempts to obtain financing, but has not been able to obtain any loans, extension of credit, or financing other than the offer being made by Enron.

After the clean-up, the County's lien will be improved to the extent of the cost for the clean-up, i.e., $300,000–$400,000. The clean-up would enable the Debtor to commence operating and as an operating business, all of the Debtor's assets would increase in value. Although it is not clear what that value would be, it certainly would be of a greater value than the value of the Debtor's property in its present state. Debtor's sole shareholder testified that its value as an operating, ongoing concern could be worth several million dollars.

In light of the fact that the projected property improvements to be made with the borrowed funds will improve the value of the County's collateral to the extent of at least $300,000 and that the value of the County's lien in its present state is zero, it follows that the County's interest will not be diminished, but will be adequately protected.

In the event the Debtor cleans up the property and is able to operate, the County is in a position to recover the full value of its lien.

In the event that the Debtor utilizes the loan proceeds to clean up the property and is not successful in continuing the business, Suffolk County has had its collateral improved to the extent of the clean-up. If the raw land is valued at $275,000, that value can only be obtained if there is a clean-up and release of the DEC injunction.

DISCUSSION

11 U.S.C. §364 provides the mechanism by which a debtor may obtain credit. . . .

The Debtor has provided unrefuted testimony that the Debtor has been unable to obtain financing less onerous to his secured creditors. In fact, during the course of this case, the Court has offered to permit any party in interest, including DEC, the Landlord, Oak Re, Suffolk County, and any other party the right to clean-up the premises and obtain an administrative lien for the cost of the clean-up. No one offered to provide the costs of the clean-up on any secured basis. The Debtor has provided testimony to support the finding that the Debtor has not been able to obtain credit without priming its senior liens.

Adequate Protection

Pursuant to 11 U.S.C. §364(d), the Debtor must present evidence that the interest of the holder of an existing lien on its property is adequately protected. Adequate protection is not expressly defined. The statute confers upon "the parties and the courts flexibility by allowing such other relief as will result in the realization by the protected entity of the value of its interest in the property involved." House Report # 95-959, 95th Cong. 1st Session (1978), reprinted in 1978 U.S. Code Cong. & Admin. News 5787, 6296. The goal of adequate protection for purposes of the provision entitling a debtor to obtain financing secured by liens senior to all other interests is to safeguard the secured creditor from diminution in the value of its interests.

Section 506 of the Bankruptcy Code enacted as part of the extensive 1978 revision of the Bankruptcy Laws, governs the definition and treatment of secured claims, i.e., claims by creditors against the estate that are secured by a lien on property in which the estate has an interest. Subsection (a) of Section 506 provides that a claim is secured only to the extent of the value of the property on which the lien is fixed; the remainder of that is considered unsecured. U.S. v. Ron Pair Enterprises, Inc., 489 U.S. 235, 109 S. Ct. 1026, 103 L. Ed. 2d 290 (1989).

Since this Court has valued the secured lien of Suffolk County as of this moment at zero, or at best having a possible raw land value of $275,000, any improvement to the Debtor's real property by way of a clean-up sufficient to remove the injunction of DEC will greatly improve the value of the collateral upon which Suffolk County has a lien. Therefore, since the clean-up to the satisfaction of the DEC is a condition precedent to the loan, Suffolk County is adequately protected. There is no question in this Court's mind that the property will be improved by the clean-up since it is presently either unsaleable or has a nominal value at best, because of the restraint imposed by the DEC regulations. Without this investment and improvement to Debtor's property, the County itself may have to invest the cost of the clean-up if it wishes to have any benefit from its collateral. It is further clear to this Court that the investment made to clean-up the property will result in a benefit not only to the Debtor and its estate, but to all secured creditors and parties-in-interest.

HPL could not obtain credit secured by a lien junior to Suffolk County's secured position despite diligent efforts. The Debtor cannot obtain financing secured by a lien on unencumbered property pursuant to 11 U.S.C. §363(c)(2) because there is no property in the estate which is not already subject to a lien. The Debtor's property is encumbered by the lien of Suffolk County and Oak Re, each of which liens exceed the value of the property liened.

. . . The Debtor's motion to obtain senior priority financing pursuant to 11 U.S.C. §364(d) is granted.

Anyone who pulled out a pencil during this case probably noticed that the debtor borrowed up to $750,000, all of which bears a first priority but only $300–400,000 of which will go to clean up. Evidently the court believes that the benefits from doing the clean up through the Chapter 11 are sufficient to give adequate protection to the protesting county whose interests will slide down in priority. For obvious reasons, this sort of result, "priming" of a pre-existing lien, is thought to be rarely granted. So far as we know, however, no one has counted.

The next case presents two of the most important and controversial issues in the realm of post-petition financing: cross-collateralization and mootness. Cross-collateralization in this context involves securing a pre-bankruptcy loan with new or additional collateral granted post-bankruptcy as part of a new post-bankruptcy loan. The simplified issue is: Should a creditor's pre-petition position (often undersecured) get promoted in exchange for post-petition financing?

The second issue deals with mootness. The problem is that several key reorganization issues, notably post-petition financing, are difficult for appellate courts to review because a stay of the bankruptcy court order will often sink the company, but absent a stay, it is hard for the appellate court to unscramble the egg if it disagrees with the bankruptcy court's decision. A creditor lending new money to a business in bankruptcy would be reluctant to turn loose the cash if the bankruptcy decision approving priority repayment could be overturned on appeal. One statutory section, subsection 364(e) of the Code, creates a particular problem. It is designed to encourage post-petition lenders by assuring them that their rights will not be upset by an appeal of the order that gives them security or a priority, leaving them with a very high-risk loan.

The subsection contemplates that a party appealing a financing order must apply for a stay of the order and that the party will usually be required to post a substantial bond. Absent a stay, the lender will be protected in its security or priority even if the appellate court later decides the financing order was ill-advised or not authorized by the statute. Absent such a rule, of course, lenders might be unwilling to advance funds until all appeals had been decided, by which time the debtor would likely have expired. On the other hand, the rule often means that the action of the lower court will never be subjected to an effective review. The conflicting policy objectives can create substantial tension.

≡ SHAPIRO v. SAYBROOK MANUFACTURING CO., INC. ≡
963 F.2d 1490 (llth Cir. 1992)

Cox, Circuit Judge:

Seymour and Jeffrey Shapiro, unsecured creditors, objected to the bankruptcy court's authorization for the Chapter 11 debtors to "cross-collateralize" their pre-petition debt with unencumbered property from the bankruptcy estate. The bankruptcy court overruled the objection and also refused to grant a stay of its order pending appeal. The Shapiros appealed to the district court, which dismissed the case as moot under section 364(e) of the Bankruptcy Code because the Shapiros had failed to obtain a stay. We conclude that this appeal is not moot and that cross-collateralization is not authorized under the Bankruptcy Code. Accordingly, we reverse and remand.

I.   FACTS AND PROCEDURAL HISTORY

Saybrook Manufacturing Co., Inc., and related companies (the "debtors"), initiated proceedings seeking relief under Chapter 11 of the Bankruptcy Code on December 22, 1988. On December 23, 1988, the debtors filed a motion for the use of cash collateral and for authorization to incur secured debt. The bankruptcy court entered an emergency financing order that same day. At the time the bankruptcy petition was filed, the debtors owed Manufacturers Hanover approximately $34 million. The value of the collateral for this debt, however, was less than $10 million. Pursuant to the order, Manufacturers Hanover agreed to lend the debtors an additional $3 million to facilitate their reorganization. In exchange, Manufacturers Hanover received a security interest in all of the debtors' property — both property owned prior to filing the bankruptcy petition and that which was acquired subsequently. This security interest not only protected the $3 million of post-petition credit but also secured Manufacturers Hanover's $34 million pre-petition debt.

This arrangement enhanced Manufacturers Hanover's position vis-à-vis other unsecured creditors, such as the Shapiros, in the event of liquidation. Because Manufacturers Hanover's pre-petition debt was undersecured by approximately $24 million, it originally would have shared in a pro rata distribution of the debtors' unencumbered assets along with the other unsecured creditors. Under the financing order, however, Manufacturers Hanover's pre-petition debt became fully secured by all of the debtors' assets.

If the bankruptcy estate were liquidated, Manufacturers Hanover's entire debt — $34 million pre-petition and $3 million post-petition — would have to be paid in full before any funds could be distributed to the remaining unsecured creditors. . . .

V. DISCUSSION

A. Mootness

We begin by addressing the lenders' claim that this appeal is moot under section 364(e) of the Bankruptcy Code. . . . The purpose of this provision is to encourage the extension of credit to debtors in bankruptcy by eliminating the risk that any lien securing the loan will be modified on appeal.

The lenders suggest that we assume cross-collateralization is authorized under section 364 and then conclude the Shapiros' appeal is moot under section 364(e). This is similar to the approach adopted by the Ninth Circuit in Burchinal v. Central Washington Bank (In re Adams Apple, Inc.), 829 F.2d 1484 (9th Cir. 1987). That court held that cross-collateralization was "authorized" under section 364 for the purposes of section 364(e) mootness but declined to decide whether cross-collateralization was illegal per se under the Bankruptcy Code.

We reject the reasoning of In re Adams Apple and In re Ellingsen because they "put the cart before the horse." By its own terms, section 364(e) is only applicable if the challenged lien or priority was authorized under section 364. . . . We cannot determine if this appeal is moot under section 364(e) until we decide the central issue in this appeal — whether cross-collateralization is authorized under section 364. Accordingly, we now turn to that question.

B. Cross-Collateralization and Section 364

Cross-collateralization is an extremely controversial form of Chapter 11 financing. Nevertheless, the practice has been approved by several bankruptcy courts. Even the courts that have allowed cross-collateralization, however, were generally reluctant to do so. . . .

The issue of whether the Bankruptcy Code authorizes cross-collateralization is a question of first impression in this court. Indeed, it is essentially a question of first impression before any court of appeals. Neither the lenders' brief nor our own research has produced a single appellate decision which either authorizes or prohibits the practice. . . .

The Second Circuit expressed criticism of cross-collateralization in In re Texlon, [596 F.2d 1092 (2d Cir. 1979)]. The court, however, stopped short of prohibiting the practice altogether. At issue was the bankruptcy court's ex parte financing order granting the lender a security interest in the debtor's property to secure both pre-petition and post-petition debt. The court, in an exercise of judicial restraint, concluded that:

> In order to decide this case we are not obliged, however, to say that under no conceivable circumstances could "cross-collateralization" be authorized.

> Here it suffices to hold that . . . a financing scheme so contrary to the spirit of the Bankruptcy Act should not have been granted by an ex parte order, where the bankruptcy court relies solely on representations by a debtor in possession that credit essential to the maintenance of operations is not otherwise obtainable.

In re Texlon, 596 F.2d at 1098. Although In re Texlon was decided under the earlier Bankruptcy Act, the court also considered whether cross-collateralization was authorized under the Bankruptcy Code. "To such limited extent as it is proper to consider the new Bankruptcy Act, which takes effect on October 1, 1979, in considering the validity of an order made in 1974, we see nothing in §364(c) or in other provisions of that section that advances the case in favor of 'cross-collateralization.'" In re Texlon, 596 F.2d at 1098 (citations omitted).

Cross-collateralization is not specifically mentioned in the Bankruptcy Code. We conclude that cross-collateralization is inconsistent with bankruptcy law for two reasons. First, cross-collateralization is not authorized as a method of post-petition financing under section 364. Second, cross-collateralization is beyond the scope of the bankruptcy court's inherent equitable power because it is directly contrary to the fundamental priority scheme of the Bankruptcy Code. See generally Charles J. Tabb, A Critical Reappraisal of Cross-Collateralization in Bankruptcy, 60 So. Cal. L. Rev. 109 (1986).

Section 364 authorizes Chapter 11 debtors to obtain secured credit and incur secured debt as part of their reorganization. . . . By their express terms, sections 364(c) & (d) apply only to future — i.e., post-petition — extensions of credit. They do not authorize the granting of liens to secure pre-petition loans. . . .

Given that cross-collateralization is not authorized by section 364, we now turn to the lenders' argument that bankruptcy courts may permit the practice under their general equitable power. Bankruptcy courts are indeed courts of equity and they have the power to adjust claims to avoid injustice or unfairness. This equitable power, however, is not unlimited. . . .

Section 507 of the Bankruptcy Code fixes the priority order of claims and expenses against the bankruptcy estate. Creditors within a given class are to be treated equally, and bankruptcy courts may not create their own rules of superpriority within a single class. 3 Collier on Bankruptcy §507.02[2] (15th ed. 1992). Cross-collateralization, however, does exactly that. As a result of this practice, post-petition lenders' unsecured pre-petition claims are given priority over all other unsecured pre-petition claims. . . .

. . . Rehabilitation is certainly the primary purpose of Chapter 11. This end, however, does not justify the use of any means. Cross-collateralization is directly inconsistent with the priority scheme of the Bankruptcy Code. Accordingly, the practice may not be approved by the bankruptcy court under its equitable authority.

VI. Conclusion

Cross-collateralization is not authorized by section 364. Section 364(e), therefore, is not applicable and this appeal is not moot. Because *Texlon*-type cross-collateralization is not explicitly authorized by the Bankruptcy Code and is contrary to the basic priority structure of the Code, we hold that it is an impermissible means of obtaining post-petition financing. . . .

Reversed and remanded.

Owner Financing

While some debtors go to new lenders and some return to their pre-petition lenders, other debtors turn to the old equity holders as another source of funds. Sometimes the pre-bankruptcy owners are willing to make additional investments in the business to keep it running. Often, however, these investors do not use the priority and superpriority provisions discussed here. Instead, in return for their investment they want continued ownership of the post-bankruptcy business.

The Bankruptcy Code restricts the participation of old equity in the post-bankruptcy corporation. The Code generally follows the rule that equity cannot retain value unless all the creditors have been paid in full, the so-called Absolute Priority Rule. But some courts have created a judicial exception to the rule (what's the fun of a rule without a complicated exception?). When equity provides new value that can't be obtained elsewhere to finance the reorganization, the court may permit equity to retain ownership if it is convinced that the bargain is fair and that creditors will be benefited.

The practice has been sharply criticized, principally by mortgage holders of apartment complexes and office buildings who would like to see the Chapter 11 case dismissed, leaving them free to repossess the property and deal with it themselves. A split among the circuits prompted the Supreme Court to review such a case in Bank of America National Trust and Savings Assoc. v. 203 N. LaSalle St. Partnership, 526 U.S. 434 (1999). The court held that the real estate partnership could not simply buy the equity in the business as part of its plan confirmation without giving others an opportunity to bid. The case ducked larger questions concerning when old equity could refinance the business in return for retaining ownership, and further litigation will surely follow.

In the context of a small business in which there is no business without the current owner-operator, as a practical matter the creditors may accede to continued participation by old equity. Of course, not all equity owners have either the desire or the financial wherewithal to participate in financing a reorganization. Even if they do, application of the Absolute Priority Rule, especially after *203 North LaSalle,* can be a difficult barrier. The rule and the exception are discussed in greater detail in the section on plan confirmation, infra p. 655. For now, we simply note another financing alternative that will be appropriate in some cases.

Financing Goods and Services

Dealing with suppliers is a major task for the new Chapter 11 debtor. Unless they are willing to continue to furnish necessary goods and services, the debtor is dead on arrival. Nothing in the Bankruptcy Code requires suppliers to continue to deal with the debtor, except in the cases in which the debtor has legally enforceable contracts for future goods and services, a point discussed in the next section of this chapter. Ordinary supply contracts — the company places an order and the supplier delivers it — often have just a series of orders, but no single, ongoing contract. Absent such ongoing contracts, many suppliers will be reluctant to extend any further credit despite the fact that they will be entitled to administrative priority if they do. §§503(b), 507(a)(1). Many of them will be willing to continue to ship or to work if they are paid cash in advance, although some suppliers may refuse to deal with the debtor on any basis, feeling betrayed by its default on pre-petition obligations or determined to forge new relationships with more reliable customers. Getting suppliers to participate in the Chapter 11 process is a central focus of the early part of a reorganization.

A combination of case law developments and the 2005 Amendments have greatly improved the leverage of suppliers of goods and services while adding to the burden of financing a Chapter 11 reorganization. It has always been the general rule in bankruptcy, including Chapter 11 cases, that unsecured pre-petition creditors could not be paid except through a pro rata distribution process. This is the most basic application of the maxim Equity is Equality, although there is no provision in the Code that states that rule explicitly. In particular, trade creditors who had extended credit for goods and services prior to bankruptcy had to wait to be paid any part of what they were owed on Bankruptcy Day. There had always been a large exception in Chapter 11 cases for employees. A small, occasional exception had also been found in a few cases for "critical vendors." In general terms, a critical vendor was a supplier whose continued delivery to the debtor was absolutely crucial to the success of the Chapter 11 case and who refused to supply further goods or services unless pre-petition debt was paid first. In the 1990s, the courts expanded the critical-vendor rule so that in some districts — notably Delaware and Southern New York — it became almost routine that the debtor would be allowed to pay the pre-petition unsecured debts of many vendors. These courts almost always ratified the debtors' decisions as to which vendors were critical. This doctrine gave the debtors in those districts considerable clout with suppliers, because of the debtors' de facto power to choose who got paid, but it also greatly increased the need for post-petition financing to provide the liquidity to pay large amounts of cash at the very beginning of the case.

In 2004, the Seventh Circuit stunned the Chapter 11 world by holding that the critical vendor doctrine must be very narrowly limited to vendors who were demonstrably "critical." Unless the debtor could produce evidence in court that payment to these suppliers was necessary and would substantially benefit the estate, then the pre-petition debts of the suppliers — all of the suppliers — would have to wait for disposition pro rata when the case was resolved through reorganization or liquidation. In re Kmart Corp., 359 F.3d 866 (7th Cir. 2004). It remains to be seen if the resulting circuit split will attract the attention of the Supreme Court. In the meantime, the existence or absence of a broad critical vendor rule in some districts but not others will have a great impact on where some debtors would prefer to file their cases, a point discussed at greater length later in this chapter and in the next one with regard to public-company bankruptcies.

The 2005 Amendments included another potentially important benefit for certain trade creditors, those who supply goods to a debtor. Goods suppliers have long enjoyed a special preference under the UCC: the right of reclamation. UCC §2-702. With some limitations, this right permitted the seller to get back the goods it had sold to a buyer who turned out to be insolvent. Of course, the seller could protect itself with a perfected purchase money security interest, but the reclamation right gave the seller similar protection even though it had never obtained (nor recorded) a security interest in the goods it shipped. This reclamation right was recognized in bankruptcy, but the Code severely limited that right. Because the right to reclaim amounted to the same kind of preference over other creditors as a security interest without having satisfied the Article 9 requirements of consent, notice, and filing, the Bankruptcy Code sharply limited the time available to exercise the right to reclaim the shipped goods.

In 2005, Congress gave suppliers of goods a greatly expanded right of reclamation. Under section 546(c), if the debtor receives the goods while insolvent and within 45 days of filing for bankruptcy, the seller may have a right to get the goods back if it makes a timely written demand. In addition, a seller of goods received by the debtor within the last 20 days before bankruptcy gets an automatic administrative priority, a one-hundred-cent right to payment for those goods. §503(b)(9).

These two provisions represent a great deal of leverage for this class of creditors. They also increase the debtor's need for cash at the very start of the case (to pay the suppliers immediately or to replace the reclaimed goods to keep the business running). The changes also add still more confusion to the maelstrom typical of a new Chapter 11 case, because of the potential administrative chaos in determining which suppliers are entitled to which goods. Correspondingly, this increased preference for the suppliers of goods may operate to the prejudice of other creditors, such as the suppliers of services who will have to await payment from a now-diminished pool. The provisions also increase the risk that fewer companies will be able to reorganize successfully, an outcome that can injure everyone who depends on that reorganization, from a taxing authority to a retired employee. Here, as elsewhere in bankruptcy, we are reminded that a benefit to one creditor often comes out of the pockets of other creditors who may be even less able to withstand the losses.

One last point in the careful balance among creditors: Note that the reclamation provisions work against the debtor (and, in a derivative sense, against the other general unsecured creditors). But it does not work against a secured lender who claims the newly delivered property as inventory. §506(c). The blanket security interest that covers inventory or after-acquired property will continue to operate against the supplier, negating any right to reclaim the goods. It seems that when Congress goes about rebalancing the rights of creditors, only some rights are on the potential chopping block.

First Day Orders

If there is one thing that lawyers know better than other observers of law, it is that procedure matters. Most of the issues that arise in the early days of a Chapter 11 case may be addressed in a court order typically referred to as a First Day Order — so named because often the debtor presents the order to the court and gets it signed on the same day the Chapter 11 petition is filed. Among the provisions included in many first day orders are (1) additional injunctive relief, beyond the automatic stay; (2) requirements for operating reports; (3) authorization to buy or sell outside of the ordinary course, authorization to pay employees wages due, and other operating items of that sort; (4) use of cash collateral and other matters related to cash management; (5) approval of a post-petition financing arrangement; and (6) employment of counsel for the debtor and for a creditors committee.

As the *Garland* case illustrates, the first day order is routinely entered without notice or an opportunity to be heard for many of the stakeholders in a Chapter 11 debtor. It may even be obtained *ex parte*, but more often it will be presented to the court with the attendance of a principal lender and perhaps a large creditor or crucial customer. In some cases a creditors' committee has been formed in advance of filing and its counsel will attend as well. Not surprisingly, the debtor will usually have lined up the parties most likely to support the first day order — that is, those who benefit from it or who are providing the financing and have already agreed that some of the money can be spent on the parties named in the first day order.

The order will often be temporary, expiring in a stated period of time if not renewed. Even then, however, the rights and practices established in the first day order are often difficult to alter at a later time. The money is often gone, and it can be difficult to recover. The result is that the debtor and a few other crucial players may have a decisive influence on the future of the case and the company, a control that even the court may find difficult to take back. That point is especially cogent in public-company cases and will receive further treatment in that section of this chapter.

Problem Set 21

21.1. You are the TIB for GoGo Properties, a real estate development firm that went, went. Despite its bad management and overleveraged debts, GoGo owns an excellent piece of suburban property. Although the "no growth" majority in the state legislature has adopted a statute that would make it impossible for a buyer to develop the property nearly as profitably, GoGo is the beneficiary of a "grandfather" clause that makes the restrictive statute inapplicable to existing owners and also makes it inapplicable to transferees if the property already has water and sewage service at the time of transfer. GoGo's property does not have water and sewage service and it will cost $100,000 to get them installed. The "no growth" statute provides that the time of transfer is defined as the time the property is first advertised or the first discussion is had concerning its possible transfer or sale.

Thus you cannot get a potential buyer to finance the work. How could you get someone to lend you the money to install the water and sewage service and thus greatly increase the value of the property? See §364.

21.2. Low Price, Inc. had a loan from the First State Bank for $500,000, secured by a lien on its inventory, when it entered Chapter 11. Low Price's total unsecured debt was $250,000. Low Price got a post-petition loan from Hanratty Finance of $250,000 secured by a lien on its equipment. FSB sought adequate protection by filing a stay-lifting complaint. The trustee offered an additional lien on Low Price's accounts receivable in order to provide adequate protection and the court approved, refusing to lift the stay. Unfortunately, the inventory was much depleted before FSB was successful in getting the case converted to Chapter 7, and the accounts have proven to be almost impossible to collect because of customers' warranty claims.

FSB is still owed $250,000 after sale of the inventory and collection of collectable accounts. Hanratty got only $150,000 from the sale of the equipment. There is $350,000 in other unencumbered assets. The only unpaid expense from the Chapter 11 case is the $150,000 fee for the debtor's lawyer. The Chapter 7 trustee and her lawyer are owed $50,000. How much will the trustee and her lawyer get? See §726(b). How much will FSB, Hanratty, and the debtor's lawyer get? See §§364(c)(l), 507(b).

21.3. Video Excitement, Inc., entered the "can't miss" business of video game manufacturing and distribution two years ago. It entered Chapter 11 last month. Your client, Murphy Investments, Inc., holds the $3 million first mortgage on the company's principal manufacturing facility. At the time of the loan, the appraisal indicated that the facility was worth $2 million.

The company has $1.5 million in unencumbered assets. The DIP has proposed to borrow $750,000 in operating money from the Yankee State Bank, securing the loan with a lien on the unencumbered assets of the company. Murphy had refused any further financing prior to bankruptcy and VEI entered bankruptcy because Yankee said it would facilitate its loan if it were a "DIP" loan approved by the court. Murphy tells you the interest rate Yankee proposes is "way too high" and is wondering if it should reconsider and offer to make the loan itself, at a lower rate, on the condition that all the money owed to it be secured by all of VEI's assets. What are the chances of getting court approval for Murphy's proposal, if VEI's management agrees? What if Yankee takes another look at VEI's financials and decides to find some business somewhere else — will prospects improve? See §364(c).

21.4. You filed a Chapter 11 petition almost three weeks ago for Ben's Auto Parts. Ben Sauers had a solid auto parts business in a strip mall on the main drag in town until the city started building a new overpass about three months before you filed. It tore up the street and in the process tore up the businesses in the mall. Ben explained, "I knew they were going to build the overpass, but they blocked access far more than necessary and my business just collapsed. No one could get to me." This morning Ben's bookkeeper, Myron Trout, brought you ten letters from suppliers of parts to Ben demanding return of their generators, spark plugs, wiper blades, etc., although with little documentation attached. He says he has gotten phone calls from five other suppliers with similar demands. Ben has more than 150 suppliers and expects more such letters every day, "even though I've never given any of those guys a lien or anything like that." On top of the letters, the biggest supplier, National Vehicle Wholesale Parts, arrived at the store with a letter demanding return of all "our parts" and a group of large men. They hauled off all of the National parts they could find. Ben protested, but was ignored and the police said it was up to the courts to sort it out. Myron wants to know what he should do about the letters and Ben wants to know what you will do about National. §§503(b), 546(c).

21.5. You had been mowing your yard late on Saturday afternoon, reviewing the events of your first week as a United States Bankruptcy Judge, when you received a call from counsel for Supertech Computers. Counsel asked for permission to come to your home to file a Chapter 11 petition on an emergency basis. Counsel and several officers from the company arrived a few minutes ago. Aside from feeling a bit strange about your "X-man" t-shirt amidst all the vests and ties, you are overwhelmed by the documents presented to you with the petition. There are numerous requests for orders approving certain sales and leases and the like, along with a request for approval of a "Financing Order." The FO would approve the making of a loan to the company of $100,000 by the Revere State Bank. RSB is interested in doing this because it has previously lent the company $200,000 secured by its inventory and accounts receivable. The new loan would be secured by inventory and accounts. No creditor's representative is present, although counsel represents that RSB has approved the transaction and form of order.

Counsel explains that the company has two pressing problems: (1) a creditor has just obtained a judgment against it for $50,000 and is threatening enforcement, but the company cannot afford the bond required for the appeal; and (2) a major supplier has refused to deliver unless paid in cash, and the assembly line will shut down in five hours without delivery (which the supplier can make in time if paid). If the line shuts down, it will cost $30,000 to restart it and Supertech will be forced to liquidate. On the other hand, shipping computers through next week will entitle Supertech to a $25,000 payment of withheld customer funds and enable the company to survive. Supertech, counsel says, now has 413 creditors (including RSB) owed a total of $800,000 and has assets worth only $300,000. Finally, counsel says he called some of the major creditors at their offices this morning, but could reach no one.

You ask counsel why he didn't call sooner, but his answers are evasive and unsatisfactory. It seems to you that he really knew he was going to file at least a couple of days ago. You begin to pepper counsel with questions: What are the company's assets, liabilities, and other security interests? Has the company made any projections of future income? What is the status of the RSB loan and is it validly and fully secured? What are the positions of other creditors to the extent they are known or reasonably estimated? What other questions will you ask debtor's counsel before you rule? What would you need to hear before you granted the debtor's motion?

D.   RESHAPING THE ESTATE

Although the "avoiding powers" of the TIB are equally available in consumer and business bankruptcy, the amount of money at stake and the complexity of the transactions involved make them far more important and more often asserted in business cases. Avoiding powers are important in business liquidations because they permit the TIB to undo pre-bankruptcy transactions between the debtor and certain creditors, to the benefit of all unsecured creditors. By so doing they serve the bankruptcy policies and they also police compliance with state law, especially Article 9 of the UCC.

The avoiding powers are equally important in Chapter 11 bankruptcies because bringing an avoidance action (or even threatening one) gives the TIB or DIP much greater leverage in negotiating with the defendant-creditor, which may face the loss of its security interest or an order requiring it to pay back amounts it received from the debtor shortly before bankruptcy. Obviously, a creditor facing the loss of its security interest has more reason to agree to the debtor's proposed treatment of the creditor in a reorganization plan.

Once the DIP or trustee in Chapter 11 gets the immediate cash flow problems under control and begins to stabilize the everyday operations of the business, it becomes time to assess the legal position of each of the creditors in preparation for constructing a workable plan. The potential application of the avoiding powers to various creditors is an important part of this calculation.

In the context of Chapter 11 and the avoiding powers, it is important to keep in mind the difference between the pre-bankruptcy "debtor" and the "Debtor in Possession" after the bankruptcy petition is filed. No matter how similar they may seem, the DIP is not the old debtor who filed Chapter 11. The DIP is trying to save the business as a going concern on *behalf of all the creditors*, as well as other constituencies such as employees, stockholders, and the community. When the DIP takes over the operation of the newly created business/estate, the rights of the DIP are not just the rights of the old debtor, but also the collective rights of the creditors to preserve the business's assets. Thus the DIP may avoid transactions that the old debtor would never have been allowed to challenge. In particular, the DIP will challenge any secured creditor's demand for better treatment than the unsecured creditors, until the challenged creditor establishes that the security interest under which it claims is not vulnerable to any of the avoiding powers of the DIP.

1.   *The Strong Arm Clause — Section 544(a)*

The order of priority in encumbered property is controlled largely by UCC Article 9 and state law real property priority schemes, but it is the Bankruptcy Code that determines the TIB's status in the state law pecking order. Section 544 compares the TIB to all other creditors by giving the TIB the rights and powers as of the date of the bankruptcy filing of a judicial lien creditor, an execution creditor, or, for real estate, a bona fide purchaser. This provision is known as the "strong arm clause," prosaically nicknamed to suggest its power to knock off unperfected interests.

Most students in the bankruptcy course will have had an Article 9 course and will have studied the strong arm clause as it applies to avoid unperfected security interests in personal property. In the following case, we explore the power of the TIB — and the resulting power of the DIP — in the real estate context. Note that section 544 has a special provision applicable to real estate, section 544(a)(3), and that this section gives the TIB even greater powers than against personal property interests, such as security interests under Article 9. Against a holder of a real property interest, the TIB has the status of a "bona fide purchaser" (BFP) of a real property. Because a BFP generally has much greater rights under state law than a mere lien creditor, the TIB's power to avoid real estate interests under the strong arm clause is also greater.

====== In re BOWLING ======

314 B.R. 127 (S.D. Ohio 2004)

OPINION BY: J. Vincent AUG

* * *

II. FACTS

Debtor Charles T. Bowling is the owner of the real estate located at 4340 West Street, Oxford, Ohio. The deed conveying the real estate to Mr. Bowling was recorded on September 26, 2000, and reflects that he was married at that time. The deed does not, however, include a spouse of Mr. Bowling as a grantee.

On July 12, 2001, Mr. Bowling executed a promissory note in favor of Alta Financial Corporation, predecessor to [the Mortgage Registration System — MERS, the company now holding the note] in the amount of $116,073.00. On that same date, Mr. Bowling also executed a mortgage conveying the real estate as security for the promissory note. The mortgage was recorded on August 1, 2001, in the Butler County Recorder's Office. On its face, the mortgage reflects that Mr. Bowling's signature was notarized by Sharon R. Eisenhut. By her certificate, Ms. Eisenhut certifies that Mr. Bowling executed the mortgage in her presence. Debtor Cathy Bowling did not sign the promissory note or the mortgage.

The Debtors filed their chapter 7 petition on January 21, 2003.

On July 30, 2003, the Trustee filed a complaint seeking to avoid MERS' mortgage on the basis that it was defectively executed under Ohio Revised Code §5301.01 and thus avoidable pursuant to 11 U.S.C. §§ 544 and/or 547. In an affidavit attached to the Trustee's Cross Motion for Summary Judgment, Mr. Bowling states that

The closing took place at my home, and the only parties present were my wife, Cathy J. Bowling and a gentlem[a]n named John. Sharon R. Eisenhut, the party signing the acknowledgement on the mortgage I executed at the time of closing was not present. I do not know Ms. Eisenhut, and certainly did not acknowledge the signing of that mortgage in her presence or to her at any time.

The Trustee also asserts that since Mrs. Bowling did not execute the mortgage, her dower interest in the real estate is property of the bankruptcy estate.

III. DISCUSSION

This case involves a question of the validity of a mortgage concerning real property located in Ohio. Therefore, the law of Ohio governs the Court's decision on the following issues raised by the parties' summary judgment motions.

A. Is Mrs. Bowling's inchoate dower interest in the real estate property of the bankruptcy estate?

B. Do the amendments to Ohio Revised Code §5301.01 eliminate the requirement that a notary must be present at the time the mortgage was signed?

C. If a notarized signature is required, is Mr. Bowling's testimony alone sufficient to establish that the notary was not present at the time the mortgage was executed?

* * *

[The court works its way through Ohio law, determining that the mortgage was not executed according to Ohio law.]

We now consider the Trustee's cross motion for summary judgment on the issue that the mortgage is defective because of the lack of presence of the notary at the time Mr. Bowling executed the mortgage; and, therefore, that the Trustee is entitled to avoid the mortgage pursuant to its strong-arm powers under §544(a)(3).

The Trustee must show by clear and convincing evidence that the mortgage was not signed and notarized as purported. Ford v. Osborne, 45 Ohio St. 1, 12 N.E. 526, 527 (Ohio 1887); see also Weaver v. Crommes, 109 Ohio App. 470, 167 N.E.2d 661 (Ohio Ct. App. 1959) ("The presumption of validity . . . can be overcome only by clear and convincing proof; and he who challenges it must sustain the burden of such proof."). "Clear and convincing evidence may be defined as that measure or degree of proof which will produce in the mind of the trier of fact a firm belief or conviction as to the allegations sought to be established." Yoppolo v. Household Realty Corp. (In re Winland), 276 B.R. 773, 784 (Bankr. N.D. Ohio 2001) (citing Helbling v. Williams (In re Williams), 240 B.R. 884, 888 (Bankr. N.D. Ohio 1999) and Cross v. Ledford, 161 Ohio St. 469, 477, 120 N.E.2d 118 (1954)).

MERS contests Mr. Bowling's assertion that Ms. Eisenhut was not present when Mr. Bowling signed the mortgage. However, similar to the mortgagee in *In re Collins*, MERS has presented no evidence that Ms. Eisenhut was present. MERS has presented no evidence of the general business practices of MERS' predecessor. Mr. Bowling has testified by affidavit that the refinancing was done at his home and that there was only one other person besides Mr. and Mrs. Bowling present at the closing, that being a male by the name of "John." As the court in In re Zaptocky noted, a refinancing is an extraordinary event for a consumer. It would stick out in Mr. Bowling's mind. In particular, it seems that Mr. Bowling would remember whether the person coming to close the loan was male or female. See Simon v. Zaptocky (In re Zaptocky), 231 B.R. 260 at 264; see also *In re Collins*, 292 B.R. at 848.

MERS cannot rest on its pleadings alone, "but must identify specific facts supported by affidavits, or by depositions, answers to interrogatories, and admissions on file that show there is a genuine issue for trial." *In re Gibson*, 219 B.R. at 198. MERS' mere argument that the notary was present, is not sufficient. There is no per se rule in Ohio that Mr. Bowling's testimony alone is insufficient to overcome the notary's certification. We find that in the absence of MERS' presentation of any evidence to the contrary, that the Trustee has met his burden and presented clear and convincing evidence that a notary was not present at the time Mr. Bowling executed the mortgage. The Trustee's motion for summary judgment is GRANTED.

Finally, MERS has not addressed the Trustee's argument that contrary to assertions in MERS' answer, MERS is not entitled to a lien in the real estate pursuant to §550. The Sixth Circuit has recently addressed this matter and determined that where the Trustee has avoided a mortgage pursuant to its strong-arm powers, the mortgagee's interest is preserved and becomes a part of the bankruptcy estate without the need for the trustee to resort to the recovery process pursuant to §550(a). Therefore, the statutory provisions of §550(e) providing for a replacement lien for the creditor are not triggered for the benefit of the mortgagee. Suhar v. Burns (In re Burns), 322 F.3d 421 (6th Cir. 2003). Based on this Sixth Circuit precedent and MERS' failure to address the issue in its pleadings, we further find that MERS is not entitled to a replacement lien pursuant to §550.

* * *

The Sixth Circuit affirmed a similar case, In re Huffman, 369 F.3d 972 (6th Cir. 2004), in which the mortgagee had failed to garner the three witnesses to the mortgage required by Ohio law. The bankruptcy court had ruled that the TIB could set aside the mortgage. The outraged mortgage lenders took their case to the Ohio legislature, easing the technical requirements for recording a mortgage, but the Sixth Circuit said that would work only for future cases, not for the debtors who had already filed for bankruptcy.

Debtors' attorneys in other states took note, bringing more cases to set aside mortgages. The courts acknowledged the strong arm provisions, but some then headed in a different direction. Because the TIB's status is that of a bona fide purchaser, some said the TIB is charged with the same limits as a BFP. These courts held that a purchaser who saw the mortgage — defective as it was — would have notice of the mortgage and could not attain BFP status in the purchase. By this line of reasoning, the TIB would similarly be charged (and the DIP as well), and that notice would prevent the TIB from setting aside the defective mortgage. In re Jones, 284 B.R. 92 (Bankr. E.D. Pa. 2002); In re Little Key, 292 B.R. 879 (Bankr. S.D. Ohio 2003). Other courts see it differently. Some note that in some states a defective filing does not put a buyer on notice. Others note that the BFP status is granted by federal law in section 544(a), which begins with the observation that the provisions apply without regard to the knowledge of the trustee or any creditor. Wonder-Bowl Properties v. Ha Ja Kim, 161 B.R. 831 (9th Cir. BAP. 1993).

The strong arm clause is effectively the testing portion of the Bankruptcy Code — it tests the strength of the lock that the secured creditor or lien creditor has put on the property. If the mortgagee locked up the property so that it could prevail over a bona fide purchaser, then the lock will hold in bankruptcy. But if the property remains unlocked, the creditor will find itself just one more floater in the general pool of unsecured creditors.

Other Property

Where the dispute is over personal property rather than real estate, of course, the TIB has only the "lien creditor" status of §544(a)(1)-(2). This means much less power under state law generally. The drafters of Article 9 have over the years steadily reduced the power of the lien creditor to avoid unperfected security interests by denying to the lien creditor the priority that they give to other secured parties and buyers. The explicit reason for nibbling away at the rights of lien creditors in Article 9 has been to respond to secured creditors' pressure to reduce the number of security interests that can be challenged in bankruptcy, when the TIB steps into the shoes of the lien creditor. When Article 9 was revised in 1999, the trend continued. For example, only secured parties and buyers are protected against misinformation of certain types in a filed financing statement, while the unsecured creditors represented by the TIB are bound by a defective and misleading filing even if they actually relied on it. UCC §9-338.

But the interplay between state and federal law is nowhere more evident than in this section. The judge in *Bowling* turned to Ohio law to learn the details of what was required, and judges in cases involving security interests on personal property turn to state law Article 9 — but only because federal law tells them to do so. In 2004, an amendment to the bankruptcy laws was introduced in the Senate to give the TIB bona fide purchaser status in *all* cases. Because Article 9 had been revised to shrink the power of the lien creditor, but not the power of the purchaser, the effect would have been to overturn much work by the credit industry. The amendment did not make it to a vote, but it stirred great anxiety in the creditor community as they contemplated the consequences of being required once again to meet every rule to make a security interest valid.

Federal Tax Liens

Just as the strong arm clause establishes the TIB's role in the state law priority schemes, the clause also works to establish the TIB's position regarding federal tax liens. Repayment of taxes and discharge of tax debt are controlled by the Bankruptcy Code as a part of the broader provisions relating to priority claims in section 507 and discharge in section 523. These provisions apply to all state and federal taxes owed, whether the tax claim is secured or unsecured. The Bankruptcy Code's rules on repayment priority and discharge raise fundamental bankruptcy issues that are covered elsewhere in these materials. By contrast, the tax lien provisions largely adopt the priority schemes set forth in state and other federal laws, which are studied in greater detail in secured lending courses.

A brief reminder of the priority issues may be helpful. A federal tax lien arises when an assessment is made, and it attaches to all the taxpayer's property and rights to property. Until the lien is filed, however, it is treated much like an unfiled security interest: good against the debtor, but not good against most other interested parties, including, in our case, the TIB. Before the lien is filed, the strong arm provisions permit the TIB to exercise the rights of a judgment lien creditor or bona fide purchaser of real estate on the date of filing, which gives the TIB priority over the unfiled tax lien. 26 U.S.C. §6323 (1995). After the tax lien is filed, however, the TIB must recognize the lien in bankruptcy and treat the government as it does other perfected secured parties.

Problem Set 22

22.1. Western Fliers runs a small charter airplane service. Eight months ago it bought a new ten-passenger Thunderbolt aircraft from Mitchell Aeronautics for $255,000. Western paid $25,000 in cash, and it gave a promissory note for $230,000 secured by the aircraft. When the deal was closed and Western had signed the security agreement and financing statement, MA's attorney gave the papers to her young assistant with the instructions "to file these right away." The assistant did so — in the filing cabinet drawer with the information on the Western sale.

Western Fliers has a major personal injury judgment against it, and it has just filed a Chapter 11. When MA learned of the filing, it pulled out its files on Western and discovered the security agreement and financing statement. It called you immediately. What do you advise? See §544(a), UCC §9-317(e).

22.2. Western Fliers, discussed in the previous problem, bought another plane a week before the filing. This plane was purchased from Aero for $10,000 down and a promissory note for $160,000 secured by the Aero Leader being purchased and "all Western Fliers' other planes, spare parts, and servicing equipment, including Western's ten-passenger Thunderbolt." When Aero learned of the Chapter 11, it immediately filed copies of the financing statement in all the appropriate locations. What can Aero get in the Chapter 11? See §§362(b)(3); 544(a); 546(b).

22.3. Larry Cochran was one of a number of investors who were persuaded to invest in home mortgages originated by Dynamic Investments, a relatively new local concern that promised high returns on safe loans secured by the borrowers' houses. Each investor put up the agreed amount and got a mortgage signed by the homeowner. Dynamic got a commission paid by the homeowner. Although the investors were shocked when Dynamic closed its doors and its president disappeared, they were not too concerned because their loans were secured by residential real estate. Unfortunately, Cochran got another shock this morning when he received a notice that his homeowner-borrower has gone into bankruptcy. He has come to you for reassurance that he is protected by his mortgage on the borrower's house. You sent your paralegal to the courthouse and he has just reported that the Cochran mortgage was filed in the land records of the county, but it seems to be missing the witness signatures required by state law. What is your analysis of Cochran's situation? See §544(a).

22.4. Topson Air Conditioning sold Sally's Boutique a central air conditioning system for $12,200, taking a $3,000 down payment and a lien on the system for the balance. After Sally had paid about $500 more, Topson got a notice of the Boutique's Chapter 7 bankruptcy. Topson's credit manager says its lien was promptly filed in the Secretary of State's office. He wants to know if the company's lien will stand up in bankruptcy. What do you tell him? See §544(a). UCC §9-334.

2. Preferences: The General Rules

The Code not only gives the trustee or DIP a strong position as a lien creditor or bona fide purchaser under state law, it also gives the trustee extraordinary new powers not available elsewhere in law. These powers include the ability to dismantle certain transactions between the debtor and creditors that took place within the 90 days immediately preceding the bankruptcy filing.

These new powers are designed to permit the TIB to review the activities of the debtor as it neared bankruptcy and to determine whether some creditors received preferential treatment before the bankruptcy was filed. If the court finds that such preferences have occurred, these creditors are not permitted to preserve their improved position in bankruptcy. Instead, these creditors face the trustee's demand that they surrender any preferences received from the debtor.

Section 547(b) determines what constitutes a preference. This section lists the key elements to a preference, all of which the TIB must prove before demanding return to the pre-transaction status. The following cases illustrate the operation of these sections.

========= GILBERT v. GEM CITY SAVINGS ASSN. =========
15 B.R. 565 (Bankr. S.D. Ohio 1981)

Ellis W. Kerr, Bankruptcy Judge.

FACTS

The trustee filed a complaint against the defendant-creditor, Gem City Savings Association, seeking to recover a payment of $1,079.64 made by the debtor to the creditor on the grounds that such payment constituted a preference under 11 U.S.C. §547.

The parties filed the following stipulations of facts:

That the defendant, Gem City Savings Association, held a valid mortgage lien on the debtor's real estate;

That within less than 90 days preceding the filing of debtor's petition in bankruptcy, debtor paid to defendant $1,079.64;

That debtor was insolvent at the time of payment;

That the $1,079.64 payment represented an arrearage of $823.64 plus a current monthly payment of $256.00;

That the value of the debtor's real estate is approximately $38,000.00;

That the outstanding balance of the loan as of May 9, 1980 (date of filing) was $24,160.17;

That defendant's claim was fully secured both immediately before and following the payment.

The parties have submitted the matter to the Court on the basis of the stipulations of fact and accompanying memoranda of law.

CONCLUSIONS OF LAW

... The stipulations of the parties indicate that the sole issue in the instant case concerns the last requirement of a preference, i.e., did the creditor receive more than he would receive if the case were a Chapter 7 case, the transfer had not been made and the creditor received payment to the extent provided for by the provisions of Title 11. ...

To make this determination, the Court must of necessity construct a hypothetical liquidation of the debtor's estate.

It is of primary importance to note that in the instant case the fair market value of the collateral exceeds the creditor's claim, i.e., the creditor is fully secured. If the transfer to the creditor is left undisturbed, the creditor upon a Chapter 7 liquidation would receive the full value of its claim, $24,160.17, and retain the $1,079.64 previously paid to it, for a total of $25,239.81.

If the payment of $1,079.64 had not been made, the creditor's claim would be increased to $25,239.81. Again, because the creditor is fully secured, upon liquidation in a Chapter 7 it would receive the full value of its claim, $25,239.81.

It is clear, then, that the transfer did not enable the creditor to receive more than he is entitled to. With or without the transfer of $1,079.64, the creditor receives a total of $25,239.81.

We hold that as a general rule payments to a fully secured creditor during the 90 day period preceding the filing of bankruptcy will not be considered a preferential transfer. This rule has been announced, either explicitly or implicitly, in several other jurisdictions. ...

===================== In re CALVERT =====================
227 B.R. 153 (Bankr. App. 8th Cir. 1998)

KOGER, Chief Judge.

Duenow Management Corporation ("Duenow") appeals the decision of the bankruptcy court finding that a pre-petition transfer made to Duenow by the debtors was avoidable under 11 U.S.C. §547 and ordering that the trustee, Wil L. Forker, recover from Duenow $8,875.00 plus the costs of the action.

FACTUAL BACKGROUND

On March 5, 1997, David G. Calvert and his wife, Sandra Calvert, filed a joint Chapter 7 petition in bankruptcy. Prior to that time, David Calvert had been a manager of a Kentucky Fried Chicken outlet located in Sioux City, Iowa, which was owned by Duenow. Calvert lost his job with Duenow in November 1996 because Duenow believed he had embezzled money from it. Calvert settled Duenow's claim against him in December 1996 for the sum of $11,844.90.

In December 1996, David Calvert borrowed $12,000.00 from his parents for the purpose of paying the settlement to Duenow. Specifically, on December 18, 1996, David Calvert's mother delivered $12,000.00 in cash to Calvert's wife, Sandra, who purchased a cashier's check in the amount of $11,844.90 with those funds. The cashier's check was made payable to the Calverts' attorney, Mr. Golby Uhlir. That same day, Sandra took the cashier's check to Mr. Uhlir, who used that check to purchase a money order in the same amount. Mr. Uhlir remitted the money order to Duenow in settlement of the claim.

Also on December 18, 1996, David and Sandra Calvert executed a "Mortgage Note" in favor of David Calvert's parents promising to repay $11,884.90 [sic]. They also gave Calvert's parents a mortgage against their home to secure the loan. Finally, the Calverts purportedly gave David's parents a lien on their 1992 Ford Ranger pickup truck. No security agreement regarding the pickup was offered into evidence, but a copy of the Certificate of Title was admitted showing the notation of a lien in favor of David Calvert's father, Glen Calbert [sic].

The evidence at trial showed that the Calverts' house was valued at $52,755.00. However, the bankruptcy court concluded that after considering the first and second mortgages on the house, the taxes payable on the house, and the escrow account balance, the debtors had only $17.17 equity in the house as of December 1, 1996, a little more than two weeks prior to giving David Calvert's parents the mortgage on the house.

The 1992 Ford Ranger pickup was valued at $8,875.00 and was unencumbered.

The debtors made the payment to Duenow, gave David Calvert's parents the mortgage on their residence, and had the lien noted on the Certificate of Title to the pickup all within ninety days prior to the filing of the bankruptcy petition and while the debtors were insolvent. As a result, the trustee filed an action to recover the payment to Duenow as a preferential transfer under §547(b). . . .

Section 547 of the Bankruptcy Code permits the trustee to recover certain payments made to creditors shortly prior to filing the bankruptcy petition. . . . The parties dispute the existence of only the first requirement, namely, that there was a transfer of an interest of the debtor in property in the first place. Specifically, the parties dispute whether an exception to §547(b), the earmarking doctrine, applies so as to remove the payment to Duenow from the reaches of §547(b).

"The earmarking doctrine is entirely a court-made interpretation of the statutory requirement that a voidable preference must involve a 'transfer of an interest of the debtor in property'." McCuskey v. Nat'l Bank of Waterloo (In re Bohlen Enters., Ltd.), 859 F.2d 561, 565 (8th Cir.1988). In order to satisfy the earmarking doctrine, the transaction must meet three requirements: (1) the existence of an agreement between the new lender and the debtor that the new funds will be used to pay a specified antecedent debt; (2) performance of that agreement according to its terms; and (3) the transaction viewed as a whole (including the transfer in of the new funds and the transfer out to the old creditor) does not result in any diminution of the estate. If the earmarking doctrine applies, no avoidable transfer is made because the loaned funds never become part of the debtor's property. There is no preference if the new creditor is merely substituted for the old creditor.

However, the earmarking doctrine applies only if the new and old creditor enjoy the same priority. Hence, the earmarking doctrine applies when a security interest is given for funds used to pay secured debts, but not when a security interest is given for funds used to pay an unsecured debt. If this "security interest" exception applies, the transfer is not earmarked and is therefore avoidable to the extent the transfer depleted the debtor's estate or "to the extent of the value of the collateral given up by the estate to secure the loan." Mandross v. Peoples Banking Co. (In re Hartley), 825 F.2d 1067, 1071 (6th Cir.1987) (citing Virginia Nat'l Bank v. Woodson (In re Decker), 329 F.2d 836, 839-40 (4th Cir.1964)). The trustee bears the burden of proving that the earmarking doctrine does not apply and thus bears the burden of proving the security interest exception does apply.

In the case at bar, the trustee argued before the bankruptcy court that the security interest exception applied because the debtors had given David Calvert's parents a security interest in the pickup truck.[3] In determining whether David Calvert's parents received a security interest in the pickup truck, we look to Nebraska law, as did the bankruptcy court.

Under Nebraska law, in order for a security interest to attach to goods, such as a vehicle, and to be enforceable against a third party, the collateral must either be in the possession of the secured party or the debtor must have

---

3. The parties do not dispute that the residence has no equity, so the mortgage given against it did not cause the estate to be diminished. Because the only dispute here involves the security interest given in the pickup truck, we limit our discussion to that issue.

"signed a security agreement which contains a description of the collateral." Neb. Rev. Stat. U.C.C. §9-203(l)(a)(1997). There is no dispute that the pickup in this case is not and was not in David Calvert's parents' possession, so in order to establish that the parents have a valid security interest in the pickup, the trustee must demonstrate that there was a signed security agreement containing a description of the pickup truck.

No written security agreement was offered into evidence at trial. The only written evidence tending to suggest that the debtors had given a security interest in the pickup to David Calvert's parents was the notation of David Calvert's father as lienholder on the Certificate of Title. The Certificate of Title also bears the county clerk's signature and seal. The bankruptcy court essentially found that this was sufficient, under Nebraska law, to establish that the debtors had given David Calvert's parents a valid security interest in the pickup. . . .

. . . After carefully reviewing the transcripts and documentary evidence, we believe the evidence was plainly insufficient to prove the existence of a security agreement. In fact, the trustee produced essentially no evidence, other than the lien notation on the title, to support the allegation that there had been a security agreement regarding the truck. . . .

. . . Although not specifically asked whether he signed a security agreement on the truck, David Calvert testified that in order to give his parents a security interest in the pickup, he simply delivered the title to them so that they could go get the lien noted thereon. Furthermore, Sandra Calvert testified that she had signed "some notes giving David's mother a mortgage on the house and promising to pay" which had been prepared by Mr. Uhlir. She also indicated that she and her husband had given the title to David's parents for them to hold, but she never mentioned a security agreement regarding the pickup.

We find this evidence is simply not enough to meet the trustee's burden of proving the existence of a signed security agreement regarding the truck. As a result, the trustee failed to prove that the debtors gave the parents a security interest in the truck. He therefore failed to prove the earmarking doctrine did not apply. The bankruptcy court should have found, therefore, that the earmarking doctrine applied, the payment to Duenow (from the funds loaned by the parents) was never property of the debtors' estate, and thus it was not an avoidable preference under §547(b).

. . . We therefore reverse the Decision of the Bankruptcy Court. . . .

═══════════════

Because Duenow Management Corporation can keep the pre-petition payment, it has no claim in the bankruptcy, but the debtor's mom and dad will take Duenow's place as a general unsecured creditor — with no security interest to fall back on.

The voidable preference section of the Bankruptcy Code is an important tool in reshaping the troubled business by permitting the DIP or TIB to avoid certain transfers made on the eve of bankruptcy. But its greatest importance may lie in its effect on pre-bankruptcy behavior, because some debtors may be better able to resist demands from their creditors by pointing out that the transactions could be avoided by a subsequent bankruptcy filing.

For many debtors, being able to use the voidable preference provisions has been a primary motivation to reorganize through Chapter 11 rather than attempting a workout outside bankruptcy. On the other hand, the voidable preference provisions also encourage creditors to cooperate in informal workouts. To the extent that some creditors fear that the debtor might make payments to other creditors while ignoring their interests, an involuntary bankruptcy (or the threat of one) gives the creditors the ability to ensure that the insolvent debtor is treating them fairly.

A special twist on preference law is the "indirect preference," which arises from the language of section 547(b)(2) concerning a transfer "to or for the benefit of a creditor." This language means there may be two or more persons potentially liable for a preferential transfer: the transferee and others who benefit indirectly from the transfer.

=========== In re DENOCHICK ===========
287 B.R. 632 (W.D. Penn. 2003)

CINDRICH, District Judge.

This bankruptcy appeal fulfills the old adage, "No good deed goes unpunished." It also illustrates the wisdom of Proverbs 22:26: "Be not one of those who give pledges, who become surety for debts." Revised Standard Version.

In this case, appellants agreed to guarantee a debt consolidation loan from NBOC to Sandra Krasinski's sister, Susan Lee Denochick (the debtor). The debtor made $1,713.35 in loan payments to NBOC in the year prior to filing bankruptcy. Appellants received none of this money, but the payments had the indirect effect of reducing their exposure on the guarantee they gave to NBOC. The trustee commenced an adversary action to avoid as a preference and recover from appellants the money Denochick paid to NBOC. After a trial, at which appellants did not testify, the bankruptcy court concluded by a memorandum order dated September 10, 2001 that appellants fell within the definition of "creditors" and that they had failed to establish the applicability of the "ordinary course of business" exception. Thus, the court concluded that the trustee could avoid the $1,713.35 and recover that amount from appellants.

We affirm. As the bankruptcy court thoroughly explained, the definition of a "creditor" under the bankruptcy code and Pennsylvania law is very broad and encompasses a guarantor of a debt. Appellants were "creditors," even though their claim was derivative of NBOC's and was contingent upon the debtor's default. Ms. Denochick's payments to NBOC conferred a benefit upon appellants, to the detriment of her other creditors.

=========

The concept of the indirect preference was a major focus of controversy for a number of years because of a case called Levit v. Ingersoll Rand

Financial Corp. (In re V.N. Deprizio Constr. Corp.), 874 F.2d 1186 (7th Cir. 1989). This was an ordinary dry and technical bankruptcy case, with Mr. Deprizio, the debtor's president, assassinated in a parking lot and that sort of thing. But the case attained great notoriety because it held that a payment made more than 90 days, but less than one year, before bankruptcy to a non-insider bank was a preference. How? The transfer occurred within the longer one-year preference period applicable to insiders (§547(b)(4)(B)) because it indirectly benefited an insider officer who was a guarantor of the bank debt. The *Deprizio* case, as it is popularly known, was based on the language in section 547(b)(1) covering a transfer "to or for the benefit of" a creditor. The theory was that payment of the guaranteed debt to the bank reduced the exposure of the insider who had guaranteed the debt, thus benefiting the insider. The insider was a creditor because the insider had a contingent right of reimbursement from the company; if the insider paid, the company would owe reimbursement. Thus payment to the non-insider bank was payment indirectly benefiting an insider within a year before bankruptcy.

Congress "fixed" this problem by amendments in 1994 and 2005, sections 550(c) and 547(i), which insulate the non-insider creditor from the effects of an insider benefit for transfers made more than 90 days before bankruptcy. Yet this relatively narrow approach leaves open many fascinating questions with regard to indirect preferences. It doesn't help Susan Denochick's sister who guaranteed the loan, only the bank that received the payments. Other examples reveal other twists. In the case in which a fully secured senior creditor is paid within 90 days (and the other requirements of section 547(b) are satisfied), there would seem to be no voidable preference as to the bank. But if the senior is sued by the TIB claiming that the payment benefited a second secured creditor with a junior position in the same collateral, there is a problem. The trustee admits that the payment was not a preference as to the senior creditor, because that creditor was fully secured. But, says the trustee, the junior creditor indirectly benefited because its security interest was "promoted" by the transfer. Therefore the payment was a preferential transfer as to the junior and is recoverable from the "initial transferee," the senior creditor. So long as the transaction in question took place within the 90 day voidable preference period, the bank would seem to have received a voidable preference, even under the amendments. Great fun.

The idea of indirect preferences runs through a number of cases. The Calverts' action in borrowing money from one creditor to pay to another creditor involved possible earmarking, depending on who controlled the money. If the replacement loan had been made on a secured basis, effectively substituting the new secured claim for a previously unsecured claim, it would have raised the issue of an indirect preference regardless of control, because the granting of the security interest would indirectly benefit the creditor who got paid with the resulting cash.

Voidable Preferences at State Law

We return briefly to the Uniform Fraudulent Transfer Act, discussed in detail at pp. 81, to see how state law has adjusted to the presence of a voidable preference section in the bankruptcy laws. The UFTA was drafted in the early 1980s to modernize its predecessor statute, the Uniform Fraudulent Conveyance Act. The new UFTA reflects an enhanced concern for fair treatment among creditors outside of bankruptcy. In addition to deeming a conveyance fraudulent when it was undertaken with fraudulent intent or when the insolvent debtor received inadequate consideration, the UFTA provides that a transfer is fraudulent whenever it is made in payment of an antecedent debt by an insolvent debtor to an insider who had reasonable cause to know of the insolvency. UFTA §§4, 5. This means that an insolvent debtor's repayment of debt to an insider can be set aside by other creditors without the need to file an involuntary bankruptcy.

The UFTA is notable because it highlights another aspect of the debtor-creditor relationship — in or out of bankruptcy, insiders should not be paid ahead of other creditors. By making such a provision available at state law, the UFTA undercuts some of the need to push a debtor into an involuntary bankruptcy in order to allocate the debtor's assets equitably. The provision also extends the restrictions on insider payments to organizations that are not subject to involuntary bankruptcy filings, such as charitable organizations.

The provisions of UFTA section 5(a) are not entirely coextensive with section 547(b) of the Code. The UFTA restricts only transfers to insiders. Moreover, the UFTA distinguishes between those creditors who are creditors at the time of the transfer, and who therefore have the right to set aside the transfer, and those creditors who became creditors after the transfer and have no right to set aside. The UFTA also requires that the insider who receives the transfer have had "reasonable cause to believe that the debtor was insolvent." The Bankruptcy Code draws no such distinctions. On the other hand, the UFTA has a four-year statute of limitations, while the Bankruptcy Code reaches back only one year to review transfers to insiders. Later in this section we will discuss section 544(b) of the Bankruptcy Code, which incorporates state fraudulent conveyance law into bankruptcy proceedings. A debtor in bankruptcy now may have two kinds of voidable preference actions available — those under section 547(b) of the Code and those under section 5(a) of the UFTA in the states that have adopted it.

The following problems are designed to illustrate the operation of section 547(b), the general rule of federal preference law. Additional facts might reveal exceptions to the general rule under section 547(c), but those exceptions will be studied in the next section.

Problem Set 23

23.1. Mountain Lakes Fuel Oil is an unsecured creditor of Wilson Manufacturing. Wilson owes Mountain Lakes $140,000. It makes a payment of $14,000 to Mountain Lakes 60 days before bankruptcy while Wilson is insolvent. Wilson is liquidated in bankruptcy, and the unsecured creditors receive a 10 percent pro rata distribution. Is Wilson's payment to Mountain Lakes a voidable preference under section 547(b)?

23.2. Underdown is a wildcat driller. His last three holes have been dry, and he fears he is insolvent. On October 1, one of his principal suppliers, OKC Supply, calls on him to discuss payment on a large unsecured account. OKC has been generous with Underdown and he is appreciative. Underdown suggests that OKC take some of the loose equipment still left at the warehouse and drilling sites, some of which OKC had originally sold to Underdown. On November 15, Underdown files for bankruptcy. Can the trustee get the equipment back from OKC? See §547(b).

23.3. When gasoline was scarce and prices were high, several creditors were eager to lend money to Raymond's Chevron Station for expansion. When the gasoline glut appeared last winter, one of those creditors, Iowa Commerce Bank, decided it would prefer to be a secured creditor. On February 1, while Raymond's was insolvent, the bank received a security interest for its previously unsecured debt in Raymond's previously unencumbered equipment. The bank filed and perfected on the same day. On April 25, Raymond's filed a Chapter 11 reorganization. Is there a voidable preference? See §547(b).

23.4. North Woods, Inc. is a logging concern that has been insolvent for several months. It believes that a current upturn in the construction industry will allow the company to become profitable again, and it persuades VenCap, a venture capital company, to lend it $50,000 to survive the next few months. On June 1, VenCap makes the loan and takes a security interest in North Woods' unencumbered equipment, which it perfects on July 1. On September 15, North Woods cannot meet its payroll and it declares a Chapter 11 bankruptcy. Has there been a voidable preference? See §547(b), (e).

23.5. On February 1, Hartford Baking, Inc. has two secured creditors. One, Magic Chef Co., sold Hartford four $10,000 specialized ovens a year earlier and perfected its security interest before delivery. On February 1, the loan balance was $35,000 and the value of the ovens was $30,000. The other creditor, Commercial Bank, made a loan to Hartford six months earlier. Commercial took a security interest in Hartford's other baking equipment and perfected at the time of the loan. On February 1, Commercial's loan had a balance of $40,000 and Commercial's collateral was worth $50,000. On February 2, Hartford paid each creditor $5,000. On April 2, Hartford filed for bankruptcy. Hartford was insolvent throughout, and the value of the collateral was stable. Would either creditor have a problem keeping the payment under section 547(b)?

23.6. Virginian Air Conditioning Service owes $250,000 to First Richmond Bank. The loan is secured by a perfected security interest in "all Virginian's current and after-acquired equipment," which on March 1 is worth about $150,000. On April 15, Virginian acquires another $200,000 in equipment from a supplier who sells on credit but who fails to take a security interest in these goods. On May 25, after having been insolvent for six months, Virginian files for bankruptcy. Has there been a voidable preference? See §547(b), (e)(3).

23.7. The principal asset of Clear Springs Bottling Company was a two-ton bottle-capping machine. As of June 1 last year, Clear Springs owed $280,000 to Hillside Bank. The loan was secured by a perfected security interest in the bottle-capping machine, which was then valued at $300,000.

On July 1, Clear Springs made a $20,000 payment to Hillside. On July 15, a fire swept through the bottlery and the bottle-capping machine was completely destroyed. Contrary to the requirements of the security agreement, Clear Springs had tried to save cash by permitting the insurance on the machine to lapse.

Clear Springs was already in serious financial trouble, and the fire finished them. They declared bankruptcy on August 1. Has there been a voidable preference? See §547(b).

23.8. If, in the preceding problem, Clear Springs had purchased another used bottle-capping machine after the fire using unsecured credit from the seller, and the new machine were worth $300,000, would there have been a voidable preference? See §547(b).

23.9. Court's Hardware is a small, family-owned hardware store. Two new, large home centers have moved into the same locality, and Court's has been insolvent for several months. John Court, the president, foresees disaster. He feels particularly upset about some of his creditors, including Granny Court, who made a $20,000 unsecured loan to the business, and First Oregon City Bank, which extended $30,000 in unsecured credit and whose president is a golfing buddy of John's. John doesn't feel at all bad, however, about some of his other creditors, including Minnesota Manufacturing, a materials supplier and unsecured creditor for $45,000, and Wayne King, a local painter who did extensive remodeling for Court's and who is still owed $5,000, but who got into a fight with John over paint splatters on the store's inventory.

John Court goes to New York National Bank and asks for a $50,000 loan to consolidate some of the store's debt, offering to give a lien on the company's forklift, worth about $20,000. New York National agrees, and it sends checks directly to Granny Court and First Oregon. Two months later Court's files for bankruptcy. Can the trustee recover the payments to Granny and First Oregon? See §§547(b); 541(a); UFTA §5(b).

23.10. Steven Zetillo is president and owner of 50 percent of the stock of Zetillo's Model Trains and Planes, Inc. A large highway has virtually cut off access to the model train store. The business has rocked around for several months, making some late payments, having some of the inventory repossessed, and so forth. On April 20 Zetillo, as president, repaid himself for an unsecured loan of $22,000 that he had made to the store. This transaction completely wiped out the last of the liquid assets in the business. In the ten weeks since that time, Zetillo has simply quit paying the store's bills.

A group of the train store's creditors visit you on July 15 for advice. One found out about the large payment to Zetillo, and they are ready to act. What do you advise? Does it matter whether they file an involuntary petition now or later? See §547(b), (f); UFTA §5(b).

3. The Exceptions

The Code makes it clear in section 547(b) that debtors cannot prefer certain creditors on the eve of bankruptcy and that creditors who seek such preferences will find them undone in bankruptcy. This has the effect of not only treating all like-situated creditors alike — "equity is equality" — but it also has a salutary effect on the debtor's business. For the debtor skirting the edges of financial demise, the voidable preference provisions create some disincentive for a creditor to expend time and money to extract preferential payments or security interests that will simply be avoided if the business cannot survive outside bankruptcy. The voidable preference section works to keep creditors from dismantling the ailing business, a deterrent that redounds to the benefit of all weak businesses as they deal with current creditors, whether or not the businesses ultimately enter bankruptcy.

A literal application of section 547(b) could, however, work too effectively as a disincentive to creditors in their dealings with businesses that may be on the eve of bankruptcy. If section 547 had no exceptions, then even transactions that were beneficial to the ongoing business (and ultimately to all the other creditors) or transactions that by their nature were not attempts to prefer certain creditors in anticipation of demise, would be avoided. To prevent this effect, the Code builds in eight exceptions to the rules of section 547(b). Those transactions that can be avoided under section 547(b) can sometimes be saved under section 547(c). Each of the five most commonly used subsection (c) exceptions has its own jargon: (1) "contemporaneous exchange"; (2) "ordinary course payments"; (3) "purchase money"; (4) "new value" rule; and (5) "floating lien."

The following materials work through all of these exceptions except the last one, inventory and account financing (the "floating lien"), which is reserved for additional discussion in the subsequent section.

Contemporaneous Exchange

The idea behind the contemporaneous exchange exception that is laid out in section 547(c)(1) is that a seller or lender should be able to deal with a buyer or borrower without worrying about whether the order in which the transaction took place could create a voidable preference. So, for example, a seller might hand over the good and the buyer might then hand over the cash. For that instant between the two events, the seller was technically a general unsecured creditor. The contemporaneous exchange exception makes it clear that such transactions are not subject to avoidance if the debtor declares bankruptcy within ninety days.

Of course, the fun begins when creditors use the exception for all kinds of other cases. Examples are in the next two cases.

Ordinary Course Exceptions

The ordinary course exception is laid out in section 547(c)(2). Code drafters wanted to balance competing concerns, the need to discourage preferences in favor of certain creditors pre-bankruptcy against the need to encourage pre-bankruptcy transactions that are essential to keep the business alive. The Bankruptcy Code therefore incorporated a voidable preference exception to permit some ordinary course transactions to stand, notwithstanding the fact that they permitted some unsecured creditors to be paid in full. Finding where to draw the line, however, has been difficult.

In the 1978 Code, subsection 547(c)(2) provided that a payment would be permitted to stand if (1) it was an ordinary course payment, and (2) the time between the extension of credit and the debtor's repayment did not exceed 45 days. This had the beneficial effect of limiting the exception to short-term extensions of credit, usually trade suppliers and utility companies. The rules were fairly clear, and litigation was minimal. The rule had its sharp detractors as well: Too many creditors complained that they could not fit within the strict limits of the rule, although they were sure they deserved protection because their business had continued to support the debtor. In the 1984 Amendments, Congress responded with a provision to widen the application of subsection 547(c)(2) by dropping the 45-day rule. The rule was amended again in 2005 to permit more creditors to claim an exception. The details are coming up.

===== In re STEWART =====

274 B.R. 503 (W.D. Ark. Bankr. 2002)

OPINION BY: Robert F. FUSSELL

★ ★ ★

STIPULATED FACTS

The parties filed the following stipulations of fact with the Court on December 7, 2001:

The Debtor, Gary Stewart, filed a chapter 13 bankruptcy case on April 11, 2000. . . . If the Debtor had filed a chapter 7 case without considering the preference action, the case would be considered a no asset case and no distribution would be anticipated for unsecured creditors. . . .

On January 29, 2000, the Debtor purchased cattle from [Barry County Livestock Auction, Inc. ("Barry County"), a livestock auction facility] by personal check number 4029 from the Bank of Pea Ridge, Arkansas, in the amount of $17,580.70. Check No. 4029 was issued to pay Barry County Invoice Nos. 15, 16 and 17, also dated January 29, 2000. When Check No. 4029 was returned to Barry County for insufficient funds on February 12, 2000, the Debtor tendered a cashier's check numbered 83582 drawn on the Bank of Pea Ridge in the amount of $17,580.70 on February 12, 2000, to satisfy the obligation owing from the insufficient Check No. 4029. [Same story with a second check.]

Cashier's Check Nos. 83582 and 83692 were purchased with monies belonging to the Debtor and constituted property of the Debtor.

The payments made with Cashier's Check Nos. 83582 and 83692 were made while the Debtor was presumed insolvent and was insolvent.

The payments made with Cashier's Check Nos. 83582 and 83692 were made within 90 days immediately preceding the Debtor's bankruptcy filing.

The payments made with Cashier's Check Nos. 83582 and 83692 enabled Barry County to receive more than it would have received if this case had been a chapter 7 case; if the payments had not been made; and if Barry County had received payment of its debt as allowed under the Bankruptcy Code.

Barry County and Bill Younger [owner of Barry County Livestock Auction] received notice of the Debtor's bankruptcy filing as a result of the Notice of Commencement of Case sent on April 14, 2000. The first meeting of creditors for the Debtor's case was conducted and concluded on June 6, 2000. Bill Younger, Dayne Galyen and Dayne Galyen, Jr., all representatives and officers of Barry County, attended and participated in the first meeting of creditors.

On or about the evening of June 6 or 7, 2000, Bill Younger, Dayne Galyen and Dayne Galyen, Jr., acting individually and on behalf of Barry County, went to the Debtor's residence. The parties' recollection of the events differ; however, a disagreement occurred and the Benton County Sheriff's Department was contacted and subsequently appeared on the scene. A few days later, Debtor's mother, Janet Scott, paid $15,000 to Barry County toward the Debtor's debt owing Barry County. Bill Younger then returned an insufficient check that had been received from the Debtor prior to the bankruptcy filing to the Debtor's mother.

* * *

A debt is antecedent if the debt was incurred prior to the allegedly preferential transfer. Jones Truck Lines, Inc. v. Central States, Southeast and Southwest Areas Pension Fund (In re Jones Truck Lines, Inc.), 130 F.3d 323, 329 (8th Cir. 1997). A debt is incurred "'on the date upon which the debtor first becomes legally bound to pay.'" Id. (quoting In re Iowa Premium Serv. Co., 695 F.2d 1109, 1111 (8th Cir. 1982)). In this case, Dayne Galyen Jr. testified, and the Court credits his testimony, that all buyers at the auction barn were required to pay for their purchases on the date of the sale. Therefore, the debts were incurred two weeks before the delivery of the cashier's checks and were antecedent debts.

The Court finds that Barry County Livestock Auction is a creditor for purposes of 11 U.S.C. §547(b)(1), and that cashier's checks number 83582 and 83692 were given by the debtor to Barry County Livestock Auction for antecedent debts. Because the parties have stipulated to the other elements of a preferential transfer, the Court finds that the trustee has met her burden of proof as to the preferential transfer of the two cashier's checks. The creditor may avoid preference liability if it can prove that it falls within one of the exceptions set forth in § 547(c). . . .

CONTEMPORANEOUS EXCHANGE FOR NEW VALUE EXCEPTION

To qualify for the contemporaneous exchange for new value exception under §547(c)(1), a creditor must prove that an otherwise preferential transfer was "(A) intended by the debtor and the creditor . . . to be a contemporaneous exchange for new value given to the debtor; and (B) in fact a substantially contemporaneous exchange." 11 U.S.C. §547(c)(1). "New value" is defined as "money or money's worth in goods, services, or new credit, or release by a transferee of property previously transferred to such transferee in a transaction that is neither void nor voidable by the debtor or the trustee under any applicable law, including proceeds of such property, but does not include an obligation substituted for an existing obligation." 11 U.S.C. §547(a)(2).

Before the Court can determine whether the payments made by the debtor with cashier's checks payable to Barry County Livestock Auction were contemporaneous exchanges for new value under the bankruptcy code, the Court must determine as a matter of law when the transfer of cattle occurred. If the transfer of the cattle did not occur until the cashier's checks were presented to Barry County Livestock Auction, the transactions may have been contemporaneous exchanges for new value. If, on the other hand, the transfer of the cattle occurred on the day of the sale, two weeks before the debtor presented the cashier's checks to Barry County Livestock Auction, the Court must determine whether the subsequent delivery of the cashier's checks to replace the insufficient funds checks constituted contemporaneous exchanges for new value.

. . . . The Court finds that under the UCC, title to the cattle passed upon delivery of the cattle on the day of the respective sales. At best, Barry County Livestock Auction retained only a security interest in the cattle.

Having found that the transfer of cattle occurred on the date of the sale, the Court must now determine whether the delivery of the cashier's checks two weeks after the transfer of the cattle is a contemporaneous exchange for purposes of §547(c)(1). The legislative history of § 547(c)(1) specifically references transactions in which checks are involved:

> Normally, a check is a credit transaction. However, for the purposes of this paragraph, a transfer involving a check is considered to be "intended to be contemporaneous," and if the check is presented for payment in the normal course of affairs, which the Uniform Commercial Code specifies as 30 days, U.S.C. §3-503(2)(a), that will amount to a transfer that is "in fact substantially contemporaneous."

Goger v. Cudahy Foods Co. (In re Standard Food Serv., Inc.), 723 F.2d 820, 821 (11th Cir. 1984) (quoting S. Rep. No. 989, 95th Cong., 2d Sess. 88, reprinted in 1978 U.S.C.C.A.N. 5787, 5874); accord Walsh v. Smythe Buick Isuzu (In re Gaildeen Indus., Inc.), 71 B.R. 759, 763 (9th Cir. B.A.P. 1987). The debtor's payment by personal check constituted a contemporaneous transfer only if the check was presented and paid within a reasonable time. Hall-Mark Electronics Corp. v. Sims (In re Lee), 179 B.R. 149, 163 (9th Cir. B.A.P. 1995). Had the debtor's personal checks cleared, Barry County Livestock Auction's argument that a contemporaneous exchange for value occurred would prevail.

However, other portions of the legislative history indicate that the bank's dishonor of the personal checks changed the nature of the transaction:

> Contrary to language contained in the House report, payment of a debt by means of a check is equivalent to a cash payment unless the check is

dishonored. Payment is considered to be made when the check is delivered for purposes of sections 547(c)(1) and (2).

Standard Food Serv., Inc., 723 F.2d at 821 (quoting 124 Cong. Rec. H11,097 (daily ed. Sept. 28, 1978); 124 Cong. Rec. S17,414 (daily ed. Oct. 6, 1978)). A contemporaneous exchange defense cannot involve a dishonored check. *Lee,* 179 B.R. at 163. When the checks were dishonored by the bank, the transactions became credit transactions and created an antecedent debt. Id.; Standard Food Serv., Inc., 723 F.2d at 821. Any subsequent payment, no matter how quickly made, would satisfy that antecedent debt. *Lee,* 179 B.R. at 163 (quoting In re Barefoot, 952 F.2d 795, 800 (4th Cir. 1991)). When the debtor delivered the cashier's checks to Barry County Livestock Auction, the cashier's checks satisfied the antecedent debt, and were not contemporaneous exchanges for new value. Hence, Barry County Livestock Auction's contemporaneous exchange for new value exception fails.

ORDINARY COURSE OF BUSINESS EXCEPTION

Barry County Livestock Auction also raised the ordinary course of business exception pursuant to § 547(c)(2). To qualify for the ordinary course of business exception, a creditor must prove that the transfer was "(A) in payment of a debt incurred by the debtor in the ordinary course of business or financial affairs of the debtor and the transferee; (B) made in the ordinary course of business or financial affairs of the debtor and the transferee; and (C) made according to ordinary business terms." 11 U.S.C. §547(c)(2).

The parties did not specifically stipulate that the transfers were in payment of a debt incurred by the debtor in the ordinary course of business between the debtor and Barry County Livestock Auction. However, the parties did stipulate that the debtor engaged in a business relationship with Barry County Livestock Auction in July 1997 that continued until the debtor filed his chapter 7 bankruptcy petition on April 11, 2000. They also stipulated that in the course of their business relationship, the debtor purchased cattle from Barry County Livestock Auction and was required to pay for the cattle purchased the same day of the purchases. Because the payments were made to satisfy debts that the debtor incurred in the ordinary course of his business dealings with Barry County Livestock Auction, the Court finds that Barry County Livestock Auction meets the [first] elements of subsection (c)(2).

[The second element] deals with the way the parties actually conducted their business dealings. According to the Eighth Circuit Court of Appeals, a court must engage in a "peculiarly factual analysis" to determine whether payments made by the debtor during the 90 day preference period were made in the ordinary course of business. Lovett v. St. Johnsbury Trucking, 931 F.2d 494, 497 (8th Cir. 1991). Specifically, the court must look at the "consistency of the transaction in question as compared to other, prior transactions between the parties." Concast Canada, Inc. v. Laclede Steel Co. (In re Laclede Steel Co.), 271 B.R. 127, 131 (8th Cir. B.A.P. 2002) (citing *Lovett*, 931 F.2d at 497). Sufficient alteration of any one of four factors may be sufficient for a court to conclude that a payment was made outside the ordinary course of business. 271 B.R. at 132. The factors are,

> (1) the length of time the parties were engaged in the transactions at issue; (2) whether the amount or form of tender differed from past practices; (3) whether the debtor or the creditor engaged in any unusual collection or payment activity; and (4) whether the creditor took advantage of the debtor's deteriorating financial condition.

Id. n.3. The Eighth Circuit has found that the timing of the payments to the creditor to be of overriding importance, and stated that review of the 12 months preceding the 90 day preference period and the 90 day period itself was an appropriate standard for determining the ordinary course of business. *Lovett*, 931 F.2d at 498.

The Court will first look at all of the dealings the debtor had with Barry County Livestock Auction. The Court received into evidence as Exhibit 8, a "Summary of Invoices/Payments From July 19, 1997 – January 8, 2000"; and as Exhibit 15, a "Schedule of Invoices/Payments January 15, 2000 – March 4, 2000."

* * *

The debtor only presented one check during the 12 month period preceding the 90 day preference period that was dishonored by the bank when presented for payment. In fact, that was the only check that was not honored when presented to the bank during the entire 42 months the debtor had been purchasing cattle from Barry County Livestock Auction prior to the preference period. That one check was written within three weeks of the preference period, and the debt was paid three days before the preference period. On the other hand, the debtor presented four checks during the preference period that were dishonored by the bank when presented for payment, two of which were later paid by cashier's checks. Despite the one dishonored check right before the preference period, the Court finds that the ordinary course of business between the debtor and Barry County Livestock Auction was that the debtor paid for his purchases with a personal check on the date of sale that was honored when presented for payment. The payments by personal checks made during the preference period that were dishonored by the bank when presented for payment, but later paid with cashier's checks, were not sufficiently consistent with the payments made during the prior 12 months. Because of this, the Court finds that Barry County Livestock Auction has failed to meet the [second] element of subsection (c)(2).

Subsection (c)(2)(C) requires that the transfers be made according to ordinary business terms; in other words, "whether the transaction was ordinary pursuant to terms in the industry." *Laclede Steel Co.*, 271 B.R. at 133.

To make this determination, the Court must compare the payment record of the debtor with the general practice in the industry regarding time of payment. *Lovett*, 931 F.2d at 499. The only testimony presented regarding the general practice in the industry was from Dayne Galyen Jr. He testified that cattle purchases were always paid on the day of purchase and that this practice was typical in the industry. Upon cross examination, he again stated that "by law," a buyer is required to pay on the day of the sale. Based on Mr. Galyen's testimony, which the Court credits, and in the absence of any contrary evidence, it is clear that payment by cashier's check two weeks after the date of sale is not typical in the industry. Because of this, the Court finds that Barry County Livestock Auction has failed to meet the elements of [the third] subsection (c)(2).

Based on the above findings of facts and conclusions of law, the Court finds that the payments made by the debtor to Barry County Livestock Auction with cashier's check number 83582 and cashier's check number 83692, in the total amount of $46,749.55, were preferential transfers in favor of Barry County Livestock Auction.

COUNT 2—VIOLATION OF AUTOMATIC STAY

By separate order, the Court has set a hearing on Count 2 of the plaintiffs' complaint on March 1, 2002, at 9:00 a.m. in the United States Bankruptcy Court, Fayetteville, Arkansas.

We would like to get a look at the Barry County Auction management team. They seem to have found some very persuasive ways to encourage both the debtor and the debtor's mother to come up with quick cash, although they may be returning that too — perhaps with a considerable kicker in the form of a cash award for contempt.

As we noted in the introduction to *Stewart*, the ordinary course of business exception that Barry County tried to invoke has been repeatedly amended. After In re Stewart was decided, Congress changed what a creditor must show in order to keep an otherwise avoidable transfer under the 547(c)(2) exception. The first element, that the debt be incurred in the debtor's ordinary course of business remained the same, but now the creditor need only prove the second element (that the transfer was in the ordinary course of the debtors' business) *or* the third element (that the transfer was made according to ordinary business terms. The law applicable at the time of *Stewart* required Barry County to prove *both* the second and third elements. It failed on both counts, however, so the outcome in *Stewart* would be the same even after the 2005 Amendments.

As *Stewart* notes, the contemporaneous exchange exception of section 547(c)(1) is designed in part to protect sellers who take checks. These transactions are often treated as same-as-cash, and 547(c)(1) protects that expectation — if the check clears when it is first deposited. If the check bounces, then the seller has become a creditor — a reluctant creditor, no doubt, but a creditor all the same. Cases like *Stewart* are a reminder that it is not the intent of the parties alone that governs, but that the transaction must in fact be contemporaneous as well.

The contemporaneous exchange exception comes up in another context, policing delayed filings. The next case illustrates the issue, along with another effort by a creditor to raise an earmarking defense. The grace period for delayed filings under section 547 has changed from 10 days (1978) to 20 days (1994) to 30 days (2005). We have inserted brackets to indicate a grace period — whatever it happens to be — so that we minimize the chances of driving you nuts. Think of it as an ever-changing state of grace.

================= In re SHREVES =================
272 B.R. 614 (Bankr. N.D. W.Va. 2001)

OPINION BY: L. Edward FRIEND II

* * *

I. FACTS

The facts of this case center on three distinct transactions: first, the purchase of the vehicle by David A. Shreves and Linda L. Shreves ("debtors") financed by United National Bank ("United"); second, the subsequent refinancing agreement between the debtors and [Valley National Bank ("Valley")]; and third, the perfection of Valley's interest during the preference period.

Sometime prior to April 3, 2000, the debtors obtained a loan from United for the purpose of purchasing a 1997 GMC Jimmy, and granted United a security interest in the vehicle. However, on April 3, 2000, before United perfected its interest, the debtors refinanced this loan through Valley. Valley executed a check on April 5, 2000 and sent it to United.

United recorded its lien on the West Virginia motor vehicle title on April 21, 2001. Ten days later, on May 1, 2000, United released this lien. The West Virginia Department of Motor Vehicles ("DMV") did not record Valley's lien on the title until August 11, 2000. Consequently, from May 1, 2000, until August 11, 2000, no lien was recorded on the vehicle title.

The reason for the late recordation appears to be delay by both Valley and the debtors. Sometime in June 2000, Valley sent a "Request for Title" and an "Application to Record Lien" form for the debtors to execute and return. Sometime in July 2000, Valley received the title and the executed application form from the debtors. On August 8, 2000, Valley submitted its application to record the lien to the DMV, and on August 11, 2000, the DMV issued a title recording Valley's lien. On October 18, 2000, the debtors filed a petition under Chapter 7 of the Bankruptcy Code. . . . [O]n December 11, 2000, the trustee filed this adversary proceeding to set aside Valley's security interest.

* * *

II.   Discussion

The trustee seeks to avoid Valley's lien perfection as preferential under 11 U.S.C. §547(b). Valley raises three defenses: first, under 547(c)(1), the "substantially contemporaneous exchange" exception; second, the state law doctrine of equitable subrogation; and third, the earmarking doctrine.

A.   *Substantially Contemporaneous Exchange Defense*

* * *

Under the Code, Valley must first prove that the transfer was intended by the parties to be a contemporaneous exchange for new value given to the debtor, and further that the transfer was in fact a substantially contemporaneous exchange. The grant of the security interest at the time of the refinancing is sufficient evidence of the intent of Valley and the debtors to make a contemporaneous exchange for new value. More problematic for Valley, however, is the demonstration that the transfer was actually substantially contemporaneous, since the perfection of the security interest occurred more than four months after the security agreement.

This Court has had a number of occasions to consider preference cases where a creditor has not timely perfected its security interest. Most often, these cases arise where there has been an "enabling loan" creating a purchase money security interest that was ultimately perfected more than ten or twenty days after the debtors acquired the collateral, but within ninety days of bankruptcy. These cases arose following the Fourth Circuit Court of Appeals decision in Wachovia Bank and Trust Co. v. Bringle (In re Holder), 892 F.2d 29 (4th Cir. 1989), and the United States Supreme Court case of Fidelity Financial Services, Inc. v. Fink, 522 U.S. 211, 139 L. Ed. 2d 571, 118 S. Ct. 651 (1998).

In *Holder*, the debtor purchased a truck on July 27, 1987, signing a security agreement with Wachovia Bank & Trust Co. ("Wachovia") in exchange for a loan. 892 F.2d at 29. Wachovia delivered the necessary paperwork to the North Carolina Division of Motor Vehicles nineteen days later, on August 12, 1987, and the lien was recorded on the same day. Id. Eighty-two days after the debtor received possession of the truck, the debtor filed for relief under Chapter 13 of the Bankruptcy Code. Id. The trustee filed a motion to avoid Wachovia's lien as preferential, and Wachovia asserted §547(c)(1), the "contemporaneous exchange" defense. See 892 F.2d at 30.

The sole question before the Fourth Circuit was whether §547(c)(1) is applicable to protect purchase money security interests perfected more than ten days after the debtor receives possession of the vehicle. 892 F.2d at 30. At the time of the transfer in question, §547(c)(3) provided that to qualify for the enabling loan exception, the security interest must be perfected on or before ten[2] days after the debtor's receipt of possession. The court

---

2. In 1994, §547(c)(3) was amended to the current twenty-day grace period; prior to 1994, the grace period was ten days. [Eds. note: 547(c)(3) has been amended again to extend the grace period to thirty days.]

concluded that the contemporaneous exchange exception did not apply to purchase money security transactions perfected more than ten days after the debtor received possession of the collateral.

Subsequent to *Holder*, the United States Supreme Court considered, in *Fidelity Financial Services, Inc. v. Fink*, 522 U.S. 211 (1998), the §547(c)(3) "enabling loan" exception to the trustee's preference avoidance power as it related to state law relation-back periods. In a non-bankruptcy context, state law often allows for a longer relation-back or grace period.

The issue in *Fink* was whether a creditor who performs the acts necessary to perfect its interest outside the §547(c)(3) [grace] period, but within the otherwise applicable state law relation-back period can invoke the "enabling loan" exception provided by §547(c)(3). The Court held that a transfer of a security interest is "perfected" under §547(c)(3) on the date the necessary state law perfection steps are taken, but that a creditor may invoke the enabling loan exception only by satisfying the state law perfection requirements within the [grace] period provided by the Bankruptcy Code.

* * *

In the instant case, Valley did not make an enabling loan to the debtors, but rather refinanced the debtors' previous loan from United. Since the enabling loan exception is applicable only to purchase money security transactions, this defense is not available to Valley. However, the law pertaining to the enabling loan exception is crucial to the analysis of Valley's contemporaneous exchange defense.

Valley requests that this Court adopt a more lenient standard under the contemporaneous exchange defense for the perfection of non-purchase money liens than the one clearly established for purchase money security loans under the enabling loan defense. Valley advocates the adoption of a flexible definition of "substantially contemporaneous" for purposes of preference action defenses. Although some courts have adopted such a standard, others, including the United States Court of Appeals for the Sixth Circuit, have declined to do so.

The Sixth Circuit considered the adoption of a flexible approach to §547(c)(1) in *Ray v. Security Mutual Finance Corp. (In re Arnett)*, 731 F.2d 358 (6th Cir. 1984). The court declined to adopt a flexible standard, and determined that the perfection of a security interest in the debtors' car that occurred thirty-three days after the security agreement was not substantially contemporaneous with the loan transaction for purposes of excepting it from the trustee's avoidance power.

The bankruptcy court and the district court both held that the lien was not a preference. Id. The Sixth Circuit reversed, however, stating:

> Although there can be no doubt that the parties' clear intent to effectuate a contemporaneous exchange was frustrated, the statute nonetheless requires that the exchange in fact be contemporaneous. Section 547(c)(1)(B). The lower courts' interpretation places too little emphasis on the necessity of temporal proximity between the loan and the transfer of the security interest.

731 F.2d at 364.

Although the Fourth Circuit has not addressed the use of a flexible standard under §547(c)(1), it did address the issue under §547(c)(3). In *Holder*, discussed supra, the Fourth Circuit could have applied a flexible test under §547(c)(3), but elected not to do so. If this Court now adopts a more flexible standard in the instant case, it would result in non-purchase money security interests having more flexibility than purchase-money security interests.

Valley and the debtors entered into the security agreement on April 3, 2000. Valley sent a check dated April 5, 2000, to United, thus fulfilling its part of the agreement. United's lien was released on May 1, 2000. The DMV received Valley's application almost three months later, between August 8 and August 11, 2000. By its own admission, Valley did not even request the certificate of title from the debtors until sometime in June 2000. Valley's perfection of its security interest was not "in fact substantially contemporaneous" with the transfer as required by §547(c)(1)(B). Therefore, Valley may not invoke the §547(c) defense to the trustee's avoidance power.

C.   The Earmarking Doctrine

The final defense raised by Valley is that of the earmarking doctrine. Under this doctrine, Valley asserts that it lent money to the debtors upon refinancing specifically for the purpose of paying off United and that consequently, Valley steps into United's secured position.

The Fourth Circuit has not addressed the issue of earmarking as it relates to the perfection of a refinancing loan during the preference period. Valley relies on the Eighth Circuit Bankruptcy Appellate Panel case of Krigel v. Sterling National Bank (In re Ward), which allowed an earmarking defense to a preference action where the debtor refinanced a vehicle loan during the preference period. See 230 B.R. 115. In *Ward*, the debtor refinanced its vehicle loan on April 23, 1997, and the original lien was released five days later on April 28, 1997, but the refinancing lien was not perfected until June 6, 1997, forty-four days later. 230 B.R. at 116-117. On July 23, 1997, eighty-three days after the refinancing agreement, the debtors filed a petition under Chapter 7 of the Bankruptcy Code. 230 B.R. at 117. The court allowed an earmarking defense on the grounds that there was an agreement between the new lender to pay a pre-existing debt of the debtor, that this agreement had been performed according to its terms, and the transfer did not diminish the amount of the debtors' estate available for distribution to creditors. See *id.* 230 B.R. at 119-120.

In the factually similar case of Vieira v. Anna National Bank, (In re Messamore), 250 B.R. 913 (Bankr. S.D. Ill. 2000), the United States Bankruptcy Court for the Southern District of Illinois specifically declined to follow the *Ward* reasoning. The court in *Messamore* acknowledged that the earmarking doctrine "is clearly applicable in a refinancing situation to determine whether the debtor's payment of an existing creditor with funds borrowed from a new creditor constitutes a preferential transfer — that is, whether such payment is a transfer of the debtor's "interest in property" to pay the debt owed to the first creditor." *Id.* at 916. The court distinguished the issue before it, however, because the "transfer" at issue was not the transfer of funds to the initial creditor, but the transfer that occurred when the new creditor perfected its lien more than ten days after the parties' loan agreement. Id. The court explained that "although the debtors' transfer to [the new lender] arose in the context of a refinancing arrangement, it did not involve the payment of funds by a third party or, indeed, the payment of borrowed funds at all. For this reason, the earmarking doctrine has no logical relevance to such transfer." Id.

This Court finds the *Messamore* Court's reasoning persuasive, and declines to follow *Ward*. The earmarking doctrine is inapplicable under the facts of the instant case.

III. Conclusion

Valley's failure to timely perfect its interest within ten days as required by §547(e)(2)(B) precludes the relation back of the transfer to the initial loan date. Since the lien perfection is a transfer occurring during the preference period, and because Valley has no valid defenses, the Court hereby sets aside the transfer of the security interest in the 1997 GMC Jimmy and declares said lien VOID.

It is accordingly SO ORDERED.

═══════════

Note that Valley could have protected itself completely by getting United to transfer its security interest to Valley at the time of payment, if United had been willing to do so. In that case, there would have been no transfer "of an interest of the debtor in property" because the transfer would have been of United's interest (i.e., a perfected security interest) in the property.

There has long been a controversy about the appropriate treatment of secured creditors who make delayed filings during the preference period. One position is that it is a mistake to police delayed filing of security interests through the preference power. See, e.g., C. Robert Morris, Bankruptcy Law Reform: Preferences, Secret Liens and Floating Liens, 54 Minn. L. Rev. 737 (1970). Accordingly, the section 547(c)(1) exception should be used to protect security interests that are perfected by tardy financing statements, thereby eliminating or reducing the effects of section 547(b) when the creditor has not filed within the statutory periods. Delayed filings are almost always accidents rather than intentional efforts to "hide" the security interest, and the parties almost always intended a contemporaneous filing within the terms of (c)(1). Any risk of abuse would be minimal because parties who delay filing to conceal the existence of the security interest from other creditors could not avail themselves of the (c)(1) exception, which requires an intention to engage in a contemporaneous transaction, that is, an intention to file promptly.

The counter to these arguments focuses on the possibility that other creditors, especially unsecured creditors, may have extended credit on the basis of the public record prior to the late filing. The preference rules are designed to protect these creditors against the carelessness of the delayed filer. Further, if (c)(1) created an exception for late filing, debtors might persuade secured parties to delay public disclosure of the security interest so the debtor could attract more unsecured credit while promising to "tip off" the secured parties if bankruptcy becomes imminent, giving the secured party time to file and perfect. This intentional abuse would clearly fail to satisfy (c)(1), but it would be difficult to prove, especially since both parties would have incentives to dissemble. Only a requirement of a contemporaneous public filing would force the parties to make public their intentions.

Another argument in favor of using the preference power against late perfection is the prevention of fraud. We sometimes forget that the hostility of common law courts to security interests in personal property was based largely on their fear that dishonest debtors would give liens on the same collateral to many different creditors. The UCC perfection requirements are designed to make such fraud much more difficult by giving notice of prior liens to every diligent subsequent creditor. Preference avoidance of security interests perfected shortly before bankruptcy substantially increases the importance, and therefore the likelihood, of creditor compliance with those requirements. Article 9 sanctions alone are less powerful, since a deceitful or careless creditor could rush to perfect when financial trouble arises and under the UCC would have an unavoidable security interest so long as perfection occurs before the date of bankruptcy.

The effect of ignoring perfection requirements was illustrated in the 1985 collapse of a Florida dealer in U.S. securities, E.S.M. Securities, in which a number of businesses, banks, and municipalities lost many millions of dollars. These investors had made loans to E.S.M. that they understood to be secured by government securities. The creditors had not perfected their security interests by taking possession of the collateral. The result was that E.S.M.'s officers were able to repledge the same collateral over and over. If all the investors had insisted on delivery of the securities — the only method of permanent perfection then available for such collateral under Article 9 of the UCC — relatively little would have been lost. Multiple pledges cannot happen if the first lender demands delivery and gets it, and if subsequent lenders refuse to lend without obtaining physical possession. The E.S.M. situation also illustrates the lack of equity there would be in permitting one of several careless lenders to perfect on the eve of bankruptcy (perhaps because of an insider relationship with the debtor) leaving the other foolish-but-innocent creditors out in the cold.

The Purchase Money Exception

For those conversant with Article 9 of the UCC, the easiest voidable preference exception to understand is subsection 547(c)(3). This subsection provides that purchase-money creditors will receive special protection in bankruptcy, just as they do under the UCC scheme. The policy reasons are similar: Of all the transactions regarded as beneficial to the estate, those that bring in new property are regarded as the most beneficial and therefore deserve the greatest protection.

As in Article 9, there are also strict limitations on the scope of the protection for purchase money lenders. As noted above, like the ordinary course exception, the purchase money exception has been repeatedly modified. In 1978, the Code provided that a PMSI creditor would be protected only if the creditor filed within ten days of the debtor's acquisition of the property. In 1994 the time limit was expanded to 20 days, in keeping with the UCC rules in a majority of states that protected PMSI lenders who filed their interests within 20 days. In 2005, the rules were amended once again, this time giving the PMSI creditor who files within 30 days full protection against a voidable preference.

The problem with this latest time extension, of course, is that the UCC hasn't kept pace, with most states providing a 20 day window for PMSI filing priority. So the PMSI lender who may be able to beat a Trustee in Bankruptcy on a voidable preference claim may have considerably more difficulty beating a previous creditor with an after-acquired property clause. Congress seems to have forgotten that its effort to help one creditor may just create a tangle with another.

The New Value Exception

Subsection 547(c)(4), the "new value" preference exception, is one of the most difficult parts of section 547. The difficulty comes from the fact that the (c)(4) exception only "shelters" preference payments that come *before* a particular extension of new value. The Code does not permit all preferential payments and new credits during the preference period to be netted out. Instead, the (c)(4) exception only applies on a payment-by-payment basis.

The mechanics of (c)(4) are as follows:

1. Identify a payment (or other transfer) that is preferential under section 547(b). (This is the first step because otherwise there is no reason to look to the section 547(c) exceptions.)
2. See if the avoidable amount of the preference can be reduced by the amount of later-advanced new value that qualifies under (c)(4) (which says "to the extent that . . ."). For example, if a creditor received a $1,000 preferential payment, then made a $700 delivery of new supplies on credit, when the debtor filed bankruptcy a preference of $1,000 would exist. Under (c)(4) the $1,000 preference should be reduced by the $700 new value, leaving only $300 to be avoided.
3. Test new value for qualification under (c)(4) by determining whether under (c)(4)(A) and (B) it was accompanied by a payment (or other transfer or was secured), which payment was itself unavoidable. For example, a creditor received a $1,000 preference and then delivered $700 of new supplies that were paid for in cash on delivery. When the debtor filed bankruptcy the new value would not qualify since it was accompanied by the full $700 payment at time of delivery. The second payment was not avoidable as a preference because it was made at the moment the debt was created and therefore was not paid on an antecedent debt under

section 547(b). Since the payment is unavoidable, it disqualifies the $700 of new value under (c)(4)(B).

This last point rests on the very basis for the (c)(4) exception and the (c)(4)(A) and (B) qualification of that exception. The exception rests on the premise that we should not extract repayment of preferences from a helpful creditor who, after the preferential payment, extended new, unsecured credit to the debtor and who will suffer in bankruptcy as an unsecured creditor to the extent of that new credit. The notion is at least arguably consistent with the idea that preference policy is designed to encourage creditors to work with a financially troubled debtor. On the other hand, if the creditor made the debtor pay cash for the new delivery of goods, protected under section (c)(4)(B), or made the debtor give an enforceable security interest for the new delivery or advance, protected under section (c)(4)(A), then there is no burning equity against the recapture of the earlier preferential payments to that creditor. The creditor should not get "new value" credit against prior preferences when the debtor paid for (or gave security for) that new value.

A comprehensive approach to (c)(4), and one that some people find easier to follow, is to start by working forward chronologically from the ninetieth day to Bankruptcy Day, identifying each payment (or other transfer) that qualifies as preferential under section 547(b). After the preferential transfers are located, work backward from each grant of new value to determine whether it is subsequent to a given preference with the same creditor having advanced unsecured credit to the debtor. Any advance of unsecured credit after the preference will work to trigger section 547(c)(4), but the dollars of each advance can be counted only once (e.g., two preferences of $1,000 each, followed by an extension of $1,500 in unsecured credit, will permit the creditor to keep $1,500 of the two preferences, not the full $2,000). There are alternate approaches that will yield the same results. So long as the computation accounts for all the elements of (b)(4), the amount saved by the exception will be the same.

The Other Exceptions

Four other exceptions to the voidable preference rules round out the provision. Subsection 547(c)(6) permits statutory liens that violate the voidable preference provisions to survive if they are otherwise unavoidable under section 545. In effect, this provision means that statutory liens will be dealt with in section 545, notwithstanding their implications in section 547(b).

The next two exceptions are applicable only in consumer settings. Subsection 547(c)(7) makes it clear that alimony and support payments, although made to an unsecured creditor, will not be recoverable as voidable preferences even when made during the preference period. This provision was added to the Code in 1994 as part of an overall effort both to improve the recovery of those who collect alimony and support payments and to make certain they keep what they collect. It was redrafted and strengthened in the 2005 Amendments.

Subsection 547(c)(8) and (c)(9) were added at the insistence of creditors who did not want to have to fight voidable preference actions for modest amounts of money. In effect, the provisions permit creditors to keep value transferred to them preferentially if the amount in question is less than $600 in consumer cases and less than $5,000 in business cases. The justification is not principled so much as a claim by the creditors that they can't afford to litigate. Some argue that the reason for these exceptions is a bit more nefarious: in no-asset or small-asset cases, setting aside a few of these low-value voidable preferences can fund the trustees' further investigation of the dealings between the debtor and creditor; without some certainty of recovery, there is nothing there to support the TIB's active involvement. Whatever the reason for the change, there seems to be a lesson in human behavior: creditors often lobby for the relaxation of the voidable preference rules, evidently focused intently on those times when they had to give up money as a VP rather than on the times they received larger distributions because their fellow creditors had to give something back.

Problem Set 24

24.1. Fun City Go-Karts was in failing financial condition and legally insolvent. Its chief supplier, Exaco, knew of the difficulties and told Fun City it would only make gasoline deliveries for cash payments. Fun City and Exaco completed about two deliveries per week for about $2,400 each during the 90 days preceding bankruptcy. Three times during that period, however, the delivery truck arrived and Fun City did not have cash available. Rather than take Fun City's check, the Exaco driver agreed simply to collect payment on his next delivery, which was accomplished each time. When Fun City files for bankruptcy within 90 days of these transactions, can the trustee recover any payments made to Exaco? See §547(b), (c)(1), (c)(8).

24.2. Big Rig Equipment is an Oklahoma rental company that has been insolvent for several months. It decided to take a final gamble and order ten new pieces of heavy equipment, begin an aggressive advertising campaign, trim its office staff, etc. The John Deere dealership was willing to finance the sale of ten new pieces of industrial and farming equipment to the business, taking a purchase-money security interest in the new equipment. The deal worked as follows: Big Rig placed the order for the equipment (specifications in the contract) on July 1. Big Rig agreed to pay $300,000, giving John Deere a security interest in the new equipment. On July 12 the equipment was identified to the Big Rig contract at the JD factory. On July 20 custom work was completed, and on July 24 the equipment was delivered to the local dealer. On July 28 the dealer delivered the equipment to Big Rig. On August 21 the JD dealership filed a financing statement in the Office of the Secretary of State (which was the correct form of perfection in Oklahoma).

Big Rig's new plans never got off the ground. On September 30, Big Rig filed for bankruptcy. The only valuable assets in the estate are the new equipment. Oklahoma has adopted the standard version of Article 9. Who gets the equipment? See §547(b), (c)(3), (e)(2). Would your answer change if Liberty National Bank had had an outstanding, perfected security interest in all of Big Rig's equipment, current and after-acquired for more than a year before the bankruptcy filing? §551; UCC §9-317(e).

24.3. GoldenView Nursing Home filed for bankruptcy in September. The trustee later reviewed the books and found among the entries evidence of the following transactions:

1. $14,200 in utility bills were paid four weeks before filing. It seems that GoldenView had been more than three months behind in its utility payments, and when the power company threatened to shut them off, GoldenView took a large portion of the August receipts and paid them off in full.

2. The June, July, and August mortgage payments were due on the first, but made between the twentieth and twenty-fifth of each month and each included a $50 late penalty charge. The mortgage is undersecured.

3. Solid State Bank received a payment in full of a $10,000 unsecured, six-month loan. The payment was made on July 15, the date it was due.

4. Jack Meloy, the principal stockholder of GoldenView, was repaid on the due date of a 30-day loan of $6,000 made to help the business meet its payroll.

Which of these payments can the trustee recover? See §547(b), (c)(2), (c)(8); UFTA §§5(b), 8(f).

24.4. Odd Notions is a button manufacturer that specializes in fine bone and shell buttons. It has been insolvent since January 1, but it has continued to operate based on an unsecured line of credit from the Des Moines People's Bank. The arrangement has been that whenever Notions needs money to make its payroll or pay bills, it will call on its line of credit and whenever Notions receives payments from its buyers, it deposits them directly to pay down the DMPB loan balance.

The current year's accounts between Notions and DMPB can be summarized as follows:

Date	Transaction	Amount	Balance owed to DMPB
1/1	beginning balance	$80,000	
1/3	payment from Notions	5,000	$75,000
1/15	new credit from DMPB	4,000	79,000
2/10	payment from Notions	2,000	77,000
2/28	new credit from DMPB	8,000	85,000
3/4	new credit from DMPB	9,000	94,000
3/10	payment from Notions	1,000	93,000
3/17	new credit from DMPB	6,000	99,000
3/20	payment from Notions	10,000	89,000
4/1	payment from Notions	9,000	80,000
4/10	Notions files bankruptcy		

How much of the payments from Notions can DMPB keep? See §547(b), (c)(4).

4.   More on the Exceptions: The "Floating Lien"

In the debates leading to the 1978 Code, no preference problem received more attention than did the inventory and receivables financing problem. The difficulty ultimately was resolved in §547(c)(5).

As many students may recall from studies of Article 9 of the UCC and secured lending, the conceptual difficulties presented in inventory and receivables financing often made the statutes and cases that predated Article 9 confusing. A financer relying on inventory or accounts receivable as collateral could not lend with complete confidence in the protection of its position. The difficulty arose from the fact that the lien on inventory or accounts covered a mass whose actual identity shifted over time. How could someone take a security interest in a tube of toothpaste on the shelf if that tube might be sold this afternoon and a new tube might replace it tomorrow? Modern inventory and account financing could progress only after the acceptance of the "floating lien" concept that covers categories such as inventory or receivables regardless of the particular goods or accounts that happened to be in the business at any particular time.

Just as secured lending concepts had some difficulty stretching to include inventory and accounts, bankruptcy law similarly struggled to accommodate inventory and account lending within the preference concept. The idea that creditors should not be receiving new value (including new property covered by old security interests) within the preference period blocked protection for inventory and receivables financers when a bankruptcy was filed. Potential lenders argued that their collateral was valuable inventory and that they should not be demoted to unsecured status simply because the physical identity of the inventory had changed (substitution of one tube for another) since the security agreement had been signed.

By the mid-1960s the debate had reached a crescendo. The early cases that held that new property coming within the reach of the security interest within the preference period created voidable preferences and took that collateral away from inventory and account financers were being challenged. The landmark case that re-set the law, Grain Merchants v. Union Bank and Savings Co., 408 F.2d 209 (7th Cir. 1969), cert. denied, 396 U.S. 827 (1969), gave vitality to the "modern" position that inventory and receivables financers should have their security interests protected in bankruptcy through application of the Article 9 floating lien. The court in *Grain Merchants* used the "relation back" doctrine to deem the interest in all inventory transferred back when the original security agreement attached, rather than dating the transfer to the later time that the new inventory was actually acquired. By this analysis, any new acquisition of inventory or receivables was no longer a "transfer" within the preference period.

Grain Merchants and its well-known cousin, DuBay v. Williams, 417 F.2d 1277 (9th Cir. 1969), which was read as going even further in protecting security interests in after-acquired property against preference attack, were hailed as innovations that ratified modern lending practices and would encourage their continued development. The "modernization" move was not without its detractors, however. A sizeable number of commentators argued that *Grain Merchants* and *DuBay* would eliminate the application of preference law to all after-acquired property.

A point that received less attention, but which was more difficult to correct, was the enhanced possibility for abuse under *Grain Merchants* and *DuBay*. Even if the application of these cases were limited to inventory and receivables financing by doctrinal analysis or by statute, *Grain Merchants* and *DuBay* omitted all review for preferential treatment of what is often the debtor's most important creditor. A powerful creditor — as the inventory and account creditors often are — could "encourage" the debtor to pour assets into the acquisition of inventory or the development of accounts at the expense of using those assets to pay other creditors who weren't paid or whose collateral was liquidated. These inventory lenders could thereby fatten themselves during the preference period unchecked by the preference constraint.

This debate came under review by the National Bankruptcy Conference, an influential private group, which referred the problem to its Committee on Coordination of the Bankruptcy Act and the Uniform Commercial Code, chaired by Professor Grant Gilmore. That committee recommended a compromise that was ultimately adopted as sections 547(e)(3) and 547(c)(5) of the Code. The committee's position was stated in its report:

> The [compromise statutory provision] rejects the analysis which may have been followed in *[DuBay]*. Under that case . . . it appears that no perfected Article 9 after-acquired property interest in inventory, receivables *or any other type of property can* ever be set aside in bankruptcy. If that is the proposition for which *Dubay* stands, it goes beyond need or reason. . . . On the other hand, the time has long since passed when it would have been possible to outlaw either inventory financing or receivables financing.

[Emphasis in original.] National Bankruptcy Conference, Report of the Committee on Coordination of the Bankruptcy Act and the Uniform Commercial Code 15 (1970), reprinted in 4 Collier on Bankruptcy 471 (15th ed. 2000).

The language of section 547(e)(3) represents a firm rejection of the "relation back" approach by flatly forbidding for preference purposes any dating of a security interest in a piece of property prior to the debtor's acquisition of an interest in that property. Under that section, the time of the "transfer" of a security interest in after-acquired property is the date the debtor acquired the property, regardless of an earlier perfection. As a result, the lender's security interest in every piece of property acquired after the filing, including most of the inventory and accounts receivable, is to be deemed "transferred" to the lender within the 90-day preference period, because virtually all the inventory would have been acquired and all accounts would have arisen within that period. Because of the operation of section 547(e)(3), the lender's security interests in inventory and receivables will almost always be preferences under section 547(b), and therefore the security interests would be voidable but for section 547(c)(5), which grants an exception for inventory and receivables.

Security interests in inventory and account receivables — but not in any other type of after-acquired property — are saved by section 547(c)(5) from avoidance as preferences under constraints that go to the second objection to *Grain Merchants*. Here the Code tempers the protection for inventory and receivable lenders with an "improvement in position" formula. This formula makes improvement in the secured party's position during the preference period potentially avoidable by the trustee. The result is that inventory and receivables financers are protected when the debtor acquires property preceding the bankruptcy, but they are not permitted to enhance their position during the critical pre-bankruptcy period.

The floating-lien exception has given rise to a great deal of discussion, but remarkably few reported cases. Given that "asset-based" financing (financing secured by inventory and accounts) is commonplace, the issue must arise often, but it is evidently not being litigated in reported cases. It may be that the very complexity of the provision and of the transactions it governs has made the parties regard litigation as unpredictable and expensive, so there is a consensus to settle. A case that illustrates that difficulty is Batlan v. TransAmerica Commercial Finance Corp., 237 B.R. 765 (D. Ore. 1999). The TIB attacked some $12 million of payments to a secured creditor during the 90 days before bankruptcy. It was stipulated that all the elements of section 547(b) were satisfied except for the "better off" requirement of section 547(b)(5). The court regarded the key question to be whether the secured party was oversecured or undersecured on Bankruptcy Day. Furthermore, the secured creditor's debt and collateral value on the ninetieth day and on Bankruptcy Day were stipulated. Despite all that stipulating, the TIB apparently did not argue section 547(c)(5) and it was ignored in the court's opinion.

Disregarding some mathematical anomalies in the opinion and recognizing that some relevant facts may not have been stated, it is interesting to apply the law to the facts that were stated. It was stipulated that on the ninetieth day, the secured party was owed $13,410,032.25 and its inventory at wholesale was worth $12,708,605.96, leaving a deficiency of $701,426.29. On the date of the filing of the petition, the court found the secured party was owed $10,728,809.96 and its inventory at wholesale was worth $10,828,004.36, so the creditor was oversecured by $99,194.40 and there was no deficiency. Application of the floating lien formula yields an improvement in position of $701,426.29 (the deficiency at the ninetieth day minus zero, which was the deficiency at Bankruptcy Day, equals $701,426.29), so the TIB should have been entitled to avoid the amount it would take to put the secured creditor $701,426.29 in the hole. In this case, the secured creditor would not be entitled to inventory worth $800,620.69 (that is, the over-security of $99,194.40 and the amount the creditor must be undersecured of $701,426.29). Removing $800,620.69 of collateral from the Bankruptcy Day total of $10,828,004.36 leaves $10,027,383.67. (The other way to reach the same result is to say that the oversecured amount naturally goes to the estate, because the secured party cannot recover more than it is owed, leaving $10,728,809.96 in collateral, then subtract collateral equal to the preference of $701,426.29, leaving the same $10,027,383.67.) Upon that avoidance, the creditor would be undersecured by $701,426.29 on Bankruptcy Day, creating a strong argument that at least some of the payments were preferences. Having not been requested to make this analysis, the court found the creditor oversecured on Bankruptcy Day and therefore concluded that there had been no preference. It should be comforting to students to realize that bankruptcy law is hard for everyone.

The following case provides yet another twist in the floating-lien calculation, ultimately posing the eternal question: Does the sun shine for the benefit of the unsecured or the secured creditor?

In re NIVENS
22 B.R. 287 (Bankr. N.D. Tex. 1982)

BRISTER, Bankruptcy Judge.

Arville Calvin Nivens and Danny Calvin Nivens, father and son, conducted a farming business as a partnership under the name of Nivens and Nivens. Each filed petition for order for relief under Chapter 7 of Title 11, United States Code, on March 18, 1982. The 1981 crop year was the last year in which they operated the farming partnership. As a result of the farming in the 1981 crop year they became entitled to receive "deficiency" payments totalling $36,648.70 and "low yield" or "disaster" payments totalling $912.05 from the Department of Agriculture under the 1981 support programs for upland cotton. The First State Bank of Abernathy ("Bank"), the Small Business Administration ("SBA") and the trustee are competing for those government support payments, represented by checks in the possession of the trustee.

[Since the right to the federal support checks "derived" from rights in the farmer's crop, priority in those checks would go to the one who had priority in the crop. The bank had a valid security interest in the crop, but the TIB contended that the bank had benefited from an improvement in position from the increase in the crop's value during the ninety days before bankruptcy, so that part of its interest in crop and support checks was voidable as a preference under section 547(b), (c)(5).]

[The trustee] contends that the recognition of a lien on behalf of the bank and SBA in the subsidy checks would result in an improvement of position by those creditors within ninety days of bankruptcy and, to the extent that the security interest has increased in value, there is an avoidable preference.

Pre-Code cases clearly indicated that a secured party maintained rights in after acquired inventory or receivables. DuBay v. Williams, 9th Cir. 1969, 417 F.2d 1277; Grain Merchants of Indiana, Inc. v. Union Bank and Savings Company, 7th Cir. 1969, 408 F.2d 209. *DuBay* and its progeny were overruled in the Code by the provisions of §547(c)(5), applicable to secured creditors claiming security interests in inventory and in accounts receivable, and §553(b), applicable to any creditor who would otherwise have right of setoff under §553(a). Crops are categorized as "inventory" by §547(a)(1). Under §547(c)(5) a preference will not result to the holder of a perfected security interest in inventory, including crops, unless and to the extent the holder improves his position during the ninety day period before bankruptcy.

The nature of a farm crop is unlike that of other types of inventory. For instance, the inventory of a grocery store might change in value from time to time, but the physical nature of the individual items comprising the inventory does not change. It is an easy matter to inventory a grocery store on separate dates and determine whether there has been an increase or decrease in inventory and in value. A lien does not exist until the property against which it is affixed comes into existence. Thus where there is an increase in the volume of the inventory of a grocery store within ninety days of bankruptcy the lien against that increase becomes fixed within the prohibited period and is avoidable. However, if there is only an increase in *value* of the inventory due to market fluctuations, without an accompanying increase in volume of inventory, there is no avoidable preference.

A crop as "inventory" is different from the grocery store inventory example. A crop is continuously undergoing change. Its existence commences as soon as the seed is planted and starts to germinate. It undergoes daily change until it finally matures and is ready for harvest. The lien which was initially fixed against the crops in its embryonic stages continues against the crop in all stages of development. It is the same lien and the same crop. Although the crop is increasing in value the crop was in existence at all relevant times. While there might be an increase in the value of the crop between the different stages of its development, the "inventory" itself is not increased. There is nothing added within the prohibited period which would mandate avoidance of lien against increase.

[The court held that there was no improvement in position and therefore no voidable preference.]

The court in *Nivens* seems clearly correct in saying that a mere increase in value of collateral does not generate an improvement in position under section 547(c)(5). More precisely, an increase in value, whether from a rising market or a good rainfall, does not involve a transfer and therefore cannot constitute a preference under section 547. On the other hand, the crop in *Nivens* did not increase in value merely by the bounty of nature. In addition to the natural increase in its value, there was value added to it by the labor of the farmers and the application of fertilizers and various other farming supplies. That additional value raises some subtle and interesting questions.

The first point involves additions to the estate by the farmers. There is little question that the farmers' labor, following the filing of bankruptcy, belongs to the farmers — not the estate. If the farmers worked during the pending Chapter 7, the work should have been compensated by the TIB out of other assets of the estate. Otherwise, the farmers have made contributions to the estate without compensation, something the creditors have no right to expect. See the earlier discussion on post-filing income, p. 123.

The second point involves more complex voidable preferences in the Chapter 7. If the farmers used cash to buy fertilizer and pesticide for the crop, the farmers executed a transfer (payment for the goods) to enhance the value of the crop. If the enhanced value of the crop goes exclusively to the secured creditor, then a preferential transfer on behalf of that creditor has occurred (in effect, the value of the cash was transferred to the secured creditor). This creates the conceptual knot of how to divide the increases in value and apportion them among the creditors. As Judge Brister said, the increase in crop value that is attributable to good fortune and sunshine does not involve a transfer and so can be kept by the creditor with a security interest in the crop. But the increase in crop value that is attributable to transfers of the debtor's cash during the preference period belongs to all the creditors on a pro rata basis — not to the secured creditor exclusively. And to the extent that, after bankruptcy, estate money is used to pay the farmers for their labor, the increases attributable to their work should also be used for the benefit of all the creditors and not the secured creditor alone.

Even this relatively simple application gives some idea of the complexities in tracing voidable preferences under section 547(c)(5) and in sorting out which creditors should benefit from which increases in value.

Setoff Preferences

We noted earlier that the right of setoff has much the same effect as a security interest (see pp. 451–457). It is therefore not surprising that the drafters of the Code had the same sort of concern about an improvement in a lender's setoff position as they did about an improvement in position by the holder of a floating lien on inventory and accounts. They adopted an analogous constraint in section 553(b), which empowers the trustee to recover from an offsetting creditor the amount by which the creditor's setoff position improved during the 90 days before bankruptcy. The formula in section 553(b) is similar in concept to that in section 547(c)(5), but not identical in detail. The most important point to note is that the avoidance power applies only if the creditor offsets before bankruptcy. The creditor who waits and exercises its right of setoff after bankruptcy, with the permission of the court under section 362, is not required to surrender any improvement in setoff position obtained during the 90-day period. The policy decision at work here remains, shall we say, opaque. Nonetheless, the banks that use setoffs are disinclined to give up this provision in their favor. Also worthy of brief note is the long line of exclusions from the operation of section 553. All of the referenced sections deal with financial contracts whose traders have persuaded Congress must be excluded from most all bankruptcy provisions lest the markets crash and the sky falls.

As with section 547(c)(5), there are relatively few cases reported under section 553(b), although application of the section must be implicated in many bankruptcies each year. The following opinion is satisfyingly straightforward.

===================== In re WILD BILLS, INC. =====================
206 B.R. 8 (Bankr. D. Conn. 1997)

Alan H. W. Shiff, Chief Judge.

The Trustee seeks to recover $101,020.84 from Union Trust Bank n/k/a First Union Bank of Connecticut ("Union Trust"), representing the amount by which Union Trust allegedly improved its position in contravention of §553(b).

BACKGROUND

The relevant facts of this adversary proceeding are substantially undisputed and are set out in the Stipulation of Facts ("Stipulation"), Pl. Exh. A, filed with this court on February 28, 1996, which provides in relevant part:

1.   This case was commenced by the filing of a Petition by Debtor, Wild Bills, Inc. ("Wild Bills"), on April 23, 1990 under Chapter 11 of [the] Bankruptcy Code, and was converted to Chapter 7 of [the] Bankruptcy Code on May 12, 1992.
2.   Prior to filing such Petition, Union Trust made the following loans to Wild Bills, which loans were outstanding in 1990 (Collectively referred to herein as the "Loans"). . . .
6.   On January 23, 1990 (90 days prior to the filing of the Petition), the account statements indicated an opening balance for all Wild Bills bank accounts in the amount of $211,094.01, as follows:

ACCOUNT NO.	OPENING BALANCE
31-139-045-7	394.93
31-688-947-6	126.96
33-339-844-7	26,268.29
31-088-997-0	21,816.09
31-588-699-6	162,487.74
TOTAL	$211,094.01

7.   At some time later in the day of January 23, 1990 . . . $130,025.82 was deposited into Wild Bills bank account number 31-588-699-6.
8.   The amount owed for the Loans on January 23, 1990 was $1,433,057.40, stated as follows:

LOAN NO	PRINCIPAL	INTEREST	TOTAL
83	93,500.00	638.52	94,138.52
75	20,000.10	367.38	20,367.48
42	110,000.00	718.07	110,718.07
59	1,200,000.00	7,833.33	1,207,833.33
TOTAL	$1,423,500.10	$9,557.30	$1,433,057.40

9.   On January 25, 1990 (88 days prior to the filing of the Petition), Union Trust declared the Loans in default. [By letter dated January 26, 1990, Union Trust informed Wild Bills that it had exercised its right of setoff as a result of several problems that had become apparent from a meeting on January 24, 1990 with representatives

of Wild Bills, including that "Wild Bills, Inc. would be unable to pay its indebtedness to [Union Trust]," that the value of the indebtedness to Union Trust was "substantially" more than the collateral, that Wild Bills was unable to service its trade debts, and that Wild Bills "saw no realistic alternative" but to seek bankruptcy protection. Pl. Exh. P; Def. Exh. 19.] . . .

12. At all times between January 23, 1990 and April 23, 1990, the claim of Union Trust for repayment of the Loans was undersecured. . . .

DISCUSSION

The Trustee commenced this action, asserting that Wild Bills made preferential transfers to Union Trust in violation of §547(b). Union Trust raised the affirmative defense that it held a valid right of setoff under §553 which it properly exercised. The Trustee now contends that the proceeding should be analyzed under §553 because Union Trust raised that section as an affirmative defense and courts under that scenario have resolved the issues under §553.

The Trustee's right to avoid a transfer must be tested against any right of Union Trust to a pre-petition setoff. If that right is established, the court does not reach §547 but makes its decision solely under §553. Other courts have relied upon legislative history to conclude that a setoff is not a "transfer" within the meaning of §101(54), thus transfer avoidance issues involving setoffs should be properly addressed under §553. Still other courts have reasoned that since §553(a) does not specifically list §547 as one of the provisions of the code that would affect a creditor's right of setoff, §553 is the appropriate section for analysis. For the reasons that follow, it is concluded that Union Trust held a valid right of setoff and therefore the analysis of the Trustee's right to recover funds set off by Union Trust is examined under §553(b).

Right of Setoff

[Although the TIB asserted that certain accounts were "special purpose" accounts as to which setoff was not permissible under state law, the court held that the trustee had not made a persuasive case and therefore all the accounts were subject to setoff under state law.]

Account 6

The Trustee does not dispute the amount available for setoff in Account 6 on January 25. He does dispute the amount that was available on January 23, alleging that only the opening balance of that account was eligible for setoff on the 23rd and not amounts that were deposited or credited to the account during the balance of that day.

Relevant Time Period of the Ninetieth Day

The Trustee argues that the court must determine "when the 'ninetieth day' begins." He claims that for purposes of §553(b), the court must ascertain what debtor/creditor relationship existed at 12:00 A.M. on the ninetieth day. Based on that inquiry, Treasury Notes in the aggregate amount of $130,025.82 and an additional amount of $8,506.10, which were credited to Wild Bills' account at some point after 12:00 A.M. would be excluded from setoff. Union Trust counters that the court must assess the account for the entire ninetieth day to arrive at the correct setoff amount.

Union Trust is correct. As noted, the parties have agreed that January 23rd was the ninetieth day prior to the filing of the petition. See Rule 9006(a) Fed. R. Bankr. P. The only method to establish that date would be to count back from the filing of the petition on April 23rd. It follows then that the debtor/creditor relationship at the end of January 23rd, the ninetieth day, must include the amounts deposited and credited to the account throughout the day. . . . The Trustee's argument would only account for 89 days and the first measurable moment of the ninetieth day. Further, the requirement that the insufficiency that existed "90 days before the date of the filing of the petition," 11 U.S.C. §553(b)(l), be calculated, indicates that the code is not concerned with a particular time of day, but rather the entire day.

Improvement in Position Calculation

January 25, 1990 — Date of Setoff

The debt owed to Union Trust on January 25, 1990 was $1,433,887.77. Union Trust setoff $339,213.51 from all of Wild Bills' accounts. The insufficiency on January 25, 1990 ($1,433,887.77 – $339,213.51) was therefore $1,094,674.26.

January 23, 1990 — Ninetieth Day

The parties agree that the sum owed by Wild Bills on January 23, 1990 was $1,433,057.40. On January 23, 1990, the total amount of all of the Wild Bills' accounts with Union Trust was $349,625.93. The resulting insufficiency on January 23, 1990 ($1,433,057.40 – $349,625.93) was $1,083,431.47. Since the insufficiency of $1,094,674.26 on January 25, 1990, the date of setoff, was more than the insufficiency of $1,083,431.47 on January 23, 1990, the ninetieth day prior to the bankruptcy filing, Union Trust did not improve its position.

ORDER

The Trustee may not recover the amounts setoff by Union Trust from Accounts 6 and 7, judgment shall enter accordingly. . . .

Problem Set 25

25.1. Precision Instruments is a manufacturer of fine watches that ultimately sell under various trade names. Precision maintains a line of credit for $4.8 million with Chase Investors. The credit is secured by all of

Precision's inventory, including work-in-progress. On February 14 the outstanding loan balance was $4.0 million and the inventory on hand was valued at $4.2 million. During the next 90 days, Chase extended another $600,000 in new value and the inventory worth increased by $1 million.

Unfortunately, the unsecured creditors, including a patent infringement claimant, have swamped the company, and the records reveal that Precision has technically been insolvent for at least 120 days. On May 14 the company files for bankruptcy, and you are appointed TIB. Can you make a preference attack against Chase Investors? See §547(b), (c)(5).

25.2. After a further review of the Precision Instruments files, you discover it had made two payments to Chase Investors during the 90 days preceding bankruptcy for $100,000 each. Is there a voidable preference action against Chase Investors?

25.3. On September 10, Restaurant Supply has an inventory valued at $450,000 and a loan of $430,000 from Nowlin Investors secured by that inventory. Active sales during September deplete the inventory to $300,000, but threats from other creditors cause all the cash raised to go elsewhere and no payments are made to Nowlin. Following threats from Nowlin, Restaurant Supply replenishes its stock, so that on December 10 the inventory is valued at $500,000, with the loan still $430,000. Restaurant Supply has been insolvent throughout. If it files bankruptcy on December 10, does Nowlin face a voidable preference problem? See §547(b), (c)(5).

25.4. Metal Traders, Inc. is a buyer and seller of gold and silver. It currently owes $1,000,000 to SpecVest, a capital investment company specializing in speculative industries. SpecVest has a perfected security interest in Metal Traders' inventory, which on April 1 is worth $800,000. Because of a federal investigation into allegations that Metal Traders was involved in an investment scam, there was a freeze on all of Metal Traders' operations so that no gold or silver was bought or sold. The good news is that the freeze resulted in a bonanza to Metal Traders: The price of gold jumped 42 percent in the interim. The bad news is that the Feds figured out the scam. The business filed for bankruptcy on June 30. Assuming it was insolvent throughout, can the trustee sue SpecVest for a preference? See §547(b), (c)(5).

25.5. Your firm represents Consolidated Bank. Sharon Sharp is the bank's loan officer for Johnny Sugar's Major Mobile, Inc., a local mobile-home dealer that is in financial trouble. Sharon calls the partner you work for, explaining that she is about to set off against the company's account with Consolidated in order to stem its likely loan losses, but thought she should check with the firm first. The partner has transferred the call to you. What questions should you ask Sharon? Be ready to advise her when she answers them.

25.6. You represent Liberty Bank, working chiefly with its commercial accounts. Liberty consults you about an open line of credit it has maintained with Tulsa Pool Supplies and Service. The current balance on the loan is $90,000 and Tulsa Pool is four months behind on its payments. The loan is secured by Tulsa Pool's inventory of pool chemicals and supplies.

The bank officials monitoring the loan have tried to pressure Tulsa Pool into paying on the loan by threatening to call the loan. Tulsa Pool points out that it is now barely the "pool season" (it is June), but that they have geared up for an active summer. In late April they were able to make an extremely favorable purchase of pool chemicals on unsecured credit (which the bank officials feel sure has not been paid). The purchase boosted the value of the inventory on hand from $30,000 to $100,000, most of which still remains in the store.

The bank analysts think that the business has been insolvent for quite some time and that it is not going to survive. They see that the business's checking account is overdrawn and that two paychecks have just been dishonored. Because the loan payments are late, the analysts have recommended that the bank call the loan and foreclose on the collateral. They ask for your help in the foreclosure proceedings. What do you advise?

Barney's Problem — Part III

Note: Unless otherwise indicated, the day this part of Barney's Problem is discussed in class is "deemed to be" March 1 of this year. This part of the problem, like the rest, is to be analyzed in "real time," i.e., as if you as counsel obtain the information or take the action indicated on the day (and the deemed date) the problem is to be discussed in class. All previous parts of the problem are incorporated into this part as of the day (and the deemed date) it is discussed in class, as if you were a sole practitioner in a town called Aloysius and this small drama were real.

On reflection, you do not let Barney Thornaby go home, but drag him to his company's offices for a review of its books. You assign your paralegal to examine each unusual payment, lien, or transfer of property the company has made since the beginning of the last calendar year (its fiscal year started June 1, last year). Below is his initial list.

1.   The Aloysius State Bank has a lien on all of the company's inventory and accounts receivable pursuant to a security agreement dated May 17, last year, securing a $400,000, 10 percent term loan. Barney's files include a photocopy of a letter from ASB to the Secretary of State enclosing the related financing statements for filing. The accounts receivable have increased greatly on the books because of delayed progress payments on the company's big county courthouse job.

2.   Last January 3, the company bought three used bulldozers for a job it has at Enormous State University and gave the seller, Darby's Dozers, a lien on the equipment for 80 percent of the price paid (price: $10,000 per bulldozer). A UCC financing statement was mailed by Barney to the Secretary of State's office on February 5. This obligation has been assigned to the Aloysius State Bank.

3.   On March 20 of last year, the company repaid an outstanding loan to the bank's executive vice president, Egbert Souse, who also sits on the company's board of directors. At the same time, the

company redeemed half of the preferred stock owned by various people, including Barney's uncle and Souse.

As you review the files, Barney mentions that his suppliers are demanding that the company give them a security interest in all the company's property, if it wants them to keep shipping. Back in early December they had gotten together and had threatened to halt deliveries, but relented on the basis of the company's payment of $50,000 on account.

Barney mentions that the next monthly bank payment of $11,500 is due March 5.

What further information will you instruct the paralegal to obtain? What action will you take or plan to take as company counsel? What effect, if any, does this new information have on your overall approach?

5.   *Executory Contracts*

a.   **The Economic Decision**

As the trustee or DIP begins to work to restructure the business, its ongoing contracts — those negotiated before the filing for which performance is continuing or is due in the future — become a central concern. As the trustee decides what direction the ongoing business should take, a review of the pending contracts becomes essential. Some of the debtor's pre-bankruptcy contracts may have been good bargains, while others may have been bad. Even among the good bargains, some may be worth more to someone else than they are to the debtor.

The following problems introduce the choices that the Code gives to the trustee in the disposition of the debtor's pre-bankruptcy contracts.

Problem Set 26

26.1. PetroCo, Inc. is an independent oil refinery. Bad market predictions and excessive overhead have caused the company to lose money for the past several consecutive quarters. Finally it has filed a Chapter 11. Indicative of its difficulties in the highly volatile market for fuel oil is its contract with ConEd. This contract provides that PetroCo will furnish 100,000 barrels of oil, nearly six months' output from the small refinery, for $30 a barrel, a price that looked lucrative when it was proposed eleven months ago. Now, two weeks from delivery, the contract appears to be a disaster. Tension in the Middle East and a strengthening OPEC have caused the price of oil once again to surge, so that if PetroCo could sell that six-month supply of oil on the current market, it would be able to get $50 per barrel. What should PetroCo do? See §365(a). Assuming PetroCo will ultimately pay its unsecured creditors 30 cents on the dollar, what will ConEd get if PetroCo rejects? Recall general contract principles and see section 502(g). What will PetroCo get from rejection? In a Chapter 7 liquidation of PetroCo, who would have received that benefit? In PetroCo's Chapter 11, who will receive that benefit? Is there a general principle that supports the result?

26.2. Jameson's Fruit Distributors has long specialized in supplying citrus fruits from Florida throughout the country. High interest rates and some bad market predictions have put Jameson's into a very tenuous financial position and it has recently filed in Chapter 11. At the time of filing, Jameson's has one large contract outstanding: It has agreed to buy 750,000 bushels of oranges for $1.02 per bushel from Florida Growers, a Tallahassee co-op.

Speculation on the futures market for oranges is active right now. No one is sure how big this year's crop will be, but the citrus count (a federal census of the oranges currently on the trees) will be announced next Monday. Jameson's president asks you, as bankruptcy counsel to the company, what will happen when the census is revealed. A high orange count will result in orange prices below the $1.02 in his contract, whereas a low count will result in a price well above $1.02. What are Jameson's options?

Florida Growers is also concerned about the effect of the orange count. They have asked another attorney what will happen if the count is high and Jameson's does not want the fruit. If that lawyer is even half as good as you are, what will she have explained to Florida Growers about their economic position? See §365(a) and (d)(2). (Do not worry about §§765 and 766.) In what important way does section 365(d) add to the DIP's options?

26.3. Farr's Manufacturing is a small concern that produces the canvas and metal slings used by the armed forces to carry canteens. Because there is little civilian use of canteens (most consumer users prefer lighter holders), Farr's deals almost exclusively with the federal government. Currently, Farr's has a three-year contract to supply 18.3 million slings on a cost-plus basis. Farr's has begun performance and is currently on schedule.

Farr's has suffered through two strikes and a fire at its factory. It now has things under control, but increased expenses and interrupted income have forced Farr's into a Chapter 11. The owner of Farr's explains to you that without the government contracts, it will not be able to survive. He wants to know if the government can cancel its contract now. Your research has disclosed no federal law against assignment of this contract and no federal law terminating a government contract because of bankruptcy. The government contract, however, includes both a "no assignment" clause and a "bankruptcy termination" clause. What do you tell Farr's? See §§541(c)(1); 365(a), (c), and (e).

26.4. American Molding & Manufacturing has long been a manufacturer of plastic parts for industrial uses (lids, radio knobs, brackets, etc.). Three years ago it decided the future was in MP3 players, and it began an aggressive campaign to expand into manufacturing for the music industry. Unfortunately, AM&M did not count on the fact that as the orders rolled in, AM&M would need new equipment and experienced people, and it had neither. Hasty expansion decisions led to serious losses, and it has just filed a Chapter 11.

AM&M plans to try the music market again, but now it is struggling for survival. It has decided to retrench in Chapter 11, and then, with a firm base, to try expansion later. Among AM&M's current contracts are several potentially profitable contracts to manufacture player parts for delivery in the near future. AM&M cannot perform them, even though they are good, profitable contracts. What should AM&M's DIP management do? See §365(a), (c), and (f).

26.5. Last year's hottest new fast-food franchise was Don's Duck Enchiladas. It became the darling of Wall Street because it had an upscale market and could expand quickly by offering franchisees very generous terms: "All they supply is the hard work." Jane Stover got the coveted franchise for northern Contra Costa County, in the San Francisco suburbs. Her franchise contract provided for (a) her purchase of the store and the land it sits on from Don's, Inc., the franchisor, for 5 percent down and the rest of the purchase price on a 20-year mortgage; (b) her purchase of food and other supplies from Don's on easy credit terms for the first two years (no payment for 90 days and a low interest rate); and (c) her option after the first year to borrow up to $100,000 from Don's at a low interest rate, repayable in easy installments. The contract provided that she would lease the store for the first year and then complete the real estate purchase. Unfortunately, only six months after she signed the contract and opened for business, a "tremor" damaged her store and closed it for several weeks. Now she has reopened, but her insurance was inadequate and she is almost out of working capital. She is current on her high franchise fees to Don's, but her bank is pressing her and she is afraid Don's will terminate on any excuse. Can she keep the franchise contract in Chapter 11? See §365(a), (c).

b.   The Statute

To an ever-increasing extent, the wealth of our society is in contracts, and valuable contracts are found in every aspect of economic life. Perhaps for that reason, section 365 is one of the longest and most detailed in the Code. So many specifics have been added that the section is very hard to parse. The analysis begins, as does the conceptual analysis of all executory contracts, not in the section devoted specifically to executory contracts, but instead to the even more fundamental section 541(a), which brings all property of the debtor, of whatever kind and wherever held, into the estate. Once the contract is in the estate, then section 365 deals with the rules surrounding rejection, assumption, and assignment. These rules effectively determine the claims that can be leveled against the estate for breach of the contract and the rights of the estate to enforce the contract and to realize its economic value either by performance or by assignment to another party.

Although it is very long, section 365 fails to state certain key rules. The first is that a contract may not be assumed if it was terminated prior to bankruptcy under nonbankruptcy law. The counterparty to a contract with the debtor often argues that its contract was history before the debtor filed and therefore may not be assumed.

In re KRYSTAL CADILLAC-OLDSMOBILE-GMC TRUCK, INC.
142 F.3d 631 (3d Cir. 1998)

MANSMANN, Circuit Judge.

In this appeal involving bankruptcy law, we are asked to decide whether a franchise agreement involving a vehicle dealership had been terminated prior to the filing of the bankruptcy petition. Because we find that the franchise agreement was still in effect when the petition was filed, it follows a fortiori that the vehicle franchise was an asset of the bankruptcy estate. We further find that the post-petition adjudications by the state administrative board and the Pennsylvania Commonwealth Court, effectively ordering the termination of the franchise agreement, were made in violation of the automatic stay provision of 11 U.S.C. §362(a)(3) and, thus, were not binding on the bankruptcy court. Accordingly, we will reverse the order of the district court affirming the order of the bankruptcy court.

I

The resolution of the dispute before us turns, in large part, on certain events which occurred prior to the commencement of the bankruptcy proceeding. We reiterate the pertinent facts here.

Krystal Cadillac-Oldsmobile-GMC Truck, Inc. ("Krystal Cadillac" or the "Debtor"), a licensed vehicle dealer in the Commonwealth of Pennsylvania, owned and operated a GMC dealership in Gettysburg, Pennsylvania. General Motors Corporation is a licensed vehicle manufacturer in the Commonwealth of Pennsylvania and the appellee in this consolidated appeal.

Krystal Cadillac operated the GMC dealership pursuant to the General Motors Corporation (Oldsmobile Division) Dealer Sales and Service Agreement, which went into effect on November 1, 1990. . . .

In October of 1991, General Motors Acceptance Corporation withdrew its line of credit financing. Consequently, Krystal Cadillac found itself lacking the necessary financing to purchase new GM vehicles. To no avail, it made numerous attempts to obtain alternative financing. On March 6, 1992, GM notified Krystal Cadillac that it was in breach of the franchise agreement for failing to maintain a line of credit and for failing to purchase new vehicles. Based on the continued breach, GM gave notice on May 10, 1993 that the franchise would terminate in sixty days, that is, on July 13, 1993. At Krystal Cadillac's request, GM extended the termination date to August 12, 1993.

On August 11, 1993, the day before the franchise agreement would have expired, Krystal Cadillac filed an appeal with the Pennsylvania Board of Vehicle Manufacturers, Dealers and Salespersons (the "Vehicle Board"), requesting a hearing on the merits of the termination. Approximately one year later, on August 2, 1994, the Vehicle Board conducted a hearing to review the propriety of GM's notice of termination. Before the Vehicle Board rendered its determination, Krystal Cadillac filed a voluntary petition for relief under Chapter 11 of the Bankruptcy Code on September 8, 1994. Thereafter, on September 27, 1994, the Vehicle Board entered an

Order and Decision allowing GM to terminate the franchise agreement. Subsequently, Krystal Cadillac appealed the order of the Vehicle Board to the Pennsylvania Commonwealth Court, which affirmed the Vehicle Board's decision on November 6, 1995. The Pennsylvania Supreme Court denied Krystal Cadillac's petition for allowance of appeal.

While this appeal was pending before the Pennsylvania Commonwealth Court, the bankruptcy court appointed Lawrence V. Young as the Chapter 11 Trustee. The Trustee, in turn, filed a motion to sell the Debtor's assets, including the GM franchise, free and clear of liens and encumbrances. . . .

[O]n April 15, 1996, the bankruptcy court entered an order denying the Debtor's motion to assume and assign the franchise. . . . [T]he Trustee filed a motion to assume and to sell the franchise agreement to a qualified buyer for the price of Five Hundred Thousand Dollars ($500,000). On that same date, the Debtor filed a Plan of Reorganization with the bankruptcy court, which provided for the sale of the GM franchise as a means to pay creditors. GM filed an objection to the Plan on July 10, 1995, arguing that since the franchise had been validly terminated in the state proceedings, the franchise was not an asset of the bankruptcy estate available for sale. . . .

. . . The district court affirmed the order of the bankruptcy court on February 3, 1997, holding that the proceeding before the Vehicle Board did not fall within the scope of the automatic stay provided by 11 U.S.C. §362 and, therefore, the Vehicle Board's order allowing GM to terminate the franchise agreement was valid and the termination was effective. Accordingly, the district court held the franchise agreement was not an asset of the bankruptcy estate. The Debtor and the Trustee filed timely but separate appeals, which we consolidated for purposes of briefing and disposition.

II

The outcome of this appeal hinges on whether the franchise agreement should have been included as an asset of the bankruptcy estate. . . . If, in fact, the franchise agreement was still in force on the date Krystal Cadillac filed its bankruptcy petition, the franchise agreement, by statute, became an asset of the bankruptcy estate. . . .

In October 1990, the Debtor and GM executed the Oldsmobile Division Dealer Sales and Service Agreement ("Oldsmobile Agreement"), which went into effect on November 1, 1990. . . .

The Oldsmobile Agreement . . . provided, in Paragraph Thirteen, for the incorporation of GM's Standard Provisions, Dealer Sales and Service Agreement (GMMS 1013) ("Standard Provisions"), as part of the franchise agreement. Article 13 of the Standard Provisions addresses breaches and the remedy procedures. Where the breach has gone uncorrected, Article 13.1.13 provides:

> If, however, Dealer's response does not demonstrate that the breach has been corrected, or explain the circumstances to [GM's] satisfaction, termination is warranted and [GM] may terminate this Agreement upon written notice to

Dealer. Termination will be effective 60 days following Dealer's receipt of the notice.

... Our inquiry does not end with an examination of the terms of the franchise agreement, however, since the agreement between the Debtor and GM is governed by the Pennsylvania Board of Vehicles Act. ... Under the Act as amended in 1996, section 818.13 sets forth the provisions governing termination of franchises. In particular, the Act states that any manufacturer who terminates or fails to renew the franchise of any vehicle dealer "unfairly, without due regard to the equities of said dealer and without just cause," has violated the Act. Id. §818.13(a). Section 818.13(c) requires the manufacturer to give the dealer a minimum of sixty days advance notice of the termination or failure to renew the franchise agreement, although subsection (c) allows a shorter notice period in certain circumstances not present here. Id. §818.13(c). Of particular relevance to this case is the subsection on appeals:

> At any time before the effective date of such termination or failure to renew, the dealer or distributor may appeal to the board for a hearing on the merits, and following due notice to all parties concerned, such hearing shall be promptly held. No such termination or failure to renew shall become effective until final determination of the issue by the board.

Id. §818.13(d). ...

Reading the franchise agreement and the Act together, as we must, we conclude that the franchise agreement was not terminated, but rather, was in force on the date the Debtor filed the petition in bankruptcy. The Act makes clear that once a dealer has appealed the notice of termination, that termination shall not become effective until the Vehicle Board issues its decision. Indeed, counsel for GM conceded at oral argument that Krystal Cadillac retained a viable legal interest in the GM franchise at the time Krystal Cadillac filed a notice of appeal with the Vehicle Board. Moreover, the Vehicle Board had not rendered its decision as of the date of the bankruptcy filing on September 8, 1994. Accordingly, we find that termination of the franchise agreement had not been effectuated on September 8, 1994, and, therefore, that the franchise became an asset of the bankruptcy estate on that date.

III

We further conclude that the subsequent determinations by the Vehicle Board and the Pennsylvania Commonwealth Court, effectively ordering the termination of the franchise agreement, were made in violation of the automatic stay provisions of 11 U.S.C. §362(a) and, thus, were not binding on the bankruptcy court. ...

IV

In sum, we find that Krystal Cadillac's property interest in a viable GMC franchise is an asset of the bankruptcy estate and that the Trustee is entitled to cure any defects, and to assume and assign the franchise for the benefit of all of the Debtor's creditors. Accordingly, we will reverse the judgment of the district court affirming the order of the bankruptcy court.

═══════

The debtor in *Krystal* did not plan to keep and operate the valuable GM franchise contract, but, like the *Krystal* TIB, planned to assign it to someone else for a consideration. It is not surprising that GM fought hard for the right to choose Krystal's successor itself — and to reap the benefits of selling the franchise. It is fairly common in bankruptcy to find the DIP or TIB anxious to sell a contract and the counterparty anxious to prevent the sale. Real estate leases, especially in a hot real estate market, are one of the most common examples. The statute provides the debtor with some powerful assistance.

═══════ In re JAMESWAY CORP. ═══════
201 B.R. 73 (Bankr. S.D.N.Y. 1996)

James L. GARRITY, Jr., Bankruptcy Judge.

FACTS

The facts are not disputed. On October 18, 1995 ("petition date"), Jamesway and its affiliates (collectively, the "debtors") filed separate petitions for relief under chapter 11 of the Bankruptcy Code in this district. At that time, debtors operated discount department stores under the "Jamesway" name. Debtors are in possession of their businesses and properties as debtors-in-possession pursuant to §§1107 and 1108 of the Bankruptcy Code.

As of the petition date, Jamesway and Mass Mutual, as successor-in-interest to Valley Green Mall Co., were parties to an agreement dated July 16, 1986, as amended (the "Newberry Lease"), whereby Jamesway, as tenant, leased certain retail space located in the Newberry Commons shopping center in Etters, Pennsylvania. Paragraph 17 of that lease states in relevant part that:

> [i]f Tenant assigns this Lease ... then during the first twenty (20) years ... Tenant shall pay Landlord 50% of the "profits" received by Tenant from the assignee or sublessee. Thereafter, Tenant shall pay Landlord 60% of such profits. ...

Newberry Lease ¶17. On or about February 9, 1996, Jamesway moved under §365 of the Bankruptcy Code to assume and assign the Newberry Lease to Rite Aid of Pennsylvania, Inc. ("Rite Aid") for $100,000 (the "Rite Aid Motion"). Over Mass Mutual's objection, we granted the motion. ...

[Two other leases had similar provisions and the court had permitted their assignment as well.]

DISCUSSION . . .

Section 365(a) of the Bankruptcy Code authorizes a debtor-in-possession to assume or reject, subject to the court's approval, any executory contract or unexpired lease of the debtor. 11 U.S.C. §365(a). A debtor-in-possession may assign an unexpired lease of the debtor only if it assumes the lease in accordance with §365(a), and provides adequate assurance of future performance by the assignee, whether or not there has been a default under the lease. See 11 U.S.C. §365(f)(2). Except as otherwise provided in the Bankruptcy Code, an executory contract or unexpired lease is assumed cum onere. . . . Jamesway contends that the subject lease provisions are void and unenforceable under §365(f)(1) because they limit its ability to realize the full economic value of the Leases for the benefit of all unsecured creditors. . . .

Mass Mutual argues that §365(f)(1) does not empower us to nullify the profit sharing provisions in the lease, but merely permits us to authorize the assignment over its objection. It argues that our power to invalidate lease provisions is limited by §365(f)(3) to "ipso facto" or forfeiture provisions and that to hold otherwise will read §365(f)(3) out of the statute. Courts do not have carte blanche to rewrite leases under §§365(f)(1) and (f)(3) or any provision of the statute. Simpson, Leases and the Bankruptcy Code: Tempering the Rigors of Strict Performance, 38 Bus. Law. 60, 75 (cited hereinafter as "Simpson"). However, §365 reflects the clear Congressional policy of assisting the debtor to realize the equity in all of its assets. Toward that end, §365(f)(1) permits assignment of an unexpired lease despite a clause in the lease prohibiting, conditioning or restricting the assignment. Subsection (f)(3) goes beyond the scope of subsection (f)(1) by prohibiting enforcement of any clause creating a right to modify or terminate the contract because it is being assumed or assigned, "thereby indirectly barring an assignment by the debtor." In re Howe, 78 B.R. at 226 (citing In re J.F. Hink & Son, 815 F.2d at 1317-18; In re Sapolin Paints, Inc., 20 B.R. 497, 509 (Bankr. E.D.N.Y. 1982)). "The essence of Subsections (1) and (3) is that all contractual provisions, not merely those entitled 'anti-assignment clauses' are subject to the court's scrutiny regarding their anti-assignment effect." Id. at 229-30 (citing Matter of U.L. Radio Corp., 19 B.R. 537, 543 (Bankr. S.D.N.Y. 1982)). While they operate in tandem to promote the Congressional policy favoring a debtor's ability to maximize the value of its leasehold assets, subsections (f)(1) and (f)(3) deal with different problems; (f)(1) with provisions that prohibit, restrict or condition assignment, and (f)(3) with provisions that terminate or modify the terms of a lease because it has been assumed or assigned. For this reason, construing the former to invalidate provisions that directly or indirectly restrict the debtor's ability to assign the subject lease does not render §365(f)(3) superfluous.

Moreover, Mass Mutual's literal construction of §365(f)(1) makes nonsense of the statute while undermining its purpose. For Mass Mutual, even if assignment of an assumed lease were expressly conditioned upon the payment of a portion of the proceeds realized upon assignment to the lessor, §365(f)(1) would permit assignment but would not affect any lease term associated with the condition. As applied herein, it would mean that

Jamesway could assign the Leases provided it paid the Landlords the relevant percentages of the profits realized through the assignments. In other words, Jamesway would be complying with the very condition that subsection (f)(1) was designed to invalidate. This is not the correct reading of the statute.

In furtherance of Congressional policy favoring the assumption and assignment of unexpired leases as a means of assisting the debtor in its reorganization or liquidation efforts, we interpret §365(f)(1) to invalidate provisions restricting, conditioning or prohibiting debtor's right to assign the subject lease. No court has read the statute as narrowly as Mass Mutual. Rather, lease provisions conditioning a debtor-in-possession's right to assignment upon the payment of some portion of the "profit" realized upon such assignment are routinely invalidated under §365(f)(1).

Mass Mutual distinguishes those cases arguing that ¶17 is enforceable under §365(f)(1) because it does not prevent Jamesway from assigning the Newberry Lease to Rite Aid, does not alter any term in the lease based upon the assignment and is not triggered by the filing of Jamesway's chapter 11 case. It urges that the only effect of ¶17 is to allocate funds between Jamesway and the landlord upon assignment of the lease and that it is relevant only as it may impact on Jamesway's business judgment in electing to assume or reject the leases. The practical effect of the profit sharing clause in the Newberry Lease is the same as those at issue in the cited cases: it limits Jamesway's ability to realize the intrinsic value of the lease. . . .

Finally, the *Tri-State* and *Monticello* landlords contend that §365(f)(1) bars enforcement of profit sharing provisions that are so burdensome as to constitute penalties. They urge that we should conduct a balancing test and enforce the provisions at issue here as reasonable fees payable upon assignment. Some cases contain language leaving open the possibility that the courts might have ruled differently had the amounts payable by the debtor upon assignment been less. None of these courts ruled that the contract provisions in question would be enforced if the debtors had to pay a "reasonable" percentage of the assignment proceeds. Nothing in §365(f)(1) supports the Landlord's position.

CONCLUSION

We grant debtor's request for an order declaring that the profit sharing provisions of the Leases are unenforceable and direct that the $50,000 currently held in escrow from the assignment proceeds of the Newberry Lease be released to debtor.

For every case in bankruptcy in which the debtor has a great lease that it wants to assign to someone else, there are surely many other debtors who are stuck in bad bargains with leases from which they hope to escape.

The statute favors the debtor and the other creditors in the rejection context as well. Section 365(g) couples with section 502(g) to say that rejection damages for any contract are calculated as a pre-bankruptcy unsecured claim, regardless of when rejection occurs. And landlords suffer further grief because section 502(b)(6) caps landlords' damage claims following rejection and the landlord remains subject to the duty under state law to mitigate damages by re-leasing the premises as soon as possible. The cap applies to the allowed amount of the claim and then the amount is paid, as with other contracts, in tiny Bankruptcy Dollars. Depending on state law and the economic circumstances of a particular case, the opportunity to reject leases and limit damages in this way may be a major advantage of a Chapter 11 filing to a debtor with many retail locations that are losing money.

One other statutory constraint must be mentioned. Section 365(c)(1) forbids assumption of a contract that could not have been assigned by the debtor under nonbankruptcy law. The classic example was the personal services contract. If an actor (hypothetically, Leonardo DiCaprio) had a contract to play the lead in a movie (say, *Titanic*), state law would not permit the actor to assign the rights under that contract to some balding, middle-aged, but wealthy guy who would pay top dollar to appear in a feature film (perhaps after his high-priced trip in a Russian rocket). If the actor were to file Chapter 7 bankruptcy, the Code would similarly forbid the balding, middle-aged trustee in bankruptcy to assume and perform the contract. But if the actor filed a Chapter 11 case, what would be wrong with his assuming the contract and performing as contracted, even if the producer wanted to renegotiate?

Although the language of section 365(c)(1) can be read to permit a DIP to assume and perform, the courts are divided about its effect. In particular, some highly controversial decisions forbid assignment of patents, on the ground that federal nonbankruptcy law (the law of patents) forbids those assignments outside of bankruptcy and therefore a patent license is unassumable even by the same company that entered into the license, acting as a DIP. In re Catapult Entertainment, Inc., 165 F.3d 747 (9th Cir. 1999). A circuit split may send the issue to the Supreme Court. Stay tuned.

Problem Set 27

27.1. Jacky Pell has a small electronics repair shop in town. His shop is in rented space in a small office building. He has come to you because he has just received notice of cancellation of the lease from his landlord. Although the notice says "vacate immediately," you have read the lease and it provides for a five-day "notice and cure" period prior to final cancellation. He explains that he has fallen two months behind on the rent on his shop (a total of $1,800) because of a fire that damaged the repair room and destroyed some of his equipment. He had to use the rent money to fix the room and replace the tools. He has offered to "catch up" on the rent over the next three months, but the landlord told him "I don't trust you anymore, now that I know you didn't keep insurance like the lease says." Jacky admits he had slipped up and forgotten the insurance, but says he has already reinstated the policy by making the back premium payments.

Although Jacky is otherwise "all right" financially, he says that eviction would destroy his business and "I'd probably never be able to build it back." What good would bankruptcy do Jacky? What would you try to do in bankruptcy to save the lease? What arguments would the landlord's attorney make against you, and how could you reply? See §365(b)(1), (3), and (c)(3). An hour after he left your office, you are going through the documents he gave you when you find he is also leasing a diagnostic machine for locating defects in appliances. You can see that the lapse of the insurance breached that lease as well. Does that present a different problem for Jacky in a bankruptcy? §365(b)(1)-(2).

27.2. Rancho Industries was in the business of raising horses and other livestock on its 10,000-acre ranch. About a year ago, it leased 1,000 acres for a five-year term to your client, Fledgling Breeders, Inc., for similar purposes. The agreed rent was $50,000 per year. Rancho promised in the lease to ensure a steady supply of water from its wells through the existing irrigation system to FB land. Rancho has recently filed a Chapter 7 petition. There is no water on the land FB leases and it would cost $60,000 per year to bring the necessary water by truck. What remedies will FB have if the lease is rejected? See §365(h).

27.3. Novelty Industries leased a manufacturing facility from Alfred Bucks for a 20-year term at $200,000 per year. Novelty's president tells you that the lease also provided that

1. it terminated automatically upon Novelty's making an assignment for benefit of creditors or entering receivership or bankruptcy;
2. it could be assigned only with the written approval of Bucks;
3. it could be terminated if Novelty's outstanding debts ever exceed twice its equity investment, upon ten days' written notice of termination from Bucks.

Shortly after Novelty sent Bucks its most recent financial statement (as required by the lease), Bucks sent a notice of termination based on the statement's revelation that Novelty's debts exceed twice its equity. Novelty has come to seek your advice since the ten days provided in the notice expire today. Just before coming to your office, Novelty's president talked to Bucks about an assignment of the lease to Monster Toys, who would be willing to pay $300,000 per year for the space. Bucks said he would agree to the assignment if he got all of the increase. Novelty has decided to get out of the toy business and will not have a further need for the facility. What can you advise Novelty? §365(b), (e), (f).

27.4. When you had a chance to read the Novelty lease yourself, you discovered that provision (2) above permitted free assignability, but required that Bucks get one-half of any increase in rent. Does your analysis change?

27.5. As you peruse the Novelty lease even more closely, you discover that the original lease had a further benefit for Novelty: In the lease Bucks agreed to make a $100,000 loan to Novelty at the beginning of the fourth year of the lease, which would be next January 1. The loan would be at an interest rate well below the current rate charged by banks. Could Novelty assume this right if it filed bankruptcy? §365(c)(2). Does the presence of the provision change the result in Problem 27.3 or the lease as a whole?

27.6. On March 1, Stan Freegate filed a Chapter 7 petition. While Stan's farming operations had always been successful, his amateurish flirtations with the commodities markets were disastrous. Aside from trading on exchanges, he had entered into a contract with Paul Plotsky, a neighbor, to buy Paul's May wheat for $2.35 a bushel. Paul came to see you on the morning of April 28. He wants you to call the TIB for Freegate and find out what is happening, since Paul has heard nothing about the wheat deal. Paul mentions that the price of wheat has risen to $3.25 since the recent drought in Canada and is going higher. How do you handle this? §365(d).

c. Extra-statutory Constraints on the Trustee's Right to Assume or Reject

To understand the case law constraints on the right to assume or reject contracts, a brief review of the fundamentals of section 365 may be useful. Every pre-bankruptcy contract that a debtor brings into bankruptcy consists of both the debtor's rights and the debtor's obligations under that contract. A debtor's pre-bankruptcy contract rights come into the estate under section 541(a), like all other property. We have seen that section 541(c)(1) invalidates anti-assignment and bankruptcy clauses that would otherwise prevent those rights from passing to the estate (see Problem 26.3). By the same token, the debtor's obligations to the other party to the contract become claims against the estate under section 502(b), (g). Thus both aspects of a contract have passed to the estate before we reach section 365(a), which states that the trustee may assume or reject that contract and its attendant bundles of rights and obligations.

Section 365 also imposes certain constraints on the trustee's right to assume or reject (perform or breach) a pre-bankruptcy contract. Three constraints on assumption are especially important. The trustees may not assume a contract if its assignment is forbidden under applicable nonbankruptcy law. §365(c)(1). Even as to assumable contracts, the trustee must cure or arrange to cure most defaults as a condition of assumption. §365(b). Finally, the trustee or its assignee (in the case of assumption and assignment under section 365(f)) must also provide "adequate assurance of future performance." §365(b)(1)(C), (f)(2)(B). The Code here tries to provide some protection for the other party if the debtor's estate plans to assume the benefits of the contract.

In this section we consider an additional, extra-statutory constraint on the trustee's right to assume or reject a pre-bankruptcy contract of the debtor. For well over a century, the courts have held that the trustee may not either assume or reject a contract unless that contract is "executory." This threshold requirement for assumption or rejection has never been codified in the statute, but it has achieved great prominence in the case law. It has created severe difficulties because the courts have never been able to explain clearly the elements that make up the quality of "executoriness" that a contract must have before it is deemed eligible for assumption or rejection.

It is obvious that a contract must be executory to be assumed or rejected, if the term is used in its ordinary sense to mean merely that there are aspects of the contract that were not fully performed or satisfied on the date of the filing of the bankruptcy. But a requirement that a contract be "executory" in that commonsense way would be a trivial one. Obviously the trustee need not, and could not, assume or reject a contract fully performed a year before bankruptcy — nor would anyone dream of doing so. Speaking of a nonexecutory contract in that sense is like discussing a sunset after dark.

It is clear by their holdings that the courts did not limit the meaning of the term "executory" to such a commonsense application. Under the Bankruptcy Act, courts held many contracts to be nonexecutory and therefore not subject either to assumption or to rejection, even though the contracts were not fully performed or satisfied prior to bankruptcy. Despite their holdings, the courts had not articulated an intelligible statement of what made some unperformed contracts executory and others nonexecutory. So matters rested until Professor Vern Countryman published his seminal articles on executory contracts in the mid-1970s. Countryman, Executory Contracts in Bankruptcy: Part I, 57 Minn. L. Rev. 439 (1973); Part II, 58 Minn. L. Rev. 479 (1974).

To understand the situation prior to these articles, consider the simplest example: a pre-bankruptcy contract in which the debtor agreed to sell 100 bushels of onions to the counterparty buyer for $1 per bushel. Neither party had performed as of the bankruptcy filing, and there were no defaults by either. Section 365 (and its predecessor) would permit the trustee to assume or reject. As we saw in Problems 26.1 and 26.2, if the market for onions is up, the trustee will reject, sell for the higher market price, and pay contract damages to the counterparty in little, pro rata bankruptcy dollars. If the market is down, the trustee will assume, hold the counterparty to the contract, and sell the onions under the contract for the now above-market contract price of $1 per bushel. Although the estate has the same state law contract position as the debtor, it has much greater opportunity to profit by rejection because it pays only a small percentage of breach damages. If a nonbankruptcy seller breached and sold at a higher market price, that seller would likely profit little because it would have to pay the counterparty its expectancy, including the contract-market differential, as contract damages. Because the trustee pays (in bankruptcy dollars) only a small percentage of those damages by making pro rata payments on claims, the estate can benefit by breaching a contract far more often than can a nonbankrupt party.

Naturally, in the onion example the trustee would say the contract is executory so that the estate may enjoy these attractive options. Naturally, too, the counterparty would like to deny the estate these options so that it would claim the contract was somehow nonexecutory and thus not subject to assumption or rejection. Hard as it may be to believe, the consequences of a contract being found nonexecutory were almost completely unaddressed — and still are today. But the counterparty would figure it must somehow be better off if the contract were not executory so as to deny the trustee those profitable options, and it would argue the contract was nonexecutory. In a fair number of cases, the counterparty would claim that the effect of nonexecutoriness was that the trustee had to perform (here, had to deliver the onions at the contract price) and many courts seemed implicitly to agree. The unstated rationale was that the trustee could not reject and therefore must be bound. In other cases, when the market was down and the counterparty did not want the onions, it would argue that the contract was nonexecutory, which meant that the trustee could not bind the counterparty to it (here, not forcing onions on the counterparty at above-market prices). This argument proceeded from the other side of the street, positing that the trustee must in some way lose the contract because it could not be assumed. Some courts seemed to accept this opposite conclusion as well.

Both of the arguments of the counterparty are nearly frivolous. There is no basis in the statute for forced assumption or for denying the trustee a bundle of contract rights inherited from the debtor. Yet trustees often make an equally shaky argument when they claim that an executory contract can be rejected right out of existence, so that the obligations of the debtor can simply be ignored rather than dealt with as claims against the estate. As obviously wrong as these positions are, they have often been urged and fairly often accepted in litigation because there has been no clear idea what happens to a nonexecutory contract.

In the face of this intellectual morass, Professor Countryman's articles distilled the mass of case law and provided the first persuasive explanation of the meaning of the threshold test of executoriness. He proposed this test:

> [A] contract under which the obligation of both the bankrupt and the counterparty to the contract are so far unperformed that the failure of either to complete performance would constitute a material breach excusing the performance of the other.

Vern Countryman, Executory Contracts in Bankruptcy: Part 1, 57 Minn. L. Rev. 439, 460 (1973).

The "material breach" test became the most widely adopted scholarly contribution to bankruptcy law in its history. It virtually became the law in most circuits and was cited favorably in the legislative history to the Bankruptcy Code, even though it was not actually codified in the statute. H.R. Rep. No. 595, 95th Cong., 1st Sess. 347 (1977). It seems clear that the Countryman test dramatically improved the courts' analyses of these problems and eliminated many cases from the reporters. Applying the test to the simple example given above, it is apparent that at the time of filing both parties have material obligations to perform, the contract is executory, and the trustee may assume or reject.

Unfortunately, it has become clear that many contemporary bankruptcy contract problems cannot be resolved by the material breach analysis. The case that follows is one such example. It also illustrates the exercise of the court's power to approve or disapprove the debtor's business decision to assume or reject a contract under section 365(a).

═══════════════ In re RIODIZIO, INC. ═══════════════

204 B.R. 417 (Bankr. S.D.N.Y. 1997)

Stuart M. BERNSTEIN, Bankruptcy Judge.

Riodizio, Inc. (the "debtor") seeks, inter alia, to reject a stock option agreement and a shareholders agreement, both entered into in June, 1995. Riodizio Company, LLC ("LLC"), the optionee as well as a party to the shareholders agreement, opposes the motion.

The motion thrusts us into the "psychedelic" world of executory contracts, Jay Lawrence Westbrook, A Functional Analysis of Executory Contracts, 74 Minn. L. Rev. 227, 228 (1989) ("Westbrook"), and reinforces the prophecy that the time that litigants and the courts spend searching for "executoriness" can be put to better use analyzing the benefits and burdens of the contract itself.

Facts

The debtor commenced this chapter 11 case on August 19, 1996. It owns and operates a Brazilian grill restaurant (called a "Riodizio" in Brazil) at 417 Lafayette Street in New York, New York. Prior to commencing business, the debtor and its two shareholders, Alan Berfas and Frank Ferraro, entered into numerous agreements with LLC to secure financing and equipment for the restaurant. These included a Loan and Lease Agreement, dated June 1, 1995 (the "Loan and Lease"), a Shareholders Agreement, dated June 23, 1995 (the "Shareholders Agreement"), and an undated stock option (the "Warrant") that the debtor granted to the LLC.

1.   The Loan and Lease

Under the Loan and Lease, LLC advanced $200,000.00 to the debtor to operate the business. The terms of the loan, as evidenced by a promissory note, called for 15% interest, with principal and interest payable in 42 monthly installments. As security for the advances, the debtor gave LLC a priority security interest in all office equipment including, without limitation, computer equipment, kitchen equipment, fixtures, mailing lists, bank accounts, Transmedia agreements and proceeds, and accounts receivable. Berfas and Ferraro also provided a limited guaranty by depositing into escrow, in favor of LLC, their respective shares in the debtor, general stock powers, and their resignations as officers, directors and employees.

The Loan and Lease also provided that LLC would purchase and then lease kitchen and other equipment valued at $150,000.00 to the debtor. Previously, however, the Court denied the debtor's motion to reject this equipment lease. First, the equipment lease was not a true lease, but rather, a security financing arrangement involving a self-amortizing loan under which the debtor paid the entire purchase price, including interest, in forty-two monthly installments of $4,612.36 each. Second, the equipment lease was part of the single Loan and Lease agreement, and the debtor could not "cherry pick" and reject unfavorable provisions contained in an integrated agreement.

2. The Warrant and Shareholders Agreement

As part of the underlying transaction, the debtor also executed the Warrant.[1] It states, in its entirety, as follows:

> Riodizio, Inc. (the "Corporation") hereby grants to the holder of this warrant the right to purchase all or part of an aggregate of 93 common shares of the Corporation for the consideration of one dollar ($1.00) per share.
> This warrant may be exercised for a period of twenty f[i]ve years.

The Warrant was signed on behalf of the debtor by Berfas and Ferraro, each of whom own 33 shares of the debtor's common stock. If LLC exercises its warrant (and the debtor delivers the shares), LLC will own approximately 60% of the debtor's outstanding shares based upon an additional investment of only $93.00.

Finally, the debtor, Berfas, Ferraro and LLC entered into the Shareholders Agreement. According to the introductory "WHEREAS" clauses, they did so at LLC's request "as an additional safeguard to its collateral." Further, LLC is made a party "solely for the purpose of granting the Company the legal and equitable right to sue for the enforcement of the agreement and/or seek damages for the breach of this Agreement; and to protect the value of the warrants." The Shareholders Agreement protects LLC's financial stake in the debtor, or otherwise benefits it, in several ways. First, it requires Berfas and Ferraro to establish a four person board of directors which will include two LLC nominees in addition to themselves. Second, it requires a two-thirds shareholders vote to take certain "extraordinary" actions. If LLC exercises its warrants and controls nearly 60% of the outstanding stock, it will be able to veto these "extraordinary" actions.[2] Third, if the shareholders open a different type of restaurant, they must first offer LLC the right to participate in the venture.

The balance of the Shareholders Agreement concerns rights and obligations running between the debtor and the shareholders. For example, Berfas and Ferraro cannot open a similarly-styled restaurant within ten miles of any restaurant operated by the debtor unless the debtor gives its written consent. Under those circumstances where they can operate a similarly-styled restaurant, they must first offer the debtor the right to participate in the venture. The debtor must purchase Key Man Life Insurance on the lives of the individual shareholders. Finally, the Shareholders Agreement contains a series of provisions relating to the sale or transfer of the shares, giving the non-selling shareholder and/or the debtor a right of first refusal.

---

1. Although the Warrant and Shareholders Agreement were executed in connection with the lending transaction, both parties treat them as separate, independent agreements for purposes of section 365.

2. Article 9.2 of the Loan and Lease grants LLC many of these same veto powers, and does not depend upon LLC becoming a shareholder.

DISCUSSION

1. Introduction

Section 365(a) states that "the trustee, subject to the court's approval, may assume or reject any executory contract or unexpired lease of the debtor." 11 U.S.C. §365(a). The Bankruptcy Code does not define the term "executory contract." The legislative history regarding this section states that "[t]hough there is no precise definition of what contracts are executory, it generally includes contracts on which performance remains due to some extent on both sides." H.R. Rep. No. 95-595, at 347 (1977); S. Rep. No. 95-989, at 58 (1978), U.S. Code Cong. & Admin. News 1978, pp. 5787, 5844, 6303. Finding this definition too broad and sweeping, most courts have adopted Professor Countryman's definition of an executory contract as

> a contract under which the obligation of both the bankrupt and the counter-party to the contract are so far unperformed that the failure of either to complete performance would constitute a material breach excusing performance of the other.

Vern Countryman, Executory Contracts in Bankruptcy: Part 1, 57 Minn. L. Rev. 439, 460 (1973).

Under Countryman's "material breach" test, a prepetition contract is executory when both sides are still obligated to render substantial performance. Where such performance remains due on only one side, the contract is non-executory, and hence, neither assumable nor rejectable. The materiality of the breach is a question of state law. Thus, if applicable non-bankruptcy law permits either party to sue for breach because of the counterparty's failure to perform, the contract is executory. . . .

Some have found the Countryman "material breach" test too constraining and static. In Chattanooga Memorial Park v. Still (In re Jolly), 574 F.2d 349 (6th Cir.), cert, denied, 439 U.S. 929 (1978), a pre-Code case, the Court observed:

> [The Countryman] definition[ ] [is] helpful, but do[es] not resolve th[e] problem. The key, it seems, to deciphering the meaning of the executory contract rejection provisions, is to work backward, proceeding from an examination of the purposes rejection is expected to accomplish. If those objectives have already been accomplished, or if they can't be accomplished through rejection, then the contract is not executory within the meaning of the Bankruptcy Act.

Id. at 351.

In this same vein, some advocate a functional analysis which eliminates the requirement of executoriness. See Westbrook, supra, 74 Minn. L. Rev. 227; see also Michael T. Andrew, Executory Contracts in Bankruptcy: Understanding Rejection, 59 U. Colo. L. Rev. 845 (1988) ("Andrew I"); Michael T. Andrew, Executory Contracts Revisited: A Reply to Professor Westbrook, 62 U. Colo. L. Rev. 1 (1991) ("Andrew II"). Under the functional approach, "the question of whether a contract is executory is determined by the benefits that assumption or rejection would produce for the estate." Sipes v. Atlantic Gulf Communities Corp. (In re General Dev. Corp.), 84 F.3d 1364, 1375 (llth Cir. 1996) (affirming on the basis of the district court's opinion, 177 B.R. 1000 (S.D. Fla. 1995)); accord *Drexel*, 138 B.R. at 696 (synthesizing the Westbrook and Andrew articles, and concluding that a threshold requirement of executoriness is misplaced; rather, the proper analysis is whether rejection will produce a benefit to the estate).

The functional approach does not repudiate the Countryman rule; it merely recognizes its limitations. It also conserves the time and effort that the parties and the court otherwise spend resolving the question of executoriness. But it has its critics. To be subject to assumption or rejection, the statute, 11 U.S.C. §365, expressly requires that the contract be executory. Ignoring executoriness rewrites the statute in a fundamental way. See In re Child World, Inc. 147 B.R. at 851 ("Manifestly, th[e functional] approach ignores the statutory requirement that the contract to be assumed or rejected must be 'executory.'").

2. *The Warrant*

Options agreements, such as the Warrant, demonstrate the shortcomings of the Countryman definition. "[A]n option contract is essentially an enforceable promise not to revoke an offer." In re III Enterprises, Inc. V, 163 B.R. 453, 460-61 (Bankr. E.D. Pa.), aff'd, 169 B.R. 551 (E.D. Pa. 1994). It is a unilateral contract until exercised; upon exercise, it becomes a bilateral contract.

An option contemplates performance by both parties but requires it from only one. The optionor must keep the offer open. The optionee may but need not exercise the option; if he does, each party must perform its obligations under the resulting bilateral contract. The optionee's failure to exercise the option constitutes a failure of condition rather than a breach of duty. The failure to perform a condition which is not also a legal duty cannot give rise to a material breach, and hence, an option contract is not executory under the Countryman definition.

Most courts, however, consider an option contract to be executory although they reach their conclusions through different routes. In In re Waldron, 36 B.R. 633 (Bankr. S.D. Fla. 1984), aff'd without op., (S.D. Fla.), rev'd on other grounds, 785 F.2d 936 (11th Cir.), cert, dismissed, 478 U.S. 1028 (1986), the debtors granted a real estate option to the Shell Oil Company. The debtors subsequently filed a joint chapter 13 petition in order to reject the contract since the value of the property exceeded the option price.

The *Waldron* court held that the option was executory, but relied on the "some performance due" standard cited in the legislative history rather than the more rigorous Countryman test. . . .

The option cases that came after *Waldron*, but adopted the Countryman definition, faced a dilemma. The optionor's obligation — to keep the option open — was substantial, but the optionee did not owe any substantial obligation that could result in a material breach. Andrew II, supra, 62 U. Colo. L. Rev. at 32. To fit the option contract within the "material breach" test, they conflated the option contract with the contingent bilateral contract, finding the optionee's duty of substantial performance in the contingent obligation to perform under the bilateral contract created by the exercise of the option.

The case law confirms that executoriness lies in the eyes of the beholder. Despite the contrary case law discussed above, the Warrant, an option contract, is not an executory contract under Countryman's "material breach" test. The debtor granted the option to LLC as additional consideration for the loan. LLC fully performed any legal obligation in connection with the Warrant when it funded the loan. While the exercise of the Warrant is a condition to the debtor's obligation to deliver the shares to LLC, LLC is not legally obligated to exercise the Warrant or do anything (or refrain from doing anything).

If the "some performance due" test in the legislative history is overly inclusive, the Countryman test excludes too much. It imposes a "material breach" requirement, raising the threshold of executoriness above what Congress seemed to intend.[5] In the case of options, it excludes contracts under which the debtor has benefits and burdens, each party must still perform as a condition to the counterparty's performance, and assumption or rejection may confer a net benefit on the estate. Under the circumstances, we should question the test rather than condemn the contract to a "legal limbo" in which it can be neither assumed nor rejected. See Westbrook, supra, 74 Minn. L. Rev. at 239.

A test less exclusive than Countryman's that takes into account the mutual performance requirement embodied in the legislative history should be substituted. Under this test, a contract is executory if each side must render performance, on account of an existing legal duty or to fulfill a condition, to obtain the benefit of the counterparty's performance. Weighing the relative benefits and burdens to the debtor is the essence of the decision to assume or reject; if each party must still give something to get something, the contract is executory, and the debtor must demonstrate whether assumption or rejection confers a net benefit on the estate. If the debtor has done everything it needs to do to obtain the benefit of its bargain, assumption serves no purpose, and the debtor may simply sue to enforce its rights. Similarly, if the counterparty has done everything necessary to require the debtor to perform, the debtor's performance adds nothing to the estate, the debtor will not assume the contract, and the counterparty can file a prepetition claim. Here, the Warrant is executory; each party must perform under the Warrant in order to obtain the benefits under the contingent bilateral contract of sale. To sell the shares and receive payment, the debtor must keep the offer open. To make payment and acquire the shares, LLC must first exercise the option granted under the Warrant.[7]

---

5. The Second Circuit has never expressly adopted the Countryman test, and in its most recent pronouncement, In re Ionosphere Clubs, Inc., 85 F.3d 992, it referred instead to the legislative history for the proper standard. Id. at 998-99.

7. If the Warrant is not executory, the debtor's effort to reject it is a superfluous act. See Drexel, 138 B.R. at 709 (quoting Andrew I, supra, 59 U. Colo. L.R. at 17). Thus, if LLC has fully performed under the Warrant, it is in no different position than the trade vendor who sold onions to the debtor prepetition, and never received payment; the seller has a damage claim, but must await a pro rata payment with the other unsecured creditors. Westbrook, supra, 74 Minn. L. Rev. at 269.

Having concluded that the Warrant is executory, the Court must determine whether its rejection will benefit the estate. While a court will ordinarily defer to the business judgment of the debtor's management, Berfas and Ferraro have an interest in preventing LLC from exercising the option and diluting their personal stakes in and control over the debtor. Consequently, the debtor cannot rely on the presumptions of [the] business judgment rule to support its decision.

The Court's independent review nevertheless confirms that rejection benefits the estate without any significant downside. Proper business reasons for rejecting a contract include the following: (1) the contract is uneconomical to complete according to its terms; (2) the contract is financially burdensome to the estate . . . and (5) in the case of a stock option contract, the debtor can market the shares and receive a higher or better price than the option offers.[9]

The Warrant provides a de minimis benefit to the debtor, granting it the right to receive $93.00 if LLC exercises its option. On the other hand, it deprives the debtor of the possibility that it can sell the same shares for more money to another investor during the next twenty-three years of its remaining life. It does not matter whether this hypothetical investor exists; a $93.00 payment is so de minimis that the mere possibility outweighs any benefit in performing the Warrant.

Breaching the Warrant through rejection produces a minimal, adverse effect on the estate. Rejection constitutes a breach of contract immediately prior to the petition date. 11 U.S.C. §365(g)(1). At the outset, the Warrant does not create any property interest in LLC's favor that would survive rejection. See *Drexel*, 138 B.R. at 709 (rejection does not terminate rights in specific property created by the rejected contract) (quoting Andrew I, supra, 59 U. Colo. L. Rev. at 17). A breach leaves LLC with a claim for damages equal to the difference between the option price and the market value of the shares at the time of the breach. If LLC suffered any damage, this goes far to proving the wisdom of rejection; the debtor can sell the shares (to LLC or a third party) for more than the per share price of $1.00, and pay LLC's claim in tiny bankruptcy dollars.[10] Further, LLC's claim is arguably subordinated under 11 U.S.C. §510(b) to the payment of its other unsecured creditors.

3. The Shareholders Agreement

Consideration of the Shareholders Agreement is far more straight forward. Manifestly, it is executory. It subjects both the debtor and the shareholders to substantial obligations discussed above. For example, the shareholders cannot compete within ten miles, they must offer the debtor the chance to participate in any similarly-styled restaurant, and the debtor

---

9. Some courts refer to a balancing of equities, suggesting that rejection should be refused if it will cause disproportionate harm to the non-debtor party. The right to assume or reject an executory contract is designed to permit the debtor to shed its obligations under burdensome and uneconomical contracts. Section 365 does not require any balancing of the equities.

10. This assumes that the shares are at least as valuable today or in the future as they were on the petition date. But even if they are not, the option price is so low as to confer no meaningful benefit on the estate.

enjoys a right of first refusal if any shareholder decides to sell his shares. On the other hand, the debtor must maintain key man life insurance on the lives of the individual shareholders. In its opposition papers, LLC does not take much issue with executoriness, focusing instead on the lack of any benefit accruing to the debtor from rejection.

The record is insufficient, however, to determine whether the debtor should be permitted to reject this contract. Having outlined only some of the relevant benefits and burdens of the Shareholders Agreement, the Court must leave it to the parties to quantify these rights and obligations, and provide an evidentiary basis to support the decision to reject. For instance, the parties have not revealed the cost of the insurance. It may represent a burdensome administrative expense. On the other hand, the existence of the restrictions on competition and the rights of first refusal may enhance the value of the debtor to a potential investor.

Not surprisingly, both parties instead focus their attention on the corporate governance issues rather than the debtor's rights and obligations. The debtor seems to assume that rejection will relieve the debtor of LLC's management control, and moreover, that this is good for the debtor. Conversely, LLC argues that the debtor's management is incompetent, or worse, and the debtor is better off if LLC can impose limitations on management's control.

Neither argument merits consideration in the context of the present motion. In essence, each asks the Court to decide which managers and management limitations are best for the debtor. In the absence of "clear abuse," a bankruptcy court will not ordinarily interfere in corporate governance issues involving the debtor. If LLC believes that current management is incompetent or dishonest, it can move for the appointment of an operating trustee. See 11 U.S.C. §1104(a).

CONCLUSION

The Court grants the debtor's motion to reject the Warrant, and directs the parties to contact chambers to schedule an evidentiary hearing. . . .

The executoriness requirement is infinitely flexible. As the *Riodizio* court notes, any contract that has any consequence for the bankruptcy case will have something about it that is unperformed, especially if one is willing to count obligations NOT to do something. (The court adopts a test that might be described as Countryman Lite.) Thus a court may be tempted to resolve a host of equities involving contracts in bankruptcy by invoking the executoriness requirement. Three classes of cases have been particularly prominent, in addition to the option cases like *Riodizio*. One involves covenants against competition. A debtor franchisee or employee files bankruptcy and rejects the franchise or employment contract, claiming that the rejection frees the debtor from the covenant. A second category includes the license contracts, where a debtor-inventor files for bankruptcy and rejects the intellectual-property license it granted to a licensee, claiming the rejection gives it the right to revoke the license and grant it to another. A third type of case is the contract for sale of real estate, where the seller goes into bankruptcy and claims its rejection of the sales contract leaves it free to sell the land to the highest bidder. The second and third categories have been addressed by Congress, although only partially solved. §365(h)–(j), (n).

There are two conceptual points that are especially important in wrestling with these and other contemporary problems. The first point has to do with specific performance. Generally, it is difficult to prevail on a request for specific performance under nonbankruptcy law. As a general rule, it is even harder to prevail against the bankruptcy estate, because specific performance would be 100 percent performance (payment) to one unsecured creditor while all the other creditors are likely getting 10 cents on the dollar. However, where there is an especially strong countervailing policy of state law or bankruptcy law, the estate might be subject to specific performance. One approach is to say that where state law makes the promise a property right, an interest in a specific asset of the debtor, then bankruptcy law will enforce it. Thus the party purchasing real estate may argue for specific performance after equitable conversion against a debtor in bankruptcy, although a party purchasing onions has no similar protection. Another approach is to find a federal bankruptcy policy that requires enforcement in particular kinds of cases. Arguably, section 365(i) is such a policy, requiring conveyance of real estate to another party who is in possession prior to bankruptcy, without regard to any specific property rights granted at state law. That is, Congress could be understood to have decided that where a party entered into a contract to purchase real estate before bankruptcy and took possession of that real estate, the party's interest in the real estate should be protected as a matter of federal commercial policy against the risk of a bankruptcy filing, regardless of state law as applied to particular facts.

Secondly, some cases construe contract rejection in a way that seems to create an avoiding power. For example, the debtor who is able to revoke an earlier conveyance under the argument that the contract of conveyance is still executory is avoiding a pre-bankruptcy transaction through section 365. The commentators are virtually unanimous in saying that debtors should not be permitted to use contract rejection in this way. The cases permitting debtors to do so can perhaps best be explained by the fact that bankruptcy contract issues frequently involve a pre-bankruptcy transfer that also may implicate the traditional avoiding powers, such as the strong arm clause and the preference power. The contract and avoiding power issues can become intertwined, leading to judicial confusion about which is operating as to specific issues.

If and when the courts adopt the idea of abandoning executoriness as a threshold test, a whole new set of problems will be revealed. For example, that test has often been used as a cover for the application of bankruptcy policies, especially pro-reorganization policies, in the face of state law results that might prevent or hinder outcomes favored under the Code. If that device is abandoned, the courts will have to face squarely what to do when state law commands a result arguably inconsistent with bankruptcy policy. For example, suppose state law (UCC Article 2) were changed to make an ordinary sale of goods contract specifically enforceable. Should the bankruptcy courts permit such a preference for suppliers over other unsecured creditors? Questions like these will likely be at the cutting edge as the courts begin to move beyond executoriness.

Problem Set 28

28.1. Your client is Roxanna Gonzales, the Trustee who was appointed in the PetroCo case (Problem 26.1) after it failed and was converted to a Chapter 7, despite the cash infusion resulting from rejection of the ConEd contract and resale of the oil at the market price. While going through the PetroCo records, she has found a contract whereby PetroCo agreed to sell its Queens office building to J-Mart, a large local retailer. The sale price was $175,000, but Gonzales thinks the building would bring at least $250,000 in the overheated market that has resulted from the construction of new luxury apartments in the area. Under the contract, the closing was to take place on June 5, but the Chapter 11 was filed on June 1, and nothing has been done since. The Chapter 7 conversion took place 55 days ago, so the Trustee is anxious to decide what to do. Can she reject the contract? Can she resell the building? What arguments will J-Mart likely make? What do you need to learn about state law to resolve this issue? What other economic facts might be important? To prepare for your meeting with Gonzales, come up with a list of issues, questions to be resolved, and possible outcomes. See §365(a), (i).

28.2. CL, Inc., patented a new bug exterminating chemical, "Death Spray," which combined high toxicity to insects with safety to humans to an unparalleled degree. Its CEO, Calvin Looper, came to you 18 months ago to represent CLI in licensing negotiations with FuturVista Technologies, a growing mini-conglomerate. In the negotiations, FuturVista agreed to pay CLI a small initial fee, plus a royalty based on net profits of its exterminator division, in exchange for a 20-year license that would be exclusive for only one year, i.e., after a year CLI would be free to license to other companies as well. In addition to the patent, CLI licensed FuturVista to use its trademark, a dead bug with an aerosol can through its heart. (Calvin had made the trademark famous in a series of talk show appearances.) In the license contract CLI agreed it could not assign its patent or the FuturVista contract to any other entity, directly or through merger or acquisition, for the life of the contract.

Calvin was very tough in the negotiations. FuturVista wanted CLI to agree to defend any suits attacking its patent or at least to cooperate in their defense. Although you told him that such agreements by inventors were standard, he refused to permit CLI to assume that or any other obligation. CLI also refused to agree to license future improvements. The contract thus provided "Licensor shall have no other or further obligation whatsoever and no defect in its patent shall be any defense to its rights under this contract."

Calvin came to see you this morning about a new deal. Gigantic Oil has acquired a pest-extermination service and has heard about Death Spray. It has offered CLI a very large royalty fee for a license for both patent and trademark, but is only interested in an exclusive license. "If CLI can just junk those jerks at FuturVista, our stock will skyrocket," Calvin explained in asking you how CLI can get the deal with Gigantic. He also explained that FuturVista has yet to turn a profit on Death Spray, although he thinks they will do so in the next year or two.

You have done some research in your state's contract law since Calvin left and found that it is very hard to prove and recover future profits ("too speculative," the cases say), although in licensing cases specific performance or other equitable relief is often granted. What advice should you give Calvin and why? Would Calvin be better or worse off if he had been less tough in the negotiations with FuturVista? Should you recommend further negotiations with FuturVista at this time? See §365(n).

28.3. Sweet Sarah Kaminsky is one terrific cook. She ran her restaurant, Sweet Sarah's, for many years, making it the center of neighborhood dining in the Clarksville neighborhood of Austin. Three years ago Sarah sold out to Harold Bonker, who bought the restaurant for $250,000. The contract of sale included a covenant that Sarah would not compete in the restaurant business in Austin or its suburbs for five years. Sadly, within six months both Sarah and Hank, her husband, were struck by cancer. After two years of massive medical intervention, she made it but he didn't. The medical bills beyond the insurance coverage were enormous. Sarah now finds herself broke and seeking a job doing the only thing she knows how to do, cooking. She's been offered a high-paying job as head chef at an upscale downtown café. Harold heard about the offer and came to you, saying "My business is doomed if Sarah works downtown, because all of her old friends and customers will want to help her out by going over there." You did some research and determined the covenant would likely be considered reasonable and enforceable under state law precedents. At Harold's request, you sent a letter warning Sarah not to violate her covenant. This morning you got a notice of her Chapter 11 bankruptcy filing. What can you tell Harold about his chances of preventing Sarah from taking the job? §§365(a), 1141(d)(1)-(2), (5).

Barney's Problem — Part IV

Note: Unless otherwise indicated, the day this part of Barney's Problem is discussed in class is deemed to be March 1 of this year. This part of the problem, like the rest, is to be analyzed in real time, i.e., as if you as counsel obtain the information or take the action indicated on the day (and the deemed date) the problem is to be discussed in class. All previous parts of the problem are incorporated into this part as of the day (and the deemed date) it is discussed in class, as if you were a sole practitioner in a town called Aloysius and this small drama were real.

As your paralegal continues to wade through the company's files, you question Barney closely on the events that have left his once-profitable company at the brink of bankruptcy.

Barney says that the company has a number of excellent contracts, but payroll and financing costs have stripped it of cash while a very rainy fall and winter prevented work and thus stopped progress payments. His big courthouse project is behind schedule, but otherwise going well. The civic center contract he just won in a close bidding contest will be enormously profitable, but will require mobilization costs he can no longer finance, even if he can still get the city to make the mobilization payment due the company next week. Down in Newton, he has almost completed his most prestigious job, the paving over of the last blade of grass at Enormous State University. His men have finished the punch-list, and he has only to deliver a certified list to the architect to get final approval and the $75,000 in retentions. However, this contract is terminable "in the event of Contractor's insolvency." Finally, the company is losing big money on the Tune Inn motel project because of cost overruns.

As he told you earlier, the Aloysius Bank yesterday said it could not grant any further credit or extensions in payment. Barney is also very worried about not meeting his next payroll.

What further opportunities and risks do you now see for the company in a bankruptcy proceeding of some kind? How does this new information fit into your overall strategic thinking?

6.   *Statutory Liens*

As the DIP aims toward a workable reorganization plan, the large creditors generally continue negotiations on the shape that plan should take. The creditors exert leverage during this process based in large part on their relative status in bankruptcy, so that general unsecured creditors have little leverage, while those with valid security interests on critical property are accorded significantly more deference.

In the preceding sections we saw the DIP demote the status of several creditors through its avoiding powers — brushed away like flies once it was clear that they couldn't do much damage to the debtor. Some creditors lost earlier advantages when the DIP invoked section 547 and voided security interests or caused them to return payments. Others lost benefits conferred by contracts with the pre-bankruptcy debtor when the DIP rejected executory contracts. Section 545 gives the DIP yet another weapon in the fight to equalize the rights of the creditors. By using the powers granted in that section, the DIP may avoid certain liens created automatically by operation of state law.

Although the section is entitled "Statutory Liens," it does not make voidable all liens created by state statutes, but only certain kinds of liens that Congress disfavors. The two principal categories of disfavored liens are landlords' liens and what we will call "bankruptcy priority liens." Subsections 3 and 4 of section 545 permit the DIP to void landlords' liens, which Congress felt gave too much of the debtor's estate to landlords to the detriment of other creditors. It is useful to compare this treatment with the limitation on landlords' claims in section 502(b)(6).

"Bankruptcy priority liens" are liens created by state law that Congress believes to be phony in the sense that the states do not intend to create real liens for all purposes, but rather to use the device of liens to impose special priority advantages for certain creditors in bankruptcy. Subsections 1 and 2 of section 545 set forth certain tests for state liens, tests that Congress hopes will trap state liens that are really hidden bankruptcy priority statutes and permit the DIP to avoid their effect. The court addressed that sort of question in the following case, in which a statutory lien protected farmers who put their grain in state-regulated storage facilities.

═══════════MERCHANTS GRAIN, INC. v. ADKINS═══════════
184 B.R. 52 (S.D. Ind. 1995)

Larry J. McKinney, District Judge.

. . . The Bankruptcy Court has found, and no one disputes, that MGI owned and operated grain storage facilities in six different states. The Ohio facility located in Columbus, Ohio, is the focus of this action. Resolving this matter involves examining the Ohio statutes that provide the means for dealing with failing or failed grain dealers. That comprehensive statutory scheme was undoubtedly designed to protect Ohio farmers from the consequences of dealing with a poorly managed grain elevator. An important issue in this case is whether Ohio's attempt to solve this problem is in reality an effort to distribute the assets of an insolvent grain dealer to farmer creditors, which effort would be superseded by federal bankruptcy law.

A crucial section of that Ohio law is §926.021(B) which states as follows:

A lien shall exist on all agricultural commodity assets of a failed agricultural commodity handler in favor of any of the following: (1) Claimants, including lenders, who possess receipts covering grain owned or stored by the handler; (2) Claimants who possess written evidence of ownership other than a receipt disclosing a storage obligation of the handler, including tickets; (3) Claimants who surrendered receipts as part of an agricultural commodity sales transaction but were not fully paid for the agricultural commodity and the handler failed within twenty days after the surrender; (4) Claimants who possess any other written evidence of the sale of agricultural commodities to the failed handler for which they were not fully paid.

The statute goes on to say in §926.021(C) that:

The lien which shall secure all claims described in division (D) of this section, shall arise at the time of the delivery of the agricultural commodity for sale, commencement of the storage obligation, or when funds are advanced by the lender, and shall terminate when the liability of the agricultural commodity handler to the claimant is discharged. . . .

The appellees in this matter, the individual farmers (the "Farmers"), are all holders of delayed price contracts. The delayed price contract itself says:

> The fixing of the price of grain is deferred, and may be established by seller at any time, but not later than _____, and upon demand by seller, the buyer is obligated to pay his regular bid price upon the date of demand for the commodities being priced by the seller. If no such notice is given by seller by the date established in the preceding sentence, the buyer's offered price on that date shall control and the buyer shall promptly give seller written notice of that price, unless a renewal has been written prior to the above expiration date covering the same grain covered by this contract and agreed upon by both buyer and seller.

The agreements also contain the crucial language that in various and sundry wordings, depending on the contract, the Farmer fully understand(s) that upon delivery I am transferring title to the Merchants Grain & Transportation and become a creditor of the Merchants Grain & Transportation for the market value of commodities so delivered until the price is established and settlement is completed. If the Merchants Grain & Transportation defaults in its obligation for settlement, I am a common creditor of the Merchants Grain & Transportation for the value of commodities not settled for. Thus the Farmers, by contract, agreed that by contracting for a delayed price with MGI they would be considered as common creditors. They also agreed that Merchants Grain & Transportation would own the grain at the time of its delivery to MGI.

The Ohio statute, however, extends the sellers' rights beyond those conferred upon them by the delayed price contract. The statutory scheme gives the Farmer a lien, arising on the date of delivery of the grain, on all the agricultural commodity assets of a failed agricultural commodity handler. Agricultural commodities are defined to include all grains that are deposited with the handler. Ohio Revised Code ("O.R.C.") §926.02. An agricultural commodity handler is defined in §926.01(c) as: "any person who is engaged in the business of agricultural commodity handling." Applying simple principles of statutory interpretation indicates that the statute grants to the Farmers, upon their delivery of grain to MGI, and in spite of the acknowledgement in the contract of the Farmers' status as common creditors, a statutory lien on the grain that they deposited as of the date of the deposit.

As long as the elevator is solvent, matters will go smoothly. If, however, statutory financial requirements are not met, the Director of Agriculture (the "Director") may refuse to grant, or may conditionally suspend, a handler's license. These financial requirements are stricter than the federal notion of bankruptcy. That is, grain dealers will be in trouble with the state regulators long before their debts exceed their assets. See O.R.C. §926.06(B), §926.10.

In this case, the MGI facility in Ohio fell below the statutory financial standard. [The court describes the financial failure of the facility, including an investigation by state regulators that was triggered when the government received a hot check from the facility. The court then explains the regulators' subsequent disposition of the facility's funds on hand.]

MGI filed for bankruptcy on May 9, 1991, which established the "petition date" for purposes of §547(b)(4) of the Bankruptcy Code. At certain times within ninety days of the petition date, the Farmers received payoffs of their claims under the deferred payment contracts. The original complaint in this matter was filed by the Trustee in order to avoid those transfers and to bring the amounts of money transferred back into the bankrupt estate. At issue is whether the statutory scheme that enabled the Department to direct the above-described transaction constitutes an attempt by Ohio to distribute the assets of an insolvent grain dealer in violation of the policies behind federal bankruptcy law. If that is the case, then the transfers of money from the escrow accounts, within ninety days of the petition date, would be considered preferential transfers and would be subject to avoidance by the Trustee.

[The court describes the activities of the regulators, noting that they acted to enforce the lien created by the Ohio statute cited above.]

The Trustee, on the other hand, argues that this lien is not valid, because it could be avoided under §545(1) of the Bankruptcy Code, thereby making the payments which went to the Farmers, payments on unsecured debts. . . . The question, of course, is whether the Ohio statutory lien becomes effective against the debtor when an insolvency proceeding concerning the debtor is commenced, or when the debtor becomes insolvent, or when the debtor's financial condition deteriorates to a specified level.

The Trustee argues that the Ohio statute describes the existence of the lien only in the context of a "failed" agricultural commodity handler, and concludes from that reference that the lien becomes effective upon the insolvency or other financial deterioration of the debtor's business. In support of this argument, the Trustee refers to the definition of "failure" in the Ohio statute. Failure is defined as including the inability to financially satisfy claimants, a public declaration of insolvency, the revocation of the commodity handler's license when it owes money to claimants, or other circumstances relating to maintaining a valid license. O.R.C. §926.021(A)(2). However, inferring that the legislature meant the lien to arise only when the commodity handler becomes financially distressed would not be reasonable, because it would render a more specific portion of the statute superfluous. Moreover, fundamental principles of statutory construction require that the more specific provision takes precedence over the more general. See Green v. Bock Laundry Mach. Co., 490 U.S. 504 (1989).

The Ohio statutory scheme specifically states that the lien becomes effective at the time of the delivery of the grain to the grain handler. O.R.C. §926.021(C). It also goes on to say, "In the event of a failure, the director of agriculture shall enforce the lien claims and allocate the proceeds. . . ." O.R.C. §926.021(D). This more specific delineation of the inception of the statutory lien takes precedence over any general reference to a lien coming into existence when the commodity handler has failed.

The statute also specifically denotes when the lien ceases to exist. The statutory lien is extinguished upon the payment of the obligation to the depositor. The Ohio statutory scheme is unlike any other scheme from any other state cited by the Trustee. By statute, the State of Ohio gives a lien to the grain depositor that arises from the time the grain is placed in the elevator

and is extinguished at one of two times, either after the grain elevator operator falls below the prescribed financial standard and the claim is paid through
the Department of Agriculture, or at the time the elevator operator pays the
depositor.

In this Court's view, the Ohio statutory lien is not voidable under
§545(1) of the Bankruptcy Code, because it becomes effective at the time
the grain is deposited rather than at the time the insolvency is suspected.
The Ohio statutory scheme is quite different from the scheme in Illinois
cited in Gorenz v. State of Illinois Dept. of Agriculture, 653 F.2d 1179 (7th
Cir. 1981).

In that case, acting pursuant to Illinois Revised Statute, Chapter 127,
§40.23 (1979), the Illinois Department of Agriculture seized grain in the
possession of John Gorenz and subsequently sold the grain and retained the
proceeds of the sale. The trustee attempted to avoid those transfers and
bring the resultant $38,000.00 back into the bankruptcy estate. Section
40.23 gives the Illinois Department of Agriculture the power:

> To control surety bonds and trust funds and to establish trust accounts and
> bank accounts in adequately protected financial institutions, to hold monies
> received by the Director of Agriculture when acting as trustee, to protect the
> assets of licensees for the benefit of claimants, to collect and disburse the pro-
> ceeds of such bonds and trust funds when acting as trustee on behalf of
> claimants without responsibility for the management and operation of dis-
> continued or insolvent businesses, such funds or additions thereto in which
> the state of Illinois has no right, title or interest.

The bankruptcy court and the district court in *Gorenz* held that the
Department was required to surrender the proceeds of the grain sale to the
trustee. The appellate court overturned that decision, finding insufficient
evidence of the ownership of the grain that was seized. If the bankrupt was
found to own the grain, the Department could not resist the jurisdiction of
the bankruptcy court, because the action of the State of Illinois would have
been an attempt to distribute assets of an insolvent grain dealer to farmer
creditors and would thus be superseded by federal bankruptcy proceedings.

In the case before this Court, however, even though the contracts seem
to indicate that the owner of the deposited grain is MGI, the State of Ohio
impressed a statutory lien upon that property, which removes it from a
bankruptcy consideration as "property of the debtor." The point is, the
deposited grain was not wholly the property of the debtor under Ohio law.
This finding would be true regardless of whether there was a bankruptcy
proceeding pending.

The State of Ohio selected this method by which to protect its farmers
from financially troubled warehousers. It has done so in a different fashion
than did the State of Illinois. Illinois impressed no liens upon the grain, and
the liens at issue here are not avoidable by the trustee pursuant to the very
language of the Bankruptcy Code. The Bankruptcy Court was therefore correct in its assessment and in its denial of the Trustee's complaint for avoidance of preferential transfers. If the Ohio statute had provided that the lien
arose on the event of financial difficulty, this case would be different.

The reasoning of In re Loretto Winery Limited, 898 F.2d 715 (9th Cir. 1990), is similar to that used in this matter. Therein a statutory lien was upheld against the trustee's attack, which lien arose on the delivery of product to the processor. The California and the Ohio statutes are based on very similar policies. As in the situation in which a mechanics lien arises, the farmer has applied his labor and resources to produce the product that then increased the value of the debtor's estate. This places the farmer in a different class than general creditors, who have only a pecuniary interest in the estate. To allow general creditors to share equally with the farmers in the estate would unjustly enrich the general creditors at the expense of the farmer's labor. Consequently, the California and Ohio legislatures have successfully endeavored to place the farmers in a different class of creditors than the general creditors, which is a class analogous to secured creditors.

[The court upheld the lien.]

The Seventh Circuit affirmed with another long discussion of why the statute in question did not quite trigger on bankruptcy or insolvency and thus violate the Bankruptcy Code.

The policy expressed in section 545 and reflected in *Merchants Grain* illustrates the warring impulses of bankruptcy law: It defers to states' decisions to prefer some creditors over others, but it insists that the states make those creditors preferred both in and out of bankruptcy.

Because the federal Bankruptcy Code is clear about voiding statutory liens that are triggered on bankruptcy or near-bankruptcy conditions, it would seem reasonable that states would not enact such laws. Reasonable, but wrong. Some states, including Arkansas, California, and North Carolina, have adopted laws to impose liens on continuing care health facilities (once known as nursing homes) only on bankruptcy, insolvency, or receivership. Statutes such as these, which would readily be avoided in bankruptcy, may have the perverse effect of encouraging financially troubled facilities to file for bankruptcy if a party attempts to file a lien. These statutes serve as a reminder, however, that statutory liens reflect the political clout of groups within a state and may not be well integrated into other parts of the commercial law scheme.

Section 545 serves another function in the bankruptcy scheme. In part (2) it voids all statutory liens that are not properly perfected or fixed as of the time of the bankruptcy filing. As such, it functions much like the strong arm provisions of section 544, with the focus in section 545 on voiding statutory liens. One frequent use of this provision is to eliminate tax liens that arise by operation of law but that have some perfection requirement that has not yet been met at the time when the debtor files for bankruptcy. In *Merchants Grain*, the trustee argued that the statutory lien was subject to set-aside because the statute provided no means to perfect the lien. The court made short work of that argument, however, designating the lien automatically perfected at the instant it arose. For statutes that provide a means of perfection, however, the party that fails to follow the necessary steps will find its lien voided in bankruptcy.

Problem Set 29

29.1. You have filed a Chapter 11 petition on behalf of Torrey's TV Repair, Inc. Although its principal owner, Joe Torrey, has been quite ill (his illness, indeed, was a major cause of the company's financial decline), he has come to consult with you about the company's bankruptcy position.

The company's shop is in two adjacent buildings, one of which it owns. It leases the second building from Star Properties, Inc. The rent on the leased building was two months in arrears before bankruptcy. Not only does your state law give a landlord a lien for unpaid rent on all personal property within the leased premises, but the Torrey-Star lease has a similar provision as well. The leased building houses several of the company's most expensive machines.

There are also some difficulties in connection with the building the company owns. Frank Gonzales, a former stockholder and employee of Torrey, has obtained a $25,000 judgment against the company in a lawsuit over his disputed salary claim. The judgment was recorded almost six months ago, although Frank has not sought to enforce it pending settlement discussions with Joe. In addition, the company owes Clarence Plumbing about $13,500 for work done in the building after last winter's severe freeze. Clarence has demanded payment, but has not filed a notice of lien in the land records. Under your state law, a mechanic's lien for work done is prior to that of a judgment lien creditor, but it loses to a bona fide purchaser for value because of the failure to file a notice of lien.

You are helping Joe put together a plan of payment for Chapter 11. To do so you must know if the company has to treat Star Properties, Frank Gonzales, or Clarence Plumbing as secured creditors. What do you think and why? See §§545(2), (3); 101(53), (51), (37).

7. *Fraudulent Conveyance and Other State Avoidance Laws in Bankruptcy*

Back in Part I, we explored state fraudulent conveyance law. See pp. 79–99 for a review. These laws, whether statutory enactments in the form of the Uniform Fraudulent Transfer Act or common law adaptations, hold that the transfer of assets by an insolvent debtor for less than reasonably fair equivalent value is regarded as an injury to all creditors that they may request a court to set aside. Section 544(b) of the Code preserves those state law rights, but gives them to the TIB (or DIP acting as a TIB) to set aside fraudulent conveyances on behalf of all the creditors in a bankruptcy action, making state fraudulent conveyance law an important part of the TIB's tools for reshaping the estate. Note, however, that the TIB's rights are derivative in the sense that there must be an actual unsecured creditor (creditor with an unsecured claim under §502) who could have brought the avoidance action under state fraudulent conveyance law. The TIB steps into that creditor's shoes.

In addition to embracing state avoidance laws through section 544(b), the Bankruptcy Code provides its own fraudulent conveyance provisions in section 548. While state laws tend to be very similar and the adoption of the

Uniform Fraudulent Transfer Act in 41 states has provided even more convergence, there remain some variations in the remaining nine states and in states that adopt non-uniform amendments to the UFTA. Section 548 creates a federal fraudulent conveyance law that is designed to ensure baseline protection in bankruptcy for all creditors, regardless of underlying state law.

The two approaches to avoiding fraudulent conveyances come back together in the avoidance remedies section of the Code, section 550, which provides the remedies for avoidance actions under all the avoiding powers, including both sections 544(b) and 548.

a. Transfers Among Related Entities

While some transactions are deemed fraudulent because they are made with intent to hinder, delay, or defraud creditors, a number are fraudulent solely because they constitute a transfer (1) when the debtor is insolvent (2) for a consideration less than "reasonably equivalent value." UFTA §§4, 5; §548(a)(l). Typically, the lack of REV occurs when the transferee gives too little value, such as a transferee who buys a piano with a market value of $10,000 for $10. But, as the following case shows, a transfer may fail the test of REV because even though plenty of value was given, it was given to the wrong party.

This case also illustrates the advantage of having two bites at the fraudulent conveyance apple, sections 544 and 548.

In re IMAGE WORLDWIDE, LTD.
139 F.3d 574 (7th Cir. 1998)

Opinion by: ESCHBACH.

Image Worldwide, Ltd. guaranteed loans paid to an affiliate corporation, Image Marketing, Ltd. Both corporations were owned by the same person, but only Image Marketing received funds from the loan. The Image Worldwide's bankruptcy trustee filed suit to avoid the guarantees as a fraudulent transfer, alleging that the guarantees made Image Worldwide insolvent, and that Image Worldwide did not receive reasonably equivalent value in exchange for its guarantees. . . .

Richard Steinberg was the sole shareholder, sole officer, and sole director of Image Marketing, Ltd. (IM), an Illinois corporation incorporated in June 1991. IM was in the commercial printing business, primarily dealing in wholesale sales of music and sports merchandise. IM leased space from FCL Graphics, a printing company that did all of the printing for IM.

In 1992, IM obtained a line of credit from Parkway Bank secured by a first lien against substantially all of IM's assets (IM loan). The line of credit allowed IM to borrow against up to 70% of its eligible accounts receivable, and required IM to reduce its indebtedness to 70% of its accounts receivable in the event that its eligible accounts receivable declined. By June 1993, IM had borrowed $300,000 on its line of credit.

At the end of 1993, IM was several hundred thousand dollars in debt to trade creditors. So in December 1993, Steinberg incorporated a new Illinois corporation, Image Worldwide, Ltd. (IW). Steinberg was the sole shareholder, officer, and director of IW as well. IW leased the same space from FCL as IM, used the same suppliers, and had many of the same customers. In early 1994, Steinberg liquidated IM. Parkway knew of and cooperated in the liquidation of IM. Instead of demanding that IM pay off its loan under the terms of the agreement, however, Parkway allowed Steinberg to use the money obtained from the liquidation of IM to pay down IM's trade debts. Parkway never required IM to pay off its loan, even when its accounts receivable declined to zero in 1994.

Instead, Parkway demanded that IW guarantee IM's $300,000 debt. IW executed the guarantee on May 27, 1994. The guarantee was secured by a first lien on substantially all of IW's assets. IW never borrowed any money from Parkway on its own. Parkway's consideration for the guarantee was its allowing IW to stay in business. Between May 27, 1994 and when IW was forced into bankruptcy, IW paid principal and interest on the loan as it became due.

Even after IM was wound down, IM still owed $200,000 to FCL Graphics. Parkway lent $200,000 to Steinberg to pay this debt (Steinberg loan). The bank paid the proceeds from this loan directly to FCL.[1] The loan was secured by all of IW's accounts receivable. As of the date of its bankruptcy, IW had paid down $72,076.49 in principal and $26,863.45 in interest on the loan.

IW was no more successful than IM. At trial, Parkway stipulated that the guarantees made IW insolvent. In August 1995, FCL stopped doing work for IW, and filed an involuntary chapter 7 petition for bankruptcy against IW. David Leibowitz was appointed as the trustee of IW's bankruptcy estate. Over the trustee's objection, Parkway obtained relief from the automatic stay, and collected IW's accounts receivable to pay down the debts guaranteed by IW. All told, Parkway collected $444,507.55 from IW, including the amounts paid prior to the bankruptcy.

The trustee instituted this adversarial proceeding in July 1996 to recover the amounts transferred to Parkway. Pursuant to 11 U.S.C. §544(b), the trustee charged that the transfers to Parkway were fraudulent transfers in violation of the Uniform Fraudulent Transfer Act (UFTA), 740 ILCS 160/5, because IW never received reasonably equivalent value for its guarantees to Parkway. . . .

The federal fraudulent transfer statute, 11 U.S.C. §548, contains a one year statute of limitations that barred the trustee from using that section to avoid the transfer. However, under the strong-arm provision of the Bankruptcy Code, 11 U.S.C. §544(b), the trustee can avoid any transaction of the debtor that would be voidable by any actual unsecured creditor under state law. The trustee need not identify the creditor, so long as the unsecured creditor exists. Thus, the trustee proceeded against Parkway under

1. The Bankruptcy Court found that "FCL Graphics was an important customer of Parkway Bank and its sole shareholder, Frank Calabrese, was also a shareholder of Parkway Bank."

the constructive fraud provision of the UFTA [§5a]. Because Parkway has stipulated that the transaction rendered IW insolvent, the key issue in this case is whether IW, as guarantor, received reasonably equivalent value for its guarantee when the direct benefits of the transaction were received by a third party, IM. Parkway argues that its allowing IW to stay in business constituted reasonably equivalent value for IW's guarantee of IM's debt. Parkway also attempts to argue that IM and IW were the same entity.

A

Because the UFTA is a state law, we must predict how the Illinois courts would handle Parkway's claims. The Illinois courts have not yet elaborated on what "reasonably equivalent value" is for purposes of §160/5. . . . Thus, we can look to interpretations of "reasonably equivalent value" from §548 cases, as well as cases from courts interpreting other states' versions of the UFTA for assistance in predicting what an Illinois court would do.

B

The bankruptcy court determined as a matter of law that "a conveyance by a corporation for the benefit of an affiliate is not regarded as given [sic] fair consideration to the creditors of the conveying corporations," citing Rubin v. Manufacturers Hanover Trust Co., 661 F.2d 979 (2d Cir. 1981). This determination is an overly narrow statement of law, and misreads the holding of *Rubin*. Nevertheless, under the appropriate law, the bankruptcy court did not clearly err in ruling that the guarantees were fraudulent transfers.

The transactions in question are known in corporate law lingo as an "intercorporate guarantee." These fall into three types: "upstream," "downstream," and "cross-stream." An upstream guarantee is when a subsidiary guarantees the debt of its parent; a downstream guarantee is when a parent corporation guarantees a debt of its subsidiary; a cross-stream guarantee is when a corporation guarantees the debt of an affiliate. See Jack F. Williams, The Fallacies of Contemporary Fraudulent Transfer Models as Applied to Intercorporate Guaranties: Fraudulent Transfer Law as a Fuzzy System, 15 Cardozo L. Rev. 1403, 1419-20 (1994) [hereinafter Williams, Fallacies]. IW's guarantees in this case were cross-stream guarantees.

Intercorporate guarantees are a routine business practice, and their potential voidability creates a risk for unwary lenders. See generally Blumberg, Intragroup Guarantees; Williams, Fallacies, 15 Cardozo L. Rev. at 1418-20; Barry L. Zaretsky, Fraudulent Transfer Law as the Arbiter of Unreasonable Risk, 46 S.C. L. Rev. 1165 (1995); Scott F. Norberg, Comment, Avoidability of Intercorporate Guarantees Under Sections 548(b) and 544(b) of the Bankruptcy Code, 64 N.C. L. Rev. 1099 (1986). Intercorporate guarantees are common because they benefit both the creditor and debtor in a loan transaction. Within a corporate group, some units will often have better credit ratings than others. The units which are perceived as credit risks by lenders will be either unable to obtain loans, or able to obtain a loan only at a higher interest rate. However, when the corporate group exploits the units with good credit ratings by having them guarantee the debt of the weaker unit, the weaker unit will benefit from either obtaining the loan, or getting the loan at a better rate. The creditor benefits from greater security in repayment. So between creditor and debtor, the guarantee is a win-win situation.

However, the creditors of the guarantor making a cross-stream guarantee can sometimes lose out in the transaction, because the guaranteeing corporation may not receive a direct economic benefit from the guarantee. See *Rubin*, 661 F.2d at 991. Should the guarantee push the guarantor into insolvency, these transactions will be scrutinized under a fraudulent transfer analysis. Fraudulent transfer law seeks to preserve assets of the estate for creditors. Some courts applying traditional fraudulent transfer rules to intercorporate guarantees therefore found that the guarantor had not received reasonably equivalent value for the guarantee, because from the standpoint of the unsecured creditor, the guarantor had received no consideration for the guarantee.

However, requiring a direct flow of capital to a cross-guarantor to avoid a finding of a fraudulent transfer "is inhibitory of contemporary financing practices, which recognize that cross-guarantees are often needed because of the unequal abilities of interrelated corporate entities to collateralize loans." TeleFest, Inc. v. Vu-TV Inc., 591 F. Supp. 1368, 1379 (D. N.J. 1984). Often, these guarantees are legitimate business transactions, and not made to frustrate creditors. In recognition of this economic reality, courts have loosened the old rule that transfers primarily for the benefit of a third party invariably give no consideration to the transferor. Thus, even when there has been no direct economic benefit to a guarantor, courts performing a fraudulent transfer analysis have been increasingly willing to look at whether a guarantor received indirect benefits from the guarantee if there has been an indirect benefit. See, e.g., *Xonics*, 841 F.2d at 201; *Rubin*, 661 F.2d at 991-92; *TeleFest*, 591 F. Supp. at 1377-81. "One theme permeates the authorities upholding guaranty obligations: that the guaranty at issue was the result of arm's length negotiations at a time when the common enterprise was commercially viable." Williams, Fallacies, 15 Cardozo L. Rev. at 1438.

Generally, a court will not recognize an indirect benefit unless it is "fairly concrete." See Heritage Bank Tinley Park v. Steinberg (In re Grabill Corp.), 121 B.R. 983, 995 (N.D. Ill. 1990). The most straightforward indirect benefit is when the guarantor receives from the debtor some of the consideration paid to it. See *Rubin*, 661 F.2d at 991; *Grabill*, 121 B.R. at 995-96. But courts have found other economic benefits to qualify as indirect benefits. For example, in Mellon Bank, N.A. v. Metro Communications, Inc., 945 F.2d 635, 646-48 (3d Cir. 1991), the court found reasonably equivalent value for a debtor corporation's guarantee of an affiliate's debt when the loan strengthened the corporate group as a whole, so that the guarantor corporation would benefit from "synergy" within the corporate group. The *Mellon* court stated that indirect benefits included intangibles such as goodwill, id. at 647, and an increased ability to borrow working capital. Id. at 648.

TeleFest indicated that indirect benefits to a guarantor exist when "the transaction of which the guaranty is a part may safeguard an important source of supply, or an important customer for the guarantor. Or substantial indirect benefits may result from the general relationship" between affiliates. 591 F. Supp. at 1380-81 (quoting Normandin, "Intercorporate Guarantees and Fraudulent Conveyances," in Personal Property Security Interests Under the Revised UCC 361, 370-71 (1977)). In *Xonics*, we recognized the ability of a smaller company to use the distribution system of a larger affiliate as an indirect benefit as well. See *Xonics*, 841 F.2d at 202. . . .

The Steinberg loan presents a [close] case, because IW may have received an indirect benefit from this guarantee. FCL Graphics was IW's printer, and thus its most important supplier. FCL also allowed IM and FW to operate their business on FCL's premises. At trial, Steinberg testified as follows about the benefits to IW from the Steinberg loan:

Q: What, if any, benefit was there to Image Worldwide for you to pay FCL Graphics $200,000? . . .
A: It was allowed to continue doing business remaining on FCL's premises and having FCL as a supplier.
Q: Is it your testimony that if you hadn't paid FCL the $200,000, it would have put Image Worldwide out of business?
A: Yes.
Q: It would have moved Image Worldwide off the premises?
A: Yes.
Q: It would not have supplied product to Image Worldwide?
A: Yes.

Transcript at 44-45, Leibowitz v. Parkway Bank & Trust Co., 210 B.R. 298 (Bankr. N.D. Ill. 1997) (No. 97 C 923). If the Steinberg loan had not been made to pay off IM's debt to FCL, FCL Graphics clearly posed a substantial threat to IW because of its ability to evict IW and discontinue providing services to IW. *TeleFest* states that:

> [Some courts have] rationalized upholding various transfers against fraudulent conveyance challenges by finding that sufficient consideration passed to the transferor because an opportunity had been given to it to avoid bankruptcy through the strengthening of an affiliated corporation that received the benefit of the transfer. Such an approach seems indisputably proper when a weak but still solvent entity is rendered insolvent only because of the inclusion of the guaranty on the liability side of the balance sheet. This permits the analysis to focus upon economic reality in the appropriate factual context without rewarding legal laxity or inflexibly ignoring real benefits merely because they have no place on the company's balance sheet.

TeleFest, 591 F. Supp. at 1379 (quoting Rosenberg, Intercorporate Guarantees and the Law of Fraudulent Conveyances: Lender Beware, 125 U. Pa. L. Rev. 235, 245-46). Under the broad reading of the indirect benefit doctrine laid down in cases like *TeleFest*, IW received an indirect benefit from the payment of the Steinberg loan because the loan kept FCL Graphics from kicking Steinberg and his companies off of FCL's property, and from refusing to do business with Steinberg. True, the balance sheet showed that IW was insolvent after taking on the IM loan and the Steinberg loan, but IW was not finished as a going concern, as IW was able to remain in business for 17 months after guaranteeing the Steinberg loan.

On the other hand, the circumstances of this case do not fit the circumstances when indirect benefits from a guarantee are found to constitute reasonably equivalent value. As indicated above, courts that uphold cross-stream guarantees generally do so when the transaction strengthens the viability of the corporate group. In this case, though, there were not two functioning corporations that benefitted mutually from the loan. By the time IW guaranteed the Steinberg loan, IM had been wound down. Even though it was not officially dissolved, the company had been liquidated and was inactive. IW became insolvent to pay an inactive affiliate's debts. Indeed, while IW was able to timely pay the bank pursuant to the loans for a time after guaranteeing the loans, IW eventually fell behind in payments to trade creditors just like IM had. In effect, by paying off IM's debts, IW kept IM out of bankruptcy by bankrupting itself. This shift of risk from the creditors of the debtor to the creditors of the guarantor is exactly the situation that fraudulent transfer law seeks to avoid when applied to guarantees. See *Rubin*, 661 F.2d at 991. Thus, while IW received an indirect benefit from the transaction, it did not receive reasonably equivalent value.

We therefore hold that indirect benefits to a guarantor may be considered when determining whether a corporation receives reasonably equivalent value for a guarantee. However, we do not believe that the bankruptcy court clearly erred when it found that IW did not receive reasonably equivalent value for its guarantees. Thus, the judgment of the district court is affirmed.

Steinberg and Parkway Bank seem to have forgotten that there are multiple consequences to dealing in separate corporate shells. The individual companies cannot be run entirely to benefit the common owner. Instead, the creditors of each separate entity can insist that the transactions of that entity be made only for reasonably equivalent value for that entity. As complex corporate structures proliferate and "creative" financing and business deals come to life, the mess to be untangled following the failure of a multi-part enterprise becomes monumental. Also, note that if the short limitation period of section 548 (one year before petition) had not run, the guarantee would likely have been avoidable under federal law as well, because the involuntary bankruptcy was not filed until August 1995. If the same facts arose in the future, however, the trustee in bankruptcy could take advantage of the 2005 Amendments that extended the reach-back period in section 548 to two years.

At the other end of the business spectrum from the multi-part conglomerate is the owner and his solely owned business. No matter. With two entities, the issue of matching up benefits and burdens for each entity reappears. This time the transferee gives up on whether the bankrupt business received REV, but it fights it out on the issue of whether the transfer was made directly to itself or whether it was first made to the owner of the business.

======================== In re VIDEO DEPOT, LTD. ========================
127 F.3d 1195 (9th Cir. 1997)

D. W. NELSON, Circuit Judge.

Kenneth Schafer, the trustee of Video Depot, Ltd., brings this fraudulent conveyance action to recover the proceeds of a cashier's check purchased by Video Depot and paid to the Las Vegas Hilton in partial satisfaction of gambling debts incurred by Jeffrey Arlynn, Video Depot's principal. Hilton appeals the district court's decision affirming the bankruptcy court's judgment in favor of the trustee. We have jurisdiction pursuant to 28 U.S.C. §1291, and we affirm.

FACTUAL AND PROCEDURAL BACKGROUND

Most of the relevant facts are not in dispute. Jeffrey Arlynn was the president of Video Depot, a consumer electronics company. Arlynn controlled virtually all of Video Depot's operations.

Arlynn was also an active gambler. Between 1985 and 1990, he made approximately 60 trips to the Las Vegas Hilton. Initially, Arlynn gambled on funds he brought with him, or against credit that Hilton extended to him for the duration of each individual trip. In 1987, however, Arlynn obtained a permanent line of credit with Hilton in the amount of $50,000, which was increased to $75,000 in 1990.

Prior to 1990, Arlynn regularly repaid his losses in full either at the end of each stay or at the beginning of the next trip. While he occasionally retained a balance, the balance was always substantially less than his credit limit. In addition, Arlynn carefully controlled the size of his accumulated credit losses. Until 1990, Arlynn's balance only twice exceeded $100,000 and never exceeded $125,000.

In early May of 1990, however, Arlynn incurred a debt of $225,000, and he did not make a payment towards this debt before he left Las Vegas. On June 15, Video Depot purchased a cashier's check payable to Hilton in the amount of $65,000. The check clearly indicated that Video Depot was the purchaser. When Arlynn returned to Las Vegas on June 16, he gave two checks to Hilton: the $65,000 cashier's check from Video Depot, and a personal cashier's check in the amount of $10,000. Arlynn had never before presented either a cashier's check or a check purchased by Video Depot to cover his gambling losses.

Video Depot commenced bankruptcy proceedings on September 14, 1990, and the trustee was appointed shortly thereafter. The trustee then filed suit against Hilton to recover the proceeds of the $65,000 cashier's check. After an initial round of litigation, both parties stipulated that the check was a fraudulent transfer within the meaning of 11 U.S.C. §548, and the bankruptcy court proceeded to determine whether Hilton was an initial transferee under 11 U.S.C. §550(a) or a subsequent transferee lacking good faith knowledge of the voidability of the transfer within the meaning of 11 U.S.C. §550(b). . . .

The central issue before us is whether Hilton was the initial transferee of the $65,000 cashier's check purchased by Video Depot.

The Statutory Scheme

The parties have stipulated that the $65,000 payment to Hilton was a fraudulent transfer within the meaning of 11 U.S.C. §548. Once a transfer has been determined to be voidable as a fraudulent conveyance under section 548, the trustee of the debtor may recover it from either

(1) the initial transferee of such transfer or the entity for whose benefit such transfer was made; or
(2) any immediate or mediate transferee of such initial transferee.

11 U.S.C. §550(a). The distinction between the two, however, is a critical one. The trustee's right to recover from an initial transferee is absolute. On the other hand, the trustee may not recover from a subsequent transferee if the subsequent transferee accepted the transfer for value, in good faith, and without knowledge of the transfer's voidability. 11 U.S.C. §550(b). Subsequent transferees therefore have a defense unavailable to initial transferees.

The purpose of this scheme is to protect creditors "from last-minute diminutions of the pool of assets in which they have interests," while at the same time to guard against "the waste that would be created if people either had to inquire how their transferors obtained their property or to accept a risk that a commercial deal would be reversed for no reason they could perceive at the time." Bonded Fin. Servs., Inc. v. European American Bank, 838 F.2d 890, 892 (7th Cir. 1988). Section 550 balances these two goals by imposing on the initial transferee the "burden of inquiry and the risk if the conveyance is fraudulent." Id. While the initial transferee is in the best position to monitor the transaction, "subsequent transferees usually do not know where the assets came from and would be ineffectual monitors if they did." Id. at 892-93.

In this case, the bankruptcy court determined, and the district court agreed, that Hilton was the initial transferee. On appeal, Hilton makes two arguments to the contrary. First, Hilton contends that Arlynn, not Hilton, was the initial transferee because Arlynn controlled Video Depot and directed that the funds be transferred to Hilton. Alternatively, Hilton argues that Arlynn was the initial transferee because Video Depot's ledger appears to indicate that the cashier's check was a "loan" to Arlynn. We address each of these arguments in turn.

I. Arlynn's Control over Video Depot

While the Bankruptcy Code does not define "transferee," it is widely accepted that a transferee is one who, at a minimum, has "'dominion over the money or other asset, the right to put the money to one's own purposes.'" In re Bullion, 922 F.2d at 548 (quoting Bonded Fin. Servs., 838 F.2d at 893). The bankruptcy court determined that Arlynn did not have dominion over the $65,000. The court reasoned that although Arlynn controlled Video Depot's operations and arranged for the check to be issued, the check was a direct transfer from Video Depot to Hilton. Once the check was issued, Arlynn no longer had legal control over the funds, even if he retained physical control over them. Arlynn therefore did not have the right to use the money for any other purpose than to give it to Hilton. Hilton maintains that Arlynn had dominion over the $65,000 because he was Video Depot's principal and, in that capacity, directed Video Depot to purchase the cashier's check.

The bankruptcy courts are split on the question of whether the principal of a debtor corporation necessarily is the initial transferee of corporate funds used to satisfy a personal obligation. . . . In Nordberg v. Arab Banking Corp. (In re Chase &. Sanborn Corp.), 904 F.2d 588 (llth Cir. 1990), on which the bankruptcy court in the present case relied, the Eleventh Circuit held that a bank was the initial transferee of loan payments made by a corporation even though the corporation's principal directed the transfer and the loan was the principal's private debt. Id. at 599-600. The court determined that "the extent of [the principal's] control over [the corporation] generally, and over [the corporation's] actions in transferring the disputed funds to [the bank] in particular, is entirely irrelevant to the 'initial transferee' issue." Id. at 598.

Since the bankruptcy court's decision, two other circuits, citing *Lucas Dallas* and the district court's opinion in this case, also have concluded that a principal who directs a debtor corporation to issue a certified check to pay for a personal debt is not an initial transferee. See Bowers v. Atlanta Motor Speedway, Inc. (In re Southeast Hotel Properties Limited Partnership), 99 F.3d 151 (4th Cir. 1996); Rupp v. Markgraf, 95 F.3d 936 (10th Cir. 1996). These courts have held that a principal or agent does not have "dominion and control" over funds unless he or she has "legal dominion and control, " in other words, the "right to put those funds to one's own purpose." *Bowers*, 99 F.3d at 155 (emphasis in original); see also *Rupp*, 95 F.3d at 941. The mere power of a principal to direct the allocation of corporate resources does not amount to legal dominion and control:

> Many principals presumably exercise de facto control over the funds of the corporations they manage. They can choose to cause their corporations to use those funds appropriately or inappropriately. The distinction is only relevant to the question whether the principal's conduct amounted to a breach of duty to the corporation.

Bowers, 99 F.3d at 156 (citing *Rupp*, 95 F.3d at 941).

Other circuit courts have held that a principal may establish legal control and dominion by first directing a transfer into his or her personal bank account and then making the payment from his personal account to the creditor. *Rupp*, 95 F.3d at 939 (citing *Bonded Fin. Servs.*, 838 F.2d at 892). In the present case, however, Video Depot purchased a cashier's check payable to Hilton, with Video Depot listed as the purchaser. Legal control over the funds consequently passed directly from Video Depot to Hilton.

Hilton contends that this view elevates form over substance. Whether Video Depot, at Arlynn's direction, purchased a cashier's check payable directly to Hilton or, instead, issued the funds to Arlynn, enabling him then to write a personal check for the sum, there is, so the argument goes, the same result — that Arlynn used corporate funds to satisfy a personal debt. What Hilton's argument fails to acknowledge, however, is the basic rationale for distinguishing in section 550 between initial and subsequent transferees. An initial transferee is exposed to stricter liability than a subsequent transferee because an initial transferee is in the best position to evaluate whether the conveyance is fraudulent. Where, as here, a transferee receives funds directly from a debtor, the transferee's capacity to monitor — and, accordingly, its burden to monitor — is at its greatest. Thus, Hilton's receipt of a cashier's check clearly purchased by Video Depot subjects it to a burden of inquiry that it may not have had upon receipt of a check from Jeffrey Arlynn's personal account.

Moreover, the rule advocated by Hilton would have the anomalous result that every agent or principal of a corporation would be deemed the initial transferee when he or she effected a transfer of property in his or her representative capacity. See *Bowers*, 99 F.3d at 156. Such a rule "gives too much power to an unscrupulous insider to effect a fraudulent transfer . . . without allowing a trustee to have the means for avoiding the transfer for the benefit of the debtor's creditors." In re Mitchell, 164 B.R. at 128. While the Sixth Circuit has expressed tentative support for this approach, see IRS v. Nordic Village, Inc. (In re Nordic Village), 915 F.2d 1049 (6th Cir. 1990), rev'd on other grounds, 503 U.S. 30 (1992), no circuit court has based a decision on it, and we decline to depart from the considered judgment of the other circuits today. Thus, we conclude that Arlynn's control over the business operations of Video Depot does not, in itself, compel a finding that Arlynn had dominion and control over the funds transferred from Video Depot to Hilton.

II.   Video Depot's "Loan" to Arlynn

Hilton next contends that the transfer of funds from Video Depot constituted a loan to Arlynn, giving Arlynn control over how the funds were spent and making him, not Hilton, the initial transferee. The bankruptcy court rejected this argument, citing insufficient evidence. Because we find nothing in the record to support a finding that Arylnn had dominion over the funds after they were disbursed by Video Depot, we agree with the bankruptcy court.

Hilton's argument rests on two documents that it submitted in support of its motion for summary judgment: excerpts from a ledger that appear to track payments by Video Depot on Arlynn's behalf and an affidavit from Arlynn. In the affidavit, Arlynn maintains:

> On or about June 15, 1990, I borrowed the sum of $65,000.00 from Video Depot and caused this loan transaction to be recorded in the records of the corporation. The $65,000.00 in corporate funds was used to purchase a cashier's check in the amount of $65,000 made payable to the Las Vegas Hilton in partial satisfaction of a debt I owed. . . . Prior to the commencement of involuntary bankruptcy proceedings against Video Depot, I repaid this specific loan to the corporation.

The ledger lists payments to Jeffrey Arlynn in the amount of $10,000 and $65,000 on June 15. On the credit side of the ledger, a $75,000 payment from Arlynn is shown.

Simply referring to the transfer as a "loan" in the company ledger does not suffice, however, to demonstrate that at any point in time Arlynn exercised independent control over the funds. So long as the money remained in Video Depot's account, Arlynn's legal right to it was circumscribed by his duties to the corporation and its creditors. Once the funds were disbursed, Arlynn could use them only to pay Hilton. Regardless of how Hilton chooses to characterize the transfer, Hilton has failed to explain how Video Depot's issuance of a check earmarked expressly for the purchase of a cashier's check to the Las Vegas Hilton gave Arlynn dominion over the funds.

Arlynn was a courier, not a transferee. Particularly in view of the fact that Arlynn, as principal of Video Depot, could direct that the transfer be called anything he pleased in the company ledger, we require more substantial evidence that he exercised independent control over the funds after they left Video Depot's account. The bankruptcy court gave Hilton ample opportunity to present such evidence, and Hilton failed to do so.

CONCLUSION

The bankruptcy court had adequate grounds for determining that Hilton was an initial transferee under section 550(a). Accordingly, we affirm the district court's decision affirming the bankruptcy court. Since we find Hilton to have been an initial transferee, we do not reach Hilton's section 550(b) argument.

Affirmed.

For many, the idea that corporate form carries any implications other than limited liability and altered tax status is shocking. That the reminder should come from a statute that has its origins in Elizabethan England (remember *Twyne's Case*?) seems to them positively perverse. The problem of matching up the entity that gave value with the entity that received value is at the heart of why leveraged buyouts can often be challenged as fraudulent conveyances. See discussion at pp. 86–98.

b.   The Extraordinary Powers of the TIB

The concept that underlies fraudulent conveyance law has its roots in protecting creditors from the unscrupulous acts of debtors, and courts have been quick to hold that the debtor-fraudulent conveyancer may not take advantage of the ability to set aside fraudulent transfers. The courts agreed that the debtor conveying fraudulently could not later rescind the transaction on those grounds — analogous to the principle of *in pari delicto*. In Chapter 11, however, we no longer have the debtor attempting to set aside its own transfer. Now it is the TIB or the DIP acting for the benefit of all the creditors and trying to save the business. For several TIBs and DIPs this has raised the unexpected possibility of setting aside transfers to reclaim property that as plain old debtors they could not reach, and, interestingly enough, attacking transfers that, as debtors, they made involuntarily. While it may be conceptually unsurprising that the DIP can act on behalf of all the creditors to reclaim property given away by the debtor or sold for less than fair consideration, some of the implications of this principle have startled the legal community.

=========== In re BAKERSFIELD WESTAR, INC. ===========
226 B.R. 227 (9th Cir. BAP 1998)

RUSSELL, Bankruptcy Judge. . . .

Bakersfield Westar, a California corporation ("Bakersfield"), provided air and ground ambulance services in Kern County, California. Bakersfield's president, appellee Craig R. Saunders, and his wife, appellee Jodie K. Saunders, co-owned 100% of Bakersfield's stock as community property.

On January 1, 1992, Craig Saunders submitted to the Internal Revenue Service an election to have Bakersfield treated as a subchapter S corporation for federal income tax purposes,[2] beginning with tax year 1992. On February 1, 1994, Mr. Saunders submitted to the IRS a statement of revocation of Bakersfield's subchapter S election, together with a statement of the Saunders' consent to the revocation of the election. The legal effect of the statement of revocation, which the IRS deemed effective as of February 1, 1994, was to make Bakersfield a "C" corporation (i.e., a separate taxable entity) for federal income tax purposes.

The Saunders filed a voluntary chapter 7 petition on February 14, 1994. The trustee in the Saunders' bankruptcy case filed a voluntary chapter 7 petition on behalf of Bakersfield (hereinafter the "debtor") on March 4, 1994. Due to the prepetition revocation of the debtor's subchapter S election (the "Revocation"), the debtor's bankruptcy estate did not succeed to the debtor's subchapter S tax attributes because the attributes had already passed through to the Saunders.

Appellant Randell Parker was appointed as the trustee in the debtor's case (the "trustee"). The trustee filed an adversary proceeding in March 1996 against the Saunders, the Saunders' bankruptcy trustee, and the IRS, seeking to avoid the Revocation as a fraudulent transfer under §§544(b) and 548, and Cal. Civ. Code §3439 et seq.

The complaint alleged that the Saunders submitted the Revocation to the IRS with the intent to shift to the debtor the significant capital gains tax burden that would arise from the future sale or other disposition

---

2. Such an election has the effect of characterizing the corporation as a "pass through" entity, with all items of income, loss, deduction, and credit flowing through the corporation to be reported on the personal tax returns of the corporation's principals.

In this case, the election authorized Bakersfield's taxable income to "pass through" to its principals, the Saunders, and any taxes due on the debtor's income were the Saunders' obligation and were reported on their personal tax returns. The election also permitted the Saunders to use the debtor's net operating losses and other tax attributes as an offset to their personal taxable income.

(e.g., foreclosure) of the debtor's assets, and with the actual intent to hinder, delay, and defraud creditors. The complaint alleged in the alternative that the debtor received less than a reasonably equivalent value in exchange for the Revocation. The Saunders' and the IRS's answers to the complaint denied the material allegations, and the IRS's answer contended that applicable treasury regulations provided the exclusive means by which a taxpayer's revocation of a subchapter S election could be rescinded or set aside.

In October 1996, the trustee moved for partial summary judgment to avoid the Revocation as a fraudulent transfer under §548(a)(1) on the grounds that the debtor's right to make or revoke its subchapter S election was "property," and the Revocation of that election was a "transfer" within the meaning of §548. The motion included the IRS as a respondent because the trustee requested an order directing the IRS to disregard the Revocation and reinstate the debtor's subchapter S status, retroactive to the date the Revocation was deemed effective, in order to restore the status quo ante.

The trustee analogized the "property" in this case to a debtor's right to carry forward a net operating loss ("NOL"),[4] which he contended has been recognized as "property" by several courts. He analogized the "transfer" in this case to a debtor's election to carry forward NOLs, which he contended those courts have recognized as a "transfer" of property.

The trustee contended that the debtor's election to be treated as a subchapter S corporation constituted a valuable property right because its corporate status allowed the debtor to pass its (and hence the bankruptcy estate's) tax liabilities through to its shareholders, the Saunders. He argued that the specific value of the election consisted of the debtor's ability to pass to the Saunders the debtor's estate's capital gains taxes resulting from the sale of over $230,000 in assets and from the future disposition of approximately $2 million in assets through foreclosure.

The trustee asserted that the Revocation constituted a "transfer" because it caused the debtor to "dispose" of its right (and thus the estate's right) to pass its tax liabilities through to the Saunders. As a result of the Revocation, the estate's substantial capital gains tax liabilities remained an obligation of the estate and its creditors, rather than an obligation of the Saunders.

The trustee also argued that the Revocation was made with the actual intent to hinder, delay, and defraud creditors. He contended that the following "badges of fraud" demonstrated the necessary intent: the debtor's failure to receive any direct or indirect value or benefit from the Revocation; the lack of any consideration received for the Revocation; the fact that the

---

4. NOLs are created when a taxpayer's deductible business expenses for a given year exceed its net income for that year. Once NOLs are sustained, the taxpayer may carry the loss back three years and use it as a deduction in that year. NOLs that remain are applied to the next two years and deducted accordingly. If any loss remains at the end of the three year carry back period, it is carried forward and deducted from the taxpayer's income over the next fifteen years (or until it is exhausted), beginning with the year after the loss was initially sustained. Alternatively, the Internal Revenue Code allows the taxpayer to forgo the carry back option and instead use the NOLs exclusively in future years. Such an election, once made, is irrevocable for that tax year. In re Russell, 927 F.2d 413, 415 (8th Cir. 1991) (citations to applicable Internal Revenue Code provisions omitted).

transferee, Mr. Saunders, was an officer of the debtor; and the debtor's insolvency (which the trustee inferred from the timing of the Revocation, i.e., about two weeks before the filing of the Saunders' bankruptcy case, and about one month before the filing of the debtor's bankruptcy case).

The IRS's opposition acknowledged that several courts have recognized the right to exercise NOL elections as "property" within the meaning of the Code, but argued that the right to make or revoke a corporation's subchapter S election cannot constitute "property" under §548 because it has no present value to a taxpayer,[6] is not referenced in the Code, and has not been recognized by any court to constitute "property." The IRS emphasized that a taxpayer's revocation of a subchapter S election has merely the prospective economic impact of changing the tax ramifications of future corporate transactions, and that the Revocation in this case did not deprive the debtor-corporation (or the bankruptcy estate) of anything of economic value, in contrast to the immediate tax consequences which arise from the exercise of NOL elections. The IRS again asserted that the Tax Code provides the exclusive means by which a corporation's subchapter S election may be revoked.

The Saunders' opposition and counter-motion for summary judgment argued that the trustee could not avoid the Revocation under §548(a) because only a corporation's shareholders could elect or revoke a corporation's subchapter S status. They also claimed that Mr. Saunders lacked the necessary actual fraudulent intent because the Revocation was made on the advice of professionals.

The trustee's response asserted that the Revocation deprived the bankruptcy estate of tax attributes it would have otherwise enjoyed, which he argued was similar in nature to the decision to carry forward NOLs, and that the amount of funds available to pay the estate's creditors would be substantially diminished due to the significant tax liabilities caused by the Revocation. . . .

IV.   DISCUSSION . . .

1.   *Whether a Corporate-Debtor's Prepetition Right to Make or Revoke Its Election to be Treated as a Subchapter S Corporation for Federal Income Tax Purposes Constitutes "Property" or an "Interest of the Debtor in Property" within the Meaning of §548(a)*

Section 548(a)(1) of the Code, under which the trustee brought his motion for partial summary judgment, allows a trustee to avoid any fraudulent "transfer" of "an interest of the debtor in property." The IRS acknowledges

---

6. Notwithstanding this argument, the IRS's opposition acknowledged that the Revocation in this case placed the burden of any future tax liability arising from the debtor's liquidation of assets on the debtor, rather than on the Saunders, as would have been the case if the subchapter S election had not been revoked.

that the Code does not define "interest of the debtor in property." Opening Brief for Appellee the United States of America ("IRS's Brief"), p.9. However, the IRS repeats its argument from the proceedings below that a debtor's prepetition right to revoke its election under I.R.C. §1362, n.10 to be treated as a subchapter S corporation, is not an "interest of the debtor in property" within the meaning of §548, because the right has no present value to a taxpayer, and has not been recognized by any court as constituting "property." I.R.C. §1362, n.11. In contrast, a debtor-corporation's right to use NOLs has a present monetary value (namely, a claim for a tax refund, which can be used by an estate to satisfy creditors), and has long been recognized by courts as "property."

We disagree. This argument unduly limits the definition of "property" to those rights which have a quantifiable "present value." Even if the definition were limited to this extent, the right in question has value to a debtor's estate and is therefore properly characterized as "property." In addition, the IRS's assertion that the right has not been recognized as "property" under the Code is incorrect.

In the absence of federal law, state law determines whether a debtor possesses an interest in property. However, a debtor's subchapter S status is a creation of I.R.C. §1362, and federal law therefore determines whether a debtor holds a "property" interest in its subchapter S status.

The United States Supreme Court has defined an "interest of the debtor in property" as "that property that would have been part of the estate had it not been transferred before the commencement of bankruptcy proceedings." Begier v. I.R.S., 496 U.S. 53, 58 (1990) (interpreting "interest of the debtor in property" under §547). *Begier* pointed to §541 for guidance in determining the parameters of the definition. Id. at 58. Section 541 includes "all legal or equitable interests of the debtor in property as of the commencement of the case" as property of the bankruptcy estate. 11 U.S.C. §541(a).

"Property of the debtor" is also defined broadly under Ninth Circuit case law. In re Bullion Reserve of North America, 836 F.2d 1214, 1217 (9th Cir. 1988), cert, denied sub nom. 486 U.S. 1056 (1988). "Generally, property belongs to the debtor for purposes of §547 if its transfer will deprive the bankruptcy estate of something which could otherwise be used to satisfy the claims of creditors." Id. at 1217. See also In re Kimura, 969 F.2d 806, 810 (9th Cir. 1992) (defining property as "generally characterized as an aggregate of rights; 'the right to dispose of a thing in every legal way, to possess it, to use it, and to exclude everyone else from interfering with it.'") (quoting Black's Law Dictionary 1095 (5th ed. 1979)). . . .

The ability to not pay taxes has a value to the debtor-corporation in this case. It is estimated that the debtor passed through to the Saunders approximately $2,359,109.00 in taxable losses from its operations during the period between September 30, 1992, and January 1, 1994, while holding its subchapter S status. It is further estimated that the debtor's estate will sustain approximately $400,000.00 in capital gains taxes from the sale and other disposition of its assets during bankruptcy as a result of the Revocation of that status.

The debtor's estate will be required to pay the capital gains taxes on an administrative expense priority basis, and its payment of the taxes will diminish the amount of monies that would otherwise be available to satisfy claims of the debtor's remaining creditors. If the Revocation had not occurred, the Saunders (and thus the creditors of their bankruptcy estate) would have been responsible for payment of these tax liabilities.

Accordingly, we hold that the debtor's prepetition right to make or revoke its subchapter S status constituted "property" or "an interest of the debtor in property" within the meaning of the Code.

2. Whether the Debtor's Prepetition Revocation of Its Corporate Status Election Constitutes a "Transfer" That May be Avoided by a Trustee under §548(a) . . .

In this case, the Saunders claim that there was no indication that the debtor had incurred or would incur any capital gains tax liabilities when the Revocation was made. They contend that their bankruptcy trustee filed the debtor's bankruptcy case without their consent, and that it would be unfair and inequitable to impose the debtor's unforeseen tax liabilities upon them when they had no control over the disposition of the debtor's assets.

The Saunders concede, however, that their decision to revoke the corporation's subchapter S status was based upon the recommendation of their professionals. The Revocation was made approximately two weeks prior to their filing personal bankruptcy. It is highly unlikely that the Saunders' professionals would have failed to inform them of the effect of the Revocation on their personal tax obligations and those of the corporation. It is equally difficult to believe that the Saunders's professionals would have failed to discuss with them the possibility that the corporation would also be forced to file bankruptcy and, if that were to happen, that a trustee might sell the debtor's assets and incur significant capital gains taxes as a result.

Thus, the decision to revoke the debtor's subchapter S status appears to reflect careful tax planning, and the Revocation appears to represent an effort by the Saunders to manipulate the bankruptcy system to their personal advantage under the guise of professional tax planning.

The rationale and holdings of *Russell* and *Trans-Lines*, as well as the broad definition of "transfer" under the Code, compel the conclusion that the trustee in this case has the power to avoid the debtor's revocation of its subchapter S status. This result is consistent with the underlying purpose of §548.

3. Whether the Tax Code Provisions Governing Subchapter S Elections Limit a Trustee's Avoiding Powers under §548(a)

The IRS contends that application of §548 would directly conflict with the Tax Code provisions that regulate subchapter S elections. It insists that the general provisions of §548 should not be read to override the specific provisions of the Tax Code regarding revocation of subchapter S elections, absent some specific statutory provision granting bankruptcy trustees rights that are not otherwise found in the Tax Code. IRS's Brief, pp. 14-15. The IRS and the Saunders both contend that courts have strictly construed the Tax Code provisions regarding subchapter S corporations, and rejected all efforts to expand their scope and application.[15]

However, courts have long held that Code provisions may override provisions of the Tax Code, even absent specific Congressional or statutory authorization to do so. See, e.g., *Russell*, 917 F.2d at 417 (rejecting IRS's argument that bankruptcy trustees could not avoid irrevocable NOL carry forward elections under the Tax Code absent specific Congressional authorization); *Feiler*, 218 B.R. at 963 (rejecting contention that more recent and specific provisions of I.R.C. §1398 limit more general provisions of §548).

Furthermore, the cases cited by the IRS and the Saunders regarding restrictive interpretation of the Tax Code's subchapter S provisions concern the effect of the subchapter S provisions on shareholders' individual tax obligations outside of bankruptcy. The cases have no relevance to a trustee's power to avoid a revocation under §548.

The IRS and the Saunders also both argue that revocation of a corporation's subchapter S election can only be made with the consent of the corporation's shareholders. They argue that a trustee does not succeed to a corporation's statutory right to make the revocation when the corporation files bankruptcy and, if the Saunders had not made the revocation in this case, the trustee would not have succeeded to their right to do so. In contrast, a bankruptcy estate is specifically authorized under the Tax Code to succeed to a debtor's right to waive NOL carry backs.

This argument fails to distinguish between "avoidance" under the Code in the bankruptcy context, and "revocation" of an otherwise irrevocable election under the Tax Code outside of bankruptcy. The Eighth Circuit Court of Appeals, concluding in *Russell* that a trustee could seek to avoid a debtor's otherwise irrevocable NOL election, stated:

> This ability [to avoid a debtor's irrevocable election under 26 U.S.C. §172(b)(3)(C)] allows a trustee to avoid an election, not revoke it. Once an election is avoided, however, it is as if it has never been made, and a trustee is free to act as she sees fit.

Russell, 927 F.2d at 417.

The IRS also expressed fears that "administrative havoc" will ensue if trustees are allowed to avoid revocations of subchapter S elections. . . . [T]he IRS complains that it might be forced to adjust shareholders' personal income tax returns if trustees are allowed to avoid otherwise valid subchapter S elections. An S corporation may now have more than 75 shareholders in any given year, and the IRS could "conceivably" be forced to adjust all of their personal tax returns, regardless of whether they were parties to the §548 action or the fraud alleged by the trustee. The IRS contends that the situation would be particularly problematic if avoidance of the election

---

15. The IRS argues that these restrictions are intended to prevent improper manipulation of the Tax Code by unscrupulous taxpayers, in addition to providing the IRS with administrative certainty. IRS's Brief, pp. 15-16. The Revocation in this case appears to reflect the very type of manipulation which the IRS claims the Tax Code restrictions are intended to prevent. See Section B, above.

under §548 were to conflict with the Tax Code's statute of limitations for adjustments to corporate and individual tax returns.

This argument is unpersuasive. The IRS acknowledges that the concern is speculative. It routinely adjusts individual and corporate tax returns in the ordinary course of its business. The possibility that the IRS might be required to amend an unknown (and possibly limited) number of additional tax returns in any given year is not an unusual occurrence and certainly will not create "administrative havoc.". . .

V.   Conclusion

The bankruptcy court based its denial of the trustee's motion for partial summary judgment on the erroneous determination that the debtor's right to make or revoke an election to be treated under the Tax Code as a subchapter S corporation for federal income tax purposes did not constitute an "interest of the debtor in property," and the debtor's prepetition revocation of its subchapter S election did not constitute a "transfer" of property, within the meaning of §548(a). The IRS was a proper defendant and the trustee's action was not precluded by the terms of §2201. We reverse and remand for further proceedings consistent with this decision.

———————

Mr. and Mrs. Saunders may not have fully grasped the implications of filing for bankruptcy and ceding control over their property — including their wholly owned corporation — to a trustee in bankruptcy. We're sure they have a clearer picture now, as they become the involuntary recipients of all that nondischargeable tax liability.

As *Bakersfield Westar* illustrates, fraudulent conveyance law may be a creature of state law, but in the hands of a TIB the possibilities for using fraudulent conveyance expand beyond the state law boundaries. The trustee, or the DIP acting as a trustee, acts on behalf of all the creditors and therefore can do things that the debtor itself could never have done. That power is even greater than it appears at first glance. Moore v. Bay, 284 U.S. 4 (1931). Because a TIB must stand in the shoes of an actual creditor to invoke section 544(b), it would be reasonable to suppose that the TIB could avoid a transfer or obligation only to the extent of that actual creditor's claim. The Supreme Court in Moore v. Bay held to the contrary: The TIB could avoid the transaction completely, even though the resulting liability might be much larger than the claim of the creditor in whose stead the TIB sued. Furthermore, the transaction was avoided for the benefit of all unsecured creditors, not just that class of creditors who could have brought the avoidance action under state law. This result has long seemed extreme to many scholars in the bankruptcy field, but the debate has quieted with the relative disuse of section 544(b) in contexts where the doctrine really mattered.

However, the Moore v. Bay controversy may be dormant rather than dead. Douglas J. Whaley, The Dangerous Doctrine of Moore v. Bay, 82 Tex. L. Rev. 73 (2003). Professor Whaley suggests that the issue may take on new vitality because of the increasing number of state and federal laws that permit avoidance of certain kinds of transactions under circumstances different from the traditional categories.

The impact of the TIB's role in fraudulent conveyance law is not limited to the scope of the avoidance. The involvement of the federal courts, through a collective proceeding, has the constant potential to enlarge the substantive reach of the avoidance power. The power of the TIB to set aside transactions that could not be touched by the pre-bankruptcy debtor was sharply expanded in 1980 when the Fifth Circuit dropped a judicial bombshell, Durrett v. Washington National Insurance Co., 621 F.2d 201 (5th Cir. 1980). The court had ruled that a legally conducted, nonjudicial foreclosure sale that had brought a low price was a "transfer" for "less than reasonably equivalent value," the language employed in section 548. This created the anomaly that permitted a debtor who had lost a piece of property in a state foreclosure proceeding to reclaim the property from the buyer if the debtor filed for bankruptcy and suddenly became (much like Superman emerging from the telephone booth) the Debtor in Possession. Now acting on behalf of all the creditors, the DIP could, within the fraudulent conveyance statute of limitations, pay off the small price paid by the buyer and reclaim valuable property for the estate.

The case stimulated great consternation — and differences among the circuits. Congress amended section 548, but failed to solve the problem. Then the Supreme Court decided BFP v. Resolution Trust Corporation, 511 U.S. 531 (1994). Amidst a hot dispute among themselves, the Court ruled 5–4 that "reasonably equivalent value" should be conclusively deemed to have been given at any judicial foreclosure sale that was noncollusive and properly conducted under state law. Market value, said Justice Scalia, "has no applicability in the forced sale context."

We confess to having been very critical of *Durrett* when it was decided, but we aren't so confident anymore — now that such dissenting views are irrelevant. Justice Souter offered a thoughtful dissent, pointing out that bankruptcy policy might reasonably trump state law interests at stake in a judicial foreclosure action, a point that seems to have escaped Justice Scalia. The underlying issue in *Durrett* has always been whether federal or state law would control the pre-bankruptcy disposition of the debtor's assets, and Justice Scalia seems to see only the state half of that argument.

BFP is also notable for its "dueling plain meanings" (played to the tune of "Dueling Banjos"), in which both the five members of the majority and the four dissenters claim to be simply reading the plain meaning of the statute that the other side is presumably too obtuse to see.

Aiding and Abetting

A number of recent cases have involved a claim that a third party "aided and abetted" a corporation's officers in some wrongdoing. In either case, there may be injury, directly or indirectly, to the corporation. The most famous example is Enron, where the reports of the Examiner provide lurid examples of financial institutions and others allegedly aiding and abetting frauds perpetrated by that company's officers, examples that seem more telling now that many of those institutions have paid billions of dollars in settlement of claims based on allegations of exactly that sort.

The liability to *creditors* of individual officers and others for participating in a debtor's pre-bankruptcy fraud is well established. E.g., In re Calypso Zamias, L.P., 293 B.R. 668 (Bankr. W.D. Pa. 2003). The difficulty arises when the TIB sues on behalf of the debtor corporation. In such cases, the courts routinely deny recovery to the TIB for fraud by corporate officers because they were typically acting on behalf of the corporation and therefore the corporation is held to be *in pari delicto* with the officers.

Two recent cases in the Second Circuit illustrate the problem. Official Committee v. Coopers & Lybrand, 322 F.3d. 147 (2d Cir. 2003); In re Bennett Funding Group, Inc., 336 F.3d 94 (2d Cir. 2003). In both cases, officers of the corporation and its professionals were allegedly involved in fraudulent conduct, and the professionals were charged with failing to report to the board negative information about an ongoing fraud. In each case, it was alleged that the corporation, not just third parties, suffered damage from the fraud. In each case, the court held that the corporation's claim was barred by *in pari delicto* (or "imputation"). Because the corporation had no claim, neither did the TIB as successor. In each case, the trustee was unsuccessful in urging exceptions to the general rule.

In cases such as *Coopers* or *Bennett Funding,* assuming proof on the merits, it would appear that all the creditors of the corporation were equally hurt by a malfeasance that is claimed to have sunk the enterprise. The damages that the corporation could not claim, and its shareholders should arguably not share, should in such cases be shared by all the creditors. If that is true, why shouldn't that kind of case be brought by the TIB, just as an avoidance case would be? After all, the doctrine of *in pari delicto* is noticeably absent in voidable preference and fraudulent conveyance cases because the TIB is conceived to have causes of action independent from any the debtor passed on to the estate and therefore is not barred by the debtor's misconduct.

Outside of bankruptcy, the fraudulent conveyance action belongs not to the debtor, but to the creditors of the debtor under state fraudulent conveyance statutes. Will the courts decide that the Bankruptcy Code gives the estate a cause of action for aiding and abetting fraud, another action that also belongs to the creditors? We suspect that there will be more cases raising variations on this issue.

Problem Set 30

30.1. For 26 years, Burt DiAngelo has owned and operated Be Well, Inc., a health products manufacturing concern. Burt now employs 106 people ("all like family"), but Burt is the business. He makes all the decisions, keeps the books, runs the show. After years of successful operation, last year was a disaster. Bad press over rodent droppings seemed to be the principal problem, and Burt has taken the company into Chapter 11.

As you and Burt are plotting strategies, Burt mentions ruefully that only six months ago today he spent nearly $40,000 cash from the business to take his extended family on a cruise to celebrate his parents' fiftieth wedding anniversary. He knew that the business was faltering, but he thought it would recover. He can't believe that a few bad news stories have brought him so low so fast.

You are getting a tingling feeling in the back of your neck. What's wrong? See §548(a)(1), (2).

30.2. Ben Goldberger organized a start-up company to take advantage of the opportunities in the rapidly expanding personal communications service industry. At an FCC auction for the licenses, he was high bidder at $5 billion for 63 C block licenses, putting 20 percent down and agreeing to pay the balance in six months. At the time of the bid, unbeknownst to Goldberger or any of the other bidders, the FCC had scheduled the sale of thousands more licenses, so that the value of what Goldberger bought was actually about $1 billion. When this became known a week later, Goldberger's investors backed out. Goldberger says his business idea is still golden, but not if he pays $5 billion for the license. What advice do you have for him?

30.3. You are counsel to the TIB for Advant Advertising, Inc., which has filed a Chapter 7 petition. Advant had grown rapidly under the leadership of its dynamic chief executive, Cheri Schneider, who made money by a combination of clever ad copy and wheeling and dealing with her clients. Unfortunately, Cheri's "golden touch" eventually turned to lead and the company was forced to file for bankruptcy.

Jefferson and Jefferson, a CPA firm that the court has appointed to investigate the chaotic records of the company, has sent you a file on one of Cheri's deals. In this transaction, Cheri traded a small office building that the company owned for stock in Sure Fire Investments, a local development company for which Advant did the advertising. What Cheri did not know was that Sure Fire was in financial trouble when the trade was made and the stock Advant got was worth only $90,000. In all fairness, however, it must be said that the management of Sure Fire was also unaware of its financial problems. The Sure Fire management thought it was giving stock actually worth $900,000, which was the appraised value of the building at the time of the building-for-stock swap.

Sure Fire got the building about six months before Advant filed its Chapter 7. Sure Fire wanted the building in order to renovate and sell it. It spent about $300,000 on renovations, but the real estate market turned down and it was only able to get $1,000,000 for the building. The buyer of the building was S. Eric Wang, a real estate genius who made his first million playing professional hockey in Detroit.

What action should you take on behalf of the TIB? Against whom will you take it and what relief will you ask for? See §§548(a), (c); 550.

30.4. Yesterday Diana Saliceti Moran, one of the partners of Commercial Investors, called you to ask about an investment that has clearly gone sour. It appears that Barry Held, the president of Held Real Estate, has gone completely round the bend. Barry has had a severe alcohol abuse problem, and he let the company fall to pieces. Although Held's second-in-command, a frightened young bookkeeper, managed to keep paying the company's creditors, including your client, during most of the decline, the business has fallen apart. Brokers have left, income is off sharply, and the business is essentially over. CI's collateral, accounts receivable, is virtually worthless.

The only substantial, unencumbered asset was the office building where the business operated. Moran says the building was worth about $850,000. She is outraged to find that the building was sold last Tuesday at a sheriff's auction. It seems that the business had failed to pay a plumber's bill of $1,600. The plumber got a judgment, and the property was auctioned off last Tuesday. The only bidder was the plumber who had brought the action, and he bid in the unpaid bill of $1,600. The bookkeeper remembers getting some kind of notice for the sale, which he gave to Held, but Held didn't even show up for the sale.

The partner says that CI will gladly pay the plumber the $1,600 plus expenses and share the value obtained from the business with the other unsecured creditors. Without that building, CI is staring at a $1.2 million loss on its loan. What advice do you give Moran?

30.5. Illinois Vacuum is an old client of yours, a long-time manufacturer of high quality cleaning equipment. The Credit Director, Shirley Lo, has come to you this afternoon because of a serious credit problem with Springfield Appliances and Aluminum Siding, a major customer of IV. IV has sold vacuum cleaners to Springfield for a long time on open account. Springfield has been suffering from competition in two new malls and has been in increasing financial difficulty. It is now 90 days behind in its payments to IV, with a total owed of about $30,000.

Lo claims the troubles at Springfield really go back to the retirement of Sam Kirwin, the principal owner of the business, and the takeover of operations by his son Scott. Lo recently talked with Sam at his new Florida retirement home. Sam refuses to believe that the business is in trouble, citing the very substantial dividend he had just received as the owner of 75 percent of the common shares. The news of this dividend hit Lo really hard and she has come to you to seek advice. Aside from the numerous other questions you would have, advise Lo about the possible remedies available to IV with regard to the dividend. Would your analysis be any different if the dividend were a regular preferred stock dividend in the amount provided for by the terms of the preferred stock (e.g., $100 to be paid per share each year, cumulatively)?

8. *Equitable Subordination*

The final avoiding power available to the TIB, equitable subordination, originated with the courts and was later incorporated by reference in section 510(c). Prior to the Code, these words did not even appear in the statute. Section 510(c) of the Code merely ratifies continued judicial development of this power.

It is quite impossible to capture this murky, rambling doctrine in a few words, but some observations may be helpful. First, the result of application of the doctrine is to postpone or "subordinate" payment of a particular creditor's claim until some or all other creditors have been paid in full.

The subordinated creditor is sent to the back of the line of creditors and will be paid last, if any money is left. Often, of course, the practical effect is that the creditor gets nothing, although in theory the claim is merely reduced in priority.

Second, the most simple and basic application of the doctrine is to the owners of a company who capitalize it by a very small equity investment plus much larger amounts "lent" to the company. If the equity investment was obviously too small for the business contemplated, the bankruptcy court may find that the purported loans should be treated as if the money had been used to purchase stock in the company, as it should have been. In that case, the loans are treated as equity investments, and equity investments receive nothing until all true creditors are paid in full. On this basis, the court will subordinate the loans, so that they will not be paid from the estate until the other creditors have been paid. This aspect of the equitable subordination doctrine is important to the analysis in the case that follows, *Carolee's Combine*.

Beyond this basic level, the doctrine is generally applied where there is an allegation of wrongdoing and the wrongdoer is in some sense an "insider," such as an officer or principal stockholder. Where the wrongdoer is not a literal insider, the doctrine is not likely to be applied unless the wrongdoer exercised "control" over the debtor, thus making itself an insider in one sense. It is in this second situation that bank lenders have sometimes been equitably subordinated when they have begun to manage the operations of their debtors. For that reason banks and other large lenders are very sensitive to the risks of this doctrine.

Conversely, the wrongdoing that triggers the doctrine is often conduct that would not be wrongful if it had been done by someone other than an insider who could exercise control. For example, a debtor might choose any suppliers, even higher priced ones, and if the debtor thought this was a good business decision, the creditors would have no grounds for complaint (other than the general, "how could he be so dumb" complaint that all creditors are entitled to voice). But if a lender persuaded a debtor to use suppliers who charge higher prices because the suppliers are owned by the lender, the other creditors might well complain. This lender's actions could raise an issue of subordinating the lender's debt to the other unsecured creditors who were injured by the debtor's failure to run the business to maximize profits.

Closely related is the fact that equitable subordination cases frequently have the flavor that the creditor was "taking advantage" of an inside or control position. Where a bank or other nominally outside creditor is involved, there is also a sense that if the creditor acts like an owner — for example, by taking control — then the courts will treat it like an owner. Owners, of course, get paid last in bankruptcy.

Finally, it should be noted that equitable subordination is more often asserted than applied. It is often threatened by TIBs because its limits are unclear and its power awesome, but there seems to be only a modest number of cases each year in which a creditor is subordinated. This may suggest that the real effect of equitable subordination is in negotiations with insiders and with creditors who have arguably overstepped the creditor role and who may be more amenable to a "reasonable" deal.

===== In re CAROLEE'S COMBINE =====
3 B.R. 324 (Bankr. N.D. Ga. 1980)

ROBINSON, Bankruptcy Judge.

This case arises out of a no-minimum, no-reserve auction venture conducted by the bankrupt Carolee's Combine, Inc., in Atlanta, Georgia, on October 8 and 9, 1976. The auction failed, grossing only $625,000.00 against liabilities of $850,000.00. Because the only assets of the bankrupt were the items sold at the auction, it was insolvent both before and after the auction. . . .

Carolee's Combine, Inc., was organized by Carolee W. Davies as a Georgia corporation for the purpose of conducting an auction of architectural antiques in Atlanta, Georgia, on October 8 and 9, 1976. The corporation planned to acquire architectural antique merchandise (generally old building materials and fixtures such as columns, staircases, railings, bars, chandeliers, windows, and the like which are suitable for incorporation into other structures), either by purchase or consignment, transport the items to Atlanta, Georgia, for restoration and refinishing, and then sell the merchandise at a no-minimum, no-reserve auction. Because Carolee Davies, the sole officer and shareholder of the bankrupt, contributed little capital, if any, to the auction venture, and because the venture could not raise substantial amounts of cash through more conventional means, it was necessary to overcome the problem of incurring substantial expense to acquire, transport and refurbish inventory, all before the proceeds from the auction sale would provide the only cash flow. In particular, the bankrupt needed cash to acquire merchandise because "point sources" — the persons in the architectural antique industry engaged in locating and salvaging merchandise from old buildings and selling it to be auctioned — normally insisted on cash payment. To solve this problem, the bankrupt used two procedures employed at least twice previously by other auction companies in which Carolee Davies and her husband, R. D. Davies, were involved: to wit, an inventive money raising scheme and maximum possible deferral of all obligations.

Between May 7, 1976, and October 4, 1976, Carolee Davies and her husband, R. D. Davies, raised $329,050.00 by promising the persons and entities who advanced such money, in writing, that on the first day of the two-day auction the amount advanced would be returned with ten percent annual interest, and that a bonus in the amount of a flat ten percent of the principal amount of the advance (styled a "Finder's Fee") would be paid at the same time. These obligations were evidenced by two documents, one styled a "Promissory Note" and the other a "Finder's Fee" letter. This device had been used to raise money for the previous auctions conducted by Carolee Davies through Carolee's Architectural Combine, Inc., a California corporation which had held an auction earlier in 1976 in Los Angeles, California, and the Golden Movement Emporium, an auction company owned by John Wilson and R. D. Davies in which Carolee Davies had been involved. Many of the 23 investors from whom the $329,050.00 was raised by the bankrupt had made similar investments in these prior ventures. The net effect of the arrangement was to provide for repayment of the investors from initial cash flow at the auction, thereby transferring the risk of loss and insolvency to the general creditors.

As part of the overall plan, Carolee's Combine, Inc. deferred as many as possible of its obligations for labor, materials, rent, and utilities until after the auction. Thus, laborers were sought who would work as "subcontractors" (thereby eliminating state and federal unemployment and withholding taxes) and who would agree to wait for payment at least in large part until the conclusion of the auction. Likewise, many suppliers of other goods and services were convinced to wait for payment until after the auction — or given post-dated checks. In addition, a few sellers of merchandise agreed to accept post-dated checks, and rent and utilities in the amount of $3,953.13 were deferred. The "floating" of these obligations allowed the bankrupt to decrease its operating expenses, thereby maximizing the purchase of merchandise with the money acquired through the fund-raising contracts.

As a result of these procedures, the bankrupt arrived at the day of the auction insolvent, having obligations of $363,623.97 to the investors on the contracts described above, an obligation of $35,561.35 to the First National Bank of Atlanta, and owing $268,940.15 to trade creditors, laborers, and others. Moreover, at the auction's conclusion, an additional $184,284.30 was owed to consignors as their 60 percent share (after deduction of expenses) of the proceeds from the sale of their merchandise. These obligations total $852,409.77. Since the auction proceeds were only $624,469.00, and since the other assets amounted to only $32,368.84, the auction failed to break even by $195,570.93.

Despite this substantial shortfall, $313,764.32 was returned to investors in advance of other creditors who received nothing. This result was assured by the fact that on October 7, 1976, the day before the auction, the bankrupt wrote checks totaling $363,623.97 for delivery to investors on the first day of the auction, October 8, 1976. The bankrupt began that day with an overdraft of $326.44 in its only bank account.

Defendant was one of the persons who received his check at the auction and was repaid his investment. The Trustee contends that this transfer represented a return on an investment of an equity nature such that it was not entitled to be paid in priority to general creditors and that it should be returned for distribution in accordance with the Bankruptcy Act. In this regard, the Trustee contends further that it should be subordinated to the claims of unsecured creditors. This Court agrees.

The evidence in this case establishes that the monies advanced pursuant to the investment contracts described above provided the "seed money" for the bankrupt's auction enterprise and constituted virtually all of its capital. The evidence also established that the extra flat ten percent "Finder's Fee" was not a finder's fee at all, since in the commercial context a finder's fee is normally paid (1) to a third party other than the lender (2) at the time the loan is arranged. Neither of these facts is present with regard to the purported "Finder's Fee" arrangement in these contracts, providing compelling evidence that the characterization of the obligation as a "Finder's Fee" was using a euphemism to disguise what, in economic terms, was, an agreed return on risk capital. The fact that the advances were risk capital or "seed money" is further evidenced by the high return which on an annual basis ranged from 60 percent to over 520 percent. Such returns are generally associated only with equity positions in investments such as stock or fixed assets, and not debt instruments; for example, during this same period of time, the bankrupt was able to obtain loans from the First National Bank of Atlanta at an interest rate of only ten percent. Further, while the return on a debt obligation increases with the risk, the guaranteed payment from initial cash flow of the corporation's auction sale clearly shifted the risk away and belies the debt nature of the obligation; in other words, the high rate of return cannot be justified as being consistent with a debt obligation on the basis of risk because, as a practical matter, there was little risk.

Based on the foregoing analysis of the investments, this Court concludes that the defendant's advance of money was an investment of an equity nature and its return must be postponed until general obligations of the bankrupt are paid. Consequently, the defendant herein must return the $1,500.00 transfer and the Trustee is entitled to a judgment in that amount.

The Trustee's ability to recover this transfer stems from two independent sources. First, it is clear that this Court, as a court of bankruptcy and equity, has the power to subordinate the claim of one creditor to the claims of other creditors "where subordination is necessary to prevent the consummation of conduct which is inequitable." Central States Corp. v. Luther, 215 F.2d 38 (10th Cir. 1954). It is well established under Pepper v. Litton, 308 U.S. 295 (1939), that obligations of a bankrupt which, under state law, are "loans" may nevertheless be treated as capital contributions for purposes of the Bankruptcy Act and the rights of the holders of such loans subordinated to the claims of general creditors. In this case, therefore, it is plain that, if the defendant had never been paid on his investment any claim with regard to that investment would, under the analysis set forth above, be subordinated to the claims of general creditors. Similarly, the principle of equitable subordination requires persons who are paid be placed in the same position as persons who are not paid. Accordingly, if equitable subordination is proper, the fact that the defendant was paid does not prevent this Court from subordinating his claim against the bankrupt and, as a necessary corollary to that subordination, requiring him to return that which he has received.

The most recent discussion of equitable subordination in this circuit is In re Mobile Steel Co., 563 F.2d 692 (5th Cir. 1977), where the Court set forth three standards which must be met for equitable subordination to be appropriate. They are (1) the subordinated creditor must have engaged in some type of inequitable conduct; (2) such conduct must have resulted in injury to other creditors of the bankrupt or conferred an unfair advantage on the subordinated creditor; and (3) equitable subordination must not be inconsistent with the provisions of the Bankruptcy Act.

The Trustee has met his burden of proof on all of these issues. The conduct of defendant, like the other investors, was clearly inequitable since the provisions of their contracts for prior payment injured trade creditors and conferred an unconscionable advantage on them in exchange for which they were promised and received an extraordinarily high return. These investors advanced monies to a speculative venture for the promise of a high return (certainly not in itself inequitable) but shifted the risk of that speculation to general creditors by arranging to be paid in advance. In essence, the investors shifted the risks, normally associated with "seed money" investments which yield the high returns they were seeking, to trade creditors. In essence, they secured a secret first claim on the assets of the corporation. Consistent with the Bankruptcy Act, this Court's equity powers are properly invoked to avoid this result.

Since for the reasons discussed above the defendant's participation in the bankrupt's auction enterprise must properly be viewed as a proprietary interest, there is another theory supporting the Trustee's claim. As an ownership interest, the defendant's claim comes within the definition of a "share" under Georgia corporate law, which defines shares as "units into which the proprietary interests in a corporation are divided." Ga. Code Ann. §22-102(e). Clearly, one cannot withdraw capital from a corporation without first arranging for the payment of its valid debts, Ga. Code Ann. §22-512(a). Since the transfer amounts to a voidable conveyance under Georgia law, the Trustee is entitled to recover it under Section 70e [predecessor to §547] of the Bankruptcy Act.

In summary, therefore, the Trustee is entitled to judgment in the amount of $1,500.00 plus interest at the statutory rate of 7 percent from the date of the transfer.

In addition to the investment transaction referred to above, defendant was a consignor and "subcontractor" who, at the end of the auction, was owed $15,158.43 for expenses and services he supplied and $14,739.65 as his share of the proceeds of goods he consigned for a total of $29,898.08. On October 17, 1976, auction personnel held a meeting with several consignors, including defendant, at which Carolee Davies, president of the bankrupt, announced that the auction had only enough money to pay each of the consignors about one-half of what they were owed. Thereafter, defendant received $5,931.00 in cash on October 20; $1,000.00 in cash on October 21; and a $9,000.00 check, dated October 21, which was paid on October 22. The Trustee contends that he is entitled to recover these transfers, in the total amount of $15,931.00, as a preference voidable under Section 60 of the Bankruptcy Act.

The Trustee has shown all elements of a preference, as defined in Section 60a of the Bankruptcy Act, in that the bankrupt transferred property to the defendant, who was a creditor, for or on account of an antecedent debt, within four months of a filing of a petition against it. Since defendant was a general creditor, and numerous other general creditors received nothing, he necessarily received a greater percentage of his debt than others of the same class. Accordingly, defendant received a preference within the meaning of Section 60a....

Finally, under Section 57g [predecessor to §502(d)], the Trustee is entitled to a judgment disallowing the defendant's claim until the amount of the transfers which he is entitled to recover are returned to the estate....

───────────────

Carolee's Combine puts two interesting twists on traditional equitable subordination doctrine. The first is that the ownership or insider element was not control, but rather the economic position in which the favored creditors put themselves. Although the origins of equitable subordination suggest it applies when justice requires treating a fund given the debtor as equity rather than debt regardless of whether the investor acted wrongfully at some point following funding, more recent cases have emphasized wrongdoing as the triggering event.

The second twist has to do with the remedy for equitable subordination. It is bad enough for a creditor to have to repay money it was paid before bankruptcy (the usual avoiding power remedy). But the subordinated creditor has its claim demoted to the back of the line, behind the other unsecured creditors (the traditional equitable subordination remedy). As the opinion reveals, the transfer thus avoided was equally avoidable under standard preference doctrine. By using equitable subordination, however, the court did not just "demote" the putative investors to equal status with all the other creditors, as avoiding a preferential transfer would have done. Instead, the effect of the subordination was that those who tried to come first ended up last. Substantially more money was thus available for repayment of the general unsecured creditors.

Contractual Subordination

Equitable subordination — that is, subordination imposed by the courts — should not be confused with contractual subordination. In the latter, which is governed by section 510(a), one party may agree that it will take satisfaction of its debt only after another creditor is satisfied on its debt. By agreement, creditors who are equal in status may become first and second, or a lower-ranked creditor may beat a higher-ranked creditor. The ordinary rules of priority are displaced by agreement. These agreements are enforceable both as a matter of contract law and of Article 9 of the UCC.

With contractual subordination, a creditor typically makes an agreement with another creditor that it will take payment from the debtor only after the other creditor has been paid in full first. The subordinated creditor also usually agrees that if by some bizarre chance it receives some payments, it will give those payments to the other creditor until the other creditor has been paid in full.

Subordination agreements are not unusual, particularly when both a debtor and an earlier-in-time creditor want a new creditor to come on board, bringing its new infusion of cash. Section 510(a) confirms that subordination agreements that are effective under state law are also effective once the debtor files for bankruptcy.

Equitable Subordination and State Law

The following case has two elements that may be unfamiliar to some students. The first is the nature of the plaintiff, an "indenture trustee." That phrase describes a trust, invariably a bank, that acts on behalf of bondholders who have lent money to the debtor by buying its bonds. The financing agreement under which the bonds are sold is called an "indenture" and the indenture trustee has certain limited but important responsibilities to bondholders in the event of a default on the bonds under the terms of the indenture. In effect, the lenders (bondholders) have an agent (trustee) who has agreed in advance to watch out for them and to take certain steps on their behalf. The second point is that the case involves a "negative pledge clause," which can be simply stated in this case as a promise by the debtor to lender number one that it will not grant a security interest to another creditor unless an equal and pro rata security interest is granted to lender number one. In general, negative pledges are just variations on a promise to a lender that the borrower won't go out and take on more debt of some particular description (secured, over a certain total, etc.).

In re EPIC CAPITAL CORPORATION
307 B.R. 767 ((Bankr. D. Del. 2004)

FARNAN, District Judge

* * *

The appeal and cross-appeal arise in connection with the Adversary Complaint filed by BNY against USA Capital and the Debtor, Epic Resorts-Palm Springs Marquis Villas, LLC ("Epic Palm Springs"). BNY is the successor indenture trustee under the Indenture dated July 8, 1998 and supplemented on January 7, 1999 and February 3, 1999. Under the terms of the Indenture, Epic Resorts, LLC ("Epic Resorts") and Epic Capital Corp. ("Epic Capital") issued $130 million in Senior Secured Redeemable Notes due 2005 (the "Bonds"). The holder of the majority of the Bonds is a group of Bondholders that refer to themselves as the Highland Funds.

The Indenture also provided that Epic Resorts and Epic Capital would grant BNY a deed of trust in property known as the Palm Springs Resort. The Palm Springs Resort is on land administered by the United States Department of Interior, Bureau of Indian Affairs ("BIA"). As a result, BIA approval was required to grant BNY a deed of trust under the terms of the Indenture. However, BIA approval was never obtained for the Palm Springs Resort.

Two years after closing on the Indenture, Epic Resorts Palm Springs Marquis Villas, LLC ("Epic Palm Springs"), the subsidiary of Epic Resorts which operates the Palm Springs Resort, borrowed $11.5 million from USA Capital. As security for the loan, Epic Palm Springs granted USA Capital a security interest in substantially all of its assets including the Master Lease and time shares related to the Palm Springs Resort. The BIA approved the security interest granted to USA Capital.

Epic Palm Springs eventually defaulted on its loan with USA Capital, and Epic Resorts and Epic Capital defaulted on their obligation to make an $8.45 million interest payment to their Bondholders. As a result, the Highland Funds filed involuntary bankruptcy petitions against Epic Resorts, Epic Capital and Epic Palm Springs.

A.   The Appeal by BNY

By its appeal, BNY contends that the Bankruptcy Court erred in failing to equitably subordinate the claims of USA Capital to its own claims. BNY contends that it can establish the three part test for equitable subordination, and that the Bankruptcy Court erred in adding a fourth element requiring egregious conduct. BNY also contends that the Bankruptcy Court erred in concluding that USA Capital entered into the loan transaction with Epic Palm Springs in good faith. Specifically, BNY contends that USA Capital had actual knowledge of the contents of the Prospectus, referring to the proposed leasehold mortgage on the Palm Springs Resorts, and the Indenture, including the negative covenants precluding Epic Resorts and Epic Capital from incurring additional indebtedness or encumbering their property, and that USA Capital ignored the provisions of these documents by recording a lien against the Palm Springs Resort. BNY contends that USA Capital's conduct was purposefully aimed to harm the contractual relationship between the Debtors and the Bondholders, and that the Bankruptcy Court should have found that USA Capital's conduct was purposeful and constituted tortuous interference with the contractual rights of BNY. Thus, BNY maintains that the Bankruptcy Court erred as a matter of law in concluding that the equities did not weigh in favor of BNY.

III.   DISCUSSION

A.   Whether the Bankruptcy Court Erred in Denying BNY's Motion for Summary Judgment Seeking Equitable Subordination of USA Capital's Claim

Pursuant to Section 510(c) of the Bankruptcy Code, the Bankruptcy Court may, after notice and a hearing, subordinate for purposes of distribution all or part of an allowed claim to all or part of another allowed claim under the principles of equitable subordination. 11 U.S.C. §510(c). To apply equitable subordination, three requirements must be met: (1) the claimant engaged in some type of inequitable conduct; (2) the misconduct resulted in injury to other creditors and conferred an unfair advantage on the claimant; and (3) equitable subordination of the claim is not inconsistent with the provisions of the Bankruptcy Code. Citicorp Venture Capital, Ltd. v. Committee of Creditors Holding Unsecured Claims, 160 F.3d 982, 986 (3d Cir.1998) (citing In the Matter of Mobile Steel Co., 563 F.2d 692, 699-700 (5th Cir.1977)).

By its appeal, BNY contends that the Bankruptcy Court erroneously applied this test by requiring BNY to show egregious conduct. However, the applicable case law indicates that where, as here, the respondent is not an insider or fiduciary of the company, the party seeking to apply equitable subordination bears a higher burden of proof in which he or she must show that the respondent engaged in egregious conduct such as fraud, spoilation or overreaching. The Bankruptcy Court recognized this principle in its decision and correctly applied a heightened standard of review to BNY's claim. Accordingly, the Court cannot conclude that the Bankruptcy Court erred in its decision.

BNY next contends that the Bankruptcy Court erred in failing to conclude that the facts of this case warrant equitable subordination. BNY contends that USA Capital was on actual notice, or at the least, inquiry notice, of the Prospectus and the negative covenants in the Indenture, such that USA Capital should be said to have acted inequitably and purposefully to injure the Bondholders by entering into the loan agreement with Epic Palm Springs. The Bankruptcy Court thoroughly analyzed the facts of this case and found that despite USA Capital's actual knowledge of the restrictive covenants in the Indenture, USA Capital did not intend to harm any relationship between the Debtors and the Bondholders, and its conduct did not rise to the level required to equitably subordinate the claim of a non-insider. As the Bankruptcy Court pointed out, Epic Palm Springs represented and warranted to USA Capital that the secured loan transaction would not result in a breach of the Indenture, USA Capital obtained an opinion letter from Epic Palm Spring's counsel confirming this point, and USA Capital confirmed that no other liens existed on the property. The information USA Capital obtained is consistent with the Prospectus, which expressly states that if approval from the BIA is not obtained, "the subsidiary guaranty of Epic Resorts Palm Springs Marquis Villas, LLC will not be secured by any mortgage on such leasehold." In light of these circumstances, the Court agrees with the Bankruptcy Court's conclusions that the equitable subordination of USA Capital's lien is not warranted in this case.

As the Bankruptcy Court recognized, equitable subordination is an extraordinary remedy which is applied sparingly. The Bankruptcy Court's decision is consistent with this principle and with the case law requiring a more egregious level of inequitable conduct to warrant the equitable subordination of a non-insider's claim. Accordingly, the Court will affirm the Bankruptcy Court's Order denying BNY's motion for summary judgment to the extent that BNY sought equitable subordination of USA Capital's claim.

* * *

The bondholders discovered that it is a dog-eat-dog world out there, and sometimes you get bit even with a big dog on your side.

Whether or not the court in this case reached the right answer, the important point is that conduct of the sort involved in *Epic* could lead to equitable subordination of another lender under the right circumstances, including the possibility of effectively avoiding a security interest like the one held by USA Capital in this case. Especially interesting is the fact that this basis for equitable subordination would also support a suit for tortuous inducement of breach of contract under state law. The theory would be that USA Capital had wrongfully induced the debtor to grant a security interest in violation of the debtor's known contractual obligations to the bondholders.

It is often the case that claims of equitable subordination parallel various causes of action, generally in tort, that are available under state law. Another example is a lender liability suit, a state law action in which the debtor claims the lender took some wrongful act against the debtor and should pay damages. A classic example would be a claim that the lender had taken action under a security agreement in bad faith without notice or proper cause. Nothing in bankruptcy should change the substance of these tort claims or the ability of the debtor to collect. Because of the bankruptcy filing, however, the claims against the creditor become property of the estate, and any collections will necessarily affect either the reorganization effort or the distributions made to other creditors.

To the extent that a debtor may have some action against a creditor in a tortious inducement or lender liability suit, the DIP or TIB can be expected to pursue that action to fund the debtor's reorganization. But it is also possible that a claim for equitable subordination will be pursued in addition to, or in lieu of, the state law tort action.

Along the continuum of bad news for the creditor is the voidable preference (disgorge money received), then equitable subordination (get paid last), and finally tort liability (pay money to the debtor who originally borrowed money). The facts will sometimes support more than one option. The possibility for an affirmative recovery through a tort action obviously increases the DIP's leverage in negotiating with the lender in question. On the other hand, it is important to realize that these sorts of tort actions or equitable subordination actions brought by trustees or DIPs have been threatened far more than they have been brought and won.

The range of avoiding powers, including the exercise of state law actions either under section 544 or as property of the estate, give the DIP the opportunity to reexamine the pre-bankruptcy relationship between the debtor and each of its creditors. If some creditors have received more than the Bankruptcy Code or state law determines is their equitable share, then the DIP has the opportunity to reconfigure the relationships by using the powers outlined in this section. Not surprisingly, exercise of these powers is one of the central tools available to reorganize a failing business or to impose liquidation distributions that may differ from the position of the parties at the time of collapse.

The following intriguing article from the International Financial Law Review, a journal that provides a sophisticated audience with news about current international practice, is a good illustration of the tangled webs that are spun around control. For those who have not read about EuroDisney's beginnings, the project became infamous because in its planning to build a Disneyworld complex on the other side of the Atlantic, apparently the Disney management had failed to notice that northern France is considerably colder than Florida much of the year or that the French might be reluctant to spend the day at a place that did not offer alcohol of any kind. The consequence was that this Disney subsidiary got into serious financial difficulty almost from the opening day. At first, its American parent seemed to distance itself, suggesting that the European lenders and bondholders would just have to cope as best they could.

European terminology differs from that in the United States. A "de facto director" (or in the United Kingdom, a "shadow director") is an owner or lender who exercises such control as to be treated as if it were a director, leading often to results like those we associate with alter ego, piercing the corporate veil, or equitable subordination.

====== JOHN MCGRATH, THE LAWYERS ======
WHO REBUILT EURODISNEY

XIII   International Financial Law Review No. 5, p. 10 (1994)

Between March 4 and March 14 of this year, the Paris offices of Cleary, Gottlieb, Steen and Hamilton hosted a series of negotiations over the future of the loss-making theme park Euro-Disneyland and its operating company EuroDisney. . . .

Those at Cleary gave themselves until the end of March to reach an agreement over the park's future or face the consequences of closure. The time was not needed. A restructuring agreement was ready by the end of the second week in March. The negotiators offer several reasons for the swift conclusion of the talks: Disney's desperation to salvage its reputation for success, the banks' determination not to be left as operators of a theme park; and the French government's need to save the park it had fought so hard to open are most often cited.

One alternative explanation credits the judge and prosecutor at the court in Marne-la-Vallee, where EuroDisney is situated, with bringing the parties to the table. According to a lawyer involved in the talks, the judge telephoned the chief negotiators at Disney and the banks almost daily for six weeks prior to the March 14 agreement, to arrange dates for preliminary hearings on EuroDisney's insolvency.

LIABILITY

However, Disney's reluctance to negotiate at the end of 1993 provoked a response which may also have led to a prompt agreement on the restructuring. Then, Eisner locked out the banks' auditing team and threatened to close EuroDisney. For Georges Berlioz, founding partner of Paris law firm Berlioz &. Co, Eisner's stance was ill-advised. "If it was a negotiating technique, it was a very poor one. The first rule of negotiation is never threaten anything which could damage you more than the party you are threatening," he says. The penalties for breaking this rule rapidly became clear. Inflamed by Eisner's stance a small group of fund managers who held a large stake in the 1991 EuroDisney warrant issue contacted Berlioz. They asked him whether, as bondholders, they had a right to be represented at the negotiations and whether Disney was bound, by legal obligation, to respect the debts of EuroDisney.

According to Berlioz, this request could be reduced to a single question: "Is the fact that Disney is a minority shareholder, protected by EuroDisney's financial structure, sufficient to exonerate it from liability?"

The results of the Berlioz investigation were published on January 31, six weeks before the signing of the heads of the agreement. "What we showed," says Berlioz, "was that there were direct sources of liability under corporate law and banking law as well as under securities law because of the contractual management, technical assistance and so on. It is not only a question of de facto management but also of direct liability under the different legal relationships." Such liability, he stresses, would apply both outside and in the case of bankruptcy. That the report reached such conclusions is no surprise — one Paris lawyer says: "Berlioz has a reputation for taking strong positions and in this case that is exactly what the bondholders wanted him to do." However, although expected, the report's conclusions may have had a broader impact on the negotiations.

THE REPORT

Commenting on the labeling of Disney as a *de facto* director, one Paris-based project finance expert says: "This is always a problem, especially during a restructuring. The parent company and banks have to be very careful not to become too deeply involved or else they will assume the role of de facto directors. The Berlioz *Rapport Adam* considers this possibility with considerable clarity and the banks may have welcomed this as a negotiating tool." ...

According to the report, Disney assumed the role of director very early on in the development: "Throughout the whole process of negotiation with the government and in the promotion of the park, the direct involvement of the Walt Disney Company has always been very clear. Michael Eisner clearly showed his direct involvement from signing the letter of intention with the French state in 1985 until the opening ceremony in 1992, just as he did when he spoke of the eventual closing of the park."

The *Rapport Adam* considers Disney as *de facto* and *de jure* director to have committed several acts which would cause it to assume liability for EuroDisney's losses. These range from an ill-advised choice of site to over-optimistic evaluation of the property market to omissions and errors in the June 1991 offering circular for the FF42.265 billion convertible bond issue.

The June 1991 offering circular [bond prospectus — Eds.] is a worrying document. It relies, with very few amendments, on the financial projections which were used in 1989 for the share offer. The circular mentions proposed expansions in the theme park, upgrading of the hotels and other Phase 1 facilities, acceleration of the opening of the second theme park, the effect of the bonds on the company's profit projections and an analysis of actual pre-opening costs. It does not mention the collapse of the French property market, changes in the resort's cost structure and the Europe-wide recession. In addition, Berlioz says that two versions of the section on modification of the bonds were printed. Each contained differing information about the voting rights of bondholders and procedures for altering the condition of repayment. Disney has now agreed to honor only the version which is most favorable to the bondholders.

THE IMPACT OF THE RAPPORT ADAM

For Berlioz the best way to gauge the success of the report is to ask whether it achieved its goals. The report was intended to save the bondholders from a rescheduling of the repayment date or from an interest rate cut. It did this. Berlioz confirms that very soon after receiving copies of the

Rapport Adam Disney assured the bondholders that they would not be involved in the restructuring.

For Deckers at Slaughter and May the *Rapport Adam* was "instrumental in persuading Disney to deal because it brought out the potential liability of Disney. When Disney told the banks that they were not taking its position seriously it allowed the banks to reply that Disney was not taking its own liability seriously."

Others are eager to downplay the significance of *Rapport Adam.* For Terray, the lack of inside information must make the Berlioz report "more a journalist's paper than a lawyer's paper . . . it is very interesting and imaginative but it is not based on hard information about the company." Terray cites an audit carried out for the banks by consultants and accountants KPMG Peat Marwick as far more accurate. "Berlioz only had the press and the various offering circulars to rely on, whereas KPMG looked at the returns, interviewed staff and wrote its own account of the company."

The KPMG report, prepared for the banking syndicates by London-based corporate reconstruction partner Michael Wheeler, was intended to look at the financial structure of the company. Tim Roberts at KPMG in London stresses that Wheeler's findings remain confidential but does confirm that management consultants from the tourism consultancy group assisted Wheeler.

Deckers adds: "Part of KPMG's mandate was to investigate whether there was any evidence the banks could use to invoke Disney's liability. It was very much on the same wavelength as George Berlioz's investigations. That is why Disney's accountants Price Waterhouse were preventing them accessing documents."

However, Terray, who was asked to consider the KPMG report's legal implications says that it presents a very different picture from that offered by *Rapport Adam.* "The auditor's report does not express any conclusion that Disney would be liable as a de facto director in the case of bankruptcy," says Terray.

THE RESTRUCTURING CONTINUED

Neither Disney, EuroDisney nor their outside counsel were prepared to comment on any aspect of the *Rapport Adam. . . .*

———————

As an introduction to the Chapter 11 plan material coming next, here is the article's summary of the deal thus negotiated:

The heads of agreement signed on March 14, 1994 undertake to find an extra 12 billion francs ($2.09 billion) for EuroDisney to continue its operations. Under the agreement, 6 billion francs are expected to be raised from investors subscribing to a new share issue. The issue will be underwritten by some of the same banks that backed Disney in the original financing of the park and Disney will buy 49 percent of the shares. In addition the banks have agreed to an 18-month moratorium on loan repayments and a three-year interest holiday. In turn, Disney has agreed to waive its management fees and not to take its royalties on entrance fees and souvenir sales for five years. Disney will also buy and lease back two of the park's attractions, Discovery Mountain and the Temple of Doom.

The parties successfully negotiated a restructuring, but the business continued to struggle. By 2005 they were back into a new set of negotiations to reorganize the finances of the park. We can only hope to get as interesting an inside view the next time around.

Recharacterization and the Intersection of State and Federal Law

A common assertion in a number of bankruptcy contexts is that the bankruptcy court should recharacterize a transaction, a property right, or a contract, looking through its legal form to its substance. Perhaps the most common instance arises when a contract or lease is claimed to be a security interest in disguise, but there are many other examples as well. In most cases, the issue involves a bundle of rights created under state law that in turn are given important consequences in bankruptcy law.

An intriguing example is a case called In re Vanguard Airlines, Inc., 298 B.R. 626 (Bankr. W.D. Mo. 2003), in which the debtor claimed that a creditor with a purported security interest in certain aircraft was really a co-venturer (i.e., equity partner) with the debtor and not a true secured party. The issue in that case was whether the creditor was entitled to repossess airplanes under the special provisions of section 1110, which gives extraordinary protections to secured creditors (and certain others) with regard to aircraft held as collateral and states that these powers are "not limited or otherwise affected by any other provision of this title or by any power of the court." Despite this sweeping language the court held:

> Pursuant to the express wording of the statute, the prohibition on the Court's power is limited to actions by the secured party, lessor or conditional vendor to take possession of the equipment, enforce its rights and remedies against the equipment as provided in the underlying agreement, and to dispose of the equipment. There is no prohibition in the statute preventing the court from exercising its equitable power to recharacterize a creditor's interest as something other than a secured party, lessor, or conditional vendor.

The power to recharacterize is very potent indeed and therefore dangerous as well, because parties have often relied on the form of their legal agreements in their conduct, which includes lending large amounts of money. On the other hand, if recharacterization were not permitted, commercial law would become a sort of sport in which clever lawyers would practice at making a racehorse look like a milk cow.

The recharacterization cases also illustrate another point that runs through all of bankruptcy law. Many questions in bankruptcy lie at the intersection of nonbankruptcy law (usually state law) and bankruptcy law. For example, we learned in the consumer section of this book (p. 253) that whether a payment is a "domestic support obligation," including alimony, and therefore entitled to priority under section 507(a)(1) is a mixed question of state and federal law. State law determines the spouse's entitlement to the payments (and provides contrast with other arrangements between ex-spouses that are not part of a support order, such as property divisions or plain old contracts stemming from business partnerships). But it is federal law that determines the category into which that state law "bundle of rights" may fall for section 507 priority purposes. Thus in a state like Texas, where alimony is theoretically forbidden but payments serving that function are routinely awarded to spouses by Texas courts, federal law characterizes the payment as alimony for bankruptcy purposes even if a state court would never call it that.

This example is a good one precisely because it is one of the few that is easy to understand. Separating the issues of state and federal law in bankruptcy cases is frequently quite difficult. The problem is often exacerbated by the fact that a particular question may have one sort of importance in a typical dispute under state law but a different sort of importance in the context of bankruptcy. In some cases, the state law issue rarely arises at all, but may have all crucial impact on bankruptcy cases and bankruptcy policy. There are extreme instances were state law may actually be so constructed that it will virtually never be applied except in bankruptcy, another instance in which state legislatures may be trying to make bankruptcy law through the back door. Ronald Mann, The Rise of State Bankruptcy-Directed Legislation, 25 Cardozo L. Rev. 1805 (2004).

Problem Set 31

31.1. Limber Lumber was a medium-sized lumber wholesaler owned by Paul and Janet Logan, both of whom worked in the business. The Hamilton State Bank lent the company the money for the purchase of the company's assets and for operating capital. The bank loan was secured by a security interest in the company's accounts.

Paul and Janet have come to see you because the company's affairs are in desperate shape and you were the lawyer who first incorporated them and gave them some initial tax and pension advice. The recent housing slump has seriously hurt their sales, just at the time when preexisting contracts forced them to buy more inventory than they needed. The company missed its last two payments on its bank loan. About six weeks ago, Paul and Janet met with Bull Trout, who was introduced as the bank's "workout man." Trout was very loud and abusive. He demanded and got a second security agreement from the company covering the company's inventory and equipment. At a second meeting a week later, he also demanded a personal guarantee from Paul and Janet secured by their home and all their personal possessions. When they refused, he gave them a letter of foreclosure on the bank's liens.

Over the ensuing five weeks, Trout has been physically occupying the company's offices. All receivables are being collected directly by the bank. They have been told that Trout has assured the Lumberman's Credit Bureau, which represents nearly every supplier in the business, that Limber was not insolvent and would pay its bills. Yet Trout, who has taken over payment of all checks, has been paying creditors only when payment would enhance the chance of an account being collected, as, for example, when payment would keep a project going and thus make the owner willing to pay the company. The bank has ignored all other company obligations, including sales taxes. Since the bank took over, it has lent a substantial amount of additional money to the company, all of which has been used to pay bills to improve receivable collections or to pay employees being used in the liquidation process.

The bank has now advertised a sale of all the company's inventory. It was apparently willing to "go public" with the company's problems because nearly all accounts have been collected and the inventory is about as large as it could plausibly be. Paul and Janet have little hope for the survival of the business, but are very upset that virtually nothing will be left for the suppliers and customers who trusted them and for the members of their family who lent "start up" money to the company to help them out. What advice can you give them about the benefits, if any, that some kind of bankruptcy proceeding might bring?

Barney's Problem — Part V

Note: Unless otherwise indicated, the day this part of Barney's Problem is discussed in class is "deemed to be" March 1 of this year. This part of the problem, like the rest, is to be analyzed in "real time," i.e., as if you as counsel obtain the information or take the action indicated on the day (and the deemed date) the problem is to be discussed in class. All previous parts of the problem are incorporated into this part as of the day (and the deemed date) it is discussed in class, as if you were a sole practitioner in Aloysius and this small drama were real.

As you and your legal assistant continue to review the books of the Thornaby company, you find a new balance sheet Barney gave to the Aloysius State Bank. Barney warns that it is incomplete and may be inaccurate, since his bookkeeper is a Toyota salesman who took the bookkeeping course by mail.

Thornaby Co. Balance Sheet
(unaudited)
February 28

	Assets	
Current Assets		
Cash	$ 875	
A/R	407,000	
Work in Progress	50,000	
Supplies and Materials	110,000	
Equipment (at cost)	150,000	
Note Receivable —		
Whipsnade	50,000	
Total Current Assets		$767,875

Other Assets
  BAM Stock (at cost) $1,250,000
  Office Lease in shopping
    center (5 yr.)   25,000
  Construction Yard (at cost)   300,000
Total Other Assets $1,575,000
Total Assets $2,342,875

Liabilities and Net Worth

Current Liabilities
  A/P $385,000
  Payroll (3/5)   150,000
  Bank Loan — current   100,000
  Equipment Loans   89,000
Total Current Liabilities $ 724,000
  Other Liabilities
  BAM Guarantee   550,000
  Lease — Office   25,000
Construction Yard Mortgage   250,000
  Bank Loan (3 yr.)   300,000
  Subordinated Loans   325,000
Total Other Liabilities $1,450,000
Total Liabilities $2,174,000
  Net Worth
  Preferred Stock ($100/share)   150,000
    Common Stock
    (1,000 shares — $1 par)   1,000
  Retained Earnings   17,875
Net Worth (Stockholder's Equity) $ 168,875
Total Liabilities and Net Worth $2,342,875

There have also been two judgments against the company, one unrecorded but executed against one of the Darby "Dozer" dozers last week and the other recorded but unexecuted. Barney says a third judgment was executed against a tank of asphalt oil, but the creditor agreed to release the lien at a Christmas party while filled with Barney's excellent scotch. The creditor took payment of $500 in cash and the company's promise to pay the remaining $1,500 in 60 days; the promise was secured by a lien on all of the company's tools. Meanwhile the rent on the office is in arrears, and the landlord is making threatening gestures. The company has also received demands for return of ten tons of gravel delivered last week and for return of 12 cases of scotch the company bought on account for its Christmas party.

What instructions do you have for your legal assistant? What is your analysis and planning? Are you closer to final conclusions about the situation? Why?

E. NEGOTIATING AND CONFIRMING THE PLAN

The attorney who has worked through the debtor's financial condition and reviewed the legal tools available to reshape the emergent reorganized company should develop some view of a plan of reorganization. Key elements may include working out financing and a canny assessment of the places where the debtor should be able to exercise maximum leverage. The next step is negotiating a plan to repay the creditors and determine how the debtor will emerge from bankruptcy.

In this section we consider the requirements for confirmation of a plan in a Chapter 11 case set out in section 1129. One of the most important requirements is that a statutory majority of each class of creditors must vote in favor of the plan for the plan to be confirmed. §§1126, 1129(a)(8). Thus, before presenting a plan, a debtor must negotiate with the creditors to arrive at a plan that is acceptable to most creditors. The negotiations may be formal, through the creditors' committee (if there is one), or more informal. In the process of the negotiations, the other requirements for confirmation under section 1129 and related sections serve as constraints within which the developing plan must be shaped. Moreover, development of a plan requires interrelated negotiations. For example, a demand by one unsecured creditor for a larger payment than the other unsecured creditors will receive can create a legal problem — fair classification of creditors under section 1122(a), in addition to the practical problem of strong resistance from the other unsecured creditors.

1. Negotiation

a. The Process

We have one prelude to the legal requirements for a confirmable plan: a narrative of the largest out-of-court workout in American history. Chrysler Motor Corporation very nearly went bankrupt in the late 1970s. The story of its rescue is the best published account of the restructuring of a large public company that we have seen.

Today this giant corporation almost certainly would have gone into Chapter 11, but in 1980 bankruptcy law was in transition from the old Bankruptcy Act to the new Code, which became effective for cases filed after October 1, 1979. The new law was untried and had many important changes from prior law. Everyone anticipated that there would be unforeseen problems with it. Above all, the huge bankruptcies that began in the mid-1980s, in which companies almost as enormous as Chrysler succeeded in Chapter 11, still lay in the future.

For these reasons, Chrysler argued that it was far too risky for it to use bankruptcy to resolve its financial problems. It convinced Congress, many of its creditors, and its unions that it should be bailed out by a combination of private concessions and government guarantees. It claimed that the alternative was its collapse, producing the loss of hundreds of thousands of jobs and billions of dollars, the devastation of entire communities, and a significant weakening of the United States as a manufacturing nation.

Although Chrysler did not file for bankruptcy, the negotiations that are described below give a flavor of the kinds of negotiations that go on in a Chapter 11. A Chapter 11 is, after all, merely a formalized and rule-bound "workout," and the negotiations are much the same as they would be in an informal workout where debtor and creditors hope to reach agreement without bankruptcy. It is true that the federal government rarely plays a key role in a Chapter 11, as it did in the Chrysler negotiations, but for our purposes it is just one more player, along with the creditors, management, unions, and stockholders. Even today, many big Chapter 11 cases involve various governmental units. For example, state environmental agencies are frequently key players in the Chapter 11 of a polluting company and both state and federal regulatory authorities may be at the table demanding that the debtor comply with their edicts. Some debtors also try to follow Chrysler's model of drawing in the federal government to foot a large part of the bill. So far the asbestos companies have been largely unsuccessful, but the airlines have received a somewhat warmer reception. Regardless of the particular details, the dynamics recounted below are much the same in contemporary restructurings.

M. MORITZ AND B. SEAMAN, GOING FOR BROKE: THE CHRYSLER STORY
Chapter 13 (1981)

PATIENCE AND PRUDENCE

Bankers function by reference to prudence. It's imprudent for them to do anything until they have to.

— *Brian Freeman, Executive Director*
Chrysler Loan Guarantee Board

Unlike the cars that littered Detroit's parking lots, Chrysler's bankers were invisible. They did not rust in winter, sink to their ankles in mud or have weeds growing in their pockets — but the bankers were as deeply mired in Chrysler's rot as any sales bank auto that ever spent a week shivering in the Michigan state fairgrounds. Headquarters in twenty different countries and in almost every major city — banks or insurance companies held $4.75 billion worth of debt issued by Chrysler or Chrysler Financial. The loan agreements were written in English and French, Spanish and German, Italian and Japanese — even Persian.

In New York, bankers muttered about Chrysler around the locker rooms of the University Club and the Racquet and Tennis Club. Others fretted in the nation's regional money centers: inside Chicago's Loop, along Chestnut Street in Philadelphia, on Montgomery Street in San Francisco and in downtown Los Angeles. There were frowns in Atlanta and Houston and St. Louis and Denver. There were fervent debates about the virtues of free enterprise at monthly board meetings held in small towns across America: in Shreveport, Louisiana; in Gulfport, Mississippi; in Darlington, South Carolina; and in Sheboygan, Wisconsin. Abroad, bankers in Toronto and Ottawa, London and Frankfurt, Paris and Tokyo watched the tapping of their Telex machines. Almost everywhere people congregated to talk about money, Chrysler's name was mud.

Yet the key to the loan guarantees lying in the government vault was clasped by the banks. To be sure, other parties had to grant concessions before Chrysler could draw down on its loans, but no group proved as obdurate as the financial community. Within weeks of President Carter signing Public Law 96-185, the United Auto Workers had pared $462.5 million from its contract. Chrysler representatives fanned out to badger officials from state and local governments, trooping into offices in Lansing, Michigan; Springfield, Illinois; Dover, Delaware; Indianapolis, Indiana; Albany, New York; Jefferson City, Missouri; and Columbus, Ohio. Others traveled to Ottawa, the Canadian capital, to win aid from the government of Prime Minister Joe Clark. In Highland Park, the legal staff drew up yet another prospectus — this time for a private stock offering among the company's dealers and suppliers. Purchasing agents tried to shave more dollars off contracts with suppliers, while other negotiators drove down Woodward Avenue to bargain with Detroit Mayor Coleman Young. While all this was going on, it was the bankers who, for close to six months, seemed nearly as impassable, immovable and insurmountable a competitor as General Motors itself.

The initial restructuring of Chrysler's debt was, according to Treasury Secretary William Miller, the most complicated financial restructuring ever undertaken in the United States. It took Chrysler longer to obtain $655 million in concessions from its four hundred lenders than it did to win the $1.5 billion in loan guarantees from the 535-member United States Congress. Compared to Lockheed, which had dealt with only twenty-four banks, Chrysler's task was a nightmare. The banks were the one remaining vestige of the company's worldwide empire. The parent company dealt with 160 banks and had $1.18 billion worth of debt outstanding, while Chrysler Financial had dealings with 282 banks holding $2.5 billion. The parent company alone had lenders involved in twelve different agreements, and the total involvement of the banks ranged from the $163,000 lent by a combination of three small banks to the $211,895,000 extended by Manufacturers Hanover Trust. Some of the banks were only involved with Chrysler, others just with Chrysler Financial, and some with both. Chrysler had to grapple with the whims and wishes of two thousand lenders and negotiators. "We were proposing the preposterous," said Chrysler's senior financial officer, Jerry Greenwald, "to assume that all our lenders would stick together." After six months of intrigue, with negotiating sessions and parlous accords given names that sounded like those of battles and peace agreements from some nineteenth-century European war, Chrysler managed to persuade its lenders to sign on four hundred dotted lines. On occasion the company skirted bankruptcy by no more than a couple of hours, but finally, together with the banks and the Treasury Department, Chrysler sorted out terms far removed from the instructions of Congress: terms equally uncomfortable for all.

The Chrysler restructuring raised questions about the way in which some of the country's most prestigious banks monitor their substantial customers and about the propriety of a bank's involvement with a client. The negotiations forced to the surface many of the jealousies and rivalries that existed between the banks and finally caused all to ponder whether there might not be a more efficient way to deal with a large, sickly customer — or, indeed to deal with enterprise as a whole.

For the most part, the banks had not been all that interested in Chrysler while it continued to pay its interest and principal on time. Over the years the company had assiduously courted the financial community at home and abroad, and had turned to the banks to finance Lynn Townsend's global dreams. In 1971, when a dozen of Chrysler's twenty-three directors were also directors or trustees of major banks or financial institutions, the Wall Street Journal, in a masterpiece of understatement, noted that "Chrysler has strong bank ties." In 1979, of the thirteen outside directors on Chrysler's sixteen-member board, ten had affiliations with banks and other financial companies. . . .

As Chrysler began its tussle with the banks, one senior Treasury official remarked, "The real question is how the banks ever let Chrysler get into the position it reached." As Chrysler's debilitating losses slopped from one quarter to the next, it became startlingly clear that there was something strangely lacking in the bankers' credit analysis. "None of the bankers seriously thought that this major corporation was going to flop on its belly," said Ed Lord, an assistant vice-president at Barclay's Bank International. . . .

The bankers treated Chrysler much like any other major company. Although they gossiped among themselves that Chrysler had what they politely called "a distinct personality," they were content enough with the quarterly statements, annual reports and the SEC's more detailed 10-K forms issued by the company. . . .

Relying on Chrysler's own financial projections was, as the Treasury Department discovered in the fall of 1979, a dangerous habit. Jerry Greenwald admitted, "There wasn't the depth of the understanding in Chrysler of the depth of the problem." When the roof caved in, Greenwald observed, "The banks didn't even know what questions to ask." By the morning of December 21, 1979, just hours after the House and Senate Joint Conference Committee had sorted out the final terms of the aid package, the banks were beginning to shape some tough questions. Most had been holding their breath, waiting to see what would roll down Capitol Hill. Few had followed the congressional debate closely and scarcely any were intimately familiar with the role that they were being asked to play.

Congress had stated its case plainly enough. Indeed, the provisions of the Loan Guarantee Act that applied to the financial community were beguilingly simple, thanks largely to officials from the Treasury Department, who were determined to retain the maximum amount of flexibility. The U.S. banks and financial institutions were asked to make concessions of $500 million — $400 million in "new loans" and $100 million in "concessions" with respect to outstanding debt. The foreign banks were asked to provide $150 million in "new loans or credits." Both the domestic and foreign financiers were informed by Congress that the $650 million they were to provide was to come on top of all loans committed to Chrysler and Chrysler Financial before October 17, 1979, the date Chrysler's final operating plan had been sent to the Treasury Department.

To bankers and lawyers long used to poring over the fine print of loan agreements, the terms of the act were comfortingly vague. The thirteen lines that applied directly to the banks did not define "concessions" and made no reference to how the burden should be split. The bankers did not know whether concessions referred to deferrals of interest payments or outright gifts. They didn't know whether the Loan Guarantee Board could modify the act or what sort of conditions they could make before granting any aid. "Congress doesn't understand finance," said Steve Miller, then Chrysler's assistant treasurer, who headed the banking negotiations. "Congress understands politics." Chrysler's lenders were faced with a choice: they could either force a bankruptcy and let their lawyers salvage some of the loans in the musty confines of a bankruptcy court, or they could make concessions.

It was Greenwald who spelled out what concessions the company wanted in "the pit," a second-floor conference room at Manufacturers Hanover's New York headquarters. Greenwald had bad news for the representatives of the U.S. banks sitting around the conference table. He briefly explained the terms of the Loan Guarantee Act, barely concealing his impatience when some of the bankers asked questions about clauses which had formed part of the House and Senate bills from the start of the congressional debate. Noting that Congress had refused to provide a loan to bridge the period before the federal guarantees started to flow, Greenwald asked for an immediate $500 million loan to tide the company over. He had $800 million of bills to pay within the month and $100 million left in the till. He stuck by his projections that Chrysler would soon be plumb out of cash, and offered the Trenton engine plant, the New Process gear plant in Syracuse, 1.8 million shares of Peugeot stock and an inventory of unsold cars as security. The bankers scoffed at the notion of security. A secured credit, they argued, was only as good as the claim on the assets, and the government had established a senior claim on all but $400 million of Chrysler's assets. A last-minute clause in the bill, the result of an explosive burst of lobbying, allowed the Loan Guarantee Board to give equal claims on up to $400 million of the company's assets. In addition, the banks wanted to know what an engine plant would be worth without a company that produced cars.

The bankers were not feeling charitable. Most hooted at the act, calling it "The Suppliers Loan Guarantee Act." The future of Chrysler, the bankers were convinced, was for the benefit of suppliers and workers. The banks, they quietly murmured, were innocent victims. Chrysler had, after all, made mincemeat of all its loan agreements. All the cleverly devised ratios, interest coverages and working-capital balances had been shredded. Chrysler not only had stopped paying debts that were coming due, it was also expected to violate what was supposedly a sacred undertaking in the world of international finance: a credit agreement with a group of Japanese banks who financed the import of Mitsubishi cars. (In the middle of January 1980, Chrysler actually stopped payments to the Japanese.)

Greenwald dropped his final bomb when he asked Steve Miller and a Los Angeles bankruptcy expert, Ron Trost, to explain the details of a ten-page "Memo for Liquidation" which had been frantically prepared in a suite at the Carlyle Hotel during the previous few days. The tersely worded memo was

Chrysler's own doomsday pamphlet, and it dealt a blow to what for some banks had become a part of the company folklore: that the assets of Chrysler Corporation and Chrysler Financial were separable in a bankruptcy. The bankers were told that the situation was so complex that both the parent company and the subsidiary would tumble into the same barrel. Even more disconcerting was Chrysler's opinion that the banks, all unsecured creditors to Chrysler Financial, would, during the course of lengthy bankruptcy proceedings, only be entitled to the low "legal" rate of 6 percent interest. To top things off, Chrysler told the bankers that the Pension Benefit Guarantee Corporation would probably have a senior claim to the company's assets. For the bankers, who had three times as much tied up in the finance company as in the parent corporation, the news was something they had privately feared but had never before heard directly from the company. Furthermore, they disagreed with Chrysler's analysis. Instead of salvaging all their loans to the finance arm, they stood to win as little as seventy-five cents on the dollar if the court battles lasted for five years. That, together with the expectation of a payoff as low as ten cents on the dollar for loans extended to Chrysler Corporation, shattered the bankers' decorum. They started to interrupt Greenwald, snorting with derision at some of the arguments and insinuating that Chrysler had purposely concealed the news. The banks desperately wanted to separate Chrysler from CFC so that the former could be pushed into bankruptcy without jeopardizing loans to the latter. When Chrysler announced that both the parent and CFC would fall together, it was not just an analysis but a threat. Altogether it was an unpleasant and inauspicious start.

The bankers already knew enough about Chrysler Financial, which had felt tremors from Chrysler's chronic condition long before Washington started to quake. Pleased with the experience of joint ventures in Europe with France's largest finance company, Sobac (controlled by the investment banking firm of Lazard Freres), and in Britain with the Mercantile Credit Company, Gordon Areen, the cherubic president of the financial subsidiary, had, in the spring of 1978, started tentative discussions about the possibility of joint ventures in other countries, including the United States. The talks had formed one part of John Riccardo's efforts to raise money to finance Chrysler's spending program. Although the finance company helped Chrysler sell cars both to dealers and to retail customers, it was an expensive operation. Chrysler had twice the amount (in relative terms) plowed into Chrysler Financial than GM had invested in General Motors Acceptance Corporation and Ford in Ford Motor Credit. Toward the end of 1978, Areen had made a further attempt to slice off part of his company, but negotiations stalled with the turmoil following the arrival of Lee Iacocca and the devastating events of the spring of 1979. The irony did not escape Areen: with $48.5 million in profits, 1978 was the best year ever for the company he had headed since 1964.

Easter week of 1979 brought disaster. Confronted with reports of the parent company's losses, the two credit-rating agencies, Moody's and Standard and Poors, lowered Chrysler Financial's debt ratings and commercial paper ratings. (Like all similar companies, Chrysler Financial depended on good credit ratings to borrow money at rates that allowed it to make profits from its loans.) Chrysler Financial could not, despite its impeccable record, be given ratings higher than those awarded Chrysler, on whom it depended for future business. For the first time ever, both agencies had lowered all their ratings for both Chrysler and the finance company. "Once the ratings were lowered," Areen recalled, "the banks knew it was raining." Two bankers knew that it was pouring cats and dogs. Chemical Bank's Benjamin McCleary and Morgan Guaranty's Richard Flinthoft dashed to Washington to brief the Treasury Department while an official at the Federal Reserve Board in New York monitored Chrysler Financial's every move.

Deprived of access to the short-term debt market and the commercial paper market, the finance company was thrown back on the more expensive credit lines it had painstakingly negotiated with each of its 282 lenders over the previous few years. The credit lines were designed as a form of insurance to cover temporary instability in the short-term paper market or a disruption within Chrysler or the auto industry. The loss of the ratings marked the start of what was a perpetual theme throughout the restructuring of Chrysler. Some of the smaller banks had seen enough and were so terrified by the sight of Chrysler Financial borrowing $50 million-a-day that they abruptly canceled their credit lines and fled. The First National Bank of Atlanta, for one, used a deposit of Chrysler Financial to reduce the size of its loan to the company — an action that provoked an angry response from bankers whose obligations to Chrysler were too large to seize without provoking an immediate bankruptcy. Indeed, Areen and his staff couldn't even draw down on all their credit lines lest they violate conditions of some of the loan covenants which, in turn, would accelerate the maturity of debt repayments and threaten the stability of the entire company. It was largely to quell the fears of the small lenders and shore up his company's rapidly crumbling buttresses that Areen turned to other alternatives.

One of the first stops was with other finance companies, and here the ties of the trade were more than helpful. One morning Bob Baker, a Chrysler Financial vice-president as well as president of the National Consumer Finance Association, took a telephone call from Gilbert Ellis, chairman of the Executive Committee of the association. Thinking that the call concerned the association's affairs, Baker was delighted to discover that Ellis, who doubled as the chairman of Household Finance, the third-largest financial company in the United States, was offering help. Areen and Baker grabbed at the offer and within days teams of officials from Household Finance were scouring records at Chrysler Financial's headquarters and its branch offices. After Ellis and the president of Household Finance, Donald Clark, had lunched with John Riccardo and Lee Iacocca, the sale of $500 million of accounts receivable (the payments owed by dealers and car buyers) was set. In a separate agreement, Areen sold another $230 million to General Motors Acceptance Corporation. The sales shrank Chrysler Financial by one-third, reduced its borrowing needs and allowed Areen and his colleagues to start mollifying the bankers.

The banks were more difficult to please than some finance companies eager to expand their business by snapping up some high-quality loans. At the end of July 1979, while John Riccardo was gearing up for his $1 billion pitch for tax relief, Areen was preparing an appeal of his own. He outlined his plan at a meeting with representatives of twenty-six of the nation's leading banks, held in Manufacturers Hanover's Park Avenue office. It was here that the tensions and anxieties within the banking community and many of the arguments used repeatedly during the restructuring of Chrysler were voiced for the first time. Areen asked the bankers to substitute a revolving credit agreement for the lines of credit they had extended to Chrysler Financial. The choice of Manufacturers Hanover as a venue was natural enough. Manny Hanny, as it is familiarly called, was the largest correspondent bank in the United States and had long had ties with Chrysler. It had been the automaker's agent bank for years, acting as a financial shepherd to the ever-expanding flock of banks. In 1970 and 1974, when Chrysler had previously encountered stormy weather Manny Hanny had launched the lifeboats. In the first crisis, which occurred after the collapse of the Penn Central, the bank's vice-chairman, John McGillicuddy, had flown all over the country with Gordon Areen and Lynn Townsend, pacifying nervous bankers. Four years later, McGillicuddy and Manny Hanny had played a prominent role in establishing a $455 million revolving credit agreement. In 1979, McGillicuddy, invited to appear before both House and Senate Committees, testified strongly in favor of federal aid. "We are not a bank that wants to close down plants and run for the hills," said senior vice-president William Langley.

Some of the other U.S. banks were suspicious about Manny Hanny's relationship with Chrysler. "There was a perception that the bank was soft on Chrysler," said one lawyer involved in the restructuring. "They had rescued Chrysler originally and were heroes. They had a vested interest in seeing that the rescue didn't collapse into failure." Some other bankers were less charitable. Noted Barclay's Ed Lord, "They were asleep at the switch. They should have been sounding the red alert earlier." The fact that McGillicuddy's predecessor as chairman, Gabriel Hauge, was a Chrysler director and that Hauge's predecessor, Robert McNeill, had also sat on Chrysler's board did not go unnoticed. Indeed, Lynn Townsend had been a director of Manufacturers Hanover for nine years.

While McGillicuddy testified in support of Chrysler, other bankers, especially Citibank's Walter Wriston and A. W. "Tom" Clausen, president of the Bank of America, voiced their opposition to a federal bailout and thereby underlined Manny Hanny's isolation. Manufacturers Hanover, the other banks felt, had far more riding on its relationship with Chrysler than the $246.3 million it had committed. At the August meeting, Manufacturers Hanover proposed to the other banks that they all extend their lending commitments to Chrysler Financial for one year as a show of support and a rallying point for the banks that had canceled their credit lines. The other New York banks — especially Citibank, Morgan Guaranty and Chemical — would have no part of any such deal. If Chrysler hoped to get a revolving credit agreement, all the banks that had fled would have to participate. The New Yorkers were contemptuous of the smaller banks, many of whom had scuttled away to the corners during previous credit crunches. Said one banker, "It's as if you put four hundred people in a skyscraper office with just one window and the whole place catches fire. If you tell them that only four can get out the window, it just won't work." By October 17 the debt had been restructured. Chrysler Financial Corporation had agreed to a 35-percent reduction in the banks participating in its revolving credit agreement and CFC also agreed to maintain $94 million in lines of credit with some of the banks that had refused to join the revolving credit system. In exchange for these concessions, the banks had to settle for a revolving credit arrangement that included only 200 of the company's 282 banks and that had shrunk from $1.8 billion to $919 million. The banks had also cannily changed some of the terms of the agreement, to prevent the siphoning off of money from Chrysler Financial into the gulping parent company — a ploy designed to help isolate Chrysler Financial in the event of a bankruptcy.

Though some of the terms of the renegotiated credit for Chrysler Financial had been specially worded to insulate it from the problems of the parent company, the Memo for Liquidation that was read to the bankers on the Friday before Christmas 1979 set the tone for the following weeks. The bankers assumed that Chrysler would try to sell part, or all, of the financial subsidiary and for the succeeding weeks they concentrated on the parent company. In early January 1980, the banks suffered another set of shocks when Chrysler outlined the form it would like the financial community's concessions to take.

Steve Miller asked the banks to lower the rate of interest on all the loans outstanding to one percent, extending this relief to the parent company for four years and to the financial company for one year. The savings, Chrysler reckoned, would amount to more than $400 million during the first year alone. The banks, not surprisingly, refused the proposal and added that they certainly would not consider making new loans to the company as required in the Loan Guarantee Act. Nothing had changed since Manny Hanny's John McGillicuddy had noted in his congressional testimony, "We don't lend money in circumstances in which we don't expect to be repaid, and that's where Chrysler Corporation is."

Chrysler also asked the banks to restore $159 million of the $567.5 million U.S. revolving credit agreements, which had been frozen when the losses started to heap up in the summer of 1979. During the Washington debate, senators and congressmen had used the $159 million of frozen credit to illustrate (depending on their inclinations) either the obduracy of the banks or the futility of Chrysler's cause. The majority of the U.S. banks had been in favor of canceling the entire $567.5 million credit agreement (though there was little hope of getting the money back) but heavy lobbying by Manny Hanny in the fall of 1979 had ensured that the credit agreement (including the frozen $159 million) remained. The other lenders, the foreign banks and the insurance companies, had squinted at the haggling of the U.S. banks. Cancellation of the agreement would have been interpreted as a signal that the banks were reconciled to bankruptcy proceedings, but the nature of the final equivocal verdict meant that the U.S. banks had given their tacit, if grudging, approval for a restructuring.

However, the American banks formed just one part of Chrysler's panoply of lenders. With the start of the restructuring, the financial community had to decide how to distribute the burden. In circles where it was notoriously tricky to convince ten people that the sun rises in the east, it became a hideous task. The sharing of the burden became a test of strength, fragile alliances and organization. The U.S. banks, however, did manage to gain one early advantage over other lenders. They had already organized a committee of representatives to deal with the rejuggling of Chrysler Financial's debt. In the middle of January 1980, a recast committee, chaired by Garry Scheuring, a vice-president of Continental Illinois, was separated into working groups to investigate Chrysler's remaining sources of funds, the shape of a possible restructuring and the prospects for bankruptcy. Though the smaller and larger banks disagreed vehemently about the depth of their commitments to Chrysler, they all were united on one issue: Congress, they felt, had dealt them a raw hand. The contributions required from U.S. financiers represented a doubling of their outstanding loans to the company and saddled them with two-thirds of the aid being sought from the world financial community, even though they held only about one-third of the credit commitments made by Chrysler. Foreign banks, which had eagerly fought to provide two-thirds of the total lines, were only asked to contribute a small part of the package.

The European lenders, on the other hand, came from countries that spoke different languages [and] had diverse financial customs and private economic worries. . . . Both the European and the Japanese lenders believed that the Americans were playing a waiting game and would eventually settle Chrysler's problems among themselves. . . .

For Chrysler, already choking on debt and struggling to cope with interest rates around 20 percent, the banks' refusal to furnish fresh loans was an oblique act of charity. For close to three months the company and its lenders batted about alternative suggestions centering on the interest Chrysler owed on its debts. The committees representing U.S. and European lenders struggled to design a package that would reduce the rate of interest and allow some deferral of interest payments. Each time one party made a suggestion, the other lenders immediately wanted to know the overall effect. To help speed negotiations, Scott Taylor, a Chase Manhattan vice-president, programmed his own Radio Shack computer to spit out various plans. Meanwhile, Chrysler's Steve Miller was engaged in the same pursuit with his Apple II computer in the den of his Michigan home.

The arduous talks with the banks developed their own characteristic pattern. Every morning a facsimile of Chrysler's daily cash statement was electronically transmitted to the company's New York lawyers. Each day Miller and his associates pored over the five-page statement, which became a measure of the fading corporate pulse, to see if there was enough money left to pay the Friday wage bills. Twice a month, on the tenth and the twenty-fifth, Miller had to gear up for the average $400 million in payments owed to suppliers. For Miller, who had joined Chrysler in October 1979 at the invitation of his former boss at Ford Venezuela, Jerry Greenwald, it was baptism by the numbers. Known to the bankers as "Little Miller" (to distinguish him from Treasury Secretary G. William Miller), the 220 pound, 6-foot-4-inch Harvard and Stanford graduate had been hired as an assistant treasurer. Within weeks, he was Chrysler's direct and tenacious mouthpiece to the international financial community.

Every Friday, Miller would wing back to Detroit for brutal all-day meetings with Greenwald. Starting at 7:30 in the morning, the pair, along with colleagues, would listen to fifteen-minute reviews from each of the twenty-two task forces appointed to nail down one piece of the package Chrysler needed to qualify for the loan guarantees. Each task force would give a terse progress report on its negotiations with state and local governments, the suppliers, Mitsubishi and all the other parties. On Tuesdays, Brian Freeman, the executive director of the Chrysler Loan Board, would fly to Detroit to monitor Chrysler's progress. Through this grueling process, Chrysler slowly developed useful operating and cash-flow plans that had been absent when Riccardo first went to Washington.

Miller, Greenwald and the banks all had dates ringed on their calendars, which later became known as "D-D Days" (Drop-Dead Days). On several occasions the company picked a date on which, it told its lenders, there would be no cash left in the till. The first D-D Day occurred in the middle of January and was avoided by a delay of payments to suppliers. The second was avoided when Chrysler suspended its payments to the Japanese banks that financed the import of Mitsubishi vehicles. Chrysler's third D-D Day was its most important. Having secured a $100 million loan from Peugeot by pledging its 1.8 million shares of the French automaker, Chrysler needed the banks to agree to waive their rights to the stock. The banks' subsequent compliance provided the first sign of unanimity.

Toward the end of March, as the self-imposed April 1 deadline for qualifying for federal aid loomed and rumors of stinging inquisitions from the Senate and House banking committees began to circulate, the bankers began to feel the pressure. For their part, the banks, in a glittering convention of twenty-five chief executive officers, had explained to Robert Carswell, the Deputy Secretary of the Treasury, and to Elmer Staats, the Comptroller of the Currency, that they would not be able to comply with the letter of the Loan Guarantee Act. As March drew to a close, representatives of the four major groups of lenders — the U.S. banks, the Europeans, the Canadians and the insurance companies — were summoned to thrash out a compromise that could be presented to the Loan Guarantee Board. It had taken three months for representatives of all the lenders to meet around the same table. While the silver market crashed and the Hunt Brothers lost a fortune, the lenders met in the Chrysler boardroom on the 54th floor of the Pan Am Building. Even a take-out order to a local delicatessen underlined the fragility of the talks. On learning that the order came from Chrysler's lenders, the deli demanded payment before it agreed to deliver the sandwiches. Finally, after two inconclusive days of bargaining, a group of eight American and European bankers adjourned for dinner at the Waldorf-Astoria to hammer out what was later known as "The Waldorf Agreement."

The financial concordat, reached over rounds of English stout and Heineken, modified the concessions to be given by the European banks, allowing them to save face in return for having been squeezed by the Americans into providing a greater share of the overall financial contribution. Satisfied that a deal was at hand, Michael Rayfield, a flamboyant senior vice-president from Britain's Barclay's International, bade the maitre d' open a $200 magnum of Dom Perignon '54 — "the kind that James Bond drinks." Although the Americans nervously protested that the unofficial gathering hadn't agreed to anything, they sipped champagne, wondering all the while whether the other lenders would agree to the latest deal.

Hours after Rayfield and his colleagues had downed the last drop of champagne, Steve Miller had a nasty shock for the bankers as they filed into the Chrysler boardroom for a meeting where contributions from the various parties were to be settled once and for all. An unusually subdued Miller started with an announcement. The management of Chrysler, he told the financiers, had pored over projections for the economy, the automobile industry and the company in hours of meetings the day before. After a detailed review, the senior management had decided that Chrysler stood no chance of survival, and a small group of directors had concurred. As a result, Miller continued, in a room that was quieter than a vault, Chrysler had filed for bankruptcy earlier that morning. Pencils and pens crashed to the oak boardroom table as Miller politely thanked the bankers for all their efforts over the previous months.

Jerry Greenwald, sitting in on the meeting, was as astonished as the bankers. Gauging the impact of his remarks, Miller began to bluster. "It's April Fool's Day. It's a joke," he said. The room filled with nervous mirth as the glum group erupted into cheers. "It wasn't very damn funny," said one banker. "We believed him." Miller's idea of humor served a purpose: it convinced the bankers of the need to complete as quickly as possible the restructuring of the parent company. However, two days after a compromise had been reached, the lenders were hit with another piece of bad news. Negotiations for the sale of Chrysler Financial had capsized in the turbulent wake of the Federal Reserve Board's credit crunch of mid-March. Prior to the hike in interest rates, Chrysler Financial president Gordon Areen had conducted further talks with his counterparts at Household Finance. The finance company had stated its willingness to purchase 31 percent of Chrysler Financial, provided that the banks purchase another 20 percent. Leery of dealing with a bevy of partners, Household Finance wanted to limit the partnership to one or two banks. For their part, the banks were skeptical about the legal implications of holding stock in a company to which they had loans outstanding. It was largely on the hazy relationship between stockholder and creditor that the talks snagged. For the rest of the lenders, it meant yet another bout of bone-wearying days and nights restructuring the debt of Chrysler Financial before Steve Miller could announce to a meeting of four hundred bankers in Detroit on April 17 that Chrysler had finally reached agreement with its banks.

The Treasury Department, however, was not under the impression that an agreement had been reached. Ever since the start of the negotiations, members of the Treasury's office of Chrysler Finance had stayed on the sidelines, watching while the lenders tussled, but after Chrysler presented its restructuring plan, the Treasury Department minutely examined the precisely worded language of the loan covenants, peering at phrases and clauses that would determine whether the fate of Chrysler and Chrysler Financial was in the hands of the government or the banks.

As Treasury officials explained their misgivings to the bankers convened in the echoing Treasury cash room, it became clear that there was plenty of tough bargaining left. For a start, the men at the Treasury were unhappy that the banks had failed to take an equity stake in the company. A bank purchase of stock, the government officials believed, offered the only manageable way for Chrysler to reduce its crippling load of debt and offered a slim chance that the company might eventually be able to sell new debt. The Treasury, in short, wanted the banks to buy $750 million of Chrysler stock and wanted an increase or extension of the credit available to Chrysler Financial.

For yet another eight days, teams of bankers and lawyers camped out in the plush surroundings of Washington's Madison Hotel, negotiating separately and ponderously on Chrysler and Chrysler Financial. Messages were shuttled between the banks and the Treasury Department, where Roger Altman, an assistant secretary, held arrogant court. Finally the banks agreed to purchase Chrysler equity by exchanging delayed interest payments for stock. The loans to the financial arm were extended and the Treasury Department successfully enforced clauses that prevented the banks from draining money from Chrysler to the finance company. After the agreement was hammered out, another three weeks were consumed as the Canadian, Japanese and European banks sought to make deals of their own. The Canadians especially, negotiating with Chrysler's Canadian subsidiary, proved defiant. For close to two weeks, it looked as if the Canadians would steal a march by collecting interest from Chrysler almost three years before the other lenders. For their part, the Europeans disliked the prospect of being forced to take an equity stock in a fading American automaker. After Chrysler and Treasury negotiators played shuttle diplomacy in Toronto and around the major cities of Europe, the most complicated part of the concessions needed to qualify for the loan guarantees was completed.

As for the rest of the package, many of its features bore barely any resemblance to the terms laid down by Congress. The banks, after all, had not come forward with any new loans. Besides, though the UAW had conceded $462.5 million and Chrysler's non-union employees had forgone the appropriate $125 million, Chrysler had not completed the necessary sale of assets, had been unable to sell additional equity and had not been able to stimulate the level of support stipulated for suppliers and dealers. Any resemblance between the Chrysler plan and the requirements of Congress was difficult to detect.

With the Canadian bankers finally pacified, Chrysler started work on the final agreement. Lawyers representing more than fifty law firms helped the investment bankers draft the documents to be signed by every bank. The legal and financial help did not come at cut-price rates. Chrysler eventually paid financial and legal fees of more than $20 million. To get the agreements printed as quickly as possible, the work was split between Sorg Printing Company and Bowne and Company, the two largest financial printing firms in the country, who were more used to dealing with evening drop-offs and morning pick-ups of corporate stock issues. The printing bill: $2 million. Before the banks could be asked to sign the legal documents, Steve Miller had to sign on behalf of Chrysler. He spent an entire day at the printers', signing each of the four thousand documents. One assistant opened each document to the proper page, another stamped in Miller's title, while a third counted and stored the signed papers. Stacked on top of each other, the boxes of documents would have topped seventy feet. As each box was filled, it was trundled off to the three New York metropolitan area airports for shipment to the banks.

By June 10, Chrysler had run out of a $150 million loan from the State of Michigan furnished six weeks before and could not pay the $50 million of supplier bills that were coming due. Every hackneyed automotive cliché could not describe Chrysler's condition. The road had never been rockier, nor the lanes narrower. The gas gauge pointed to empty and even the fumes had dried up. Chrysler had stopped. Some banks were now threatening to let the air out of the corporate tires.

Twenty banks — some foreign, some domestic, most small and all with relatively minor loans to Chrysler outstanding — were refusing to sign the loan agreements. All wanted their money and all hoped that some of the major banks would pay them off on the courthouse steps, but the reasons for their reluctance varied. For some, it was a matter of national pride. For others, shaky financial conditions or belligerent shareholders and directors handcuffed executives. In other cases, there had been a change in management since the loans had been made. Although the "recalcitrants," as Chrysler immediately called them, only held $33 million of the total $4.75 billion debt, they threatened the aid package to such an extent that the meeting of the Loan Guarantee Board where all was to be finalized had to be postponed three times.

Chrysler had no time for niceties and needed four hundred pinstriped ducks lined up in an unwavering row. On June 13, Steve Miller met with senators and members of the House in Washington, clutching a list of twenty banks. The list included the West German Deutsche Genossenschaftsbank, which had seized an $8 million payment heading from Volkswagen to Chrysler. Meanwhile, Banque Bruxelles Lambert of Belgium had filed suit for a $10 million loan Chrysler had failed to repay. In the United States, the Bank of the Southwest in Houston, York Bank and Trust in York, Pennsylvania, the Whitney National Bank of New Orleans and the Peoples Trust of Fort Wayne, Indiana, felt slighted by the major banks.

Once more Chrysler marshaled its battalions of lobbyists. With the aid of its top banks, yet another computerized list was assembled. This time it contained the business connections and names of every officer and director of the banks encircling the financial stockade. Calls were made by John McGillicuddy from Manufacturers Hanover and by William Miller from the Treasury Department. Richard Cummings, the vice-chairman of one of Chrysler's staunchest allies, the National Bank of Detroit, took to the road to persuade some of his nervous colleagues. As Gordon Areen left Chrysler Financial's headquarters to lend his muscle, subordinates joked that they were sending the gorilla out again. Steve Miller, who had made 116 flights during the restructuring, took to the air.

Standing almost in the shadow of Chrysler's truck-assembly plant in St. Louis, the Crestwood Metro Bank felt the heat. Citing, like many of the other dissidents, prudent banking management, Crestwood stood fast, but finally the resistance crumpled. "We realize we're nowhere without Chrysler in business," said a Crestwood official. "We're somewhere with them still in business." By far the toughest nut to crack was David W. Knapp, the bespectacled president of the American National Bank and Trust Company of Rockford, Illinois. Steve Miller, Gordon Areen and Wendell Larsen all flew to Rockford to try to persuade Knapp to join the club. Circling the town on June 18 they finally found the city hall, where the meeting with Knapp had been convened in the mayor's office, parked their Dodge Omni at the foot of the steps and were promptly met by a gaggle of reporters, TV cameras and photographers. Knapp remained unmoved by the arguments. "If you take a loan, you pay it back," he told the Chrysler men. Even a barrage of telephone calls from the mighty of the financial world left him undaunted. "Their crystal ball tells them this solves the problem," Knapp countered. "Mine doesn't." Knapp, who seemed to revel in the attention, told reporters that his bank was "just not interested" in saving Chrysler.

Following their unsuccessful meeting, Miller held a press conference, snippets of which played on that night's network newscasts. Miller predicted that Chrysler would be bankrupt in a matter of days if Knapp refused to sign. Within hours, the people of Rockford, many of whom worked at the nearby Chrysler Belvidere plant, started to picket the bank and withdraw deposits. It was the withdrawals, which could have turned into a run on the bank, and what Knapp, in a masterful understatement, called "a certain divisiveness in the community," that helped him change his mind. Threatening phone calls and a bomb scare finally convinced the president of the American National Bank and Trust Company of Rockford to let Chrysler live to fight another day.

On June 20, the final domestic holdout, the Twin City Bank of North Little Rock, Arkansas, was treated to a Chrysler double act. Steve Miller arrived after flying through the night and Gordon Areen ducked in beneath a heavy bank of fog in a propeller-driven Queen-Air. The bank, which had $78,000 loaned to Chrysler, buckled and was followed shortly afterward by West Germany's DG Bank.

All that remained was the final act of any loan agreement: the closing. Even that nearly failed. Chrysler's first problem was to locate documents stuck in an airport strike in Beirut. With a $15,000 chartered plane standing by in Paris to whisk the documents to an airport for an international flight to New York, they were finally taken to a local American consulate, from where their authenticity was conveyed to the Loan Guarantee Board. The night before the closing, though, the documents, the loan agreement, the federal aid package and Chrysler all nearly went up in smoke.

On June 23, as dusk settled over Manhattan, Chrysler's lawyers were putting the finishing touches on the loan agreement, thirty-three floors above Park Avenue in the office of Debevoise, Plimpton, Lyons and Gates, when wisps of black smoke started to curl past the windows. The lawyers and bankers trooped down an emergency staircase with some joking that the fire was "Rockford's Revenge," but what started in the Bank of America's computer center quickly caught hold, melted the aluminum stair railings and sent buckling sheets of glass cascading to the street below. Jerry Greenwald was strolling toward the law office when he bumped into Steve Miller, heading for a local restaurant. "Can you imagine if that was our building?" Greenwald asked Miller as he looked at the fire trucks pulling up to the Westvaco Building. It was.

The fire, fought by 125 firemen, was the worst skyscraper blaze in New York for twenty years. At 2 A.M., a small group of diehard bankers and lawyers argued their way past police barricades, struggled through the smoke that obscured the ends of hallways and stuffed the soot-covered documents into fifty cardboard boxes and twelve metal mail carts. At 2:30 A.M., hours before the deal was due to close, a straggling caravan wheeled Chrysler's future up Park Avenue and over to the Citicorp Center law offices of Shearman and Sterling.

Ten hours later, a hundred people jammed the conference room where the documents had been hastily reassembled. Speaker phones lined the walls and Debevoise lawyer Richard Kahn began to call the roll. Other law offices in New York said they were ready; from Washington, the three members of the Loan Guarantee Board said they were ready. From Paris and Toronto, there were similar responses. Finally, Steve Miller was asked whether Chrysler was ready. At 12:26 P.M. on June 24, eleven months after John Riccardo had asked for tax relief and six months after President Carter had signed the Loan Guarantee Act, Chrysler had permission to draw down its first $500 million of guaranteed loans.

Once the negotiation was concluded, Chrysler acquired a new asset named Lee Iacocca and the rest is history — a very successful reorganization. It is interesting to note that the Chrysler deal had all the key elements of a Chapter 11 reorganization, including a "standstill" agreement among creditors that provided a consensual automatic stay, an acceptance of "haircuts" that equaled a discharge, equality of treatment among similarly situated creditors that was like pro rata distribution, and commercial pressures that "crammed down" the deal on the creditors who wanted to say no. Chrysler illustrates how all parties operate in the shadow of the law to create non-bankruptcy bankruptcies, if they have the time and money to negotiate for such a solution. For the remainder of this chapter we turn to the much more common case in which the law provides the structure — and the clout — that Chrysler enjoyed by virtue of sheer size.

b. Working Through the Tax Implications

Every plan negotiation implicates many areas of the law in addition to Title 11 of the U.S. Code. The shape of the plan may be influenced by labor laws, environmental laws, laws regulating the debtor's business, even zoning ordinances. One constant, however, in virtually every Chapter 11 is the influence of U.S. income tax law. Here we identify a few of the most important aspects of federal tax law as it affects the development of a plan. The details of tax law are beyond the scope of these materials, but it is important to know that certain key tax issues may threaten the viability of the plan.

In general the tax rules used to be much more favorable to a reorganizing company than they are today. As a result, at least some of the reorganization techniques used in past years may be less useful today because of changes in the tax treatment of reorganizations. In the 2005 Amendments, Congress advanced the same trend, generally improving the collection rights of the taxing authority vis-à-vis those of competing creditors or the reorganizing debtor.

The principal respect in which a plan's success may be threatened by tax consequences is that the forgiveness of debt by the creditors under a plan may be treated as "income" to the debtor. At first it may seem strange to speak of a debtor-taxpayer deriving "income" from the forgiveness of debt or its legal discharge. Certainly the disappearance of an obligation does not increase the debtor's bank account, as more common forms of income do. Nonetheless, a moment's reflection will reveal why the cancellation of a debt obligation must be considered "income" and therefore subject to income taxation.

The cancellation of debt is income because it increases the debtor's wealth as surely as if the debtor had won the lottery. We all understand that if Jane wins $10,000 in the Massachusetts lottery, she must pay income tax on the winnings. The win increased her net wealth by $10,000 and that is taxable income. On the other hand, if Jane borrows $10,000, the loan does not constitute income because it has to be paid back. The debt she owes balances out the cash she receives, so there is no net increase in Jane's wealth. But suppose Jane's creditor calls her and says, for whatever reason, "Jane, forget about paying me back." At that moment, Jane has $10,000 in the bank with no offsetting obligation to pay it back. The disappearance of the debt has increased her net wealth by $10,000, and that increase is economically identical to winning the lottery. (In fact, after that call she may go out and celebrate, just as if she had won the lottery.) The cancellation of the debt means that she will not have to take $10,000 out of her future income to pay back the debt — with the same boost to her future economic outlook as if she received lottery winnings in installments over the next several years. The cancellation of the debt is income and taxable as such. This sort of income is often called "Cancellation of Debt Income" or "COD."

Of course, it is commonplace in bankruptcy reorganization for creditors to cancel, voluntarily or otherwise, some part of the debts owed to them by the debtor. The cancellation is given effect by the bankruptcy discharge that accompanies confirmation of a Chapter 11 plan under section 1141 of the Code. Because the canceled debts constitute income economically, it follows that the debtor risks having to pay income tax on the value it has realized from the cancellation. Even if the tax impact is deferred to future years, the effect might be that more income tax will have to be paid in the future, so that the income stream available for creditors under the plan will be reduced. Thus the avoidance or mitigation of income tax liability arising from debt cancellation is an important part of the structuring of any plan of reorganization.

Sections 108 and 1017 of the Internal Revenue Code govern how to treat income generated by a bankruptcy discharge. In general, the income arising from discharge of indebtedness in bankruptcy is excluded from gross income, so that current tax does not have to be paid on it, but an amount equal to that exclusion must be offset against other tax advantages. The debtor may elect either of two approaches: It may reduce its tax "attributes," such as net operating loss carryovers ("NOLs") and tax credits, or it may reduce its basis in its assets, such as the tangible assets, the value of which can be deducted over the years via depreciation. In either case, the effect is to increase the taxes that the debtor may have to pay in future years by reducing credits or deductions that the debtor would otherwise have been able to use to reduce taxes on its future income. As a result, the debtor avoids immediate taxation on COD income at the risk of increased taxation in later years, if it returns to profitability.

To the extent that a debtor can retain NOLs after accounting for COD income, other amendments to the Internal Revenue Code have made the use of NOLs much more problematic and complex. Section 382 of the IRC imposes rules that can severely reduce the value of the NOLs of a reorganized company emerging from bankruptcy if the effect of the plan is an "Ownership Change," as therein defined. A bankruptcy reorganization will frequently involve an ownership change because of a buyout by a new investor or the giving of stock to preexisting creditors. The rules are complicated, but the effect of an ownership change will often be the loss of virtually all of the NOLs. See generally, Jacobs, The Chapter 11 Corporate Tax Survival Kit or How to Succeed as Guardian Ad Litem of a Corporate Debtor's NOLs, 42 Tax Law. 3 (1988).

It is much more difficult to "sell" a bankrupt's NOLs than it used to be. Nonetheless, it is possible that a reorganized debtor can acquire a profitable corporation and shelter its profits with the debtor's NOLs. Being in a position to operate tax-free for a time, it may be able to offer a higher price for the business than another buyer. To the extent that NOLs can be preserved, they represent a unique sort of "asset" that can make an important contribution to a successful reorganization.

2. Confirmation

In most Chapter 11 cases, confirmation of a plan is the point of the whole game. The tools we have studied up to this point are of little value if the debtor cannot get a plan confirmed and successfully emerge from the bankruptcy courthouse, no longer a DIP. Some debtors manage to solve their problems with their creditors and dismiss their cases without confirming a plan, but most need to confirm a plan and bind all the parties at once.

a. Reorganization Structures

For those students who have not been exposed to business and finance courses, it will be useful to describe briefly some of the most common structures adopted in those Chapter 11 reorganizations in which something more than just extension and reduction of debt is necessary. In such cases, the debtor may wish to issue stock to some of its creditors because it does not foresee a cash flow large enough to allow sufficient cash payments to them. In other cases, the best return for creditors may be found in the sale of the debtor as an operating unit, i.e., on a "going concern" basis. These and other common transactions may be structured in a variety of ways, depending on both legal and economic considerations. Legal considerations include the Bankruptcy Code, state corporate law, and federal and state tax laws.

It is commonplace for a reorganization to involve the issuance of new stock in the debtor company (common stock, preferred stock, or both), as well as "warrants" to purchase more stock in the future. In some cases, stock distribution may be inevitable: If the debtor cannot generate enough assets to pay the lowest priority class of creditors, that class can be crammed down only by giving lower classes (usually the present stockholders) nothing. The lowest creditor class then becomes the owner of the company by receiving securities in lieu of payment. In other cases, the old common shareholders may retain an interest, but their interest may be diluted by the issuance of additional common stock to some or all classes of creditors. Such an issuance is often a "sweetener" to these creditors, promising them not only partial payment, but also some hope of profit if the debtor eventually does well. Another possibility is the issuance of warrants, which are (roughly) options to buy stock at a fixed price. By accepting warrants, the creditor avoids the responsibilities of share ownership (e.g., reporting requirements), but can hope to exercise the warrants, and sell the stock thus acquired, if the company does well and the stock develops value.

Often the best solution in a Chapter 11 is sale of the company as a going concern to some new investor, with the proceeds to be distributed to creditors. Such a transaction might occur by a sale of assets, including copyrights, trademarks, and goodwill, or it might occur by a sale of stock. Some deals involve both, as when a new corporation is formed to which all of the debtor's assets are transferred and the stock of the new corporation is then issued to the purchaser. The purchaser will sometimes want to "purchase" existing management, including employment contracts binding key personnel, while in other cases old management is the last thing the purchaser wants.

Other possibilities are the sale of tangible assets as a package, but without sale of the company as a whole (i.e., without the personnel and intangibles that make the company a going concern), or, of course, the sale of the assets piecemeal. Even more common is the sale of part of the debtor's business or assets, either the sale of a profitable division to generate necessary cash or the sale of a loser that the purchaser thinks can be turned around by new management.

Just as leveraged buyouts have been fashionable in recent years for taking over profitable companies, they have also been used as devices to restructure businesses trying to emerge from Chapter 11. The continuing popularity of LBOs in bankruptcy carries a certain irony since the LBOs of many successful corporations seem to have been the events that put them on the road to bankruptcy a few years later.

The structure of an LBO in Chapter 11 works just as it did outside Chapter 11, which was discussed on pp. 86-98. The company or a division is sold, with the purchase price provided largely by bank loans or commercial paper secured by the assets being purchased. The purchasers in such transactions are often the management and employees of the business or division being sold, although not invariably so. The frequency of such moves has added some leverage to managements' and employees' negotiating positions in Chapter 11. Sometimes they threaten to take over the emerging corporation, seizing control of the corporation from current equity or some competing management group. Other times they are the newest version of the white knight, willing to run the corporation and make some repayments to the creditors when the alternative looks like liquidation and low payouts. Not surprisingly, LBOs of businesses in bankruptcy are often accompanied by employee agreements to work for less or to terminate bitter strikes in order to save jobs and give the company a reasonable shot at successful reorganization. In any case, the success of an LBO will depend on whether management can secure financing to confirm a Chapter 11.

In any Chapter 11 reorganization, whether prepackaged, employee-financed, or whatever, the eventual structure of the confirmed plan is often tax-driven. Once the parties have decided on the basic economic transaction to be attempted in Chapter 11, the details are likely to be governed by how parties can maximize the tax benefits (or minimize the tax costs) associated with a particular deal. For more on tax planning, see the discussion on pp. 607–609.

b.   Best Interests of the Creditors and Feasibility

In general, the achievement of consensus — the acceptance of a financial plan by majorities in each class of creditors — is the heart of the Chapter 11 process. Most of the requirements for confirmation under section 1129 relate to the acceptance process. Two of them, however, are flat legal requirements that must be satisfied even if the majority of creditors of each class approve the plan: The plan must be in the "best interests" of each individual creditor who does not agree to it and the plan must be found feasible even if every creditor does agree to it. We consider those two requirements first. We then turn to the standards relating to acceptance by classes of creditors and, where a class does not accept, the availability of "cramdown" to force acceptance under certain circumstances.

The phrase "best interests" and the word "feasibility" nowhere appear in the statute itself. They are the jargon used to describe the requirements of section 1129(a)(7) and (11), respectively. The jargon is derived from the pre-Code cases in which these two doctrines were developed. We will consider feasibility first and then best interests.

The central fact about the "feasibility" test of section 1129(a)(11) is that no very general statements can be made about it. Feasibility goes to the likelihood that the plan will succeed — that the business will survive and prosper at least long enough to make the scheduled payments. The test is applied on a case-by-case basis and reflects the best business judgment of the bankruptcy judge based on the testimony (often including expert testimony) of witnesses.

In one sense it could be argued that the feasibility requirement is undesirable; if most creditors believe that the business can succeed, they should be permitted to go forward under the plan. On the other hand, a dissenting creditor will regard feasibility as the ultimate protection against the hopeless naïvete of fellow creditors. Since the feasibility test must be satisfied even if *all* creditors have approved the plan, however, it is undeniably paternalistic. It requires the court to join in the creditors' judgment that the business has a reasonable prospect of survival under the terms of the plan. As a practical matter, however, if no one challenges a plan's feasibility, the court's limited time and resources will tend to constrain judicial inquiry.

Operating in the protective arms of Chapter 11 can give a debtor a chance to recover. It also creates a track record that helps the court evaluate whether the debtor in fact can do what it says it can do. Here the motel debtor had great projections but fell short in practice.

=========== In re MALKUS, INC., DEBTOR. ===========
2004 Bankr. LEXIS 2120 (Bankr. M.D. Fla. 2004) 2004 WL 3202212

OPINION BY: George L. PROCTOR

* * *

FINDINGS OF FACT

1. On July 30, 2003, Malkus, Inc. ("Debtor") filed a voluntary petition under Chapter 11 of the Bankruptcy Code.

2. Debtor's sole asset and business operation is the ownership and operation of a 113-unit Howard Johnson Express Motel in Deland, Florida (the "Motel"). The Motel is operated by one of its 50% shareholders, Charles Malkus ("Malkus"). Malkus' wife, Judith ("Judith") owns the other 50%. The Motel is an exterior corridor, approximately 30-year-old concrete block facility located outside the city limits of Deland, Florida.

3. At the time Debtor entered into its lending relationship with LaSalle National Bank ("LaSalle"), the Motel operated under a franchise agreement with Choice Hotels Franchising, Inc. as a Quality Inn. In April 2001, Debtor's franchise with Choice Hotels Franchising, Inc. was terminated.

4. After termination of the franchise agreement with Quality Inn, Debtor entered into a franchise agreement with Howard Johnson's International, Inc., the flag under which it continues to operate. In the Motel's most recent quality assurance audit, the Motel received a score of 373 out of a possible score of 500; a score below 370 constitutes a failing score. (LaSalle's Ex. 47)

5. On August 20, 1998, the Debtor executed in favor of Archon Financial, LP (the "Original Lender") a Mortgage Note in the amount of $2,700,000.00 (the "Note"). The Note was secured by a first priority mortgage lien upon and security interest in all of the real and personal property comprising the Motel. As of the petition date, the outstanding principal balance due on the Note, exclusive of any interest, prepayment or yield maintenance amount, and fees and costs, was $2,422,980.21. (LaSalle's Ex. 5) The Original Lender's interest in the Note and other loan documents was subsequently assigned to LaSalle.

6. The lending relationship between the Debtor and LaSalle, is a securitized, pooled financing arrangement, or a commercial mortgage backed securities transaction ("CMBS financing").

7. In December 2000, notwithstanding the prohibition against any junior financing contained in paragraph eight (8) of the Mortgage, Debtor executed a second mortgage in favor of First Community Bank as security for a personal debt of Malkus and Judith. (LaSalle's Ex. 53). The First

Community Bank second mortgage was undertaken without the written consent of LaSalle. (LaSalle's Ex. 53)

8. On October 1, 2002 Debtor defaulted under the Note and other Loan Documents. Debtor also stopped making the required tax and insurance escrow payments, as well as the capital improvement and replacement reserve payments required under the terms of the Loan Documents.

9. On February 20, 2003, Lender started a foreclosure proceeding to foreclose its first priority mortgage lien and security interest in the Motel. (LaSalle's Ex. 48) In order to prevent the grant of summary judgment, and appointment of a receiver in the foreclosure case, Debtor filed this Chapter 11 case on July 30, 2003, the day of the summary judgment hearing. (LaSalle Ex's 48, 50 and 51)

10. On September 5, 2003, Debtor and LaSalle entered into a Stipulation Authorizing Debtor's Use of Cash Collateral and Providing Adequate Protection to Lender (the "Stipulation"). (LaSalle's Ex. 11) The Stipulation required Debtor to pay LaSalle at the end of every month the net cash generated from the operation of the Motel, less the actual approved expenditures and the operating reserves; and to escrow $3,941.00 monthly in order to pay the post-petition real estate taxes. (LaSalle's Ex. 11) On September 25, 2003, the Court approved the Stipulation.

11. Notwithstanding the Stipulation, Debtor failed to operate within the agreed budget, failed to escrow the required real estate tax amounts, and failed to deliver to LaSalle the monthly net income for months during which a positive net income was derived.

12. On November 4, 2003, the Court entered an order that required Debtor to comply with the budget, to escrow $3,941.00 per month for taxes, and to otherwise comply with the Stipulation. (LaSalle's Ex. 12) When Debtor still failed to comply with the Stipulation, the Court entered an Order lifting the automatic stay to permit LaSalle to proceed with the foreclosure case through the entry of final judgment, with no sale to occur without further Court order. (LaSalle's Ex. 13).

13. In the Fall of 2003, Malkus "loaned" a variety of funds to the Debtor in order to keep the Motel operating, and also had the Debtor repay such "loans" without any authorization or approval by the Court.

14. Debtor's Plan is comprised of twelve (12) classifications of claimants. Class One (1) addresses Administrative Claims, Class Two (2) addresses Priority Claims, Classes Three (3) though Ten (10) address the treatment of secured claims, Class Eleven addresses the treatment of unsecured claims and Class Twelve (12) addresses Equity Interests.

. . . [The court explains various features of the plan.]

17. In February, 2004 Debtor made an adequate protection payment to LaSalle in the amount of $20,000. Since the pendency of the case no other adequate protection payments to LaSalle have been made.

CONCLUSIONS OF LAW

[After considering other objections to the plan, the court moved on to feasibility.]

C.   The Plan Fails to Comply with §1129(a)(11)

Pursuant to §1129(a)(11) a plan of reorganization must be feasible. "Although success does not have to be guaranteed, the Court is obligated to scrutinize a plan carefully to determine whether it offers a reasonable prospect of success and is workable." In re Yates Development, 258 B.R. 36, 44 (Bankr. M.D. Fla. 2000).

§1129(a)(11) of the Bankruptcy Code provides, in pertinent part, that the Court shall confirm a plan only if:

> (11) Confirmation of the plan is not likely to be followed by the liquidation, or the need for further financial reorganization, of the debtor or any successor to the debtor under the plan, unless such liquidation or reorganization is proposed in the plan.

"Visionary schemes are not sufficient to make a plan feasible." *In re Sovereign Oil Co.*, 128 B.R. 585, 587 (Bankr. M.D. Fla. 1991). A debtor's past performance is one of the most important measures of whether a debtor's plan will succeed.

LaSalle argues that Debtor's expenses, during the post-petition period of operations, exceeded Debtor's own budget in virtually every month (once adjusted for budgeted items — such as payments to the Lender (that were not made) — are figured in). In addition, LaSalle asserts that Debtor even lost money in two of the months that were projected by the Debtor to be successful, revenue producing months.

Although Debtor's revenues have risen during the months of July, 2004, August, 2004 and September, 2004, Debtor's dismal track record spanning over the pendency of Debtor's case has clearly shown that the projections relied upon in the Plan are unreasonable and unachievable. The Court cannot simply overlook the motel's historical poor operating results because of a few months in which the Debtor was either able to meet or surpass the motel's projected revenues. Based upon the above the Court finds Debtor's plan is not feasible.

CONCLUSION

The Court finds the Debtor has failed to carry its burden, as the proponent of the Plan. Debtor has failed to prove the requirements of Sections 1129(a)(2), (a)(3) and (a)(11). Therefore, the plan cannot be confirmed and the Court will dismiss the case. The Court will enter a separate order consistent with these Findings of Fact and Conclusions of Law. Ordered in Jacksonville, Florida this 15 day of November, 2004.

George L. Proctor
United States Bankruptcy Judge

Sometimes the debtor just can't pull the plan together. For Made in Detroit, the inability to pin down strong plan financing doomed the debtor's plan.

══════════ In re MADE IN DETROIT, INC., DEBTOR ══════════
299 B.R. 170 (Bankr. E.D. Mich. 2003)

OPINION BY: Marci B. McIvor

* * *

I   Undisputed Facts

In 1997, the Debtor, Made in Detroit, Inc., purchased approximately 410 acres of real property (the "Property") for the purpose of development. The Property is located on the Detroit River in both Gibraltar and Trenton, Michigan, and it is the Debtor's only significant asset. For the next five years, the Debtor attempted to develop the Property. Due to problems in obtaining permits, the development was delayed. As a result of the long delay, the costs associated with pursuing the permits, and because Debtor was not generating income, the Debtor became delinquent in payments to secured creditors. In 2002, the primary secured creditor, Standard Federal, commenced a foreclosure action against the Debtor. As a result, on October 23, 2002, the Debtor filed for bankruptcy protection under Chapter 11 of the Bankruptcy Code.

On July 15, 2003, the Debtor filed its Third Amended Combined Plan and Disclosure Statement (the "Debtor's Plan"). The Plan provides that it will be funded via a nine million dollar loan from Kennedy Funding, Inc. and that the Kennedy loan is contingent on certain conditions precedent, including a $270,000 commitment fee and a $15 million valuation of the Property. Specifically, the Plan states:

> On July 8, 2003, the Debtor received a draft of a Loan Commitment from Kennedy Funding for a loan in the amount of $9,000,000.00. The Debtor will receive a firm loan commitment from Kennedy Funding when the Debtor deposits $270,000.00 in an escrow account. The Debtor intends to obtain these funds through loans or capital contributions from shareholders and/or loans from other persons. Based upon willingness expressed by its shareholders, the Debtor does not anticipate any difficulties in obtaining the funds necessary for this transaction. The monies in the escrow account will be applied towards the closing fee if the Debtor fails to close the loan. Otherwise, the fees will be paid from the loan proceeds. Kennedy Funding also intends to obtain an updated appraisal of the Real Property after the escrow account is funded. In order to issue a loan commitment for $9,000,000.00, Kennedy Funding has stated that it requires that the appraisal indicate an "as is, quick sale" value for the real property of at least $15,000,000.00.

Debtor's Plan at 20-21.

The terms of the proposed loan from Kennedy are set forth in a July 8, 2003, loan commitment letter, admitted as Creditors' Exhibit 1 at the confirmation hearing. It sets forth three basic conditions that must be fulfilled prior to funding the loan: 1) the payment of a commitment fee; 2) a property valuation of at least fifteen million dollars on an "as is" quick sale basis; and 3) the participation in the loan of investors.

First, the loan commitment requires the payment of a $270,000 commitment fee:

> The commitment and all of its terms and conditions will become effective only upon delivery to this office of a signed copy of this commitment, duly accepted by the Borrower, accompanied with the commitment fee in the amount of Two Hundred Seventy Thousand Dollars ($270,000.00) which is non-refundable and earned for among other things, the commitment to provide funds.

★ ★ ★

Second, the loan commitment provides for funding of the loan based on an "as is" quick sale value of $15 million.

> . . . Quick sale is defined as a ninety (90) day to one hundred twenty (120) day sale to a cash buyer. The Borrower understands that KFI will inspect the Collateral and, in its sole discretion, determine both the "as is" and "as completed" valued of the Collateral based upon all plans, budgets, specifications, approvals, etc. provided by Borrower detailing the proposed improvements. Borrower acknowledges that KFI will not at any time lend or advance more than Sixty Percent (60%) of the quick sale of the real estate Collateral at that time . . .
>
> If KFI's determination of the value of the property is disputed by the Borrower, Borrower may reject the Loan Offer and elect to engage the services of a third party appraiser. If Borrower makes this election, the Borrower and KFI shall mutually agree upon a third party MAI appraiser, with proper credentials, contracted by KFI, and any fees for said appraiser to be reimbursed by KFI by borrower prior to the appraisal being performed . . .

Creditors' Exhibit 1 at 4-5 (lines 111-43). The commitment letter provides that Kennedy will advance 60% of the "as is" quick sale value of the Property. Thus, for Debtor to obtain a nine million dollar loan, the "as is" quick sale valuation of the property would need to be at least fifteen million dollars. Under the terms of the commitment letter, the value is to be determined by Kennedy, in its sole discretion. If the Debtor/Borrower disagrees, then the parties will mutually agree on a third party appraiser. "As is" value is the value of the unimproved land as it currently exists. "Quick sale" is defined as a cash sale to a buyer with a short, ninety to one hundred twenty day, marketing period.

Third, the commitment letter provides that Kennedy will bring participants (investors) into the transaction. If Kennedy is unable to bring in such participants, then Kennedy can cancel its obligation to loan the funds

The Debtor's Plan provided that once the nine million dollar loan was obtained, the secured creditors and administrative claimants would be paid in full, the unsecured creditors would receive an initial distribution of $750,000 (with the balance of claims to be paid from the proceeds of the sale of lots), and equity shareholders would retain their interest.

The Official Committee of Unsecured Creditors (the "Committee") and Wayne County Treasurer filed objections to confirmation of the Debtor's Plan. In addition, on July 9, 2003, the Committee filed its own plan of reorganization (the "Committee's Plan"). The Committee's Plan provided that it would be financed by an "as is" immediate cash sale of the property to the Trust for Public Land for $4,800,000.

II   FINDINGS OF FACT AND CONCLUSIONS OF LAW

* * *

A.   Feasibility

Debtor's Plan fails to meet the requirement that a plan must be feasible. Feasibility is a mandatory requirement for confirmation. . . . Section 1129(a)(11) of the Bankruptcy Code provides that a plan can be confirmed only if "confirmation of the plan is not likely to be followed by the liquidation, or the need for further organization, of the debtor or any successor to the debtor under the plan, unless such liquidation or reorganization is proposed in the plan." 11 U.S.C. §1129(a)(11).

Section 1129(a)(11) prevents confirmation of visionary schemes which promise creditors more than the debtor can possibly attain after confirmation. Travelers Ins. Co. v. Pikes Peak Water Co. (In re Pikes Peak Water Co.), 779 F.2d 1456, 1460 (10th Cir. 1985). A plan that is submitted on a conditional basis is not considered feasible, and thus confirmation of such a plan must be denied. *Sis*, 120 B.R. at 94.

The plan does not need to guarantee success, but it must present reasonable assurance of success. Kane v. Johns-Manville Corp., 843 F.2d 636, 649 (2d Cir. 1988). To provide such reasonable assurance, a plan must provide a realistic and workable framework for reorganization. Crestar Bank v. Walker (In re Walker), 165 B.R. 994, 1004 (E.D. Va. 1994). See also In re Howard, 212 B.R. 864, 879-80 (Bankr. E.D. Tenn. 1997) (like Chapter 11 plan, Chapter 12 plan must be realistic, not mere wishful thinking; debtors must be able to do what they are proposing). The plan cannot be based on "visionary promises;" it must be doable.

> Sincerity, honesty and willingness are not sufficient to make the plan feasible, and neither are visionary promises. The test is whether the things which are to be done after confirmation can be done as a practical matter under the facts.

In re Hoffman, 52 B.R. 212, 215 (Bankr. D.N.D. 1985).

In *Hoffman*, the debtor's plan proposed to pay creditors within two years from the sale of real property. However, there was no potential purchaser and the plan did not set forth the terms of the proposed sale. The court found that the plan was not feasible because the proposed sale of the real estate was not "sufficiently concrete to assure either consummation within the two-years or that even if sold within the two-year period the price obtained would be sufficient" to pay the secured creditor. Id.

Similarly, in In re Walker, 165 B.R. 994 (E.D. Va. 1994), the court also found a plan based on funding through a speculative sale of real estate was not feasible. There, the district court reversed the bankruptcy court's confirmation of a plan because the plan was not feasible. The plan proposed to pay creditors from the sale of two parcels of real estate. However, the plan did not provide any time frame within which the properties would be sold, did not set forth the terms of the proposed sale, and did not set forth a plan for the liquidation of other properties if the proceeds from the sale of the two identified properties was insufficient to pay creditors. Based on these deficiencies, the court held that the proposed plan was not feasible. *Id.* at 1005.

Likewise, in In re Thurmon, 87 B.R. 190 (Bankr. M.D. Fla. 1988), the court found that a plan conditioned on a sale of property which in turn was conditioned on financing was not feasible. In *Thurmon,* the plan proposed that funding would be obtained through a lease purchase agreement. The lease purchase agreement provided that a buyer would lease property from the debtor and would then purchase 147 acres from the debtor. The closing of the land sale was conditioned on the buyer's ability to obtain financing on favorable terms. The buyer had not yet applied for the financing but testified that he would do so within 30 days. The court found that the plan was not feasible because it was not reasonably likely that the money to fund the plan would come from the buyer.

While Debtor in this case is sincere, honest, and willing, the Debtor's Plan of Reorganization is not realistic, as it does not provide a reasonable assurance of success. The Plan is based on "wishful thinking" and "visionary promises." As a practical matter, the Debtor's Plan is not sufficiently concrete as to be feasible because it is contingent on exit financing from Kennedy and there is no reasonable assurance that the Kennedy loan will ever close or that the Property will be appraised at a value high enough to provide a $9 million loan. Like in *Hoffman, Walker,* and *Thurmon,* it is not reasonably likely that Debtor's Plan will be funded. The conditions precedent to Kennedy's funding of the loan were not satisfied as of the date of the confirmation hearing. Further, the evidence did not show that the satisfaction of such conditions was reasonably likely in the foreseeable future.

The $270,000.00 loan commitment fee was never put into an escrow account or paid to Kennedy Funding. At the hearing, Debtor argued that the Court prevented it from paying the commitment fee. The Debtor previously attempted to pay the fee by obtaining Court approval of a loan from shareholders, which loan was to be repaid as an administrative expense. On May 23, 2003, the Debtor brought a motion for additional unsecured debt under 11 U.S.C. §364(b), which authorizes the payment of unsecured debt as a first priority administrative expense. The motion sought court approval to borrow $240,000 from Debtor's shareholders to pay a commitment fee in that amount to Kennedy Funding, Inc. The Debtor proposed that repayment of the shareholder loan would be due on the Effective Date of the Second Amended Plan, and would have administrative priority under 11 U.S.C. §503(b)(1) and 507(a)(1).

On July 3, 2003, the Court denied the Debtor's motion under 11 U.S.C. §364(a) because the Debtor's proposed shareholder loan for the purpose of paying the commitment fee was not a post-petition ordinary-course-of-business debt. Further, the Court denied Debtor's request to incur the proposed loan as unsecured debt under 364(b), which required Court approval, because the loan was not a proper administrative expense as it did not directly and substantially benefit the estate. Debtor did not meet its burden of showing benefit to the estate, because the Kennedy loan was contingent. There was no guarantee that Kennedy would ever fund the loan. Also, even if Kennedy did fund the loan, the Debtor's Plan might not be confirmed. Thus, there was no showing that payment of the loan commitment fee would benefit the estate. Further, Debtor did not meet its burden of showing that the funding was a loan that could be classified as an administrative expense because, under the totality of the circumstances, the funding appeared to constitute capital contributions, not a loan. In sum, the Court denied Debtor's request to have the commitment fee classified as an administrative expense which is entitled to first priority repayment. However, this ruling did not "prevent" Debtor from paying the commitment fee. Debtor could have paid the fee via capital contributions or loans that would not be entitled to repayment ahead of other creditors.

* * *

In summary, the Debtor failed to show at confirmation that it had exit financing to fund its plan. The proposed financing had so many contingencies that Debtor's Plan was conditional at best. Thus, the Debtor's Plan is not feasible under 1129(a)(11), and the Court must deny confirmation of Debtor's Plan.

━━━━━━━━━━━━━━

The best interests test, like its cousin the feasibility test, can be raised by a single creditor. Especially important is the fact that the section 1129(a)(7) standard applies to each creditor — not to each class, but to each and every creditor individually. This means that unless a creditor has individually voted in favor of the plan, the best interests test requires a finding that the objecting creditor will receive at least as much under the plan as that creditor would have received in a liquidation under Chapter 7. The consequence is that the court must do a liquidation analysis, estimating the amount that could be obtained by selling each asset of the estate and then calculating the resulting dividend that would be paid to the nonaccepting creditor.

The following case, like so many in bankruptcy, turns on valuation. If the value of the assets is as the plan proponent asserts, then the plan meets the best interests test because it matches or betters what the creditors are promised in Chapter 7. But if the value of the assets is higher, then the plan as written cannot be confirmed.

━━━━━ SK-PALLADIN PARTNERS, L.P., Plaintiff, v. ━━━━━
PLATINUM ENTERTAINMENT, INC.

2001 U.S. Dist. LEXIS 20710 (N.D. Ill. 2001)

OPINION BY: Suzanne B. CONLON
OPINION: MEMORANDUM OPINION AND ORDER

* * *

BACKGROUND

As a public company, Platinum's primary business was the production, distribution, marketing, and sale of recorded music. On June 30, 2000, Platinum's board of directors held its final meeting. Prior to that meeting, Platinum's obligations to First Source Financials, Inc. ("First Source"), its secured lender, had fully matured. Platinum had defaulted on that obligation and was at risk of forfeiture. Platinum was not actively operating its business and most of its employees had been terminated. The board authorized Thomas Leavens, a Platinum officer, to effect an orderly transfer of Platinum's assets to First Source, and take other appropriate action including the filing of a bankruptcy petition. Immediately thereafter, the directors resigned from the board, and new directors were never appointed.

Platinum filed its Chapter 11 bankruptcy petition on July 26, 2000. The bankruptcy court authorized Platinum to retain Tudor Management Group ("Tudor"), the board's prior consultant, to render management and consulting services to Platinum. Platinum and Tudor prepared offering memorandum for the assets, placed advertisements in entertainment industry publications, and retained a publicity agent to conduct marketing for the assets. Platinum received only two written expression of interests for its music catalog, which did not result in a sale because the catalogue had been inactive for 18 months. Consequently, Platinum determined the catalogue's liquidation value at $15 million.

Meanwhile, Platinum commenced settlement negotiations with The Harry Fox Agency, Inc. ("Harry Fox") to resolve pre-bankruptcy class action suits. Harry Fox initiated those suits on behalf of copyright owners when Platinum failed to pay its royalties. Platinum and Harry Fox reached a settlement agreement conditioned on the approval of class members and subject to confirmation of the joint plan. Platinum and the committee proposed the joint plan, which called for: (1) reorganization of Platinum's legal and financial affairs; (2) resumption of Platinum's business; (3) immediate deposit of $1 million for payment of unsecured claims; and (4) payment of $2 million to fund the Harry Fox settlement. First Source agreed to fund the joint plan.

On July 18, 2001, Palladin, a Class 3 holder of unsecured claims, objected to the joint plan. Palladin argued the joint plan was proposed in violation of Delaware law, and the joint plan did not serve the best interest of creditors under 11 U.S.C. §1129(a).

[The court then dispensed with the Delaware claim, ruling in favor of the plan proponents.]

II.   Best Interests of Creditors

Palladin contends the joint plan fails to satisfy the best interest of creditors under 11 U.S.C. §1129(a)(7). Pursuant to §1129(a)(7), each of the creditors in a Chapter 11 reorganization must receive at least as much as they would under a Chapter 7 liquidation. Specifically, Palladin asserts the Harry Fox class action suits diminished the value of Platinum's music catalogue. According to Palladin, the bankruptcy court erred by closing discovery and denying the admission of appraisals that purportedly demonstrated the value of the music catalogue was higher; and not taking into account the music catalogue value after settlement of the Harry Fox class action suits.

The bankruptcy court's decision to exclude evidence is reviewed for abuse of discretion. General Elec. Co. v. Joiner, 522 U.S. 136, 140, 139 L. Ed. 2d 508, 118 S. Ct. 512 (1997). The bankruptcy court excluded appraisals prepared by Kagan Media Appraisals, Inc. ("Kagan") at the confirmation hearing over Palladin's objections. The court determined the Kagan appraisals were hearsay, and Palladin failed to designate the appraiser as a witness. See Waddell v. Commissioner, 841 F.2d 264, 267 (9th Cir. 1988) (appraisal is hearsay when no foundation is provided for business record exception). Palladin argues the bankruptcy court arbitrarily closed discovery on July 26, 2001, making it impossible to depose the appraiser. The joint plan was filed on June 15, 2001. The bankruptcy court allowed discovery to proceed until July 26, 2001. Three days before the hearing, Palladin served Platinum with a document request seeking nineteen categories of documents. Palladin appeared at the hearing on July 26, 2001 and stated appraisals were forthcoming from Platinum. Tr., Vol. VII, Ex. 14, at 19. Palladin requested an extension of discovery. When the bankruptcy court asked Palladin for an estimated discovery time, Palladin responded: "It's not something I don't think that can be done in two weeks, six weeks or even two months." Id. The court asked Palladin if it had retained valuation experts. Palladin stated it had not. The court responded: "Your casual reference to the need for months to take discovery runs completely contrary to the manner in which bankruptcy cases are pursued." Id. at 20. The bankruptcy court denied an extension of the discovery schedule because Palladin had been "less than diligent" in pursuing discovery. Id. at 19. Palladin failed to request timely discovery of the Kagan appraisals, retain its own valuation experts, depose a Kagan witness, and request extension of the discovery period before the scheduled confirmation hearing. Id. at 19-20. Nevertheless, the court delayed the hearing until August 21, 2001 to allow Palladin to review documents produced in response to its discovery request.

Palladin's assertions on appeal are meritless. The bankruptcy court's finding that Palladin failed to perform discovery with due diligence has some support in the record. That resulted in Palladin's inability to offer the Kagan appraisal at the hearing. Nor did Palladin offer its own expert testimony on the value of Platinum's music catalogue. Indeed, the court noted Palladin was aware of Platinum's position on the music catalogue prior to July 26, 2001. Id. at 21. Palladin had one month to conduct necessary discovery. Without a Kagan witness, the appraisals were correctly barred as inadmissible hearsay. A court may reverse discretionary evidentiary rulings when "no reasonable person could agree with the bankruptcy court." In re Geraci, 138 F.3d at 319. Palladin fails to make that showing on appeal. Consequently, the bankruptcy court's ruling was not an abuse of discretion. The bankruptcy court's factual determinations on the value of Platinum's assets are reviewed for clear error. Fed. R. Bankr. P. 8013. Palladin asserts the bankruptcy court improperly valued the music catalogue at $15 million when the Kagan appraisals listed them at $60 million. However, the Kagan appraisals were properly excluded as hearsay. Palladin did not offer admissible evidence to support its asserted value of the music catalogue. Nor does Palladin point to any record evidence in its appellate brief. Instead, Palladin offers unsupported assertions that the music catalogue's value must be higher because the Harry Fox class action suits were settled. The bankruptcy court noted First Source's $33 million secured claim and all administrative claims must be paid before other creditors. Extensive efforts to sell Platinum's assets proved fruitless. The bankruptcy court determined that was a "strong indication that the assets were not worth more than $33 million." Moreover, the bankruptcy court relied upon the only evidence of valuation presented at the hearing — Platinum's submission that the music catalogue was worth $15 million. Because Platinum's submissions were uncontroverted, the bankruptcy court reasonably relied on that evidence. Consequently, the bankruptcy court's factual finding was not clear error.

CONCLUSION

The motion to dismiss the appeal is denied. Palladin has failed to show the bankruptcy court's factual findings were clearly erroneous, its evidentiary rulings were an abuse of discretion, or that its conclusions of law were in error. Accordingly, the bankruptcy court's order of August 28, 2001 confirming the First Amended Joint Plan of Reorganization of Platinum Enterprises, Inc. is affirmed.

═══════════

The tension here was tight: Was the objecting party simply trying to delay, or did it believe that valuable assets were about to be sold off at bargain basement prices? Bankruptcy courts are called on to make a lot of very fine judgments. Once there was an objecting creditor, the burden was on the proponent of the proposed plan (the debtor) to show the liquidation value of the company in order to determine how much the creditor would get in a Chapter 7. Here the debtor made such a showing and the creditor failed to rebut it. Also note that the nature of bankruptcy is such that the courts are often impatient with leisurely litigators; assets need to be sold, customers need to be serviced lest lost, and so on — right now.

Problem Set 32

32.1. Country Smokes, Inc., is a manufacturer of corn cob pipes for the souvenir trade. Although it has been in business for over 50 years, it has been badly wounded by the most recent hike in the price of gasoline: Decreased vacation driving has seriously depressed souvenir sales. It filed its Chapter 11 petition on June 1 of this year and has now proposed its Plan of Reorganization.

Your client is Pany Chemicals, which supplies the various chemicals needed in the production of Country's pipes. Country owes Pany $1,000,000 on an unsecured basis. Talbert Pany, the president of Pany, came storming into your office this morning waving a copy of Country's proposed plan. He was furious because Country proposes to pay only 50 cents on the dollar to the unsecured creditors. You explained that Pany could vote against the plan, but Talbert was sure the other unsecured creditors will vote for it, because they are afraid of losing Country as a customer if it liquidates. Since the other unsecureds are owed a total of $4,000,000, the plan could be adopted even if Pany dissents.

Talbert was especially annoyed because Country never told him that it had a $10,000,000 working capital loan from the First State Bank or that the loan was secured by a lien on all of Country's equipment. The equipment, which is worth about $2,500,000, is Country's only important asset, other than some real estate that is encumbered for its full value. The plan provides that First State will keep its lien on the equipment and the remaining balance of its loan will be paid in full.

Talbert said that the bank is really calling the shots in the Chapter 11, because of its secured position. He feels that Country would never have been forced into Chapter 11 in the first place except that First State insisted on payment of $7,500,000 of the $10,000,000 loan in April, just when Country needed cash to start acquiring inventory. That is why the bank is only owed $2,500,000 now. He can't understand "how a bank can force a company into bankruptcy and then get paid in full while the rest of us get only 50 percent."

Talbert asked you to call the bank's lawyer and "insist" (his word) on a better deal for the unsecureds. You know the bank's lawyer will tell you to get lost unless you have some potent legal ammunition. What have you got to say?

c. Classification and Voting

The most important check on a debtor is the requirement that the plan be approved by a majority of the creditors. Creditors are divided into classes for purposes of voting and distribution, with those in a class sharing similar legal status and pro rata distribution. A class votes in favor of a plan only when a two-part majority is achieved. Section 1126(c) requires approval by both a simple majority in number of creditors and a two-thirds majority in amount of debt. Because voting is by class, the debtor is particularly interested in how the classes are constructed. The Code gives the debtor some flexibility in designating the classes, and in some cases debtors may classify creditors in part with an eye to creating favorable majorities in each class, a kind of financial gerrymandering arguably present in the next case.

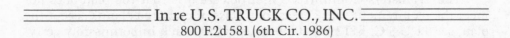

In re U.S. TRUCK CO., INC.
800 F.2d 581 (6th Cir. 1986)

Cornelia G. KENNEDY, Circuit Judge. . . .
Underlying this appeal is the Teamsters Committee's claim that U.S. Truck is liable to its employees for rejecting a collective bargaining

agreement between the local union and U.S. Truck. After filing its petition for relief under Chapter 11 of the Bankruptcy Code on June 11, 1982, U.S. Truck, a trucking company primarily engaged in intrastate snipping of parts and supplies for the automotive industry, sought to reject the collective bargaining agreement. U.S. Truck rejected the agreement with the approval of then-Bankruptcy-Judge Woods, in December 1982. Judge Woods found that rejection of the agreement was "absolutely necessary to save the debtor from collapse." Memorandum Opinion and Order, December 6, 1982, at page 8. New agreements have been negotiated to the satisfaction of each participating local union. Such agreements have been implemented over the lone dissent of the Teamsters Joint Area Rider Committee. Under the most recently mentioned agreement in the record (due to have expired in March 1985), U.S. Truck was able to record monthly profits in the range of $125,000 to $250,000. These new agreements achieved such results by reducing wages and requiring employees to buy their own trucking equipment, which the employees then leased to the company.[1]

The parties agreed to an estimate of the size of the Teamsters Committee claim against U.S. Truck so that the confirmation plan could be considered. The District Court held a hearing to consider the plan on January 23, 1985. The court considered three objections by the Teamsters Committee to the plan. Consideration of the objections, and the court's treatment of them, requires an understanding of the statutory scheme for approval of a chapter 11 reorganization plan.

II

Section 1129 contains two means by which a reorganization plan can be confirmed. The first way is to meet all eleven of the requirements of subsection (a), including (a)(8) which requires all impaired classes of claims or interests to accept the plan. The other way is to meet the requirements of subsection (b), which, first, incorporates all of the requirements of subsection (a), except for that contained in subsection (a)(8), and, second, imposes two additional requirements. Confirmation under subsection (b) is commonly referred to as a "cram down" because it permits a reorganization plan to go into effect over the objections of one or more impaired classes of creditors. In this case, U.S. Truck sought approval of its plan under this "cram down" provision.

III

The Teamsters Committee's first objection is that the plan does not meet the requirement that at least one class of impaired claims accept the plan, see 11 U.S.C. §1129(a)(10), because U.S. Truck impermissibly gerrymandered the classes in order to neutralize the Teamsters Committee's dissenting vote. [The court then focused on whether Class XI, the only clearly

---

1. This is referred to by the parties as the owner/operator system.

impaired class to accept the plan, was properly constituted. Class XI was composed of unsecured creditors, excluding the labor union claimant.]

The issue raised by the Teamsters Committee's challenge is under what circumstances does the Bankruptcy Code permit a debtor to keep a creditor out of a class of impaired claims which are of a similar legal nature and are against the same property as those of the "isolated" creditor. The District Court held that the Code permits such action here because of the following circumstances: (1) the employees represented by the Teamsters Committee have a unique continued interest in the ongoing business of the debtor, (2) the mechanics of the Teamsters Committee's claim differ substantially from those of the Class XI claims, and (3) the Teamsters Committee's claim is likely to become part of the agenda of future collective bargaining sessions between the union and the reorganized company. Thus, according to the court, the interests of the Teamsters Committee are substantially dissimilar from those of the creditors in Class XI. We must decide whether the Code permits separate classification under such circumstances.

Congress has sent mixed signals on the issue that we must decide. Our starting point is 11 U.S.C. §1122. . . . The statute, by its express language, only addresses the problem of dissimilar claims being included in the same class. It does not address the correlative problem — the one we face here — of similar claims being put in different classes. Some courts have seized upon this omission, and have held that the Code does not require a debtor to put similar claims in the same class.

> We think the courts erred in holding that section 1122(a) prohibits classification based on the presence of a co-debtor. Section 1122(a) specifies that only claims which are "substantially similar" may be placed in the same class. It does not require that similar claims *must* be grouped together, but merely that any group created must be homogenous. Although some courts have held that section 1122(a) prohibits classification based on any criterion other than legal right to the debtor's assets, the plain language of the statute contradicts such a construction. Moreover, section 1122(a) so interpreted would conflict with section 1322(b)(1), which specifically authorizes designation of more than one class of unsecured creditor, each presumably with equal legal rights to the debtor's estate.

Barnes v. Whelan, 689 F.2d 193, 201 (D.C. Cir. 1982) (emphasis in original) (holding that Chapter 13 debtor may group his unsecured debtors according to whether or not a co-debtor is present).

Further evidence that Congress intentionally failed to impose a requirement that similar claims be classified together is found by examining the "classification" sections of the former Bankruptcy Act. The applicable former provisions were 11 U.S.C., sections 597 (from former Chapter X) and 751 (from former Chapter XI). . . . Section 597 was interpreted to require all creditors of equal rank with claims against the same property to be placed in the same class. Congress' switch to less restrictive language in section 1122 of the Code seems to warrant a conclusion that Congress no longer intended to impose the now-omitted requirement that similar claims be classified together. However, the legislative history indicates that

Congress may not have intended to change the prior rule. The Notes of the
Senate Committee on the Judiciary state:

> This section [1122] codifies current case law surrounding the classification of
> claims and equity securities. It requires classification based on the nature of
> the claims or interests classified, and permits inclusion of claims or interests
> in a particular class only if the claim or interest being included is substantially
> similar to the other claims or interests of the class.

S. Rep. No. 989, 95th Cong., 2d Sess. 118, reprinted in 1978 U.S. Code
Cong. & Ad. News 5787, 5904.

It is difficult to follow Congress' instruction to apply the old case law to
the new Code provision. The old case law comes from two different sources.
Chapter X of the old Act was designed for thorough financial reorganizations of large corporations. It imposed a very formal and rigid structure to
protect the investing public. Chapter XI was designed for small nonpublic
businesses, did not permit the adjustment of a secured debt or of equity, and
thus contained few investor-protection measures. The idea behind Chapter
11 of the Code was to combine the speed and flexibility of Chapter XI with
some of the protection and remedial tools of Chapter X. Thus, Congress has
incorporated, for purposes of interpreting section 1122, the case law from
two provisions with different language, that were adopted for different purposes, and that have been interpreted to mean different things.

In this case, U.S. Truck is using its classification powers to segregate
dissenting (impaired) creditors from assenting (impaired) creditors (by
putting the dissenters into a class or classes by themselves) and, thus, it is
assured that at least one class of impaired creditors will vote for the plan
and make it eligible for cram down consideration by the court. We agree
with the Teamsters Committee that there must be some limit on a debtor's
power to classify creditors in such a manner. The potential for abuse would
be significant otherwise. Unless there is some requirement of keeping similar claims together, nothing would stand in the way of a debtor seeking out
a few impaired creditors (or even one such creditor) who will vote for the
plan and placing them in their own class.

We are unaware of any cases that deal with this problem as it arises in
this case. As we noted above, the legislative history of the Code provides little assistance in determining what limits there are to segregating similar
claims. Nevertheless, we do find one common theme in the prior case law
that Congress incorporated into section 1122. In those pre-Code cases, the
lower courts were given broad discretion to determine proper classification
according to the factual circumstances of each individual case.

The District Court noted three important ways in which the interests of
the Teamsters Committee differ substantially from those of the other
impaired creditors. Because of these differences, the Teamsters Committee
has a different stake in the future viability of the reorganized company and
has alternative means at its disposal for protecting its claim. The Teamsters
Committee's claim is connected with the collective bargaining process. In
the words of the Committee's counsel, the union employees have a "virtually unique interest." See 47 B.R. at 939. These differences put the Teamsters

Committee's claim in a different posture than the Class XI claims. The Teamsters Committee may choose to reject the plan not because the plan is less than optimal to it as a creditor, but because the Teamsters Committee has a noncreditor interest — e.g., rejection will benefit its members in the ongoing employment relationship. Although the Teamsters Committee certainly is not intimately connected with the debtor, to allow the Committee to vote with the other impaired creditors would be to allow it to prevent a court from considering confirmation of a plan that a significant group of creditors with similar interests have accepted. Permitting separate classification of the Teamsters Committee's claim does not automatically result in adoption of the plan. The Teamsters Committee is still protected by the provisions of subsections (a) and (b), particularly the requirements of subsection (b) that the plan not discriminate unfairly and that it be fair and equitable with respect to the Teamsters Committee's claim. In fact, the Teamsters Committee invokes those requirements, but as we note in the following sections, the plan does not violate them. . . .

While the emphasis in Chapter 11 is on consensus, it is important to underline the fact that creditors accept by classes, not individually. The individual creditor is protected by the best interest and feasibility tests, but otherwise it is the will of the majority of each class (as defined) that binds all. This rule is highly important, because it addresses a fundamental problem of debt restructuring: eliminating the incentive to hold out. Recall that in the Chrysler workout there was a great temptation to be the last one to agree and then hold out for better treatment than everyone else. Such incentives can make agreement impossible to reach, leaving aside the risk of pure cussedness on the part of one creditor or a small group. Every bankruptcy system around the world that contemplates court-approved workouts provides for some form of majority rule. It is the lack of such a rule that often defeats attempts at out-of-court workouts. It is this fact that makes classification so important.

Difficulties arise in the area of classification because the Code is silent on when a plan proponent may separately classify groups of creditors. While *U.S. Truck* and similar cases conclude that debtors may divide creditors into groups, other courts have been quite resistant to what they see as a gerrymandering of classes. The statute is clear about two elements of classification — permission to separate the small creditors into a separate class for convenience and prohibition on combining differently situated creditors into a single class. But it offers no guidance on when — or if — legally similar creditors might be allocated to separate classes. §1122(a), (b).

The National Bankruptcy Review Commission wrestled with this question and concluded that "Section 1122 should be amended to provide that a plan proponent may classify legally similar claims separately if, upon objection, the proponent can demonstrate that the classification is supported by a 'rational business justification.'" NBRC Recommendation 2.4.16 (1997). While "rational business justification" does not provide an obvious checklist for parties and courts to use, such an amendment would make it clear that separate classification of legally similar claims is permissible, and it would provide a direction for the courts to look in as they evaluate different classification schemes. The recommendation has not become part of the statute, but some courts have already applied it.

════════ In re BERNHARD STEINER PIANOS USA, INC. ════════
292 B.R. 109 (Bankr. N.D. Tex. 2002)

Harlin D. HALE, Bankruptcy Judge.

I.   EVENTS LEADING UP TO THE PLAN

Bernhard Steiner Pianos was established in Europe in 1886. In 1903, the company moved operations to South Africa. Bernhard Steiner Pianos was a part of the Kahn Pianos Group, a family business owned by the Kahn family. The Kahn family enjoys an international reputation in the piano industry, with Ivan Kahn being the fourth generation of piano makers in the family.

In 1976, Ivan Kahn and members of his family relocated to the United States and established Bernhard Steiner Pianos USA, Inc. ("Debtor") in North Dallas. The company deals in the sale and service of new and used pianos of all descriptions. The company sells new pianos, consigns used pianos, and repairs and refurbishes pianos. By 2001, annual sales had reached over $3.3 million.

Unfortunately, the Kahn family also entered into other areas of commerce in Africa. Ivan Kahn's father and mother contracted with the Nigerian government relating to certain construction. The Kahn family was to provide services and the Nigerian government would then submit payment for those services. Apparently, after some political upheaval in Nigeria, the new government refused to pay the debts of the old government. Much time, energy, and money has been spent by the Kahn family to remedy that situation.

★ ★ ★

In a self-described "misguided" attempt to aid his family, Kahn began borrowing funds from the Debtor without repaying on a timely basis, if at all. To further compound the situation, the events of September 11, 2001 were far-reaching and even impacted negatively a piano store in Dallas, Texas. After the terrorist attacks, piano sales fell dramatically for Mr. Kahn. In late 2001 and early 2002, sales were also dismal. Due to the Debtor's cash crunch, funds were not turned over to the lenders providing the floor plan financing. The collateral for the floor plan lenders was exceeded by the debt owed to those entities. Debtor, and Kahn, found themselves out of trust with the floor plan lenders.[2]

---

2. Although the Court has approved the Plan, such approval does not extend to the unauthorized use of cash collateral of the Objecting Creditors.

Debtor filed this bankruptcy proceeding on March 14, 2002. Debtor remained open for business during the pendency of this bankruptcy. Early in the case, the Objecting Creditors obtained relief from the automatic stay, and repossessed their remaining collateral.

During this bankruptcy case, Debtor entered into a Court-approved agreement with a third party whereby the third party would provide pianos to Debtor and would also pay for the cost of operations for a 90 day period. In return, Debtor and the third party split the profits from the sale. During this 90 day period, Debtor sold $1 million worth of pianos and netted $45,000. Thereafter, Debtor entered into another Court-approved agreement with another third party who presently provides pianos to Debtor for sale.

Debtor filed its Debtor's Plan of Reorganization dated September 13, 2002 (the "Plan"). The Plan contemplates repayment of Debtor's creditors on a 100% basis. Kahn testified that in order for Debtor to repay its creditors, Debtor must maintain a successful operation. Kahn further testified that Debtor's ability to continue successfully in business will require that the Debtor attract good consignment pianos; the sale of new pianos alone will not suffice.

Typically, consignment pianos come from individual owners. Most of the consignment business is by word of mouth. In the piano industry, if a consignee gets the reputation that it is unwilling or unable to pay consignors, the consignee won't be able to attract good consignment pianos. Kahn testified that it would be very difficult to supplement any lost consignment income through other operations. Kahn testified that the quicker the Debtor repays the consignment class, the quicker they will get new consignment pianos.

Kahn testified that he will remain the president of the company after confirmation. Largely speaking, Mr. Kahn is all that is left of the Debtor. The company's only tangible assets are some desks and some old wood. At the confirmation hearing, the parties were complimentary of Mr. Kahn's heroic efforts at keeping the Debtor in operation. Through his management during the pendency of the bankruptcy, Kahn singlehandedly managed to keep the Debtor's doors open. The Bernhard Steiner Pianos name is closely associated with Kahn and the Kahn family in the minds of the piano-buying public. The public identifies the Debtor and Mr. Kahn as one and the same.

The Plan was ultimately approved by all the impaired classes except for Class 6, of which the Objecting Creditors, the floor plan lenders, are members.

II. Analysis

A. Separate Classification of Certain Unsecured Creditors

The Plan separately classifies creditors whose claims arose from consigned goods and general unsecured claims, including the claims of the floor plan lenders. The floor plan lenders object to this separate classification. Both classes are unsecured creditors.

The consignment creditors, Class 4, will be repaid over a term of 10 months beginning on the effective date of the plan. The floor plan lenders are part of the allowed general unsecured class, Class 6. Under the Plan, as originally drafted, their scheduled payments begin after full payment to Class 4 (and the convenience class, Class 5), approximately one year after the effective date. Under an agreed modification made in Court after the effective date, the Class 6 creditors will also begin to receive a portion of excess cash flow. Based on the record, the excess cash flow payments should begin before the Class 4 consignment claims are paid in full. Despite the favorable change in the payment schedule, the Objecting Creditors still object and argue that both Class 4 and Class 6 should be placed in the same class.

All unsecured claims outstanding as of the commencement of the case, and claims arising from the rejection of executory contracts or unexpired leases, may be classified together as general unsecured claims. 7 *Collier on Bankruptcy* ¶1122.03[4][a] (15th ed. rev.2000). However, the Code does not require that all such claims be placed within a single class.

The Fifth Circuit has taught that, as a general premise, substantially similar claims, or those which share common priority and rights against the debtor's estate, should be placed in the same class. Small unsecured claims may be classified separately from their larger counterparts if the court so approves for administrative convenience. *Id.* Substantially similar claims are not permitted to be separately classified "in order to gerrymander an affirmative vote on a reorganization plan." *Id.*

Nevertheless, in this Circuit, separate classification is permitted for "good business reasons." Heartland Fed. Sav. & Loan Ass'n v. Briscoe Enterprises, Ltd., II (In re Briscoe Enterprises, Ltd., II), 994 F.2d 1160, 1167 (5th Cir.1993) (citing Matter of Greystone, 995 F.2d 1274 (5th Cir.1991), *cert denied*, 506 U.S. 821, 113 S.Ct. 72, 121 L.Ed.2d 37 (1992)). In *Briscoe*, the Court found that where a continuing relationship with an unsecured creditor who had a distinct interest in the debtor's business was essential to the continued operations of the debtor, separate classification of that creditor was for a good business reason.

In the present case, the Debtor has met the good business reason test. Selling consigned pianos has historically been an important part of the Debtor's business and is contemplated to be an integral part of the Debtor's future. Debtor presented evidence, which was not rebutted, that its consignment business had suffered significantly since word had leaked out that Debtor did not remit the proceeds from the sale of consigned pianos. Kahn testified that the consignment market is local and small, and adverse local community opinion affected whether pianos would be consigned to the Debtor or to its competitors. Kahn also testified that competitors were informing potential consignors that Debtor had failed to remit the sale proceeds to its past consignors. The undisputed testimony is that the Class 4 consignment creditors were separately classified so as to accelerate repayment to them so Debtor could begin expeditiously to repair its tarnished consignment name in a small market. Improving the consignment public's perception of this Debtor and restoring trust in the Debtor among potential consignors as soon as possible is important to the success of the reorganization overall.

No evidence of gerrymandering was offered at the confirmation hearing. Debtor's principal, Mr. Kahn, testified that the development of future consignment business was necessary to its successful reorganization and accordingly, for the repayment of its creditors. Further, the Plan, on its face, treats the consignment class and the general unsecured class differently. The Debtor has presented a good business reason for the separate classification and treatment of consignment creditors in Class 4 from the claims of the general unsecured creditors; therefore, the Court overrules the classification objection.

---

i.   Classification and the Single Asset Case

While the DIP may enjoy fairly wide latitude in classifying claims under a plan when there are many different creditors, one type of case has caused courts endless headaches — and has caused some to rethink the law of classification. The single-asset real estate case typically involves a debtor that is a corporation or a partnership formed for the purpose of operating a single property, such as an apartment house or an office building. In a single-asset real estate case (or SARE, in the jargon of the trade), the debtor has usually borrowed a large sum to finance the purchase of the real estate, the market has crashed, and the debtor takes the operation into bankruptcy to avoid foreclosure of the mortgage and to strip down the mortgage to the current value of the property, which it plans to repay over time. The mortgage lender, frequently a bank or commercial lender, often resists, preferring to foreclose and remarket the property itself.

Some courts have taken an aggressive stand against SARE cases, holding that filing bankruptcy to deal with one large creditor is a bad-faith filing and dismissing the cases out of hand. Chapter 11s of SARE companies in the Eleventh Circuit, for example, are routinely dismissed with little inquiry into the facts of the case. But other courts cannot find any indication in the Code that such cases are ineligible for bankruptcy relief.

Nonetheless, many courts remain hostile to the use of Chapter 11 for little more than stripping a commercial mortgage. Typically, the principal creditor, a commercial lender who will have a deficiency judgment that often amounts to millions of dollars, pledges to vote "no" on the plan. In order to confirm a plan against the wishes of a single large creditor, the DIP will need a class of accepting creditors. Enter the trade debt. Typically, the apartment house or office building project will owe a fairly modest amount of money to suppliers, trade creditors, employees, and the like. If the latter can be formed into a class, they will often vote "yes" because they want to continue to do business with the SARE debtor. In that case, at least one class accepts the plan, so that the plan can be confirmed. §1129(a)(10).

In cases such as the SARE, the ability to group together small claimants to create a separate, accepting class is crucial to the reorganization. When the small creditors are lumped together with the single big deficiency creditor in a single class, they may vote "yes," but the class — by dollar amount — will not accept the plan. Only if the small creditors are separately classified can there be an accepting class.

Some courts have been extremely hostile to the creation of a separate class of unsecured creditors for the apparent purpose of obtaining the necessary approval from one impaired class. An example is a Fifth Circuit case in which the debtor partnership owned an apartment house and proposed to "cram down" a badly undersecured mortgage lender by creating a small class of trade creditors. In re Greystone III, 948 F.2d 134 (5th Cir. 1991). At the same time, other courts have insisted on just such a separate classification when unsecured claimants have differing interests. In re Woodbrook Associates, 19 F.3d 312 (7th Cir. 1994). In any case, classification, once thought to be a minor provision in the Code, has assumed major proportions in some types of cases.

The use of Chapter 11 by SAREs has produced such strong opposition that Congress was moved to address them in the 1994 Amendments and again in the 2005 revision. The amendments were aimed to constrict access to Chapter 11 for SAREs. §362(d)(3)-(4). For a more detailed discussion, see pp. 668–669.

ii. Impairment

"Impairment" refers to whether a creditor class will be completely protected under the plan. It is an aspect of the acceptance process in the sense that a debtor is excused from obtaining the acceptance of the plan from a class that is not impaired. §1129(a)(8)(B). By operation of law, an unimpaired class is "deemed" to have accepted the plan. §1126(f). In addition, if a class is unimpaired, by definition the best interests test of section 1129(a)(7) has been met and need not be separately explored.

The logic behind this special treatment for unimpaired classes of creditors is fairly obvious. If creditors in a class are not being deprived of their nonbankruptcy rights by the plan, why should their approval of the plan be required? Yet in operation the proper contours of the impairment concept are much harder to fix than at first appears.

Impairment figures into voting and confirmation as a plan proponent determines which classes of creditors must vote. Sometimes the bargain with a creditor will not be left exactly the same, and a dispute may arise over whether this creditor has been impaired and therefore may vote. A central question is whether impairment refers to legal impairment, economic impairment, or some combination of the two. If a creditor's legal rights are left exactly the same, is the creditor unimpaired under the following exemplary circumstances?

1. The company that emerges from Chapter 11 has one quarter the assets and revenues of the company to which the creditor lent.
2. Certain powerful creditors are given security — or are given additional security — by the plan, while this creditor is left unsecured, with fewer unencumbered assets left to pay this creditor should liquidation eventually result.
3. The creditor is given collateral of the same value as its original collateral, but the new collateral is of a type that is less important to the debtor, leaving it with much less leverage over the debtor for ultimate collection.

The last of these three examples also illustrates the fact that economic "impairment" shades into legal impairment, since it is a nice question whether substitution of collateral of equal dollar value is an impairment of legal rights.

By the same token, legal impairment may result even without economic impairment. For example, a creditor might be given additional security for its debt, which leaves it far more confident of payment than before. At the same time, the creditor might be subjected to a "cure" period before it can foreclose, whereas before it could have foreclosed immediately. An economist might say that the creditor's economic condition has improved, even though its bundle of legal rights has been reduced or impaired.

The choice between looking for legal or for economic impairment is related to the "absolute priority" and "cramdown" rules we will shortly consider, as well as the best interests test we have already covered. Those rules require valuation of assets for their application; judicial valuation is a very time-consuming and expensive activity. The drafters of the Code wanted very much to avoid valuations whenever possible. The desire to avoid valuation favors focusing solely on legal impairment, because measurement of economic impairment will often require valuation. On the other hand, to ignore economic impairment would risk elevating form over substance. It might permit subversion of the economic protection required by the acceptance requirement of section 1129(a)(8) coupled with the requirements in section 1129(b) for "cramdown" of classes that do not accept the plan. In the same way, it would threaten the protection provided by the best interests requirement of section 1129(a)(7).

While the debtor sometimes wants to declare a creditor unimpaired in order to avoid giving that creditor the right to vote, in cramdown cases the plan proponent will need at least one impaired class to vote its acceptance. This means that the party proposing the plan walks a tightrope — it must offer favorable enough treatment to attract a yes vote, but it must impair the claims of the class in order for the class to have any voting rights.

The following opinion illustrates both the importance of impairment and the jockeying among the parties in a hotly disputed Chapter 11 case.

In re PPI ENTERPRISES (U.S.), INC.
324 F.3d 197 (3d Cir. 2003)

SCIRICA, Circuit Judge.

I.

Sheldon Solow owns a Manhattan office tower at 9 West 57th Street. On August 9, 1989, he leased 10,000 square feet to PPI Enterprises ("PPIE"), a Delaware corporation, for its corporate headquarters. The lease ran for ten years, requiring annual payments (in monthly installments) of $620,000 for five years and $650,000 thereafter. Polly Peck International, PLC, a United Kingdom corporation and the indirect corporate parent of PPIE, guaranteed these commercial lease obligations. Sanwa Bank issued a standby letter of credit to Solow, on behalf of PPIE, in the amount of $650,000.

Over time, Polly Peck's financial status unraveled and insolvency proceedings commenced in Great Britain. On October 25, 1990, the Chancery Division of the High Court of Justice entered an administration order[2] for Polly Peck and appointed three administrators for the company. As Polly Peck's subsidiary, PPIE faced credit cancellations and defaults exceeding $17 million.

In September 1991, PPIE abandoned its corporate headquarters in Manhattan and ceased paying rent to Solow. On October 8, 1991, Solow delivered PPIE written notice of default under the lease. After PPIE failed to cure the default, Solow gave notice on October 21, 1991, of his intent to terminate the lease. Remaining rent due under the leasehold agreement totaled approximately $5.86 million. Solow subsequently drew on Sanwa Bank's letter of credit, applying it in lieu of monthly rent payments between October 1991 and July 31, 1992. By the latter date, the letter of credit was exhausted.

PPIE filed for Chapter 11 bankruptcy in Delaware. PPIE stated it had four objectives: (1) concluding the Polly Peck "wind-down"; (2) "liquidating" PPIE; (3) invoking provisions to reject a restriction on its ability to sell the Del Monte stock; and (4) limiting Solow's lease termination damages under Bankruptcy Code §502(b)(6).

On August 9, 1996, Solow filed a proof of claim with the Bankruptcy Court, reducing his alleged damages to $4,757,824.94. Then, in December 1996, Solow moved to dismiss the Chapter 11 filing for bad faith. Solow alleged PPIE's bankruptcy was a sham filing designed to create value for Polly Peck and its creditors at his expense, and that the bankruptcy served no legitimate purpose. According to Solow, PPIE did not intend its bankruptcy filing to effectuate a corporate reorganization, because the company had no ongoing business, only one remaining employee, and "no assets other than stock certificates representing a 2% interest in Del Monte Foods Company." After an evidentiary hearing, the Bankruptcy Court in January 1997 denied the motion without prejudice.[5]

On March 31, 1998, PPIE filed its bankruptcy plan ("Plan"), dividing administrative claims and priority tax claims into four classes.[6]

The Plan treated Solow's claim as a "Class 2 non-insider general unsecured claim." PPIE contended Plan approval by the classes of creditors was

2. Administration under the Insolvency Act of 1986 is the closest analogue in British law to Chapter 11 bankruptcy relief.
5. In the meantime, Del Monte agreed to re-purchase its stock from PPIE for $1.6 million, subject to higher offers. Solow objected, arguing stock transfer restrictions inhibited bidding by third parties. After Del Monte lifted the restriction, Del Monte and Solow engaged in an exchange of bids, with Solow eventually winning at a price of $11 million. A few months later, Solow resold the Del Monte stock for at least $30 million to Texas Pacific Group, generating a profit that exceeded $19 million.
6. Class 1 consisted of "priority claims"; Class 2 included "non-insider general unsecured claims." Members of Classes 1 and 2 were to be paid, at 100 cents on the dollar, in "cash and other consideration as required." Class 3, encompassing "affiliate claims," and Class 4, encompassing "interests," were to be paid in "remaining cash and the assignment of certain debtor claims or causes of action." Those with Class 3 "affiliate claims," Solow alleges, were the "insiders" owing more than $50 million to PPI Holdings B.V., PPIE's direct corporate parent, and Polly Peck.

unnecessary since none were impaired. Nonetheless, PPIE solicited votes from Classes 1, 2, and 3. Only two of seven ballots were returned from Class 2 — Solow's "no" vote and one "yes" vote. With no clear majority, Solow contends Class 2 effectively rejected the Plan.

On December 30, 1998, the Bankruptcy Court determined Solow's claim was subject to the statutory cap of 11 U.S.C. §502(b)(6) and reduced by application of the letter of credit; the bankruptcy was filed in good faith; and as an "unimpaired creditor," Solow was deemed to have accepted the plan. In re PPI Enters., 228 B.R. 339 (Bankr. D. Del.1998) (Walsh, J.).

III.

The central issue on appeal is whether the doctrine of impairment precludes Solow from having voting rights against PPIE's Chapter 11 bankruptcy plan.

* * *

The Bankruptcy Court here began by reviewing 11 U.S.C. §502(b)(6). The court determined the Plan did not impair Solow's legal, equitable, and contractual rights, since the limitation on Solow's potential recovery was dictated by §502(b)(6), which was independent of the Plan. Solow contends application of §502(b)(6) alters his claim and entitles him to vote against the Plan's confirmation. The question is whether the impairment sections of the Bankruptcy Code require such a result.

A.

1.

We begin with the language of the Bankruptcy Code. As noted, §1124(1) provides that a claim is impaired unless the plan "leaves unaltered the legal, equitable, and contractual rights to which such claim . . . entitles the holder of such claim." Under §101(5), a "claim" refers broadly to a creditor's right to recovery.

Solow contends a broad definition of "claim" requires a finding of impairment whether the source of impairment is the plan or a statute. The Bankruptcy Court rejected Solow's argument, finding he "confuse[d] two distinct concepts: (i) plan impairment, under which the debtor alters the 'legal, equitable, and contractual rights to which [the] claim entitles the holder of such claim,' and (ii) statutory impairment, under which the operation of a provision of the Code alters the amount that the creditor is entitled to under nonbankruptcy law." *PPI Enters.*, 228 B.R. at 353.

* * *

A closer inspection of the language employed in Section 1124(1) reveals "impairment by statute" to be an oxymoron. Impairment results from what the *plan* does, not what the statute does. A plan which "leaves unaltered" the legal rights of a claimant is one which, by definition, does not impair the creditor. A plan which leaves a claimant subject to other applicable provisions of the Bankruptcy Code does no more to alter a claimant's legal rights than does a plan which leaves a claimant vulnerable to a given state's usury laws or to federal environmental laws. The Bankruptcy Code itself is a statute which, like other statutes, helps to define the legal rights of persons, just as surely as it limits contractual rights. Any alteration of legal rights is a consequence not of the plan but of the bankruptcy filing itself.

* * *

In sum, PPIE's Chapter 11 Plan intends to pay Solow his "legal entitlement" and provide him with "full and complete satisfaction" of his claim on the date the Plan becomes effective. Solow is only "entitled" to his rights under the Bankruptcy Code, including the §502(b)(6) cap. Solow might have received considerably more if he had recovered on his leasehold claims before PPIE filed for bankruptcy. But once PPIE filed for Chapter 11 protection, that hypothetical recovery became irrelevant. Solow is only entitled to his "legal, equitable, and contractual rights," as they now exist. Because the Bankruptcy Code, not the Plan, is the only source of limitation on those rights here, Solow's claim is not impaired under §1124(1).

* * *

VI.

For the foregoing reasons, we will affirm the District Court.

═══════════════

The court went on to hold that filing for Chapter 11 primarily to take advantage of the rent cap is not per se a bad faith use of bankruptcy law, distinguishing its own decision finding bad faith in a premature filing in *SGL Carbon* (see pp. 430–434).

The courts continue to pursue different philosophies about the proper use of Chapter 11, particularly in SARE cases, and those differences manifest themselves in technical disputes over such terms as impairment. In one SARE case, the debtor offered to pay the unsecured claims in full 60 days after confirmation; the unsecured creditors voted in favor of the plan, but the real estate mortgage lender strenuously objected. In re Windsor on the River Associates, Ltd., 7 F.3d 127 (8th Cir. 1993). Judge Morris Arnold deemed the payment plan to the unsecured creditors "artificial impairment" as he decried the "manipulation of claims in a reorganization proceeding."

It appears that the problems of artificial impairment and artificial classification have much in common. Artificial classification tends to arise where the principal creditor in a single-asset reorganization is undersecured. The extent to which the creditor's claim exceeds its security interest in the single asset of the debtor should be treated, absent the debtor's manipulation, as unsecured credit, and classified with the rest of the unsecured creditors. To achieve "cramdown" under section 1129(a)(10), however, many debtors have attempted to classify the often large unsecured portion of the principal creditor's claim separately from small unsecured trade claims. This is done to prevent the principal creditor from blocking approval of the debtor's plan, which a slightly impaired class of trade claimants might be persuaded to give, in light of the alternative specter of liquidation. See In re Sandy Ridge Dev. Corp., 881 F.2d 1346 [5th Cir. 1989); see also Meltzer, Disenfranchising the Dissenting Creditor, 66 Am. Bankr. L.J. at 281.

Similarly, artificial impairment has arisen most commonly in single-asset reorganizations. The difference is that the debtor is dealing with an oversecured, rather than undersecured, creditor. Because the lender is oversecured, there is no unsecured portion of the claim to classify along with the unsecured trade creditors. The problem, however, is that the approving class of unsecured trade claimants must hold impaired claims. Impairment in such cases is more difficult, since the value of the asset exceeding the secured claim is often sufficient to satisfy the much smaller unsecured trade claims in full.

The possible effects of confirmation under such circumstances are somewhat unsettling. Confirmation might encourage similarly situated debtors to view the bankruptcy code as an alternative to refinancing. First, debtors with projects lacking the fiscal promise necessary to gain refinancing on the open market might resort to section 1129(a)(10) as the mechanism by which they might draft their own loans from existing lenders. Second, the very threat of such an alternative might coerce lenders into extensions of credit terms that might otherwise not be called for by market conditions.

Finally, such an outcome would directly undermine one of the primary functions of bankruptcy law: to discourage "side dealing" between the shareholders of a corporation and some creditors to the detriment of other creditors. See Posner, Economic Analysis of Law 375. A similarly situated debtor, with the knowledge that impairment under section 1129(a)(10) might be manufactured, would be encouraged to make arrangements with small, unsecured creditors, and to seek their approval when a plan is filed that leaves their interests only marginally affected. It is exactly such "side dealing" that prompted the adoption of a bankruptcy code, and to allow it would defeat "'the purposes Congress sought to serve.'" *Norfolk Redevelopment*, 464 U.S. at 36, quoting *Chapman*, 441 U.S. at 608. Accordingly, we hold that, for purposes of 11 U.S.C. §1129(a)(10), a claim is not impaired if the alteration of rights in question arises solely from the debtor's exercise of discretion.

Id. at 131-132. Judge Arnold then reversed the bankruptcy court's confirmation of the plan, holding that there was no impaired class voting in favor of the plan. When the plan fails, the way would be paved for the secured creditor to lift the stay and foreclose on the building. Of course, if the property is sold at foreclosure, the unsecured creditors will be paid only if the proceeds exceed the value of the outstanding mortgages. This possibility illustrates once again the O. Henry quality of bankruptcy, because the unsecured creditors were receiving payment in full under the plan, but they risk getting nothing at all when the debtor is liquidated.

As *PPI Enterprises* and *Windsor on the River Associates* illustrate, grouping together classes of creditors and negotiating their treatment is done with a keen eye on plan confirmation, whether the debtor aims for a consensual plan or a cramdown.

d.   Claims Trading

In *OBT Partners*, the big creditor purchased and voted the claims of several other classes of creditors. The court made the following notation:

> The Debtor filed "Debtor's Objections to Claims and Motion to Designate Claims as Excluded from Balloting in Connection with Debtor's Amended Plan of Reorganization" alleging that the claims purchased by Principal should be designated under 11 U.S.C. §1126(e) since Principal purchased and voted the Class 8 claims in bad faith. This motion remains pending before this court. The parties have agreed that those objections should be held in abeyance pending this decision on the cross-motions for summary judgment.

In re OBT Partners, 214 B.R. at 866 n.3. Because the plan was confirmed even if all the ballots purchased by the creditor were counted, the court never reached the question of whether all those claims could be separately voted.

A single, large creditor is not the only one that may be interested in buying the claims of creditors in bankruptcy cases. Outside investors, people who had no special connection to the company before the bankruptcy filing, may want to buy the claims of creditors in a reorganization proceeding. The process of buying these bankruptcy-based obligations is known as claims trading.

For some investors, claims purchase may be a way to buy at discount. So, for example, an investor may offer to buy claims at a fraction of their face value, knowing that they can make substantial returns on their investments if some of those claims result in substantial payoffs in confirmed Chapter 11 plans. Other investors may purchase claims in order to take a more aggressive role: buying claims at a discount in order to get a seat at the negotiating table for the Chapter 11 reorganization to enhance the repayment to the newly purchased class of claims. Still other investors see claims purchase as a way to buy companies. For an insolvent business that may soon wipe out all its equity, the class of unsecured creditors are in line to become the equitable owners of the business. A Chapter 11 may effectively put a business "in play" for a takeover, and a claims trader stands to profit in the same way that a shareholder profits in a corporate takeover.

The bankruptcy courts struggle with policy issues about how claims trading may affect the Chapter 11 reorganization. The footnote from *OBT Partners* is an example of the issue. Can a party to the bankruptcy buy claims with the intent of changing the Chapter 11 outcome? Is vote-buying when only economic interests are at stake acceptable? Is a purchase to block a confirmation the same as a purchase to assist in a confirmation? While claims trading has moved from millions of dollars in annual activity to billions of dollars, the courts have only begun to wrestle with these questions. The Ninth Circuit faced some of these questions in the next case.

====== In re FIGTER LTD. ======
118 F.3d 635 (9th Cir. 1997)

FERNANDEZ, Circuit Judge:

Figter Limited, a Chapter 11 debtor and owner of Skyline Terrace, an apartment complex, appeals from the district court's affirmance of the bankruptcy court's decision that Teachers Insurance and Annuity Association of America (Teachers), the holder of a $15,600,000 promissory note secured by a first deed of trust on Skyline Terrace, bought twenty-one unsecured claims in good faith and that it could vote each one separately. We affirm.

BACKGROUND

Figter filed a voluntary petition under Chapter 11 of the Bankruptcy Code. It owns Skyline Terrace, a 198-unit residential apartment complex located in Los Angeles. Teachers is a creditor. It holds a $15,600,000 promissory note executed by Figter. The note is secured by a first deed of trust on Skyline Terrace and by $1,400,000 of cash on hand. In fact, Teachers is Figter's only secured creditor and is the only member of Class 2 in a reorganization plan proposed by Figter. The plan contemplates full payment of Teachers' secured claim, but at a disputed rate of interest. Thus, under Figter's plan, Teachers' claim is not impaired. The plan calls for the impairment of Class 3 unsecured claims by payment at only 80% of their face value.

Teachers has opposed Figter's reorganization plan from its inception because, among other things, that plan contemplates the conversion of Skyline Terrace Apartments into condominiums, with payment to and partial releases by Teachers as the units sell. That could easily result in a property that was part condominium and part rentals, if the plan ultimately fails in operation.

Teachers proposed a plan of its own, which provided for the transfer of Skyline Terrace and the cash collateral to Teachers in satisfaction of its secured claim, as well as a payment of Class 3 unsecured claims at 90%. Teachers' plan was premised on the assumption that its claim was partly unsecured. However, on May 31, 1994, before the purchases of other claims took place, the bankruptcy court determined that Skyline Terrace had a value of $19,300,000. Thus, Teachers' claim in the amount of $17,960,000 was fully secured. It did not thereafter pursue its plan. From October 27, 1994 until October 31, 1994, Teachers purchased twenty-one of the thirty-four unsecured claims in Class 3 at one hundred cents on the dollar, for a total purchase price of $14,588.62. Teachers had made the same offer to all of the Class 3 claim holders, but not all accepted it. The offer remained open. Teachers then filed notices of transfer of claims with the court, as is required under Bankruptcy Rule 3001(e)(2). Those notices were served on all affected parties, including Figter. No objections were filed by the unsecured creditors. The district court upheld the bankruptcy court's determination regarding Teachers' purchase of the unsecured claims. As a result, Figter's plan is unconfirmable because it is unable to meet the requirements of 11 U.S.C. §1129(a)(10); there will not be an impaired, consenting class of claims. That will preclude a "cram down" of Teachers' secured claim under 11 U.S.C. §1129(b). Figter has appealed in an attempt to avoid that result. . . .

DISCUSSION

Figter asserts that Teachers should be precluded from voting its purchased Class 3 claims because it did not buy them in good faith. Figter also asserts that even if the claims were purchased in good faith, Teachers cannot vote them separately, but is limited to one total vote as a Class 3 creditor. If Figter were correct in either of its assertions, it could obtain Class 3 approval of its plan and enhance its chances of cramming down Teachers' Class 2 claims. But Figter is not correct.

A.   Good Faith

The Bankruptcy Code provides that "on request of a party in interest, and after notice and a hearing, the court may designate any entity whose acceptance or rejection of [a] plan was not in good faith, or was not solicited or procured in good faith or in accordance with the provisions of this title." 11 U.S.C. §1126(e). In this context, designate means disqualify from voting. The Bankruptcy Code does not further define the rather murky term "good faith." That job has been left to the courts.

The Supreme Court brought some clarity to this area when it decided *Young v. Higbee Co.*, 324 U.S. 204 (1945). In *Young*, the Court was discussing the predecessor to §1126(e) when it declared that if certain persons "had declined to accept [the] plan in bad faith, the court, under section 203 could have denied them the right to vote on the plan at all." Id. at 210-11. It went on to explain that the provision was intended to apply to those "whose selfish purpose was to obstruct a fair and feasible reorganization in the hope that someone would pay them more than the ratable equivalent of their proportionate part of the bankrupt assets." Id. at 211. In other words, the section was intended to apply to those who were not attempting to protect their own proper interests, but who were, instead, attempting to obtain some benefit to which they were not entitled. While helpful, those reflections by the Court do not fully answer the question before us. Other courts have further illuminated the area.

If a person seeks to secure some untoward advantage over other creditors for some ulterior motive, that will indicate bad faith. But that does not mean that creditors are expected to approach reorganization plan votes with a high degree of altruism and with the desire to help the debtor and their fellow creditors. Far from it.

If a selfish motive were sufficient to condemn reorganization policies of interested parties, very few, if any, would pass muster. On the other hand, pure malice, "strikes" and blackmail, and the purpose to destroy an enterprise in order to advance the interests of a competing business, all plainly constituting bad faith, are motives which may be accurately described as ulterior. That is to say, we do not condemn mere enlightened self interest, even if it appears selfish to those who do not benefit from it.

Thus, if Teachers acted out of enlightened self interest, it is not to be condemned simply because it frustrated Figter's desires. That is true, even if Teachers purchased Class 3 claims for the very purpose of blocking confirmation of Figter's proposed plan. That self interest can extend even further without being an ulterior motive. It has been held that a creditor commits no wrong when he votes against a plan of a debtor who has a lawsuit pending against the creditor, for that will not, by itself, show bad faith. It has also been held that no bad faith is shown when a creditor chooses to benefit his interest as a creditor as opposed to some unrelated interest. And the mere fact that a creditor has purchased additional claims for the purpose of protecting his own existing claim does not demonstrate bad faith or an ulterior motive. "As long as a creditor acts to preserve what he reasonably perceives as his fair share of the debtor's estate, bad faith will not be attributed to his purchase of claims to control a class vote." In re Gilbert, 104 B.R. 206, 217 (Bankr. W.D. Mo. 1989).

Courts, on the other hand, have been sensitive to situations where a company, which was not a preexisting creditor, has purchased a claim for the purpose of blocking an action against it. They have seen that as an indication of bad faith. The same has been true where creditors were associated with a competing business and desired to destroy the debtor's business in order to further their own. And when the debtor had claims against itself purchased by an insider or affiliate for the purpose of blocking a plan, or fostering one, that was seen as a badge of bad faith. Figter would have us add that in a single asset bankruptcy, claim purchasing activities, like those of Teachers, are in bad faith. It cites no authority for that, and we see no basis for establishing that as a per se rule.

In short, the concept of good faith is a fluid one, and no single factor can be said to inexorably demand an ultimate result, nor must a single set of factors be considered. It is always necessary to keep in mind the difference between a creditor's self interest as a creditor and a motive which is ulterior to the purpose of protecting a creditor's interest. Prior cases can offer guidance, but, when all is said and done, the bankruptcy court must simply approach each good faith determination with a perspicacity derived from the data of its informed practical experience in dealing with bankrupts and their creditors.

Here, the bankruptcy court did exactly that. It decided that Teachers was not, for practical purposes, the proponent of an alternate plan when it sought to purchase the Class 3 claims. Nor, it found, did Teachers seek to purchase a small number of claims for the purpose of blocking Figter's plan, while injuring other creditors, even if it could do that in some circumstances. Rather, Teachers offered to purchase all Class 3 claims, and only some of those claimants' refusals to sell precluded it from doing so. Moreover, Teachers was a lender, not a competing apartment owner. It acted to protect its interests as Figter's major creditor. It reasonably feared that it could be left with a very complex lien situation, if Figter went forward with its plan. Instead of holding a lien covering the whole of the property, it could have wound up with separate fractured liens on various parts of the property, while other parts were owned by others. That could create a very undesirable mix of owners and renters and of debtors and nondebtors.

Added to that was the actual use of cash, which was collateral for the debt owed to Teachers. It cannot be said that Teachers' concerns were irrational.

Based on all that was before it, the bankruptcy court decided that in this case Teachers was a creditor which acted in a good faith attempt to protect its interests and not with some ulterior motive. We cannot say that it erred in making that ultimate determination.

B.   Voting

Figter's fallback position is that even if Teachers did act in good faith, it must be limited to one vote for its twenty-one claims. That assertion is answered by the language of the Bankruptcy Code, which provides that:

> A class of claims has accepted a plan if such plan has been accepted by creditors . . . that hold at least two-thirds in amount and *more than one-half in number of the allowed claims* of such class held by creditors . . . that have accepted or rejected such plan.

11 U.S.C. §1126(c) (emphasis added). That language was interpreted in *Gilbert*, 104 B.R. at 211, where the court reasoned:

> The formula contained in Section 1126(c) speaks in terms of the number of claims, not the number of creditors, that actually vote for or against the plan. . . . Each claim arose out of a separate transaction, evidencing separate obligations for which separate proofs of claim were filed. Votes of acceptance . . . are to be computed only on the basis of filed and allowed proofs of claim. . . . [The creditor] is entitled to one vote for each of his unsecured Class X claims.

That same view was iterated in Concord Square Apartments of Wood Cty, Ltd. v. Ottawa Properties, Inc. (In re Concord Square Apartments of Wood Cty., Ltd.), 174 B.R. 71, 74 (Bankr. S.D. Ohio 1994), where the court held that a creditor with "multiple claims, has a voting right for each claim it holds." We agree. It would not make much sense to require a vote by creditors who held "more than one-half in number of the allowed claims" while at the same time limiting a creditor who held two or more of those claims to only one vote. If allowed claims are to be counted, they must be counted regardless of whose hands they happen to be in. . . .

Of course, that is not to say that a creditor can get away with splitting one claim into many, but that is not what happened here. Teachers purchased a number of separately incurred and separately approved claims (each of which carried one vote) from different creditors. There simply is no reason to hold that those separate votes suddenly became one vote, a result which would be exactly the opposite of claim splitting.

Therefore, the bankruptcy court did not err. . . .

========

The hard question facing the parties to a negotiation after *Figter:* How sharp are the edges in the Ninth Circuit opinion? Are all purchases to further one's own economic interests "in good faith"? Or has Judge Fernandez left lots of wiggle room for courts to reduce the voting rights attached to the claims if the circumstances differ from those in *Figter*? The next year, the Third Circuit found that a quiet purchase by an insider of the debtor was in bad faith in a case based on the bankruptcy of Papercraft Corporation. Citicorp Venture v. Committee of Creditors Holding Unsecured Claims, 160 F.3d 982 (3d Cir. 1998). The insider ultimately decided not to try to vote his claims, but the court recognized that he nonetheless was in a powerful position and subordinated his claims against the debtor, which means that the insider-buyer would collect nothing until all the other creditors had been paid in full.

Bankruptcy Judge Lief Clark presided over a case in which both the debtor and a creditor proposed competing plans. In re Applegate Property, Ltd, 133 B.R. 827 (Bankr. W.D. Tex. 1991). An affiliate of the debtor began to buy up claims, which it then voted to block the creditor's plan. Judge Clark disallowed the votes:

> The purchasing of claims by an affiliate or insider of the Debtor for the sole or principal purpose of blocking a competitor from purchasing such claims is an obstructionist tactic done in contemplation of gaining an unfair advantage over other creditors. Such conduct cannot, as a matter of law, be in good faith. This court is unable to ascertain any independent, legitimate interest which would justify the purchase of these claims by Daseke than to obstruct the competing plan proponent. The sole purpose was to ensure the confirmability of their own plan, partly by locking in an affirming impaired class . . . and partly by blocking an acceptance by that same impaired class in the RTC's plan. That purpose will not withstand the "good faith" hurdle imposed by Section 1126(e).
>
> The evil of an insider's acquiring a blocking position is especially insidious in the context of competing plans, as is the case here. The Code contemplates that, when two or more plans are before the court,
>
>> The court may confirm only one plan. . . . If the requirements of subsections (a) and (b) of this section are met with respect to more than one plan, the court shall consider the preferences of creditors and equity security holders in determining which plan to confirm.
>
> 11 U.S.C. §1129(c). Thus, when the court is forced to make the choice under Section 1129(c), one of the groups that has input into the decision is the creditors. One may reasonably infer, from the structure of Section 1129 generally, that Congress had in mind the considerations of independent third parties when it directed courts to accede to the desires of creditors in Section 1129(c), rather than the wishes of an insider. When the debtor, in the context of competing plans, buys up blocking claims in an important "swing class" consisting of such independent third parties (whether directly or indirectly, as here), it is effectively stacking the deck on the Section 1129(c) issue, undercutting the ability of the court to properly "consider the preferences of creditors" as directed by the statute. See In re Allegheny International, Inc., 118 Bankr. at 299; see also In re MacLeod, 63 Bankr. at 656 (competitor acquired blocking position for ulterior purpose of destroying or injuring the debtor, so that the interests of its competing business would be furthered).
>
> Sanctioning claims acquisition for purposes of blocking an opponent's plan would also ignite a scramble for votes conducted almost entirely outside the Code's carefully developed structure (plan, disclosure statement, equal treatment, regulated solicitation, court-supervised confirmation), leaving creditors to select not the best plan but the best deal they might be able to

individually negotiate. Creditors would be paid, no doubt, but not equally, and not on the basis of accurate information. Such a wild free-for-all may appeal to the entrepreneurial capitalist, but it also issues a gilt-edged invitation to fraudulent and corrupt practices, to say nothing of the ramifications of buying claims in exchange for forbearance, a potential violation under the federal criminal code. See 18 U.S.C. §152; see also In re Featherworks Corp., 25 Bankr. 634, 641 (Bankr. E.D.N.Y. 1982). Needless to say, such an invitation cannot responsibly be issued by this court.

The argument that "we needed to do it to them before they did to us" is flawed in at least two respects. First, the conduct on the part of RTC could have earned similar condemnation and disqualification, for precisely the same reasons, i.e., their sole purpose, as the evidence indicated at the hearing, would have been to defeat the confirmability of Debtor's Plan.[7] Second, such a rationale, if accepted, would no doubt become the favorite excuse to justify such tactics in the future. Courts would be forced into speculating about what some other party was "going to do." What should a court do under such an inquiry if it determines that the debtor honestly held the fear, but that the fear was not justified? The question itself suggests the futility of such a legal standard.

Accordingly, pursuant to Section 1126(e), the votes cast by Daseke are disallowed for purposes of the RTC Plan as such votes were neither acquired nor voted in good faith.

Id. at 835-836.

Papercraft and *Applegate* suggest a second issue that lurks in claims trading: Should there be any regulations on the sale of claims? When parties buy and sell publicly traded stock, they do so subject to the rules of stock exchanges, federal and state securities laws, and the oversight of the SEC or other agencies. When parties buy and sell claims against companies in bankruptcies, they may be trading in what is effectively the residual ownership of the business. Many of the same market problems that prompt regulation of stock markets also exist when the subject of the sale is a bankruptcy claim. What should be the regulations governing secret purchases, failure to buy all the shares in a class, strategic purchases at different prices, disclosure, blocking positions, control positions? All the issues that arise in the sales of securities can arise in the sale of claims, for all the same reasons. The difference is that in Chapter 11 there is no equivalent to the SEC and the securities laws to protect traders in these markets. Instead, the courts are left to fashion a common law of regulation around the Bankruptcy Code.

Problem Set 33

33.1. Talbert Pany is back in your office (see Problem Set 32, pp. 622–623). Although your phone call to the bank's lawyer was successful, Talbert is

---

7. Certainly Debtor's counsel would have no way of determining in advance how this court might rule on such an issue and their advice to purchase such claims would seem to be a proper method of handling the problem, given such uncertainty. In the future, such advice would be unwise. This is not to say, however, that there are never legitimate grounds for buying claims. Under the proper circumstances, the purchasing of claims may well be a legitimate tactic. What those legitimate grounds are is not presently before the court nor is the court inclined to embark on such a discussion.

madder than ever. The debtor has proposed an amended plan that offers exactly 60 cents on the dollar to the unsecureds, although it offers the possibility of full payment if certain profit levels are reached in future years. Talbert says the profit levels required for any additional payments are utterly ridiculous ("Couldn't make that if they put a pipe in every mouth in America"), so effectively the plan only offers 60 percent plus interest. He trumpets, "If those deadbeats are going to give me the same amount as if they closed down, then let's close 'em down and let 'em look for honest work."

Talbert also has a practical objection to the amended plan: His tax lawyer says he would be better off getting paid 60 percent now and writing off the rest as a bad debt against this year's income. Because of the possible payment in full under the plan (even though it is illusory), the IRS might challenge any attempt to write off the unpaid 40 percent of the debt until the plan is completed.

Talbert has been out "working the electorate" to defeat the amended plan. He tells you that he has found one other unsecured creditor who agrees with him and is now willing to vote against the amended plan. This other creditor is owed $600,000. Talbert also says that the holder of the mortgage on Country's real estate might be talked into voting against the plan, but that holder has been classified separately under the plan as unimpaired because the plan will cure the default, deaccelerate the debt, and pay it according to its original terms.

Talbert has been further upset by "Country's latest maneuver." Of the total unsecured debt of $5,000,000 (of which Pany Chemicals is owed $1,000,000 and the other dissenting creditor $600,000), some $300,000 consists of a number of small claims of less than $1,000 each. Talbert has talked to some of these small creditors and reports that Sam Pickens, the president of Country, has personally guaranteed these debts in order to convince these small creditors to vote for the plan. Talbert says, "This is just the sort of cheap trick a snake like Pickens would pull."

Talbert wants to know if he can "stop this steamroller." What is your strategy and on what theories does it rest? (Ignore any question of "cramdown" under section 1129(b) for now.)

33.2. You have been called into a conference with Alice Sharp, the executive director of the National Credit Planning Association. Because of your firm's prominence in the bankruptcy field, it is often employed by government agencies and trade associations to develop new commercial legislation. Because you are the brightest and most imaginative associate in the firm, you have been called on to work with Ms. Sharp on a legislative reform that NCPA is considering.

NCPA's concern is with section 1122(a) of the Bankruptcy Code. A number of its members have been involved in Chapter 11 cases in which there have been disputes about classification of creditors. Many feel that this section is too vague and leaves too much to the court's discretion. As one creditor-member wrote to Ms. Sharp:

> In approving this unfair and arbitrary classification of our claim, the judge said that classification must be decided "on a case by case basis." As near as

I can tell, that means the judge can do what he wants, unless another judge later decides he didn't want right. Since the bankruptcy judges love debtors anyway. . . .

Ms. Sharp asks you to develop an amendment to section 1122(a) for circulation to the membership and possible submission to Congress. She emphasizes that she has no preconceived idea about its contents. The NCPA thinks of itself as a law-reform organization and is proud of its reputation for having no axe to grind. Thus she asks you to write the proposal as you think it should be; the only requirement is that it establish a fair and reasonably precise standard well suited to the purposes of Chapter 11. For your presentation to her board of directors next Monday, she wants: (a) your proposals for a study of the problem (how one would go about such a study and so forth) and an estimate of the cost of such a study, and (b) the reform amendment you would propose in case the board is not prepared to finance a study.

e. Solicitation and Disclosure

It is easy to assume that the technical requirements for solicitation and disclosure are simply that: requirements to be met, but not deserving much attention. In fact, the disclosure requirement can produce heated litigation. Most often, as in the following case, a creditor claims the debtor failed to disclose important financial and business information that was necessary for an informed vote on the plan. In other instances, litigation ostensibly challenging the disclosure statement may actually be challenging the debtor's conduct on other grounds. For example, a creditor may assert that the proposed plan has a fatal flaw that will prevent confirmation and that the disclosure statement is defective for failing to "disclose" that the plan cannot be confirmed. This permits a confirmation issue to be raised prior to solicitation.

i. Required Disclosures

The following case offers an especially clear list of what information must be included in a disclosure statement. Just as businesses differ and plans for how to resuscitate or liquidate them differ, the details of what must be included in a disclosure statement also differ.

In re MALEK
35 B.R. 443 (Bankr. E.D. Mich. 1983)

GRAVES, Bankruptcy Judge.

The above-entitled cause came before the Court on Monday, May 16, 1983, for a hearing on the Debtor's disclosure statement. Pursuant to 11 U.S.C. §1125(a)(l) and (b) the Court rejects and denies approval of the

Debtor's disclosure statement for its failure to provide adequate information as defined by the Bankruptcy Reform Act of 1978.

The Debtor, filing his Chapter 11 petition as an individual, is nonetheless bound by the requirements of 11 U.S.C. §1125(a)(l) and must provide a disclosure statement in conformity with the letter and spirit of the Code. The Debtor is required, at a minimum, to provide a disclosure statement containing the following information:

* * *

A.   Description of Business

The Debtor must furnish information describing the nature of the business being reorganized under Chapter 11. This analysis must include the competitive conditions in the industry and the Debtor's role in that industry. He must disclose whether or not he is dependent upon one or more customers or clients. Where the Debtor is a licensed professional whose income is derived from providing services that are billed on an hourly rate, the Debtor must provide information giving the creditor a good faith estimate of the number of clients, the anticipated services, the hourly rate, and the anticipated annual billings that will provide the source of his income. The Chapter 11 Debtor should provide a description of the service to be rendered, location of principal and branch offices, employee staff and payroll, salaries of officers and directors. Any special property interests, such as patents, trademarks, licenses, or franchises should be disclosed and described.

B.   A History of the Debtor Prior to Filing

The Chapter 11 Debtor should describe, in detail, his activities before filing, including the reasons for filing the Chapter 11. This history should be provided in a neutral, objective and noninflammatory manner. Litigation issues are to be described in an objective professional tone, free of any mischaracterizations of the issues to be resolved in such litigation. Where possible, the Debtor should provide an evaluation of the probable success of any litigation and its effect on the Debtor's business or his plans for reorganization under Chapter 11.

C.   Financial Information

The Debtor must provide a statement of assets and liabilities together with a profit and loss analysis prior to the filing of his Chapter 11 petition. The Debtor must also provide financial information sufficient to inform the creditors of all liens, encumbrances, security interests, loans or other financial obligations which may impair the Debtor or his assets.

D. Description of the Plan

The plan of reorganization must be described in sufficient detail to give the creditors enough information to determine how their rights will be affected.

E.   How the Plan is to be Executed

F.   Liquidation Analysis

G.   Management to be Retained and the Compensation
of the Personnel Retained

H.   Projection of Operations

The Debtor should provide the projection of operations subsequent to confirmation so that the Court may determine the feasibility of the plan. The Debtor is required to make a full, clear, and complete disclosure of all underlying assumptions. The Debtor must provide sufficient financial information to determine if the projections for operations subsequent to confirmation are feasible. If the plan assumes an increase in income, the basis for this assumption must be set forth. If the future operations contain a risk of loss of income or anticipated financial instability, the factors that may cause a loss or diminution of income should be set forth.

I.   Litigation

All pending or contemplated litigation of whatever nature must be described fully, completely, and in detail. Trial dates, where known, must be disclosed. Appeals, filed or contemplated, must be disclosed. The disclosure statement must include a professional evaluation of the probable success of any pending or contemplated litigation.

J.   Transactions with Insiders

The disclosure statement must describe fully, completely, and in detail all transactions with insiders. If there are no such transactions Debtors must so state.

K.   Tax Consequences

The disclosure statement must reveal the probable tax consequences if the Chapter 11 plan is confirmed. If there are no tax consequences, the disclosure statement must contain an affirmative statement of that fact.

The Court grants the objection of Stricoff and Okray to the disclosure statement for the statement's failure to provide the information set forth in this Order.

* * *

Disclosure statements for large, publicly traded companies may run into thousands of pages. For a small business, disclosure may be accomplished in a few pages. In either case, however, creditors are free to complain if they feel that the debtor has not provided enough information and courts are often quick to send the debtor back to amend a disclosure statement to add more information. In a hotly contested case, it is not uncommon to see a Second Amended Disclosure Statement, Third Amended Disclosure Statement, and so on.

Because it is the basis on which the creditors vote, the disclosure statement is a central document in a Chapter 11 reorganization. In a study of 201 large firms that completed Chapter 11 reorganizations between 1982 and 1993, Professors Betker, Ferris, and Lawless concluded that there was a "significant optimistic bias in the earnings projections" of the disclosure statements:

> The annual pretax and post tax incomes of reorganized firms are systematically overestimated for each of the four years following plan confirmation. . . . By the fourth year following plan confirmation, the cumulative forecast error for pretax income (e.g., EBIT) is 170% of the average annual projected income examined in the study.

Brian Betker, Stephen Ferris, and Robert Lawless, "Warm with Sunny Skies": Disclosure Statement Forecasts, 73 Am. Bankr. L.J. 809, 834 (1999). The title of their article says it all. The authors recommend that those who rely on disclosure statements "should discount the projected income figures prior to a determination of the plan's ultimate feasibility." Of course, as one side increases the discount factor, the other may just ratchet up the gloriousness of the projections.

The problem with inaccurate disclosure is not limited to overstated value. Management may sometimes understate the value of the debtor company in order to persuade creditors to accept payouts that are lower than those they would be entitled to if the firm were correctly valued. If the firm is undervalued, of course, the effective distribution to the equity owners of the emerging business will have been far in excess of their legal entitlement. In the Chapter 11 case of National Gypsum Corporation, for example, a short time after the Chapter 11 plan was confirmed, a group of creditors sued management and equity. The creditors alleged that the business was grossly (and fraudulently) undervalued in the Chapter 11 documents, causing the creditors to settle for too little money. The problem of management *under*valuation was documented in Stuart Gilson, Edith Hotchkiss, and Richard Ruback, Valuation of Bankrupt Firms, 13 Review of Financial Studies 43 (2000).

ii. The "Safe Harbor" Rule

When a business attempts to reorganize in Chapter 11, it makes statements about the operations of the company, projections, and proposed distributions of stock for money or for forgiveness of debt. Depending on whether the business is large enough or in certain lines of work, those statements and distributions could be subject to SEC regulations governing such matters. Bankruptcy laws displace the SEC regulations governing disclosure as part of the solicitation for a Chapter 11 plan. This exemption is referred to as a "safe harbor," that is, an area in which companies can make disclosure and solicit votes exempt from SEC regulations. Section 1125(e) states the safe harbor rule: No person connected with the solicitation of plan acceptances and rejections is liable for a violation of the securities laws, so long as that person acts in good faith and in compliance with Title 11. The general purpose of section 1125 is to avoid the impact of the strict disclosure requirements of the securities laws. The exemption from SEC and state registration requirements of section 1125(d) is similar to exemptions provided in other specialized fields, but the exemption from fraud liability given by section 1125(e) is more unusual.

The legislative history explains the rationale for the safe harbor rule:

> The purpose of the provision is to protect creditors, creditors' committees, counsel for committees, and others involved in the case from potential liability under the securities laws for soliciting acceptances of a plan by use of an approved disclosure statement. The securities laws generally provide for absolute liability of a person that offers or sells securities if there was the failure to state a material fact in connection with the offer or sale. The Supreme Court has recently held, however, that the civil liability for damages provided under section 10(b) of the Securities Exchange Act of 1934 and Rule 10b-5 do not extend to good faith, though negligent, omissions or misstatements. [Ernst & Ernst v. Hochfelder, 425 U.S. 185 (1976).]
>
> The safe harbor provision codifies the *Hochfelder* case for solicitations in connection with a bankruptcy reorganization. If a creditor or creditors' committee relies on an order of a Federal bankruptcy court that the disclosure statement contains adequate information, that is, states all material facts that should be stated under the circumstances, and meets any other applicable requirement of chapter 11, then that creditor or committee should not be held liable for soliciting acceptances based on a securities law theory that he failed to disclose adequately. Such liability would gut the effectiveness of the disclosure section, and require compliance with all securities laws in spite of the pendency of the reorganization case. As noted above, this would render the reorganization chapter far less valuable to distressed debtors than it would otherwise be.
>
> It has been suggested that the provision seriously jeopardizes the protections to which public investors are entitled, and permits fraud.
>
> Fraud under the securities laws is defined to include honest, open, good faith omission to state a material fact. Thus, even if the person potentially liable did not know of the existence of a material fact, and had no way of knowing of its existence, if he failed to state that fact in connection with the purchase or sale of a security, then he would be guilty of securities fraud. That is what is contemplated by absolute liability in the securities law context, and that is why the safe harbor provision in the strictest sense of the securities laws "codifies fraud." However, in a more realistic sense, the person soliciting acceptances of a plan will have been told by an order of the court that the disclosure statement contains adequate information. If that person thereafter solicits acceptances in good faith and in compliance with the provisions of chapter 11, he should not be held liable for fraud. . . .
>
> The provision also releases a solicitor from injunctive liability on application of the S.E.C., as well as from legal (damages) liability. Injunctive liability

could have the same chilling effect on the participation in reorganization cases as the absence of a civil damages exemption could have. When the S.E.C. obtains an injunction against an attorney for having committed fraud, his reputation is severely diminished, and he may be subject to disbarment. The threat of an injunctive proceeding by the S.E.C. may be leverage that could be used to frustrate the disclosure policy contained in the section.

H.R. Rep. No. 595, 95th Cong., 2d Sess. 230, 231, reprinted in 1978 U.S. Code Cong. & Admin. News 6189, 6190.

It is worth noting that if the *Hochfelder* case stands for the proposition that good faith misrepresentations never give rise to a damage action, as the committee report asserts, then the principal effect of the section 1125(e) exemption is to block SEC injunctive actions, in which the SEC seeks to enjoin a defendant "from further violations of the securities laws." The legislative history is unusually candid in stating that its authors feared not merely the adverse effects of such an injunctive action, but also the "leverage" that the SEC had derived from threatening such actions. Creditors complained that the SEC entered cases, threatening to tie the debtor in regulatory knots but offering to drop its requirements if the debtor would agree to better payments for certain public bondholders and shareholders — parties that were legally subordinated to the creditors. One reason that certain creditor groups supported the 1978 Bankruptcy Code was to prevent what they considered the SEC's overzealous representation of public debtholders and stockholders to the prejudice of private creditor interests.

Not everyone is satisfied with this arrangement, however. When the parent corporation of Drexel Burnham Lambert, a huge stockbrokerage house that was once home to Michael Milken, filed for bankruptcy, there was renewed discussion of a role for the SEC in Chapter 11 cases. At the time of the filing, Milken was facing 98 racketeering counts, and Drexel Burnham had already agreed to pay multimillion dollar fines for its activities. Actually, there was nothing special about the Drexel Burnham case to make it a vehicle to discuss SEC participation in bankruptcy on behalf of the debtor's stockholders. Drexel Burnham's customers were fully protected, in part to the credit of the SEC's aggressive supervision as the company sank into trouble. The equity owners of Drexel were the ones injured, just as they are in most other business bankruptcies. SEC participation in bankruptcy cases was an idea that had been circulating for some time anyway, and the Drexel Burnham case simply made a convenient — if confusing — focus to raise the issue of SEC regulation. Nonetheless, the SEC continues to lobby from time to time for a role in bankruptcies to watch out for equity shareholder interests. If Congress makes such a change, it will have a noticeable impact on plan negotiations in Chapter 11s for publicly traded corporations.

iii. Prepackaged Bankruptcies

Yet another reorganization approach that grew in importance during the 1990s is the "prepackaged 11." A prepacked plan straddles a workout, which never goes into bankruptcy, and an ordinary Chapter 11, with full post-petition negotiations. According to its proponents, prepacks pick up the best of both worlds. A prepack takes most of the process outside the courthouse and outside the rules studied so far, including solicitation and disclosure. It is a parallel road to the one we have been walking, with the steps largely the same, but accomplished privately rather than by court order.

In the prepackaged plan the debtor and several key creditors have worked out a refinancing structure for the debtor, often involving substantial forgiveness of debt, infusion of new capital, and a promise of future credit. To make the deal work, however, the debtor takes the corporation through Chapter 11, taking advantage of whichever provisions of federal reorganization may be needed: e.g., compelling a dissenting creditor to come along by majority vote of each class, discharging contingent pre-bankruptcy liabilities, or recapturing substantial preferential transfers.

A prepackaged 11 can move with amazing rapidity, perhaps proposing and confirming a plan within weeks of the bankruptcy filing. Southland, Inc. confirmed one of the most visible of the prepackaged 11s — entirely fitting that the parent corporation of 7-Eleven convenience stores would show the world the way to get into and out of Chapter 11 with no waiting in line. The speed of a prepack makes it particularly attractive to companies that are concerned that the announcement of a bankruptcy could trigger a series of new problems. So, for example, a company with a number of foreign ties may plan to enter bankruptcy, announce its plan of reorganization and funding for that plan, and emerge from bankruptcy — all before its foreign creditors and business partners feel compelled to seize foreign property or cease doing business with the bankrupt debtor.

The essential feature of a prepack is the prebankruptcy negotiation with an eye toward moving the company into bankruptcy once the details are confirmed among the major players. Two questions arise: first, what law governs solicitations, e.g., SEC or bankruptcy law, and second, will pre-filing solicitations be adequate for post-filing confirmations? The bankruptcy code answers the two issues together. Section 1126(b) deems these pre-petition votes to be effective in the bankruptcy proceedings so long as the pre-petition solicitation complied with all applicable disclosure laws and regulations. If there are no applicable SEC or similar laws, then the solicitations will be effective if they comply with section 1125(a) solicitation requirements in the Bankruptcy Code. If the plan proponent chooses to solicit post-bankruptcy, then the ordinary rules of 1125 apply, but the case will be slowed down by the need to seek court approval of the disclosure statement.

The use of prepacks grew with astonishing speed among large companies in the early 1990s. In 1993 about 21 percent of the bankruptcies of publicly traded companies were prepacks, with 1994 not far behind at 17 percent. 2004 Bankruptcy Yearbook 162. But the numbers have leveled off since then, now down to an estimated 4 percent of all filings, suggesting that this fabulous new idea may be last year's model.

Empirical research suggests that the pre-packs may not be living up to their advertised advantages. Prepackaged cases have been significantly more likely to collapse back into bankruptcy for a second time than non-prepackaged cases. Lynn M. LoPucki and Joseph W. Doherty, Why Are

Delaware and New York Bankruptcy Reorganizations Failing?, 55 Vanderbilt L. Rev. 1933, 1973 (2002). Moreover, the little evidence that is available suggests that the failures of prepackaged cases are more costly than the failures of non-prepackaged cases. Operating losses average about 23 percent for prepacks that are pushed back into bankruptcy, compared with operating losses of about 11 percent for other companies that are forced to refile. Lynn M. LoPucki, Can the Market Evaluate Legal Regimes? A Response to Professors Rasmussen, Thomas, and Skeel, 54 Vanderbilt L. Rev. 331, 336-338 (2001).

Many of the 2005 Amendments made it more difficult or more expensive for Chapter 11 debtors to confirm plans of reorganization, but Congress took a different tack with prepacks. New rules facilitate pre-filing disclosure and solicitation, keeping the fast-moving Chapter 11s speeding right along. Before the amendments, dissenting creditors determined to stop a prepackaged plan could file an involuntary petition or begin a state law foreclosure or other proceeding that would push the debtor into bankruptcy. Once in bankruptcy, the ordinary rules of Chapter 11 would govern, the begun-but-incomplete solicitation would be set aside, and the court and creditors would be involved in approval of the disclosure statement and other solicitation steps. Such a move effectively derailed the prepack, requiring that the work already done be repeated. But after the amendments, a debtor that began solicitation pre-petition may continue apace if the solicitation complies with applicable non-bankruptcy law, typically the securities laws. 11 U.S.C. §1125(g). Now creditors opposing a prepack will need to push a debtor into bankruptcy before solicitation begins or the creditor may discover that the prepack is complete before the creditor has a chance to speak up. Similarly, the 341 meeting of creditors is waived in prepacks whenever the debtor has solicited pre-petition. 11 U.S.C. §341(e). Yet another Chapter 11 speedbump is removed.

Because public disclosure of information is one of the core principles of bankruptcy, one of the most surprising findings in the Business Bankruptcy Project was that many publicly traded companies in the sample did not file asset and debt schedules — the basic information that is eventually woven into the disclosure statement.

> On going back to the files, we found that six [of the ten] public companies in our sample had been excused from filing schedules by the bankruptcy court. All of these companies filed in Delaware and all were "pre-packaged" filings. Although section 521(1) of the Code says that the court may excuse the filing of schedules, we had understood that schedules are almost always required. It appears we were wrong. Although these were Delaware "pre-packs," the Southern District of New York adopted a new General Order contemplating a similar concession to pre-packaged cases, perhaps in response to the Delaware phenomenon. It seems to us this development raises policy questions about the exercise of public power without public scrutiny as to important data about the party obtaining relief. We are especially interested in the position of the dissenting creditors who may be forced to acquiesce by the bankruptcy filing.

Financial Characteristics 499 (1999).

The creditors that are rolled over in a prepackaged plan sometimes face a difficult task to fight a steamroller confirmation, much to their consternation. The data from the Business Bankruptcy Project raise questions about the quality of the disclosure of information that forms the basis of multimillion dollar decisions. Other cases seem to give away the farm to a whole host of creditors, planning to slip them through on First Day Orders. So, for example, it was an alert bankruptcy judge who slowed down a prepack in which part of the deal was to pay $2.3 million to 27 critical vendors who supported the plan. In re Coserv, L.L.C., 273 B.R. 487 (Bankr. N.D. Texas 2002). Indeed, Professor LoPucki declares that the principal attraction of prepacks is that they provide little opportunity for opposition to form before the whole process is over.

But those consenting to the plan see prepacks as Chapter 11 at its best: reorganizing a company and increasing its chance for survival with a minimum of court involvement. The benefits are said to be savings in legal fees and time, although a study of that issue hasn't yet been done. Whether or when it is beneficial to avoid court procedures, including court scrutiny and control, as well as transparency to the public and to the public markets, is an unanswered question. What is clear is that it is in the interests of many of the players to keep the process close to their collective chests.

Problem Set 34

34.1. You are still representing Pany Chemicals (see Problem Sets 32 and 33). Your negotiations with the bank and the debtor went quite well, due to the power of your legal arguments blended with your winning smile, and a plan of reorganization for Country Smokes paying 70 percent to the unsecured creditors has been confirmed.

You were therefore startled when Talbert Pany, the president of Pany Chemicals, burst into your office yesterday, the veins on his neck like tree trunks. He is upset because he has just been sued by the debtor, Country, to recover $250,000 that Country paid to Pany on March 15 of this year. "They are stiffing me for 30 percent of what they owe me and now they say I am a *preferred* creditor," as Talbert put it. He could not believe that Country could get approval of its plan without saying a word about recovering any preferences and then "sandbag me."

Talbert, of course, remembered your alternative strategy to force a suit against the bank for its preference and demanded you immediately take such steps. Talbert said he would feel better about having to pay if the bank did too. You explained that the plan, for which Pany voted, expressly released the bank from any liability for the preferential payment. Talbert demanded to know why the plan didn't release Pany too. You reminded him, gently, that you didn't know about the payment to Pany. "You didn't ask," Talbert replied. There followed a long and painful silence.

You and Talbert finally agreed that you would try to think of a way to defend the preference action and call him back today. Talbert told you as he left that he was particularly upset about the whole situation because he has learned that Country's backlog of orders was actually considerably less than had been claimed in the solicitation materials. He said he isn't sure if Country's president, Sam Pickens, is "a liar or a dummy," but either way the prospects for a successful payout seem dimmer than ever. What should you do?

f. Cramdown*

Even if a plan satisfies the best interests test of section 1129(a)(7) as to every nonaccepting creditor and meets the test of feasibility, it nonetheless must be accepted by the statutory majority of creditors in each impaired class under section 1129(a)(8). If any class rejects the plan, then the plan cannot be confirmed as a consensual plan under 1129(a). There is, however, one more shot at confirmation: If the plan satisfies the further tests set forth in section 1129(b), it may be confirmed. The requirements for confirming a plan under these circumstances are referred to as "cramdown." (Once again, the word "cramdown" is jargon that does not appear in the statute.)

The classification issues discussed earlier figure heavily in a typical cramdown. Because creditors vote by class, and because a plan is consensual if all classes accept the plan, sometimes a plan proponent will try to create multiple classes of creditors where dissenters can be outvoted. Whether creditors can engage in such creative classification is a matter of hot dispute. Sometimes the debtor knows there will be a dissenting class, as in the case of the SARE in which a single large creditor votes both the secured and the unsecured portion of its claim against the plan. The debtor knows that the plan cannot be consensual with a dissenting class, which the creditor will surely provide, so the debtor will plan a cramdown from the beginning. In other cases, negotiations may go badly so that a debtor unexpectedly faces the possibility of a cramdown.

To qualify for a cramdown, the plan must attract at least one consenting class of impaired creditors. Without that consenting class, a plan cannot be confirmed, even by cramdown. §1129(a)(10). But with it, if the debtor can meet the other requirements of 1129(b), the debtor may confirm a plan even over the vigorous objections of one or more classes.

i. Absolute Priority and the Participation of Old Equity

A cramdown plan must meet additional statutory requirements. Section 1129(b)(1) permits cramdown of the rejecting class only if the plan does not discriminate unfairly between classes *and* is "fair and equitable." The latter phrase effectively incorporates a long line of cases defining "fair and equitable" treatment of dissenting creditor classes under the old Chapter X reorganization provisions.

Section 1129(b)(2) sets forth minimum requirements for a plan to be found "fair and equitable," leaving to the courts the imposition of any additional requirements in particular cases. These minimum requirements are divided into three categories, (b)(2)(A), (B), and (C), governing the rights of secured creditors, unsecured creditors, and equity holders, respectively.

---

*In this section, as throughout the Chapter 11 materials, the discussion refers to a corporate debtor unless the contrary is stated or obviously meant. For a discussion of cramdown by natural persons in Chapter 11, see pp. 684–688.

As a general rule, the liens of secured creditors must be preserved by the plan, and the creditors must be paid the "present value" of their allowed secured claims, i.e., they must receive payment of the full value of the collateral, plus a market interest rate. §1129(b)(2)(A). (This is essentially the same rule as the one governing the treatment of secured creditors in Chapter 13. See pp. 285–306.) Unsecured creditors and senior stockholders are protected by a very different cramdown rule. It is different both from the secured creditor rule and from the rule in Chapter 13 (the disposable income test). In addition to the best interests test of section 1129(a)(7), which must still be met, a class of unsecured creditors and senior stockholders that votes against a plan are protected by the "absolute priority" rule. If a class votes against the plan, it must be paid in full or the plan must provide that any parties "junior" to them will get nothing. So, in the classic instance, unsecured creditors who have as a class rejected the plan cannot be crammed down unless all of the equity owners are getting nothing under the plan. §1129(b)(2)(B). By the same token, preferred stockholders must receive the full value of their preferred position or they cannot be crammed down unless the common stockholders get nothing. §1129(b)(2)(C). The protection against cramdown for unsecured creditors and senior interest holders is called the absolute priority rule because, unless the creditors waived their rights by voting for the plan, the higher priority takers (e.g., the unsecured creditors) must be paid in full before the lower priority takers (e.g., the owners) get anything.

On the face of it, that rule means the equity owners must get the unsecured creditors to support the plan or equity loses everything. Many cases so hold. But equity owners need not give up so easily. For equity owners who want to own the emerging Chapter 11 business and who cannot manage a full repayment plan or count on acceptance of the plan by all classes of creditors, there is yet another possibility that does not appear in the Code.

Recall that in the early sections dealing with Chapter 11 the debtor had several devices to deal with post-petition financing to resuscitate the failing business. In addition to seeking business loans in return for security interests or the like, the debtor may look for a new investor to put money into the business and become the new equity owner. And, not surprisingly, that new equity owner who will provide the cash for the reorganization attempt is often the old equity owner, still running the show. For an appropriate infusion of badly needed cash, old equity can become post-bankruptcy new equity, even in a cramdown.

Not surprisingly, whether old equity should be permitted to participate by means of a contribution to the estate is often hotly contested. The creditors fear that equity is buying its interest at a bargain price, valuing the business low, paying the creditors pennies on the dollar, and then scooping up the real value with a modest infusion of cash. Moreover, in many cases they see that if old equity can be shut out, the reorganization will fail and the creditors will be able to liquidate the business — a prospect that sometimes becomes more appealing as enmity between the parties grows.

The issue finally worked its way to the Supreme Court, which dealt it only a glancing blow. Note that in this case the main incentive for old equity was not its assessment of the long-term value of the business, but the risk of major tax liability if the ownership of the real estate changed.

BANK OF AMERICA NATIONAL TRUST & SAVINGS ASSN. v. 203 NORTH LASALLE STREET PARTNERSHIP
526 U.S. 434 (1999)

Justice SOUTER delivered the opinion of the Court.

The issue in this Chapter 11 reorganization case is whether a debtor's prebankruptcy equity holders may, over the objection of a senior class of impaired creditors, contribute new capital and receive ownership interests in the reorganized entity, when that opportunity is given exclusively to the old equity holders under a plan adopted without consideration of alternatives. We hold that old equity holders are disqualified from participating in such a "new value" transaction by the terms of 11 U.S.C. §1129(b)(2)(B)(ii), which in such circumstances bars a junior interest holder's receipt of any property on account of his prior interest.

I

Petitioner, Bank of America National Trust and Savings Association (Bank), is the major creditor of respondent, 203 North LaSalle Street Partnership (Debtor or Partnership), an Illinois real estate limited partnership. The Bank lent the Debtor some $93 million, secured by a nonrecourse first mortgage[3] on the Debtor's principal asset, 15 floors of an office building in downtown Chicago. In January 1995, the Debtor defaulted, and the Bank began foreclosure in a state court.

In March, the Debtor responded with a voluntary petition for relief under Chapter 11 of the Bankruptcy Code, 11 U.S.C. §1101 et seq., which automatically stayed the foreclosure proceedings, see §362(a). The Debtor's principal objective was to ensure that its partners retained title to the property so as to avoid roughly $20 million in personal tax liabilities, which would fall due if the Bank foreclosed. The Debtor proceeded to propose a reorganization plan during the 120-day period when it alone had the right to do so, see 11 U.S.C. §1121(b); see also §1121(c) (exclusivity period extends to 180 days if the debtor files plan within the initial 120 days). The Bankruptcy Court rejected the Bank's motion to terminate the period of exclusivity to make way for a plan of its own to liquidate the property, and instead extended the exclusivity period for cause shown, under §1121(d).[5]

The value of the mortgaged property was less than the balance due the Bank, which elected to divide its undersecured claim into secured and unsecured deficiency claims under §506(a) and §1111(b).[6] Under the plan, the Debtor separately classified the Bank's secured claim, its unsecured defi-

---

3. A nonrecourse loan requires the Bank to look only to the Debtor's collateral for payment. But see n.6, infra.

5. The Bank neither appealed the denial nor raised it as an issue in this appeal.

6. Having agreed to waive recourse against any property of the Debtor other than the real estate, the Bank had no unsecured claim outside of Chapter 11. Section 1111(b), however, provides that nonrecourse secured creditors who are undersecured must be treated in Chapter 11 as if they had recourse.

ciency claim, and unsecured trade debt owed to other creditors. See §1122(a).[7] The Bankruptcy Court found that the Debtor's available assets were prepetition rents in a cash account of $3.1 million and the 15 floors of rental property worth $54.5 million. The secured claim was valued at the latter figure, leaving the Bank with an unsecured deficiency of $38.5 million.

So far as we need be concerned here, the Debtor's plan had these further features:

(1) The Bank's $54.5 million secured claim would be paid in full between 7 and 10 years after the original 1995 repayment date.[8]

(2) The Bank's $38.5 million unsecured deficiency claim would be discharged for an estimated 16% of its present value.[9]

(3) The remaining unsecured claims of $90,000, held by the outside trade creditors, would be paid in full, without interest, on the effective date of the plan.[10]

(4) Certain former partners of the Debtor would contribute $6.125 million in new capital over the course of five years (the contribution being worth some $4.1 million in present value), in exchange for the Partnership's entire ownership of the reorganized debtor.

The last condition was an exclusive eligibility provision: the old equity holders were the only ones who could contribute new capital.[11]

The Bank objected and, being the sole member of an impaired class of creditors, thereby blocked confirmation of the plan on a consensual basis. See §1129(a)(8). The Debtor, however, took the alternate route to confirmation of a reorganization plan, forthrightly known as the judicial "cramdown" process for imposing a plan on a dissenting class. §1129(b).

There are two conditions for a cramdown. First, all requirements of §1129(a) must be met (save for the plan's acceptance by each impaired class of claims or interests, see §1129(a)(8)). Critical among them are the conditions

---

7. Indeed, the Seventh Circuit apparently requires separate classification of the deficiency claim of an undersecured creditor from other general unsecured claims. See In re Woodbrook Associates, 19 F.3d 312, 319 (1994). Nonetheless, the Bank argued that if its deficiency claim had been included in the class of general unsecured creditors, its vote against confirmation would have resulted in the plan's rejection by that class. The Bankruptcy Court and the District Court rejected the contention that the classifications were gerrymandered to obtain requisite approval by a single class, In re 203 N. LaSalle Street Limited Partnership, 190 B.R. 567, 592-593 (Bkrtcy. Ct. ND Ill. 1995); Bank of America, Illinois v. 203 N. LaSalle Street Partnership, 195 B.R. 692, 705 (ND Ill. 1996), and the Court of Appeals agreed, 126 F.3d at 968. The Bank sought no review of that issue, which is thus not before us.

8. Payment consisted of a prompt cash payment of $1,149,500 and a secured, 7-year note, extendable at the Debtor's option.

9. This expected yield was based upon the Bankruptcy Court's projection that a sale or refinancing of the property on the 10th anniversary of the plan confirmation would produce a $19-million distribution to the Bank.

10. The Debtor originally owed $160,000 in unsecured trade debt. After filing for bankruptcy, the general partners purchased some of the trade claims. Upon confirmation, the insiders would waive all general unsecured claims they held.

11. The plan eliminated the interests of noncontributing partners. More than 60% of the Partnership interests would change hands on confirmation of the plan. See Brief for Respondent 4, n.7. The new Partnership, however, would consist solely of former partners, a feature critical to the preservation of the Partnership's tax shelter. Tr. of Oral Arg. 32.

that the plan be accepted by at least one class of impaired creditors, see §1129(a)(10), and satisfy the "best-interest-of-creditors" test, see §1129(a)(7). Here, the class of trade creditors with impaired unsecured claims voted for the plan, and there was no issue of best interest. Second, the objection of an impaired creditor class may be overridden only if "the plan does not discriminate unfairly, and is fair and equitable, with respect to each class of claims or interests that is impaired under, and has not accepted, the plan." §1129(b)(l). As to a dissenting class of impaired unsecured creditors, such a plan may be found to be "fair and equitable" only if the allowed value of the claim is to be paid in full, §1129(b)(2)(B)(i), or, in the alternative, if "the holder of any claim or interest that is junior to the claims of such [impaired unsecured] class will not receive or retain under the plan on account of such junior claim or interest any property," §1129(b)(2)(B)(ii). That latter condition is the core of what is known as the "absolute priority rule." . . .

We granted certiorari, 523 U.S. 1106 (1998), to resolve a Circuit split on the issue. The Seventh Circuit in this case joined the Ninth in relying on a new value corollary to the absolute priority rule to support confirmation of such plans. See In re Bonner Mall Partnership, 2 F.3d 899, 910-916 (CA9 1993), cert. granted, 510 U.S. 1039, vacatur denied and appeal dism'd as moot, 513 U.S. 18 (1994). The Second and Fourth Circuits, by contrast, without explicitly rejecting the corollary, have disapproved plans similar to this one. See In re Coltex Loop Central Three Partners, L.P., 138 F.3d 39, 44-45 (CA2 1998); In re Bryson Properties, XVIII, 961 F.2d 496, 504 (CA4), cert, denied, 506 U.S. 866 (1992).[15] We do not decide whether the statute includes a new value corollary or exception, but hold that on any reading respondent's proposed plan fails to satisfy the statute, and accordingly reverse.

II

The terms "absolute priority rule" and "new value corollary" (or "exception") are creatures of law antedating the current Bankruptcy Code, and to understand both those terms and the related but inexact language of the Code some history is helpful. The Bankruptcy Act preceding the Code contained no such provision as subsection (b)(2)(B)(ii), its subject having been addressed by two interpretive rules. The first was a specific gloss on the requirement of §77B (and its successor, Chapter X) of the old Act, that any reorganization plan be "fair and equitable." 11 U.S.C. §205(e) (1934 ed., Supp. I) (repealed 1938) (§77B); 11 U.S.C. §621(2) (1934 ed., Supp. IV) (repealed 1979) (Chapter X). The reason for such a limitation was the danger inherent in any reorganization plan proposed by a debtor, then and now, that the plan will simply turn out to be too good a deal for the debtor's owners. See H.R. Doc. No. 93-137, pt. I, p.255 (1973) (discussing concern with

15. All four of these cases arose in the single-asset real estate context, the typical one in which new value plans are proposed. See 7 Collier on Bankruptcy ¶1129.04[4][c][ii][B], pp.1129-1113 (15th ed. rev. 1998). See also Strub, Competition, Bargaining, and Exclusivity under the New Value Rule: Applying the Single-Asset Paradigm of Bonner Mall, 111 Banking L.J. 228, 231 (1994) ("Most of the cases discussing the new value issue have done so in connection with an attempt by a single-asset debtor to reorganize under chapter 11").

"the ability of a few insiders, whether representatives of management or major creditors, to use the reorganization process to gain an unfair advantage"); ibid. ("It was believed that creditors, because of management's position of dominance, were not able to bargain effectively without a clear standard of fairness and judicial control"); Ayer, Rethinking Absolute Priority After *Ahlers*, 87 Mich. L. Rev. 963, 969-973 (1989). Hence the pre-Code judicial response known as the absolute priority rule, that fairness and equity required that "the creditors . . . be paid before the stockholders could retain [equity interests] for any purpose whatever." Northern Pacific R. Co. v. Boyd, 228 U.S. 482, 508 (1913). See also Louisville Trust Co. v. Louisville, N.A. & C.R. Co., 174 U.S. 674, 684 (1899) (reciting "the familiar rule that the stockholder's interest in the property is subordinate to the rights of creditors; first of secured and then of unsecured creditors" and concluding that "any arrangement of the parties by which the subordinate rights and interests of the stockholders are attempted to be secured at the expense of the prior rights of either class of creditors comes within judicial denunciation").

The second interpretive rule addressed the first. Its classic formulation occurred in Case v. Los Angeles Lumber Products Co., in which the Court spoke through Justice Douglas in this dictum:

> "It is, of course, clear that there are circumstances under which stockholders may participate in a plan of reorganization of an insolvent debtor. . . . Where the necessity [for new capital] exists and the old stockholders make a fresh contribution and receive in return a participation reasonably equivalent to their contribution, no objection can be made. . . .
>
> "We believe that to accord 'the creditor his full right of priority against the corporate assets' where the debtor is insolvent, the stockholder's participation must be based on a contribution in money or in money's worth, reasonably equivalent in view of all the circumstances to the participation of the stockholder."

308 U.S. at 121-122.

Although counsel for one of the parties here has described the *Case* observation as "'black-letter' principle," Brief for Respondent 38, it never rose above the technical level of dictum in any opinion of this Court, which last addressed it in Norwest Bank Worthington v. Ahlers, 485 U.S. 197 (1988), holding that a contribution of "'labor, experience, and expertise'" by a junior interest holder was not in the "'money's worth'" that the *Case* observation required. 485 U.S. at 203-205. Nor, prior to the enactment of the current Bankruptcy Code, did any court rely on the *Case* dictum to approve a plan that gave old equity a property right after reorganization. See Ayer, supra, at 1016; Markell, Owners, Auctions, and Absolute Priority in Bankruptcy Reorganizations, 44 Stan. L. Rev. 69, 92 (1991). Hence the controversy over how weighty the *Case* dictum had become, as reflected in the alternative labels for the new value notion: some writers and courts . . . have spoken of it as an exception to the absolute priority rule, while others have characterized it as a simple corollary to the rule.

Enactment of the Bankruptcy Code in place of the prior Act might have resolved the status of new value by a provision bearing its name or at least unmistakably couched in its terms, but the Congress chose not to avail itself of that opportunity. [The court explores the ambiguity of the legislative history in some detail.]

The upshot is that this history does nothing to disparage the possibility apparent in the statutory text, that the absolute priority rule now on the books as subsection (b)(2)(B)(ii) may carry a new value corollary. Although there is no literal reference to "new value" in the phrase "on account of such junior claim," the phrase could arguably carry such an implication in modifying the prohibition against receipt by junior claimants of any interest under a plan while a senior class of unconsenting creditors goes less than fully paid.

III

Three basic interpretations have been suggested for the "on account of" modifier. The first reading is proposed by the Partnership, that "on account of" harks back to accounting practice and means something like "in exchange for," or "in satisfaction of," Brief for Respondent 12-13, 15, n.16. On this view, a plan would not violate the absolute priority rule unless the old equity holders received or retained property in exchange for the prior interest, without any significant new contribution; if substantial money passed from them as part of the deal, the prohibition of subsection (b)(2)(B)(ii) would not stand in the way, and whatever issues of fairness and equity there might otherwise be would not implicate the "on account of" modifier.

This position is beset with troubles, the first one being textual. Subsection (b)(2)(B)(ii) forbids not only receipt of property on account of the prior interest but its retention as well. See also §§1129(a)(7)(A)(ii), (a)(7)(B), (b)(2)(B)(i), (b)(2)(C)(i), (b)(2)(C)(ii). A common instance of the latter would be a debtor's retention of an interest in the insolvent business reorganized under the plan. Yet it would be exceedingly odd to speak of "retaining" property in exchange for the same property interest, and the eccentricity of such a reading is underscored by the fact that elsewhere in the Code the drafters chose to use the very phrase "in exchange for," §1123(a)(5)(J) (a plan shall provide adequate means for implementation, including "issuance of securities of the debtor . . . for cash, for property, for existing securities, or in exchange for claims or interests"). It is unlikely that the drafters of legislation so long and minutely contemplated as the 1978 Bankruptcy Code would have used two distinctly different forms of words for the same purpose.

The second difficulty is practical: the unlikelihood that Congress meant to impose a condition as manipulable as subsection (b)(2)(B)(ii) would be if "on account of" meant to prohibit merely an exchange unaccompanied by a substantial infusion of new funds but permit one whenever substantial funds changed hands. "Substantial" or "significant" or "considerable" or like characterizations of a monetary contribution would measure it by the Lord Chancellor's foot, and an absolute priority rule so variable would not be much of an absolute. Of course it is true (as already noted) that, even if old equity holders could displace the rule by adding some significant amount of cash to the deal, it would not follow that their plan would be entitled to adoption; a contested plan would still need to satisfy the overriding condition of fairness and equity. But that general fairness and equity criterion would apply in any event, and one comes back to the question why Congress would have bothered to add a separate priority rule without a sharper edge.

Since the "in exchange for" reading merits rejection, the way is open to recognize the more common understanding of "on account of" to mean "because of." This is certainly the usage meant for the phrase at other places in the statute, see §1111(b)(1)(A) (treating certain claims as if the holder of the claim "had recourse against the debtor on account of such claim"); §522(d)(10)(E) (permitting debtors to exempt payments under certain benefit plans and contracts "on account of illness, disability, death, age, or length of service"); §547(b)(2) (authorizing trustee to avoid a transfer of an interest of the debtor in property "for or on account of an antecedent debt owed by the debtor"); §547(c)(4)(B) (barring trustee from avoiding a transfer when a creditor gives new value to the debtor "on account of which new value the debtor did not make an otherwise unavoidable transfer to . . . such creditor"). So, under the commonsense rule that a given phrase is meant to carry a given concept in a single statute, the better reading of subsection (b)(2)(B)(ii) recognizes that a causal relationship between holding the prior claim or interest and receiving or retaining property is what activates the absolute priority rule.

The degree of causation is the final bone of contention. We understand the Government, as amicus curiae, to take the starchy position not only that any degree of causation between earlier interests and retained property will activate the bar to a plan providing for later property, Brief for United States as Amicus Curiae 11–15, but also that whenever the holders of equity in the Debtor end up with some property there will be some causation; when old equity, and not someone on the street, gets property the reason is res ipsa loquitur. An old equity holder simply cannot take property under a plan if creditors are not paid in full. Id., at 10–11, 18.

There are, however, reasons counting against such a reading. If, as is likely, the drafters were treating junior claimants or interest holders as a class at this point,[24] then the simple way to have prohibited the old interest holders from receiving anything over objection would have been to omit the "on account of" phrase entirely from subsection (b)(2)(B)(ii). On this assumption, reading the provision as a blanket prohibition would leave "on account of" as a redundancy, contrary to the interpretive obligation to try to give meaning to all the statutory language. One would also have to ask why Congress would have desired to exclude prior equity categorically from the class of potential owners following a cramdown. Although we have some doubt about the Court of Appeals's assumption that prior equity is often the only source of significant capital for reorganizations, old equity may well be

---

24. It is possible, on the contrary, to argue on the basis of the immediate text that the prohibition against receipt of an interest "on account of" a prior unsecured claim or interest was meant to indicate only that there is no per se bar to such receipt by a creditor holding both a senior secured claim and a junior unsecured one, when the senior secured claim accounts for the subsequent interest. This reading would of course eliminate the phrase "on account of" as an express source of a new value exception, but would leave open the possibility of interpreting the absolute priority rule itself as stopping short of prohibiting a new value transaction.

in the best position to make a go of the reorganized enterprise and so may be the party most likely to work out an equity-for-value reorganization.

A less absolute statutory prohibition would follow from reading the "on account of" language as intended to reconcile the two recognized policies underlying Chapter 11, of preserving going concerns and maximizing property available to satisfy creditors. Causation between the old equity's holdings and subsequent property substantial enough to disqualify a plan would presumably occur on this view of things whenever old equity's later property would come at a price that failed to provide the greatest possible addition to the bankruptcy estate, and it would always come at a price too low when the equity holders obtained or preserved an ownership interest for less than someone else would have paid.[26] A truly full value transaction, on the other hand, would pose no threat to the bankruptcy estate not posed by any reorganization, provided of course that the contribution be in cash or be realizable money's worth, just as *Ahlers* required for application of *Case*'s new value rule.

IV

Which of these positions is ultimately entitled to prevail is not to be decided here, however, for even on the latter view the Bank's objection would require rejection of the plan at issue in this case. It is doomed, we can say without necessarily exhausting its flaws, by its provision for vesting equity in the reorganized business in the Debtor's partners without extending an opportunity to anyone else either to compete for that equity or to propose a competing reorganization plan. Although the Debtor's exclusive opportunity to propose a plan under §1121(b) is not itself "property" within the meaning of subsection (b)(2)(B)(ii), the respondent partnership in this case has taken advantage of this opportunity by proposing a plan under which the benefit of equity ownership may be obtained by no one but old equity partners. . . . At the moment of the plan's approval the Debtor's partners necessarily enjoyed an exclusive opportunity that was in no economic sense distinguishable from the advantage of the exclusively entitled offerer or option holder. This opportunity should, first of all, be treated as an item of property in its own right. While it may be argued that the opportunity has no market value, being significant only to old equity holders owing to their potential tax liability, such an argument avails the Debtor nothing, for several reasons. It is to avoid just

26. Even when old equity would pay its top dollar and that figure was as high as anyone else would pay, the price might still be too low unless the old equity holders paid more than anyone else would pay, on the theory that the "necessity" required to justify old equity's participation in a new value plan is a necessity for the participation of old equity as such. On this interpretation, disproof of a bargain would not satisfy old equity's burden; it would need to show that no one else would pay as much. See, e.g., In re Coltex Loop Central Three Partners, L.P., 138 F.3d 39, 45 (CA2 1998) ("Old equity must be willing to contribute more money than any other source" (internal quotation marks and citation omitted)); Strub, 111 Banking L.J., at 243 (old equity must show that the reorganized entity "needs funds from the prior owner-managers because no other source of capital is available"). No such issue is 'before us, and we emphasize that our holding here does not suggest an exhaustive list of the requirements of a proposed new value plan.

such arguments that the law is settled that any otherwise cognizable property interest must be treated as sufficiently valuable to be recognized under the Bankruptcy Code. See *Ahlers*, 485 U.S. at 207-208. Even aside from that rule, the assumption that no one but the Debtor's partners might pay for such an opportunity would obviously support no inference that it is valueless, let alone that it should not be treated as property. And, finally, the source in the tax law of the opportunity's value to the partners implies in no way that it lacks value to others. It might, indeed, be valuable to another precisely as a way to keep the Debtor from implementing a plan that would avoid a Chapter 7 liquidation.

Given that the opportunity is property of some value, the question arises why old equity alone should obtain it, not to mention at no cost whatever. . . .

It is no answer to this to say that the exclusive opportunity should be treated merely as a detail of the broader transaction that would follow its exercise, and that in this wider perspective no favoritism may be inferred, since the old equity partners would pay something, whereas no one else would pay anything. If this argument were to carry the day, of course, old equity could obtain a new property interest for a dime without being seen to receive anything on account of its old position. But even if we assume that old equity's plan would not be confirmed without satisfying the judge that the purchase price was top dollar, there is a further reason here not to treat property consisting of an exclusive opportunity as subsumed within the total transaction proposed. On the interpretation assumed here, it would, of course, be a fatal flaw if old equity acquired or retained the property interest without paying full value. It would thus be necessary for old equity to demonstrate its payment of top dollar, but this it could not satisfactorily do when it would receive or retain its property under a plan giving it exclusive rights and in the absence of a competing plan of any sort.[27] Under a plan granting an exclusive right, making no provision for competing bids or competing plans, any determination that the price was top dollar would necessarily be made by a judge in bankruptcy court, whereas the best way to determine value is exposure to a market. See . . . Markell, 44 Stan. L. Rev., at 73 ("Reorganization practice illustrates that the presence of competing bidders for a debtor, whether they are owners or not, tends to increase creditor dividends"). This is a point of some significance, since it was, after all, one of the Code's innovations to narrow the occasions for courts to make valuation judgments, as shown by its preference for the supramajoritarian class creditor voting scheme in §1126(c), see *Ahlers*, supra, at 207 ("The Code provides that it is up to the creditors — and not the courts — to accept or reject a reorganization plan which fails to provide them adequate protection or fails to honor the absolute priority rule"). In the interest of statutory coherence, a like disfavor for decisions untested by competitive choice

---

27. The dissent emphasizes the care taken by the Bankruptcy Judge in examining the valuation evidence here, in arguing that there is no occasion for us to consider the relationship between valuation process and top-dollar requirement. Post, at 5 n.7. While we agree with the dissent as to the judge's conscientious handling of the matter, the ensuing text of this opinion sets out our reasons for thinking the Act calls for testing valuation by a required process that was not followed here.

ought to extend to valuations in administering subsection (b)(2)(B)(ii) when some form of market valuation may be available to test the adequacy of an old equity holder's proposed contribution.

Whether a market test would require an opportunity to offer competing plans or would be satisfied by a right to bid for the same interest sought by old equity, is a question we do not decide here. It is enough to say, assuming a new value corollary, that plans providing junior interest holders with exclusive opportunities free from competition and without benefit of market valuation fall within the prohibition of §1129(b)(2)(B)(ii).

The judgment of the Court of Appeals is accordingly reversed, and the case is remanded for further proceedings consistent with this opinion.

It is so ordered.

Concur: Justice THOMAS, with whom Justice SCALIA joins, concurring in the judgment.

I agree with the majority's conclusion that the reorganization plan in this case could not be confirmed. However, I do not see the need for its unnecessary speculations on certain issues and do not share its approach to interpretation of the Bankruptcy Code. I therefore concur only in the judgment.

                                         I

Our precedents make clear that an analysis of any statute, including the Bankruptcy Code, must not begin with external sources, but with the text itself. The relevant Code provision in this case, 11 U.S.C. §1129(b), does not expressly authorize prepetition equity holders to receive or retain property in a reorganized entity in exchange for an infusion of new capital.

. . . Unfortunately, the approach taken today only thickens the fog.

Dissent: Justice STEVENS, dissenting.

Prior to the enactment of the Bankruptcy Reform Act of 1978, this Court unequivocally stated that there are circumstances under which stockholders may participate in a plan of reorganization of an insolvent debtor if their participation is based on a contribution in money, or in money's worth, reasonably equivalent in view of all the circumstances to their participation.[1] As we have on two prior occasions, we granted certiorari in this case to

---

1. As Justice Douglas explained in Case v. Los Angeles Lumber Products Co., 308 U.S. 106 (1939): "It is, of course, clear that there are circumstances under which stockholders may participate in a plan of reorganization of an insolvent debtor. This Court, as we have seen, indicated as much in Northern Pacific Ry. Co. v. Boyd [, 228 U.S. 482 (1913),] and Kansas City Terminal Ry. Co. v. Central Union Trust Co. [, 271 U.S. 445 (1926)]. Especially in the latter case did this Court stress the necessity, at times, of seeking new money 'essential to the success of the undertaking' from the old stockholders. Where that necessity exists and the old stockholders make a fresh contribution and receive in return a participation reasonably equivalent to their contribution, no objection can be made. . . .

"In view of these considerations we believe that to accord 'the creditor his full right of priority against the corporate assets' where the debtor is insolvent, the stockholder's participation must be based on a contribution in money or in money's worth, reasonably equivalent in view of all the circumstances to the participation of the stockholder." 308 U.S. at 121-122 (footnote omitted).

decide whether §1129(b)(2)(B)(ii) of the 1978 Act preserved or repealed this "new value" component of the absolute priority rule. I believe the Court should now definitively resolve the question and state that a holder of a junior claim or interest does not receive property "on account of" such a claim when its participation in the plan is based on adequate new value....

I

Section 1129 of Chapter 11 sets forth in detail the substantive requirements that a reorganization plan must satisfy in order to qualify for confirmation. In the case of dissenting creditor classes, a plan must conform to the dictates of §1129(b). With only one exception, the requirements of §§1129(a) and 1129(b) are identical for plans submitted by stockholders or junior creditors and plans submitted by other parties. That exception is the requirement in §1129(b)(2)(B)(ii) that no holder of a junior claim or interest may receive or retain any property "on account of such junior claim or interest."

When read in the light of Justice Douglas' opinion in Case v. Los Angeles Lumber Products Co., 308 U.S. 106 (1939), the meaning of this provision is perfectly clear. Whenever a junior claimant receives or retains an interest for a bargain price, it does so "on account of" its prior claim. On the other hand, if the new capital that it invests has an equivalent or greater value than its interest in the reorganized venture, it should be equally clear that its participation is based on the fair price being paid and that it is not "on account of" its old claim or equity.

Of course, the fact that the proponents of a plan offer to pay a fair price for the interest they seek to acquire or retain does not necessarily mean that the bankruptcy judge should approve their plan. Any proposed cramdown must satisfy all of the requirements of §1129 including, most notably, the requirement that the plan be "fair and equitable" to all creditors whose claims are impaired. See §1129(b)(1). Moreover, even if the old stockholders propose to buy the debtor for a fair price, presumably their plan should not be approved if a third party, perhaps motivated by unique tax or competitive considerations, is willing to pay an even higher price. Cf. §1129(c).

In every reorganization case, serious questions concerning the value of the debtor's assets must be resolved.... I believe that we should assume that all valuation questions have been correctly answered....

It would seem logical for adherents of this view also to find participation by junior interests in the new entity not "on account of" their prior interest, if it were stipulated that old equity's capital contributions exceeded the amount attainable in an auction, or if findings to that effect were not challenged.

Perhaps such a procedural requirement would be a wise addition to the statute, but it is surely not contained in the present text of §1129(b)(2)(B)(ii). Indeed, that subsection is not a procedural provision at all. Section 1129 defines the substantive elements that must be met to render plans eligible for confirmation by the bankruptcy judge after all required statutory procedures have been completed. Cf. §1121 (Who may file a plan); §1122 (Classification of claims or interests); §1125 (Postpetition disclosure and solicitation); §1126 (Acceptance of plan); §1127 (Modification of plan). Because, as I discuss below, petitioner does not now challenge either the procedures followed by the Bankruptcy Judge or any of his value determinations, neither the record nor the text of §1129(b)(2)(B)(ii) provides any support for the Court's disposition of this case.

II

As I understand the Court's opinion, it relies on two reasons for refusing to approve the plan at this stage of the proceedings: one based on the plan itself and the other on the confirmation procedures followed before the plan was adopted, in the Court's view, the fatal flaw in the plan proposed by respondent was that it vested complete ownership in the former partners immediately upon confirmation, ante, at 18, and the defect in the process was that no other party had an opportunity to propose a competing plan.

These requirements are neither explicitly nor implicitly dictated by the text of the statute. As for the first objection, if we assume that the partners paid a fair price for what the Court characterizes as their "exclusive opportunity," I do not understand why the retention of a 100% interest in assets is any more "on account of" their prior position than retaining a lesser percentage might have been. Surely there is no legal significance to the fact that immediately after the confirmation of the plan "the partners were in the same position that they would have enjoyed had they exercised an exclusive option under the plan to buy the equity in the reorganized entity, or contracted to purchase it from a seller who had first agreed to deal with no one else." Ante, at 19.

As to the second objection, petitioner does not challenge the Bankruptcy Judge's valuation of the property or any of his other findings under §1129 (other than the plan's compliance with §1129(b)(2)(B)(ii)). Since there is no remaining question as to value, both the former partners (and the creditors, for that matter) are in the same position that they would have enjoyed if the Bankruptcy Court had held an auction in which this plan had been determined to be the best available. . . .[5]

Nevertheless, even after proposing their plan, the partners had no vested right to purchase an equity interest in the post-reorganization enterprise until the Bankruptcy Judge confirmed the plan. They also had no assurance that the court would refuse to truncate the exclusivity period and allow other interested parties to file competing plans. As it turned out, the Bankruptcy Judge did not allow respondent to file its proposed plan, but the bank did not appeal that issue. . . .

When the court approved the plan, it accepted an offer by old equity. If the value of the debtor's assets has been accurately determined, the fairness of such an offer should be judged by the same standard as offers made by

---

5. It goes without saying that Congress could not have expected the partners' plan to include a provision that would allow for the Bankruptcy Judge to entertain competing plans, since that is a discretionary decision exclusively within the province of the court. See §1121(d).

newcomers. Of course, its offer should not receive more favorable consideration "on account of" their prior ownership. But if the debtor's plan would be entitled to approval if it had been submitted by a third party, it should not be disqualified simply because it did not include a unique provision that would not be required in an offer made by any other party, including the creditors.

Since the Court of Appeals correctly interpreted §1129(b)(2)(B)(ii), its judgment should be affirmed.

Accordingly, I respectfully dissent.

As Justice Thomas predicted, the fog seems only to have thickened. Practitioners representing debtors are busy developing new ways to satisfy *203 North LaSalle* while old equity continues its participation in the business. Meanwhile practitioners representing large, secured creditors are busy fighting them. Each side can recite its own version of what the majority in *203 North LaSalle* really meant.

The National Bankruptcy Review Commission proposed to resolve the debate over equity participation in the post-reorganization business with two amendments. The first was to amend section 1129(b)(2)(B)(ii) to make it clear that a junior class could purchase a new interest in the reorganized debtor. The second was to amend section 1121 to provide that if the debtor moved to cram down a plan that provided for the sale of an interest in the business to old equity then exclusivity should be terminated so that any party in interest could propose a competing plan. NBRC Recommendation 2.4.15. The proposal addressed much the same concern expressed in *203 North LaSalle,* but the remedy was fashioned in a different way.

One problem with the emergent case law on absolute priority is that many of the opinions have involved two related peculiarities: The debtors are SAREs, and the principal objector is a secured creditor who can repossess the property in liquidation but who gets its voting power from the unsecured portion of its claim. In such cases, there are often few general unsecured creditors who will be affected, and, after voting against the plan, the secured creditor will typically take control of the property. According to the data collected for the Business Bankruptcy Project, in the mid-1990s, SARE cases comprised about 7 percent of all business bankruptcies. Calculated from *Financial Characteristics* at 521, table 1; 543, table 10. The majority in *203 North LaSalle* noted that all four of the circuit court cases producing the conflict that caused them to take the case were SARE cases. Indeed, a huge proportion of the classification and cramdown cases reported at any level are SARE cases. These cases may make it to published opinions more often in part because they are frequently large enough to have substantial assets at stake that make litigation worthwhile. But they are also litigated because, unlike most ongoing businesses, they often have no continuing working relationships that are essential to the survival of the business. In these cases, the war of litigation is far more acceptable than in many other kinds of cases. As a result, much of the law of Chapter 11s is written in the context of SARE cases.

SARE cases are important, but they are aberrational in some very important ways. Often they involve huge amounts of debt owed to one creditor, with very little debt owed to anyone else. The implications of this fact echo through the difficulties the courts have with classification, impairment, voting, and absolute priority. The creditor with a bifurcated claim may vote its unsecured claim and thereby dominate the class of unsecured creditors or be separately classified and create a dissenting class and thereby prevent a consensual plan. Even though the power that these creditors exercise is in their capacity as unsecured creditors, they often have little in common with the general unsecured creditors. The creditor with the bifurcated claim will get all the assets of the business, and when it votes its unsecured debt it is voting for benefits it will receive as a secured creditor. The general unsecured creditors, by contrast, usually get nothing if the plan is not confirmed. They may object strenuously to their interests being represented by a creditor who in fact will fare very differently in liquidation.

On the other hand, the amount of general unsecured debt is often so small that the SARE case often can be classified as a two-party dispute. In such a case, it is harder to articulate the policy reasons for moving a two-party action out of state law and into the mechanism of collective resolution designed for the bankruptcy system.

But the most troubling aspect of making law in the areas of classification, impairment, voting, and absolute priority in the context of new value cases is that the law that emerges applies to other kinds of cases as well, including sole proprietorships and large, diversified businesses. The glory of the common law has long been that decisions are shaped and refined through different facts before generally applicable principles emerge. In Chapter 11, much of the law is written in the context of a small subset of cases that involve very different considerations than most other cases in the business bankruptcy system.

The distortion caused by SARE cases in the areas of classification and cramdown is even more pronounced now that Congress has found other ways to squeeze those cases out of the system. With the advent of the 2005 Amendments, sections 101(51B) and 362(d)(3) will mean that only SARE cases with substantial cash flow can survive in bankruptcy for more than a short time. But the case law that these cases spawned may live on for decades.

There is a tendency for lawyers, as well as for students, to focus on cramdown in Chapter 11 because it is a legal *rule*, and to ignore the negotiation that leads to creditor acceptance of a plan because it is a messy, idiosyncratic *process*. Yet negotiated consent is the essence of the Chapter 11 scheme, particularly outside the SARE context. The exclusive right to propose a plan and the possibility of cramdown represent the leverage that the debtor brings to the negotiating table, but agreement is the larger theme. Chapter 11 is descended from both of the reorganization chapters, Chapters X and XI, under the old Act, but more from the latter than the former. Consent was the essence of Chapter XI (for mom-and-pop operations), while absolute priority was the central focus of Chapter X (for publicly traded companies). When they were combined into Chapter 11, the absolute priority rule was modified to permit equity participation if creditor consent was obtained. Thus consent remains the heart of Chapter 11. For a fascinating discussion of the history of these developments, see John Ayer, Rethinking

Absolute Priority after *Ahlers,* 87 Mich. L. Rev. 963 (1989), cited by the Court in *203 North LaSalle.*

In most cases, the key to retaining ownership is section 1126, which controls the voting process by which creditors approve a plan. The absolute priority rule comes into play only if the creditors are crammed down, that is, if the majority does not vote approval of a plan.

ii.   *Cramdown Against the Secured Creditor*

The Code provides that the secured creditor receive the present value of its allowed secured claim, i.e., that it get interest at an appropriate rate on an amount equal to the value of its collateral. §1129(b)(2)(A)(i)(II). We have covered computation of the allowed secured claim at pp. 225–227 and again at pp. 297–306. The *Till* case in the Supreme Court set down rules for a cramdown interest rate in Chapter 13 and would seem to apply to very similar language in section 1129. See pp. 298–305. The cramdown rule for secured creditors is essentially the same in section 1129(b)(2) as it is in Chapter 13, so that each secured creditor can demand the present value of its allowed secured claim as an absolute condition of confirmation. Only one additional element requires extensive discussion.

The additional element is important to the undersecured creditor. The Bankruptcy Code, in effect, bifurcates the claim of the undersecured creditor, giving it full value for the secured portion and putting its unsecured portion in with the unsecured claims, a process often referred to as "lien-stripping." We have seen the policy questions that lien-stripping creates in Chapter 13 cases. The commercial context of a business case presents another set of complications. Congress has responded to some of those complications by giving secured creditors a device that may improve their negotiating positions in Chapter 11 cases. This device does not appear to be frequently used, perhaps in part because of the sheer difficulty of reading it in the Bankruptcy Code. The device is called the "1111(b) election." Its importance as a method of blocking certain kinds of debtor plans is considerable, even if it is not often formally invoked. Its primary use to date has been in SARE cases.

This election benefits secured creditors that are undersecured. The undersecured creditors that may benefit from the election are in two distinct legal circumstances. The first type is the usual undersecured creditor that has both an allowed secured claim and an allowed unsecured claim under section 506(a). The second type of beneficiary is the nonrecourse undersecured creditor, one that has only a secured claim at the outset of the case with no unsecured claim permitted for any deficiency. We first consider the usual undersecured creditor with its combined secured-unsecured claim.

By using section 1111(b)(1)(B), the undersecured creditor can waive any deficiency or unsecured claim that would result from the creditor's undersecurity and thus waive any participation in the plan as an unsecured creditor. In exchange, the debtor is forced to pay the secured creditor over time the full number of dollars that the creditor is owed, even though the creditor is undersecured and even though unsecured creditors may be getting only a fractional payment. But the debtor is *not* required to pay the present value of the entire claim, only the present value of that portion of the claim equal to the value of the collateral. Note that the election is in section 1111(b)(1)(B), but the two-part payment test stated in the last two sentences is found in section 1129(b)(2)(A)(i)(II), which should be read AS IF it said the following:

> "(II) that each holder of a claim of such class receive on account of such claim deferred cash payments **(1)** totaling at least the allowed amount of such claim, **and (2)** of a value, as of the effective date of the plan, of at least the value of such holder's interest in the estate's interest in such property;" (clarifying additions in boldface)

The effect of an 1111(b) election can be illustrated as follows. A creditor is owed $1,000,000 secured by a building worth $500,000. In the normal course under section 506, the creditor has a secured claim for $500,000, which is the allowed secured claim, and an unsecured deficiency claim for the remaining $500,000. If the plan calls for all payments to be made at the end of one year and the applicable rate of interest at the time is 10 percent, then the creditor must be paid $500,000 plus 10 percent interest ($550,000) at the end of the year. If unsecured creditors are receiving a 20 percent pay-out also at the end of one year, the creditor will get an additional $100,000 from its deficiency claim, for a total of $650,000 paid in the bankruptcy.

If the secured creditor instead makes an 1111(b) election, it waives its unsecured claim, but it gets a secured claim for $1,000,000. As to that claim, it must be paid $1,000,000 by the end of the plan — in our example, one year. As to the $500,000 value of its collateral, it is guaranteed not less than $50,000 interest for the one-year period under the plan, for a total of $550,000. Thus if it gets $1,000,000 by the end of the year, both tests will have been fulfilled: The number of dollars it received was equal to the full number of dollars in its claim ($1,000,000) and was at least as great as the value of collateral plus interest for the period ($550,000).

Because section 1129(b)(2)(A)(i) is structured as two tests (I-II) that must be satisfied rather than two amounts that must be paid, the debtor can stretch out an electing creditor's payments over a long period and thus pay that creditor much less on a present value basis than the full claim. Suppose the debtor agrees to pay our exemplary creditor $1,000,000 over 10 years. The payment of $1,000,000 in nominal dollars satisfies the first test — payment of the face value of the note. Because $1,000,000 is equal to $500,000 plus 10 percent interest for ten years (ignoring the declining balance, $50,000 interest per year equals $500,000, for a total amount due of $1,000,000), the second test is also satisfied — payment of the present value of the allowed secured claim. Because the unsecured claim is waived in an 1111(b) election, the creditor in this case is actually worse off with the election and a ten-year payout because it missed the 20 percent payment on the unsecured claim that it would have had at the end of the first year. In addition, the creditor that made the 1111(b) election lost its ability to vote as an unsecured creditor and perhaps to force a liquidation of the business and the resulting seizure of its collateral.

On the other hand, the undersecured creditor that waives its deficiency under 1111(b) gains an advantage against a debtor that confirms a plan and must pay off the loan in a short time frame. If some economic circumstance forces the debtor to repay the loan in a year or two, the requirement that it pay the full number of dollars of the creditor's claim will result in a payment greater than an amount equal to the value of the collateral plus interest. As in our previous example, a debtor that pays over just one year must pay $1,000,000, which is much more than the $500,000 value of the collateral plus interest for one year. The jargon of the trade is that the debtor cannot "cash out" the creditor for just the collateral value, discharging the rest against a small payment to unsecureds. Generally, this situation will arise where the debtor sells or refinances the property within a fairly short time after bankruptcy.

The second type of undersecured creditor that may benefit from section 1111(b) is the nonrecourse creditor. A loan is nonrecourse if the original security agreement provided that the creditor would look only to the collateral for payment, with no right to sue the debtor for any deficiency (the phrase often used is "the debtor had no personal liability"). For a variety of economic reasons, this sort of loan is fairly common in real estate development. (Recall from footnote 3 in *203 North LaSalle* that the creditor had originally had a nonrecourse loan.) Absent section 1111(b)(1)(A) the result in bankruptcy would be that the nonrecourse creditor ordinarily could claim against the collateral, but not against the estate. It would have only an allowed secured claim, with no claim against the remaining assets of the estate for the shortfall in the value of its collateral. But section 1111(b)(1)(A) gives the nonrecourse creditor a full recourse claim in bankruptcy. Such creditor can then assert the usual secured-unsecured claims or make the 1111(b) election described above.

Although section 1111(b)(1)(A) (which we call the "recourse rule") appears on its face to be an inexplicable preference for nonrecourse lenders that makes their rights comparable to recourse lenders, the move was a deliberate congressional choice. The congressional debates raised the concern that corporate debtors with a single asset, such as an apartment building that is often purchased with nonrecourse financing, would take advantage of temporarily depressed markets to strip down the mortgages. If the debtor had borrowed the full value of the collateral at purchase, but the value declined by 30 percent in a bad real estate market, a debtor who did not face the recourse rule could make a very shrewd move: The debtor could declare Chapter 11 and have the allowed secured claim reduced to the current value of the property, which the debtor would pay off over time. The deficiency would be erased without any payment by the estate, and without the ability to vote and block the plan or demand imposition of the absolute priority rule. (Remember that on a nonrecourse loan the creditor gets no deficiency claim — only a claim against the collateral, which has now declined in value.) The debtor could continue to manage the property and, when the payments were made (and the market had recovered), would own the same property outright for considerably less than the repayment of the amount it used to buy the property. The recourse rule stopped that practice, saying, in effect, that if the debtor wants to keep the property for a payout over time, the creditor can at least claim the full loan balance.

The recourse rule for a nonrecourse creditor was also intended to give the creditor a say under the absolute priority rule. If its allowed secured claim was badly underestimated because the bankruptcy court seriously undervalued the collateral, in the absence of the recourse rule they would have no unsecured claim and therefore no vote in the unsecured class of claims. But the recourse rule gives the nonrecourse creditor a claim against the estate, and that claim will actually be made larger by any undervaluation of the secured claim. The creditor may therefore be able to block acceptance of the plan by the unsecured class and force application of the absolute priority rule under section 1129(b)(2)(A). The Supreme Court decision in *203 North LaSalle* shows just how important that claim can become.

If the nonrecourse creditor sees no advantage in having an unsecured claim, it has the right to make the same 1111(b) election as the undersecured creditor who was a recourse creditor all along. That is, the nonrecourse creditor can elect to force the debtor to pay the full number of dollars of its entire claim, although like the recourse creditor it cannot require payment of the present value of the whole claim, only of the value of the collateral. In short, it can elect to be treated just like the undersecured recourse creditor who makes the 1111(b) election as explained in the first part of this section.

The 1111(b) election can only do so much for creditors because the election also has some important restrictions. If the debtor is selling off some of its collateral in an attempt to downsize and reorganize the business, it will be cashing out the secured creditors with security interests in the collateral. The Code provides that if property is sold under section 363, the creditor cannot use the election. §1111(b)(1)(A)(ii), (B)(ii). The reason is fairly obvious. An undersecured creditor cannot turn its undersecurity into a demand for full payment at a bankruptcy sale by using the election. Otherwise, a debtor planning to sell as part of its reorganization effort would be stymied whenever it had undersecured creditors with interests in the property, and nonrecourse creditors would be in a better position than ordinary secured creditors who would receive only the value of the collateral and an unsecured claim for the remainder.

The new twists in strategy introduced by the 1111(b) election add another dimension to the negotiation of a Chapter 11 plan. Notwithstanding its obvious power, not every undersecured creditor will want to make an 1111(b) election. Sometimes the participation as an unsecured creditor is more valuable than the payment over time without an allowance for present value. Other times, undersecured creditors with huge unsecured portions to their loans may decide to stay in the plan as unsecured creditors in order to preserve their voting rights. It is not uncommon for the parties to engage in an odd shadow dance in which the debtor indicates the terms of the plan and the secured creditor then decides whether to make an 1111(b) election, at which time the debtor readjusts the plan. The parties might go to court, each demanding that the other go first, so that they can maximize the consequences of an election or non-election.

We have often described Chapter 11 as an invitation to a negotiation, and this section should show just how complex that negotiation may be.

Problem Set 35

35.1. You are still counsel to Pany Chemicals in the Chapter 11 proceeding of Country Smokes, Inc. (see Problem Sets 32–34), largely because Talbert Pany was mollified by your successful motion to revoke confirmation of Country's Plan under section 1144.

Ironically, less than two weeks after your motion was granted, Country got a big contract with a corporation that owns a number of theme parks around the country and Country's prospects have improved dramatically. As a result, Country has amended its disclosure document, which now looks even better because of the big contract. It is proposing the same plan as before, the bank to be paid in full, with interest, and the unsecureds to get 70 cents on the dollar.

Talbert remains furious with Country and with Sam Pickens, its president, and is determined to defeat the plan. Although Talbert's objection to the plan — that Country can now afford to pay more than 70 percent on unsecured claims — is a plausible one, his reaction is also emotional, because of the "sandbagging" preference action. Talbert believes that enough other unsecured creditors now agree with him that the plan can be defeated.

He wants to know if the plan could be confirmed even over the protest of a majority of the unsecureds. Although you continue to urge Talbert to let you use his "electoral" leverage to negotiate a better deal, he insists on knowing if "this cramdown stuff" will work against him here. What is the answer, as things stand now? If the bank agreed to less than full payment, might the analysis change? What position might Country take with the unsecureds who are threatening to vote no? What leverage does Pany have? What deal might you propose to the bank and Country on behalf of Pany, based on that leverage?

Barney's Problem — Part VI: Overview

Note: Unless otherwise indicated, the day this part of Barney's problem is discussed in class is "deemed to be" March 1 of this year. This part of the problem, like the rest, is to be analyzed in "real time," i.e., as if you as counsel obtain the information or take the action indicated on the day (and the deemed date) the problem is to be discussed in class. All previous parts of the problem are incorporated into this part as of the day (and the deemed date) it is discussed in class, as if you were a sole practitioner in Aloysius and this small drama were real.

Your legal assistant brings over the "Construction Yard" file and points out that there is a mortgage of $250,000 on the property, but no corresponding note from the Thornaby Construction Company. Barney explains that in November of last year, he personally bought the property adjacent to the yard and then leased it to the company, because it needed the additional room. He paid $250,000 for the property, the money having been borrowed and the loan secured by a mortgage on both properties.

Shortly thereafter, Barney discovered that the neighboring turkey farmer had an easement allowing his turkeys to cross the property, making it useless to the company. Barney was able, however, to buy out the easement for $60,000, using $20,000 of the company's money, $20,000 he had just received in preferred stock dividends from the company, and $20,000 that the company borrowed from Barney's uncle. The latter loan, along with the $100,000 Barney had previously borrowed from his uncle and invested in the company, was subordinated, but it was secured by a second lien on the company's accounts receivable. (A copy of the financing statement is on p.676.)

Barney cuts off your further questions, pointing out that the more immediate problem is generating cash to pay the crews, who have agreed to a two-week deferral. He made a start this week by selling a large number of tools for $45,000. He originally got the tools for $30,000 at an auction last December, where the company paid no cash, but merely gave the auction company a security interest covering the tools. (A copy of that financing statement is on p. 677.)

Because it was so sweet a deal, Barney bought the tools even though he wasn't sure the company would really need them this year, figuring he could always sell them prior to April 1, when the purchase price would be due.

At your suggestion, Barney talked to Aloysius Construction, the other bidder on the civic center. It would be willing to pay $400,000 for the contract, but wouldn't be able to advance the cash until June 1. However, the owner says his lawyer won't approve the deal anyway, because the civic center contract has a non-assignability clause.

In addition, Barney received a letter this morning from the lawyer for Frederick Trinsic and Barney's Auto-Mow, Inc. BAM was formed to develop and market a programmable lawn mower invented by Trinsic. It is a joint venture company whose stock is owned 50-50 by Thornaby Construction and Trinsic. Trinsic licensed the patent to BAM for $50,000 per year during development, with a royalty once production began. The license contract is guaranteed by Thornaby Construction. Barney says the lawn mower is a terrific idea, which is why he wanted it to bear his name: "Can you imagine sitting on the porch watching my mower mow your lawn all by itself?" Unfortunately, the software development has hit snag after snag and a competing mower has made its appearance. Thornaby Construction has poured money into the joint venture, but the mower has made no progress in two years and the chief programmer has quit in despair: "The thing does nothing but eat money and garden hoses." Barney has finally concluded the idea will never become practical, but the contract has no termination provision. The lawyer's letter he got this morning insists that BAM must continue the payments to Trinsic until development is complete and cites a recent state court opinion so interpreting a similar contract. The letter reminds Thornaby Construction that it has guaranteed performance of this obligation.

What issues would these new facts present in a case under the Code?

Finally, Barney tells you that Wheeler Cogburn will offer any one of the following: to buy the yard for $650,000, or all the common stock of the

UCC FINANCING STATEMENT
FOLLOW INSTRUCTIONS (front and back) CAREFULLY

| A. NAME & PHONE OF CONTACT AT FILER [optional] |
| Emily Kadens |

B. SEND ACKNOWLEDGMENT TO: (Name and Address)

Auction Unltd., Ltd.
Brady, Mx 00000

Filed:

01/15/ this year
9:00 A.M

Secretary of State

THE ABOVE SPACE IS FOR FILING OFFICE USE ONLY

1. DEBTOR'S EXACT FULL LEGAL NAME - insert only one debtor name (1a or 1b) - do not abbreviate or combine names

1a. ORGANIZATION'S NAME				
Thornaby Co.				

OR 1b. INDIVIDUAL'S LAST NAME	FIRST NAME	MIDDLE NAME	SUFFIX

1c. MAILING ADDRESS	CITY	STATE	POSTAL CODE	COUNTRY
P. O. Box 00	Aloysius	Mx	00000	U. S.

1d. SEE INSTRUCTIONS	ADD'L INFO RE ORGANIZATION DEBTOR	1e. TYPE OF ORGANIZATION	1f. JURISDICTION OF ORGANIZATION	1g. ORGANIZATIONAL ID #, if any
				☐ NONE

2. ADDITIONAL DEBTOR'S EXACT FULL LEGAL NAME - insert only one debtor name (2a or 2b) - do not abbreviate or combine names

2a. ORGANIZATION'S NAME				

OR 2b. INDIVIDUAL'S LAST NAME	FIRST NAME	MIDDLE NAME	SUFFIX

2c. MAILING ADDRESS	CITY	STATE	POSTAL CODE	COUNTRY

2d. SEE INSTRUCTIONS	ADD'L INFO RE ORGANIZATION DEBTOR	2e. TYPE OF ORGANIZATION	2f. JURISDICTION OF ORGANIZATION	2g. ORGANIZATIONAL ID #, if any
				☐ NONE

3. SECURED PARTY'S NAME (or NAME of TOTAL ASSIGNEE of ASSIGNOR S/P) - insert only one secured party name (3a or 3b)

3a. ORGANIZATION'S NAME				
Auction Unltd., Ltd.				

OR 3b. INDIVIDUAL'S LAST NAME	FIRST NAME	MIDDLE NAME	SUFFIX

3c. MAILING ADDRESS	CITY	STATE	POSTAL CODE	COUNTRY
	Brady	Mx	00000	U. S.

4. This FINANCING STATEMENT covers the following collateral:

Equipment

5. ALTERNATIVE DESIGNATION [if applicable]:	☐ LESSEE/LESSOR	☐ CONSIGNEE/CONSIGNOR	☐ BAILEE/BAILOR	☐ SELLER/BUYER	☐ AG. LIEN	☐ NON-UCC FILING

6. ☐ This FINANCING STATEMENT is to be filed [for record] (or recorded) in the REAL ESTATE RECORDS. Attach Addendum [if applicable]	7. Check to REQUEST SEARCH REPORT(S) on Debtor(s) [ADDITIONAL FEE] [optional]	☐ All Debtors	☐ Debtor 1	☐ Debtor 2

8. OPTIONAL FILER REFERENCE DATA

FILING OFFICE COPY — UCC FINANCING STATEMENT (FORM UCC1) (REV. 05/22/02)

International Association of Commercial Administrators (IACA)

UCC FINANCING STATEMENT
FOLLOW INSTRUCTIONS (front and back) CAREFULLY

A. NAME & PHONE OF CONTACT AT FILER [optional]

B. SEND ACKNOWLEDGMENT TO: (Name and Address)

R. L. Thornaby
1 Main Street
Nowton, Mx 00000

Filed:

03/20/ last year
2:00 P.M

Secretary of State

THE ABOVE SPACE IS FOR FILING OFFICE USE ONLY

1. DEBTOR'S EXACT FULL LEGAL NAME - insert only one debtor name (1a or 1b) - do not abbreviate or combine names

1a. ORGANIZATION'S NAME				
Thornaby Co.				
OR 1b. INDIVIDUAL'S LAST NAME	FIRST NAME		MIDDLE NAME	SUFFIX

1c. MAILING ADDRESS	CITY	STATE	POSTAL CODE	COUNTRY
P. O. Box 00	Aloysius	Mx	00000	U. S.

1d. SEE INSTRUCTIONS	ADD'L INFO RE ORGANIZATION DEBTOR	1e. TYPE OF ORGANIZATION	1f. JURISDICTION OF ORGANIZATION	1g. ORGANIZATIONAL ID #, if any
				☐ NONE

2. ADDITIONAL DEBTOR'S EXACT FULL LEGAL NAME - insert only one debtor name (2a or 2b) - do not abbreviate or combine names

2a. ORGANIZATION'S NAME				
OR 2b. INDIVIDUAL'S LAST NAME	FIRST NAME		MIDDLE NAME	SUFFIX

2c. MAILING ADDRESS	CITY	STATE	POSTAL CODE	COUNTRY

2d. SEE INSTRUCTIONS	ADD'L INFO RE ORGANIZATION DEBTOR	2e. TYPE OF ORGANIZATION	2f. JURISDICTION OF ORGANIZATION	2g. ORGANIZATIONAL ID #, if any
				☐ NONE

3. SECURED PARTY'S NAME (or NAME of TOTAL ASSIGNEE of ASSIGNOR S/P) - insert only one secured party name (3a or 3b)

3a. ORGANIZATION'S NAME				
OR 3b. INDIVIDUAL'S LAST NAME	FIRST NAME		MIDDLE NAME	SUFFIX
Thornaby	R. L.			

3c. MAILING ADDRESS	CITY	STATE	POSTAL CODE	COUNTRY
1 Main Street	Nowton	Mx	00000	U. S.

4. This FINANCING STATEMENT covers the following collateral:

Accounts Receivable

5. ALTERNATIVE DESIGNATION [if applicable]:	☐ LESSEE/LESSOR	☐ CONSIGNEE/CONSIGNOR	☐ BAILEE/BAILOR	☐ SELLER/BUYER	☐ AG. LIEN	☐ NON-UCC FILING

6. ☐ This FINANCING STATEMENT is to be filed [for record] (or recorded) in the REAL ESTATE RECORDS   Attach Addendum   [if applicable]
7. Check to REQUEST SEARCH REPORT(S) on Debtor(s) [ADDITIONAL FEE]   [optional]   ☐ All Debtors ☐ Debtor 1 ☐ Debtor 2

8. OPTIONAL FILER REFERENCE DATA

FILING OFFICE COPY — UCC FINANCING STATEMENT (FORM UCC1) (REV. 05/22/02)   International Association of Commercial Administrators (IACA) company for $150,000, or all the assets for $2,000,000. Considering, of course, prior problems as well, what is your overall advice and plan? Why?

Barney also gave you the following notes he made while you were reviewing the files and the financing statements.

Barney's Projections

To 6/1 —
   If can use current contract payments and materials — Break even with courthouse and some smaller existing contracts.
   6/1 on —
   Can return to prior profit levels (brother-in-law just got 10-year term as Chairman County Contracting Bd.).
   Maybe more —
   If pending bill establishes a branch of ESU, ESU-Aloysius, double profits starting year 3.

g.   Small Business Reorganization

As we noted in the introduction to the bankruptcy portion of this book, the differences between business bankruptcies and consumer bankruptcies are myriad. Even when the formal legal structures are the same — automatic stay, property of the estate, plans of reorganization — both the practical and the policy differences between the two kinds of cases are enormous. But the huge difference between business and consumer cases can obscure another difference — a staggering variety within each of the two classifications. Business cases include Tina's Tax Preparation & Tanning Salon, a Tupperware party planner, and a lawn service guy who has lost his mower (all companies in our Business Bankruptcy Project sample) along with somewhat better-known companies such as Enron, Worldcom, Alephia, and perhaps every major airline carrier in the country. These tiny little businesses and great big businesses face many of the same formal provisions when they try to reorganize in Chapter 11, but the practical realities facing these businesses may be very different.

Although an Enron filing may dominate the headlines, far more small businesses than big businesses enter Chapter 11 each year. The data from the Business Bankruptcy Project show that the median business debtor in Chapter 11 had total liabilities of a modest $351,000. *Financial Characteristics* 499, at 538, table 8. Only 9.7 percent of the businesses in Chapter 11 had liabilities in excess of $5 million. Id. at 529, figure 3. Unlike their shareholder-owned and investor-owned counterparts in the multimillion or even billion-dollar range, it is likely that most of these smaller businesses are owner-operated. The resources available for attorneys' fees and accountants' reports make even the basic paper management different in two side-by-side filings, both of which are formally designated as business Chapter 11s.

One Chapter or Three?

During the Great Depression, when bankruptcy laws were expanding beyond the simple Chapter 7 liquidation model, Congress recognized that very small operations might face different pressures as they tried to reorganize. As a result, Congress adopted Chapter X for the big, publicly traded companies, Chapter XII for the SAREs, and Chapter XI for the smaller mom-and-pops, as they were affectionately known. While the central ideas were the same in all three chapters — try to reorganize the business and pay off debts over time — Chapter XI had several provisions that made reorganization easier for the struggling debtor to accomplish. These differences reflected a deliberate congressional decision that helping small businesses stay on their feet would be good for the national economy and good for the families that depend on these businesses. Congress also understood that a small outfit might not have the same access to capital markets or the same professional services, and they might need a little more leeway to keep a struggling business on its feet. It also saw that a complex reorganization machinery might sink little businesses that otherwise could survive.

When Congress rewrote the bankruptcy laws in 1978, Chapters X, XI, and XII were merged into a single reorganization chapter. The resulting Chapter 11 retained the complex apparatus necessary to reorganize a huge corporation, but it also adopted many of the small debtor–friendly aspects of the old Chapter XII.

Over time, the unification of the three kinds of business cases has begun to unravel. As we noted earlier, the reorganization of SAREs has been made extremely problematic by amendments to the automatic stay and short deadlines that apply only to these real estate cases. In addition, the 2005 Amendments include an extensive set of provisions that are designed to apply only to "small business debtors," a new term defined by the Bankruptcy Code.

Compared to the Congress of the Great Depression that put in special breaks for mom-and-pops in Chapter XI, the Congress of 2005 took a very different approach to small businesses. The 2005 Amendments include new provisions, applicable only to small businesses, to make Chapter 11 reorganization far more difficult. New paperwork requirements and greater supervision from the Office of the United States Trustee will drive up the costs of operating in Chapter 11 for small businesses, and shorter deadlines and decreased discretion for the judges will increase the leverage of the creditors and make it more challenging for small businesses to emerge from Chapter 11 successfully.

For a small business in Chapter 11, the material we have already studied remains relevant. Small businesses, like their giant counterparts, follow the same general path of struggling to maintain the protection of an automatic stay, negotiating financing, evaluating and challenging claims against the estate, recalling voidable preferences, assuming and assigning contracts, and, most of all, negotiating a plan that they can confirm so they can emerge from Chapter 11. But there are other twists to explore that appear when a small business files for bankruptcy.

Who Is a Small Business Debtor?

The 2005 Amendments created a new classification of debtor: the Small Business Debtor. 11 U.S.C. §101(51D). The 1994 Amendments had defined small businesses and made a few new rules for them, but because the rules were applied only at the debtor's election — and because almost no debtor ever selected them — the earlier provisions had virtually no effect on the system. Those rules have now been repealed. The new rules that replaced them are mandatory, which means that a careful look at which debtors are — and are not — subject to their application is important. Now every "person engaged in commercial or business activities" must take a close look to see if the regular rules of Chapter 11 apply or if this debtor will be further constrained by treatment as a small business debtor. §101(51D)(A). (Recall, of course, that the Bankruptcy Code defines a "person" to include partnerships and corporations. §101(41). Alice should feel right at home in this Wonderland.)

We can start with the numbers. Size can be measured in a number of ways. The SBA, for example, measures many businesses by the number of employees. For purposes of many public accommodation laws, landlords are measured by the number of rental units. Dow Jones reports classify companies by annual revenues. Stockbrokers talk about market capitalization. Accountants think about assets minus liabilities. But for companies that are broke, companies in which liabilities routinely exceed assets, only a few of these measures would separate Tina's Tax & Tanning from Enron. So Congress looked elsewhere.

In bankruptcy, the measure of "small" is not by how big the debtor is, but by how big are the bills that are coming due. A small business debtor is one that "has aggregate noncontingent liquidated secured and unsecured debts as of the data of the petition . . . in an amount not more than $2,000,000." §101(51D). Debts to insiders or affiliates are excluded from the total, probably to keep a strategic owner-operator from lending money to his own business on the eve of bankruptcy just to keep it out of the small business designation.

Why debts? They are certainly much easier to count than trying to figure out the value of the used typewriters and stock of paperclips in the business. Even so, debt presents it own tricky elements. The "noncontingent liquidated" debt concept has appeared before, showing up in the definition of eligibility for Chapter 13. 11 U.S.C. §109(e). Its close cousin, "noncontingent undisputed" debt appeared as the trigger for involuntary petitions. 11 U.S.C. §303. Clearly Congress had some notion that counting the dollar value of the debts would be a fairly routine matter, and, for the majority of businesses with either huge debts or very modest debts, that is undoubtedly true. But, as in much of life, the margins can be a little tricky. Is a plain old bank loan a noncontingent, liquidated debt, even if the interest and penalties haven't been calculated? What if the debtor plans to contest the amount owed?

For the small but well-advised debtor, the presence of a specific dollar amount of debt that will determine whether the debtor will be shuffled into a far more hostile Chapter 11 is an invitation to engage in some pre-bankruptcy planning. The debtor who is somewhere under the magic $2 million can quit paying the utilities, stop making the promised pension plan contributions, and hit the company credit cards. That $2 million number may be in a struggling debtor's mind as he or she decides that this might be a good time to buy a new truck, renovate the back office, or draw down on the line of credit.

Can an attorney advise the small businessperson to take on more debt in order to improve the business's position in bankruptcy? Under the 2005 Amendments, no attorney can tell an "assisted person" to run up debts, but the definition of "assisted person" is restricted to someone who owes "primarily consumer debts" and whose non-exempt property is valued at less than $150,000. §§526(a)(4), 101(3). That seems to leave out most small businesses. There is, of course, the general constraint on filing in good faith, as Mr. Reed, proprietor of Triple BS, learned in the Fifth Circuit (see pp. 199–205). Some courts also showed great creativity in tossing out SARE cases under a general good faith standard, long before they had any statutory rope with which to hang these debtors.

The size of the debts is not the only criteria to declare a business "small." Only cases in which no creditors' committee has been appointed or in which the committee is "not sufficiently active and representative to provide effective oversight of the creditor" will be tagged for treatment as a small business. §101(51D)(A). Most small business cases don't have creditors' committees because the unsecured creditors are insufficiently interested to form such a committee. Many creditors may ask themselves why they should take the time to serve if all they will receive is a pro rata share of a very small estate. Moreover, committees may provide oversight, but that oversight comes at a cost — attorneys' fees, accounting fees, etc. Those costs are borne by the estate, leaving less for distribution to the creditors. Once again, however, a well-advised debtor may have friends and family in the creditor body and they may be willing to serve on a committee, if only to keep the business out of the small business category.

The New Rules for the Little Guys

The first thing a lawyer handling a small business Chapter 11 will notice is that the paperwork is different. In addition to the forms and disclosures required in all Chapter 11 cases, the small business debtor must attach additional information to its voluntary petition. Section 1116 requires management to append a balance sheet, statement of operations, cash flow statement, and federal income tax returns or file a statement, under penalty of perjury, that no such documents have been prepared. During the course of the bankruptcy, small business debtors will be required to file periodic financial and other reports containing information with respect to the debtor's profitability and the debtor's projected cash receipts and disbursements. §308. The amendments also direct the Judicial Conference of the United States to prescribe standard form disclosure statements and plans of reorganization for small business debtors. It isn't clear whether such forms will be mandatory. If they are mandatory, little businesses will no longer be permitted to use specially tailored plans to meet their specific needs, the way the big businesses can, nor can they fall back on the cheap templates their lawyers have used for years. On the other hand, standardized forms may provide a degree of guidance to inexperienced lawyers and help creditors evaluate plans quickly. The impact of moving small businesses toward a one-size-fits-all model remains to be seen.

In addition to the duties of TIBs or DIPs laid out in sections 1106 and 1107, the small business debtor in Chapter 11 must add the duties in section 1116. So, for example, management must attend meetings with the United States Trustee, "including initial debtor interviews, scheduling conferences, and meetings of creditors convened under section 341 unless the court, after notice and a hearing, waives that requirement upon a finding of extraordinary and compelling circumstances." §1116(2). The debtor is specifically instructed to file all required schedules, file tax returns, and maintain insurance. While these are usually thought of as appropriate business practices for any debtor in Chapter 11, the point of spelling them out is to provide clearer grounds for dismissal of debtors who slip deadlines or can't assemble the paperwork.

Small business cases will also be subject to greater monitoring by the United States Trustee. The UST will be required to conduct an initial debtor interview "as soon as practicable" after filing. 28 U.S.C. §586(a)(7). The UST is instructed to investigate the debtor's viability, inquire about the debtor's business plan, explain the debtor's obligations to file monthly operating reports and other required reports, attempt to develop an agreed scheduling order, and inform the debtor of other obligations. The UST may also become a roving investigator, checking into the debtor's viability and making inquiries in the business community and visiting the debtor's business to "ascertain the state of the debtor's books and records, and verify that the debtor has filed its tax returns." 28 U.S.C. §586(a)(7)(B). The UST is also charged with reviewing and monitoring the debtor's activities, to identify as promptly as possible "whether the debtor will be unable to confirm a plan." This represents a potentially important shift toward involving the UST in business operations as well as case administration.

Modified solicitation and disclosure rules will apply in small business cases. 11 U.S.C. §1125(f). The biggest change, however, is likely to come from the change in exclusivity rules. A small business debtor will have the exclusive right to propose a plan of reorganization for 180 days and the plan, whenever proposed, must be approved within 300 days of the bankruptcy filing or the case will be dismissed. §1121(e). Courts may not extend those periods unless the debtor demonstrates that it is "more likely than not" that the court will confirm a plan within a reasonable period of time, a new deadline is imposed at the time the extension is granted, and an extension order is signed before the existing deadline has expired. The burden is on the moving party, usually the debtor, to show that it will propose a confirmable plan within a reasonable time period.

The time limits imposed on plan confirmation have drawn particular fire. The available empirical evidence suggests that they are both too long and too short. That is, for the cases in which there is little hope of a reorganization, permitting the debtor to drift in Chapter 11 for six months (180 days) is wasteful and the statute does little to push these hopeless cases out faster than the judges were managing before the changes came into play. In a study focused on small business cases filed in Chicago in 1998, professors Douglas Baird and Edward Morrison determined that 91.5 percent of unsuccessful cases are resolved within 345 days of filing, the greatest number being resolved in the first two months. By contrast, successful cases took longer; more than a third of all the cases that eventually confirmed a plan of reorganization did so after 345 days. Our data from the Business Bankruptcy Project indicate that in 2002 75 percent of all Chapter 11 cases were resolved in less than a year and 90 percent in less than 18 months.

Is it a big deal if the debtor cannot confirm a plan and the case is dismissed or if the plan is confirmed and the business cannot regain its footing? After all, Professor LoPucki has talked at length about "Chapter 22s," that is, Chapter 11 filings that confirmed a plan but ended up back in Chapter 11 a second time. Can the debtors just come back and try again? They can, but only if they can prove some things that their bigger cousins need not talk about. A small business debtor hoping to take a second bite at Chapter 11 within two years of the first filing must prove to the court that its bankruptcy resulted from circumstances beyond the debtor's control that were not foreseeable at the time the case was filed and that it is more likely than not that the court will confirm a plan of reorganization (as opposed to a liquidating plan). If the small debtor cannot make that proof, then there is no automatic stay available to protect the debtor. 11 U.S.C. §362(n)(1)(D). The latter point raises yet another policy question: Why would Congress prefer that a debtor struggling with a failed reorganization attempt another reorganization rather than a Chapter 11 liquidation? More mysteries.

Indeed, the whole notion of a statute that singles out small businesses for heightened scrutiny has a somewhat otherworldly quality. There is no systematic evidence to suggest that small business bankruptcies are rife with fraud, abuse, or even heavy partying. Ironically, the general unsecured creditors who extend credit to these small debtors, represented by their trade group the Commercial Law League of America, vigorously opposed these changes, arguing that they would increase the leverage of the big banks and push more businesses into liquidation, leaving nothing for the trade debt, the suppliers and other smaller creditors. They lobbied against the bill but were unable to persuade Congress that the system was working all right in the small business cases.

The small business provisions raise yet another question: If the provisions here are good policy — more disclosures, limits on refiling — then why don't they apply to all businesses filing for bankruptcy? One possible explanation dates to the National Bankruptcy Review Commission, established by Congress in 1994 to review the bankruptcy laws and make recommendations for change. From the beginning, the commission was split into two camps, one that generally supported the bankruptcy system as it worked and one that was convinced that debtors of all stripes — business and consumer — were abusing their creditors. See Report of the National Bankruptcy Review Commission, Chapter 5: Individual Commissioner Views, Dissent of the Honorable Edith Jones and Commissioner James I. Shepard (1997). To attack a wide range of problems, the commissioners decided to form working groups. The strongest critics of the debtors hoped to make substantial amendments to Chapter 11, but they ended up on the small business working group instead of the Chapter 11 working group. Big business lenders and the elite bankruptcy bar combined to persuade the commission that trying to make life tougher for debtors would not help anyone, but there was no strong constituency to speak on behalf of small businesses. The proposals from the commission's small business working group became the basis for the small business amendments that Congress ultimately adopted. See Report of the National Bankruptcy Review Commission, Chapter 2: Small Business Proposals 2.5.1 (1997).

Who Will Own the Reorganized Small Business?

There is one more crucial question that is special to small business, a question that was not affected by the 2005 Amendments: Who will own the small business as it emerges from Chapter 11? After all, if John Pottow is going to go through the strain of bankruptcy, he probably wants to know up front whether Pottow's Pottery will belong to Pottow and all the little Pottows to come.

The absolute priority issues facing small owner-operated businesses are very different from those facing SAREs or big, diversified companies. Often the owner-manager of a small business in Chapter 11 has already exhausted all the cash and property resources and personal credit available from any source, pouring everything into setting the business up initially and trying to prevent its collapse in bankruptcy. Nothing else is available to help purchase the equity outright, so the owner-manager looks for some other contribution to secure equity ownership. One such device is "sweat equity," the promise of future labor as a contribution to purchase the equity ownership.

Unfortunately for the owner-operators, the Supreme Court has explicitly rejected sweat equity as new value for cramdown purposes. In re Ahlers, 485 U.S. 197 (1988). The case involved farmer-debtors trying to save their family farming operation. The Court once again engaged in close statutory reading and minimal policy analysis. It held that no implied exception or modification of the absolute priority rule was available for sweat equity cases, while expressly reserving whether the new-value rule has survived. Calling the debtor's proposed contribution "intangible, inalienable, and in all likelihood unenforceable," the Court found that "a promise of future services cannot be exchanged in any market for something of value to the creditors today." 485 U.S. at 204. Without the approval of their creditors as a class, said the Court, the debtors still had to meet the absolute priority rule.

The debtors in *Ahlers* made another argument as well, claiming they were not retaining any value because the security interests attached to the farm far exceeded the farm's value, rendering the value of the farm zero. If the equity was worth nothing, then the debtors could not be violating the absolute priority rule, they argued. The Court also rejected this approach, saying that there is always some value in the control of an enterprise and in the possibility that the property will rebound — and the debtor who keeps it without paying violates the absolute priority rule.

With no source for cash to buy the right to continue to own and operate their business, and no ability to earn the right through sweat equity, it would seem that most small business owners will be forced simply to liquidate their businesses. But creditors are not always so eager in these cases to see the business fold. Because the owner and manager are the same, the creditors often recognize that unless the manager stays on, the business is worthless. Antoinette's Tonight, Home of Antoinette LaPierre's Genuine Authentic Handpacked Blackened Redfish, may be worth very little if Antoinette is out and Sam Bump is in. In other cases, the equity owner is critical because the owner's business connections are what make the business go. Sportco's Athletic Supply Equipment depends on having Red Holstrom, a former all-pro tight end and retired state champion high school coach, around to make calls on the high school coaches. And Pottow's Pottery depends on the artistic hand of the Great Pottow himself. Sometimes the relationships are even more tangled, so that it may be the owner-manager's father-in-law who owns the warehouse that the business leases at favorable rates or the wife who does all the accounting and billing for free, benefits that will not be available to strangers who try to take over the business.

In these and other cases, the creditors have the chance to make a deal. They can vote for confirmation despite their impairment if they believe they will do better in the reorganization than they would trying to liquidate or sell the business. They understand the comparative advantages decision: They can lose a lot in a liquidation right now, or they can possibly lose much less if they let a Chapter 11 play out with the owner-operator in place. For unsecured creditors who often will get only a trivial amount in a liquidation, the option to permit the Chapter 11 looks fairly attractive.

The consequence of a decision such as *203 North LaSalle* in such a case may depend on the perceived self-interests of key creditors. So long as they want to work with the debtors, a consensual plan in which the owner-operator stays around is likely. But the *LaSalle* decision increases the power of any class of creditor to object. It seems clear that a small business debtor who cannot convince most of the suppliers to go along with a feasible plan does not have much of a chance of survival in any case. But the risk is that most creditors will want to see the debtor try to survive, while one creditor will resist. If that creditor cannot be included in a larger class, then cramdown may be impossible. Increased leverage may translate into better treatment for the creditor who figures this out, thus undermining the equality principle among creditors

Not all the creditors may have the same perspective, as Mr. Johnston learned in the next case.

In re MJ METAL PRODUCTS, INC.
292 B.R. 702 (D. Wyoming 2003)

OPINION BY: Peter J. McNiff

* * *

1. The debtor is a close corporation owned by Mark Johnston and his former spouse, Alicia Hickson. The debtor is engaged in the manufacture of food servicing equipment. According to the approved disclosure statement, the debtor's prepetition liabilities exceed the debtor's assets and there is no evidence before the court to the contrary. The debtor has net equity before consideration of unsecured claims of $30,000;

2. Under the proposed chapter 11 plan, the debtor will pay general unsecured creditors (Class 8) a total of $80,000. The scheduled unsecured claims (of approximately 80 creditors) total approximately $132,000. The scheduled claims do not include monetary amounts for the claims of Kelly Martin, Leslie Newcombe, Brian Johnson, or of the National Labor Relations Board (NLRB);

3. The NLRB filed a timely proof of claim for $48,423, based on a judgment in its favor by the Tenth Circuit Court of Appeals affirming an administrative order, MJ Metal Products, Inc. v. N.L.R.B., 267 F.3d 1059 (10th Cir. 2001). The underlying basis of the money judgment was back wages due Kelly Martin, Leslie Newcombe, and Brian Johnson. The claim sets forth the amount of those back wages as $9,319, $11,104, and $28,000, respectively;

4. In the plan, the debtor proposes that all common stock will be cancelled on the effective date of the plan. New stock in the reorganized debtor will be sold to the highest bidder by sealed bids. The right to participate in the bidding is limited to "former shareholder(s)," i.e., Mr. Johnston and Ms. Hickson;

5. The debtor submitted a ballot report, absent the actual ballots, prior to the hearing. The ballots were introduced at the request of the court. The ballots show that 10 of the voting Class 8 creditors elected to accept the plan, and one, the NLRB, did not. Mr. Newcombe submitted a ballot, but did not state the amount of his claim on the ballot.

The total dollar amount of the Class 8 creditors accepting the plan is $62,727.04. The total dollar amount of the creditor's claim rejecting the plan is $58,503. In other words, 52% of the voting Class 8 creditors accepted the plan without counting Mr. Newcombe's ballot.

CONCLUSIONS OF LAW

Under 11 U.S.C. §1129(a), the court is required to confirm a chapter 11 plan if the proposed plan satisfies certain statutory requisites. Among those requirements, each class of claims must either accept the plan, or the treatment of that class must be unimpaired. 11 U.S.C. §1129(a)(8). In this case, the debtor's plan is not confirmable under §1129(a)(8). Class 8 is an impaired class of claims because it is not receiving payment in full, and "two-thirds in amount" of the voting creditors did not accept the plan. 11 U.S.C. §1126(c).

A plan proponent may obtain confirmation of a plan which does not satisfy §1129(a)(8) if that class of unsecured claims is paid in full (which in this case it is not), or if the plan complies with the absolute priority rule, i.e., no holder of an interest junior to the claims in the class will receive an interest in any property under the plan. 11 U.S.C. §1129(b)(2)(B)(ii). In this case, the plan proposes that one or the other shareholder will receive stock in the reorganized debtor, in direct violation of the absolute priority rule.

The debtor contends, however, that because there is no creditor in Class 8 raising the issue of the absolute priority rule, the court should confirm the plan regardless of whether or not the rule is satisfied. The debtor is wrong. The court has an independent duty to determine whether a plan complies with §1129.

Second, the debtor contends that the NLRB should be precluded from voting the claims of the wage claimants, whose back wages are detailed in the NLRB proof of claim. If the NLRB vote is stricken, the debtor will have the necessary acceptances in Class 8.

The debtor argues the NLRB violates Fed. R. Bankr. P. 2019(a). Under Rule 2019(a), an entity representing more than one creditor is required to file a statement detailing the authority of that entity to act on behalf of those creditors. Rule 2019(b) authorizes the court to sanction any entity violating Rule 2019(a) by invalidating a plan rejection, among other things.

In this case, the Tenth Circuit Court of Appeals affirmed a decision in favor of the NLRB, not a judgment in favor of the individual wage earners. The NLRB is the party in interest entitled to enforce the judgment. The debtor has not objected to the NLRB proof of claim, and did not file a motion on proper notice under Rule 2019(b). The debtor's argument is opportunistic and unconvincing.

The debtor also urges the court to include Mr. Newcombe's claim as an acceptance, and to deduct the amount of his "claim" from the NLRB's rejection vote. Regardless of the legal authority for this proposition, such adjustments will not help the debtor. Even by such calculations, only 63% of the voting creditors in Class 8 could be deemed to have accepted the plan.

Last, the debtor contends that the absolute priority rule is satisfied because the provision providing for a sale of the reorganized debtor's stock to the existing shareholders satisfies the new value exception to the rule. The United States Supreme Court has not specifically stated that a new value contribution by equity holders is an exception to the absolute priority rule, although in the case of Bank of America Nat. Trust and Sav. Ass'n v. 203 North LaSalle St. Partnership, 526 U.S. 434 (1999), the Court discussed the exception at length.

In *North LaSalle*, the Court found the debtor's proposed plan unconfirmable because the plan vested equity in the reorganized business in the debtor's partners "without extending an opportunity to anyone else either to compete for that equity or to propose a competing reorganization plan." Id. at 1422. The Court also stated that "plans providing junior interest holders with exclusive opportunities free from competition and without benefit of market valuation" violate §1129(b)(2)(B)(ii). Id. at 1424. In other words, if a new value contribution exists as an exception to the rule, exposure to the market is essential to obtain that new value. The cases cited by the debtor either predate the decision in *North LaSalle* or are not on point.

The plan in this case did not preclude other parties from proposing a plan. However, the plan does provide an exclusive right to the existing shareholders to bid for shares in the reorganized debtor. That exclusivity is, in this court's view, directly contrary to the intent of the Supreme Court in the *North LaSalle* case, and the plan is not confirmable.

Ms. Hickson objects that the plan is not proposed in good faith, but evidence to that effect was notably lacking. She also argues that her shares in the existing company should not be cancelled, and she should not be required to participate in any bidding process. Her argument is directly contrary to the provisions of §1129 and therefore, must be rejected.

In this case, the debtor retains many options which may result in a confirmable plan. The debtor can expose the sale of reorganized shares to the market, the debtor can attempt to obtain additional accepting votes in Class 8, or the debtor can pay the unsecured creditors in full. Other options are undoubtedly available.

According, IT IS ORDERED that confirmation of the debtor's amended chapter 11 plan is denied; and FURTHER ORDERED that any proposed plan or amended plan shall be filed within 30 days of the date of this order.

═══════════════

MJ Metal Products is a firm reminder that the multiparty element of Chapter 11 — even in modestly sized cases — can add new layers of complications that make it very hard to get to yes.

Problem Set 36

36.1. Katie and Matt Porter have built Bassett Babies, an online retailer specializing in Bassett Hound–themed clothing, toys, and knickknacks, into a thriving business with $4 million annual revenues. But when a scandal erupted over Linus, their prize-winning hound and the model for the signature trademark on all their merchandise, business took a nosedive. A losing competitor in the Westminster finals sued Linus's legal owner, Bassett Babies Inc., alleging that Linus had had cosmetic surgery (in violation of Westminster rules) and that his lineage papers were forged. As the lawsuit has dragged on, Katie and Matt have fallen behind on all their payments. When they come to see you, they have about $1.7 million in debts. They absolutely did not fiddle with Linus's beautiful snout, but the very wealthy woman who is suing is suffering from bruised pride and is unwilling to let go of the litigation. They are fairly certain they can win the pending suit eventually, but legal fees are mounting up, and they really need to launch a public relations blitz to win back their clients right away. They are afraid that if they don't declare bankruptcy soon, creditors will seize their inventory and the business will be over. When Katie, Matt, and Linus come to see you, what do you recommend? See §§101(51D), 1121(e).

36.2. Melissa Jacoby is a patient woman, but when her patience is gone, it is gone. And right now, she has run out of patience with On-the-Mark Car Repair. As a parts supplier, Melissa is owed about $100,000, which makes her the largest unsecured creditor in On-the-Mark's Chapter 11. Melissa heads up the creditors' committee, but the other creditors aren't interested in investing much time in participating in a bankruptcy that is unlikely to yield much of anything; they are willing to follow her recommendation. She can't see that Mark is making much progress, she's tired of fooling around with him, and she's sick of spending time on the committee work. She calls you to ask what are her options to get the case resolved promptly. What do you suggest? See §101(51D).

36.3. Mukesh Tyagi has been a senior counsel with the Office of the United States Trustee for several years. He watched the debates over the bankruptcy bill with interest, and he has been instrumental in designing supervision protocols for small business cases in Chapter 11 and ways to monitor the required paperwork. Last week Mukesh was catching up on his law review reading when he noticed Lawless and Warren, The Myth of the Disappearing Business Bankruptcy, 93 California L. Rev. 745 (2005). The authors provide data to show that about 13 to 17 percent of all bankruptcy filings currently denominated "non-business" are in fact tied to a failed owner-operated business. That means more than 250,000 self-employed or formerly self-employed debtors a year are filing in Chapter 7 or Chapter 13. Mukesh starts getting a very uncomfortable feeling that his organizational plans for dealing with the 2005 Amendments may be inadequate. You serve as general counsel to the UST. What advice do you have when Mukesh calls? See §§101(51D)(A), 308, 707(b)(1); 28 U.S.C. 586(a)(7).

36.4. When Adam Levitan's baby daughter was ill, Adam set aside everything to be with his family. After several frightening months, the child recovered, but Adam's dental practice, Happy Smiles, Inc., did not. Adam tried to resuscitate the business through Chapter 11, but all the assets are tied up with security interests, and he is concerned that his creditors may be difficult to deal with, particularly the rival dentist who sold Adam two X-ray machines on credit and who has made it clear he would like to put Adam out of business. Adam says he has nothing to offer but his hands — everything else has already gone into the business. Adam is sure he can start again, but he needs the lease, the customer list, the trade name, and the equipment from his office. Adam has a new bank, First Wave, which is willing to lend Adam about $500,000 if it can have a first lien against all the assets. Half a million is a fair liquidation price for these assets. What do you advise? See §§363(f), 1129(b).

3. *The Reorganization of Public Companies*

There are not nearly so many big Chapter 11s as small ones, but each of the big cases has disproportionate economic impact. In 2003, 143 public companies filed for bankruptcy with a total $97.5 billion in assets, averaging $686 million per case. The 2004 Bankruptcy Yearbook and Almanac 36. The biggest employers in the 1994 bankruptcy sample, for example, were among the largest cases. *Financial Characteristics* at 548. In 2003, K-Mart filed with its 232,000 employees and there were many other filings by companies employing thousands of workers. Stock in such companies is often widely held, and resolution of a big Chapter 11 case may affect communities and industries throughout the country — or throughout the world.

Most of the largest companies are public companies, but by no means all of them. Some large companies are closely held and have never issued stock or bonds to the investing public. Unlike public companies, private companies are not required to register their securities with the Securities and Exchange Commission in Washington or to file the numerous reports and financial statements required of public companies. Because of this lack of information, very little systematic research has been done on such companies. (There are many in-between and specialized cases, even among public companies. For example, companies like the New York Times Company and the Ford Motor Company are public companies, but their management remains controlled by their founding families through special classes of stock with special voting power.) In this section, we will discuss only public companies, even though some of the phenomena discussed are relevant to all large companies.

The central distinguishing characteristic of public companies, as noted earlier, is that in most such corporations management is separated from ownership. The people who run the company are not the owners or even the principal owners; typically the shareholders are a large group of investors, most of whom have little say in how the company is run. The first important consequence of these facts in the bankruptcy context is that the ownership of the company is irrelevant to its operating success. That is, it will succeed or fail regardless who owns the stock, in sharp contrast with Antoine's Redfish Restaurant, which likely expires if Antoine leaves. The second important consequence flows from the first: The interests of management and shareholders may be inconsistent. There is a huge literature on this second point, which is said to be the central focus of all of corporate law (that "corporate governance" of which you may have read). Suffice for present purposes to note that the management of a public company may have a much greater interest in the survival of management jobs and perks than in the maintenance of shareholder equity. Especially under conditions of financial distress, the best decision from management's point of view may not be the best from the perspective of shareholders — or creditors.

Because many public companies are large, their sheer size makes their encounters with financial distress quite different from smaller companies. The management of a huge workout or Chapter 11 case (think of United Airlines or K-Mart) is an enormous task, requiring battalions of lawyers and other professionals, along with huge supporting staffs and thousands of the debtor's regular employees. The shareholders and the creditors of such companies are also numbered in the thousands and scattered across the nation and the world. The consequent problems of notice and adequate representation make these cases very different from the bulk of Chapter 11 proceedings.

Finally, public company workouts and bankruptcies attract the most sophisticated players in the bankruptcy field, from workout champions at major banks to top turnaround specialists to high-visibility bankruptcy lawyers. It is not surprising that various important subgenres of Chapter 11 have arisen from the bankruptcies of public companies. The functioning of Chapter 11 can be quite different in many of these cases from the traditional pattern discussed earlier. In particular, it is by no means certain that survival of the company is the DIP's objective and it may be hard to predict on whose behalf the DIP is negotiating.

Control

Control lies at the heart of all bankruptcy systems. In the United States in Chapter 7 and Chapter 13, as in most bankruptcy systems around the world, public or governmental control is given to a trustee in bankruptcy, albeit under judicial supervision. In Chapter 11, management is in control, because it makes the decisions for the DIP, which is given the same rights and duties as a trustee in bankruptcy. Because control in a public company usually lies with management and the managers are not the principal owners of the company, control in bankruptcy is separated from the equity interests, making it possible that any of a number of different corporate stakeholders might exercise the DIP's control through their influence on management. Jay Lawrence Westbrook, The Control of Wealth in Bankruptcy, 82 Tex. L. Rev. 795 (2004).

Naturally, each constituency in a financially distressed corporation is anxious to advance its own interests. They are more likely to be the winners at the end if they have control of the process. The three cases in this section illustrate three important aspects of that struggle for control. The first is that some creditors may exercise control through obtaining security interests in most of the debtor's assets or through making DIP loans at the start of a bankruptcy case and making those loans conditional upon strict covenants in their favor in a first day order. The resulting control may be exercised in ways unfavorable to equity and to other creditors who are unsecured. The second is that management, divorced from equity in a public company, has interests of its own that creditors may be better able to satisfy. The third is the role of the valuation of the company's worth in determining who will be in control of the wealth that emerges from a Chapter 11 under a confirmed plan. Because of the system of priorities, from secured creditors on top through layers of unsecured creditors with various priorities down to equity at the bottom, the higher the valuation the more groups have a legitimate stake in the debtor company, in or out of bankruptcy. The lower the valuation, the more power flows to those at the top of the priority tree.

A nonbankruptcy legal idea that is quite relevant in this context is that when the debtor enters "the zone of insolvency" directors acquire a duty to creditors under state corporate law instead of or in addition to their duty to shareholders. The classic opinion is found in Credit Lyonnais Bank Nederland, N.V. v. Pathe Communications Corp., 1991 WL 277613 (Del. Ch. Dec. 30, 1991). This concept has generated some following in the courts, but mostly criticism from academics. See generally, Jonathan C. Lipson, Directors' Duties to Creditors: Power Imbalance and the Financially Distressed Corporation, 50 U.C.L.A. L. Rev. 1189 (2003).

One group that necessarily has an important role in Chapter 11 consists of the banks (or other lending institutions) that have provided financing to the debtor. Very often in public companies such creditors are unsecured, because those companies are attractive customers for banks but the companies would prefer to avoid tying up their assets by granting security interests. At the same time, bankers are more comfortable in lending unsecured to such companies, so competitive pressures often lead to large unsecured loans.

As a result, it is not uncommon that a company entering a period of financial distress has mostly unencumbered assets. At that point, the lenders are very apt to demand security, sweetening the demand with an offer of "fresh money" over and above what is already owed. Thus a company whose assets were mostly free of security interests prior to the period of financial distress may be highly encumbered by the time it files for bankruptcy. Even if it is not, the company will still need DIP financing and often will be required to give broad security interests to secure that financing. So, just before or just after bankruptcy, the lenders may acquire security that gives them great influence over the management /DIP. The result may be what we have called the SPIP or Secured Party in Possession.

In the late 1980s, Professors LoPucki and Whitford conducted a series of painstaking interviews and analyses of behavior of the management of large companies that had filed for bankruptcy during the decade. They concluded that only about 20 percent of the DIP managers aligned themselves with equity in their decision-making, while about a third clearly aligned with creditors; the remainder were scattered in some general (and sometimes conflicting) sense of "maximizing the estate" or "preserve the company." Lynn LoPucki and William Whitford, Corporate Governance in the Bankruptcy Reorganization of Large, Publicly Held Companies, 141 U. Penn. L. Rev. 669, 735, Table VII (1993). Management may be running the show, but the data suggest that in a number of cases the show may be run for the benefit of a subgroup of creditors.

The SPIP bankruptcy has many advantages for lenders over an out-of-bankruptcy resolution. Among other things, it means that their security interests are confirmed by court order and any disposition of the collateral also receives judicial blessing, giving the lenders additional legal protection throughout the process.

In those situations, the lenders may demand extensive protective covenants in the first day order and, as noted earlier, that order is often subject to relatively little scrutiny by the other stakeholders in a public company case. Generally, the victories won by the debtor and the key creditors in that order are hard to reverse. Thus the following decision surprised a lot of bankruptcy experts, especially those who felt that the Delaware bankruptcy bench was too friendly to lenders. The opinion also provides a view into the jockeying for control in a bankruptcy, with a secured creditor and debtor who seem to be working things out, and a pesky unsecured creditors' committee that wants to check things out as well. The unsecured creditors were out of luck unless they could find a basis for whittling away at the control exercised by the lenders. At least on the face of this opinion, it appears that the DIP/trustee was squarely on the side of the lenders. And equity is nowhere to be seen.

═══════ In re CHANNEL MASTER HOLDINGS, INC. ═══════

309 B.R. 855 (Bankr. D. Del. 2004)

Mary F. WALRATH, Chief Judge.

Before the Court are the final chapter 11 fee applications for the professionals of the Debtors and the Official Unsecured Creditors' Committee ("the Committee"). An Objection was filed by Comerica Bank, as agent for the pre-petition and post-petition lenders ("the Lenders"), to the fees of the Committee's professionals.

I. Factual Background

On October 2, 2003, Channel Master Holdings, Inc., and its two affiliates (collectively "the Debtors") filed voluntary petitions under chapter 11 of the Bankruptcy Code. The cases have been administratively consolidated. Prior to the filing, the Debtors had negotiated an agreement to sell substantially all their assets to the Andrews Corporation ("Andrews") for $17 million, which was substantially less than the balance due to the Lenders. On the filing date, the Debtors filed a motion for approval of bid procedures in connection with that sale. The Debtors also filed a Motion for approval of financing and use of cash collateral ("the DIP Financing Motion"). An Interim Order was entered on October 3, 2003, and a final hearing was held on the DIP Financing Motion on October 21, 2003. In the interim, the Committee was formed and selected counsel.

At the final hearing on the DIP Financing Motion, the Debtors presented a budget which capped the fees of the Committee's professionals at $75,000. (Exhibit P-1) The budget also capped fees for the Debtors' professionals ($990,000) and the Lenders' advisors ($350,000). (*Id.*) There was also a miscellaneous category for chapter 11 expenses of $225,000. (*Id.*) The Committee objected to the cap on its professional fees, asserting that it was insufficient especially compared to the caps for the Debtors' and Lenders' professionals. The Lenders argued that, since they were under-secured, the unsecured creditors had no stake in the case and the Lenders should not be required to pay more than minimal fees for the Committee's participation. We granted the DIP Financing Motion and approved the budget but held that we had the authority to allocate the budgeted fees among the professionals on a pro-rata basis.

The Debtors proceeded with the sale process. On November 20, 2003, we entered an order approving the sale of substantially all the Debtors' assets to Andrews for $18.1 million. The sale closed the next day. After applying the proceeds to the Lenders' claims, there remains due to them over $25 million. The parties were thereafter unable to agree upon a wind-down budget. As a result, the case was converted to chapter 7 on December 3, 2003.

The professionals for the Debtors and the Committee filed final fee applications for all services rendered prior to conversion. The fees requested are as follows:

Pepper Hamilton (Debtors' attorneys): Fees of $331,330.25; expenses of $32,404.28; and retainer of $100,475.79.

FTI Consulting, Inc. (Debtors' financial advisors): Fees of $262,606; expenses of $15,208.75; and retainer of $59,870.30

SG Cowen Securities Corp. (Debtors' investment bankers): Monthly fees of $100,000; expenses of $14,425.87; and success fee of $605,000 to be paid from sale proceeds.

Traub, Bonacquist & Fox (Co-counsel to Committee): fees of $144,966 and expenses of $3,401.65.

Monzack and Monaco, P.A. (Co-counsel to Committee): Fees of $23,790.50 and expenses of $2,480.92.

J.H. Cohn LLP (Committee's financial advisors): fees of $98,970.50 and expenses of $6,531.60.

* * *

The Lenders objected to fees sought by the Committee's professionals in excess of the $75,000 carve-out in the budget attached to the DIP Financing Order. The Lenders also objected to the fees sought as excessive for the tasks that the Committee was required to perform. They argue that the Committee's professionals were cognizant of the fact that the unsecured creditors were "out of the money" and should have restricted their services accordingly.

A hearing was held on the fee requests on March 5, 2004, after which we permitted supplemental submissions to be filed by the parties. Supplemental objections to specific time entries were filed by the Lenders on March 12, and a response was filed by the Committee on March 19, 2004.

III.   DISCUSSION

A.   *Application of Cap in DIP Financing Order*

The Lenders assert that the DIP Financing Order precludes the Court from approving any fees in excess of the $75,000 cap on fees of the Committee's professionals. The Committee argues that the cap is not binding and that the Court so ruled at the time of the DIP Financing Order. It asserts that its cap is particularly outrageous when compared to those allowed for the Debtors' and Lenders' professionals ($990,000 and $350,000, respectively). The Committee argues that, even if the $75,000 cap is enforceable, any excess fees requested by its professionals would, nonetheless, be payable from the budget's miscellaneous category ($225,000).

We agree with the Committee that the existence of a cap on fees for Committee's professionals in the DIP Financing Order does not limit allowance or payment of fees to those professionals. A court has the inherent power to direct disgorgement of fees by any professional and to redistribute those disgorged fees among all professionals in order to assure that none receives more than its pro rata share. See, e.g., In re Unitcast, Inc., 219 B.R. 741, 753 (6th Cir. BAP 1998) ("disgorgement is a remedy within the discretion of bankruptcy judges as the final arbiters of professional fee requests under [sections] 330 and 331 of the Code"); Specker Motor Sales Co. v. Eisen, 300 B.R. 687, 691 (W.D. Mich. 2003) (holding that disgorgement "honors the intent of the Code and the classification of the remaining creditors as equal, none having a superpriority over another"); In re Penn State Clothing Corp., 204 B.R. 161, 164 (Bankr. E.D. Pa. 1997) (noting that, where Chapter 11 plan has been confirmed prior to conversion, disgorgement is not necessary, but payments have to be deducted from total amount of remaining claim); In re Lockwood Corp., 216 B.R. 628, 636 (Bankr. D. Neb. 1997) (explaining that interim compensation is subject to disgorgement when estate is administratively insolvent); In re Metropolitan Elec. Supply Corp., 185 B.R. 505, 511-12 (Bankr. E.D. Va. 1995) (finding chapter 7 trustee's request for disgorgement of chapter 11 professional fees appropriate to the extent that payments exceed professionals' pro rata distribution amount).

We stated at the hearing on the DIP Financing Order our intent to consider disgorgement of fees, despite the carve-out caps in the budget, in the event it became appropriate. It has now come to pass that, indeed, the estate is administratively insolvent and reallocation of fees may be warranted. If we were to allow all requested fees and enforce the carve-out caps as the Lenders argue we should, the Debtors' professionals would receive 100% of their fees, while the Committee's professionals would receive approximately 27%. After first applying the $160,346.09 retainers they held as of the petition date, the fees and expenses requested by the Debtors' professionals total $595,629.06 against a cap of $990,000. In contrast, the Committee's professionals seek $282,141.17 against a cap of $75,000. After applying that cap, the Committee's professionals are still owed $207,141.17.

However, there are sufficient funds available from the $225,000 cap for miscellaneous expenses to cover the fees of the Committee's professionals even without invading the $394,370.94 balance of the Debtors' cap. Therefore, we find it unnecessary to require the Debtors' professionals to disgorge any fees.

B. Review of Fee Requests Generally

Even if there are no objections, we have an independent duty to review all fee requests of professionals retained in a chapter 11 case to assure that the services rendered were necessary and appropriate and that the fees requested are reasonable.

* * *

C. Objection to Fees of Committee's Professionals

The Lenders assert that the fees requested by the Committee's professionals must be reduced because they performed many unnecessary services and because the value of the necessary services performed is substantially less than requested. From the inception of the case, the unsecured creditors appeared to be entitled to nothing: the Debtors filed a motion to sell substantially all their assets to Andrews for far less than the secured creditors were owed. Given these circumstances, the Lenders argue, the Committee's professionals should not have performed services that were neither designed nor likely to result in a recovery for their constituency.

The Committee's professionals assert, however, that the services they rendered in this case were in furtherance of their fiduciary duty and were designed to enhance the possibilities of a recovery for unsecured creditors. The fact that they were not successful should not mandate denial of their fees.

We agree with the Committee that success is not a prerequisite to allowance of fees in chapter 11. However, we do not think that chapter 11 is a license to perform services and generate fees in a vacuum without considering the possibilities of recovery for the professional's constituents.

In this case, we conclude that a reasonable professional representing the Committee would have performed many of the services performed by the professionals in this case, but not to the extent that the professionals did in this case.

1.   Key Employee Retention Plan

The Lenders state that the Committee spent too much time analyzing and objecting to the Key Employee Retention Plan ("KERP") proposed by the Debtors because any reduction in the cost of that plan would not have benefited the unsecured creditors until an additional $25 million was received by the estate and paid to the Lenders. We disagree. It was reasonable for the Committee to review and oppose the KERP. Such plans often propose excessive bonuses for senior management of the Debtors, on the theory that the bonuses are necessary to retain competent employees with knowledge of the Debtors' operations. Often Committees are successful in reducing the amounts paid under such plans by arguing that the number of employees covered or the amount to be paid is excessive. Reductions in the amounts paid under those plans typically free additional working capital to allow the Debtors to survive, thereby enhancing recovery for all creditors. Further, because the KERP was proposed early in this case, the Committee was not able to wait until after the sale (when it became clear that unsecured creditors would get no recovery) to oppose the motion.

However, under the circumstances of this case, where the Debtors were proposing a quick sale of their businesses for substantially less than half what the Lenders were owed, it was unlikely that any reduction in the KERP payments would have resulted in a recovery for unsecured creditors. The cost of the KERP was essentially being borne totally by the Lenders. In fact, after extensive investigation and negotiation, the Committee was able to achieve only a facial change to the benefit of unsecured creditors (reducing the KERP by $250,000 only if the Lenders were paid in full). In fact, the Lenders were not paid in full and the reduction was never effective. Yet, the efforts of the Committee professionals in getting this "reduction" totaled almost $34,000. We find this excessive and conclude that a reasonable professional in these circumstances would have spent no more than $5,000 in reviewing the KERP. Consequently, we will allow only 15% of the fees requested by the Committee professionals relating to the KERP motion. The disallowance will be done pro rata based on the amount of time spent by all professionals on this matter.

2.   Sale

The Lenders also complain that the Committee's professionals spent excessive time (over $103,000) in connection with the sale process. They argue that, since the initial bid was approximately 40% of the secured debt, it was highly unlikely that there would have been any recovery for unsecured creditors from the sale. We disagree with the Lenders on this point. Although the initial bid was less than the Lenders' claims, we are aware of situations where an auction in bankruptcy has resulted in substantially increased bids. We have even had cases where the ultimate sale resulted in a recovery for unsecured creditors (and even shareholders) although it was originally thought that those constituencies had no chance for a distribution. Such results have often come through the efforts of the Committee in insisting upon bid procedures that are fair and in seeking to locate additional interested bidders. Thus, we are not prepared to conclude that these efforts were unwarranted; in fact, they were part of the fiduciary duty owed by the Committee to its constituents. We will, therefore, allow fees for this work.

5.   Analysis of Lenders' Liens

The Lenders assert that Monzack and Monaco spent too much time analyzing the perfection of the Lenders' liens, especially since the task was not completed by the time the case was converted. The entries identified by the Lenders total $14,287.50.

We disagree with the Lenders. It was the duty of the Committee's professionals[6] to analyze and, if appropriate, contest the liens of the Lenders. If the liens were avoided, it would have resulted in a recovery for the unsecured creditors. The fact that the task was not completed because of the conversion is no reason to disallow the fees incurred for this work; Monzack and Monaco note that they have turned over their work on this task to the chapter 7 Trustee for completion. We find this an appropriate task for the Committee's professionals to perform, and the amount of time spent was not excessive. As a result, we will allow these fees.

* * *

IV.   Conclusion

We will allow the fee requests of the professionals for the Debtors and the Committee for the reasons and in the amounts stated above.

Note that a security interest in most of the debtor's assets means that there may be no source of payment for the debtor's professionals or those hired by the creditors' committee, unless the secured party consents. The facts in the *Channel Master* case reinforces the common sense prediction that lenders are unlikely to be happy about the idea that their collateral should be used to finance an attack on their security interests or otherwise employed to defeat their goals. Yet the court clearly regarded protection of unsecured creditors, through the committee counsel, as an essential element of bankruptcy law not subject to being ceded to the private parties in the case. Judge Walrath's decision may be a reaction to a specific case of overreaching or it could be a judicial shot across the bow of lenders who seek to use the bankruptcy courts while continuing to call the shots as if bankruptcy had not been filed.

---

6. The Debtors had conceded the validity of the Lenders' liens in the DIP Financing Order, reserving to the Committee the right to contest them.

How Long Will the Debtor Have to Reorganize?

Companies that file for Chapter 11 have an exclusive period of time in which to propose and confirm a plan of reorganization. Section 1121(b) gives the debtor 120 days in which to propose its own plan of reorganization and section 1121(c)(1) gives 180 days to solicit votes to confirm the plan. Both times are measured from the date of filing and overlap each other. During these times, no other party in interest can propose or solicit a different plan of reorganization.

The idea behind giving the DIP the first crack at proposing a plan is multileveled. Partly, it encourages management to file by assuring them that they will stay in the driver's seat for a period of time. Presumably management knows the most about the circumstances of the debtor's difficulties, and management may be best situated to propose a plan to solve them. Exclusivity also prevents a bankruptcy filing from turning into immediate chaos as different parties put forth their plans. By providing some stability and continuity, companies are spared a plunge into an immediate fight among multiple claimants. It also makes the company the central point for bringing together all the parties for negotiation.

In big reorganizations, those with thousands of outstanding contracts and leases, complex financial structures, and far flung operations, 120 days of exclusivity was unlikely to provide the time needed to reorganize the business. Prior to the 2005 Amendments, the courts had the power to extend exclusivity indefinitely. The courts might require a showing that the debtor was making good progress toward a plan and just needed more time to bring it together. Exclusivity might be extended because the debtor needed more time to sell off a division, to renegotiate contracts, or to settle a labor dispute. If a debtor could show that a recalcitrant creditor was the cause for delay, a court might extend exclusivity. Whether — and how long — to extend exclusivity was entirely within the province of the bankruptcy court, and rarely overturned in any appeal. As a consequence, the discretion of the bankruptcy court figured heavily in the confirmation of big, complex Chapter 11 plans.

A second impact of exclusivity has been its effect on leverage in the great Chapter 11 negotiations. The possibility of languishing in bankruptcy month after month, with interest no longer running on the loan while the debtor remains protected by the automatic stay, brings many creditors to the bargaining table. They may not like it, but they are ready to take a haircut, get what they can and move on. Sometimes the debtor who can credibly threaten to stay in Chapter 11 can herd the creditor cats into some semblance of a negotiated deal.

The 2005 Amendments changed the dynamic. Now, no matter the reason for delay, no matter how complex the case or how outrageous the creditors' behavior, section 1121(d)(2) imposes a cap on judicial discretion of 18 months to propose a plan and 20 months (again overlapping dates) to solicit votes. The debtor faces a firm deadline: get your plan confirmed or face the possibility that every creditor in the case will propose less attractive alternatives. For those who believe that debtors had too much running room — or, more accurately, that bankruptcy judges were giving debtors too much running room by continuing to protect them with repeated extensions of exclusivity — this change is welcome. For those who believe that judges used extensions of exclusivity and the threat of lifting exclusivity to move cases along, this change seems quite wrong-headed. Certain creditors can watch the calendar as closely as the debtor, knowing that if they can string the bankruptcy out for another few months, they can propose their own liquidating plans, grab what they can, and leave the debtor in ruins. Such a threat may cause a debtor to negotiate a reorganization package that appears to be more favorable to those creditors but that is doomed to failure.

Either way, these revisions are likely to have a powerful impact on cases — particularly the larger, more complex cases and the ones in which the food fights among the creditors were well underway by the time of the bankruptcy filing. The days when LTV Steel could take seven years to confirm a plan of reorganization are over. According to the data reported in http://lopucki.law.ucla.edu/corporations, the average time to confirm a plan for a big, publicly traded debtor is 510 days, but the standard deviation is another 436 days — suggesting that some did it very quickly and a substantial number took a very, very long time. Whether the caps on judicial discretion to grant extensions in exclusivity will herald a new day of faster reorganizations or simply a time of really large liquidations is a question to be answered by the next round of empirical studies. Stay tuned.

Liquidating Plans and Asset Sales

Increasingly Chapter 11 cases are producing liquidating plans. Generally, a liquidating plan is one in which the tasks remaining may be limited to selling assets, resolving disputes, collecting debts through lawsuits, and distributing the proceeds obtained according to an agreed formula. Since 1978, the Code has always permitted liquidating plans. §1123(b)(4). However, the use of Chapter 11 rather than Chapter 7 for liquidation has grown greatly in recent years. Data from the 2002 portion of the Business Bankruptcy Project shows that more than 10 percent of confirmed plans are liquidating plans. Sometimes the liquidating plan provides for the mechanism by which assets will be sold over time. A typical example would be the conveyance of some or all of the estate's assets to a liquidating trust managed by a trustee appointed through the plan.

Often, however, the sale of assets is accomplished under section 363(b)(1) (sale out of the ordinary course) before any plan has been approved. In those cases, a principal reason for filing bankruptcy may be to use section 363(f) to give the buyer the comfort of a clean title, free and clear of all liens. Buyers will often pay more for that comfort, particularly where there may be some disputes lurking in the background that could give rise to later challenges. A sale free and clear under section 363(f) gives a federal court's blessing to a transfer, which is exactly what the buyer wants. In those cases, the plan proposed and confirmed after the sale may be for the sole purpose of paying professionals and distributing any remaining proceeds.

Again *Channel Holdings* illustrates the point. It appears that the major purpose of the bankruptcy filing in that case was to sell the debtor's major asset free and clear. The parties intended after the sale to approve a plan to wrap up the case and distribute the proceeds. Only when they did not agree on a confirmable plan did the case convert to the traditional liquidation chapter, Chapter 7. The case illustrates the trend toward increasing use of liquidating plans and section 363 asset sales. This trend is not limited to public companies, but its effects are most important in that context.

Management Change

The idea that the word bankruptcy is a synonym for "it cuts both ways," is nowhere better illustrated than in the problem of compensating management. A major difficulty for a distressed public company is retention of effective and experienced managers to guide it through a workout or Chapter 11. Such managers have many options and often will not stay with a company unless offered guarantees of compensation in amounts sufficient to balance the risks, including accepting or remaining in a job that might terminate all too soon. On the other hand, creditors facing losses, employees disgusted with what they see as management mistakes, and other stakeholders are likely to be skeptical about the idea of large payoffs for the boss proposed by the boss. We saw in *Channel Holdings* that counsel for the creditors' committee was anxious to scrutinize the KERP plan proposed for management. The resulting tensions and the dynamics of clashing constituencies are captured in the following case.

In re GENEVA STEEL CO.

236 B.R. 770 (Bankr. D. Utah 1999)

Opinion by: Glen E. CLARK.

Geneva Steel Company's Motion for Order Authorizing Implementation of Employee Retention Program ("Motion") . . . seeks leave of court to implement an employee retention program designed to provide an incentive for 36 key employees of Geneva to remain with Geneva through the reorganization process. The retention program affects six senior executives and 30 managers (collectively referred to as "key employees") and is made up of two parts: a severance plan for the six senior executives, and an emergence bonus for the six senior executives and the managers.

The severance plan entitles each of the six senior executives to severance pay equal to six months salary if terminated by Geneva for any reason other than death, disability or cause prior to the date of substantial consummation of a plan of reorganization, and for severance pay equal to nine months salary if terminated within 90 days after the date of substantial consummation of a plan of reorganization. Severance benefits would be payable 30 days after the executive is terminated.

The emergence bonus entitles all key employees to a bonus if they are still employed on the date of substantial consummation of Geneva's plan of reorganization. Senior executives would receive a bonus of 50% of their annual salary. Managers would, in the discretion of Geneva's management, receive a bonus of up to 25% of their salary.[3]

Geneva argues that the retention program is critical to its business success and ongoing vitality. It contends that there is a real danger that key employees will be enticed away by other companies if a retention plan is not implemented, and that, without the services of these key employees, it will be difficult to stabilize, preserve, and successfully reorganize Geneva's business. Geneva further argues that the proposed retention program is based on its board's sound business judgment. Geneva's board of directors approved the retention program based upon the recommendations of management, The Blackstone Group, Geneva's outside financial advisor, and William M. Mercer, Inc., Geneva's expert on corporate compensation.

The Motion is supported by the Official Committee of Unsecured Creditors and the Official Committee of Bondholders. At the hearing, Geneva introduced uncontested evidence that (1) key employees are difficult to replace because talented job candidates often avoid working for a company in Chapter 11; (2) an executive search firm would likely need to be retained and their fees usually are 30% of the key employees' base salaries and bonuses; (3) signing bonuses, reimbursement for relocation expenses and above market salaries would be required to induce qualified candidates to accept employment with a Chapter 11 debtor; (4) the loss of key employees often leads to additional resignations of other key employees; and (5) a committee of "outside" (nonemployee) directors approved the retention program proposed in the Motion.

The United States Trustee and the Steelworkers object to the Motion. The United States Trustee argues that more detail regarding Geneva's Motion should be provided, including a more precise definition of the term "substantial consummation," and that severance payments under the retention program may be entitled to an inappropriately high priority if the case is converted to Chapter 7.

The Steelworkers argue that the retention program sends the wrong message to Geneva's work force, that the emergence bonus may be payable to key employees even if a Chapter 11 liquidating plan is confirmed, that the severance plan contains no provision for mitigation in the event an executive finds other work after termination, and that Geneva did not consult the Steelworkers prior to submitting the retention program to the court. In support of its objection, the Steelworkers placed into evidence a petition signed by over 900 Geneva employees opposing the retention program.

CONCLUSIONS OF LAW

Business Judgment

Geneva argues that the decision to offer the retention program is the sound business judgment of its board of directors. The court finds that to

---

3. At the hearing, Geneva indicated that it was management's intention to immediately commit to paying all managers the full 25% emergence bonus thereby eliminating any uncertainty created by leaving the amount of each manager's emergence bonus to the sole discretion of Geneva's management.

propose this retention program without first having discussed its provisions with the Steelworkers is not an example of sound business judgment. This is particularly true in light of the circumstances faced by Geneva today. Management may appropriately reserve decisions on executive benefits to itself and its directors when all is well, but when the continued existence of the business is in question and the executive benefits are subject to court approval, the dynamics of the decision making process must change. Mr. Cannon expressed profound surprise at the depth of the Steelworkers' opposition to the proposed retention program. This is not the type of surprise that the court expects to find at the hearing on such a motion.[4]

While there is evidence that retention of the key employees is critical to Geneva's survival, there is also evidence that granting the Motion as prayed may jeopardize the continuing support of the Steelworkers in Geneva's reorganization process. Indeed, evidence was presented that some plumbers and electricians have already left Geneva's employment. The court views the support and participation of the Steelworkers as being equally critical to Geneva's successful reorganization as the support and participation of the key employees. The tension created by these opposing interests creates a significant dilemma for the court. To deny the Motion in full increases the risk that Geneva's management team may be lost or further reduced. However, to grant the Motion in full risks alienating the Steelworkers and their support of Geneva's efforts to reorganize. In an effort to fashion a compromise between these competing interests, the court will comment on the relative merits of the proposed retention program and invite Geneva to renew its Motion if it so desires.

Severance Plan

The severance plan is justified in part by Geneva's argument that its executives are in need of a "cushion" to fall back upon in the event that they are terminated. When viewed strictly as a "cushion," it makes sense for Geneva to provide a severance benefit for its senior executives to assist them through a period of unemployment. It is only with great deference to Geneva's business judgment that the court partially defers to Geneva's opinion that because the senior executives' services are highly sought after by competing employers they must be protected from prolonged periods of unemployment. Yet, it does not make sense to use the severance plan to provide the senior executives with a windfall. To be acceptable to this court, the severance plan must contain a mitigation provision that reduces the amount payable in the event the executive obtains other employment during the six or nine month reimbursement period.

The severance plan provides that all severance payments shall be made within 30 days following the executive's termination. Because the severance payments are offered by Geneva in consideration for the senior executives'

---

4. If Geneva's management had consulted with the Steelworkers while formulating its retention program, the resulting program might have accommodated the Steelworkers' objections, might have been submitted to the court unopposed, and might have been approved by the court as filed.

continued employment during the bankruptcy proceeding, the severance payments are entitled to administrative priority. In re Amarex, Inc., 853 F.2d 1526 (10th Cir. 1988) (the crucial issue is what consideration supports the bonus, and whether such consideration, or a portion of it, was pre-petition services). To be entitled to priority treatment in the event the case is converted to a case under Chapter 7, the severance plan must be approved by the court after notice and hearing. In re Buyer's Club Markets, Inc., 5 F.3d 455 (10th Cir. 1993). Because the severance plan provides that severance payments are payable if the employee is terminated after the case is converted to Chapter 7 and that all severance payments shall be made within 30 days of the executive's termination, it appears that the severance payments are intended not to be subject to §726(b) subordination. Such a severance plan is unacceptable because of the adverse impact the provision could have on the administration of the case in Chapter 7.[5] To be approved by this court, the severance plan must provide that in the event the case is converted to a case under Chapter 7, severance payments shall be treated as Chapter 11 administrative expense claims, and shall be paid by the Chapter 7 trustee as promptly as practicable on a pro rata basis with all other Chapter 11 administrative expense claims.

Emergence Bonus

The emergence bonus proposes to pay senior executives 50% of their emergence bonus in stock,[6] and 50% in cash. However, the court believes that the approach voluntarily taken by Mr. Cannon to accept the entire emergence bonus in stock is the better approach, and it should apply to each of the six senior executives.

The emergence bonus proposes to pay key employees a bonus upon confirmation and substantial consummation of a plan of reorganization. Because the Motion specifically refers to a "plan of reorganization," the court will construe the Motion as proposing to pay the emergence bonus only in the event that a "plan of reorganization" is confirmed, and not a Chapter 11 liquidating plan.

Based upon the foregoing and other good cause showing, it is hereby

Ordered that Geneva's Motion for authorization to implement an employee retention program is denied without prejudice, and it is further

Ordered that Geneva is granted leave of court to set a hearing on ten days notice to parties present at the hearing of June 23, 1999, for approval of a retention program consistent with this order.

The competition among the competing claimants in *Geneva Steel* illustrates problems that pervade nearly every Chapter 11 reorganization. Current management wanted to make sure that if the business collapsed

---

5. Severance payments total as high as $1,035,351.
6. The court applauds Mr. Cannon's willingness to voluntarily take 100% stock instead of 50% stock and 50% cash.

they would get paid in the subsequent conversion to Chapter 7. Judge Clark was equally keen to make sure that if things went wrong the management team would not pick all the meat off the carcass of the failed business. Running a business in Chapter 11 consists of equal parts optimism for the upward swing and pessimism in the contemplation of liquidation. We can also be sure that each company constituency was fighting for control, even if the union was more public in its struggle than some of the rest. The DIP has to decide which constituencies are key and win their support for its plans, plans that will inevitably be influenced by the personal interests of the managers. If that sounds like a political campaign, remember that at the end is a vote.

In the 2005 Amendments, Congress jumped into the fray, no doubt influenced by all the scandals at Enron, WorldCom, and elsewhere. In addition to hearing about blatant scandal, it was told that many executives were just getting fat managing companies in Chapter 11 while the creditors and others suffered. The response was twofold, in sections 503 and 548. Section 503(c) imposes very strict limits on KERPs and other compensation programs for executives. Section 548(a)(1)(B)(ii)(IV) provides for recovery of pre-bankruptcy transfers made to insiders at a time when the debtor was insolvent. Unfortunately, this text clearly reflects the difficulties that arise when a deep suspicion of the judiciary provokes very detailed language while a lack of knowledge of the problem to be solved makes the language inapposite. Many observers were concerned that these provisions would make it difficult to retain good managers and would make Chapter 11 even more unattractive to management, thus making it even harder to solve the problem of initiating a reorganization in sufficient time to save value.

Treatment of Equity

Traditionally it was assumed that management would act on behalf of the owners of the company, the equity shareholders. Increasingly, however, equity receives little or nothing in the reorganization of a public company. Instead, Chapter 11 in a number of publicly held cases has become a mechanism for sale of the company as a going concern or a turnover of its ownership to existing creditors. Where the company is sold, the plan that is confirmed may be devoted solely to determination of the terms of distribution of proceeds under a liquidating plan. One report of the results for equity in 2003 suggests that equity holders in many public companies receive little or nothing in a plan of "reorganization." The 2004 Bankruptcy Yearbook and Almanac 280-281.

One area in which equity owners have fought back is valuation. When the company is going forward operationally, but the reorganization plan proposes to turn its ownership over to creditors, that result is justified by the assertion that the shareholders are "under water" or "out of the money" — which just means that the company is insolvent. Because there is no net worth, there is no value for equity, the people who get paid last. The response of equity in some recent cases has been a claim that the company's true value is being artificially depressed or misrepresented. Properly valued, equity may claim, the company is worth enough to pay its debts over time and still produce value for its owners.

========= In re LORAL SPACE & COMMUNICATIONS, LTD. =========
2004 WL 2979785 (S.D.N.Y.) 2004)

PATTERSON, J.

The Appellants, Loral Stockholders Protective Committee (the "LSPC"),[1] appeal *pro se* the September 2, 2004 judgment of the United States Bankruptcy Court for the Southern District of New York (the "Bankruptcy Court"), denying their motion for the appointment of an examiner under Sections 1104(c)(1) and (2) of the Bankruptcy Code

I. PROCEDURAL BACKGROUND

Based on the Bankruptcy Court's opinion, the following is the procedural history of this proceeding. Loral Space & Communications Ltd. ("Loral") and its affiliated debtors and debtors in possession (with Loral, the "Debtors") filed their Chapter 11 petitions on July 15, 2003. The LSPC, which proceeds *pro se* here as it did in all related proceedings in the Bankruptcy Court, moved for the appointment of an official shareholders' committee in September 2003, after learning that the U.S. trustee did not intend to appoint such a committee on its own. The Bankruptcy Court denied this motion after a hearing on September 19, 2003. The LSPC moved again for the appointment of an official shareholders' committee on October 27, 2003. Finding that the Debtors were hopelessly insolvent, the Bankruptcy Court denied the LSPC's second motion at a December 2, 2003 hearing.

On May 2, 2004, after learning of the Debtors' agreement with the Official Committee of Unsecured Creditors (the "Creditors' Committee") that the Chapter 11 plan would provide for no recovery by common shareholders,[2] the LSPC moved for a third time for the appointment of an official shareholders' committee. In support of its motion, the LSPC argued that an official shareholders' committee could conduct a valuation of Loral that would support its view that the Debtors and Creditors' Committee had valued Loral at several hundreds of millions of dollars lower than its true value.[3] After a hearing on May 21, 2004, the Bankruptcy Court denied the motion for the appointment of an official shareholders' committee by order dated May 28, 2004. The LSPC's appeal of this order is pending.

On August 5, 2004, the LSPC moved for the appointment of an examiner under 11 U.S.C. §§1104(c)(1) and (2). The LSPC argued that an examiner

---

1. The Bankruptcy Court referred to the LSPC as the "Ad Hoc Committee." According to the Bankruptcy Court, the LSPC represents approximately 8.4 percent of the outstanding common shares of Loral.

2. Under the terms of the plan, the equity of the post-bankruptcy corporation would be split between the corporation's managers and its creditors.

3. The LSPC also argued that an official shareholders' committee was necessary because the Debtors' management had engaged in numerous misrepresentations and self-dealing.

was necessary "to provide a complete appraisal of the Debtor assets and lia-bilities in question." The Bankruptcy Court held a hearing on August 19, 2004, at which the LSPC made the same arguments in support of the exam-iner motion as it had previously made in support of its motion for the appointment of an official shareholders' committee: the LSPC argued (1) that the Debtors were undervaluing many of their most valuable assets; and (2) that the Debtors and Creditors' Committee were improperly colluding to depress the valuations of Loral. The Court rejected the LSPC's motion at the August 19, 2004 hearing and issued a memorandum decision on September 2, 2004.

On December 7, 2004, this Court received a letter from the LSPC requesting an expedited appeal of the Bankruptcy Court's denial of its motion to appoint an examiner pursuant to 11 U.S.C. §1104(c)(2) and stat-ing that it would rely on the papers it had already filed. This Court issued an Order the following day, December 8, 2004, that the Appellees file opposing briefs by December 15, 2004 directed "at least in part to the issue of whether Judge Drain was correct in determining that an independent exam-iner should not be appointed for the limited purpose of investigating whether the debtors' and the creditors' committees' professionals had fol-lowed the proper procedures in conducting their valuation analyses of the going concern value of Loral Space & Communications Ltd., including the orbital space slots." The Court heard argument on December 17, 2004. At the conclusion of the hearing, this Court reversed and remanded the Bankruptcy Court's decision to deny the LSPC's motion for the appoint-ment of an examiner and ordered the Bankruptcy Court to appoint an exam-iner within ten (10) days.

* * *

III. Discussion

Judge Drain recognized in his opinion, filed September 5, 2004, that the debtors fixed, liquidated, unsecured debts, other than debts for goods, ser-vices, or taxes, or owing to an insider, exceed $5,000,000. He also acknowl-edged that Loral was a public company and that the legislative history of 11 U.S.C. §1104(c)(2) indicates that the purpose of establishing the threshold figure of $5,000,000 was to protect equity holders of public companies. Judge Drain further recognized that the majority view of Section 1104(c)(2) requires appointment of an examiner if the $5,000,000 threshold is met. He then cited *In re Revco D.S., Inc.*, 898 F.2d 498 (6th Cir.1990), which recog-nized that if the debt threshold is met, appointment of an examiner is mandatory. Judge Drain also noted that under *In re Revco*, the Bankruptcy Court has discretion to "prescribe the parameters of examiners' investiga-tions as is appropriate." *In re Loral*, 313 B.R. at 586.

The Bankruptcy Court, however, departed from the "majority view" to state, without citation to any legal authority: "[I]t is not at all clear that the court should go the extra mile under section 1104(c)(2) to try to conceive of an appropriate investigation if the movant has sought a wholly inappropriate one." *Id.* at 587. Thus, the Bankruptcy Court decided not to prescribe the parameters of the examiner's investigation, as allowed by Section 1104(c). Judge Drain concludes, "notwithstanding the legislative history of section 1104(c)(2) of the Bankruptcy Code, the appointment of an examiner pursuant to the terms of sections 1104(c)(1) and (c)(2) of the Bankruptcy Code to conduct a going concern valuation of the Debtors should be denied." *Id.* at 588.

* * *

The Bankruptcy Court's decision is reversed. On its face, Section 1104(c)(2) mandates the appointment of an examiner where a party in interest moves for an examiner and the debtor has $5,000,000 of qualifying debt. Furthermore, as Judge Drain noted prior to denying the LSPC's motion, "the legislative history of Section 1104(c)(2) reflects Congress's desire to provide extra protection to stockholders of public companies through the mechanism of an independent functionary." In re Loral, 313 B.R. at 585 (quoting In re Gilman Servs., Inc., 46 B.R. 322, 327 (Bankr. D. Mass. 1985); see also 7 Collier ¶1104.03[2][b] at 1104-39 (reviewing legislative history of 11 U.S.C. §1104(c)).

The Second Circuit has not yet considered whether this provision of the Bankruptcy Code is in fact mandatory. However, the Sixth Circuit, as well as a number of bankruptcy courts, has stated that it is. See In re Revco D.S., Inc., 898 F.2d 498, 500-01 (6th Cir.1990) (holding that appointment of examiner is mandatory in view of the phrase "the court shall order"). In In re Revco, the Sixth Circuit reviewed the two alternatives created by Section 1104(c) and concluded that unless paragraph (c)(2) requires appointment of an examiner in cases exceeding the debt threshold, "it becomes indistinguishable" from paragraph (c)(1).[7] In re Revco, 898 F.2d at 501.

In light of the straightforward language and legislative history of 11 U.S.C. §1104(c)(2), this Court holds that the Bankruptcy Court had no discretion to deny appointment of an examiner where, as here, the $5,000,000 debt threshold is met and shareholders of a public company have moved for appointment of an examiner. See In re Revco, 898 F.2d at 501.

* * *

[T]he Bankruptcy Court may exercise its discretion to limit the scope of the examiner's investigation and the compensation and expenses available to the examiner.

IV.   Conclusion

For the foregoing reasons, the Bankruptcy Court's denial of the LSPC's motion to appoint an examiner is reversed and remanded to the Bankruptcy

---

7. A recent decision by the Bankruptcy Court for the Northern District of Illinois makes this conclusion clear when it observes: "[I]f paragraph (c)(2) were not mandatory, then §1104(c) would have the following meaning: 'If specified debt is less than $5 million, it is in the court's discretion to appoint an examiner; and if specified debt is more than $5 million, it is in the court's discretion to appoint an examiner.' " In re UAL Corp., 307 B.R. at 85 n. 2.

Court to appoint a qualified independent examiner. In this Court's view, the examiner should have an adequate budget and expertise to review whether appropriate procedures were followed in valuing Loral's assets, particularly the space-based assets.

═══════════

While this decision was procedural, focused on the mandatory appointment of an examiner in a case involving more than $5 million in liabilities, the central focus is the proper valuation of the company and the rights of equity, if any, after such a valuation. That focus in turn highlights issues of control. Of course, the ad hoc committee of shareholders could have hired its own valuation experts and hoped for cooperation from management's employees, but that would be a very difficult, if not impossible task and a very expensive one. The examiner will be compensated from the estate. That expense will be a dead loss as far as the creditors and management are concerned, but a fundamental protection of shareholder rights in the eyes of the owners (or former owners) of the company. The role of the examiner is one of several issues that relate indirectly to the question of control of the proceeding and the influence of various Chapter 11 constituencies. Another is selection of a venue for the proceeding, a subject discussed in the next chapter of this book.

Problem Set 37

37.1. Reggie McFlintock is deeply divided about what to do. A year ago he was a fast-rising star in the electronics industry when he was offered the job of CEO of XKX Industries. XKX is a large publicly owned telecommunications company that survived the brutal shakeout of 2000, but only by a hair. He knew there was a serious risk that XKX was beyond saving, so he asked for a $2 million signing bonus and a $500,000 salary with big performance incentives added. The XKX board was deeply divided by his offer. Bill Finley, a nonmanagement board member, said, "Given a little time to get our new products to market, this company will be worth easily $150 million but Reggie is the only guy who can do it." However, Ethel Cinchley, another independent director, thought such compensation for a CEO of a deeply troubled company made no sense and that the company should accept a recent offer from Maximum Cap of $50 million for all its assets, "which would pay all our debts and leave something for the shareholders." Bill carried the day and Reggie got the job. Ethel and her supporters resigned.

Now, a year later, they both appear to have been right. The first of the new products has gone to market and is doing very, very well. On the other hand, overall revenue is down and losses are mounting. It is not clear if the company is solvent on a balance sheet basis, although it is paying its bills.

Recently, Maximum Cap, Inc. has made a new offer of $20 million for all the XKX assets, tying the lower price to the continued decline in XKX's financials. The $20 million would pay all creditors in full, although with nothing left for shareholders. Maximum also promised to take over Reggie's contract and make him the head of its new XKX division, although Reggie notes that Maximum executives don't seem to have much job security.

Bill Finley is firmly opposed to the offer, telling Reggie that turnaround is just ahead, "although we on the board will support whatever decision you finally make, even though it will be a terrible disappointment to the shareholders if you sell and you will be giving up a lot personally under your contract incentives." Reggie agrees there is a good chance of recovery, but the company's bank lenders are pressing him hard to accept the deal. They want to be paid off. Because of revenue problems, XKX might miss a payment and face default anytime in the next six months, likely forcing the company to go into Chapter 11 to hold off the banks and other creditors.

Reggie got a call this morning from the lawyer for the bank group emphasizing his fiduciary duty to creditors and urging him "not to take any stupid risks when you've got $20 million on the table in front of you." Now Reggie has called you as the company's outside general counsel. First, he wants to know what legal considerations should affect his decision. Secondly, he especially wants you to explain to him whose interests he is supposed to put first. §§503(c); 548(a)(1); 1121(d)(2).

4. *Negotiating with Special Claimants*

a. Introduction

Nowhere is the collective process of bankruptcy clearer than it is at the point where the DIP tries to put together a plan that accounts both for the legal rights of its creditors and for what will persuade creditors to support the plan. To bring the business successfully through bankruptcy, the DIP must find a way to deal with the creditors that satisfies most — or at least critical majorities — of them.

The invitation to a bankruptcy negotiation goes to all the creditors. Most of the invited creditors fit neatly within the legal boxes of secured and unsecured (or, perhaps within the smaller boxes of oversecured and undersecured creditors, priority unsecured and general unsecured creditors). In fact, however, creditors with similar legal positions but different functional positions may influence the plan process in a number of ways. Trade creditors, for example, may hope to continue to do business with the debtor, unlike a debtor's tort victims who wish only to be paid and never see the debtor again. Banks and taxing authorities may both have enforceable liens against property, but their willingness to wait for repayment or to negotiate for refinancing may differ markedly. To understand the progress of any Chapter 11 toward liquidation or reorganization, it is important to understand something about the creditors as well as the debtors.

In this section, we pause to look beyond the formal categories of creditors to some creditors who pose very special problems in business reorganizations. We focus on three: environmental claimants, mass tort claimants, and regulatory claimants. We identify these three because each kind of claimant presents particularly acute social policy questions. Both environmental and mass tort claimants present conceptual problems about when their claims arise and how (or whether) they can be resolved in a business reorganization, while bankrupt companies that face extensive regulatory oversight, such as utilities or airlines, face special challenges in which the bankruptcy court and the regulatory agency may struggle over control. The problems in this section are among the most interesting — and most challenging — in the reorganization field.

Big Liabilities

Environmental problems and mass tort problems often result in a financial crisis for a business, and so it is not uncommon to see a company with a substantial environmental problem or a mass tort problem file for bankruptcy protection. The Bankruptcy Code could be amended to deny businesses with such problems any access to bankruptcy, but that would not cause any of the problems to go away; it would merely remove a forum for dealing collectively with the problem. If the environmental or tort problems are serious, at some point the claims on the debtor's resources will trigger a competition between the business creditors and the special environmental or tort claimants. Outside bankruptcy, few mechanisms are available to supervise the business and, in particular, to monitor the distribution of its assets. In bankruptcy the conflict is highlighted and all the parties can be represented in the negotiations that will decide the repayment structure and the fate of the business. Bankruptcy may not provide ideal solutions, but it provides a better structure to find solutions than do most of the alternatives.

The policy questions presented when a failing debtor owes commercial lenders and trade creditors *and* has a huge clean-up bill or product liability obligations are not hard to see. Every dollar that goes to an environmental clean-up is a dollar that does not go to the banks and suppliers; every dollar that goes to a commercial creditor or vendor is a dollar that does not go to someone injured by the debtor. In a world of businesses with more obligations than dollars, this is a distributional issue in its starkest form.

Because the distributional claimants include both creditors who voluntarily engaged in business with the debtor and those who did not consent to become the debtor's environmental claimants or tort victims, traditional analysis can be very unsatisfactory. The clean lines of division that separate secured from unsecured and priority from general creditors leave the environmental claimants and tort victims in a general unsecured class with the least protection and the lowest likelihood of repayment. The fact that those who will be paid first are often the most sophisticated creditors and the ones most able to spread the risk of losses among several different borrowers compounds the discomfort.

Congress could establish a special priority in bankruptcy for the payment of environmental claims and mass torts. So far, it has not. Even with the 2005 Amendments that ran to several hundred pages, Congress carefully stayed away from specifying the distributional priorities among competing claimants in mass tort or environmental cases. Instead, the courts are left to fashion distributional schemes as best they can using the generic tools available in the Bankruptcy Code.

The distributional questions in bankruptcy are made even more diffi-cult by a complicating fact: Environmental claims and mass tort claims are often temporally different from ordinary loans and sales on credit. These claims often span the pre- and post-filing period. Timing matters in bankruptcy because the heart of the system is the sharp cleavage separating the debtor's pre-filing past and the debtor's post-filing future. Pre-filing cred-itors are grouped together for a collective resolution of the claims against the debtor. Post-filing creditors are creditors of the new estate and, when the estate is closed, of the emergent debtor. Those post-filing claims are fully enforceable against the estate and the post-bankruptcy debtor, unlike the pre-filing claims that may be entitled only to pro rata distributions.

Throughout these materials we have emphasized that the definition of "claim" is extraordinarily broad, encompassing not only all current obliga-tions, but any "right to payment, whether or not such right is reduced to judgment, liquidated, unliquidated, fixed, contingent, matured, unma-tured, disputed, undisputed, legal, equitable, secured, or unsecured." §101(5)(A). This broad definition explains why debts are accelerated and the bankruptcy deals with the total amount outstanding, rather than just the payments currently due.

The inclusion in the 1978 Code for the first time of contingent and unliquidated obligations was necessary to achieve the goal of clearing the debtor's financial decks, but it meant that bankruptcy cases must deal with obligations such as guarantees and warranty promises that may not come to fruition until years hence — if ever. The Code grants the bankruptcy judge a unique power with which to address such elusive and uncertain liabilities in section 502(c), which permits the estimation of claims. Nonetheless, a great intellectual and practical burden arises from the requirement to address such claims. The burden is greater because of the lack of guidance from the state law that theoretically creates liabilities, because these are claims that could not be litigated under state law until a cause of action arose.

Many of the questions considered in this section go to the scope of the Chapter 11 discharge in section 1141. For corporations, this discharge is the broadest known to our law, so logically it would seem that a discussion of the discharge would come at the end of the section on the Chapter 11 plan process. They address basic issues such as who are the claimants, what are their entitlements, and who can speak for them.

b.   Environmental Claims

The public's concern with the presence of hazardous and toxic waste sites that endanger the environment and public health has prompted gov-ernments at all levels to enact legislation designed to protect the environ-ment. Such laws now exist at every level: local, state, and federal. Businesses may run afoul of these laws in any number of ways. They may dispose of their waste improperly; they may release toxins into the air; they may fail to return land or water to a safe condition. Some businesses have obvious and long-standing environmental issues, such as strip miners and chemical manufacturers. Others may operate businesses for decades before they discover that their trash or their energy source contains substances that subject them to environmental regulations. Still others may inherit environmental obligations when they buy already-polluted land.

The policies embedded in the environmental regulations reflect the goal of protecting public health and safety by imposing financial responsibility on principally responsible parties. The difficulty, as we routinely point out in this book, is that some businesses do not have the financial resources to meet all their obligations. The question then becomes how to deal with these financial obligations along with all the others that may be facing the debtor.

The principal timing difficulty with environmental claims is that the obligations tend to cover both a pre- and post-filing period. A business is not supposed to spill toxic waste any time *and* it is supposed to clean up any toxic waste it spills. A spill that occurs pre-petition clearly creates a pre-petition obligation; a spill after filing creates a post-petition obligation. A pre-petition clean-up obligation creates a pre-petition claim, but if that clean-up obligation continues post-petition, does it also create a post-petition claim? The answers to these questions will be important to determine both what claims survive bankruptcy and what is the payment priority within bankruptcy.

The following case involves a company that filed for Chapter 11, but was converted to Chapter 7 and then liquidated. In Chapter 7, the corporation did not receive a discharge, but with no assets left, there is little point for any claimants to pursue it. In this case, however, the live human beings who owned and operated the company are still around and they share liability for the environmental obligations of their company under federal statutes that make owners and operators principally responsible parties (PRPs in the environmental lingo). The question that now faces Mr. and Mrs. Jensen, just as it would have faced the Jensen Lumber Business if it had successfully reorganized in Chapter 11, is whether the environmental obligations were discharged in bankruptcy.

=========================== In re JENSEN ===========================
127 B.R. 27 (9th Cir. BAP 1991)

Opinion by: ASHLAND. . . .
The Jensens individually wholly-owned Jensen Lumber Company ("JLC"), whose manufacturing process included dipping logs in fungicide tanks. [The State of California Department of Health Services ("DHS")] generally seeks indemnity for cleanup costs incurred related to the fungicide tanks, which remained on property (the "site") leased and later abandoned in bankruptcy by JLC. The California Regional Water Quality Control Board (the "Board") inspected the site on January 25, 1984 and issued a letter, received by the Jensens on February 2, stating a hazardous waste problem existed at the site. The Jensens thereafter individually filed bankruptcy under Chapter 7 on February 13, 1984. They did not list any claim for hazardous waste cleanup. The DHS later became involved in March, 1984 but did not expend funds for hazardous waste cleanup until substantially after that time.

Following the determination that no assets were available for distribution to creditors, the Jensens received a discharge on July 16, 1984. The Jensens filed an adversary proceeding on April 24, 1989, to determine that the DHS's claim for cleanup costs was discharged in the Jensen's individual bankruptcy, after the DHS had taken steps seeking recovery under the federal and state "Superfund" statutes, CERCLA[1] and HSA[2] respectively. . . .

ISSUE PRESENTED

This case requires us to determine when claims arise for purposes of bankruptcy, specifically claims under CERCLA and HSA.

As a preliminary matter, we note the DHS does not contend its claim is excepted from discharge. Rather, the DHS asserts its claim arose postpetition and *is* therefore not discharged. Thus, the sole issue as framed by the parties, and as addressed by the bankruptcy court concerns when DHS's claim arose for purposes of bankruptcy. . . .

DISCUSSION

A.   11 U.S.C. §101(4) Defines Claims for Bankruptcy Purposes and Legislative History Mandates a Broad Interpretation of This Definition

Congress has expressed a clear intention that the definition of claim be interpreted broadly. H.R. Rep. No. 595, 95th Cong., 1st Sess. 309, reprinted in 1978 U.S. Code Cong. & Admin. News 5963, 6266, states: "The bill contemplates that all legal obligations of the debtor, no matter how remote or contingent, will be able to be dealt with in the bankruptcy case." The Senate commented similarly. "The effect of the definition is a significant departure from present law. . . . By this broadest possible definition and by use of the term throughout the title 11 . . . the bill contemplates that all legal obligations of the debtor, no matter how remote or contingent, will be able to be dealt with in the bankruptcy case. It permits the broadest possible relief in the bankruptcy court." S. Rep. No. 989, 95th Cong., 2d Sess. 21-22, reprinted in 1978 U.S. Code Cong. & Admin. News 5787, 5807-08. While all courts generally acknowledge the definition of claim should be interpreted broadly, the issue remains exactly how broad.

B.   The Supreme Court Precedents Do Not Address the Discrete Issue of When a Claim Arises for Purposes of Bankruptcy

The parties and the bankruptcy court rely to varying degrees on two recent Supreme Court cases addressing environmental issues in the context

---

1. The Comprehensive Environmental Response, Compensation and Liability Act, 42 U.S.C. §§9601-9657.
2. The Hazardous Substance Account Act, Cal. Health and Safety Code, §25300 et seq.

of bankruptcy. In Ohio v. Kovacs, 469 U.S. 274 (1985), the State of Ohio had obtained, prior to debtor's bankruptcy, an injunction ordering the debtor to clean up hazardous waste residing on debtor's property. After the debtor filed the petition, the State filed a complaint against the debtor seeking a declaration that the debtor's obligation under the injunction was not dischargeable. The State argued the injunction did not constitute a "debt" or "liability on a claim" as defined in the Bankruptcy Code and thus was not dischargeable. The Supreme Court rejected this argument, holding the State sought the equivalent of a monetary payment within the definition of claim, and the obligation was thus dischargeable in bankruptcy. Id. at 283. While holding the environmental obligation constituted a dischargeable claim, *Kovacs* nevertheless did not address when such claims arise for bankruptcy purposes. Id. at 284. We find *Kovacs* inapposite for this reason.

Midlantic National Bank v. New Jersey Dept. of Environ. Protection, 474 U.S. 494 (1986), also involved environmental obligations in bankruptcy. At issue in *Midlantic* was whether the trustee's powers permitted abandonment of property of the debtor contaminated with hazardous waste. Id. at 496. The Supreme Court examined the scope of the trustee's powers in light of Congressional intent and case precedent. The court held that a trustee in bankruptcy may not abandon property in contravention of a state statute or regulation that is reasonably designed to protect the public health and safety, here state environmental laws. Id. at 506-507. The Supreme Court concluded the property must be either sold or cleaned up. The Court took a narrow view of the trustee's powers to force cleanup of the hazardous waste. However, this interpretation of the trustee's powers does not decide when a bankruptcy claim arises. For this reason, we find *Midlantic* to be likewise inapposite.

G.   Three Points of Origination Find Authoritative Support

Authority generally supports three points of origination for claims, each of which is advocated by one or the other parties in the present case. The cases hold bankruptcy claims may arise: (1) with the right to payment; (2) upon the establishment of the relationship between the debtor and the creditor; or (3) based upon the debtor's conduct. Following the foregoing examination of each theory, we hold the DHS's claim arose for purposes of the Jensens' bankruptcy at the time of actual or threatened release of the hazardous waste, or based upon the debtors' conduct.

1.   The Claim Arises with the Right to Payment

DHS contends and the bankruptcy court held that DHS's claim did not arise until DHS incurred costs for hazardous waste cleanup. DHS argues and the bankruptcy court held that §101(4) specifically requires a "right to payment" before a claim cognizable in bankruptcy arises. The argument then proceeds that the right to payment under CERCLA or HSA does not arise until cleanup costs are incurred. DHS thus argues that until cleanup costs are incurred, no right to payment, and no cognizable claim, exists for bankruptcy purposes.

This theory has been adopted by at least one circuit court. In In re Frenville, 744 F.2d 332 (3rd Cir. 1984), cert., denied, 469 U.S. 1160 (1985), a creditor appealed a district court order holding the creditor's indemnity action against the Chapter 7 debtor was barred by the automatic stay. While the debtor's acts underlying the indemnity occurred prepetition, the suit against the creditor was filed postpetition; prompting the indemnification action. In determining when the claim originated, the Third Circuit first noted the Bankruptcy Code does not clearly define when a "right to payment" arises, and therefore applied state law. Id. at 337. The relevant state law declared a right to payment on an indemnity arises upon payment of the judgment flowing from the act. The *Frenville* court then concluded the suit against the creditor had been filed post-petition, the creditor's claim therefore arose postpetition, and the automatic stay did not apply. Id. . . .

However, *Frenville* has been roundly criticized by several courts. As stated in In re A.M. Robins Co., 63 Bankr. 986, 992 (Bankr. E.D. Va. 1986), the *Frenville* court confuses "a 'right to payment' for federal bankruptcy purposes with the accrual of a cause of action for state law purposes." Indeed, under *Frenville* and *Union Scrap Iron* [123 Bankr. 831 (D. Minn. 1990)] we can perceive no difference between claims inside or outside bankruptcy. Such an interpretation simply is unwarranted from a reading of §101(4), which includes contingent and unmatured rights to payment, as well as those having been reduced to judgments.

Further, holding that the cause of action, or in the present case, the statutory right to payment, triggers recognition of the bankruptcy claim contravenes the overriding goal of the Bankruptcy Code to provide a "fresh start" for the debtor. In a no-asset Chapter 7 case, like the one at hand, manipulation will surely result. The creditor, aware of a debtor's precarious financial situation, will delay expenditures in anticipation of the debtor's bankruptcy, thereby preventing discharge of the creditor's claims. Additionally, debtors having attentive creditors will be denied the benefit of bankruptcy's fresh start, although enjoyed by other debtors similarly situated but whose creditors are less well-informed. Such untenable results cannot be endorsed.

* * *

2. The Claim Arises upon the Establishment of the Relationship between the Debtor and the Creditor

[The court concludes that cases supporting this approach equally support the third approach, that a claim arises at the time of the debtor's conduct.]

3. The Claim Arises Based upon the Debtor's Conduct

The final theory, that the bankruptcy claim arises based upon the debtor's conduct, we believe most closely reflects legislative intent and finds the most support in the case law. These cases have generally held the bankruptcy claim arises upon conduct by the debtor which would give rise to a cause of action, if other elements may later be satisfied. A brief review of frequently cited cases supporting this approach follows.

In In re Johns-Manville Corp., 57 Bankr. 680 (Bankr. S.D.N.Y. 1986), creditors, not asbestos-related, seeking indemnity or contribution from debtor Johns-Manville, moved for relief from the stay to pursue their claims in state court. This necessitated interpreting §101(4) as to when bankruptcy claims arise. The bankruptcy court denied the relief from stay, noting ". . . the focus should be on the time when the acts giving rise to the alleged liability were performed. . . ." Id. at 690. The court found the operative time to be the sale of the defective goods by Johns-Manville to the creditors, which occurred prepetition. Id. Significantly, the *Johns-Manville* court was concerned with the policy of basing timing of claims on factors other than the debtor's conduct. "Procedural and extraneous factors such as the timing of the filing of a summons and complaint by a third party, which is not associated with the underlying nature of the cause of action . . . simply should not determine the existence or nonexistence of a 'claim'." Id.

The bankruptcy court in In re A.H. Robins Co., 63 Bankr. 986 (Bankr. E.D. Va. 1986), reached a similar conclusion. There, a Dalkon Shield claimant sought a declaration that her claim against the debtor manufacturer was postpetition and thus not subject to the automatic stay. The claimant had been inserted with the shield prepetition, but perceived no injury until postpetition. In analyzing when the bankruptcy claim arose, the *A.H. Robins* court rejected the reasoning in *Frenville* and found the definition of claim articulated in *Edge* broader than necessary to give effect to Bankruptcy Code goals. Id. at 993. The court then adopted the theory in *Johns-Manville*, that a "right to payment," and therefore a claim, arises at the time when the acts giving rise to the alleged liability were performed. Id. The *A.H. Robins* court held the right to payment arose at the time the shield was inserted. Id.

One bankruptcy court has applied the reasoning of *Johns-Manville* and *A.H. Robins* to environmental claims. In In re Chateaugay Corp. ("LTV"), 112 Bankr. 513 (Bankr. S.D.N.Y. 1990), the United States and New York State sought declaratory judgments regarding dischargeability of environmental claims in bankruptcy. The bankruptcy court examined the language of CERCLA, which requires as a predicate to liability "[a] 'release' or a 'threatened release' of a 'hazardous substance' . . . at the site." Id. at 518. The *LTV* court held so long as a prepetition triggering event has occurred, i.e. the release or threatened release of hazardous waste, the claim is dischargeable, regardless of when the claim for relief may be in all respects ripe for adjudication. Id. at 522. As the *LTV* court states, very frequently only one part of a tort occurs prepetition, with the injury occurring postpetition, yet such claims should be considered dischargeable. Id. Accord In re Hudson Oil Co., 100 Bankr. 72, 77 (Bankr. D. Kan. 1989).

We adopt the reasoning propounded in *Johns-Manville* and *A.H. Robins*, as applied in *LTV*. DHS attempts to distinguish *LTV* by noting an extensive relationship existed between the *LTV* parties prior to the bankruptcy filing. This argument is unpersuasive and overlooks the plain holding of *LTV* that a claim arises for purposes of discharge upon the actual or threatened release of hazardous waste by the debtor. *LTV* is directly analogous to the present case and we subscribe to its sound reasoning. This conclusion gives effect to the important bankruptcy goal of providing a fresh start to the debtor and discourages manipulation of the bankruptcy process.

D. *Environmental Policy Considerations May Not Control the Bankruptcy Code in the Absence of Clear Legislative Intent*

The bankruptcy court and DHS further contend that important public policy supporting environmental cleanup requires that environmental claims be treated differently from other claims. This argument ignores the only Ninth Circuit authority in this area, In re Dant & Russell, Inc., 853 R2d 700 (9th Cir. 1988). At issue there was whether private claims against the debtor under CERCLA could be accorded administrative expense priority. In holding the priority sought not merited, the Ninth Circuit sounded a strong policy against according preference to particular claims. "Although [the creditor] asserts that public policy considerations entitle its claims for cleanup costs to administrative expense priority, we acknowledge that Congress alone fixes priorities . . . (citation omitted). Courts are not free to formulate their own rules of super or sub-priorities within a specifically enumerated class." Id. at 709. While not addressed in determining the timing of a claim, the *Dant* court's language clearly discourages according preference to particular claims.

CONCLUSION

Based upon the Board letter dated February 2, 1984, threatened release of the hazardous waste involved here clearly occurred prior to filing of the Jensens' individual bankruptcy on February 13, 1984. Because we hold claims in bankruptcy arise based upon the debtor's conduct, we conclude that DHS's claim arose in this case prepetition, and was therefore discharged in the Jensens' bankruptcy. The decision of the bankruptcy court is reversed.

In effect, the court in *Jensen* determined that the California Department of Health Services should have filed a claim in the Jensens' Chapter 7 and in Jensen Lumber's Chapter 11 and collected whatever it could. The strategy of collecting nothing in the bankruptcy and waiting for a post-bankruptcy collection did not work in this case.

If the California DHS had filed a claim, what could it have expected to collect? Mr. and Mrs. Jensen were in a no-asset Chapter 7, so DHS could not have collected anything from the bankrupt estate. But many debtors that file for bankruptcy, particularly operational businesses in Chapter 11, have substantial remaining assets at the time of filing. Would an environmental claim be just another general unsecured claim, or would it have been entitled to a special priority? If the business is struggling to confirm a Chapter 11, the difference is great between dealing with a multimillion dollar clean-up claim as an administrative expense priority (which must be paid in full at confirmation under section 1129(a)(8)) or as a general unsecured debt (which receives only pro rata treatment with other unsecured creditors under section 1129(a)(7)). In some cases, the classification of the environmental claim will determine whether the business can be reorganized in Chapter 11 or whether it will simply be liquidated in Chapter 7.

The next case gives one court's view of how the clean-up claims should be characterized.

In re VIRGINIA BUILDERS, INC.
153 B.R. 729 (Bankr. E.D. Va. 1993)

Opinion by: Douglas O. TICE, Jr. . . .

FINDINGS OF FACT

In 1984, London Bridge Industrial Park II ("LBII"), a Virginia general partnership, purchased the property, London Bridge Industrial Park. . . .

Shortly after the LBII purchase, Virginia Builders, Inc. ("Virginia Builders"), began operating on the property with full consent of LBII. Virginia Builders stored and maintained over 30 vehicles, including heavy equipment, on the property. The maintenance consisted primarily of refueling and oiling. Fuel tanks containing diesel and waste oil were located throughout the property. On the eastern side of the property stood a tin shed with a concrete floor. Virginia Builders used the shed to repair vehicles and store tools.

In 1988, plaintiff First Virginia Bank of Tidewater extended loans to LBII, secured in part by a first priority deed of trust on the property and in part by a security interest in unrelated property owned by LBII. In May 1990, the LBII loans were in default. In light of impending foreclosure, the bank ordered a Phase I environmental study to determine the extent of any environmental contamination. [The first report suggested no need for remediation, but conditions on the property continued to deteriorate as Virginia Builders steam cleaned and refueled their heavy equipment on the site.] . . .

On July 31, 1991, the bank foreclosed on the property. However, the debtor continued to occupy and operate on the property. On October 1, 1991, the debtor filed its petition for chapter 11 bankruptcy. Despite repeated requests and negotiations with the debtor's principals, the bank resorted to formal letters demanding the debtor to stop operations and remove debris from the property. The debtor did not cease operations and vacate the property until May 1992.

Although debtor insists that the environmental contamination on the property occurred prepetition, the contamination was incessant, occurring both prepetition and postpetition. Despite testimony by Hughes [the president of Virginia Builders] that no vehicles or equipment were refueled or maintained on site after September 25, 1991, the balance of evidence indicates the debtor did not cease but continued to refuel on the property through the time of its withdrawal in May 1992.

On April 29, 1992, the bank received an anonymous letter alleging a possible environmental hazard on the property. (Plaintiff's Exhibit 2). Bank officials immediately inspected the premises, finding debris on the property, the area around the fuel tanks stained, significant standing diesel fuel on the ground, and the shed floor heavily stained with petroleum. A drainpipe leading from the shed to a nearby ditch revealed petroleum residue. The bank immediately ordered McCallum [Laboratories] to perform a Phase II environmental study. The Phase II environmental study tested both soil and groundwater samples from the site and confirmed that the property had drastically deteriorated since the 1990 Phase I study. . . .

Although the bank did not report the violation to the [State Water Control Board (SWCB)] in accord with state regulations and the recommendation of McCallum, the bank proceeded to clean up ("remediate") the property. Due to the level of contamination, the evidence indicated that the SWCB would likely have directed remediation by the bank. . . .

Position of the Parties

First Virginia Bank of Tidewater

Plaintiff asserts that Virginia Builders caused the contamination of approximately 300 cubic yards of soil on London Bridge Industrial Park property. Plaintiff relies on the two environmental studies performed by McCallum Laboratories to pinpoint the timing of the contamination. Plaintiff further relies on the stipulation agreement entered into between the parties to prove ongoing contamination. Plaintiff contends that since the contamination occurred prepetition and postpetition, plaintiff is entitled to an administrative expense priority for costs of compliance to cure environmental damage.

Virginia Builders, Inc.

Virginia Builders argues that it is not liable for the environmental damage and that the Bank has no cause of action arising out of the condition of the property. Debtor argues that plaintiff does not allege any federal or state law violation. Further, debtor asserts that the remediation was superfluous because the bank never notified the appropriate regulatory agency and thus did not know if remediation was necessary.

Debtor further asserts that the plaintiff should not receive administrative expense priority for its clean up costs. Debtor argues that any contamination occurred prepetition. Debtor also contends that since it did not own but was merely a trespasser on the property, the bank's clean up did not benefit the estate of the debtor and therefore should not be accorded priority under 11 U.S.C. §503(b)(1)(A).

Discussion and Conclusions of Law

The issues before the court center on the environmental contamination of the property on which debtor operated its business. First the court must determine whether Virginia Builders, operating on the bank's property, is responsible for the environmental contamination. If so, the court must then determine whether the remediation costs are allowable as an administrative expense under 11 U.S.C. §503(b)(l)(A) or whether such costs constitute a general unsecured claim.

The evidence is uncontroverted that Virginia Builders was the sole responsible party for the environmental contamination found on the property. . . .

The obligation to remediate the property must arise out of state or federal environmental law. If there is no obligation under non-bankruptcy law, then under bankruptcy law there is no duty to clean up the property. The debtor's contamination of the property was in violation of Virginia law, and the debtor was obligated to clean it up.[6] Furthermore, the statute provides that the SWCB has the authority to contain and clean up the site[7] and charge the responsible parties for the necessary costs.[8] Debtor contends that the bank should not recover because the SWCB was not formally notified, and therefore remediation may have been unnecessary. Notwithstanding the bank's failure to formally notify the SWCB, its recovery is not precluded. The evidence indicated that SWCB relies heavily on private industry to determine the magnitude of contamination and based upon those recommendations, determines whether clean up is necessary. Testimony indicated that due to the gravity of contamination, the SWCB would have ordered remediation in this case. The pollution caused by Virginia Builders was in excess of state regulations and in violation of state law; the fact that formal action did not compel clean up does not affect the liability of Virginia Builders or the claim of the bank.

Certain claims are entitled to administrative expense priority by virtue of 11 U.S.C. §503(b)(l)(A). Since there is no specific provision in §503 (b) giving priority to environmental claims, the general rule has been to accord environmental claims general unsecured status. However, environmental claims have been conferred administrative status based on three grounds: (1) the timing of the damage; (2) the provisions of 28 U.S.C. §959(b) (Supp. 1991), which direct trustees and debtors in possession to act within bounds of state law; and (3) the judicially created exception found in Midlantic Nat'l Bank v. New Jersey Dept. of Environmental Protection, 474 U.S. 494 (1986). I find that the bank's actual costs incurred in cleaning up the property qualify for administrative expense priority on all three grounds.

Courts have consistently construed the language of §503(b)(l)(A) broadly. In Reading Co. v. Brown, 391 U.S. 471, 485 (1968), the Court found that negligence damages inflicted post-petition gave rise to necessary costs of administering the estate, thus elevating the claim to administrative status. In In re Charlesbank Laundry, Inc., 755 F.2d 200 (1st Cir. 1985), the Second Circuit relied on *Brown* and held that a civil compensatory fine for a debtor's violation of an injunction qualified for first-priority treatment as

---

6. The discharge of oil upon state lands is strictly prohibited. . . . Va. Code Ann. §62.1-44.34:18 (Michie 1992).

7. In the event of such discharge or threat of discharge, if it cannot be determined immediately the person responsible therefor, or if the person is unwilling or unable to promptly contain and clean up such discharge or threat of discharge, the Board may take such action as is necessary to contain and clean up the discharge or threat of discharge, including the engagement of contractors or other competent persons. . . . Va. Code Ann. §62.1-44.34:18(B) (Michie 1992).

8. Va. Code Ann. §62.1-44.34:18(C) (Michie 1992).

an administrative expense, even though the injunction arose from proceedings involving nuisance rather than negligence. The court stated that:

> If fairness dictates that a tort claim based on negligence should be paid ahead of pre-reorganization claims, then a fortiori, an intentional act which violates the law and damages others should be so treated. . . .

Charlesbank Laundry, Inc., 755 F.2d at 203.

Environmental damages occurring postpetition have also fallen within the necessary costs of preserving the estate and have been afforded administrative expense priority.

However, some courts have denied administrative expense priority in situations in which environmental contamination took place prepetition.

Other courts have held that prepetition release of hazardous wastes as defined in 42 U.S.C. §9601(14) (Supp. 1988) or under state law will be entitled to administrative priority. . . .

Dant & Russell involved a claim for prospective costs of cleaning up toxic waste released by a debtor prepetition. The court denied administrative priority because the property was not owned by the bankruptcy estate. However, the court noted that, "quite a different result . . . is warranted when the clean up costs result from monies expended for the preservation of the bankruptcy estate." Dant & Russell, 853 F.2d at 709.

The bank's position in this case is that its actual costs of clean up should be given administrative priority since the estate was benefitted by having an obligation performed on its behalf. The estate benefitted to the extent that a potentially massive liability has been alleviated, and preserved to the extent that debtor will not be liable for additional civil penalties for its environmental violations. Therefore, in my view the bank's actual clean up costs satisfy the administrative priority standard of §503(b)(l)(A), and to the extent Dant & Russell may be inconsistent with this analysis I find it unpersuasive.

Most environmental claims encompass a hybrid of prepetition and postpetition damage. The contamination usually begins as a result of a debtor's prepetition activities and continues causing further property damage postpetition. Courts generally hold that the entire remediation cost qualifies as an administrative expense in these hybrid scenarios. Moreover, one commentator suggests that simply allowing the property to remain contaminated postpetition is a new harmful act sufficient to elevate clean up costs to administrative expense priority. See Kathryn R. Heidt, The Automatic Stay in Environmental Bankruptcies, 67 Am. Bankr. L. J. 69, 124 (1993).

The environmental contamination caused by debtor in this case occurred both prepetition and postpetition. The evidence indicated that contamination began at some point in 1991, and the parties apparently stipulated that Virginia Builder's operations continued through May 1992. The bank incurred the cost to remedy the contamination, and in my view these costs qualify as administrative expenses.

Although the Supreme Court has not specifically ruled on the priority status of environmental claims, it has addressed the relationship between the Bankruptcy Code and environmental law. In Ohio v. Kovacs, 469 U.S. 274, 283 (1985), the Court held that a debtor's obligation to clean up hazardous waste under a state injunction was dischargeable. However, the Court limited its decision by stating:

> We do not question that anyone in possession of the site . . . must comply with the environmental laws of the State. . . . Plainly that person or firm may not maintain a nuisance, pollute the waters of the State, or refuse to remove the source of such conditions. . . .

Kovacs, 469 U.S. at 285.

The Court's emphasis on compliance with state law was further expressed in *Midlantic,* where the Court recognized an exception to the general rule treating environmental clean up obligations as general unsecured claims. *Midlantic* involved a chapter 7 trustee who sought to abandon property pursuant to 11 U.S.C. §554(a) which contained waste oil contaminated with PCBs. The Court stated 28 U.S.C. §959(b) evidences congressional intent that trustees and debtors in possession are not to have carte blanche to ignore non-bankruptcy law. *Midlantic,* 474 U.S. at 505. Thus, a trustee could not abandon property in violation of a state statute or regulation reasonably designed to protect the public health or safety from identified hazards. *Midlantic,* 474 U.S. at 507. In essence, the Court found that the priorities of the bankruptcy code must acquiesce to laws designed to protect the public health and safety. *Midlantic,* 474 U.S. at 507; see also In re Stevens, 68 Bankr. 774, 783 (D. Me. 1987).

Cases following *Midlantic* grant administrative priority for environmental clean-up costs by relying either on compliance with state law via 28 U.S.C. §959(b) or the Court's emphasis on public health and safety.

I find this case substantially similar to In re Wall Tube, which involved a debtor/lessee that operated a manufacturing plant. The Tennessee Department of Health and Environment found prepetition environmental damage from the hazardous waste by-products of manufacturing and assessed violations of both state and federal environmental law. In re Wall Tube, 831 F.2d at 122. The state cleaned up the site and sought reimbursement under the Comprehensive Environmental Response Compensation and Liability Act ("CERCLA") 42 U.S.C. §§9601-9607 (1983 & Supp. 1992). The court relied on the special emphasis in *Kovacs* and *Midlantic* regarding the importance of complying with state law and protecting public health and safety. Since the State of Tennessee, in the absence of compliance by the debtor's estate, was entitled by state law to expend funds to remediate the contamination, those expenses were actual and necessary to preserve the estate so as to keep it in compliance with state law and to protect the public health and safety.

In this case, the debtor could not have avoided liability imposed by Virginia law if the Commonwealth had directed the clean up, and the weight of the evidence suggests the SWCB would have mandated clean up due to the high level of contamination.

Moreover, the debtor is liable under Virginia law to private parties for negligently or intentionally causing property damage arising from environmental contamination. The bank expended funds to clean up the site which in the court's view were actual and necessary to bring the estate in compliance with state law, and to eliminate a threat to public health and safety. Accordingly, the court must conclude the actual costs of remediation incurred by the bank are entitled to administrative expense priority.

The court will enter judgment in favor of plaintiff by a separate order. The amount of the claim will be determined by the court after plaintiff submits appropriate documentation. The court also defers ruling on plaintiff's request for attorney fees until an itemized statement is submitted.

As the preceding cases should make clear, the courts are struggling toward a coherent treatment of environmental obligations. They have not yet arrived.

c. Mass Torts

The phrase "mass tort" has come into the legal lexicon in the past two decades to highlight the special circumstances of injuries to a large number of people, sometimes over a long period of time. With widespread distribution of manufactured products and provision of services to great numbers of people, a defective product can affect the safety of thousands or even millions of people. The popular culture has become saturated with the shorthand references to events and products that endangered countless numbers of people. The Dalkon Shield, Bhopal, breast implants, asbestos, PCBs, Love Canal, DES, Fen-Phen, and thalidomide are among the products and places that have joined the mass injury hall of fame.

The mass-tort bankruptcy case sprang forth full grown, like Athena from the head of Zeus, after the adoption of the 1978 Code. The reason is that the new definition of claim was not merely broad, but eliminated the ancient concept of "provability," which had previously excluded certain claims from being asserted in bankruptcy. The most important category of "unprovable" claims was a tort claim. The bad news for a tort victim was that no distribution could be had in the bankruptcy case; the good news was that the victim's cause of action was also not discharged. If the case was a corporate Chapter 7, then, the news was all bad. If it was a personal bankruptcy or a corporate reorganization, however, the news was often good, because the victim could sue the post-discharge debtor and collect in full-sized, post-petition dollars. When Congress decided to expand the definition of claim, it knew of the great expansion of products liability law and decided that tort claims had to be resolved in bankruptcy along with everything else. As usual, the courts were left to sort it out.

Not all businesses facing mass tort liability end up in bankruptcy. Some settle with their victims out of court. Others fight lengthy battles, one at a time, through the civil court system and survive intact. Others are subjected to massive class action suits, but their resources are adequate to meet the burdens. But a fair number end up in bankruptcy, and even those that have not filed still conduct their business under the long shadow of a Chapter 11.

Not all of those are in bankruptcy because of financial distress. The role of bankruptcy in some of these cases is not simply its traditional one of formulating solutions to the problems of a general default. Some of the companies that file for bankruptcy because of mass-tort problems are not in immediate financial trouble and might be able to survive in the long term as well. They file because of the serious weaknesses in the current class-action system that make it very difficult for a defendant to resolve all claims in one lawsuit. In Amchem Products v. Windsor, 521 U.S. 591 (1997), for example, the Supreme Court voided a class action asbestos settlement (known as the *Georgine* settlement) that had been reached in January 1993 and that imposed case number and dollar caps on the claims of class members that could be paid over a ten-year period. Faced with litigation costs in hundreds or thousands of cases that could exceed $1 million per year, defendants in *Amchem* and similar cases were desperate to find a substitute procedural "joinder" device that would avoid the difficulties presented by non-bankruptcy procedures. Bankruptcy, which brings all litigation together from across the nation, or even across the world, presents the opportunity for a "global" resolution of their problems. In this section, we focus on companies whose financial existence is threatened, although those companies may benefit from the joinder factor as well.

The presence of a class of mass tort claimants in a Chapter 11 reorganization profoundly changes the negotiations among the parties. Commercial creditors and tort creditors often view each other with great suspicion, as bank lawyers and tort lawyers are forced to work together in unfamiliar ways.

The huge question that faces a business with massive tort liability for a single accident or a single type of product defect is whether all of the claimants can be dealt with in a single reorganization. Once again, the temporal problem reasserts itself. A company may produce a product, such as asbestos, that was widely distributed over a long period of time. Who has been exposed and what will be the consequences of that exposure may not be known. Can a Chapter 11 reorganization bind every claimant — those with judgments against the company, those with pending claims, those who have been exposed but are not yet sick, and those who do not even know of their exposure?

Outside bankruptcy, each plaintiff could line up and sue when his or her cause of action ripened under state tort law. The first claimants to discover their problems would be paid in full, but, if the magnitude of the problem is sufficiently large, at some point the business will run out of money. That means that even though it engaged in the same wrongful behavior that injured each potential victim, some victims would be fully compensated while others would receive nothing.

If the debtor has filed for Chapter 11, it will try to confirm a plan of reorganization to deal with all the claimants at once — both those currently known and those who will make themselves known in the future. When all claimants are collected together, the payment is likely to be smaller to the present claimants than under first-come, first-served state law rules. Of course, the payment will likely be much larger for those claimants who would have been left at the end of the line with nothing. Depending on how they assess the business's long-term economic prospects, all the tort claimants may resist group treatment. The present claimants do not want money put aside for the future claimants, instead insisting that everything be paid out now. The future claimants, when they discover their problems later and also discover a solvent, post-reorganization business, will want to make claims against that post-bankruptcy business, without regard to whatever proportional settlement was worked out in the Chapter 11.

The following case involves Johns-Manville, once the world's largest manufacturer of asbestos. When asbestos was linked with a potentially fatal lung disease that occurs a number of years after exposure, Manville faced an onslaught of civil suits. Ultimately, Manville became one of the most publicized bankruptcy cases filed during the 1980s.

It is significant in this context to note that Manville did not run to the bankruptcy court as its first alternative to deal with its mounting tort problems. Instead, as American companies often do, Manville gathered other manufacturers of asbestos and all their insurers and headed for Congress. They made a powerful case, arguing that back in the 1940s and 1950s no one had known that asbestos was a potentially lethal product (a hotly disputed point), that Manville and others had done a huge share of their asbestos-handling work for the government, and that asbestos was so ubiquitous that victims would have a nearly impossible time proving legal causation linked to any one manufacturer. The asbestos manufacturers proposed that Congress treat the disease asbestosis as a kind of national plague and establish a fund to care for the victims. Many asbestosis sufferers joined this lobbying effort, seeing Congress as a more reliable source of compensation than piecemeal litigation against recalcitrant companies. Congress, with its hands full over budget deficits and inflation at the time and infused with a new national spirit of privatization, politely declined the invitation. The solution, said Congress, would have to come from the companies that made asbestos. For Manville and a number of other large companies that dealt with asbestos, bankruptcy was the result. After its bankruptcy filing, Manville went back to Congress for relief, apparently believing that the dramatic step of filing in Chapter 11 would force congressional action. It was again disappointed.

When Manville filed for bankruptcy, critics charged that it was simply trying to evade its responsibility to its victims and find a way to protect its substantial business revenues. After all, said the critics, Manville had assets far in excess of its liabilities at the time of filing. The first victims to prevail against Manville could expect to collect millions without seriously denting the company's profitability. By going into bankruptcy the corporation was throwing yet another roadblock into the path of the victims' long-thwarted attempts to collect.

Without speaking to the question of corporate motivation, it should be pointed out that by filing bankruptcy Manville squarely raised the question of dealing equitably with both the early and the later claimants. In the piecemeal one-at-a-time litigation of state tort law, the first successful claimants against Manville might expect to collect millions. But if Manville's projections were right about the number of people exposed and the extent of their injuries that would appear over time, at some point some injured parties would find themselves with judgments against Manville and no assets left to satisfy them. Bankruptcy has the potential to smooth out the collection process, with all the injured parties taking proportionate shares, in a way that state collection law cannot.

In addition to the potential inequity of the first-come, first-served approach, there was a great risk that Manville would fail as a business, despite its apparent profits. The reason was that banks and investors were growing increasingly apprehensive about the long-term future of the company in light of the massive litigation against it and the uncertainties of future litigation. They were becoming unwilling to provide necessary funds to Manville as long as its financial future was so filled with unknowns. If the result was that Manville was unable to continue as a going concern, the greatest losers would be its creditors, including all those tort claimants, a dramatic illustration of the fact that in a tort system based on money damages, the victim has a great stake in the prosperity of the tortfeasor.

The consequence was that all claims against Manville had to be resolved in some way in order to provide protection for future claimants and to provide the necessary certainty for financing its ongoing business. In addition, there was an obvious need to find ways to determine claims (existing claims and those arising in the future) as economically as possible.

As difficult as it might be to cope with the many thousands of claims of people who were sick from asbestosis, the greater difficulty was presented by "future claimants," the victims of exposure to asbestos who had not yet developed symptoms (and who may not have even known that they had been exposed, much less injured). In trying to resolve all of Manville's troubles in a single forum, the bankruptcy court faced the difficult conceptual problem of confirming a plan to delineate the interests of claimants who did not yet know they were interested parties in the *Manville* case, but who would have their rights adjudicated in the bankruptcy action as part of the resolution of contingent and unmatured claims. The question was whether the court could find a legally acceptable way to represent these claimants and to resolve their rights. In Kane v. Johns-Manville Corp., the Second Circuit reviewed the bankruptcy court's confirmation of a plan of reorganization for Manville. The court dealt with the same issues that can arise in any Chapter 11 confirmation (claims, voting, good faith) but in the special context of future claimants and injuries yet to be discovered.

KANE v. JOHNS-MANVILLE CORP.
843 F.2d 636 (2d Cir. 1988)

Jon O. NEWMAN, Circuit Judge:

This appeal challenges the lawfulness of the reorganization plan of the Johns-Manville Corporation ("Manville"), a debtor in one of the nation's most significant Chapter 11 bankruptcy proceedings. Lawrence Kane, on behalf of himself and a group of other personal injury claimants, appeals from an order of the District Court for the Southern District of New York (Whitman Knapp, Judge) affirming an order of the Bankruptcy Court (Burton R. Lifland, Chief Judge) that confirmed a Second Amended Plan of

Reorganization (the "Plan"). Kane and the group of 765 individuals he represents (collectively "Kane") are persons with asbestos-related disease who had filed personal injury suits against Manville prior to Manville's Chapter 11 petition. The suits were stayed, and Kane and other claimants presently afflicted with asbestos-related disease were designated as Class-4 creditors in the reorganization proceedings. Kane now objects to confirmation of the reorganization Plan on several grounds: it discharges the rights of future asbestos victims who do not have "claims" within the meaning of 11 U.S.C. §101(4) (1982), it was adopted without constitutionally adequate notice to various interested parties, the voting procedures used in approving the Plan violated the Bankruptcy Code and due process requirements, and the Plan fails to conform with the requirements of 11 U.S.C. §1129(a) and (b) (1982 & Supp. IV 1986). We determine that Kane lacks standing to challenge the Plan on the grounds that it violates the rights of future claimants and other third parties, and we reject on the merits his remaining claims that the Plan violates his rights regarding voting and fails to meet the requirements of section 1129(a) and (b). The order of the District Court affirming the Bankruptcy Court's confirmation of the Plan is affirmed.

[In the face of mounting asbestos lawsuits, Manville found its access to credit drying up and its business turning into full-time litigation. It filed for Chapter 11, eventually proposing a plan of reorganization that included a trust to compensate victims, funded by more than half of the Manville stock. In negotiations, the future claimants — that is, those who would learn about their asbestos-related illnesses in the future — were represented by a court-appointed Legal Representative.]

... Manville was directed to undertake a comprehensive multimedia notice campaign to inform persons with present health claims of the pendency of the reorganization and their opportunity to participate. Potential health claimants who responded to the campaign were given a combined proof-of-claim-and-voting form in which each could present a medical diagnosis of his asbestos-related disease and vote to accept or reject the Plan. For voting purposes only, each claim was valued in the amount of one dollar. Claimants were informed that the proof-of-claim-and-voting form would be used only for voting and that to collect from the Trust, they would have to execute an additional proof of claim establishing the actual value of their damages.

The notice campaign produced a large number of present asbestos claimants. In all, 52,400 such claimants submitted proof-of-claim-and-voting forms. Of these, 50,275 or 95.8% approved the Plan, while 2,165 or 4.2% opposed it. In addition to these Class-4 claimants, all other classes of creditors also approved the Plan. Class 8, the common stockholders, opposed the lan. . . . On December 18, 1986, the Bankruptcy Court issued a Determination of Confirmation Issues in which it rejected all objections to confirmation. . . .

DISCUSSION

A. Standing

The Legal Representative of the future claimants challenges Kane's standing to bring this appeal. The Legal Representative contends that Kane is not directly and adversely affected by the confirmation order and that his appeal improperly asserts the rights of third parties, namely the future claimants. We conclude that Kane is sufficiently harmed by confirmation of the Plan to challenge it on appeal but that his appeal must be limited to those contentions that assert a deprivation of his own rights. . . .

. . . The question we must consider is whether on this appeal of the confirmation order, Kane may assert claims of these third parties. We conclude that he may not. . . .

Prudential concerns weigh heavily against permitting Kane to assert the rights of the future claimants in attacking the Plan. First, Kane's interest in these proceedings is potentially opposed to that of the future claimants; both Kane and the future claimants wish to recover from the debtor for personal injuries. To the extent that Kane is successful in obtaining more of the debtor's assets to satisfy his own claims, less will be available for other parties, with the distinct risk that the future claimants will suffer. Thus, we cannot depend on Kane sincerely to advance the interests of the future claimants. Second, the third parties whose rights Kane seeks to assert are already represented in the proceedings. Though it is true, as Kane points out, that the future claimants themselves are not before the Court, they are ably represented by the appointed Legal Representative. Therefore, it is not necessary to allow Kane to raise the future claimants' rights on the theory that these rights will be otherwise ignored. The Bankruptcy Court appointed the Legal Representative specifically for the purpose of ensuring that the rights of the future claimants would be asserted where necessary. Certainly as between Kane and the Legal Representative, there is no question that the latter is the more reliable advocate of the future claimants' rights, and we may confidently leave that task entirely to him. Finally, and significantly, the Legal Representative has expressly stated in this appeal that he does not want Kane to assert the future claimants' rights. This is precisely the situation where the third-party standing limitation should apply. . . .

Kane argues that he ought to be permitted at least to challenge the Injunction because his claim is "inextricably bound up with" the rights of the future claimants. Kane reasons that his own recovery from the Trust depends upon Manville's financial stability, which in turn could be jeopardized by a future claimant's successful challenge to the Injunction. If future claimants are not bound by the Injunction, then, Kane predicts, they will sue Manville's operating entities directly, Manville will be unable to meet its funding commitments to the Trust, and Kane will lose his rights to compensation under the Plan. Kane therefore contends that he should be able to test the validity of the Injunction as to the future claimants now so as to avoid a successful challenge detrimental to him in the future.

Though we recognize that future claimants may at some later point attempt to challenge the Injunction, we do not believe that Kane's interests are so "inextricably bound up with" those of the future claimants in such a suit as to warrant third-party standing. Even if we assume that future claimants would at some later time be permitted to advance a position contrary to that taken by the Legal Representative in this litigation and assume further that the future claimants' objections to the Injunction are upheld, matters upon which we express no opinion, Kane has failed to show a sufficient likelihood that he would be harmed by such a successful challenge. The flaw in Kane's analysis is that it assumes that an onslaught of future victims' suits could impair the Trust before Kane is paid. Such is not the case. Kane and the other present claimants are, by definition, currently afflicted with asbestos disease. They may all initiate claims against the Trust immediately after confirmation. Resolution and payment of these claims is expected to take approximately ten years. The bulk of the future victims, in contrast, are not presently afflicted with disease. Many of them will not become ill until well into the 1990's or later. While some of the last of the present claimants may overlap with the first of the future claimants in presenting their damage claims, the claims of these groups will be presented essentially consecutively. By the time enough future claimants develop asbestos-related disease, challenge the Injunction, and, if successful, collect damages directly from Manville to an extent sufficient to impair the long-term funding of the Trust, Kane will have had years to enforce his own claims. Kane's concern that he will be precluded from collecting from the Trust because of future claimants' suits against Manville is therefore too speculative a basis on which to grant third-party standing. . . .

Manville broke ground in the bankruptcy arena and earned itself a place in commercial law history. On the face of it, the parties in *Manville* had untied the Gordian knot, had solved the unsolvable problem. But like so many other bankruptcy cases, *Manville* has its own O. Henry twist.

Less than two years after the plan was confirmed, serious difficulties arose in the operation of the Manville trust, the most important being that the trust was running out of cash as settlements were achieved (one of Kane's claims). Amidst recriminations all around, there was sharp criticism of the management of the trust and of the large payments going to claimants' lawyers. These concerns were accompanied by a growing realization that the Manville settlement had to be coordinated with the massive remaining litigation against other asbestosis defendants. (Very few people had been careful to breathe only Johns-Manville's asbestos, and other manufacturers wanted contribution from Manville.)

Manville showed the way that others followed. (When Dow Corning decided to seek a bankruptcy solution to the thousands of breast-implant lawsuits filed against it, does anyone doubt that the Dow Corning lawyers had dog-eared copies of all the *Manville* opinions as they worked for years to confirm a reorganization plan in that case?) But Manville could not rely on the Code and the courts for its solution. While the preceding case solved the problem of confirming a plan of reorganization, it did so on an issue of standing. That leaves open the question about what would happen if a future claimant sues the company directly years after the bankruptcy case was closed. Manville's lawyers continued to worry about whether it had adequate jurisdictional reach to solve its problems, particularly in the broad reach of the injunctions issued as part of its plan that forced victims to deal with the trust and prevented them from suing Manville's insurers and co-defendants directly. These injunctions were crucial to the economic functioning of both the trust and the company; they were the cornerstones of the insurance companies and co-defendants' contributions to the Manville trust. Without the assurance that they could not be sued elsewhere, they wanted to save their money for distribution to individual victims who might sue them.

Manville's lawyers continued to lobby for special legislation to sanction its class action treatment of its victims. The effort was rewarded in the 1994 Amendments, which added a special section for those claiming "personal injury, recovery for damages allegedly caused by the presence of, or exposure to, asbestos or asbestos-containing products." 11 U.S.C. §524(g). While the statute by its own terms is intended to affect asbestos cases, it cannot escape the attention of any court that perhaps the Code does not accomplish all that the courts hoped it would in the *Manville* case.

Even after the 1994 Amendments, the number of asbestos claims reported each year continued to climb. In 1982, the best available research estimated that about 21,000 people would file claims related to asbestos liability. By 2003, the Institute for Civil Justice at RAND put that number at 600,000. But RAND notes that every estimate of liability has been low, and that 27 million workers were employed in high-risk industries and were likely exposed.

As victims looked for new companies to compensate them for their injuries, more companies began to feel pressure. Owens Corning, W.R. Grace, and other industrial giants that faced exposure to asbestos litigation found themselves in Chapter 11. When automobile manufacturers were sued by employees who installed brake pads, companies whose asbestos contact was limited to using asbestos-laced products discovered they were not safe. Alarm about the potential range of lawsuits drove renewed calls for legislation to insulate the companies and to compensate the victims. Congress is currently considering a national asbestos trust, funded by contributions from companies that have potential asbestos liability and their insurers, with the government (taxpayer) agreeing to make up the shortfall if funds run short.

Asbestos may have taught lawyers that bankruptcy presented one option to dealing with mass tort liability, but the innovations were far from complete. In the following case, Fairchild Aircraft, once a proud producer of some of America's finest aircraft, was in Chapter 11 and about to be liquidated when a new buyer came along with cash and a plan. The buyer would renovate the factory, streamline operations, and continue manufacturing planes, thereby preserving 700 jobs in San Antonio and, the buyer hoped, revitalizing the company as a profitable business. The buyer worked out the financial terms of the sale, which would pay all the creditors far more than they had dreamed when it appeared the company would be sold off piecemeal, but the buyer insisted on one condition: The new, post-reorganization company would take responsibility for any defects in the planes it manufactured, but it could not assume liability for planes manufactured years earlier by the old, pre-bankruptcy Fairchild. As a condition of purchase, the buyer asked for a release from the future claims of people who might be injured by defects in the planes sold years earlier. The liquidating trustee loved the plan, as did the creditors and the employees. The judge was enthusiastic, the release was signed, the plan was confirmed, and Fairchild reopened for business.

Then tragedy struck. An old Fairchild plane crashed in Tennessee. Unlike the case in *Manville*, now there was a future claimant initiating a suit against the post-bankruptcy company.

In re FAIRCHILD AIRCRAFT CORP.
184 B.R. 910 (Bankr. W.D. Tex. 1995)

Leif CLARK, Bankruptcy Judge.

BACKGROUND FACTS

The facts surrounding this matter span over a decade, beginning sometime before 1985 and ending with the filing of this adversary proceeding in August 1994. As they relate to the resolution of the present controversy, the facts are undisputed.

Fairchild Aircraft Corporation manufactured and sold commuter aircraft, one a 19-seat passenger aircraft sold to civilians as a Metro III and to the military as the C-26, and the other a smaller aircraft sold as the Merlin II and III or the Fairchild 300. This case concerns the crash of one these smaller aircraft, a Fairchild 300. FAC stopped production of the Fairchild 300 in 1982. FAC continued to sell the aircraft as late as 1985, because it held several of the airframes in inventory. It is undisputed that the aircraft in question in this case was manufactured no later than 1982 and sold no later than 1985 — five years before FAC's later chapter 11 bankruptcy.

FAC filed for chapter 11 relief on February 11, 1990. Shortly after the filing, a chapter 11 trustee was appointed (the "Trustee"), with full authority to operate the debtor's business. The Trustee, Bettina M. Whyte, decided that reorganization was not a viable option for the estate, and solicited a buyer for the company's assets, which she proposed to sell as a going concern. On August 14, 1990, the Trustee entered into an asset purchase agreement with a group of investors who formed a corporation for the purpose of the acquisition, called appropriately enough Fairchild Acquisition, Inc. FAI was to pay $5 million in cash and was to assume liability for FAC's secured debt to Sanwa Business Credit, in the range of $36 million. The estate was to retain some cash, its estate causes of action (including preference actions), and a share of an anticipated tax refund. The asset purchase agreement also contained the following provision, which the acquiring entity maintains was an essential element of the bargain and induced the seller to purchase the assets for as much as it did:

> Purchaser shall not assume, have any liability for, or in any manner be responsible for any liabilities or obligations of any nature of Seller or the Trustee, including without limiting the generality of the foregoing: . . . (ii) any occurrence or event at any time which results or is alleged to have resulted in injury or death to any person or damage to or destruction of property (including loss of use) or any other damage (regardless of when such injury, death or damage takes place) which was caused by or allegedly caused by (A) any hazard or

alleged hazard or defect or alleged defect in manufacture, design, materials or workmanship. . . .

The sale took place as part of the confirmation of the Trustee's First Amended Plan of Reorganization and was of course subject to the approval of the bankruptcy court. On September 17, 1990, the court confirmed the Trustee's Plan and the asset sale agreement which was its central feature. The confirmation order expressly stated that the assets were sold "free and clear of all liens, claims, and encumbrances," except for those liens and encumbrances assumed by the buyer under the plan. See 11 U.S.C. §1141(c). The order further stated that the purchaser would not "assume, have any liability for, or in any manner be responsible for any liabilities or obligations of any nature of Debtor, Reorganized Debtor, the Trustee or the Fiscal Agent." Finally, the order enjoined and stayed "all creditors, claimants against, and persons claiming or having any interest of any nature whatsoever" from "pursuing or attempting to pursue, or commencing any suits or proceedings at law, in equity or otherwise, against the property of the Debtor's estate . . . the proceeds of the sale . . . or any other person or persons claiming, directly or indirectly, including the Purchaser under the Asset Purchase Agreement. . . ."

The court found that the consideration to be paid by FAI (the cash and the assumption of secured debt) was "fair and adequate and fully representative of the maximum value that can be realized at this time for Debtor's Property." The court also made a finding that the notice provided concerning the plan and disclosure statement was reasonable under the circumstances. The Trustee had published notice of the disclosure statement, plan of reorganization and confirmation hearing in the Weekly News of Business Aviation, and in two local newspapers, the San Antonio Light and the San Antonio Express-News.

The Trustee made no provision in her plan for claimants in the position of these defendants. Indeed, the debtor had not even listed any of the owners or operators of FAC aircraft in its bankruptcy schedules, though their identities were available and ascertainable from the records of FAC.[9] The Trustee made no particular effort to reach these persons in the plan process, and the plan itself made no particular provision for these persons.

On April 1, 1993, a Fairchild 300 aircraft, originally sold and manufactured by FAC crashed near Blountville, Tennessee. Four individuals lost their lives. Multiple lawsuits were of course filed on the heels of this crash, in both federal and state courts in Georgia, Tennessee and South Carolina. Three of the plaintiffs were persons suing both individually and on behalf of estates of the individuals killed in the aircraft crash. The plaintiffs also included Eastern Foods, Inc. and Hooters of America, Inc., the owners of the airplane, as well as Insurance Company of North America, the owner's insurance carrier. The plaintiffs named FAI as one of the defendants, alleging that the aircraft was defectively manufactured by FAC, and that FAI is

---

9. One of the defendants in this case had purchased the aircraft in question prepetition, and his identity was known to the company. Of course, as of the filing, the aircraft had not crashed.

now liable for the manufacture and sale of a defective product on a successor liability theory. FAI filed this adversary proceeding as a preemptive strike, seeking an order for declaratory and injunctive relief premised on the provisions of the plan, the asset purchase agreement, and the court's order confirming the plan. As such, the plaintiffs in the products liability lawsuits find themselves as defendants in this action for declaratory relief.

Discussion

I.   Framing the Issue

The legal issues presented can be stated simply. FAI claims that the provisions of the asset purchase agreement and order confirming the plan "cleansed" the property acquired of any liability for the acts of FAC, including any successor liability growing out of the sale of those assets to FAI by the trustee of FAC's bankruptcy. FAI says that the sale was free and clear of this sort of liability, and that the bankruptcy court should here so declare. FAI also contends that any lawsuit to force liability on FAI based upon its acquisition of assets would violate the bankruptcy court's injunction contained in the confirmation order, and asks the court to enforce that injunction.

FAI would like to stop the defendants in their tracks without ever having to defend against a successor liability lawsuit. It is not hard to understand why. Even if FAI believes the successor liability allegation to have little merit (and that is its position), it must still incur the cost of defense and risk the uncertainty of litigation. Moreover, there are still other FAC aircraft out there, and if another one crashes, an adverse outcome in this litigation could all but assure an adverse outcome in other litigation as well. Rather than endure these risks, FAI would like to rely on what it believes to have been the effective protections built into the court-supervised sale process, protections for which it believes it bargained. If those protections prove to be worthless, then it will not have received the benefit of its bargain, a result with consequences reaching far beyond this litigation not only for FAI but also for bankruptcy estates in general. . . .

B.   The Concept of a Bankruptcy Claim . . .

Courts have struggled to give content to the extraordinarily broad definition of claim found in the Code, with an eye on the impact that bankruptcy now has on a given creditor who is held to have a "claim" in the bankruptcy case. On the one hand, all recognize that Congress fully intended to move away from the relatively restricted definition in the Act, toward a concept that would permit the bankruptcy process to accord broad and complete relief to debtors. After all, what's the point in having a remedy for financial restructuring that leaves a substantial portion of the debt outside the process? By the same token, however, more and more courts and commentators also recognize that the concept must have some limits. Due process, fundamental fairness, and the limits of subject matter jurisdiction all seem to mark the outer boundaries of the concept. Courts are still struggling with a formulation that reconciles these competing considerations. . . .

An early effort at defining the reach of the Code's concept of claim offers an example of how easily the decisional process can get off track. The Third Circuit adopted what might be classified as a "state law accrual" test in *Frenville*, reasoning that the term "right to payment" found in the statute itself was synonymous with accrual of a right to be paid under state law. Avellino & Bienes v. M. Frenville Co. (Matter of Frenville Co., Inc.), 744 F.2d 332, 335-36 (3d Cir. 1984), cert, denied, 469 U.S. 1160 (1985). *Frenville's* reliance upon state law has been rightly criticized by other courts as being inconsistent with the intended breadth and scope of the statute and seems to have been rejected in all circuits save its place of origin.

This criticism has also led to the formulation of a second test, often called the "conduct" test, because it looks to the conduct which gave rise to the claim to determine whether a bankruptcy claim has arisen. Under this test, a claim will arise for bankruptcy purposes when the conduct which gave rise to the liability occurs, even though the injury resulting from that conduct may not occur or be manifested until after the commencement of the bankruptcy proceeding.

Concerned about the broad sweep of the "conduct" test and its adverse impact on notions of fundamental fairness, several courts have devised yet a third approach, characterized as the "relationship" or "conduct plus" test. The "relationship" test looks not merely to the conduct of the debtor, but to whether the purported claimant had a specific and identifiable relationship with the debtor prepetition. It is not enough that the claimant's injury can be traced to the debtor's prebankruptcy conduct. The court must also inquire into the relationship of the debtor and the alleged claimant. A claim for bankruptcy purposes will exist only where "some prepetition relationship, such as contact, exposure, impact, or privity, between the debtor's prepetition conduct and the claimant" is established. *Piper*, 162 Bankr. 619 at 627. . . .

This is an entirely new and different approach to the problem of future claims. It starts, true enough, by looking at the events that give rise to the claim, but it finishes by focusing less on the claim and more on the claimant. At the beginning of the inquiry, we are attentive to the clearly expressed intentions of the statute that the bankruptcy process sweep broadly and completely, to maximize the possibility of achieving an effective result. But by the end of the inquiry, we find ourselves most attentive to the other side of the dialectic, that of assuring that the process, whatever else it be, be fair.

This concern for procedural fairness is not new. A number of courts have been talking about it, though not perhaps in so many words. Without a doubt, that somewhat hidden agenda has influenced their resolution of what should and what should not be classified as a bankruptcy claim. . . .

"Claim" ought not do what is "not possible" in a court of law — it may not authorize courts to ride roughshod over due process and notions of fundamental fairness, for example. The bankruptcy process, after all, has its antecedents in equity. Courts have an affirmative duty to assure that the process, within the confines of the law, achieve a fair and equitable result.

The immediate limitation this suggests is that, of necessity, no treatment which violates the due process rights of a claimant can be permitted to stand, regardless the purported breadth of the definition of bankruptcy claim (to say nothing of the breadth of provisions such as section 1141(c)). Even more important for our analysis, in addition to these constitutional constraints (which would be applicable regardless of the dialectic), the bankruptcy process ought to be fair in the broader, equitable sense. Not every conceivable obligation finding its source in the debtor's pre-bankruptcy past is necessarily an obligation that can be fairly handled by the bankruptcy process. . . . [A] debtor in a given case will have to be able to sufficiently identify contingent liabilities such that the holders of such claims could be afforded some degree of procedural fairness before a court will call the claim a bankruptcy claim, i.e., one which not only has its antecedents in the debtor's prebankruptcy past but which also can be dealt with fairly by the bankruptcy process. . . .

We have posited the "legal representative" as one device for assuring fundamental fairness for future claimants. It may not be the only way, of course. Each case will turn on its own facts. We know, for example, that a non-party could be bound to a prior judgment, where the non-party's inter-ests have been represented in the proceeding by a person with similar rights or interests. A non-party may also be bound to the issues resolved in a prior suit where the non-party's interests were "so closely aligned with the inter-ests" of a party that the non-party's interests can be held to be "virtually represented." *Meza*, 908 F.2d at 1266. The point is not that one or another method is guaranteed to achieve fundamental fairness, but rather that whatever method is chosen to meet the peculiar circumstances must, in the process, achieve fundamental fairness in the manner in which it deals with remote claims such as these.

. . . The definition of bankruptcy claim under section 101(5), as con-strued by the Fifth Circuit in *Lemelle*, must be sufficiently broad to include liabilities first manifesting themselves post-confirmation where the con-duct which caused the injury occurs prepetition. But the selfsame defini-tion is also restricted to those claims to which it is also possible to accord fair representation of their interests in the course of the case. *Lemelle* requires a debtor to take affirmative steps to bring these types of claimants into the bankruptcy process with appropriate protections to assure a level of procedural fairness. The debtor must demonstrate to the bankruptcy court that it had sufficient knowledge of the nature and scope of the claims to be obligated to fairly anticipate having to provide for them as part of its finan-cial restructuring, that these types of claims were indeed bankruptcy claims because it was practically and equitably possible to deal with such liabilities as claims, and that such claims were in fact dealt with fairly and responsibly. This is what we take the Fifth Circuit to have meant when it insisted that the debtor demonstrate a prepetition "relationship" with the potential victims such that it was possible for the court to practically deal with the claimants in the bankruptcy. . . .

In the present case, there is no dispute that the injuries alleged arose out of the prepetition conduct of FAC. The basis for successor liability is the debtor's manufacture and sale of allegedly defective aircraft, which must have occurred at least five years prior to the bankruptcy (if it occurred at all). Nor is there any dispute that the injuries occurred post confirmation and that the manifestation of those injuries occurred simultaneously with the injury. The undisputed facts also show that the debtor (actually in this case, the trustee) did not take the necessary steps to establish these liabilities as claims in the bankruptcy proceeding either directly or indirectly (though perhaps they could have been included). No claims were ever filed on behalf of these persons, and at no time did any party attempt to have a legal representative appointed. These claimants could have been claimants in the bankruptcy sense, for the debtor certainly had enough information to know that some of its planes might fall out of the sky, and that people injured or killed in those crashes would likely attempt (perhaps justifiably) to hold FAC responsible. The debtor could have, with a fair amount of precision, even estimated the number of such aircraft likely to crash, and the number of persons likely to be injured as a result. And the trustee could have then taken the steps that were taken in *A.H. Robins* and *Johns-Manville* to appoint a legal representative for these interests whose task it would have been to assure that appropriate steps were taken to protect or provide for those interests.[27]

> Because these steps were not taken, though they could have been, these alleged claims cannot, at the end of the day, be treated as "bankruptcy claims." . . .

Regretfully, the successor in this case cannot enjoy the fruits of our analysis. That is really no one's fault. How, after all, could any of the litigants in this case know how these issues would shake out back in 1990, before the Fifth Circuit had ever spoken on the issue. Yet it is the nature of the beast that, in all likelihood, it will never be possible for a debtor emerging from bankruptcy (or any successor entity), to know of a certainty that the provisions of a given plan will effectively cut off claimants such as these unless and until a challenge is mounted. In no other way can the due process rights of such claimants be fully vindicated.

The order of sale did not insulate FAI, and this court lacked the jurisdiction to enjoin these claimants, because they did not hold "bankruptcy claims" as defined in this decision. Summary judgment must be denied to plaintiffs, and entered in favor of defendants. An order will be entered consistent with this decision.

---

27. It is not necessary here to spell out what those steps might have been. Each case must turn on its own facts, and will be affected in no small part by the nature of the reorganization proposed. The defendants in this case suggested that FAC might have, as part of its plan, arranged for some sort of insurance as part of the sale. FAI contends that such insurance, if required, would have chilled the purchase or have substantially reduced the sales price obtained. That is probably true, but then that is simply a reflection of the economic reality that, for the debtor to have obtained effective relief vis-à-vis these particular kinds of bankruptcy claims, it would have been obligated to make some sort of provision for their interests. What result would ultimately have been negotiated is, at this point, gross speculation, for we do not know how the parties might have behaved had they had to deal with a legal representative zealously representing the interests of its constituents.

The next chapter in *Fairchild* also had its own twists. The company appealed to the district court, where the case languished for nearly three years. In the meantime, the new management was making a success of the revitalized Fairchild. The crash victims' families and Fairchild continued to negotiate and finally struck a deal, the terms of which remain undisclosed. As part of the deal, however, the parties asked the bankruptcy court to vacate its decision in *Fairchild*, so that no precedent would be on the books to pin post-bankruptcy liability on the company. The bankruptcy court agreed, but was that proper? 220 B.R. 909 (1998). Another bankruptcy case, settled out while awaiting a hearing in the Supreme Court, established the proposition that settlement and vacator cannot be used to junk a precedent. U.S. Bancorp Mortgage Co. v. Bonner Mall Partnership, 513 U.S. 18 (1994). Just when everything seems settled, bankruptcy cases have a way of playing out like modern murder mysteries, with one more issue cropping up at the last minute.

In another mass-tort case, In re A. H. Robins, the manufacturer of the Dalkon Shield intrauterine contraceptive device found its way into bankruptcy court. 880 F.2d 769 (4th Cir. 1989). In the *Robins* case, the company used bankruptcy in part to stop the mounting punitive damage awards that were accompanying the successful claims against the corporation. Victims claimed not only that the company had produced a device that injured millions of women, but that when they knew the device was dangerous, company officials deliberately covered up the information and continued selling their product. Like Manville, Robins also established a trust to compensate its victims. And like Manville, Robins was embroiled in a number of other acrimonious disputes during the course of the bankruptcy. After some charges of serious irregularities, Robins' management was largely ousted, and control and ownership of the business passed to new hands. Robins confirmed a plan and began settlement through its trust fund to resolve its tort liability. For a scathingly critical discussion of the Robins case, see R. Sobel, Bending the Law (1989).

Since *Robins*, companies in other industries have successfully used bankruptcy trusts to pay those injured by their products, which has helped support a developing specialty among the practicing bar. National Gypsum, another manufacturer of products that contained asbestos, faced claims estimated to run from $270 million to $3.7 billion. The DIP settled with its insurers to fund a trust to pay $1 billion over the next decade. The trust is administered by the Center for Claims Resolution, a company established in Princeton, New Jersey, to handle this type of dispute. And so another new industry is born.

d.   Regulatory Claimants

As experience with Chapter 11 has expanded, many different kinds of companies have turned to it to try to solve their financial crises and restructure their businesses. Some of those companies are deeply regulated, and, in some cases, their regulatory agencies end up trying to collect money from them. Regulators have special powers over the regulated. They can often revoke licenses, take away landing slots, or otherwise make it impossible for the company to operate. When the regulator says it is owed money, it may demand payment as a condition of permission to continue to operate. The regulator, of course, argues that it is simply regulating commerce, as state or federal law requires it to do. The debtor, however, may claim that the regulator is attempting to collect on a debt or otherwise violating the bankruptcy laws.

The next case involves a start-up that started itself right into Chapter 11. In the space of a few short years, the value of a broadcast license took more ups and downs than a roller coaster ride. NextWave, one of the winners in an early FCC auction to buy some of those licenses, saw its value plummet when the FCC held a subsequent auction that flooded the market with more licenses. NextWave lost its financing and could not pay for the licenses it had won. As the market absorbed the new licenses (and some were not issued), supply and demand swung back again to make them valuable. In the meantime, the FCC was to re-auction the licenses that it had earlier sold to NextWave but for which NextWave had never paid. By the time this case went to the Supreme Court, NextWave had offered to pay the purchase price of the license in full, but the FCC said it was too late — the license was gone and could be re-sold to someone else. The case raises the question whether, at least in these circumstances, the FCC is like any other creditor or whether its status as a regulatory agency permits it to use its administrative powers to trump the debtor's efforts in bankruptcy.

FCC v. NEXTWAVE PERSONAL COMMUNICATIONS, INC.
537 U.S. 293 (2003)

Justice SCALIA delivered the opinion of the Court.

In these cases, we decide whether §525 of the Bankruptcy Code, 11 U.S.C. §525, prohibits the Federal Communications Commission (FCC or Commission) from revoking licenses held by a debtor in bankruptcy upon the debtor's failure to make timely payments owed to the Commission for purchase of the licenses.

In 1993, Congress amended the Communications Act of 1934 to authorize the FCC to award spectrum licenses "through a system of competitive bidding." 48 Stat. 1085, as amended, 107 Stat. 387, 47 U.S.C. 309(j)(1). It directed the Commission to "promot[e] economic opportunity and competition" and "avoi[d] excessive concentration of licenses" by "disseminating licenses among a wide variety of applications, including small businesses [and] rural telephone companies." 309(j)(3)(B). [To accomplish that goal, Congress encouraged the FCC to sell on credit to small enterprises, which the FCC did. NextWave was one such enterprise that won bids for several of the licenses.] NextWave was awarded 63 C-Block licenses on winning bids totaling approximately $4.74 billion, and 27 F-Block licenses on winning bids of approximately $123 million. In accordance with FCC regulations, NextWave made a downpayment on the purchase price, signed promissory notes for the balance, and executed security agreements that the FCC perfected by filing under the Uniform Commercial Code. The security agreements gave the Commission a first "lien on and continuing security interest in all of the Debtor's rights and interest in [each] License." Security Agreement between NextWave and FCC 1 (Jan. 3, 1997), 2 App. to Pet. for Cert. 402a. In addition, the licenses recited that they were "conditioned upon the full and timely payment of all monies due pursuant to . . . the terms of the Commission's installment plan as set forth in the Note and Security Agreement executed by the licensee," and that "[f]ailure to comply with this condition will result in the automatic cancellation of this authorization." Radio Station Authorization for Broadband PCS (issued to NextWave Jan. 3, 1997), 2 App. to Pet. for Cert. 388a.

[NextWave, along with several other successful bidders, could not pay, and rather than forfeit the licenses,] NextWave filed for Chapter 11 bankruptcy protection in New York. It suspended payments to all creditors, including the FCC, pending confirmation of a reorganization plan. NextWave initiated an adversary proceeding in the Bankruptcy Court, alleging that its $4.74 billion indebtedness on the C-Block licenses was avoidable as a "fraudulent conveyance" under 544 of the Bankruptcy Code, 11 U.S.C. §544, because, by the time the Commission actually conveyed the licenses, their value had declined from approximately $4.74 billion to less than $1 billion. The Bankruptcy Court agreed ruling in effect that the company could keep its C-Block licenses for the reduced price of $1.02 billion, and the District Court affirmed. NextWave Personal Communications, Inc. v. FCC, 241 B.R. 311, 318-319 (S.D.N.Y.1999). The Court of Appeals for the Second Circuit reversed, holding that, although the Bankruptcy Court might have jurisdiction over NextWave's underlying debts to the FCC, it could not change the conditions attached to NextWave's licenses. In re NextWave Personal Communications, Inc., 200 F.3d 43, 55-56 (1999) (per curiam). The Second Circuit also held that since, under FCC regulations, "NextWave's obligation attached upon the close of the auction," there had been no fraudulent conveyance by the FCC acting in its capacity as creditor. Id., at 58.

Following the Second Circuit's decision, NextWave prepared a plan of reorganization that envisioned payment of a single lump sum to satisfy the entire remaining $4.3 billion obligation for purchase of the C-Block licenses, including interest and late fees. The FCC objected to the plan, asserting that NextWave's licenses had been canceled automatically when the company missed its first payment deadline in October 1998. The Commission simultaneously announced that NextWave's licenses were "available for auction under the automatic cancellation provisions" of the FCC's regulations. . . . [The Second Circuit ruled that the DC Circuit had exclusive jurisdiction to review the regulatory issues at stake in the dispute.]

* * *

[The DC Circuit held] that the FCC's cancellation of NextWave's licenses violated 11 U.S.C. §525: "Applying the fundamental principle that federal agencies must obey all federal laws, not just those they administer, we conclude that the Commission violated the provision of the Bankruptcy Code that prohibits governmental entities from revoking debtors' licenses solely for failure to pay debts dischargeable in bankruptcy." 254 F.3d 130, 133 (2001). We granted certiorari.

II

* * *

A

The FCC has not denied that the proximate cause for its cancellation of the licenses was NextWave's failure to make the payments that were due. It contends, however, that §525 does not apply because the FCC had a "valid regulatory motive" for the cancellation. In our view, that factor is irrelevant. When the statute refers to failure to pay a debt as the sole cause of cancellation ("solely because"), it cannot reasonably be understood to include, among the other causes whose presence can preclude application of the prohibition, the governmental unit's motive in effecting the cancellation. Such a reading would deprive 525 of all force. It is hard to imagine a situation in which a governmental unit would not have some further motive behind the cancellation, assuring the financial solvency of the licensed entity, e.g., Perez v. Campbell, 402 U.S. 637 (1971); In re The Bible Speaks, 69 B.R. 368, 374 (Bkrtcy. D. Mass. 1987), or punishing lawlessness, e.g., In re Adams, 106 B.R. 811, 827 (Bkrtcy. D.N.J. 1989); In re Colon, 102 B.R. 421, 428 (Bkrtcy.E.D.Pa.1989), or even (quite simply) making itself financially whole. Section 525 means nothing more or less than that the failure to pay a dischargeable debt must alone be the proximate cause of the cancellation, the act or event that triggers the agency's decision to cancel, whatever the agency's ultimate motive in pulling the trigger may be.

Some may think (and the opponents of §525 undoubtedly thought) that there ought to be an exception for cancellations that have a valid regulatory purpose. Besides the fact that such an exception would consume the rule, it flies in the face of the fact that, where Congress has intended to provide regulatory exceptions to provisions of the Bankruptcy Code, it has done so clearly and expressly, rather than by a device so subtle as denominating a motive a cause. There are, for example, regulatory exemptions from the Bankruptcy Code's automatic stay provisions. 11 U.S.C. §362(b)(4). And even §525(a) itself contains explicit exemptions for certain Agriculture Department programs, see n. 2, supra. These latter exceptions would be entirely superfluous if we were to read §525 as the Commission proposes, which means, of course, that such a reading must be rejected.

B

Petitioners contend that NextWave's license obligations to the Commission are not "debt[s] that [are] dischargeable" in bankruptcy. 11 U.S.C. 525(a). First, the FCC argues that "regulatory conditions like the full and timely payment condition are not properly classified as 'debts' " under the Bankruptcy Code. Brief for Petitioner FCC 33. In its view, the "financial nature of a condition" on a license "does not convert that condition into a debt." Ibid. This is nothing more than a retooling of petitioners' recurrent theme that "regulatory conditions" should be exempt from 525. No matter how the Commission casts it, the argument loses.

★ ★ ★

C

Finally, our interpretation of §525 does not create any conflict with the Communications Act. It does not, as petitioners contend, obstruct the functioning of the auction provisions of 47 U.S.C. §309(j), since nothing in those provisions demands that cancellation be the sanction for failure to make agreed-upon periodic payments. Indeed, nothing in those provisions even requires the Commission to permit payment to be made over time, rather than leaving it to impecunious bidders to finance the full purchase price with private lenders. What petitioners describe as a conflict boils down to nothing more than a policy preference on the FCC's part for (1) selling licenses on credit and (2) canceling licenses rather than asserting security interests in licenses when there is a default. Such administrative preferences cannot be the basis for denying respondent rights provided by the plain terms of a law.

★ ★ ★

For the reasons stated, the judgment of the Court of Appeals for the District of Columbia Circuit is
Affirmed.

[Concurring opinion of Justice Stevens and dissenting opinion of Justice Breyer omitted.]

═══════════════

Problem Set 38

38.1. Strosnider Sunrise Farm, Inc., has been in Kim Strosnider's family for three generations, growing into a 1,600-acre fruit and vegetable operation. Kim works hard and the business is profitable, but Kim is worried. The state EPA has found contamination in the soil and water on her property. Kim explains that she can't even begin to list the pesticides and chemical fertilizers they have used on the crops over the past 60 years. The EPA has told her to clean it up and explained that if she doesn't, they will clean it up and send her a bill for about $1.1 million. Kim says that the business can't pay that kind of money. "It might as well be $1.1 trillion — we can't even make interest payments on a million dollars. The land and the equipment are already over-mortgaged. We make a profit some years, but only because I work eighteen hours a day." She asks for your help. What do you tell her?

38.2. You are still working for Congresswoman Herring. She is looking for a "new" environmental issue. She has been asked to cosponsor a new superfund bill. The bill is based on one recently passed by the state of Alabama that creates a lien to cover the fees, interest, and penalties imposed for the disposal of hazardous waste. The lien enjoys the same priority as state revenue liens — which gives these liens priority over all other liens on the property, even preexisting ones. The proposed bill would cover all clean-up costs. Spell out the implications of this bill for the congresswoman. What is your advice?

38.3. You have been Chris Rosekrans's chief legal advisor as he has taken on one business challenge after another. He's put together a group of investors to buy Kewanee Boiler, a 70-year-old company that specialized in heavy industrial boilers. The company has fallen on hard times; the plant is shuttered and in Chapter 11. Current management has abandoned the business, and the liquidating trustee had recommended a piecemeal sale. Rosekrans is willing to invest $40 million to revitalize the factory and shift its output to a more varied industrial supply output. The 550 workers who would be recalled are delighted to see high skill, high wage jobs return, creditors see the promised 50 percent repayment as an unexpected windfall, and the mayor sees this as a chance to turn around a decaying part of the city. The only hitch is that Rosekrans has read *Fairchild Aircraft.* He knows about the old problems with the Kewanee boilers produced back in the 1970s. Forty-six of the 10,000 sold that were manufactured from 1971 to 1975 have simply blown up, averaging about two a year once the boilers were ten years old. Rosekrans says his investors are willing to take full responsibility for every product they produce, but not for the products manufactured long before they took over. He says that unless you can guarantee that if a boiler blows up and someone gets hurt, he won't face a judge who later decides that Kewanee is liable, then he won't invest. Everyone — investors, creditors, employees, the mayor — awaits your answer.

38.4. Universal Chips is a major supplier of standard microchip circuits for various purposes. One market niche that it dominates is production of thermostat control units for home heating and cooling systems.

After years of rapid growth, however, UC is now in financial trouble. Its difficulties arise not only from its slowness to adopt some of the most recent technical advances, a mistake its R&D department is rapidly correcting, but also from a failure of quality control during a two-year period of over-rapid expansion. During that period, UC produced a number of defective chips for the thermostat market. The company's engineers estimate that about 30 percent of the chips produced during that period are subject to sudden, unpredictable failure, with varying consequences ranging from a simple need for replacement to serious damage to an entire home heating system. Because the central microchip is a unit with an expected lifespan far greater than the system as a whole, it is installed in a way that makes it difficult and expensive to remove.

UC recently filed in Chapter 11. In general its prospects for reorganization look good, except that its principal lenders and the public debt markets are very concerned about its potential long-term liabilities arising from the thermostat chip problem. You have been retained by the National Association of Home Heating Repair Persons (NAHHRP) as bankruptcy counsel. NAHHRP members have installed hundreds of thousands of the thermostats with suspect chips. To replace them all would cost at least $50 million, and much of that cost would be wasted, at least in the sense that many of the chips will last the normal 20 years with no problem. On the other hand, NAHHRP sees the likelihood of expensive replacement costs and warranty claims from members' homeowner customers for years in the future. Unfortunately, it is very hard to predict what those costs will be or when they will be incurred. (For example, the experts are bitterly divided over the likely "peak" failure year; some say year five after installation, while others think it will be year nine.)

What claim will you file on behalf of NAHHRP members? How might the court rule on the claim? How might your members be treated in a plan of reorganization? Do homeowners have a claim? If some lawyer representing a small group of potentially affected homeowners should file a purported "class" claim, how should you react on behalf of NAHHRP members? Should you support or oppose? If you or the company opposes the class claim, what arguments can be made against it, and how will counsel for the class respond?

38.5. Mark Herring, CEO and largest shareholder of Herring Homes, has built the company into the second largest residential builder in the state. A sudden spike in mortgage rates, coupled with a military base closing and two rounds of layoffs at the area's largest employer has pushed local housing into a terrible slump. Already highly leveraged, HH has collapsed into Chapter 11. Mark has cut back sharply, but he has continued to build homes and he thinks he has worked out a good plan with substantial creditor support. The problem is the state's licensing board. It seems that when HH failed to pay several skilled tradespeople last year, the state agency took over the claims and successfully sued HH on their behalf. In addition, the agency sent HH notice six months ago that annual licensing fees of $20,000 were past due. Now that both claims have remained unpaid for six months, the state agency takes the position that HH's contractor's license has automatically been terminated. HH can reapply, but, according to the agency, it must pay all outstanding dues and other claims in full before a license can be issued. The agency points to explicit language in the state statute providing for automatic termination of the license whenever a contractor owes money for more than six months to the agency for fees or to settle claims and that prohibits issuance of a new license to anyone who has unpaid obligations to the agency. Without a license, HH cannot conduct business. What do you advise?

5.   Post-confirmation: Life after Chapter 11

As we discussed in the section on "future" claims, in 1978 Congress greatly expanded the concept of "claim" with the purpose of making confirmation of a Chapter 11 plan as broad a "fresh start" as possible, especially for a corporation that will be continuing in business. The flexibility of Chapter 11 rules and procedures also enables a sweeping resolution of financial and legal issues. Nonetheless, it is not always possible to resolve every single issue in the plan confirmation. This section discusses some of the most important issues that remain after everyone's had the cake and champagne in the law-firm library following the confirmation hearing. Midnight indigestion comes when a lawyer realizes there were more problems that should have been addressed before confirmation.

One set of problems arises from claims by the post-confirmation debtor against other entities. To what extent have those claims against third parties been resolved in the confirmation process? This question is usually addressed under the doctrinal heading "res judicata."

A second set of problems relates to claims against the debtor (or the estate): Have all the claims been discharged? Two important types of issues under this heading are timing and notice. The timing problem arises because section 1141 discharges almost all debts up to the moment of confirmation. Whenever bankruptcy law makes something important turn on timing, there is a question about when an obligation comes into existence. We have seen this issue arise when it was necessary to determine when a property interest arose so that something of value would or would not be declared "property of the estate." Similarly, we revisited the issue when it was necessary to determine whether an environmental claim arose pre-petition or thereafter in order to determine its repayment status in bankruptcy. Those are just two instances of a host of possible legal outcomes that will turn on timing questions. There is a serious and continuing split among the circuits about when claims arise for the purposes of the discharge.

The second type of issue concerning claims against the debtor, the notice problem, rests on the simple fact that the Constitution requires due process and due process requires notice. In this case, the notice required is notice of the Chapter 11 case and its plan of reorganization. Disputes about notice are a second occasion to determine whether certain creditors' claims against the debtor have or have not been discharged.

The third post-petition set of problems is occasioned by the claim by a third party, often an insider of the debtor, that the plan has discharged the liabilities of the third party as well as those of the debtor.

In addition to these problems of "claim preclusion," a fascinating set of issues arises from attempted solutions to the very practical problem that it often takes years to sort out the affairs of a Chapter 11 debtor, but it would be harmful, if not fatal, to keep the debtor in bankruptcy all that time. One important solution that has emerged in recent years is the liquidation trust. One type of trust is devoted to selling properties over a period of years to maximize returns to the estate and, in turn, to the creditors. Another type is a litigation trust, which represents a store of value in the form of claims against various parties. The trust may pursue the claims itself, may sell them to others, or may enter into a joint venture with others to pursue them. This "disembodied" litigation is creating a host of questions for the courts.

In this section we explore each of these problems, and then we close with a brief Chapter 11 coda about the companies that return to bankruptcy after confirmation of a plan. We observe that these post-confirmation concerns also implicate important questions about the continuing jurisdiction of the bankruptcy courts after confirmation, but we reserve discussion of those issues to the next Part of the casebook.

a. Effects of Confirmation: Claims Against the Debtor

Whether a claim against the debtor survives confirmation and discharge turns on timing and notice. The first point, timing, depends on the time period to which a claim is assigned, pre-confirmation or post-confirmation. (Remember that claims that arose during bankruptcy are also discharged by plan confirmation in Chapter 11.) Naturally, claims that arise after the debtor emerges from bankruptcy are not somehow prospectively discharged, making the former debtor bullet-proof against liabilities to which the rest of society is subject. Yet sometimes claims arise post-confirmation that have roots in the pre-confirmation past, creating issues analogous to the "future claims" issues discussed earlier. The problems of allocation are similar, so we just identify the point here and move on.

The next case illustrates an aspect of another common discharge issue: Did the claimant receive sufficient notice of the bankruptcy?

══════════════════ In re U.S.H. CORP. ══════════════════
223 B.R. 654 (Bankr. S.D.N.Y. 1998)

Burton R. Lifland, Bankruptcy Judge.

U.S. Home Corporation ("US Home"), moves to dismiss the complaint filed by a group of homeowners (the "Plaintiffs") which seeks an order (a) determining that the Plaintiffs are not bound by this Court's order confirming U.S. Home's plan of reorganization and (b) permitting Plaintiffs to pursue prepetition claims against U.S. Home.

Background

On April 15, 1991, U.S. Home, together with certain affiliated entities (collectively, the "Debtors"), filed petitions under chapter 11. In the course of the Debtors' chapter 11 proceedings, by order dated October 22, 1991 (the "Bar Order"), this court fixed December 23, 1991 (the "Bar Date") as the last date by which all claims (with certain exceptions not relevant here) against the Debtors were to be filed. By order dated May 24, 1993 (the "Confirmation Order") the Debtors' reorganization plan was confirmed.

The Debtors are primarily builders of single family homes doing business in eleven states. From 1989 through 1991, U.S. Home developed and built, among other things, numerous townhomes in Country Place subdivision ("Country Place") in Brazoria County, Texas which is in proximity to the Gulf of Mexico. The Plaintiffs are homeowners who reside in Country Place.

In June of 1995, the Country Place townhome owners association (the "Association") attempted to buy windstorm insurance to cover their homes in Country Place because the insurance company which had previously provided its insurance policy had withdrawn from the Texas market. In the course of seeking to purchase such insurance with another company, the Association allegedly was required to produce certificates verifying that the buildings were in compliance with the building code requirements of the Texas Catastrophe Property Insurance Association ("CAT-POOL"). CAT-POOL was formed by a group of insurance companies along with the Texas State Board of Insurance because of the catastrophic, hurricane-related losses which have occurred along the Texas Gulf Coast. According to the Plaintiffs, the purpose of CAT-POOL was to insure that homes built in counties immediately bordering the Gulf of Mexico would be built in such a manner as to reasonably withstand hurricane-force winds and thus, be insurable, at a reasonable rate, against the risk of hurricanes and windstorms.

The Association hired a structural engineer, Howard Pieper, to conduct an inspection of the property in order to obtain the required certification. He subsequently determined that the homes were not built to CAT-POOL standards. According to an affidavit of Mr. Pieper, he had previously been hired by U.S. Home in March of 1991 to assure and certify that a home being built in the Country Place subdivision met the CAT-POOL standards. Mr. Pieper states that he did not find the construction met those standards and in April 1991, informed U.S. Home of the requirements necessary to meet such standards. In May 1991, Mr. Pieper also "prepared a simplified document for use by U.S. Home and its subcontractors."

On August 1996, Plaintiffs sent demand letters to U.S. Home apparently in accordance with the Texas Deceptive Trade Practices Act.

U.S. Home responded that the Confirmation Order permanently enjoined litigation against U.S. Home based on prepetition claims. Plaintiffs then commenced this action seeking an order determining that they are not bound by the Confirmation Order because they were not given formal notice of the bankruptcy proceeding.

In moving to dismiss the complaint, U.S. Home argues, first, that the CAT-POOL guidelines are voluntary and, therefore, the Plaintiffs have failed to state a claim upon which relief may be granted. Second, U.S. Home argues, as unknown creditors who received constructive notice by publication of the bankruptcy proceeding, the Plaintiffs' claims are barred by the discharge provisions contained in the Confirmation Order, Plan and section 1141(d) of the Bankruptcy Code. It is undisputed that the claims at issue arose prior to confirmation of the Plan. All of the homes were built and sold by U.S. Home prior to the effective date of the Plan. . . .

Discharge of Prepetition Claims

Ordinarily, an order confirming a reorganization plan operates to discharge all unsecured debts and liabilities, even those of tort victims who were unaware of the debtor's bankruptcy. See 11 U.S.C. §§1141 and 524 (1998). Once confirmed, the plan binds the debtor and all creditors, whether or not a creditor has accepted the plan. See 11 U.S.C. §1141(a).

Discharge under the Bankruptcy Code, however, presumes that all creditors bound by the plan have been given notice sufficient to satisfy due process. Whether a creditor received adequate notice depends on the facts and circumstances of each case. Due process is met if notice is "reasonably calculated to reach all interested parties, reasonably conveys all of the required information, and permits a reasonable amount of time for response." Mullane v. Central Hanover Bank, 339 U.S. 306 (1950). In *Mullane*, the Supreme Court held that "[a]n elementary and fundamental requirement of due process in any proceeding which is to be accorded finality is notice reasonably calculated, under all circumstances, to apprise interested parties of the pendency of the action and afford them an opportunity to present their objections." *Mullane*, 339 U.S. at 313-14, 70 S. Ct. 652. Thus, if a creditor is not given reasonable notice of the bankruptcy proceeding and the relevant bar dates, its claim cannot be constitutionally discharged. What constitutes "reasonable notice," however, varies according to the knowledge of the parties.

When a creditor is unknown to the debtor, publication notice of the claims bar date may satisfy the requirements of due process. See *Mullane*, 339 U.S. at 317-18. However, if a creditor is known to the debtor, notice by publication is not constitutionally reasonable, and actual notice of the relevant bar dates must be afforded to the creditor. . . .

The Bar Order required the Debtors to notify all known claimants by mail and unknown claimants by publication of the Bar Date. In addition to publishing notices in the national editions of The New York Times, U.S.A. Today and The Wall Street Journal, the Debtors published notice of the Bar Date in, among other regional papers and publications, the Dallas Morning News, the Austin American Statesman, the Amarillo Globe Times, the Houston Chronicle, the San Antonio Express News, the Fort Worth Star Telegram, the Lubbock Avalanche, the Harlingen Valley Star, the El Paso Herald Post, the Wichita Falls, the Midland/Odessa Group, and the Abilene Reporter. The Debtors' publication notices were more than sufficient to satisfy due process requirements and hence, if the Plaintiffs were "unknown" creditors at the time of the Bar Order, their claims are now barred. If, however, the Plaintiffs were "known" creditors at the time of the Bar Order and failed to receive actual notice, their claims may not be discharged.

Known versus Unknown

As characterized by the Supreme Court, a "known" creditor is one whose identity is either known or "reasonably ascertainable by the debtor." Tulsa Professional Collection Serv., Inc. v. Pope, 485 U.S. 478, 490 (1988). An "unknown" creditor is one whose "interests are either conjectural or future or, although they could be discovered upon investigation, do not in due course of business come to knowledge [of the debtor]." *Mullane*, 339 U.S. at 317.

A creditor's identity is "reasonably ascertainable" if that creditor can be identified through "reasonably diligent efforts." Mennonite Bd. of Missions v. Adams, 462 U.S. 791, 798 n.4 (1983). Reasonable diligence does not require "impracticable and extended searches . . . in the name of due process." *Mullane*, 339 U.S. at 317. . . .

. . . Debtors cannot be required to provide actual notice to anyone who potentially could have been affected by their actions, such a requirement

would completely vitiate the important goal of prompt and effectual administration and settlement of debtors' estates.

Plaintiffs assert that they are not bound by the U.S. Home bankruptcy
discharge because they were known contingent creditors who were not
given formal notice of the chapter 11 proceeding. Plaintiffs argue that they
were "known" creditors because U.S. Home knew that it sold homes to
Plaintiffs that were not built in accordance with the CAT-POOL guidelines
and knew that it had an obligation to disclose this information to potential
buyers, but failed to do so. U.S. Home argues that there was no law in Texas
that required U.S. Home to build in accordance with the voluntary guidelines of CAT-POOL, and no case law, statute, rule or regulation or other
legal authority for the proposition that a failure of a builder to construct a
home in accordance with voluntary CAT-POOL guidelines is a breach of
duty. Moreover, the property at issue was insured for several years and,
according to an affidavit filed by U.S. Home, is still readily insurable
whether or not the homes were built to CAT-POOL standards.

Given the pleadings and arguments presented to this court, there are no
set of facts under which I could find the Plaintiffs were known creditors of
U.S. Home before or at the time of confirmation. The Plaintiffs do not
counter the crucial contention pled and affirmed by affidavit by U.S. Home,
that there is no building code, standard or law which required U.S. Home to
build according to CAT-POOL standards. Without the linchpin of a duty of
U.S. Home to build in accordance with CAT-POOL standards, U.S. Home
could not have been expected to discover any potential claim of the
Plaintiffs prior to confirmation, particularly one so remote. It was not the
duty of U.S. Home to search out "each conceivable or possible creditor." If
the Plaintiffs were to be considered known creditors at the time of the confirmation, the universe of creditors entitled to actual notice would defeat
the purpose of title 11's expedited and cost effective claims resolution process. . . . The motion to dismiss is granted.

═══════════

This opinion also illustrates that the notice and merits issues are frequently intertwined or, some would say, entangled.

b.   Claims by Debtors

Liquidating Trusts

Because there may be good reasons for taking months or years to complete the process of financial reorganization, various devices have been
developed to grant the luxury of time, while getting the debtor more
promptly back into the commercial world. One common instance arises
when time is needed to finish developing and selling assets that do not fit
into the debtor's new business plan or its management's capabilities. The
asset, an office building, for example, may be transferred to a trust as part of
the Chapter 11 confirmation, the sale may be completed months later, and

the money from the sale is then distributed according to the terms of the trust (e.g., pro rata to the unsecured creditors). By use of this device, the estate can maximize the value of the assets without holding the debtor in bankruptcy longer than necessary.

Another increasingly common device is the litigation trust. With a litigation trust, instead of assets such as real estate, the estate contributes causes of action that the debtor had against other parties. The estate might be paid immediately for this property and the money distributed to creditors. The trust may get this money by selling shares to third parties or to some subset of creditors. The trust then litigates or settles the suits, and whatever it recovers is distributed to the trust shareholders. Sometimes the estate receives a contingent percentage of whatever the trust ultimately recovers, with the trust responsible for funding the litigation expenses.

One recent case serves as a fairly typical example of a litigation trust. The basic dispute was among an Irish bank that had lent to a joint venture that developed a hotel that failed; the debtor, which had guaranteed part of the joint venture's loan; and two investors who had agreed to indemnify the debtor against losses on the guarantee. The dispute had generated two lawsuits in the United States and one in England. The debtor's TIB proposed, in effect, to sell the debtor's indemnification rights to the bank in exchange for (a) the bank's agreement to fund a defense in New York and an attack in England and (b) a percentage of any recovery in England. The putative indemnitors objected. The court held that they had no standing to object, because they were really adverse parties. Alternatively, it held that the agreement was really a settlement that the bankruptcy court properly approved under Bankruptcy Rule 9019 relating to court approval of the settlement of claims by and against the estate. In re Ashford Hotels, Ltd., 235 B.R. 734 (S.D.N.Y. 1999).

Ashford is a fairly plain-vanilla example (although the number of transnational parties and multiplicity of suits makes it look like vanilla with sprinkles). But the litigation-trust device is becoming ever more structurally complex and, perhaps, problematic. One reason is that Wall Street's endless creativity has spawned the possibility of public offerings of securities that are essentially contingent interests in bankruptcy litigation trusts. At some point, questions about champerty must reappear. Another reason is that increasingly trustees and debtors are assigning lawsuits that are unique to bankruptcy, like the power to recover a preference. Although the motive is the same as in the sale of a pre-petition cause of action arising under nonbankruptcy law — to generate recoveries for creditors — the separation of bankruptcy actions from the special context in which they arise may lead to serious problems of legal concept and public perception.

Res Judicata

Debtors who contemplate bringing lawsuits after bankruptcy have one important point to bear in mind: making sure that the cause of action survives the court order granting confirmation of a plan. While claims by the debtor (as opposed to claims against the debtor) are not discharged under section 1141, other legal doctrines may bar them.

======================= In re HOWE =======================
913 F.2d 1138 (5th Cir. 1990)

KING, Circuit Judge:

* * *

I. BACKGROUND.

Maxcy Gregg Howe and Dena Crawford Howe ("the Howes") instituted voluntary Chapter 11 bankruptcy proceedings in 1982. They negotiated a plan of reorganization with their creditors and the bankruptcy court
confirmed the plan on January 28, 1983. Five years later, the Howes filed
in state court lender liability claims that were removed to federal court
and referred to the bankruptcy court. The Howes' creditors, principally
Premier Bank ("Premier") (formerly First National Bank of Shreveport)
and Benjamin Vaughan ("Vaughan"), moved to dismiss the claims on the
basis of res judicata, prescription, or equitable or judicial estoppel. The
Howes, in turn, moved to abstain and remand, arguing that their claims
concerned issues of evolving state law better left to the state courts. The
bankruptcy court granted Premier's motion to dismiss The district court
affirmed.

After the Howes first instituted Chapter 11 proceedings, Premier filed
a proof of claim on two promissory notes executed in 1980 totaling
$2,122,622.20. The notes were secured by a collateral mortgage covering
1,200 acres of the Howes' farm and dairy operations and a chattel mortgage
on their house, farm equipment and cattle. The Howes responded by filing a
complaint seeking, for various reasons, to have the chattel mortgage
declared null and void and contending that the rate of interest charged by
Premier was usurious. As a condition for Premier's loan to the Howes in
1980, the Howes' hired Vaughan as a consultant for their dairy operation at
$1,000.00 per month. In the reorganization proceedings, the Howes filed an
application to reject Vaughan's management contract as an executory contract that overcharged for management services. Premier opposed this
application and, following a hearing, the parties entered into a stipulated
order whereby Vaughan would continue in a lesser management role and at
a reduced compensation level.

On June 18, 1982, the Howes filed their disclosure statement and initial plan of reorganization. Premier filed objections to the disclosure statement and plan and also filed a motion to dismiss the reorganization
proceedings as unfeasible. The Howes filed a second and a third disclosure
statement and plan. Premier withdrew its objections and its motion to dismiss "subject to settlement and agreement." The parties negotiated andset-
tled on a Fourth Amended Plan of Reorganization and Disclosure
Statement, dated January 17, 1983. The Howes' lender liability claims that
are the subject of this appeal were not scheduled as an asset of the estate,
nor were they disclosed or treated in the Fourth Amended Plan of
Reorganization and Disclosure Statement. The bankruptcy court confirmed this plan on January 28, 1983.

The plan specifically treated the Howes' indebtedness to Premier as an allowed claim, partially secured and partially unsecured.

Approximately five years after confirmation of the plan, the Howes brought this lender liability action based on the 1980 loan transaction. They claim that Premier, Vaughan and others induced the Howes to incur substantial indebtedness without regard to their ability to repay the borrowed sum. The aim, according to the Howes, was to drive the Howes into financial ruin so that the defendants could obtain a certain tract of the Howes' land for commercial development. They also alleged that Premier requested, as a condition for the loan, that the Howes hire Vaughan as a consultant, and that Vaughan thereafter took total control of their operations. The Howes claimed violations of fiduciary and contractual duties, Louisiana securities laws, and state law fraud. Damages were sought in the amount of $14,250,000.00.

* * *

III.   RES JUDICATA.

The Howes contend that the district court erred in affirming the bankruptcy court's dismissal of their state law claims on res judicata grounds. The law in this circuit is well settled that a plan is binding upon all parties once it is confirmed and all questions that could have been raised *pertaining to such plan* are res judicata. This circuit's test for res judicata requires that:

(1) The parties be identical in both suits,
(2) A court of competent jurisdiction rendered the prior judgment,
(3) There was a final judgment on the merits in the previous decision, and
(4) The plaintiff raises the same cause of action or claim in both suits.

The Howes concede that the first three elements of the test are met. They contend, however, that their claim does not involve the same cause of action as the earlier bankruptcy proceeding because "there was not an order in the bankruptcy proceeding ... specifically addressing the relationship which existed by and among" the parties.

A.   Was It the Same Claim?

The *Nilsen* court adopted for the Fifth Circuit the transactional test of the *Restatement (Second) of Judgments* for determining whether two suits involve the same claim for res judicata purposes. Under this approach, the critical issue is not the relief requested or the theory asserted but whether plaintiff bases the two actions on the same nucleus of operative facts. The rule is that res judicata "bars all claims that were or *could have been* advanced in support of the cause of action on the occasion of its former adjudication, ... not merely those that were adjudicated."

The seminal case in this circuit on the res judicata affect of a confirmation order is Southmark Properties v. Charles House Corp.[12] In Southmark, we held that a district court's order confirming a trustee's sale of Southmark's property barred the debtor's later claim that the creditor engaged in fraudulent and extortionate activities leading to that sale. Southmark claimed that the creditor's improper activities concerning its construction loan caused it to default and led to the creditor's foreclosure action. The foreclosure action, in turn, led to Southmark's bankruptcy filing and, finally, to the trustee's sale of the property. The court noted that a common nucleus of operative facts informed the district court's order approving the reorganization sale and the debtor's subsequent claim that the creditor's activities caused that sale. The central transaction in both instances, the court reasoned, was the passing of title to the property in exchange for the cancellation of the mortgage debt.

The loan transaction at the heart of the present litigation was also the source of Premier's claim against the estate. The Howes vigorously contested the validity of Premier's lien in adversary proceedings in the bankruptcy court and contended that Premier's loan was usurious. Premier's loan was the only major claim against the estate and was the subject of extensive negotiations prior to confirmation of the plan of reorganization. We cannot escape the conclusion that the Howes' present allegations merely assert new theories based on the same nucleus of operative facts that informed their earlier bankruptcy proceedings. The two actions, therefore, constitute the same claim or cause of action for res judicata purposes.

* * *

The Howes argue that they should be allowed to pursue their claims because, although they may have been aware of the basic facts underlying their claims, they were not aware of the significance of those facts. We find the Howes' ignorance an inadequate excuse for their failure to raise their claims in the earlier proceedings. They do not suggest that the facts forming the basis of those claims were undiscoverable until after those proceedings. Nor do they suggest that the adversary proceedings lacked the procedural mechanisms that would have allowed them to bring their claims.

* * *

Based on the foregoing reasons, we AFFIRM the judgments in case number 89-4548 and case number 89-4513.

═══════════════

c.   Discharge of Non-debtors

Because modern legal systems permit the creation of new corporate entities freely and cheaply, a considerable range of choice may exist as to which affiliates in a group go into bankruptcy. In an interrelated group,

---

12. 742 F.2d 862 (5th Cir. 1984).

however, persons and entities other than the debtor may contribute money or talent that is essential to a reorganization. Often, they will want to be released from future liability in return for their contributions. The following case presents an example of the resulting difficulties and sets forth the contrasting positions taken by various courts. These issues are also related to jurisdictional questions that we will address in the next Part.

In re ARROWMILL DEVELOPMENT CORP.
211 B.R. 497 (Bankr. D.N.J. 1997)

William H. GINDIN, Chief Judge.

PROCEDURAL HISTORY

This dispute, between two nondebtors, comes before the court as a motion by Stefano Delliturri ("Delliturri"). . . . Delliturri and John, Mary, Joan and Vincent Caglianone (the "Caglianones") were parties to a state court fraudulent conveyance action. . . . Delliturri asserted that John Caglianone fraudulently transferred real property to his wife Mary and their children. The state court, Hon. Wilfred Diana, found that the reorganization plan of debtor, Arrowmill Development Corp. ("debtor"), discharged John Caglianone from all debts against him, including the debt of Delliturri.

On December 12, 1996 the Appellate Division issued a decision reversing Judge Diana ("Dreier Opinion"). The Appellate Division raised several issues concerning the propriety of discharging a nondebtor through a reorganization plan. The Dreier Opinion thus directed the state trial court to supervise the parties' submission of the present dispute to the bankruptcy court. Judge Diana communicated with this court concerning the matter and thereafter advised the parties that this court would undertake to resolve the issues raised by the Appellate Division.

FACTS

Movant, Stefano Delliturri, leased space for his pizzeria and restaurant in debtor's shopping center. Delliturri sued debtor and John Caglianone in a separate state court action seeking damages for fraudulent inducement to enter into a commercial lease. John Caglianone is an equity holder of debtor, and negotiated the lease with Mr. Delliturri on debtor's behalf. The state court action was the object of a settlement in which Delliturri was to receive $102,000 from the defendants, jointly and severally. On April 7, 1994, after a default and in accordance with the terms of the settlement, a judgment in the same amount was entered in Delliturri's favor. The judgment was later amended on March 3, 1995 to adjust the amount to $77,555. . . .

Delliturri filed a timely proof of claim in debtor's chapter 11 proceeding in March 1994. . . . Delliturri took no position with regard to the plan and did not participate in negotiations. The third amended plan was eventually confirmed by this court. . . .

DISCUSSION

Jurisdiction . . .

Having found that [this] court did possess subject matter jurisdiction to entertain a release of nondebtor, John Caglianone, the court must now consider the issue of discharge.

Discharge of Nondebtors

A discharge in bankruptcy is an involuntary release by operation of law of creditor claims against an entity (both asserted and unasserted) which is enforced by the court. Since a discharge is an extreme remedy, stripping a creditor of its claims against its will, it is a privilege reserved for those entities which file a petition under the bankruptcy code and abide by its rules. Simply put, "the enjoyment of the benefits afforded by the code is contingent on the acceptance of its burdens." [Judith R. Starr, Bankruptcy Court Jurisdiction to Release Insiders from Creditor Claims in Corporate Reorganizations, 9 Bankr. Dev. J. 485, 498 (1993)].

A chapter 11 debtor receives a discharge upon confirmation of a plan, pursuant to 11 U.S.C. §1141(d)(l). That discharge is specifically limited, however, by 11 U.S.C. §524(e). Section 524(e) provides that, "[e]xcept as provided in subsection (a)(3) of this section, discharge of a debt of the debtor does not affect the liability of any other entity on, or the property of any other entity for, such debt." 11 U.S.C. §524(e). . . .

The circuit courts are divided over the issue of nondebtor discharge. Emerging from such decisions are three lines of cases. The first line of cases holds that reorganization plans may discharge nondebtors even over the objection of creditors.

The second line of cases holds that the bankruptcy court may never discharge or release a nondebtor.

The third line and majority view is that bankruptcy courts may "discharge" or release nondebtors from their debts only if the affected creditors consent. . . .

Keeping in mind the Third Circuit's analysis that section 524(e) specifically limits the scope of the discharge, and that the Bankruptcy Code does not contemplate a discharge of nondebtors, this court holds that plans of reorganization may not contain provisions which discharge nondebtors. While the court agrees that there may be very good policy reasons for providing a discharge to a nondebtor, the court is constrained by the plain language of 11 U.S.C. §524 and persuaded by the policy reasons against a blanket discharge of nondebtors. . . .

. . . As cautioned by a commentator, nondebtor discharge has "potential for abuse, in which corporate bankruptcy becomes a form of insurance for insiders and thus creates a moral hazard . . . because insiders may be tempted to engage in high risk behavior by the knowledge that they can protect themselves from its consequences by taking the corporation [and not themselves] into chapter 11." [Judith R. Starr, Bankruptcy Court Jurisdiction to Release Insiders from Creditor Claims in Corporate Reorganizations, 9 Bankr. Dev. J. 485, 499 (1993).]

Consent to Release of Liability of Nondebtor by Affected Creditor

When a release of liability of a nondebtor is a consensual provision, however, agreed to by the affected creditor, it is no different from any other settlement or contract and does not implicate 11 U.S.C. §524(e). A voluntary, consensual release is not a discharge in bankruptcy. As indicated above, a discharge is an involuntary release of a creditor's debt by operation of law. Where the creditor consents to the release, and presumably receives consideration in exchange for that agreement, it has not been forced by virtue of the discharge provisions of the code, to accept less than full value for its claim. . . .

Accordingly, it is not enough for a creditor to abstain from voting for a plan, or even to simply vote "yes" as to a plan. (See *McAteer*, "a creditor's approval of the plan cannot be deemed an act of assent having significance beyond the confines of the bankruptcy proceedings." 985 F.2d at 118). Rather the "validity of the release . . . hinge[s] upon principles of straight contract law or quasi-contract law rather than upon the bankruptcy court's confirmation order." Peter E. Meltzer, Getting out of Jail Free: Can the Bankruptcy Plan Process Be Used to Release Nondebtor Parties?, 71 Am. Bankr. L.J. 1, 40 (1997). Thus, the court must ascertain whether the creditor unambiguously manifested assent to the release of the nondebtor from liability on its debt.

In this case, creditor Delliturri did not vote for the plan and clearly did not manifest any assent to have his claim against John Caglianone released. Accordingly, paragraphs 1.17 and 2.3 of the reorganization plan do not release Mr. Caglianone from any liability he may have had to Mr. Delliturri.

CONCLUSION

For all of the above reasons, this court finds that the court had the subject matter jurisdiction pursuant to 28 U.S.C. §1334(b) to enter relief between nondebtors Stefano Delliturri and John Caglianone. The court did not have the authority, however, to enter a discharge of John Caglianone of all debts against him, as that relief is prohibited by 11 U.S.C. §524(e). The court further finds that Mr. Delliturri did not voluntarily assent to the release of his debt against John Caglianone. Therefore a contractual release was not achieved; and paragraphs 1.17 and 2.3 of the reorganization plan do not operate as a release of his debt. Mr. Delliturri's claim against John Caglianone was not affected by the bankruptcy proceedings.

We met Ivan Kahn earlier as he successfully overcame an objection to the classification of creditors in the reorganization plan of his family's century-old piano business in Dallas. A later portion of the opinion addresses his personal future as the company struggles to survive.

In re BERNHARD STEINER PIANOS USA, INC.
292 B.R. 109 (Bankr. N.D. Tex. 2002) Debtor.

Harlin D. HALE, Bankruptcy Judge.

* * *

B. THE EFFECT OF CONFIRMATION UPON CLAIMS AGAINST THIRD PARTIES: THE REACH OF 11 U.S.C. §524(E)

Textron and Transamerica objected to Plan ¶¶10.03, 10.04 and 12.04 Debtor subsequently modified the Plan in open court on November 20, 2002, by omitting paragraph 10.04 and replacing 10.03 with the following language:

> 10.03 NOTWITHSTANDING ANYTHING CONTAINED HEREIN TO THE CONTRARY, NEITHER DEBTOR, REORGANIZED DEBTOR, THE OFFICERS, GUARANTORS, AND DIRECTORS OF THE DEBTORS NOR THE SHAREHOLDERS SHALL BE DISCHARGED AND RELEASED FROM ANY LIABILITY FOR CLAIMS AND DEBTS UNDER THIS PLAN, HOWEVER, ABSENT FURTHER COURT ORDER UPON NOTICE AND HEARING, THE EXCLUSIVE REMEDY FOR PAYMENT OF ANY CLAIM OR DEBT SO LONG AS THE PLAN IS NOT IN DEFAULT SHALL BE THE PLAN. TO THE EXTENT NECESSARY, ANY APPLICABLE STATUTE OF LIMITATIONS AGAINST COLLECTION FROM ANY THIRD PARTY IS SPECIFICALLY TOLLED FROM THE PERIOD OF TIME FROM THE BANKRUPTCY PETITION DATE UNTIL THE DATE UPON WHICH THE DEBTOR FAILS TO CURE ANY WRITTEN NOTICE OF DEFAULT AS SET FORTH IN THE PLAN.

(Debtor's Plan of Reorganization Dated Sept. 13, 2002 and attached to Order Confirming Debtor's Plan of Reorganization, as Modified at 8-9.) The Confirmation Order provides for a ten day cure period and relief from modified ¶10.3 upon "changed circumstances." (Order Confirming Debtor's Plan of Reorganization, as Modified ¶16.)

Textron and Transamerica are not satisfied with the modification and continue to argue that modified ¶10.3 of the Plan (hereinafter "¶10.3") violates §524(e) to the extent it acts as a release of their claims against Debtor's principal, Kahn.

1. Availability of the Relief Requested

Generally, a plan of reorganization cannot be confirmed if the Plan purports to release guarantors of the debtor's debts and a creditor objects to the release. Paragraph 10.3 specifically states that guarantors are not discharged or released from any liability under the plan. Therefore, on its face, the Plan does not purport to grant a release for third parties, such as Mr. Kahn. Further, nothing in ¶10.3 affects Kahn's ultimate liability under any guaranty agreement. Instead, ¶10.3 merely controls the timing of when a claim, if any, against Kahn, can be brought. And, under the Plan, as modified, the temporary stay could lift upon uncured default under the plan, or upon a change in circumstances for Mr. Kahn, i.e. recovery of the Nigerian Funds. If the Objecting Creditors are not paid under the Plan, they may pursue their guarantor, Mr. Kahn. If his circumstances improve, or if the situation warrants, the Objecting Creditors can seek relief from the stay imposed by the Plan.

On the issue of the effect of confirmation on the claims against third parties, this Court does not write on a clean slate. The Fifth Circuit has held that post-confirmation *permanent injunctions* that effectively release a non-debtor from liability are prohibited. Feld v. Zale Corp. (In re Zale Corp.), 62 F.3d 746, 761 (5th Cir.1995). However, temporary injunctions may be proper under unusual circumstances. These circumstances include (1) when the non-debtor and debtor enjoy such an identity of interest that the suit against the non-debtor is essentially a suit against the debtor, and (2) when the third-party action will have an adverse impact on the debtor's ability to accomplish reorganization. *Id.*

* * *

The *Zale* unusual circumstances test has been met in this case. The success or failure of the Debtor lies mainly, if not exclusively, with the efforts, reputation, and dedication of Mr. Kahn. For all practical purposes, at this time, he is the Debtor. This Debtor will survive and creditors will be paid under the plan only if Mr. Kahn is allowed to conduct the business of the Debtor without distraction. Debtor and Kahn enjoy such an identity of interest that the prosecution of the claims, or attempted collection of any judgments against Kahn would be tantamount to prosecuting and/or seeking collection from the Debtor. Further, Textron and Transamerica's pursuit of judgment or recovery against Kahn individually would have an adverse impact on the successful reorganization of the Debtor.

2. Stay versus Temporary Injunction

Section 362 of the Bankruptcy Code provides for an automatic stay. The §362 automatic stay, however, terminates once the plan is confirmed and the property of the estate vests in the debtor.

It appears that although ¶10.3 is not precisely couched as a temporary injunction it has the effect of one. Thus, the Court must treat ¶10.3 as a temporary injunction and Debtor must meet the evidentiary burden of obtaining an injunction. In order to obtain injunctive relief, the moving party must show: (1) a substantial likelihood that the movant will prevail on the merits; (2) a substantial threat that the movant will suffer irreparable injury if the injunction is not granted; (3) that the threatened injury to the movant outweighs the threatened harm an injunction may cause to the party opposing the injunction; and (4) that the granting of the injunction will not disserve the public interest.

The Court finds that the foregoing factors are met.

The Code gives Debtor the right to attempt reorganization. Debtor has shown that, given the opportunity, it can likely reorganize successfully. The Debtor will suffer irreparable injury, *i.e.*, it will not successfully reorganize, if Transamerica and Textron are permitted to pursue their individual guaranty claims and/or judgments against Kahn, Debtor's largest asset at the outset of Debtor's reorganization. Debtor's inability to reorganize will not only harm Debtor, but also Debtor's creditors since any liquidation in this case would result in little to any recovery for any creditor. The harm to Transamerica and Textron, on the other hand, is simply that they are not being repaid as quickly as they would like. They are free to pursue Kahn on his guaranties in the event Debtor defaults on its Plan payments and the default is not cured within 10 days. At that time, they need only to obtain an order from this Court lifting the "stay" and allowing them to proceed against Kahn directly. The harm to Debtor far outweighs the harm to Transamerica and Textron.

Finally, the granting of a temporary injunction or "stay" does not disserve the public interest. Accordingly, Paragraph 10.3 and the Plan as modified, are approved.

Mass tort cases often involve claims against debtors by thousands of currently unnamed people who will someday discover their injuries and want to sue the responsible party. They may also want to sue others, such as the responsible party's insurance company. So, for example, the Chapter 11 of an asbestos manufacturer may be structured to deal with all of the asbestos claims — both current and future, and to protect both the asbestos manufacturer and its insurance company from further liability in the future. The issues are complex and tangled, but a more sophisticated version of the device used in *Bernhard Steiner Pianos* is put to work in those cases. Trusts are set up, funded by the debtor and the proceeds of the insurance policy, and the claimants — both present and those who come along in the future — are required to seek funding first from the trust. An injunction remains in place to protect both the debtor and the insurance company, while the claimants use a faster claims process for compensation. The approach is referred to as a "channeling injunction," and it suggests that liability may someday in the far distant future come back to rest on the protected party, but most (or all) of the claimants will be paid as the plan prescribes.

d.   Chapter 22

Despite a court's finding of feasibility and the approval of creditors, all too often companies emerge from Chapter 11 only to fail again. In the jargon of the trade, these Chapter 11 repeaters are in "Chapter 22." Data in the Bankruptcy Research Database show that about one in four of the publicly traded companies that confirmed a Chapter 11 plan ended up back in bankruptcy. See http://lopucki.law.ucla.edu. These repeated failures raise a host of difficult legal issues. In particular, the relationship between the earlier case and the new one is often unclear. For example, are contracts assumed in the earlier case entitled to special treatment in the later one? Can a debtor reopen the earlier case so as to maintain previously eschewed preference actions, rather than filing a new case? Would the reopening give debts incurred since the last case administrative priority? As more and more ex–Chapter 11 debtors reenter the marketplace, these issues will continue to multiply. Recently a new group of cases have begun hitting the courts. You guessed it: Chapter 33s.

Aside from these legal questions, these Chapter 22 cases lead to a concern that the courts are finding feasibility where it does not exist. See Stuart Gilson, Transaction Costs and Capital Structure Choice: Evidence from Financially Distressed Firms, 52 J. Fin. 161 (1997). A very interesting article reported that Delaware and the Southern District of New York, which attract a disproportionate number of the largest public company Chapter 11 cases, have substantially higher rates of Chapter 22s than courts elsewhere. Lynn M. LoPucki and Sarah D. Kalin, The Failure of Public Company Bankruptcies in Delaware and New York: Empirical Evidence of a 'Race to the Bottom,' 54 Vanderbilt L. Rev. 231 (2001). The authors speculate that these two jurisdictions approve riskier plans and thus attract filings by debtors who seek approval of plans they know are marginal. It seems at least equally plausible that the debtors are pressured to file in such a jurisdiction by creditors unwilling to accept a sufficient "haircut" to permit the business to survive. Whatever the answer may be, there remains the concern that plans are being approved that leave debtors too burdened with debt to survive. Whether those cases "should have been" resolved by liquidation or by a greater creditor willingness to face reality will have to be the object of further study. We discuss these issues further in the later section on venue.

Problem Set 39

39.1. Suppose in Problem 38.4 neither consumers nor the contractors' association (the NAHHRP) knew of the problem with the home thermostats at the time of UC's Chapter 11 filing. The debtor published a notice of the bankruptcy and the bar date for filing claims in all major newspapers around the country and there were many news stories about the filing as well. A year after confirmation, the NAHHRP discovered the problem with the thermostats. They come to you as counsel to the association asking (a) Can their members sue UC for their damages for replacement of the chips in response to the demands of their customers, the homeowners? (b) Can the homeowners sue the contractors, even if the contractors cannot sue UC? Does either question turn on whether UC knew about the problem? Would it matter if there were some low-key news stories about a possible problem with the thermostats? See §§1141, 523(a)(3), 524.

39.2. You represent RiverMist Homes, Inc., one of the most successful developers in the St. Louis area. The recent dramatic increase in interest rates has virtually shut down the residential market and RiverMist is one of many home builders to file for Chapter 11. Unlike many others, however, RiverMist and its president, Mozambique Evans, have a whole community of devoted lenders and suppliers who believe in its long-term future. You have managed to negotiate a very complex restructuring of the company's debt, with sacrifices from a number of contractors and suppliers and new financing from the Missouri Gold Standard Mortgage Company (MGSMC). The plan of reorganization has been approved by all classes of creditors, but there is a major problem. The plan provides that Evans will put up substantial assets to back the company's obligations under the plan. He is willing to do that, but only if he is released from all his personal guarantees on the pre-bankruptcy debt. Evans has made a lot of money in real estate, but has given much of it to his children and his foundation, and he says, "I'm not willing to risk dying broke." If the plan fails, he will just retire on his large pension fund and other exempt assets. The hearing on confirming the plan is scheduled for next week.

One major creditor, Tiffany Mortgage, voted against the plan. It holds substantial guarantees from Evans. It was recently taken over by Titanic Homes, a major competitor of RiverMist. Neither Thorton Hedgely, president of Titanic, nor his lawyer will return your calls. As the housing recession deepens, MGSMC and the other supporters of the plan are getting very nervous and may head for the exits. Can you do anything to get a reorganization plan confirmed?

39.3. Evelyn Brewer of the Missing Children Foundation called you this morning in shock. The foundation has been sued by Morris Mangle, the former president of Associated Fundraisers (AF), for return of money the foundation had received from AF. AF was a company that raised money for charities by telephone solicitations until it went into Chapter 11 last year. The reorganization failed and converted into a Chapter 7. Evelyn explains that the foundation was paid $35,000 by AF about a month before AF's Chapter 11 filing. The money had been owed for nine months after completion of a successful money-raising campaign by AF for the foundation. "I only got it by threatening to go to the newspapers and I was so relieved after the bankruptcy that we were out of it and didn't have to make a claim," Evelyn told you. A phone call to one of the lawyers involved in the case has gotten you the explanation for the lawsuit: Mangle made a deal with the Chapter 7 trustee that he would pay the trustee $10,000 in return for an assignment of all the preference and fraudulent conveyance actions the estate might have. The TIB distributed the money, net of her fee, to the creditors who had filed claims and closed the case. As a result of the deal, Mangle not only keeps whatever he can get, but now doesn't have to worry about being sued for the real estate he transferred from AF to his daughter Susan six months before the bankruptcy. What can you do for the foundation?

F. ETHICAL ISSUES

1. *Compensation and Disclosure*

We have considered a number of issues important both to the academic study of bankruptcy and to preparation for a bankruptcy practice. It would be misleading, however, to conclude that the essential elements of managing a business reorganization could be raised without some careful attention to the ethical aspects of representing parties in Chapter 11 proceedings. An understanding of these issues, many of which are not raised directly in the Code, is essential both theoretically and practically.

Ethical issues in Chapter 11 (including lawyer compensation) are sufficiently complex to merit separate study. Bankruptcy practice raises many of the same ethical issues as any complex legal negotiation process, but some factors make the bankruptcy practice more heavily littered with hidden snares. Chapter 11 practice is fast-moving, and delayed decisions often mean a significant change in legal position — and in the likelihood that the business will survive or a debt will be repaid. Chapter 11 negotiations take place in a dynamic, multiparty environment in which parties with similar interests often combine to share strategies and support, only to find that a slight shift in circumstances makes them intensely competitive adversaries. Parties initiate negotiations with a blend of hard facts, shrewd guesses, and unfounded hopes; the progress of negotiations may take them closer to or further from reality. Moreover, negotiation always takes place directly in the shadow of the courthouse. Once a business is in Chapter 11, the negotiations in the halls and the representations and requests in court begin to interact in ways matched in few other areas of the law.

One of the first differences an attorney representing a debtor in bankruptcy notices is that the court has a much more active role in supervising the attorney-client relationship than it does in ordinary litigation. The attorney represents a new legal entity — the DIP — and court supervision of the attorney is closely akin to supervision of attorneys of decedent's estates and of minors.

Every attorney representing a debtor in bankruptcy is, of course, subject to all the canons and rules of ethics applicable to the legal profession. Back in the discussion of consumer bankruptcy we explored the special obligations imposed on attorneys when they advise assisted persons (consumer debtors with property valued at less than $150,000) and certain constraints in the advice attorneys may give to consumers. See pages 166. In addition, we pause to note the provision of the Bankruptcy Code that may be most shocking to consumer attorneys: Section 330 excludes any compensation from the estate for the debtor's attorney. Lawyers were so surprised by this 1994 Amendment to the Bankruptcy Code that the argument went all the way to the Supreme Court, which promptly said, in effect, "Yup, that's what the statute says." In re Lamie, 540 U.S. 526 (2004). For attorneys representing individuals in small bankruptcies the provision forced them to demand payment up front — although that was a practice that prudence may have already required. But counsel to DIPs and TIBs escaped with their access to payment intact (note the restriction was only on debtor's counsel, not DIP's counsel), so the furor over *Lamie* mostly bypassed the business bankruptcy bar.

In this section, we focus on the role of the attorney in a business setting, typically as counsel to the DIP. The Bankruptcy Code requires that counsel can serve only with court approval (§327(a)), that counsel's fees be approved by the court (§§328(a), 329(b), 330(a)), that only "disinterested persons" may serve as counsel (§327(a)), and that the representation and fee arrangements must be disclosed to the court and creditors (§329(a)). These statutory provisions are not explicitly limited to business cases, but they take on a new importance on the business side that is rarely found in smaller consumer cases.

In the following case, Judge Bufford reviews the appointment of the debtor's choice of counsel.

=================== In re LEE ===================
94 B.R. 172 (Bankr. CD. Cal. 1989)

AMENDED OPINION DENYING APPOINTMENT OF COUNSEL
Samuel L. BUFFORD, Bankruptcy Judge.

I.   FACTS

Debtors Chile B. Lee and Hae Sook Lee filed this voluntary Chapter 11 bankruptcy case on August 23, 1988. They are apparently the sole shareholders of Seoul Corporation, whose Chapter 11 bankruptcy case was filed in this Court on August 16, 1988. Seoul Corporation is engaged in the sale of general merchandise and costume jewelry at wholesale. Chile Lee is the president and Hae Sook Lee is the secretary of Seoul Corporation. Presumably the debtors are also the only directors of Seoul Corporation, although this is not disclosed in the papers filed with the Court. Both of the petitions were signed by Jang W. Lee, as counsel for debtors.

A brief review of the schedules filed by the Lees and Seoul Corporation discloses that there is a substantial overlap of creditors for the individuals and for the corporation. However, it appears that a number of creditors are not shared.

The debtors in each case have filed an application for the appointment of the law firm Lee, Scott & Young ("LSY"), in which Jang W. Lee is a partner, as general counsel for the debtors, pursuant to Bankruptcy Code §327.

Jang W. Lee states that he has received a retainer of $2,500 to represent Chile B. Lee and his wife in this case, and that he has received no retainer for representing Seoul Corporation. However, the retainer is not disclosed in the employment application in this case.

The employment applications also make no disclosure whatever of the relationship between these two cases, or that LSY is seeking employment in both of them, notwithstanding the conflicts that such employment could raise. The declaration of Jang W. Lee in the employment application in each case states:

1. To the best of my knowledge, I am not connected with the debtors, their creditors, or any other party in interest except I am the attorney for the debtors in this Chapter 11 case. . . .
2. No member or associate of this law firm represents any interest in this estate, adverse or otherwise, except the interest of the applicants.

The parallel applications for appointment as legal counsel came to the Court's attention because they arrived in chambers and were reviewed on the same day. If this had not occurred, the problem would likely not have come to the Court's attention.

After noting the similar employment applications in the two cases, the Court obtained and reviewed the respective bankruptcy case files and thus learned of the conflicting interests that LSY seeks to represent. The Court then issued an order to show cause why LSY should not be disqualified in both cases because of its failure to disclose the parallel employment applications. In response to the order to show cause, LSY disclosed for the first time its retainer in this case.

II.   ANALYSIS

This is not an isolated instance of a potential conflict in interest by prospective counsel for related debtors. This Court has received similar applications for appointment as counsel for related debtors from many law firms in Los Angeles that represent bankruptcy debtors.

The failure to disclose the potential conflict is also not an isolated instance. In this Court's experience, prospective counsel infrequently discloses that appointment is sought in a related case.

This is also not an isolated instance of the failure to disclose in an employment application the amount or source of a retainer. Many applications for employment do not disclose the receipt of a retainer, and few disclose the source of such funds. However, the Court has reason to believe that retainers are quite common in bankruptcy cases in this district.

A.   *Retainer*

The obligation to disclose a retainer is based on Bankruptcy Rule 2014(a). . . . The application in this case clearly does not comply with Rule 2014, because it does not disclose the retainer of $2,500. Thus it fails to set forth part of applicant's proposed arrangement for compensation.

The requirement to disclose "any proposed arrangement for compensation" includes a requirement to disclose any retainer received by or promised to the applicant. . . .

LSY's application is totally silent as to the retainer agreement. Thus it fails altogether to make the required disclosure. The retainer agreement was disclosed only in response to the order to show cause.

B.   Parallel Employment Applications

LSY's parallel employment applications in this case and in the *Seoul Corporation* case raise two problems. First, the failure to disclose the parallel applications is a violation of Rule 2014(a). Second, appointment of LSY in both cases would result in its representation of conflicting interests, which is prohibited.

1.   Non-Disclosure

LSY's failure to disclose its application to represent Seoul Corporation is also a violation of Rule 2014(a). Rule 2014(a) requires the disclosure in an application for employment of "all the [applicant's] connections with . . . any other party in interest. . . ." Disclosure is required of any application to represent more than one related party, including the representation of debtors in related cases. All facts that may be relevant to a determination of whether an attorney is disinterested or holds or represents an interest adverse to the debtor's estate must be disclosed.

The purpose of such disclosure is to permit the Court and parties in interest to determine whether the connection disqualifies the applicant from the employment sought, or whether further inquiry should be made before deciding whether to approve the employment. This decision should not be left to counsel, whose judgment may be clouded by the benefits of the potential employment.

It appears to the Court that such nondisclosure usually results from an intentional effort to prevent the Court from noticing that counsel is seeking appointment in related cases that may raise conflicts of interest. Thus in most if not all cases the deception is deliberate.

The failure to disclose the employment application in a related case is alone a sufficient basis for disqualifying counsel in both cases. While the Court does not impose total disqualification in this case, it will not hesitate to disqualify counsel in the future in all related cases, or to impose other appropriate sanctions, for similar nondisclosure.

2.   LSY's Adverse Interests

LSY does not meet the requirements of Bankruptcy Code §327(a), for the appointment of attorneys in both of these cases. Section 327(a) authorizes a trustee to employ "one or more attorneys . . . that do not hold or represent an interest adverse to the estate, and that are disinterested persons. . . ." Section 1107(a) gives a debtor in possession the rights and powers of a trustee (with certain exceptions not material here), including the power to employ attorneys.

Section 327 requires the application of a two-pronged test for the employment of professional persons. A debtor in possession or trustee may employ attorneys with court approval only if (1) they do not hold or represent an interest adverse to the estate, and (2) they are disinterested persons.

Both prongs of this test must be met. LSY fails to meet the first of these requirements.

The term "adverse interest" is not specifically defined in the Bankruptcy Code. The reported cases have defined what it means to hold an adverse interest as follows:

(1) to possess or assert any economic interest that would tend to lessen the value of the bankrupt estate or that would create either an actual or potential dispute in which the estate is a rival claimant; or

(2) to possess a predisposition under circumstances that render such a bias against the estate.

To "represent an adverse interest" means to serve as agent or attorney for entities holding such adverse interests. . . .

Seoul Corporation has an interest adverse to the estate of the debtors in this case because, according to the schedules filed in the respective cases, there is joint liability on many of the debts owing by the respective estates. Thus it is in the interest of Seoul Corporation, as debtor in possession, to have these debts paid by the estate of the Lees. In contrast, it is in the interest of the debtors in this case to have Seoul Corporation's estate pay these debts. If LSY is appointed to represent the debtors in both cases, it will be representing these conflicting interests. . . .

3. Counsel's Response

Jang W. Lee contends that the representation of the debtors in the two cases does not involve the representation of conflicting interests, because Seoul Corporation is not a creditor of Chile B. Lee, and Lee is willing to waive any claims he has against the corporation.

First, Chile B. Lee does not have the power unilaterally to waive a claim of his estate against the corporation. The filing of a bankruptcy case creates an estate, which includes all legal and equitable interests of the debtor in property as of the commencement of the case. Bankruptcy Code §541. This property includes all causes of action that belong to the debtor on the date of filing. Thus any claim available to Chile B. Lee against the Seoul Corporation belongs to his estate, and presumptively to his creditors. As a debtor in possession he has a fiduciary duty to assert any such claim on their behalf. The filing of the bankruptcy case terminated his power unilaterally to waive claims, including any claims that he may have against Seoul Corporation.

Second, it is too early to determine whether Seoul Corporation has any claim against Chile B. Lee, its shareholder and president (and presumably also a director). Careful scrutiny of Chile B. Lee's actions as a shareholder, director and officer is necessary before such a determination can be made. The financial status of the corporation makes it quite likely that such a claim may be available to the corporation.

Third, inter-debtor claims are not the only grounds for conflicts of interest. Substantive consolidation, for example, which is a possibility in this case, is another issue where the lack of separate counsel for related debtors may cause substantial harm because of conflicts of interest. LSY simply ignores the many other ways in which conflicting interests may arise, including those in this case, that preclude multiple representation.

Fourth, and most important . . . in this case LSY has been dishonest and has hidden the conflict from the Court. This fact alone justifies the disqual-ification of LSY as counsel in both cases. . . .

LSY also pleads that the debtors in these two cases cannot afford sepa-rate counsel. This rationale has often been used in the past to justify the appointment of counsel to represent related debtors. However, lack of financial resources is no justification for representing conflicting interests.

Lack of financial resources is often a reason for waiving a conflict of interest. Rule 5-102 permits an attorney to represent conflicting interests upon the written consent of all parties concerned. An attorney who desires to represent a debtor in possession and a conflicting interest must obtain a written waiver from the debtor, all creditors and the United States trustee. No such waiver has been offered in this case. . . .

IV. CONCLUSION

The Court has the power to disqualify counsel in both of these cases, on each of the following grounds: (1) failure to disclose the retainer; (2) failure to disclose the parallel employment applications; (3) the attempt to repre-sent debtors with interests in actual conflict. However, because the trans-gressions in this case are commonly shared by the bar in this district, the Court declines to impose this drastic remedy on LSY. Instead, the Court exercises its discretion in this case to deny appointment in one case, and to permit LSY to represent the other debtor. However, the Court will not hesitate to impose stiffer sanctions in the future for the violation of these standards.

Counsel has informed the Court that LSY prefers that employment be authorized in the *Seoul Corporation* case, if it is not authorized for both cases. The court will so order.

In the next case, the bankruptcy court disqualified the law firm and denied all compensation. The bankruptcy court opinion is based largely on findings of fact that revealed conflicts of interest and attorney nondisclo-sure. Note that the latter ground alone would have been sufficient in itself for disqualification, but Judge Hillman had more to say. Note also that this sort of nightmare is not limited to small and obscure law firms. The largest and best-regarded firms in the country face the same risks, every day.

In re FILENE'S BASEMENT, INC.
239 B.R. 850 (Bankr. D. Mass. 1999)

William C. HILLMAN, Chief Judge.

I. INTRODUCTION

On August 23, 1999, Filene's Basement, Inc. and Filene's Basement Corp. (the "Debtors") filed voluntary chapter 11 petitions. Accompanying the petitions (which I subsequently ruled would be jointly administered) were applications to employ Attorney Paul P. Daley ("Daley") and the law firm of Hale and Dorr LLP ("H & D" or "the Firm") which I allowed on August 24, 1999. On September 3, 1999, T.A.C. Group, Inc. ("T.A.C.") filed a motion for reconsideration of the appointment of H & D as Debtors' counsel (the "Motion"). In it, T.A.C. alleges that H & D is not a disinterested person as required under the Bankruptcy Code, has a conflict of interest due to representation of T.A.C., and holds interests potentially adverse to the Debtors' estate. . . .

. . . For the reasons stated below, I grant the motion for reconsideration and vacate the prior order appointing H & D as counsel to the Debtor and deny the application to employ.

II. FACTUAL ASSERTIONS

Daley's Rule 2014(a) statement (the "Statement") accompanying the application seeking employment of H & D (called "the Firm" in the Statement) contained the following averments:

> 2. Neither I, the Firm, nor any partner, counsel or associate thereof, insofar as I have been able to ascertain, holds or represents any interest adverse to the estate of [the Debtors].
>
> 3. I have caused the Firm to compare the Debtors' list of their 20 largest unsecured creditors, the Debtors' secured lenders, the Debtors' landlords, and list of officers, directors and 5% shareholders, with the Firm's client database to identify creditors or shareholders with which the Firm has any connection and made reasonable inquiry regarding whether any partners or employees of the Firm own any equity interest in the Debtors. Such comparisons, searches and inquiries have revealed the following:
>
>> a. The Firm has represented the Debtor prepetition, since July 1998, as its general counsel in connection with various corporate, litigation and other matters as specifically assigned by the Debtors. The Firm has been paid currently for all services rendered.
>>
>> b. Certain creditors (or affiliates thereof), shareholders and individuals are clients of the Firm as revealed during the inquiries described in Section 2 [sic]. Attached hereto as Exhibit A is a listing of the clients and a description of the Firm's services to such clients.[1] The billings to any one client or the aggregate group is not material to the Firm's

---

1. Surprisingly, T.A.C. does not appear on Exhibit A.

revenues. Individually, no client represented more than 1% of the Firm's total billings, and the aggregate group represented less than 1.1% of the total billings, of the Firm for calendar year 1998.

c.   The Firm has and continues to represent T.A.C. Group, Inc. ("T.A.C.") in connection with discrete financing and corporate matters entirely unrelated to the Debtors. T.A.C. is a plaintiff in a lawsuit naming the Debtors as defendants. The Firm does not represent either party in such lawsuit and will not provide representation to T.A.C. in connection with any matters or dealings in these Chapter 11 cases.

The litigation between T.A.C. and the Debtors described in the Statement (the "State Court Action") also names as a defendant James McGowan ("McGowan"), a former president of T.A.C. and present vice president of the Debtors. In the Motion, T.A.C. describes the litigation, and H & D's involvement with its subject matter as follows:

In the State Court Action, which arises out of the Debtor's employment of McGowan, T.A.C. alleges harm caused by the Debtor's and McGowan's use of T.A.C.'s trade secrets and confidential business information in violation of, among other things, a confidentiality and nondisclosure agreement drafted by Hale and Dorr in its capacity as General counsel to T.A.C.

T.A.C. further describes its relationship with H & D in this way:

6.   Hale and Dorr has been T.A.C.'s general counsel for approximately 18 years. In fact, with a few exceptions, Hale and Dorr represents T.A.C. on all of its legal matters, including real estate, corporate, financing, labor and employment, trademark, and intellectual property matters. T.A.C. relies on Hale and Dorr not simply to handle discrete assignment [sic] that T.A.C. assigns to it, but many of the matters that Hale and Dorr handles for T.A.C. are of an ongoing nature and have been ongoing for many years. T.A.C. relies on Hale and Dorr to alert T.A.C. to legal issues affecting T.A.C.'s business and to bring legal problems to T.A.C.'s attention on the many ongoing matters that Hale and Dorr handles. Thirty-four Hale and Dorr lawyers, and 23 other time charging professionals at Hale and Dorr, have done legal work for T.A.C. in the last three years alone. As set forth in the Doxer Affidavit [q.v.], by any measure, T.A.C. is a substantial client of Hale and Dorr.

7.   At least one Hale and Dorr attorney who has appeared for the Debtors in this case, Mitchel Appelbaum, is working for T.A.C. on an on-going bank financing matter and TAC [sic] anticipates that it will need to continue to use Mr. Appelbaum on this matter.

8.   Hale and Dorr represented T.A.C. in connection with the termination of McGowan's employment. Without T.A.C.'s

knowledge or consent, Hale and Dorr also represented the Debtor in connection with the Debtor's later hiring of McGowan, which gave rise to T.A.C.'s litigation against the Debtor. Indeed, as set forth in the Doxer Affidavit, Hale and Dorr was negotiating the Debtor's employment agreement with McGowan while McGowan was still on T.A.C's payroll under an agreement that Hale and dorr [sic] negotiated for T.A.C. . . .

10. Three Hale and Dorr senior partners have been deposition witnesses and will be trial witnesses in T.A.C.'s lawsuit against Debtor, offering testimony that will impeach statements made under oath by officers of the Debtor.

In response to these allegations, H & D tendered these rejoinders:

6. Hale and Dorr has represented TAC in various matters beginning about 1981. Hale and Dorr denies that it has been TAC's "general counsel" for 18 years: denies that is [sic] represents TAC on all its legal matters and admits that it handles discrete legal assignments from TAC, some of which may be "ongoing" in the sense that follow-on work may be needed. Hale and Dorr has not been retained as "general counsel" by TAC nor has Hale and Dorr been engaged to alert TAC to legal issues affecting TAC's business or to bring legal problems to TAC's attention, except for issues arising in a specific assignment about which TAC seeks legal advice.

Hale and Dorr admits that a number of lawyers and paralegals have done legal work for TAC in the last three years, but only four lawyers and one paralegal worked an average of 17 hours or more a year for TAC during that three-year period. TAC's billings, over both the 18-year period (which totaled not the $2,000,000 to $3,000,000 alleged by Mr. Doxer but $1,510,045) and the last three years, average less than 0.1 % of Hale and Dorr's annual billings. Hale and Dorr denies that TAC is a "substantial client" as that term would normally be used by lawyers evaluating the importance of a given corporate client to a firm.

The Debtors further state that in each of the last several years (including 1999), TAC requested that Hale and Dorr furnish its auditor an audit letter. In each audit letter, Hale and Dorr responded to TAC's auditor that it did not represent TAC on a regular basis and that its engagement was limited to specific matters as to which Hale and Dorr was consulted by TAC, i.e., a special counsel not a general counsel audit letter. Mr. Doxer received a copy of each audit letter. Copies of the audit letters in redacted form for the years 1994-1999 are attached to the Affidavit of Mitchel Appelbaum as Exhibit A.

7. Mr. Appelbaum worked for TAC on bank financing documents prior to August 11, 1999. Since that date he has done no work for TAC. He commenced work for Debtors on August

16, 1999. At no time did he work on TAC's and Debtors' matters simultaneously. TAC's loan documentation matter on which Mr. Appelbaum worked has nothing to do with the Debtors or these proceedings. Hale and Dorr denies the remaining allegations in paragraph 7.

8.   Hale and Dorr drafted Mr. McGowan's severance agreement dated June 19, 1999. Subsequent to the signing of that agreement, Hale and Dorr was asked by Debtors to draft an employment agreement with Mr. McGowan and drafts were exchanged with Mr. McGowan's counsel. The terms were negotiated by the Debtors and Mr. McGowan. Hale and Dorr did not advise the Debtors with respect to Mr. McGowan's severance agreement with TAC, his post-severance obligations, if any, to TAC, or his status, if any, on or off TAC's payroll. Mr. McGowan's severance agreement, which Debtors were provided by Mr. McGowan, had no non-competition clause, a fact obvious from the document and independently known to Debtors. Ultimately, Mr. McGowan's severance agreement was an Exhibit to Mr. McGowan's employment contract with Debtors. Hale and Dorr denies the remaining allegations in paragraph 8.

9.   Hale and Dorr agrees that it was unable to represent either TAC or the Debtor in the State Court Action and asserts that each party obtained separate counsel. Hale and Dorr denies that there is any conflict preventing Hale and Dorr from vigorously representing the Debtors in these proceedings. Hale and Dorr denies that the existing TAC/Filene's State Court Action is a conflict preventing Hale and Dorr from representing Debtors. Mintz, Levin has been retained to and will litigate that claim on behalf of the Debtors and Hale and Dorr has no conflict.

10. Three senior partners of Hale and Dorr were deposition witnesses in the State Court Action. Hale and Dorr has not been informed by either party that those three partners will be witnesses in the litigation and does not believe they will be witnesses. If they were to be called as witnesses (which is entirely speculative at this point) they would merely be fact witnesses and the weight and impact of their testimony as fact witnesses were to be given [sic], it would not be hostile or adverse to either party but a recitation of facts to be weighed and evaluated by the trier of fact. Hale and Dorr denies the remaining allegations in paragraph 10.

III.   Discussion

A.   *The Disclosure Requirements of 11 U.S.C. §327(a) and Fed. R. Bankr. P. 2014*

The Bankruptcy Code allows a trustee to retain professionals, subject to court approval, "that do not hold or represent an interest adverse to the estate, and that are disinterested persons, to represent or assist the trustee in carrying out the trustee's duties under this title." 11 U.S.C. §327(a). As the Court of Appeals for the First Circuit has observed, the thrust of §327 is to "ensure that all professionals appointed pursuant to §327(a) tender undivided loyalty and provide untainted advice and assistance in furtherance of their fiduciary responsibilities." Rome v. Braunstein, 19 F.3d 54, 57 (1st Cir. 1994).

The Federal Rules of Bankruptcy Procedure require that an applicant file a verified statement disclosing "the person's connections with the debtor, creditors, any other party in interest, their respective attorneys and accountants, the United States trustee, or any person employed in the office of the United States trustee." Fed. R. Bankr. P. 2014(a) passim. "The purpose of the disclosure requirements is to provide the court with information necessary to determine whether the professional's employment meets the broad test of being in the best interests of the estate." In re Lincoln North Assoc., 155 B.R. 804, 807 (Bankr. D. Mass. 1993).

It has been held that the requirements of the rule transcend those of §327(a), as they mandate disclosure of all connections with the named parties, rather than being limited to those which deal with disinterestedness. Failure to be forthcoming with disclosure provides the bankruptcy court with an independent ground for disqualification.

The Statement revealed that H & D "has [represented] and continues to represent T.A.C. Group, Inc. ("T.A.C.") in connection with discrete financing and corporate matters entirely unrelated to the Debtors." The Motion and the Firm's response thereto demonstrate a continuing relationship over 18 years, resulting in the payment by T.A.C. to the Firm of over $1,500,000 in fees,[2] although it denies T.A.C.'s contention that it serves as its general counsel.

More troublesome is the Firm's description of the litigation between T.A.C. and the Debtors, which appears above, but which I repeat here for convenience:

> T.A.C. is a plaintiff in a lawsuit naming the Debtors as defendants. The Firm does not represent either party in such lawsuit and will not provide representation to T.A.C. in connection with any matters or dealings in these Chapter 11 cases.

"[C]oy or incomplete disclosures which leave the court to ferret out pertinent information from other sources are not sufficient." In re Saturley, 131 B.R. 509, 517 (Bankr. D. Me. 1991). I now know that the litigation involves McGowan, once president of T.A.C. and now an officer of Debtors, and that the plaintiff asserts violation by McGowan and the Debtors of certain rights of T.A.C. I further have been made aware that H & D represented T.A.C. in connection with the termination of McGowan's employment; that it represented the Debtors in connection with the hiring of McGowan; and that three partners in the Firm have given depositions in connection with the

---

2. Since this is less than 1/10 of 1% of the Firm's annual billings in recent years, it does not consider T.A.C. a "substantial client."

litigation. T.A.C.'s contention is that the three partners will be called as witnesses and will give testimony questioning the veracity of statements by officers of the Debtors. The Firm's rejoinder, that the attorneys would merely recite facts if called as witnesses, strikes me as a bit disingenuous.

Other facts not disclosed in the Statement include the fact that T.A.C. is a competitor of the Debtors and that the Debtor's business plan calls for it to open a series of stores strikingly similar in concept to T.A.C.'s operations. The mere fact of competition between two clients is not disqualifying where the two parties do not hold or assert claims against each other and do not "assert competing claims to an economic interest." In re Caldor, Inc., 193 B.R. 165, 171 (Bankr. S.D.N.Y. 1996). This case contains additional disqualifying elements.

Based upon the matters quoted and cited above, I conclude that the Statement fails to satisfy the Firm's obligation to make full disclosure of connections with parties in interest as required by the rule. This could, under the authorities cited above, result in disqualification or fee reduction.

B.   The Disinterested and Lack of Interest Adverse Requirements of 11 U.S.C. §327(a) and Fed. R. Bankr. P. 2014

The First Circuit observed in *Rome* that the Bankruptcy Code requires "rigorous conflict-of-interest restraints upon the employment of professional persons in a bankruptcy case." *Rome*, 19 F.3d at 57. The Code does not define "adverse interest." In *Rome* the First Circuit described "interest adverse" as the "possess[ion] or assert[ion] [of] mutually exclusive claims to the same economic interest, thus creating either an actual or potential dispute between rival claimants as to which . . . of them the disputed right or title to the interest in question attaches under valid and applicable law; or (2) [the possession of] a predisposition or interest under circumstances that render such a bias in favor of or against one of the entities." *Rome*, 19 F.3d at 58 n.l (quoting In re Roberts, 46 B.R. 815, 826-27 (Bankr. D. Utah 1985)). The term "interest adverse to the estate" may in fact be broader than it appears. In *Granite Partners*, the Bankruptcy Court for the Southern District of New York found that "adverse interest" pertains to "any interest, however slight, 'that would even faintly color the independence and impartial attitude required by the Code and Bankruptcy Rules.'" See In re Granite Partners, 219 B.R. at 33 (quoting In re Roberts, 46 B.R. at 828 n.26).

The Code defines "disinterested person" as including any person that "does not have an interest materially adverse to the interest of the estate or of any class of creditor or equity security holders, by reason of any direct or indirect relationship to, connection with, or interest in, the debtor. . . ." U.S.C. §101(14)(E).

By its terms, §327 appears to envision a two prong analysis of "adverse interest" and "disinterestedness," but the courts have observed that such an approach is redundant. *Martin* at 175, 179 n.4; In re Granite Partners, 219 B.R. at 33. Many courts, including the First Circuit, have favored a single determination of "whether any competing interest of a court-appointed professional 'created a meaningful incentive to act contrary to the best interest of the estate and its sundry creditors — an incentive sufficient to place those parties at more than acceptable risk — or the reasonable perception of one.'" *Rome*, 19 F.3d at 58 (quoting *Martin*, 817 F.2d at 180). While combining the stated two elements into one, the *Martin* formulation enunciates the long-standing additional test relating to the appearance of impropriety; that is, even if there is not in fact a competing interest of the type described above, if there is a reasonable perception of such an interest, the applicant should be disqualified. "Section 327 is intended . . . to address the appearance of impropriety as much as its substance. . . ." *Martin* at 180.

1.   Actual Conflict of Interest

Stated most simplistically, the Firm is regularly engaged by T.A.C. to handle legal matters of various kinds, and has been for almost a score of years. T.A.C. is now engaged in litigation against the Debtors, whom H & D serves as general counsel. While it is true that the Firm is technically aloof from the conflict, in that it represents neither of the antagonists, it is a part of the proceedings, as the litigation will involve contracts drawn by H & D for both sides; the interpretation of those contracts; and possible testimony of partners in the Firm regarding various related matters. Further, the chief executive officer of the Debtors has testified that the Debtors' business plan is based in large part on the establishment of stores which adopt the techniques used by T.A.C. One obvious purpose of the litigation is to retard Debtors' learning curve in this regard.

Under these circumstances, I find that there is an actual adverse interest in the Firm's continued representation of T.A.C. while it seeks to represent the Debtors. When there is an actual conflict of interest, disqualification is mandatory.

2.   Perception of Conflict

Even if I were to determine that the conflict is not yet ripe, but merely incipient; that I do not know the outcome of the State Court Action nor the extent to which that outcome may affect the possibility of success for Debtors' plan or reorganization, I would nonetheless hold that there is an obvious appearance of impropriety in the dual representation.

Consider hypothetically things which might occur: If the Debtors prevail in the State Court Action because of the content of the agreement whereby McGowan's employment by T.A.C. was terminated, T.A.C. might feel compelled to bring a malpractice action against the Firm. Contrawise, if the final result should be success for T.A.C., with Debtors held liable because of their employment of McGowan, it might be the debtors who seek indemnity from H & D because it was upon the Firm's advice that it entered into an employment contract with McGowan. If T.A.C. should be awarded large amounts of damages, payment might adversely affect the feasibility of any plan Debtors might propose, and on whose lap would the blame be laid? If Debtors should be enjoined from utilizing the services of McGowan, and those services should be critical to the reorganization, where might the finger of blame be pointed? If Debtors' reorganization should fail, would this benefit the Firm in its ongoing representation of T.A.C.?

Even if there is no present adverse interest, both the potential for a conflict and the perception that there might be such are clear to me. A potential conflict constitutes a ground for disqualification under §327. *First Jersey Securities*, supra.

IV.   Conclusion

I hold that H & D has failed fully to disclose its connections with parties in interest as required by Rule 2014 and that it lacks disinterestedness in this case either because of an actual present adverse interest or the appearance of one.

The First Circuit has most correctly noted, in considering the sanction to be imposed, that "the bankruptcy court cannot always assess with precision the effect the conflict may have had either on the results achieved or the results that might have been achieved by following 'the road not taken.'" *Rome*, 19 F.3d at 62. It is early in this case. A change of counsel at this point, while inconvenient, will eliminate more serious problems down the path. As a result, I grant the motion for reconsideration and vacate my prior order. Writing anew, I deny the Debtors' application to employ H & D, and direct that the retainer paid be returned to the Debtors forthwith. H & D may file an application for reimbursement of actual and necessary expenses which it has incurred.

═══════════════

It is important to focus on the fact that the law firm in the preceding case got into a serious tangle between long-term clients in litigation even before the bankruptcy filing. The bankruptcy process exposed a problem that existed even without the bankruptcy, but in the context of creditor interests and heightened disclosure obligations, the problem exploded.

In one sense, the firm in the preceding case was lucky: The problem surfaced and was resolved early in the case. In other cases, the firms have poured in thousands of hours when the conflict finally comes to light, forcing them to disgorge millions in fees. E.g., In re Keller Financial Services of Florida, Inc., 248 B.R. 859 (Bankr. M.D. Fla. 2000).

A theme that arises again and again in these cases is the problem of retaining a debtor's long-time general counsel as its bankruptcy counsel. If the lawyer has sat on the company's board of directors and suits might be filed against the directors, or if the firm is owed large amounts of money for fees at the time of bankruptcy, the courts may well find the firm disqualified as bankruptcy counsel. In that case, the company may be forced to educate new counsel in complex operations and pending lawsuits just at the moment of extreme financial emergency. Balancing competing policy interests in this context is excruciating.

In the following case the conflict addressed by the court is even more central to the attorney-client relationship — and virtually impossible to avoid in any case. *Martin* raises a conflict that is so central to the attorney-client relationship everywhere that it is largely unseen: the conflict over payment. Attorneys want to be paid and clients would like to pay less or not at all. Like nearly all conflicts, this one can heat up with surprising speed in a bankruptcy. Clients may not be able to pay as the bills are presented, and attorneys are often struggling to work out a way that will compensate them for their time without pushing the debtor over a financial cliff.

In the following case, the attorney tried to deal with the problem of adequate assurance of future payment by doing what many other businesses do at the inception of a business relationship: take a security interest to ensure future payments. That may be fine for a bank or a supplier, but is it acceptable for a lawyer?

═══ In re MARTIN ═══
817 F.2d 175 (1st Cir. 1987)

SELYA, Circuit Judge.

This case deals with the right of a lawyer, preliminary to submitting a client's petition under chapter 11 of the 1978 Bankruptcy Code (Code), to take security for the payment of attorneys' fees to be incurred while representing the client in connection with the bankruptcy proceedings. It likewise inevitably deals with the propriety of such an act. Apropos of the central point at issue, directly pertinent precedent ranges from slim to none. So, we write on what amounts to a clean slate.

I.   BACKGROUND

On November 27, 1984, Larry T. Martin and Cynthia J. Martin, then husband and wife, sought the advice of Verrill & Dana (V & D), a law firm. The chief reason for the consultation was that the Martins found themselves in precarious financial straits because of the poor performance of their restaurant business. The outcome of this and a subsequent meeting was the debtors' election to file a chapter 11 petition to reorganize the business in bankruptcy court. But, they were unable to muster sufficient ready cash to pay V & D the $5000 retainer which the law firm demanded.

A bargain was struck between lawyers and clients whereby the Martins invested a mere $500 in a cash retainer and signed an open-ended demand note (Note) payable to V & D for $100,000. The Note provided for the payment of all indebtedness of the makers to the payee existing prior to (or created simultaneously with) execution and delivery, as well as all indebtedness to be incurred *in futuro* by reason of legal services to be rendered. The Note was secured by a second mortgage (Mortgage) on certain improved real estate owned by the debtors, located at 258 Summit St., Portland, Maine. These premises were used neither as the debtors' principal residence nor for any business purpose associated with the running of the restaurant. According to their counsel, the land and buildings on Summit St. comprised property which the debtors did not intend to liquidate in the anticipated course of the chapter 11 reorganization. The bankruptcy court found that the debtors "enjoyed a substantial equity" in this real estate.

On December 11, 1984, not by coincidence, two events occurred: the Mortgage was recorded and V & D escorted Mr. and Mrs. Martin through the portals of chapter 11. Acting through the attorneys, the petitioners then sought permission from the bankruptcy court to employ V & D to represent them as debtors in possession. The application made a clean breast of the terms and conditions of the retainer and the other accoutrements of the fee arrangement as required by Bankruptcy Rule 2016(b). The particulars of the Note and Mortgage were revealed fully. On December 14, 1984, the bankruptcy court issued an order (Engagement Order) authorizing the employment of counsel "under general retainer of $500 at . . . usual hourly rates." The court did not mention the Note or Mortgage at that time. And, V & D proceeded to undertake the assignment without any reiteration to the bankruptcy judge of the request that the Mortgage be sanctioned.

The debtors' flirtation with chapter 11 was short-lived. Within six months, they voluntarily converted the action to a straight bankruptcy proceeding under chapter 7 of the Code. A trustee was appointed. Then, a flurry of activity took place as the parties in interest struggled to wind up the aborted chapter 11 case and to process the neoteric chapter 7 case. Among other things, V & D applied for interim fees anent the services it had rendered. The trustee, apparently believing that the Summit St. property was bereft of equity (if one counted the Mortgage as value), sought permission to abandon it. The creditors' committee objected.

The bankruptcy court found that the Mortgage constituted an interest adverse to the bankrupts' estate. Accordingly, the court reasoned, V & D ran afoul of the mandate of §327(a) of the Code which (with certain exceptions not germane to this case) allows the "employ[ment of] one or more attorneys . . . that do not hold or represent an interest adverse to the estate, and that are disinterested persons." . . . 11 U.S.C. §327(a) (1978).[1] The court concluded that V & D was not "disinterested" and "should not have been employed as attorney[ ] for the debtors in possession . . . without divesting itself of its interest in the debtors' property." Though invalidating the Note and Mortgage, the court allowed V & D's application for compensation and reimbursed expenses in large part, deleting only such items as were unreasonable, unnecessary, or prohibited (such as services and disbursements directly related to the preparation and recordation of the Note and Mortgage). . . .

. . . If the Mortgage is upheld, the law firm will presumably be entitled to the now excluded fees for time spent on the Note and Mortgage. It will also have an improved chance of being paid whatever it has earned. Without the Mortgage, the priority accorded to an administrative expense item may not be enough. If the real estate equity must be shared with other administrative expense claimants, the bankrupt estate could prove insufficient to pay all of V & D's fees. A preferred position vis-à-vis the Summit St. property would afford V & D an appreciably better likelihood of full payment.

---

1. Although §327(a), by its terms, speaks of representing "the trustee," 11 U.S.C. §1107(a) (1978) makes §327(a) applicable to attorneys appointed to assist chapter 11 debtors in possession. (See Matter of Triangle Chemicals, Inc. 697 F. 2d 1280, 1284 (5th Cir. 1983) [§1107(a) "places the debtor in possession in the shoes of a trustee in every way"].)

II. Discussion . . .

The asseveration that the debtors, by failing to appeal from the Engagement Order, somehow lost the right to complain of the subsequent invalidation of the Mortgage, is jejune. The Engagement Order merely authorized the employment of V & D "under general retainer of $500 at [the firm's] usual hourly rates." It did not purport to pass directly or indirectly on the propriety of the Mortgage. Although the appellee argues that the "implication" of the Engagement Order was to deny the debtors' request for approval of the Mortgage, the implication — like many implications — lies mainly in the mind of the implier. It is based on the sheer gossamer of speculation and surmise, without the slightest record support. . . .

Though it might seem evident that 11 U.S.C. §327(a) controls the question of whether or not the Mortgage is enforceable, the debtors dare to differ. They advance a rather curious argument to the effect that §§328 and 329 of the Code "presuppose" that an attorney may take a security interest in a debtor's property to ensure the payment of legal fees, thereby removing such a transaction from the rigors of §327. Their logic is totally unconvincing.

It is true, as the appellants intone, that §328(a) allows the employment of counsel "with the court's approval . . . on any reasonable terms and conditions." But, adverting to that statute begs the question: the reasonableness of a pivotal "condition" of employment is precisely what is at issue in this case. Nothing in §328(a) insinuates that the engagement power conferred thereunder exempts attorneys so appointed from passing through the disinterestedness checkpoint erected by §327(a). . . .

We turn, then, to a fuller consideration of §327(a). At first blush, this statute would seem to foreclose the employment of an attorney who is in any respect a "creditor." But, such a literalistic reading defies common sense and must be discarded as grossly overbroad. After all, any attorney who may be retained or appointed to render professional services to a debtor in possession becomes a creditor of the estate just as soon as any compensable time is spent on account. Thus, to interpret the law in such an inelastic way would virtually eliminate any possibility of legal assistance for a debtor in possession, except under a cash-and-carry arrangement or on a *pro bono* basis. It stands to reason that the statutory mosaic must, at the least, be read to exclude as a "creditor" a lawyer, not previously owed back fees or other indebtedness,[5] who is authorized by the court to represent a debtor in connection with reorganization proceedings — notwithstanding that the lawyer will almost instantaneously become a creditor of the estate with regard to the charges endemic to current and future representation.

When construed in this fashion, the twin requirements of disinterestedness and lack of adversity telescope into what amounts to a single hallmark. Phrasing the standard in terms of the case at bar, the bankruptcy court was bound to inquire whether the acceptance of the Mortgage by V & D created either a meaningful incentive sufficient to place those

---

5. The performance of standard prepetition services, i.e., preliminary work routinely undertaken to facilitate an upcoming chapter 11 filing, will not serve to disqualify an otherwise eligible attorney.

parties at more than acceptable risk — or the reasonable perception of one. The test is not dependent upon the presence of connivance or over-reaching. Malfeasance has not been suggested, let alone shown. No one contends that, in this case, the chicken coop had been entrusted to the fox, or that V & D had impure motives, or that the firm was swayed in its judgments or actions by the existence of the Mortgage. There is nothing to indicate that counsel's attention to the concerns of the debtor's estate was somehow diminished. Section 327 is intended, however, to address the appearance of impropriety as much as its substance, to remove the temptation and opportunity to do less than duty demands. . . .

We acknowledge that the Code is less than explicit in mapping the contours of the disinterestedness requirement. Although it is easy to spot situations which fall at either end of the spectrum, see, e.g., In re Whitman, 51 B.R. 502 (Bankr. D. Mass. 1985) (security agreement taken by law firm, covering debtor's equipment, invalidated because of overreaching and failure to disclose), there is a scumbled area in the center which cannot easily be color-coded. We realize that any attorney — other than one working purely as a volunteer — has a financial interest in the matters entrusted to his care, so in that sense, there is always some danger that the lawyer's judgment will be shaded by his own economic welfare. Yet, that risk, standing alone, seems acceptable. At the opposite pole, we find it strikingly evident that §327(a) would be drained of its meaning if bankruptcy counsel were free, willy-nilly, to set aside for themselves the most promising assets of the estate as a precondition to handling a chapter 11 proceeding. That risk is, of course, anathema.

Once this tension is acknowledged, it is a small step to recognize that 11 U.S.C. §327(a) will not support, either by its terms or by its objectives, a bright-line rule precluding an attorney at all times and under all circumstances from taking a security interest to safeguard the payment of his fees. It will sometimes be difficult to obtain competent counsel in anticipation of a bankruptcy proceeding unless the lawyer's financial wellbeing can be assured to some extent. All too often, debtors — who are, almost by definition, prone to be in somewhat straitened circumstances — may be unable to furnish cash retainers. Even if it is theoretically possible for a particular debtor to do so, such an outlay may siphon off needed funds in such a way as to hamstring legitimate efforts to reorganize under chapter 11. Conversely, the fundamental objectives of chapter 11 may be thwarted if property essential to a reorganization is tied up by an attorney's lien, or if a particular security arrangement (or the perception which it naturally engenders) impairs fair treatment either of creditors or of administrative expense claimants. Reason requires that a balance be struck. . . .

This inquiry is of necessity case-specific. There must be at a minimum full and timely disclosure of the details of any given arrangement. Armed with knowledge of all of the relevant facts, the bankruptcy court must determine, case by case, whether the security interest coveted by counsel can be tolerated under the particular circumstances. . . .

III. Conclusion

We hold that the issue pertaining to the propriety of the secured retainer agreement entered into between the debtors and V & D was properly preserved for appellate review. The Martins did not waive the right to complain concerning invalidation of the Mortgage by failing to press an appeal at an earlier stage.

Having reached the merits of the appeal, we do not find that the grant of the Mortgage to the law firm as security for the payment of its fees was impermissible *per se*. We hold, however, that the bankruptcy court, in the exercise of its sound discretion, must assess the appropriateness of the Mortgage against the backdrop of the litigation. Accordingly, remand is indicated. We do not imply that remand will or will not alter the result; that is not for us to say. We vacate the judgment of the district court and return the case to it for further proceedings not inconsistent herewith.

Vacated and remanded. No costs.

————————————

Often attorneys ensure that they will be paid for future services by taking a retainer and then billing the client against that retainer. When the retainer is exhausted, the attorney may ask for another retainer before work continues, or the attorney may decide to bill the client as services are performed, expecting payment after the fact. The retainers are a familiar device for attorneys in all kinds of practice, including criminal law, family practice, and corporate practice. Not surprisingly, attorneys in bankruptcy practice use them extensively.

Bankruptcy courts routinely recognize the validity of retainer agreements, although most courts require that the agreement be disclosed as part of the general requirements for disclosure of fee arrangements, as Judge Bufford required in *Lee*. §329(a); Bankruptcy Rule 2014(a). Most courts also make it clear that if the attorneys want to draw against the retainer, they must still seek court approval before taking as fees the money in the retainer account. Conceptually, many courts treat retainer agreements as if they were security interests in the cash held by the attorney. The attorney has first call on the retainer for approved fees, and unused retainers are returned to the estate for distribution to the creditors. Not surprisingly, this structure encourages the creditors to review the attorney's fee charges to make certain that the attorney is not depleting the retainer at the expense of the creditors.

It is interesting to speculate whether the attorneys in the *Martin* case would have been in a less vulnerable economic position if they had simply demanded a $100,000 cash retainer and the Martins had sold their Portland real estate to fund it. If that approach was unobjectionable, then we are truly puzzled about form and substance. Perhaps Alice can explain it to us when she returns from Wonderland.

2. *Privilege and Conflict of Interest*

The final case in this section illustrates the special difficulties arising because of the attorney's representation of the company, rather than of the corporate officers, and the complications that develop when a TIB later demands disclosure of earlier officer-attorney conversations. Attorneys who are not sensitized, before beginning practice, to the special ethical difficulties they will face in bankruptcy run the risk of making serious mistakes that prejudice those who come to them for help — long before anyone sees the problem developing.

════════════COMMODITY FUTURES TRADING════════════
COMMISSION v. WEINTRAUB
471 U.S. 343 (1985)

Justice MARSHALL delivered the opinion of the Court.

The question here is whether the trustee of a corporation in bankruptcy has the power to waive the debtor corporation's attorney-client privilege with respect to communications that took place before the filing of the petition in bankruptcy.

I

The case arises out of a formal investigation by petitioner Commodity Futures Trading Commission to determine whether Chicago Discount Commodity Brokers (CDCB), or persons associated with that firm, violated the Commodity Exchange Act, 7 U.S.C. §1 et seq. CDCB was a discount commodity brokerage house registered with the Commission, pursuant to 7 U.S.C. §6d(l), as a futures commission merchant. On October 27, 1980, the Commission filed a complaint against CDCB in the United States District Court for the Northern District of Illinois alleging violations of the Act. That same day, respondent Frank McGhee, acting as sole director and officer of CDCB, entered into a consent decree with the Commission, which provided for the appointment of a receiver and for the receiver to file a petition for liquidation under Chapter 7 of the Bankruptcy Reform Act of 1978 (Bankruptcy Code). The District Court appointed John K. Notz, Jr., as receiver.

Notz then filed a voluntary petition in bankruptcy on behalf of CDCB. He sought relief under Subchapter IV of Chapter 7 of the Bankruptcy Code, which provides for the liquidation of bankrupt commodity brokers. 11 U.S.C §§761-766. The bankruptcy court appointed Notz as interim trustee and, later, as permanent trustee.

As part of its investigation of CDCB, the Commission served a subpoena duces tecum upon CDCB's former counsel, respondent Gary Weintraub. The Commission sought Weintraub's testimony about various CDCB matters, including suspected misappropriation of customer funds by CDCB's officers and employees, and other fraudulent activities. Weintraub appeared for his deposition and responded to numerous inquiries but refused to answer 23 questions, asserting CDCB's attorney-client privilege. The Commission then moved to compel answers to those questions. It argued that Weintraub's assertion of the attorney-client privilege was inappropriate because the privilege could not be used to "thwart legitimate access to information sought in an administrative investigation."

Even though the Commission argued in its motion that the matters on which Weintraub refused to testify were not protected by CDCB's attorney-client privilege, it also asked Notz to waive that privilege. In a letter to Notz, the Commission maintained that CDCB's former officers, directors, and employees no longer had the authority to assert the privilege. According to the Commission, that power was vested in Notz as the then-interim trustee. In response to the Commission's request, Notz waived "any interest I have in the attorney-client privilege possessed by that debtor for any communications or information occurring or arising on or before October 27, 1980" — the date of Notz's appointment as receiver.... Frank McGhee and his brother, respondent Andrew McGhee, intervened and argued that Notz could not validly waive the privilege over their objection.[1] The District Court rejected this argument and, on July 27, entered a new order requiring Weintraub to testify without asserting an attorney-client privilege on behalf of CDCB.

The McGhees appealed from the District Court's order of July 27 and the Court of Appeals for the Seventh Circuit reversed. 722 F.2d 338 (1984). It held that a bankruptcy trustee does not have the power to waive a corporate-debtor's attorney-client privilege with respect to communications that occurred before the filing of the bankruptcy petition. The court recognized that two other Circuits had addressed the question and had come to the opposite conclusion. We granted certiorari to resolve the conflict. 469 U.S. — (1984). We now reverse the Court of Appeals.

II

It is by now well established, and undisputed by the parties to this case, that the attorney-client privilege attaches to corporations as well as to individuals. Both for corporations and individuals, the attorney-client privilege serves the function of promoting full and frank communications between attorneys and their clients. It thereby encourages observance of the law and aids in the administration of justice.

The administration of the attorney-client privilege in the case of corporations, however, presents special problems. As an inanimate entity, a corporation must act through agents. A corporation cannot speak directly to its lawyers. Similarly, it cannot directly waive the privilege when disclosure is in its best interest. Each of these actions must necessarily be undertaken by individuals empowered to act on behalf of the corporation. In *Upjohn Co.*, we considered whether the privilege covers only communications between counsel and top management, and decided that, under certain circumstances, communications between counsel and lower-level employees are also covered. Here, we face the related question of which corporate actors are empowered to waive the corporation's privilege.

The parties in this case agree that, for solvent corporations, the power to waive the corporate attorney-client privilege rests with the corporation's

---

1. The Court of Appeals found that Andrew McGhee resigned his position as officer and director of CDCB on October 21, 1980. 722 F.2d 338, 339 (1984). Frank McGhee, however, remained as an officer and director.

management and is normally exercised by its officers and directors.[4] The managers, of course, must exercise the privilege in a manner consistent with their fiduciary duty to act in the best interests of the corporation and not of themselves as individuals.

The parties also agree that when control of a corporation passes to new management, the authority to assert and waive the corporation's attorney-client privilege passes as well. New managers installed as a result of a takeover, merger, loss of confidence by shareholders, or simply normal succession, may waive the attorney-client privilege with respect to communications made by former officers and directors. Displaced managers may not assert the privilege over the wishes of current managers, even as to statements that the former might have made [to] counsel concerning matters within the scope of their corporate duties.

The dispute in this case centers on the control of the attorney-client privilege of a corporation in bankruptcy. The Government maintains that the power to exercise that privilege with respect to pre-bankruptcy communications passes to the bankruptcy trustee. In contrast, respondents maintain that this power remains with the debtor's directors.

III

As might be expected given the conflict among the courts of appeals, the Bankruptcy Code does not explicitly address the question before us. Respondents assert that 11 U.S.C. §542(e) is dispositive, but we find reliance on that provision misplaced. Section 542(e) states:

> *Subject to any applicable privilege,* after notice and a hearing the court may order an attorney, accountant, or other person that holds recorded information, including books, documents, records, and papers, relating to the debtor's property or financial affairs, to disclose such recorded information to the trustee (emphasis added).

According to respondents, the "subject to any applicable privilege" language means that the attorney cannot be compelled to turn over to the trustee materials within the corporation's attorney-client privilege. In addition, they claim, this language would be superfluous if the trustee had the power to waive the corporation's privilege.

The statutory language does not support respondent's contentions. First, the statute says nothing about a trustee's authority to waive the corporation's attorney-client privilege. To the extent that a trustee has that power, the statute poses no bar on his ability to obtain materials within that privilege.

---

4. State corporation laws generally vest management authority in a corporation's board of directors. See e.g., Del. Code Ann. Tit. 8, §141 (1983); N.Y. Bus. Corp. Law §701 (McKinney Supp. 1983-1984); Model Bus. Corp. Act §35 (1979). The authority of officers derives legally from that of the board of directors. See generally Eisenberg, Legal Models of Management Structure in the Modern Corporation: Officers, Directors, and Accountants, 63 Calif. L. Rev. 375 (1975). The distinction between the powers of officers and directors are not relevant to this case.

Indeed, a privilege that has been properly waived is not "applicable" as against the trustee. For example, consistent with the statute, an attorney could invoke the personal attorney-client privilege of an individual manager.

The legislative history also makes clear that Congress did not intend to give the debtor's directors the right to assert the corporation's attorney-client privilege against the trustee. . . . Rather, Congress intended that the courts deal with this problem:

> The extent to which the attorney client privilege is valid against the trustee is unclear under current law and is left to be determined by the courts on a case by case basis. 124 Cong. Rec. 32400 (1978) (remarks of Rep. Edwards); id., at 33999 (remarks of Sen. DeConcini).

The "subject to any applicable privilege" language is thus merely an invitation for judicial determination of privilege questions.

In addition, the legislative history establishes that §542(e) was intended to restrict, not expand, the ability of accountants and attorneys to withhold information from the trustee. Both the House and the Senate Report state that §542(e) "is a new provision that deprives accountants and attorneys of the leverage that they ha[d], . . . under State law lien provisions, to receive payment in full ahead of other creditors when the information they hold is necessary to the administration of the estate." S. Rep. No. 95-989, p.84 (1978); H.R. Rep. No. 95-595, pp.369-370 (1977). It is therefore clear that §542(e) was not intended to limit the trustee's ability to obtain corporate information.

IV

In light of the lack of direct guidance from the Code, we turn to consider the roles played by the various actors of a corporation in bankruptcy to determine which is most analogous to the role played by the management of a solvent corporation. Because the attorney-client privilege is controlled, outside of bankruptcy, by a corporation's management, the actor whose duties most closely resemble those of management should control the privilege in bankruptcy, unless such a result interferes with policies underlying the bankruptcy laws.

A

The powers and duties of a bankruptcy trustee are extensive. Upon the commencement of a case in bankruptcy, all corporate property passes to an estate represented by the trustee. . . .

As even this brief and incomplete list should indicate, the Bankruptcy Code gives the trustee wide-ranging management authority over the debtor. In contrast, the powers of the debtor's directors are severely limited. Their role is to turn over the corporation's property to the trustee and to provide certain information to the trustee and to the creditors. §§521, 343. Congress contemplated that when a trustee is appointed, he assumes control of the business, and the debtor's directors are "completely ousted." See H.R. Rep. 95-595, pp.220-221 (1977).

In light of the Code's allocation of responsibilities, it is clear that the trustee plays the role most closely analogous to that of a solvent corporation's management. Given that the debtor's directors retain virtually no management powers, they should not exercise the traditional management function of controlling the corporation's attorney-client privilege, unless a contrary arrangement would be inconsistent with policies of the bankruptcy laws.

B

We find no federal interests that would be impaired by the trustee's control of the corporation's attorney-client privilege with respect to prebankruptcy communications. On the other hand, the rule suggested by respondents — that the debtor's directors have this power — would frustrate an important goal of the bankruptcy laws. In seeking to maximize the value of the estate, the trustee must investigate the conduct of prior management to uncover and assert causes of action against the debtor's officers and directors. See generally 11 U.S.C. §§704(4), 547, 548. It would often be extremely difficult to conduct this inquiry if the former management were allowed to control the corporation's attorney-client privilege and therefore to control access to the corporation's legal files. To the extent that management had wrongfully diverted or appropriated corporate assets, it could use the privilege as a shield against the trustee's efforts to identify those assets. The Code's goal of uncovering insider fraud would be substantially defeated if the debtor's directors were to retain the one management power that might effectively thwart an investigation into their own conduct.

Respondents contend that the trustee can adequately investigate fraud without controlling the corporation's attorney-client privilege. They point out that the privilege does not shield the disclosure of communications relating to the planning or commission of ongoing fraud, crimes, and ordinary torts. The problem, however, is making the threshold showing of fraud necessary to defeat the privilege. Without control over the privilege, the trustee might not be able to discover hidden assets or looting schemes, and therefore might not be able to make the necessary showing.

In summary, we conclude that vesting in the trustee control of the corporation's attorney-client privilege most closely comports with the allocation of the waiver power to management outside of bankruptcy without in any way obstructing the careful design of the Bankruptcy Code.

V

Respondents do not seriously contest that the bankruptcy trustee exercises functions analogous to those exercised by management outside of bankruptcy, whereas the debtor's directors exercise virtually no management functions at all. Neither do respondents seriously dispute that vesting control over the attorney-client privilege in the trustee will facilitate the recovery of misappropriated corporate assets.

Respondents argue, however, that the trustee should not obtain control over the privilege because, unlike the management of a solvent corporation, the trustee's primary loyalty goes not to shareholders but to creditors, who elect him and who often will be the only beneficiaries of his efforts. . . .

. . . [R]espondents' position ignores the fact that bankruptcy causes fundamental changes in the nature of corporate relationships. One of the painful facts of bankruptcy is that the interests of shareholders become subordinated to the interests of creditors. In cases in which it is clear that the estate is not large enough to cover any shareholder claims, the trustee's exercise of the corporation's attorney-client privilege will benefit only creditors, but there is nothing anomalous in this result; rather, it is in keeping with the hierarchy of interests created by the bankruptcy laws. See generally 11 U.S.C. §726(a).

Respondents also ignore that if a debtor remains in possession — that is, if a trustee is not appointed — the debtor's directors bear essentially the same fiduciary obligation to creditors and shareholders as would the trustee for a debtor out of possession. Wolf v. Weinstein, 372 U.S. 633, 649-652 (1963). Indeed, the willingness of courts to leave debtors in possession "is premised upon an assurance that the officers and managing employees can be depended upon to carry out the fiduciary responsibilities of a trustee." Id., at 651. Surely, then, the management of a debtor-in-possession would have to exercise control of the corporation's attorney-client privilege consistently with this obligation to treat all parties, not merely the shareholders, fairly. By the same token, when a trustee is appointed, the privilege must be exercised in accordance with the trustee's fiduciary duty to all interested parties.

To accept respondents' position would lead to one of two outcomes: (1) a rule under which the management of a debtor-in-possession exercises control of the attorney-client privilege for the benefit only of shareholders but exercises all of its other functions for the benefit of both shareholders and creditors, or (2) a rule under which the attorney-client privilege is exercised for the benefit of both creditors and shareholders when the debtor remains in possession, but is exercised for the benefit only of shareholders when a trustee is appointed. We find nothing in the bankruptcy laws that would suggest, much less compel, either of these implausible results.

VI

Respondent's other arguments are similarly unpersuasive. First, respondents maintain that the result we reach today would also apply to individuals in bankruptcy, a result that respondents find "unpalatable." But our holding today has no bearing on the problem of individual bankruptcy, which we have no reason to address in this case. As we have stated, a corporation, as an inanimate entity, must act through agents. When the corporation is solvent, the agent that controls the corporate attorney-client privilege is the corporation's management. Under our holding today, this power passes to the trustee because the trustee's functions are more closely analogous to those of management outside of bankruptcy than are the functions of the debtor's directors. An individual, in contrast, can act for himself; there is no "management" that controls a solvent individual's attorney-client privilege. If control over that privilege passes to a trustee, it must be under some theory different from the one that we embrace in this case.

Second, respondents argue that giving the trustee control over the attorney-client privilege will have an undesirable chilling effect on attorney-client communications. According to respondents, corporate managers will be wary of speaking freely with corporate counsel if their communications might subsequently be disclosed due to bankruptcy. But the chilling effect is no greater here than in the case of a solvent corporation, where individual officers and directors always run the risk that successor management might waive the corporation's attorney-client privilege with respect to prior management's communications with counsel. . . .

Finally, respondents maintain that upholding trustee waivers would create a disincentive for debtors to invoke the protections of bankruptcy and provide an incentive for creditors to file for involuntary bankruptcy. According to respondents, "[i]njection of such considerations into bankruptcy would skew the application of the bankruptcy laws in a manner not contemplated by Congress." The law creates numerous incentives, both for and against the filing of bankruptcy petitions. Respondents do not explain why our holding creates incentives that are inconsistent with congressional intent, and we do not believe that it does.

VII

For the foregoing reasons, we hold that the trustee of a corporation in bankruptcy has the power to waive the corporation's attorney-client privilege with respect to prebankruptcy communications. We therefore conclude that Notz, in his capacity as trustee, properly waived CDCB's privilege in this case. The judgment of the Court of Appeals for the Seventh Circuit is accordingly reversed.

The issues in *Weintraub* have split the two authors of this book fairly sharply, with one of us agreeing with Justice Marshall's analysis that the trustee is "successor management," as with any corporate takeover, while the other argues that the trustee only inherits the property of the corporation and the right to control that property, not the right to control its governance or to control any rights that it has in the bankruptcy independent of its property.

It is particularly interesting in this conceptual context to wonder how the Court would rule on the question it specifically reserved: the trustee's waiver of the privilege in an individual's bankruptcy. The bankruptcy courts have not had the luxury of ducking that question. The cases are rare — but they are beginning to arise — in which the bankruptcy trustee attempts to waive the privilege of the individual debtor in order to determine what happened to the assets of the estate. It is no surprise that the courts themselves differ over the final answer. Compare In re Williams, 152 B.R. 123 (Bankr. N.D. Tex. 1992) (individual debtor's privilege can be waived by trustee of liquidating trust established by debtor's Chapter 11 reorganization), with In re Hunt, 153 B.R. 445 (Bankr. N.D. Tex. 1993) (individual debtor's privilege cannot be waived by trustee). Two Texas bankruptcy courts, same issue, different results.

Although the issue of privilege may be one of the most attention-getting aspects of potential conflicts in representing a company considering a Chapter 11, Professor LoPucki points out that the potential conflicts between a corporation and its owner or manager are far more fundamental and pervasive. In the following excerpt from LoPucki, Teacher's Manual for the Debtor Creditor Game 71 (West 1984), he demonstrates the difficulty in seeing and explaining the conflicts and in trying to find a reasonable representation position for the attorney.

LoPUCKI, THE DEBTOR'S LAWYER AS TROJAN HORSE

Shares is the sole shareholder of Corps, a corporation which is now in financial difficulty; He comes to Lawyer for advice. Shares describes the problems of the business, and after some discussion they conclude that the corporation should file for reorganization under chapter 11 of the Bankruptcy Code. Among the papers which Lawyer prepares for that filing is the standard "Application of Debtor-In-Possession to Employ Attorney." The "Debtor-in-Possession" referred to is, of course, the corporation; the attorney to be employed is Lawyer. Included in the application is the usual recitation that Lawyer "represents no interest adverse to the estate." See Bankruptcy Code §327(a).

Shortly after the proceeding is filed, Lawyer comes to three very disturbing realizations. First, the heart of Corps' problem may be that Shares is a poor manager. Second, it is in the corporation's best interests to have the Court seriously consider replacing Shares as manager. Third, Shares would be a fool to voluntarily step down, since if he does creditors will seize control of the proceedings and oust him from his ownership position. He will lose everything. What should Lawyer do?

Since Lawyer, in this example, led Shares to believe that he would represent Shares' interests as well as those of the corporation, and those interests are now in direct conflict, Lawyer probably is bound to withdraw from both representations. He has lost his clients and the fees he might have earned during the remainder of the proceedings. If Lawyer had been conscious of the likelihood of such a conflict from the beginning could he have reached a better result? Let's give Lawyer another try.

Shares comes to Lawyer for advice about the Corps' financial difficulties. Lawyer carefully explains that here is a potential conflict of interest between Shares and Corps, and that he should not represent both. Since it is Corps which needs to file the chapter 11 proceeding, he suggests that he should represent Corps before filing as "debtor" and after filing as "debtor-in-possession." Lawyer advises Shares that, should an actual conflict of interest arise, he will notify Shares and Shares can then obtain separate counsel. He also cautions Shares that while Shares' communications to him will be protected by the attorney-client privilege, the privilege will be owned by the corporation, not by Shares. A trustee appointed at some later time could compel Lawyer to disclose Shares' communications to Lawyer, over the objection of both Lawyer and Shares.

Shares is absolutely astounded. "I brought my legal problem to you and asked for help. You seem to be telling me not only that you cannot help me, but that you may be 'ethically' bound to work against my interests. And you expect to be paid out of the corporation that I own 100 percent of! If that is correct, wouldn't I (or any other owner of a closely held corporation in financial difficulty) be a fool to authorize the hiring of an attorney for the corporation?"

"That's certainly a problem," says Lawyer, "but a corporation is a person, a separate legal entity, and needs to have the undivided loyalty of its attorney, just as you would want to have the undivided loyalty of your attorney." (If Lawyer is conscious of any irony, his face does not betray it.)

"You may *say* that a corporation is a 'person,' but that doesn't make it so," Shares responds. "I started the business, I supplied the capital, I hired the people who did the work. There is no one in the business but a bunch of short-term employees and me. There is no other person who might be injured by your loyalty to me."

"What about the creditors?" Lawyer replies.

"Are you supposed to represent them?" Shares asks. "Most of them already have their own attorneys and wouldn't be interested. The law purports to be worried about the interests of the corporation, but a corporation is nothing but a legal fiction. There's nobody in this corporation except me." Shares pauses, grins, then adds, "And you, of course, if I were dumb enough to let you in."

Lawyer is obviously offended. "I don't make the rules," he says. "But as an attorney I have ethical obligations to the Court as well as to the client." The sound of these familiar words enables Lawyer to regain his composure. He continues, "If you don't want me in your corporation, possibly working against you, you'll just end up with somebody else doing the same thing. Worse yet," Lawyer chuckles, "you might get some lawyer who's not as ethical as I am!"

Shares ignores Lawyer's attempt at humor. "Since I'm ultimately going to be paying your fees anyway, couldn't I just hire you as my attorney — and let the corporation be the one without counsel?"

Lawyer thought about that for a few minutes. "I don't think that will work unless the corporation is also represented. Who would sign the pleadings? Who would make the arguments in court? Oh, I suppose it could be done, but it would be very clumsy. I've never heard of anyone else doing it. It would be very unusual for a corporate debtor in a chapter 11 proceeding to have no attorney. The creditors and the Bankruptcy Judge wouldn't like it. They would think we were up to something, and in a way, they would be right. You'd run a very high risk that a trustee would be appointed. If that happened, you'd probably lose your ownership interest in the business."

There is a long silence before Shares speaks. "So then the real problem isn't that the corporation needs an attorney. It's that the creditors and the Judge want it to have one. Then aren't you telling me that the lawyer for a debtor-in-possession is really a sort of Trojan horse — brought in by a shareholder like myself for the ostensible purpose of representing my interests — but whose real function is to spy on me for the creditors and the court?"

"That's not really a fair description," Lawyer protests. "We also do a lot of other things. . . ."

Shares interrupts. "This is ridiculous," he fumes. "I read in a newspaper article that about 90 percent of all corporations that file under chapter 11 are owned and managed by a single owner or a family, and that in about 90 percent of the cases the cause of the debtor's problems is that the businesses have bad managers. What you are telling me is that your Code of Professional Responsibility requires that their lawyers work in the interests of the corporations even if it means working against the men or women who hired them. Why that means that in at least 81 percent of all chapter 11 proceedings in this country the attorney for the debtor-in-possession has an 'ethical' duty to work to oust his own client from control!"

"Almost correct," says Lawyer, "but that guy he's ousting *isn't* his client."

Some lawyers would try to avoid the hard issues in this dialogue by saying that management competence is not a legal issue. Aside from the fact that such "business" issues are often intertwined with legal issues, unavoidable conflicts of a purely legal sort are commonplace with closely held companies in financial distress. Insider preference and fraudulent conveyance issues are obvious examples, and they routinely arise despite the lack of any evil motive or sense of wrongdoing on the part of the owner-officer of the business. Paying suppliers to keep the business afloat or asking dad to lend money very short term to the business in order to make payroll are business decisions with powerful legal implications if the company heads into bankruptcy. Perhaps the most important lesson to be drawn from Professor LoPucki's story is that it is the lawyer — not the client — who is responsible for dealing with these conflicts.

Problem Set 40

40.1. You are part of one of the most successful bankruptcy boutiques in Minneapolis. Your firm has a thriving debtor practice, but the firm is barely able to break even and is paying very little in partnership profits. A review of your books shows the reason: More than 30 percent of the hours and expenses the firm bills in bankruptcies are never paid. This compares most unfavorably with a bad debt rate of less than 5 percent on estate work completed and less than 10 percent on general corporate work undertaken by comparable firms in the city. A major meeting is called for later this month to decide what direction the firm should take. What do you recommend?

40.2. Your firm has represented Summer Enterprises for over a decade. Summer is a large conglomerate (sales exceeding $2.3 billion last year) that generates over a million dollars in yearly revenue for the firm. Your experience with failing firms and workouts has brought you to the attention of Ella Roland, the senior partner managing the Summer account. Roland calls you in to ask you to take on a very important assignment: Go over the Summer books, interview the employees, and try to determine if some nefarious activity is afoot that is causing Summer's devastating quarterly losses despite record sales. The chairman of the board of Summer says that you are to be given carte blanche by the company, bringing in your own accounting team and any other assistance you need. No one else is to know of your task, except that you are working under the chairman's authority.

You make a preliminary review of the records and you see that Summer may have a high-placed embezzler. In the alternative, you think there may be irregularities in Summer's government contracts (perhaps kickbacks?) or in their accounting practices. You have identified a large group of employees to interview. What will you say to the employees as you begin your interviews? Does it matter whether Summer seems to be on sound financial footing despite the problems under investigation?

40.3. Jesse's Jet Clean, a state-wide chain of car washes, has been a client of the firm since the first location opened 22 years ago. You have been in charge of Jesse's account for about a year. Recently, you've been consulting with Jesse over a possible Chapter 11 filing. You have been a little slow in billing the company since you took over, so it owes about $300,000 to the firm for work over the last six months. It looks as if the company will file in the next couple of weeks. Do you foresee any problem in the firm's handling the bankruptcy? You've gotten to know Jesse pretty well working on his retirement plan and real estate investments, as well as the company's problems, and you know he would faint at the thought of getting a new lawyer at this point. If there is a problem, how best to solve it?

40.4. You have been with your firm for 12 years now and, as the head of Reorganizations and Workouts, have become a partner moving into an important leadership role in the firm. Because of increasing director liability, the corporate law department has asked for a special management meeting on the issue of whether firm members should continue to be permitted to serve on the boards of directors for different clients. You have been invited to the meeting along with several other partners who have developed long associations with clients and who have sat on boards for years. In preparation for the meeting, make your own notes about the arguments you are likely to hear in the meeting, aside from the liability issues raised by the corporate people. Also, think about the position you will take in advising your colleagues.

THE FUNCTIONS AND BOUNDARIES OF BANKRUPTCY LAW

CHAPTER 9

DOMESTIC JURISDICTION

We title Part IV after a notable book about modern bankruptcy law, Professor Thomas Jackson's *The Logic and Limits of Bankruptcy Law* (1986). Although we disagree with Professor Jackson in important ways, his book is a landmark in modern theorizing about bankruptcy because it is an attempt to define the proper scope of bankruptcy law by understanding its functions. Part IV is an introductory exploration of the functions of bankruptcy law and its proper place within the larger scheme of the law.

As is our wont, we begin with the concrete doctrinal problems created by the bizarre jurisdictional scheme Congress has created for bankruptcy matters, a scheme that in its complexity reflects the mixed feelings and purposes with which Congress approaches this subject. We then give the discussion a wider scope by exploring the interaction of national bankruptcy laws with a globalizing world market, an interaction that reveals some fundamental issues about the functions of bankruptcy and its relationship to a host of other laws and policies. Finally, we provide an introduction to the robust academic debate about the nature of bankruptcy and the role of bankruptcy scholarship.

A. THE 1978 CODE

The 1898 Act contemplated that many matters relating to the bankrupt debtor's affairs would continue to be resolved in state court. As a result, the federal courts were not given broad jurisdiction over all disputes related to bankruptcy, but only over the bankruptcy case itself. Related disputes were resolved in state court unless the district court had independent, non-bankruptcy jurisdiction of a particular dispute, such as diversity jurisdiction. The bankruptcy jurisdiction was called "summary jurisdiction," while matters outside summary jurisdiction were called "plenary" and were litigated in the state or federal court where they would have been brought if no bankruptcy petition had been filed. An elaborate jurisprudence developed concerning which types of cases fell within each category.

The distinctions that developed were arcane and confusing, to say the least. Thus a state law claim by the bankrupt debtor against a third party might be within the summary jurisdiction of the district court because the

793

creditor had asserted a claim of its own in the bankruptcy and had thus "consented" to bankruptcy jurisdiction. This "consent" approach became so extended and artificial as to be dubbed "jurisdiction by ambush." On the other hand, an action as central to the bankruptcy process as the recovery of a preference usually was a "plenary" suit, which had to be brought in state court unless independent federal jurisdiction could be established. Enormous amounts of time and money were spent litigating questions of jurisdiction under the 1898 Act. The frequency with which debtors were forced to divert their attention from reshaping their businesses and negotiating a successful plan in order to concentrate on expensive and time-consuming jurisdictional litigation contributed to the belief that the bankruptcy laws were not effectively structured to save businesses in distress.

Over time, more and more of the summary jurisdiction of the district court was in fact exercised in the first instance by the bankruptcy referees (the precursors to the bankruptcy judges), rather than the district judges. This process culminated in the 1973 Rules, which made the referees' factual findings subject to attack only if they were "clearly erroneous," giving them the same dignity accorded by the appellate courts to the findings of the district judges. In addition, the referees acquired the title of "Bankruptcy Judges" and began to wear robes in the courtroom. Affording the bankruptcy court proceedings some of the trappings and power of typical plenary court proceedings laid the groundwork for subsequent jurisdictional changes.

Despite these developments, there continued to be expensive and time-consuming jurisdictional litigation. It is important to understand that this litigation involved two distinct, although related, questions as to each dispute: (a) Is this dispute within the federal bankruptcy jurisdiction, as opposed to the general jurisdiction of a state court or the nonbankruptcy (federal question and diversity) jurisdiction of a federal court? (b) If the dispute is within bankruptcy jurisdiction, is the district judge the only one who can hear the matter or may the bankruptcy judge decide it?

As bankruptcy jurisdiction disputes became oppressively complex and costly, some reckoned that the resources diverted to these issues could make the difference between success and failure for some tottering reorganizations. Overhaul of the jurisdictional requirements was an important impetus in the call for reform of the bankruptcy system. In the debate over the 1978 Reform Act, the House and Senate agreed that federal bankruptcy jurisdiction should be extended broadly. Bankruptcy jurisdiction was expanded to include all disputes "related to" the bankruptcy in order to eliminate the costly, time-consuming litigation over summary and plenary matters. The houses differed, however, in their proposed assignment of this expanded jurisdiction. The House wanted to create separate bankruptcy courts in which the bankruptcy judges would be appointed for life by the president under Article III of the Constitution, just like the district judges. The Senate, reflecting the views of the sitting Article III judges, proposed to leave the bankruptcy judges in an inferior role as assistants to the district judges, appointed by them for a term of years. The Reform Act compromised these views by authorizing the president to appoint the bankruptcy judges, but only for a term of years, and by giving bankruptcy judges virtually all of the bankruptcy jurisdiction, but only as "adjuncts" to the district court.

This jurisdiction scheme was challenged as violating Article III of the Constitution in the landmark case of Northern Pipeline Construction v. Marathon Pipe Line Co., 458 U.S. 50 (1982). The reorganization debtor, Northern Pipe Line, sued Marathon in bankruptcy court, alleging breach of contract, misrepresentation, and coercion. The defendant protested that such a case could not be heard by a court that did not have Article III status. Justice Brennan, writing for a four-person plurality, emphasized the importance of Article III status and the lifetime appointments for federal judges. Northern Pipe Line pointed out that other Article I courts, such as territorial courts, courts martial, and legislative courts and administrative agencies "created by Congress to adjudicate cases involving 'public rights'" all operated without challenge. Many scholars had believed that "public rights" analysis would furnish the rubric under which the constitutionality of the Bankruptcy Code jurisdiction would be sustained, but the Court was unpersuaded:

> Appellants argue that a discharge in bankruptcy is indeed a "public right," similar to such congressionally created benefits as "radio station licenses, pilot licenses, and certificates for common carriers" granted by administrative agencies. But the restructuring of debtor-creditor relations, which is at the core of the federal bankruptcy power, must be distinguished from the adjudication of state-created private rights, such as the right to recover contract damages that is at issue in this case. The former may well be a "public right," but the latter obviously is not. Appellant Northern's right to recover contract damages to augment its estate is "one of private right, that is, of the liability of one individual to another under the law as defined." Crowell v. Benson, 285 U.S., at 51.
>
> Recognizing that the present case may not fall within the scope of any of our prior cases permitting the establishment of legislative courts, appellants argue that we should recognize an additional situation beyond the command of Art. III, sufficiently broad to sustain the Act. Appellants contend that Congress' constitutional authority to establish "uniform Laws on the subject of Bankruptcies throughout the United States," Art. I, §8, cl. 4, carries with it an inherent power to establish legislative courts capable of adjudicating "bankruptcy related controversies." In support of this argument, appellants rely primarily upon a quotation from the opinion in Palmore v. United States, 411 U.S. 389 (1973), in which we stated that both Congress and this Court have recognized that . . . the requirements of Art. III, which are applicable where laws of national applicability and affairs of national concern are at stake, must in proper circumstances give way to accommodate plenary grants of power to Congress to legislate with respect to specialized areas having particularized needs and warranting distinctive treatment. Id., 407-408.
>
> Appellants cite this language to support their proposition that a bankruptcy court created by Congress under its Art. I powers is constitutional, because the law of bankruptcy is a "specialized area," and Congress has found a "particularized need" that warrants "distinctive treatment." . . .
>
> The flaw in appellants' analysis is that it provides no limiting principle. It thus threatens to supplant completely our system of adjudication in independent Art. III tribunals and replace it with a system of "specialized" legislative courts. True, appellants argue that under their analysis Congress could create legislative courts pursuant only to some "specific" Art. I power, and "only when there is a particularized need for distinctive treatment." They therefore

assert that their analysis would not permit Congress to replace the independent Art. III judiciary through a "wholesale assignment of federal judicial business to legislative courts." Ibid. But these "limitations" are wholly illusory. For example, Art. I, §8, empowers Congress to enact laws, inter alia, regulating interstate commerce and punishing certain crimes. Art. I, §8, cls. 3, 6. On appellants' reasoning Congress could provide for the adjudication of these and "related" matters by judges and courts within Congress' exclusive control. . . .

Justices Rehnquist and O'Connor concurred in the result, but they avoided the larger constitutional question by saying only that this particular exercise of jurisdiction was beyond the scope of the bankruptcy judge. The dissenters thought there was adequate authority for the exercise of the bankruptcy court's jurisdiction, with Chief Justice Burger arguing that these bankruptcy courts derived their authority as adjuncts of the district courts in which they sat.

The opinion has been read and re-read by a generation of bankruptcy practitioners and students, but the decision remains opaque, perhaps in part because there are six opinions, with shifting concurrences and dissents, making it impossible even to pin down the holding with precision. But there was little time to work out the intellectual reasoning. The bankruptcy system was in crisis, and the complexity of the practical issues was multiplying.

B.   THE 1984 AMENDMENTS

Although the Supreme Court twice stayed application of its holding in *Marathon* in order to permit Congress to recast bankruptcy jurisdiction, Congress was unable to act promptly and *Marathon* went into effect on Christmas Eve 1982. The Judicial Conference, comprised of sitting federal district and circuit court judges, acted through the Administration Office of the Courts to provide interim guidance by the issuance of an "Emergency Rule," which each district court was urged to adopt. The Emergency Rule was adopted across the country and governed reference of matters to bankruptcy judges until the passage of the 1984 Amendments Act.

As we discussed in the introduction to consumer bankruptcy, the 1984 Amendments Act was the focus of substantial political pressures from the consumer credit industry, organized labor, and various other interests, and made extensive changes in the substantive provisions of the 1978 Code. Nonetheless, the resolution of the jurisdictional issues created by *Marathon* and by the Emergency Rule was the central problem that the 1984 Amendments had to address.

The actors squared off as they had during debates over the 1978 Code. The House of Representatives wanted to resolve the *Marathon* issue by creating Article III bankruptcy judges, while the existing Article III judges and their Senate supporters were adamant that bankruptcy judges should remain mere adjuncts to the district court. There was also a backlash in the legal community against the expanded bankruptcy jurisdiction of the federal courts, since many commercial and tort litigators had found themselves dragged into a bankruptcy court for the first time in their careers. They were unsure about the quality of those courts and worried about the courts' alleged pro-debtor bias. These latter concerns were manifested in proposals to reduce the power of the federal courts in bankruptcy by requiring abstention in favor of the state courts in many instances, even though a particular matter might be "related to" a bankruptcy. They were also reflected in proposals to restrict the matters that a bankruptcy court could hear on a final, "clearly erroneous" basis, a position given powerful impetus by *Marathon*.

The political battle over bankruptcy jurisdiction and the role of the bankruptcy judges was hard fought, with compromises achieved only in the final hours. Two unfortunate consequences resulted from this struggle. First, very little useful legislative history accompanied the passage of the amendments, and second, the language finally adopted is, at best, inartful.

On the whole, the Senate approach prevailed. Bankruptcy judges would not become Article III judges. Instead, to satisfy the limits on the reach of Article I judges, their jurisdiction would be curtailed. The 1984 Amendments required abstention by the federal courts in matters involving state law claims and limited the matters that bankruptcy judges could decide on a "clearly erroneous" basis. As explained in detail below, the new provision designated certain matters as "core proceedings" that may be heard by bankruptcy judges, subject to the unlimited discretion of the district judges to withdraw any matter from the bankruptcy court at any time. 28 U.S.C. §157. On the other hand, the House succeeded in changing much of the original Senate language to leave considerable room for the courts in drawing the relevant lines.

From the start, it was unclear whether the 1984 Amendments had cured the *Marathon* problem. The Supreme Court's discussion in the following case is ostensibly limited to the question of entitlement to jury trial under the Seventh Amendment, but it raises serious questions about the constitutionality of the entire jurisdictional edifice concocted by the 1984 Act.

GRANFINANCIERA, S.A. v. NORDBERG
492 U.S. 33 (1989)

Justice BRENNAN delivered the opinion of the Court.

The question presented is whether a person who has not submitted a claim against a bankruptcy estate has a right to a jury trial when sued by the trustee in bankruptcy to recover an allegedly fraudulent monetary transfer. We hold that the Seventh Amendment entitles such a person to a trial by jury, notwithstanding Congress' designation of fraudulent conveyance actions as "core proceedings" in 28 U.S.C. §157(b)(2)(H) (1982 ed., Supp. IV).

I

The Chase & Sanborn Corporation filed a petition for reorganization under Chapter 11 in 1983. A Plan of Reorganization approved by the United

States Bankruptcy Court for the Southern District of Florida vested in respondent Nordberg, the trustee in bankruptcy, causes of action for fraudulent conveyances. In 1985, respondent filed suit against petitioners Granfinanciera, S.A. and Medex, Ltd. in the United States District Court for the Southern District of Florida. The complaint alleged that petitioners had received $1.7 million from Chase & Sanborn's corporate predecessor within one year of the date its bankruptcy petition was filed, without receiving consideration or reasonably equivalent value in return. Respondent sought to avoid what it alleged were constructively and actually fraudulent transfers and to recover damages, costs, expenses, and interest under 11 U.S.C. §§548(a)(1) and (a)(2), 550(a)(1) (1982 ed., Supp. V). . . .

The Court of Appeals for the Eleventh Circuit . . . found that petitioners lacked a statutory right to a jury trial, because the constructive fraud provision under which suit was brought — 11 U.S.C. §548(1)(2) (1982 ed., Supp. V) — contains no mention of a right to a jury trial and 28 U.S.C. §1411 (1982 ed., Supp. IV) "affords jury trials only in personal injury or wrongful death suits." 835 F.2d, at 1348. The Court of Appeals further ruled that the Seventh Amendment supplied no right to a jury trial. . . .

III

Petitioners rest their claim to a jury trial on the Seventh Amendment alone.[3] The Seventh Amendment provides: "In Suits at common law, where the value in controversy shall exceed twenty dollars, the right of trial by jury shall be preserved. . . ." We have consistently interpreted the phrase "Suits at common law" to refer to "suits in which *legal* rights were to be ascertained and determined, in contradistinction to those where equitable rights alone were recognized, and equitable remedies were administered." Parsons v. Bedford, 3 Pet. 433, 447 (1830). Although "the thrust of the Amendment was to preserve the right to jury trial as it existed in 1791," the Seventh Amendment also applies to actions brought to enforce statutory rights that are analogous to common-law causes of action ordinarily decided in English law courts in the late 18th century, as opposed to those customarily heard by courts of equity or admiralty.

The form of our analysis is familiar. "First, we compare the statutory action to 18th-century actions brought in the courts of England prior to the merger of the courts of law and equity. Second, we examine the remedy sought and determine whether it is legal or equitable in nature." The second stage of this analysis is more important than the first.

If, on balance, these two factors indicate that a party is entitled to a jury trial under the Seventh Amendment, we must decide whether Congress

3. The current statutory provision for jury trials in bankruptcy proceedings — 28 U.S.C. §1411 (1982 ed.,. Supp. IV), enacted as part of the Bankruptcy Amendments and Federal Judgeship Act of 1984 (1984 Amendments) — is notoriously ambiguous. . . .

Petitioners therefore appear correct in concluding that, "absent any specific legislation in force providing jury trials for cases filed before July 10, 1984, but tried afterwards, [their] right to jury trial in this proceeding must necessarily be predicated entirely on the Seventh Amendment." Brief for Petitioners 33, n.7.

may assign and has assigned resolution of the relevant claim to a non–Article III adjudicative body that does not use a jury as factfinder.[4]

A

There is no dispute that actions to recover preferential or fraudulent transfers were often brought at law in late 18th-century England. As we noted in Schoenthal v. Irving Trust Co., 287 U.S. 92, 94 (1932) (footnote omitted), "[i]n England, long prior to the enactment of our first Judiciary Act, common law actions of trover and money had and received were resorted to for the recovery of preferential payments by bankrupts." . . .

Respondent does not challenge this proposition or even contend that actions to recover fraudulent conveyances or preferential transfers were more than occasionally tried in courts of equity. He asserts only that courts of equity had concurrent jurisdiction with courts of law over fraudulent preference actions. While respondent's assertion that courts of equity sometimes provided relief in fraudulent preference actions is true, however, it hardly suffices to undermine petitioners' submission that the present action for monetary relief would not have sounded in equity two hundred years ago in England. . . .

B

The nature of the relief respondent seeks strongly supports our preliminary finding that the right he invokes should be denominated legal rather than equitable. Our decisions establish beyond peradventure that "[i]n cases of fraud or mistake, as under any other head of chancery jurisdiction, a court of the United States will not sustain a bill in equity to obtain only a decree for the payment of money by way of damages, when the like amount can be recovered at law in an action sounding in tort or for money had and received." Buzard v. Houston, 119 U.S. 347, 352 (1886), citing Parkersburg v. Brown, 106 U.S. 487 (1883).

Indeed, in our view Schoenthal v. Irving Trust Co., 287 U.S. 92 (1932), removes all doubt that respondent's cause of action should be characterized as legal rather than as equitable. In Schoenthal, the trustee in bankruptcy sued in equity to recover alleged preferential payments, claiming that it had no adequate remedy at law. As in this case, the recipients of the payments apparently did not file claims against the bankruptcy estate. The Court held that the suit had to proceed at law instead, because the long-settled rule that suits in equity will not be sustained where a complete remedy exists at law, then codified at 28 U.S.C. §384, "serves to guard the right of trial by

---

4. We consider this issue in Part IV, infra. Contrary to Justice White's contention, see post, at 2809-2810, we do not declare that the Seventh Amendment provides a right to a jury trial on all legal rather than equitable claims. If a claim that is legal in nature asserts a "public right," as we define that term in Part IV, then the Seventh Amendment does not entitle the parties to a jury trial if Congress assigns its adjudication to an administrative agency or specialized court of equity. The Seventh Amendment protects a litigant's right to a jury trial only if a cause of action is legal in nature and it involves a matter of "private right."

jury preserved by the Seventh Amendment and to that end it should be liberally construed." Id., at 94. . . .

IV

Prior to passage of the Bankruptcy Reform Act of 1978, "[s]uits to recover preferences constitute[d] no part of the proceedings in bankruptcy." Schoenthal v. Irving Trust Co., supra, at 94-95. Although related to bankruptcy proceedings, fraudulent conveyance and preference actions brought by a trustee in bankruptcy were deemed separate, plenary suits to which the Seventh Amendment applied. While the 1978 Act brought those actions within the jurisdiction of the bankruptcy courts, it preserved parties' rights to trial by jury as they existed prior to the effective date of the 1978 Act. 28 U.S.C. §1480(a) (repealed). The Bankruptcy Amendments and Federal Judgeship Act of 1984 (1984 Amendments), however, designated fraudulent conveyance actions "core proceedings," 28 U.S.C. §157(b)(2)(H) (1982 ed., Supp. IV), which bankruptcy judges may adjudicate and in which they may issue final judgments, §157(b)(1), if a district court has referred the matter to them. §157(a). We are not obliged to decide today whether bankruptcy courts may conduct jury trials in fraudulent conveyance suits brought by a trustee against a person who has not entered a claim against the estate, either in the rare procedural posture of this case . . . or under the current statutory scheme. See 28 U.S.C. §1411 (1982 ed., Supp. IV). Nor need we decide whether, if Congress has authorized bankruptcy courts to hold jury trials in such actions, that authorization comports with Article III when non–Article III judges preside over them subject to review in or withdrawal by the district courts. We also need not consider whether jury trials conducted by a bankruptcy court would satisfy the Seventh Amendment's command that "no fact tried by a jury, shall be otherwise re-examined in any Court of the United States, than according to the rules of the common law," given that district courts may presently set aside clearly erroneous factual findings by bankruptcy courts. Bkrtcy. Rule 8013. The sole issue before us is whether the Seventh Amendment confers on petitioners a right to a jury trial in the face of Congress' decision to allow a non–Article III tribunal to adjudicate the claims against them.

A . . .

. . . [O]ur decisions point to the conclusion that, if a statutory cause of action is legal in nature, the question whether the Seventh Amendment permits Congress to assign its adjudication to a tribunal that does not employ juries as factfinders requires the same answer as the question whether Article III allows Congress to assign adjudication of that cause of action to a non–Article III tribunal. For if a statutory cause of action, such as respondent's right to recover a fraudulent conveyance under 11 U.S.C. § 548(a)(2), is not a "public right" for Article III purposes, then Congress may not assign its adjudication to a specialized non–Article III court lacking "the essential attributes of the judicial power." And if the action must be tried under the auspices of an Article III court, then the Seventh Amendment affords the parties a right to a jury trial whenever the cause of action is legal in nature.

B

Although the issue admits of some debate, a bankruptcy trustee's right to recover a fraudulent conveyance under 11 U.S.C. §548(a)(2) seems to us more accurately characterized as a private rather than a public right as we have used those terms in our Article III decisions. In Northern Pipeline Construction Co., 458 U.S., at 71, the plurality noted that the restructuring of debtor-creditor relations in bankruptcy "may well be a 'public right.'" [11] But the plurality also emphasized that state-law causes of action for breach of contract or warranty are paradigmatic private rights, even when asserted by an insolvent corporation in the midst of Chapter 11 reorganization proceedings. The plurality further said that "matters from their nature subject to 'a suit at common law or in equity or admiralty'" lie at the "protected core" of Article III judicial power. There can be little doubt that fraudulent conveyance actions by bankruptcy trustees — suits which, we said in Schoenthal v. Irving Trust Co., 287 U.S., at 94-95 (citation omitted), "constitute no part of the proceedings in bankruptcy but concern controversies arising out of it" — are quintessentially suits at common law that more nearly resemble state-law contract claims brought by a bankrupt corporation to augment the bankruptcy estate than they do creditors' hierarchically ordered claims to a pro rata share of the bankruptcy res. See Gibson, Jury Trials in Bankruptcy: Obeying the Commands of Article III and the Seventh Amendment, 72 Minn. L. Rev. 967, 1022-1025 (1988). They therefore appear matters of private rather than public right.[12]

Our decision in Katchen v. Landy, 382 U.S. 323 (1966), under the Seventh Amendment rather than Article III, confirms this analysis. . . . We read Schoenthal and Katchen as holding that, under the Seventh Amendment, a creditor's right to a jury trial on a bankruptcy trustee's preference claim depends upon whether the creditor has submitted a claim against the estate, not upon Congress' precise definition of the "bankruptcy estate" or upon whether Congress chanced to deny jury trials to creditors who have not filed claims and who are sued by a trustee to recover an alleged preference. Because petitioners here, like the petitioner in Schoenthal, have not filed claims against the estate, respondent's fraudulent conveyance action does not arise "as part of the process of allowance

11. We do not suggest that the restructuring of debtor-creditor relations is in fact a public right. This thesis has met with substantial scholarly criticism, and we need not and do not seek to defend it here. Our point is that even if one accepts this thesis, the Seventh Amendment entitles petitioners to a jury trial.

12. See Northern Pipeline Construction Co. v. Marathon Pipe Line Co., 458 U.S. 50, 71 (1982) (opinion of Brennan, J.):

[T]he restructuring of debtor-creditor relations, which is at the core of the federal bankruptcy power, must be distinguished from the adjudication of state-created private rights, such as the right to recover contract damages that is at issue in this case. The former may well be a "public right," but the latter obviously is not.

and disallowance of claims." Nor is that action integral to the restructuring of debtor-creditor relations. Congress therefore cannot divest petitioners of their Seventh Amendment right to a trial by jury. Katchen thus supports the result we reach today; it certainly does not compel its opposite. . . .

It may be that providing jury trials in some fraudulent conveyance actions — if not in this particular case, because respondent's suit was commenced after the bankruptcy court approved the debtor's plan of reorganization — would impede swift resolution of bankruptcy proceedings and increase the expense of Chapter 11 reorganizations. But "these considerations are insufficient to overcome the clear command of the Seventh Amendment." Curtis v. Loether, 415 U.S., at 198.

V

We do not decide today whether the current jury trial provision — 28 U.S.C. §1411 (1982 ed., Supp. IV) — permits bankruptcy courts to conduct jury trials in fraudulent conveyance actions like the one respondent initiated. Nor do we express any view as to whether the Seventh Amendment or Article III allows jury trials in such actions to be held before non–Article III bankruptcy judges subject to the oversight provided by the district courts pursuant to the 1984 Amendments. We leave those issues for future decisions.[19] . . .

Justice SCALIA concurring in part and concurring in the judgment.
I join all but Part IV of the Court's opinion.

* * *

Justice WHITE dissenting. . . .
How does the Court determine that an action to recover fraudulently conveyed property is not "integrally related" to the essence of bankruptcy proceedings? Certainly not by reference to a current statutory definition of the core of bankruptcy proceedings — enacted by Congress under its plenary constitutional power, see U.S. Const. Art. I, §8, to establish bankruptcy laws. As discussed in the preceding paragraph, this vision of what is "integrally related" to the resolution of creditor-debtor conflicts includes the sort of action before us today. See 28 U.S.C. §157(b)(2)(H) (1982 ed., Supp. V). Nor does the Court find support for its contrary understanding in petitioners' submission, which concedes that the action in question here is brought to "recover monies that are properly part of the debtor's estate and should be ratably distributed among creditors," and that fraudulent

19. Justice White accuses us of being "rather coy" about which statute we are invalidating, post, at 2806, n.2, and of "preferring to be obtuse" about which court must preside over the jury trial to which petitioners are entitled. Id., at 2811. But however helpful it might be for us to adjudge every pertinent statutory and constitutional issue presented by the 1978 Act and the 1984 Amendments, we cannot properly reach out and decide matters not before us. The only question we have been called upon to answer in this case is whether the Seventh Amendment grants petitioners a right to a jury trial. We hold unequivocally that it does.

transfers put at risk "the basic policy of non-discriminatory distribution that underlies the bankruptcy law." This, too, seems to belie the Court's view that actions to set aside fraudulent conveyances are not "integrally related" to reforming creditor-debtor relations.

Nor is the Court's conclusion about the nature of actions to recover fraudulently transferred property supportable either by reference to the state of American bankruptcy law prior to adoption of the 1978 Code, or by reference to the pre-1791 practice in the English courts. If the Court draws its conclusions based on the fact that these actions were not considered to be part of bankruptcy proceedings under the 1800 or 1898 Bankruptcy Acts (or, more generally, under federal bankruptcy statutes predating the 1978 Code), it has treated the power given Congress in Art. I, §8, as if it were a disposable battery, good for a limited period only — once the power in it has been consumed by use, it is to be discarded and considered to have no future value. The power of Congress under this clause is plainly not so limited: merely because Congress *once* had a scheme where actions such as this one were solely heard in plenary proceedings in Article III courts — where the Seventh Amendment attached — does not impugn the legality of every other possible arrangement.

Perhaps instead the Court rests its conclusion on the practice of the 18th-century English courts. I take issue with this view of the old English law, below. But even if this were correct, I do not see why the Article I, §8, power should be so restricted.

B

The above is not to say that Congress can vitiate the Seventh Amendment by assigning any claim that it wishes to a specialized tribunal in which juries are not employed. Cf. Atlas Roofing, supra, at 461, n.16. Our cases require a second inquiry — the one that the Court focuses exclusively upon — concerning the nature of the claim so assigned. . . .

In sum, I do not think that a fair reading of the history — our understanding of which is inevitably obscured by the passage of time and the irretrievable loss of subtleties in interpretation — clearly proves or disproves that respondent's action would have sounded in equity in England in 1791.[9]

With the historical evidence thus in equipoise — and with the nature of the relief sought here not dispositive either — we should not hesitate to defer to Congress' exercise of its power under the express constitutional grant found in Art. I, §8, cl. 4, authorizing Congress "[t]o establish . . . uniform Laws on the subject of Bankruptcies." Congress has exercised that power, defining actions such as the one before us to be among the "core" of bankruptcy proceedings, triable in a bankruptcy court before a bankruptcy judge, and without a jury. I would defer to these decisions.

* * *

9. Nor do I think it clear, as the Court seems to, that simply because the remedy sought by respondent can be expressed in monetary terms, the relief he seeks is therefore "legal" in nature, and not equitable. . . .

Justice BLACKMUN with whom Justice O'CONNOR joins, dissenting. . . .

The uncertainty in the historical record should lead us, for purposes of the present inquiry, to give the constitutional right to a jury trial the benefit of the doubt. . . .

I agree with Justice White, that it would be improper for this Court to employ, in its Seventh Amendment analysis, a century-old conception of what is and is not central to the bankruptcy process, a conception that Congress has expressly rejected. To do so would, among other vices, trivialize the efforts Congress has engaged in for more than a decade to bring the bankruptcy system into the modern era.

There are, nonetheless, some limits to what Congress constitutionally may designate as a "core proceeding," if the designation has an impact on constitutional rights. Congress, for example, could not designate as "core bankruptcy proceedings" state-law contract actions brought by debtors against third parties. Otherwise, Northern Pipeline would be rendered a nullity. In this case, however, Congress has not exceeded these limits.

Although causes of action to recover fraudulent conveyances exist outside the federal bankruptcy laws, the problems created by fraudulent conveyances are of particular significance to the bankruptcy process. . . .

In sum, it must be acknowledged that Congress has legislated treacherously close to the constitutional line by denying a jury trial in a fraudulent conveyance action in which the defendant has no claim against the estate. Nonetheless, given the significant federal interests involved, and the importance of permitting Congress at long last to fashion a modern bankruptcy system which places the basic rudiments of the bankruptcy process in the hands of an expert equitable tribunal, I cannot say that Congress has crossed the constitutional line on the facts of this case. By holding otherwise, the Court today throws Congress into still another round of bankruptcy court reform, without compelling reason. There was no need for us to rock the boat in this case. . . .

═══════════════

As the dissenting justices made clear, *Granfinanciera* involved both the immediate question of jury trials in bankruptcy court and the much larger question of the validity of the entire jurisdictional scheme. As to the narrower point, a subsequent preference-avoidance case confirmed that the jury-trial rights protected in *Granfinanciera* would be deemed waived by a creditor who had voluntarily come into bankruptcy court to assert its remaining claims. Langenkamp v. Culp, 498 U.S. 42 (1990). But the case left open the more fundamental jurisdictional issues. In the 1994 Amendments, Congress weighed in with a provision authorizing jury trials in bankruptcy court, but only if (a) the matter is otherwise within the bankruptcy court's jurisdiction, (b) the district court expressly authorizes it, and (c) the court has the consent of all parties. 28 U.S.C. §157(e). The 2005 Amendments added a provision that slightly bolsters the status of the bankruptcy courts by permitting direct appeals from bankruptcy court to the Court of Appeals in limited circumstances. 28 U.S.C. 158(d). Otherwise, seeing no pressing problems on the horizon, Congress shied away from any general jurisdictional issues.

Each term since *Granfinanciera,* observers have expected the proverbial other shoe to drop and the Court to declare the 1984 jurisdictional scheme unconstitutional. However, year after year has gone by with no action while the membership of the Court has changed.

If the Supreme Court strikes down the whole system, Congress will have to accept Article III bankruptcy judges or create yet another jurisdictional crazy quilt. In the meantime, so long as something like the current jurisdictional arrangement continues, it is necessary to understand something of its structure, as any new system will likely evolve from the existing one.

It is important to emphasize that the statute vests a very broad "related to" bankruptcy jurisdiction in the district courts. 28 U.S.C. §1334(b). It then limits the actual operation of that jurisdiction by provisions for discretionary or mandatory abstention in favor of state courts. §1334(c)(1) and (2).

Within the federal district courts, the statute gives the district judges in each district the collective right to refer some or all of the court's bankruptcy jurisdiction to the bankruptcy judges. §157(a). Every federal district has adopted a "local" rule referring all bankruptcy cases to the bankruptcy court, so the discussion that follows applies everywhere.

Section 157 defines those matters that a bankruptcy judge may hear for review on a "clearly erroneous" basis and those concerning which bankruptcy judges can only act as "masters" recommending findings of fact and conclusions of law to the district judges. The statute divides bankruptcy matters into three categories: (a) proceedings that arise *under* Title 11, (b) proceedings that arise *in* Title 11 cases, and (c) proceedings that are *related to* Title 11 cases. These categories are undefined, and their significance is unclear in many respects. The first two categories, arising "under" and arising "in," are the two types of cases that a bankruptcy judge might be able to hear on a "clearly erroneous" basis. Whether a particular "under" or "in" proceeding can be so heard by the bankruptcy judge depends upon its further categorization as a "core proceeding." "Core proceedings" may be heard by bankruptcy judges, while "noncore proceedings" will go to the district court.

Core proceedings are also undefined, but section 157(b) lists matters that are *included* among core proceedings. Not only does this approach leave open arguments for including other matters as core proceedings, but some of the listed categories are so broad that almost any "under" or "in" proceeding might arguably qualify. See, e.g., §157(b)(2)(o).

Cases that are merely "related to" may also be heard by the bankruptcy judge, but only as a master making recommendations to the district judge, unless the parties consent to bankruptcy judge jurisdiction. §157(c).

Personal injury and wrongful death claims *against* the estate receive special — and strange — treatment. On the one hand, they are not subject to the core jurisdiction of the bankruptcy judge, §157(b)(2)(B), but on the other hand they are not subject to mandatory abstention under section 1334(c)(2). §157(b)(4). As a result, such cases that are related to a bankruptcy case will be tried by the district judge, unless the parties consent to bankruptcy jurisdiction, §157(c)(2), or the district court abstains on a discretionary basis and permits a state court to try the case. §1334(c)(1).

Finally, the district court has the power to take away any bankruptcy matter from the bankruptcy judge at any time. §157(d). Furthermore, the district judge *must* take over any matter involving federal statutes "regulating organizations or activities affecting interstate commerce," which describes a very substantial part of the United States Code.

The courts have had to face the very real difficulties of giving specific meaning to this host of undefined terms. There are two problems overall. Will the case be decided by a state or a federal judge? If by a federal judge, will it be the Article III judge or the Article I bankruptcy judge? In this section we have one case addressing each of these questions. The first case addresses the question of federal jurisdiction or not:

(a) Is a matter sufficiently related to bankruptcy to justify federal jurisdiction?

(b If there is federal jurisdiction, is the federal court (i) required or (ii) permitted to abstain in favor of a state court?

Neither question arises under the *Marathon* case, because neither addresses whether the matter will be heard by an Article I or an Article III judge. So long as an Article III judge sits in the district court, both questions are issues of interpretation of the statutes by which Congress has conferred bankruptcy jurisdiction on the federal courts.

In re DOW CORNING CORP.
86 F.3d 482 (6th Cir. 1996)

Boyce F. MARTIN, Jr., Circuit Judge.

This is an appeal to determine the subject matter jurisdiction of federal district courts, sitting as bankruptcy courts, over proceedings "related to" a case filed under Chapter 11 of the Bankruptcy Code, and the ability of federal district courts to transfer such proceedings to the district court in which the bankruptcy case is pending. The principal issue presented is whether the district court erred, as a matter of law, in its determination that claims for compensatory and punitive damages asserted in tens of thousands of actions against numerous nondebtor manufacturers and suppliers of silicone gel breast implants could have no conceivable effect upon, and therefore were not related to, the bankruptcy estate of The Dow Corning Corporation. The district court held that it did not have "related to" jurisdiction over those claims pursuant to 28 U.S.C. §1334(b) and concluded that they could not be transferred to it pursuant to 28 U.S.C. §157(b)(5). For the following reasons, we reverse and remand for further proceedings consistent with this opinion.

I

Until it ceased their manufacture in 1992, Dow Corning was the predominant producer of silicone gel breast implants, accounting for nearly 50% of the entire market. In addition, Dow Corning supplied silicone raw materials to other manufacturers of silicone gel breast implants. In recent years, tens of thousands of implant recipients have sued Dow Corning, claiming to have been injured by autoimmune reactions to the silicone in their implants. Dow Chemical Company, Corning Incorporated, Minnesota Mining and Manufacturing Company, Baxter Healthcare Corporation and Baxter International Incorporated, and Bristol-Myers Squibb Company and Medical Engineering Corporation are other manufacturers and suppliers of silicone gel-filled implants, and are codefendants with Dow Corning in a large number of personal injury actions.

On June 25, 1992, prior to Dow Corning's filing of its Chapter 11 petition, the Federal Judicial Panel on Multidistrict Litigation ordered the consolidation of all breast implant actions pending in federal courts for coordinated pretrial proceedings, and transferred those actions to Chief Judge Pointer of the Northern District of Alabama. On September 1, 1994, Chief Judge Pointer certified a class for settlement purposes only, and approved a complex agreement between members of the class and certain defendants that contemplated the creation of a $4.25 billion fund to cover, among other things, the costs of treatment and other expenses incurred by breast implant recipients. Each class member was given the opportunity to opt out of the class and to pursue her individual claims separately. Several thousand plaintiffs opted out of the settlement class, while approximately 440,000 elected to register for inclusion in the Global Settlement.

Due to the litigation burden imposed by what is one of the world's largest mass tort litigations, and the threatened consequences of the thousands of product liability claims arising from its manufacture and sale of silicone breast implants and silicone gel, Dow Corning filed a petition for reorganization under Chapter 11 of the Bankruptcy Code on May 15, 1995, in the United States District Court for the Eastern District of Michigan. The district court had jurisdiction over that proceeding pursuant to 28 U.S.C. §1334(a). As a result of Dow Corning's Chapter 11 filing, all breast implant claims against it were automatically stayed pursuant to 11 U.S.C. §362(a). Claims against Dow Corning's two shareholders, Dow Chemical and Corning Incorporated, and the other nondebtor defendants were not stayed. Dow Chemical, Corning Incorporated, Minnesota Mining, Baxter and Bristol-Myers Squibb subsequently removed many opt-out claims in which those companies were named defendants with Dow Corning from state to federal court pursuant to 28 U.S.C. §1452(a).

On June 12, 1995, Dow Corning filed a motion pursuant to 28 U.S.C. § 157(b)(5) to transfer to the Eastern District of Michigan opt-out breast implant claims pending against it and its shareholders, Dow Chemical and Corning Incorporated.[6] Dow Corning's motion covered claims that had been removed to federal court and were pending in the multidistrict forum,

---

6. Dow Corning's motion sought a transfer of lawsuits against it and its shareholders which were not part of the global settlement. Dow Corning, Dow Chemical and Corning have stated that "[t]housands of the suits against Dow Corning have included claims against Dow Chemical and Corning, even though neither of those companies designed, manufactured, tested, or sold breast implants." Brief for Dow Corning Corporation, The Dow Chemical Company, and Corning Incorporated at 9. . . .

as well as claims pending in state courts which were in the process of being removed to federal courts pursuant to 28 U.S.C. §1452(a). Dow Corning envisioned its transfer motion as the first step in ensuring a feasible plan of reorganization, and indicated that it would seek to have the transferred actions consolidated for a threshold jury trial on the issue of whether silicone gel breast implants cause the diseases claimed. Dow Chemical and Corning Incorporated joined in Dow Corning's motion.

On June 14, 1995, Minnesota Mining, Baxter, and Bristol-Myers Squibb also moved, pursuant to Section 157(b)(5), to transfer to the Eastern District of Michigan the opt-out cases in which those manufacturers were named as defendants with Dow Corning.[7] In their Section 157(b)(5) motions, Minnesota Mining, Baxter, and Bristol-Myers Squibb also asked the district court to order that the claims at issue be transferred to the district court in which the bankruptcy case is pending so that the court could conduct a consolidated trial on the issue of causation.

On September 12, 1995, the district court issued two opinions and companion orders regarding the Section 157(b)(5) transfer motions. With respect to opt-out breast implant cases pending against Dow Corning, the district court asserted jurisdiction under Section 1334(b) and permitted transfer pursuant to Section 157(b)(5). The district court, however, denied the remainder of the transfer motions on the ground that, as a matter of law, it lacked subject matter jurisdiction over the claims sought to be transferred because they were not "related to" Dow Corning's bankruptcy proceeding pursuant to 28 U.S.C. §1334(b). . . .

. . . In addressing these issues, we begin, as we do in any case involving a question of statutory construction, with the express language of the statute at issue and an examination of Congressional intent. In addition, we recognize that our decision will significantly impact the future course of this massive litigation. Realizing that we cannot satisfy all competing interests perfectly, our primary goal is to establish a mechanism for resolving the claims at issue in the most fair and equitable manner possible. In seeking to achieve that goal, we are called upon to balance four different, and frequently competing, interests: those of the individuals who have brought and will bring breast implant claims; Dow Corning's interests with regard to its attempt to formulate a successful reorganization plan; Dow Chemical and Corning Incorporated's interests as shareholders of Dow Corning; and the judicial system's interest in allocating its limited resources effectively and efficiently. . . .

III

The first issue to be resolved is whether the district court has subject matter jurisdiction over breast implant claims pending not only against the debtor, Dow Corning, but also over certain claims pending against the nondebtor defendants. . . .

---

7. The Minnesota Mining, Baxter, and Bristol-Myers Squibb motions were limited to personal injury actions in which Dow Corning was a named codefendant with one or more of those parties and the plaintiffs had opted out of the Global Settlement. . . .

In addressing the extent of a district court's bankruptcy jurisdiction under Section 1334(b) over civil proceedings "related to" cases under title 11, we start with the premise that the "emphatic terms in which the jurisdictional grant is described in the legislative history, and the extraordinarily broad wording of the grant itself, leave us with no doubt that Congress intended to grant to the district courts broad jurisdiction in bankruptcy cases." In re Salem, 783 F.2d at 634. Although "situations may arise where an extremely tenuous connection to the estate would not satisfy the jurisdictional requirement" of Section 1334(b), Robinson v. Mich. Consol. Gas Co., Inc., 918 F.2d 579, 584 (6th Cir. 1990), Congressional intent was "to grant comprehensive jurisdiction to the bankruptcy courts so that they might deal efficiently and expeditiously with all matters connected with the bankruptcy estate." Celotex Corp. v. Edwards, 514 U.S. 300, —, 115 S. Ct. 1493, 1499 (1995) (citations omitted).

The definition of a "related" proceeding under Section 1334(b) was first articulated by the Third Circuit in *Pacor*. As stated in that case, the "usual articulation of the test for determining whether a civil proceeding is related to bankruptcy is whether the outcome of that proceeding could conceivably have any effect on the estate being administered in bankruptcy." *Pacor*, 743 F.2d at 994. An action is "related to bankruptcy if the outcome could alter the debtor's rights, liabilities, options, or freedom of action (either positively or negatively) and which in any way impacts upon the handling and administration of the bankrupt estate." Id. A proceeding "need not necessarily be against the debtor or against the debtor's property" to satisfy the requirements for "related to" jurisdiction. Id. However, "the mere fact that there may be common issues of fact between a civil proceeding and a controversy involving the bankruptcy estate does not bring the matter within the scope of section [1334(b)]." Id. (stating also that "[j]udicial economy itself does not justify federal jurisdiction"). Instead, "there must be some nexus between the 'related' civil proceeding and the title 11 case." Id. Our Circuit adopted the *Pacor* test for determining whether a civil proceeding is "related to" a bankruptcy proceeding under Section 1334(b) in *Robinson*, 918 F.2d at 583 (noting in doing so that circuit courts have "uniformly adopted an expansive definition of a related proceeding under section 1334(b)"). The majority of our sister circuits have likewise adopted the *Pacor* test for "related to" jurisdiction.

In addition, the Supreme Court recently cited *Pacor* with approval in addressing the broad scope of the jurisdictional grant in Section 1334(b). The Court stated:

> Congress did not delineate the scope of "related to" jurisdiction, but its choice of words suggests a grant of some breadth. The jurisdictional grant in [Section] 1334(b) was a distinct departure from the jurisdiction conferred under previous acts, which had been limited to either possession of property by the debtor or consent as a basis for jurisdiction. We agree with the views expressed by the Court of Appeals for the Third Circuit in *Pacor* that "Congress intended to grant comprehensive jurisdiction to the bankruptcy courts so that they might deal efficiently and expeditiously with all matters connected with the bankruptcy estate," and that the "related to" language of [Section] 1334(b) must be read to give district courts (and bankruptcy courts

under [Section] 157(a)) jurisdiction over more than simple proceedings involving the property of the debtor or the estate.

Celotex, 514 U.S. at — - — , 115 S. Ct. at 1498-99 (citations omitted) (recognizing at the same time that a bankruptcy court's jurisdiction cannot be limitless). The Court also stated that proceedings "related to" a bankruptcy proceeding include "suits between third parties which have an effect on the bankruptcy estate." Id. at — n.5, 115 S. Ct. at 1499 n.5 (citing 1 Collier on Bankruptcy ¶3.01[1][c][iv], pp.3-28 (15th ed. 1994)). . . .

1. Claims for Contribution and Indemnification

Dow Corning, Dow Chemical and Corning Incorporated argue that the district court erred in its determination that "related to" jurisdiction does not exist over certain breast implant claims asserted against Dow Chemical and Corning Incorporated because, in addition to the claims asserted by the personal injury claimants, Dow Chemical and Corning Incorporated have asserted cross-claims against each other and Dow Corning in the underlying litigation, which will have an effect on the bankruptcy estate. Minnesota Mining, Baxter, and Bristol-Myers Squibb argue that, despite the fact that they have not yet filed contribution and indemnification claims or proofs of claim relating to implant litigation in Dow Corning's bankruptcy case, they have contingent claims for contribution and indemnification that will have a conceivable effect on the bankruptcy proceedings. Minnesota Mining, Baxter, and Bristol-Myers Squibb therefore argue that the breast implant claims covered by their Section 157(b)(5) motions will give rise to thousands of claims against Dow Corning for indemnification and contribution. In addition, the nondebtor defendants claim that Dow Corning may itself have claims against them for contribution and indemnification under theories of joint and several liability. The companies argue that these claims need to be resolved as part of Dow Corning's bankruptcy proceedings and reorganization plan, and certainly will affect the debtor's rights, liabilities, options, and freedom of action in the administration of its estate.

Pacor involved John and Louise Higgins' claim against the Philadelphia Asbestos Co. (Pacor) in state court seeking damages allegedly caused by Mr. Higgins' work-related exposure to asbestos supplied by the company. In response, Pacor filed a third-party complaint impleading the Johns-Manville Corporation, which Pacor claimed was the original manufacturer of the asbestos. After Johns-Manville filed for Chapter 11, a dispute ensued as to whether the Higgins-Pacor action was "related to" the Manville bankruptcy so that the entire controversy could be removed to bankruptcy court. The Third Circuit held that the primary Higgins-Pacor action would not affect the Manville bankruptcy estate, and therefore was not "related to" the bankruptcy proceedings. The court stated that the Higgins-Pacor action was, "[a]t best, a mere precursor to the potential third party claim for indemnification by Pacor against Manville," and held that, because all issues with regard to Manville's possible liability would be resolved in a subsequent third party impleader action, "there would be no automatic creation of liability against Manville on account of a judgment against Pacor." Pacor, 743 F.2d at 995 (stating also that "[t]here would therefore be no effect on administration of the estate, until such time as Pacor may choose to pursue its third party claim"). Thus, the court in Pacor viewed the absence of "automatic" liability on the part of the debtor as dispositive in determining that Section 1334(b) "related to" jurisdiction did not exist.

It has become clear following Pacor that "automatic" liability is not necessarily a prerequisite for a finding of "related to" jurisdiction. The Third Circuit itself has emphasized that:

> A key word in [the] test is "conceivable." Certainty, or even likelihood, is not a requirement. Bankruptcy jurisdiction will exist so long as it is possible that a proceeding may impact on "the debtor's rights, liabilities, options, or freedom of action" or the "handling and administration of the bankrupt estate."

In re Marcus Hook Dev. Park Inc., 943 F.2d 261, 264 (3d Cir.1991) (citation omitted).

Our Circuit has held that Section 1334(b) "does not require a finding of definite liability of [an] estate as a condition precedent to holding an action related to a bankruptcy proceeding." In re Salem, 783 F.2d at 635. . . .

The degree of identity between debtor and nondebtor co-defendants was an important factor in *A.H. Robins Co. I*, a mass tort case involving the Dalkon Shield, an intrauterine contraceptive device. . . . A.H. Robins . . . sought injunctive relief restraining the prosecution of the actions against its codefendants. The district court granted a preliminary injunction, holding that all actions that might be satisfied from proceeds of the debtor's products liability policy with Aetna Casualty and Insurance Company were stayed, and enjoined further litigation in eight civil actions. . . .

In discussing the propriety of the stay issued against A.H. Robins' non-debtor codefendants, the Fourth Circuit stated that, although Section 362(a)(1) is generally available only to a debtor, proceedings against non-bankrupt codefendants may be stayed by a bankruptcy court where there are "unusual circumstances." . . .

Based on the principles outlined above, we believe the district court has "related to" subject matter jurisdiction over the breast implant claims pending against the nondebtor defendants in this case. Thousands of suits asserted against Dow Corning include claims against the nondebtors, and the nature of the claims asserted establishes that Dow Corning and the various nondebtor defendants are closely related with regard to the pending breast implant litigation. Dow Chemical and Corning Incorporated have already asserted cross-claims against each other and Dow Corning in the underlying litigation, and the other nondebtor defendants have asserted repeatedly throughout their briefs, motions, and oral arguments that they intend to file claims for contribution and indemnification against Dow Corning, and we have no reason to doubt the veracity of those assertions at this time.

We find that it is not necessary for the appellees first to prevail on their claims against the nondebtor defendants, and for those companies to establish joint and several liability on Dow Corning's part, before the civil actions pending against the nondebtors may be viewed as conceivably impacting Dow Corning's bankruptcy proceedings. The claims currently pending against the nondebtors give rise to contingent claims against Dow Corning which unquestionably could ripen into fixed claims. The potential for Dow Corning's being held liable to the nondebtors in claims for contribution and indemnification, or vice versa, suffices to establish a conceivable impact on the estate in bankruptcy.

Claims for indemnification and contribution, whether asserted against or by Dow Corning, obviously would affect the size of the estate and the length of time the bankruptcy proceedings will be pending, as well as Dow Corning's ability to resolve its liabilities and proceed with reorganization. In addition, we believe there is a qualitative difference between the single suit involved in *Pacor* and the overwhelming number of cases asserted against Dow Corning and the nondebtor defendants in this case. A single possible claim for indemnification or contribution simply does not represent the same kind of threat to a debtor's reorganization plan as that posed by the thousands of potential indemnification claims at issue here.

2. Joint Insurance

Dow Corning, Dow Chemical, and Corning Incorporated also argue that "related to" jurisdiction exists as to claims pending against the shareholders because the three companies share joint insurance. We believe this argument provides additional support for the existence of "related to" jurisdiction under the unique facts of this case, but address it only briefly because we have already concluded that Section 1334(b) jurisdiction exists over breast implant claims pending against Dow Corning and one or both of its parents.

Dow Corning, Dow Chemical, and Corning Incorporated are co-insured under various insurance policies, which together provide over $1 billion in coverage. Dow Corning's interest in the policies is one of the largest assets of its bankruptcy estate. In addition, Dow Corning recently entered into ten new insurance settlements under which the estate will receive, if approved by the bankruptcy court, approximately $350 to $450 million in cash. Most of these settlements involve policies under which Dow Chemical or Corning Incorporated is a co-insured.

Dow Corning, Dow Chemical, and Corning Incorporated claim that the district court's order, by allowing thousands of claims to proceed separately against Dow Chemical and Corning Incorporated, will diminish the value of this major bankruptcy asset to the extent that settlements, judgments and defense costs incurred by the shareholders will exhaust policy limits otherwise available to Dow Corning, its creditors, and individuals asserting claims in the bankruptcy proceedings. In addition, all three co-insureds argue that the policies will be further diminished if and when payments must be made to Minnesota Mining, Baxter, or Bristol-Myers Squibb. Dow Chemical has already notified insurers that it is asserting claims against the jointly-held policies on the ground that, as a co-insured, it is entitled to recover from the insurers all of its defense costs, as well as any settlements or judgments paid by it in litigating breast implant claims. The concern, then, is that permitting scores of trials against the shareholders to go forward while litigation against the debtor is stayed may result in the shareholders making claims for insurance and seeking and obtaining payment from the insurers before Dow Corning is able to make any claims of its own...

Dow Corning's interest in the insurance policies at issue is property of its estate under the expansive definition set forth in 11 U.S.C. §541(a)(l). The threat posed to those insurance policies if claims pending against Dow Chemical and Corning Incorporated are permitted to go forward in a separate manner supports a finding of "related to" jurisdiction under Section 1334(b). The prospect of Dow Chemical and Corning Incorporated being able to assert mature, liquidated claims against the insurance proceeds if litigation pending against them is permitted to go forward demonstrates a conceivable impact on the bankruptcy proceedings. If it is determined that Dow Chemical or Corning Incorporated has a priority to the insurance proceeds, even if the bankruptcy court has the power to prevent payments of the proceeds while Dow Corning is in bankruptcy, the risk remains that the insurance coverage may be eviscerated when the proceeds are eventually distributed. In addition, certain of the policies cover defense expenses, and those costs alone may significantly reduce the pool of coverage available to Dow Corning if the claims pending against Dow Chemical and Corning Incorporated are allowed to proceed separately. In addition, the bankruptcy court has yet to determine whether it has the power to prevent Dow Corning's co-insureds from receiving proceeds of the jointly-held policies while Dow Corning is in bankruptcy. Resolution of the dispute over the right to proceeds alone will have a conceivable effect on Dow Coming's bankruptcy proceedings.

IV

[The court found that 28 U.S.C. §157(b)(5) authorized a transfer of venue to the bankruptcy court.]

V

Finally, a Section 157(b)(5) motion "requires an abstention analysis." In re Pan Am Corp., 950 F.2d 839, 844 (2d Cir.1991) ("In re Pan Am Corp. II"). The abstention provisions of 28 U.S.C. §1334(c) qualify Section 1334(b)'s broad grant of jurisdiction. In re Salem, 783 F.2d at 635. It is for the district court to "determine in each individual case whether hearing it would promote or impair efficient and fair adjudication of bankruptcy cases." Id.

Section 1334 provides for two types of abstention: discretionary abstention under 28 U.S.C. §1334(c)(1) and mandatory abstention under 28 U.S.C. §1334(c)(2), ...

For mandatory abstention to apply, a proceeding must: (1) be based on a state law claim or cause of action; (2) lack a federal jurisdictional basis absent the bankruptcy; (3) be commenced in a state forum of appropriate jurisdiction; (4) be capable of timely adjudication; and (5) be a non-core proceeding. Non-core proceedings under Section 157(b)(2)(B) (i.e. liquidation of personal injury tort or wrongful death case) are not subject to Section 1334(c)(2)'s mandatory abstention provisions pursuant to 28 U.S.C. §157(b)(4).

The district court in this case determined that Section 157(b)(4) rendered exempt from the mandatory abstention requirement all personal injury tort claims pending solely against Dow Corning, and decided not to abstain discretionarily with regard to those claims at this time. . . . Because we believe the district court is in a better position to make the necessary abstention determinations, as to both mandatory and discretionary abstention, we remand the case to the district court for further proceedings on this issue. . . .

In most instances, once the Supreme Court refused to review the case, the Sixth Circuit opinion would end the matter. But the district court judge in the Dow Corning case remained reluctant to take on the massive and complex package just handed to her by the circuit court. The district court abstained, citing both the mandatory and permissive absention provisions. The circuit court was not amused.

In re DOW CORNING CORP.
113 F.3d 565 (6th Cir. 1997)

Boyce F. MARTIN, Jr., Chief Judge.

Before the Court is an appeal and petition for writ of mandamus by Dow Corning; its shareholders, The Dow Chemical Company and Corning Incorporated; and other manufacturers of silicone products that have been named as co-defendants with Dow Corning in product liability suits relating to silicone implants. These parties contest the district court's denial of their motion to transfer to the Eastern District of Michigan breast-implant claims brought in various jurisdictions by claimants who have chosen not to join the global settlement pool. The district court, upon remand from this Court, exercised discretionary and mandatory abstention in declining to transfer the claims against the shareholders and the co-defendants. For the reasons stated herein, we issue a writ of mandamus ordering the district court to transfer the claims against the shareholders to the Eastern District of Michigan and to evaluate each claim individually to determine whether mandatory abstention applies.

The Official Committee of Tort Claimants initially contend that we are without jurisdiction to review the district court's decision. Indeed, Congress has significantly curtailed the courts of appeals' ability to review a district court's decision to exercise mandatory or discretionary abstention under 28 U.S.C. §1334(c)(1), (2). . . . However, we conclude for two reasons that we have jurisdiction in mandamus to review the district court's decision.

First, this is not the ordinary situation in which the district court, either on motion of a party or on its own motion, determines that abstention under 28 U.S.C. §1334(c) is appropriate. Rather, the district court was instructed by this Court, in an order remanding this matter for the explicit purpose of determining whether abstention was proper, to undertake a case-by-case review of these tort claims and to determine, as to each case, whether to abstain. The district court did not comply with our order of remand. The issuance of a writ of mandamus is therefore necessary and appropriate to require the district court to conduct the abstention analysis in strict compliance with the requirements of §1334 and our order of remand.

Second, §1334(d) does not mention this Court's ability to review such determinations pursuant to our mandamus authority under 28 U.S.C. §1651. . . . Because of the significant risk posed to Dow Corning's estate by the multi-forum breast-implant litigation, this case is one of those rare instances where mandamus relief is appropriate. . . .

The district court's decision applying mandatory abstention to the proceedings against the shareholders is, in generous terms, inadequate. The requirements for mandatory abstention dictate that each case must be examined individually. The district court, in its three-page discussion of mandatory abstention, failed to make the necessary case-by-case inquiry. No hearing was conducted, and no evidence was accepted by the district court. It is undisputed that some of the cases do not meet the requirements of mandatory abstention. Indeed, in many of the cases, there does not even appear to have been a motion for abstention filed by the plaintiff in the proceeding. Moreover, the number of cases requiring mandatory abstention is impossible for us to determine because of the paucity of evidence on the record. Thus, the district court's decision employing §1334(c) to abstain globally without examination of a single individual claim cannot stand.

The district court's exercise of discretionary abstention is equally troubling. . . .

As an initial matter, it makes little practical sense to transfer the claims against Dow Corning while refusing to transfer those against the shareholders. . . .

The district court also overlooked the risks to Dow Corning's estate that were clearly articulated in our prior decision. Failing to transfer the claims against the shareholders will likely affect the size of the estate and the length of time the bankruptcy proceedings will be pending, as well as Dow Corning's ability to resolve its liabilities and proceed with reorganization. . . .

Accordingly, we issue a writ of mandamus ordering the district court to transfer the claims against Dow Chemical and Corning Incorporated to the Eastern District of Michigan. Once transfer has been accomplished, the cases should be indexed and cross referenced so that, in any proceeding in which a motion for abstention is filed, the district court may make the required abstention determinations and adequately state its reasoning as to each such proceeding. Because we find it unnecessary to transfer any other pending proceedings to the district court at this time, we deny the non-debtor manufacturers' petition for writ of mandamus.

Mandamus is an extraordinary proceeding in any federal action, whether it involves bankruptcy or not. But a case encompassing thousands of separate lawsuits is also extraordinary, so perhaps it is not unusual for all the parties to test the limits of the law.

The next case addresses the question that arises *within* the federal courthouse. It is the *Marathon* question, as seen through 28 U.S.C. §157, Congress's attempt to solve the problem of allocating jurisdiction between the federal district court and the bankruptcy court. Although the following case is a mass-tort Chapter 11, the issue presented this time is a contract question involving interpretation of policies of insurance. In 1993, in an opinion referred to in the following case, the Second Circuit was seen as greatly narrowing the "core" jurisdiction of the bankruptcy courts in contract matters. Orion Pictures Corp. v. Showtime Networks, Inc. (In re Orion Pictures Corp.), 4 F.3d 1095 (2d Cir. 1993). In the case that follows, six years after *Orion*, the judges of that circuit court disagree considerably about the proper articulation of the applicable rule, although they all agree on the result in the case presented.

In re UNITED STATES LINES, INC.
197 F.3d 631 (2d Cir. 1999)

WALKER, Circuit Judge:

The United States Lines, Inc. and United States Lines (S.A.) Inc. Reorganization Trust (the "Trust") sued in the Bankruptcy Court for the Southern District of New York (Francis G. Conrad, Bankruptcy Judge) seeking a declaratory judgment to establish the Trust's rights under various insurance contracts. The bankruptcy court held that the action was within its core jurisdiction and denied the defendants' motion to compel arbitration of the proceedings. The District Court for the Southern District of New York (Sidney H. Stein, District Judge), reversed and held that the insurance contract disputes were not core proceedings. After ordering arbitration to go forward, the district court certified its order for interlocutory appeal pursuant to 28 U.S.C. §1292(b). We now reverse and remand.

BACKGROUND

. . . On November 24, 1986, United States Lines, Inc. and United States Lines (S.A.) Inc., as debtors, filed a voluntary petition for bankruptcy relief under Chapter 11 of the Bankruptcy Code, 11 U.S.C. §§101 et seq. The Trust is their successor-in-interest pursuant to a plan of reorganization that was confirmed by the bankruptcy court on May 16, 1989.

Among the creditors are some 12,000 employees who have filed more than 18,000 claims, most of which are for asbestos-related injuries sustained while sailing on different ships in debtors' fleet over four decades. Many additional claims are expected to mature in the future. The Trust asserts that these claims are covered by several Protection & Indemnity insurance policies (the "P & I policies") issued by four domestic and four foreign mutual insurance clubs ("the Clubs"). . . . All of the P & I policies were issued before the debtors petitioned for bankruptcy relief.

The proceeds of the P & I policies are the only funds potentially available to cover the above employees' personal injury claims. At the heart of each of the P & I policies is a pay-first provision by which the insurers' liability is not triggered until the insured pays the claim of the personal injury victim. The deductibles for each accident or occurrence vary among the different policies, ranging from $250 to $100,000.

On December 8, 1992, the Bankruptcy Court entered a stipulation of conditional settlement between the Trust and an initial group of 106 claimants, and on January 5, 1993, the Trust began this action as an adversarial proceeding in bankruptcy, pursuant to 28 U.S.C. §2201, seeking a declaratory judgment of the parties' respective rights under the various P & I policies. Nine of the ten counts in the complaint seek a declaration from the court of the Clubs' contractual obligations under the P & I policies in light of the stipulation of conditional settlement. The tenth claim seeks punitive damages for creating an "insurance maze."

I. Whether the Declaratory Judgment Action Is "Core"

The Bankruptcy Code divides claims in bankruptcy proceedings into two principal categories: "core" and "non-core." . . . With respect to non-core claims, unless the parties otherwise agree, the bankruptcy court can only recommend findings of fact and conclusions of law to the district court. . . .

The origin of the core/non-core distinction is found in Northern Pipeline Construction Co. v. Marathon Pipe Line Co. . . .

. . . [U]nder Marathon, . . . [p]roceedings can be core by virtue of their nature if either (1) the type of proceeding is unique to or uniquely affected by the bankruptcy proceedings, see, e.g., id. at 706 (claim allowance), or (2) the proceedings directly affect a core bankruptcy function. . . .

We now turn to the question of whether the underlying insurance contract claims are core. Some arguments for deeming the contract claims core are unavailing. While "[t]he debtors' rights under its insurance policies are property of a debtor's estate," St. Clare's Hosp. & Health Ctr. v. Insurance Co. of N. Am. (In re St. Clare's Hosp. &. Health Ctr.), 934 F.2d 15, 18 (2d Cir. 1991), the contract claims are not rendered core simply because they involve property of the estate. "The issue [in the contract claims] is the scope of the insurance policies, an issue of contractual interpretation, not their ownership." In re United States Brass Corp., 110 F.3d 1261, 1268 (7th Cir. 1997). A general rule that such proceedings are core because they involve property of the estate would "create[ ] an exception to Marathon that would swallow the rule." Orion Pictures Corp. v. Showtime Networks, Inc. (In re Orion Pictures Corp.), 4 F.3d 1095, 1102 (2d Cir. 1993).

The Trust argues that the proceedings are core because not all of the insurance claims have been fully developed pre-petition. However, the critical question in determining whether a contractual dispute is core by virtue of timing is not whether the cause of action accrued post-petition, but whether the contract was formed post-petition. The bankruptcy court has core jurisdiction over claims arising from a contract formed post-petition under §157(b)(2)(A). But a dispute arising from a pre-petition contract will usually not be rendered core simply because the cause of action could only arise post-petition. In Orion, for example, we held to be non-core Orion's cause of action for anticipatory breach of a pre-petition contract that sought declaratory and other relief from Showtime even though the event that triggered Orion's claim occurred post-petition. See In re Orion Pictures Corp., 4 F.3d at 1097, 1102.[1]

Notwithstanding that the Trust's claims are upon pre-petition contracts, we conclude that the impact these contracts have on other core bankruptcy functions nevertheless render the proceedings core. . . . [R]esolving disputes relating to major insurance contracts are bound to have a significant impact on the administration of the estate. In Orion, we concluded that where the insurance proceeds would only augment the assets of the estate for general distribution, the effect on the administration of the estate was insufficient to render the proceedings core. See Orion, 4 F.3d at 1102 ($77 million potential debt which admittedly would ease administration and liquidation of the estate still encompassed by Marathon prohibition). Resolving the disputes over the P & I policies here has a much more direct impact on the core administrative functions of the bankruptcy court.

The insurance proceeds are almost entirely earmarked for paying the personal injury claimants and represent the only potential source of cash available to that group of creditors. However, under the pay-first provisions of the P & I policies, those proceeds will not be made available until the Trust has paid the claims. . . . The insolvent insured is therefore often forced to satisfy the pay-first requirement by means of complex, creative payment schemes. In addition to the difficulties involved in paying the claims, the Trust faces a significant risk that the payment scheme ultimately employed will be deemed not to satisfy the pay-first requirement. . . .

III. Annulment of the Arbitration Clauses

The parties have entered into valid agreements to arbitrate their contract disputes, some of which call for international arbitration. Arbitration is favored in our judicial system. . . . The arbitration preference is particularly strong for international arbitration agreements. . . . The Clubs therefore argue that the bankruptcy court cannot enjoin arbitration of the proceedings. We disagree. . . .

. . . In the bankruptcy setting, congressional intent to permit a bankruptcy court to enjoin arbitration is sufficiently clear to override even international arbitration agreements.

Thus, there will be occasions where a dispute involving both the Bankruptcy Code, 11 U.S.C. §101 et seq., and the Arbitration Act, 9 U.S.C. §1 et seq., "presents a conflict of near polar extremes: bankruptcy policy

---

1. This paragraph expresses the views of the author. Each of the other members of the panel has filed a concurring opinion setting forth his separate views.

exerts an inexorable pull towards centralization while arbitration policy advocates a decentralized approach towards dispute resolution." Societe Nationale Algerienne Pour La Recherche, La Production, Le Transport, La Transformation et La Commercialisation des Hydrocarbures v. Distrigas Corp., 80 B.R. 606, 610 (D. Mass. 1987).

Such a conflict is lessened in non-core proceedings which are unlikely to present a conflict sufficient to override by implication the presumption in favor of arbitration. Core proceedings implicate more pressing bankruptcy concerns, but even a determination that a proceeding is core will not automatically give the bankruptcy court discretion to stay arbitration. . . . However, there are circumstances in which a bankruptcy court may stay arbitration, and in this case the bankruptcy court was correct that it had discretion to do so. . . .

Jon O. NEWMAN, Circuit Judge, concurring:

I concur in the result and in all aspects of Judge Walker's opinion except his individual statement of the view that whether a lawsuit alleging a post-petition breach of a pre-petition contract is a core proceeding depends on the impact the contract has on core bankruptcy functions. In my view, the efficient functioning of the bankruptcy system will be better served by a bright-line rule that treats as core proceedings all suits alleging post-petition breaches of pre-petition contracts.

This Circuit's approach to the issue of whether post-petition breaches of pre-petition contracts are core has not been consistent. . . .

On this inconclusive state of the law in the Second Circuit, I believe the issue of whether a suit for a post-petition breach of a pre-petition contract is core remains open. . . . I agree, as Judge Walker's opinion demonstrates, that this suit affects core functions and, for that reason, can be considered core, but I would deem it core simply because it involves a post-petition breach.

. . . There can be nothing unconstitutional in permitting a non–Article III bankruptcy court to adjudicate a cause of action for a post-petition breach of a pre-petition contract, a cause of action that did not exist until the jurisdiction of the bankruptcy court attached. . . .

Since a cause of action for a post-petition breach can constitutionally be considered core, it always should be in order to promote the efficient functioning of the bankruptcy system. That efficiency will be substantially impeded by injecting into numerous bankruptcy proceedings the fact-specific and somewhat nebulous issue of whether a particular post-petition breach of a pre-petition contract has a sufficient impact on core functions to render the cause of action core. . . .

CALABRESI, Circuit Judge, concurring:

I too "concur in the result and in all aspects of Judge Walker's opinion except the portion indicating that whether a lawsuit alleging a post-petition breach of a pre-petition contract is a core proceeding depends on the impact the contract has on core bankruptcy functions." Judge Newman's Concurrence at 1. But my reasons for not joining fully in that part of Judge Walker's opinion are different from Judge Newman's. . . .

Were I to reach the question, I would be inclined to favor a case-by-case approach. But since we do not need to resolve the issue to decide the case before us, I would defer the matter to another day and to a case that raises the question squarely. Like Judges Walker and Newman, I have no doubt that this particular post-petition breach of a pre-petition contract is core. That is all I need to decide the instant case. . . .

Why so much bother over locating the insurance-contract dispute within the core jurisdiction of the bankruptcy judge, when the Article III district judge could just take over the dispute and resolve it in the usual way?

Venue

Despite the jurisdictional uncertainty, the bankruptcy courts exercise enormous judgment and influence in the cases that come before them. When has a creditor shown that it is not "adequately protected"? When has a debtor shown that it is providing "adequate assurance of future performance"? When has the U.S. Trustee shown that replacement of management will be "in the best interests of the debtor"? Given the degree of range of decision-making open to bankruptcy judges, it is unsurprising that some debtors and creditors who may be headed to bankruptcy court look very hard at the particular judge who will decide their economic fate. Once again, the bankruptcy system offers some surprising turns.

For the typical individual or small business faced with a financial crisis, the bankruptcy judge who will hear the matter is whatever judge happens to be sitting in the district where the soon-to-be-debtor lives. 28 U.S.C. §1408(a). But for a big business, the alternatives listed in the statute provide the possibility of shopping for the court that the debtor finds most congenial. A debtor may file in its "domicile, residence, or principal place of business." For many large companies with operations spread across several states and incorporation papers filed in some distant location, the immediate possibilities are more than one: the place where the debtor is incorporated and the place or places where the debtor has substantial assets and operations. In addition, section 1408(b) adds another option: a debtor may file wherever an affiliate, general partner, or partnership has already filed. This means, for example, that when Ionosphere Clubs (the frequent flier club of Eastern Airlines) filed in New York where it was incorporated, Eastern Airlines, incorporated and located mainly in Florida, could file in New York just minutes later.

Venue is never locked in. Even if a filing is properly located in one jurisdiction, the court may transfer a case to another district "in the interest of justice or for the convenience of the parties." 28 U.S.C. 1412. With so many choices, it would be reasonable to assume that there are many hard-fought lawsuits over venue. Reasonable, but wrong.

In fact, if a party protests the venue choice of the debtor, experience shows that courts are very unlikely to transfer the case elsewhere. Enron was a company born, bred, and managed in Texas, with operations all over the world. By the time of Enron's spectacular crash, it had 7,500 employees in Houston, including its entire management team and an extensive operations center. Another 17,500 were scattered around the globe. By contrast, there were a total of 63 employees in New York. But Enron chose a New York filing, despite the vigorous protests of Enron's employees, many Texas-based creditors, and the Texas state attorney general. The parties immediately moved to have the case transferred back to the Lone Star State.

═══════════════ In re ENRON CORP. ═══════════════
274 B.R. 327 (Bankr. S.D.N.Y. 2002)

Opinion by J. GONZALEZ

The issue before the Court is whether venue of these bankruptcy cases should be transferred from the Southern District of New York to the Southern District of Texas. Motions to transfer venue were filed by Dynegy, Inc. (and its affiliates), Statex Petroleum, Inc., Packaged Ice, Inc. (and its affiliates) and EC Power (collectively, "Dynegy"); Petro-Hunt, L.L.C., Tenaska Marketing Ventures, Pioneer Resources USA, Inc., Pure Resources, Inc., Spinnaker Exploration Company, Equiva Trading Company, Shell Chemical Risk Management Company, Shell Chemical LP, and Dunhill Resources I, LLC (collectively, "Dunhill"); Pamela M. Tittle, Thomas O. Padgett and Gary S. Dreadin, on behalf of themselves and a class of other persons similarly situated; Southern Ute Indian Tribe d/b/a Red Willow Production Company; and joinder motions filed by Reliant Energy Services, Inc.; Anning-Johnson Company, Contour Energy Co., PDM Strocal and Phillips Petroleum Company; El Paso Merchant Energy L.P.; the Texas Comptroller of Public Accounts, Texas Workforce Commission, Texas General Land Office and Texas Natural Resource Conservation Commission; the Florida State Board of Administration; and EXCO Resources, Inc. (in the aggregate, the "Movants").

Opposition and statements in support of opposition to transfer venue were filed by the Debtors (as defined hereinafter); the Official Committee of Unsecured Creditors; JP Morgan Chase Bank & Co.; Citibank, N.A. and Citicorp USA, Inc.; Barclays Bank Plc and Barclays Physical Trading Limited; Industrial Bank of Japan Trust Company; Sumitomo Mitsui Banking Corporation; Westdeutsche Landesbank Girozentrale; Abu Dhabi International Bank Inc.; Dresdner Bank A.G.; The Bank of New York; KBC Bank NV; Fleet National Bank; First Union National Bank; IntesaBci S.p.A.; Banca Nazionale Del Lavoro; Bank of Tokyo-Mistsubishi, Ltd.; Bank Hapoalim B.M.; St. Paul Fire and Marine Insurance Company, Continental Casualty Company, National Fire Insurance Company of Hartford, Federal Insurance Company, Fireman's Fund Insurance Company, Travelers Casualty & Surety Company, Travelers Indemnity Company, Liberty Mutual Insurance Company, Safeco Insurance Company of America, Hartford Fire Insurance Company, and Lumbermens Mutual Casualty Company.

* * *

[The debtors consist of 18 affiliated companies, collectively known as "Enron."] Enron is a large, multifaceted national and international corporation with operations, financial interests, creditors and stockholders across the United States and around the world. Enron Corp., an Oregon corporation, is a holding company of subsidiaries engaged in the wholesale and commodity market business, telecommunications and insurance. The Debtors divide their business operations into five primary business units: Enron Wholesale Services, Enron Retail Services, Enron Transportation Services, Enron Global Services and Enron Broadband Services. Enron's wholesale business unit, which includes marketing and trading of energy and other commodities, is Enron's core operation and main profit driver. During the past year, Enron maintained the world's largest online energy trading site (EnronOnline) and was the world's largest trader of electricity and natural gas.

Enron is currently directing those interested in doing business with Enron to make trades strictly via telephone and has temporarily suspended internet trading operations. These telephones are all operated in Portland, Oregon and Houston, Texas. None of the Debtors own real property located in New York. With the exceptions of Garden State Paper Company, LLC, EMC and Operational Energy Corp., all of the Debtors have identified their principal place of business as being Houston, Texas.

With two exceptions, the Debtors are organized under the laws of Oregon, California or Delaware. One Debtor is organized under the laws of Texas and another is organized under the laws of Pennsylvania. None of the Debtors is organized under the laws of New York.

All or substantially all of certain of the Debtors' corporate books and records (such as corporate minute books) are located at the corporate headquarters of Enron Corp. in Houston.

The Debtors' Pending Litigation And Investigations

There were 27 litigation matters pending against Enron in New York at the time of Enron's most recent 10K disclosure. None of those matters were listed by Enron under the section requiring disclosure of material litigation.

On December 2, 2001, an adversary proceeding in these cases entitled Enron Corp., Enron Transportation Services Co., CGNN Holding Co., Inc. and MCTJ Holding Co. LLC v. Dynegy Inc. and Dynegy Holdings Co., Inc. was commenced in New York. On December 3, 2001, Dynegy countersued in a Texas State Court in Houston. Both suits are breach of contract actions involving contracts governed by the laws of the State of Texas.

On November 13, 2001, a class-action lawsuit was filed against Enron and others in the United States District Court for the Southern District of Texas on behalf of the participants in the Enron Corp. Savings Plan (the "Enron 401(k) Plan"). The action is styled and numbered Tittle et al. v. Enron Corp., et al., Case No. H-01-3913, and has been consolidated with at least eight other ERISA class actions filed against Enron Corp. in Texas (the "ERISA Action"). In the Tittle lawsuit, the plaintiffs allege, among other things, that under ERISA: (1) Enron is a fiduciary of the Plan; and (2) Enron and the other fiduciaries breached their duties to the participants and beneficiaries of the Plan in a variety of ways. The Enron 401(k) Plan that is the subject of the Tittle lawsuit provides that "all provisions of the Plan shall be construed in accordance with the laws of Texas except to the extent preempted by federal law." The ERISA Action is stayed as to Enron Corp. pursuant to the automatic stay imposed by Section 362 of title 11 of the United States Code (the "Bankruptcy Code").

A number of Congressional committees, federal agencies, commissions, and departments have requested information and are conducting hearings and investigating Enron.

The Debtors' Management, Officers And Directors

Approximately fifty-five current or former officers of Enron Corp. reside in Houston, Texas or in the Southern District of Texas. Among the Debtors, only the Board of Enron Corp. includes outside directors. All of the directors of the other Debtors are inside directors who are also employees of one or more of the Debtors. Most of these inside directors hold the title of Director for numerous Enron entities and most inside directors reside in Houston, Texas or elsewhere in the Southern District of Texas.

The Creditors

The Debtors provided to Movants the best available accounts payable listing from their business records showing vendors of the Debtors who were owed money and their locations. The category of vendors is one of several general categories of creditors. The listing was subject to correction and does not contain other types of creditors, including the following:

1. counterparties to swaps, hedges and physical contracts;
2. bank and lending debt;
3. Enron corporation's public bond debt;
4. former employee claims; and
5. governmental unit claims

Further, the listing contains inter-company debt. The parties each presented summary charts related to this information to the Court.

Enron Corporation's largest unsecured creditor is JP Morgan Chase (formerly Chase Manhattan Bank, at times referred to interchangeably) with an unsecured claim of $1.907 billion. At the time the debt was incurred, the office of Chase Manhattan Bank, in Houston, had responsibility for the loan. Chase Manhattan Bank's principal offices are in New York City and it is represented in the bankruptcy proceedings by New York counsel. Beginning at least several weeks before the Chapter 11 filing, the New York office of Chase assumed responsibility for the loan.

The Official Committee of Unsecured Creditors (the "Committee") is comprised of fifteen members. Of those fifteen members, six are located in New York City and three are located in Texas. The other six members of the Committee are located in Ohio, Canada, Minnesota, Maryland, California and Oklahoma. Wells Fargo Bank Minnesota, N.A., as Indenture Trustee, located in Minneapolis, and The Williams Companies, Inc., located in Tulsa, Oklahoma, are the co-chairs of the Committee.

Enron Corporation's two largest secured creditors, Citibank, N.A. and Chase Manhattan Bank (now, JP Morgan Chase), have offices located in Houston, Texas, which had responsibility for administering the credit facility.

Enron Corporation has obtained a new $1,000,000,000 secured line of credit from JP Morgan Chase & Co. and Salomon Smith Barney secured by the assets of Transwestern Pipeline Company and Northern Natural Gas Company.

Enron Corp. lists seventeen largest creditors, which are comprised of ten creditor listings in New York, three in the United Kingdom, two in South Dakota, one in Minnesota, one in Italy and none in Texas. The ten creditor listings for New York include multiple listings of the Bank of New York, as Indenture Trustee with respect to several separate indentures, each of which has a separate group of bond or noteholders, who are located across the country.

THE DEBTORS' EMPLOYEES

As of December 2, 2001, the bankruptcy petition date, Enron Corp. and its affiliates employed approximately 25,000 full and part time employees worldwide (approximately 7,000 hourly wage employees and approximately 18,000 salaried employees). Just before the petition date, as of December 1, 2001, over 7,500 employees worked at the Debtors' Houston headquarters and resided in the Southern District of Texas. Approximately 7,000 employees worked worldwide. Of these employees, 5,496 were employees of the Debtors in these cases. Of these employees of the Debtors, 4,681 worked in Houston, and sixty-three of these employees of the Debtors worked in New York.

On December 3, 2001, Enron and its affiliates discharged approximately 60% (4,200) of their Houston employees. Since December 3, 2001, Enron has discharged an additional 200 of its Houston employees. Most of the Enron employees so discharged in the United States were employed in Houston. Enron has discharged twelve New York employees.

Currently, Enron and its affiliates employ a total of approximately 19,000 persons worldwide and approximately 3,000 of those employees work in Houston, Texas. Of these various employees, 1,687 are employed by the Debtors in Houston and fifty-seven are employed by the Debtors in New York. The remainder of the employees of the Debtors are located elsewhere.

Enron plans to provide severance benefits in an amount equal to $4,500 per severed employee, which will serve as a credit against accrued and unpaid wages, amounts due under the severance plan Enron had in place at the time of termination of employment, and any Enron obligation pursuant to the Worker Adjustment Retraining Notification Act. The $4,500 severance benefit has been paid to those employees discharged on December 3, 2001. The severance payment of $4,500 is less than the monthly salary of some of the Houston employees who were laid off.

Approximately 12,000 of Enron's employees participated in the Enron 401(k) Plan. As of January 2001, the Enron 401(k) Plan was composed mostly of Enron stock (61% of the 401(k) plan). Many employees have lost more than $100,000 of value in their 401(k) plans. Those persons whose retirement funds are in the Debtors' 401(k) Plan are among the Debtors' creditors. The Labor Department is investigating Enron's handling of employee 401(k) plans. In addition, as previously noted, the ERISA Action is pending in Texas.

On November 30, 2001, Enron Corp. and/or its affiliates paid $55 million in bonuses to 587 of its "key employees." The vast majority of these key employees are located in Houston.

Most of the Debtors' real property is located in Houston. Subsidiaries of the Debtor, Enron Corp., own interstate pipelines. The amount of ad valorem taxes owed to Texas taxing authorities by Enron is $139,878,630.

THE BANKRUPTCY PROCEEDINGS

As part of its "first day" orders, the Debtors obtained an order from the Court authorizing the Debtors to enter into certain postpetition credit agreements (the "DIP Financing") in order to, inter alia, provide outside parties confidence in the Debtors that will enable and encourage them to resume ongoing credit relationships with the Debtors. The Debtors have not needed to borrow any funds under the DIP Financing.

* * *

THE DEBTORS' PROFESSIONALS

Debtors have retained the law firm of Weil, Gotshal and Manges LLP ("WGM") to represent them in connection with their bankruptcy. WGM has its principal law offices in New York and also has offices in Houston and Dallas. WGM's principal bankruptcy and restructuring department is based in New York. Both WGM's Houston and Dallas offices have a corporate restructuring section and experienced bankruptcy practitioners.

The Debtors have employed Leboeuf, Lamb, Greene & MacRae, LLP ("LLG&M") as special counsel. LLG&M has its principal office in New York and has an office located in Houston.

The Debtors have employed Andrews & Kurth LLP as special counsel to represent the Debtors in their bankruptcy. Andrews & Kurth's principal office is located in Houston where it employs over 200 attorneys. Andrews & Kurth also has offices in New York.

Prior to their bankruptcy, the Debtors employed 145 lawyers in their Houston offices. As of May 2001, if Enron's legal department in Houston were a private firm, it would have been Houston's sixth-largest. Arthur Andersen LLP ("Arthur Andersen") has worked as Enron's outside auditor for more than ten years. Arthur Andersen accountants and consultants used to occupy an entire floor at Enron's headquarters in Houston, Texas. Last year Arthur Andersen earned over $50 million for audit and consulting work it performed for Enron. The Houston office of Arthur Andersen has conducted the Enron audits since at least 1997.

FOREIGN INSOLVENCY PROCEEDINGS

A number of Enron affiliates are in insolvency, bankruptcy or administration proceedings worldwide.

ACCESSIBILITY OF NEW YORK

New York is one of the world's most accessible locations. New York is served by three airports with international flights, as well as major rail stations making it accessible to parties in interest located worldwide. It is convenient with respect to both the diversity of locations served and the frequency of service provided.

New York is located over 1,600 miles from Enron's corporate headquarters in Houston which is located a few blocks from the United States Bankruptcy Court for the Southern District of Texas. A roundtrip flight from Houston to New York takes approximately seven hours. The average price of a roundtrip ticket from Houston to New York, full coach fare, is $1,807.85. No flights departing from Houston, Texas arrive in New York prior to 10:00 a.m. Eastern Time.

DISCUSSION

Under §1408(1), a prospective debtor may select the venue for its Chapter 11 reorganization. Specifically, venue is proper in any jurisdiction where the debtor maintains a domicile, residence, principal place of business or where its principal assets are located for at least 180 days before the filing of the bankruptcy petition. Pursuant to 28 U.S.C. §1408(2), venue is also proper for any affiliate that files a bankruptcy petition within a venue where there is already a bankruptcy case pending under §1408(1).

* * *

The burden is on the movant to show by a preponderance of the evidence that the transfer of venue is warranted. The decision of whether to transfer venue is within the court's discretion based on an individualized case-by-case analysis of convenience and fairness.

Transferring venue of a bankruptcy case is not to be taken lightly. [Commonwealth of Puerto Rico v. Commonwealth Oil Refining Co. (In re

Commonwealth Oil Refining Co.), 596 F.2d 1239, 1241 (5th Cir. 1979) ("CORCO")] ("the court should exercise its power to transfer cautiously") (citation omitted); In re Pavilion Place Associates, 88 B.R. 32, 35 (Bankr. S.D.N.Y. 1988) ("Transfer is a cumbersome disruption of the Chapter 11 process.") (citations omitted).

A debtor's choice of forum is entitled to great weight if venue is proper. "Where a transfer would merely shift the inconvenience from one party to the other, or where after balancing all the factors, the equities leaned but slightly in favor of the movant, the [debtor's] choice of forum should not be disturbed." *Garden Manor*, 99 B.R. at 555 (citing 1 James Wm. Moore et al., Moore's Federal Practice P 56.10 (2d ed. 1988); In re Great American Resources, Inc., 85 B.R. 444 (Bankr. N.D. Ohio 1988) ("venue decisions should not merely shift the inconvenience from one party to another") (citations omitted). The decision to transfer requires an examination of a broad array of factors, and a bankruptcy court's decision denying or transfer-ring venue will only be reversed if the court's decision constitutes an abuse of discretion.

Pursuant to 28 U.S.C. §1412, the Court must grant relief if it is estab-lished that a transfer of venue would be proper if it is in (1) the interest of justice or (2) the convenience of the parties. In considering the convenience of the parties, the Court weighs a number of factors:

1.   The proximity of creditors of every kind to the Court;
2.   The proximity of the debtor to the Court;
3.   The proximity of the witnesses necessary to the administration of the estate;
4.   The location of the assets;
5.   The economic administration of the estate; and
6.   The necessity for ancillary administration if liquidation should result.

CORCO, 596 F.2d at 1247. The factor given the most weight is the pro-motion of the economic and efficient administration of the estate. Id.

When considering the "interest of justice," the court applies a broad and flexible standard. *Manville*, 896 F.2d at 1391. The court considers whether transfer of venue will promote the efficient administration of the estate, judicial economy, timeliness, and fairness. Id.

* * *

Convenience of the Parties

The proximity to the court of the creditors and necessary witnesses

In considering the proximity of creditors, this Court must examine both the number of creditors as well as the amount of claims held by such creditors. See *CORCO*, 596 F.2d at 1248 ("both number and size are of equal significance in gaining acceptance of a plan and should be of equal signifi-cance in considering the convenience of creditors"). The Debtors' cases have been referred to as the largest bankruptcy ever filed. Creditors exist worldwide with claims ranging in amount from thousands to billions of dollars.

In examining the list of top twenty creditors, and the numerous other creditors that have sought various forms of relief within the early stages of this case (as discussed hereinafter), it is evident to the Court that while some creditors would best be served by this bankruptcy case being located in Texas, for the remainder of creditors — national and worldwide, Texas provides no better venue, and perhaps may be more inconvenient, than New York. See *Industrial Pollution Control*, 137 B.R. at 181 (retaining venue of case in Pennsylvania where transfer to Ohio would be more convenient to Ohio creditors while less convenient to others). The Debtors' multifaceted business enterprises affect parties throughout the nation and world. New York's accessibility for all creditors (and stockholders) weighs in favor of a New York venue. *CORCO*, 596 F.2d at 1248 (considers proximity of creditors and stockholders).

In considering creditors of all kinds, the Court finds it relevant to weigh the position of the Committee in its statutory role as a fiduciary to and representative body of the unsecured creditors. The Committee consists of representatives of all of the creditor constituencies, including a former employee representative. As such, the position of the Committee, while not dispositive, is something that should be considered by the Court. Counsel for the Committee has indicated the Committee's strong opposition to a transfer of the bankruptcy case, and the Committee filed pleadings in support of retention of the case in New York.

Furthermore, the Debtors' largest creditors — the banks (holding debt in their own name and serving as Indenture Trustees for publicly traded notes and bonds for more than twenty-five indentures, both foreign and domestic) oppose transfer of venue in these cases. JP Morgan and Citibank also oppose transfer of venue in their capacity as debtor in possession lenders.

In the five weeks this case has been pending, there has been significant and diverse creditor participation — diverse both as to the nature of the claim and the location of the claimant. Indeed, more than 225 entities have either sought, or responded to, relief requested before the Court. It is clear that those who are participating in these cases are not as localized as the Movants argue. Although the business relationship between the Debtors and the creditors may have been initiated from a desk in Houston, its impact is far reaching and geographically diverse.

With respect to the parties necessary to appear in court, the Movants argue that the largest aggregation of certain creditors, such as employees and trade vendors, is in Texas. The parties presented charts and documentary evidence representing the location of various creditors, presumably in order to show their nexus, or lack thereof, to New York and Texas. The Movants emphasize that an overwhelming percentage of trade and vendor creditors are located in Texas. However, the Movants' numbers take into consideration inter-company debt. If the debts owed to inter-company Debtors are removed, the percentage of debt owed to Texas entities drops from approximately 90% to 34%, with the balance (66%) being held by non-Texas entities. Of the 66% representing trade and vendor debt not in Texas, 20% is owed to creditors in New York and 46% is owed to creditors outside of both New York and Texas. If the same analysis is applied with respect to the creditors in terms of number versus amount, the percentage in number located in Texas is 33%, and the percentage of creditors located outside of Texas is 67%.

If the Court were to accept Movants' argument that inter-company debt should be considered, then approximately 88% of the trade and vendor debt in amount would be held by Texas entities. However, in that case 90% would be held by Debtor entities who oppose transfer of venue. Finally, there is a large percentage of overall debt owed to banks located in New York and a significant amount of bond and noteholder debt located worldwide.

Concerning Enron's former employees, the Court is sympathetic to their concerns and the fact that if venue remains in New York many of them would find it burdensome to attend hearings. However, it is not certain that all the issues that the former employees may want addressed, such as the factors that led to Enron's collapse and those who may have been responsible for the collapse, will be brought before the bankruptcy court. Yet it is clear that such issues will certainly be addressed by Congressional investigations and the investigations by federal departments and agencies. The major issues impacting former employees involve the 401(k) Plan. Whether they are resolved in the ERISA Action or in the claims resolution process in the bankruptcy cases, and regardless of where the cases are venued, these issues are best addressed by a former employee representation approach. This would generally not require the claimants to actually appear in court to have their rights protected and concerns raised. To the extent the former employees' concern is that it would be burdensome to follow the progress of this case, the Court will address that issue as discussed hereafter.

While substantially all of the Debtors' officers are located in Houston, most will not be required to attend hearings before this Court. Rather, the certain participants in the proceedings before this Court will be the professionals retained in these cases. Subject to court approval, appearances required by the officers (or other management) can be addressed by telephonic and video conferencing capabilities. The limited appearances that may be required of the principals will nevertheless allow them to continue with the management of the businesses.

The Attorney General of Texas has filed its support for transfer of venue. There are also many Texas state and local authorities that have an economic interest to be protected. However, the non-judicial administration of these claims will take place in Texas. To the extent that judicial intervention is required, these departments and agencies, like other parties who find it burdensome to travel to attend hearings, can utilize alternative methods of participation [such as teleconferencing].

Economic and Efficient Administration of the Estate

* * *

In *In re Garden Manor Associates*, the court retained venue of a single asset real estate debtor, whose sole asset was located in another jurisdiction, after taking into consideration the fact that New York was the location where the debtor could most successfully reorganize. 99 B.R. 551, 554-55 (Bankr. S.D.N.Y. 1988). This is the ultimate purpose of a Chapter 11 bankruptcy case. The court in *Garden Manor* found that the case turned on the debtor's ability to raise capital, renegotiate loan terms, locate a potential purchaser, or execute a potential cram down of its major secured creditor. Id. While the general partner and managing agent were located in New York, the court also found it relevant that the parties most likely to be a source of capital were located in New York. Therefore, the court found that efforts to reorganize could best be carried forth in New York.

* * *

One must examine the realities of this case. It is the largest bankruptcy case ever filed, the complexities of which are yet to be fully appreciated. Its reorganization will depend in great part on the ability of the Debtors' advisors and senior managers to achieve a financial restructuring that will result in the capital markets regaining confidence in the Debtors, thereby affording the Debtors full and complete access to those markets. New York is a world financial center and, as such, has the resources that will be required to address the Debtors' financial issues. Most of the entities and individuals expected to be responsible for the financial restructuring and development of a plan of reorganization in this case are located in New York or have ready access to New York, including most of the Debtors' legal and financial advisors as well as the legal and financial advisors to the Committee and the lenders. Those members of the financial community that provide access to capital necessary to the Debtors' financial restructuring are located in New York. Furthermore, while the Debtors' management and operations are predominantly in Houston, New York is a more convenient location for those responsible for negotiating and formulating a plan of reorganization. The Court finds that New York is the more economic and convenient forum for those whose participation will be required to administer these cases. Accordingly, New York is the location which would best serve the Debtors' reorganization efforts — the creation and preservation of value.

* * *

Interest of Justice

The interest of justice prong is a broad and flexible standard that is applied based on the facts and circumstances of each case. In evaluating the interest of justice, the Court must consider what will promote the efficient administration of the estate, judicial economy, timeliness and fairness. The Court finds that the considerations involved with the interest of justice are intertwined with the economic and efficient administration of the estate. As already discussed, the administration of this estate will be best promoted by retaining venue in this Court. In addition, in considering both the efficient administration of the estates and judicial economy, it is also necessary to take account of the "learning curve." The learning curve analysis involves consideration of the time and effort spent by the current judge and the corresponding effect on the bankruptcy case in transferring venue.

* * *

This Court has gained familiarity with many of the issues that have and will continue to arise in these cases. A substantial number of motions have been filed and were scheduled to be heard within the first month of these cases. Some of them have already been held and concluded. While other matters previously scheduled to have taken place by this date have subsequently been adjourned, the Court had already familiarized itself with many of the pleadings filed in those matters. In addition, the Court has been required to educate itself on a variety of issues to provide interim relief on an emergent basis.

The Movants argue that since they timely filed their motions to transfer venue, the "learning curve" should not be considered. However, the importance of maintaining stability in these bankruptcy cases required the Court to direct its immediate attention to the proper administration of these cases. A review of the docket shows that many requests for shortened notice were filed for matters to be heard concerning a myriad of issues, including claims that supplies of energy were to be imminently discontinued. These issues had to be immediately addressed.

Maintaining the stability of these cases and ensuring their proper administration had to take precedence over the request for an expedited venue hearing. This is especially true in light of the fact that these cases were properly venued pursuant to 28 U.S.C. §1408. Thus, although the Movants filed a timely request for the transfer of venue, diverting the Debtors' and Committee's attention to the motion for transfer of venue would have been counterproductive to the needs and interests of these cases during the initial stages of these cases. Moreover, although certain of the Movants initially requested a shortened time frame for notice of a hearing, that request was subsequently withdrawn while certain Movants pursued discovery. Thus, while the Movants were not dilatory, the necessities of this case resulted in an accrual of knowledge by the Court.

Further, as previously discussed, the learning curve that has been established in the Enron Debtors' cases contributes to judicial economy. A transfer at this time would not promote judicial economy as it would only delay pending matters while a transferee court familiarized itself with the intricacies of these cases.

These Debtors' cases have a global presence. Indeed, affiliated entities have already filed insolvency proceedings in various countries. Further promoting judicial economy is the fact that this Court has familiarity with Cross-Border Insolvency cases, having presided over (i) cases regarding parallel proceedings in Canada and the United States, and (ii) 11 U.S.C. §304 proceedings involving insurance insolvencies in Australia. This Court has experience in developing a protocol to facilitate the coordination of proceedings in this Court and the proceedings conducted in a foreign jurisdiction. Moreover, this Court conducted video hearings regarding the foreign proceedings referred to above. Thus the interest of justice also supports retention of venue in this district.

The goal of these chapter 11 cases is the reorganization of the Debtors. The parties most essential to that purpose are located in New York. The Debtors, whose finances are extremely complex, will need access to the capital markets and financial experts available in New York. The negotiation and confirmation of a plan of reorganization necessitate substantial involvement by the professionals retained by the Debtors, the Committee, and the financial institutions, which are all primarily located in New York. Thus, the significant financial and legal decisions concerning the efforts to restructure the Debtors will be made in New York. The fact that New York is a financial center and the presence in New York of those who will participate on a consistent basis in these cases make New York the most efficient forum for administering these cases.

The Court finds that in considering matters of judicial economy, timeliness and fairness as well as the efficient administration of the estate, the interest of justice is served by retaining jurisdiction.

———

The evidence that big companies have filed for bankruptcy in places distant from their home offices is striking. The data collected by Professor Lynn LoPucki (http://lopucki.law.ucla.edu/) documents the location of the main business operations and the bankruptcy filings for all the large, publicly traded companies that have filed for bankruptcy since 1980. The results? About two-thirds of all the big businesses in Chapter 11 have filed in a forum other than their principal place of business.

The big winner in this migration is Delaware. In the early 1980s, no big cases were filed there. By the mid-1990s, Delaware had an 87 percent market share. By the mid-2000s, New York and Delaware together took about half of all the cases that were shopped out of other locations around the country.

Does it matter? Professor LoPucki notes that the refiling rate — that is, the number of big companies that file for Chapter 11 then come back to file again — is about 42 percent for cases filed in Delaware, 19 percent in New York, and 4 percent in all other courts combined. He argues that the courts are not pressing the companies to make the hard moves that are necessary for a successful reorganization. Defenders of Delaware and New York claim the cases filed there are different, but so far no one can identify a difference that can be documented. By every obvious comparison — size, debt, number of employees, industry, etc. — the cases are similar; the only major variable seems to be the venue chosen to hear the cases.

In *Enron* the fight over forum pitted Texans against New Yorkers, but it did not make a clean split between debtor and creditors. The creditors' committee and several large creditors liked the choice of the New York court, while many smaller creditors, employees, and state officials opposed it. The court notes particularly that the creditor putting up $1 billion in post-petition financing is happy with New York. This division among creditors is a reminder not only that bankruptcy is a creditor-versus-creditor world, but also that a big Chapter 11 filing may be well-wired in advance, with certain in-the-know creditors called in to help make key decisions — such as forum selection.

Why would the people who decide where to file a bankruptcy choose Delaware or New York over the local jurisdiction? Some debtors may want to escape unhappy employees who can march around in front of the courthouse or the scrutiny of the local press. Others may be looking for judges who are sympathetic to debtors on first day orders or who will readily extend debtor exclusivity. Perhaps it is the expertise and efficiency of the Delaware courts that attracts big cases. See, e.g., Marcus Cole, 'Delaware Is Not a State': Are We Witnessing Jurisdictional Competition in Bankruptcy? 55 Vand. L. Rev. 1845 (2002). Or maybe the big case lawyers who are disproportionately located in New York and Delaware are calling the shots. Or perhaps, as one Delaware supporter claimed in hearings before the National Bankruptcy Review Commission, it is the proximity to the Philadelphia airport. Perhaps.

A big case bankruptcy generates lawyers' and professionals' fees, along with hotels, meals, messenger services, stenography, and enough other services that Chapter 11 is now estimated to be a $2 to $4 billion a year industry. Moreover, a big case can secure a national reputation for a bankruptcy judge. Professor LoPucki concludes that pressures on judges to make decisions that favor the people who decide where the cases will be placed forces courts into a destructive competition. His book, Courting Failure: How Competition for Big Cases Is Corrupting the Bankruptcy Courts (2005) makes for lively reading. If you want to start a shouting match in New York or Delaware, just mention the book.

Many who disagree with the tone or some of the specific allegations in *Courting Failure* nonetheless concur that the current system of forum shopping produces powerful pressures on the judicial process. It is hard to see how any judge could be completely unmindful, if only subconsciously, that a particular decision could result in the gain or loss of millions of dollars in fees and other economic benefits for the bar and the community where that judge lives. If a ruling against management or a powerful creditor interest would have the effect of driving away the big cases and their economic benefits, a subtle but powerful pressure to avoid such a ruling seems to many observers to be inevitable.

Problem Set 41

41.1. As counsel for the TIB in a Chapter 7 liquidation bankruptcy of the Mullen Company, you have been reviewing the claims filed by creditors. One is a claim by Atlantic Supply for goods it sold under contract to Mullen. On examining the Mullen files, you have concluded that the goods were defective and that substantial damages may be due Mullen from Atlantic. What action may you take, in what court, and before what judge? What if Atlantic had not filed a claim in the bankruptcy case? If you also find a basis for an antitrust action against Atlantic in connection with these transactions, how would that affect the answers to the foregoing question? See 28 U.S.C. §§157(b)(2)(C), 1334(a), (c)(2).

If Mullen had filed a Chapter 11 reorganization, reconsider your position. As attorney for the DIP, you recognize that no plan can be confirmed until these disputes with the Atlantic company are resolved. It would take six months to get to trial in bankruptcy court, eighteen months in state court, and two-and-a-half years in federal district court. How would these facts affect your litigation decisions? See 28 U.S.C. §§157(b), 1334(c)(2).

41.2. You represent the TIB for Ingrid Schupbach, who recently filed in Chapter 7. Ingrid appears to have had valid pre-petition claims against her former employer, who fired her after she asserted that he had sexually harassed her. In addition to a Title VII civil rights claim, she probably had an action for breach of her employment contract. She also had a truth in lending claim against her bank and an assault suit against her former husband. These claims belong to the trustee. Can these claims be brought in federal court and, if so, before which judge? Would it matter if the defendants also wanted to be in federal court and before the same judge you want? See 28 U.S.C. §§157, 1334(c)(2).

41.3. On July 1, 2001, Fred Lancy filed a Chapter 7 bankruptcy petition. Fred's schedules indicated that his was a "no asset" case. You were appointed TIB in four cases filed about that same time and examined the debtors in those cases routinely on September 5, 2001, when they appeared for their section 341 meetings. By pushing hard during the examination, you extracted the fact that on April 1, 2000, Fred Lancy conveyed his 250-acre farm to his sister, Rita, for $1. Your state fraudulent conveyance law has a two-year statute of limitations, so you could attack the conveyance under section 544(b) even though you could not do so under section 548.

You know from your general civil practice that a suit filed in your state court will not get to trial for at least two years and therefore you would prefer to take some action with regard to the farm in bankruptcy court. Does the federal court have jurisdiction? If so, will you be before a bankruptcy judge or a district judge? If your opponent seeks delay, what positions might she take? If she loses, will she ever be able to get appellate review of her arguments on these points? Is there a theory on which she might get the Supreme Court to hear the case? See 11 U.S.C. §§544(b), 548; 28 U.S.C. §§157(b)(2)(H), 1334(c)(2).

41.4. Stan Johnson had enough financial trouble even before he was sued in state court by Ethel Cannon. Ethel had blocked Stan's car in a mall parking lot. He got mad and deliberately backed into her car, breaking several of her favorite bones. Feeling the pressure mounting, he bought a book called "Doing Your Own Bankruptcy and Auto Body Repairs" and filed a Chapter 7. He has now received a notice of trial in Ethel's case against him and has decided to ask a lawyer where he stands. When he asks you, what do you tell him? Before you answer, check §523(a)(6); 28 U.S.C. §§1334(c)(2), 157(b)(2)(B).

41.5. No one is quite sure how to describe what Alden Industries does anymore. The old chemical company and its two dozen subsidiaries have morphed into a consumer electronics, cattle feed, and industrial fasteners business — just to name a few. In fact, maybe that's why the billion-dollar company is in enough trouble to be thinking about a Chapter 11 filing. You have just made partner at your firm, and you have been asked to put together a strategy meeting — beginning with where to file. As you put together your notes for the agenda, what is on your list?

CHAPTER 10

TRANSNATIONAL BANKRUPTCIES

A. INTRODUCTION

An increase in the number of multinational companies leads inevitably to an increase in the number of multinational bankruptcies. Because it was often seen as a last chance to reap value from a soon-to-be-liquidated business, bankruptcy traditionally has been one of the most parochial and nationalistic areas of the law. Each nation has followed a "grab rule" approach: seizing local assets and distributing them to the claimants in a local proceeding, with little concern for the overall result for the company or for claimholders outside the domestic jurisdiction. However, increasing experience with global bankruptcy cases, the emergence of academic theories supporting a global perspective, and a burst of interest by international law reform organizations have combined to produce a dramatic shift in viewpoints and a number of international initiatives that seemed unlikely just a few years ago.

There were two main theoretical approaches to international bankruptcy: territorialism and universalism. Territorialism justified the "grab rule" on the grounds that local creditors had legitimate expectations that any financial crisis would be resolved applying local policies and preferences. Its proponents argued that those expectations gave rise to vested local rights that should be respected. Universalism rests on the fact that bankruptcy is a collective proceeding that must extend to all of a debtor's assets and all the stakeholders. In effect, universalism holds that a bankruptcy resolution must be symmetric to a debtor's market. In liquidation, this is the only approach that will maximize the collection of assets and permit a distribution of those assets in accord with a coherent and fair set of rules. Moreover, reorganization is nearly impossible without one central, supervising court. Just as a national market (such as the United States) requires a national bankruptcy regime, a globalizing world requires a globalizing bankruptcy regime.

The globalizing forces affect many areas of the law. In an era in which General Electric cannot merge with Honeywell without the approval of the Commission of the European Union, it is pointless to talk about territorial application of the antitrust laws. Similarly, when the great Korean car manufacturer Daewoo trembled on the brink of collapse, with huge lawsuits by creditors in numerous courts around the world and stalled negotiations with banks and bondholders from nearly every developed country, the idea of restructuring within a territorial bankruptcy system becomes nonsensical. It seems inevitable that the task of the legal architects of our economic future is to construct a global solution as soon as possible.

The great majority of experts in the field agree that universalism is the right long-term approach. They also agree that it will take some time to achieve, even in a globalizing world. (Experts disagree sharply as to how long.) Some urge that modified territorialism is the best interim solution, because they believe it is not possible to construct a workable universalist system in the absence of a full, undiluted universalism with one court and one law. Lynn M. LoPucki, Courting Failure (2004).

Most experts, however, are more inclined to "modified universalism," which, as its name suggests, starts from the opposite perspective. This is the view adopted by the American Law Institute, which explains modified universalism in its recently adopted Principles for Cooperation as "universalism tempered by a sense of what is practical at the current stage of international legal development. . . ." American Law Institute, Transnational Insolvency Project, Principles of Cooperation in Transnational Bankruptcy Cases Among Members of the North American Free Trade Agreement at 1, n.2 (2003).

The key difference between the two approaches is that modified universalism takes a worldwide perspective, seeking solutions that come as close as possible to the ideal of a single-court, single-law resolution, while territorialism is defined by a conviction that local creditors have vested rights in whatever assets can be seized by their courts when insolvency looms. Various aspects of these two approaches will be revealed in the cases and text that follow.

The problem of the management of the general default of a multinational company (called a "bankruptcy proceeding" in the United States and an "insolvency proceeding" in most of the world) has two central aspects: choice of forum and choice of law. The two are often confused in the literature and in the cases. The main reason for this confusion is that traditionally each national court thought only to apply its local bankruptcy law to all aspects of the case before it, so there was no attention to the difference between choosing a court to manage the case and choosing a law to apply to certain issues in the case. Indeed, it will often be correct to apply the managing court's law to various issues, but it will also be necessary to apply other national laws to particular transactions or claims, so it is important to remember the distinction between "Which court should have primary management of the case?" and "Which law should be applied to this issue?"

The discussion that follows is divided along just those lines. The next section deals with choice of forum and the section after that with choice of law, which includes the more difficult and less-developed issues in the field.

B.   CHOICE OF FORUM

By hypothesis, the problem of choice of forum arises only in a system of modified universalism. In a territorial system every court administers the assets it controls, while in a fully realized universalist system the administering court is chosen by some internationally agreed set of rules. Even so, choice of forum in a universalist system does not mean that only one court is involved in the case, because it is necessary to obtain cooperation from every court that has control over important segments of the company's assets. Choice of forum means choice of a primary forum, the lead court in administering the case. That court is the court in the jurisdiction that is deemed to be the company's "home" country, typically the situs of the "center of its main interests." The home-country court will have pending before it a full-fledged bankruptcy proceeding under its law. The other courts involved in the case may also have bankruptcy cases pending. Where other courts have full bankruptcy cases involving the same company, we speak of "parallel proceedings" in the home country and the cooperating country. Alternatively, the proceedings in other courts may be limited to "ancillary proceedings" that are designed solely to assist the primary court. Either approach can be used to cooperate in a system of modified universalism, although the ancillary approach is more efficient at meeting universalist objectives.

In the absence of a legal framework for cooperation, a practice of creating "protocols" has begun to emerge (see In re Maxwell, infra). Protocols are agreements among major stakeholder groups as to how a multinational bankruptcy will be managed. In regimes in which the debtor remains in possession, the debtor will be one of those major stakeholders in the negotiations, but in other legal regimes, transnational reorganizations or liquidations may take place by agreement among all the creditors. The development of these protocols has not only facilitated the resolution of the cases concerned, but it is also creating a database of experience highly useful to those seeking to fashion an improved international regime. The ALI Principles of Cooperation has an appendix that includes the text of some of these protocols.

Conceptually, the first step in understanding these issues is to study the way that various countries treat the foreign assets of "home country" companies. In the United States, for example, a U.S. court may need to decide how to deal with the problem of a U.S. company in Chapter 11 with assets located all over the world. Once we have seen how the home country addresses the problem, we can turn the telescope around and explore the question of cooperation from the perspective of a court that controls assets belonging to a company with its home in another country.

1. Home Court: United States

It is difficult for other countries to defer to U.S. bankruptcy courts if U.S. courts do not assert worldwide jurisdiction over the assets of U.S. bankrupts. In fact, the 1978 Code exerts just such a broad reach as to the assets of the debtor. §541(a)(l). The legislative history to that subsection's predecessor in the old Act makes it clear that the Code asserts jurisdiction over the assets of the bankrupt "wherever located" in the world. A number of other countries employ the same rule. See, e.g., Insolvency Act

§436 (United Kingdom); Trib. Comm. Seine 2 Fev. 1882 (France); American Law Institute, Transnational Insolvency Project, International Statement of Canadian Law at 24, n.6 (2003).

The following case illustrates both the broad reach of U.S. jurisdiction claims with respect to the debtor's property and the serious practical difficulties of enforcement. Although the style of the case is "In re McLean Industries, Inc.," the principal operating company among the bankrupt group of corporations was United States Lines, one of the largest shipping companies in the world. We provide excerpts from two opinions in the case.

<hr>

In re MCLEAN INDUSTRIES, INC.
68 B.R. 690 (Bankr. S.D.N.Y. 1986)

DECISION AND ORDER

Howard C. BUSCHMAN, III, Bankruptcy Judge.

United States Lines, Inc., a debtor herein (the "debtor") seeks from this Court a preliminary injunction restraining defendant GAC Marine Fuels Ltd. ("GAC Marine") from taking any action to arrest or interfere with vessels and other property of this estate. It further seeks an order holding GAC Marine in civil contempt for violating both the automatic stay applicable to this proceeding by the filing of the petition, 11 U.S.C. §362, and the restraining order issued by this Court. GAC Marine, although essentially admitting the underlying facts, opposes these motions, declaring that it, as a non-domiciliary corporation organized under the laws of the United Kingdom and with a principal place of business in London, is not subject to the in personam jurisdiction of this Court. The Debtor disputes this assertion and thus, the principal issue to be resolved by this Court is whether GAC Marine is subject to in personam jurisdiction before this Court.

The debtor filed a voluntary petition for relief under Chapter 11 of the Bankruptcy Code, 11 U.S.C. §§101 et seq. (1984) (the "Code") on November 24, 1986. On that date, this Court issued an order, which restated the automatic stay provided by §362(a) of the Code and not excepted by §362(b) of the Code. The Debtor has remained in possession and continues to operate its trans-Pacific and western hemisphere cargo shipping services. It is in the process of terminating its around the world and North Atlantic services.

The facts are not in dispute. On December 4, 1986, ten days after the petition was filed, GAC Marine commenced an in rem admiralty action in the Supreme Court of Hong Kong against the debtor, pursuant to a Writ of Summons, for the payment of $173,750 allegedly owed it for fuel oil delivered on board the *American Utah*, a vessel owned by the debtor, in October 1986 in Khorfakkan Port, United Arab Emirates. On December 9, 1986, upon application of GAC Marine, the Hong Kong court issued a warrant of arrest against the *American California*, also owned by the debtor. As a result, this vessel has since been restrained from leaving Hong Kong harbor.

On December 8, 1986, GAC Marine commenced an admiralty proceeding in the High Court of the Republic of Singapore against the debtor as the owner of the *American Oklahoma*. This proceeding was commenced to recover $69,500 allegedly owed by the debtor to GAC Marine for fuel oil delivered on the vessel *American Washington* on November 5, 1986, also in Khorfakkan Port. The Singapore court issued, on December 8, 1986, a warrant of arrest directed at the *American Oklahoma*, also owned by the debtor.

GAC Marine took these actions with knowledge of the debtor's filing of its reorganization petition and the resultant automatic stay provided by §362 of the Code, and after being informed by the debtor that such actions would be improper, carried out a threat contained in a telex from GAC Marine to the debtor dated November 28, 1986. That telex stated:

> As outlined below, our invoices nos. AG86/10/010 and AG86/ 10/011 fell due for payment on the 27th November 1986. On request by agents for payment of these invoices, we have been informed of your refusal to settle all outstandings as your company has filed for bankruptcy under Chapter 11 of the U.S. Law.
>
> Accordingly, all invoices as set out hereunder and [sic] applicable to the following ships must be settled immediately. . . .
>
> Chapter 11 procedure in the USA is not enforceable in foreign jurisdictions. Therefore we are entitled to arrest any U.S. Lines ship abroad and unless prompt settlement is made to us, we will have no recourse other than to take such action as is deemed necessary by our lawyers for the protection of our interests. We will therefore arrest your ships one-by-one unless settlement is made immediately. . . .

GAC Marine is, we are told by its counsel, a subsidiary of a Liechtenstein corporation, apparently known as Gulf Agency Company ("GAC") which has its central office in Athens, Greece. GAC Marine's principal offices are located in London, England but its invoices state that it also has offices in Hong Kong, Norway, United Arab Emirates and Basking Ridge, New Jersey. The New Jersey office is apparently located in the same office as that of G.A.C. Shipping (North America) Ltd. ("GAC Shipping"), another GAC subsidiary. That office is staffed by one Norman Schmidt, Georgianne Temple and Marilyn Taylor, who are paid by GAC Shipping with funds supplied by GAC. But Schmidt styles himself as manager of GAC's U.S. office and his business card is under the name of the defendant GAC Marine. GAC and GAC Marine, according to Schmidt, "apparently are run by the same people." Schmidt describes his duties for GAC Marine as "sales and contact and follow through." As this description implies, he and his fellow workers do more than merely solicit business from potential American customers seeking to purchase marine fuel (bunkers) for delivery overseas. . . .

IV

[We now turn] to consideration of whether the defendant is subject to in personam jurisdiction here on these causes of action and generally.

The limits of such in personam jurisdiction are apparently conceded by both sides to be tested by due process. This is not a case in diversity where state law concepts govern the extent of personal jurisdiction. Rather, this is a case involving the violation of a federal statute and related court order. There is nothing that indicates that Congress sought to assert in personam jurisdiction on any standard other than due process in an action concerning a breach of the automatic stay through arresting, seizing or attaching estate property.

Two grounds for the exercise of such jurisdiction consistent with due process are asserted here: (i) transactional jurisdiction as set forth in 1 Restatement (Second) of Conflicts of Laws §47(1) (1971) (the "Restatement") and (ii) general "doing business" jurisdiction as set forth in §47(2) of the Restatement.[4]

Here it is clear that the defendant transacts business in the United States. It regularly affords, in the United States, quoted prices and terms for delivery of bunkers abroad. Agreements for the same are reached in the United States upon the acceptance of the quoted prices and terms. Its representative in the United States is apparently empowered to sign letters and to deliver documents on its behalf with respect to U.S. customers. It repeatedly holds itself out to the world as having an office in the United States.

It is also clear that the second half of the test, i.e., that the cause of action asserted arose from business done here, has also been satisfied even though the acts complained of, the procuring of the Hong Kong warrant and the Singapore arrest, took place abroad. While the term "arising from" the business transacted in the state might convey the implication that the business transacted must itself give rise to the claim, the courts have construed the phrase far more broadly, holding, in effect, that the claim need only relate to that business in a general way. All that has been required is a relationship between the underlying controversy and the forum state. A. von Mehren & D. Trautman, Jurisdiction to Adjudicate: A Suggested Analysis, 79 Harv. L. Rev. 1121, 1148-51 (1966). Consequently, the Supreme Court has recently taken to expressing the formula in terms of claims that "arise out of or relate to" forum business activities or activities directed at residents of the forum. Burger King Corp. v. Rudzewicz, 471 U.S. 462 (1985). . . .

Here, both a strict relevance test and a historical connection test are satisfied. It is undisputed that the New Jersey agreements to obtain bunkers in Sharjah concern the same subject matter, i.e., the debts, upon which the Hong Kong and Singapore proceedings were based. Further, they are relevant to the cause of action asserted at least insofar as it is claimed that those proceedings are attempts to collect pre-petition debts. Those debts are the matters negotiated and agreed to in New Jersey and where consideration in the form of payment of antecedent debts was delivered. The defendant is thus subject to in personam jurisdiction here on those claims. . . .

---

4. No claim is made on this motion that in personam jurisdiction may be posited on the notion that the interest of the United States in administering bankruptcy proceedings of domestic corporations is so strong as to justify the right of its courts, in the exercise of exclusive jurisdiction over the property of the estate afforded by 28 U.S.C. §1334(d), to enjoin attempts to divest them of that jurisdiction and to determine the rights of all creditors wherever they may be. Nor is any claim made on this motion that jurisdiction may be found on the basis that the warrant and arrest of the two vessels had a substantial, direct and foreseeable effect on the administration of this estate of exactly the type that 11 U.S.C. §362(a) was designed to prevent. Those highly interesting issues are left to another day.

Furthermore, GAC's contention that it is not subject to jurisdiction under the general "doing business" test of §47(2) of the Restatement is without merit. That section provides:

> A state has power to exercise judicial jurisdiction over a foreign corporation which does business in the state with respect to causes of action that do not arise from the business done in the state if this business is so continuous and substantial as to make it reasonable for the state to exercise such jurisdiction.

Although the relationship between GAC Marine and GAC Shipping is apparently structured to enable GAC not to have bank accounts here, it is nevertheless clear that the business of GAC in New Jersey is business done "not occasionally or casually, but with a fair measure of permanence and continuity." Tauza v. Susquehanna Coal Co., 220 N.Y. 259, 115 N.E. 915 (1917). The seven to fifteen transactions per month negotiated in a fashion similar to the transactions at issue here, the receipt of checks in New Jersey, the use of its letterhead by personnel located in New Jersey, the assertions of having a New Jersey office, all show GAC Marine's continued presence here. While GAC Marine claims that GAC Shipping lacks the power to confirm agreements, Schmidt's testimony that confirmations are rarely given from abroad and that the arrangements nevertheless proceed shows that such are not usually required or material.

It is beyond cavil that the mere presence of even a wholly owned subsidiary does not afford jurisdiction over the parent. Restatement §52, Comment b. But

> [i]f a subsidiary corporation does an act, or causes effects, in the state at the direction of the parent corporation or in the course of the parent corporation's business, the state has judicial jurisdiction over the parent to the same extent that it would have if the parent had itself done the act or caused the effects.

Ibid. Accordingly, a corporate parent or affiliate is present for jurisdictional purposes not because of the affiliation but rather because of the intercorporate relationship which is characterized by services in the forum for the parent by the subsidiary beyond mere solicitation, and by frequent communication between them. . . .

For these reasons, finding jurisdiction need not rely on GAC Marine's description of itself as having an office in New Jersey at the address occupied by GAC Shipping. But that it has so described itself makes clear what this record demonstrates: anyone wanting to do business with GAC Marine here need only telephone it in New Jersey by dialing the number it states on its letterhead and invoices.

IV

We thus find that, with the debtor's success on the merits being virtually conceded on this motion and with its injury being, and deemed to be,

irreparable, a preliminary injunction should issue since in personam jurisdiction is established. We further find that a contempt citation should
issue since all that need be shown is a knowing violation of the automatic
stay. Although willfulness is not required in view of the remedial nature of
the remedy, the brazenness of GAC Marine's conduct makes that remedy
particularly appropriate.

===

An injunction and finding of contempt notwithstanding, the fish continued to wiggle on the hook.

In re McLEAN INDUSTRIES, INC.
76 B.R. 291 (Bankr. S.D.N.Y. 1987)

DECISION AND ORDER

Howard C. BUSCHMAN III, Bankruptcy Judge.

United States Lines, Inc. (the "Debtor") seeks an interlocutory judgment finding GAC Marine Fuels Ltd. ("GAC Marine") to be in continuing
civil contempt and requiring GAC Marine to pay to the Debtor all accrued,
unpaid contempt sanctions for the period from December 23, 1986, through
February 3, 1987, as set forth in an order of this Court dated December 29,
1986. GAC Marine, in opposition, principally insists that it is impossible
for it to comply because it assigned its pre-petition claims against the
Debtor to another entity. Upon these claims it had instituted foreign proceedings and obtained warrants of arrest against vessels operated by the
Debtor. It further contends that the order should not have been entered.

I . . .

At the hearing on [the previous order], the only disputed issue was
whether GAC Marine was subject to the in personam jurisdiction of this
Court. No claim was made that the order would be ineffectual, that the
injury was not irreparable or that the automatic stay was not violated.
Even though GAC Marine now claims to have assigned its claims on
December 22, 1986, apparently in either Vaduz, Liechtenstein or Sharjah,
United Arab Emirates, no evidence of the assignment was introduced. The
evidence at the hearing indicated that GAC Marine owned the claims and
was actively protecting them in the foreign proceedings. If the assignments
occurred on December 22, given the six hour time difference between New
York and Vaduz and the nine hour time difference between New York and
Sharjah, GAC Marine could seemingly have telefaxed the assignment to
counsel, prior to the hearing. Upon the closing of the record, counsel for
GAC Marine was given until the morning of December 29, 1986, to file a
brief addressing that issue. No brief was filed and the Court announced its
decision that afternoon. . . .

At trial on the instant matter, the parties stipulated to the evidence. That evidence indicates that on December 23, 1986, the Debtor received a telex from International GAC Marine Fuels Limited which informed it of an assignment of the claims underlying the foreign proceedings to FAL Bunkering Company Limited of Sharjah, United Arab Emirates ("FAL"). Apparently, GAC Marine occasionally transacts business with FAL. In consideration of the transfer of these claims, FAL granted GAC Marine a discharge of 50% of the debt owed by GAC Marine for bunkers sold to it by FAL which GAC Marine had sold to the Debtor.

The following day, GAC Marine's counsel made an ex parte application to the Supreme Court of Hong Kong, on behalf of GAC Marine and FAL, to have FAL substituted as plaintiff in place of GAC Marine and thereby continue the arrest proceeding commenced by GAC Marine. The Hong Kong court entered such an order on that date. On December 26, 1986, GAC Marine's counsel made a similar ex parte application to the High Court of Singapore, which also was granted with the same effect. As stipulated by the parties, the vessels originally arrested by GAC Marine continue to be restrained at Hong Kong and Singapore ports, at least through February 3, 1987.

A notice of motion in the name of GAC Marine was filed in the Singapore court requesting that court to direct a judicial sale of a vessel belonging to the Debtor, known as the *American Oklahoma*, which was scheduled to be heard on January 23, 1987. . . .

III

GAC Marine's principal argument on this motion is that the assignment renders it impossible to comply with the December 29th order. . . .

. . . [N]o evidence was offered to show that GAC Marine cannot buy back the claim from FAL; FAL did not testify that it would not retransfer the claim. On this score, nothing more than assertions of counsel were made. These bald assertions do not amount to the plain and unmistakable evidence contemplated by the Second Circuit in considering this defense. . . .

Indeed, GAC Marine does not even assert, much less prove, that it could not obtain orders from the Hong Kong and Singapore courts vacating the orders it obtained, whereby the arrest proceedings were continued for the benefit of FAL. Thus, instead of taking steps to discontinue those arrest proceedings as the contempt decree required, GAC Marine took the active steps of ensuring their continuation. GAC Marine thus violated 11 U.S.C. §§362(a)(1), (a)(4) and (a)(6) anew. It appears that even today GAC Marine would prefer to continue to harass the Debtor, as it continued to carry out the threat, announced in its telex of November 28, 1986, of keeping the Debtor's vessels arrested "one-by-one" until it was paid its pre-petition debts.

IV

Failing to sustain its defense of inability to comply, GAC Marine makes the further assertions (i) that the Court is somehow "extending" its jurisdiction by holding in contempt those who would seize foreign assets of a United States debtor, (ii) that the assignments here are permitted by Rule 3001 of the Rules of Bankruptcy Procedure, and (iii) that the contempt decree is "ineffectual" because it will not free the debtor's vessels since other foreign creditors have joined the arrest proceedings. These points are of no merit, even if they could be considered as excuses for GAC Marine's violations of the automatic stay. . . .

With GAC Marine having conceded the bankruptcy court's power to enter a contempt decree upon a violation of the automatic stay codified in 11 U.S.C. §362(a), its assertion of an "extension" of jurisdiction is premised on the notion that contempt should not be found where the violation takes place overseas. That notion is belied by both 28 U.S.C. §1334(d) and 11 U.S.C. §541 which speak of the debtor's property "wherever located" and vest the district court, and the bankruptcy court on reference pursuant to 28 U.S.C. §157(a), with exclusive jurisdiction over it. . . .

Further, GAC Marine did not, it must be stressed, lack a remedy if its interests were unfairly prejudiced by the automatic stay. Pursuant to 11 U.S.C. §362(d), it could have sought modification of the stay and introduced evidence of cause for modification, as that section requires. Indeed, this Court, in this bankruptcy case, has entered orders permitting entities having pre-petition maritime liens that are actually secured by value in a vessel, see 11 U.S.C. §506(b), to join in foreign arrest proceedings commenced by others so that those liens could be protected in those proceedings. Instead of availing itself of the opportunity to demonstrate cause and asserting that it has a lien secured by value, GAC Marine flouted 11 U.S.C. §362(a) by starting an arrest proceeding for one vessel and joining in an arrest proceeding for another. Those acts cannot be excused.

GAC Marine's claim that all it did was assign a claim, as permitted by Rule 3001, also cannot be sustained. As this record shows, it did far more in petitioning the Hong Kong and Singapore courts to enable FAL to step into its shoes as an arresting party. . . .

Also without substance is the assertion that the December 29th contempt decree is "ineffectual" because it does not achieve the goal of freeing the Debtor's vessels from arrest, as other foreign creditors were also parties to the arrest proceedings and are not subject to this Court's jurisdiction. While the arrests would remain, as GAC Marine points out, even if GAC Marine were to withdraw, the purpose of the contempt decree was to secure compliance by GAC Marine, which is subject to in personam jurisdiction, with §362 of the Bankruptcy Code. All GAC Marine need concern itself with is obedience to United States law as it affects business transacted here. The participation of foreign creditors in those arrest proceedings affects only the question of damages claimed by the Debtor — a question to be resolved at the ultimate trial on the merits. . . .

The evidence being clear that GAC Marine has not purged itself of civil contempt and has continued to act in violation of the automatic stay, the Debtor's motion must be, and hereby is granted to the extent that an order is to be entered in favor of plaintiff and against defendant declaring defendant in further contempt of 11 U.S.C. §362(a), ordering defendant to pay accrued sanctions as set forth in the Order of December 29, 1986 through February 3,

1987, and further ordering that judgment against defendant and in favor of plaintiff in that sum be entered if defendant fails to make such payment of such sum within five days after the date of such order. It is so ordered.

═══════════

In this case, the recalcitrant creditor had enough contacts with the United States to permit enforcement of the stay. Where that is not true, restraint of creditors will depend on the cooperation of foreign courts. If that cooperation is not forthcoming, reorganization or an orderly, value-maximizing liquidation may be impossible. Conversely, the extension of the stay to overseas assets to the extent the U.S. courts have personal jurisdiction over creditors creates a serious risk of conflict with other countries. Our frequent interactions with Canada are illustrative. The large Canadian banks have operations in the United States and therefore can be effectively prevented from undertaking collection actions in Canada, a fact that has led to considerable resentment at U.S. "overreaching." On the other hand, the courts in the two countries routinely cooperate with each other, so that conflict has generally been avoided. The ALI Principles of Cooperation set down specific rules designed to avoid a conflict in stays and to give the parties guidelines as to which stay applies when. ALI Principles, Procedural Principle 4: Stay Upon Recognition, at 56.

2.   Home Court: Elsewhere

Obviously we cannot do a survey of foreign cases in which a home country court tries to deal with foreign assets and claims. There are far too many countries with far too many rules, and the variations are complex. But the following example offers some insight. It comes from an annual report and commentary on Netherlands law, so the statement of the case, as well as the commentary, are as reported by a scholar in the Netherlands, Titia M. Bos, of the University of Amsterdam.

═══════ X v. SCHENKIUS (receiver for Y) ═══════
Court of Appeal of 'S-Hertogenbosch, 6 July 1993
KG 1993, 406; NIPR 1993 No. 469; NJ 1994, 250
Reported in 42 Netherlands International Law Review 121 (1995)

THE FACTS

On 6 June 1988 the *Arrondissementsrechtbank* (District Court) of the Hague granted a divorce to *X* and Y. *X* petitioned the same court to declare *Y* bankrupt. The bankruptcy order was rendered on 18 July 1988 and Schenkius was appointed receiver. The divorce decree was officially registered on 6 December 1988.

X and *Y* had been married in community of property under the Dutch Civil Code. Their joint estate included a plot of land with two villas in

Spain. In summary proceedings before the President of the District Court of 's-Hertogenbosch, the receiver demanded that *X* be ordered to cooperate in the sale of this real estate for the benefit of the bankrupt estate. For this purpose the receiver required, among other things, a power of attorney for the sale signed by *X* and the original title deeds. *X* disputed this, arguing that since her former husband's bankruptcy had been declared in the Netherlands, its territorial effect was restricted to those parts of the estate located in the Netherlands. On 7 September 1992, the President of the District Court of 's-Hertogenbosch ordered *X* to cooperate in the sale of the Spanish property. In doing so, the President took into account that a bankruptcy declared in the Netherlands comprises the entire estate, thereby obliging the debtor (in this case *Y*) as far as possible to place any foreign property at the disposal of the receiver. The legal force of the bankruptcy attachment as such may be restricted to the Netherlands, but property located abroad is nevertheless part of the bankrupt estate and the bankrupt is obliged to cooperate so as to enable the receiver to include this property in the liquidation. This applies equally to *X* as the ex-wife of the bankrupt, since *X* and *Y* were married in community of property and their divorce was not yet final (had not been entered in the civil register) at the time when the bankruptcy was declared.

On appeal against this judgment at the *Gerechtshof* (Court of Appeal) of 's-Hertogenbosch, *X* submitted the following objections:

(1) The judgment was incorrect in assuming that the bankruptcy comprised the entire estate, including those items of property located abroad.

(2) The President had incorrectly based his decision on a supposed distinction between the bankrupt estate, on the one hand, and the bankruptcy attachment, on the other, so that the debtor's property abroad is seen as belonging to the bankrupt estate.

(3) The President had incorrectly ruled that the bankrupt was obliged to cooperate so as to enable the receiver to include this foreign property in the liquidation of the estate, and that this obligation applied equally to *X* as the ex-wife of the bankrupt to whom she was married in community of property under the Civil Code.

THE JUDGMENT

The Court of Appeal affirmed the judgment of the President of the District Court. The Court of Appeal concurred with the President's judgment, that the bankruptcy comprised the entire estate and that this included all property belonging to the joint estate arising from the bankrupt's community of property marriage contract. A bankruptcy commenced in the Netherlands is assigned territorial effect out of respect for the sovereignty of other countries and in the absence of reciprocity in recognizing bankruptcies declared elsewhere. Despite this, the receiver may attempt to liquidate, for the benefit of the bankrupt estate, any property belonging to the bankrupt that is located abroad. . . .

[COMMENTARY]

... The Insolvency Code ... states that the bankruptcy comprises the bankrupt's entire estate, a provision that implies a pretension to international force for a bankruptcy commenced in the Netherlands. In other words, items of property located abroad which belong to a debtor who has been declared bankrupt in the Netherlands, are considered to be part of the bankrupt estate. ...

... The impression that Dutch international insolvency law is characterized by a "negative attitude to foreign bankruptcy decrees" and is based on "the principle of territoriality" needs to be refined in the light of more recent case law in the Netherlands. ...

This case reflects both the traditional, highly territorial view of bankruptcy common in much of the world for a long time and the modern stirrings of a more cosmopolitan view in the Netherlands and elsewhere. There are countries that adopt the territorial view so strictly that they make no claim whatsoever to overseas property. Japan has been an example of this, although its new legislation is beginning to change that rule. Others, like the Netherlands, try to overcome the disadvantages of that doctrine when they are the home country by forcing cooperation from the debtor, thus avoiding the need for foreign judicial recognition of their insolvency proceedings. In both countries, and throughout the world, scholars are leading a movement toward a less territorial and more cooperative rule.

C. COOPERATING WITH THE HOME COUNTRY COURT

1. Cooperating Court: United States

The United States has taken a leadership role in encouraging international cooperation by frequently deferring to proceedings in other countries as to companies not based in the United States. An eminent scholar, Professor Stephen Riesenfeld convinced Congress to include in the 1978 Code sections 303(b)(4), 304–306, which were designed to permit and encourage U.S. bankruptcy courts to cooperate with home country bankruptcy courts abroad. (The shorthand reference to these provisions collectively is "section 304.") This unilateral initiative did not require reciprocity and did not attract much reciprocity at first, a point illustrated by the seizure of U.S. Lines ships all over the world with little or no reference to the U.S. bankruptcy court.

Over time, however, other courts began to respond to this initiative and to a growing belief in international financial circles that some better solution to multinational bankruptcy should be found. These converging beliefs led in turn to promulgation by the UN in 1997 of a Model Law of Cross-Border Insolvency for international cooperation in bankruptcy matters. The development of the Model Law is outlined *infra* at pp. 860–861. The United

States was a very active participant in the development of the Model Law and the National Bankruptcy Review Commission almost immediately recommended to Congress that the United States adopt it. Although adoption was delayed by the long political struggle over other aspects of the pending bankruptcy legislation, the Model Law was adopted as part of the 2005 amendments, becoming Chapter 15 of the Bankruptcy Code.

The adoption of Chapter 15 was intended to encourage enactment of the Model Law in countries around the world. It was not intended to change greatly United States law as it had developed under section 304. It retains the common law approach of using an ancillary proceeding as the vehicle of cooperation, but it also permits parallel proceedings. The process of negotiation required the inclusion of provisions that give some primacy to local parallel proceedings (called "concurrent" proceedings" in section 1529), but the legislative history and the amendment to section 305 make it clear that the court has broad discretion to dismiss the local United States case in favor of an ancillary approach in deference to the foreign proceeding where it is pending in the home country of the debtor.

Chapter 15 contemplates cooperation with foreign "main" proceedings, which are proceedings in the country where is located the "center of main interests" of the debtor, a test taken from the European Union Regulation discussed below. §§101(23), 1502(4). A "foreign representative" (section 101(24)) may file for recognition of a foreign proceeding in the United States under section 1515 and recognition will be granted quickly in most cases using various presumptions. §§1515-17. Upon recognition, an automatic stay goes into effect with the same force and same limitations as under section 362 and the court is given broad powers, including the grant of additional injunctive relief, the use of U.S. discovery tools, and the turnover of assets within its control to the foreign representative, who is also empowered to operate the debtor's business. §§1520(a)(3), 1521(a)-(b). Foreign nonmain proceedings (that is, proceedings in countries other than the "main" one) are granted only quite limited recognition and cooperation. §1521(c). The foreign representative is required to make full disclosure to the United States bankruptcy court of the status of proceedings elsewhere in the world and to keep that information up to date.

Chapter 15 excludes cases of natural persons whose debts are below the Chapter 13 levels established in section 109(e) if the debtors are citizens or permanent residents of the United States.

Some of the cases decided under section 304 will remain important sources of guidance to the courts in applying Chapter 15. This next case is among the first to reflect the dynamics of a reorganization negotiation rather than a struggle over the results of a liquidation.

=== In re BOARD OF DIRECTORS OF MULTICANAL S.A. ===
314 B.R. 486 (Bankr. S.D.N.Y. 2004)

Allan L. GROPPER, Bankruptcy Judge.

Multicanal S.A. ("Multicanal"), a cable company located in Argentina, has filed a petition under §304 of the Bankruptcy Code seeking recognition in the United States of an *acuerdo preventivo extrajudicial* ("APE") proceeding in the Republic of Argentina. At the commencement of the proceeding, Multicanal also moved to enjoin a large United States holder of its Notes, Argentinian Recovery Company LLC ("ARC"), from continuing to pursue two lawsuits in New York State Court in which ARC sought a judgment for overdue amounts on the Notes. ARC is an entity formed to hold Multicanal Notes owned by certain clients of WRH Partners Global Securities, L.P. ("Huff"), an investment manager whose clients include pension funds, charitable foundations, research institutions and universities (for convenience, ARC and Huff will hereafter collectively be called "Huff"). Huff has opposed the §304 petition and in addition, together with two affiliated Noteholders, filed an involuntary Chapter 11 petition against Multicanal under §303 of the Bankruptcy Code.

FACTS

Background

Multicanal S.A. is a *sociedad anonima* organized under Argentine law, with principal offices in Buenos Aires. It is a wholly-owned subsidiary of Grupo Clarin ("Clarin"), an Argentine media conglomerate that owns, among other properties, the largest circulation newspaper in Argentina. About 90% of Multicanal's operations are in Argentina, with virtually all of the remainder in Paraguay and Uruguay. Its revenues are derived primarily from monthly subscription fees for cable service, connection fees and advertising. Although it purchases goods and materials from this country, it has no ongoing business in the United States. As of January 28, 2004, the date that the involuntary petition was filed, its sole U.S.-based assets were three bank accounts with an aggregate balance of approximately $9,500.

Multicanal's restructuring can be traced to Argentina's recent economic collapse. This debt, representing substantially all of Multicanal's debt for money borrowed, includes Bank debt and five series of U.S. dollar-denominated notes (the "Notes") in an aggregate principal amount of U.S. $509 million. It also represents about 97% of Multicanal's total debt.

There are two principal means of restructuring under the Argentine insolvency laws. The first is by a *concurso preventivo*, which seeks to reorganize a debtor's business and avoid liquidation of the estate. In a *concurso* the debtor continues to manage its business under the supervision of a court-appointed supervisor and a creditors' committee. Creditor consents for the restructuring are obtained after the debtor has filed for relief with the court. An automatic stay is triggered by the filing of a *concurso*, and transactions outside of the ordinary course of business require prior court authorization.

The second means of restructuring is by an *acuerdo preventivo extrajudicial*, or APE, which is generally much less expensive and time-consuming than a *concurso*. An APE is a privately negotiated debt restructuring, supported by a qualified majority of a debtor's creditors, that is submitted to an

Argentine court for judicial approval. An APE proceeding gives rise to judicial oversight after creditor approval has been solicited, from the time of the filing for confirmation. An APE may only affect claims of unsecured creditors; those claims that are not affected by the APE remain unimpaired.

* * *

In the third quarter of 2002, Multicanal approached known institutional holders of its debt, including Fleet National Bank, Citibank, Deutsche Bank, Credit Suisse First Boston, Credit Lyonnais, Toronto Dominion, TIAA-CREF, Fintech Advisory Ltd., Orix Capital Markets LLC, Dolphin Fund Management and Huff, to commence discussions on the possibility of a restructuring. Certain of these holders, who collectively held in excess of 25% of Multicanal's Notes, formed an informal Negotiating Group. The Group retained Argentine counsel, whose fees and expenses were paid by Multicanal.

[Multicanal went through a process of negotiation with its creditors. The Huff group at all times opposed the terms of the restructuring proposed by the company and a hard-fought battle ensued, with threats of lawsuits and criminal actions in both the United States and Argentina. Eventually, Multicanal offered a plan with options with mixes of cash and securities that was accepted by 94% of the creditors and approved by the Argentinian court. Huff then filed suit on its notes in the United States courts. Multicanal responded with a request for an injunction against those suits under section 304 and Huff then filed an involuntary bankruptcy petition in the United States against Multicanal under section 303 of the Bankruptcy Code. The court granted a preliminary injunction and here addresses the merits of both the section 304 petition and the involuntary petition after trial.]

DISCUSSION

I. *Standards and Prerequisites for Granting Relief Under §304.*

The Supreme Court made clear over a century ago that in contracting with a foreign entity, a person subjects himself to those laws of the foreign government "affecting the powers and obligations of the corporation with which he voluntarily contracts." Canada S. Ry. Co. v. Gebhard, 109 U.S. 527, 537, 3 S.Ct. 363, 27 L.Ed. 1020 (1883). U.S. courts have recognized that foreign courts have an interest in presiding over the insolvency proceedings of their own domestic business entities to promote the systematic distribution of a debtor's assets.

* * *

Only a "foreign representative" has standing to seek relief under §304. Huff contends that Multicanal's board of directors fails to satisfy the definition of "foreign representative," as it is not a "trustee" or other independent fiduciary. A board of directors may be an appropriate representative in a §304 case, however, if it plays a role similar to that of a debtor in possession under the U.S. Bankruptcy Code, where management remains in control of the reorganizing debtor and an independent trustee is not ordinarily appointed.

* * *

Once the prerequisites are established, §304(c) provides "guidelines" for the exercise of the Court's discretion in determining whether to grant relief. Section 304(c) provides:

> In determining whether to grant relief under subsection (b) of this section, the court shall be guided by what will best assure an economical and expeditious administration of such estate, consistent with —
> (1) just treatment of all holders of claims against or interests in such estate;
> (2) protection of claim holders in the United States against prejudice and inconvenience in the processing of claims in such foreign proceeding;
> (3) prevention of preferential or fraudulent dispositions of property of such estate;
> (4) distribution of proceeds of such estate substantially in accordance with the order prescribed by this title;
> (5) comity; and
> (6) if appropriate, the provision of an opportunity for a fresh start for the individual that such foreign proceeding concerns.

11 U.S.C. §304(c). Notwithstanding the delineation of those factors, under the statute, the touchstone is "an economical and expeditious administration" of the foreign estate, and the factors in subsection (c) are guidelines, not requirements.

Many decisions have also held that the fifth factor, comity, is preeminent in determining whether relief should be granted. In re Treco, 240 F.3d at 156-57 ("We do not quarrel with the view . . . that comity is the ultimate consideration in determining whether to provide relief under §304.")

II. Huff's Opposition to the APE

Huff has opposed recognition of Multicanal's APE as prejudicial and unfair to U.S. creditors on three principal grounds. First, Huff argues that the APE is a form of private insolvency regime not subject to adequate judicial control and not entitled to recognition under the general standards of §304(c). Second, Huff contends that the vote taken in favor of the APE was coerced and unfair, and that a lack of judicial oversight (among other things) led Multicanal to engage in abusive practices that created an atmosphere of coercion and intimidation. Third, Huff alleges that Multicanal discriminated against U.S. retail investors in its restructuring.

* * *

A.   Is the APE a Form of Insolvency Proceeding
Entitled to Recognition Under §304?

Argentina has detailed and comprehensive laws relating to both liquidations (*quiebra*) and reorganizations (*concurso*).

Huff attacks the APE in principle as providing uncontrolled discretion to a debtor and as having too truncated a statutory underpinning.

The absence of a detailed statutory framework for the APE is not fatal. For example, the Canadian Companies' Creditors Arrangement Act ("CCAA") has only three parts, yet they provide the underpinning for a reorganization law that is recognized under §304 and routinely granted comity.

As for the alleged lack of judicial oversight during the period of solicitation and voting, the APE bears a strong resemblance to U.S. prepackaged plans of reorganization ("Prepacks"), which in one form or another have been an established means of restructuring in the United States for many years.[8]

In both an APE and a U.S. Prepack the debtor continues in possession of its property and operates its business, and Argentine and U.S. courts, respectively, may enjoin or restrict the disposition of a debtor's assets. Once a case is filed, U.S. courts exercise supervisory and oversight powers in a U.S. Prepack; Argentine courts do the same in an APE. Moreover, in many U.S. Prepacks, as in Multicanal's APE, there is no need for a claims administration or reconciliation process because affected claims are admitted and all other creditors are generally paid on confirmation of a plan or in the ordinary course of the debtor's business.

* * *

In connection with Huff's charges that Multicanal's plan provides too small a recovery to unsecured creditors, it should be emphasized that the Bankruptcy Code does not require rejection of a consensual plan that has received the requisite vote because the debtor could "pay more." Chapter 11, like the APE, is based on the principle that a plan should, if possible, be negotiated and then ratified by a creditor vote. The members of the Negotiating Group that agreed to support the APE were large, sophisticated, well-represented institutions. Huff's assertions that the APE amounted to a give-away for Clarin's benefit insults these creditors.[10]

* * *

B.   The Voting and Solicitation Procedures
Used by Multicanal in the APE

Huff has identified certain practices and procedures in connection with the voting on the APE that it alleges were coercive and unlawful and

---

8. They are also used in other countries in different forms. See, e.g., Jacques Henrot & Emmanuel Fatome, Pre-Bankruptcy and Bankruptcy Processes in France, 1998-1999 Ann. Surv. Bankr.L. 619, 630-36 (1999) (discussing the reglement amiable procedure under the French Law of 1984); John A. Barrett, Jr., Mexican Insolvency Law, 7 Pace Int'l L.Rev. 431 (1995) (discussing Mexico's suspension of payments law).

10. Huff asserted that some of the members of the Negotiating Group supported the APE only because they were more interested in the future of Multicanal's shareholder, Clarin, with which they also had a debtor-creditor relationship.

should cause the Court either to withhold recognition of the APE or require a new vote. Huff charges that these practices were inconsistent with those that would prevail in a United States insolvency case and resulted in a denial of due process to U.S. creditors.

[The court examined each of these points and found that the procedures, although different in some respects from U.S. procedures, were consistent with due process and not coercive in the commercial context of these sorts of negotiations.]

5.   IMPROPER PRESSURE AND THREATS BY MULTICANAL

Finally, Huff contends, Multicanal pressured creditors, offered improper consideration for votes and facilitated vote distortion by assisting "yes" voters but not negative voters.

In its opposition to the APE, Huff took very extensive discovery in accordance with the procedures that prevail in the United States, including the depositions and the production of tens of thousands, if not hundreds of thousands of pages of documents. Huff established on this record that Multicanal vigorously pursued the APE, attempting to garner support and to keep Notes out of the hands of Huff, which was also increasing its holdings and had announced itself as a firm opponent of the APE.

Huff uncovered no indication that Multicanal offered improper inducements to any entity to support the APE. Tensions were high between the parties, but there was no impediment to Huff's effective opposition to the APE, which it has continued to fight in the courts of Argentina and the United States.

One act involving Huff, however, requires further examination. In November 2003, Urricelqui, a director of Multicanal, filed criminal charges against several representatives of Huff for allegedly demanding that Multicanal provide Huff treatment under the APE which would be better than that available to all other creditors.

This Court has no authority or desire to review the actions of a criminal court in Argentina. Nevertheless, Multicanal is seeking affirmative relief in our courts for its restructuring, a matter in which the interest of the United States is not incidental. Notes in principal amount of over $500 million were issued in New York, governed by New York law, and about 80% of the Notes are held by U.S. entities, most visibly by Huff and its clients.

Accordingly, prior to entry of a final order under §304 , Multicanal will have to establish in this proceeding justification for its commencement of a criminal prosecution in Argentina against Huff and its representatives.

C.   Discrimination against U.S. Retail Noteholders

Huff's final contention is that Multicanal discriminated against U.S. retail Noteholders . . . in its APE. For the reasons discussed below, the Court finds that the APE discriminated against the U.S. . . . Noteholders, and that such discrimination must be remedied if the APE is to receive recognition under §304.

1.   THE DISCRIMINATORY TREATMENT

There is not much dispute about the fact that U.S. retail holders received different treatment from other Noteholders. These figures lead to the conclusion that, although the U.S. retail holders held the same Notes as the QIBs and were placed in the same class by Multicanal for APE voting purposes, they were provided with a distribution of significantly lesser value.

2.   ASSERTED JUSTIFICATION FOR THE DISCRIMINATION

Multicanal did not dispute the disparate treatment given to U.S. retail holders. It argued principally that the difference in treatment resulted from the effect of the U.S. securities laws and that the treatment was justified.

* * *

A foreign proceeding cannot discriminate against U.S. creditors and expect recognition under §304. Multicanal has not adequately explained why it did not take appropriate steps to eliminate the disadvantageous aspects of the discrimination.

This is especially true in that there were at least four alternatives available to Multicanal that would have allowed it to offer substantially the same distribution to . . . [noteholders] in the United States as it did to other Noteholders.

This Court will not in the first instance direct a remedy without hearing from the parties, but the discrimination must be eliminated before final relief is entered herein.

III.   THE INVOLUNTARY CHAPTER 11 PROCEEDING

* * *

A.   Section 305(a)(2)

Section 305(a)(2) provides that a Court may dismiss a case if there is a foreign proceeding pending and the factors set forth in §304(c) warrant dismissal. As discussed above, Multicanal's APE is a "foreign proceeding" and, with certain caveats, the §304(c) factors have been satisfied. Thus the Court may, in its discretion, dismiss the involuntary petition pursuant to this section.

In the instant case, the economical and expeditious administration of the foreign estate is best served by proceeding with its §304 petition and dismissing the involuntary Chapter 11 petition.

A U.S. Chapter 11 proceeding to run concurrently with the existing APE, one alternative proposed by the involuntary petitioners, would hinder rather than advance an equitable distribution in this case.

CONCLUSION

Multicanal's APE may be recognized and enforced in the United States pursuant to 11 U.S.C. §304 and the involuntary Chapter 11 dismissed, subject to the following. Multicanal shall within 30 days file and serve (i) a proposed cure for the discrimination against U.S. retail Noteholders and (ii) sufficient information about the criminal proceedings in Argentina so that a determination may be made that those proceedings are substantially justified.

─────────────

Cases like this one, in which the involuntary parallel proceeding was dismissed under section 305 in favor of ancillary cooperation with the main proceeding in Argentina, will likely remain important precedents under the new Chapter 15. On the other hand, the continued relevance of cases denying cooperation under section 304 is less clear. In particular, U. S. courts struggled with the contradictions inherent in section 304 when security interests or other alleged interests in property were at issue, because section 304 created a mechanism for cooperation at the same time that it required protection of U.S. creditors in language much more specific than that of section 1522, which is clearly designed to give the courts more discretion in the context of a mandate to cooperate. Compare §304(c) with §§1522, 1525-1527. Subsection (c) of section 304 could be read to mean we would cooperate only when the provisions of the other law were not different in any way that would adversely affect some U.S. creditor, which would mean we would rarely cooperate. On the other hand, it could be understood as requiring only a general similarity to our law, a similarity that may be found in the laws of a number of other countries. As so often happens, faced with two conflicting policy goals — international cooperation and protection of U.S. creditors — Congress simply incorporated them both and left it to the courts to sort out.

One key question under section 304(c) is whether secured creditors, the law's darlings, can be sent off to foreign climes when they lend money to a foreign debtor. If a creditor has collateral in the United States, can it ignore Chapter 15, except perhaps for a temporary delay in repossession and sale? Some observers thought so after the decision announced in a case called *In re Treco*, 240 F.3d 148 (2d Cir. 2001). The Bank of New York claimed a security interest in certain accounts belonging to an African bank that had gone into liquidation in the Bahamas, where it was incorporated. The Bahamian liquidators applied for a section 304 order turning over the accounts to them. The Second Circuit panel refused, holding that Bahamian law was too different from United States law to satisfy section 304(c).

The key to the decision was that Bahamian law (like the law of the United Kingdom and a number of other countries) permits administrative expenses to trump the bank's security interest, while of course United States law would not permit any use of the bank's collateral to pay the costs of the bankruptcy case unless a direct benefit to the bank was shown. Of considerable importance in *Treco* was the fact that administration expenses, including fees for the professionals in the Bahamas, had already consumed $8 million of the $10 million in the bankruptcy estate, with the case not half over. Furthermore, fees and expenses were being approved by a court official, not a judge. The panel believed that if the New York money was turned over, it would disappear into that maw. The court emphasized that section 304(c) required individual consideration of the foreign law's effect in each case. Here that effect was too drastic.

Some commentators have argued that *Treco* shows that the collateral of secured creditors is largely exempt from any turnover under section 304. Others believe that the emphasis of the *Treco* court on a case-by-case approach highlights the importance in that case of the stunning level of administrative charges, 80 percent of the total in the estate with no supervision over fees by a judge! When we compare Chapter 15 to section 304, Chapter 15 does provide for the protection of creditors at every stage in the process, but in much more general terms. §1522. It is noteworthy, that it does not single out secured creditors for special protection nor require substantial similarity to American law in the distribution of the estate.

Chapter 15 has eliminated the section 304(c) requirements except in one unusual respect. Section 1507 re-enacts section 304, including subsection (c), but only insofar as the court wishes to use it to grant additional assistance. Thus cases like *Treco* that refuse cooperation will not be controlling under the new provisions. On the other hand, section 1507 ensures that cases granting cooperation under section 304 will continue as possible sources of authority for cooperative actions.

Perhaps the most far-reaching change in the Model Law, in the United States and elsewhere, is the adoption of provisions expressly encouraging direct communication between courts in multinational bankruptcy cases. §§1525-1526. These sections also authorize direct communication between courts and bankruptcy trustees. In both situations, appropriate notice and supervision are also required. These provisions are not merely pious hopes. Even before Chapter 15 was adopted, in a case in which the United Kingdom and the United States had gotten at cross purposes, a transatlantic telephone call between a British judge and an American judge enabled the courts and parties to avoid an unpleasant and costly conflict between these generally friendly court systems. In re Cenargo Int'l, Plc, 294 B.R. 571 (Bankr. S.D.N.Y. 2003). The idea of judges talking directly to each other took a little getting used to, but the ALI Principles eventually gave a strong endorsement to such communications, providing a set of guidelines for courts and lawyers to use. ALI Principles of Cooperation Among the NAFTA Countries Proc. Prin. 10, 57 and App. B (2003). The International Insolvency Institute is in the process of translating the ALI Guidelines into a number of languages for use all over the world. http://www.iiiglobal.org/international/guidelines.html.

2.   *Cooperating Court: Elsewhere*

Slowly but surely, courts in other jurisdictions have begun to respond to the section 304 initiative. Independently, often in cases not involving the United States, courts in several countries have shown a willingness to cooperate with a home country court. The following example from Canada illustrates this trend. Once again, it is one of the huge mass-tort cases that makes new law.

≡ ROBERTS v. PICTURE BUTTE MUNICIPAL HOSPITAL ≡
[1999] 4 W.W.R. 443 (Alberta QB)

1. This is an application by the Defendant Dow Corning Corporation ("DCC") for a permanent stay of proceedings against it. DCC is now the only remaining Defendant in this action, as the actions against the other four Defendants were dismissed on the basis of having been commenced outside of the applicable limitation periods. DCC applies for a permanent stay of these proceedings on the grounds that this Court should recognize the jurisdiction of the United States Bankruptcy Court for the Eastern District of Michigan, Northern Division. The Plaintiffs, Wanda and Alan Roberts, argue that a stay is inappropriate.

Background

2. The female Plaintiff underwent surgery in 1981 for bilateral fibrocystic disease and mammary dysplasia in both breasts. Also in 1981, she received silicone gel breast implants manufactured by McGhan Medical Corporation ("McGhan"), a former Defendant. After problems with those implants, they were replaced in June 1983 with silicone gel implants manufactured by DCC. Soon after, one implant was found to have ruptured, necessitating surgery to clean up as much silicone as possible from her system.

3. Since that time, the female Plaintiff alleges widespread pain and problems, which she blames on the silicone gel released into her body. For this application, it is not necessary nor appropriate for me to comment on her symptoms or their cause.

4. The Plaintiffs started this action on August 31, 1989. There was also class action litigation in the U.S. which coordinated all claims arising out of the failure of both McGhan and DCC implants. That class action collapsed when DCC sought bankruptcy protection on May 15, 1995 under Chapter 11 of the United States Bankruptcy Code (the "U.S. Bankruptcy Code"). Section 362 of the U.S. Bankruptcy Code imposes an automatic stay on all actions or proceedings against DCC to recover claims that arose before the claims bar date.

5. The U.S. Bankruptcy Court set February 14, 1997 as the foreign claims bar date (the deadline for filing claims in the bankruptcy proceedings). The Plaintiffs filed proofs of claim in that U.S. proceeding on January 17, 1997. More than 700,000 proofs of claim were filed from many countries, including more than 30,000 by Canadian residents.

Legislation

6. DCC is asking that this Court recognize the proceedings in the U.S. Bankruptcy Court. The U.S. Bankruptcy Code provides for an automatic stay once bankruptcy proceedings are commenced in the U.S.

7. . . . [T]he stay purports to be extra-territorial, applying, for example, in Alberta. It is then up to this Court to decide whether the principles of

comity favour upholding the stay in this jurisdiction. As the Plaintiffs emphasize, comity is a discretionary matter. I am not bound by the stay imposed by the U.S. Bankruptcy Act.

8. I note that the Canadian legislation has a similar provision (Bankruptcy and Insolvency Act ("BIA"), R.S.C. 1985, c. B-3).

9. The Plaintiffs accept that the U.S. Bankruptcy Code governs DCC's estate, and that the Plaintiffs are creditors under the jurisdiction of the U.S. Bankruptcy Court.

PLAN OF REORGANIZATION

10. DCC filed a Plan of Reorganization (the "Plan") with the Bankruptcy Court on August 25, 1997. The Bankruptcy Court rejected this Plan, and an amended plan was presented on February 17, 1998. The Bankruptcy Court approved that Plan, which now has to be voted upon by the various classes of creditors. . . .

11. Breast implant claimants would have four settlement paths, based on their history, symptoms and past and proposed treatment. Any claims not settled by agreement under the Plan process would go to common issue trials. Any claims remaining after common issue trials would undergo individual claims review and mediation. The last resort would be individual litigation. These individual trials would be held in the U.S., dismissed in favour of litigation in the claimant's home jurisdiction, or held in the U.S. using the law of the claimant's home jurisdiction. The Plan is designed to solve as many claims as possible in an orderly and expeditious manner. . . .

ANALYSIS

General Principles

16. Where an appropriate forum must be chosen, the Courts may grant a stay of proceedings. In the words of the Supreme Court of Canada: "This enables the court of the forum selected by the Plaintiffs (the domestic forum) to stay the action at the request of the Defendant if persuaded that the case should be tried elsewhere." (Amchem Products Inc. v. British Columbia (Workers' Compensation Board), [1993] 1 S.C.R. 897 (S.C.C.), at 912). This decision is completely discretionary. I am not bound to defer to the U.S. bankruptcy proceedings.

17. *Amchem* also discusses the vital principle of comity. . . .

18. After cautioning against abusing the power to enjoin foreign litigation, the S.C.C. in *Amchem* outlined the test for restraining foreign proceedings. Although a case on anti-suit injunctions, the first part of the test also relates to stays. The Court must determine if there is a forum other than the domestic forum which is "clearly more appropriate" (at 931). If not, the domestic forum should refuse to stay the domestic proceedings. At 931-932, the S.C.C. continued:

> In this step of the analysis, the domestic court as a matter of comity must take cognizance of the fact that the foreign court has assumed jurisdiction.

If, applying the principles relating to forum non conveniens outlined above, the foreign court could reasonably have concluded that there was no alternative forum that was clearly more appropriate, the domestic court should respect that decision and the application should be dismissed. When there is a genuine disagreement between the courts of our country and another, the courts of this country should not arrogate to themselves the decision for both jurisdictions. In most cases it will appear from the decision of the foreign court whether it acted on principles similar to those that obtain here, but, if not, then the domestic court must consider whether the result is consistent with those principles.

19. As La Forest J. stated in Morguard Investments Ltd. v. De Savoye (1990), 76 D.L.R. (4th) 256 (S.C.C.) at 268, modern states "cannot live in splendid isolation." They must follow comity, which is "the deference and respect due by other states to the actions of a state legitimately taken within its own territory."

20. Comity and cooperation are increasingly important in the bankruptcy context. As internationalization increases, more parties have assets and carry on activities in several jurisdictions. Without some coordination, there would be multiple proceedings, inconsistent judgments and general uncertainty.

21. I also note that U.S. Courts have shown themselves willing to grant comity in similar circumstances. For example, a Bankruptcy Court granted comity in Tradewell Inc. v. American Sensors & Electronics Inc., 1997 WL 423075 (U.S. S.D.N.Y. 1997). In that case, all proceedings against the Defendant Canadian corporation were stayed under the Companies' Creditors Arrangement Act. The Defendant successfully applied to the U.S. Bankruptcy Court for a stay in the U.S. based on comity. That Court stated that U.S. public policy should recognize the foreign proceedings, thus facilitating the "orderly and systematic distribution" of the debtor's assets. This was especially true for Canada, which has similar procedures and procedural safeguards.

DISCUSSION

* * *

25. The Plaintiffs argue that foreign claimants are not treated fairly by the proposed Plan because their settlement package would be at a discount from that given to U.S. claimants. However, there are several safeguards to prevent unfairness. First, the Plaintiffs, along with the rest of the class, have the opportunity to vote against the Plan. If, as a class, they vote against it, the U.S. Bankruptcy Court can only confirm the Plan if it feels the Plan does not "discriminate unfairly" against classes which rejected it. I understand this to mean that treatment can be fair across classes without being equal, as long as there is equality within the class itself. Second, the Plaintiffs are not obliged to settle under the Plan. They may proceed to trial. Third, this Plan actually protects creditors. If there were no stay and no Plan, only the first to trial and judgment would receive any compensation

at all, and trials could potentially drag on for many years. Under the Plan, each creditor will receive something and will receive it much sooner. . . .

ORDER

31. In the circumstances of this case, the U.S. Bankruptcy Court has apparently decided that fairness among creditors is achieved without having complete equality across all classes of creditors. The Plaintiffs attorned to that jurisdiction. However, even had there been no attornment, I find that common sense dictates that these matters would be best dealt with by one Court, and in the interest of promoting international comity it seems the forum for this case is in the U.S. Bankruptcy Court. Thus, in either case, whether there has been an attornment or not, I conclude it is appropriate for me to exercise my discretion and apply the principles of comity and grant the Defendant's stay application. I reach this conclusion based on all the circumstances, including the clear wording of the U.S. Bankruptcy Code provision, the similar philosophies and procedures in Canada and the U.S., the Plaintiffs' attornment to the jurisdiction of the U.S. Bankruptcy Court, and the incredible number of claims outstanding. Lastly, while not determinative, I found it significant that there has been acceptance of the Plan in Ontario and Quebec. This not only suggests that the Plan proposes a reasonable offer, but it also suggests that the parties affected in these provinces have accepted the principle that international comity should be recognized in these proceedings. Application granted.

═══════════

It is particularly interesting that the Alberta court went out of its way to avoid relying on the filing of a claim in the United States as the sole ground for binding these plaintiffs, but instead emphasized the role of comity regardless of "attornment" to the foreign jurisdiction.

D. INTERNATIONAL LAW REFORM

A number of international institutions — notably the International Monetary Fund and the World Bank — have gotten interested in reform of bankruptcy laws, both domestic and international. Law reform organizations have also developed projects in international bankruptcy cooperation. These projects have not addressed choice of law, our next subject, but have focused on cooperation among courts in managing international cases.

We discussed earlier the Model Law on Cross-Border Insolvencies promulgated by the United Nations Commission on International Trade Law (UNCITRAL), the law that is the basis for Chapter 15 of the Bankruptcy Code. Unlike a treaty or convention, a model law is offered for adoption by each country in the hope that its adoption by a number of countries will begin the process of cooperation and, eventually, harmonization. The Model

Law will come into effect in the United Kingdom in 2006 and has been adopted in Japan, Mexico, Poland, Romania, and South Africa, among other countries.

The Transnational Insolvency Project of the American Law Institute was also mentioned earlier. Its purpose is to go the next step beyond the model law to improve cooperation among the three NAFTA countries, Canada, Mexico, and the United States, in multinational insolvencies. The project has produced authoritative summaries of the bankruptcy laws of each of the three countries and a statement of Principles of Cooperation. At the heart of the ALI Principles is the idea of a global perspective. Each principle is designed to encourage the courts and the parties to look at such cases overall, seeking the best results for the creditors regardless of local advantage.

Finally, the European Union has adopted a bankruptcy "regulation," which is a law issued at the European level that is binding on all member countries and enforceable in their courts. Effective May, 2002, over time it will tend to improve cooperation and coordination in trans-EU cases, although it does not go as far in the cosmopolitan direction as many observers had hoped. Its most important feature may simply be the fact that it is an EU regulation and therefore will be subject to uniform interpretation through the European Court of Justice. It thus will offer the first example of a truly international bankruptcy regime.

E.   CHOICE OF LAW

As we noted earlier, choice of forum and choice of law are closely intertwined issues in the bankruptcy field and the analyst must keep them sharply distinct while simultaneously remaining aware of their close interaction — a difficult business at best. The following cases reflect several key points: (a) choice of law is often a distinct issue; (b) choice of law is always related to which country is the home country and therefore to choice of forum; (c) choice of law for application of avoidance law is in many ways the single most important question in international insolvency, at least from a litigant's point of view. It should be noted that we are discussing choice of which *bankruptcy* law to apply. In any cross-border bankruptcy case the court will also be required to choose which *nonbankruptcy* law to apply to a particular dispute. Thus, for example, if a TIB in such a case attacks the enforceability of a security interest, the court must ascertain first which jurisdiction's secured-credit law applies to determine the validity of the security interest (e.g., in the United States, whether the creditor has met the obligations imposed by Article 9 of the UCC), and second, which nation's bankruptcy avoidance provisions apply (e.g., in the United States, does section 544 or 547 of the Bankruptcy Code void an otherwise enforceable security interest?). The permutations multiply, if, for example, Canadian nonbankruptcy law applies to determine the underlying substantive right (e.g., validity of a contract), then German insolvency law determines the effect of the right once the debtor has filed for bankruptcy (e.g., treatment of executory contracts).

Although there are many issues in a bankruptcy case that may require determination of the applicable bankruptcy law, three areas are most crucial: avoiding powers, distribution (priority) rules, and discharge. There are very few cases (much less statutory provisions) anywhere in the world addressing choice of law for any of the three. Chapter 15 is silent on the subject. In this section we discuss the avoiding powers.

Both of the next two cases arise from the Maxwell bankruptcy. One legal point is key to the dispute: Unlike United States preference law, British insolvency law requires that a payment is not avoidable unless the debtor had a desire to prefer the creditor. The consequence was that the preference under attack in these cases was likely to be avoidable under section 547 of the U.S. Bankruptcy Code, but likely to be unavoidable under section 239 of the English Insolvency Act 1986. (Note also that an "overdraft facility" is simply a type of loan.)

BARCLAYS BANK P.L.C. v. HOMAN AND OTHERS
Court of Appeal (Civil Division)
[1993] BCLC 680, [1992] BCC 757 (8 October 1992)

GLIDEWELL, L.J.

THE PARTIES

Maxwell Communications Corporation plc is an English company which was controlled by the late Mr Robert Maxwell. It is registered in England, and until its collapse last December was quoted on the London Stock Exchange and managed by a board of directors in London. However, its principal assets were and are in the United States. They are shares which Maxwell Communications owns, indirectly through two wholly-owned subsidiary companies, in Macmillan Inc and Official Airline Guides Inc, American companies with American subsidiaries. The total assets in the United States are worth many times the value of the assets outside America, which are estimated to be worth less than £100m.

Barclays Bank plc is an English bank, with the majority of its branches in the United Kingdom. In the United States Barclays has branches in the state of New York and offices in other major cities.

THE FACTS

Until November 1991 Maxwell Communications had an agreement with Barclays for an overdraft facility at the bank's branch in Holborn, London. The limit on the facility was expressed in sterling, but drawings could be made in any convertible currency. The agreement provided that drawings in foreign currencies were to be repaid to 'such bank or branch of the bank as the bank shall specify.' By October 1991 $US30m[illion] had been drawn against this facility. As is now well-known, by that date it was apparent to their creditors that Maxwell Communications and other companies in which the late Mr Robert Maxwell was interested were in severe financial difficulties. Barclays started to express concern about the extent of Maxwell Communications' overdraft drawings.

On 5 November 1991 Mr Robert Maxwell died. Shortly before that, on 1 November 1991, MacMillan Inc had sold one of its subsidiary companies, QUE, to Prentice-Hall Inc for $US157.5m. The purchase price was paid by Prentice-Hall to National Westminster Bank plc in New York, where it was credited to a suspense account on 18 November. On the following day it was credited to Maxwell Communications' $US account with National Westminster in London. . . .

On 26 November 1991 Mr Pelly met Mr Kevin Maxwell in London and again threatened action if the $30m was not paid. On the same day a payment was made of the $30m plus accrued interest from the NatWest dollar account to Barclays' branch in New York, through which all payments in dollars to Barclays are routed. It was then credited to pay off the overdraft account at the Holborn branch.

PROCEEDINGS IN THE UNITED STATES AND ENGLAND

On 16 December 1991 Maxwell Communications by its directors filed a petition in the United States Bankruptcy Court in the Southern District of New York under ch 11 of the US Bankruptcy Code. Although Maxwell Communications is an English company, it is not disputed in this court that the United States court has jurisdiction to entertain the petition on the ground that Maxwell Communications has property in the United States. The effect of presenting the petition was under §362 of the code to bring into operation an automatic stay on all proceedings against Maxwell Communications by creditors subject to the jurisdiction of the United States court. However, this did not prevent action being taken in England by other creditors.

On 17 December 1991 Maxwell Communications presented a petition to the High Court in England for an administration order. On 20 December 1991 Hoffmann J appointed the first three respondents to this appeal as administrators. On the same day the United States bankruptcy judge in New York, the Hon Tina L Brozman, ordered the appointment of an examiner under §1104 of the code. Subsequently, Mr Richard A Gitlin, a distinguished Connecticut lawyer, was appointed examiner.

The administrators in England and the examiner in New York, subject to the respective jurisdictions of their courts, have carried on the administration of Maxwell Communications in co-operation with each other. . . .

THE PRESENT PROCEEDINGS

On 6 July 1992 Millett J, on an ex parte application made on behalf of Barclays, granted them an interim injunction restraining the respondents . . .

(b) in particular . . . from making a claim against the Applicant for payment or the return of the relevant payment in any proceedings under the Bankruptcy Code of the United States of America. . . .

. . . On 28 July 1992, after a hearing *inter partes*, Hoffmann J dismissed the motion by Barclays and struck out their application. It is against this decision that Barclays now appeal.

THE PRINCIPLES TO BE APPLIED

. . . In Societe Nationale Industrielle Aerospatiale v Lee Kui Jak [1987] 3 All ER 510, [1987] AC 871, the plaintiff's husband was killed in a helicopter accident in Brunei. The helicopter had been manufactured by Aerospatiale, a French company, which carried on business in Texas. The plaintiff started actions both in Brunei and Texas for damages. The Judicial Committee of the Privy Council, in a judgment delivered by Lord Goff of Chieveley, granted an injunction restraining her from proceeding in the courts of Texas. . . .

In my view, in relation to the circumstances of the present case, the principles to be derived from the judgment of the Privy Council in *Aerospatiale* can be summarised as follows: (i) If the only issue is whether an English or a foreign court is the more appropriate forum for the trial of an action, that question should normally be decided by the foreign court on the principle of *forum non conveniens*, and the English court should not seek to interfere with that decision. (ii) However if, exceptionally, the English court concludes that the pursuit of the action in the foreign court would be vexatious and oppressive and that the English court is the natural forum, i.e. the more appropriate forum for the trial of the action, it can properly grant an injunction preventing the plaintiff from pursuing his action in the foreign court. (iii) In deciding whether the action in the foreign court is vexatious and oppressive, account must be taken of the possible injustice to the defendant if the injunction be not granted, and the possible injustice to the plaintiff if it is. In other words, the English court must seek to strike a balance. . . .

At a later stage in his judgment, [Judge Hoffman] considered the extent to which the facts disclosed a connection with the jurisdiction of the United States Bankruptcy Court. He took into account in particular the fact that, although Barclays received the repayment of the overdraft at their branch in Holborn, in practice the money derived from the proceeds of the sale of QUE in the United States.

The reasoning which led the judge to his main conclusion was as follows. He said:

> "It seems to me probable that an English court would regard the transaction as sufficiently connected with England to justify assuming jurisdiction under §239. But it does not follow that it would be unjust or unconscionable for a United States court to assume jurisdiction under §547. I do not think it necessary for me to express a view on whether an English court, faced with the mirror image of the facts of this case and exercising its discretion in accordance with the guidelines in Re Paramount Airways Ltd [1992] BCLC 710, [1992] Ch 160, would accept or decline jurisdiction.

The fact that a United States court might take a different view of the weight of the relevant connecting factors is not in itself a ground upon which this court would grant an injunction. This was made clear by Lord Goff of Chieveley in Aerospatiale [1987] 3 All ER 510, [1987] AC 871, when he dealt with what seems to me the analogous case of the discretion to stay proceedings on grounds of *forum non conveniens:* '. . . in a case in which there is simply a difference of view between the English court and the foreign court as to which is the natural forum, the English court [cannot] arrogate to itself, by the grant of an injunction, the power to resolve that dispute.' In other words, the normal assumption is that the foreign judge is the best person to decide whether an action in his own court should proceed. Comity requires a policy of non-intervention not only for the same reason that appellate courts are reluctant to interfere with the exercise of a discretion, namely that in the weighing of the various factors, different judges may legitimately arrive at different answers. It is also required because the foreign court is entitled, without thereby necessarily occasioning a breach of international law or manifest injustice, to give effect to the policies of its own legislation. . . ."

The judge also considered, I believe as a secondary matter in coming to his conclusion, that if he did grant an injunction in the circumstances of the present case, it might well be futile. He said:

"It seems to me, therefore, that an injunction (were I otherwise disposed to grant it) could serve no purpose except to antagonise the United States court and prejudice the co-operation which has thus far prevailed between the ch 11 and the English administration. If the United States judge does not think that there is a sufficient connection with America to justify a preference action against Barclays, she will dismiss the company's suit. If she does think so, she will not be deflected from securing the prosecution of that claim by any injunction I may make." . . .

Finally, Mr Merriman argues that because Barclays are or may be at a disadvantage under §547 of the United States Code as compared with their position under §239 of the Insolvency Act, this of itself makes proceedings in America against them oppressive or vexatious. I do not accept that this is correct. I have already indicated that the authorities require the disadvantage to Barclays to be balanced against the advantage to the administrators/the examiner, acting on behalf of the creditors of Maxwell Communications. While it is true that American law differs from English law in this respect, of itself there is nothing inherently oppressive about the difference. . . .

For the reasons I have sought to set out, I agree with the conclusion which the learned judge reached. I would therefore dismiss this appeal.

MANN, L.J.

I have had the advantage of reading in draft the judgments of Glidewell and Leggatt LJJ. I agree with them and for the reasons which they give I also would dismiss this appeal.

LEGGATT, L.J.

On behalf of Barclays Bank plc (the bank) Mr Nicholas Merriman QC contends for two main principles: (1) The primary insolvency proceeding is that which takes place in the insolvent company's country of incorporation, and (2) the recovery of assets as preferences (and possibly as fraudulent transfers) must be judged according to the law of the country of incorporation or of the natural forum for the recovery of preferences.

In the insolvency of MCC in which both assets and creditors are distributed worldwide, it cannot sensibly be suggested that any one forum is the natural forum, that is, the forum in which exclusively proceedings should be brought. If proceedings are legitimately brought and maintained in another jurisdiction, both forums are to be regarded as natural, and there is no need for this court to seek to interfere with the conduct of the foreign proceedings. . . .

In this case the presence in the United States of substantial creditors, of assets and of moneys derived from assets, coupled with the absence of any challenge to the ch 11 proceedings, suffice to explain the assumption of jurisdiction by the United States court, and militate against the conduct of them being regarded as unconscionable according to English notions. . . .

For myself I would want no part in any order, the intended effect of which would be to recommend to Judge Brozman what orders to make in her own court. That would represent unacceptable hubris. For the reasons given by Glidewell LJ and in this judgment I reject Mr Merriman's propositions. I see no reason to disturb the even tenor of the way projected by Hoffmann J, and I too agree that the appeal should be dismissed.

Disposition: Appeal dismissed. Leave to appeal to the House of Lords refused.

The administrators proceeded to file their preference actions in the United States, with the following result.

In re MAXWELL COMMUNICATION CORP. PLC
93 F.3d 1036 (2d Cir. 1996)

CARDAMONE, Circuit Judge:
The demise of the late British media magnate Robert Maxwell and that of the corporation bearing his name, the Maxwell Communication Corporation plc, followed a similar and scandalous path, spawning civil and criminal litigation in England and around the world. This case illustrates that some positive consequences have resulted from these parallel demises. From Maxwell's mysterious death, which forced his international corporation into bankruptcy, was born a unique judicial administration of the debtor corporation by parallel and cooperative proceedings in the courts of the United States and England aimed at harmonizing the laws of both countries and also aimed at maximizing the benefits to creditors and the prospects of rehabilitation.

We have before us a small but significant piece of the swirling legal controversy that followed the collapse of Robert Maxwell's media empire.

The question to be addressed is whether Maxwell Communication, as a debtor estate in Chapter 11, may recover under American law millions of dollars it transferred to three foreign banks shortly before declaring bankruptcy. . . .

BACKGROUND

A.   Events Preceding the Dual Filings . . .

Maxwell alleges that in the fall of 1991, less than 90 days before its Chapter 11 filing, it made several transfers — transfers it now seeks to avoid — to three European banks (collectively, the banks) with whom it had credit arrangements. Two of these banks are Barclays Bank plc (Barclays) and National Westminster Bank plc (National Westminster), both of which have their headquarters in London and maintain an international presence, with branches in New York and elsewhere. The other bank is Societe Generale, a French Bank headquartered in Paris with offices, among other places, in London and New York. . . .

[The court described the payments to the three banks, which were similar to that described in the *Barclays* opinion: payments in London that may have derived from sale of U.S. subsidiaries, for a total paid to the three during the 90 days of approximately US$100 million.]

B.   The Dual Insolvency Proceedings

On December 16, 1991 Maxwell filed a petition for reorganization under Chapter 11 of the United States Bankruptcy Code in the Bankruptcy Court for the Southern District of New York. The next day, it petitioned the High Court of Justice in London for an administration order. Administration, introduced by the Insolvency Act 1986, is the closest equivalent in British law to Chapter 11 relief. Acting under the terms of the Insolvency Act, Justice Hoffman, then of the High Court (now a member of the House of Lords), appointed members of the London office of the accounting firm of Price Waterhouse as administrators to manage the affairs and property of the corporation.

Simultaneous proceedings in different countries, especially in multiparty cases like bankruptcies, can naturally lead to inconsistencies and conflicts. To minimize such problems, Judge Brozman appointed Richard A. Gitlin, Esq. as examiner, pursuant to 11 U.S.C. §1104(c), in the Chapter 11 proceedings. The order of appointment required the examiner, inter alia, to investigate the debtor's financial condition, to function as a mediator among the various parties, and to "act to harmonize, for the benefit of all of [Maxwell's] creditors and stockholders and other parties in interest, [Maxwell's] United States Chapter 11 case and [Maxwell's] United Kingdom administration case so as to maximize [the] prospects for rehabilitation and reorganization."

Judge Brozman and Justice Hoffman subsequently authorized the examiner and the administrators to coordinate their efforts pursuant to a

so-called Protocol, an agreement between the examiner and the administrators. In approving the Protocol, Judge Brozman recognized the English
administrators as the corporate governance of the debtor-in-possession. As
the bankruptcy judge later explained, this recognition was motivated not
only by the need for coordination but also because Maxwell was "incorporated in England and run . . . by [Maxwell] executives out of Maxwell
House in London subject to the direction of an English board of directors."
Maxwell I, 170 B.R. at 817. Justice Hoffman reciprocated, granting the
examiner leave to appear before the High Court in England.

These joint efforts resulted in what has been described as a "remarkable
sequence of events leading to perhaps the first world-wide plan of orderly liquidation ever achieved." Jay Lawrence Westbrook, The Lessons of Maxwell
Communication, 64 Fordham L. Rev. 2531, 2535 (1996). . . . The mechanism
for accomplishing this is embodied in a plan of reorganization and a scheme
of arrangement, which are interdependent documents and were filed by the
administrators in the United States and English courts respectively.

. . . The plan and scheme treat all of Maxwell's assets as a single pool
and leave them under Maxwell's control for distribution to claimants.
They allow any creditor to submit a claim in either jurisdiction. And, in
addition to overcoming many of the substantive differences in the insolvency laws of the two jurisdictions, the plan and scheme resolve many
procedural differences, such as the time limits for submitting claims.

. . . [T]hey did not address the instant dispute regarding the debtor's
ability to set aside pre-petition transfers to certain creditors.

C.   British Denial of Anti-Suit Injunction . . .

Following a hearing, Justice Hoffman . . . declined to interfere with
the American court's determination of the reach of our avoidance law. . . .
This ruling was affirmed by the Court of Appeal, and leave for further
review by the House of Lords was denied. . . .

II.   INTERNATIONAL COMITY

A.   The Doctrine

Analysis of comity often begins with the definition proffered by Justice Gray in Hilton v. Guyot, 159 U.S. 113 (1895): " 'Comity,' in the legal
sense, is neither a matter of absolute obligation, on the one hand, nor of
mere courtesy and good will, upon the other. But it is the recognition
which one nation allows within its territory to the legislative, executive
or judicial acts of another nation, having due regard both to international
duty and convenience, and to the rights of its own citizens or of other persons who are under the protection of its laws." Although *Hilton* addressed
the degree to which a foreign judgment is conclusive in a court of the
United States, the principle expressed is one of broad application.

. . . The doctrine does not impose a limitation on the sovereign power
to enact laws applicable to conduct occurring abroad. Instead, it guides our

interpretation of statutes that might otherwise be read to apply to such conduct. When construing a statute, the doctrine of international comity is best understood as a guide where the issues to be resolved are entangled in international relations. . . .

Moreover, international comity is a separate notion from the "presumption against extraterritoriality," which requires a clear expression from Congress for a statute to reach non-domestic conduct. . . .

Comity is exercised with reference to "prevalent doctrines of international law." *Lauritzen*, 345 U.S. at 577. The management of transnational insolvencies is concededly underdeveloped. However, certain norms shared among nations are relevant to the present case. . . .

The factors enumerated in the [Restatement (Third) of United States Foreign Relations Law] correspond to familiar choice-of-law principles. The analysis must consider the international system as a whole in addition to the interests of the individual states, because the effective functioning of that system is to the advantage of all the affected jurisdictions.

B.   Applicability of the Doctrine to the Case at Hand

Because Congress legislates against a backdrop that includes those international norms that guide comity analysis, absent a contrary legislative direction the doctrine may properly be used to interpret any statute. Comity is especially important in the context of the Bankruptcy Code for two reasons. First, deference to foreign insolvency proceedings will, in many cases, facilitate "equitable, orderly, and systematic" distribution of the debtor's assets. Cunard S.S. Co. v. Salen Reefer Servs. AB, 773 F.2d 452, 458 (2d Cir. 1985). Second, Congress explicitly recognized the importance of the principles of international comity in transnational insolvency situations when it revised the bankruptcy laws. See 11 U.S.C. §304; see S. Rep. No. 989, 95th Cong., 2d Sess. 35, reprinted in 1978 U.S.C.C.A.N. 5787, 5821 (explaining §304). . . .

III.   PROPRIETY OF DISMISSAL BY THE BANKRUPTCY COURT

A.   Standard of Review

Having established that the doctrine of comity applies, we now explain why we think dismissal was warranted, that is to say, why the statute was properly construed not to reach the pre-petition fund transfers to the defendant banks. . . .

B.   Primacy of English Law

England has a much closer connection to these disputes than does the United States. The debtor and most of its creditors — not only the beneficiaries of the pre-petition transfers — are British. Maxwell was incorporated under the laws of England, largely controlled by British nationals, governed by a British board of directors, and managed in London by British executives. These connecting factors indicated what the bankruptcy judge called the "Englishness" of the debtor, which was one reason for recognizing the administrators — who are officers of the High Court — as Maxwell's corporate governance. These same factors, particularly the fact that most of Maxwell's debt was incurred in England, show that England has the strongest connection to the present litigation.

Although an avoidance action concededly affects creditors other than the transferee, because scrutiny of the transfer is at the heart of such a suit it is assuredly most relevant that the transfers in this case related primarily to England. The $30 million received by Barclays came from an account at National Westminster in London and, while it was routed through Barclays' New York branch like all payments received in U.S. dollars, it was immediately credited to an overdraft account maintained in England. Plaintiffs claim no particular United States connection to the other alleged transfers to Barclays, all of which were denominated in the amended complaint in pounds sterling. Similarly, the transfers to National Westminster and Societe Generale were made to and from accounts maintained in Great Britain.

Further, the overdraft facilities and other credit transactions between the transferee banks and the debtor resulted from negotiations that took place in England and were administered primarily there. English law applied to the resolution of disputes arising under such agreements. We recognize that some of the money transferred to the banks came from the proceeds of the sale of Maxwell subsidiaries in the United States, which is a subject we discuss in a moment. In almost all other respects, however, the credit transactions were centered in London and the fund transfers occurred there.

C.   Relative Interests of Forum and Foreign States

Given the considerably lesser American connection to the dispute, the bankruptcy court believed its forum's interests were "not very compelling." *Maxwell I,* 170 B.R. at 818. Virtually the only factor linking the transfers to the United States — that the sale of certain Maxwell subsidiaries in the United States provided the source of some of the funds — is not particularly weighty because those companies were sold as going concerns. Hence, the potential effect that such sales might have had on local economies is not here implicated. . . .

Because of the strong British connection to the present dispute, it follows that England has a stronger interest than the United States in applying its own avoidance law to these actions. Its law implicates that country's interest in promoting what Parliament apparently viewed as the appropriate compromise between equality of distribution and other important commercial interests, for instance, ensuring potentially insolvent debtors' ability to secure essential ongoing financing. In addition, although complexity in the conduct of transnational insolvencies makes choice-of-law prognostication imprecise, we agree with the lower courts that English law could have been expected to apply. . . .

D. Cooperation and Harmonization: Systemic Interest

In addition to the relative strength of the respective jurisdictional interests of England and the United States, there is a compelling systemic interest pointing in this instance against the application of the Bankruptcy Code. These parallel proceedings in the English and American courts have resulted in a high level of international cooperation and a significant degree of harmonization of the laws of the two countries. The affected parties agreed to the plan and scheme despite differences in the two nations' bankruptcy laws. The distribution mechanism established by them — beyond addressing some of the most obvious substantive and procedural incongruities — allowed Maxwell's assets to be pooled together and sold as going concerns, maximizing the return to creditors. And, by not requiring a creditor to file its claim in both forums, the arrangement eliminated many of the inefficiencies usually attendant in multi-jurisdiction proceedings.

Taken together, these accomplishments — which, we think, are attributable in large measure to the cooperation between the two courts overseeing the dual proceedings — are well worth preserving and advancing. This collaborative effort exemplifies the "spirit of cooperation" with which tribunals, guided by comity, should approach cases touching the laws and interests of more than one country.

Where a dispute involving conflicting avoidance laws arises in the context of parallel bankruptcy proceedings that have already achieved substantial reconciliation between the two sets of laws, comity argues decidedly against the risk of derailing that cooperation by the selfish application of our law to circumstances touching more directly upon the interests of another forum. . . .

Conclusion

. . . [I]n this unique case involving cooperative parallel bankruptcy proceedings seeking to harmonize two nations' insolvency laws for the common benefit of creditors, the doctrine of international comity precludes application of the American avoidance law to transfers in which England's interest has primacy. We decline to decide whether, setting aside considerations of comity, the "presumption against extraterritoriality" would compel a conclusion that the Bankruptcy Code does not reach the pre-petition transfers at issue. Thus, we express no view regarding the banks' contention that the Bankruptcy Code never applies to non-domestic conduct or conditions. . . .

Accordingly, for the reasons stated, the order appealed from is affirmed.

Among the important lessons in *Maxwell* are these:

(a) Every international bankruptcy case requires both a choice-of-forum and a choice-of-law analysis, unlike most litigation in which only a choice-of-law problem is presented. The result of the forum selection decision (e.g., deference because of comity) may change the resolution of formal legal issues such as choice of law, so that choice-of-law results are difficult to predict. Indeed, they cannot be reasonably predicted except in combination with predictions about choice of forum.

(b) Protocols of cooperation in the administration of an international case are crucial to the achievement of a satisfactory result in the absence of effective legal rules. The converse, of course, is that any substantial stakeholder involved in a case may be able to block cooperation, with no legal mechanism available to substitute for agreement.

(c) Politeness matters.

When the founders of our country gathered in Philadelphia to make a Constitution, the achievement of free trade and national enterprise among the former colonies was a central concern. In that context, they took it as a given that the new national market required that the national legislature be empowered "to Establish . . . uniform Laws on the subject of Bankruptcies throughout the United States." U.S. Const., Art. I, §8, cl. 4. Just as surely, the growth of international trade and transnational enterprise requires the achievement of international agreement on the rules of transnational insolvency. If the U.S. precedent illustrates the need, it also illustrates the difficulty, because it took our ancestors 100 years to fulfill the constitutional command, failing to enact a permanent bankruptcy law until 1898. We must hope that the international community will not be so long delayed.

Problem Set 42

42.1. Maple Leaf Components, Inc., a consumer electronics company based in Calgary, had a plant there and in York, Ontario, along with warehouses in several other Canadian cities and four U.S. locations. Maple Leaf filed liquidation bankruptcy in Calgary yesterday under the Bankruptcy and Insolvency Act. Your client, CompuTech, Inc., based in Detroit, wants to obtain pre-judgment attachments against each of the U.S. warehouses to secure payment of the $775,000 Maple Leaf owes to it. Jim Parsons, the CompuTech general counsel, has lots of questions. Does the Canadian stay affect our client's right to seize the inventory? What is the likely next step by the Canadian bankruptcy trustee for Maple Leaf? What effect will it have on our client? Overall, Jim wants to know our take on their likelihood of success in grabbing the inventory. See §§ 1501, et seq.

CHAPTER 11

THE FUNCTIONS
OF BANKRUPTCY LAW

A. INTRODUCTION

Only now, as the days left in the bankruptcy class dwindle down to a precious few, do we turn to a separate discussion of the theory of bankruptcy law. In one sense, we have examined the theory of bankruptcy in virtually every section in this book, examining the purposes and functions of separate pieces of the law and how they relate to each other. But now we back up for the larger picture, for an overview of what the bankruptcy system is trying to accomplish.

If the theory of bankruptcy law were well-settled, it would have made sense to describe it early on, so the student could evaluate separate issues from the perspective thus provided. But comprehensive bankruptcy theories are nascent and highly controversial. Even the approach is in dispute. For some scholars, bankruptcy theories present highly abstract intellectual issues best understood through models, while others see the theories deeply grounded in a hard, practical reality. So we have waited until the end to introduce these theories, now that the student knows something about the subject and can begin to critique the various notions that have been put forward.

Bankruptcy theory is intrinsically interesting, like the life cycle of the honey bee or the moons of Jupiter, but it also serves a function. If we could understand the purpose and function of bankruptcy law, we could better evaluate proposals for its reform and arrive at a better resolution of issues presented under the law as it is. Above all, we could place bankruptcy accurately in the larger universe of the law and more clearly draw the policy boundaries between it and other legal fields.

There is a rich and robust debate in progress about these questions. In a casebook already burdened with substantial citations and readings, we can only offer an introduction to that debate. We must ignore a number of excellent contributions and many interesting riffs and twists on the central arguments. Our hope is that we can provide an overview of the debate that will seduce the student into exploring it further.

The discussion that follows is limited to the bankruptcy of legal persons, primarily corporations. We have already pointed out the furious policy debate about consumer bankruptcy. To this point, however, that debate has not threatened the traditional idea that the central purpose of bankruptcy for natural persons is the discharge and the fresh start, with a minor theme sounding in the orderly repayment of debt. Although we now have a means tests and other limitations on the discharge, no serious challenge to the fundamental idea of the discharge has been raised. In this section, we focus the discussion on theoretical questions about legal-person bankruptcy.

One point arises in various contexts and therefore deserves mention at the start. Some theorists believe that bankruptcy has a merely procedural function, rather than invoking any policy goals of its own. On that ground, they argue that bankruptcy should rarely, if ever, disturb the rights of creditors and other stakeholders under nonbankruptcy law. Because this argument is derivative of its proponents' underlying theories, its persuasiveness depends on the plausibility of those theories. Nonetheless, the point is often advanced on a stand-alone basis, so to speak, making it necessary to identify it to the student.

From a private newsletter, June 22, 2000: Cheval Golf & Country Club in Tampa filed Chapter 11 last week. The club says it has no financial difficulty but is using bankruptcy to change its governing bylaws which specify that any changes must be approved unanimously by the membership. The club blames its problems on a former lawyer who drafted the original documents.

B.   EXCLUSIONS FROM BANKRUPTCY

Empiricists that we are, we naturally preface a discussion of theory with a brief review of the areas that are at the boundaries of bankruptcy, just outside the walls, but excluded from its operation under existing law. An inquiry as to why these areas are excluded casts some light on the issues presented by theory.

Banks and insurance companies are excluded from ordinary bankruptcy in most countries. (We include any deposit-taking entity in the term "banks.") They go broke, but not bankrupt, because they have their own specialized insolvency systems. Although these systems resemble bankruptcy law in many ways, the key difference is that they provide government guarantees or complete distributional priority to one preferred class of creditors — depositors and policyholders, respectively. The other stakeholders — ordinary creditors and stockholders, for example — may lose all they had risked when one of these entities fails, but everything possible is done to protect the preferred classes. Without exploring all the reasons for this differentiation, suffice it to say that it is assumed that these actors are very risk-averse and that ensuring them of nearly perfect security is therefore central to the smooth working of the country's financial system. In the case of banks, of course, the protection is iron-clad because of the deposit insurance provided by state and federal governments, while state laws often provide for compulsory compensation funds to cover policyholder losses in insurance insolvencies.

Interestingly, the third industry that contributes to the vast capital market thus protected by the law is the securities industry. Therefore, we are not surprised to find that the Securities Investors Protection Act gives coverage to brokerage customers who deposit their stocks and bonds with the broker. The "SIPC" system looks like the protection offered bank depositors by the FDIC, although there are some indications that it is not so good. These customers are presumably thought willing to take the risk of the markets, but not the risk of the financial mismanagement or venality of the brokers themselves. Consistent with that thought, stockbrokers are put in a sort of insolvency ghetto within the Bankruptcy Code. They are not permitted to file for Chapter 11 at all, and special rules apply to a stockbroker (or commodity broker) bankrupt who files under Chapter 7. §§741-766. In particular, as with banks and insurance companies, the customers who leave stock deposited with a stockbroker represent a preferred class of creditors in a stockbroker bankruptcy. §752.

Finally, the railroads are also given special treatment in the case of financial default. They are forbidden from filing in Chapter 7 (§109(b)) and are governed by a separate subchapter in Chapter 11.

While these entities are given special treatment, all of them are subject to specialized laws for the management of a general default. Railroads and financial brokers are covered by Title 11, but governed by quite different rules within the Code. Banks and insurance companies in default are governed by laws, federal and state, that look much like Title 11 and include many similar provisions; in effect, they have special rules under a specialized bankruptcy regime. None of them are simply exempted from bankruptcy-type laws completely.

Why are these businesses exempt from the ordinary laws of bankruptcy? The Bankruptcy Code governs an incredible range of businesses across our multi-trillion-dollar economy; In this book, we have gone from jukebox operators to steel mills to "riodozios," from traveling auctions to hog farms to single-asset real estate companies. It is true that all of the excluded companies but railroads are essentially financial companies, but many financial companies are not excluded from bankruptcy. Indeed, in a development that should keep the irony-specialists busy for a long time, the so-called "sub-prime" lenders (that is, companies that lend to bad credit risks) have been filling the bankruptcy courts in recent years.

All the excluded companies except for railroads are characterized by two distinctions: They hold large amounts of value deposited (as opposed to invested) by the public and they are heavily regulated at all times, not just when they become financially distressed. We can explain the lone exception, railroads, on historical grounds, since all other common carriers are eligible for bankruptcy and many have used it (for example, Continental Airlines, United Air Lines, U.S. Lines (ocean shipping), Greyhound, U.S. Truck). Thus, the common thread for exclusion from the ordinary bankruptcy rules would be "highly regulated financial institution that takes deposits of money or valuables from the public."

That brings us to hedge funds and a company called Long Term Capital Management (LTCM). The term "hedge fund" is not well defined, legally or otherwise. In financial terms, to "hedge" is to make somewhat offsetting investments such that one investment is apt to go up while the other goes down, thus buffering risk. Sun tan lotion and raincoats might be a homey example. If one is doing badly, the other is probably doing well. If a company has major operations in Ruritania and is worried that the Ruritanian currency it earns might be devalued against the dollar, it might buy a "currency swap" that goes up if the Ruritanian money goes down, thus balancing its currency risk. Many hedge funds engage in transactions of that sort, but with an idea to making a gain on the transaction rather than simply hedging a risk. Thus a hedge fund might be the "counterparty" to the currency swap with the company worried about currency fluctuations, as the fund bets that the value of the currency will either remain steady or decline. However, the term "hedge fund" is not limited to such transactions. It has come to include investment companies with many different investment strategies. Perhaps the central theme for all of them is "leverage" (lots of borrowed money in relation to the equity at risk) and the fact that no investor should consider investing in one unless he or she is highly sophisticated and truly rich.

Hedge funds are almost entirely unregulated and take investments, not deposits, so they are just the opposite of the companies that have been excluded from the ordinary bankruptcy laws. Thus one would assume they would not be excluded from bankruptcy. And one would be right, in a simple, technical sense. A hedge fund is eligible to file for bankruptcy. Yet they are effectively excluded, because a bankruptcy filing for them would be pointless. The financial instruments in which they deal — including exotica such as "swaps" and "repos" — are exempt from the automatic stay and the avoiding powers. This means that virtually all of their assets would be effectively seized by the "counterparties" to these instruments at the moment of bankruptcy or shortly thereafter, leaving nothing for a bankruptcy court to administer. See, e.g., §§362(b)(6)-(7), (17); 559-560. Each of the creditor "counterparties" would then be in a position to sell its reclaimed asset. (We spare the student the mechanics.) There would be nothing left to do with the debtor hedge fund except sell the office furniture and dissolve the corporate charter. Thus, the general default of many hedge funds is effectively excluded from bankruptcy.

LTCM was the mother of all hedge funds. Its leading partners included a legendary bond trader and two Nobel Prize winners, who had become celebrated for extraordinary breakthroughs in mathematical methods of analyzing investments. LTCM made very complex investments all over the world, investments that were designed to be very safe and yet generate remarkable yields well above what most safe investments yield. (Ah, the eternal promise: low risk and high returns.) On the strength of its partners' credentials, leading banks, pension funds, and other major investors poured more than $4 billion into LTCM. It borrowed billions more, so that its portfolio was more than 20 times as much as its equity, a very high level of "leverage." A series of financial difficulties in Russia and Asia caused the value of its investments to drop rapidly and visibly, raising fears that all of its "counterparties" might grab and sell their financial instruments at the same time, causing global markets to collapse and imposing huge, sudden losses on leading banks and securities firms. Some believed that the entire world economy might be at risk if the dominoes fell.

The consequence was that the New York Federal Reserve "invited" a number of the leading banks and securities firms to a meeting at its offices. The invitees agreed to invest billions more, collectively, in the equity of LTCM in order to prevent a run on its assets. The markets quieted and recovered. The rescuing firms got back their investments and more. Some of the original partners even got a few million to take home from the wreck.

The key point to this story is the role of the Fed. A White House investigation and other reports denied that the Fed had provided anything more than a meeting place. Many observers found that story implausible. It seemed more plausible that political pressure had been applied to save a company that was "too big to fail." From the perspective of a bankruptcy specialist, the obvious problem was that there was no bankruptcy law to impose a moratorium freezing the assets and permitting an orderly resolution of the problem, including a new equity investment. The political intervention seems a highly undesirable interference in the market — unreliable, unpredictable, and subject to either the appearance or the reality of political favoritism. In short, the intervention had many of the characteristics that the United States likes to criticize in developing economies.

Notwithstanding this critique, there is a strong movement to increase financial exemptions of this sort, adding more financial instruments to swaps and repos on the list of assets excluded from bankruptcy protection and providing exclusion from bankruptcy of a major new form of secured financing, called "asset securitization." Asset securitization is a sale or secured transaction in which the subject matter of the transaction is a debtor's accounts receivable and the funds obtained by the debtor come from a sale of securities on the capital markets. The exclusion means that the debtor's accounts would be excluded from protection by the automatic stay, and transfers that would otherwise be avoidable (for example, a near-bankruptcy transfer that would be a preference) would be exempted from avoidance. Because exemption of a transaction from bankruptcy represents an enormous advantage for the exempted creditor, we may expect to see increasing demands for this treatment for all sorts of transactions.

These developments should cause us to ask if it would be better as a general matter to permit the parties to various financial transactions to exempt themselves from the bankruptcy laws and adopt their own rules for a general default. If Congress is going to exempt a growing number of transactions from bankruptcy protection, it might be desirable to simply deregulate the field and let debtors and creditors manage general defaults as they like, with bankruptcy law little more than an option for those who do not specify alternative approaches. If one prefers the abstraction, we could say that we might leave the management of general defaults to the market. Some theorists say just that.

C.   ALTERNATIVE APPROACHES TO BANKRUPTCY

The goals traditionally ascribed to bankruptcy law were to ensure equality of distribution and to prevent fraud and unravel its effects. See, e.g., Garrard Glenn, The Law Governing Liquidation (1935); Harold Remington,

A Treatise on the Bankruptcy Law of the United States (1908); Ian Fletcher, The Law of Insolvency (2d Ed. 2002) (British law).

As we have seen, the goal of equality is often honored in the breach. The consequence of the priority systems found in virtually every bankruptcy law around the world is that general unsecured creditors receive little or nothing in liquidations, with most of the assets going to secured creditors and priority unsecured creditors. It would not be difficult to make the argument that equality is a lost cause as a fundamental goal, and that bankruptcy policy would be better served if it were recognized that it has merely the small role of equalizing the distributions within priority classes, including the class of general unsecured creditors. Of course, one who favored the equality principle would argue that a better solution would be the abolition or reduction of priorities. In fact, bankruptcy reform movements around the world in the last decade have exhibited some tendency to do just that, except for the priorities for secured creditors and employees. But the larger point is that it is not surprising that academics would begin to propose entirely new theories for the management of general default.

Although there has been little support for fundamental change in our bankruptcy laws from the mercantile community, a number of academics have proposed such changes. In the last decade or so, the leading proponents for radical change have divided into two groups. The first in time advocated an approach that might be called automated bankruptcy. The second, and currently the most visible, are contractualists. The summaries that follow are very simplified and do not do justice to the many, many pages of argument that elaborate and support them, but they serve as an introduction.

Automated bankruptcy rests on the idea that it would be useful to separate the purely economic function of bankruptcy from the litigation aspects, so that a business could be rapidly and inexpensively liquidated, sold, or placed under new management, without the cost and delay associated with litigation over issues such as fraud, mismanagement, and lender liability. It derives from an article by Professor Bebchuk. Lucian A. Bebchuk, A New Approach to Corporate Reorganizations, 101 Harv. L. Rev. 775 (1988). His proposal had two central components. The courts would enforce absolute contractual priority in both liquidation and reorganization, and the control over the deployment of the assets of a firm in general default would be determined by a sort of reverse "bidding-in" by existing creditors or equity holders. Each class of equity or debt (predefined by contract) would either purchase all the interests above it at face value or forfeit the interests of their class. Any class that elected to purchase would own the company. If no lower class bought the debt above it, the highest class of debt would own the company outright. The new owner would then decide how to deploy the assets, whether through sale of assets or continuing operation of the business. In Professor Bebchuk's original conception, the process would not require much court involvement. The process would be completely controlled by creditors. In later proposals, the court would have some role to play. Barry E. Adler, A Theory of Corporate Insolvency, 72 N.Y.U. L. Rev. 343 (1997); Philippe Aghion et al., Improving Bankruptcy Procedure, 72 Wash. U. L.Q. 849, 850 (1994). This approach attracted considerable attention in the middle 1990s, but has been less prominent since that time.

The contractualist approach has endured longer. It begins with the Coase Theorem, which proposes that a legal rule that alters the bargains of economic actors is inherently inefficient. Ignoring transaction costs, it follows that most legal rules are economically inefficient, beyond the fundamental commitment to enforce whatever the parties have agreed upon. Given that general premise, the contractualists propose eliminating or narrowing bankruptcy law so that it contains a minimum of mandatory rules and permits economic actors to construct their own rules to manage general default. The range of proposals runs from virtually complete contractualization of bankruptcy to a broad tolerance of waivers of bankruptcy rules by debtors.

One of the first articles proposing a more-or-less complete contractualization of bankruptcy was written by Professor Robert Rasmussen. His basic idea is a "bankruptcy menu" from which a firm chooses the bankruptcy provisions that would be best for it and its creditors. The choice would be made at the inception of the firm and would be included in its corporate charter. It would be unalterable without the agreement of all creditors, with certain exceptions. Thus each creditor would know from the start the bankruptcy regime that would apply to the debtor and would extend credit priced on that basis. Therefore the firm could decide to what extent it wished to exchange future bankruptcy protection for lower present interest costs, producing the most efficient result. This excerpt summarizes his proposal:

> When a firm is formed, it would be required to select what courses of action it wishes to have available if it runs into financial difficulties down the road. The virtue of standardized options is that they reduce transactions costs and make communication to third parties easy. One can still allow parties to write their own contract if none of the options available suit their needs, though a well-crafted set of options should ensure that most firms prefer one of the options to the cost of creating a brand new bankruptcy procedure. The existence of a known menu of bankruptcy choices thus answers the transaction-cost argument for treating bankruptcy as a mandatory rule.
>
> A menu approach can handle the strategic-manipulation problem as well. An approach that limits the firm's ability to change its selection after it has incurred debt ensures that the threat of the firm amending its bankruptcy choice so as to transfer wealth from the creditors to the equity holders is eliminated. A full discussion of such limitations is postponed until the choices on the menu have been delineated. For now, the important point is that these limitations ensure that a firm can publicly announce what bankruptcy option it would choose, and all future creditors would be able to rely on the option that the firm specifies.
>
> A menu approach to corporate bankruptcy law creates another benefit as well; it would aid the owners of a firm in deciding which option they should choose. By offering a discrete set of choices, the menu would enable banks and other creditors to anticipate the interest-rate adjustments that would be made for each option. They could then communicate to those establishing the firm the true cost of selecting one bankruptcy provision over another. The benefit of this communication is increased by the fact that, as discussed in the next Part of this Article, choosing the optimal bankruptcy term may turn on the preferences of the firm's owners. Such owners, not Congress or the courts, are in the best position to assess these preferences, and the menu approach allows the owners to compare each option's benefits with its costs.

It is thus clear that as far as those who choose to deal with a firm are concerned, the law of corporate reorganization should be a default rule. However, involuntary creditors should be subject to a mandatory rule. Persons such as tort creditors have in no meaningful sense contracted with the firm. If their rights could be set by the investors of the firm, their rights would most likely be nonexistent. Since the firm does not need their consent, the equity holders have an incentive to foist on them the harshest terms possible. Stated differently, given the inability of nonconsensual creditors to contract with the firm ex ante, a default-rule approach would encourage consensual creditors to shift the costs of insolvency onto nonconsensual creditors. If the firm could assign the lowest possible priority to nonconsensual claimants, it could thus increase the return to consensual claimants, thereby lowering the firm's cost of credit.

This problem is easily remedied. It is beyond peradventure that mandatory rules can be justified as protecting third parties. It is clear that nonconsensual creditors need such protection. They do not, however, need the protection of a mandatory bankruptcy regime. The question of the appropriate treatment of nonconsensual claimants when a firm is insolvent is the subject of a rich literature. This Article does not, and need not, enter this debate. Rather, once policymakers decide the optimal treatment of nonconsensual creditors, this treatment should be unalterable by any debt contract. In other words, the priority status of tort claimants should not depend on which bankruptcy option a firm selects. Thus, a bankruptcy regime consisting primarily of default rules can readily accommodate the existence of nonconsensual claimants.

Robert K. Rasmussen, Debtor's Choice: A Menu Approach to Corporate Bankruptcy, 71 Tex. L. Rev. 51, 66-67 (1992).

Another prominent proponent of contractualization has been Professor Alan Schwartz. Professor Schwartz recognizes one concern with a menu approach or any other contractualist regime, which is that the circumstances of the debtor change over time, so that the most efficient choice of bankruptcy regime at one moment in the life of the firm may not be the most efficient at a later point in its development. He proposes that there be a rolling readjustment in the bankruptcy regime to reflect these changes. Each new creditor would negotiate a bankruptcy bargain with the debtor. If the bargain was different than the one made with the first creditor, the first creditor would automatically shift to the new bargain.

Professor Schwartz believes that the principal obstacle to the most efficient choice of bankruptcy solutions (e.g., liquidation versus reorganization) is the "private" benefit that those controlling the firm may gain from the choice (e.g., reorganization and another paycheck). This benefit may motivate those in control to choose a strategy that is suboptimal for the firm's creditors. He proposes therefore that a payment to those in control be provided as part of the bankruptcy bargain. By paying management to make the optimal decision, Schwartz believes that managers will have less incentive to make a decision that benefits them solely, such as a continuing effort to revive a failing business that would offer greater returns to creditors if it were liquidated but that offers a continuing paycheck to management so long as it remains open. One of his critics, Professor LoPucki, characterizes

[handwritten margin note: Recognizes a Problem w/ the "Bankruptcy Menu" Approach →]

this payment as a "bribe." Professor Schwartz summarized a major aspect of his proposed approach in response to a critique:

(A) The only goal of a business bankruptcy law should be to reduce the cost of debt capital, which the law best does by maximizing the debt investors' insolvency state payoff.

(B) Regarding mandatory bankruptcy systems:

(i) Requiring parties always to use the mandatory state system increases a borrowing firm's cost of capital over the cost that would obtain in a world in which the firm and its creditors could contract for an alternative bankruptcy.

(ii) If the rule against contracting for a preferred bankruptcy system were relaxed, parties would write "bankruptcy contracts" that would induce a borrowing firm to choose the system that would be optimal for it and its creditors were it to become insolvent.

(C) There should be few mandatory rules within bankruptcy systems.....

My model assumed that two bankruptcy systems existed. One system, denoted L, resembled the current Chapter 7, and the other, denoted R, resembled the current Chapter 11. For the purposes of this Response, the parties in my model could write two types of bankruptcy contracts. The first would not deal explicitly with bankruptcy at all, leaving the insolvent firm free to choose the bankruptcy system it preferred ex post. Since creditors are legally entitled to the full monetary return from a bankruptcy procedure, the firm would not consider this return in making its choice. Rather, the firm's owners/managers would choose the bankruptcy system that maximized their private benefits. The parties, however, could renegotiate after insolvency to induce the firm to choose the bankruptcy system that generated the highest monetary return when that system did not also maximize the firm's private benefits. The model assumed that a firm always gets greater private benefits in the reorganization system R because the managers get to run the firm for a longer time in that system and also have some chance of saving the business. Hence, the parties would renegotiate only when the liquidation system L turned out to generate a higher monetary return than the reorganization system R. The creditors then would pay the firm a sum to forgo the R system's greater private benefits and instead enter liquidation.

The second contract I discussed — and the one Professor LoPucki considers — authorized the firm to keep a portion of the monetary return that would be generated by whatever bankruptcy system it chose. If this portion — the "bribe" — were set appropriately, the sum of the private benefits and cash payments the firm would get if it chose the optimal system always would exceed the firm's total payoff from choosing suboptimally. This contract was called renegotiation-proof because the parties would have no need to renegotiate later: The firm would choose the efficient bankruptcy system if the contract bribe was correctly specified.

One or the other of these contracts would maximize the creditors' insolvency-state payoff and thereby minimize the firm's cost of capital, depending on the relevant economic parameters. For example, the renegotiation contract would often be best when the reorganization system had a higher expected return than the liquidation system. The creditors do not pay a bribe under this contract and thus could keep the entire high return that system R would generate; the firm would choose R without a bribe because it would get greater private benefits in that system. If the liquidation system generated the higher expected return, on the other hand, the renegotiation-proof contract often would be best. The firm then would have to he bribed to choose liquidation. The ex post bribe would exceed the contractual bribe because ex post it is known with certainty that the firm will choose the inefficient system; hence, the firm could exploit its bargaining power to capture most of the monetary gain from choosing optimally. Though one or the other of these contracts can be efficient, depending on the economic parameters, only renegotiation contracts can be written under current law. This restriction thus reduces welfare.

My model assumed that creditors could observe and verify to a court the actual monetary return that a bankruptcy procedure would generate. Thus, if the lending agreements promised the firm, say, 30% of the monetary return from bankruptcy, the creditors could recover the remaining 70% in a bankruptcy proceeding. The creditors, however, could not verify to a court, and might be unable to observe, all of the firm's private benefits. This would not preclude bankruptcy-contracting, because the firm offers creditors the bankruptcy contract, and it knows what its private benefits would be; hence, it could select the contract — renegotiation or renegotiation-proof — that would maximize the creditors' insolvency-state return (and thereby lower the firm's capital costs). Creditors would sign whatever contract the firm offered because, in a competitive credit market, creditors earn zero profits in all equilibria and so would be indifferent to the contract the firm chose, the interest rate would reflect the effect of that contract.

A renegotiation-proof contract would have to be modified in those cases in which the creditors lent at different times because the optimal bribe could change with changes in the relevant economic parameters. The contract thus would need a conversion term, such that if the optimal bribe later changed, the bribes in all prior contracts would be updated to equal the newly optimal bribe: the portion of the bankruptcy return from whatever system the insolvent firm chose that would be sufficient to induce the firm to choose optimally. The initial creditor would sign a contract in which the bribe could change because the contractual bribe would not change in expectation.

Alan Schwartz, Bankruptcy Contracting Reviewed, 109 Yale L.J. 343, 344-348 (1999).

Some of the contractualists have a more limited agenda. They propose that bankruptcy law remain as it is, but that to some extent the rules become default rules rather than mandatory ones. That is, the parties would be free to waive the default rules. Professor Marshall Tracht is one proponent of such a regime. Marshall E. Tracht, Contractual Bankruptcy Waivers: Reconciling Theory, Practice, and Law, 82 Cornell L. Rev. 301 (1997). He argues that waivers are already being enforced in response to market forces. He believes that value maximization will most often be achieved by private bargains and that only in rare cases will other possible goals of bankruptcy law (for example, saving an unsophisticated debtor from an overreaching creditor) be prejudiced by such bargains. Therefore he favors using a strong presumption in favor of enforcing such bargains while reserving to the courts the possibility of refusing enforcement, and applying the bankruptcy law as written, in unusual cases.

Professor Steven Schwarcz also favors some bankruptcy waivers and "procedure contracts," but is much more detailed and selective in analyzing which sorts of waivers are consistent with bankruptcy policy and which are not. He concludes that enforcement of certain kinds of waivers would promote economic efficiency without serious prejudice to important bankruptcy policies. His central argument is that pre-bankruptcy waivers will permit debtors to obtain the liquidity necessary to avoid bankruptcy. That is, a debtor in financial distress is more likely to get credit, and to pay less for it, if it agrees to waive the automatic stay and other bankruptcy protections. A debtor for whom that credit would not be enough to survive will rationally file Chapter 11 instead of accepting the credit with the waiver. Assuming debtors act rationally and can accurately assess their needs and predict the future, most such waivers will therefore be efficient. A contractual solution would not be permitted if it produced "a secondary material impact," which is defined as "unreasonable harm to the interests of creditors." He would also protect against serious debtor miscalculation as to its own interest by requiring that a debtor must get "reasonably equivalent value" in the form of a good chance to survive. His proposal is summarized as follows:

> Provisions of the Code sometimes should be viewed as default — not mandatory — rules. A prebankruptcy contract that is unlikely to result in a secondary material impact neither offends the bankruptcy policy of equality of distribution nor creates an externality that should be unenforceable under contract law. This determination can be made ex ante, at the time of contracting.
>
> A risk still remains that the prebankruptcy contract could impair the debtor's ability to rehabilitate. A court could assess that risk by observing ex post whether or not the debtor's ability to reorganize in bankruptcy has, in fact, been impaired by the prebankruptcy contract. If parties to a prebankruptcy contract cannot determine its enforceability until the debtor is in bankruptcy, however, creditors would be discouraged from offering valuable consideration for the contract, thereby making it more difficult for the debtor to reorganize outside of bankruptcy and impeding the policies of debtor rehabilitation and economical administration. Therefore, an ex ante solution to this problem is preferable. I have proposed as a solution that prebankruptcy contracts be enforceable only if the debtor receives value that is reasonably equivalent to the value of the contract. This requirement would promote debtor rehabilitation by providing the debtor with value that could help it reorganize and by permitting enforceability to be judged ex ante, at the time the prebankruptcy contract is formed. Therefore, a prebankruptcy contract for which the debtor receives reasonably equivalent value should be enforceable if, viewed ex ante, it is unlikely to result in a secondary material impact and does not manifestly impair a debtor's ability to be rehabilitated.
>
> As a corollary of this rule, however, if the debtor does not receive reasonably equivalent value, the policy of debtor rehabilitation may be implicated even if the prebankruptcy contract has no secondary material impact. Therefore, a bankruptcy court should be able to consider the enforceability of such contracts ex post and, as appropriate, enforce them or not based on whether the contract has impaired the debtor's ability to reorganize in bankruptcy. By the same token, if the prebankruptcy contract, at the time of contracting, is likely to (and later does) cause a secondary material impact, it may be unenforceable even if the debtor receives reasonably equivalent value. Of course, if the prebankruptcy contract is likely to (and does) cause a secondary material impact, and the debtor does not receive reasonably equivalent value, the contract clearly violates bankruptcy policies and should not be enforced.

Steven L. Schwarcz, Rethinking Freedom of Contract: A Bankruptcy Paradigm, 77 Tex. L. Rev. 515, 584-585 (1999).

These theories have been criticized on various grounds. One notable critique comes from Professor Lynn LoPucki. He argues that the basic model proposed by Professor Alan Schwartz lacks both internal logic and a mathematical basis. He concludes his critique with this observation:

> The case for freedom of contract rests squarely on the assumption that each party chooses the contract because the contract makes that party better off. Because each party is better off, all parties are better off in the aggregate. That aggregate then becomes a proxy for "social welfare." In the bankruptcy context, this theory holds that thousands of correct decisions by a debtor and each of its creditors and shareholders will generate one correct decision — the bankruptcy contract — in the aggregate. That decision will maximize social welfare.
>
> The principal problem in attempting to apply this theory in the context of bankruptcy is that most creditors' interests are too small to warrant their active, knowledgeable participation. The task of bankruptcy-contract promoters is to find justifications for treating these creditors as if they had participated knowledgeably. Thus, Alan Schwartz would bind every earlier creditor to the contract made by the last, on the theory that the earlier one would have made the same decision; Steven Schwarcz would bind creditors to bankruptcy-procedure contracts on the basis of actual agreement by "representative members of a similarly situated class," on the theory that "distributional effects on other members of the class are likely to be small"; and Marshall Tracht would bind unsecured creditors to the stay waivers contracted by debtors with their secured creditors on the theory that the recoveries of unsecured creditors would have been de minimis anyway. Only Robert Rasmussen seems to contemplate requiring the agreement of all creditors for the validity of a bankruptcy contract, and even he would imply it from the existence of the contract on the public record for a specified period before bankruptcy.
>
> Relaxing the requirement for active, knowledgeable participation by all creditors in bankruptcy contracting reduces transaction costs. At the same time, however, it exposes the interests of nonparticipating creditors to the redistributional impulses of the active, knowledgeable participants. One cannot simply assume that if the redistributions thus achieved are small, the accompanying declines in efficiency will be small as well. William Whitford and I have shown that there is no necessary relationship between the two. The strength of the redistributional impulses evident in the current pattern of bankruptcy contracting, combined with the largely unexplored potential for even small redistributions to have large adverse effects on efficiency, should give pause to future bankruptcy-contracting theorists. Solutions that purport to take account of the preferences of all creditors without actually doing so may be both redistributional and inefficient.

Lynn LoPucki, Contract Bankruptcy: A Reply to Alan Schwartz, 109 Yale L.J. 317 (1999).

The larger debate is summarized by Professor Susan Block-Lieb, who offers her own critique as well. Susan Block-Lieb, The Logic and Limits of Contract Bankruptcy, 2001 Ill. L. Rev. 503. While we will not attempt the difficult feat of digesting the criticisms in far less space, it is important to note a central obstacle to all the contractualist proposals: the collective nature of the bankruptcy process. Each of these theorists has been required to wrestle with the work of Thomas Jackson, who, along with his frequent co-author Douglas Baird, argues that the sole function of bankruptcy is to solve a "collective-action problem" among creditors. Actions by each creditor to collect tend to harm the value of the debtor's assets and are in themselves costly and inefficient. Therefore there is a "common pool problem," by analogy to a pond fished by a number of fishermen whose competition for the fish will empty the pond and ruin the fishing for the future. Thomas Jackson, The Logic and Limits of Bankruptcy Law (1986). The purpose of bankruptcy is to provide a common, collective response to this problem, thus maximizing the value of the debtor's assets and providing the most efficient method of realizing on those assets and distributing the proceeds to the creditors. The ideal bankruptcy law enacts the bargain that these creditors hypothetically would have struck among themselves at the inception of the lending relationship, so it is often called the "creditors' bargain" theory. From this perspective, to the extent that parties can advantage themselves by avoiding the collective treatment, the bargain fails.

Against the intuitive appeal of this collectivist analysis, the contractualists must construct models that permit a number of creditors contracting with the debtor over time to achieve a contract-based result. Each of the theorists discussed above has tried to overcome this fundamental problem.

The obstacles to contractualism represented by the collective nature of bankruptcy were highlighted in a recent empirical study. Elizabeth Warren and Jay Lawrence Westbrook, Contracting Out of Bankruptcy: An Empirical Intervention, 118 Harv. L. Rev. 1197 (2005). The reported data are from a sample of business bankruptcy cases first filed in 1994 and followed for six years, along with additional data from cases filed in 2002. The data showed an average of 19 unsecured claimants per bankruptcy case, ignoring the large cases in which unsecured creditors number in the thousands. Given that these claimants are only the creditors still around on Bankruptcy Day, not those who were once creditors but were paid off and have now moved on, it is apparent that a large number of negotiations of bankruptcy contracts and changes in bankruptcy contracts would be required under any of the contractualist systems. Of course, because it is hard to know in advance which companies would eventually end up in bankruptcy, the negotiations would also be necessary for a much wider swath of the American economy. All in all, the negotiations over possible bankruptcy clauses involve potentially huge transaction costs and a battle of the forms beyond anything taught in Contracts class. Furthermore, in the course of the debate scholars have identified types of creditors who are "non-adjusting," that is, they could not negotiate even if they wanted to. Lucian Arye Bebchuk and Jesse M. Fried, The Uneasy Case for the Priority of Secured Claims in Bankruptcy, 105 Yale L. J. 857, 864, 881 (1996). These non-adjusting creditors include involuntary creditors (e.g., tort victims), quasi-involuntary creditors (e.g., hospitals, utilities), and creditors with contracts too small to be worth negotiating *ex ante* to protect against a risk of bankruptcy (e.g., a $5,000 supply contract). The data from "Contracting Out" show that such creditors make up a very substantial percentage of the claimants in a typical bankruptcy case, meaning that they would be at the mercy of whatever contracts were drafted by the creditors that were in a position to negotiate. Instead of adjusting bankruptcy contract terms, they would have to set their prices on worst-case assumptions that would likely produce substantial efficiency losses.

There is a second problem with all of the theorists discussed to this point — automated, contractualist, and creditors' bargain — which is the missing-debtor problem. Starting with Professor Jackson, all of these theorists have assumed that the debtor and its stockholders have no legitimate interest in the outcome of a bankruptcy proceeding. They have also assumed that debtors will go willingly to the sacrifice, rather than manipulating or secreting assets and filing lawsuits. On that basis, most of the theorists have assumed that the debtor's exclusive interest will be in reducing borrowing costs by offering creditors the best possible bankruptcy regime at the start in exchange for having no rights when the business encounters financial distress. Thus we have Professor Schwartz asserting that the reduction of debt-capital costs is the only legitimate goal of bankruptcy law (see above), while not explaining why the cost and availability of equity capital is unimportant and irrelevant.

A related consequence is that the automated bankruptcy theorists are able to assume a machine that goes of itself. The filing decision, for example, is presumed to be selfless, automatic, and rational at all times. Similarly, some theorists assume no substantial transaction or litigation costs as each tranche of creditors bids for the business or passes the bid to the next tranche. By this theory, the reorganization of a company such as Federated Department Stores (owner of Bloomingdale's, among other stores) and its 66 affiliates presumably would yield no disputes over the complex corporate arrangements. Nor would Federated's 45,000 creditors who were divided into 77 separately identified classes of debt, including a large number of debt arrangements replete with contractual subordination agreements, prompt any disputes that might slow down the automatic offer to each class to buy-or-be-wiped-out.

Earlier we discussed a growing school of thought that proposes that control of the general default process is the central concept in bankruptcy law, whatever system of priorities for various interests might be adopted. (See pp. 409–410.) In work cited earlier, Professor Jay Westbrook has argued that contractualists have failed to consider the methods of control that would be necessary to implementation of a plausible contractualist regime. He asserts that contractualism can work only if based on a system of dominant security interests tying up most if not all of a debtor's assets, a general-default system similar to that found in the United Kingdom. He points to the work of professors Baird, Rassumusen, and Skeel as providing examples of secured parties effectively privatizing the bankruptcy process through the use of security interests, although those authors do not describe their findings in that way. On that basis, the debate about contractualism is really a debate about certain categories of creditors using security interests to control the recovery process for their own benefit. He questions whether such a system is likely to be either fair or efficient.

From a policy perspective, a number of bankruptcy scholars have rejected the contractual or automatic bankruptcy theories, believing that bankruptcy laws serve interests beyond those of maximizing value to creditors or producing the lowest cost of borrowing. Professor Elizabeth Warren has written extensively about the policies that underlie the bankruptcy system. She is deeply skeptical that a single theory — and therefore a single-minded revision — will capture all the interests that a bankruptcy system must serve. In a debate with Professor Baird, she wrote:

> I see bankruptcy as an attempt to reckon with a debtor's multiple defaults and to distribute the consequences among a number of different actors. Bankruptcy encompasses a number of competing — and sometimes conflicting — values in this distribution. As I see it, no one value dominates, so that bankruptcy policy becomes a composite of factors that bear on a better answer to the question, "How shall the losses be distributed?"

Elizabeth Warren, Bankruptcy Policy, 54 U. Chi. L. Rev. 775, 777 (1987).

A few years later she articulated some of the competing goals of the Chapter 11 system, which we summarize as follows:

> *Enhance Value.* By creating specialized collection rules to govern in the case of multiple default and by requiring collective rather than individual action, the value to be gleaned from the failing business can be increased while the expenses of collecting that value are decreased. Bankruptcy rules can also preserve going concern value while they can cabin many forms of strategic behavior that would otherwise waste collective resources.
>
> *Establish an Orderly Distribution Scheme.* By moving away from the race of the diligent at state law, there can be a considered judgment of who should receive preferences in the event that not all parties' expectations can be met. Distribution to parties with different legal rights can be settled in a legislative arena. Parties with no formal rights to the assets of the business, such as employees who will lose jobs and taxing authorities that will lose ratable property, may profit from a second chance at restructuring debt and giving the business a chance to survive *in situ.*
>
> *Internalize the Costs of Default.* A viable Chapter 11 system reduces the pressure on the government to bail out failing companies, thus forcing creditors to make market-based lending decisions and to monitor their debtors more closely.
>
> *Establish a Privately Monitored System.* The initiation decision in bankruptcy is one of the hardest. A system that provides sufficient incentives for debtors to choose it voluntarily or for creditors to force their debtors into it avoids the high costs that come with a publicly monitored system, both in terms of the costs of errors (decisions to place a company in bankruptcy that come too quickly or too slowly) and the costs of monitoring. Such a system also avoids the potential politicalization of such decisions.

Elizabeth Warren, Bankruptcy Policymaking in an Imperfect World, 92 Mich. L. Rev. 336 (1993).

Perhaps the biggest dispute among those debating different approaches to bankruptcy is the starting point. Again, Professor Warren:

> We must consider bankruptcy policies in light of their application to cases that arise in the real world. It is therefore critical to note that the markets bankruptcy affects are not perfect and that they contain substantial

transaction costs, information asymmetries, and ambiguities about the property rights of the parties. While one might make this blanket warning to constrain any policy debate, it is a particularly pertinent limitation in the bankruptcy area for two reasons: bankruptcy policy is itself grounded in market imperfections, and critics have ignored market imperfections in constructing a hypothetical system that is superior to the current bankruptcy system.

The basis for bankruptcy policy is so deeply rooted in market imperfections that any attempt to discuss such policy in a perfect market is a Zen-like exercise, much like imagining one hand clapping. Bankruptcy laws are created to deal with the problems of market imperfections. If, in fact, markets were perfect — if debtors and their creditors had perfect information about the market generally and each party's position within it; if debtors and creditors could costlessly monitor, renegotiate, and enforce their agreements; if the legal rights of parties were always unambiguous and clear to all actors — then bankruptcy laws undoubtedly would take a different form. Many features of the bankruptcy system, for example, are intended to deal with creditors' inadequate information and the high costs of gathering the information they need to make collection decisions. Debtors must disclose substantial information about their business operations so that all creditors will have low-cost, accurate information to inform their oversight and strategic decisionmaking during the bankruptcy process. If creditors had perfect, costless information, these provisions would be superfluous. Like other laws, bankruptcy laws take their shape from the problems with which they were created to cope. . . .

Not surprisingly, to test the vitality of a number of economic principles, researchers often begin their analysis with the familiar incantation of a perfect market: a world without those transaction costs, information asymmetries, or ambiguous property rights to muddy the analytic waters. . . .

It is interesting to imagine what kind of market would produce enough failure to stimulate an interest in a bankruptcy system but would be so perfect that a hypothetical bankruptcy system could operate without concern for market imperfections. While some tests of allocative efficiency may reasonably begin with the presumption of a perfectly functioning market, a policy discussion should not begin in such a state of grace. To do so limits the sweep of the policy inquiry to questions of allocative efficiency and precludes alternate avenues of exploration at the inception of the journey. Bankruptcy policy discussions should provide ample opportunity to test allocative efficiency hypotheses, but they should provide a framework for considering a number of other functions of the bankruptcy system as well. . . .

Ink has spilled freely in the past few years as a number of critics have called for the reform or outright abolition of the bankruptcy system, claiming that it has failed and offering some other method for dealing with business failures. The critics reassert the theoretical justifications for the bankruptcy system by implication, focusing on how the system has failed to meet some thinly articulated goals.

It is important to expose the inefficiencies, inadequacies, incentives, and errors of the bankruptcy system. Its shortcomings may be many, and its operation is sufficiently important to both debtors and creditors to warrant thorough academic study and strong public debate. The chapter 11s; of large, publicly traded cases that have fueled much of the debate are important, particularly as these cases become the fora for the resolution of a multitude of critical social issues. No one should sit back comfortably, assured that we have a well-functioning business bankruptcy system.

In the march through the details of the rules and the attention to the megacase, however, it is essential that the larger impact of the system not be lost. The bankruptcy system is designed to serve critical functions to preserve the value of failing businesses, to distribute that value according to deliberately defined policies, and to internalize the costs of business failure. The system assists a variety of businesses, more than ninety-nine percent of which are not publicly traded. It also serves literally millions of different creditors and other interested parties affected by the bankruptcy laws. Because the functions of the bankruptcy system are deeply intertwined, a single change has the potential to create multiple effects throughout the system. Moreover, changes pursued for one end may simultaneously move the system further away from a number of other objectives.

It is appropriate to end this essay by repeating the initial call for caution. Debates about bankruptcy policy must be more carefully framed to expose their policy presumptions, and any proposal for reform should be accompanied by a thoughtful evaluation of its impact on the competing policy concerns. It is also appropriate, however, to end with a call for a wider exploration of the problems of the system — particularly the kinds of problems that do not fit neatly within established paradigms. We remain woefully short on reliable empirical data about the operation of the system, particularly with respect to the routine cases. Our theoretical grasp of the incentives at work for competing parties is primitive at best, and it certainly deserves elaboration. In short, there is much to learn. In learning, however, there is much known that we should not forget.

Id. at 387.

Not surprisingly, those conclusions reflect, in a general way, the viewpoints of the current authors.

Problem Set 43

43.1. You have been invited to compete for an academic prize consisting of an opportunity to study bankruptcy law for a year, all expenses paid, in several very congenial venues, starting with Paris. The winner will be selected after a debate among students representing the various theoretical viewpoints discussed above. Choose (or be assigned) a position advocating one of those views. Be prepared to discuss its strengths and weaknesses and to cite data, statutory provisions, or cases you have studied in this course to support your position. Think about whether any empirical data might be available or might be developed to support your position or the position of others, but also be ready to make efficiency arguments in the law and economics mode. Because you have not been presented with the details of the theories discussed, you are spared having to address them. You should focus instead on the fundamentals, such as (a) the market efficiencies available in the contract approaches as against the difficulty of negotiating among a number of creditors over time; and (b) the claim that bankruptcy should serve debtor interests as against the Bankruptcy Code rules that seem to confirm that creditors have the overriding rights in bankruptcy (e.g., the absolute priority rule in section 1129(b)).

43.2. The country of Ruritania has recently emerged from a dictatorial, quasi-socialist period and has installed a democratic government committed to a regulated free-market system like that found in the United States.

On the strength of your success in the theoretical competition described above, after your year of study, you have received a contract from USAID and the World Bank to advise the Ruritanian government on a new bankruptcy code for business bankruptcy cases. (Another group is working on a consumer system.) Among the issues that concern the government in that regard is whether any bankruptcy system established should include state-owned enterprises, which are being privatized slowly because of the harsh impact of the loss of the many jobs they supported. The country's prior bankruptcy law emphasized criminal penalties for officers and directors of failed companies and made no provision for discharge of entrepreneurs or consumers. The government is now committed to encouraging an entrepreneurial climate, but recognizes that a major cultural shift will be required. The country's government is unitary (i.e., not federal) and it has no specialized judiciary, so that bankruptcy matters have traditionally been handled by the ordinary judges of the civil courts. What else do you need to know about Ruritania before making recommendations for a bankruptcy law? In particular, what else do you need to know about its legal system? Sketch out your initial thoughts on what system you will propose and why.

DISCHARGED

TABLE OF CASES

TABLE OF STATUTES
AND REGULATIONS

INDEX